Macmillan
Encyclopedia of
Architects

Editorial board

Macmillan Encyclopedia of

Architects

ADOLF K. PLACZEK, *editor in chief*

Volume 2

THE FREE PRESS
a division of Macmillan Publishing Co., Inc.
New York
COLLIER MACMILLAN PUBLISHERS
LONDON

THE FREE PRESS
A Division of Macmillan Publishing Co., Inc.
866 Third Avenue, New York, N. Y. 10022

Collier Macmillan Canada, Inc.

Library of Congress Catalog Card Number: 82-17256

Printed in the United States of America

printing number

2 3 4 5 6 7 8 9 10

Library of Congress Cataloging in Publication Data
Main entry under title:

Macmillan encyclopedia of architects.

    Includes bibliographies and indexes.
    1. Architects—Biography.   I. Placzek, Adolf K.
II. Title: Encyclopedia of architects.
NA40.M25   1982   720′.92′2 [B]   82-17256
ISBN 0-02-925000-5 (set)

EADS, JAMES BUCHANAN

In the Eads Bridge (1867–1874) in St. Louis, Missouri, James Buchanan Eads (1820–1887), a self-educated engineer and inventor who was born in Lawrenceburg, Indiana, made the first major application of structural steel and devised tension and compression tests of this little-known material. Piers of the then world's largest bridge were built within the country's first and deepest under-water pneumatic caissons. For Union forces in the Civil War, he built a fleet of ironclad gunboats at a St. Louis boatyard. He died in Nassau, the Bahamas, where he was promoting a ship-carrying railroad across the Isthmus of Tehuantepec, Mexico.

GEORGE McCUE

WORKS

*c.1861–1865, Ironclad Gunboats (for the United States Navy); 1867–1874, Eads Bridge; St. Louis, Mo. 1875–1879, Jetties, South Pass Ship Canal, Mississippi River.

BIBLIOGRAPHY

Various papers of James Buchanan Eads can be found in the collection of the Missouri Historical Society, St. Louis.

DORSEY, FLORENCE 1947 *Road to the Sea: The Story of James B. Eads and the Mississippi River.* New York: Rinehart.
HOW, LOUIS 1900 *James B. Eads.* Boston: Houghton Mifflin.
McHENRY, ESTILL (editor) 1884 *Addresses and Papers of James B. Eads, Together with a Biographical Sketch.* St. Louis, Mo.: Slawson.
SCOTT, QUINTA, and MILLER, HOWARD S. 1979 *The Eads Bridge.* Columbia: University of Missouri Press.
VOLLMAR, JOSEPH E., JR. 1974 *James B. Eads and the Great St. Louis Bridge.* St. Louis, Mo.: Engineers Club.
WOODWARD, CALVIN M. 1881 *A History of the St. Louis Bridge.* St. Louis, Mo.: G. I. Jones.

EAMES, CHARLES O.

Charles Ormand Eames (1907–1978) ranks as one of the most important American architectural designers of his generation. Although the scope of his work included urban planning, buildings, interiors, furniture, stage and movie sets, photography, motion pictures, graphics, industrial products, exhibitions, and teaching, he nonetheless considered himself "an architect who considers everything as architecture and has practiced architecture in all his work" (Eames, 1967, p. 3).

Eames was born in St. Louis, Missouri. He began his architectural studies at Washington University in St. Louis in 1924 and interspersed them with work in a local architectural firm, Trueblood and Graf. As a student, Eames is thought to have been particularly interested in the work of FRANK LLOYD WRIGHT, but his interest in modern architecture was considerably broadened on a trip to Europe in 1929 where he saw the work of the International style architects.

In the following year, Eames established the firm of Gray and Eames in St. Louis. The Great Depression was not the most opportune time for a young architect to begin his career, and Eames's work during the 1930s included a variety of commissions: theater sets, churches, stained glass, mosaics, textiles, furniture, and ceramics. His versatility as a designer was thus established very early. Perhaps his two most noted commissions in this period were for the John Philip Meyer Residence in St. Louis (c.1935–c.1938), a rather modern design, and the Aloe Plaza (only partially executed) for Carl Milles's fountain, *Meeting of the Waters*, in St. Louis (1938–1940).

The turning point in Eames's career was the award of a fellowship in 1938 to Cranbrook Academy in Bloomfield Hills, Michigan, then under the direction of ELIEL SAARINEN and one of the most important design centers in America. It was at this time that Eames established his close relationship with a fellow faculty member, EERO SAARINEN, who had been appointed a design instructor for 1939–1941. The two collaborated on an exhibit of the work of the Cranbrook staff (1939); in this early show may be seen many of the seminal ideas that Eames was to develop over the next three decades in numerous expositions. Their other collaboration was for three-dimensionally molded plywood chairs in the Organic Design in Home Furnishings Competition held at the Museum of Modern Art, New York, in 1940–1941; Eames and Saarinen received two first prizes and established their international reputations at the ages of thirty-four and thirty respectively.

In 1941, Eames moved to California with his second wife, Ray Kaiser, who was a noted sculptor and painter in her own right; together, they formed an extraordinary design team, and it is virtually impossible to distinguish what is husband or wife in their projects.

The decade of the 1940s was a period when Eames's work took many directions and when he made great strides toward becoming a mature artist. His work, like Saarinen's, seemed to have been based on a systems approach, which involved a detailed analysis of a design problem and a search for the latest technology to solve the problem. It was this design approach—rather than a predilection for a particular stylistic mode—which allowed Eames to work in many media with equal agility

and which accounts in part for the startling changes in his work.

One of Eames's early California projects was for a City Hall for the *Architectural Forum* (May 1943), which marked a decisive break from his St. Louis work and illustrated how much he had learned from the Saarinens and ALVAR AALTO. During the 1940s, Eames continued his experiments with molded plywood, resulting in a remarkable series of furniture designs for Herman Miller after 1946. His interest in photography quickened, and about 1944, Eames developed the fast-slide technique which was to be so integral in later exhibits and films. This interest in film was a natural outgrowth of his employment in the art department at Metro-Goldwyn-Mayer Studios after his move to the West Coast.

The two buildings on which Eames's international reputation as an architect is based were begun in 1945, with Eero Saarinen, as Case Study Houses No. 8 and No. 9 for *Arts and Architecture.* They were built respectively as the Eames residence (1945–1949) and the John Entenza residence (1945–1950) in Pacific Palisades, California. The initial design for the Eames house was for a cantilevered "bridge house" and was derived from a sketch (c.1934) by LUDWIG MIES VAN DER ROHE. As redesigned by Eames in 1949, it was changed to two prefabricated steel-framed pavilions separated by a patio. To the post-World War II generation, the executed design seemed to be an important alternative to the wood-framed tract house. It was also categorized as being quite Miesian, though the only similarities were in the frank expression of the steel frame as a modulating gridwork. Since most viewers saw the building only in black and white periodical illustrations, they were unaware of the exuberance and richness of the wall panels: transparent (clear and wire glass), translucent (fiberglass), and opaque (wood, grey asbestos, aluminum-colored metal siding, and blue, red, earth, white, black, and gold-leafed plaster) walls provided a complex relationship between interior and exterior. Eames's design took full advantage of the California light and the dramatic site, a meadow overlooking the Pacific Ocean. In the interiors, his conception of space as a "variable container" for objects and living—one of his most important contributions to modern design—reached its ultimate development. In contrast to the starkness of many International style interiors, Eames's interiors were increasingly filled with distinctive arrangements of furniture, rugs, flowers, pillows, toys, candles, shells, and other collectibles that approached a High Victorian clutter. This preference for rich interior decoration, a deep respect for nature, and his sensitivity to the building site perhaps reflected a continued admiration for his collegiate idol, Frank Lloyd Wright. As with Wright, also, Eames's conception of form and space had decidedly Japanese overtones.

With the completion of the two Case Study Houses, Eames's accomplishments were significant enough to constitute a style that was recognized internationally. He continued to work on architectural projects through the mid-1960s, though buildings per se clearly occupied less of his time. One of the few commercial commissions executed during this period was the Herman Miller Showroom in Beverly Hills (c.1947–1949). A residence envisioned for Billy Wilder in Beverly Hills (1949–1951) would have been the greatest of the Case Study House's, and its loss for American architecture must rank with Wright's unbuilt McCormick House (1907).

Eames's style was disseminated through a series of public installations: a room at the exhibit "For Modern Living" at the Detroit Institute of Arts (1949); the Good Design Shows at the Merchandise Mart in Chicago (1949) and the Museum of Modern Art (1950); and numerous showroom installations for Herman Miller into the 1960s. The last major interior design project executed by his office was a lobby in the Time/Life Building in New York (c.1959–1960).

If there were fewer architectural projects, the output of the studio up until Eames's death in 1978 was nonetheless phenomenal. Fiberglass and aluminum were employed in a series of innovative furniture designs. More than fifty films were produced on subjects ranging from architecture, furniture, toys, statesmen, to computers. Eames's energies in his later years, however, seemed to have been devoted mainly to a series of traveling exhibitions. In examining subjects such as the computer (1971), Copernicus (1972), or Franklin and Jefferson (1975–1976), he sought to communicate ideas about our society and where it was going.

It is thus somewhat ironic that for a man who did not have a formal architectural degree, Charles Eames perhaps more than any American of his generation claimed such universal reponsibilities for the architect in twentieth-century society. As Edgar Kaufmann, Jr., saw so clearly in 1950, "Eames designs are carriers of a new look at life, of a new concept of the designer as a craftsman of the modern tradition who unites technology and artistry in a fresh concept of living" (Kaufmann, 1950, p. 40).

R. CRAIG MILLER

WORKS

c.1935–c.1938, John Philip Meyer Residence; c.1938–1940, Aloe Plaza for the Meeting of the Waters Fountain (with Carl Milles); St. Louis, Mo. 1945–1949, Charles Eames Residence (with Eero Saarinen); 1945–1950, John Entenza Residence (with Saarinen); Pacific Palisades, Calif. c.1947–1949, Herman Miller Showroom, Beverly Hills, Calif.

BIBLIOGRAPHY

"Case Study Houses 8 and 9 by Charles Eames and Eero Saarinen, Architects." 1945 *Arts and Architecture* 62, no. 12:43–51.
"Case Study Houses No. 8 and No. 9, Architects, Charles Eames and Eero Saarinen." 1948 *Arts and Architecture* 65, no. 3:39–41.
"Case Study House for 1949: Designed by Charles Eames." 1949 *Arts and Architecture* 66, no. 12:26–39.
"Dallo studio di Eames." 1963 *Domus* no. 402:26–42.
DREXLER, ARTHUR 1973 *Charles Eames: Furniture from the Design Collection.* New York: Museum of Modern Art.
"Eames Celebration." 1966 *Architectural Design* 36, no. 9:432–471.
EAMES, CHARLES 1941 "Design Today." *California Arts and Architecture* 58, no. 9:18–19.
EAMES, CHARLES 1971 "General Motors Revisited." *Architectural Forum* 134:21–28.
GOLDBERGER, PAUL 1978 "The Keen, Loving Eye of Charles Eames." *Art News* 77, no. 8:135–136.
KAUFMANN, EDGAR, JR. 1950 "Chairs, Eames and Chests." *Art News* 49, no. 3:36–40.
McCOY, ESTHER 1973 "An Affection for Objects." *Progressive Architecture* 54:64–67.
McCOY, ESTHER 1975 "Charles and Ray Eames." *Design Quarterly* 98–99:21–29.
NOYES, ELIOT 1946 "Charles Eames." *Arts and Architecture* 63:26–44.

EAMES, WILLIAM S.

William S. Eames (1857–1915), in partnership with Thomas C. Young, had a prolific practice in St. Louis, Missouri, from 1885. The firm was responsible for several United States penitentiaries, the Education Building at the 1904 St. Louis Exposition, and many skyscrapers, both in St. Louis and further west.

GWEN W. STEEGE

WORKS

c.1892, Cupples Station; c.1903–1908, Cupples Warehouses; c.1903–1908, Frisco Building; c.1903–1908, Liggett Building; c.1903–1908, Wright Building; 1904, Education Building, Louisiana Purchase Exposition; St. Louis, Mo. 1906–1911, United States Custom House, San Francisco. 1907, Penitentiary, Leavenworth, Kan. 1913–1914, Boatman's Bank and Office Building, St. Louis, Mo.

BIBLIOGRAPHY

CROLY, HERBERT 1912 "The Building of Seattle."

Architectural Record 32, no. 1:1–21.

"Examples of Architecture in St. Louis." 1896 *Architectural Record* 5:393–410.

HERBERT, WILLIAM 1908 "Some Business Buildings in St. Louis." *Architectural Record* 23:391–396.

McCUE, GEORGE (1964)1967 *The Building Art in St. Louis.* St. Louis: American Institute of Architects.

STURGIS, RUSSELL 1908 "Some Recent Warehouses." *Architectural Record* 23:373–386.

EBERSTADT, RUDOLPH

Rudolph Eberstadt (1856–1922), born in Worms, Germany, was trained as an economist, and his doctoral dissertation, on the development of legislation and taxation of the crafts in France, reveals the influence of Gustav Schmoller and economists of the historical school; his standing as an economist was recognized with his appointment to a chair at the University of Berlin. Eberstadt's interests were diverse. His publications include studies of the origins of the guild system in France and Germany and an extended investigation of the capital market in Germany. But he is remembered above all for his writings on housing. His numerous publications in this field include studies of the taxation of urban land, municipal land policies, the provision of capital for the housing market, and investigations of housing in Holland, England, and the Rhineland; in 1910, his entry, with Bruno Mohring and Petersen, in the competition for the plan for Greater Berlin, won third prize. His most important work, *Das Handbuch des Wohnungswesens und der Wohnungsfrage* (1909), was regarded as the standard work on the housing question in the years immediately before World War I.

Eberstadt's first publication on housing, *Städtische Bodenfragen* (1894), which offered an analysis of the relationship between housing form and land values, immediately attracted the attention of housing reformers and established his reputation in the field. Dismissing the idea that the tenement block or *Mietskaserne,* the high-density form of housing then current in German cities, was the result of high land values, Eberstadt claimed to offer evidence that it was, on the contrary, the expected return from this dense form of housing that determined the price of land. This was hailed by housing reformers, particularly the members of the Verein für öffentliche Gesundheitspflege, as vital support for the campaign for stricter control on the density of residential development and a clear argument for the introduction of zoning regulations.

In *Das Handbuch des Wohnungswesens,* Eberstadt not only reviewed the whole field of housing but also extended and generalized his attack on the *Mietskaserne* form of residential development. This he denounced as a product of a malign form of speculation, based not on normal economic processes, but on the unhealthy manipulation of mortgages and capital for building. He argued that this damaging state of affairs was made possible by two developments. First, the supply of land was artificially restricted by the land companies and others speculating in land. Second, he maintained that the absence of any distinction between money borrowed for the purchase of land and that used for construction, coupled with the fact that residential builders were invariably men without capital, placed the unscrupulous developer—typically a broker for building land—in a position of unnatural influence. In this way, the structure of the housing market gave free rein to those with a vested interest in raising the price of land and encouraged the unhealthy *Mietskaserne* form of housing. This interpretation was vigorously challenged by Andreas Voigt who, in *Kleinhaus und Mietskaserne* (1905), defended the *Mietskaserne* as a rational means of reducing housing costs where land values had been inflated as a result of the competition for land between commercial and other interests which could afford to pay a higher rate of return than residential development. After bitter controversy, the consensus of opinion favored the views of Eberstadt and his followers in their condemnation of the failings of the existing situation.

Eberstadt naturally regarded the reform of specific failings of the existing system of providing land and capital for housing as the most effective approach to solving the problems of housing. Unlike the more radical members of the housing reform movement, he dismissed the work of the nonprofit sector and the co-operative housing movement as insignificant and stressed the importance of reforming private enterprise as the only way of securing sufficient supply of housing to improve housing conditions and lower rents. Although a fourth and final edition of *Das Handbuch* was published in 1922 (the year of his death), Eberstadt's views were regarded as increasingly irrelevant in the changed climate brought about by government intervention in the housing market after 1914.

N. O. A. BULLOCK

ECKBO, GARRETT

Garrett Eckbo (1910–) was born in New York and raised in California. He attended the University of California, Berkeley, from 1932 to 1935 and earned a B.S. in landscape design. He received an M.L.A. from the Harvard University Graduate School of Design under Walter Chambers in 1938. During his early career, Eckbo worked for Kastner and Berla, architects, and designed with NORMAN BEL GEDDES the landscape of the General Motors exhibit at the New York World's Fair of 1939. His major work consists of gardens, urban landscape designs, and development plans for public buildings, private homes, and institutions located primarily in California. Eckbo's work expresses his belief in uniting natural and man-made elements in the urban environment. His firm, Eckbo and Kay Associates, has won numerous awards.

Besides his professional practice, Eckbo has held several university positions including chairman of the department of landscape architecture at the University of California from 1965 to 1969. In addition, Eckbo has established himself as an influential author with the publication of six books pertaining to the theory and practice of landscape architecture as well as innumerable articles on related topics in *Architectural Record, Landscape Architecture,* and other professional journals. As a designer of outdoor environments, teacher, and author, Eckbo has made a substantial and instructive contribution to our knowledge of landscape architecture.

LEAH NESS

WORKS
*1939, General Motors Building, World's Fair, New York. 1956, El Caballero Country Club (landscaping), Calif. 1958, Bellehurst Community Development (landscaping), Calif. 1960, Harper Humanities Garden, University of Denver, Colo. 1961, Mount Sinai Hospital Playground, Los Angeles. 1963, El Paso International Airport (landscaping), Tex. 1968, Lodi Park Master Plan, New Delhi. 1970, The Villages (housing), San Jose, Calif. 1973, Denver Botanic Garden, Colo. 1974–1978, Bayhill Office Building (landscaping), Calif. 1977, Student Union Square, University of New Mexico, Albuquerque. 1978, Sand Bay Village Condominiums (landscaping), Calif. 1978, Baylands Master Plan (with Kenneth Kay), Palo Alto, Calif.

BIBLIOGRAPHY
BULL, HENRIK 1974 "Northstar." *Architectural Record* 155, Jan.:142–147.
ECKBO, GARRETT 1949 "Landscape Design in the U.S.A." *Architectural Review* 105:25–32.
ECKBO, GARRETT 1950 *Landscape for Living.* New York: Architectural Record.
ECKBO, GARRETT 1956 *The Art of Home Landscaping.* New York: Dodge.
ECKBO, GARRETT 1964 *Urban Landscape Design.* New York: McGraw-Hill.
ECKBO, GARRETT 1969 *The Landscape We See.* New York: McGraw-Hill.
ECKBO, GARRETT 1971 *Environment and Design.* Tokyo.
ECKBO, GARRETT 1978 *Public Landscape.* Berkeley: Institute of Government Studies, University of California.
STREATFIELD, DAVID 1972 "The Landscape We See." *Landscape Architecture* 62, no. 2:148–151.

ECKEL, E. J.

A native of Strasbourg, France, and 1868 *diplomate* of the Ecole des Beaux-Arts, Edmond Jacque Eckel (1845–1934) developed a varied architectural practice in Saint Joseph, Missouri, with a number of partners: George R. Mann, 1880–1892; Walter Boschen, 1908–1910; and Will S. Aldrich and George R. Eckel, his son, starting in 1910.

WESLEY I. SHANK

WORKS
*1885–1888, Pottawattamie County Courthouse, Council Bluffs, Iowa. 1889, German–American Bank Building; *c.1890, Wheeler–Motter Dry Goods Company Building; Saint Joseph, Mo. 1894–1895, City Hall, St. Louis, Mo. c.1904, Auditorium, Saint Joseph, Mo.

BIBLIOGRAPHY
BRYAN, JOHN ALBURY (compiler and editor) 1928 *Missouri's Contribution to American Architecture.* Mo.: St. Louis Architectural Club.
"Contemporary Architects and their Works: E. J. Eckel, F.A.I.A." 1911 *Western Architect* 17:79–84.
MANN, GEORGE R. (1893)1971–1972 *Selections from an Architect's Portfolio.* Reprinted in "American Architectural Books: Based on the Henry Russell Hitchcock Bibliography." New Haven: Research Publications.

ECOCHARD, MICHEL

Michel Ecochard (1905–) studied architecture in Paris, where he was born, but most of his career as an architect and urbanist took place outside of France. From 1932 to 1945, he worked in Syria where he built the remarkable museum of Damascus (1943) and prepared the master plans for Damascus (1936) and Beirut (1943). In Rabat from 1946 to 1953, he directed the Moroccan service of urbanism and architecture. A man of scrupulous integrity, Ecochard found himself in conflict with speculators and opportunists. His uncompromising character and convictions made him undesirable to an administration all too ready to give in to all types of pressures and compromises.

A civil servant, Ecochard was transferred to France and condemned to a depressing inactivity.

By opening a private studio for architecture and urbanism, however, he was able to continue to work in the Middle East which he knew well and to which he had always remained sentimentally attached. In collaboration with French and Lebanese colleagues, he built several schools in Lebanon and established master plans for Junieh and Byblos as well as the new plan for Beirut. In 1960, his very interesting entry in the international competition for the museum of Kuwait won a well-deserved first prize, but it was never realized. On a UNESCO mission to Pakistan, Ecochard prepared plans for a beautiful university. Unfortunately, this project had to be modified, and not for the better, following the change of generals at the head of the government.

Enthusiastic, always ready to fight for his ideal of a progressive and humanistic architecture, Ecochard knew more disappointments than successes. This man of rare professional and moral merit deserved better.

PIERRE VAGO
*Translated from French by
Richard Cleary*

WORKS

1931, Museum, Antioch, Turkey. 1936, Damascus Master Plan. 1936, Museum, Damascus. 1943, Beirut Master Plan. 1961, Hospital (with others), Beirut. 1962–1978, University of the Ivory Coast, Abidjan. 1963, College of Further Education, Brazzaville, Congo. 1963, University of the Federation of the Cameroons, Yaounde. 1964, Damascus Master Plan. 1964, Primary School, Martigues, France. 1969, French Embassy, Yaounde, Cameroons. 1978, Beirut Master Plan.

BIBLIOGRAPHY

VAGO, PIERRE 1980 "Ecochard, Michel." Pages 226–227 in Muriel Emanuel (editor), *Contemporary Architects*. New York: St. Martin's.

EDBROOKE, FRANK E.

Frank E. Edbrooke (1840–1918) in 1879 began a thirty-five-year career as one of late nineteenth-century Denver's leading architects. His commercial architecture, in particular, set a sophisticated standard for the downtown section of the city. His Chamber of Commerce Building (1884), with its round arches and tripartite vertical division, placed Edbrooke firmly in the mainstream of those commercial designers influenced by H. H. RICHARDSON and LOUIS H. SULLIVAN. In several of his commercial blocks, such as the People's National Savings Bank (1889–1890), Edbrooke used a stone base with the more delicate scale of brick for the upper stories; this combination was widely imi-

tated in Denver. Edbrooke's best known building is probably the Brown Hotel (1890–1892), a nine-story sandstone triangle with gracefully curved corners. Strongest in the commercial field, Edbrooke nevertheless also designed residences, mainly in the Queen Anne style, as well as some institutional buildings, such as the Richardsonian Romanesque Central Presbyterian Church (1890–1892).

GWEN W. STEEGE

WORKS

*1879–1880, Tabor Block; *1879–1880, Tabor Grand Opera House; *1883, First Baptist Church; *1884, Chamber of Commerce Building; *1887, Unity Temple; *c.1888, Frank C. Young House; 1889, Masonic Temple; 1889–1890, Metropole Hotel (now Cosmopolitan Hotel); *1889–1890, People's National Savings Bank; 1890–1891, College of Loretto; 1890–1892, Brown Palace Hotel; 1890–1892, Central Presbyterian Church; *1892, California Building; *1892, Club Building; 1892, Warren House; 1893, Frank E. Edbrooke House; 1894, Denver Dry Goods Company Building; Denver, Colo.

BIBLIOGRAPHY

BRETELL, RICHARD R. 1973 *Historic Denver: The Architects and the Architecture, 1858–1893*. Colo.: Historic Denver.
MORRIS, LANGDON 1979 *Denver Landmarks*. Denver, Colo.: Cleworth.
ROBERTS, EDWARD 1888 "The City of Denver." *Harper's Monthly* 76:944–957.

EDBROOKE, W. J.

Willoughby J. Edbrooke (1843–1896), born in Evanston, Illinois, first practiced in Chicago, in 1868, and eventually formed a partnership with Franklin P. Burnham. Among their major commissions were the Georgia State Capitol (1884–1889) and the Mecca Apartments (1891–1892) in Chicago. Edbrooke served as the superintendent of construction of Chicago and as supervising architect of the Treasury Department for which he initiated the design of at least forty government buildings.

MARJORIE PEARSON

WORKS

1879–1882, Main Building; 1883–1886, Edbrooke Science Hall; Notre Dame, Ind. 1884–1889, Georgia State Capitol (with Franklin P. Burnham), Atlanta. 1888, Sorin Hall (with Burnham), Notre Dame, Ind. 1891–?, Courthouse, Custom House, and Post Office, Omaha, Neb. 1891–?, Post Office, Dallas, Tex. *1891–1892, Mecca Apartments (with Burnham), Chicago. 1891–1896, Post Office, Courthouse, and Custom House (not completed until 1899), Milwaukee, Wis. 1891–1896, Post Office (not completed until 1899), Washington. 1892–?, Courthouse and Post Office, Wilmington, Del. 1892–?, Post Office and Courthouse, Kansas City, Mo. *1892–1893, U.S. Government Building, World's Columbian Exhibition, Chicago. 1892–1896, U.S. Appraisers Warehouse (not completed until 1899; partial redesign by William Martin Aiken), New York. 1892–1896, Post Office, Courthouse, and Custom House (not completed until 1900), Saint Paul, Minn.

BIBLIOGRAPHY

BROWN, GLENN 1894 "Government Buildings Compared with Private Buildings." *American Architect and Building News* 44, Apr. 7:2–12.

CRAIG, LOIS ET AL. 1978 Pages 195–205 in *The Federal Presence: Architecture, Politics, and Symbols in United States Government Building.* Cambridge, Mass.: M.I.T. Press.

HITCHCOCK, H. R., and SEALE, WILLIAM 1976 *Temples of Democracy: The State Capitols of the U.S.A.* New York: Harcourt.

U.S. SUPERVISING ARCHITECT OF THE TREASURY DEPARTMENT 1891–1892 *Annual Report.* Washington: U.S. Government Printing Office.

VAN BRUNT, HENRY 1969 "Architecture at the World's Columbian Exposition." Pages 225–288 in William A. Coles (editor), *Architecture and Society: Selected Essays of Henry Van Brunt.* Cambridge, Mass.: Belknap.

"W. J. Edbrooke." 1891 *Architecture and Building* 14:215–216.

EDELMANN, JOHN

Raised in Cleveland, Ohio, of German parentage, John Edelmann (1852–1900) joined Burling, Alder (see ADLER AND SULLIVAN), and Company of Chicago in 1872. In 1873, he became the foreman of William Le Baron Jenney's atelier where he met LOUIS H. SULLIVAN. The ornamental design of both benefited from Jenney's library. Edelmann taught Sullivan aesthetics and German metaphysics, introducing him to his theory of "suppressed functions." He was the partner of Joseph C. Johnson in 1874. After a hiatus, he returned to Adler in 1880, bringing Sullivan with him. He designed several buildings in Cleveland for Coburn and Barnum (1881) and J. B. Perkins (1882–1883) which evolved from polychromatic Victorian toward a Chicago functionalism. He worked for SOLON S. BEMAN in 1884, but by 1887, he was permanently located in the New York–New Jersey area. Unsuccessful in private practice, he worked for others such as ALFRED ZUCKER for whom he designed the Decker Building (1892–1893), New York. Edelmann never reconciled his many talents and dissipated his energies in radical politics.

THEODORE TURAK

WORKS

*1874, Moody Tabernacle, Chicago. 1881, Blackstone Building; 1881, Perkins–Power Block; 1882–1883, Gilman Building; *1882–1883, Stephens and Widlar Building; *1882–1883, Wilshire Building; Cleveland, Ohio. 1892–1893, Decker Building; New York. 1894, John Edelmann House, Kearny, N.J.

BIBLIOGRAPHY

CONNELY, WILLARD 1960 *Louis Sullivan as He Lived: The Shaping of American Architecture.* New York: Horizon.

EGBERT, DONALD D., and SPRAGUE, PAUL E. 1966 "In Search of John Edelmann, Architect and Anarchist." *Journal of the American Institute of Architects* 45:35–41.

MORRISON, HUGH (1935)1971 *Louis Sullivan: Prophet of American Architecture.* Westport, Conn.: Greenwood.

PAUL, SHERMAN 1962 *Louis Sullivan, An Architect in American Thought.* Englewood Cliffs, N.J.: Prentice-Hall.

SPRAGUE, PAUL E. 1968 "Architectural Ornament of Louis Sullivan and His Chief Draftsman." Unpublished Ph.D. dissertation, Princeton University, N.J.

SULLIVAN, LOUIS H. (1924)1956 *The Autobiography of an Idea.* Reprint. New York: Dover.

TURAK, THEODORE 1974 "French and English Sources of Sullivan's Ornament and Doctrine." *Prairie School Review* 11, no. 4:5–28.

EDIS, R. W.

A minor master of the Queen Anne school of English architecture, Robert William Edis (1839–1927) came in his youth under the spell of WILLIAM BURGES and of French Gothic but took to Queen Anne in the 1870s. His prosperous and increasingly conservative practice included warehouses, hotels, clubs, galleries, and houses for the artistically respectable. Edis was also a London politician and the formidable commander of the Artists' Rifles. His social pretensions were rewarded with royal patronage and, in 1919, a knighthood.

ANDREW SAINT

WORKS

*1865, Warehouses, Wood Street; 1872, Warehouses, 91–93 Southwark Street; 1873, Joseph Lancaster Junior School, Harper Road, Southwark; 1879–1881, 31 and 33 Tite Street; London. 1883, 1891–1892, Sandringham House (additions), Norfolk, England. *1884–1886, Constitutional Club, London. *1887–1891, Byrkley Lodge, Staffordshire, England. 1890–1891, Junior Constitutional Club; 1897–1899, Great Central Hotel; London.

BIBLIOGRAPHY

EDIS, R. W. (1881)1973 *Decoration and Furniture of*

Town Houses. Reprint. New York: British Book Center.

GIROUARD, MARK   1977   *Sweetness and Light.* Oxford University Press.

"Obituary"   1927   *The Builder* 13, July 1:26.

"Obituary"   1927   *Journal of the Royal Institute of British Architects* 34:639.

EFFNER, JOSEPH

Joseph Effner (1687–1745), one of the leading artistic personalities in Munich in the first third of the eighteenth century, is noteworthy for his instrumental role in introducing Bavaria to the latest French architecture and decoration. Son of the court gardener at Schloss Dachau, he learned his father's profession at an early age. In 1706, when Elector Max Emanuel was forced into political exile, Effner accompanied his patron to Paris. There, he studied gardening and architecture, probably under GERMAIN BOFFRAND. He returned to Munich in 1715, after Max Emanuel's restoration, and was appointed court architect in charge of the electoral country palaces, notably Schloss Nymphenburg (1664–c.1750) and Schloss Schleissheim (1702–1726) near Munich.

Orchestrating the contributions of the large, international corps of artisans that Max Emanuel had assembled at his court, Effner supplied designs not only for architecture and decoration, but also for gardens, furnishings, and court festivities. He made his greatest impact in the field of interior decoration. Through his collaboration with the talented stuccoer Johann Baptist Zimmermann (at Schleissheim, 1720–1726, and the Reiche Zimmer in the Munich Residenz, 1726–1729) and with woodcarver Johann Adam Pichler (at Nymphenburg, 1716–c.1725, as well as at Schleissheim and the Reiche Zimmer), Effner contributed significantly to the creation of a brilliant, indigenous rococo style. At the height of this development in the 1730s and 1740s, notably in the work of FRANÇOIS CUVILLIÉS at the Amalienburg (1734–1739, Nymphenburg Park), the Bavarian rococo far surpassed its French models in playful whimsy, elusive surface effects, and freedom from architectural constraint. Effner prepared comprehensive plans for the completion of Nymphenburg (1715) and Schleissheim (1719), but only the lateral wing blocks (1715–c.1750) and the Rondell (1728–1758) of the former were realized. His most successful architectural works were the Pagodenburg (1716–1719) and the Badenburg (1718–1721), small pavilions in the Nymphenburg Park. Both were influential in the later development of this building type in Germany. In their classical restraint, they remained, like most of his exterior architecture, rigorously French. His Palais Preysing (1723–1728) in Munich, with its overlay of exuberant relief ornament, is an important exception. Beginning around 1730, Effner gradually lost his artistic pre-eminence to Cuvilliés, the favorite architect of Elector Karl Albrecht, and became increasingly involved with administrative duties.

SAMUEL J. KLINGENSMITH

WORKS

1715–1717, Schloss Dachau, Germany. 1715–1717, Schloss Fürstenried; 1715–c.1750, Schloss Nymphenburg; 1716–1719, Pagodenburg, Nymphenburg Park; 1718–1721, Badenburg, Nymphenburg Park; 1719–1726, Schloss Schleissheim; 1723–1728, Palais Preysing; 1725–1728, Magdalenenklause, Nymphenburg Park; 1726–1729, Reiche Zimmer, Residenz; 1728–1758, Rondell, Schloss Nymphenburg; *1734, Gelbes Jagdhaus, Forstenried Park; Munich.

BIBLIOGRAPHY

HAGER, LUISA   1955   *Nymphenburg: Schloss, Park und Burgen.* Munich: Hirmer.

HAGER, LUISA, and HOJER, GERHARD   (1965)1976   *Schleissheim: Neues Schloss und Garten.* 4th ed., rev. Munich: Bayerische Verwaltung der staatlichen Schlösser, Gärten und Seen.

HAUTTMANN, MAX   1913   *Der kurbayerische Hofbaumeister Joseph Effner: Ein Beitrag zur Geschichte der höfischen Kunstpflege, der Architektur und Ornamentik in Deutschland zur Anfang des 18. Jahrhunderts.* Strasbourg, France: Heitz.

HEMPEL, EBERHARD   (1965)1977   *Baroque Art and Architecture in Central Europe.* 2d ed. New York: Viking.

HITCHCOCK, H. R.   1968   *German Rococo: The Zimmermann Brothers.* Baltimore: Penguin.

KREISEL, HEINRICH   1969   "Régence Furniture in Munich." *Apollo* 90:390–403.

LIEB, NORBERT   1941   *Münchener Barockbaumeister: Leben und Schaffen in Stadt und Land.* Munich: Schnell & Steiner.

THON, CHRISTINA   1977   *Johann Baptist Zimmermann als Stukkator.* Munich and Zurich: Schnell & Steiner.

VITS, GISELA   1973   *Joseph Effners Palais Preysing: Ein Beitrag zur Münchener Profanarchitektur des Spätbarock.* Berne: Lang; Frankfurt: Lang.

EGAS, ENRIQUE

Enrique Egas (?–1534) was one of the major architects in Castile in the last years of the fifteenth and first decades of the sixteenth century. His style is transitional, falling between the bold and splendid late Gothic style of his master JUAN GUAS and the younger masters of the new Plateresque style, ALONSO DE COVARRUBIAS, DIEGO DE SILOÉ, and others, who adopted Italianate forms of decoration and planning. Egas simplified the decorative forms of Juan Guas but he never completely came to terms with the new manner. His career exemplifies the continuing vigor of medieval architectural modes into the sixteenth century in Spain.

Enrique Egas was a descendant of a family of architects and sculptors who came from Brussels. His father, Hanequin, and his father's brother, Egas Cueman, settled in Toledo where they were working on the cathedral by 1448. Enrique and his brother Antón Egas both became architects, but Antón's career is not well known, apart from his collaboration with Enrique. Enrique had at least three children: Enrique, who became an architect and worked with Alonso de Covarrubias at the Alcázar in Toledo; Diego, who was a sculptor; and Juan, a painter and decorator. It used to be thought, incorrectly, that María Gutiérrez de Egas, the wife of Alonso de Covarrubias, was Enrique's daughter; but she may have been a relative. This continuity of families is typical of the artistic and building professions in Spain in the fifteenth century and it is a significant factor in defining architectural practice. Most architects, like Egas, were the sons of architects. Enrique succeeded his father Hanequin as master of the works at Toledo in 1498, a position he held until his death in 1534.

The Cathedral of Toledo was begun in 1227 on the model of French cathedrals such as Bourges and Le Mans. By 1497, it was largely complete. Egas was responsible for continuing construction, and he was nominally in charge of overseeing all architectural and decorative projects; however, a number of chapels by other architects were built during his tenure at the cathedral. Egas himself supervised the remodeling of the sanctuary (Capilla Mayor) from 1500 to 1504 with Pedro de Gumiel and others, including the well-known sculptor Felipe Bigarny. From 1504–1512, Egas and Gumiel also designed and built the entrance to the chapter room (Sala Capitular). Egas's most striking work in the cathedral is his design for the new Chapel of the Mozarabic Rite (Capilla Mozárabe) in 1519.

Egas is usually cited in documents as the "master of the works" at Toledo, clear evidence that this position established him professionally; but he is best known for other works. A significant number of Egas's designs are for royal commissions from the Spanish kings and, in this, his career resembles that of his teacher Juan Guas.

Egas most probably worked at the royal foundation, San Juan de los Reyes, in Toledo after the death of Juan Guas; the simple, open-well staircase is attributed to him. The first of Egas's royal buildings, however, was the Royal Hospital at Santiago

de Compostela in Galicia. The hospital was founded in 1499. From 1501 to 1511, Enrique Egas, working in collaboration with Antón, provided designs and approved construction of the main façade (1501–1511), the two courtyards behind it (1509–1513), and the hospital chapel (begun in 1511). The main portal was executed by French sculptors from 1518, but since Enrique Egas was in Santiago in 1517 to inspect construction, it is not unreasonable to assume that he designed the main portal.

The Santiago hospital was the first royal general hospital and Egas's cruciform plan was widely influential. The cruciform idea may have been adumbrated earlier in Spain at the Hospital General in Valencia which was begun in 1493 and described as cruciform when the program was reconstituted in 1512. The motif ultimately derives from the Italian type of general hospital. At Santiago, long open wards form a T with the chapel in the central arm. The entire complex is enclosed and two courtyards are placed on either side of the chapel. In the eighteenth century, two more courtyards and wards were added at the rear of the building. The closest Italian precedents for this arrangement are the hospital of Santa Maria Nŭova in Florence (fourteenth and fifteenth centuries), Santo Spirito in Sassia in Rome (1476–1483) built for Sixtus IV, and a group of north Italian hospitals, the most famous of which is IL FILARETE's Ospedale Maggiore in Milan (begun in 1456). This building was incomplete but Filarete's designs were known from his *Trattato di Architettura,* written about 1465. There is no evidence that Egas

Egas.
Royal Hospital.
Santiago de Compostela,
Galicia, Spain.
1501–1517

Egas.
Chapel, Royal Hospital.
Santiago de Compostela,
Galicia, Spain.
1501–1517

Egas.
Royal Chapel.
Granada, Spain.
1506–1507

knew any of these buildings directly, but it is likely that the plan type was widely known, especially by patrons.

Egas's style in the hospital chapel is still late Gothic; but the façade of the hospital is simple and organized around its central portal in a manner used by later Plateresque architects. The portal itself is a rectilinear composition of decorated pilasters framing a series of statues, standing under Gothic canopies. A round central arch is framed by relief ornament and small figures on the archivolts. In the portal and the main cornice, Egas adopted a vocabulary which included many motifs (particularly foliage) of classical origin but he combined them without regard for classical syntax.

Egas is considered to have been responsible for two other cruciform hospital designs. In 1494, Cardinal Pedros González de Mendoza, archbishop of Toledo and councillor to the Spanish kings, provided for the foundation of a general hospital in Toledo on a site near the Alcázar. Construction on the Hospital of the Holy Cross began in 1504 and continued to 1515 but little was built, partly because the cathedral, which administered the project, was reluctant to provide the funds. Egas's role

is not documented, but it is assumed that he provided the plans since he was then architect of the cathedral. The plan is a Greek cross and Egas is thought to have built the four interior halls. The decoration is simple; there is no elaborate sculpture, but the two-storied crossing and decorated wooden ceilings make an impressive interior. The main façade, the entrance portal to the courtyard, and the courtyard and staircase were all designed by Alonso de Covarrubias at a later date.

Even less was built of Egas's cruciform design for the Royal Hospital in Granada, which was founded in 1504 and under construction until 1511. The interior halls and a portion of a courtyard were completed later in the sixteenth century.

The hospitals are Egas's most modern buildings. The institution was not medieval and the programs and plans were of Italian inspiration. Partly because of these buildings, Egas was once viewed as one of the founders of Spanish early Renaissance style, known as the Plateresque. Egas's other works, however, are chiefly ecclesiastical and they belong to the late medieval style.

In 1498, Egas began construction at the new Cathedral of Plascencia, but he was replaced in 1513 by Francisco de Colonia who, in 1521, was replaced by Juan de Alava, the architect responsible for the present church. It is not known why Egas left the works but it may be that other commissions were more pressing.

In 1506, he was ordered to Granada to assume control of the building of the Royal Chapel, the royal burial chapel of the Spanish kings, which was to be attached to the cathedral. Egas was not the original designer of the building and, in 1509, he objected to the plans that he was expected to follow, saying that they were small and mean. Agreement was reached in 1510, and Egas continued to supervise the work but Gallego y Burín (1952) does not believe that the basic design of the chapel was by Egas. In plan, the chapel is a rectangular box, two stories tall, with shallow side chapels off the nave and a shallow transept and polygonal apse. Its style is usually described as Isabelline Gothic. The simple mural surfaces are enlivened on the exterior by a strip of intricate open-work tracery and by an elaborate portal which leads from the interior of the present cathedral to the chapel. The Capilla Real is most famous for its Renaissance sculpture and decoration but there is no evidence that Egas himelf contributed to these designs.

In December 1521, Egas went again from Toledo to Granada to prepare plans for its new cathedral, adjacent to the royal chapel. Construction began with the assistance of Sebastián de Alcántara. In 1528, Egas was paid for a lengthy visit to Granada and for a set of projects and plans for the church (Rosenthal, 1961). Only a few days later, however, a request was made for a master of the "Roman" style, and by June 1528, Diego de Siloe had replaced Egas as master of the works. It was once thought that Egas's foundations determined much of Siloe's plan but Rosenthal has shown that Egas's construction affected only the width of the church, the outer walls of the chevet, and the position of the transept. No drawings by Egas have survived to give a more precise notion of his plan but it is generally thought that he had submitted a design based upon the thirteenth-century plan of the Cathedral of Toledo. By 1528, this must have seemed old-fashioned.

In spite of his dismissal from Granada, Egas continued to play an important role in Spanish architectural projects. Long after the new Plateresque or "Roman" style (as it was called) was popular in Castile, Egas was still advising at major projects. He was a consultant at Seville Cathedral in 1512 and 1515, at the new cathedral project at Malaga in 1528, in Segovia in 1529. His activity at the building of the new cathedral in Salamanca has been documented by Chueca (1951): he criticized the works in 1523, 1530, and in 1534. Egas's most brilliant pupil was Alonso de Covarrubias who rejected Egas's Gothic ornament but kept something of his taste for elaborate, active decoration which brought figural sculpture, relief carving, and ornamented structure into dense and active compositions.

CATHERINE WILKINSON

WORKS

1500–1504, Cathedral (sanctuary); Toledo, Spain. 1501–1517, Royal Hospital, Santiago de Compostela, Galicia, Spain. c.1504, Monastery of San Juan de los Reyes (staircase); 1504–1512, Cathedral (entrance to Chapter Room); 1504–1515, Hospital of the Holy Cross (completed by Alonso de Covarrubias); Toledo, Spain. 1506–1507, Royal Chapel; 1506–1517, Royal Hospital (remained incomplete); Granada, Spain. 1519, Chapel of Mozarabic Rite, Cathedral, Toledo, Spain. 1521–1528, Cathedral (foundations only; completed by Diego de Siloe), Granada, Spain.

BIBLIOGRAPHY

AZCÁRATE, JOSÉ MARÍA DE 1957 "La Labor de Egas en el Hospital Real de Santiago de Compestela." Pages 15–23 in *Miscellanea Profesor Dr. D. Roggen de Bikkel.* Antwerp, Belgium: De Sikkel.

AZCÁRATE, JOSÉ MARÍA DE 1958 *La Arquitectura Gótica Toledana del Siglo XV.* Madrid: Instituto Diego Velasquez, Consejo Superior de Investigaciones Cientificas.

CHUECA GOITIA, FERNANDO 1951 *La Cathedral Nueva de Salamanca.* Spain: University of Salamanca.

CHUECA GOITIA, FERNANDO 1953 *Arquitectura del Siglo XVI.* Madrid: Plus Ultra.

GALLEGO Y BURIN, ANTONIO 1952 *La Capilla Real de Granada.* Madrid: Consejo Superior de Investigaciones Cientificas.

LLAGUNO Y AMÍROLA, EUGENIO, and CEAN-BERMUDEZ, JUAN AUGUSTIN (1829)1977 *Noticias de los Arquitectos y Arquitectura de España.* Madrid: Ediciones Turner.

ROSENTHAL, EARL 1961 *The Cathedral of Granada: A Study in the Spanish Renaissance.* N.J.: Princeton University Press.

EGGERICX, JEAN J.

An architectural educator and journalist as well as a designer of both individual buildings and building groups, Jean J. Eggericx (1884–1963) was a leading figure in the Modern movement in Belgium. During the decade following World War I he was responsible for planning a number of garden-city housing estates, mostly around Brussels. In these designs, Eggericx relied mainly on English precedents and worked closely with LOUIS VAN DER SWAELMEN. His architecture of this period also bears comparison with certain contemporary Dutch work, especially in the sensitive use of traditional materials. During the 1930s, Eggericx assimilated the influence of the International style. He designed many types of buildings throughout his career but remains best known for his small- and large-scale residential projects and planning work.

ALFRED WILLIS

WORKS

1919–1921, Cité de Comines, Zonnebeke, Elverdinghe, Belgium. 1921–1963, Floréal and Le Logis Housing Estates, Watermael-Boitsfort, Brussels. 1925, Van der Perre House, Uccle, Belgium. 1925–1926, Wolfers

House, Brussels. 1927, Children's Home, Bredene-Oostende, Belgium. 1929, Chapel, Virton, Belgium. 1929, Les Trois Tilleuls Housing Estate (with amenities), Boitsfort; 1931, Health Center, Boitsfort; 1936–1938, Léopold and Albert Apartment Buildings; Brussels. *1937, Belgian Pavilion, World's Fair, Paris.

BIBLIOGRAPHY

BEKAERT, GEERT, and STRAUVEN, FRANCIS 1971 *La Construction en Belgique 1945–1970.* Brussels: Confederation Nationale de la Construction.

CULOT, MAURICE, and TERLINDEN, FRANÇOIS (editors) 1969 *Antoine Pompe et l'effort moderne en Belgique.* Belgium: Musée d'Ixelles.

DE KONINCK, L. H. 1963 "J. J. Eggericx: 1884–1963." *Architecture* no. 52:210–213.

PUTTEMANS, PIERRE 1976 *Modern Architecture in Belgium.* Brussels: Vokaer.

SCHMITZ, MARCEL 1937 *L'architecture moderne en Belgique.* Brussels: Editions de la Connaissance.

SCHOONBRODT, RENÉ 1979 *Sociologie de l'habitat social.* Brussels: Editions des Archives d'architecture moderne.

SMETS, MARCEL 1977 *L'avènement de la Cité-Jardin en Belgique.* Brussels: Mardaga.

EGGERS and HIGGINS

Otto R. Eggers (1882–1964) and Daniel Paul Higgins (1886–1953) formed the partnership of Eggers and Higgins in 1937. Since 1922, they had both been partners in the office of JOHN RUSSELL POPE; upon Pope's death, they continued their practice. Barred from using Pope's name, the firm continued as Eggers and Higgins, Eggers taking responsibility for the designs and Higgins for administration and sales representation. The firm grew to be one of the largest in the country in the 1950s.

Eggers, born in New York, received his architectural education at Cooper Union as well as in the atelier of HENRY HORNBOSTEL at the Beaux-Arts Institute of Design in New York.

Higgins began work in Pope's office around the same time as Eggers, working as an accountant. In his spare time, he studied architecture at New York University.

The firm is best known for its designs of large institutional projects, particularly hospitals and university buildings. In 1976, the firm became known as the Eggers Group, with David L. Eggers as its senior partner.

STEVEN MCLEOD BEDFORD

WORKS

1937, National Gallery of Art, Washington. 1939, Schaefer Building, New York World's Fair. 1941, Cardinal Hayes High School, Bronx, N.Y. 1943, Naval Training Station, Bainbridge, Md. 1945, Church of Our Lady of Victory, New York. 1948, Veteran's Administration Hospital, Albany, N.Y. 1951, New Rochelle High School, N.Y. 1952, SS United States. 1952, New York University Law School. 1955, Canada House; 1955, General Grant Houses; New York. 1956, Federal Reserve Bank, Buffalo, N.Y. 1966, Banque Continentale, New York. 1970, Avco Corporation Headquarters, Greenwich, Conn. 1971, Pace College, New York. 1973, Indiana Law School, Indianapolis. 1974, Lehigh Valley Brewery, Allentown, Pa. 1975, Staten Island High School, N.Y. 1978, Saint Joseph Mercy Hospital, Ann Arbor, Mich.

BIBLIOGRAPHY

LAMPL, PAUL 1977 "Higgins, Daniel Paul." Supplement 5, pages 300–301 in *Dictionary of American Biography.* New York: Scribner's.

"Obituary." 1964 *New York Times,* Apr. 24, p. 34.

EHRENSVAERD, CARL AUGUST

Carl August Ehrensvaerd (or Ehrensvärd) (1745–1800) has been called an original Swedish aesthetician and early functionalist. He was born in Stockholm of noble birth. His father was commander-in-chief of the fortress of Sveaborg in Finland, then belonging to Sweden, and Ehrensvaerd grew up there. He continued his studies in Sweden, entering a military career, which culminated with his being appointed colonel in the Swedish navy. Abruptly, he determined to break his career and started on a stimulating journey to Italy.

This journey had as a result two of the most individual works in the Swedish literature of the eighteenth century: "Journey to Italy 1780, 1781, 1782" (1786) and "Philosophy of the Free Arts" (1786) as well as a large number of drawings and watercolors. In these two works we meet many of the new ideas of that time, including neoclassicism and physiognomy, and theories of climate. The major importance of these works, however, is that many ideas later encountered in modern functionalism—above all the ideas of LE CORBUSIER—were presented in polemical form to the architects of Ehrensvaerd's own time. His sketches also prove that he was as radical as were ETIENNE LOUIS BOULLÉE or CLAUDE NICOLAS LEDOUX in their contemporary projects. The Storehouse in Karlskrona, built in 1784, is pure functionalism, the earliest executed example in Sweden and perhaps in Europe.

HOLGER FRYKENSTEDT

BIBLIOGRAPHY

The Age of Neo-Classicism. 1972 London: The Arts Council of Great Britain.

Ehrensvaerd.
Storehouse.
Karlskrona, Sweden.
1784

EHRENSVAERD, CARL AUGUST 1786 *De fria konsters philosophi.* Stockholm: Tryckt I Kongl Tryckeriet.

EHRENSVAERD, CARL AUGUST (1786)1948 *Resa til Italien 1780, 1781, 1782.* Reprint. Stockholm: Sällskapet Bokvännerna.

EHRENSVAERD, CARL AUGUST 1922–1925 *Skrifter.* Edited by Gunhild Bergh. 2 vols. Stockholm: Bonniers.

FRYKENSTEDT, HOLGER 1965 *Carl August Ehrensvaerd (1745-1800): An Original Swedish Aesthetician and an Early Functionalist.* Uppsala, Sweden.

FRYKENSTEDT, HOLGER 1965 *Studier i Carl August Ehrensvaerds författarskap.* Stockholm: Almquist & Wilksell.

HONOUR, HUGH (1968)1977 *Neo-Classicism.* Rev. ed. Harmondsworth, England: Penguin.

JOSEPHSON, RAGNAR 1963 *Carl August Ehrensvaerd.* Stockholm: Norstedt.

NILSSON, STEN Å. 1964 "Pyramid på Gustav Adolfs torg." *Konsthistorisk Tidskrift* 33:1–20.

ROSENBLUM, ROBERT 1967 *Transformations in Late Eighteenth-Century Art.* N.J.: Princeton University Press.

WARBURG, KARL 1893 *Karl August Ehrensvaerd.* Stockholm: Beijer.

EIDLITZ, CYRUS

Cyrus Lazelle Warner Eidlitz (1853–1921), son of LEOPOLD EIDLITZ, was educated in Geneva, Switzerland, and Stuttgart, Germany, before entering his father's office as a draftsman in 1871. Stylistically eclectic, Eidlitz's work demonstrated a particularly fine use of decorative and textural effects and command over difficult design challenges. Important early buildings which brought him national attention were Dearborn Station, Chicago (1885), and the Buffalo, New York, Public Library (c.1884–1887), a Romanesque building designed for an extremely irregular site. His outstanding achievement is usually considered the original New York Times building (1903), designed with Alexander Mackenzie, for a trapezoidal site located over an old subway station in New York.

GWEN W. STEEGE

WORKS

1878, Saint Peter's Church (reconstruction), Westches-ter Square, N.Y. c.1879, Railway Station, Detroit, Mich. c.1884–1887, Public Library, Buffalo, N.Y. 1885, Dearborn Station, Chicago. c.1887, Metropolitan Telephone Building, Cortland St.; 1889, Western Electric Building; 1890, Metropolitan Telephone Building, Broadway; 1891, Racquet and Tennis Club; 1894, Bank for Savings; 1894, Fidelity and Casualty Company; 1896, Bar Association; 1896, Townsend Building; 1903, New York Times Building; New York.

BIBLIOGRAPHY

"Obituary." 1921 *The New York Times* Oct. 6, p.17.

SCHUYLER, MONTGOMERY 1896 "Cyrus L. W. Eidlitz." *Architectural Record* 5, no. 4:411–435.

SCHUYLER, MONTGOMERY 1903 "The Evolution of a Skyscraper." *Architectural Record* 14, no. 5:329–343.

WODEHOUSE, LAWRENCE 1976 *American Architects from the Civil War to the First World War.* Detroit, Mich.: Gale.

EIDLITZ, LEOPOLD

Leopold Eidlitz (1823–1908) was one of the founding members of the American Institute of Architects and an untiring advocate of the functional-organic approach to architecture. An ardent, but also a Gothic, structuralist, he believed in that essential Gothic unity between architecture and engineering. Structure, he felt, must always be clearly expressed, it being the chief generator of all significant architecture; buildings must be organized in ways analogous to nature; and only natural materials must be used.

As much of his work has not survived, Eidlitz has been long neglected, but there is no denying the integrity and, at his best, the almost animal strength of his buildings. Architecture, he wrote, should be able "to perform acts . . . of muscular and nerve motion . . . equivalent to actual motion arrested" (Eidlitz, 1881, p. 222). Influenced by Ralph Waldo Emerson, he compared a building to the body of a lion—both are constructed for a specific purpose and with "a beauty . . . expressive of the nature of [their] structure (Eidlitz, 1858, p. 141). This kinesthetic view, which he developed in his book, *The Nature and Function of Art* (1881), was to influence in particular FRANK FUR-

Eidlitz.
Saint George's.
New York.
1846–1848

NESS and, through him, LOUIS H. SULLIVAN in their development of an architecture evoking physical gesture. But Eidlitz, though certainly no formalist imitator of the past, was at heart a romantic medievalist for whom the Romanesque and Gothic vocabulary as well as the structural principles of the thirteenth century sufficed. The architectural development he had influenced, which could be carried out only in steel, led into a world he was unwilling to enter.

Eidlitz was born in Prague. He never studied architecture formally but was trained at the Vienna Polytechnic to be a land-steward, whose concern was the construction of utilitarian buildings for estate administration. He emigrated to New York in 1843, soon followed by his brother Marc (who became his builder), and went to work as a draftsman for RICHARD UPJOHN. Montgomery Schuyler, who knew him well, reported that from the beginning of his career Eidlitz admired the architecture of the Bavarian Romanesque Revival, especially that of FRIEDRICH VON GÄRTNER. The influence of Upjohn's contemporary Romanesque work can also be felt in Eidlitz's early churches, particularly in their towers. His first commission, for which he went into partnership with Charles Blesch, a Bavarian with the architectural training Eidlitz lacked, was Saint George's, New York, a twin-towered *Rundbogenstil* hall, for many years the largest interior space in the city. It was to be his only large church of this kind, for he then moved more and more in the direction of Upjohn's ecclesiological Gothic. When in 1865 a fire left only its walls and towers standing, Eidlitz rebuilt Saint George's, his second interior enlivened with polychroming, now lost, which served to focus the huge space, lending added thrust to its enfolding gallery and to the exposed beams of the roof.

Following Saint George's, Eidlitz and Blesch designed a new building for the First Church of Christ in New London, Connecticut. It is entered through a central stone tower, part of a massive Romanesque west front; one passes through its tunnellike transverse corridor into a different world of slender wood columns and pointed arches—Eidlitz's first Gothic Revival interior. Wood construction provided him the opportunity to develop his penchant for exposed structure, which he was to continue with particular success in his Willoughby House (1854) in Newport, Rhode Island. In this large chalet, exterior communicates with interior by means of first- and second-story balconies that wrap around the house, holding it deftly together, so that one can step out-of-doors from almost every room.

In the 1850s, Eidlitz built a series of five Gothic churches, all with open-timbered roofs, in which he made a gradual transition from the New London galleried hall and apse to the cruciform, clearstoried designs he produced for the Broadway Tabernacle in New York (1858–1859) and Christ Church, St. Louis, Missouri (1859–1867). It was not academic Gothic that interested him, however, as the flush, undecorated arch of the west door of his Second Congregational Church in Greenwich, Connecticut, or the octagonal piers at Christ Church, branching into arches in smooth lines uninterrupted by capitals, demonstrate. These churches do have a solid, workmanlike quality about them, an angularity at times quite awkward, which prompted Schuyler to comment that it looked "as if an inspired village mason, aided, or even possibly impeded, by a manual of German geometric Gothic, had piled up stone" (Schuyler 1908). But Eidlitz's primary concern was to have his buildings admit how they worked, even if this was to "attempt . . . forms which are less pleasing" (Eidlitz, 1881, p. 70). Crude form was "not to be entirely annihilated; . . . through all the modelling the mass must be felt" (ibid., p. 417).

All but one of Eidlitz's public and commercial buildings in New York are now gone, but they constituted an important part of his work. The Continental and American Exchange Banks had Renaissance façades with powerful stone cornices and an almost equal ratio of glass to stone. Their impression of massiveness and strength was achieved by the modeling of the full thickness of wall in the window reveals. For the Produce Exchange, however, Eidlitz was able to design a fully free-standing building, almost square and fitted cleverly onto its irregular site by means of slightly projecting transepts. By giving it no principal façade and only the simplest main entrance, he invited its being experienced in the round. The Exchange room, lit by huge windows and unobstructed except for four brownstone piers that supported the exposed timbers of the roof, took up the entire main floor, the ground level occupied by offices which opened directly onto the street.

In his Brooklyn Academy of Music, Eidlitz attempted an almost didactic exterior expression of interior arrangements, lining up along the street its various components: entry, foyer, auditorium, stage, green room, and even dressing rooms. Whatever its failings, it must be acknowledged as one of the earliest attempts at functional auditorium design. The Dry Dock Savings Bank in New York, whose vaulted hall was a prototype of the Albany Assembly Chamber, was lit by bands of pointed windows in an almost Venetian array. It can perhaps be seen as a kind of high Victorian celebration of money, particularly as its author was soon to publish a book called *Big Wages and How to Earn Them.* The last of these New York buildings, and the only one to survive, was the addition Eidlitz made to John Kellum's "Tweed" Courthouse. Threatened with demolition since the turn of the century, it has never been modernized, and the courtroom with its polished granite columns, tiled floor and Romanesque fireplace is still intact, used now for offices and storage.

In his post-Civil War buildings, perhaps because his command of structure was now more secure, Eidlitz allowed himself a romantic eclecticism he had before eschewed. The commission for Temple Emanu-El in New York, which he shared with HENRY FERNBACH, unleashed his innate sense of color and decoration. Its tremendous round arches he celebrated with repeated Saracenic patterns, and on the outside turrets sprouted from every possible corner. It was followed, only a block away, by the Church of the Holy Trinity whose exterior he completely covered in Victorian decoration, but whose tower was one of his most powerful statements: the columns of its aerial porch interrupting its upward thrust with the weight of the huge pyramid above.

From 1875 to 1885, together with H. H. RICHARDSON and FREDERICK LAW OLMSTED, Eidlitz worked on the completion of the Capitol in Albany. His share of the work included the Assembly Stair, the Senate Corridor, the short-lived Golden Corridor with its formal simplicity and resplendent coloring, and the Assembly Chamber which was to be his most completely developed transeptual space, rising in a hierarchy of bays and vaulting, the decoration perfectly subordinated to its clearly expressed structure. Unfortunately, its great groined vault, the widest ever built, was not adequately supported; it soon began to crack and had to be taken down in 1888 and replaced with a flat wooden ceiling, thereby ruining what Schuyler (1908) called "perhaps the noblest monument of the Gothic revival in America." In the mean time,

Eidlitz.
Produce Exchange.
New York.
1860–1861

Eidlitz.
State Capitol Assembly
Chamber (with
Richardson and Olmsted).
Albany.
1875–1885

however, Eidlitz had built his magnificent Senate Staircase which, with its half-arches and inscribed circles, is one of his boldest and most inventive designs. He had so made Gothic construction his own, that he was now able to create within it fresh, original work.

In the mid-1880s Eidlitz undertook the reconstruction of Cooper Union in New York (1884–1885), and designed the Clergy House for Saint George's (1886–1888), a powerful conception whose carefully arranged windows give accurate account of its interior arrangement. This was his last commission of any size, and, standing close to the church which was his first, and its rectory, today provides a view of the development in architectural expressiveness that had taken place in his work over the forty years that separate them.

STEPHEN S. GARMEY

WORKS

1846–1848, Saint George's; 1847, Wooster Street Synagogue; New York. *1848, P. T. Barnum House, Bridgeport, Conn. 1849–1854, First Church of Christ, New London, Conn. *1851, Eidlitz Residence; *1851–1852, Fifth Avenue Presbyterian Church; 1851–1852, Saint George's Rectory; 1853–1855, Saint Peter's; New York. 1854, Willoughby House, Newport, R.I. *1854–1855, City Hall, Springfield, Mass. *1856–1857, Continental Bank, New York. 1856–1859, Second Congregational Church, Greenwich, Conn. *1857, American Exchange

Bank, New York. *c.1858, Hamilton Ferry House, Brooklyn, N.Y. *1858–1859, Broadway Tabernacle, New York. 1859–1867, Christ Church, St. Louis, Mo. *1860–1861, Brooklyn Academy of Music, N.Y. *1860–1861, Produce Exchange, New York. *1865, Masonic Temple, Troy, N.Y. *1866–1868, Temple Emanu-El (with Henry Fernbach); 1867–1868, Saint Peter's Chapel; New York. 1868–1870, Parish House and Church of the Pilgrims (additions); *1869, Brooklyn Union Building, Brooklyn, N.Y. *1870, Decker Building; *1870, 1875, Church of the Holy Trinity; *1872, Children's Aid Society, Newsboys' Lodging House; *1872, Saint George's Chapel; *1875, Dry Dock Savings Bank; New York. 1875–1885, State Capitol (with H. H. Richardson and Frederick Law Olmsted), Albany, N.Y. 1876–1878, "Tweed" Courthouse (south wing); 1886–1888, Saint George's Clergy House; 1884–1885, Cooper Union (reconstruction); *1890, Asylum, Ward's Island, N.Y. *1890, Asylum Buildings, Central Islip, N.Y.

BIBLIOGRAPHY

BROOKS, H. ALLEN 1955 "Leopold Eidlitz: 1823–1908." Unpublished M.A. thesis, Yale University, New Haven.

EIDLITZ, LEOPOLD 1858a "Christian Architecture." *Crayon* 5 2:53–55.

EIDLITZ, LEOPOLD 1858b *Crayon* 5 4:109–111. Eidlitz's speech at the first annual dinner of the American Institute of Architects.

EIDLITZ, LEOPOLD 1858c "On Style." *Crayon* 5 5:139–142.

EIDLITZ, LEOPOLD 1859a "Cast Iron and Architecture." *Crayon* 6 1:20–24.

EIDLITZ, LEOPOLD 1859b "The Architect." *Crayon* 6 3:99–100.

EIDLITZ, LEOPOLD 1859c *Crayon* 6 5:150–151.

EIDLITZ, LEOPOLD 1861 "On Aesthetics in Architecture." *Crayon* 8 4:89–91; 5:111–113.

EIDLITZ, LEOPOLD (1881)1977 *The Nature and Function of Art; More Especially of Architecture.* Reprint. New York: Da Capo.

EIDLITZ, LEOPOLD ("A. Foreman") 1887 *Big Wages and How to Earn Them.* New York: Harper.

EIDLITZ, LEOPOLD 1892 "The Vicissitudes of Architecture." *Architectural Record* 1, no. 4:471–484.

EIDLITZ, LEOPOLD 1894a "The Architect of Fashion." *Architectural Record* 3, no. 4:347–353.

EIDLITZ, LEOPOLD 1894b "Competitions—The Vicissitudes of Architecture." *Architectural Record* 4, no. 2:147–156.

EIDLITZ, LEOPOLD 1897 "The Educational Training of Architects." *Journal of the Royal Institute of British Architects* Series 3 4:213–217, 462–468.

EIDLITZ, LEOPOLD and SERRELL, JOHN W. 1870 *A Viaduct Railway for the City of New York.* New York.

ERDMANN, BIRUTA 1977 "Leopold Eidlitz's Architectural Theories and American Transcendentalism." Unpublished Ph.D. dissertation, University of Wisconsin, Madison.

LEVINE, NEIL A. 1967 "The Idea of Frank Furness' Buildings." Unpublished M.A. thesis, Yale University, New Haven.

McFARLAND, H. H. 1871 "History and Descriptive Sketch of the Church of the Pilgrims." *Congregational Quarterly,* Jan.

ROSEBERRY, CECIL R. 1964 *Capitol Story.* Albany: State of New York.

SCHUYLER, MONTGOMERY 1879 "The Capitol of New York." *Scribner's Monthly* 19, no. 2:161–178.

SCHUYLER, MONTGOMERY (1908)1961 Pages 136–187 in William H. Jordy and Ralph Coe (editors), *American Architecture and Other Writings.* Cambridge, Mass.: Belknap.

EIERMANN, EGON

Egon Eiermann (1904–1970) was a prominent German architect of the rationalist school. Born in Neuendorf near Berlin, he studied under HANS POELZIG at the Technische Hochschule in Berlin-Charlottenburg (1923–1927). He began his career working for the department store chain Karstadt and the Berlin electric utility company. In 1930, he established a private practice in Berlin, designing private residences in collaboration with Fritz Jaenecke. In 1936–1937, Eiermann worked on Hitler's exhibition and film, *Gebt mir vier Jahre Zeit,* and from 1936 on he designed the first of many administrative and production facilities for major corporations.

Accepting a professorship in Karlsruhe in 1947, Eiermann established private practice in that southwest German city. Most of his numerous corporate commissions of the 1950s and 1960s were carried out in collaboration with Robert Hilgers. Influenced by SKIDMORE, OWINGS, and MERRILL in the postwar years, Eiermann produced works that may be characterized as formalistic, mechanistic, expressive of a regular structural frame, and meticulously detailed. Among his widely published corporate designs were the Burda-Moden Warehouse in Offenburg (1953–1955) and the Neckermann Mail-Order Building in Frankfurt (1958–1961).

Eiermann built for international exhibitions, including an apartment block for the Interbau housing exhibition in Berlin (1957); but most noteworthy was his German Pavilion for the Brussels World's Fair in 1958 (with Sep Ruf). This steel-and-glass structure, with wrap-around balcony, was repeated in type in the Chancery of the German Embassy in Washington (1958–1964). The Kaiser Wilhelm Memorial Church in the heart of West Berlin (1957–1963) aroused comment and controversy. Retaining the bombed-out shell of the old, neo-Romanesque church tower, Eiermann chose to flank it with stark, mechanical-looking geometric prisms faced with countless, identical, perforated, precast-concrete squares, thus earning for the structure the popular epithet *die Eierkiste* (the egg crate).

An influential figure in Germany during the 1960s, Eiermann was frequently the center of controversy and was characterized by some as authoritarian and choleric. Three major high-rise structures of the decade were his Members' Building for the Bundestag in Bonn (1965–1969), the headquarters for IBM-Germany in Stuttgart-Vaihingen (1967–1972), and the administrative and development center for Olivetti-Germany in Frankfurt (1968–1972). Falling within the realm of international modernism, these buildings show a certain elegance and plasticity, a lightness and expression of structural function that give them a distinction among the glass boxes of the period.

Eiermann was dean of the faculty of architecture in Karlsruhe until his death. He was the recipient of numerous recognitions and awards.

RON WIEDENHOEFT

Eierman.
Kaiser Wilhelm Memorial Church.
Berlin.
1957–1963

WORKS

1929–1930, Berlin Electricity Company Transformer Station; 1931–1932, The Growing House (with Fritz Jaenecke); 1931–1942, Private Residences (with Jaenecke); 1934–1937, Grieneisen Undertakers Quarters; Berlin. 1936–1939, Foerstner AG (expansion), Apolda, Germany. 1937–1939, Dega AG Buildings, Berlin. 1939–1941, Märkische Metallbau GmbH Buildings, Oranienburg, Germany. 1948–1952, Ciba AG Buildings (with Robert Hilgers), Wehr, Germany. 1949–1951, Handkerchief Weaving Mill (with Hilgers), Blumberg, Germany. 1950–1953, Vereinigte Seidenweberei AG (with Hilgers), Krefeld, Germany. 1951, Merkur Store (with Hilgers), Heilbronn, Germany. 1951–1960, Merkur Store (with Hilgers), Stuttgart, Germany. 1951–1965, Experimental Generating Station (with Hilgers), Technische Hochschule, Karlsruhe, Germany. 1952, Merkur Store (with Hilgers), Reutlingen, Germany. 1952–1956, Matthaus Church (with Hilgers), Pforzheim, Germany. 1953–1955, Burda-Moden Buildings, Offenburg, Germany. 1954, German Section, Triennale Exhibition, Milan. 1955–1957, Volkshilfe Lebensversicherung AG Offices (with Hilgers), Cologne, Germany. 1956–1960, Essener Steinkohlenbergwerke AG Administration Building (with Hilgers), Essen, Germany. 1957, Apartment Block (with Hilgers), Interbau Housing Exhibition; 1957–1963, Kaiser Wilhelm Memorial Church; Berlin. *1958, German Pavilion (with Sep Ruf), Brussels World's Fair. 1958–1960, Hardenberg House (with George Ollich), Baden-Baden, Germany. 1958–1960, Horten Store (with Hilgers), Heidelberg, Germany. 1958–1961, Neckermann KG Mail Order Facilities (with Hilgers), Frankfurt. 1958–1961, Steel Works Administration Building (with Hilgers), Offenburg, Germany. 1958–1964, German Embassy Chancery (with Eberhard Brandl), Washington. 1959–1960, Egon Eiermann House, Baden Baden, Germany. 1961–1963, Dea-

Scholven Refinery (with Hilgers), Karlsruhe, Germany. 1965–1969, Bundestag Member's Building, Bonn. 1966–1968, Hochtief AG Office Building (stage 1), Frankfurt. 1967–1970, International Business Machines German Headquarters (not completed until 1972), Vaihingen, Stuttgart, Germany. 1968–1970, Olivetti German Administration and Development Center (not completed until 1972), Frankfurt.

BIBLIOGRAPHY

EIERMANN, EGON, and KUHLMANN, HEINZ 1967 *Planungsstudie Verwaltungsgebäude am Beispiel für die IBM-Deutschland.* Stuttgart, Germany: Krämer.
"Headquarters of IBM Germany." 1974 *Architecture & Urbanism* 4, no. 6:100–103.
"Headquarters of Olivetti Germany." 1974 *Architecture & Urbanism* 4, no. 6:91–99.
"The Olivetti Story." 1973 *Architecture Plus* 1, no. 8:21–61.
ROSENTHAL, H. WERNER 1971 "Egon Eiermann 1904–1970." *Journal of the Royal Institute of British Architects* 78, Jan.:41.

EIFFEL, GUSTAVE

Gustave Eiffel (1832–1923), creator of the 300 meter (967 foot) tower in Paris that bears his name, was born in Dijon, France. At the age of eighteen, he entered the Collège Sainte-Barbe in Paris in preparation for the Ecole Polytechnique. Failing its entrance examinations, he opted for the Ecole Centrale des Arts et Manufactures, initially following a course in chemistry but subsequently turning to a study of metal construction. Begin-

Eiffel.
Eiffel Tower.
Paris.
1887–1889

ning in 1856, he held a series of positions with firms constructing railroad equipment or engaged in building railroads themselves. At this time, he constructed his first metal bridge over the river Garonne near Bordeaux. In 1865, while supervising the delivery of locomotives to Egypt, he had an opportunity to observe the construction of the Suez Canal and, perhaps, to view the pyramids of Giza, whose lithic monumentality represented the absolute structural antithesis of his future skeletal masterpieces in iron and steel. Established as an independent consultant by 1864, he set up his own metal-working ateliers at Levalois-Perret, a Paris suburb, by 1876.

Eiffel built numerous bridges, chiefly for railroads, during the next two decades, working not only in France but throughout Europe, South America, and even in Indochina. He gradually developed a type of metal structure combining broad, gracefully arched spans of several hundred feet flanked by tall, spidery pylons. This formula was brought to perfection in the dramatic railroad viaduct over the Truyère at Garabit, 1885–1888, situated near Nîmes and not far from the famed Roman masonry-arched Pont du Gard of the first century A.D. Together, they form a dramatic pair, illustrating the contrasting engineering accomplishments of two powerful, technologically oriented civilizations. The 165 meter span of the arch over the Garabit, together with delicate, open volumes of the accompanying pylons point directly to the conception of the renowned tower that was planned as the central feature of the Paris International Exposition of 1889.

Previously, Eiffel had been involved as a consultant for the metal construction of two earlier Paris Exhibitions, those of 1867 and of 1878. His contribution in 1867 was of more than momentary importance, since for that structure he made a theoretical study of the elasticity of wrought iron so that an efficient design based upon unusually precise calculations resulted. In 1876, moreover, Eiffel had been associated with LOUIS-AUGUSTE BOILEAU and his son in the construction of the pioneering Paris department store Bon Marché, and in 1885 he had provided the internal skeleton for Bartholdi's Stature of Liberty when it was erected in New York harbor.

Eiffel's tower, for which Stephen Sauvestre provided the initial architectural conception and Maurice Koechlin and Emile Nougier the engineering calculations, was first conceived in 1884. However, an official competition, with over one hundred entries, was not held until 1886. Eiffel's reputation as a successful bridge builder led him to triumph over a number of intriguing if impractical schemes, not to mention the nonsensical ones that open competitions frequently invite. The foundations were begun on January 26, 1887. Once underway, the project provoked skepticism and scorn. Important opposition in the form of a petition against the tower's erection was signed by CHARLES GARNIER, the painters Bouguereau and Meissonier, the composer Gounod, and writers such as Dumas *fils* and de Maupassant. Evoking the biblical Tower of Babel, this document went on to castigate the tower "which even commercial America would not have" as "without a doubt the dishonor of Paris." In spite of this and other distractions the structure was successfully completed and opened to the public on May 15, 1889, almost if not exactly on time. By the time the Exhibition closed later that year, nearly two million people had visited the Eiffel Tower, attesting to its popular appeal.

Its success as an engineering and architectural venture was due to Eiffel's genius in producing a strong lightweight structure assembled from many small components. Because of its open, perforated form he was able to solve the problems of wind resistance that had been recognized as a special challenge for structures of this height. However, the tower's shape is not exclusively determined by engineering considerations. The conspicuous round arches that appear to bind together the four inclined pylons just below the first platform are a complete concession to form and design. They play no contributory role in the structural stability of the work, being suspended from above. These arches are evidence of a certain conventionality of contour that Eiffel must have felt necessary in order to make the tower acceptable to a broad and technically uninformed public.

Eiffel's career was subsequently marred by his association with the scandal surrounding Ferdinand de Lesseps's ill-starred Panama Canal venture, though he was finally cleared of wrongdoing upon judicial appeal in 1893. From this time until his death in 1923, Eiffel built nothing, even choosing to retire from his Levallois-Perret firm which had fabricated the structural parts of the tower. The remaining decades of his life were devoted to experiments, many of which were carried out in his private laboratory atop the tower and related to the future study of aerodynamics which the construction of the tower and its antecedent bridges had engendered in the first place.

JOHN JACOBUS

WORKS

1876, Bon Marché (with Louis-Auguste Boileau), Paris. 1877–1878, Maria Pia Bridge over the Douro, Oporto, Portugal. 1880–1884, Bridge over the Truyère, Garabit, France. 1884, Dome of the Observatory, Nice, France.

1885, Statue of Liberty (internal structure), New York. 1887–1889, Eiffel Tower, Paris.

BIBLIOGRAPHY

BESSET, MAURICE 1957 *Gustave Eiffel.* Paris: Hatier.
HARRISS, JOSEPH 1975 *The Tallest Tower: Eiffel and the Belle Epoque.* Boston: Houghton Mifflin.
PONCETTON, FRANÇOIS 1939 *Eiffel: Le magicien du fer.* Paris: Tournelle.
PRÉVOST, JEAN 1929 *Eiffel.* Paris: Reider.

EIGTVED, NIKOLAJ

Nikolaj Eigtved (1704–1754), whose name is also spelled Nicolai Eigtwedt and Niels Eigtved, was born in Eigtved, Denmark. In his youth, he traveled extensively across Europe studying architecture in Vienna, Rome, and Paris. He worked briefly in Warsaw and Dresden, Germany. He settled back in Copenhagen in 1735 and became one of the three most prominent architects in Denmark along with the German E. D. Hauser and his Danish counterpart Laurids de Thurah. Eigtved often collaborated with de Thurah; in 1750, they designed the Ledreborg Residens in Roskilde, Denmark. From 1751 until his death in 1754, Eigtved directed the Academy of Arts in Copenhagen.

Following his travels, Eigtved became court architect to Frederik V and was largely responsible for the rebuilding of Copenhagen on a grand and heroic scale. Specifically, he was commissioned with the entire renovation of the Frederiksstaden quarter, the focal point of which was the octagonally shaped Amalienborg Square and its surrounding palaces (1750–1754).

In addition, Eigtved designed many private residences in Copenhagen as well as the Royal Theater (1750) and the Frederik Hospital (1752) founded by Frederik V. He also designed the Christians Kirke (1755–1756) in Copenhagen and the bridge and entrance pavilions of the Christiansborg Palace (1755–1756) in Copenhagen.

PETER L. DONHAUSER

WORKS

1750, Ledreborg Residens (with Laurids de Thurah), Roskilde, Denmark. *1750s, Royal Theater; 1750–1754, Amalienborg Square (and surrounding palaces); *1755–1756, Christiansborg Palace (interior), Copenhagen.

BIBLIOGRAPHY

NORBERG-SCHULZ, CHRISTIAN 1974 Pages 38–39, 46, 344, 385 in *Late Baroque and Rococo Architecture.* New York: Abrams.
VOSS, KNUD 1971 *Arkitekten Nicolai Eigtved: 1701–1754.* Copenhagen: Busck.

EISENLOHR, LUDWIG

Ludwig Eisenlohr (1851–?) was an architect prominent in southwest Germany before World War I. Born in Nürtingen near Stuttgart, he studied architecture in Stuttgart and Berlin, developing a style of historical classicism in a variety of public buildings for Stuttgart and surrounding cities and in a great number of private houses and villas. Eisenlohr was associated in practice originally with C. Weigle and from 1909 with Oskar Pfennig. In his later works, under the influence of THEODOR FISCHER, he reduced the overt historicism and tended toward an expression of simple tectonic form, especially the well-crafted bearing wall of stone masonry.

RON WIEDENHOEFT

EISENMANN, JOHN

John Eisenmann (1851–1924), in collaboration with George H. Smith, designed the Cleveland Arcade (1888–1890). This dramatic complex consists of two nine-story Romanesque office buildings, with Richardsonian (see H. H. RICHARDSON) entrance arches. They are joined by a five-story skylighted arcade whose open truss and tiered galleries boldly demonstrate innovations in iron and steel construction.

GWEN W. STEEGE

WORK

1888–1890, Cleveland Arcade, Ohio.

BIBLIOGRAPHY

HUXTABLE, ADA LOUISE 1956 "Progressive Architecture in America: The Cleveland Arcade." *Progressive Architecture* 37:139–140.
SCHOFIELD, MARY-PEALE 1966 "The Cleveland Arcade." *Journal of the Society of Architectural Historians* 25:281–291.
SCHOFIELD, MARY-PEALE 1967 "Cleveland Arcade." *Architectural Forum* 127:60–65.

EISLER, OTTO

Otto Eisler (1893–1968) was a Czech architect who since 1923 worked in Brno. Most of his designs were intended for the building enterprise of his brothers, Arthur and Mořic Eisler, who also built the Tugendhat Villa designed by LUDWIG MIES VAN DER ROHE. Eisler's work shows the influence of two architectural schools: the Vienna school, represented by cubic volumes and the role of plain nonarticulated surfaces, and the Berlin school with its elegant proportions of window and door recesses, with houses opening to gardens. Eisler used exotic and rare plants. Well known is the "House of Two Brothers" designed as a residence for him and his brother Mořic. During World War II, Eisler lived in exile in Norway and spent some time in concentration camps. After the war, he directed his attention primarily to garden architecture. He designed Brno Zoological Garden (1953), as well as gardens for a number of hospitals designed by his friend, BEDŘICH ROZEHNAL.

VLADIMÍR ŠLAPETA

WORKS

1925–1939, Houses, Shops, Apartments; 1930, Otto Eisler Residence, Pisaiky; 1946–1953, Hospital Garden, Černá pole; Brno, Czechoslovakia. 1946–1953, Hospital Garden, Dačice, Czechoslovakia. 1946–1953, Hospital Garden, Kyjov, Czechoslovakia. 1953, Brno Zoological Garden; Brno, Czechoslovakia.

BIBLIOGRAPHY

"Büro- und Geschäftshäuser in der Tschecho-Slowakei." 1930 *Bauwelt* 21, no. 19:1–18.

EISLER, MAX 1930 "Otto Eisler, Brünn, Verwaltungsgebäude des Phönix und Miethaus in Brünn." *Moderne Bauformen* 29:304–306.

EISLER, MAX 1932 "Ein Wohnhaus für zwei Junggesellen." *Moderne Bauformen* 31:261–263.

HITCHCOCK, H. R., and JOHNSON, PHILIP (1932)1966 *The International Style: Architecture Since 1922.* 2d ed. New York: Norton.

"Neue Wohnhäuser in der Tschechoslowakei." 1930 *Baumeister* 28:142–149.

ŠLAPETA, VLADIMÍR 1978 "Otto Eisler." *Československý architekt* 24, no. 17:2.

ELDEM, SEDAT HAKKI

Sedat Hakki Eldem (1908–) is the most renowned and prolific architect of Republican Turkey. Belonging to a wealthy and upper class family, he had a completely Western education in his childhood, partly in European countries, and graduated from the Academy of Fine Arts in Istanbul in 1928. He met and was influenced by AUGUSTE PERRET and LE CORBUSIER and spent two years in Berlin. In 1931, he became an assistant professor at the Academy. From that time until the 1960s, his social standing, talent, and position in the Academy made him one of the most authoritative voices in the development of architectural styles in Turkey.

In the early 1930s, going against the Beaux-Arts tradition still strong in the schools and in practice, he was, with a small number of other architects, a proponent of early functionalism, which was strongly expressed in his building for the SATIE (1934), the Administration of Electricity, and, although stylistically less characteristic, in his General Directorate of Customs and Monopoly in Ankara (1937–1938).

However, the influence of European nationalism in the postwar period and the strongly nationalistic atmosphere of the early Republic strengthened his tendency toward a nationalistic style, which became dogma in education in the late 1930s and lasted until the early 1950s. Eldem has been interested in the history of vernacular architecture throughout his teaching and professional life, particularly in the palaces and houses of the late Ottoman period. He was a diligent connoisseur of the late Domestic architecture, and the study of Turkish houses and palaces became a major prerequisite for his students. Thus during the 1940s, elements of classical Ottoman architecture became common themes of design in his hands and those of his followers. Buildings such as the Faculty of Literature and Sciences of the University of Istanbul and the Faculty of Sciences of the University of Ankara, built in collaboration with Emin Onat, are characterized by this historicist monumentalism and away from his short-lived functionalism. For example, his project for the mausoleum of Kemal Atatürk in Ankara was rather a variation of a Seljuk tomb tower.

Eldem built a series of houses in Istanbul practically imitating plans of old Turkish houses but giving to their exterior a modern touch with the use of concrete structure and a functionalist geometry. His most direct and rather well-received attempt for a complete revival of an old scheme was the Café House of Taslik in Istanbul (1948), a replica of the old reception room of the Grandvizir Köprülü Hüseyin Pasha's mansion on the Bosphorus.

After 1950, however, Eldem reached another stage in his style: he tried to integrate the functionalist vocabulary and the basic elements of the traditional vernacular with a delicate sense of balance, but structural expression—which according to him comes from Perret—remained preponderant. This period started with the winning project of the Palace of Justice in Istanbul (1950), in collaboration with Onat. Eldem also was partly responsible for the final design of the Istanbul Hilton (1955) by SKIDMORE, OWINGS, AND MERRILL.

Among the well-known examples of his later work are the Social Security Complex at Zeyrek (1962–1964), Akbank at Findikli (1971), both in Istanbul; the embassies of Pakistan (1960s), India (1960s), and the Netherlands (1960s) in Ankara; and more recently, the strongly formalistic design of Koç Library in Istanbul (1972–1974).

For Eldem, creation of a modern national style remained a supreme goal, which led him to emphasize form rather than function in his design. He has always remained a sensitive designer of façades and details.

Since his retirement in 1978, he has been publishing materials on Turkish traditional domestic architecture.

DOĞAN KUBAN

WORKS

*1934, SATIE Building; 1937–1938, General Directorate of Customs and Monopolies; Ankara. 1940s, Faculty of Literature and Sciences (with Emin Onat), University of Istanbul, Turkey. 1940s, Faculty of Sciences (with Onat), University of Ankara. 1948, Café House of Taslik; 1955, Istanbul Hilton (with Skidmore, Owings, and Merrill); Istanbul, Turkey. 1960s, Embassy of India; 1960s, Embassy of the Netherlands; 1960s, Embassy of Pakistan; Ankara. 1962–1964, Social Security Complex, Zeyrek, Turkey. 1971, Akbank, Findikli, Turkey. 1972–1974, Koç Library, Istanbul, Turkey.

BIBLIOGRAPHY

ASLANOĞLU INCORPORATED 1923–1938 *Erken Cumhuriyet Dönemi Mimarliği.* n. p.

CEZAR, M. (editor) 1973 *Devlet Güel Sanatlar Akademisinin 90 Yılı: 1883–1973.* Istanbul, Turkey.

ELDEM, SEDAT HAKKI 1939 "Millî Mimari Meselesi." *Arkitekt* 9, nos. 9–10:220–223.

ELDEM, SEDAT HAKKI 1940 "Yerli Mimariye Doğru." *Arkitekt* 10, nos. 3–4:69–74.

ELDEM, SEDAT HAKKI 1978 "Toward a Local Idiom: A Summary History of Contemporary Architecture in Turkey." Pages 89–99 in *Conservation as Cultural Service.* Istanbul, Turkey.

SOZEN, METIN, and TAPAN, METE 1973 *Elli Yılın Türk Mimarisi.* Istanbul, Turkey: Türkiye Is Bankasi.

ELLIS, HARVEY

Although the architectural designs of Harvey Ellis (1852–1904) are inventive manifestations of numerous styles prevalent in the United States during the late nineteenth and early twentieth centuries, his particular place in architectural history rests on his seminally important perspective renderings, which were published in *American Architect and Building News* and *Northwestern Architect* during his lifetime and in *Architectural Review* and *Western Architect* during the first decade after his death.

Born in Rochester, New York, Ellis had neither much formal education beyond high school nor much office apprenticeship before joining his brother Charles in an architectural partnership which lasted from 1879 to 1885. Seemingly, he simply drifted into this association as he would continue to drift in and out of other professional architectural situations for the rest of his life. These were years of expansion for Rochester, and the firm, with Harvey in charge of design, produced a large number of buildings ranging from the Alexander B. Lamberton House (1883), modeled on the Queen Anne work of R. NORMAN SHAW, to the Richardsonian (see H. H. RICHARDSON) Romanesque United States Court House and Post Office Building (1885–1890). During these years Ellis was also an active member of the Rochester Art Club contributing numerous watercolors and drawings of conservative, realistic vein to its annual exhibitions. Only when one keeps in mind his love of drawing and painting as well as his casual approach to the architectural profession, can his mature work be fully understood.

The first phase of his career ended in 1885 when Charles was charged with bribery in attempting to secure a public commission. Harvey, after catapulting to national fame in the same year with his published competition design for a monument to General Grant, left Rochester to wander and work for a decade, mainly in the Midwest, as a designer and delineator of imaginative residential and commercial buildings for other architects. His work for Leroy Sunderland Buffington of Minneapolis, Minnesota, and Eckel and Mann of St. Joseph and St. Louis, Missouri, is particularly noteworthy.

Although he varied specific styles from one project to another, his designs exhibit certain basic similarities—irregular silhouettes, steeply pitched roofs, windows grouped in horizontal or vertical units, sheltered entrances, and a rich variety of surface textures deriving from both material and ornamentation. During this period, Ellis randomly and eclectically combined and simultaneously reworked motifs from the Victorian Gothic, the Shingle style, the Richardsonian Romanesque, the Scottish Baronial, the Châteauesque, and even, after 1891, the Beaux Arts styles. Each style and even each specific stylistic motif was subjected to his imaginative interpretation and, dominating the whole synthesizing creative process was the sensitive, romantic, pictorial vision of an artist.

As a delineator, Ellis typifies the architect's artist whose job was to produce beautiful perspective renderings for presentation or publication. Many of these renderings were pictures of buildings never intended to be built. In spite of erratic personal conduct caused by alcoholism, Ellis's design and rendering virtuosity kept him in steady demand in the Midwest, and during these years nearly two dozen of his signed pen and ink renderings were published.

Although the perspective renderings of Ellis and his emulators long have been admired, their architectural designs often have been judged undisciplined paraphrases or unfortunate misunderstandings of the mature style of H. H. Richardson. A more sympathetic view is that these designers had different, neo-Picturesque goals in mind.

By 1895, Ellis, by then a reformed alcoholic, had returned to Rochester, and for the next seven years he occasionally designed buildings for his brother and other local architects. However, during this phase of his life he mainly produced commercial designs for posters, magazine covers, book plates, stained glass, and furniture. Stylistically, his artistic work had become moderately avant-garde showing the influence of non-illusionistic modes. In 1902, Gustav Stickley recruited Ellis as the editor for *The Craftsman* magazine, a position he held until his death. He also designed unusually elegant furniture for The Craftsman Workshops which influenced Stickley and others.

EILEEN MANNING MICHELS

WORKS

1883, Alexander B. Lamberton House (with Charles Ellis); 1885–1890, United States Courthouse and Post Office Building; Rochester, N.Y. 1887–1889, Pillsbury Hall, University of Minnesota; *1888, Samuel C. Gale House; Minneapolis, Minn.

BIBLIOGRAPHY

Many articles written by Harvey Ellis appeared in The Craftsman *from 1903 to 1904. Many plates of Ellis's pen and ink renderings appeared in* Western Architect *from 1912 to 1913.*

BRAGDON, CLAUDE 1897 "Harvey Ellis." *Brochure Series of Architectural Illustration* 3:139–146.

CHRISTISON, MURIEL 1944 "How Buffington Staked His Claim." *Art Bulletin* 26, no. 1:13–24.

"Competition Design for a Memorial to General Grant." 1885 *American Architect and Building News* 28, supplement.

GARDEN, HUGH M. G. 1908 "Harvey Ellis, Designer and Draughtsman." *Architectural Review* 15:184–188.

KENNEDY, ROGER G. 1966 "The Long Shadow of Harvey Ellis." *Minnesota History* Fall:97–108.

KENNEDY, ROGER G. 1968 "Long, Dark Corridors: Harvey Ellis." *Prairie School Review* 5, nos. 1–2:5–18.

MANNING, EILEEN 1953 "The Architectural Designs of Harvey Ellis." Unpublished M.A. thesis, University of Minnesota, Minneapolis.

MEMORIAL ART GALLERY OF THE UNIVERSITY OF ROCHESTER, and MARGARET WOODBURY STRONG MUSEUM 1972 *A Rediscovery—Harvey Ellis: Artist, Architect.* Rochester, N.Y.

"A Revival of Pen and Ink Rendering: The Work of Harvey Ellis." 1912 *Western Architect* 18:36–37.

SWALES, FRANCES 1924 "Master Draughtsman, III: Harvey Ellis, 1852–1907 (sic)." *Pencil Points* 7, July:49–55, 79.

TSELOS, DIMITRI 1944 "The Enigma of Buffington's Skyscraper." *Art Bulletin* 26, no.1:3–12.

ELLIS, PETER

Peter Ellis (1804–1884), a relatively obscure figure, has become well known in recent years for his radical functionalist designs for office buildings in Liverpool, the city where he practiced. Oriel Chambers (1864), with a cast-iron frame, shallow brick arched floors modeled on earlier warehouses, and uncompromising elevations, broke away from the current neoclassical British tradition for commercial buildings and foreshadowed the Modern movement. The building at 16 Cork Street (1866) continues this idea; its courtyard elevations are remarkable, particularly the cantilevered spiral staircase. Ellis received adverse contemporary criticism for his work and it may be because of this that he appears to have practiced subsequently more as a civil engineer. No other buildings by him have been authenticated.

J. N. TARN

WORKS

1864, Oriel Chambers Office Building, Water Street; 1866, Office Building, 16 Cork Street; Liverpool, England.

BIBLIOGRAPHY

HITCHCOCK, H. R. (1958)1977 *Architecture: Nineteenth and Twentieth Centuries.* 4th ed. Baltimore: Penguin.

HUGHES, JAMES QUENTIN 1964 *Seaport.* London: Lund Humphries.

PEVSNER, NIKOLAUS 1969 *The Buildings of England: Lancashire: The Industrial and Commercial South.* Harmondsworth, England: Penguin.

ELMES, HARVEY LONSDALE

One of the most talented British neoclassical architects, Harvey Lonsdale Elmes (1814–1847) studied first with his father, James Elmes, and from 1831 at the Royal Academy. Between 1834 and 1837, he assisted Henry E. Goodridge and his father. He won the 1839 and 1840 competitions for Saint George's Hall, Liverpool, begun 1841. In poor health, he was twice forced to relinquish the commission, first in 1842 when he toured Belgium and Germany, and again in 1847, traveling to Jamaica, where he died.

R. WINDSOR LISCOMBE

WORKS

1840–1851, Saint George's Hall and Assize Courts (structure completed 1847–1851 by R. Rawlinson, and interior, 1851–1854, by CHARLES R. COCKERELL); 1840–1843, The Collegiate Institution; Liverpool, England. 1845, Raby Hall, Birkenhead, England. 1845, Redcliffe Villa, New Brighton, England. 1846?–1847,

Thingwall Hall (now Saint Edward's Orphanage), Knotty Ash, near Liverpool, England. *1847?, Allerton Tower, Lancashire, England. 1847–1851, Lancashire County Lunatic Asylum (executed by W. Moseley), Rainhill, England.

BIBLIOGRAPHY
BAYLEY, STEPHEN 1975 "A British Schinkel." *Architectural Association Quarterly* 7, no. 2:28–32.
HUGHES, QUENTIN 1964 Pages 96–102 in *Seaport: Architecture & Townscape in Liverpool.* London: Lund Humphries.
HUGHES, QUENTIN 1973 "Neo-Classical Ideas and Practice: St. George's Hall, Liverpool, by Harvey Lonsdale Elmes." *Architectural Association Quarterly* 5, no. 2:36–44.
JONES, RONALD P. 1904 "The Life and Work of Harvey Lonsdale Elmes." *Architectural Review* 15:230–245.
KILPIN, J. T. 1869 "The Late Mr. Elmes and St. George's Hall." *Transactions of the Historic Society of Lancashire and Cheshire* New Series 9.
TANNER, J. A. 1917 "A Contemporary Account of St. George's Hall." *Architectural Review* 41:122–125.
WAINWRIGHT, DAVID 1959 "Elmes." *Architectural Review* 125:349–350.
WATKIN, DAVID 1974 Pages 237–240 in *The Life and Work of C. R. Cockerell.* London: Zwemmer.

ELMSLIE, WILLIAM C.

See PURCELL and ELMSLIE.

ELSAESSER, MARTIN

Martin Elsaesser (1884–1957) was a prominent architect and educator in Germany of the 1920s and 1950s. Born in Tübingen, he was of the same generation as WALTER GROPIUS, LUDWIG MIES VAN DER ROHE, and BRUNO TAUT, and achieved success already before World War I. A pupil of THEODOR FISCHER and PAUL BONATZ in Stuttgart, Elsaesser developed in his architecture the link between traditional styles and expression of social stratification in the prewar era and the *Sachlichkeit,* economic constraints, and social consciousness of the Weimar period. Many of his buildings are characterized by pitched roofs, simple tectonic form, and the rich color and texture of brick.

Elsaesser began his career as an educator early. An assistant at the Stuttgart Technische Hochschule (1907–1912), he lectured there from 1912 to 1920, became professor and director of the Kunstgewerbeschule in Cologne in 1920, whence he was called in 1925 to become simultaneously building director of the city of Frankfurt and professor of the Kunstgewerbeschule there. He left Germany to work in Ankara, Turkey, during the 1930s, and in 1947 returned to become professor of design at the Technische Hochschule in Munich, where he remained until his death. His principles were published as *Einführung in das Entwerfen* (1950) and *Wohnung und Lebensgefühl* (1955).

In 1933, a substantial book of Elsaesser's designs and commissions from the period 1924–1932 was published. Included in the impressive array are villas, schools, Protestant churches, swimming pools, hospitals, and other buildings for the public sector. Among the most important of these was the large Central Market of Frankfurt, a spacious reinforced shell construction.

Late in life, Elsaesser contributed articles on schools, universities, kindergartens, and youth hostels to the *Handbuch der modernen Architektur* (1957).

RON WIEDENHOEFT

EMBERTON, JOSEPH

Joseph Emberton (1889–1956) was born in Audley, Staffordshire. He won a scholarship to the Royal College of Art in London. World War I took him to Egypt where he was influenced by Suleiman architecture as is evident from his work at the British Empire Exhibition (1924–1925). His enthusiasm for the logic and exact science of the artillery led to an architecture of logic and reason. His Royal Corinthian Yacht Club (1930–1931), a steel-framed structure on a reinforced concrete base, was shown at the International Style Exhibition in 1932. Simpson's Store (1936), Piccadilly, London, which has a pioneer welded steel frame, is ornamented with colored light. The travertine stair and Mendelsohnian (see ERIC MENDELSOHN) light fitting reappear at the H.M.V. Store, Oxford Street, London (1939) and at Blackpool Casino (1939).

ROSEMARY IND

WORKS

*1924–1925, Lion Kiosk; Nobel Hall; State Express House; Main Avenue Kiosk; and Lakeside Kiosk; British Empire Exhibition (with P. J. Westwood), Wembley, England. 1925–1926, House, Weybridge, Surrey, England. *1928, Madelon Chaumet Shop, Berkeley Street; 1929–1930, Olympia, Hammersmith Road; London. 1930–1931, Royal Corinthian Yacht Club, Burnham on Crouch, Essex, England. 1934–1950, Blackpool Pleasure Beach, England. 1936, Simpson's Store, Piccadilly; 1939, Blackpool Casino; 1939, H.M.V. Store, Oxford Street; London.

BIBLIOGRAPHY
IND, ROSEMARY 1976 "The Architecture of Pleasure:

Joseph Emberton's Work at Blackpool." *Architectural Association Quarterly* 8, no. 3:51–59.

IND, ROSEMARY 1982–1983 *Joseph Emberton.* London: Scolar. Forthcoming publication.

REILLY, CHARLES H. 1931 "Some Younger Architects of Today: Joseph Emberton." *Building* Aug.:348–356.

EMERSON, WILLIAM RALPH

William Ralph Emerson (1833–1917) was an important figure in the development of late nineteenth-century American domestic architecture. Although his career spanned more than fifty years, its most characteristic phase was the period of the late 1870s and 1880s, when he was one of the earliest and finest designers of Shingle style country and suburban houses.

Emerson was born in Alton, Illinois, where his father, William Samuel, a native of Maine and distant cousin of Ralph Waldo Emerson, had gone to speculate in land. His boyhood was spent in Kennebunk, Maine, and in Boston, where he lived with his uncle, the educator and botanist, George Barrell Emerson. After leaving the Boston public schools, Emerson worked for Jonathan Preston, a local builder. He was in partnership with Preston from 1857 to 1861, with Carl Fehmer from 1864 to 1873. He practiced alone in 1862–1863 and from 1874 to 1909. Around 1880, his draftsmen included Albert Winslow Cobb, later partner of JOHN CALVIN STEVENS. Emerson was a charter member of the Boston Society of Architects.

Little is known of Emerson's earliest work. The M. H. Sanford House in Newport, Rhode Island

Emerson.
Charles G. Loring House.
Pride's Crossing,
Massachusetts.
1881

(1869–1870), a mansard-roofed house with fine stencilled decoration on the interior, is an important commission by Emerson and Fehmer.

In 1873 Emerson married Sylvia Hathaway Watson of Milton, Massachusetts. He eventually designed more than twenty buildings for Milton clients, including the Misses Forbes House (1876), a Stick-style masterpiece, and the William Ellery Channing Eustis House (1878), a large masonry dwelling with Queen Anne details, a dramatic stairhall and an impressive open plan. Clusters of important Emerson buildings are also found in the resort communities of Bar Harbor, Maine, and the north shore of Massachusetts.

Historians have considered Emerson one of the inventors of the Shingle style, a short lived but uniquely American domestic idiom. It was he who designed the first completely shingled house of the 1870s, without the first floor of clapboards, brick or stone characteristic of the English-inspired Queen Anne: the C. J. Morrill House in Bar Harbor (1879).

Emerson became one of the most popular domestic architects in the northeast. His work was increasingly marked by open plans and imaginative treatment of interior space, by a feeling for materials and a playful and unpedantic use of both Queen Anne and Colonial Revival detail. He was exceptionally sensitive to natural surroundings, siting his buildings carefully and placing windows to frame important views. Perhaps the quintessential Emerson building of the early 1880s is the General Charles G. Loring House (1881) in Pride's Crossing, Massachusetts. Perched on a crag overlooking the sea, this free-form, shingle and stone house with its piazzas and window seats embodies the exuberance of Emerson's best work.

The prevailing academicism of the 1890s was foreign to Emerson's temperament. Although his later buildings are always well designed, they lack his earlier inventiveness. Emerson's last great building may well have been the gambrel-roofed, shingled house (1886) in Milton that he designed for himself.

CYNTHIA ZAITZEVSKY

WORKS

1869–1870, M. H. Sanford House, Newport, R.I. 1876, Frances Cornelia and Margaret Perkins Forbes House; 1878, William Ellery Channing Eustis House; Milton, Mass. 1879, C. J. Morrill House, Bar Harbor, Maine. *1880, Colonel Robert H. Stevenson House, Stable, and Coachman's House, Milton, Mass. *1880–1881, Church of Saint Sylvia, Bar Harbor, Maine. 1880–1881, Alexander Cochrane House; 1881, General Charles G. Loring House; Pride's Crossing, Mass. *1881, R. B. Scott House, Bar Harbor, Maine. 1881–1882, Boston Art Club. 1882–1883, Augustus Hemenway House, Canton, Mass. 1883, Mary Hemenway House, Manchester-by-the-Sea, Mass. 1886, William Ralph Emerson House, Milton, Mass. *1888, William Caleb Loring House, Pride's Crossing, Mass. 1893, Thomas Bailey Aldrich House, Tenant's Harbor, Maine. 1896, Frederick Law Olmsted House, Deer Isle, Maine.

BIBLIOGRAPHY

SCULLY, VINCENT J., JR. (1955)1971 *The Shingle Style and the Stick Style*. Rev. ed. New Haven: Yale University Press.

SCULLY, VINCENT, J., JR. 1970 "American Houses: Thomas Jefferson to Frank Lloyd Wright." Pages 163–209 in Edgar Kaufmann, Jr. (editor), *The Rise of an American Architecture*. New York: Praeger.

ZAITZEVSKY, CYNTHIA 1969 *The Architecture of William Ralph Emerson, 1833–1917*. Cambridge, Mass.: Fogg Art Museum.

EMMETT, JOHN T.

John T. Emmett (1828–1898) was the author of a series of articles attacking, with sensational effect, the architecture of mid-Victorian England. In "The State of English Architecture" (1872), he pilloried the leading Gothic Revivalists as purveyors of "art-manufactured gee-gaws" and lashed the "childish sensuality of the public, the professional vanity of the clergy and the vulgar luxury of the rich." The ideas in Emmett's explosive journalism derived mainly from JOHN RUSKIN; he believed that true architecture could come only from the hands of the honest working craftsman. His own buildings, all antedating his written works, were mild transcriptions of fourteenth-century English Gothic, which he held to be the only valid basis for a modern English architecture. They included a few churches and New College, Finchley Road, London (1851).

JOHN SUMMERSON

BIBLIOGRAPHY

EMMETT, J. T. 1867 "Courts of Justice Commission: Instructions for the Competing Architect." *Quarterly Review* 123:93–118.

EMMETT, J. T. 1872 "The State of English Architecture." *Quarterly Review* 132:295–335. This article is reprinted in *Six Essays*.

EMMETT, J. T. (1891)1972 *Six Essays*. Reprint edition edited with an introduction by J. Mordaunt Crook. New York: Johnson.

ENDELL, AUGUST

August Endell (1871–1924) was an architect, theorist, and Arts and Crafts designer active in Germany. His works clarify some of the ways in which *Jugendstil* and *Kunstgewerbe* (Arts and Crafts) ideals contributed to the development of modern architecture during a period of stylistic diversity and change. As with many other contemporary artists, the range of Endell's Arts and Crafts designs was extensive and included furniture, fabrics, carpets, and jewelry. He was one of a circle of artists associated with the Vereinigte Werkstätten für Kunst im Handwerk founded in Munich in 1897. Designs of his were included in the famous 1897 international art exhibition at the Munich Glaspalast along with items by HERMANN OBRIST, RICHARD RIEMERSCHMID, Bernhard Pankok, BRUNO PAUL, Otto Eckmann, and PETER BEHRENS. He was also represented in the equally significant 1899 exhibition of the Munich Secession (founded in 1892). Endell's first architectural work, the Elvira Photographic Studio in Munich (1896–1897) embodied his ideas on the empathetic potential of artistic forms. His later architectural works, although perceptibly different from those of his *Jugendstil* period, continued to manifest many of his early theoretical ideas.

Endell was born in Berlin, the son of Karl Friedrich Endell, a municipal architect. Endell studied philosophy, psychology, and aesthetics, first at Tübingen and after 1892 in Munich under Theodor Lipps, whose ideas on empathy were to become the core of Endell's architectural theory. In Munich, he encountered Obrist through whom he was introduced to other members of the Arts and Crafts circle. Endell's first publication on aesthetics was a pamphlet, *Um die Schönheit* (1896), in which he called upon the reader to yield to the emotional content of art rather than to rely upon intellect alone. Principles of beauty, he suggested, were to be found in nature's forms and colors and especially in flowers (the orchid was the symbol of the pamphlet). Through contemplation of nature one could broaden and refine artistic feelings and creativity.

Endell's theories on perception and the psychology of art, elaborated in three articles between 1897 and 1900, were the basis for his design of the Elvira Studio. The project, involving the renovation of an existing building, transformed wall surfaces essentially through systems of ornament and proportion. Consonant with Endell's derivations of empathy theory, the studio consisted of linear configurations wherein length and thickness of line, directional thrust, frequency of occurrence, and geometric shape established varied eurythmic patterns, tempos, and tensions. On the façade, one of the popular images of the Art Nouveau, Endell's sober theoretical aims were seemingly overshadowed by a delightful yet bizarre composition. Above an asymmetrical arrangement of entrance and windows was a smooth wall expanse over which swarmed stucco reliefs of small marine forms and a giant wave-creature colored in strident tones of turquoise and red. On the interior, spatial effects were expressed through those factors important to Endell—the proportional relationship of planes and lines; the size, shape, and placement of apertures; and ornament of changing form and scale employed to enliven space by accenting intervals, junctures, and terminals. Endell shared with other architects and Arts and Crafts designers of the time a desire to control all aspects of an interior in order to achieve a coherent effect and a unified movement of forms.

In 1901, Endell returned to Berlin, and in the following years he developed a successful practice. His decorative schemes for Ernst von Wotzogen's Buntes Theater (1901) and cabaret revue of that year was the ultimate realization of his ideas on controlled interior design. Endell brought renewed focus to his beliefs in what is probably his most important publication, *Die Schönheit der grossen Stadt* of 1908. Influenced by his mentor, Obrist, he called for a sensitivity to the "spiritual" essence underlying the material world and spoke of the bounding and vivifying of space as the true music of architecture. His role within the Deutscher Werkbund, of which he was a charter member, was a central one. In the famous 1914 controversy over the issue of standardization presented by HERMANN MUTHESIUS versus individualism presented by HENRY VAN DE VELDE, he vociferously supported the latter position, rejecting the notion of a homogeneous cultural style and calling for artists to be assured equal status with the manufacturers of their designs. After the war, in 1918, Endell was appointed director of the Breslau Academy of Art and held that post until the year of his death. Endell's entire career, and not the early works alone, reflects his pursuit of what he believed to be the far-reaching poetic possibilities of architecture and design.

EUGENE A. SANTOMASSO

WORKS

*1896–1897, Elvira Photographic Studio, Munich. 1898, Sanatorium, Wyk auf Föhr, Germany. 1901, Buntes Theater; 1904, Schule für Formkunst; 1905–1906, Neumannsche Festival Hall; 1906–1907, Apartment House, 32 Kastanienallee, Westend; 1908, Apartment House, 17 Eichenallee, Westend; 1909, Salamander Shops (interiors), Westend; 1910–1911, Apartment House Kühl, 14 Akazienallee, Westend; 1912–1913, Racetrack, Mariendorf; Berlin. 1914, Railway Dining Car, Werkbund Exposition, Cologne, Germany.

BIBLIOGRAPHY

ENDELL, AUGUST 1896 *Um die Schönheit: Eine Paraphrase über die Münchener Kunstausstellung in 1896.* Munich: Franke.
ENDELL, AUGUST 1897–1898 "Möglichkeit und Ziele einer neuen Architektur." *Deutsche Kunst und Dekoration* 1:141–153.
ENDELL, AUGUST (1898)1975 "Formenschönheit und dekorative Kunst." Pages 20–26 in Tim Benton, Charlotte Benton, and Dennis Sharp (editors), *Architecture and Design: 1890–1939.* New York: Whitney Library of Design.
ENDELL, AUGUST 1900 "Architektonische Erstlinge." *Die Kunst* 2:297–317.
ENDELL, AUGUST 1908 *Die Schönheit der grossen Stadt.* Stuttgart, Germany.
FUCHS, GEORG 1901–1902a "Das 'Bunte Theater' von August Endell." *Deutsche Kunst und Dekoration* 9:275–289.
FUCHS, GEORG 1901–1902b "Originalität und Tradition." *Deutsche Kunst und Dekoration* 9:290–296.
HEUSS, THEODOR 1918 *Das Haus der Freundschaft in Konstantinopel: Ein Wettbewerb Deutscher Architekten.* Munich: Bruckmann.
KILLY, HERTA ELISABETH; PFANKUCH, PETER; and SCHEPER, DIRK 1965 *Poelzig-Endell-Moll und die Breslauer Kunstakademie: 1911–1932.* Berlin: Akademie der Künste. Exhibition catalogue.
WEISS, PEG 1979 Pages 34–40 in *Kadinsky in Munich: The Formative Jugendstil Years.* N.J.: Princeton University Press.

ENGEL, CARL LUDWIG

Although Carl Ludwig Engel's (1778–1840) career was almost wholly spent in Finland, where he did most to establish the neoclassical style that dominated Finnish architecture for a hundred years, he was a German, not a Finn, and acquired his mastery of the neoclassical language in Russia.

Born in Charlottenburg, Berlin, and trained at the Berlin Institute of Architecture under the influential neoclassicist FRIEDRICH GILLY, Engel served briefly as town architect of Tallinn, Estonia, before moving to Petersburg. In 1812, on a visit to Finland, he met Johan Albrekt Ehrenström, the aristocrat and amateur of the arts responsible for drawing up a town plan for Helsinki. Chosen by the Russians—who in 1809 had become the rulers of Finland—as the grand-duchy's new capital in place of the ancient capital Turku, it had been largely destroyed by fire the previous year. Impressed by Engel's talent, Ehrenström persuaded Czar Alexander I to appoint him architect for the reconstruction of the city.

Engel moved to Helsinki in 1816 and became the leading architect in Finland, never leaving the country. Of his many buildings in Helsinki, implementing Ehrenström's plan, the most notable are those surrounding Senate Square, all in the disciplined neoclassical style he had learned in Petersburg. They include the Senate House (1818–1822), the Main Building of the University of Helsinki (1828–1832), the domed University Library (1836–1845), and, on a high terrace occupying the whole northern side, the Lutheran Cathedral (1830–1840).

Engel designed many other important buildings in Helsinki, including the City Hall (1827–1833). In 1824 he was appointed to the highly responsible post of controller of public works in succession to Carlo Francesco Bassi. As a result, his influence—and his neoclassical vocabulary—were distributed all over Finland; for he set up an office in which designs for churches and official buildings in many country towns were produced as well as standard patterns on which builders in the latter could model designs, adapting them to local needs. His output was immense. Among Finnish towns possessing town halls by Engel, or supervised by him, are Pori (1840), Lappeenranta, Kajaani, and Kokkola. He built or supervised a number of churches outside Helsinki, notable among which are the cruciform, domed Church at Lapua (1827) and the Orthodox Church (1840) in the central square at Turku, completed after his death. In addition to his official duties Engel conducted a private practice, building, in his formal neoclassical style, the largest private mansion in Finland at Vuojoki, near Rauma (1836).

Since Finland's only building stone is a hard, unworkable granite, Engel's buildings are of brick or timber covered with plaster, a type of construction with which he had become familiar in Tallinn and Petersburg. From these cities he no doubt derived the practice of painting his façades in strong colors with details depicted in white. His work is largely responsible for the elegance and consistency of the part of Helsinki surrounding the south harbor. He retained the post of controller of public works until his death and to his influence may be attributed the restraint characteristic of Finnish architecture up to the end of the nineteenth century and even beyond.   J. M. RICHARDS

WORKS

1818–1822, Senate House; 1822, Guards' Barracks, Kasarmitori Square; 1824–1826, Holy Trinity Church; 1826, Venha (old) Church; Helsinki. 1827, Church, Lapua, Finland. 1827–1833, City Hall; 1828–1832, Main Building, University of Helsinki; 1830–1840, Lutheran Cathedral; Helsinki. 1836, Country House, Vuojoki, Finland. 1836–1845, Library, University of Helsinki. 1840, Town Hall (not completed until 1841), Pori, Finland. 1840, Orthodox Church (not completed until 1845), Turku, Finland.

BIBLIOGRAPHY

RICHARDS, J. M. 1978 *800 Years of Finnish Architec-

Engel.
Senate House.
Helsinki.
1818–1822

ture. Newton, Abbot, England: David and Charles.
SUOLAHTI, EINO E. 1973 *Helsinki: A City in a Classic Style.* Helsinki: Otava.
WICKBERG, NILS ERIK 1962 *Finnish Architecture.* Helsinki: Otava.

ENSINGEN, ULRICH VON

Ulrich von Ensingen (1350?–1419) was born in southern Germany, probably in Ensingen near Ulm, and was the progenitor of the Ensingen family of craftsmen that included his son MATTHÄUS ENSINGEN. In 1391, Ulrich was invited to Milan by the cathedral authorities; there he refused and went to Ulm as master mason of the cathedral (1392–1417). He moved to Strasbourg in 1399 to work on the single tower designed as a precise geometrical sequence. The virtuoso effect of the Strasbourg tower is achieved by a cage of tracery and several open spiral stairways in the turrets. Ulrich died in Strasbourg before the spire was completed.

JEANINE CLEMENTS STAGE

WORKS

1392–1417, Ulm Cathedral (choir, towers, and Besserer Chapel), Germany. 1399–1419, Strasbourg Cathedral (west tower; completed after Ensingen's death), Germany. 1409, Maria Magdalena Nunnery, Pforzheim, Germany.

BIBLIOGRAPHY

CARSTANJEN, FRIEDRICH 1893 *Ulrich von Ensingen.* Munich: Ackerman.
KOEPH, HANS 1980 "Die Esslingen Frauenkirche." *Eslinger Studeen* 19:271.
PFLEIDERER, RUDOLF 1905 *Das Münster zu Ulm.* Stuttgart, Germany: Wittwer.
VELTE, MARIA 1951 *Die Anwendung der Quadratur und Triangulatur bei der Grund- und Aufrissgestaltung der gotischen Kirchen.* Basel: Birhhäuser.
WORTMANN, REINHARD 1969 "Der Westbau der Strassburger Munsters und Meister Erwin." *Bonner Jahrbuch* 169:290–318.

ENSINGER, MATTHÄUS

Son of ULRICH VON ENSINGEN and member of a family of South German architects, Matthäus Ensinger (1390?–1463) trained under his father at Strasbourg Cathedral (c.1400) and Ulm Cathedral. Matthäus repeatedly used the basilica plan of the latter cathedral, for example, in the Cathedral of V. Vincent, Berne, Switzerland (begun 1421 but completed c.1588 by Daniel Heintz of Prismell). In 1429, Matthäus became master mason at the Frauenkirche at Esslingen, Germany, and recommended HANS BÖBLINGER the elder in 1440 as his successor. Matthäus returned to Ulm and became master of the works in 1446 and worked there until his death in 1463. Three of his sons became masons and continued the Ensinger dynasty of masons.

JEANINE CLEMENTS STAGE

WORKS

1419–1429, Frauenkirche, Esslingen, Germany. 1420–1446, Cathedral of Saint Vincent, Berne. 1424–1425, Tomb of the Dukes of Neuchâtel, Switzerland. 1435–1436, Ripaille Church of Notre Dame and Tomb of Amadeus VIII of Savoy (never finished), Germany. 1449–1450, Strasbourg Cathedral, France. 1440–1463, Ulm Cathedral, Germany.

BIBLIOGRAPHY

KOEPF, HANS 1980 "Die Esslinger Frauenkirche." *Esslinger Studien* 19.
MOJON, LUC 1967 *Der Münsterbaumeister: Matthäus Ensinger.* Bern: Beutel.

EOSANDER, JOHANN FRIEDRICH

Johann Friedrich Eosander (1670?–1729), called Freiherr von Goethe, was born in Denmark. He was employed as an apprentice at the construction of the Riga fortress where his father, Nils Eosander, was an engineer. In 1699, he became King Friedrich's court architect. Eosander designed coronation decorations and city gates in Berlin (1701). For the next several years, Eosander renovated castles in the Berlin area. From 1713 to 1715 he was in the military service of Charles XII of Sweden. From 1724 to 1726, Eosander was employed by Count Flemming near Dresden to build a luxurious castle. He died as a lieutenant general in Dresden.

JEANINE CLEMENTS STAGE

WORKS

1704, Charlottenburg Castle (expansion of main wing and addition of cupola and chapel), Germany. 1708, Monbijou Castle (central wing; altered after 1710), Berlin. *1709, Atlandsberg Castle, Germany. 1724–1726, Castle (for Count Flemming), near Dresden, Germany.

ERDMANNSDORFF, FRIEDRICH WILHELM VON

The work of Friedrich Wilhelm Freiherr von Erdmannsdorff (1736–1800) marks a turning point in German architecture between late baroque and classicism. Through the patronage of Prince Leopold Friedrich Franz of Dessau, the most enlightened German prince of his time, Erdmannsdorff had the opportunity, on joint study trips to England (1763) and Italy (1761–1763, 1765–1766, and 1770–1771), to become acquainted with the modern architectural movements of his day—the English landscape garden, Palladianism (see ANDREA PALLADIO), and the Roman avant-garde of Johann Winckelmann, GIOVANNI BATTISTA PIRANESI and JACQUES-LOUIS CLÉRISSEAU. These experiences were applied in the castle and park buildings commissioned by Prince Franz in Wörlitz (Saxony) and in the park itself, the first German landscape garden modeled after Kew and Stowe. In Wörlitzer Castle, his most important work, Erdmannsdorff succeeded in synthesizing a Palladian clarity in the building elements with a subtly Pompeian decorative style in the interiors.

EBERHARD DRÜEKE
Translated from German by Beverley R. Placzek

WORKS

1769–1773, Wörlitzer Castle, Wörlitz, Germany. 1777, Court Theater, Dessau, Germany. 1795, Town Hall, Wörlitz, Germany.

BIBLIOGRAPHY

HARKEN, MARIELUISE 1973 *Erdmannsdorff und seine Bauten in Wörlitz.* Wörlitz, Germany: Orienbaum & Luisium.
RIESENFELD, ERICH PAUL 1913 *Erdmannsdorff, der Baumeister des Herzogs Leopold Friedrich Franz von Anhalt-Dessau.* Berlin.

ERICKSON, ARTHUR

Arthur Charles Erickson (1924–), whose bold architectural forms, exploiting the effects of various materials and structural systems, have dramatized houses, office towers, and university campuses, studied architecture at McGill University. After traveling extensively in Europe and the Far East, he returned to practice in his native Vancouver, B.C. (1953). Erickson/Massey Associates was formed in 1963 after Erickson and Geoffrey Massey won a competition for Simon Fraser University (near Vancouver), planned along a mountaintop pedestrian walkway with a central covered mall. The plan (1969) for the University of Lethbridge similarly fostered places for community interaction, here sheltered by concrete megastructures in a harsh prairie environment. Concurrently, carefully sited houses reflected Erickson's interest in Japanese culture with their trabeated wood or concrete frames and their merging of building and surrounding landscape.

Since 1972, as principal of Arthur Erickson Architects, Erickson has continued the search for striking large-scale images, as previously found in the massive concrete MacMillan Bloedel Building (1968–1969), Vancouver, and the angular, mirrored Canadian Pavilion, Osaka, Japan (1970). A new spatial complexity appears in the Museum of Anthropology (1974–1976) in Vancouver, where Erickson's typically elemental detailing and neutral colors set off artifacts and plants seen by people in movement. The Provincial Government Offices and Courthouse (1974–1979), also in Vancouver, introduce a multi-use complex of buildings, with an outdoor pedestrian spine reminiscent of Erickson's university projects, into an established urban context.

THOMAS G. BEDDALL

WORKS

1962, Graham House, West Vancouver, British Columbia. 1964–1965, Transportation Center and Central Mall (with Jeffrey Lindsay), Simon Fraser University, Burnaby, British Columbia. 1967, Craig House, Kelowna, British Columbia. 1967, Theme Building (with Lindsay), Expo '67, Montreal. 1968–1969, MacMillan Bloedel Building, Vancouver, British Columbia. 1970, Canadian Pavilion (with Lindsay), Expo '70, Osaka, Japan. 1970–1971, University of Lethbridge, Alberta. 1974, Eppich House, West Vancouver, British Columbia. 1974, Hillborn House, Cambridge, Ontario. 1974–1976, Museum of Anthropology, University of British Columbia; 1974–1979, Provincial Government Offices and Law Courts, Robson Square; Vancouver, British Columbia. 1974–1980, Bank of Canada Building (with Marani, Rounthwaite, and Dick), Ottawa. 1977, Eglinton West and Yorkdale Rapid Transit Stations, Toronto.

BIBLIOGRAPHY

DUBOIS, MACY 1974 "Erickson." *Canadian Architect* 19, no. 11:32–38.
ERICKSON, ARTHUR 1966 "The Architecture of Japan: The Roots." *Canadian Architect* 11, no. 12:28–36.
ERICKSON, ARTHUR 1968 "The University: The New Visual Environment." *Canadian Architect* 13, no. 1:24–37.
ERICKSON, ARTHUR 1975 *The Architecture of Arthur Erickson.* Montreal: Tundra.
IGLAUER, EDITH 1981 Seven Stones: A Portrait of Arthur Erickson, Architect. Seattle, Wash.: Harbor/University of Washington Press.
NAIRN, JANET 1980 "Vancouver's Grand New Government Center." *Architectural Record* 168, no. 8:65–75.
ROGATNICK, ABRAHAM 1968 "Simon Fraser University, British Columbia." *Architectural Review* 143, no. 854:263–275.
SCHMERTZ, MILDRED F. 1977 "Spaces for Anthropological Art." *Architectural Record* 161, no. 5:103–110.
"The University of Lethbridge: Project One." 1973 *Architectural Record* 153, no. 5:115–124.

ERICSON, SIGFRID

Sigfrid Ericson (1879–1958) studied first at the Chalmers Technical Institute in Göteborg, Sweden, and then at the Royal Academy in Stockholm, from which he graduated in 1902. In 1903, he began teaching, first at the Slöjdförenings skola in Göteborg, and then, in 1906, at the Chalmers Institute. He returned to the Slöjdförenings skola in 1913 as its director, a position which he held until 1945.

Ericson was a founding member of the Ares Consortium in 1919; this group was responsible for building Göta-place, the Göteborg Fine Arts Museum, and for planning the 1923 Jubilee Exhibition at Göteborg. This exhibition was an internationally influential display of the latest in Swedish modern architecture and decorative art. With ARVID BJERKE, Ericson designed the pavilions of this exhibition in a simplified neoclassical style.

The Masthuggs Church, Göteborg (1910–1914), is Ericson's most striking building. Here, he used traditional Scandinavian styles with such expressive force that the effect is modern.

JUDITH S. HULL

WORKS

1910–1914, Masthuggs Church, Göteborg, Sweden. 1917–1918, House, Vargaslättan, Sweden. 1919–1923, Exhibition Hall (with Arvid Bjerke), Jubilee Exhibition; 1919–1923, Museum of Fine Arts (with Bjerke); 1937–1938, Communal Middle School; 1940, Johannesberg Church; Göteborg, Sweden.

BIBLIOGRAPHY

BJERKE, ARVID, and ERICSON, SIGFRID 1930 *Göteborgs jubileum, 1923, Utställningens arkitektur.* Stockholm: Generalstabens litografiska anstalt.
MJÖBERG, HARALD 1958 "Sigfrid Ericson—arkitekt, 1879–1958." *Byggmästaren Arkitektur* 37:197–199.
NYMAN, THURE 1942 "Sigfrid Ericson." Volume 2, page 430 in *Svenska Män och Kvinnov.* Stockholm: Bonniers.

ERSKINE, RALPH

Ralph Erskine (1914–), a Swedish–British architect, was born in London and educated at the Regent Street Polytechnic there (1932–1938). As a pacifist, he settled in Sweden in 1939, just a few months before the outbreak of World War II. After the war and after further study at the Academy of Arts in Stockholm, he developed his very personal, organic, and expressive architecture, partly inspired by Swedish New Empiricism and British community planning. For small industrial communities, he designed both dwellings and work shops, such as Gyttorp in the province of Närke (1945–1955), Hammarby in Gästrikland (1947–) and Fors in Dalecarlia (1950–1953), with its famous cardboard factory building in gracefully modeled brick. He became strongly interested in finding a special housing architecture for the Nordic subarctic conditions and experimented with different kinds of buildings, for example, at Kiruna (1961–1962) and Svappavaara (1963), both in Lapland. During the 1960s, he also designed several distinguished housing areas, such as Brittgården at Tibro (1959–1961) and Esperanza at Landskrona (1969–1970), followed by Nya Bruket at Sandviken (1973–1978). He also obtained commissions in Great Britain, among others, College Clare Hall at Cambridge (1969–1970), Eaglestone at Milton Keynes (1973–1977), and above all the total renewal of Byker at Newcastle-on-Tyne (1969–1982). Typical of Erskine's architecture is a great variety of forms and materials and a contrast between heavy and light elements, as well as a "human" attitude and a wish to create a socially working unit with participation from the tenants. Among his latest works are the Student Center and Library at Stockholm University and the housing area Malminkartano in Helsinki, Finland.

FREDRIC BEDOIRE

BIBLIOGRAPHY

Architectural Design. 1977 47, nos. 11–12. Double issue devoted to Erskine.
Arkitektur. 1981 81, no. 7. Special issue devoted to Erskine.

ERVI, AARNE

Aarne Ervi (1910–1977) belongs to the generation of architects who made Finnish architecture world-famous. After graduating from the Helsinki University of Technology, Ervi worked in ALVAR AALTO's office for a few years before establishing his own practice in 1938. Following World War II, Ervi designed several industrial buildings and power stations; the first and most handsome power station, with its powerful cubic mass, is at Pyhäkoski, Finland (1949). Aalto's functionalism of the 1930s influenced Ervi's early work, particularly two university projects: the Porthania (1950–1957) for Helsinki University, the first building in Helsinki constructed with prefabricated reinforced concrete; and for Turku University, the library, the main building, and the Institute of Natural Sciences (1952–1956). His major achievement was, however, as the planner and architect of Tapiola, the internationally famous garden city in Finland. Not only did he win the competition for the overall plan in 1954, but he also designed the major buildings: the administrative and shopping centers (1961), the Swimming Hall (1964–1965), the Heikintori Department Store (1968), and the Tapiola Garden Hotel (1974). His sensitivity to detail and understanding of nature is best seen in his houses, the best example being his own house and studio in Kuusisaari, Helsinki (1950, studio 1961). Concurrently with his own practice, he worked as the director of the Helsinki City Planning Office (1965–1986).

PIRKKO-LIISA LOUHENJOKI

WORKS

1933–1937, Library Extension, Helsinki University. 1940, Office and Restaurant Building, Heinola, Finland. 1947–1953, Voimatalo Commercial and Office Building (with Tapani Nironen), Helsinki. 1949–1957, Oulujoki Oy Power Plants and Housing (Pyhäkoski [1949], Jylhämä [1950], Nuojua [1957], and Utanen [1957]), Finland. 1950, Ervi House, Kuusisaari, Helsinki. 1950–1957, Porthania, Helsinki University. 1951, Country Club, Otaniemi, Finland. 1952–1956, Library, Main Building, and Institute of Natural Sciences, Turku University, Finland. 1954, High School, Lohja, Finland. 1954, Tower House; 1955, Oravanpesä Apartment House; 1955, Shopping Center Mäntyviita; Tapiola, Finland. 1957, Hotel and Restaurant School, Helsinki. 1958–1971, Power Plant, Naantali, Finland. 1961, Administrative and Shopping Center, Tapiola, Finland. 1961, High school, Lehtikuusentie; 1961–1962, Apartment House, Myllytie; 1962, Atelier Ervi, Kuusisaari; Helsinki. 1964, Terrace Houses (with Heikki Koskelo and Markus Tavio), Itäranta; 1964–1965, Swimming Hall; Tapiola, Finland. 1965, Kauppa-Häme Commercial Building, Tampere, Finland. 1967, Institute of Natural Sciences Building II, Turku University, Finland. 1968, Heikintori Department Store, Tapiola, Finland. 1968, Swimming Hall, Kemi, Finland. 1969, Kaleva Insurance Company, Espoo, Finland. 1969, Töölö Library, Helsinki. 1974, Tapiola Garden Hotel, Finland.

BIBLIOGRAPHY

RICHARDS, J. M. 1978 *800 Years of Finnish Architecture.* London: David & Charles.
SALOKORPI, ASKO 1970 *Modern Architecture in Fin-*

land. London: Weidenfeld & Nicolson; New York: Praeger.

TEMPEL, EGON 1968 *New Finnish Architecture.* Translated by James C. Palmes. London: Architectural Press; New York: Praeger.

WICKBERG, NILS ERIK (1959)1962 *Finnish Architecture.* Helsinki: Otava.

WHITTICK, ARNOLD 1980 "Ervi, Aarne." Pages 240–241 in Muriel Emanuel (editor), *Contemporary Architects.* New York: St. Martin's.

ERWIN VON STEINBACH

Architect of the west façade and the Chapel of the Virgin of the Cathedral of Notre-Dame at Strasbourg, France, between 1275 (1277?) and 1318, Erwin von Steinbach (?–1318) is known through six medieval documents, the earliest being a German text of 1284 in which he is called *Meister Erwin Werkmeister,* meaning Master of Work (at Strasbourg). In 1316, Erwin completed a Chapel of the Virgin that contained until 1682 (when the chapel was destroyed by the architect Hans George Heckler) a balustrade inscription stating that "Master Erwin built this work." This inscription is now preserved in the Musée de l'Oeuvre Notre-Dame at Strasbourg. The third contemporary mention of Erwin is in an inscription on the tombstone of his wife, Husa, who died on July 21, 1316. On January 17, 1318, Erwin died, and he was buried beside the cathedral under a tombstone that read "In the Year of the Lord 1318, [on] the 16th of the kalens of February, died Master Erwin, Governor of the Fabric of the Church of Strasbourg" (ANNO DOMINI M.CCC.XVIII XVI KALENDAS FEBRUARII OBIIT MAGISTER ERWINUS GUBERNATOR FABRICAE ECCLESIAE ARGENTIENSIS). On March 18, 1338, Master Johann died, and he was buried beside Erwin and Husa. His tomb inscription stated that he was Filius Erwini, Erwin's son (or possibly his grandson).

It is the sixth medieval reference to Erwin that tells of his principal work and provides the surname Steinbach. However, this inscription is lost and its date is uncertain. On the vault behind the north portal of the west façade at Strasbourg there was (until the nineteenth century?) a painted inscription that read: In the Year of the Lord 1277 on the Day of the Blessed Urban [May 25] this glorious work was begun by Master Erwin of Steinbach" (ANNO DI M.CC.LXX.VII IN DIE BEATI URBANI HOC GLORIOSUM OPUS INCHOAVIT MAGISTER ERWINUS DE STEINBACH). Since the date of this inscription is unknown, its accuracy cannot be verified. It is known that the foundations of the Strasbourg façade were begun on February 2, 1276, thus the façade proper could have been begun by Erwin on May 25, 1277. But the basis of the claim that his surname was "von Steinbach," or that he was from the small village of that name in the neighboring Duchy of Baden, may be entirely legendary. It is thus by tradition and habit, rather than by documentation, that Erwin's surname has become affixed in history.

More than anyone else, it was the poet Johann Wolfgang von Goethe (1749–1832) who did this affixing. Indeed, Goethe did more to assure Erwin's fame than Erwin did through his own architectural work. Between 1770 and 1773, Goethe was a student at Strasbourg and wrote his celebrated essay praising German Gothic architecture which he dedicated to the spirit of Erwin: *Concerning German Architecture, to the Blessed Spirit of Erwin von Steinbach* (*Von Deutscher Baukunst, D[ivis] M[anibus] Ervini a Steinbach*).

Goethe later renounced this essay as youthful exuberance and refused to include it in his collected writings, but it has survived and more than anything else has assured Erwin's fame. In brief, Goethe laments being unable to locate Erwin's tomb, although he knew its precise inscription— Erwin's tomb inscription was rediscovered in 1816 by Sulpice Boisserée and Maurice Engelhard—and vows to erect a suitable monument to Erwin. But Goethe quickly realizes that Erwin already has his monument: "Of what use is a memorial to you? You have erected to yourself the most glorious one; and although the ants who crawl there worry little about your name, you have the same fate as the architect who piled up the mountains to the clouds."

Goethe inaccurately attributed the entire Gothic cathedral to Erwin. However, Erwin appears to have been responsible only for the Chapel of the Virgin, the west façade, and possibly some repairs to the nave after a fire in 1298. It is not possible to determine precisely the extent of Erwin's contribution to the west façade. It is documented that the north tower octagon was built by ULRICH VON ENSINGEN between 1399 and 1419 and that the famous open-work spire of that tower was built between 1420 and 1459 by JOHANNES HÜLTZ. Erwin may have intended a twin-towered façade, but his work does not extend above the block of the façade proper.

In the Musée de l'Oeuvre Notre-Dame at Strasbourg are preserved two project drawings for the Strasbourg façade, both of which have at one time or another been attributed to Erwin. However, neither drawing can be proved to be from his hand. The earlier of the two drawings, Strasbourg "A," dates from around 1255/1260 and may have been by Erwin's predecessor at Strasbourg and the architect of the nave, a Master Rudolf. Strasbourg

"B" is a large drawing (274 cm. or 8.89 ft. tall) termed by Georg Dehio "the most beautiful thing devised in the Gothic world." This drawing dates from around 1275. Both contain features based on French Court style architecture, but Drawing "B" goes beyond French features and of the two more nearly corresponds to the Strasbourg façade. Thus it is possible, although not provable, that Strasbourg "B" is by Erwin himself.

The principle of Erwin's façade concept was to employ three portals with gables but to erect, from the tops of the portals themselves, a freestanding vertical tracery screen set some 60 cm in front of the gables. Erwin thus built what Paul Frankl termed "autonomous tracery," establishing counterplay and tension between horizontals and diagonals of the façade proper and the verticals of his tracery screen. Some have criticized the scheme as too complex, a tour de force in stonework. It is possible that the design reflects in an unconscious sense the scholasticism of the *Summa* of the Strasbourg theologian Ulrich Engelberti, written between 1262 and 1272 but, in the summary by Paul Frankl, "there exists [between text and façade] no immediate causal relationship."

No other works can be attributed to Master Erwin, although his Strasbourg façade influenced a number of later German Gothic designs, most notably the Pieterskirche at Wimpfen im Tal. Tradition has it that Erwin founded the masons' lodge in Strasbourg in 1275. A charming but entirely spurious legend reports that Erwin's daughter, Sabina, was a sculptor at Strasbourg. A certain Sabina did carve at least one statue (now destroyed) on the south transept façade of Strasbourg, but this work dated from around 1230, a full generation before Erwin is known to have had any connection with Strasbourg. The misassociation of Sabina with Erwin derives from misinterpretation of the inscription GRATIA DIVINAE PIETATIS ADESTO SAVINAE DE PETRA DURA PER QUAM SUM FACTA FIGURA as "Sabina of Hard Stone (=Steinbach) by whom I [the statue] have been made" rather than "Sabina, by whom I have been made from hard stone."

CARL F. BARNES, JR.

BIBLIOGRAPHY

AARON, LUCIEN [George Delahache] 1910 *La cathédrale de Strasbourg.* Paris: Longuet. Includes information on medieval texts concerning Erwin.

FRANKL, PAUL 1959 *The Gothic: Literary Sources and Interpretations Through Eight Centuries.* N.J.: Princeton University Press.

FRANKL, PAUL 1962 *Gothic Architecture.* Baltimore: Penguin.

GALL, ERNST 1959 "Erwin de Steinbach." Volume 2, pages 38–39 in Pierre Francastel (editor), *Les archi-tectes célèbres.* Paris: Mazenod.

GOETHE, JOHANN WOLFGANG VON (1947)1958 "Of German Architecture, D. M. Ervini a Steinbach." Volume 2, pages 360–369 in Elizabeth G. Holt (editor), *A Documentary History of Art.* Garden City, N.Y.: Doubleday.

RECHT, ROLAND 1981 "Sur le dessin d'architecture gothique." *Etudes d'art médiéval offertes à Louis Grodecki.* Edited by Summer McK. Crosby. Paris: Editions Ophrys.

ESHERICK, JOSEPH

Joseph Esherick (1914–) has practiced primarily in the San Francisco area and has been integral to the establishment of the Bay Area tradition in architecture. A native of Philadelphia, he studied architecture at the University of Pennsylvania, graduating in 1937. Although educated in the Beaux-Arts tradition, an early Crafts influence through association with his uncle, Wharton Esherick, a sculptor and wood craftsman, coupled with admiration for the work of LE CORBUSIER and LOUIS I. KAHN formed the foundation for Esherick's strict philosophy of architecture. His theory purports that architecture is a process that brings both obvious and unapparent needs together in relation to reality. He feels that there is confusion between the process and the end product. The end product is not the building, but man living in and using a space. Critical of the aesthetic theory of design, Esherick is committed to the idea that it is not important how a building looks, but to what degree it functions for the client and how it is used.

After working for GEORGE HOWE in Philadelphia, Esherick moved to San Francisco where he worked part-time for Walter Steilberg. Through this association, Esherick was introduced to the early architects working in the woodsy Bay Area tradition. During the late 1930s, trips into the northern coastal areas gave him a firsthand introduction to the barns, mining sheds, and other examples of rural vernacular architecture, which made a strong impression on him. Later, the California vernacular became a prevalent form in his work, enabling him to integrate a building successfully into a given environment. Esherick's early concern for the utilitarian aspect of design, his desire to have his buildings reflect and merge with nature, and the successes with residential design using the California vernacular led to his involvement in the 1960s with the highly acclaimed Sea Ranch (1965–1967), north of San Francisco.

In 1972, Joseph Esherick and Associates became Esherick, Homsey, Dodge, and Davis, a firm practicing in San Francisco of which Esherick is president. In addition to his successful practice, Esherick has served on the faculty of the department of architecture at the University of California, Berkeley, since 1952. His commitment to architectural education, his carefully calculated theories of architecture, and his highly successful practice combine to insure a strong influence on the future of architecture.

JO ANNE PASCHALL

WORKS

1940, Esherick House, Ross, Calif. 1947, Smith House, Orinda, Calif. 1950, Squaw Valley Ski Lodge and Facilities, Sun Valley, Id. 1951, Goldman House, San Francisco. 1954, Bergin House, Kentwoodlands, Calif. 1956, Pelican Building, University of California, Berkeley. 1957, Holt Guest House, Stockton, Calif. 1961, Cary House, Mill Valley, Calif. 1961, Child Study Center, Berkeley, Calif. 1961, McIntyre House, Hillsborough, Calif. 1962, Larsen House; 1962, Lehman House, San Francisco. 1963, Bermack House, Oakland, Calif. 1965-1967, Demonstration Houses, General Store, Restaurant, Entry Marker, The Sea Ranch, Calif. 1965, Wurster Hall (with Vernon Demars and Donald Olsen), University of California, Berkeley. 1967, The Very Very Terry Jerry Dress Shop, The Cannery, San Francisco. 1968, Mini-Mod I and II, The Sea Ranch, Calif. 1971-1972, Student Center, California Polytechnic State University, San Luis Obispo.

BIBLIOGRAPHY

HEYER, PAUL (1966)1978 *Architects on Architecture: New Directions in America.* New & enl. ed. New York: Walker.
"Joseph Esherick and His Use of Form, His Use of Space, His Use of Site." 1952 *House and Home* 1, Jan.:124-135.
"Joseph Esherick: Theory and Practice." 1961 *Western Architect and Engineer* 222, no. 6:20-37.
MISAWA, HIROSHI; EHIRA, KANJI; and SUGAWARE, MICHIO 1965 "World Architects: Joseph Esherick." *Japan Architect* Mar.:79-85.

ESPERANDIEU, JACQUES HENRY

Born in Nîmes, France, Jacques Henry (also Henri) Espérandieu (1829-1874) worked first for C. A. QUESTEL, then went to Paris to study at the Ecole des Beaux-Arts (1846-1853), where he enrolled in LÉON VAUDOYER's atelier. He returned to work for Questel and then, from 1855, for Vaudoyer on the cathedral of Marseilles, succeeding him as architect in 1872. He became *architecte de la ville* in 1867 and built a great deal in Marseilles, all of a robust and grandiose kind. His most ambitious undertaking was the Palais de Longchamp, fronting a reservoir, consisting of a central pavilion with cascades and fountains below, flanked by museums of fine arts and natural history. The design of this complex was claimed as his own by the sculptor Fréderic Auguste Bartholdi, though he was finally to lose his claim for fees in 1901.

R. D. MIDDLETON

WORKS

1853-1864, Notre Dame de la Garde; 1857-1862, Monument of the Immaculate Conception; 1862-1869, Palais de Longchamp; 1864-1874, Ecole des Beaux-Arts and Library; 1867-?, Château du Pharo (designed by HECTOR M. LEFUEL), Marseilles, France.

BIBLIOGRAPHY

ESPÉRANDIEU, A., ROUSSEL, E., and GAIDAN, J. 1877 *Henry Espérandieu: Révélations posthumes, publiées par son frère et ses amis.* Nîmes, France: Clavel-Ballivet.
ESPÉRANDIEU, JACQUES HENRY 1872a *Notice du Palais de Longchamp à Marseille.* France: Imprimerie du Journal de Marseille.
ESPÉRANDIEU, JACQUES HENRY 1872b "Le sentiment et l'architecture de la forme et de la coloration des édifices." *Revue Générale de l'architecture* 29:12-18, 51-55, 107-110.
PARROCEL, ETIENNE 1883-1884 Volumes 3 and 4 in *L'Art dans le midi. Célébrités marseillaises. Marseille et ses édifices, architectes et ingénieurs du XIXe siècle.* Marseille, France: Chatagnier.
REINAUD, EMILE ALFRED 1905 *Henry Espérandieu et le Palais de Longchamp.* Nîmes, France: Chastanier.

ESSEX, JAMES

James Essex (1722-1784) was the first Gothic Revival architect seriously to study and to understand the construction techniques of medieval buildings. Although he was better known for his classical designs in and around Cambridge, England, his native town, his most significant works were his restorations of the medieval cathedrals of Ely (1757-1762) and Lincoln (1762-1765), his Gothic altarpiece for Kings College Chapel, Cambridge (1770-1775), and his small-scale but well-documented commissions from HORACE WALPOLE for his house at Strawberry Hill (1776-1777).

T. H. COCKE

ESTEY, ALEXANDER R.

Alexander R. Estey (1826-1881), resident of Framingham, Massachusetts, was trained in the offices of Richard Bond and GRIDLEY J. F. BRYANT in Boston. He designed a significant number of Romanesque and Gothic Revival churches as well as educational, commercial, and residential structures. Working primarily in New England and vicinity, Estey was also a consultant in the design of the interior of the Library of Congress in Washington.

FREDERIC C. DETWILLER

WORKS

*1851, Prospect Congregational Church; *1854, Cornerstone Baptist Church; Cambridge, Mass. 1861–1862, Emmanuel Church, Boston. 1861–1862, Methodist Church, Burlington, Vt. 1864, Saint John's Church, Framingham, Mass. 1864–1867, Saint Peter's Episcopal Church (with Woodcock and Meacham), Cambridge, Mass. 1866, Church of Our Saviour, Longwood, Brookline, Mass. 1867, Old Cambridge Baptist Church, Mass. *1869, Monk's Building, Boston. 1873–1877, Harvard Church, Cambridge, Mass. 1877, Baptist Theological School; 1877, Union Congregational Church; *1881, Boston 7 Albany Depot; Boston.

BIBLIOGRAPHY

RETTIG, ROBERT E. 1969 *Guide to Cambridge Architecture.* Cambridge, Mass.: M.I.T. Press.
TUCCI, DOUGLASS SHAND 1974 *Church Building in Boston, 1720–1970.* Concord, Mass.: Rumford Press.
TUCCI, DOUGLASS SHAND 1978 *Built in Boston.* Boston: New York Graphic Society.

EULALUIS

Eulaluis, whose birthplace is unknown, is a shadowy figure in the history of Greek architecture. He is not mentioned by any ancient author whose works survive today, and even the spelling of his name is uncertain. It is possible, although unattested, that he was connected with some of antiquity's most well-known building projects, but even here the record is obscure. His career may have been typical of those of the thousands of artists and craftsmen who bequeathed to later ages the great legacy of Greek art, while remaining themselves essentially anonymous.

B. M. BOYLE

BIBLIOGRAPHY

DRACHMANN, AAGE G. 1963 *The Mechanical Technology of Greek and Roman Antiquity.* Copenhagen: Munksgaard; London: Hafner; Madison: University of Wisconsin Press.

EUPOLEMOS OF ARGOS

A fire in 423 B.C. destroyed the primitive wooden Argive Heraion; it was replaced by the building (c.416 B.C.) designed by Eupolemos of Argos (flourished c.430–410 B.C.). Elaborate exterior dec-

orations were complemented on the interior by the chryselephantine statue of Hera, by Polykleitos. The temple itself followed an ideal schema, with six columns on the fronts, twelve on the flanks; column spacings were ten Doric feet, column diameters four, metopes three and triglyphs two. It was apparently an attempt to demonstrate the perfectability of the Doric order. Only the foundations are in place today.

B. M. BOYLE

WORK

*c.416 B.C., Second Temple of Hera, Argos, Greece.

BIBLIOGRAPHY

DINSMOOR, WILLIAM B. 1973 *The Architecture of Ancient Greece.* Reprint. New York: Biblio & Tannen.
PAUSANIAS, *Graeciae descriptio,* Book 2, chapter 17.

EVELEIGH, JOHN

Emerging from obscure beginnings, John Eveleigh (?–1802) worked for Thomas Baldwin and others until starting his own practice in Bath, England. Eveleigh designed several ranges of terraces (rowhouses) for speculative development in Bath based on the urban idea of crescent or square configurations to form an interior enclosure or garden. He employed Palladian (see ANDREA PALLADIO) motifs of rustication, a central pediment, and columns to compose a palatial façade out of smaller, individual dwellings. Failure to obtain public subscriptions to the pleasure gardens of Grosvenor Place forced Eveleigh into bankruptcy in 1793, whereupon he left Bath and designed the Guildhall at Plymouth (1800).

RICHARD LORCH

WORKS

1786, Portland Place (front façades); 1786–1793, Grosvenor Place; 1788, Camden Crescent; 1790, Sion Row; c.1790, Somerset Place; Bath, England. 1800, Guildhall, Plymouth, England.

BIBLIOGRAPHY

GREEN, NOWBRAY 1904 *The Eighteenth Century Architecture of Bath.* Bath, England: George Gregory.
ISON, WALTER 1948 *The Georgian Buildings of Bath from 1700 to 1830.* London: Farber.

EYRE, WILSON

With his roots in Philadelphia and childhood spent in Europe, and through his innate artistry and taste, Wilson Eyre (1858–1944) created a body of architecture, important in its own right, which coalesced the understated, comfortable, eclectic Philadelphia residential style—still a regional phenomenon. Starting as a master of the late Queen Anne Revival or Shingle style and designing more than 350 commissions in his lifetime, he merged the simplicity and straightforward craftsmanship of the Pennsylvania farmhouse, the sometimes awkward Philadelphia Georgian, the Arts and Crafts, and the then current Anglo-American eclecticism with a personality and wit that was as extraordinary as his skill as delineator and artist. His greatest gift lay in domestic design, which constituted the bulk of his work, although commissions included museums, churches, hospitals, and office and college buildings. An instructor in architecture and drawing, he was also a founder and, from 1901 to 1905, an editor of *House and Garden* magazine and was active in professional and civic affairs. He retained a small office, capable of handling "only as much work as he could personally design and study over to his satisfaction."

Eyre was born in Florence, where his father was in the foreign service. Schooled in Europe, Canada, and Newport, Rhode Island, and with one year in the architecture program at the Massachusetts Institute of Technology, he joined the office of James Peacock Sims in Philadelphia in 1877. He assumed control of this firm, upon the death of the principal in 1882. After a brief partnership with a coworker, William Jackson (the office remained in Eyre's name alone until 1912), a partnership with John Gilbert McIlvaine began, lasting until McIlvaine's death in 1939. A small New York branch office existed from 1901 to 1915. Little was done after the 1929 Depression; and by Eyre's death he was a fondly recalled but distant presence, noted mostly for his rendering skills.

The high point of Eyre's career came between about 1890 and World War I, when in various combinations he merged the Queen Anne with indigenous American and English forms. He featured the work of the artisan in subtly creative ways with attention to small details. Although evocation of the past was of interest, it was always to be in the context of current needs and usage, so that a new American architecture might ultimately emerge.

Eyre was a founder of the pioneering Philadelphia T-Square Club in 1883 and was its president from 1887 to 1888. Through his varied teaching commitments and his status as a major architect, his influence on generations of Philadelphia architects was great. He also had an influence on architecture as a whole, largely through the frequent publication of his works in the architectural press and regular participation in annual architectural exhibitions. Among those affected were Edmond

Eyre.
J. Cooke III House and Gardens (Brookfield).
Philadelphia.
1909–1914

Gilchrist, GEORGE HOWE, and perhaps CHARLES F. A. VOYSEY.

Eyre was also president of the Philadelphia Chapter of the American Institute of Architects for several years and was made a Fellow of the institute in 1893. He received an honorary doctor of fine arts from the University of Pennsylvania in 1926.

A tall, patrician man with biting wit but great charm, he epitomized in many ways the late Victorian gentleman bohemian architect and artisan, but he was at the same time American and Philadelphian.

EDWARD TEITELMAN

WORKS

*1883, John Ashurst House, near Philadelphia. Begun 1883, Charles Potter House (Anglecot), Philadelphia. 1885, Henry Genet Taylor House and Office, Camden, N.J. *Begun 1887, John W. Petter House and Gardens (Fairacres), Jenkintown, Pa. *Begun 1888, Casino, Bar Harbor, Maine. *1889, Percifer Roberts House, Philadelphia. Begun 1890, Charles Lang Freer House, Detroit. 1890, Clarence Moore House; 1891, Neil and Mauran Houses; Philadelphia. *1891, Newcomb College (chapel); *1893, Newcomb College, Arts Building; New Orleans, La. 1893–1926, Free (University) Museum of the University of Pennsylvania (with COPE and STEWARDSON, and FRANK MILES DAY); 1894, Joseph Leidy House and Office; begun 1894, Mask and Wig Clubhouse; Philadelphia. 1903, Roland R. Conklin House (Rosemary Farm), Huntington, N.Y. *Begun 1904, Second John W. Pepper House, Jenkintown, Pa.

1907, Second William Turner House (Lycoming); 1909–1914, J. Cooke III House and Gardens (Brookfield); Philadelphia. 1911–1924, Horatio Gates Lloyd House (Allgates), Haverford, Pa. 1914, John F. Townsend House and Gardens (Montrose), Radnor, Pa. Begun 1914, William White House, Waterford, Conn. 1916, John J. Jefford House (Hunting Hill Farm), Media, Pa. 1924, Swann Memorial Fountain, Parkway, and Logan Square, Philadelphia.

BIBLIOGRAPHY

Primary repositories for Willison Eyre material are the Avery Architectural Library, Columbia University, New York, and the Furness Library of the University of Pennsylvania, Philadelphia, which contain hundreds of drawings and some original source materials.

CAYE, ROGER 1913 "The Office and Apartments of a Philadelphia Architect, Mr. Wilson Eyre, at 1003 Spruce Street." *Architectural Record* 34, July:78–88.

EYRE, WILSON 1896 "From Liverpool to London." *Architectural Review* (Boston) 4, no. 1:3–5.

EYRE, WILSON 1898 "The Surroundings of the Country House." *Brochure Series of Architectural Illustration* 4:189–197.

EYRE, WILSON 1908 "The Planning of Country Houses." *American Architect and Building News* 93:107–108, 115–116.

EYRE, WILSON 1913 "My Ideal for a Country Home: A House Expressing Domesticity." *Country Life in America* 24:35–36.

EYRE, WILSON 1931 "Modern Art." *T-Square Club Journal of Philadelphia* 1, no. 12:10–13.

FAHLMAN, BETSY 1980 "Wilson Eyre in Detroit: The Charles Lang Freer House." *Winterthur Portfolio* 15:257–270.

GITHENS, ALFRED MORTON 1900 "Wilson Eyre, Jr.: His Work." Pages 121–184 in Albert Kelsey (editor), *Architectural Annual, 1900*. Philadelphia: Architectural Annual.

MILLARD, JULIAN 1903 "The Work of Wilson Eyre." *Architectural Record* 14:279–325.

PRICE, C. MATLACK 1912 "The Development of a National Architecture: The Work of Wilson Eyre." *Arts and Decoration* 3, Nov.:16–19.

TEITELMAN, EDWARD 1971 "Wilson Eyre, Jr., and the Arts and Crafts in Philadelphia." *Journal of the Society of Architectural Historians* 30:245–246. Abstract of a 1971 typescript.

TEITELMAN, EDWARD 1980 "Wilson Eyre in Camden: The Henry Genet Taylor House and Office." *Winterthur Portfolio* 15:229–255.

TEITELMAN, EDWARD, and FAHLMAN, BETSY "The Furniture and Furnishings of Wilson Eyre." In Kenneth Ames (editor), *Furniture in Victorian America*. Watkins Glen, N.Y.: American Life Foundation. Forthcoming publication.

WALLICK, FREDERICK 1910a "'Fairacres' and Some Other Recent Country Houses by Wilson Eyre." *International Studio* 40, no. 158:29–36.

WALLICK, FREDERICK 1910b "The Rational Art of Wilson Eyre, An Architect Who Designs Houses to Meet the Needs and Express the Qualities of Today." *Craftsman* 17:537–551.

FABIANI, MAX

The Slovenian architect Max Fabiani (1865–1962) was born in Cobdil in the Karst region, in what is now Yugoslavia. As one of OTTO WAGNER's most eminent pupils, he developed and continued Wagner's teachings. He built important buildings in Vienna and in Ljubljana, in Gorizia and in Trieste. Upon graduation from the Vienna Technical University, he was employed there as a teacher's assistant; he also traveled widely throughout Europe. Later (1894–1898), he collaborated with Otto Wagner and from 1899 on was in charge of Wagner's office. From 1910 to 1920, he was professor of interior and ornamental design at the Technical University in Vienna.

His most important Viennese building is the department store of Portois and Fix (1899), a strict formulation of Otto Wagner's ideas. The upper three stories of its smooth façade are surfaced in green, with only sparse Secessionist decorative additions. The Artaria (1900), an apartment and commercial building also in Vienna, is less severe, with English bow windows, a two-story base and smooth upper stories articulated only by moldings. Echoes of Tuscan Renaissance architecture appear here, as they do in all Fabiani's later buildings. This intermediate stylistic position between *Sezession* and historicism made him an appropriate personal adviser on architectural matters to the heir to the throne, Archduke Francis Ferdinand. After World War I, Fabiani lived in Gorizia. As a planner, he drew up significant master plans for the Isonzo Valley, Gorizia, Ljubljana, and other cities. His drawings recall those of LEONARDO DA VINCI, as do his similarly wide-ranging interests, which reached into traffic engineering and aerodynamics.

SOKRATIS DIMITRIOU

WORKS

1899, Portois and Fix Interior Design Firm; 1900, Artaria Apartment and Commercial Building; Vienna. *1901, Austrian Pavilion, International Exhibition, Paris.

BIBLIOGRAPHY

HITCHCOCK, H. R. (1958)1963 *Architecture: Nineteenth and Twentieth Centuries*. Baltimore: Penguin.
POZZETTO, MARCO 1966 *Max Fabiani Architetto*, Gorizia, Italy: Comune di Gorizia.
POZZETTO, MARCO 1979 *La Scuola di Wagner: 1894–1912*. Trieste, Italy: Comune di Trieste.

FABRIS, EMILIO DE

Emilio de Fabris (1808–1883) was born in Florence of humble background and orphaned at an early age. A student of Gaetano Baccani, he won a prize to study in Rome at the age of thirty. After three years, he returned to Florence and soon gained the patronage of Leopold II, the grand duke of Tuscany, who took him on trips to Naples and Sicily to paint views of antiquity. The major undertaking of de Fabris's career was the Florence Duomo façade (1867–1886), a commission he obtained after three competitions. Completed after his death by his successor, Luigi Del Moro, it is an academic work of the Gothic Revival designed to harmonize with the polychromy of the Trecento Campanile and Duomo lateral walls. De Fabris was a professor of architecture and perspective at the Florentine Academy of Fine Arts and later became its president. He designed the domed tribune (1882) in the Gallery of the Academy for the display of MICHELANGELO's *David*.

JOY M. KESTENBAUM

WORKS

1867–1886, Duomo (façade); 1882, Tribune of Academy of Fine Arts; Florence.

BIBLIOGRAPHY

BELTRAMI, LUCA 1900 *Storia della Facciata di S. Maria del Fiore in Firenze.* Milan: Allegretti.
DE FABRIS, EMILIO 1967 *Del Sistema Tricuspidale per il Coronamento della Facciata di Santa Maria del Fiore, Seguito alle Considerzione Pubblicate nel 1864.* Florence: Barbera.
MEEKS, CARROLL L. V. 1966 *Italian Architecture 1750–1914.* New Haven and London: Yale University Press.

FAHRENKAMP, EMIL

After studying at the Technische Hochschule in Aachen, Germany, Emil Fahrenkamp (1885–1966) became assistant to WILHELM KREIS at the Applied Arts School in Düsseldorf and succeeded Kreis as professor there and at the Academy of Art in Düsseldorf. His years of greatest activity were under the Weimar Republic, when he received many commissions for industrial and office buildings in the Rhineland, and began to establish a practice in Berlin. Like Kreis's, Fahrenkamp's buildings were recognizably modern but retained reminiscences, such as vertically oriented windows, of historicism. Under the Third Reich, Fahrenkamp withdrew from teaching but continued to practice. After 1945, he returned to his professorship and was made an honorary member of the Academy of Art in Vienna.

BARBARA MILLER LANE

WORKS

1923–1927, Factory and Administration Buildings, Rhine Steel Works, Berlin; Duisburg; Düsseldorf; Frankfurt am Main; Nuremberg, Stuttgart; Germany. 1924, Ballin Estate, Schmargendorf, Berlin. 1924, Benz Store, Düsseldorf, Germany. 1924, Lochner House, Aachen, Germany. 1924–1925, City Hall (interior remodeling), Mühlheim am Ruhr, Germany. 1926, Café Monopol, Cologne, Germany. 1926, Catholic Church, Hamborn, Germany. 1926, Evangelical Church, Düsseldorf, Germany. 1926, Rheinisch-westfälische Zeitung Offices, Essen, Germany. 1926–1927, Hotel Breidenbacher Hof, Düsseldorf, Germany. 1927, Evangelical Church, Essen, Germany. 1927, Emil Fahrenkamp House, Duisburg, Germany. 1927, Factory, Leverkausen, Germany. 1927, Housing Development (Sonne), Duisburg, Germany. 1927, Palais des Nations (project; with Albert Deneke), Geneva. 1933–1945, Housing, Braunschweig, Germany. 1933–1945, Office Building, Fehrbelliner Platz, Berlin. 1937, Exposition Buildings, Düsseldorf, Germany. 1945–1956, I. G. Farben Power Station, Frankfurt am Main, Germany. 1945–1956, Office Buildings, Renenia-Ossag, Berlin. 1945–1956, Resort Hotel (Monte Verita), Ascona, Switzerland.

BIBLIOGRAPHY

BENDER, EWALD 1938 "Kronenburg und seine Meisterschule." *Zentralblatt der Bauverwaltung* 58:1131–1136.
BENDER, EWALD 1939a "Das Deutsche Haus aus der internationalen Wasserausstellung in Lüttich 1939." *Zentralblatt der Bauverwaltung* 59:779–787.
BENDER, EWALD 1939b "Das Ehrenmal des Baues Essen." *Zentralblatt der Bauverwaltung* 59:1093–1096.
CREMER, PAUL JOSEPH 1931 "Kurhotel 'Monte Verita' in Ascona." *Zentralblatt der Bauverwaltung* 51:69–72.
HOFF, AUGUST 1928 *Emil Fahrenkamp: Ein Ausschnitt seines Schaffens aus den Jahren 1924–1927.* Stuttgart, Germany: J. Hoffmann.
RITTICH, WERNER 1938 *Architektur und Bauplastik der Gegenwart.* Berlin: Rembrandt.
"Schaffendes Volk: Die Düsseldorfer Austellung." 1937 *Monatshefte für Baukunst und Städtebau* 21:205–209.

FAIRBAIRN, WILLIAM

Sir William Fairbairn (1789–1874) was a leading industrialist of the first half of the nineteenth century who played a major role in the development of iron framing for buildings. He was born in Kelso, Scotland, and apprenticed in Newcastle as a millwright. After further experience, he established his own works in Manchester with James Little, who later withdrew. From the manufacture of machinery for mills, he turned to the erection of whole mills, iron-framed, and to building locomotives, ships, and bridges. He sponsored extensive experimental researches (by Eaton Hodgkinson) on the structural uses of iron and collaborated with ROBERT STEPHENSON in developing the tubular iron bridge. He published widely the fruits of his researches.

ROWLAND MAINSTONE

WORKS

1845–1850, Conway and Britannia Tubular Bridges (with Robert Stephenson), North Wales. 1851–1853, Salt Mill, Saltair, near Bradford, England.

BIBLIOGRAPHY

FAIRBAIRN, WILLIAM   1849   An Account of the Construction of the Britannia and Conway Tubular Bridges. London: Weale.
FAIRBAIRN, WILLIAM   (1854)1870   On the Application of Cast and Wrought Iron to Building Purposes. 4th rev. ed. London: Longmans.
FAIRBAIRN, WILLIAM   (1861)1869   Iron—Its History, Properties, and Processes of Manufacture. 3d rev. ed. Edinburgh: Black.
FAIRBAIRN, WILLIAM, and POLE, WILLIAM   (1877)1970   The Life of Sir William Fairbairn. Reprint. Newton Abbot, England: David & Charles.

FALCONETTO, GIOVANNI MARIA

Giovanni Maria Falconetto (1468–1535) was born in Verona, Italy, and died in Padua, where he had been municipal architect since 1524. Although he spent twelve years in Rome during the early part of his career training as a painter, Falconetto undertook his major works in the Veneto and other areas of northern Italy. In spite of this, his work retains the strong imprint of Renaissance Rome. In painting, Falconetto is compared to such central Italian artists as Melozzo da Forli and Pietro Perugino, while in architecture his work reflects the classicism of DONATO BRAMANTE and RAPHAEL. It is in terms of this classicism that Falconetto's architecture is most important: he is an early practitioner of this style in the strongly Gothic north of Italy. With his introduction of classical design to the north, Falconetto sets the stage for the later sixteenth-century developments of JACOPO SANSOVINO and ANDREA PALLADIO in Venice.

SARAH E. BASSETT

WORKS

1524, Alvise Cornaro Logia; 1528, Porta di San Giovanni; 1530, Porta di Savonarola; 1533, Chapel of Saints, Church of Sant'Antonio; Padua, Italy.

(A)c.1535, Vescovi Villa (executed by ALVISE CORNARO), Luvigliano, near Padua, Italy.

BIBLIOGRAPHY

FIOCCO, GIUSEPPE   1930   "Le architetture di Giovanni Maria Falconetto." Dedalo 11:1203–1241.
HEYDENREICH, LUDWIG H., and LOTZ, WOLFGANG   1974   Architecture in Italy: 1400–1600. Baltimore: Penguin.
VENTURI, ADOLFO   1930   "Edifici di un umanista e Padova." L'Arte 33:265–279.

FALUDI, EUGENIO GIACOMO

Eugenio Giacomo Faludi (1899–) was born in Budapest. He graduated from the Scuola Superiore di Architettura in Rome in 1924. He was a member of the Italian Rationalist movement during the 1920s and 1930s. Since 1940, he has lived in Canada and has been active in Canadian town planning.

DENNIS DOORDAN

WORKS

1929, Villa Rossi, Mestre, Italy. *1933, Model Houses, V Triennale, Milan. 1943, Master Plan, Toronto. 1947, Master Plan, Hamilton, Canada.

BIBLIOGRAPHY

CENNAMO, MICHELE   1973   La Prima Esposizione Italiana di Architettura Razionale. Naples: Fausto Fiorentino.
"Eugene Giacomo Faludi."   1975   Volume 13, page 324 in The Canadian Who's Who. Toronto: Tunnell.
FALUDI, EUGENIO G.   1939   Architetture di Eugenio Faludi. Milan: Officine Grafiche Esperia.

FAMIN, AUGUSTE

A student of Charles PERCIER AND Pierre Leonard FONTAINE, Auguste Pierre Sainte-Marie Famin (1776?–1859?) won the Prix de Rome in 1801. His studies of ancient and Renaissance monuments in Italy were exhibited in 1806. He later published, with AUGUSTE GRANDJEAN DE MONTIGNY, Architecture toscane . . . (1815), which became an important reference work.

LISA B. REITZES

WORKS

1809–1824, Château at Rambouillet (restoration), France. 1844–1846, Collège Rollin, Paris.

BIBLIOGRAPHY

HAUTECOEUR, LOUIS   1943–1957   Histoire de l'Architecture classique en France. 7 vols. Paris: Picard.

FANCELLI, LUCA

Born in Settignano, near Florence, Luca Fancelli (c.1430–1495?) is best known as the architect who supervised the construction of LEONE BATTISTA ALBERTI's Mantuan churches San Sebastiano (begun c.1460) and Sant'Andre for which he prepared a wooden model in 1471. Fancelli's early training is uncertain, but he absorbed the Florentine early Renaissance manner of FILIPPO BRUNELLESCHI and MICHELOZZO MICHELOZZI. He seems also to have studied sculpture. GIORGIO VASARI's statement that Fancelli was responsible for the Palazzo Pitti in Florence must be rejected. In 1450, Luca Fancelli settled in Mantua in north Italy, having been recommended to Lodovico II Gonzaga by Cosimo de' Medici; the majority of his architectural work was accomplished in that city and its environs.

Fancelli's early works in Mantua include the Ospedale Grande, authorized by Pope Nicholas V in 1449 but not put into use until 1472, and the Gonzaga Palazzo at Révere, a project which he seems to have taken over soon after his arrival. For the Gonzaga family, Fancelli undertook restorations of the Castello di San Giorgio, and in 1480, he began work on the massive new wing of the family stronghold, the Domus Nova, only one range of which was built. The Domus Nova features corner towers and pilasters expressed in an Albertian giant order.

Documentary evidence indicates that Luca Fancelli was ill-tempered and seems to have indulged in petty thievery, but he was indispensable in Mantua, for it was felt that he was the only architect capable of faithfully carrying out the ideas and plans of Alberti. In addition to directing the building of San Sebastiano and Sant'Andrea, Fancelli also oversaw the construction of the Torre dell'Orologio, which was completed in 1473. He also worked for many of Mantua's wealthy families building domestic structures in the town and in the surrounding countryside.

Fancelli's first Gonzaga patron, Lodovico II, died in 1478, and his successor Federico I died in 1484. The new marquis of Mantua, Francesco II, gave Fancelli little support, and after having lived there for over thirty years the architect began to travel extensively. He was called to Milan by Giangaleazzo Sforza in 1487, and after a return to Mantua he went to Naples in 1491, having been recommended to Alfonso II by Lorenzo de' Medici. In September of that year, Fancelli was appointed *capomaestro* of the Florentine Duomo; in November, he wrote to Mantua saying that he was working on a model for the cathedral's façade. Between 1492 and 1494, Luca Fancelli was present in both Florence and Mantua, and he is last documented in Florence in 1494. The full importance of this architect is yet to be realized for he was a key figure in the dissemination of Tuscan architectural ideas in north Italy.

SHERYL E. REISS

WORKS

c.1450–1472, Ospedale Grande, Mantua, Italy. 1450s, Gonzago Palazzo, Révere, Italy. 1460–?, San Sebastiano (according to plans by Leon Battista Alberti); 1461–1462, Palazzo Vecchio (restoration); 1472–?, Sant'Andrea (according to plans by Leon Battista Alberti); 1473–?, Castello di San Giorgio (restoration); 1480–1484, Domus Nova; Mantua, Italy.

BIBLIOGRAPHY

BRAGHIROLLI, W. 1876 "Luca Fancelli, scultore, architetto e idraulico del secolo XV." *Archivio storico Lombardo* 3:610–638.

BROWN, CLIFFORD M. 1972 "Luca Fancelli in Mantua: A Checklist of His 185 Letters to the Gonzaga." *Mitteilungen des Kunsthistorischen Instituts in Florenz* 16, no. 2:153–166.

BURNS, HOWARD 1981 "The Gonzaga and Renaissance Architecture." Pages 27–38 in David Chambers and Jane Martineau (editors), *Splendors of the Gonzaga*. London: Victoria and Albert Museum. Exhibition catalogue.

CARPEGGIANI, PAOLO 1971 "Luca Fancelli: architetto civile nel contado Gonzhagesco." *Arte Lombarda* 16:37–44.

CARPEGGIANI, PAOLO 1978 "I Gonzaga e l'arte: la corte, la città, il territorio (1444–1616)." Pages 167–190 in *Mantova e i Gonzaga nella civiltà del Rinascimento*. Milan: Editgraf.

FOSTER, PHILIP 1981 "Lorenzo de' Medici and the Florence Cathedral Façade." *Art Bulletin* 63:495–500.

JOHNSON, EUGENE J. 1975 *S. Andrea in Mantua: The Building History*. University Park: Pennsylvania State University Press.

LAMOUREUX, RICHARD E. 1979 *Alberti's Church of San Sebastiano in Mantua*. New York and London: Garland.

MARANI, ERCOLANO 1965 "Luca Fancelli." Pages 63–115 in *Mantova: Le Arti II*. 3 vols. Mantua, Italy: Istituto Carlo d'Arco.

VASIC VATOVEC, CORINNO 1979 *Luca Fancelli, architetto. Epistolario Gonzhagesco*. Florence: Uniedir.

WITTKOWER, RUDOLF (1949)1971 *Architectural Principles in the Age of Humanism*. New York: Norton.

FANZAGO, COSIMO

Cosimo Fanzago (1591–1678), born in Clusone near Bergamo, Italy, dominated the architectural scene in Naples during the seventeenth century. Four years after his arrival in Naples, in 1612, he joined forces with the Florentine sculptor Angelo Landi. After Landi's death around 1620, Fanzago began his architectural career. He received commissions for numerous projects ranging from small-scale works, such as pulpits, to altars, chapels, churches, and palaces, while continuing his sculptural practice. Since the execution of many of these extended over long periods of time, a typological approach to his work seems most appropriate.

Fanzago developed a new type of high altar: a free-standing structure, placed well forward from the apse wall, which created a retrochoir. He first experimented with the idea in San Nicola al Lido, Venice (1629–1634). The Neapolitan altars of Santa Maria degli Angeli alle Croci (1639–1640) and Santa Maria di Costantinopoli (1645) are more elaborate with columnar superstructures and low walls with portals flanking the mensas. The high altar of the Gesù e Maria, Pescostanzo (1640?–1645), is similar in conception. The most complex altar is found in Santa Maria La Nova (1645–1647) in Naples where a transparent *serliana* replaces the solid superstructures of the earlier designs. The high altar of San Lorenzo in Lucina, Rome (1650–1652), constructed anew by Carlo Rainaldi in 1675, was probably also a screen type, as was the contemporary one in San Domenico Maggiore, Naples (1650). Two more traditional altars deserve mention. A drawing of the high altar of the Abbey at Montecassino (1645), destroyed during the bombing of 1943, shows a scheme almost identical to that constructed for the Benedictines of Santi Severino e Sosio in Naples (1635–1641). The elaborate scrollwork decoration above the mensas is characteristic of Fanzago.

The chapels decorated by Fanzago most clearly exhibit his varied skills. The monumental wall retable designed for the Church of the Augustinian Nuns in Salamanca (1633–1634) is the least complex. In the chapels of Sant'Ignazio and San Francesco Saverio (1637–1650) in the transepts of the Gesù Nuovo in Naples he integrated the architectural, sculptural, and decorative elements into a harmonious whole in contrast to the additive appearance of his model—the Cappella Fornaro (1600–1602) in the same church. Fanzago reduced the plastic elements to a minimum, allowing the rich coloristic effects of the polychrome marbles and floral inlays to dominate in the chapels of Sant'Antonio di Padova (1638–1649) and the Cacace family (1643–1645) in San Lorenzo Maggiore, Naples. Two chapels in Santa Teresa degli Studi (after 1637) and Santa Maria delle Anime del Purgatorio (1664), which are related in design, are considerably less sumptuous.

In Naples, Fanzago constructed a series of façades for pre-existing churches. The earliest entirely by his hand is the modest façade of the Santissima Trinità delle Monache (1630). For the new façade of the Certosa di San Martino (1623–1656) he employed a triumphal-arch elevation. The façade of Santa Maria della Sapienza (1638–1653) is a highly original, classicizing variation of the Certosa design. A three-arch loggia, raised on a high basement, is flanked by rectangular openings which give access from the street level to the double-ramp staircase behind the façade. For the façade and entrance vestibule of Santa Maria degli Angeli alle Croci (1639–1640), Fanzago, instead, used a series of *serlianas*. The façade of Santo Spirito dei Napoletani (1649) in Rome, which was rebuilt in 1853, represents an attempt to superimpose the horizontal terminations of his Neapolitan façades on a structure designed to carry a pediment.

Fanzago's preferred church plan was a Greek cross, covered by a tall dome, which was enclosed either in a square or rectangular block, often with an extension on the east for a retrochoir. He employed this type for the Ascensione a Chiaia (1622/1624–1657), Santa Maria dei Monti (1628–1678), San Giuseppe dei Vecchi a San Potito (1634–1678), Santa Teresa a Chiaia (1650–1662), and Santa Maria Maggiore, called La Pietrasanta (1653–1678), in Naples. The most inventive scheme is found in Santa Teresa a Chiaia where four monumental *serliana* support the cupola. Fanzago accented the center of the longitudinal plan of San Giorgio Maggiore (1640–1678) by placing a dome over the middle of the nave and by slightly projecting the contiguous side chapels. In San Giuseppe degli Scalzi a Pontecorvo (1643–1660), also in Naples, Fanzago designed a rectangular core, covered by a coved vault, with shallow transepts in the center. For the façade of this church, the best preserved of those constructed *ex novo* by the architect, he again employed an internal staircase and externally used his favorite motifs—the triumphal arch and the *serliana*. Santa Maria Egiziaca a Pizzofalcone (1651/1661–1678) is the most problematical of his works. Lacking documentation, the date of the origin of the project and its relationship to Sant'Agnese in Piazza Navona in Rome cannot be determined. As it stands today, the church was constructed between 1698–1717. However, Fanzago's plan, which is mentioned in a document of 1665, seems to have been adopted, at least in its main outlines.

Fanzago also completed works begun by other architects and was active as a restorer. Between 1623 and 1631, he finished the large cloister of the Certosa di San Martino, which was started by Giovanni Antonio Dosio. Beginning in 1631, he was involved in converting the Gothic church of the same monastery. Following a quarrel with the Certosini in 1656, work was suspended and not taken up again until the eighteenth century. His participation in Santa Maria delle Anime del Purgatorio (1620?–1638), Santa Maria degli Angeli alle Croci (1639–1640) excluding the façade and altar, and San Ferdinando (1660?) seems to have been limited to decoration. Between 1649 and 1652, Fanzago restored Santa Maria in via Lata in Rome. Despite alterations made under Pope Pius IX (1853), his hand can still be seen in the side portals, the pavement, the ceiling, the clearstory, and the embellishment of the nave walls. Of his intervention in San Lorenzo in Lucina, Rome (1650–1652), only the pulpit, the holy water basin, and part of the pavement remain.

Time has not treated Fanzago's palaces very well. The Palazzo Caviano (begun 1632) and the Palazzo Stigliano (after 1647) were remodeled in the eighteenth and nineteenth centuries respectively. Around 1652, he added the portal, staircase, and loggia to the Palazzo Maddaloni, which was severely damaged in 1943. The Palazzo Donn'Anna (1642–1644), which was left incomplete and now is in a poor state of repair, is the most original of Fanzago's designs for palaces in Naples. A monumental belvedere of three stories of loggias dominates the impressive seaward façade; unparalleled in palace design are the beveled corners of the building.

Fanzago was also involved in a number of minor projects. In addition to that in San Lorenzo in Lucina, Rome, he executed pulpits in the Church of the Augustinian Nuns (1636) in Salamanca and in Santa Maria degli Angeli alle Croci (1639–1640) in Naples. In Naples, he completed one fountain, the Fontana Medina (1634–1639) and constructed two others, the Fontana Sellaro (1650–1653) and the Fontana del Sebeto (1658). Between 1637 and 1660, he carried out the fanciful Guglia di San Gennaro, a commemorative monument, in Naples.

Fanzago was not especially interested in creating complex spatial units as were his contemporaries in Rome. In fact, his style is rooted in the sixteenth century and he seems to have been drawn particularly to ANDREA PALLADIO from whom he borrowed on more than one occasion. The relative simplicity of the articulation of his interiors and their clarity of design serve as perfect foils for the rich decoration. The impact of his scintillating polychrome inlays and of the abstract marble work on Neapolitan architects has long been recognized, but Fanzago's influence spread beyond Naples and its immediate surrounds. During his sojourn in Naples, FILIPPO JUVARRA seems to have taken note of Fanzago's decorative repertory.

Moreover, the capricious play of antithetical curving volutes seems to have played a major role in the development of the rococo in southern Germany. Fanzago's contribution, however, was not limited to decorative motifs. The Greek cross and cupola scheme, which he used so frequently, set the standard for sacred architecture in Naples until the 1720s. The staircase-vestibules of Santa Maria della Sapienza (1638–1653) and San Giuseppe degli Scalzi a Pontecorvo (1643–1660) served as precedents into the next century. The most notable examples are San Giuseppe dei Ruffi (1715–1725) by Marcello Guglielmelli and San Francesco Scariano (finished 1721) by Giovanni Battista Nauclerio. The screen-type high altar introduced by Fanzago continued to be employed as late as the 1760s. Despite his successful career as a sculptor, decorator, and architect, Fanzago died in a state of near destitution.

CATHIE C. KELLY

WORKS

1620?–1638, Santa Maria delle Anime del Purgatorio (façade and interior decoration); 1622/1624–1657, Ascensione a Chiaia; 1623–1656, Certosa di San Martino (cloister, façade, and interior); 1628–1678, Santa Maria dei Monti (not completed until 1714); Naples. 1629–1634, San Nicola al Lido (high altar), Venice, Italy. 1630, Santissima Trinità delle Monache (façade); begun 1632, Palazzo Caviano; Naples. 1633–1634, Church of the Augustinian Nuns (high altar), Salamanca, Spain. 1634–1639, Fontana Medina; 1634–1678, San Giuseppe dei Vecchi a San Potito (not completed until 1724); 1635–1641, Santi Severino e Sosio (high altar); Naples. 1636, Church of the Augustinian Nuns (minor altars, pulpit, and portal), Salamanca, Spain. 1637–1650, Chapels of Sant'Ignazio and San Francesco Saverio, Gesù Nuovo; 1637–1660, Guglia di San Gennaro; after 1637, Chapel of Santa Teresa, Santa Teresa degli Studi; 1638–1649, Chapel of Sant'Antonio di Padova, San Lorenzo Maggiore; 1638–1653, Santa Maria della Sapienza (façade); 1639–1640, Santa Maria degli Angeli alle Croci (high altar and façade); Naples. 1640?–1645, Gesù e Maria (high altar), Pescostanzo, Italy. 1640–1678, San Giorgio Maggiore; 1642–1644, Palazzo Donn'Anna; 1643–1645, Cappella Cacace, San Lorenzo Maggiore; 1643–1660, San Giuseppe degli Scalzi a Pontecorvo; Naples. *1645, Abbey Church (high altar), Montecassino, Italy. 1645, Santa Maria di Costantinopoli (high altar); 1645–1647, Santa Maria La Nova (high altar); after 1647, Palazzo Sitgliano; Naples. *1649, Santo Spirito dei Napoletani (façade); 1649–1652, Santa Maria in via Latia; Rome. 1650, San Domenico Maggiore (high altar), Naples. 1650–1652, San Lorenzo in Lucina (decoration and *high altar), Rome. 1650–1653, Fontana Sellaro; 1650–1662, Santa Teresa a Chiaia; 1651/1661–1678, Santa Maria Egiziaca a Pizzofalcone (not completed until 1717); after 1652, Palazzo Maddaloni; Naples. 1653–1678, Santa Maria Maggiore (La Pietrasanta); 1658, Fontana del Sebeto; 1660?, San Ferdinando (façade);

1664, Mastrelli Chapel, Santa Maria delle Anime del Purgatorio; Naples.

BIBLIOGRAPHY

BLUNT, ANTHONY 1975 *Neapolitan Baroque & Rococo Architecture.* London: Zwemmer.

BÖSEL, RICHARD 1977 "Anthony Blunt, *Neapolitan Baroque & Rococo Architecture.*" *Zeitschrift für Kunstgeschichte* 40:81–87.

BÖSEL, RICHARD 1978 "Cosimo Fanzago a Roma." *Prospettiva* 15:29–40.

BRAUEN, FRED 1976 "Fanzago's Commission as Royal Chief Engineer." *Storia dell'arte* 26:61–72.

CANTONE, GAETANA 1969 "Il complesso conventuale di S. Maria Egiziaca a Pizzofalcone." *Napoli nobilissima* 8:93–106.

DOMINICI, BERNARDO DE' 1742–1743 *Vite de' pittori, scultori, et architetti napoletani.* 3 vols. in 2. Naples: Ricciardo.

EIMER, GERHARD 1970–1971 *La Fabbrica di S. Agnese in Navona: Römische Architekten, Bauherren, und Handwerker im Zeitalter des Nepotismus.* 2 vols. Stockholm: Almquist & Wiksell.

FOGACCIA, PIERO 1945 *Cosimo Fanzago.* Bergamo: Istituto italiano d'arti grafiche.

MADRUGA REAL, ANGELA 1975 "Cósimo Fanzago en las Agustinas de Salamanca." *Goya* 125:291–297.

PANE, ROBERTO 1939 *Architettura dell'età barocca in Napoli.* Naples: Editrice Politecnica.

PORTOGHESI, PAOLO (1966)1970 *Roma Barocca: The History of an Architectonic Culture.* Cambridge, Mass.: M.I.T. Press. Originally published in Italian.

SALERNO, LUIGI; SPEZZAFERRO, LUIGI; and TAFURI, MANFREDO 1973 *Via Giulia: Una utopia urbanistica del '500.* Rome: Staderini.

TASSI, FRANCESCO MARIA (1793)1969–1970 *Vite de' pittori, scultori, e architetti bergamaschi.* 2 vols. Reprint. Milan: Edizioni Labor.

WEISE, GEORG 1974–1977 "Il repertorio ornamentale del Barocco napoletano di Cosimo Fanzago e il suo significato per la genesi del Rococò (I–V)." *Antichità viva* 13, no. 4:40–53, no. 5:32–41; 14, no. 1:24–31, no. 5:27–35; 16, no. 5:42–51.

WINTHER, ANNEMARIE 1973 *Cosimo Fanzago und die Neapler Ornamentik des 17. und 18. Jahrhunderts.* Bremen, Germany: Hauschild.

WITTKOWER, RUDOLF (1958)1980 *Art and Architecture in Italy 1600 to 1750.* 3d ed., rev. Reprint. Harmondsworth, England: Penguin.

FARQUHARSON, DAVID

Born and trained in Scotland, David Farquharson (1827–1914) designed major buildings in San Francisco and Sacramento, California. Most famous was the Bank of California, a deliberately small-scaled, many-columned brick structure with stone façade after JACOPO SANSOVINO. His clients included the City of Sacramento, a subscription library, the University of California, and several powerful bankers. Through correspondence and subscriptions, he kept abreast of distant architectural developments, early on using iron girders and bearing columns, following GEORGE BROWNE POST's Western Union Building with his own Stock Exchange (1876–1877). Locally influential, he trained apprentices and helped found the West Coast's first architectural society. Later, he became a banker.

ANNE BLOOMFIELD

WORKS

*1854, Courthouse; *1856, Dawson House; Sacramento, Calif. *1865, Cosmopolitan Hotel (addition with Henry Kenitzer); *1865, Nucleus Hotel (with Kenitzer); *1867, Bank of California (with Kenitzer); *1867–1868, Mercantile Library (with Kenitzer); *1870, Tuckerville Houses; San Francisco. 1870–1873, South Hall; *1873, North Hall; University of California, Berkeley. *1873, London and San Francisco Bank; *1875, Nevada Bank; *1876–1877, Real Estate Associates Building; *1876–1877, Stock Exchange; *1878, Saint Ann's Building; *1880, Holbrook Block; *1881, Arizona Block; San Francisco.

BIBLIOGRAPHY

BLOOMFIELD, ANNE 1980 "David Farquharson: Pioneer California Architect." *California History: The Magazine of the California Historical Society* 59, no. 1:16–33.

FARQUHARSON, DAVID (collator) n.d. "Scrapbooks of Public Buildings." Documents Collection, College of Environmental Design University of California, Berkeley.

"San Francisco Chapter, A.I.A." 1909 *Architect & Engineer* 17, no. 3:96.

FATHY, HASSAN

Hassan Fathy (1900–)—philosopher, teacher, architect, artist, poet, champion of the poor—represents the antithesis of the blind drive toward technology in cultures undergoing rapid modernization by advocating tradition alloyed with today's technology. Fathy is known primarily for his book, *Architecture for the Poor,* and for the characteristic signature of his work: mud brick, vault, and dome.

Fathy was born to a family of modest wealth in cosmopolitan Alexandria at a time when Egypt was dominated culturally by the French and financially by the British. Typical was Heliopolis, a suburb of Cairo built in 1904, which was financed by the Belgians and designed by a French architect in the favored Italianate style. But despite the veneer of European culture among the upper class urban Egyptians, most of the country was largely rural. The vast majority lived in villages, barely changed since the Pharaohs. Fathy's father derived his modest wealth from fairly large land holdings worked by tenant farmers, and he visited his lands rarely. Fathy was educated on the pattern of well-to-do families. He was taught in French and was heavily indoctrinated in European culture. His university studies were in architecture at the School of Engineering in Giza, on the outskirts of Cairo. In his book, he indicated that he wanted to study agriculture but failed the entrance examinations and changed to engineering. His architectural education followed the Beaux-Arts traditions, for the French and other European cultures permeated all aspects of Egyptian life.

Fathy graduated in 1926, and his first employment was with the Department of Municipal Affairs in Cairo, where he dealt with various small projects for the government. In 1927, according to his own account, he first set foot on his father's estate, where he was shocked by the harsh realities of the *fellahen* (farmers). He was overwhelmed by the "horrible squalor and ugliness." Driven to rebuild the farm, he came upon mud brick as the natural building choice with potential as a universal housing material. He experimented with the use of sun-dried mud brick, and the publicity he gained provided the chance to build several houses—ironically, mostly for very wealthy clients.

Since the turn of the century, there had been interest throughout Egypt in improving the plight of the *fellah*. Many model village designs were proposed and experiments were undertaken with construction materials, redesign of dwellings and vil-

lages, and more efficient ovens and sanitary latrines. By 1937, an Administration for Village Affairs was established, followed in 1939 by a Ministry of Social Affairs whose goal was to provide rural improvements. The model villages tended to be sterile which barracks-type designs that generally disregarded local traditions. Some experimentation was done with mud brick, and Fathy may have been involved in these initial studies which provided a reference for his later work.

The outbreak of World War II cut off supplies of timber and steel—the primary materials for roofing—and Fathy's early experiments with mud brick became focused. On a fortuitous trip south to Aswan in Upper Egypt he discovered the traditional vault and roofing typical in the area, patterned after ancient shrines and tombs dating from the tenth century.

Returning to Cairo, he completed a farm project at Bahtim for the Royal Society of Agriculture in which he first used traditional domes and vaults, built by Aswan masons who were still following skills handed down from father to son. This project was the first full expression of his philosophy of low-cost housing using mud brick walls and formwork-free mud brick vaults for the roof. Such housing was of very low cost: the materials were readily available, and the necessary construction skills were minimal and readily learned. He felt that now craftsman and architect could work in harmony in re-establishing long lost traditions.

In 1945, Fathy was given a three-year leave of absence from his teaching position at the School of Fine Arts in Cairo and started what would become his best known project, New Gourna in Luxor. His task for the Ministry of Antiquities was to relocate a complete village situated on the Tombs of the Nobles outside of Luxor, where the people made their livelihood by stealing and selling tomb artifacts. A particularly audacious theft of a rock carving brought about the Ministry's determination to move the village, thus giving Fathy the chance to put into practice the philosophy on which his reputation rests. In designing the village, he felt that his task was to restore the aesthetic qualities of the indigenous style to the *fellahen* and to recapture the Egyptian character which had been lost through the vicissitudes of time. In New Gourna, although it was never entirely completed, Fathy's use of mud brick and the vault and dome reached maturity. Driven by cost constraints, Fathy realized the inherent harmony of these elements to the fullest and with a wonderful variety, ranging from simple dwellings to schools, markets, and mosques. Here also, he effectively used traditional concepts and designs for cli-

Fathy.
Ceramics Factory.
Garagos, Egypt.
1948

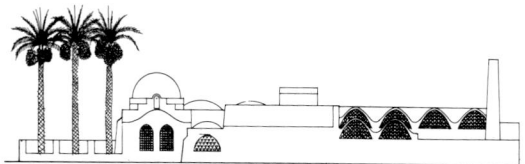

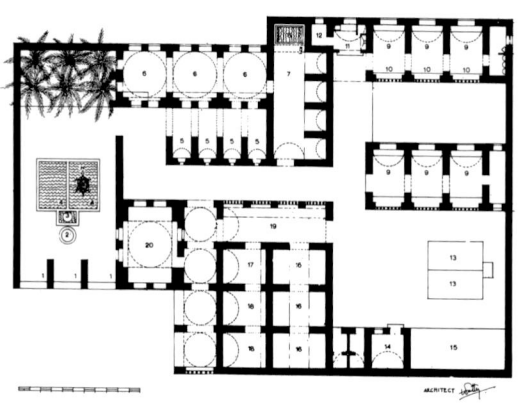

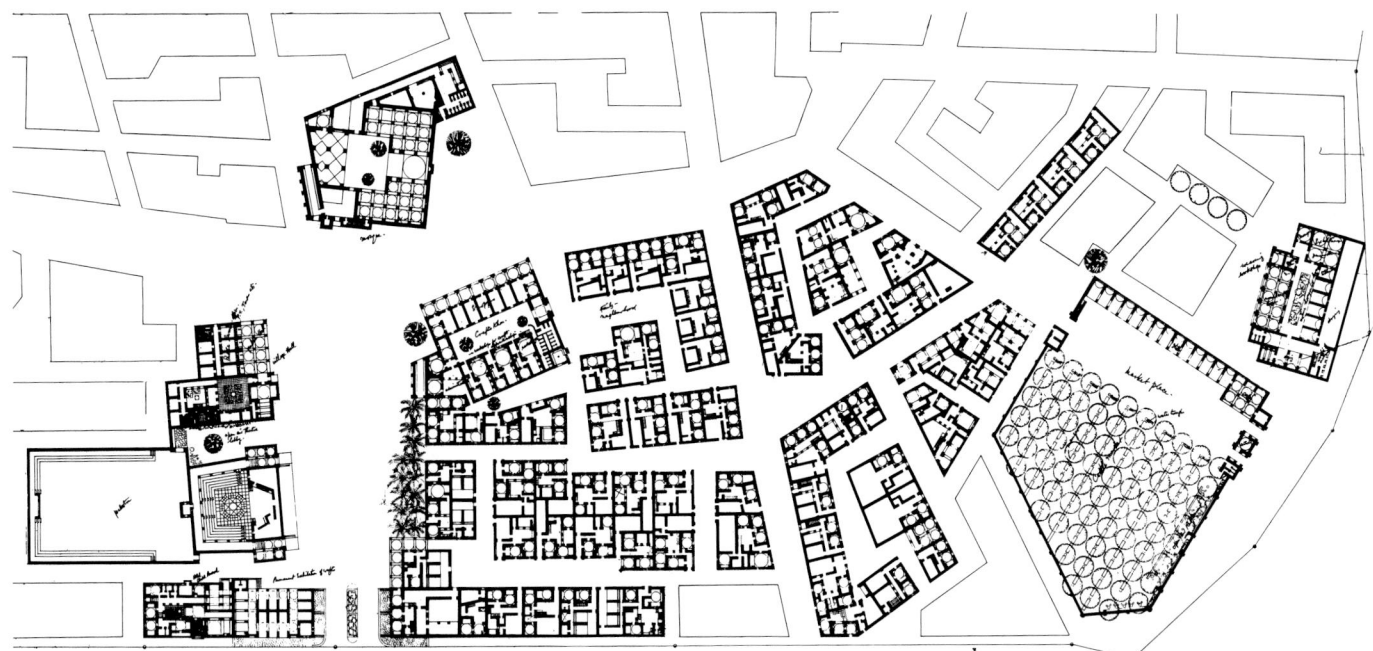

Fathy.
New Gourna Village
(partially built).
Luxor, Egypt.
1945-1948

matic control, for example, *malkafs* (windcatchers) with the addition of wetted traps to cool the air in the rooms of the buildings. However, he was not tied by traditions, for he introduced the Austrian *Kachelofen* as a more efficient source of heat and for cooking. In planning, he reinforced the traditional *badana* (family group), and he kept the narrow lanes for natural cooling and the traditional four quarters of a village structure. Not limiting himself to architecture alone, he also dealt with the problem of retaining the villagers, who lacked skills other than grave-robbing, and with *bilharzia*, a water-borne parasitic disease. Construction was done in the traditional cooperative system, which lowered costs, trained workers in new skills, and transmitted building techniques to future generations. He viewed his project and its process of development as an experiment toward a national rural development program.

But best intent often does not coincide with result, and not unexpectedly the villagers refused to move and used all their devices to sabotage the project. There was little official support for Fathy's design, and after nine months of construction, work was suspended. In 1948, Fathy left the partially completed village and returned to teaching, writing, and promoting his architectural philosophy.

In 1954, the Ministry of Social Affairs asked Fathy to be a consultant to the committee reconstructing the village of Mit-el-Nasara. He turned to the ideas learned in Gourna, and this time the villagers were cooperative and eager to respond. The government, however, ignored his advice and gave the work to another Ministry, who speci-

fied concrete buildings and construction by contractors.

In 1954, Nasser took control of Egypt, sequestered foreign property, and ejected Western influences. In 1957, during the unsettled times, Fathy moved to Athens, where he became a consultant to Doxiadias Associates. He continued his experiments in rural housing, this time in Iraq, and participated in a two-year study on a "City of the Future."

The government's emphasis had shifted to helping the *fellahen*, and land distribution and rural improvement programs were initiated. In 1962, Fathy returned to Cairo and directed research on various experimental houses for the Housing Research Ministry, testing traditionally built structures following scientific procedures.

He continued his technical experiments in re-evaluating traditional methods by testing various mud brick designs for their heat transfer characteristics and optimum *malkaf* arrangements. He tested several of his ideas at the Building Research Center in 1963-1965.

Fathy undertook several designs in the 1960s for the Ministry of Culture and the Ministry of Tourism. Fathy's use of indigenous construction techniques and materials and of non-Western designs were particularly appropriate, since Egypt was drained by heavy military expenses and rejected Western influences.

Most of his designs in this period were not solely mud brick and vault and dome but also made use of traditional Middle Eastern motifs and materials other than mud brick. A particular design of note is the Institute of Folk Art (1965)

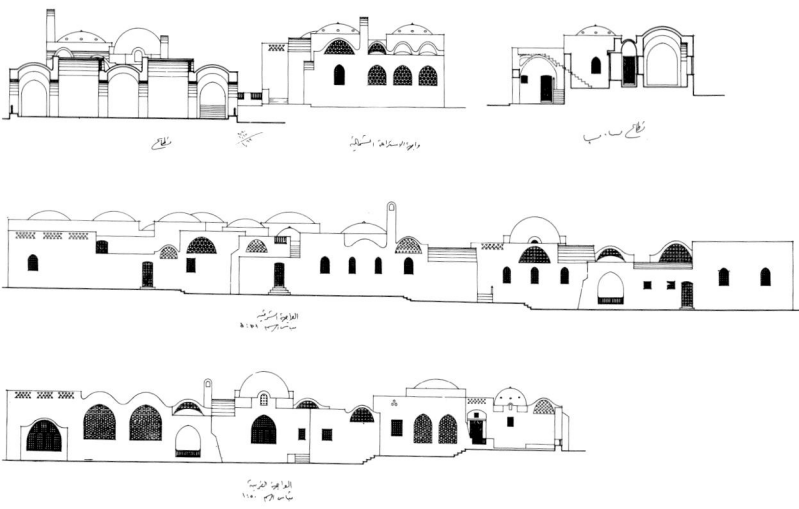

Fathy.
Sidi Crier (partially built.)
Mediterranean Coast,
Egypt.
1971

Fathy was awarded the Egyptian National Prize for Arts and Letters in 1969, a time when things Egyptian were praised and reinforced. National morale was low, and extensive self-doubt existed in the country because of a brief, ill-fated war. At this time, he also completed his book documenting the development of New Gourna, which is considered by some a seminal handbook on development. Initially published by the Ministry of Culture as *Gourna: Tale of Two Villages,* it did not become widely read until it was reissued as *Architecture for the Poor* in English and French translations. In many ways, Fathy was more accepted internationally than in his native Egypt, and his appointment in 1969 as a fellow at the Adlai Stevenson Institute of International Afairs in Chicago furthered this recognition.

In the early 1970s, Anwar Sadat regained the Suez Canal, and a renewed self-respect and interest in Egyptian history swept the country. Coupled with the world's focus on the oil-rich Middle East, all things Islamic became of international interest. In this atmosphere, Fathy designed several projects including a VIP villa project in Tabuk, Saudi Arabia (1974); the Mushrabeya Hotel Center project in Giza (1976); the Nile Festival Island Resort project in Luxor (1978); and the Rebat Hotel project in the Kharga Oasis (1978). All of these projects departed from the dome, vault, and mud brick idiom and used traditional Islamic concepts, decorative motifs, and other materials. Again, Fathy put a heavy emphasis on natural means of climatic and light control with *malkafs* and *mushrabeyas* (lattice windows). His most developed design was the VIP Villa in Saudi Arabia, where cost was not a factor and where the full richness and expression of Arabic decorative motifs can be seen.

which he conceived as a "walk through time," with each room in turn representing a different century and designed and decorated in the prevailing style.

In 1964, Fathy's other village project—Bariz ("Paris") in the Kharga Oasis—was prepared for the government organization responsible for the development of deserts and oases. Fathy's plan elaborated on his concepts from Gourna. However, since no village models existed in the oasis, he chose as a basic image a Tunisian desert village which he superimposed on his neighborhood structure. Lack of funds curtailed the project and only the market was built.

Fathy's reputation and ideas spread, and in 1966 he was asked to serve as a United Nations consultant for rural housing in Saudi Arabia. He used the village of El Dareeya as a model and proposed modern versions of traditional dwelling designs, respecting the local traditions while providing for modern needs. He also continued his interest in teaching, first at the Faculty of Fine Arts and later at Al-Azhar University. His courses on Islamic architecture became legendary, and his walks through the Mamluk sections of Cairo became the highlight for his many students.

Fathy returned to teach young architects at Cairo University, focusing on issues of rural housing. In 1977–1978, Fathy proposed his International Institute of Appropriate Technology, which he intends as a setting for combining education and practical training. It is envisioned as a testing

Fathy.
Mushrabeya Hotel Center
(theater-craft center).
Giza, Egypt.
1976

Fathy.
Kazeroni House.
Giza, Egypt.
n.d.

ground for his ideas of cooperative efforts combining architect, craftsmen, and users in community development projects.

In 1980, Fathy was the recipient of the Chairman's Award in the first Aga Khan Awards for Architecture for his lifelong contribution and commitment to architecture in the Muslim world.

Recently, in the wave of user participation in housing and appropriate technology, Fathy was asked by a group of American converts to the Muslim faith to demonstrate his ideas in building a community near Santa Fe, New Mexico. Again following his experience in Gourna, he brought Nubian masons to the site to work with local artisans and built part of a planned community which he had been commissioned to design.

The realities of Egypt and the world make traditional craftsmen and their techniques scarce and expensive. Despite the silt-rich land in the delta of Egypt, official policy prohibits use of agricultural soil (the material for Fathy's mud bricks) for construction because the Aswan dam has ended the annual renewal of silt, and the spread of urban areas has taken additional scarce land from cultivation. Fathy strongly disputes his critics and claims that there is enough soil for all uses.

Today, Egypt is overwhelmed by a rapid population growth, and Cairo especially has been flooded with migrants since the 1950s. Illegal, informal housing (built of fired brick and concrete floors) is spreading on the outskirts, and government attempts to mass-produce housing have generally not succeeded. There has been a renewed interest in Fathy's ideas, which in essence promote informal construction but with the inclusion of the architect as technical and aesthetic arbiter. Fathy has continued to insist that only through the revival of indigenous techniques, which releases the potential of the people, can the housing shortage be solved.

Although he has received numerous awards, Fathy has never been fully accepted in his own country, for he is considered a romantic with good but impractical ideas. In his work he is a perfectionist and he demands the utmost of his craftsmen and clients. Costs—despite the inherent low cost of the basic material—tend to be forgotten in the process, and he would rather cancel a project than see a redesigned solution implemented.

Fathy's few buildings are clearly beautiful and

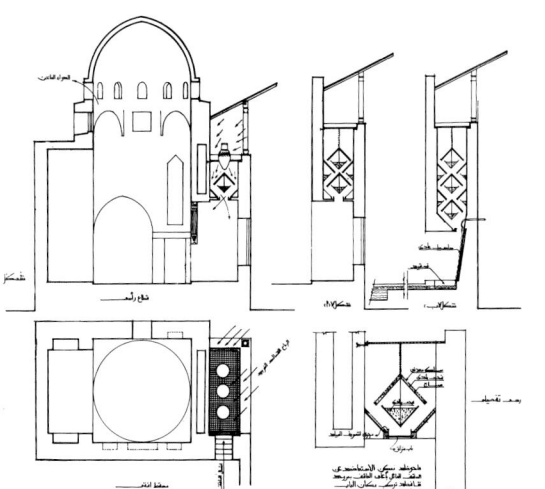

Fathy.
Detail of windcatcher with
*   evaporative cooling.*
n.d.

harmonious and reveal him to be a designer of elegance. His greatest influence, however, is in his philosophy and in his crusade for vernacular tradition coupled with technology.

REINHARD GOETHERT
with MARGARET DE POPOLO

WORKS

1930's, Rest Houses, Safaga, Egypt. 1937, Royal Society of Agriculture Farm, Bahtim, Egypt. 1942, Taher Omari Farm, Sedmant el Gabal, Fayum, Egypt. 1942-1945, Hamed Said House, Marq, Egypt. 1945?, School, Fares, Egypt. 1945-1948, New Gourna Village (partially built), Luxor, Egypt. 1948, Ceramics Factory, Garagos, Egypt. 1964, Bariz Village (partially built), Kharga Oasis, Egypt. 1971, Sidi Crier (partially built), Mediterranean Coast, Egypt. 1980, Dar el Islam Community (partially built), N.M. n.d., Kallini House, Menia, Egypt. n.d., Kazeroni House, Giza, Egypt. n.d., Fouad Riad House, Saqqarah Road, Egypt. n.d., Akeel Samy House, Giza, Egypt. n.d., Stoprail House, Luxor, Egypt.

BIBLIOGRAPHY

CLARK, FELICIA 1980 "Appropriate Invention." Architectural Record 167:187, 189, 195.
COUSIN, JEAN-PIERRE 1978 "Hassan Fathy." L'Architecture d'Aujourd'Hui 195:42-78.
DEPOPOLO, MARGARET, and GOETHERT, REINHARD 1981 Hassan Fathy—Architect: An Exhibition of Selected Projects. Cambridge, Mass.: M.I.T. Exhibition catalogue.
FATHY, HASSAN 1962 "Rural Self-Help Housing." International Labour Review 85, no. 1:1-17. Abstracted in Ekistics 13, no. 80:398-401.
FATHY, HASSAN (1963)1973 "Planning and Building in the Arab Tradition: The Village Experiment at Gourna." Pages 210-229 in Monroe Berger (editor), The New Metropolis in the Arab World. Reprint. New York: Octagon.
FATHY, HASSAN 1964 "An Ekistic Approach to the Problem of Roofing in Peasant House-building." Ekistics 17, no. 103:391-398.
FATHY, HASSAN 1966 "Model houses for El Dareeya, Saudi Arabia." Ekistics 21, no. 124:214-219.
FATHY, HASSAN (1969)1973 Architecture for the Poor: An Experiment in Rural Egypt. University of Chicago Press. Originally published with the title Gourna: A Tale of Two Villages.
FATHY, HASSAN 1972a The Arab House in the Urban Setting: Past, Present and Future. London: Longmans.
FATHY, HASSAN 1972b "The Qa'a of the Cairene Arab House; Its Development and Some Usages for Its Design Concepts." Pages 135-152 in Colloque International Sur L'Histoire Du Caire, 1969. Proceedings. Cairo: Ministry of Culture, Arab Republic of Egypt.
FATHY, HASSAN 1973 "Constancy, Transposition and Change in the Arab City." Pages 319-334 in L. Carl Brown (editor), From Madina to Metropolis. Princeton, N.J.: Darwin.
MARQUIS, ROBERT B. 1980 "Egypt's Prophet of Appropriate Technology." American Institute of Architects Journal 69:38-39.
"Nouveau Village de Gourna, Architecte: Hassan Fathy." 1968 L'Architecture d'Aujourd'hui. 39, no. 140:12-17.
"Le Nouveau Village de Gournah, Egypte, Architecte: Hassan Fathy." 1947 L'Architecture Française 8, nos. 73-74:78-82.
SCALESSE, TOMMASO 1980 "Hassan Fathy in Egitto." Pages 240-258 in Architettura Povera. Rome: Carucci.
SCHILLING, JAKOB 1965 "Gourna: Ein architektonisches Experiment in Ägypten." Deutsche Bauzeitung 70, no. 99:46-50.

FATIO, MAURICE

Maurice Fatio (1897-1943) was born in Geneva. He graduated from the University of Zurich in 1920 and emigrated that year to the United States. He formed a partnership with William A. Treanor in 1921 (joined by Frederick G. Sulmann in 1931) with offices in New York City and Palm Beach, Florida.

Fatio ran the Palm Beach office, designing Spanish-style mansions in the footsteps of ADDISON MIZNER, and, in the 1930s, neo-Georgian and Regency houses. During World War II, the firm had commissions in Santiago, Chile, and Rio de Janeiro.

VICTORIA NEWHOUSE

WORKS

1920s, J. S. and H. C. Phipps Houses; 1930, Joseph E. Widener House; 1936, Library Society of the Four Arts; Palm Beach, Fla.

BIBLIOGRAPHY

HOFFSTOT, BARBARA D. (1974)1980 Landmark Architecture of Palm Beach. Rev. ed. Pittsburgh: Ober Park Associates.
TREANOR, WILLIAM A., and FATIO, MAURICE 1932 Treanor and Fatio: Architects. New York: Architectural Catalog Company.

FAVENTINUS

M. Cetius Faventinus (4th century) was the author of a book on domestic building closely modeled on certain sections of the work of VITRUVIUS and written probably in the first half of the fourth century. Like many works of the period, it was not an original contribution to the subject, but primarily a compilation from earlier sources. Exercises of this kind were intended to satisfy the demands of contemporary literary taste, for which form took priority over content.

B. M. BOYLE

BIBLIOGRAPHY

PLOMMER, WILLIAM HUGH 1973 *Vitruvius and Later Roman Building Manuals.* Cambridge University Press.

FAYDHERBE, LUCAS

A major figure in Belgian sculpture and architecture of the seventeenth century, Lucas Faydherbe (1617–1697) came from a family of artists. He was a friend and student of Rubens, whom he assisted between the years 1636 and 1640. After the death of his master (1640), he settled in Malines as *franc-maître*.

Because of his bold manner of execution, the richness of his pictorial effects, and his vigorous and full style which is characterized by an abundance of ringed columns rich with embossing, he is considered the leader of the Rubensian baroque.

PIERRE LENAIN
Translated from French by Shara Wasserman

WORKS

1662, Church of the Priory of Leliendael, Belgium. 1663–1681, Church of Notre-Dame de Hanswijk, Malines, Belgium. 1663–1700, Church of the Norbertine Abbey of Averbode, Belgium.

BIBLIOGRAPHY

ACKERE, JULES EMILE VAN 1972 *Baroque and Classic Art in Belgium.* Brussels: Vokaer.
LIBERTUS, FRÈRE 1938 *Lucas Faydherbe: Beeldhouwer en bouwmeester.* Antwerp, Belgium: De Sikkel.
THIBAUT DE MAISIÈRES, MAURY DIEUDONNÉ JOSEPH JULES MARIE 1943 *L'architecture religieuse en Belgique à l'époque de Rubens.* Brussels: Editions du cercle d'art.

FEDERIGHI, ANTONIO

Antonio Federighi (1420–1490) was an Italian sculptor and architect of the Renaissance. Employed extensively in Siena, Italy, his native town, by the Piccolomini family, he built for Pius II a papal loggia (1462) and aided Antonio Rossellino with the construction of the Palazzo della Papesse (1460–1495). His best work is the witty Palazzo dei Diavoli (1460) just outside Siena.

NICHOLAS ADAMS

WORKS

1460, Palazzo dei Diavoli; 1460–1495, Palazzo della Papesse (with Antonio Rossellino); 1462, Logge del Papa; 1463–1468, Capella di Piazza (additions); Siena, Italy.

BIBLIOGRAPHY

MANTURA, BRUNO 1968 "Sulla Paternità della Cappella e del 'Palazzo dei Diavoli' a Siena." *Commentari* 19:259–267.

FEILDEN, BERNARD

Bernard Melchior Feilden (1919–) was born in London and trained there at the Architectural Association. In 1954, he established a private practice in Norwich, England, and carried out a wide variety of domestic, industrial, commercial, and town planning projects while specializing in the conservation of historic religious buildings. In 1956, he commenced work on Norwich Cathedral where his innovative techniques for inspecting the endangered building and his application of contemporary structural engineering solutions to the problems of deterioration saved the building. In 1965, he began work on York Minster, the largest Gothic cathedral in northern Europe. As surveyor to York Minster, he carried out a major program to stabilize the foundations, clean the stone, and rehabilitate the landscaping. In 1969, he turned his attention to Saint Paul's Cathedral, London, where as surveyor he carried out a comprehensive inspection of the cathedral's fabric and initiated conservation of the western towers, the interior, and the organ. From 1977 to 1981, he served as the third director of the International Centre for the Study of the Preservation and Restoration of Cultural Property in Rome. In 1981, he became chairman of the United Kingdom National Committee of the International Council on Monuments and Sites.

W. BROWN MORTON III

WORKS

1956–1977, Norwich Cathedral (restoration), England. 1965–1977, York Minster (restoration), England. 1969–1977, Saint Paul's Cathedral (restoration), London.

BIBLIOGRAPHY

FEILDEN, BERNARD M. 1976 *The Wonder of York Minster.* York, England: Cerialis.
FEILDEN, BERNARD M. 1982 *Conservation of Historic Buildings.* London: Butterworth.

FELIBIEN DES AVAUX, ANDRE

Born in Chartres and having gone to Paris at the age of fourteen, André Félibien des Avaux (1619–1695) left for Rome in 1647 where he spent two years as secretary to the marquis de Fontenay-Mareuil who had been sent as ambassador to the

Holy See. A private diary of Félibien informs us about his contacts with the art of antiquity and the Renaissance and with contemporary artists such as Nicolas Poussin and Claude Lorrain. Returning to France in 1649, Félibien married and settled in Chartres.

Introduced to the Royal Court, Félibien later took several offices. He was one of the eight members of the Académie des Inscriptions et Belles-Lettres founded in 1663. Successively, Félibien became *historiographe du Roy* (1666), *historiographe des Bâtiments du Roy* (1669), and historiographer of the arts and manufactures. In 1671, he was appointed secretary to the new Academy of Architecture. He also became *garde des antiques du Palais Brion* (1673).

Besides some translations and historiographical works like his *Description sommaire du château de Versailles* (1674), Félibien published several treatises on art theory, among them the *Principles* (1676) known as one of the main documents of the classic art doctrine in France.

WALTER KAMBARTEL

BIBLIOGRAPHY

DELAPORTE, YVES 1958 "André Félibien en Italie." *Gazette des Beaux-Arts* 51:193–214.

FÉLIBIEN, ANDRÉ 1674 *Description sommaire du château de Versailles*. Paris: Deprez.

FÉLIBIEN, ANDRÉ (1676)1699 *Des Principes de l'architecture, de la sculpture, de la peinture et des autres arts*. 3d ed. Paris: Coignard.

FÉLIBIEN, ANDRÉ 1725 *Oeuvres*. Trevoux, France.

FÉLIBIEN, JEAN-FRANÇOIS 1687 *Recueil historique de la vie et des ouvrages des plus célèbres architectes*. Paris: Mabre-Cramoisy.

FONTAINE, ANDRÉ 1909 *Les doctrines d'art en France*. Paris: Laurens.

HAUTECOEUR, LOUIS 1948 *La règne de Louis XIV*. Volume 2 in *Histoire de L'Architecture classique en France*. Paris: Picard.

LAFOND, JEAN 1954 "Félibien est-il notre premier historien du vitrail? Les 'Principes de l'architecture' et l' Origine de l'art de la peinture sur verre!" *Bulletin de la Société de l'Histoire de l'Art Français* 1954:45–60.

LEMONNIER, HENRY 1911–1924 *Procès-Verbaux de l'Académie Royale d'Architecture*. Paris: Schemit.

FELIBIEN DES AVAUX, JEAN FRANÇOIS

Born in Chartres, the second son of ANDRÉ FÉLI-BIEN DES AVAUX, secretary of the Académie d'Architecture, Jean François Félibien des Avaux (c.1656–1733) eventually succeeded his father in this position. Appointed historian to the Bâtiments du Roi and treasurer of the Académie des Inscrip-

tions, he resigned in 1716 as a result of charges of dishonesty; and he was acquitted in 1722. Seeking to emulate his father's work on the lives of famous painters, he published a book on architects' lives (1687), which was thought unreliable by his contemporaries. Still, it was significant as the first attempt to outline a history of Gothic architecture, recognizing "Gothique ancien" and "Gothique moderne," corresponding roughly to Romanesque and Gothic, and also noted the importance of Abbot Suger. Félibien des Avaux later suggested that early medieval architecture derived from the imagery of caves, Gothic itself from forest groves.

R. D. MIDDLETON

BIBLIOGRAPHY

FÉLIBIEN DES AVAUX, JEAN FRANÇOIS 1687 *Recueil historique de la vie et des ouvrages des plus célèbres architectes*. Paris: Mabre-Cramoisy.

FÉLIBIEN DES AVAUX, JEAN FRANÇOIS 1699 *Les plans et les descriptions de deux des plus belles maisons de campagne de Pline le consul, avec des remarques sur tous les bâtimens et une dissertation touchant l'architecture antique et l'architecture gothique*. Paris: Delaulne.

FÉLIBIEN DES AVAUX, JEAN FRANÇOIS 1702 *Description de la nouvelle église de l'hostel royal des Invalides*. Paris.

FÉLIBIEN DES AVAUX, JEAN FRANÇOIS 1703 *Description sommaire de Versailles ancienne et nouvelle*. Paris: Chrétien.

MERLET, K. LUCIEN VICTOR CLAUDE 1882 *Bibliothèque chartraine antérieure au XIXe siècle*. Orléans, France: Herluison.

MIDDLETON, ROBIN DAVID 1962 "The Abbé de Cordemoy and the Graeco-Gothic Ideal: A Prelude to Romantic Classicism." *Journal of the Warburg and Courtauld Institutes* 25, nos. 3–4:299–302.

FELLNER, FERDINAND

Ferdinand Fellner (1847–1916) was born in Vienna, the son of a theater architect. Working first with his father and then in collaboration with Hermann Gottlieb Helmer, he was active from Switzerland to Russia, from north Germany to Bulgaria, but above all in Austria-Hungary. In all, he built forty-eight theaters, concert halls, and meeting halls and planned others, as well as erecting numerous other buildings. The theaters were mostly free-standing gallery and box theaters, more or less richly decorated, depending on the client. They continued the sculptural, rich form language of GOTTFRIED SEMPER, starting with Renaissance and baroque forms and later, with the change in contemporary taste, turning to the *Jugendstil*.

SOKRATIS DIMITŘIOU

WORKS

1888–1889, Deutsches Volkstheater, Vienna. 1898–1899, Arbeitertheater, Berndorf, Austria. 1898–1899, Stadttheater, Graz, Austria. 1909–1910, Stadttheater, Klagenfurt, Austria.

BIBLIOGRAPHY

FELLNER, FERDINAND, and HELMER, HERMANN 1914 *Sammelwerk der ausgeführten Bauten und Projekte: 1870–1914.* Vienna: Privately printed.
HOFFMANN, HANS-CHRISTOPH 1966 *Die Theaterbauten von Fellner und Helmer.* Munich: Prestel.
WAGNER-RIEGER, RENATE 1970 *Wiens Architektur im 19. Jahrhundert.* Vienna: Österreichischer Bundesverlag.
WURM-ARNKREUZ, ALOIS VON 1919 *Architekt Ferdinand Fellner und seine Bedeutung für den modernen Theaterbau.* Vienna and Leipzig: Verlag für Technik und Industrie.

FENGER, LUDVIG

Ludvig Peter Fenger (1833–1905) was born in Slotsbjergby, Denmark. As a student at the Royal Academy of Fine Arts in Copenhagen, Fenger was influenced primarily by Ferdinand Meldahl and adopted the current eclectic styles based on historical European architecture. Later, Fenger departed from this international style by using undisguised brick rather than stucco on the façade of the Polytechnic Institute, Copenhagen (1880–1882). This prominent display of brick, a material used abundantly and expressively in traditional Scandinavian architecture, heralded national romanticism, a movement which emphasized indigenous building materials, forms, and practices. Interest in Denmark's past led Fenger to write several histories of Danish architecture. He served as city architect of Copenhagen from 1886 until his death.

JUDITH S. HULL

WORKS

1871–1872, Holmens Church (restoration); 1878, Saint Jacobs and Saint Matthew's Churches; 1879, Royal Louise Hospital; 1880–1882, Polytechnic Institute; 1889–1892, Main Fire Station; Copenhagen. 1900–1901, Fire Station, Osterbo, Denmark. 1901–1902, Eastern Electric Works, Copenhagen.

BIBLIOGRAPHY

LANGKILDE, HANS ERLING 1980 "Ludwig Peter Fenger." Volume 4, pages 372–373 in Sven Cedergren Bech (editor), *Dansk Biografisk Leksikon.* Copenhagen: Gyldendal.

FENNER, BERT

See MCKIM, MEAD, and WHITE.

FERGUSSON, JAMES

James Fergusson (1808–1886) wrote the first comprehensive history of architecture, initiated in the *Illustrated Handbook of Architecture* (1855) and fulfilled in the multivolume *History of Architecture in All Countries* (1862–1867). Born in Ayr, Scotland, he toured India, completing a study of rock-temples in 1843. After returning to England in 1845, he concentrated on historical and topographical writing and also executed some designs, favoring the Italianate. A speculative theorist and dogmatic critic, he castigated copyist architecture, recommending that architects emulate but beautify engineering design. He was awarded the Royal Institute of British Architects Gold Medal (1871). After his death he was compared with VITRUVIUS.

R. WINDSOR LISCOMBE

BIBLIOGRAPHY

CRAIG, MAURICE 1968 "James Fergusson." Pages 140–152 in John Summerson (editor), *Concerning Architecture.* London: Allen Lane.
FERGUSSON, JAMES 1847a *An Essay on the Ancient Topography of Jerusalem.* London: Weale.
FERGUSSON, JAMES 1847b *Picturesque Illustrations of Ancient Architecture in Hindustan.* London: J. Hogarth.
FERGUSSON, JAMES 1849 *An Historical Inquiry into the True Principles of Beauty in Art More Especially with Reference to Architecture.* London: Longman.
FERGUSSON, JAMES 1851 *The Palaces of Nineveh and Persepolis Restored.* London: J. Murray.
FERGUSSON, JAMES (1855)1859 *The Illustrated Handbook of Architecture: Being a Concise and Popular Account of the Different Styles of Architecture Prevailing in All Ages and Countries.* 2nd ed. London: J. Murray.
FERGUSSON, JAMES (1862)1891 *A History of the Modern Styles of Architecture.* 3d ed., rev. London: J. Murray.
FERGUSSON, JAMES 1862–1867 *A History of Architecture in All Countries, From the Earliest Times to the Present Day.* 3 vols. London: J. Murray.
FERGUSSON, JAMES (1868)1873 *Tree and Serpent Worship, or Illustrations of Mythology and Art in India.* 2d ed., rev. London: India Museum.
FERGUSSON, JAMES 1872 *Rude-Stone Monuments in All Countries: Their Age and Uses.* London: J. Murray.
FERGUSSON, JAMES 1874 *A History of Ancient and Mediaeval Architecture.* London: J. Murray.
FERGUSSON, JAMES 1876 *A History of Indian and Eastern Architecture.* London: J. Murray.
FERGUSSON, JAMES 1878 *The Temples of the Jews and the Other Buildings in the Harem Area of Jerusalem.* London: J. Murray.
FERGUSSON, JAMES 1883 *The Parthenon: An Essay on the Mode by Which Light was Introduced into Greek and Roman Temples.* London: J. Murray.
MACLEOD, ROBERT 1971 Pages 70–79 in *Style and Society: Architectural Ideology in Britain 1835–1914.* London: Royal Institute of British Architects.
PEVSNER, NICHOLAUS 1972 "James Fergusson."

Pages 238–251 in *Some Architectural Writers of the Nineteenth Century*. Oxford: Clarendon Press.

WHITE, WILLIAM H. 1886 "James Fergusson: A Sketch of his Life." *Report of the Royal Asiatic Society* 1886: xxvii–xxxvii.

WINTER, ROBERT W. 1958 "Fergusson and Garbett and American Architectural Theory." *Journal of the Society of Architectural Historians* 15:25–29.

FERNÁNDEZ-SHAW E ITURRALDE, CASTRO

Castro Fernández-Shaw e Iturralde (1896–1978), born in Madrid, was a disciple and collaborator of Antonio Palacios y Ramilio and as such was one of the first to introduce modern architecture to Spain. He is one of the few visionary and utopian architects of recent Spanish culture.

His Gas Station in Alberto Aguilera Street, Madrid (1927), was constructed as a polemical work and became significant for its clear adherence to the European nationalist trends. His project for the Airport of Barajas (1929) and the House on Memendez y Pelayo Street in Madrid (1935) show a certain Mendelsohnian (see ERIC MENDELSOHN) influence.

Better known are his visionary projects in which he mixed futurist and expressionist influences. He made several versions of numerous imaginary themes, of which the most distinguished are the series of "anti-aerial architecture," "dynamic architecture," and "aerodynamic architecture."

He founded and edited the magazine *Farmhouses and Skyscrapers*.

ADOLFO G. AMEZOUETA
*Translated from Spanish by
Judith E. Meighan*

WORKS

*1927, Gas Station, Alberto Aguilera Street; 1931, Coliseum Cinema (with Pedro Muguruza); 1934, Riscal Building; 1935, Housing, 15 Memendez y Pelayo Street; Madrid.

BIBLIOGRAPHY

CABRERO GARRIDO, FELIX 1980 *Casto Fernández-Shaw*. Madrid: Colegio Oficial de Arquitectos.

FULLAONDO, DANIEL 1969 "El movimiento futurista: C. Fernández Shaw." *Nueva Forma* 38.

FERNBACH, HENRY

Henry Fernbach (1829–1883) was born in Loewenberg in Prussian Silesia (now Iwowek, Poland) and attended the Berlin Building Academy. Around 1855, he emigrated to New York and established a successful practice. Fernbach built synagogues in the *Rundbogenstil* and Moorish Revival style. In collaboration with LEOPOLD EIDLITZ, he planned and supervised the construction of Temple Emanu-El (1866–1868) in New York. He was an accomplished designer of commercial buildings in the Second Empire mode and he favored the use of cast-iron construction. Fernbach was an early member of the American Institute of Architects and was active in its New York chapter.

JOY M. KESTENBAUM

WORKS

*1864–1865, B'nai Jeshurun Synagogue; *1865–1866, Harmonie Club Building; *1866–1868, Temple Emanu-El (with Leopold Eidlitz); *1868–1869, Shaaray Tefila Synagogue; 1870–1872, Ahawath Chesed (Central Synagogue); *1870–1872, German Savings Bank (with Edward Kendall); *1871–1873, New Yorker-Staats Zeitung Building, New York. 1873–1875, Mutual Life Insurance Co. of New York Building, Philadelphia; *1876–1877, Salem Fields Cemetery Gatehouse, Brooklyn, New York; *1880, Institute for Improved Education of Deaf Mutes (Lexington School for the Deaf); 1881, 93–99 Greene Street; 1881–1882, 114–120 Greene Street; 1882–1883, 121–123 Greene Street; 1882–1883, 133–137 Greene Street; New York.

BIBLIOGRAPHY

FRANCIS, DENNIS STEADMAN 1980 *Architects in Practice, New York City, 1840–1900*. New York: Committee for the Preservation of Architectural Records.

"Henry Fernbach." (1941)1969 Volume 4, page 279 in *Universal Jewish Encyclopedia*. New York: Ktav.

KESTENBAUM, JOY 1979 "Henry Fernbach: Architect of Distinction." *News of the Jewish Historical Society of New York* June–Aug.:4.

"The Late Henry Fernbach." 1883 *Real Estate Record and Builders Guide* 32, Dec. 8:974.

NEW YORK LANDMARKS PRESERVATION COMMISSION 1973 *Soho—Cast Iron Historic District, Designation Report*. New York: The commission.

"Obituary." 1883 *American Architect and Building News* 14, no. 413:241.

VAN PELT, DANIEL 1898 *Leslie's History of the Greater New York*. New York: Arkell.

WISCHNITZER, RACHEL 1955 *Synagogue Architecture in the United States*. Philadelphia: Jewish Publication Society of America.

FEROGGIO, GIOVANNI BATTISTA

Giovanni Battista Feroggio (1723–1797) was born and died in Camburzano, Piedmont, Italy. Feroggio designed the replacement for ASCANIO VITOZZI's Spirito Santo in Turin, Italy, and the church of

Santa Caterina in Asti, Italy, both derived from the work of BERNARDO ANTONIO VITTONE. Feroggio also rebuilt the Teatro Carignano in Turin after a fire in 1787. The church of San Germano in San Germano Vercellese, long attributed to Feroggio, has recently been shown to be by Michele Ricciardi.

HENRY A. MILLON

WORKS

1764–1767, Spirito Santo, Turin, Italy. 1766–1773, Santa Caterina, Asti, Italy. 1787, Teatro Carignano (rebuilding), Turin, Italy.

BIBLIOGRAPHY

BRAYDA, CARLO; COLI, LAURA; and SESIA, DARIO 1963 *Ingegneri e architetti del sei e settecento in piemonte*. Turin, Italy: Società ingegneri e architetti.

CARBONERI, NINO 1963 Volume 1, pages 78–79 in *Architettura: Mostra del Barocco Piemontese*. Turin, Italy: Catalogo a cura di Vittorio Viale.

CARBONERI, NINO 1974 "Attribuzioni e documenti vittoniani." Volume 2, pages 286–289 in Vittorio Viale (editor), *Bernardo Vittone e la disputa fra classicismo e barocco nel settecento*. Turin, Italy.

OLIVERO, E. 1934 "La Chiesa dello Spirito Santo in Torino e il suo architetto Giov. Battista Feroggio." *Torino* 14, nos. 11–12:9–17.

FERREY, BENJAMIN

Born in Christchurch, Hampshire, England, Benjamin Ferrey (1810–1880) was articled in 1825 or 1826 to AUGUSTUS CHARLES PUGIN in London. He became a fellow pupil of Pugin's son, A. W. N. PUGIN, and drew the plates for some of their books. Hired by WILLIAM WILKINS in 1832 or 1833, he established his own office in 1834, being briefly in partnership with Thomas Larkins Walker. His first major commission (1836) was a group of villas in Bournemouth, but soon, influenced by A. W. N. Pugin and the Ecclesiological Society, he became one of the Society's favorite church architects and "one of the earliest, ablest, and most zealous pioneers of the modern Gothic school" (Eastlake, 1970, p. 220). His Saint Stephen, Westminster (1847–1850), was one of the most important new churches in London.

Ferrey's most significant buildings were his many churches—mostly Gothic but in some cases Norman in style. He also restored many medieval churches and designed schools, parsonages, public buildings, and country houses, generally in the Tudor style. He was a sensitive and capable designer rather than an innovator, and his finest works are fastidious, scholarly, and assured. However, because he resisted the widespread influence

of the Italian and early French Gothic styles in the 1850s, his work in this period looks old-fashioned.

Ferrey became a fellow of the Royal Institute of British Architects in 1839 and was twice elected vice-president. He was also a founder of the Architectural Museum, a fellow of the Society of Antiquaries (1863), and a frequent exhibitor at the Royal Academy. In 1861, he published his important *Recollections of A. W. N. Pugin*. He died in London in 1880, having been associated for several years with his son, Edward Benjamin Ferrey.

E. N. KAUFMAN

WORKS

1836, Westover Estate Villas and Hotel, Bournemouth, Hampshire, England. 1839–1859, Dorset County Hospital, Dorchester, England. 1841–1842, Holy Trinity Church, Roehampton, London. 1841–1844, Saint Nicholas, Grafton, Wiltshire, England. 1842, Cathedral (restoration), Wells; 1842–1850, Saint Mary Magdalene (restoration), Taunton; Somersetshire, England. 1843–1846, Saint James, Morpeth, Northumberland, England. 1845–1846, Christ Church, Melplash, Dorset, England. 1846, Bishop's Palace (restoration), Wells, Somersetshire, England. 1847–1849, Holy Trinity, Penn Street, Buckinghamshire, England. 1847–1850, Saint Stephen, Westminster, London. 1847–1852, Saint Peter's College, Saltley, Birmingham, England. 1853–1860, Saint Mary, Buckland Saint Mary, Somersetshire, England. 1857–1858, All Saints, Blackheath, London. 1858–1861, Wynnstay, Clwyd, Wales. 1861, Bulstrode, Buckinghamshire, England. 1861, Saint Peter, Slinfold, Sussex, England. 1865–1867, Saint Michael, Chetwynde, Shropshire, England. 1877, Bagshot Park, Surrey, England.

BIBLIOGRAPHY

CLARKE, BASIL F. L. (1938)1969 *Church Builders of the Nineteenth Century*. Reprint. Newton Abbot, England: Charles.

EASTLAKE, CHARLES L. (1870–1872)1970 *A History of the Gothic Revival*. Edited with an introduction by J. Mordaunt Crook. Reprint. Leicester (England) University Press; New York: Humanities Press.

FERREY, BENJAMIN (1861)1978 *Recollections of A. W. N. Pugin and His Father Augustus Pugin*. With an introduction and index by Clive Wainwright and Jane Wainwright. Reprint. London: Scolar.

"The Late Mr. Benjamin Ferrey." 1880 *The Builder* 39:281–283.

"The Late Mr. Benjamin Ferrey." 1880 *Building News and Engineering Journal* 39:261–262.

FERRISS, HUGH

From the 1920s through the 1950s, Hugh Ferriss (1889–1962) was America's foremost architectural delineator, and though he preferred the term "design consultant," both titles understate the scope and originality of his contribution. In his commercial work (usually elaborate perspectives of buildings commissioned by their architects) and even more in his visionary drawings, Ferriss redefined a new, more creative role for the delineator as an interpreter of the mood and message of architecture. In an essay on rendering for the *Encyclopaedia Britannica* (1929), he proposed that the delineator could serve as a guide in city planning, assist in evolving new types of architecture, and strengthen the psychological influence of architecture on human values. A licensed architect, Ferriss elected to build only on paper, yet his influence (particularly in the 1920s) on the development of a modern style for urban architecture equaled that of any contemporary.

Born and raised in St. Louis, Missouri, Ferriss received his degree in architecture from the Beaux-Arts-oriented Washington University in 1911. After two years' experience as a draftsman and with a letter of introduction to CASS GILBERT, he departed for New York, his adopted metropolis. He drew perspectives in Gilbert's office until 1915, when he began to free-lance as an architectural illustrator. His first drawings appeared in *Vanity Fair* and various newspapers, and by the early 1920s, his renderings were featured regularly in architectural periodicals in both plates and advertisements.

Through the 1920s, Ferriss's reputation rose like the skyscrapers that were his favorite and most frequent subject. His characteristic treatment of buildings as simplified, sculptural masses rendered in dramatic chiaroscuro began with the "zoning envelope studies" of 1922, a series of drawings developed in collaboration with HARVEY W. CORBETT, which depicted the setback formula for skyscrapers prescribed by the 1916 New York zoning law. These striking images revealed the elemental beauty and power inherent in the undisguised setback form; the suppression of ornament and historical allusion influenced architects who were searching for a "modern" style for the skyscraper. The zoning studies also inspired the ideal city Ferriss illustrated in *The Metropolis of Tomorrow* (1929). This book, a collection of his finest renderings of skyscrapers, predictions based on current architectural trends, and his visionary proposal for a humanistic city of the future, represents one of the most eloquent testaments of urban optimism of that ebullient decade. A keen interest in the future of architecture remained a leitmotif throughout his long career.

Ferriss often participated as both delineator and design consultant on large projects such as the New York World's Fair (1936–1939) and the United Nations Building (1946–1949). In 1941, he toured the United States sketching its most significant recent structures. These drawings, exhibited in a one-man show at the Whitney Museum in 1942, later formed the nucleus of *Power in Buildings* (1953). Active in many professional organizations, he served as the president of the New York chapters of the Architectural League and the American Institute of Architects.

CAROL WILLIS

BIBLIOGRAPHY

FERRISS, HUGH 1929 *The Metropolis of Tomorrow.* New York: Ives Washington.

FERRISS, HUGH (1929)1973 "Architectural Rendering." Volume 2, pages 310–311 in *Encyclopaedia Britannica.* Chicago: Benton. Originally published with the title "Rendering, Architectural."

FERRISS, HUGH 1953 *Power in Buildings; An Artist's View of Contemporary Architecture.* New York: Columbia University Press.

LEICH, JEAN FERRISS 1980 *Architectural Visions: The Drawings of Hugh Ferriss.* New York: Whitney Library of Design.

FERSTEL, HEINRICH VON

Heinrich von Ferstel (1828–1883) was one of the four most important architects of the Ringstrasse in Vienna (the others being FRIEDRICH VON SCHMIDT, THEOPHILUS EDUARD HANSEN, and CARL HASENAUER). Most of Ferstel's work, which is concentrated on the church, the monumental public building, the apartment building, and the design of plazas, is found in the Ringstrasse area.

Ferstel, the son of a bank official, studied at the Polytechnical Institute and at the Academy of Fine Arts in his native Vienna (1843–1851). His teachers Eduard VAN DER NÜLL AND August SICCARDSBURG deeply influenced the first period of his work. Having finished his studies, Ferstel traveled through Italy, Germany, France, the Netherlands, and England, where he was very much impressed by the housing conditions of the middle class.

In 1855 Ferstel won the competition for the Votivkirche (1856–1879), his first independent project which founded his reputation. The rules of the competition specified that the church had to be designed in Gothic Revival. Ferstel's second great project was the Bank- und Börsengebäude (1856–1860), mainly in Tuscan trecento, a very complex building with a refined inner communication system. In his following projects Ferstel proved to be a true adherent of GOTTFRIED SEMPER. Like

Semper, he preferred Renaissance Revival for his public and apartment buildings.

Twice Ferstel could extend his projects from single buildings to the design of plazas: Rooseveltplatz and Schwarzenbergplatz. Both plazas were planned to frame monuments (the Votivkirche and the monument of Prince Schwarzenberg)—a pre-Sittesque (CAMILLO SITTE) idea. As the plaza of the nineteenth century was cut through by broad streets, Ferstel tried to unite the single blocks by arcades. This would have required the cooperation of the landowners, whose antagonistic interests—the city lacking a strong planning authority—doomed the plan to failure. At Rooseveltplatz, Ferstel could shape only the space behind the Votivkirche by planning three apartment buildings and the Presbytery (1878–1879), but he could not integrate the Chemical Institute (1869–1872) and his most famous work, the University of Vienna (1873–1884). Though the program for the university was very complex, Ferstel planned a monolithic axial building in Renaissance Revival which did not entirely meet the demands of the natural scientists. For Schwarzenbergplatz Ferstel also planned arcades to connect the four corner buildings of the plaza, but even in this case he had to drop the idea. He designed the two most important buildings facing Ringstrasse: the Palace of Archduke Ludwig Viktor (1863–1869) and Wertheim Palace (1864–1868), both in Renaissance Revival, standing in the tradition of formal aristocratic housing.

In 1866, Ferstel entered the competition for the Museums of Art and Natural History but he did not win. In compensation he was asked to design the Österreichisches Museum für Kunst und Industrie (1868–1871) and the Kunstgewerbeschule (1875–1877), both in Renaissance Revival.

Throughout his life Ferstel was interested in housing reform. In a book he wrote with Rudolf von Eitelberger (1860) he attacked the average Viennese tenement building as the ruin of the family and of society. He developed the *Ganzes Haus:* one family living and working with journeymen and servants in a house of its own for well-to-do business- and tradesmen. Knowing quite well that his ideas were utopian, as in the epoch of capitalism living and working were irrevocably separated, he added a reduced program which he could realize in his apartment buildings: luxurious buildings with two or three big family apartments on each floor. Ferstel naturally failed to realize the one-family house in the city because, as his critic Ferdinand Fellner pointed out, high prices for building sites, high building densities, zoning regulations, and the conditions of mortgages would be prohibitive. But he succeeded in the suburbs: in 1872 a

Ferstel.
University of Vienna.
1873–1884

Cottageverein, following Ferstel's ideas, constructed small one-family houses of the English type for middle class owners. In 1883, Ferstel initiated the construction of Türkenschanzpark, an English park near those "cottages," thus emphasizing the need of park areas for the urban population.

As an architect Ferstel stayed within the limits of historicism, as defined by Semper, which he showed not only in his work but also in the lectures he gave as a professor at the Polytechnical Institute since 1866.

RENATE BANIK-SCHWEITZER

WORKS

1856–1860, Bank- und Börsengebäude; 1856–1879, Votivkirche; Vienna. 1860–1861, Villa Wisgrill, Traunsee, Austria. 1860–1862, Pollak Apartment Building, Vienna. 1861–1863, Bergl Palace, Brno, Czechoslovakia. 1862–1877, Catholic Church, Teplice, Czechoslovakia. 1863–1867, Protestant Church, Brno, Czechoslovakia. 1863–1869, Palace Ludwig Viktor; 1864, Villa Ferstel, Grinzing; 1864–1868, Wertheim Palace; *1868–1870, Administration Building of the State Railway Company; 1868–1870, Wertheim Apartment Building; 1868–1871, Österreichisches Museum für Kunst und Industrie; 1869–1872, Chemical Institute of the University of Vienna; Vienna. 1870–1872, Villa Wartholz, Reichenau, Austria. 1870–1872, Zentralanstalt für Meteorologie und Erdmagnetismus; 1870–1873, Leon Apartment Building, Schottenring; 1870–1873, Maximiliansgymnasium; 1871–1872, Primary School, Grinzing; Vienna. 1871–1872, Villa Tauber, Traunsee, Austria. 1872–1873, Weiss Apartment Building; 1873–1874, Casino of the *Cottageverein;* Vienna. 1873–1874, Villa Jacobson, Reichenau, Austria. 1873–1875, Apartment Building of Allgemeine Österreichische Baugesellschaft; 1873–1875, Liechtenstein Garden Palace; 1873–1884, University of Vienna; 1874–1876, Leon Apartment Building, Kärntnerstrasse; 1875–1876, Leon

Apartment Building, Wipplingerstrasse; *1875–1876,
Villa Gerbitz, Grinzing; 1875–1877, Kunstgewerbeschule; 1875–1877, Linder Apartment Building; 1875–
1877, Wiener Baugesellschaft Apartment Building;
1877–1878, Benischko Apartment Building; 1878–
1879, Presbytery of the Votivkirche; 1880–1881, Hol-
litzer Apartment Building; Vienna. 1880–1883, Administration Building of the Austro-Hungarian Lloyd,
Trieste, Italy. 1880–1884, City Hall, Tiflis, Russia.
1880–1884, Winter Palace of Archduke Ludwig Viktor,
Klessheim, near Salzburg, Austria. 1882–1884, Leon
Apartment Building, Ebendorferstrasse, Vienna.

BIBLIOGRAPHY

EGGERT, KLAUS 1976 Volume 7 in *Der Wohnbau der
Wiener Ringstrasse im Historismus 1855–1896. Die Wiener Ringstrasse—Bild einer Epoche.* Wiesbaden, Germany: Franz Steiner.

EITELBERGER, RUDOLF VON, and FERSTEL, HEINRICH
1860 *Das bürgerliche Wohnhaus und das Wiener
Zinshaus: Ein Vorschlag aus Anlass der Erweiterung der
innern Stadt Wien's.* Vienna: C. Gerold's Son.

FELLNER, FERDINAND 1860 *Wie soll Wien bauen zur
Beleuchtung des "bürgerlichen Wohnhauses" der Herren
Professor R. v. Eitelberger und Architekt Heinrich Ferstel,
mit einigen Bemerkungen über Wiener Baugesetze.* Vienna.

FERSTEL, HEINRICH VON 1877 "Denkschrift über die
kunftige bauliche Entwicklung Wiens, verfasst vom
österreichischen Ingenieur- und-Architekten-Verein
auf Anlass der Beratungen über die Verfassung eines
Generalbaulinienplanes für Wien und Umgebung."
*Wochenschrift des Österreichischen Ingenieur- und
Architekten-Vereines* 2:65–75.

FERSTEL, HEINRICH VON 1880 *Rede gehalten bei der
feierlichen Inauguration des Rektors der k.k. Technischen
Hochschule in Wien Heinrich Freih. v. Ferstel am 9.
Oktober 1880.* Vienna.

FERSTEL, HEINRICH VON 1881 *Der Dom von Parenzo.*
Vienna.

FERSTEL, HEINRICH VON 1883 *Über Styl und Mode.*
Vienna.

SCHWEITZER, RENATE 1967 "Die Cottage-Anlage in
Wien-Währing." *Wiener Geschichtsblätter* 22:240–
252.

THAUSING, MORITZ 1879 *Die Votivkirche in Wien.* Vienna: R. V. Waldheim.

WAETZOLDT, STEPHAN VON 1977 *Bibliographie zur
Architektur im 19. Jahrhundert: Die Aufsätze in den
deutschsprachigen Architekturzeitschriften 1789–1918.*
Nendeln, Germany: KTO Press.

WAGNER-RIEGER, RENATE 1970 *Wiens Architektur
im 19. Jahrhundert.* Vienna: Österreichischer
Bundesverlag.

WIBIRAL, NORBERT 1953 "Heinrich von Ferstel und
der Historismus in der Baukunst des 19. Jahrhunderts." Unpublished Ph.D. dissertation, University
of Vienna.

WIBIRAL, NORBERT, and MIKULA, RENATA 1974
*Heinrich von Ferstel. Die Bauten und ihre Architekten.
Teil 3. Die Wiener Ringstrasse—Bild einer Epoche.* Vol-
ume 8. Wiesbaden, Germany: Franz Steiner.

WURM-ARNKREUZ, ALOIS VON 1918 "Die Fran-
cisco-Josephinische Zeit der Wiener Architektur."
*Zeitschrift des Österreichischen Ingenieur- und Architekten-
Vereines* 70:159–163.

FESZL, FRIGYES

Frigyes Feszl (1821–1884) was the most original
personality in Hungarian romantic architecture,
whose main work is the Municipal Concert Hall,
Budapest (1859–1864). Feszl came from a stonecutter family. In 1839–1841 he studied at the
Academy in Munich, where he was a pupil of LEO
VON KLENZE and FRIEDRICH VON GÄRTNER.
After his study tour in Germany and Italy, he won
the first prize in the competition of the House of
Parliament of the city of Pest (not executed). Together with Károly Gerster and Lipót Kauser, he
prepared several designs in which he combined the
medieval architectural elements with oriental design of form: the Oszwald House (1846–1851),
the Glosz House (1847), and the Church and
Monastery of the Capuchins (1852), all in Budapest. The same elements can be observed in the
Jewish Synagogue (1858) on Dohány Street, Budapest, built by LUDWIG VON FÖRSTER, whose
domed sanctuary with Moorish elements was built
according to Feszl's designs.

The façade of the Municipal Concert Hall is
formed from neo-Romanesque and Moorish elements. Its interior is richly embellished with decorative paintings, frescoes, and woodcarvings.

JUDITH KOÓS

WORKS

*1846–1851, Oszwald House; 1847, Glosz House; 1852,
Calvin Square Calvinist Church (crypt of countess
Manó Zichy); *1856, Danube Steamship Company
(storage building); 1858, Dohány Street Synagogue
(domed sanctuary); 1859–1864, Municipal Concert
Hall; *1867, Coronation Mound (Rooesewelt Square);
Budapest.

BIBLIOGRAPHY

JÁNSZKY, BÉLA 1929 *A magyar formatörekvések története
építészetünkben: 1894–1914* ("History of the Hungarian Endeavors of Form in Our Architecture: 1894–
1914"). Budapest.

MERÉNYI, FERENC 1970 *Magyar építészet: 1867–1967*
("Hungarian Architecture: 1867–1967"). Budapest:
Müszaki Könyvkladó.

RADOS, JENÖ (1961)1975 *A magyar építészettörténete*
("History of Hungarian Architecture"). 3d ed. Budapest: Müszaki Könyvkladó.

VÁMOS, FERENC 1925 "Feszl Frigyes és Kora"
("Frigyes Feszl and His Age"). *Magyar Müvészet*
1925:340–357, 402–432.

VÁMOS, FERENC 1962 "Alexy Károly müve a Vigadón"

("The Work of Károly Alexy on the Municipal Concert Hall"). *Müvészettörténeti Értesitő* 11, no. 4:265–273.

VÁMOS, FERENC ʾ1963 "Az elso pesti orshágháza tervezésének előkészületei (1835–1844)" ("Preparations of the Designing of the First House of Parliament in Pest"). *Müvészettörténeti Értesitő* 12, no. 1:38–47.

FEUERSTEIN, BEDŘICH

Bedřich Feuerstein (1892–1936) received his training at the Technical University in Prague, Czechoslovakia. Although he could only rarely carry out his architectural ideas, he was, due to his absolute taste, perfect judgment, and international understanding of the problems, one of the prominent representatives of the Prague avant-garde. He was the chief designer in AUGUSTE PERRET's office for the theater at the 1925 Exhibition of Decorative Arts in Paris. Later, in Japan, in the Tokyo atelier of his compatriot ANTONIN RAYMOND, he designed the Soviet Embassy (1928) and Saint Lucas Hospital (1928–1930) in Tokyo. He also made trips to the United States, the Soviet Union, and China. His Nymburk Crematorium (1921–1923) in Czechoslovakia is an outstanding structure strongly suggestive of ETIENNE LOUIS BOULLÉE's and CLAUDE NICOLAS LEDOUX's style, which was regarded as one of the best architectural works of Czech purism of the early 1920s.

VLADIMÍR ŠLAPETA

WORKS

1921, Military Geographic Institute, Dejvice District, Prague. 1921–1923, Crematorium, Nymburk, Czechoslovakia. 1925, Perret Theater Project (with others), Exhibition of Decorative Arts, Paris. 1928, Union of Soviet Socialist Republics Embassy (with Antonin Raymond); 1928–1930, Saint Lucas Hospital (with Raymond); Tokyo.

BIBLIOGRAPHY

Bedřich Feuerstein 1936 Prague: Mánes.
MASARYKOVÁ, ANNA 1967 *Bedřich Feuerstein.* Prague. Exhibition catalogue.

FIGINI, LUIGI, and POLLINI, GINO

The association of Luigi Figini (1903–) and Gino Pollini (1903–) dates back to 1926, when both were studying at the Milan Polytechnic Institute. Together with GIUSEPPE TERRAGNI, Sebastiano Larco, Carlo Rava, and others, Figini and Pollini in 1926 formed the *Gruppo 7*. Their manifesto (published in 1926 and 1927), although limited ideologically and ambiguous in its political positions, was an essential document of Rational architecture in Italy.

After their first works, still rich with academic references, the two architects gained general recognition in 1933 with the villa-studio for an artist at Milan's Fifth Triennale. Although they were influenced by LUDWIG MIES VAN DER ROHE's Barcelona Pavilion, in this project Figini and Pollini offered autonomous Rationalism, in the way in which they combined materials and treated smooth surfaces, achieving a rapport between the built and the natural which was to be a constant in their subsequent work. Their participation in the Italian branch of the Congrès Internationaux d'Architecture Moderne (CIAM) represented their need to overcome the provincialism of Italian culture; likewise, their editorial participation in the new magazine *Quadrante* reflected their desire to include architecture in the broader field of the arts.

Meeting Adriano Olivetti in 1933 was fundamental for the careers of Figini and Pollini, as he patronized the two architects' work for more than twenty years (1934–1957). In the enlargement of the Olivetti Offices in Ivrea (1934–1945), Figini and Pollini humanized the factory and, applying the principles of the Modern movement, achieved one of the first work places that was in line with the most advanced prospects of paternalistic capitalism. The Nursery School in Ivrea (1939–1941) was one of their most significant works, for the way it fitted into the neighborhood.

In the postwar period, the work of Figini and Pollini did not deviate from the Rationalist line, although gradually abandoning their initial purist rigor. The production of these years enlarged from architecture to urbanism. Among the works during this period are the INA Casa housing quarter in via Dessié, Milan (1951), with GIO PONTI; the plan of Borgo Porto Conte in Sardinia (1951); and the social services zone for Olivetti in Ivrea (1954–1957), where the relationship between architecture and city is fully realized. They also did religious architecture, with new and original interpretations of such community spaces. The Church of the Madonna dei Poveri, Milan (1952–1954), is distinguished by its light distribution and a shrewd use of unfinished materials; the Church of Santi Giovanni e Paolo in Milan (1964), in its complexity, is functionally and spatially articulate. The Manifattura Ceramica Pozzi of Ferrandina (1962–1963) is among the most fully resolved balances between architecture and landscape. Among more recent works, the Flower Market at Pescia (1972) and the project for the Church of the Mater Ecclesiae in Rome (1978, in collaboration with others) are noteworthy. The relationship between architecture and nature continues to fascinate Figini, who has explored it with numerous villas and gardens. Pollini has taught at the university since 1936.

In more than one-half century of activity, the two architects have never betrayed the principles that animated their youthful years, demonstrating a singular coherence and continuity.

CESARE DE' SETA

WORKS

*1930, Casa Elettrica, IV International Exposition of Decorative Arts, Monza, Italy. 1931, Bar Craja (with Luciano Baldessari); *1933, Artist's Villa-Studio, V Triennale; 1933, House, via Annunciata; Milan. *1934–1942, Olivetti Offices; 1939, Low-cost Housing, Borgo Olivetti; *1939, Nursery School Olivetti; Ivrea, Italy. *1951, INA Casa Quarter (with Gio Ponti), via Dessié; *1952, Church of the Madonna dei Poveri; Milan. *1954–1956, Social Services Zone for Olivetti, Ivrea, Italy. 1956, House, via Circo; *1964, Church of Santi Giovanni e Paolo; Milan. 1972–1980, New Buildings for the Science Departments (with others), University of Palermo, Italy. *1978, Church of Mater Ecclesiae (with others), Rome.

BIBLIOGRAPHY

BLASI, CESARE 1963 *Figini e Pollini.* Milan: Edizioni di Comunità.
DE' SETA, CESARE (1972)1978 *La cultura architettonica in Italia tra le due guerre.* Bari, Italy: Laterza.
GENTILI TEDESCHI, EUGENIO 1959 *Luigi Figini e Gino Pollini.* Milan: Il Balcone.
SAVI, VITTORIO (editor) 1980 *Luigi Figini e Gino Pollini/architetti.* Milan: Electa. Exhibition catalogue.

IL FILARETE

Antonio di Pietro Averlino's exact birth and death dates are not known, but he was probably born between 1400–1410 in Florence. Although GIORGIO VASARI states that he died in Rome at age 69, there are no records of the place or date of his death. Known as Filarete (lover of virtue, or better of *virtù*), he was primarily a sculptor until 1450, when he turned his attention almost exclusively to architecture. Between 1461–1464 he composed an untitled treatise on architecture, dedicated first to Francesco Sforza and later (c.1465) to Piero de' Medici. He is best known for his central doors of St. Peter's (1433–1445) in Rome, the Ospedale Maggiore (1460–1465) in Milan, and his architectural treatise—one of three treatises written in Italy during the fifteenth century.

Filarete was probably trained first as a bronze founder and not as a goldsmith. He extols FILIPPO BRUNELLESCHI as the originator of the new "ancient" architectural style and as the model for all to follow. He apparently knew LEON BATTISTA ALBERTI, and shared his reverence for Roman antiquity and a desire to reevoke the grandeur of Rome. His planned architecture in the treatise reveals affinities with Brunelleschi's dome of the cathedral of Florence and his mathematically derived proportions. The greatest influences on his architecture were the Romanesque churches of Lombardy, Tuscany, and San Lorenzo in Milan.

Filarete's career began with a commission to execute a pair of bronze doors for the central portals of old St. Peter's in Rome. Work began in 1433 and the doors were completed and set in place in 1445. They were taken down, enlarged, and returned as the central doors of the new basilica in 1620. A number of bronze medals that can be attributed to him were probably executed at this time.

In 1447 he received his first architectural commission to execute the tomb of Cardinal Chaves of Portugal in San Giovanni in Laterano in Rome. Derived from the Arch of Janus, or the Quadrifons, near San Giorgio in Velabro, Rome, the freestanding tomb was dismantled and reconstructed during later baroque modifications to the church. The sculptural decoration was not completed, because in late 1448, Filarete was accused of attempting the pious theft of the head of John the Baptist. He wrote that he was arrested, tortured, and expelled from Rome. In February 1449 the Signoria of Florence interceded—apparently unsuccessfully—with the new pope on his behalf. He moved on to Venice after a stop in Rimini, but in December 1449, he was probably expelled from Venice with other Florentines when hostilities broke out between the two cities.

With his arrival in Milan, perhaps early in 1450, Filarete became more and more involved in architecture. He became a ducal engineer and spent the next fifteen years working on architectural projects in Lombardy. By 1451 he is documented at work on the construction and the architectural decoration of the gate tower on the Castello di Porta Giovia (now Castello Sforzesco). The gate tower was destroyed in 1521, but was later reconstructed by LUCA BELTRAMI between 1893 and 1904. In 1454 Filarete was briefly associated with work at the Cathedral of Milan, but nothing specific is known about his contribution.

In 1457 he was given leave of absence to build a new cathedral for Bergamo. Although Filarete was back in Milan in 1460, his plan for the cathedral was followed faithfully. The church was enlarged and modified by CARLO FONTANA in 1620 and was completely remodeled in 1853. The cathedral has never been studied in depth, but it is an early example of the transmission of Florentine architectural ideas to the north of Italy.

Filarete's major architectural work in Milan is the Ospedale Maggiore, now seat of the University of Milan. Construction began in 1460 and when Filarete left Milan in 1465, one part of the hospital was ready to receive patients. Work continued until approximately 1500 under the direction of Guiniforte Solari (see SOLARI FAMILY), Ambrogio da Rosate and GIOVANNI ANTONIO AMADEO with inevitable modifications in conception and detail. Only one of the two crosses of Filarete's plan was ever executed. A new plan for the remainder of the hospital was conceived by Carcano in 1587 and further modified by FRANCESCO MARIA RICCHINO in 1625. The older section of the building later underwent further modifications and restorations.

Filarete planned the building as a 5:2 rectangle. A cross of equal arms is inscribed within a square at either end of the rectangle thus leaving a 1:2 rectangle for the hospital church and its forecourt. Seen from the major façade on the Via della Festa del Perdono the unexecuted square on the left was to have been the women's wing with the square on the right reserved for men. Although the street has been raised considerably since Filarete's time, his high basement for shops and support services can still be seen. The entire structure was to have been surrounded by a portico. The interior cross subdivides the square into four smaller squares which become courtyards with porticoes on each of two stories. Each arm of the cross is a large airy ward for patients with a dome over the crossing. Filarete was concerned with introducing light and air into the wards. He also provided for the personal hygiene of the patients, for isolation wards, and for support services. This is perhaps the first modern hospital.

Architecturally the building can best be characterized as a compromise between the Brunelleschian style of Florence and the late Gothic of the Solari family and others that remained popular in Milan. Filarete was personally involved in the execution of the arms of the cross and one of the interior courtyards. In this area the columns, window and door frames, and terra cotta frieze are much more restrained than in the other three courtyards. He accepts Milanese colorism in architecture but employs the grey serrizzo stone, yellow to red Verona stone and brick and terra cotta with balanced restraint. His decoration provides a compromise between Florentine classical acanthus swags and the exuberance of Lombard Gothic rinceaux. Florence

and Milan meet in the building and create a compromise style acceptable in Lombardy, France, and Spain. Through this style, which appears in Lombard churches and villas and at the Château de Madrid and the Hospital in Santiago da Compostella, France and Spain were able to understand and to accept Italian High Renaissance architecture.

The plan of the Ospedale Maggiore had immediate and long lasting effects. DONATO BRAMANTE was commissioned to copy it for a proposed hospital in Venice. CESAREDI LORENZO CESARIANO used it to illustrate his edition of VITRUVIUS's writings. It influenced the plans of the Hospital de los Reyes Catolicos in Santiago da Compostella and of the Escorial. The plan was adopted for French hospitals of the sixteenth and seventeenth centuries and ultimately was used in Mexico. The original plan probably derives in great part from Filarete's use of mathematics and perhaps from examples at Pavia and Lodi.

Filarete's contributions to various ducal fortifications have not been identified. He is connected in an unidentified way with the important though unfinished Cà del Duca, the Sforza residence in Venice. He may also be responsible for San Sigismondo in Cremona, usually attributed to Bartolomeo Gadio. The plan is identical to one in Filarete's treatise.

Filarete is perhaps most widely known for his treatise on architecture. Its purpose was primarily to teach Francesco Sforza and his heir, Galeazzo Maria, to appreciate Florentine architecture. In the treatise Filarete plans an ideal city, called Sforzinda, which is an eight-pointed star. Its walls are a transition between medieval thin wall construction and the fully developed Renaissance bastion. Major streets lead to the center of the city where the cathedral, ducal palace and law courts are located. There are subsidiary piazze on the periphery, each with a parish church.

Filarete designed market squares, governmental buildings, and housing for the various classes of the city. Trades are located in restricted areas with the most noisome on the periphery. Sforzinda is also provided with a port, Plusiapolis. His Temple of Virtù looks forward to ETIENNE LOUIS BOULLÉE and the cathedrals of the treatise to Bramante's St. Peter's. He reevokes antiquity with a Colosseum-like structure and with a Roman circus. He invents new forms with his hospital, a private palace with an advanced twin tower façade, and an imaginary sculpture that predicts LEONARDO's unfinished equestrian statue of Francesco Sforza. The treatise contains digressions that provide a fuller understanding of fifteenth century life in Italy, allegorical conundrums, and information on contemporary building practice.

JOHN R. SPENCER

WORKS

1433–1445, Old Saint Peter's (central doors); *1447–1448, Tomb of Cardinal Chaves, San Giovanni in Laterno; Rome. *1451–1457, Castello (Sforzesco) di Porta Giovia (gate tower), Milan. 1457, Cathedral of Bergamo, Italy. 1460–1465, Ospedale Maggiore, Milan.

BIBLIOGRAPHY

Arte Lombarda New Series 38–39: entire issue. Includes articles on Filarete by Paolo Carpeggiani, Giuseppina Dal Cannon, Philip Foster, Margherita Licht, Loredana Olivato, John Onians, Carlo Perogalli, and Lionello Puppi.

BASCAPÉ, GIACOMO C. 1936 "Il progresso dell'assistenza ospedaliera nel sec. XV e gli ospedali 'a crociera.'" *Tecnica ospedaliera* 1:9–21.

BELTRAMI, LUCA 1894 Il Castello di Milano. Milan: Hoepli.

BELTRAMI, LUCA 1900 *La "Cà del Duca" sul Canal grand*. Milan: Nella Tipografia di U. Allegretti.

BIAGETTI, VINCENZINA 1937 *L'Ospedale Maggiore di Milano*. Milan: Perrella.

CAIMI, GAETANO 1857 *Notizie storiche del Grand 'ospitale di Milano*. Milan: Cogliati.

CRIPPA, G. 1971 "Inediti sul Duomo di Bergamo dal Filarete al Fontana." *Bergamo arte* 2:21–30.

DOHME, R. 1880 "Filarete's Traktat von der Architektur." *Jahrbuch der Königlich Preussischen Kunstsammlungen* 1:225–241.

FABRICZY, CORNELIUS VON 1904 "Ein Brief Antonio Averulinos, gennant Filarete." *Repertorium für Kunstwissenschaft* 27:188–189.

FILARETE, ANTONIO AVERLINO (1461–1464)1965 *Treatise on Architecture*. Translated, with an introduction and notes, by John R. Spencer. New Haven: Yale University Press.

FRANCO, FAUSTO 1939 "L'Interpolazione del Filarete trattosta fra gli artefici del Rinascimento architettonico a Venezia." Pages 267–280 in *Atti del IV Convegno nazionale di storia dell'architettura*. Milan: The Congress.

GRASSI, LILIANA 1955 "Aspetti nuovi dell'antico Ospedale Maggiore sistemato ad uso dell'Università di Milano." *Arte Lombarda* New Series 1:136–145.

HEYDENREICH, LUDWIG H., and LOTZ, WOLFGANG 1974 *Architecture in Italy*. New York: Pelican.

LANG, S. 1972 "Sforzinda, Filarete and Filelfo." *Journal of the Warburg and Courtauld Institutes* 35:391–397.

LAZZARONI, MICHELE, and MUÑOZ, ANTONIO 1908 *Filarete*. Rome: Modes.

MÜNTZ, EUGÈNE 1889 "Les arts à la cour des papes, nouvelles récherches." *Mélanges d'archéologie et d'histoire* 9:134–173.

ONIANS, JOHN 1971 "Alberti and Filarete. A Study in their Sources." *Journal of the Warburg and Courtauld Institutes* 34:96–114.

SAALMAN, HOWARD 1959 "Early Renaissance Architectural Theory and Practice in Antonio Filarete's 'Trattato di Architettura.'" *Art Bulletin* 41:89–106.

SALMI, MARIO 1936 "Antonio Averlino detto il Filarete e l'architettura lombarda del primo Rinascimento." Pages 185–196 in *Atti del Primo Congresso nazionale di storia dell'architettura*. n.p.: The Congress.

SCURATI-MANZONI, PIETRO 1969 "Lo svillupo degli edifici rinascimentale a pianta centrale in Lombardia." *Archivio storico Lombardo* 7:193–209.

SINUSI, S. 1971 "Razionalità e immaginazione in Filarete." *Reviste studi salernitani* 7:281–296.

SPENCER, JOHN R. 1958 "Filarete and Central-plan Architecture." *Journal of the Society of Architectural Historians* 17:10–18.

SPENCER, JOHN R. 1970 "The Cà del Duca in Venice and Benedetto Ferrini." *Journal of the Society of Architectural Historians* 29:3–8.

SPENCER, JOHN R. 1976 "Filarete and the Cà del Duca." *Journal of the Society of Architectural Historians* 35:219–222.

THOENES, C. 1972 "Sostegno e adornamento. Zur sozialen Symbolik der Saülenordnung." *Kunstchronik* 1972:343–344.

TIGLER, PETER 1963 *Die Architekturtheorie des Filarete*. Berlin: de Gruyter.

VASARI, GIORGIO 1878 *Le Vite . . .* Edited by G. Milanesi. 2 vols. Florence: Sansoni.

VON MOOS, STANISLAUS 1970 *Kastell, Palast, Villa: Studien zur italienischen Architektur des 15. und 16. Jh.* Zurich: Philos Diss Zurich.

ZAREBSKA, TERESA 1965 "L'abitazione colletiva nella teoria urbanistica italiana del XV e XVI secolo." *Urbanistica* 1965:31–35.

FINSTERLIN, HERMANN

Born in Munich where he later studied chemistry, physics, and medicine, Hermann Finsterlin (1887–1973) studied painting under Franz von Stuck in 1913. In 1916, he held his first exhibition of erotic painting and models. In 1918, he showed forty works on an architectural theme at an exhibition of unknown architects at the I. B. Neumann Gallery in Berlin. His work was also published by BRUNO TAUT in the magazine *Frühlicht* and by the Arbeitsrat für Kunst. He taught briefly at the Bauhaus as visiting professor (c.1930), and his paintings and drawings were exhibited in many European centers. He carried out mural paintings during the Nazi period. After the war, his reputation was resuscitated by a number of European and American architectural critics and historians. From the early 1960s on, his work received wide international publicity and he began a process of redrawing his earlier fantasy buildings. He did not, however, build any permanent buildings. A major postwar exhibition of his work was held in Stuttgart (1973), and much of his drawn work and paintings now resides in the Kunstverein there.

DENNIS SHARP

FIORAVANTI, ARISTOTELE

Aristotele Fioravanti (1415?–1486?) was perhaps the most celebrated engineer of the fifteenth century. Active as an architect, military engineer, and bronze founder in his native Bologna between 1437 and 1474, he won widespread renown in 1455 by transporting the campanile of Santa Maria del Tempio in Bologna. He was in the service of Francesco Sforza, duke of Milan, between 1458 and 1464, worked in Hungary in 1467, and tackled a variety of engineering problems at Cento, Mantua, Venice, Rome, and Naples. His last eleven years were spent in Russia, where he built the Kremlin Cathedral of the Dormition (1475–1479) in the local Byzantinizing style.

RICHARD J. TUTTLE

WORK

1475–1479, Cathedral of the Dormition (or the Assumption), Kremlin, Moscow.

BIBLIOGRAPHY

Arte lombarda 1976 44–45:entire issue. Acts of the Bologna conference "Aristotele Fioravanti a Mosca (1475–1975)."

BELTRAMI, LUCA 1888 *Aristotele da Bologna al servizio del Duca di Milano (1458–1464).* Milan: Colombo & Cordani.

BELTRAMI, LUCA 1912 *Vita di Aristotile da Bologna.* Bologna, Italy: Libreria L. Beltrami.

CANETTA, CARLO 1882 "Aristotile da Bologna: Notizie inedite tratte dal-l'Archivio di Stato di Milano." *Archivio Storico Lombardo* 9:672–697.

GUALANDI, MICHELANGELO 1870 "Aristotele Fioravanti, meccanico e ingegnere del secolo XV." *Atti e Memorie della Regia Deputazione di Storia Patria per le Provincie di Romagna* Series 1 9:57–77.

FIORENTINO, MARIO

Born in Rome, Mario Fiorentino (1918–) grew up in the circle of the Association for Organic Architecture and the *Scuola romana,* collaborating with MARIO RIDOLFI. After World War II, he applied himself to research on industrial architecture.

ANTONINO TERRANOVA

WORKS

1944–1948, Monument of the Ardeatine Caves (with others); 1949–1954, INA-CASA Tiburtino Quarter (with others); Rome. 1950, UNRRA-CASAS Village, Cutro, Italy. 1954–1957, Apartments, Villa Balestra, Rome. 1954–1958, Residential Buildings, Spine Bianche Quarter, Matera, Italy. 1959–1964, Latte Dolce Experimental Quarter, Sassari, Italy. 1960–1967, Apartments, Pietralata, Rome. 1964–1967, Vanvitelli INA-CASA Quarter (with others), Caserta, Italy.

BIBLIOGRAPHY

CONFORTO, CINA; DE GIORGI, GABRIELE; and MUNTONI, ALESSANDRA 1977 *Il dibattito architettonico in Italia 1945–1975.* Rome: Bulzoni.

GREGOTTI, VITTORIO 1968 *New Directions in Italian Architecture.* New York: Braziller.

TAFURI, MANFREDI, and DAL CO, FRANCESCO (1976)1979 *Modern Architecture.* Translated by R. E. Wolf. New York: Abrams.

FISAC SERNA, MIGUEL

Miguel Fisac Serna (1913–) graduated from the Superior Technical School of Architecture in Madrid in 1942. His intention to combine the lively Mediterranean tradition with the National Romanticism of Scandinavia bore fruit in his C.S.I.C. Bookstore in Madrid, in which the textures of the "natural" materials of brick and wood play an important role. This stage culminated in his most representative work, the Theological School of the Dominican Order in Alcobendas, Madrid (1955), which became influential as a model of religious architecture.

Fisac's work between 1955 and 1965 was characterized by experiments with the expressive nature of concrete in the brutalist form. More recently, his designs have been guided by a search for the plastic possiblities of materials, especially concrete.

MIGUEL ANGEL BALDELLOU
Translated from Spanish by
Judith E. Meighan

WORKS

1942, Chapel of the Holy Ghost of C.S.I.C.; 1950, C.S.I.C. Bookstore, 4 Medinaceli; Madrid. 1952, Apostolic College of the Dominicans, Arcas Reales, Valladolid, Spain. 1955, Theological School of the Dominicans, Alcobendas; 1956, Miguel Fisac House, Cerro del Aire; Madrid. 1958, House of Culture, Cuenca, Spain. 1958, Parish Church of the Coronation of Our Lady, Vitoria, Spain. 1960, Alter Laboratories Administration Building; 1965, College of the Congregation of the Assumption; 1965, Parish Center, Moratalaz; 1966, Computation Center, University City; Madrid.

BIBLIOGRAPHY

BENEVOLO, LEONARDO (1963)1971 *History of Modern Architecture.* 2 vols. Cambridge, Mass.: M.I.T. Press.

FLORES LOPEZ, CARLOS 1961 *Arquitectura española contemporánea.* Madrid: Aguilar.

FISCHER, JOHANN MICHAEL

Both the location, in the first chapel on the right of Munich's Frauenkirche, and the text of his gravestone attest to the high standing of Johann Michael Fischer (1692–1766) among Bavarian architects of the eighteenth century. The long inscription lauds him as artistically seasoned, honest, upright, a *Baumeister* to three Serene Highnesses, an accredited *Mauermeister* in Munich, and as one who never relaxed because "from his tireless hand came thirty-two churches, twenty-three monasteries, besides many other secular buildings."

Born in Burglegenfeld (Oberpfalz), Germany, the son of a local mason, Fischer traveled to Bohemia and Moravia in 1715–1716 and went to Munich in 1718–1719 to serve there as foreman to the city mason Johann Mayr. He became a citizen and mason in 1723, married a daughter of Mayr in 1725, and in the following year received his first major commission, the abbey church at Osterhofen. Through his marriage he became a step-brother-in-law to the brothers Johann Baptist and Ignatz Anton Gunetzrhainer, who held positions in Munich as city and court masons under the chief court architect JOSEPH EFFNER. Although these family connections undoubtedly had professional advantages, they unfortunately blocked Fischer from work in Munich itself. The only exceptions were the Hieronymite Church of Sankt Anna am Lehel, the Church of Sankt Michael at Berg-am-Lain (on the eastern outskirts of the city), some townhouses, and small churches in and around the city.

The geographical range of Fischer's active church production extends west from Munich to Ottobeuren and Zwiefalten in Swabia, south to Benediktbeuern, southeast to Rott-am-Inn, north to Ingolstadt, and east-northeast to the Danube region between Regensburg and Passau.

Burglegenfeld, Fischer's birthplace not far north of Regensburg, is in a region close enough to Franconia to have felt the influence of the Dientzenhofer family of architects (see DIENTZENHOFER BROTHERS). Indeed, the Salesian convent church at Amberg was designed by Wolfgang Dientzenhofer, as were the nearby ones of Ensdorf and (probably) Michelfeld, both later frescoed by Cosmas Damian Asam (see ASAM BROTHERS). Further afield, the Dientzenhofers flourished in Franconia, Prague, and neighboring Bohemia. On his early travels, Fischer may have seen and admired their work.

Evidence of this connection can be found in Fischer's own work following his accreditation as mason in 1723. The superposed monks' choir and sacristy of the abbey of Niederaltaich (1724), on the Danube some thirty miles above Passau, already show his preference for boldly domed spaces, assertive cornices, and coved transitions over windows that soften the intersection of side walls and cupola above. These elements often mark the work of the Dientzenhofers. At two dependencies of Niederaltaich, Rinchnach and Kirchham, Fischer further developed these tendencies. Great emphasis is placed on corner niches that frame altars placed diagonally athwart the main axis, flat behind at the earlier Kirchham (1724), but concave at Rinchnach (1727). These niches help mold a rectangular space into something approaching a rotunda effect. Although Henry-Russell Hitchcock has suggested an influence here from such small Munich-area churches as Kreuzpullach (c.1710) and Schönbrunn (1723–1724)—both of uncertain authorship—a reflection of Dientzenhofer interiors, especially at Prague, seems clear in the molded spaces, the large windows admitting a strong direct light, and in the armature of powerful baroque entablatures, imposts, and pilasters in the GIOVANNI LORENZO BERNINI tradition.

These elements receive their first definitive expression in the Premonstratensian Abbey Church at Osterhofen, midway on the Danube between Straubing and Passau and just below Niederaltaich. Rapidly constructed from 1726 to 1728, the church was decorated in 1729–1735 with stuccoes, sculpture, and frescoes by the Asam brothers. This fact warns us that Fischer was an architect, not a decorator, and that the ensemble is a collaborative venture in which ornament—and its all-important religious significance—is clearly as crucial as Fischer's architectural shell. Characteristic of the predominantly baroque flavor of the time was the choice of the Asams as decorators, just as the employment of Johann Baptist Zimmermann (see ZIMMERMANN BROTHERS), the brothers Franz Xaver Feichtmayr and Johann Michael Feichtmayr, and IGNAZ GÜNTHER and MATTHÄUS GÜNTHER in subsequent Fischer churches indicates the arrival of the rococo and the nascent neoclassical eras.

However baroque the Asams' stuccoes and frescoes, and the architectural forms of Fischer may be, the big windows flood Osterhofen's interior with a diffused light totally at variance with the mysterious darkness, dramatically spotlighted from concealed sources, in Cosmas Damian Asam's church at Weltenburg, begun in 1716 and ready for its ornamentation two years later.

Fischer's plan for Osterhofen is longitudinal, with a narrowed choir extension and no transepts. In lieu of side aisles, the nave is flanked by oval-shaped side chapels between the sturdy interior wall pillars that shoulder the main barrel vault.

Traditionally, the longitudinal church was rectangular, marked by strong horizontal tiers, and divided crosswise into bays. Fischer provided a shell that denied this tradition and molded the interior into a unified, rotundalike space. Diagonally placed altars in concave niches serve as a transition to the choir area. Colossal pilasters rise through the gallery level to the base of the nave vault, canceling any sense of division into horizontal stories. The space is further unified by the dramatic play of concave chapels against the outcurving balustrades above them—a feature, like the oval shape itself, that was standard in the designs of the Dientzenhofers. Another device, found in Christoph Dientzenhofer's friary church, at Obořiště, near Prague (1702–1712), is the stilting and convex bowing of the nave arcade arches, leading the eye both upward and into the lower curve of the vault itself. Fischer's moldings around these arches, more pronounced than Dientzenhofer's, further emphasize the spatial continuity from side wall to vault.

In similar spirit, Cosmas Damian Asam's nave fresco is a single, enveloping composition that effectively overrules the floor level division into bays; and Egid Quirin Asam's high altar, like the many side ones, is a burst of Berninesque curvatures with rich colors against white and gold to match his brother's frescoes. The white purity of Fischer's wall surfaces, deeply gouged coves, potent entablatures, and pilasters has been almost effaced by stucco incrustations, in which color again explodes. It takes an effort at Osterhofen to sense the power of Fischer's spatial continuum—more so than in most of his later churches, where the ornament is under greater restraint when it impinges on architectural elements. One would like to know what Fischer thought of the transformation of his first major achievement.

That Rinchnach (1727) could be constructed during the erection of Osterhofen comes as no surprise, for they are hardly twenty-five miles apart and, as usual, local foremen directed work on the site. But that construction of Sankt Anna am Lehel in Munich itself also began in 1727 suggests active travel on the part of a busy architect. Evidence abounds for Fischer's personal presence at building sites.

Sankt Anna am Lehel is the first important example in a long series of centrally planned churches that form the core of Fischer's oeuvre. Built from 1727 to 1729, the church was decorated during the 1730s by the Asam brothers and dedicated in 1737. In the mid-nineteenth-century era of Romanesque revivals, Fischer's façade was replaced by a heavy, Rhenish-looking entrance front by K. Voit. The nearly total destruction of the church

Johann Michael Fischer. Premonstratensian Church. Osterhofen, Germany. 1726–1728

(except for this façade) in the bombings of 1944 was followed by a painstaking rebuilding. The Asams' stuccoes and frescoes were successfully reproduced—in some cases reassembled from fragments. In 1968, it was wisely decided to replace Voit's façade by a faithful copy—developed from Fischer's preserved drawings—of the original. Around 1960, with little of the Asams' decoration as yet reinstalled, one could admire Fischer's shell unadorned. Nevertheless, it is important to note that the higher proportions of the interior, as compared with Osterhofen, in themselves guaranteed a less overpowering impact of stucco and fresco work. In plan, Sankt Anna am Lehel consists of an ovoid nave, developed from two intersecting circles, and a three-quarter round (horseshoe-shaped) choir. Beyond, but invisible from the church proper, is a semicircular chapter room. Support for the cupola is provided by interior wall pillars whose faces terminate in fluted pilasters. At the vestibule and choir ends, however, these piers are set diagonally to the main axis in order to bend the space toward its ovoid shape. On each side are three side chapels—the outer ones deeply niched—set between the wall pillars. Each central chapel is wider than its neighbors, and the enframing arch higher, so that the effect of a truncated Greek cross is established. Asam's fresco further unifies the interior space. Large windows over the side altars provide a brilliant light for Fischer's wall surfaces, elegant pilasters, and aggressive entablature blocks above the ornately stuccoed capitals. Light from the side windows subtly molds the tall diagonal niches. The horseshoe shape of the choir—really only an altar space, with the circle completed by the altar railing—has the advantage over a normal semicircular apse of concealing the apsidal side windows until one is well within the nave. Clarity, elegant proportions, evenly diffused light from generous wall perforations are contrary to traditional baroque practice. Despite baroque elements in the Asams' decoration, an important step has been taken here in the direction of a new rococo architecture. In the same year, 1727, as Sankt Anna was begun—but far to the west in Swabia, at Steinhausen—another architect, Dominikus Zimmermann, was moving in his own very different way toward that goal.

As for Fischer's façade, we may describe it as a preparation for his façade at Diessen. Colossal pilasters enframing the round-arched portal rise to the base of an attic story, here topped by a framed niche that projects from the hipped roof as a dormer. Below it is a slightly irregular oval window, somewhat echoing the shape of the nave within.

Fischer's next major project, the Augustinian Priory Church at Diessen, built 1732–1734 on the west side of the Ammersee, was preceded in 1731 by a trip with the energetic prior, Herkulan Karg, to visit Bavarian churches, including Fischer's own and Osterhofen in particular. In 1733, the prior made a second journey as far as the South Tyrol, in search of decorators. Here we have striking evidence of Fischer's personal commitment, but also of the dominating role so often played by the patron, and, perhaps most important of all, of the separation of architect and decorator in much of eighteenth-century building.

A longitudinal plan was decided upon, one clearly indebted to that of the Jesuit Sankt Michaelskirche in Munich (1583–1590) and to the array of South German wall pillar churches of the Vorarlberg type that it had helped engender during the late seventeenth century. As Osterhofen followed in this tradition in its basic plan and structure, Fischer was well qualified to undertake the Diessen commission, even though it meant a departure from his growing concern for centrally planned church design.

Behind a much improved Sankt Anna façade, Diessen opens through a generous vestibule beneath an organ loft to a four-bay rectangular nave separated from a large choir by a triumphal arch and ending in a semicircular high altar space. Substantial wall pillars provide room for rectangular side chapels, but here the altars (one with a Saint Sebastian altarpiece by Giovanni Battista Tiepolo) are placed on the narrow transverse faces of the chapels rather than against the side wall as at Sankt Anna. As a result, the eye is caught by a rapid sequence of richly ornamented altars, led through the seeming proscenium formed by the triumphal

arch, and on to the sumptuous high altar at the far end, some two hundred feet from the entrance. Two transverse steps raise the level of the fourth bay into the suggestion of a transept, four more elevate the choir, and three final ones lift the high altar to its crowning position. Channeled pilasters terminate each wall pillar in the nave, but in the choir and altar spaces these give way to more aggressive columns. As at Osterhofen, the nave arcade arches, rising high above supporting entablature blocks, are stilted for greater lift, and they bend toward and up into the curve of barrel vault of the nave, some sixty-five feet high at its apex. At Diessen, the entablature blocks are doubled, with the sloping base of the upper one seeming to turn the transverse nave and choir arches into a horseshoe shape. Unlike Osterhofen, the church has no gallery. Thus the laterally marked bays gain their great height without interruption, and the nave as a whole takes on the effect of a theater auditorium. The main fresco pulls the first three bays into a single composition, but the fourth bay, marked above by a less emphatic proscenium arch than the one preceding the choir, has its own transverse fresco, thus completing the suggestion of a transept already introduced below by the change in floor level. These devices combine to form a telescoping effect, again as in a theater, but here it is a *theatrum sacrum,* no doubt inspired by theaters actually existing in such major abbeys as Ottobeuren. Through a special arrangement Diessen's high altar is equipped to serve a dramatic purpose: a concealed staircase leads behind the altar to a platform masked by its top segment. The latter also masks and diffuses light coming from a large oculus cut below the apse vault. Through a system of ropes and pulleys, the large oil painting enframed by the great altar can be rolled down and a selection from other paintings, proper to the religious season, can be rolled up to replace it.

The plan of Diessen reveals Fischer's insistence on rounding off corners and breaking up planes. In the façade there are shallow undulations, not present at Sankt Anna; the two outer corners of each side chapel are semicircular; the choir is narrowed to allow for a sacristy and other service rooms along its outer wall, but this feature also breaks up the rectangular strictness of the plan as a whole. Finally, the gradual telescoping of the space toward the east is reinforced by diagonally receding columns in the high altar itself.

Looking back from choir to entrance, one gains a better impression of Fischer's superb shell, for no side altars now appear and the wall surfaces are relatively clear of ornament.

As for Diessen's ornament, its magnificence is of a kind totally different from that of the Asams at

Osterhofen. The stuccoists chosen by Prior Karg were the brothers Franz Xaver and Johann Michael Feichtmayr and Johann George Üblherr, all of them trained at the Bavarian center of Wessobrunn—only a few miles southwest of Diessen itself. Alastair Laing has suggested that the choice was influenced by Karg's probable visit to the important Cistercian abbey of Stams, near Innsbruck in the Tyrol. Here, in 1731, Franz Xaver Feichtmayr had completed the elaborate stucco décor. The Feichtmayrs were based in Augsburg and this fact may have led to the choice of Johann Georg Bergmüller as frescoist, for he had recently been appointed director of the Augsburg art academy. Üblherr had other impressive qualifications: he had been working under Johann Baptist Zimmermann in the decoration of the Reiche Zimmer of the Munich Residenz. All these connections brought to Diessen a decorative style linked to Parisian Régence and the newly evolving rococo—and strongly divergent from the Rome-oriented baroque of the Asam brothers. By Asam standards, the decoration of Diessen, begun in 1736 and for the most part completed in time for the dedication of 1739, is much more delicate and sophisticated, blonder in color, and noticeably more intimate in scale. It is also marked by a hesitant use of asymmetry—in the side altars resolved by its mirror image across the main axis. There is considerable use of rocaille cartouches; especially fine are those attached to the pendentives supporting the choir cupola. Their appearance at Diessen, among the earliest examples in Germany, quickly followed publication through engravings by such French designers as J. A. MEISSONNIER—engravings that were immediately pirated by the printmakers of Augsburg, as Laing has pointed out.

Henry-Russell Hitchcock has a rather too pat phrase to the effect that Fischer's naves and choirs (that is, after Osterhofen and Sankt am Lehel) are "rococo overhead but baroque below the entablatures." It applies fairly well to Diessen, except that the side altars are clearly not baroque; but the great high altar, surprisingly said to have been designed by FRANÇOIS CUVILLIÉS with massive statues by Joachim Dietrich, has a pronounced Roman flavor. Hitchcock's phrase applies much better to JOHANN BALTHASAR NEUMANN's Kaisersaal at the Würzburg Residenz.

We return now to Fischer's main line of development, the centrally planned church. Two small parish examples of 1730 in the environs of Munich, Bergkirchen and Unering, are noteworthy as simple statements of the domed octagon plus a small projecting altar space. A major project of 1735–1740, the Augustinian church at Ingolstadt, destroyed in World War II, is much more complex, but at the same time more strictly on the central plan than Sankt Anna am Lehel. A domed octagonal nave with bowed transverse extensions and four large, diagonally placed oval chapels leads to a smaller square choir, brought to an octagon internally and domed, like the nave, with a shallow cupola. Closely related to Ingolstadt is the pilgrimage church at Aufhausen (near Regensburg), also designed in 1735 but not dedicated until 1751. Here, the nave rotunda has hexagonal chapels at the corners, and the square choir is balanced at the front by a squarish vestibule under the organ loft. Both these churches have galleries above the corner chapels, unlike Sankt Anna, and both are marked by extensive use of coves. The fluting of the pilasters on the main piers at Ingolstadt (as at Diessen) was given up at Aufhausen in favor of plain surfaces—a practice that Fischer followed hereafter with the single exception of Fürstenzell.

The centralized plan of the Archfraternity Church of Sankt Michael at Berg-am-Lain, on the easterly edge of Munich itself, is still more complex than those of Ingolstadt and Aufhausen. Berg-am-Lain was built under the patronage of Clemens August, duke of Bavaria and, since 1732, prince-bishop of Cologne—one of the three exalted highnesses referred to on Fischer's gravestone. A first plan submitted by Fischer in 1735 called for an octagonal domed nave plus a horseshoe-shaped choir; but local politics brought in the city mason Philip Köglsberger, who undertook a more ambitious solution. In 1739, however, Köglsberger was discharged, and Fischer was reinstated. Somewhat restricted by existing foundations, he managed to produce a masterpiece. By 1744, the church was ready for its decoration.

A strongly bowed and deeply coved façade, flanked by twin towers, leads through a transverse vestibule to the spacious octagonal nave, which has shallow arms suggesting a transept. The square choir beyond, brought internally to an octagon and spanned like the nave with a saucer dome, is smaller and at a lower level. It leads in turn to a shallow ovoid altar space that echoes the shape of the vestibule. The nave has no galleries or recessed corner chapels blocking the rise from floor to ceiling. Instead of the indirect light that filters through galleries at Ingolstadt and Aufhausen, Fischer daringly cut a huge window through the nave pendentives, thereby flooding his rotunda with brilliant effect. This was made possible by eliminating Köglsberger's proposal for a stone vault in favor of a plaster one hung, as it were, from the rafters. As one proceeds into the choir, a subtle variation comes into view. Here, the much smaller pendentives are treated as shallow niches for high-relief white stucco figures of the Four

Church Fathers. Light enters only from small side windows between them that are invisible from the nave. In this manner, the brilliant nave light is hushed as we look toward the high altar, likewise mysteriously lit from the side. In the nave, the top of each of the great diagonal windows—set in the angled plane of the exterior wall—is at a considerable distance from the inward curve of the pendentive. As a result, there is room for a horizontal ceiling medallion, circular like the two main cupolas. Looking straight up from the center of the nave, we have the exciting spectacle of an immense frescoed circle flanked at a lower level by four smaller ones, stuccoed white.

Below the powerful continuous main entablature, the lower story of Fischer's shell is all solemn baroque: unchanneled pilasters and engaged columns of polychromed *scagliola,* deep coves in the transverse arms of the nave. But the advanced rococo flavor of the ornament, especially in the altars and the pulpit, relates sympathetically to the new airiness, high-value color, and small scale of Zimmermann's frescoes and stucco work. The gracious statues here are by Johann Baptist Straub, the leading Munich sculptor of the day. We are far removed from the baroque density of the Asams' ornament at Osterhofen, produced over a decade earlier.

During the 1740s, Fischer received three important commissions, all much affected by prior construction on the site. All three extend longitudinally, but submit in different ways to a centralized space organization. In chronological order they are Fürstenzell, Zwiefalten, and Ottobeuren.

In 1738, the Cistercian Abbey Church of Fürstenzell, just west of Passau, was to be rebuilt; after two successive designers had been discharged, the task was given to Fischer in 1740. The contract notes that he was "famed for his great experience." A basilican plan in the Vorarlberg mode had already been established and the foundations laid. Thus, for Fischer, forced to return to the Osterhofen–Diessen line of his career, the problem of centralizing the space was considerable. Moreover, the wall pillars of the four-bay nave were especially massive and aggressive. In between were side chapels with a gallery above—precluding a Diessen solution—and these were so deep as to recall the Sankt Michaelskirche in Munich. No doubt to break up their ponderousness, Fischer, for the last time, gave the pier ends a revetment of fluted pilasters, paired and close together. Deep coves mold the side chapels, both ends of the nave ceiling, and the junction of the choir ceiling with the end wall over the high altar. Lateral arches over the chapels and above the gallery bow out in the manner we have come to expect. The unusually low and wide proportions have a Roman expansiveness, as do the great arched windows that light the gallery. Except for its twin towers, the façade is easily recognizable as a variant of Diessen's. Construction was completed by 1744. Subsequent rococo decoration of Fischer's nave was carried out by J. G. Funk, a former assistant to J. B. Zimmermann, and by the Tyrolese frescoist Johann Jakob Zeiller.

In 1742, Fischer was called to the important Benedictine Abbey of Zwiefalten, just west of the Swabian Danube and some fifty miles southwest of Ulm. This was to be the scene of his most distant activity from Munich. About two years earlier, Fischer had advised on the alteration of the abbey church, also Benedictine, of Ochsenhausen, south of Ulm. Satisfaction there may account for his being called to Zwiefalten to replace an architect whose competence failed in the construction of the specified stone vaults. Once again, Fischer inherited a building well underway but succeeded in transforming it. He was greatly limited by the fact that the former Romanesque church on the site was flanked by abbatial buildings. There was no room at the front for lateral expansion, and little behind because the newly begun church used the old foundations. Hardly five miles to the east, on the nascent Danube—here it is merely a wide stream—is the late seventeenth-century wall pillar church of Obermarchtal, one of the finest examples of the so-called Vorarlberg type, with a gabled façade and twin towers flanking the choir. Clearly, this precedent attracted, if not Fischer himelf, then the abbot of Zwiefalten. Fischer's towerless façade is an aggressive variant of his Diessen type, with giant columns in lieu of pilasters and a prominently bowed central section. Twin towers rise just beyond the slightly projecting transept arms of this very long church. The vestibule, under an organ loft, is unusually large. Beyond it stretch a four-bay nave, a spacious domed transept area, a long choir, and an altar space somewhat deeper than the vestibule. The total length is approximately three hundred feet.

The Greek-cross effect of the impressive transept area is achieved in spite of the fact that its arms project so little on the exterior. Fischer's twin towers, like those of Obermarchtal and the lesser twin towers of Ulm's Gothic cathedral, have the happy effect of seeming to shorten an extremely long and narrow rectangle.

Within, a Roman solemnity in the architecture is propelled into explosive movement by vast, illusionistic frescoes and a wild tangle of rococo stuccoes and sculpture. The substantial wall pillars, perforated by large openings for passage at the gallery level and faced with paired reddish *scagliola*

columns—for which the columned façade prepared us—miraculously take on a lightness not
seen at Fürstenzell. The bowing of the gallery
balustrades above the side chapels is emphatic. As
earlier at Osterhofen, they lead the eye rapidly toward the high altar. Mercifully, at Zwiefalten,
hardly any ornament touches Fischer's magnificent
superposed white entablatures—indispensable stabilizing elements in all this flux. Franz Johann
Spiegler's nave fresco (1751), locally known as a
"heavenly maelstrom," not only brings the four
nave bays into immediate oneness, but from the
entrance it seems literally to upend the ceiling—
until you reach its center, where the distortion resolves into a comprehensible illusion. Yet, all this
is but prelude to the great transept, narrowed as it
joins the choir beyond by a triple file of receding
columns. The pendentives are filled with magnificent rocaille cartouches, designed by Johann Michael Feichtmayr, who, with his brother Franz
Xaver, had participated in the stuccoing of Diessen.
Actual construction at Zwiefalten began in 1744,
decoration three years later; the façade dates from
1750; and completion of the vast decorating project continued until 1765. The general interior effect, therefore, is of the most advanced rococo.

Several small commissions, including a private
house in Munich, mark Fischer's activity in the
mid-1740s, but in 1748 came the opportunity to

*Johann Michael Fischer.
Benedictine Abbey Church.
Zwiefalten, Germany.
1742–1750*

build his grandest church of all: at Ottobeuren,
the great Benedictine abbey some fifty miles into
Swabia to the west of Landsberg. Under the ambitious abbot, Rupert Ness, the monastic buildings
of the venerable institution had been replaced in
1711–1724 by palatial quarters—including a
Kaisersaal and adjoining apartments to accommodate any visiting emperor. It was decided to build a
new church, not on the old site facing west—for
that had been pre-empted by the imperial
rooms—but in clear space adjoining a major stair-

*Johann Michael Fischer.
Benedictine Abbey Church.
Ottobeuren, Germany.
1748–1755*

case on the north. During the next twenty years, several architects submitted plans, including Dominikus Zimmermann. Simpert Kraemer, another architect, had actually started work in 1737, but encountered such difficulties that long delays ensued. Joseph Effner was called in for consultation in 1744 by the new abbot, Anselm Erb, and in 1749 Kraemer withdrew, it having become clear that Fischer was now in charge. How much had been built when Fischer took over is uncertain, but a strongly bowed twin-towered façade was already established, and apparently also the wide-armed cross plan lengthened by vestibule and altar spaces and terminated by apsidal transept arms. There are some connections here with the much earlier cathedral of Salzburg, of special interest when we learn that a lantern dome was at first envisaged—later reduced to the present saucer cupola on Effner's advice. (Roman lantern domes, so greatly favored in Salzburg and Vienna, are limited to only four in Bavaria and Swabia: Kempten, the Theatine church in Munich, Ettal, and Weingarten.)

What is clear is that Fischer systematically rounded off all corners, set the two large bays of the nave under an embracing oval cupola to balance the more irregularly shaped one over the equally large choir, and erected his magnificent cornices over great piers lined, as at Zwiefalten, with reddish *scagliola* columns. He placed huge, thermal-shaped clearstory windows in the nave and choir and an array of large, round-arched lights in the façade, the transept arms, and above the low side altars of the nave. These altars are set against the lateral walls, allowing a passage to be cut through from one chapel to the next—like an aisle, but at a slightly raised floor level. Entering from the great vestibule, one is astonished by the impact of three successive cupolas on pendentives, each with its superb rocaille cartouche. Seven steps raise the choir-and-altar area to a commanding position. Since there are no galleries, the vast uninterrupted space takes on the majesty of a Roman bath. Without its decoration, Ottobeuren could properly be called baroque were it not for the brilliant light everywhere apparent.

Decoration, however, vies with that at Zwiefalten in rococo virtuosity. The elegant stucco work, again by J. M. Feichtmayr, is complemented by Joseph Christian's statues and the frescoes of J. J. Zeiller—whom we have met at Fürstenzell. The two superb organ cases lining the choir are the work of Martin Hörmann, with gilded reliefs by Joseph Christian. A third organ—perhaps for antiphonal effects—was projected for the loft over the vestibule. It was not completed, but in 1957 a proper modern instrument was in-

stalled there. Following completion of the building in 1755, the decoration continued even past the dedication of 1766—the year of Fischer's death.

Flanking the choir, in spaces balancing the nave chapels, are service rooms. These connect with passages leading past the side walls enclosing the altar space to a gracious foyer behind it. To this foyer a grand abbatial staircase descends. One thinks back, by contrast, to the simple stone steps that led down from twelfth-century Cistercian dormitories to the choirs of those stark churches.

In 1750, Fischer was called to the revered Benedictine Abbey of Benediktbeuern, some fifty miles south of Munich, to design the large Anastasia-kapelle of the north transept arm of the old church. The plan is a pure longitudinal oval. On each side, the chief altar and the two flanking side altars are lit by a thermal window flanked by round-arched ones. The wall revetment consists of *scagliola* pilasters, not columns—in deference to the restricted space. Fischer's strong but lofty shell makes an admirable foil for the exquisite rococo décor. Here, the same team that ornamented Ottobeuren—Feichtmayr and Zeiller—provided what may be called Haydnesque stuccoes and frescoes. At this point, it is worth noting that the recurrence of decorators in Fischer's churches suggests that he now enjoyed some power to select them, and that the situation had gradually changed from that of the 1730s, when the abbot of Diessen alone made the choice.

During his brief campaign at Benediktbeuern, Fischer found time to execute one of his best small churches for a dependency at nearby Bichl, a vestibule in the form of two lateral ovals leads to a square domed nave with an octagonal choir beyond. Zeiller again provided the frescoes, and the sculptor Straub, who had served Fischer so well at Berg am Lain and was to do so again at Schäftlarn designed the fine small high altar with its triumphant equestrian Saint George.

In 1751, Fischer apparently took over long-delayed work on the Premonstratensian abbey church at Schäftlarn, on the Isar hardly a dozen miles south of Munich. As at Ottobeuren, it is difficult to determine how much is due to earlier designers, notably to the 1733 plan of François Cuvilliés. Under the patronage of Elector Max III Joseph, work was resumed on a revised plan submitted by J. B. Gunetzrhainer; but, as Henry-Russell Hitchcock points out, control was under a "Herr Fischer" who can hardly have been other than his step-brother-in-law and who was far more experienced. Decoration began in 1753, with especially elegant stuccoes and frescoes by J. B. Zimmermann and superb altar sculptures by Straub. Entrance through a square façade tower leads to a saucer-domed space with slightly projecting arms (similar to the Zwiefalten transept but flanked by two narrow transverse bays); then, up three steps, to a smaller domed choir and a horseshoe-shaped apse capped by a three-quarter dome. Three circular windows bring in light from the sides, as do round-arched windows in the transverse bays. There is no gallery. In short, Fischer has altered his Diessen plan to produce a centralized nave extended by choir and apse. The harmony between circular cupolas and oculus windows is especially pleasing; and the highly sophisticated ornament, in its restraint, responds sympathetically to the purity of Fischer's white surfaces. The clean pilasters—no longer engaged columns—help define an impression of neoclassicism altogether different from the interiors of Zwiefalten and Ottobeuren.

The year 1753 brought Fischer a disappointment: rejection of a plan for the great Benedictine church at Neresheim, in favor of one by Balthasar Neumann. There followed a group of ingeniously designed small churches, as well as a house in Munich for Straub. In 1759, Fischer undertook the design of a new church for the more modest Benedictine abbey of Rott-am-Inn, some forty miles southeast of Munich. It is his most exquisite creation.

To Rott-am-Inn Fischer brought as foreman Melchior Streicher, who had served him at both Benediktbeuern and Schäftlarn. Within the next year, the building was ready for decoration. Franz Xaver Feichtmayr was the stuccoist, with his son-in-law Jakob Rauch; Matthäus Günther painted the frescoes; and the elaborate program of sculptures was carried out by Ignaz Günther (no relation to Matthäus) and his assistant, Joseph Götsch. Feichtmayr had worked at Diessen, and he and Rauch had recently completed superb stuccoes for the Wilten parish church, outside Innsbruck, where Matthäus Gunther executed the frescoes. Ignaz Günther (1723–1775), a pupil of Straub, had studied in Vienna, where he caught a note of sweetness and refinement which he developed to a high pitch in his elegantly stanced figures with their sensitive faces and hands. Germany's greatest eighteenth-century sculptor, Günther created an amalgam of Parisian grace and local medieval piety. By 1763, most of the decoration was in place. The brief four-year span of operations at Rott-am-Inn accounts in part for its remarkable homogeneity.

At Rott-am-Inn, Fischer inherited the foundations of a recently pulled down Romanesque church that extended longitudinally to a pair of small towers flanking its eastern end. His new façade (1759–1760) is of the Diessen type, but flattened to a single plane. Its unfluted pilasters mark

Johann Michael Fischer. Premonstratensian Church. Schäftlarn, Germany. 1751–1753

Johann Michael Fischer. Benedictine Abbey Church. Rott-am-Inn, Germany. 1759–1760

Johann Michael Fischer.
Church.
Altomünster, Germany.
1763–1766

a surprising return to Fischer's own beginnings, as at Rinchnach. We enter a low *Vorhalle* containing monuments from the medieval past. Ahead is an extremely delicate ironwork grille by Joseph Ligner, with simple rectangular panels topped by playful curves that suggest breaking waves. Above and through it we glimpse a softly lit interior, very white, with primly pilastered piers aligned to the main axis, the whole animated by discrete spots of rococo ornament. We proceed to a true first bay, saucer-domed, and turn to discover that the organ loft extends back over the *Vorhalle* to the façade window. Ahead is the main octagonal space with its larger saucer dome and shallow transverse arms, each with an altar under a thermal window. In the four angles are galleries over rectangular chapels (as at Ingolstadt and Aufhausen, but there the chapels are oval or hexagonal). In the galleries, the light from distant windows is subtly muted, in direct contrast with the bold pendentive lighting of Berg-am-Lain. The arch over each gallery opening, smaller and lower than those on the main axes, breaks into what would here have been a much too overwhelming pendentive. Coving is more discrete than before. Capitals are reduced to dabs of rococo ornament, entablatures to a single block. No lateral or diagonal arch bows out as heretofore. The circular dome fresco rises from a continuous cornice interrupted only by small cartouches. The smaller domed choir duplicates the entrance bay; Ignaz Günther's white-and-gold high altar rises against its end wall. Only later do we discover that behind it is a sacristy as large as the choir, and that Fischer has used the base of the old eastern towers for lesser service rooms. Yet in plan, the sacristy exactly balances the *Vorhalle*. Thus we have here the perfect symmetry of main rotunda flanked by

equal domed bays, each in turn extended by *Vorhalle* and sacristy: the consummate solution of the centralized longitudinal plan.

Fischer's last important commission, the Brigittine Abbey Church (1763–1766) at Altomünster, about twenty-five miles northwest of Munich, is by all odds his most extraordinary. Stuccoes are by Jakob Rauch, whom we met at Rott-am-Inn, frescoes by Josef Mages (dated 1768). Set on a hill sloping sharply to the west, the new church followed the old Romanesque one in having a downhill entrance under a high tower with a flight of stairs leading up to the interior. A very tall façade was therefore required, and Fischer faced it with high flat pilasters. The stunning impact of a space gradually revealed is not unlike that of the Romanesque cathedral of Le Puy, in southern France.

To understand the peculiarities of Altomünster, one should remember that the Brigittine order required separate areas in the church for nuns, monks, lay brothers, and the parish congregation. To make matters even more difficult, separate circulation, some of it concealed, had to be provided for each of the three monastic communities. While the congregation attended service in the octagonal nave, the monks had their own choir at the far end of the church, behind and above the high altar. The lay brothers' choir is placed between the nave and the choir proper, but it is low-ceilinged because directly above it is the nuns' choir, overlooking the high altar to the east but with the rear opening onto the main rotunda through a grille. Of the two sets of galleries surrounding the octagonal nave, the upper one connects with the nuns' quarters, the lower one with the monks'. I omit description of these connections, but they are ingenious. Note, however, that the monks' choir is raised to the level of the lower gallery. At floor level, a narrow aisle provides circulation around the entire church as far as the high altar area. The altar itself is very complicated: above a semicircular base are three altarpieces, the flanking ones set diagonally to help define an apsidal end which in fact does not exist.

Although the nave octagon roughly approximates that of the smaller Rott-am-Inn, there are many differences that result in some artistic loss. The existence of an outer aisle, for example, and of double galleries around the entire octagon, causes all light to enter indirectly. We miss the subtle variations of Rott's lighting. Because of the aisle, too, lateral and diagonal altars in the nave were placed under shallow niches in the inner plane of the rotunda itself. Although this adds great emphasis to its octagonal shape, no recessions into transept arms or diagonal chapels whet our further interest. By Rott's standard, stuccoing of the nave is coarse; yet, the lay brothers' choir and the high altar area are most elegantly accoutered. As for Fischer's architectural members, the powerful nave entablature and the pilastered piers—set as at Rott-am-Inn parallel to the main axis—are neoclassically strict. In the choir areas beyond, entablatures are dispensed with, and in lieu of pier capitals there are simple linear moldings.

In his seventy-fifth year, on May 6, 1766, Fischer reached the end of his long career, or, as his gravestone more graciously informs us, "lay the ground stone for his last edifice, the House of Eternity." Inheriting baroque forms, Fischer opened them up, sculpturing them with white light. He rounded off angular intersections and introduced a vigorous, undulating movement. In his old age a kind of détente set in. As the first signs of French neoclassicism began to invade Germany, they coincided with a similar trend in Fischer's late work, generated, it seems clear, by a gradual evolution in his own creativeness.

S. LANE FAISON, JR.

WORKS

1724, Abbey (choir and sacristy), Niederaltaich, Germany. 1724, Church, Kircham, Germany. 1726–1728, Premonstratensian Church, Osterhofen, Germany. 1727, Church, Rinchnach, Germany. *1727–1729, Sankt Anna am Lehel (rebuilt 1950s), Munich. 1730, Church, Bergkirchen, Germany. 1730, Church, Unering, Germany. 1732–1734, Augustinian Church, Diessen, Germany. 1735–1739, Church, Aufhausen, Germany. *1735–1740, Augustinian Church, Ingolstadt, Germany. 1735–1744, Saint Michael's, Berg-am-Lain, Germany. 1740–1744, Cistercian Abbey Church (rebuilding), Fürstenzell, Germany. 1742–1750, Benedictine Abbey Church, Zwiefalten, Germany. 1748–1755, Benedictine Abbey Church, Ottobeuren, Germany. 1750, Benedictine Abbey Church, Benedictbeuren, Germany. 1750, Church, Anastasiakapelle, Germany. 1750, Church, Bichl, Germany. 1751–1753, Premonstratensian Abbey Church, Schäftlarn, Germany. 1759–1760, Benedictine Abbey Church, Rott-am-Inn, Germany. 1763–1766, Church, Altomünster, Germany. n.d., J. B. Straub House, Munich.

BIBLIOGRAPHY

FEULNER, ADOLF 1923 *Bayerisches Rokoko.* Munich: Wolff.

FRANZ, HEINRICH GERHARD 1955 "Johann Michael Fischer und die Baukunst des Barock in Böhmen." *Zeitschrift für Ostforschung.*

HAGEN-DEMPF, FELICITAS 1954 *Der Zentralbaugedanke bei Johann Michael Fischer.* Munich: Schnell & Steiner.

HAUTTMANN, MAX 1921 *Geschichte der kirchlichen Baukunst in Bayern/Schwaben und Franken/1550–1780.* Munich, Berlin, and Leipzig: Schmidt.

HITCHCOCK, H. R. 1968 *Rococo Architecture in Southern Germany.* London: Phaidon.

LAING, ALASTAIR, and BLUNT, ANTHONY 1978 "Central and Eastern Europe." Pages 165–298 in *Baroque and Rococo: Architecture & Decoration.* New York: Harper.

LIEB, NORBERT 1941 *Münchener Barockbaumeister.* Munich: Schnell & Steiner.

LIEB, NORBERT (1953)1958 *Barockkirchen zwischen Donau und Alpen.* 2d ed. Munich: Hirmer.

SCHNELL, HUGO n.d. *Gesamtverzeichnis des deutschsprachigen Schrifttums.* Munich.

FISCHER, KARL VON

Heinrich Karl Joseph von Fischer (1782–1820) was born in Mannheim, Germany. In 1796, he moved with his parents to Munich where, at age 14 he entered the workshop of the architect Maximilian von Verschaffelt. In 1799, he went to Vienna, studying at the Vienna Academy until 1806. While still in Vienna, he designed a palace in Munich which today is known as Prinz-Karl-Palais (1803–1806). This building, opposite the English Garden at the starting point of the monumental Prinzregentenstrasse, is the first mature work of classicist architecture and the first stone portico in Munich. Count Montgelas financed von Fischer's travels to France and Italy (1806–1808) which reinforced his architectural concepts and prepared the ground for his subsequent involvement in the planning of the City of Munich under King Max Joseph I. His closest collaborator in this project was the garden architect Friedrich Ludwig von Sekell. Von Fischer was appointed professor at the Academy in Munich in 1808. Before LEO VON KLENZE, Karl von Fischer was the most outstanding architect in Munich during the reign of King Max Joseph I.

During the following years, Fischer was involved in the design of the Karolinenplatz (1808–1812) and some of the palaces bordering it. His own house (designed 1809), located at the corner of Brienner and Acis Streets, was destroyed in 1937. In 1810, he provided plans for the east and west buildings of the residence; however, they remained unexecuted. His major commission was the design for the Hof- und Nationaltheater (1811–1818) which had been commissioned by the king (1810) and which should imitate the Odeon in Paris. For half a century it was the largest public opera house in central Europe. Fischer's plans for this building show his tendency away from the Viennese style toward a more classical taste developed during his travels to Italy and France. Built between 1811 and 1818, it was destroyed by fire in 1823 and subsequently rebuilt by Klenze who added the second pediment to the façade. Wings, which von Fischer had planned at the sides of the building, were not executed. The size of the building surpassed the scale of older structures and thus set a new standard for nineteenth-century architecture in Munich. For Crown Prince Ludwig, von Fischer prepared plans for a Walhalla (hall of fame) and a Glyptothek. Von Fischer died in Munich at the age of 37. Most of his drawings are preserved in the collections of the Technische Universität, Munich.

EGON VERHEYEN

WORKS

1803–1806, Prinz-Karl-Palais; *1808–1812, Karolinenplatz with *Palais Ashbeck, Palais Törring, and Palais Hompesch (much altered); *1809, Karl von Fischer House; 1811–1818, Hof- und Nationaltheater; Munich.

BIBLIOGRAPHY

FEUCHTMAYR, INGE 1966 *Das Prinz Carl-Palais in München: Gestalten und Begebenheiten.* Munich: Süddeutscher Verlag.

HEDERER, OSWALD 1942 *Die Ludwigstrasse in München.* Munich: Dietz.

HEDERER, OSWALD 1960 *Karl von Fischer: Leben und Werk.* Munich: Callwey.

KELLER, H. K. E. L. 1960 *Das Pariser Modell des Bayerischen Nationaltheaters.* Munich: Grottus-Stift.

MUNICH, STADTMUSEUM 1972 *Bayern, Kunst und Kultur.* Munich: Prestel. Exhibition catalogue.

FISCHER, THEODOR

The role of Theodor Fischer (1862–1938) as an educator is comparable to that of PETER BEHRENS. DOMINIKUS BÖHM and HUGO HÄRING attended Fischer's lectures at the Polytechnic School in Stuttgart. PAUL BONATZ was his teaching assistant and BRUNO TAUT was apprenticed to him during his Stuttgart period. ERIC MENDELSOHN and J. J. P. OUD studied with him at the Munich Polytechnic School. He was also an important leader of the young science of city planning.

Fischer, born in Schweinfurt am Main, studied with FRIEDRICH VON THIERSCH at the Munich Polytechnic School and worked as an assistant to PAUL WALLOT when the latter was building the Reichstag in Berlin. After work as an architect in Dresden and Munich, Fischer became director of the Munich city planning office in 1893 and later received a professorship at the Munich Polytechnic School in 1901. In 1903 he was invited to teach at the Stuttgart Polytechnic School. He always maintained an active private practice alongside his teaching duties. Fischer became an important founding member of the German *Werkbund* in 1907 and was its first president. In 1908 he returned to Munich to assume the Polytechnic School's new chair in city planning, remaining until 1928. Though his practice thrived throughout the 1920s, he received almost no work after 1932.

Fischer's architectural style was usually characterized in his own day as "South German." This points to a more picturesque, lighter expression than the ponderous and heavily articulated Wilhelmine style. Although Fischer made varied historical references in his buildings, he preferred to make them to the vernacular traditions of southern Germany in his smaller, domestic buildings, as in his design for the houses of Gmindersdorf (1903–1908), a factory town in a rural setting. In his designs for larger public buildings, on the other hand, Fischer did on occasion turn to a more official idiom, usually to underline their position in the urban fabric or for the sake of continuity with nearby structures. For instance, his design for an extension to the sixteenth-century University of Jena (1904–1908) is executed in a simplified middle-German Renaissance style. But whether his public buildings are medievalizing or faintly baroque, his designs are never somber or imposing and instead retain a light touch. This holds true even from 1910 onward, when, together with the general trend toward a neoclassical idiom, his style becomes somewhat more severe. It is characteristic of Fischer's work that he turned at this time to a graceful, Brunelleschian Renaissance mode rather than to the monumental, almost Doric style of Behrens. An excellent example is the Kunstgebäude in Stuttgart (1909–1912), an art center and exhibition building. Although an important and dignified public building that abuts on what was then the palace of the Kings of Württemberg, it is not a pretentious structure. Its ingenious siting makes it the pivot and linking element between two open spaces, an arrangement greatly admired by CAMILLO SITTE, whose ideas on urban planning had influenced Fischer. The Kunstgebäude illustrates that for Fischer architectural style and civic planning went hand in hand and that, even in so prestigious a location, he was concerned with the

Theodor Fischer.
Kunstgebäude.
Stuttgart, Germany.
1909–1912

spatial experience of the pedestrian rather than with some ideal, formally rigid, monumental image.

Fischer's ideas concerning city planning were articulated in *Stadterweiterungsfragen mit besonderer Rücksicht auf Stuttgart* ("City Extension Problems with Special Regard to Stuttgart" [1903]). He maintains that the characteristics of the local landscape should be enhanced, not contradicted, by the planner, and even demands that the ring of hills surrounding Stuttgart should be crowned with tall buildings. Tall structures were then being erected only in the center of Stuttgart (at the bottom of the valley) which Fischer feared would eventually eradicate the natural contours of the setting. Fischer also questions existing zoning laws reflecting an approach to architecture that presumed the erection of self-contained monuments. As an example Fischer mentions the Piazza dei Signori in Verona, where an archway covering a street provides a continuous peripheral enclosure for the urban space. Fischer's beliefs about visual linkage and the importance he gave to perceptual and experiential aspects of urban groupings were closely related to Sitte's ideas. Like Sitte, Fischer was against the categorical application of a theoretical system. Fischer's approach to planning, therefore, was completely opposed to the highly conceptual, formalistic schemes of LE CORBUSIER in the 1920s.

Fischer had a chance to apply his ideas by designing general and expansion plans for a number of German cities and towns, including Ludwigsburg (1910), Bayreuth and Dortmund (1914), Mannheim (1916), and Augsburg (1926). Although Fischer was well known as a designer of schools, museums, and churches, his involvement in the design of housing estates seems to be as important. In addition to the workers' colony at Gmindersdorf, he designed, among others, workers' housing in Stuttgart's Weberstrasse (1904–1906), a workers' colony at Langensalza (1907–1908), low-income housing at Neu-Westend in Munich (1909–1910), and the housing development Alte Haide, Munich (1918–1929). Exhibitions of his works were organized by the Munich Secession in the winter of 1901–1902 and by the Munich Kunstverein in 1914. In 1916, Karl Ernst Osthaus, well-known patron of architects and artists, together with the Association for Low-Income Housing of Greater Berlin, organized a traveling exhibit of garden city designs that comprised, among others, Fischer's Gmindersdorf as well as Bruno Taut's Falkenberg, inspired by Fischer.

In his pamphlet *Für die deutsche Baukunst* ("For German Architecture" [1917]), Fischer criticized the existing educational system in architecture

Theodor Fischer. Low-Income Housing. Neu-Westend, Munich. 1909–1910

because of its heavy academic bias: more than half of a student's time was usually occupied with the study of mathematics and the natural sciences. He also objected strongly to the great emphasis on drawing and design. Moreover, a large part of the supposed architectural training consisted of drawing after plaster models of buildings and architectural rendering had attained an existence of its own. (Much of this criticism is still valid today.) This type of learning did not, in his opinion, reveal whether a student had any aptitude for the design of three-dimensional space.

Fischer proposed instead that actual construction be studied before a student even entered architectural school, including such ordinary but crucial matters as making windows and doors. Fischer also suggested that the category of journeyman be reintroduced, an apprenticeship position which had been abandoned when architectural training had turned away from its older crafts background to embrace academia.

Fischer's approach was to be used at the Bauhaus until the mid-1920s. In fact, WALTER GROPIUS referred to Fischer's "For German Architecture" as an important source for his own pedagogical ideas.

ROSEMARIE HAAG BLETTER

WORKS

1900–1901, Girls' School, Luisenstrasse; 1900–1902, School at Elisabethplatz; Munich. 1902–1914, Municipal Theater, Heilbronn, Germany. 1903–1908, Workers' Colony, Gmindersdorf, Germany. 1904–1906, Workers' Housing, Weberstrasse, Stuttgart, Germany. 1904–1908, University of Jena (extension), Germany. 1907, Church of the Redeemer, Stuttgart, Germany. 1907–1908, Workers' Colony, Langensalza, Germany. 1907–1913, Museum, Kassel, Germany. 1908–1911, Garrison Church, Ulm, Germany. 1909, School, Hellerau, Germany. 1909–1910, Low Income Housing, Neu-Westend, Munich. 1909–1912, Kunstgebäude, Stuttgart, Germany. 1912–1915, Museum, Wiesbaden, Germany. 1914, Pavilion, Werkbund Exhibition, Cologne, Germany. 1918–1929, Alte Haide Housing Development, Munich.

BIBLIOGRAPHY

FISCHER, THEODOR 1903 *Stadterweiterungsfragen mit*

besonderer Rücksicht auf Stuttgart. Stuttgart: Deutsche Verlags-Anstalt.

FISCHER, THEODOR 1917 *Für die deutsche Baukunst.* Munich: Georg Müller.

KARLINGER, HANS 1932 *Theodor Fischer, Ein deutscher Baumeister.* Munich: Callwey.

PFISTER, RUDOLF 1968 *Theodor Fischer: Leben und Wirken eines deutschen Baumeisters.* Munich: Callwey.

FISCHER VON ERLACH, JOHANN BERNHARD

The career of Johann Bernhard Fischer von Erlach (1656–1723), Austria's greatest baroque architect, spanned the end of the seventeenth and first quarter of the eighteenth century and his *oeuvre* encompassed the major building types of that time. His style—so readily accepted by the Hapsburg imperial court as its official language—synthesized elements from the full-baroque of GIOVANNI LORENZO BERNINI, FRANCESCO BORROMINI, and PIETRO DA CORTONA; the late-baroque of DOMENICO FONTANA; and the early classicism of J. B. Mathey and others. Despite Fischer's eclectic approach, his great buildings from the Ancestral Hall of the Althan Family to the Saint Charles Borromeo Church are striking in their originality. Fischer was utopian in his mammoth first project for Schönbrunn, and imaginative and fantastic in his designs for pleasure pavilions. The architect's abiding interest in the past and present of architecture may be seen in his *Historic Architecture* (1721) and in his built works, whose singularity and grandeur are so much a part of any definition of the baroque period in Austrian architecture.

The architect, sculptor, and architectural historian, Johann Bernhard Fischer von Erlach, was born in Graz, Austria, in July 1656; he died in Vienna in April 1723. His father was the sculptor Johann Baptist Fischer (the title von Erlach was granted to the architect in 1696 when he was knighted). Fischer left Graz, in either 1670/1671 or 1674, for Rome to further his education. After more than a decade Fischer returned to Austria in 1687 to settle in the capital city of the Hapsburg Empire, Vienna.

Fischer's early reception in Rome was inhospitable and he struggled until he found a position in the studio of the painter and architect Phillip Schor, one of the members of a family of artists and decorators of German descent who had settled in Rome. Through Schor and his family, Fischer was gainfully employed, given further education, and introduced to the important artists and patrons of the Roman late-baroque period. Fischer's early and continuing interest in gardens; their palace belvederes, gates, fountains, and particularly their ornamental vases, must have been stimulated, in part, by the work of the Schor family.

In Rome, Fischer became an avid student of the history of architecture, an interest he never abandoned. Fischer sketched the ancient ruins of Rome together with the architectural monuments of the renaissance and baroque periods. His desire to understand the eternal values of architecture led him to appreciate such disparate geniuses as Bernini and Borromini, with the classical style of Bernini's architecture having the greatest influence on him. Whether or not Fischer met Bernini, who died in 1680, has been much debated and cannot be settled with absolute certainty. That he knew members of the circle of Bernini is undebatable for Fischer had access to Bernini's drawings, including unexecuted projects like that for the Louvre east façade.

Beginning in the 1680s, Fontana was the leading architect of Rome. Having worked many years as Bernini's assistant, he fell heir to the master's unfinished commissions. His was an eclectic style, much dependent upon the ideas of the previous generation including, of course, Bernini but also Borromini and Cortona. Fischer was likewise as a late baroque architect to strive for a manner of synthesis in his architecture, pulling together ideas from the ancients through the moderns for his own individualistic efforts.

Fischer's interest in French art and theory influenced his earliest works in Vienna, like the Garden Belvedere for the Liechtenstein Palace in the Rossau (1687/1688–1690). Engravings of French architecture would have been readily available to Fischer in Rome, where the French were much in evidence. Roman artists were well aware of the magnificent achievement in palace design and decoration at Louis XIV's court at Versailles, and artistic influences rather than flowing from Italy to France, as had been true in the Renaissance and early baroque periods, had begun going in the opposite direction, with Paris replacing Rome as the arbiter of European taste in the early eighteenth-century.

In 1684, Fischer went to Naples to assist Schor, who had been named court architect by the newly appointed viceroy, Don Gaspar Guzman d'Haro. He was still in Naples in 1685, but was in Graz by 1687 and in that same year in Vienna where he was to remain, except for pleasure trips and journeys to the sites of his works, until his death.

Fischer must have realized that the conditions in Vienna were auspicious for major architectural commissions. The victory of the combined forces of the emperor and King John Sobieski of Poland against the Turks in the Siege of Vienna of 1683 had breathed a spirit of confidence into the imperial court, the aristocracy, and the citizenry. Austrian patrons now believed native artists capable of achievements rivaling those of the Italians, upon whom there had been much reliance earlier in the century. Witness to this is the fact that Fischer obtained work from almost the moment of his arrival in Vienna. In 1687, the year of his return, he received two Imperial commissions and thus began his service to the crown which was to encompass the reigns of three monarchs: Leopold I, Joseph I, and Charles VI. He soon added to his imperial patronage a number of powerful protectors and patrons from the aristocracy, including members of the Dietrichstein, Salm, and Liechtenstein families.

Although Fischer left letters, drawings, and his volume on the history of architecture, and is mentioned in contemporary archival material, relatively little is known of his private life and personality. A tremendous worker, with a scholarly bent, his personal feelings were seldom injected into his letters or writings. Esteemed during his lifetime, Fischer's features were recorded several times by other artists, among the portrayals remaining are: a painted portrait (1723) by Adam Manyoki in the Imperial Oratory of the Saint Charles Borromeo Church, Vienna, and another, in relief, on a bronze medal (1719) by Benedickt Richter.

Fischer married Sophia Konstantia Morgner, a notary's daughter, in 1690. They had five children. Their second son Joseph Emanuel Fischer von Erlach (1693–1742) became an architect and in the late years of his father's life completed several of his important commissions, including the monumental Saint Charles Borromeo Church and the Imperial Library. Fischer von Erlach, a widower, was married a second time in 1705. This marriage was not successful and his wife left him.

Always a student of architecture, Fischer traveled to study and to obtain commissions. He visited Prague in 1691, where he sketched the newly erected Kreuzherrenkirche and Troja Summer Palace, both by Mathey. The restrained early classicism of the Kreuzherrenkirche, with its planar façade defined by pilasters and drafting and embellished with sculpture deeply impressed Fischer. Because of the continual antagonism between Austria and France, Fischer never experienced French architecture firsthand.

In 1704, Fischer traveled to the Prussian court of Frederick I in Berlin, seeking the patronage of that monarch. He carried with him a grandiose design for a palace (one signed drawing exists in the Albertina, Vienna)—a modification of the unbuilt first project for the Palace of Schönbrunn—but failed to interest Frederick, who already had an

excellent architect in ANDREAS SCHLÜTER, in realizing it.

Fischer's ultimate destination on his trip was England, where he arrived with a letter of introduction from Emperor Leopold I to Queen Anne. This would undoubtedly have led to a meeting with his English counterpart, CHRISTOPHER WREN, whose Saint Paul's Cathedral was then under construction. Wren was, like Fischer, an architectural theorist and, as Hans Sedlmayr has suggested, a meeting between the two men may have strengthened Fischer's resolve to write a history of architecture; he began his volume in the following year.

Yet, it was Chatsworth House in Derbyshire, rather than Wren's buildings, which seem to have impressed Fischer the most during his stay in England. The severely classical west façade, designed by WILLIAM TALMAN, had only been completed in 1703. Together with English Palladianism in general, it seem to have fired in Fischer a desire to see ANDREA PALLADIO's works and in 1707 he set off for Venice.

Fischer probably visited Venice on his first trip to Italy, but he returned with much greater dedication to understanding the architecture of Palladio. He returned to Venice once again in 1717 and to Prague in 1720, but only for brief periods.

Fischer was a man of diverse talents, the last great sculptor–architect of the renaissance and baroque periods. In the 1680s, he received commissions for sculpture, architecture, and gardens. In 1687 he designed the stucco decoration for the restoration of the decaying Mausoleum of the Emperor Ferdinand II in Graz, for Emperor Leopold I. He placed relief figures and heavy acanthus frames around narrative frescoes in the interior. Another imperial commission of the same year, for the votive Holy Trinity Plague Column, was a collaborative effort. Fischer was responsible for the design of the six bas-reliefs combining biblical and historical references at the base of the column. He began carving the marble himself, but this work was completed in 1689 by Johann Ignaz Bendl.

Fischer's first major architectural commission, a belvedere (1687–1690) for the garden of Prince Johann Adam Andreas von Liechtenstein in suburban Rossau is illustrated in Fischer's *Historic Architecture* (book 5, plate 12). A large triumphal arch sustained by columns was at the center before an open vaulted room. Low closed wings were attached at the sides. The belvedere, a single story over a low basement, rose to a horizontal roofline decorated with a balustrade and sculpture. Capitalizing on the belvedere's site at the top of the garden, Fischer created a double-stepped terrace and placed a symmetrical oval stairway at the entrance.

The delightful Liechtenstein Garden Belvedere with its combination of Italian and French sources was a work of mature and original vision.

In March 1689 Fischer reported to Prince Maximilian Jakob Moriz Liechtenstein that he was instructing Joseph, the twelve-year-old heir-apparent to the Hapsburg throne in architecture. In this way Fischer came into contact with the future emperor and the court surrounding him. Joseph came to be a valued patron, even standing as godfather to the first of the architect's children.

Joseph I became emperor on the death of his father, Leopold I, in May 1705, and on Christmas eve of the same year Fischer was made Chief Imperial Inspector of royal buildings and festivities. This position, which he held until his death, put him in a position above his rival, LUCAS VON HILDEBRANDT, who was also an imperial architect.

In connection with Joseph I, Fischer gained his first celebrity. He designed two temporary triumphal arches for Joseph's official entry into Vienna in 1690, after his coronation as King of Poland in Augsburg. The arches, both of which are illustrated in *Historic Architecture*, were elaborate constructions combining sculptured figures, emblemata, and architecture in an elaborate iconographic program lauding the Hapsburg dynasty. Several motifs which Fischer was to return to throughout his career, like the triumphal arch and the historiated column, were presented in this ephemeral architecture of 1690, which pleased the royal family and thrilled the Viennese citizenry.

Nine years later, in 1699, Fischer was again called upon to design two arches, this time to celebrate the coronation and marriage of Joseph I. In comparison to the earlier arches, the Triumphal Arch of the Foreign Merchants (*Historic Architecture*, book 4, plate 1) appears more unified, has fewer figures and is iconographically less complicated. Its lower register was defined by a large Serliana having sculpted atlantes holding the central arch. On the second register, a circle of columns formed a monopteral enclosure for an equestrian statue of Joseph I which was suspended on clouds.

Throughout his career, Fischer von Erlach was called upon to design sculptural commissions, especially altars. After 1689 he did not execute the sculpture himself, but left this to others who worked from his drawings or models. A representative altar commission was that for the Holy Trinity high altar of the important pilgrimage Church of Mariazell, Styria, Austria, which because of patronage by the Hapsburg family had a national significance. Fischer's drawing (Albertina, Vienna) for the altar dates from 1692, but the work on it done by stonemasons, sculptors, and goldsmiths took until 1704 to complete. A Berninesque scenographic grouping of free-standing columns sustain an arch and frame the altar's central vision: a crucifix suspended above a silver globe.

An exceptional altar solution was Fischer's highly successful placement of a baroque high altar into the vertical Gothic space of the chancel of the Franciscan Church in Salzburg. The Franciscans wished to replace Michael Pacher's late medieval carved altar, but to retain the venerated image of the Madonna and Child from it. Fischer's altar is placed before a column in the chancel's center, and climbs upward along it. The Madonna and Child are enthroned in a shallow illusionistic niche before a golden glory. They are framed by a diadem arch held by free-standing paired columns of red veined marble. The architect's sensitivity to the architecture and sculpture of another historic period is apparent in the Franciscan high altar.

Fischer's most grandiose architectural design was the first project for the grounds and Palace of Schönbrunn, which is illustrated in the *Historic Architecture* (book 4, plate 2) and modestly called there an "imperial hunting lodge." Perhaps Schönbrunn I was begun as early as 1688, and it may have been a presentation piece given Leopold I to enhance and secure Fischer's position with the court. There is considerable doubt as to whether Fischer believed that the gigantic scheme of terraces, cascades, ramps, arcades, and fountains climbing the hill to a palace larger in dimensions than the Palace of Versailles would ever be built by a court just out of war.

Fischer drew from many sources for the composition of Schönbrunn I, particularly the vast complexes of the ancients like the Roman Temple of Fortuna at Praeneste, which he might have studied at firsthand. At that site, terraces and ramps were used to climb a slope crowned by the temple. Fischer too had the central section of his palace suggest a temple, a Christian one, by combining elements from the façade by CARLO MADERNO for St. Peter's, Rome (the arcade, engaged giant columns, the attic, and statues) and Bernini's façade for Santa Maria at Ariccia (the arcade and pediment). The entry, with lateral low service buildings was at the bottom of the Schönbrunnerberg, on the top of which the palace was to have been built. It would then, as Fischer's caption to the engraved plate points out, have overlooked the city of Vienna and the frontiers of Hungary, a significant symbolic position. Hildebrandt was later able to position his magnificent Upper Belvedere Palace for Prince Eugen of Savoy in just such a symbolic way. The placement of Schönbrunn II, built from 1696 onward, at the bottom of the Schönbrunnerberg seems to have been the one

point about which Fischer repeatedly lamented.

The huge first court of Schönbrunn I was designed as a jousting field, with the imperial viewing tent set before the backdrop of a rocky water cascade. The second court and all further courts at Schönbrunn I were to have been on arcaded terraces, with the third and fourth courts holding fountains and embroidered floral parterres. The palace rested on the uppermost terrace, whose central oval court was placed between the curving arms of wings of the façade. Bernini's second project for the east façade of the Louvre may have suggested the use of curving wings for the palace. The giant order was used by Fischer to articulate almost the entire surface of the palace, which spreads out laterally via courts and additional wings, in a manner similiar to JULES HARDOUIN MANSART's expansion of Versailles. Clearly Fischer had set out to surpass that French model.

In 1693 Fischer was called upon for much reduced plans for Schönbrunn (*Historic Architecture*, book 4, plates 3 and 4). The garden of Schönbrunn II was begun in 1695 and the main building in 1696, the year in which Fischer was knighted. A more traditional French style palace, Schönbrunn II retained the severe low service buildings of the large project, but replaced the trajanic columns at the entrance with simpler obelisks. There is only a single large court before the main block of the palace whose sides are stepped back to give the plan a French U-shape. To either side of the court, low detached stable buildings are elegantly clad in pilasters.

A French baroque garden was laid out behind the palace ascending the Schönbrunnerberg, but not entirely as Fischer had planned it. Today Ferdinand Hetzendorf von Hohenberg's neoclassical Gloriette marks the crest of the hill, rather than the garden belvedere Fischer had projected in his engraved plate.

Fischer's original interior palace plan had a cen-

tral hall extending the width of the building, with a separate set of state apartments for the king and queen at either side. Nikolaus Pacassi, the Empress Maria Theresa's architect, made major alterations to the interiors at mid-century when the palace was redecorated in the rococo manner. On the exterior Pacassi tore down Fischer's outer stairs, and in adding a mezzanine floor to the palace's central section destroyed the focal point of the court façade. Now instead of Fischer's original five large arched openings, a tedious seventeen arches stretch across the building's central projection.

If the exuberant and original Schönbrunn I is compared with the reticent and traditional Schönbrunn II, the classicizing restraint of the latter may not be as indicative of the architect's own taste, as of court taste, just as the scale of the project was of court finances.

Rising above a steep cliff over the River Thaya in Moravia (Vrahov nad Dyji, Czechoslovakia), the Ancestral Hall of the Althan Family on their

Fischer von Erlach.
Schönbrunn Palace.
Vienna.
1696–1711 and later

Fischer von Erlach.
Grosse Galerie, Schönbrunn
*   Palace.*
Vienna.
1696–1711 and later

Frain Estate, is Fischer's most dramatically sited building and one of his richest inventions of the early years in Vienna. Built in 1688 for Johann Michael II, Count Althan, in 1695 when Johann Michael Rottmayr finished the ceiling frescoes. The entire remodeling and a later chapel (1698–1700) may have been designed by Fischer.

The exterior, defined by broad pilasters, climbs in vertical splendor, its smooth walls in sharp contrast to the jagged rock cliff on which it sits. Originally the outside walls terminated with an attic and heavy stone vases, but these were removed by Joseph Emanuel Fischer von Erlach in 1740 when he installed the present Mansard roof.

The Ancestral Hall, a bold free-standing oval in plan, is entered through a single door from an oval, horizontally placed, vestibule. An awe-inspiring interior space (26 meters long and 13 meters wide), it is the "pantheon" of the Althan family. Fischer placed an oval cupola directly over the oval walls, and punctured it with ten large oval windows deeply set into the vault.

The hall's iconographic program begins with the statues of the Althan family members in niches around the lower register and continues with accounts of their deeds and virtues in stucco and frescoes on the walls and vaults. In the Ancestral Hall at Frain, Fischer, for the first time in his *oeuvre*, integrated architecture with sculpture and painting to create a monumental unified interior (in German, a *Gesamtkunstwerk*).

This commission marked the first fruitful collaboration of Fischer with Rottmayr in what was to be a relationship extending until the architect's death. While in Rome, Fischer had seen and come to appreciate the great illusionistically painted vaults of painters like G. B. Gaulli (Church of Il Gesù, Rome [1674–1679]) and the Jesuit Father Andrea Pozzo, who had completed his ceiling fresco in the nave of S. Ignazio, Rome in 1694. In that ceiling the walls of the church continued into a grand painted scheme of architecture which appears to rise steeply for another story before opening into blue sky and clouds. The painted vault had a tremendous flowering in central Europe in Fischer's time, because of such painters. Pozzo went to Vienna in 1702, working there on frescoes and altars until his death in 1709.

The late seventeenth and especially the eighteenth century saw an exceptional number of designs for eccentrically planned palaces and churches, many of which were built. It is still somewhat surprising to find attributed to Fischer, early in his career, c.1690–1693, the uncanonical Garden Palace for Christian Johann Althan in the Rossau suburb of Vienna. The Althan Garden Palace had an X-shaped plan with a horizontally placed oval salon in the center connecting the four wings.

Fischer followed the Althan Garden Palace with a whole series of designs for garden palaces (Lustgartengebäude) some of which are illustrated in *Historic Architecture* (book 4, Plates 18 and 19; book 5, plate 10). Unfortunately none of these elegant palaces were ever executed by him, although variations were produced by other architects.

Fischer von Erlach's single greatest patron, was Johann Ernst, Thun-Hohenstein, prince-bishop of Salzburg from 1687–1709, under whose auspices he built in Salzburg: the façade and horse bath of the Archbishop's Stables (1693–1694); the Hospital and Church of Saint John the Baptist (Johannes-Spital) (1695–1704); the University Church (Kollegienkirche) (1696–1707); the Ursuline Church and Nunnery (Ursulinenkirche) (1699–1705); and Klesheim Palace (1700–1709), along with other projects. Together Fischer and his patron changed the urban milieu of the alpine city, giving it many of the lively baroque squares and churches which characterize it today.

Fischer may have known the prince-bishop when he resided in Graz, as bishop of Seckau, prior to 1687. At any rate, he seems to have worked for him beginning in c.1689–1690, when he designed the Mirabell Palace Garden with its sculptural ornamentation; a few of the stone vases and statues from this project are still *in situ*. From that time, Fischer usually was engaged with one or more projects for the archbishop until that prelate's death in 1709.

In 1693, Fischer completed the Summer Riding School (Felsenreitschule), Salzburg, a remarkable outdoor riding theater consisting of three tiers of arcades for spectator galleries carved directly into the rock of the Salzburg landmark hill, the Mönchsberg. Carving into the Mönchsberg was not so remarkable; this had been done for centuries at the ancient cemetery of nearby Saint Peter's Church to create mortuary chapels, but the monumental and unified effect that Fischer achieved was something never before seen.

Fischer then began work on refurbishing of the Archbishop's Stables and the square in front and at the side of them. Built earlier in the century, Fischer's commission was to give the stables an elegant baroque façade in keeping with its prominent place in the city —across from a major hospital. In the square directly in front, Fischer placed one of the most magnificent horse baths (Pferdeschwemme) of the baroque period. He ran a wall along the Mönchsberg side of the square, on which blind arcades frame frescos of horses. Such practical yet ornamental horse baths were not exceptional in the period and Fischer had earlier included one in his stables built for the Liechtenstein Estate in Eisgrub, Moravia (1688–1698).

The Salzburg horse bath was oval in plan and had arms on the cross axes with ramps to lead the horses through the water. In the center, on a high stone pedestal an over life-size sculptural group, a horse breaker with a rearing horse, was placed facing Fischer's stable portal. In 1732 the position of the statues was turned ninety degrees to face the street, which changed the effect of their silhouette against the wall and their interchange with the stable portal. At that time the original balustrade surrounding the bath was exchanged for the carved rococo one that is seen today.

A high point in Fischer's activities for the prince-bishop of Salzburg came in 1694, when he signed a contract for the Holy Trinity Church with its accompanying priest's residence and college, the Collegium Virgilianum; presented the first drawings for the Benedictine University Church which was to commence building in 1696; and laid the cornerstone for the Pilgrimage Church of Maria Kirchental near Lofer, Austria.

In planning the Holy Trinity complex, Fischer again had the opportunity to define an important urban space in Salzburg. The site was on a long square already occupied by an older diocesan palace and part of the medieval town wall. Fischer's plan, a rectangle with the church in the center of the long side overlooking the square, was a solution that became popular for later monasteries of the baroque period in Austria and Germany.

The church's concave center was originally held in place by two low tower bases surmounted by terminals perforated by ovals. The church had a more dynamic center because of the clearer interplay of shapes between the concavity of the Roman dome, which rose well above the other elements of the façade, and the convex lower portions. In 1757 a second register was added to the towers completely distorting Fischer's intentions, and the present disposition of the tower's caps dates only from 1818.

The Holy Trinity Church façade is often compared with Borromini's Sant'Agnese in Piazza Navona, with which it shares some features. But Fischer was much more concerned than was Borromini with the continuation of the adjacent palace façades onto the church façade in order to unify the entire elevation in the context of its role in defining the city square. The concave center of Holy Trinity Church is more emphatic than Sant'Agnese's and in this it seems closer to Bernini's second project for the Louvre Fischer's church was conceived as part of a whole, a monumental "triumphal" center to a complex of which it was only a part. Borromini's Sant'Agnese was to dominate the Piazza Navona (it had subsequently to share its place with Bernini's Fountain of the Four Rivers). The mixed metaphor of the sacred and profane which Fischer explored in the Holy Trinity and its adjacent buildings was later to be attempted by his son, in the Saint Michael's Wing (Michaelerplatz) of the Hofburg Palace, Vienna, which borrows many of its forms from the Holy Trinity Church and College.

For Holy Trinity, Fischer chose an oval for the plan and placed it longitudinally. Shallow rectangular chapels were placed on the cross axes, and niches on the diagonal axes. An oval Roman dome with slender rectangular windows in the drum rises steeply over the congregational area. The lower register of the interior is clad in giant Corinthian pilasters with a second smaller order of pilasters bundled behind them in the congregational space and continuing alone into the lower barrel vaulted cross arms. Light from the dome filters into the white interior; the only saturated color is in the three altars and the cupola fresco painted by Rottmayr.

The tall and slender proportions of the dominant central domed space of Holy Trinity Church create a vertical pull upward into Rottmayr's splendid fresco "The Coronation of the Virgin by the Holy Trinity." The cross arms, although completely separate spaces reverberate into the central room through the device of the bundled pilasters which turn the corners. In this way, the central space while soaring upward, still appears to be held in place by the arms of the cross. The church's dual iconographic focal points, Fischer's original altar and Rottmayr's fresco, were firmly established through the structure of the church and its articulation.

Rather than a blend of the parts, as Fischer had sought to achieve with the Holy Trinity Church and its square, with the commission for the Benedictine University Church (Kollegienkirche) his concern focused upon the presense of the church in the cityscape of Salzburg. Its size and placement, facing the river and on a cross axis with the white marble Cathedral by Santino Solari gave Fischer a chance to impress the church's image upon the entire city.

The University Church has a powerful façade, convex in the center with two towers at the sides, and completely dominates the narrow medieval square at the end of which it stands. The church's back, sides, and dome are all carefully articulated with pilasters and lisens. Constructed of baser material than the cathedral, and in a striking coloristic contrast to it, the plaster surface of the church is tinted in striking shades of umber and beige and its roof is a faded green. Fischer's sense of powerful external massing on a large church is first seen here; in the clarity, singularity and beauty of all the exterior parts it is reminiscent of Cortona's Saints Luca and Martina, Rome.

The three bay oval projection of the main façade forms an open porch which serves as a prelude to the interior. The lower portion of the façade, below the running entablature, is articulated by giant order Ionic pilasters. The upper façade is composed of the towers and an attic over the porch. The dome is meant to be seen in distant views from around the city, like so many domes of the Roman baroque. Fischer's device of the oval projection on the façade was to have an enormous impact on the future of ecclesiastical architecture of the baroque in Germany and Austria.

The University Church has a cross plan of uneven arms with a Roman dome over the crossing. Oval chapels on the four outside corners of the arms are devoted to the patron saints of the four faculties of the university. The chapels and arms interconnect and may be entered by separate doors in the intervals between the oval porch and towers of the main façade. In this way Fischer accommodated the university processionals, which could proceed directly from the square along the church's perimeter and into the galleries above the chapels through either the stairs in the bell towers or the double stair housed behind the high altar.

Fischer's plan somewhat resembles both Rosato Rosati's San Carlo ai Catinari, Rome (1611), and the University Church of the Sorbonne, Paris, by JACQUES LEMERCIER, but his interior proportions differ greatly from these models. Fischer's majestic church interior, one of the finest of the Austrian baroque, is lofty in the manner of

Gothic architecture. The white interior is articulated by giant Corinthian pilasters on fourteen-foot bases. Along the nave, the intervals between the pilasters contain two registers of niches filled with statues so that together with the arch openings of the chapel and gallery a triumphal arch motif is formed. An oculus is cut into the vault of each chapel and gallery so that light may enter into them an outside lantern analagous to the subsidiary lanterns in St. Peter's basilica in Rome.

The elegant stucco decorations of the interior were designed by Fischer and carried out by Diego Francesco Carlone and Paolo d'Allio, but the interior was not completely finished at the time of the dedication in 1707, and the fresco intended for the cupola of the central dome was never carried out.

Originally Fischer's magnificent circular domed tabernacle, (known from a drawing, c.1706, and *Historic Architecture,* book 4, plates 10 and 11), stood above the high altar and before the tremendous stucco glory which fills the semicircular back wall of the high altar room. Fischer framed this altar composition, with giant free-standing columns, a device used by Palladio in his church architecture. Fischer's over-all concept for the high altar derived from Bernini's Cathedra Petri, where in a preliminary design the use of lateral columns had also been foreseen.

Fischer's other projects in Salzburg, although not as grand as the University Church, posed a variety of interesting problems for the architect. In the Hospital and Church of Saint John in Mülleck near Salzburg (Johannes-Spital) (1695–1705), the high altar, its tabernacle and the side altars, with paintings by Rottmayr, are all from drawings by Fischer.

The small church is embedded in the center of the undecorated wings of the hospital. A two-register lower façade, consisting of an open porch with a fenestrated loggia above it, it divided into three bays by giant Ionic pilasters. This treatment is close to Bernini's Santa Bibiana, Rome, although the giant order was not used there.

The Saint John Hospital Church plan is unusual in one respect, the rare use by Fischer of undulating wall segments in an interior. The plan is a cross whose shallow arms surround a broad crossing covered with a ribbed quadripartite vault.

The Ursuline Church and Nunnery in Salzburg stands on a triangulated site running along the banks of the Salzach River and bordered by two streets, one of which runs along the cliff of the Mönchsberg. Fischer placed the church at the apex of the triangle at the confluence of the two streets, so that its façade became a backdrop for a lovely open square on the river's bank. The two towers of the main church façade are set back several feet

Fischer von Erlach.
Kollegienkirche.
Salzburg, Austria.
1696–1707

from it and serve as transitional elements between the church and the nunnery, which runs behind it along the two streets. Fischer's Ursuline Church recalls the Roman churches by CARLO RAINALDI and Bernini on the Piazza del Popolo, where the site and the use of the tower is analogous. The Ursuline Church was begun in 1699, the exterior and interior with a pulpit and high altar from Fischer's designs were finished in 1705; the nunnery was built between 1707 and 1726.

The definition of the Ursuline Church façade as a porch with upper loggia, is almost identical to that of the Saint John Hospital Church, and both ultimately derive from the University Church which dominated Fischer's thoughts in those years. However, on the Ursuline Church the upper portion of the façade is not set back as at Saint John's.

In his projects for garden palaces, Fischer's imagination and fantasy are everywhere evident. Nevertheless he was not to achieve the fame as a designer of garden palaces that he hoped for and was overshadowed in this ambition by Hildebrandt. At Klesheim, outside of Salzburg, Fischer did have the opportunity to build a garden palace for the prince-bishop, but not to his desired specifications. Judging from Fischer's plate of Klesheim (*Historic Architecture,* book 4, plate 17), it was to have been an elegant and airy summer residence, whose transparent center was a large open belvedere, oriented toward a view of the Salzburg mountains. Preceded by a court and fountain the palace was approached via a raised semicircular ramp leading to three arched openings on the ground floor. Begun in 1700, the death of the archbishop in 1709 halted work on the palace which was complete except for the interiors.

Klesheim Palace is much altered today; lacking is the lively sculptural ornamentation of the balustrades along the horizontal rooflines. In 1731–1732 the three central bays on the ground story were duplicated over the entry ramp to create a base for a terrace on the *piano nobile.* The terrace revived, to the detriment of the palace facade, Fischer's idea for a *plein aire* belvedere from which to view the Hohensalzburg.

In his designs for garden pavilions Fischer often explored the idea of separate sections of a building pushing away from its center. The Garden House in the park of Klesheim Palace (1700–1709) has such a plan, but unlike the Althan Garden Palace whose theme is the same, it has no important central room.

The decade just before and after the turn of the century saw a tremendous surge of palace building within the city of Vienna, most of it accomplished by the tearing down or merging of older build-ings. These city palaces for the aristocracy were built around large inner courts and had a single magnificent street façade flanked by contiguous buildings. Their entry portals were given special attention, and sculptural programs often defined their surfaces and rooflines.

Fischer contributed several fine palaces to this genre, including the Strattmann Palace, the city palace of Prince Eugen of Savoy, the Batthyány Palace, the Bohemian Chancellery, and the Gallas Palace built in Prague. As court architect Fischer also hoped to contribute significantly to the extensive alterations planned for the Imperial Hofburg Palace. He had executed interiors for the Hofburg since c.1699 (the great hall and the Indian Cabinet), but these rooms and his designs for the expansion of the palace have been lost.

The Strattmann Palace was commissioned by the Court Chancellor Theodor Althet Heinrich Strattmann in 1692, and provided Fischer with his initial opportunity to build a city palace in Vienna. Seen in its original form in an engraving by Salomon Kleiner, its nine bay façade on the Schenkenstrasse had two bay risalts on either end. The ground story had a drafted surface, while the upper level of the risalts carried giant Corinthian pilasters. On the central five bays, paired pilasters were placed between rectangular French windows, while on the third story oblong windows and paired terms were used in a treatment closely derived from Italian Mannerist palaces. The portals boldly defined by a diadem arch framed by columns, with an upper balcony before an ornate French window; this was a treatment that Fischer favored on many of his city palaces. Despite the resolute treatment of the portal, the Strattmann Palace façade is lacking in focus, a problem that Fischer was to resolve in future city palaces.

The City Palace of Prince Eugen of Savoy (1696–1697) has a more unified, monumental, and baroque appearance than the Strattmann Palace, achieved by the use of giant Ionic pilasters across the entire façade. The original façade, which Fischer was careful to claim for his own in *Historic Architecture* (book 4, plate 5) was composed of twelve bays with two portals, of which only seven, those now found in the center, were constructed by him. The palace gained ten additional bays and one portal in two building campaigns supervised by Hildebrandt (1708 and 1723), who remained faithful to Fischer's elevation.

Despite the many stories of Prince Eugen's Palace façade (five rows of windows are visible), Fischer succeeded in giving it a simple two register reading. The giant order pilasters of the central section of Bernini's Chigi Palace, Rome, may have prompted Fischer's choice of this device, but Do-

MENICO MARTINELLI had already employed giant pilasters in Vienna on his influential Liechtenstein Palace.

Because Prince Eugen's Palace was located on a narrow street, Fischer used refined sculptural detailing, rather than more plastic elements, to articulate its façade. The content of the iconographic program, designed to compliment Prince Eugen's talents as a military leader through analogies with heroes of antiquity, would not have been lost on the populace of Vienna. Prince Eugen was fast becoming a popular figure in the 1690s, and often would surpass the emperor in the affection of the people in the future years.

The stairhall of Prince Eugen's Palace, a masterpiece of its type, is entered through a low dim vestibule covered with elegant stucco decoration. A Palladian motif closes off the far end of the vestibule from a shallow interior court, whose wall fountain it frames. The stairhill, placed in a narrow space, rises first through an open flight flanked by four muscular atlantes carved by Giovanni Giuliani. The entire stairroom may be seen from this point as it rises through the height of the palace. At the first landing the stair divides and moves along the wall until at an intermediate landing it again changes direction to reach the upper balcony held by the atlantes. The rooms of the piano nobile may be entered from the balcony. The open character of the stairhall, in combination with the sculpted atlantes, and decorative balustrades were to have a profound influence on Viennese stair design of the eighteenth century.

Fischer's next important city palace was built between 1698 and 1705 for Adam Batthyány, Governor of Croatia. Its façade was recorded in an eighteenth-century engraving by Kleiner. In this work, Fischer intensified the central section of the façade, defining the five middle bays as a risalt with grand tapering pilasters and lavish decoration.

The Bohemian Chancellery Palace, Vienna, was constructed under the auspices of two successive Upper Court Chancellors of Bohemia in the years 1708-1714. It has been so much altered that today it is best studied in drawings and engravings. Its nine bay façade on the Wipplingerstrasse again showed Fischer's concern with annunciating the center of the structure. The three bay central risalt was clad with giant pilasters which now carried a classical pediment. The lateral bays acted as wings and the portal with three entrys, as at the Battyány Palace, was ornamented with over life-size sculpted terms.

The palace, built for Johann Leopold Donat, Count Trautson, must be considered in the line of development of Fischer's city palaces as it is like them in type, despite a garden at one side. Begun in 1710 and completed in c.1716, it is directly related to the Bohemian Chancellery and was built at the same time.

Because of the ample space before the Trautson palace, Fischer was able to emphatically step forward the pedimented central bays of the façade, creating a powerful and plastic center to the building. The planarity of Bernini's palace façades was being abandoned by Fischer for the relief of those of Palladio. The present closed upper balustrade which looks like an attic story is too austere; it was carved and open in Fischer's plate of the façade in *Historic Architecture* (book 4, plate 7).

The plan of the Trautson Garden Palace, on a corner site, has a series of inner courts laid out on the main axis; the principal rectangular court is closed with a monumental exedra. The new restraint and calm of the façade is carried a step further in the entrance vestibule where severe Tuscan columns and pilasters provide the basic definitions. The imposing staircase overflows from its stairroom to begin in the vestibule with sphinxes on plinths succeeded by sculptured atlantes as the stair climbs to the first landing. There it divides into two flights which rise to the grand salon in the middle risalt of the *piano nobile* above the vestibule. Unfortunately the palace's original interiors have been lost.

The last major city palace by Fischer was built not in Vienna, but in Prague: the Gallas Palace (1713-1719). Although by the time of its completion Fischer was ailing, at the time of its design he was still at the height of his powers and continuing to develop new ideas about city palaces.

The Gallas Palace project involved the integration of several older houses into one large palace with a long façade along a narrow street in the Prague Old Town. Fischer's major innovation was a façade with several focal points rather than just one in the middle. The Gallas façade is subdivided into an ornamental three bay center, a lateral wing, and end pavilion. Both the center and the pavilion rise above the wings announcing the differentiation of the parts along the roofline. The two major portals are on the pavilions and Fischer's collaborator on them was a genius of Bohemian baroque sculpture, Matthias Braun von Braun. Braun's dynamic atlantes, in pairs beside the arched entries, add an arresting tension to the portals.

The Gallas Palace concludes Fischer's career as a designer of city palaces. Brilliant and innovative until the end, he remained cognizant of the urban problems, the symbolic content, and the functional necessities of aristocratic palaces.

In his written history of architecture, Fischer was encyclopedic, paralleling eighteenth-century thinkers in other disciplines. He wished to be both inclusive and archaeologically correct, and admitted in his preface to *Historic Architecture* that he had tried to view the ruins illustrated, and when that had been impossible had relied upon the most authentic testimonies taken from contemporary historians or old medals. Yet Fischer was not a pedant and hoped to be entertaining as well as informative. His general aim, again from his preface, was that his essay would not only ". . . please the eye of the Curious, and those of the nicest Taste, but will embellish their minds; and tend toward the Cultivation of the Arts in general" (English translation by Thomas Lediard [1730]). He began preliminary work on *Historic Architecture* shortly after his visit to England and was, no doubt, under the influence of the many thinkers and architects he had known or admired in his travels and studies: Cortona, Athanasius Kircher, and Giovanni Pietro Bellori, to name but a few. Fischer von Erlach presented the manuscript of his volume to the Emperor Charles VI in 1712, shortly after Charles's assumption to the Imperial throne. Two years before the architect's death, the first printed edition with ninety plates was published in Vienna (1721).

The erudition, imagination, and wit that went into the creation of this volume make it unique among eighteenth-century architecture books. Fischer von Erlach's aim in *Historic Architecture* was to discover the eternal values of architecture, as well as its diversity. He declared in the preface: "Artists will see, that Nations differt (sic) no less in their Taste for Architecture, than in Food and Raiment," but that, "notwithstanding all these Varieties, there are certain general principles in Architecture," such as, "Rules of Symmetry; that the Weaker must be supported by the Stronger, and the like" (English translation by Thomas Lediard [1730]).

Fischer's plates, most of them executed by J. A. Delsenbach, range from the relatively accurate (Diocletian's Palace at Split and the Hagia Sophia in Constantinople) to the totally fantastic (Solomon's Temple and the Temple at Nineveh). They are inclusive enough to present Stonehenge and the fabled Seven Wonders of the Ancient World. Beginning with the Temple of Solomon, as a divinely inspired work, Fischer traced the history of civilizations as evidenced in one art, architecture. However, the wondrous and curious both in nature (the cataracts of the Nile) and in art (the Colossus of Rhodes) are also recorded. Fischer's book on Roman architecture makes it clear that the vastness and monumentality of their complexes, such as the Domus Aurea of Nero or the Baths of Diocletian, fired his imagination.

Near the end of his life, Fischer's long career of Imperial service was rewarded with two great commissions: Saint Charles Borromeo Church (Karlskirche) and the Imperial Library (Hofbibliothek), both of which came to him around the year 1715.

The Saint Charles Borromeo Church, Vienna, is both a votive church, pledged by Charles VI during the plague of 1713, and a dynastic monument bearing the name of the Emperor's patron saint. Its complicated iconographic program was orchestrated by the scholars Carl Gustav Heraeus and Conrad Adolph von Albrecht. In 1715, competitive models were commissioned for the church from Hildebrandt, Ferdinando Galli-Bibbiena, and Fischer von Erlach; the latter's was accepted in the same year. The construction of the church was done between 1715 and 1724. The decorations were completed by the time of its dedication in 1738, when it was turned over to the care of an international order, the Knights of Malta, Order of the Cross with Red Star, in the Emperor's presence.

The centralized plan of the church is an oval which is placed longitudinally to a lengthy horizontal two-towered façade. Rectangular chapels project from the cross-axis and smaller chapels with upper galleries are contained in the oval on the diagonal axes. There is an oval dome on a drum over the body of the church and a smaller dome over the choir; the cross chapels are barrel vaulted. A choir with a semicircular closure is set between sacristies with upper oratories and stairrooms. The original plan (*Historic Architecture*, book 4, plate 15) included a monk's choir behind a screen of columns, like that found in Palladio's Il Redentore, Venice, but it was never executed. There are other variances between Fischer's plates and the executed building, particularly in the dome which was built higher and given a fresco rather than coffers. It has been difficult to determine whether Fischer von Erlach sanctioned these changes, or whether they are the work of his son who completed the execution of the building.

In the eighteenth century the Saint Charles Borromeo church faced the city and the Hofburg Palace from an open site in a country suburb. For this reason, all of its exteriors were carefully delineated, as had been true with the University Church, and the same powerful sense of external massing is again evidenced.

Fischer's engraved plate does not capture the breadth and volumetric clarity of Saint Charles's façade. The low bell towers of the façade are connected to the central Roman style portico by concave wall segments before which colossal Trajanic columns stand. These columns are not only referential to Roman imperial grandeur and by infer-

Fischer von Erlach.
Karlskirche.
Vienna.
1715–1738

ence to the Holy Roman Empire of Charles VI, but also to the "pillars of Hercules," Charles's chosen mythical hero and emblem, to baroque plague columns, and to the colossal columns believed to have stood before the ancient Temple of Jerusalem (Solomon's Temple). Fischer's columns bear bas-reliefs of the life and miracles of Saint Charles Borromeo. The iconographic program continues across the exterior and into the interior, where in Rottmayr's fresco on the dome, Saint Charles is seen before the Trinity, and over the high altar a figure of the saint appears ascending into heaven. The antiquarian Heraeus maintained in a letter to Gottfried Wilhelm Leibniz that the Saint Charles Church commemorated not only Saint Charles Borromeo, but also Charles VI, Charlemagne, and Charles the Bold of Flanders. Most obviously, the Emperor Charles VI is honored by inference and by the explicit presence of many emblems: his coat-of-arms (organ gallery), the Hapsburg double-headed eagle and crown (at the tops of the façade columns), and others.

The interior of the Saint Charles Borromeo Church is only slightly more plastic in definition than are Fischer's other large churches despite the use of paired columns as framing or screening devices in the arms. Giant pilasters on high bases still dominate the oval central space, as earlier, providing the decided vertical thrust to the dome that is familiar in Fischer's church architecture. The double arches of the diagonal chapels, reminiscent of Wren's crossing in Saint Paul's Cathedral, together with the high arches of the crossing arms provide a reading suggesting Fischer's signature motif, the triumphal arch. The dim lighting and darkly veined marbles of the Saint Charles interior recall the coloration of Roman baroque churches.

The Saint Charles Borromeo Church, particularly the façade, fulfilled Fischer's most basic theoretic stance, that each new work be unique, but exist in the context of the civilizing history of architecture. It is clear from the many and divergent sources that Fischer drew upon in the creation of this church façade, among them: St. Peter's façade in Rome and also Bernini's project for it; FRANÇOIS MANSART's façade for the Eglise de Minimes, Paris; the portico of the Pantheon, Rome; and even the minarets of the Hagia Sophia, Constantinople, that he intended in its grandeur to suggest to *summa* of the history of sacred architecture.

Finally commissioned to build a major new wing for the Hofburg Palace, Fischer's plans for the Imperial Library (Hofbibliothek) were prepared between 1716–1720, but the building was not begun, due to a shortage of funds, until 1722. Unable for reasons of health to supervise the building's construction, this was left to his son, Joseph Emanuel Fischer von Erlach who adhered, in the essentials, to his father's plans.

Originally a free-standing block, the Imperial Library is today flanked by two wings built by Pacassi, which stretch out at right angles from it to form a U-shape court. The foundations from an earlier building were in place and may have necessitated the oblong plan Fischer adopted. In its middle he placed a large longitudinal oval (77 meters by 14 meters) to create a centralized hall which boldly projects from its lateral wings. An oval domical covering, to hold a complicated program in fresco, was placed over the oval hall while the wings were barrel vaulted. Paired colossal columns bisect the internal wings serving as monumental screens to separate the interior spaces and to frame a vista, as columns in Imperial Roman buildings had done. Symbolically the paired columns are, as in Saint Charles Borromeo Church, a reference to the "pillars of Hercules", and thus to the Emperor Charles VI.

The exterior, which because of restorations is harder and drier than Fischer intended, has a high fortresslike holding story defined by horizontal drafting. The upper façades of the wings and central projection are defined as variations of triumphal arches, even to their culmination in sculptural groups which are placed before separate Mansard roofs on an attic story. These triumphal motifs, with their giant pilasters and arched windows, are close in conception to the elevation of the nave of the University Church, Salzburg, and other of Fischer's works. Ultimately they are inspired by the architect's profound admiration for Roman triumphal arches, an admiration shared by many other architects of the Renaisaance and baroque period, like LEON BATTISTA ALBERTI, they constitute a *leit-motif* of Fischer's *oeuvre*. The triumphal arch was, of course, symbolically suitable for the library of a Holy Roman Emperor.

The program for the exterior and interior decorations of the Imperial Library was conceived by Conrad Adolph von Albrecht with contributions from others, including the Emperor's antiquarian, Heraeus. In essence, it seeks to present the library as a temple of wisdom and the Imperial house, in particular the Emperor Charles VI, as a protector and purveyor of wisdom.

The interior of the central hall is an ancestral gallery, a concept that Fischer had previously given form in the Ancestral Hall of the Althan Family. In the Imperial Library, Emperor Charles VI's statue is placed in the center of the oval hall, and figures of members of the Hapsburg family are placed in a circle around him. The ceiling fresco by Daniel Gran, which continues the conceit of an architectural setting illusionistically into the vault, contains allegorical figures of all types and has as its focal point representations of Hercules and Apollo holding a medallion portrait of Charles VI. In the Imperial Library, a familiar baroque rhetoric is fulfilled in paint, sculpture, and in architecture.

Much of the library's fine interior detailing must be the invention of Joseph Emanuel Fischer von Erlach, but the basic interior design, with books fit into the walls from floor to ceiling on two levels, and with a shallow gallery supported by consoles, is the elder Fischer von Erlach's idea. Spiral stairs in circular enclosures give access to the galleries, and act with the columns to define the sequential spaces of the interior. The library's rich combination of warm interior tonalities comes from the ceiling frescoes, the wood of the shelves and gallery with its gilt highlighting, and the marbles of the columns and floor.

While the Saint Charles Borromeo façade may be considered Fischer's most inventive ecclesiastical exterior of the later years, the Elector's Chapel (1716–1724) in the Cathedral of Breslau (Wroclaw, Poland) is his most inventive interior. Built as a mausoleum for the prince-bishop of Breslau and Worms, Franz Ludwig von Neuberg, the chapel was dedicated to the Holy Eucharist.

The chapel's exterior is simply delineated with lisens, while the single entry portal, on the interior of the cathedral, has an elegant aedicular surround. The plan is a longitudinal oval with shallow recesses symmetrically placed at its top and bottom for doors (only one is real, the other three are false). The altar room is approximately half as long as the chapel itself and steps back, scenographically, to the altar through three pairs of free-standing columns. The tabernacle and sculpture of the altar are brilliantly lit from side windows invisible from the chapel. This exceptional altar room owes much to Bernini's altar compositions.

The interior space of the Elector's Chapel is given an unexpected sense of movement through Fischer's treatment of the wall surfaces. He injects a pendentive zone between the oval dome and the oval ground plan. The entablature running around the room cuts sharply inward and outward, following the breaches in the oval walls created by the door recesses. Although the integrity of the oval space is maintained, and there are no overlapping spaces, a Borrominesque complexity and ambiguity are added to the interior through the reading of the walls.

In the Elector's Chapel, Fischer brilliantly combined elements from the architectural vocabulary of the two great masters of Roman baroque architecture. In this work Fischer is seen less as the harbinger of the neoclassicism of the end of the eighteenth century, as he is so often portrayed, than as an architect adhering steadfastly to the principles of the baroque and its sense of history, which was to use rather than to copy or revive it.

BEVERLY HEISNER

WORKS

1687–1689, Holy Trinity Plague column (with others); *1687–1690, Liechtenstein Palace (garden belvedere), Rossau; Vienna. 1688, Schloss Eisgrub Stables; 1688–1695, Schloss Frain (Ancestral Hall); Moravia, Czechoslovakia. (A)1689–1690, Schloss Mirabell (garden, vases, sculpture), Salzburg, Austria. 1690, Two Triumphal Arches for Joseph I, *1690–1693, Althan Garden Palace, Rossau; Vienna. 1690–1693, Summer Riding School; Archbishop's Stables, Salzburg, Austria. 1690–1696, Fountain, Krautmarkt, Brno, Czechoslovakia (A)1692–1693, Strattmann Palace; 1692–1697, Neuwaldegg Hunting Lodge; 1692–1704, Church of Mariazell (high altar; executed by E. C. Engelbrecht and J. A. Pfeffel to Fischer von Erlach's design); Salzburg, Austria. c.1693, Hunting Lodge, Engelhartstetten, Austria. 1693–1694, Archbishop's Stables and Horse Bath; 1694–1697, Cathedral (spiral staircase in north tower); 1694–1702, Dreifaltigkeitskirche (priest's house and college); Salzburg, Austria. c.1694–1709, Hospital and Church of Saint John (Johannes-Spiral), Mülleck, Austria. 1696–1700, City Palace of Prince Eugene of Savoy, Vienna. 1696–1701, Pilgramage Church of Maria Kirchenthal, Lofer; 1696–1707, Kollegienkirche; Salzburg, Austria. 1696–1711 and later, Schönbrunn Palace, Vienna. (A)1698–1700, Schloss Frain (chapel), Moravia, Czechoslovakia. 1698–1705, Batthyány Palace; 1699, Triumphal Arches (two; for Joseph I), Vienna. 1700–1709, Klesheim Palace (including garden house), Salzburg, Austria. *1702–1706, Saint Joseph's Hoher Markt; After 1708–1714, Bohemian Chancellery; 1709–1711, Dietrichstein Palace (remodeling of façade); Vienna. *c.1710–1715, Villa Huldenberg, Weidlingau, near Vienna. 1710–1716, Trautson Garden Palace; *c.1712, Schwarzenberg City Palace; Vienna. 1713–1719, Gallas Palace; 1714–1716, Saint James Church (sepulchral monument for Johann Wenzel Count Wratislaw von Mitrowitz); Prague. 1715–1738, Karlskirche, Vienna. 1716–1718, Herzogenburg Convent (central part of east wing, great hall and staircase), Lower Austria. *c.1716–1719, Hofburg Palace (project for revisions); 1716–1724, Elector's Chapel, Breslau Cathedral, Poland. 1718–1721, Herzogen Convent Church (tower), Lower Austria. 1719–1723, Imperial Stables (partially executed); c.1720, Schwarzenberg Garden Palace (alteration and interior decorations); 1722–1730, Imperial Library, Hofburg Palace; Vienna.

BIBLIOGRAPHY

AURENHAMMER, HANS 1973 *J. B. Fischer von Erlach.* London: Allen Lane.
BUCHOWIECKI, WALTER 1957 *Der Barockbau der ehemaligen Hofbibliothek in Wien, ein Werk J. B. Fischer von Erlach.* Vienna: Prachner.
FERGUSSON, FRANCES D. 1970 "St. Charles' Church, Vienna: The Iconography of its Architecture." *Journal of the Society of Architectural Historians 29,* no. 4:318–326.
FISCHER VON ERLACH, JOHANN BERNHARD (1721)1964 *Entwurfeiner historischen Architectur.* Reprint of the 2d edition of 1725 followed by the 1730 English translation of Thomas Lediard. Farnsborough, England: Gregg.
GRIMSCHITZ, BRUNO 1944 *Wiener Barockpaläste.* Vienna.
HAGEN-DEMPF, FELICITAS 1949 *Die Kollegienkirche in Salzburg.* Vienna.
HASELBERGER-BLAHA, HERTA 1955 "Die Triumphtore Bernhard Fischers von Erlachs." *Wiener Jahrbuch für Kunstgeschichte* 17:63–85.
ILG, ALBERT 1895 *Die Fischer von Erlach.* Vienna: Konegen.
KUNOTH, GEORG 1956 *Die historische Architektur Fischers von Erlach.* Dusseldorf: Schwann.
LANCHESTER, H. V. 1924 *Fischer von Erlach.* London: Benn.
MORPER, JOHANN JOSEPH 1957 "Schriftum zum Fischer von Erlach." *Das Münster* 10, nos. 1–2:49–51.
PASSMORE, EDWARD 1951 "Fischer von Erlach, Architect to a Monarchy." *Journal of the Royal Institute of British Architects* 58:452–475.
SEDLMAYR, HANS 1925 *Fischer von Erlach der Ältere.* Munich: Piper.
SEDLMAYR, HANS (1956)1976 *Johann Bernhard Fischer von Erlach.* Vienna: Herold.

FISKER, KAY

Kay Fisker (1893–1965) was a Danish architect and designer who is best remembered for his work in private and public housing. Born in Frederiksberg, Denmark, Fisker received a degree from the school of architecture at the Academy of Fine Arts in Copenhagen in 1920. Shortly thereafter, he went into private practice until 1930 when he formed a partnership with CHRISTIAN FREDERIK MØLLER. In 1936, Fisker became professor of architecture at the Academy of Fine Arts in Copenhagen, and in 1941 he became dean of the architectural school there. He was also a visiting professor and lecturer at numerous American schools, including the Harvard Graduate School of Design (1952) and the Massachusetts Institute of Technology (1952 and 1957); Tulane University (1952); and the Georgia Institute of Technology (1952). Fisker wrote several books on Danish architecture and wrote extensively for magazines. As an editor and writer, he was also a major contributor to the Danish journal *Arkitekten* between 1917 and 1960.

Characterized by formal clarity and logical planning, Fisker's architecture draws its combined inspiration from traditional regional styles and early twentieth-century German functionalism. His planning and housing designs continually reflect his struggle to marry functional propriety and aesthetic unity without sacrificing one for the other. Thus, Fisker's planning solutions in large-scale housing attempt to vary and singularize the living units with features such as windows, staircases, and balconies. On the other hand, his interest in the graphic aspects of design led him to experiment with form and materials as purely aesthetic devices. The façade of Aarhus University (1932–1945), for example, Fisker's most ambitious work, is reduced to basic and simple cubic forms expressed in the varied window placement. With traditional materials and an even, overall rhythm, the buildings are further unified in color, shape, and profile.

The essentially graphic qualities of Fisker's architecture can also be seen in his designs for furniture, silverware, and other household articles as well as in his work for various ship interiors.

PETER L. DONHAUSER

WORKS

1918–1921, Cooperative Building Society Housing, Borups Allé and Stefansgade; 1920–1922, Hornbaekhus Cooperative Society Housing, Borups Allé, Aagade and Hornbaekgade; 1924–1926, Amagerbo Housing, Englandsvej and Østerdalsgade (with S. C. Larsen); Copenhagen. *1925, Danish Pavilion, World's Fair, Paris. 1925–1927, Glaenøgaard Housing, Vognmandsmarken, 1927, Gullofshus Housing, Artillerivej and Gullofsgade; 1930, Housing, Herman Triers Plads; 1930–1932, Housing, Aaboulevarden and Rosenørns Allé; 1931, Tagensgaard Housing, Tagensvej; Copenhagen. 1932, District Hospital and Radium Center, Aarhus, Denmark. 1932–1945, Aarhus University (with Pøul Stegmann until 1937; with C. F. Møller until 1945); 1934, Natural History Museum; 1935, Jutland Trade and Agricultural Bank, Riiskov; Aarhus, Denmark. 1938, Vestersøhus II Housing, Vester Søgade; 1939–1944, Stefansgaarden Housing (with Eske Kristensen), Stefansgade, Copenhagen. 1941, State Youth Camp, Avdebo, Denmark. 1941, Shipbuilding Works (extensions and conversions), Helsingor, Denmark. 1943, Egeparken Terraced Housing, Bredevej and Lindevangen, Lyngby, Denmark. 1944, Svanholm Estate Farmworkers' Housing, Hornsherred, Denmark. 1945, Voldparken Housing and School, Husum, Denmark. 1949, Lundehøjgaard Soldiers' Home II, Høvelte Camp, Denmark. 1951, Nygaardsparken Housing and Shopping Center, Brøndbyøster, Denmark. 1955, National Council for Unmarried Mothers Administration Building and Home, Copenhagen. 1956–1957, Interbau Housing, Berlin. 1960, Multistory development (with Robert Duelund Mortensen), Göteborg, Sweden.

BIBLIOGRAPHY

FABER, TOBIAS 1966 *Arkitekten Kay Fisker: 1893–1965.* Copenhagen: Arkitektens Forlag.

FISKER, KAY 1950 "Den Funktionelle Tradition." *Arkitekten* 52:69–100.

FISKER, KAY 1948 "The History of Domestic Architecture in Denmark." *Architectural Review* 104, Nov.:219–226.

FISKER, KAY 1950 "The Moral of Functionalism." *Magazine of Art* 43, Feb.:62–67.

FISKER, KAY, and ELLING, CHRISTIAN (editors) 1961 *Danish Architectural Drawings.* Copenhagen: Gyldendalske.

FISKER, KAY, and YERBURY, F. R. 1927 *Modern Danish Architecture.* New York: Scribner.

"Kay Fisker—70 Years." 1963 *Arkitekten* 65, Feb.: special issue.

"Den Klintske Skole." 1963 *Arkitektur* 7, Apr.: special issue.

LANKILDE, HANS ERLING 1960 *Arkitekten Kay Fisker.* Copenhagen: Arkitektens Forlag.

FITCH, JAMES MARSTON

Born in Washington, James Marston Fitch (1909–) received a bachelor's degree in architecture from Tulane University in 1928. He was employed as a researcher for the Tennessee State Planning Board (1934) and as an analyst of low-cost housing for the Federal Housing Administration (1935–1936). After serving in the Army during World War II as a meteorologist, Fitch edited several architectural magazines and taught in the school of architecture at Columbia University beginning in 1954. There, he initiated a graduate program in historic preservation (1964) and began a long career as a lecturer, author, and extensive traveler. He has done research for many organizations, including the Municipal Arts Society, the Society of Architectural Historians, and the Victorian Society of America. Among his well-known books are a biography of WALTER GROPIUS, a two-volume work on American building, and a work titled *Architecture and the Esthetics of Plenty.*

LEAH NESS

BIBLIOGRAPHY

FITCH, JAMES MARSTON 1960 *Walter Gropius.* New York: Braziller.

FITCH, JAMES MARSTON 1961 *Architecture and the Esthetics of Plenty.* New York: Columbia University Press.

FITCH, JAMES MARSTON (1963)1970 Pages 17–23, 84–92, 154–163 in *Four Great Makers of Modern Architecture: Gropius, Le Corbusier, Mies van der Rohe, Wright.* Reprint. New York: Da Capo.

FITCH, JAMES MARSTON (1947–1948)1966–1972 *American Building.* 2 vols. 2d ed., rev. Boston: Houghton Mifflin.

FLAGG, ERNEST

Ernest Flagg (1857–1947) belongs to the generation of architects who, trained at the Ecole des

Ernest Flagg.
Singer Tower.
New York.
1906–1908

Beaux-Arts in Paris, returned to New York in the 1880s and 1890s to promote the principles and aesthetics of the so-called "French school." Flagg abandoned his formal education at the age of fifteen to become an office boy on Wall Street and a merchant ingenue in a number of land and building speculations with his father and brother in the 1870s and 1880s. This experience not only made Flagg ambitious and shrewd but also stimulated his interest in architecture and planning.

After a year of preparing for the entrance exams, Flagg entered the second class at the Ecole des Beaux-Arts in Paris in August 1889. He studied in the atelier of Paul Blondel where he met Walter B. Chambers, with whom he traveled and later formed a loose partnership.

From Blondel and from the writings of the mid-century theorist Charles Blanc, Flagg learned the principles and aesthetics of architectural design, including the concept of *parti* or "the logical solution of the problem from his [the architect's] dual standpoint as constructor and artist." To Flagg, *parti* reconciled in architecture the polarities of art and science, aesthetics and technology, intuition and reason, that characterized the decade of the 1890s.

Flagg's return to New York in 1891 coincided with a critical shift of taste in architecture from the English to the French. Joined by other Beaux-Arts-trained architects, including Charles F. McKim (see McKim, Mead, and White), William A. Boring, and Chambers, Flagg helped to found the Society of Beaux-Arts Architects to promote the educational values of "the French school." Flagg further allied himself to the group of recently returned *anciens élèves* of the Ecole like Carrère and Hastings, Boring and Tilton, and Trowbridge and Livingston. He called upon architects to formulate a national style that would be "architectural" and not "archaeological."

Flagg's work and interests were varied and often appeared paradoxical. His architecture embraced such disparate concerns as lavish institutions on the one hand and skyscrapers and tenements that reflected issues in urban reform, on the other. Moreover, Flagg's Beaux-Arts training and his understanding of *parti* caused him to produce custom design largely according to building type and program, stamped with a Frenchness that acknowledged diverse tendencies and available styles in France.

Flagg's *partis* for institutions reflect academic classicism and idealism. These include his early commissions for the Corcoran Art Gallery, Washington (1892–1897), Saint Luke's Hospital, New York (1892–1896), and the U.S. Naval Academy, Annapolis, Maryland (1896–1908). In domestic architecture, Flagg continued to consult specific requirements of program and architectural character while reflecting the prevailing taste for Colonial Revival. He chose Georgian–Federal Revival for his town house at 109 East 40th Street (1906–1907) and Dutch Colonial for his country house, "Stone Court," on Staten Island (1897–1899). Without any contradiction, Flagg also synthesized French and American neoclassicism in his Alfred Corning Clark House, Riverside Drive, New York (1899–1900).

Flagg remains best known for his commercial and utilitarian buildings and especially for the Singer Loft Building (1902–1904) at 561 Broadway, New York, and the Singer Building (1896–1899) and Tower (1906–1908), both in New York. Here he promoted the ethic of structural rationalism already assimilated in France through the efforts of Eugène Emmanuel Viollet-le-Duc and his followers. The Singer Loft Building illustrates Flagg's attempt to introduce to America a rational architecture by uniting the best of America—the skeletal frame—with the best of France—logical decoration. From a structural point of view, the Singer Loft Building is his most inventive achievement, even though it raises a conflict between rationalism and functionalism, between rendering the structure explicit, and at the same time, the attempt to fireproof it.

In an effort to reform urban zoning and height restriction associated with skyscraper design in the densely developed business district in lower Manhattan, Flagg designed the Singer Tower as an addition to the Singer Building. The Singer Tower, demolished in 1968, showed Flagg's conviction that a tower could be restricted to one-quarter of its site but rise indefinitely. In 1908, the 47-story Singer Tower briefly held the record as the tallest building in the world; its imagery made the Singer name associated with progress. Yet the Singer Tower was less a reflection of the French ideals of decorated structure than Flagg's earlier Singer Loft Building.

Long considered the prime mover in New York model tenement housing, Flagg was deeply committed to efforts at improving conditions for the urban poor. His light-court plan, published in 1894, served as the model for tenement house design for more than forty years. Flagg's first tenements for the City and Suburban Homes Company, the Clark Tenements, on West 68th and 69th Streets, New York (1896–1898) inaugurated the use of this plan.

During the last twenty-five years of his long career, Flagg studied Greek principles of proportion and their adaptation to small house design and construction. Four elements comprised

Flagg's aspirations for the small house: the use of module, fixed at 3 feet 9 inches, to facilitate design; a system of proportional relationships derived from Greek principles; economical methods of construction; and the possibility of self-building. He summarized his findings and presented his designs in a remarkable book entitled *Small Houses: Their Economic Design and Construction* (1922).

During most of his architectural career, Flagg was admired for his talent while mistrusted for his personal conduct. Late to achieve professional recognition, it was not until 1911 that Flagg was elected to the American Institute of Architects. His writings and buildings illustrate his concerns both for an American architecture based on Beaux-Arts principles and for better housing for city dwellers.

MARDGES BACON

WORKS

1892–1896, Saint Luke's Hospital, New York. 1892–1897, Corcoran Gallery of Art, Washington. 1894–1898, Saint Margaret Memorial Hospital, Pittsburgh. 1896–1897, Mills House Number 1 (now "The Atrium"); *1896–1898, Clark Tenements; *1896–1899, Singer Building; New York. 1896–1908, U.S. Naval Academy, Annapolis, Md. 1897–1899, Farmington Avenue Church (now Immanuel Congregational Church; with George M. Bartlett), Hartford, Conn. 1897–1899, Ernest Flagg House ("Stone Court"), Staten Island, N.Y. 1898–1899, Fire Engine Company 33; 1899, New York Fireproof Model Tenements; *1899–1900, Alfred Corning Clark House; 1899–1900, O. G. Jennings House (now Lycée Français; with Walter B. Chambers); 1902–1904, Singer Loft Building; New York. 1903–1905, Frederick G. Bourne House ("The Towers"), Dark Island, Chippewa Bay, N.Y. 1904–1906, Naval Hospital, Washington. *1905–1907, Automobile Club of America; *1906–1907, Ernest Flagg House; 1906–1908, Ernest Flagg Office; *1906–1908, Singer Tower; New York. 1906–1911, Pomfret School, Conn. 1910–1911, Princeton University Press (now Scribner Building), N.J. 1912–1913, Charles Scribner's Sons Building; New York. 1913–1914, Gwynne Building, Cincinnati, Ohio. 1917, "Bow-Cot," Staten Island, N.Y. 1918, Sun Village (Emergency Fleet Corporation Housing Project), Chester, Penn. 1933–1937, Flagg Court, Brooklyn, N.Y.

BIBLIOGRAPHY

BACON, MARDGES 1978 "Ernest Flagg: Beaux-Arts Architect and Reformer." Unpublished Ph.D. dissertation, Brown University, Providence.
BURNHAM, ALAN 1974 "Flagg, Ernest." Supplement 4, pages 280–282 in *Dictionary of American Biography.* New York: Scribner.
DESMOND, HARRY W. 1902 "The Works of Ernest Flagg." *Architectural Record* 11:1–104.
DESMOND, HARRY W. 1904 "A Rational Skyscraper." *Architectural Record* 15:274–284.

FLAGG, ERNEST 1894a "Influence of the French School on Architecture in the United States." *Architectural Record* 4:211–228.
FLAGG, ERNEST 1894b "The New York Tenement-House Evil and its Cure." *Scribner's Magazine* 16:108–117.
FLAGG, ERNEST 1908 "The Limitation of Height and Area of Buildings in New York." *American Architect and Building News* 93, no.2:125–127.
FLAGG, ERNEST 1922 *Small Houses: Their Economic Design and Construction. Essays on the Fundamental Principles of Design and Descriptive Articles on Construction.* New York: Scribner.
SEMSCH, OTTO FRANCIS (editor) 1908 *A History of the Singer Building Construction: Its Progress from Foundation to Flag Pole.* New York: Trow.

FLETCHER, BANISTER FLIGHT

Banister Flight Fletcher (1866–1953), architect and architectural historian, was born in London, the son of Banister Fletcher, professor of architecture at King's College, London. Fletcher studied at University College, London, and entered his father's office in 1884, studying also at the Royal Academy schools, the Architectural Association, and the Ecole des Beaux-Arts in Paris. He became his father's partner in 1889 and succeeded to the practice, jointly with his brother Herbert Phillips Fletcher, in 1899. Fletcher was better known as a historian, particularly for the monumental *A History of Architecture on the Comparative Method* (1896). This work has been translated into many languages and has appeared in many editions: the eighteenth edition appeared in 1975. He became the principal benefactor of the library of the Royal Institute of British Architects, to which he bequeathed his own library. He was called to the bar of the Middle Temple in 1908 and conducted arbitrations and advised on London Building Act disputes. From 1918 to 1919, he was senior sheriff of the City of London. He was knighted in 1919.

MARGARET RICHARDSON

WORKS

1897, Gosletts' Premises, 127–131 Charing Cross Road; 1899, King's College School, Wimbledon; 1905, Saint Ann's Vestry Hall, Carter Lane; 1912, 30a and 30b Wimpole Street; 1926, The Roan School (with Percy B. Dannatt), Maze Hill, Greenwich; 1927, Strawberry Hill Housing Estate; Twickenham; 1933, Hospital and Staff Quarters, Moden College, Blackheath; 1937, Gillette Factory, Great West Road, Osterley; London.

BIBLIOGRAPHY

FLETCHER, BANISTER F. (1896)1975 *A History of Architecture.* 18th ed. New York: Scribner.
HANNEFORD-SMITH, W. 1934 *The Architectural Work*

of Sir Banister Fletcher. London: Batsford.
"Obituary." 1953 Journal of the Royal Institute of British Architects 60:464–465.

FLITCROFT, HENRY

Henry Flitcroft (1697–1769) was an English architect of the Palladian (see ANDREA PALLADIO) school and a protégé of LORD BURLINGTON. The son of a laborer employed in the royal service at Hampton Court, he trained as a joiner before attracting the earl's attention with his talent for drawing. Burlington employed him as a draftsman and clerk of works, and in 1726 obtained a post for him in the Office of Works. Throughout his official career, which spanned more than forty years, Flitcroft designed no major public works but proved himself an able administrator with a sound practical knowledge of building. His private commissions included country houses, town houses, churches, and garden buildings; many of his clients held positions in government or at court, and he may have met them in the course of his official duties.

The influence of his early training under Burlington and the firsthand acquaintance with the designs of INIGO JONES and Andrea Palladio which it gave him is evident in all Flitcroft's work. His external elevations display that chaste, economical quality characteristic of Burlington's Palladianism, but he was also capable of creating, for example at Wentworth Woodhouse (1736–1764) and Woburn Abbey (1747–1761), magnificent interiors in the grandiose manner of WILLIAM KENT. Although he could on occasion throw off strict Palladian discipline to dramatic effect, as at Hoober Stand, Wentworth Woodhouse (1746–1748) and Alfred's Tower, Stourhead (1765–1769), Flitcroft was not generally an innovator but rather an able and experienced practitioner in an existing genre. His only known pupil was KENTON COUSE.

JULIET E. ALLAN

WORKS

1729, Bower House, Havering, London. c.1730–c.1760, Amesbury Abbey (garden buildings and additions to house), Wiltshire, England. *1731–1733, Montagu House, Whitehall; 1731–1734, Church of Saint Giles-in-the-Fields; 1732–1735, 36 Sackville Street; 1735–1736, 10 Saint James's Square; London. 1736–1742, Ditchley House (interiors), Oxfordshire, England. 1736–1764, Wentworth Woodhouse (east front and garden buildings), Yorkshire, England. *1738–1739, Church of Saint Olave's, Tooley Street, London. *1738–1739, Midgham House (additions), Berkshire, England. 1738–1740, House, Dover Street, London.

1740–1744, Saint Giles House (alterations and interiors), Wimborne Saint Giles, Dorset, England. c.1742–c.1744, Cumberland Lodge (alterations and offices), Windsor Great Park, Berkshire, England. 1742–1755, Wimpole Hall (external remodeling and interiors), Cambridgeshire, England. *1743–1764, 4 Grosvenor Square (alterations); 1744, 5–6 Bloomsbury Square; London. c.1744–1750, Lilford Hall (offices and interiors), Northamptonshire, England. 1744–1766, Stourhead (garden buildings, alterations to house, and interiors), Wiltshire, England. c.1745, Frognal Grove, Hampstead, London. 1746–1748, Hoober Stand, Wentworth Woodhouse, Yorkshire, England. *c.1747–c.1750, Windsor Great Park (garden buildings), Berkshire, England. 1747–1761, Woburn Abbey, Bedfordshire, England. *1748–1749, 25 Saint James's Place, London. 1748–1749, Wimpole Church, Cambridgeshire, England. 1749–1751, Milton House (south front, interiors, and offices), Northamptonshire, England. c.1750, Fort Belvedere, Windsor Great Park, Berkshire, England. *1753–1754, Villa, Clapham, London. *1755–1756, Stivichall Hall, Warwickshire, England. *1761, Villa, Putney, London. 1765–1769, Alfred's Tower (not completed until 1772), Stourhead, Wiltshire, England.

BIBLIOGRAPHY

PAPWORTH, WYATT (editor) 1852–1892 The Dictionary of Architecture. 8 vols. London: Architectural Publication Society.

FLORENCE, H. L.

Henry Louis Florence (1841–1916) was a characteristic London commercial architect of the late Victorian period. He studied at the Ecole des Beaux-Arts in Paris briefly as well as in London. Florence worked in partnership with Lewis Henry Issacs and is said to have done much of the design work. The firm specialized in hotels, generously planned and eclectic in style.

ANDREW SAINT

WORKS

*1876, Holborn Viaduct Hotel and Station; 1878–1879, Holborn Vestry Hall; 1882–1885, Northumberland House (Victoria Hotel); 1894–1896, Connaught Hotel; 1896–1900, Woodlands Stores, Knightsbridge; London. 1898, Empire Hotel, Suffolk, England. 1902, Institute of Journalists, London.

BIBLIOGRAPHY

"Obituary" 1916 The Builder 110, Feb. 25:160.

FLORIS, CORNELIS II

Cornelis Floris II or Floris de Vriendt (1514–1575), born in Antwerp, Belgium, into a family of artists, is known as sculptor of tombs and epitaphs, architect, and draftsman. From his journey to Italy he brought back to Antwerp the knowledge of Renaissance ornaments, with which he formed a new Flemish style. His Antwerp Town Hall (1561–1566), a mixture of Italian Renaissance and northern Gothic elements, had much influence in the Netherlands.

MARIET J. H. WILLINGE

WORKS

1548, Tomb of Frederic I, Sleswick, Germany. 1550–1552, Tabernacle, Zoutleeuw, Belgium. 1554, Tomb of Jan van Merode, Geel, Belgium. 1561–1566, Townhall, Antwerp, Belgium. *(A)1563, Frans Floris House; *(A)German Hansa House; Antwerp, Belgium. 1570–1573, Tomb of Duke Albrecht, Königsberg, Germany. 1573–1574, Roodscreen, Tournai, Belgium.

BIBLIOGRAPHY

GELDER, HENDRIK E., and DUVERGER, J. (editors) (1936)1954 Volume 1 in *Kunstgeschiedenis der Nederlanden.* 3d ed. Utrecht: De Haan.
GERSON, HORST, and KUILE, E. H. TER 1960 *Art and Architecture in Belgium: 1600–1800.* Harmondsworth, England: Penguin.
HEDICKE, ROBERT 1913 *Cornelis Floris und die Florisdekoration.* Berlin: Bard.
ROGGEN, D., and WITHOF, J. 1942 "Cornelis Floris." *Gentsche Bijdragen tot de Kunstgeschiedenis* 8:79–171.
VERMEULEN, F. A. J. 1931 Volume 2 in *Handboek tot de geschiedenis van de Nederlandsche Bouwkunst.* The Hague: Nijhoff.

FOLGUERA GRASSI, FRANCISCO

Francisco Folguera Grassi (1891–1960) was born in Barcelona, Spain. He obtained the title of architect in 1917. Folguera was a planner, theoretician, and writer. He published *Mechanical Foundations of Structures* (1954), *Plan for the Natural Illumination of Buildings* (1937), *Urbanism for All* (1959), and *Gaudi,* the latter in collaboration with José Francisco Ràfols (1929). He translated many other works. He was one of the constructors of the Pueblo Español (Spanish village) for the International Exposition in Barcelona in 1929, a work known throughout the world and a model in its class.

JUAN BASSEGODA NONELL
Translated from Spanish by
Judith E. Meighan

WORKS

1919, Casa Ensesa, S'Agaró, Spain. 1924, Circo Olimpia; 1930, Casa Sant Jordi; Barcelona, Spain. 1939, Church of Mollet del Vallès, Spain. 1940, Church, S'Agaró, Spain. 1941–1960, Reforma del Monasterio de Montserrat, Spain.

BIBLIOGRAPHY

BENAVENT DE BARBERÀ, P. 1970 "La Obra de F. Folguera." *M.C.* no. 68, Jan.
VILA SAN JUAN, PABLO 1968 "Francisco Folguera Grassi: El arquitecto de la serenidad." *Vanguardia Española* July 27.

FOMIN, IVAN A.

Ivan Aleksandrovich Fomin (1872–1936) attained prominence in his later years as a founder of Socialist Realism, the official Soviet style promoted during Stalin's regime.

Born in Orl (Russia), Fomin enrolled in St. Petersburg's Academy of Art (1894–1896) after being sent to Moscow to study mathematics. Influenced by Art Nouveau during a trip to France (1897), he worked for the leading Moscow Art Nouveau architect FEODORE O. SHEKHTEL before re-entering the Academy in the architectural section (1905–1909). A postgraduation travel award acquainted him with the architectural heritage of the Mediterranean and persuaded him of the perpetual vitality of classic forms. In establishing his own practice in St. Petersburg (1910–1918), the artist-architect Fomin determined to forward the development of a Russian architectural classicism inspired by the current wave of Russian nationalism and by his personal administration for the architecture of M. F. KAZAKOV.

Fomin loved monumentality, pursued the synthesis of all art forms in architecture, searched for the internal beauty in classic forms, and boldly manipulated them to suit present needs. With this approach he served the aims of the Russian aristocracy, as demonstrated by his Polovtsev's Mansion (1911–1913) in St. Petersburg and Gagarin's Estate *Kholomki* (1912–1913) near Pskov (Russia). He later offered the same values to fulfill the goals of the succeeding Soviet government, naming his stylized interpretation of classical motifs "proletarian classicism." Thus, he became the head of the first State Architecture-and-Planning Studio (1919–1928) in Petrograd (Leningrad after 1924). Called later to Moscow for the construction of his Dinamo Complex (1926–1930) there and for his Polytechnic Institute (1927–1929) in Ivanovo-Voznesensk near the capital, he continued to work, lecture, write, and head Architectural Studio 3 of the Moscow Soviets (1933–1936). His last projects, the House of the Ukrainian Soviets (1934–1938) in Kiev, Soviet Union, and two subway stations in Moscow, *Krasnye Vorota* (1934–1935) and *Ploshchad Sverdlov* (1936–1938), were acclaimed as models of Socialist Realism and publicized in the Soviet press long after his death in 1936.

MILKA T. BLIZNAKOV

WORKS

1911–1913, Polovtsev's Mansion, St. Petersburg, Russia. 1912–1913, Gagarin's Estate (*Kholomki*), near Pskov, Russia. 1912–1915, Abamelek-Lazarev's Mansion, St. Petersburg, Russia. 1926–1930, Department Store, Club, and Housing Complex (with A. Ya. Langman), Dinamo Association, Moscow. 1927–1929, Polytechnic Institute (with T. J. Fomin); 1928–1931, Library of the Polytechnic Institute (with T. J. Fomin); Ivanovo-Voznesensk, Russia. 1929–1930, Moscow Soviet of People's Commissars Headquarters (with G. K. Oltarzhevsky); 1934–1935, Krasnye Vorota Subway Station; Moscow. 1934–1938, House of the Soviets of People's Commissars of the Ukrainian Soviet Socialist Republic (with P. V. Abrosimovich), Kiev, Russia. 1936–1938, Ploshchad Sverdlov Subway Station, Moscow.

BIBLIOGRAPHY

AFANASIEV, K. N. (editor) 1970 *Iz istorii Sovetskoi arkhitektury.* Moscow: Akademiya Nauk SSSR.

BARKHIN, MIKHAIL T. (editor) 1975 Volume 1, pages 98–149 in *Mastera sovetskoi arkhitektury ob arkhitekture.* Moscow: Iskusstvo.

ERN, I. V. 1960 "Iz arkhitekturnogo nasledstva T. A. Fomina." *Arkhitekturnoe nasledstvo* 12:208–209.

FOMIN, IVAN A. 1904 "Moskovskii Klassitsizm." *Mir Iskusstva* 12:187–198.

FOMIN, IVAN A. 1933a "Iz Moego Tvorcheskogo Opyta." *Arkhitektura SSSR* 5:32–33.

FOMIN, IVAN A. 1933b "Rekonstruktsiya Klassiki: O Stile Nashey Epokhi." *Sovetskoe Iskusstvo* 19–20:6.

IL'IN, M. 1946 *Ivan Aleksandrovich Fomin.* Moscow: Akademiya Arkhitektury SSSR.

KOPP, ANATOLE 1978 *L'architecture de la période Stalinienne.* Grenoble, France: Presses Universitaires.

MINKUS, M., and PEKAREVA, N. 1953 *I. A. Fomin.* Moscow: Gos. Izd. Literatury po stroitel'stvu i arkhitekture.

USACHEVA, K. B. 1972 *I. A. Fomin: k stoletiyu so dnya rozhdeniya.* Moscow: Gos. nauchno-issledovatelskii musei arkhitektury imeny A. V. Shchuseva.

VOYCE, ARTHUR (1948)1969 *Russian Architecture: Trends in Nationalism and Modernism.* Reprint. Westport. Conn.: Greenwood Press.

FONTANA, CARLO

Born at Rancate near Como, Italy, Carlo Fontana (1638–1714) is distantly related to DOMENICO FONTANA, the famous engineer of Sixtus V. Domenico designed the pope's streets and moved four obelisks for him, notably that standing now in front of Saint Peter's. Carlo, who is assumed to have arrived in Rome in the early 1650s, trained first under PIETRO BERRETTINI DA CORTONA, whom he assisted as a draftsman in the construction of the façade and square of Santa Maria della Pace. After its completion (1655–1658), he worked with GIOVANNI LORENZO BERNINI on St. Peter's square. Timothy Kitao's statement (1977) that Fontana had no share in this project is confuted by a document and a drawing related to the concentric arrangement of part of the columns on the perimeter of the oval which have survived in Windsor Castle. In 1663, Fontana assisted Bernini in the remodeling of the Scala Regia which involved the difficult operation of keeping the parts of the Scala Regia, situated above the entrance into the stairhall, temporarily suspended in order to execute Bernini's plans designed for this area.

Although Mattia de Rossi (see DE ROSSI FAMILY) was most closely connected with Bernini as his immediate collaborator, we find Fontana frequently working under Bernini, especially on commissions connected with Pope Alexander VII (1655–1667) and his family (the Chigi), such as the palace for the Cardinal Flavio Chigi in Piazza Santi Apostoli in Rome (1664–1667) and at Ariccia, the "resort area" of the family located about twenty miles from Rome, where Fontana participated not only in the completion and remodeling of the palace, but also of the Church of the Assumption erected opposite the palace (1662–1664). With assistance, Fontana elaborated projects for the latter, of which the major one, preserved in the Vatican Library, is dated 1670. Fontana also assisted Carlo Rainaldi in the design and execution of the façade of Sant'Andrea della Valle (1662) and became involved in a forceful competition not only there but especially in the most intricate projection of the twin churches on the Piazza del Popolo, where he presented projects of his own while the first of the two churches, Santa Maria di Montesanto, on the left, was under construction (c.1664). He had to submit to Bernini's interference in 1673, which determined the present shape of the dome. In the final phase of the construction of the sister church, Santa Maria dei Miracoli, he superseded Carlo Rainaldi in 1677 and finished the interior of the church, especially the dome, according to his own intentions.

On May 15, 1667, Carlo Fontana was unanimously accepted as *accademico di merito* of the Accademia di San Luca in Rome, and about 1670 he was made *cavaliere.* He was elected *principe* of the Academy in 1686 and 1693, serving in this capacity until 1699. When Clement XI reorganized the Accademia di San Luca in 1702, the painter Carlo Maratti succeeded Fontana as lifetime *principe,* while Fontana remained in charge of architectural matters as *primo consigliere,* a position he held until his death.

From 1664, Fontana assisted Bernini as *misuratore e stimatore della Camera Apostolica* and was envisaged to follow him in this capacity; in 1666, he became *misuratore della R. Fabbrica di S. Pietro,* receiving the honored appointment as architect of St. Peter's held by Bernini in his lifetime in 1697.

One of his first works is the still somewhat undistinguished façade of Santi Faustino e Giovita (c.1664), the only original feature of which is the integration of the peculiarly shaped space for a fresco in the tympanum of the church front. The almost simultaneous façade of San Biagio in Campitelli (c.1665), however, is surprising in the manner in which Fontana conceived the upper portion of the façade with its receding bays for a spectator viewing the church laterally in the narrow street (Via Giulio Romano, which no longer exists). About the same time, Fontana was involved in his first restoration of Santo Spirito dei Napolitani (1666–1668) and began the construction of Santa Maria Maddalena with the apse (1668), but he left the commission when the execution had reached the transept (1671). One of his major works of this early period is the completion of the Cathedral of Santa Margherita at Montefiascone (1670–1674) with a dome that is distinguished by the folded impression of the surface of the exterior shell, created by the very strong ribs which spring from the eight corners of the already existing drum and which alternate with the concavely shaped intervals.

The patronage of Cardinal Paluzzo Albertoni Altieri, nephew of Clement XI, who had commissioned this work from him, did not lead to the important commission of the extension of the Palazzo Altieri on the Piazza del Gesù in Rome, the original portion of which had been executed by Giovanni Antonio de Rossi about the middle of the century and was enlarged by him under the pontificate of Clement X (1670–1676). A rather moderate commission was the remodeling of the monastery church, Santa Marta in Piazza del Collegio Romano (1670–1674), where Fontana added lateral chapels to the nave and heightened the vault. Remarkable, however, because of its connection with Bernini's style of the period, is the altar decoration with the two angels holding aloft an oval frame for a no longer extant painting. Strongly Berninian in concept is the baldachin of the main altar of Santa Maria in Traspontina of 1674, with its motive of the angels carrying the heavy bronze baldachin in the shape of a crown. The supporting structure consists of four pairs of concentrically arranged columns. The precious material and the ingenuity of the composition allows us to recognize in this altar Fontana's first real masterpiece.

From this point, works on which his fame is mainly based follow in quick succession. The Cappella Ginetti in Sant'Andrea della Valle, begun in 1671 but finished only in 1684, is one of the major monuments of its kind in which the deliberate use of colored marble plays a dominating role in the overall effect, as do the statues of the deceased cardinals of the family represented kneeling over lateral entrances in free emulation of Bernini's monument to Alexander VII, completed during those years. The highpoint of Carlo Fontana's chapel architecture is the cappella designed for Cardinal Alderano Cybo in Santa Maria del Popolo (1682–1684), where Fontana had the freedom to erect an almost free standing structure. Originally planned on a system of concentric circles, it was eventually erected on a Greek-cross plan with three shortened arms. The chromatic scheme realized for the main part relies on that of the marbles used in the Capella Ginetti, but in addition to the contrast with the white marble sculpture, the Cappella Cybo, through the harmonious blending with Carlo Maratti's altarpiece (1686: *The Church Fathers Discoursing on the Immaculate Conception*), offers a perfect example of a so-called complete work

Carlo Fontana.
San Marcello al Corso.
Rome.
1682–1684

of art (for the painting, see Dowley, 1957, pp. 167–172).

Connected with the earlier plan for the Cappella Cybo is Fontana's original scheme for the Jesuit Sanctuary at Loyola of about 1681, where the architect employed chapels of alternating depths that are concentrically oriented toward the main space. This elaborate scheme was simplified in the execution by an annular passageway with the lateral chapels positioned in niches.

One of Fontana's most famous works is the façade of San Marcello al Corso, (1682–1684), the concave front of which, articulated by full columns, steps backward in concentric layers. A most peculiar feature is the aedicula originally intended for a relief, but now empty. Twin bell towers, envisaged by Fontana in the final stage of the projection, were not executed.

When Fontana obtained the commission for the remodeling of the Baptismal Chapel of St. Peter's in a very involved competition (1692–1698), he found a situation similar to that of two decades earlier with the Cappella Ginetti at Sant'Andrea della Valle, where the room for the chapel was pre-established. To realize his conception, Fontana used greater freedom, however, by filling the entire space of the center and of the lateral sections with frescoes and by opening the sail vault to illuminate them by a window located in the upper room. In this way, he provided a source of indirect light for the pictorial representations by Carlo Maratti and his assistants with the *Baptism of Christ* in the center.

Fontana also designed the cover (*coperchio*) for the baptismal font, cast in bronze, which is suspended by an ingenious iron skeleton. Fontana was a rather prolific designer of monuments involving sculpture, the most famous of which is that executed in St. Peter's for Queen Christina of Sweden (1696–1701) which features a larger-than-life bronze medallion portrait of the queen. Fontana's cynical critic, the diarist Valesio, likened it to a clock dial. The monument to the sponsoring Pope Innocent XII, executed in 1692, was deliberately inobtrusive by will of the pontiff; it was replaced in 1747 by the present monument by Filippo della Valle.

About the turn of the century, Fontana suffered several setbacks in his career. His project of 1694 for the Jesuit Church in Frascati remained on paper, and so did a related project for the Cardinal Francesco Negroni (1697) and a project for the main façade of San Giovanni in Laterano which has survived only in a copy. His huge enlargement scheme for the square of St. Peter's also remained unexecuted; it envisaged, in the first phase, a replica of the Piazza Retta at the location of the no

longer extant Piazza Rusticucci and, in the second phase, even the clearing of the Borgo area to establish a convenient and monumental access to the Vatican basilica. He was more successful in acquiring the commission to transform and enlarge the Palazzo Ludovisi left unfinished by Bernini for the purposes of a centralized papal Curia (called henceforth the *Curia Innocenziana* [1694–1696]). To Bernini's scheme Fontana added a tripartite portico designed after the pattern of triumphal arches, and on top of the building he placed a parapet and belfry. He also executed a semicircular courtyard on the rear side of the building (after 1870 transformed into the present structure of the *Camera dei Deputati*). His remarkable urban scheme, which envisaged a semicircular forecourt on a piazza, remained unexecuted.

A more comprehensive scheme connected the Piazza di Pietra and the square in front of Sant'Ignazio, for which plans of around 1694 are mentioned in documents found by Dorothy Metzger, who assumes that the square in front of Sant'Ignazio had also been planned in the form of a half circle (Metzger, 1979).

In general, however, Fontana was less fortunate in his palace architecture than with his chapels. The Palazzo del Conte Bigazzini (c.1676–1680) which with its tripartite articulation of the center pre-empted to a degree that of the Palazzo Montecitorio, was destroyed when the Piazza Venezia was enlarged, and the Palazzo Grimani in the Via Rasella was transformed in the nineteenth century.

The project for the Liechtenstein Palace in Landskron of 1696 remained on paper, but it certainly exercised a strong influence when LUIGI VANVITELLI designed his Palazzo Reale at Casserta, which shares with Fontana's scheme the subdivision of the square courtyard into four smaller units by the device of crossing wings which contain a scenographic vestibule in the center.

The execution of Fontana's sometimes rather innovative plans for villas was also overclouded. In this respect, he was more successful at the beginning of his career. The projects for a country palace in San Quirico d'Orcia (1678–1679) for Flavio Chigi was followed by the successful modification of the Villa Cetinale (1679–1680) near Siena for Don Mario Chigi. The front of this casino is embellished by a double-ramped staircase with two landings connected with niches for sculpture and a cornice surmounted at the ends by scrolled pediments.

For Flavio Chigi's Villa Versaglia at Formello, now a ruin, Fontana contributed, among other things, the house with the open arcade of about 1681.

One of Fontana's most successful, though as far as we know, also unexecuted projects for a casino was that of 1689 which he submitted to the presumptive commissioner, the Venetian Ambassador Girolamo Landi, in two versions. One is Roman in style with a hexagonal *salone* after SEBASTIANO SERLIO and one is in a Venetian style with a circular *salone* based on ANDREA PALLADIO's Villa Rotonda.

After the turn of the century, Carlo Fontana's career began to fade. He was no longer *principe* of the Accademia di San Luca, but he held an important position as first adviser in matters of architecture. Although hampered by gout, he executed two catafalques, the first for Emperor Leopold I in Santa Maria dell'Anima (1705), the second for King Pedro II of Portugal (1707) in Sant'Antonio dei Portoghesi. Both were lavishly constructed evocations of his famous altar tempietto in Santa Maria in Traspontina, though made of perishable material appropriate for the purpose.

The major building which occupied him since the beginning of the pontificate of Clement XI (1700–1721) was the enlargement of the Ospizio di San Michele. First to be constructed was the Casa Correzionale (1701–1704) for youthful delinquents which set an example for the further development of correctional institutions, for example, by providing individual spaces for the inmates and preparing them through instruction for a return to normal life. Much admired already in its time, it was soon followed by an enlargement project for the entire hospice, begun in 1708 but interrupted by Fontana's death in 1714 when the cruciform church was almost complete. Fontana's plan can be reconstructed with two symmetrical courtyards flanking the church, only one of which has been executed according to his plans. The building was continued by NICOLA MICHETTI, who changed the plan for Fontana's second courtyard, the completion of which, with the rest of the huge building complex, continued almost until the end of the century.

Another building serving public needs, this one for entertainment and cultural activity, was also ill-fated: the Teatro Tor di Nona (1669–1671), the first structure for which had been sponsored by Queen Christina of Sweden. Shortly after it had been rebuilt on a larger scale (1695–1697), it had to be destroyed by order of Pope Innocent XII, who objected to the institution for moral reasons.

Around 1700, Fontana constructed a library in the Convent of the Dominicans of Santa Maria Sopra Minerva for Cardinal Girolamo Casanata. This room took the form of a huge barrel-vaulted hall with arches cut into the vault for windows above the bookshelves. Continued after the death of the Cardinal (1700), it associates itself with FRANCESCO BORROMINI's Biblioteca Vallicelliana in the Convento dei Filippini and with his Biblioteca Alessandrina in the Sapienza.

A building for mere utilitarian purposes was Fontana's granary (1703–1705) on the Piazza di Termini where he envisaged in the first planning phase a double-ramped staircase to be attached to the rear side of the building, in the execution, he used the nearby so-called Mausoleo, a structure belonging to the baths of Diocletian, for a four-ramped stairway with a rectangular well.

Fontana's most important building was never executed: the church to be erected at the far end of the Colosseum in commemoration of the early Christian martyrs. The project originated after the Holy Year of 1675 by order of Innocent XI, but the war against the Turks inhibited the execution at that time. Reactivated under Clement XI about 1706, similar economic and political difficulties prevented the execution *a priori*. The ground plan of Fontana's church is based on that of Bernini's Assunta at Ariccia, and the elevation was carefully adjusted to the scale of the tiers of the surrounding Colosseum structure.

Carlo Fontana.
Santa Maria in
Traspontina (high
altar).
Rome.
1674

Carlo Fontana.
Project for a church to be
erected in the Colosseum.
Rome.
1675

Moderate in scope were commissions for the remodeling of the portico and façade of Santa Maria in Trastevere (1702), and the restoration of San Teodoro al Palatino (1702–1704), which Fontana freed from the moisture coming from the Palatine Hill by means of an *intercapedine;* he also provided it with an interesting piazza forecourt accessible from the street through curvilinear stairways patterned after those of the *confessio* of St. Peter's and related structures.

A second campaign of restoration and remodeling of Santo Spirito dei Napolitani took place between 1702 and 1708, and, besides an extensive renovation of the church interior, resulted in the creation of a new chapel for the high altar. Unfortunately, the chapel was changed in the nineteenth century along with other modifications in the interior decorative ornament of the church.

The series of chapels designed by Carlo Fontana ends with the Cappella Albani (San Sebastiano fuori le mura, 1706–1712) where Clement XI's brother Orazio Albani is buried. Here, Fontana again designed a building on a Greek-cross plan reminiscent of the Cappella Cybo, but with more restraint in the decoration of the interior. It differs from Fontana's earlier work in that it terminates in an apse with a niche for a statue and has carefully designed and executed stucco decoration in the pendentives and the inner shell of the dome.

Fontana's multifaceted activities also include the modification of the Fontana Paola on the Janiculum, where he added a basin to FLAMINIO PONZIO's five-bayed fountain structure by order of Alexander VIII (1689–1691) and pierced the interval in the center where the coat of arms of the pope appears in a stagelike fashion within the frame of the opening (1690–1700). The basin repeats the shape of that of the Fontana di Trevi, left unfinished by Bernini, for which Fontana produced a series of projects in 1706, preserved in Windsor Castle.

A considerable part of Fontana's time was occupied with works of engineering. He repaired the water supply system for the Fontana Paola and occupied himself with the problem of the Tiber inundations, in the solution to which he was defeated in competition by Cornelio Mayer (1669) and again, thirty years later, by Francesco Maria Onorati. His project for the restoration of the Ponte Senatorio (1692) remained on paper, but he restored the aqueduct leading to Civitavecchia (1692–1702) and repaired the harbors of Civitavecchia and Anzio under Innocent XII. For Civitavecchia he also designed the breakwater in 1708 to protect its entrance.

The career of Carlo Fontana developed in many ways, in the manner characteristic for architects of his time in Rome. Trained by the outstanding masters of that period, da Cortona and Bernini, and endowed with a sensitivity that stimulated his curiosity of Borromini's audacious experiments, Fontana established himself in a period of economic and other difficulties, patronized by ecclesiastical dignitaries of high rank and the Roman nobility which gave him the chance to develop his talents in the direction of his natural inclinations. Chapels of highest sophistication, the Cappella Cybo in Santa Maria del Popolo and the Baptismal Chapel in St. Peter's, are landmarks in chapel design in Rome.

Fontana was also patronized by the popes, but his relationships with the pontiffs who employed him—Innocent XII and Clement XI—were always more or less tense. Innocent XII not only curtailed his projects for the palace and the Piazza di Montecitorio and showed no inclination to become involved in the costly proposals for the extension of the square of St. Peter's, but he also treated Fontana with harshness; he criticized the bell tower of the Palazzo Montecitorio on the formal occasion of the inauguration ceremony because he found it too small. In 1693, he even ordered the destruction of the model for the baptismal font on which Fontana had collaborated with the sculptor Domenico Guidi and for which he was responsible as the architect. Fontana's dignity as *principe* of the Accademia di San Luca and as a renowned professional shrunk to a minimum before the highest patron of ecclesiastical projects, who could even afford to delay payment. Even under Clement XI, a pope exceptionally devoted to the arts and architecture, Fontana's fortune was rather moderate. He had to leave his position as *principe* of the Academy to Carlo Maratti, and he had to tolerate a secondary role as first adviser in the field of architecture. The commissions given to him, with the exception of the Ospizio di San Michele, were for the most part secondary in nature. Even his own son, Francesco, was preferred over him when the delapidating early Christian basilica of Santi Apostoli had to be rebuilt.

The domineering position granted to Fontana's teacher and predecessor, Bernini, who conversed with the popes on the level of personal friendships, was certainly not given to Fontana. And yet, he was the most respected achitect of his time. Considering the number of students who trained under him, which included such distinguished architects as JOHANN BERNHARD FISCHER VON ERLACH, LUCAS VON HILDEBRANDT, JAMES GIBBS, Nicodemus Tessin (see TESSIN FAMILY), FILIPPO JUVARRA, to mention only the most famous, it is safe to say that he enjoyed what we call today a national and even international reputation.

Fontana's teaching "philosophy," known through the famous dialogue with Filippo Juvarra, is based on the reverence for the monuments of the classical past. He has been considered the administrator of the legacy of the great architects of the high baroque. His importance as an architect does not exhaust itself, however, in a merely retrospective attitude. The use of the architectural vocabulary of his masters is sophisticated and often original. In urban planning, he even played a leading role, not by inventing "ideal cities" but in terms of what would be manageable on the basis of preexisting situations, if not without enormous sacrifices. It is his personal tragedy that none of his urban ideas which later proved to be so influential were realized in his lifetime.

It would certainly be wrong to classify Fontana as the precursor of neoclassicism, although the recent interpretation by Bianca Tavassi La Greca (1977) strongly leans in this direction. This notion is confuted by Fontana's receptive attitude toward the articulative schemes of the Roman baroque and even prebaroque (Mannerism, for example) and his inclination toward the stongly contrasting chromatic effects which are characteristic of the period. Where Fontana appeared to be progressive, for example, in the imaginatively and freely decorated temporary structures, he rather showed himself as a precursor or initiator of a movement that led to a style referred to by Wittkower and others as Roman rococo, with FERDINANDO FUGA as the major exponent.

Fontana, especially in the 1690s and in the early 1700s, was a prolific writer. Most important are his books on the Basilica of St. Peter's (1694), the Palazzo Montecitorio (1694 and 1708), and the Colosseum (posthumously, 1725) in which he codifies his professional experience, demonstrates his historical interests and erudition—almost a precursor of Fischer von Erlach in this respect—and displays the wide range and fertility of his building ideas which were denied realization by adverse circumstances. Manuscript fragments with chapters relating to some of his structures have survived among his drawings at Windsor Castle and elsewhere, a sure indication of his intention to write a monograph of his own works. Age and commissions which kept him active until the last months of his long life prevented him from carrying out what seems to have been a favorite idea, especially in the final phase of his professional activity.

HELLMUT HAGER

WORKS

c.1661–1667 and later, Santa Maria dei Miracoli (with Carlo Rainaldi and Gianlorenzo Bernini), Piazza del Popolo; c.1661–1667 and later, Santa Maria di Montesanto (with Rainaldi and Bernini), Piazza del Popolo; 1664, Santi Faustino e Giovita (façade); c.1665, San Biagio in Campitelli (façade and entrance vestibule); 1666–1668, Santo Spirito dei Napolitani (remodeling of interior); 1670–1674, Santa Margherita at Montefiascone (completion); 1670–1674, Santa Marta in Piazza del Collegio Romano (remodeling and enlargement); 1671–1684, Cappella Ginetti, Sant'Andrea della Valle; 1674; Santa Maria in Traspontina (high altar); Rome. c.1675, Medieval Church (remodeling, including the façade of the Collegiata), Lanuvio, Italy. *1676–1680, Palazzo del Conte Bigazzini; *1676–1680, Palazzo Grimani (transformed); c.1680 and later, Palazzo Massimo al Campidoglio (remodeling and fountain in the courtyard); 1678–1679, San Quirico d'Orcia (palace and garden); near Pienza, Italy. 1678–1680, Santa Margherita in Trastevere, Rome. 1679–1680, Villa Cetinale, near Siena, Italy. c.1680, Villa Versaglia, Formello, Italy. 1682–1684, Cappella Cybo, Santa Maria del Popolo; 1682–1684, San Marcello al Corso (façade); *1685–1687, Cappella dell' Assunta, Collegio Clementino; Rome. 1688, Cathedral (dome), Como, Italy. 1689–1692, Cathedral (completion), Bergamo, Italy. *1692, Monument to Innocent XII, St. Peter's; 1692–1698, St. Peter's (baptismal chapel); Rome. 1692–1702, Aqueduct (restored), Civitavecchia, Italy. 1694–1696, Palazzo Ludovisi (completion); 1696–1701, Monument to Queen Christina of Sweden, St. Peter's; c.1700, Convent of the Dominicans (library), Santa Maria Sopra Minerva; Rome. 1700, Palais Martinitz, Prague. 1701–1704, Casa Correzionale; 1708–1711, Ospizio di San Michele (addition of a cortile with a hospice for the elderly); 1702, Santa Maria in Trastevere (remodeling of portico and façade); 1702–1704, San Teodoro al Palatino (restoration); 1702–1708, San Spirito dei Napolitani (second remodeling of the interior and construction of a chapel for the main altar; transformed in the nineteenth century); 1703, Santa Maria dell' Umiltà (façade); 1703, Casino Vaini; 1703–1705, Granari alle Terme; Rome. 1705, Palazzo Capponi, Florence. 1705, Palazzo Durazzo (stairhall and loggia opposite the near front), Genoa, Italy. 1706–1712, Cappella Albani, San Sebastiano fuori le mura, Rome.

BIBLIOGRAPHY

Architectural Fantasy and Reality: Drawings from the Accademia Nazionale di San Luca, Concorsi Clementini,

1700–1750. 1981–1982 University Park: Museum of Art, Pennsylvania State University. Exhibition catalogue.

BJURSTRÖM, PER 1966 *Feast and Theatre in Queen Christina's Rome.* Stockholm: Nationalmusei.

BLUNT, ANTHONY 1969 "The Drawings of Carlo Fontana in the Royal Library at Windsor Castle." *Barocco europeo, barocco italiano, barocco salentino.* Lecce, Italy: Convegno Internazionale sul Barocco.

BLUNT, ANTHONY, and COOKE, LESTER 1960 *The Roman Drawings of the XVII and XVIII Centuries in the Collection of Her Majesty the Queen at Windsor Castle.* London: Phaidon.

BONANNI, FRANCESCO 1696–1700 *Numismata summorum Pontificum Templi Vaticani fabricum.* Rome.

BONANNI, FRANCESCO 1699 *Numismata Pontificum Romanorum quae a tempore Martini V. usque ad annum M.D.C.XCIX.* 2 vols. Rome.

BRAHAM, ALLAN 1975 *Funeral Decoration in Early Eighteenth-century Rome.* London: Victoria and Albert Museum.

BRAHAM, ALLAN, and HAGER, HELLMUT 1966 "The Tomb of Christina." Pages 48–58 in *Queen Christina of Sweden: Documents and Sources.* Stockholm.

BRAHAM, ALLAN, and HAGER, HELLMUT 1977 *Carlo Fontana: The Drawings at Windsor Castle.* London: Zwemmer.

BRAUER, HEINRICH, and WITTKOWER, RUDOLF (editors) 1931 *Die Zeichnungen des Gianlorenzo Bernini.* Berlin: Keller.

BUCHOWIECKI, WALTER 1970 Volume 2 in *Handbuch der Kirchen Roms.* Vienna: Hollinek.

CATENA, CLAUDIO 1954 *Guida Storico Artistica.* Rome: Traspontina.

CHATTARD, G. P. 1762–1767 *Nuova descrizione del Vaticano, o sia Palazzo Apostolico di S. Pietro.* 3 vols. Rome: Barbienelli.

CONFORTI, MICHAEL 1980 "Planning the Lateran Apostles." *Studies in Italian Art and Architecture: Memoirs of the American Academy in Rome* 35:243–260.

COUDENHOVE-ERTHAL, EDUARD 1930 *Carlo Fontana und die Architektur des römischen Spätbarocks.* Vienna.

COUDENHOVE-ERTHAL, EDUARD 1933 "Römisches Stadtbaudenken zu Ende des Seicento." Pages 95–103 in *Hermann Egger: Festschrift zum 60. Geburtstag.* Graz, Austria: Leykam.

COUDENHOVE-ERTHAL, EDUARD 1934 "Zum Problem Carlo Fontana." *Wiener Jahrbuch für Kunstgeschichte* 23:157–158.

DONATI, UGO 1942 *Artisti ticinesi a Roma.* Bellinzona, Italy: Istituto editoriale ticinese.

DOWLEY, FRANCIS H. 1957 "Some Maratta Drawings at Düsseldorf." *Art Quarterly* 20:163–179.

ENGGASS, ROBERT 1972 "Laurentius Ottoni Rom. Vat. Basilicae Sculptor." *Storia dell' Arte* 15–16:315–342.

FALDA, GIOVANNI BATTISTA 1665–1699 *Il nuovo teatro delle fabbriche di Roma moderna.* Rome.

FASOLO, FURIO 1949 *Le chiese di Roma nel' 700, I, Trastevere.* Rome.

FASOLO, FURIO 1961 *L'opera di Hieronimo e Carlo Rainaldi.* Rome: Edizioni Ricerche.

FLEMING, JOHN 1958 "Cardinal Albani's Drawings at Windsor: Their Purchase by James Adam for George III." *The Connoisseur* 142:164–169.

FONTANA, CARLO 1692 *Discorso del Mons. Carlo Vespignano sopra la facile riuscita di restaurare il Ponte Senatorio.* Rome.

FONTANA, CARLO 1696 *Discorso sopra le cause delle inondazioni del Tevere.* Rome.

FONTANA, CARLO 1697 *Descrizione della nob. Cappella della Fonte Battesimale in S. Pietro.* Rome.

GARMS, JÖRG 1979 *Il Bambin Gesù.* Rome: Istituto di studi romani.

GIGLI, LAURA 1977 *San Marcello al Corso.* Rome: Istituto di studi romani.

GOLZIO, VINCENZO 1939 *Documenti artistici sul Seicento nell' Archivio Chigi.* Rome: Palombi.

GOLZIO, VINCENZO 1934 "Le chiese di S. Maria di Montesanto e di S. Maria dei Miracoli a Piazza del Popolo in Roma." *Archivi d'Italia* Series 2 8:122–148. 148.

GRASSI, LILIANA 1966 *Provincie del Barocco e del Rococo.* Milan: Ceschina.

HAGER, HELLMUT 1967–1968 "Zur Planungs- und Baugeschichte der Zwillingskirchen auf der Piazza del Popolo: S. Maria di Montesanto und S. Maria dei Miracoli in Rom." *Römisches Jahrbuch für Kunstgeschichte* 11:189–306.

HAGER, HELLMUT 1968 "Progetti del tardo Barocco per il terzo braccio del colonnato della Piazza S. Pietro." *Commentari* 19:299–314.

HAGER, HELLMUT 1973a "Carlo Fontana's Project for a Church in Honour of the 'Ecclesis Triumphans' in the Colosseum, Rome." *Journal of the Warburg and Courtauld Institutes* 36:319–337.

HAGER, HELLMUT 1973b "La crisi statica della cupola di S. Maria in Vallicella in Roma e i rimedi proposti da Carlo Fontana, Carlo Rainaldi e Mattia di Rossi." *Commentari* 24:300–318.

HAGER, HELLMUT 1974a "La cappella del Cardinale Alderano Cybo in Santa Maria del Popolo." *Commentari* 25:47–61.

HAGER, HELLMUT 1974b "Carlo Fontana and the Jesuit Sanctuary at Loyola." *Journal of the Warburg and Courtauld Institutes* 37:280–289.

HAGER, HELLMUT 1974c "L'intervento di Carlo Fontana per le chiese dei Monasteri di Santa Marta e Santa Margherita in Trastevere." *Commentari* 25:225–242.

HAGER, HELLMUT 1975 "On a Project Ascribed to Carlo Fontana for the Façade of San Giovanni in Laterano." *Burlington Magazine* 117:105–109.

HAGER, HELLMUT 1976 "Un riesame di tre cappelle di Carlo Fontana a Roma." *Commentari* 27:252–289.

HAGER, HELLMUT 1981 "Some Observations on Bernini's Architectural Legacy." Volume 2 in *Studies in Italian Art History.* American Academy in Rome.

INCISA DELLA ROCCHETTA, GIOVANNI 1929 "Notizie sulla fabbrica della Chiesa Collegiata di Ariccia." *Rivista dell' Istituto di Archeologia e Storia dell' Arte* 1:281–285.

JACOB, SABINE 1975 *Italienische Zeichnungen der Kunstbibliothek Berlin. Architektur und Dekoration 16.*

bis 18. Jahrhundert. Berlin.

KITAO, TIMOTHY K. 1977 "Carlo Fontana Had No Part in Bernini's Planning for the Square of St. Peter's." *Journal of the Society of Architectural Historians* 36:85–93.

MALLORY, NINA 1977 *Roman Rococo Architecture from Clement XI to Benedict XIV (1700–1758).* New York: Garland.

METZGER, DOROTHY J. 1979 *Piazza S. Ignazio, Rome in the Seventeenth and Eighteenth Centuries.* Ann Arbor: University of Michigan.

MILLON, HENRY A. 1980 "The Antamoro Chapel in S. Girolamo della Carità in Rome: Drawings by Juvarra and an Unknown Draughtsman." *Studies in Italian Art and Architecture: Memoirs of the American Academy in Rome* 35:261–289.

MISCIATELLI, PIERO 1909 "Un documento inedito dell' architetto Carlo Fontana." *Repertorium für Kunstwissenschaft* 32:247–257.

ONOFRIO, CESARE D' 1976 *Roma val bene un' abjuria: Storie romane tra Christina di Svezia, Piazza del Popolo e l'Accademia d'Arcadia.* Rome: Palombi.

PASTOR, LUDWIG VON 1953 *The History of the Popes.* London: Hodges, Kegan Paul.

ROSSI, DOMENICO D' 1702–1721 *Studio d'architettura civile.* 3 vols. Rome.

SALERNO, LUIGI 1967 *Piazza di Spagna.* Naples: Cava dei Tirreni.

SCHIAVO, ARMANDO 1971 "Notizie biografiche sui Fontana." *Studi Romani* 19:56–61.

TAVASSI LA GRECA, BIANCA 1977 "Alcuni problemi inerenti l'attivita teoricà di Carlo Fontana." *Storia dell' Arte* 29:39–59.

WITTKOWER, RUDOLF 1937 "Carlo Rainaldi and the Roman Architecture of the Full Baroque." *Art Bulletin* 19:242–313.

WITTKOWER, RUDOLF (1958)1973 *Art and Architecture in Italy: 1600–1750.* 3d ed. Harmondsworth, England: Penguin.

FONTANA, DOMENICO

Born at Melide in the Swiss canton of Ticino, Domenico Fontana (1543–1607) was the first of a group of extraordinary architects, among them CARLO MADERNO, FRANCESCO BORROMINI, and CARLO FONTANA, to come to Rome from this region. He arrived in Rome at about the age of twenty and began as a stucco worker. Within a decade, he had come into the service of Cardinal Felice Peretti Montalto, the future Sixtus V, for whom in 1576 Fontana began a suburban villa located on the Quirinal Hill in Rome. In 1581, the cardinal took up residence in the Villa Montalto, which was significantly enlarged after he was elected pope in 1585. The villa was distinguished by its huge size and by the gardens that emphasized radiating vistas and expansive paths around the relatively limited extent of the buildings.

The achievement for which Fontana is best remembered is the transfer of the Vatican obelisk from the south of Saint Peter's to the piazza in front of the basilica. The project had been discussed and repeatedly dismissed since the mid-fifteenth century; but a tract published by Camillo Agrippa in 1583, *Di trasportar la guglia in su la piazza di San Pietro,* inspired new hopes. Fontana was appointed to the legendary task in 1585. Key to the safe transport of the obelisk was Fontana's design for a double tower of huge timbers to cradle the obelisk while it was lowered, moved, and re-erected. The dedication took place in 1586. In the dramatic raising of the obelisk, 800 men, 140 horses, and forty windlasses were employed; observers were constrained behind a police cordon and ordered silent on pain of death while signals were given to the workers with bells and trumpets. The entire operation is described in detail in Domenico Fontana's *Della trasportatione dell'obelisco vaticano* (1590), the second edition of which (Naples, 1604) is our most complete guide to his entire oeuvre.

The balance of Fontana's work at the Vatican is less impressive. The Vatican Library, built between 1587 and 1590, severed the commanding space of DONATO BRAMANTE's Cortile del Belvedere and provided nothing more exciting than a group of capacious rooms frescoed by mediocre artists. The

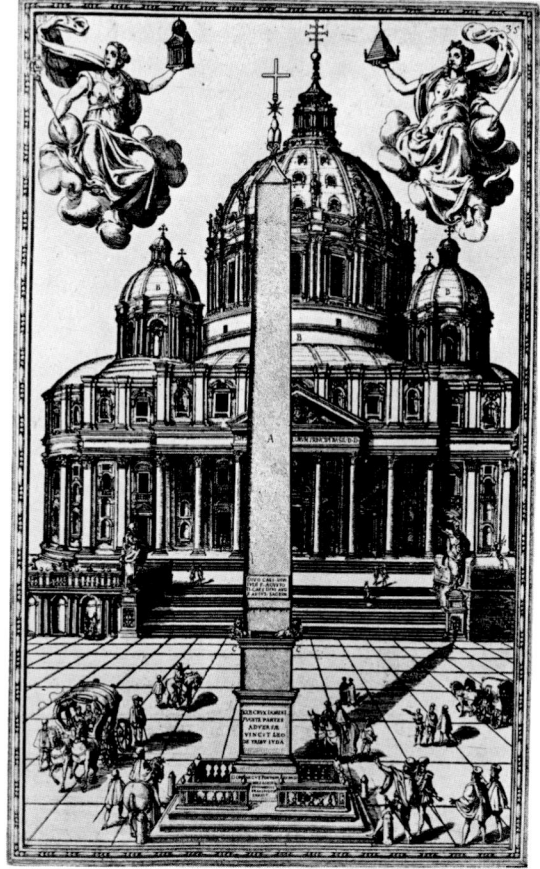

Domenico Fontana. Plate from Della trasportatione dell'obelisco vaticano. *Rome. 1590*

vaulting of the dome of Saint Peter's between 1588 and 1590 was the primary responsibility of GIACOMO DELLA PORTA, for whom Fontana merely served as executor. The Vatican Palazzo Sisto V was in fact begun under Gregory XIII (1572–1585); Fontana took up the work in 1589, built three floors of the palace, and added a fourth on the orders of Clement VIII (1592–1605).

Exorcised and Christianized, the Vatican obelisk symbolized a church triumphant and inaugurated an era of building activity that was intended to solidify papal control over the entire city of Rome. The focal point for this effort was at San Giovanni in Laterano, the cathedral of Rome. Here, Fontana brought a second obelisk, quarried from the spina of the Circus Maximus in 1587 and dedicated at the Lateran in 1588. He aligned it to the new road leading to the Colosseum for which he was responsible, and to the benediction loggia which he built at the right transept of the Lateran basilica in 1585–1587. The loggia abutted the Lateran palace, residence of the popes since the time of Constantine, which Sixtus V demolished and rebuilt to Fontana's design between 1585 and 1589. At the same time, Fontana constructed a portico in front of the Scala Santa to face the new palace. These building activities were part of Sixtus V's efforts to secure and edify the outlying districts of Rome.

This process was also underway on the Quirinal in the vicinity of the Villa Montalto and Santa Maria Maggiore, the favored church of Sixtus V. At Santa Maria Maggiore, Cardinal Montalto commissioned Fontana to build the Cappella del Presepio several months before being elected pope. The chapel, enshrining relics of the crib from Bethlehem, is a Greek cross appended to the flank of the church but so large as almost to form a separate edifice. Its completion in 1587 was accompanied by the collocation of an ancient obelisk, carted from the Mausoleum of Augustus to the apse of the church in the same year. In 1586, near the western gate of the Villa Montalto, Fontana created the Piazza delle Terme in conjunction with the head fountain (1587) for the Acqua Felice, the new aqueduct constructed by his brother Giovanni Fontana on the orders of Sixtus V.

Fontana's major building enterprises in Rome were connected by a network of new roads that changed the face of the city. The most famous artery, the Via Felice (1585–1589), originated at Santa Croce in Gerusalemme, continued past Santa Maria Maggiore and the Villa Montalto, dipping and then rising to the Trinità dei Monti. Originally, it was to go on to the Piazza del Popolo where an obelisk from the Circus Maximus was erected in 1589. Its wide path crossed that of the pre-existing Via Pia, which Fontana re-systematized. At one end of the Via Pia stood MICHELANGELO's Porta Pia; at the other end, Fontana positioned the Dioscuri, the famous horse tamers, on the newly graded Piazza del Quirinale (1589–1590). On many other occasions as well, Fontana carried out important roadwork, but in few cases (including those cited above) is it certain that the works were conceived by him. Thus, the extent of Fontana's talent as a town planner, rather than a mere executor, remains conjectural.

Fontana's architectural style never matched his unchallenged supremacy in organizational and technical matters. His buildings are generally remarkable for their grandeur of conception rather than their resourcefulness or their finesse in execution, and these qualities may have been cultivated by the spirited ambitions of his patron, Sixtus V. After the pope's death in 1590, Fontana was relegated to a minor position in the constellation of more exciting architects in Rome. In 1593, he accepted an invitation to become the royal architect in Naples but, despite an active career, he never regained the prominence he had previously enjoyed. He was buried in Sant'Anna dei Longobardi in Naples.

TOD A. MARDER

WORKS

*1576–1588, Villa Montalto; 1585–1586, Re-erection of Vatican Obelisk; 1585–1587, Benediction Loggia, San Giovanni in Laterano; 1585–1587, Cappella del Presepio, Santa Maria Maggiore; 1585–1589, Lateran Palace; 1585–1589, Via Felice; 1585–1598, Scala Santa (façade); 1586–1587, Systematization of Piazza delle Terme; 1587, Ospizio dei Mendicanti at Ponte Sisto; 1587, Re-erection of obelisk at Santa Maria Maggiore; 1587–1588, Re-erection of obelisk at San Giovanni in Laterano; 1587–1590, Systematization of Via Pia, Piazza del Quirinale, and the Dioscuri; 1587–1590, Vatican Library; 1588, Via San Giovanni in Laterano; 1588–1590, Saint Peter's (execution of dome); 1589, Re-erection of obelisk at Piazza del Popolo; 1589–1592, Palazzo Sisto V (enlargement); 1590, Catafalque of Sixtus V; Rome. 1593–1603, Church of Gesù e Maria; 1600–1602, Palazzo Reale; Naples.

BIBLIOGRAPHY

DONATO, UGO 1942 *Artisti ticinesi a Roma.* Bellinzona, Italy: Istituto.

D'ONOFRIO, CESARE 1967 *Gli obelische di Roma.* Rome: Bulzoni.

FONTANA, DOMENICO (1590)1604 *Della trasportatione dell'obelisco vaticano.* Naples, Italy.

GIEDION, SIEGFRIED 1952 "Sixtus V and the Planning of Baroque Rome." *Architectural Review* 111:217–226.

HESS, JACOB 1967 "La biblioteca vaticana: Storia della costruzione." Pages 143–152 in *Kunstgeschichtliche Studien zu Renaissance und Barock.* Rome: Storia e Letteratura.

IVERSEN, ERIK 1968 *Obelisks in Exile. The Obelisks of Rome.* Copenhagen: Gad.

LANCIANI, RODOLFO 1912 Volume 4, pages 121–175 in *Storia degli scavi di Roma.* Rome: Loescher.

MATTHIAE, GUGLIELMO 1970 "Domenico Fontana e l'idealismo sistino." *Studi romani* 18:431–444.

MUÑOZ, ANTONIO 1944 *Domenico Fontana architetto, 1543–1607.* Rome: Cremonese.

SCHIAVO, ARMANDO 1971 "Notizie biografiche sui Fontana." *Studi romani* 19:56–61.

SCHWAGER, KLAUS 1961 "Zur Bautätigkeit Sixtus V and S. Maria Maggiore in Rome." Pages 324–354 in *Miscellanea Bibliothecae Hertzianae.* Munich: Schroll.

STRAZZULLO, FRANCO 1969 *Architetti e ingegneri napoletani dal 500 al 700.* Turin, Italy: Benincasa.

WASSERMAN, JACK 1962 "The Palazzo Sisto V in the Vatican." *Journal of the Society of Architectural Historians* 21:26–35.

FONTANA, GIOVANNI

Born in Melide, Lake Lugano, in Italy, of a family of architects active in Rome and Naples, Giovanni Fontana (1540–1614) was the older brother of DOMENICO FONTANA and uncle of Giulio Cesare Fontana. He collaborated with his brother on the Benediction Loggia of the Lateran Palace (1582–1586), the Papal Palace at the Quirinale (1585), and the erection of the Obelisk (1586) at St. Peter's Square in the Vatican.

He distinguished himself as a hydraulics engineer who designed numerous water supply systems and port works. Fontana was involved in the restoration of the Aqueduct of Trajan (1608–1612), which carried water from Lake Bracciano to Rome, and collaborated on the design of its terminal fountain, the Acqua Paola. At the Villa Aldobrandini in Frascati, he designed a cascade (1603).

JUAN BASSEGODA NONELL

WORKS

1582–1586, Benediction Loggia (with Domenico Fontana), Lateran Palace; 1585, Papal Palace at the Quirinale (with Fontana); Rome. 1586, Alessandrina-Felice Aqueduct (begun by Matteo Bartolami; completed with Fontana), Italy. 1586, Obelisk at St. Peter's Square (with Fontana), Vatican City, Rome. 1603, Villa Aldobrandini (cascade; with Orazio Olivieri), Frascati, Italy. 1604, Trastevere Fountain (restoration of the Santa Maria), Rome. 1604–1622, Fountain (with CARLO MADERNO), Loreto, Ancona, Italy. 1608–1612, Aqueduct of Trajan (restoration); 1610–1612, Trajan's Aqueduct (terminal fountain on the Janiculum; with Maderno and FLAMINIO PONZIO); Italy. 1613, Fountain of Ponte Sisto (with GIOVANNI VASANZIO), Tiber River (moved from the left to the right bank in the nineteenth century), Italy.

BIBLIOGRAPHY

BRIZZI, BRUNO 1973 *Roma: Le Fontane.* Rome: Columbo.

FONTANA, DOMENICO 1590 *Della trasportatione dell'obelisco vaticano et della fabriche di nostro Signore Papa Sisto fatte dal cavallier Domenico Fontana.* Rome: Basa.

MELANI, ALFREDO (1884)1930 *L'Architettura italiana antica e moderna.* 7th ed. Milan: Hoepli.

MUNOZ, ANTONIO 1919 *Roma barocca.* Milan: Bestetti & Tumminelli.

NORBERG-SCHULZ, CHRISTIAN 1971 *Baroque Architecture.* New York: Abrams.

PORTOGHESI, PAOLO (1966)1970 *Roma Barocca: The History of an Architectonic Culture.* Cambridge, Mass.: M.I.T. Press. Originally published in Italian.

RICCI, CORRADO 1922 *Baukunst und dekorative Skulptur der Barockzeit in Italien.* Stuttgart, Germany: Hoffmann.

WOERMANN, KARL 1925 Volume 5, pages 20–21 in *Historia del Arte en todos los tiempos y pueblos.* Madrid: Editorial Saturnino Calleja.

FONT GUMA, JOSÉ

José Font Guma (1860–1922) was a Spanish architect born in Vilanova i la Geltrú. He was an assistant to Elias Rogent i Amat at the works of the University Exposition of Barcelona in 1888. He taught at the school of architecture of the University at Barcelona. A collector and student of Catalan tiles, he published *Catalan and Valencian Ceramic Tiles* (1905).

JUAN BASSEGODA NONELL
Translated from Spanish by
Judith E. Meighan

WORKS

1906, Reforma del Ateneo Barcelonés; 1914, Casa Colon, Paseo de Gracia; Barcelona, Spain. n.d., Castillo de La Geltrú (restoration), Spain. n.d., Fábrica Pirelli de Vilanova, Spain. n.d., Hospital de Sitges, Spain. n.d., Iglesia de Santa María de Cervelló, Spain.

BIBLIOGRAPHY

BOHIGAS, ORIOL 1968 *Arquitectura Modernista.* Barcelona, Spain: Lumen.

FONT I CARRERAS, AUGUST

August Font i Carreras (1846–1924) was born in Barcelona, Spain. He obtained his professional title in 1869. He was a disciple of the architect Elias Rogent i Amat. His great work in the field of restoration of monuments and buildings is very important. His principal work is the Seminary of Tarragon in Barcelona (1892–1899). He planned with the architect JOSEP ORIOL MESTRES I ESPLUGAS the neo-Gothic façade of the Cathedral of Barcelona (1887–1913). His style was eclectic with a penchant for the neo-Arabic.

XAVIER GÜELL GUIX
Translated from Spanish by
Judith E. Meighan

WORKS

1887–1913, Cathedral (façade, with Josep Oriol Mestres i Esplugas); 1892–1899, Seminary of Tarragon; Barcelona, Spain.

FONTSERÈ MESTRÈS, JOSÉ

José Fontserè Mestrès (1829–1897), son of architect José Fontserè Domenech, was born in Barcelona, Spain, where he became master of works in 1853. Fontserè's architectural works were always in the eclectic style, following a neo-Greek tendency, with relative simple lines. This was the usual style of masters of works, whose formal education was limited to three years of study of elementary subjects.

Although not qualified, Fontserè was in charge of construction of the Ciudadela Park. In 1866, he prepared a proposal for the park, and in 1868, he developed a project that also included plans for the National Museum, the Palace of Industry, and the Gardens, which he presented in an international competition. Although no first prize was awarded, the municipality gave him control of the project. In 1872, he became director of the park works, a position he held until the opening of the Universal Exposition in the park in 1887.

Within the park, Fontserè also designed the Borne Market (1873–1876) (the first covered marketplace in Spain utilizing a metallic structure), the water routes, the entrance gates, the restaurant, the Museum of Natural Science (later constructed by Rovira Trias), the cascade, the pedestal for the monument to General Prim, the dairy farm, the aviary, the dovecot, and the *Umbráculo,* all completed between 1873 and 1883. His collaborators included ANTONIO GAUDÍ I CORNET, whose involvement appears to have been decisive.

Fontserè was a man of liberal ideas, a freemason, and a major in the national militia. As master of works, he was not formally allowed to design or direct public works or monumental works of any kind.

JUAN BASSEGODA NONELL

WORKS

1854, Torre Castanyer, Olot, Spain. 1866, Puerta Nueva Gardens; 1869, Circo Barcelonés Theater (restoration); 1871, Antonio Camps House; 1873–1876, Borne Market; 1874, Ciudadela Park (water reservoir); 1874, Paseo de San Juan (balustrade); 1875, Ciudadela Park (pedestal for entrance gates); 1875, Magín Barbarà House; 1875, Saint Sebastian Convent (restoration); 1876, Ciudadela Park (candelabra for the rotunda and the external wall); 1877–1882, Ciudadela Park (cascade); 1880, Pàmias House; 1882, Ciudadela Park (aviary, restaurant, dairy farm, and pedestal for the Juan Prim Monument); 1882, Ricart House; 1883, Ciudadela Park (*Umbráculo*); 1888, Lyceum Circle Pavilion, Universal Exposition; Barcelona, Spain.

BIBLIOGRAPHY

BASSEGODA NONELL, JUAN 1971 "Arquitectos Catalanes del siglo XIX." *La Prensa* Nov. 23.
FLORENSA, A. 1961 *Miscelánea Fontserè.* Barcelona.
IGLÈSIAS Y FORT, JOSÉ 1955 Pages 107–123 in *L'escultor Joan Roig Soler: 1835–1918.* Spain: Asociación de Estudios Reusenses.
La Illustración Española y Americana 1875 39:245.
LLATAS, R. 1970 "Cien años atrás en Barcelona." *Destino* 1970:9–12.
PUIG ALFONSO, F. 1930 Pages 195–212 in *Curiositats barcelonines.* Barcelona.
RUBIÓ Y TUDURÍ, N. M. 1927 "La restauracion del parque de la Ciudadela." *Barcelona Atracción* 17. no. 192:171–182.

FOOTNER, WILLIAM

William Footner (1799–1872) was born in London, but in 1838 he emigrated to Canada, first settling in Sherbrooke, Quebec; in 1842, he established himself in Montreal. He had had a good classical training and appears to have been responsible for introducing the Greek Revival to Montreal. He worked at times with JOHN OSTELL. His major works were the Courthouse, Sherbrooke (1841), and the Bonsecours Market, Montreal (1846).

JOHN BLAND

FORBAT, FRED

Fred Forbat (1897–1972), born in Pécs, Hungary, was a student of the Bauhaus in Weimar and served as construction supervisor for the Adolf Sommerfeld House in Berlin by WALTER GROPIUS. This led to his being asked to supervise the erection of 10,000 dwellings for the Sommerfeld Company in Macedonia, Greece, and his appointment as chief architect for the company in Berlin.

Forbat assisted in the planning for the Gehag housing development in Zehlendorf, Berlin in the late 1920s, designed the easternmost buildings of the Gross-Siedlung Siemensstadt in Berlin, and also built a major portion of the Forschungs-Siedlung Haselhorst in Berlin (1930–1931). In 1932, he went with a group of German architects and planners under the leadership of ERNST MAY to the Soviet Union for a year, thence to Greece, followed by five years in his native Hungary, where he built various dwellings during the 1930s.

In 1938, Forbat was invited to Sweden to contribute to the early development of general plans for Swedish cities. Working first in Lund, he moved to Stockholm in 1942, established a consulting office, and prepared development plans for towns such as Landskrona (1951), Sölvesborg (1952), Kristinehamn (1955), and others. In the 1940s and 1950s, he published extensively on city planning in Sweden.

RON WIEDENHOEFT

FORBES, W. N.

Major-General William Nairn Forbes (1796–1855) was born in Aberdeenshire, Scotland. He joined the Bengal Engineers to become a cadet in India in 1815. He superintended the construction of machinery for the projected Calcutta Silver Mint and he designed the Mint (1824–1831) in the neoclassic style with an imposing Doric portico. His only other known work is the neo-Gothic Saint Paul's Cathedral, Calcutta (1839–1847).

PAULINE ROHATGI

WORKS

1824–1831, The Mint; 1839–1847, Saint Paul's Cathedral; Calcutta.

BIBLIOGRAPHY

COTTON, EVAN 1907 *Calcutta Old and New*. Calcutta: Newman.
NILSSON, STEN 1968 *European Architecture in India: 1750–1850*. London: Faber.
SANDES, E. W. C. 1933–1935 *The Military Engineer in India*. 2 vols. Chatham, England: Institution of Royal Engineers.

FORD, O'NEIL

O'Neil Ford (1905–1982) born in Pink Hill, Texas, attended what is now North Texas State University. With no formal architectural training other than an International Correspondence School course, Ford entered the Dallas office of David R. Williams in 1926 where his interest in early Texas structures, indigenous materials, and the integration of crafts and architecture was nurtured.

Ford established his own practice in Dallas (1930–1934, 1936) and worked on numerous government projects. The Little Chapel in the Woods at Texas Women's University (1939) constructed by the National Youth Administration was the first major commission for the firm now joined by partner Arch B. Swank. Ford subsequently moved his practice to San Antonio where he was called in 1938 to supervise the WPA restoration of La Villita, an eighteenth-century residential quarter, and entered into partnership with Jerry Rogers. In 1967, Boone Powell and Chris Carson, with Ford, formed Ford, Powell, and Carson, which continues today.

Ford first drew international attention in 1949 with pioneer use of the Youtz-Slick Lift Slab method of construction for the first buildings on the new campus of Trinity University at San Antonio, done in collaboration with Bartlett Cocke and Associates and Harvey P. Smith. Other innovative work involved the use of concrete shell construction, engineered by FELIX CANDELA of Mexico, in the design of buildings done for Texas Instruments.

MARY HOLLERS JUTSON GEORGE

WORKS

1939, Little Chapel in the Woods, Texas Women's University, Denton. 1949–present, Trinity University Campus, San Antonio, Tex. 1956–1958, Texas Instruments Semi-conductor Plant, Dallas, Tex. 1961–present, Skidmore College Campus, Saratoga Springs, N.Y. 1965, Marshall T. Steves House (with Chris Carson); 1972, Saint Mary's Hall; San Antonio, Tex.

BIBLIOGRAPHY

AMERICAN INSTITUTE OF ARCHITECTS, DALLAS CHAPTER 1962 *The Prairie's Yield.* New York: Reinhold.
BURCHARD, JOHN, and BUSH-BROWN, ALBERT 1961 *The Architecture of America.* Boston: Little, Brown.
FORD, O'NEIL 1964 "The Condition of Architecture." Pages 28–50 in Harry S. Ransom (editor), *The People's Architects.* University of Chicago Press.

FORESTIERE, BALDASARE

Using only handtools and his experience on the construction of the Boston subway, Baldasare Forestiere (1879–1946) built an underground complex of ninety rooms covering seven acres in Fresno, California. At depths ranging from 10–35 feet, he planted a citrus orchard and tunneled his home around it. Holes opened to the sky allowed for light and water.

JANET KAPLAN

WORK

1906–1946, Baldasare Forestiere House, Fresno, Calif.

BIBLIOGRAPHY

WAMPLER, JAN 1977 Pages 50–59 in *All Their Own: People and the Places They Build.* Cambridge, Mass.: Schenkman.

FORSMAN, F. G. J.

See WIMMELL and FORSMAN.

FÖRSTER, EMIL VON

Born in Vienna, Emil von Förster (1838–1909) studied at the Academy in Berlin. At first, he worked in the studio of his father, LUDWIG VON FÖRSTER, but in 1895 he went into state employment, remodeling the Burgtheater and the Hofburg in Vienna. In his numerous buildings for housing and commercial purposes throughout the Austro-Hungarian monarchy, he used a rich, decorative style with elements of the Austrian baroque.

ECKART VANCSA

WORKS

1872–1874, Allgemeine Österreichische Baugesellschaft; *1872–1874, Ringtheater; 1880–1883, Giro- und Kassen-verein; 1885–1887, Bodencreditanstalt; 1897, Burgtheater and Hofburg (remodeling); 1898–1901, Dorotheum; Vienna.

BIBLIOGRAPHY

EGGERT, KLAUS 1976 *Der Wohnbau der Wiener Ringstrasse im Historismus: 1855–1896.* Wiesbaden, Germany: Steiner.
WAGNER-RIEGER, RENATE 1970 *Wiens Architektur im 19. Jahrhundert.* Vienna: Österreichischer Bundesverlag.

FÖRSTER, LUDWIG VON

Born in Bayreuth, Germany, Ludwig von Förster (1797–1863) studied at the Academy in Munich (1816–1818) and at the Academy of Vienna under PETER VON NOBILE (1819). He was professor at the Viennese Academy from 1843 to 1846.

The importance of Förster lies in his influence on the following generation of Viennese Ringstrasse architects—in his studio worked such prominent architects as THEOPHILUS HANSEN—through the foundation of the periodical *Allgemeine Bauzeitung* in 1836 and through his fundamental ideas for the planning of Vienna's Ringstrasse.

ECKART VANCSA

WORKS

1840–1842, Palais Pereira; 1846–1849, Gustav-Adolf Church; *1850–1854, Elisabethbrücke; *1853–1859, Israelitisches Bethaus; 1864, Palais Hoyos-Sprinzenstein; Vienna.

BIBLIOGRAPHY

NIEMANN, GEORGE, and FELDEGG, FERDINAND 1893 *Theophilos Hansen und seine Werke.* Vienna: Schroll.
WAGNER-RIEGER, RENATE 1970 *Wiens Architektur im 19. Jahrhundert.* Vienna: Österreichischer Bundesverlag.

FOSCHINI, ARNALDO

Born in Rome, Arnaldo Foschini (1884–1968) was representative of the eclectic *Scuola romana* in the period immediately following World War I and of the *architettura littoria* of the fascist era.

Foschini worked mainly in Rome. In the fascist urban renewal of the old town, he carried out the plan of one important *sventramento*—a rectilinear cut in the urban texture—the Corso del Rinascimento, near Piazza Navona. He also built several monuments and buildings for the University of Rome.

After World War II, Foschini became president of the Gestione INA-Casa, the organization of the National Insurance Institute through which the government promoted a financing plan for low-cost housing in Italy. As such, Foschini was responsible for the organization's policy and for the distribution of works on the basis of competitions.

From 1924 to 1954, Foschini taught architecture at the University of Rome.

ANTONINO TERRANOVA

WORKS

1927, Supercinema Movie Theater (with others); 1931, Church of San Giacono degli Spagnoli; 1932–1935, Institute of Hygiene (entrance colonnade); University of Rome; 1935–1940, Corso del Rinascimento; 1938–1959, Farnesina Foreign Office (with others); 1955–1958, Santissima Immacolata, Via Laurentina; 1960–1968, San Giovanni Hospital (additions); 1962–1963, Santo Spirito Hospital Administration Buildings; Rome.

BIBLIOGRAPHY

ACCASTO, GIANNI; FRATICELLI, VANNA; and NICOLINI, RENATO 1971 L'architettura di Roma capitale: 1870–1970. Rome: Golem.
CEDERNA, ANTONIO 1980 Mussolini urbanista. Rome: Laterza.
DE GUTTRY, IRENE 1978 Guida di Roma Moderna, dal 1870 ad oggi. Rome: De Luca.
GREGOTTI, VITTORIO 1968 New Directions in Italian Architecture. New York: Braziller.
INSOLERA, ITALO 1962 Roma moderna. Turin, Italy: Einaudi.
ISTITUTO NAZIONALE DI URBANISTICA, ROME (1952)1954 Urbanisti Italiani. 2d ed. Rome: The institute.
MARCONI, PLINIO 1943 "Arnaldo Foschini architetto." Meridiano di Roma 15.

FOSSATI, PEDRO

Pedro Fossati (19th century) was born in the Swiss canton of Ticino, near the Italian border, a place which was to provide nineteenth-century Argentina with many of the architects and builders who arrived on its shores.

The works of Fossati were representative of the principles of academicism; they were quite close to the models of the Italian Renaissance, in particular those of ANDREA PALLADIO, SEBASTIANO SERLIO, and GIACOMO BAROZZI DA VIGNOLA.

Fossati was one of those architects whose lot it was to provide several regions of Argentina and Uruguay with the facilities that those two neighboring countries were lacking. He developed such novel architectural programs as hospitals, country houses, salting-plants, and so on. The Estancia Santa Cándida (1858) and the San José Palace (1857) built for General J. J. de Urquiza in Concepción del Uruguay, Entre Ríos—which can be traced clearly to Palladian villas—are his most outstanding works.

RAMÓN GUTÍERREZ

WORKS

1853, Italian Hospital, Montevideo. 1855, Italian Hospital; 1856, Bishop's Palace; Buenos Aires. 1857, Cathedral; 1857, San José Palace; 1858, Santa Cándida Palace and Salting Plant; Concepción del Uruguay, Argentina.

BIBLIOGRAPHY

BOSCH, BEATRIZ 1978 San José: La residencia del Organizador. Buenos Aires.
CASTRO, ANTONIO P. 1944 El palacio San José: Residencia del General Urquiza en Entre Ríos. Buenos Aires.
GIURIA, JUAN 1958 Volume 2 in La arquitectura en el Uruguay (1830–1900). Montevideo: Universal.
GUTÍERREZ, RAMÓN; PAULA, ALBERTO DE; and VIÑUALES, GRACIELA 1971 Arquitectura de la Confederacion Argentina en el litoral fluvial (1852–1862). Resistencia, Argentina: Impreso en el Departamento de Publicaciones e Impresione de la Universidad Nacional del Nordeste.
MACCHI, MANUEL E. 1969 Palacio San José: Museo y Monumento Nacional. Concepción del Uruguay, Argentina: Villa San José.
PAULA, ALBERTO DE, and GUTÍERREZ, RAMÓN 1974 La encrucijada de la arquitectura argentina. Resistencia, Argentina: Departamento de Historia de la Arquitectura, Universidad Nacional del Nordeste.

FOSTER, JOHN

John Foster (c.1787–1846) brought the new Greek Revival architectural style to his native Liverpool, England, during the 1820s and 1830s. A pupil of JEFFRY WYATVILLE, Foster spent time in Greece and Asia Minor (1810–1812) with C. R. COCKERELL. In 1824, Foster succeeded his father as official architect of Liverpool, a post he held until 1835. Foster's most notable work, the austerely dramatic Customs House (1828–1835), was destroyed in World War II.

FRANCES D. FERGUSSON

WORKS

*1816–1826, Saint Michael's Church; *1820–1822, Saint John's Market; *1822–1824, The Royal Infirmary; Liverpool, England. *1826, Garswood New Hall, Ashton-in-Makerfield, Lancashire, England. *1826–1829, Public Baths, St. George's Dock; *1828–1835, Customs House; *1829–1831, Saint Catherine's Church; Liverpool, England. *1834, Saint Gregory's Church, Bollington, England. 1834, William Huskisson Temple, St. James's Cemetery; *1835–1836, Lime Street Railway Station; Liverpool, England.

BIBLIOGRAPHY

PICTON, J. A. 1875 Volume 1, page 470 in *Memorials of Liverpool.* London: Longmans.

FOUILHOUX, JACQUES ANDRE

Jacques André Fouilhoux (1879–1945) was born in Paris. He studied at the Sorbonne and graduated as a mechanical engineer from the Ecole Centrale des Arts et Manufactures. In the United States by 1904, he founded the firm of Fouilhoux and Whiteside in Portland, Oregon, in 1908. After working for ALBERT KAHN and RAYMOND M. HOOD, among others, he became Hood's partner in 1927.

Respected for his engineering and supervisory skills, Fouilhoux worked on Rockefeller Center (1929–1941). After Hood's death, he became a partner of Wallace K. Harrison (see HARRISON AND ABRAMOVITZ). They designed the Rockefeller Apartments, general plans, and major structures for the World's Fair (1938–1939), and collaborated with others on the Fort Greene and Clinton Hill Housing Projects, all in New York City.

CAROL HERSELLE KRINSKY

WORKS

1929–1931, Rockefeller Center (with L. A. Reinhard and Henry Hofmeister, Raymond M. Hood, and Harvey Wiley Corbett, Wallace K. Harrison, and William H. MacMurray); *1938–1939, Rockefeller Apartments (with Harrison and Abramovitz); *1938–1939, Trylon and Perisphere (with Harrison and Abramovitz), World's Fair; New York.

BIBLIOGRAPHY

"J. André Fouilhoux." 1945 *Architectural Forum* 83-2:86.

KELLER, A. 1938 "Leading Architects Series 3." *New York World Telegram* Feb. 16.

KRINSKY, CAROL H. 1978 *Rockefeller Center.* New York: Oxford University Press.

FOULSTON, JOHN

John Foulston (1772–1842) set up practice in London after training in THOMAS HARDWICK's office but, apart from designs exhibited at the Royal Academy in 1794, 1804, and 1808, nothing is known of his work until 1810 when his success in a competition for a building complex, comprising a theater, a hotel, and assembly rooms, for Plymouth, England, took him to that city where he rapidly became the leading architect. An ingenious constructor, his Theatre Royal, Plymouth (1811–1813), made extensive use of cast and wrought iron in an attempt to make it completely fireproof. While at Ker Street, in nearby Devonport (formerly Plymouth Dock), he produced a unique group of buildings in different styles—"Primitive Doric" Town Hall (1821–1823), "Egyptian" Library (1823), "Hindoo" Baptist Chapel (1823–1824), and a "Greek Doric" Commemorative Column (1824). Usually, his work was in the Greek Revival style, sometimes showing the marked influence of JOHN SOANE, for example, in the Proprietary Library (1812) and Saint Andrew's Chapel (1823), both in Plymouth, but occasionally he designed in the Gothic style as at Saint Paul's Chapel, Stonehouse near Plymouth (1830–1831). An important part of his work were the urbane streets of stucco-faced terraced houses he designed for Plymouth.

About 1830, he took George Wightwick into partnership and retired from practice soon after. In 1838, he published *The Public Buildings erected in the West of England as designed by John Foulston F.R.I.B.A.*

FRANK JENKINS

WORKS

*1811–1813, Assembly Rooms; *1811–1813, Royal Hotel; *1811–1813, Theatre Royal; *1812, Proprietary Library; *1818–1819, The Athenaeum; Plymouth, England. 1818, Cornwall Lunatic Asylum, Bodmin, England. *1821, Princess Square, Plymouth, England. 1821–1823, Town Hall; 1823, Civil and Military Library (now the Oddfellows' Hall), Devonport, England. *1823, Saint Andrew's Chapel (later Saint Catherine's Church), Plymouth, England. *1823–1824, Mount Zion Baptist Chapel; 1824, The Column; Devonport, England. c.1825, Saint Michael's Terrace and Albemarle Villas, Stoke Damarel, near Plymouth, England. 1826, Saint Andrew's Church (alterations and refitting), Plymouth, England. *1830, Public Ballroom, Torquay, Devon, England. 1830–1831, Saint Paul's Chapel, Stonehouse near Plymouth, England.

BIBLIOGRAPHY

DAWE, J. W. 1971 "John Foulston." *Proceedings of the Plymouth Athenaeum.* 2.

FOULSTON, JOHN 1838 *The Public Buildings Erected in the West of England as Designed by John Foulston.* London: Williams.

JENKINS, FRANK 1968 "John Foulston and His Public Buildings in Plymouth, Stonehouse and Devonport." *Journal of the Society of Architectural Historians* 37:124–135.

RICHARDSON, A. E., and GILL, C. I. 1924 Pages 67–73 in *Regional Architecture of the West of England.* London: Benn.

FOWKE, FRANCIS

Captain in the Royal Engineers, Francis Fowke (1823–1865) was important for his role, as superintendent of buildings, in the development of the cultural complex at South Kensington, London, from 1856 to 1865. He was born in Ulster, trained at the Royal Military Academy, Woolwich, and in 1855 caught the eye of HENRY COLE, secretary to the Department of Science and Art, who was director of the South Kensington scheme. Fowke's buildings of brick and terra cotta, influenced by North Italian early Renaissance styles (via GOTTFRIED SEMPER) were the forerunners of the brick and terra cotta revival of the 1870s and 1880s.

BETTY ELZEA

WORKS

1856–1865, South Kensington Museum (galleries, courts, lecture theater); 1861–1862, Buildings for the International Exhibition of 1862, South Kensington; London.

BIBLIOGRAPHY

BRADFORD (ELZEA), BETTY 1962 "The Brick Palace of 1862." *Architectural Review* 8:15–21.
COLE, HENRY 1865 "Obituary." *Journal of the Society of Arts* 14:59–60.
PEVSNER, NIKOLAUS 1952 *London: Except the Cities of London and Westminster.* Harmondsworth, England: Penguin.
PHYSICK, JOHN, and DARBY, MICHAEL 1973 *Marble Halls.* London: Victoria and Albert Museum. Exhibition catalogue.

FOWLER, CHARLES

Charles Fowler (1792–1867) was born at Cullompton, Devonshire and was articled in 1807 to John Powning of Exeter. In 1818, he set up a London practice after four years as assistant to David Laing. Although he maintained links with Devonshire throughout his career, two major markets in London, Covent Garden (1828–1830) and Hungerford (1831–1833), made Fowler's reputation as a designer of this building type. His innovative approach was well demonstrated at Hungerford in the elegant cast-iron canopy and laminated tile flat roofs. He was closely involved with the formative years of the Royal Institute of British Architects and was its honorary secretary from 1836 to 1843.

JEREMY TAYLOR

WORKS

*1818–1821, Courts of Bankruptcy, London. *1818–1822, New Market, Gravesend, Kent, England. 1819–1825, Syon House (alterations), Middlesex, England. 1824?–1825, Teffont Evias Church, Wiltshire, England. 1826, Totnes Bridge, Devonshire, England. 1828–1830, Covent Garden Market, London. 1829–1830, Syon House (conservatory), Middlesex, England. 1829–1831, Saint John's Church, Oxford Square, Paddington; *1831–1833, Hungerford Market; *1835, Fishmarket Roof, Hungerford Market; London. 1835, Cornmarket, Tavistock; *1835–1837, Lower Market, Exeter; 1835–1838, Higher Market (completion), Exeter; 1835–1838, Saint Paul's Church, Honiton; 1838, Saint Mary's Church, Bickleigh; 1842–1845, County Lunatic Asylum, Exeter; Devonshire, England. 1848, Fever Hospital, Islington, London. 1848, Powderham Castle (alterations), Devonshire, England. *1852, Wax Chandlers' Hall, London.

BIBLIOGRAPHY

DONALDSON, T. L. 1867 "Memoir of the late Charles Fowler." *Royal Institute of British Architects, Sessional Papers* Nov. 4:1–15.
TAYLOR, JEREMY 1964 "Charles Fowler: Master of Markets." *Architectural Review* 135:174–182.
TAYLOR, JEREMY 1968 "Charles Fowler (1792–1867): A Centenary Memoir." *Architectural History* 11:57–74.
THORNE, ROBERT 1980 *Covent Garden Market: Its History and Restoration.* London: Architectural Press.

FRAGNER, JAROSLAV

Working mostly in Prague, Czechoslovakia, where he was born, Jaroslav Fragner (1898–1967) was in 1945 appointed professor of architecture at the Academy of Fine Arts there. In the early 1920s, he formed, together with KAREL HONZÍK, EVŽEN LINHART, and VÍT OBRTEL, the group called the Four Purists. His architectural works, especially his industrial and factory buildings from the end of the 1920s and the early 1930s, exhibit an exact and pure composition of volumes as well as noble details. After World War II, he devoted his time to the reconstruction of historical monuments, particularly the Carolinium House and the representative rooms of Prague Castle. In 1965, he was awarded the honorary title of National Artist for his life work.

VLADIMÍR ŠLAPETA

WORKS

1929, Pharmaceutical Plant, Dolní-Měcholupy, Prague. 1929–1931, Power Plant, Kolín, Czechoslovakia. 1932 Tatra (dwelling and shop house), Kelin, Czechoslovakia. 1932–1933, Morák Summer Villa, Nespeky, Czechoslovakia. 1934, Merkur (dwelling and shop house); 1946–1968, Carolinium House (reconstruction); 1954–1965, Prague Castle (reconstruction); Prague.

BIBLIOGRAPHY

Nový, Otakar 1969 *Jaroslav Fragner 1898–1967.* Prague: Union of Architects of ČSSR. Exhibition catalogue.

Kubiček, Alois, and Šlapeta, Vladimír 1967 "Jaroslav Fragner 1898–1967." *L'architecture d'aujourd'hui* 38, no.132:15.

FRANCESCO DI GIORGIO MARTINI

Francesco di Giorgio Martini (1439–1501) was a Sienese artist, architect, theorist, and engineer. In the 1480s and 1490s he was one of the best-known architects in Italy; his treatises continued to be influential throughout the sixteenth century. As a military engineer he is known as the inventor of the bastioned trace, the first effective defense against gunfire and the basis of postmedieval fortifications. As an architectural theorist he provided the first complete body of theory to meet Leon Battista Alberti's demand for a new, Renaissance architecture based on the architecture of the ancients.

Although there are no documents about his education, Francesco di Giorgio's artistic style suggests that he was trained by Lorenzo di Pietro called Il Vecchietta, the leading artist in Siena from the 1440s through the 1460s, and also an architect. Francesco di Giorgio's extensive knowledge of engineering was based on the treatises of Mariano di Jacopo called Il Taccola, who died after 1455 and who may have been one of his earliest teachers. During the pontificate of Pope Pius II (1458–1564) Francesco di Giorgio probably worked in Rome and Pienza. His lifelong studies of ancient architecture must have begun at that time.

By 1464, Francesco di Giorgio was established as an independent artist in Siena. In 1469, he began a three-year term as engineer of the Sienese water works. He continued to work as an artist and he began to receive small architectural commissions. In 1472 and 1473, he was probably in Urbino working on the ducal palace, although his activities in those years are undocumented. In 1474, he began his first complete church, in Siena, San Bernardino all'Osservanza, which has since been extensively altered. In late 1474 or early 1475, he presented to Federico da Montefeltro, Duke of Urbino, a book of drawings of machines, weapons, and castles, now in the British Museum. In its dedication Francesco di Giorgio hints that he could be a modern Vitruvius to the modern Caesar. The hints were well-received with the result that in 1476 Francesco di Giorgio moved to Urbino, taking with him his first complete treatise, probably the manuscript now in Turin. He remained in Urbino until 1489, serving as ducal architect and as one of the principal officers of the ducal court.

By his own count, Francesco di Giorgio received 136 commissions from the Dukes of Urbino, including bridges, mills, machines, and hydraulic works, as well as buildings and castles. Among his projects in Urbino were large additions to the Palazzo Ducale (1476–1482), a cathedral (1476–1494), a monastery (1476–1482), and a convent (1482–1489). Outside Urbino, in the Marches, he built two smaller ducal palaces and numerous castles. Of all these works, the only survivors are parts of the palaces in Urbino and Gubbio (1476–1482), the monastery and church of San Bernardino degli Zoccolanti (1482?–1498) in Urbino, and castles (1476?–1499?) in San Leo, Mondavio, Sassocorvaro, and Cagli. Meanwhile, he continued to work as an artist and theorist. With the help of scholars subsidized by Federico da Montefeltro, he made the earliest known translation of Vitruvius into a modern language, probably completed by 1482 and preserved in an autograph copy in the Biblioteca Nazionale in Florence. By 1489, he finished the first draft of his final treatise. A revised and illustrated copy of it was completed before 1492 and is now bound with the translation of Vitruvius in Florence.

Following the death of Duke Federico in 1482, Francesco di Giorgio began to receive commissions from other clients. In 1484, he designed his surviving masterpiece, the church of Santa Maria delle Grazie al Calcinaio in Cortona, completed largely according to his intentions except for the dome which was built after 1509. He also designed two town halls, the Palazzo degli Anziani (1484–1493) in Ancona and the Palazzo del Comune (1484–1503) in Iesi. It is possible that he worked in Rome in the 1480s and 1490s, although his presence there is not documented. Two Roman buildings, the church of San Pietro in Montorio, begun around 1480, and the Palazzo della Cancelleria, begun around 1484, display the characteristics of his style to such an extent that he should be considered among the most likely candidates for attribution, especially since he possessed appropriate social and political connections for these commissions.

In 1489, Francesco di Giorgio returned to Siena where he was appointed state architect and engineer, architect of the cathedral, and a member of the governing council. During the last decade of his life he received major commissions for works of art and he designed two churches in Siena, San Sebastiano in Valle Piatta (1493–1504) and Santo Spirito (1498–1509), both of which have been greatly altered. Santo Spirito is especially interesting since it contains one of the earliest examples of a barrel vault penetrated by lunette windows, a form which became common in the sixteenth century. Francesco di Giorgio also attempted to build a large dam across the Bruna River, but it failed catastrophically, partly because he was often absent from Siena and was unable to supervise the project.

During the 1490s, Francesco di Giorgio's services were solicited from near and far. Throughout the decade he made several trips to Urbino to continue projects begun earlier. In the summer of 1490 he was called as a consultant to Milan, Pavia, and Bologna. During this journey he worked with DONATO BRAMANTE and LEONARDO DA VINCI on the structural design of the *tiburio* of Milan Cathedral and on the design of Pavia Cathedral. In 1491, he made the first of three or four long journeys to Naples to plan and supervise construction of a new system of defenses. Among his adventures there was the successful mining of the Castel Nuovo in 1495 to drive out the French invaders who had captured it. In all of his travels Francesco di Giorgio continued to study and draw the remains of ancient buildings and art. Fragments of his sketchbooks are preserved in the collections of the Galleria degli Uffizi in Florence.

In 1501, Francesco di Giorgio retired to his farm near Siena, where he died in November of that year at age sixty-two. His reputation lasted through most of the sixteenth century. GIORGIO VASARI said of him that he had done more in his time to further the cause of good architecture than anyone since FILIPPO BRUNELLESCHI. However, by the end of the sixteenth century his name had become obscure and his treatises remained unpublished. In the nineteenth century he was recognized as an important figure in the history of military engineering, but only recently have scholars begun to understand his considerable importance as a civil architect and theorist.

Francesco di Giorgio's treatises are a mine of information about everything Renaissance architects did, or claimed they could do, from designing cities and all their buildings to the finer details of construction technology, machines, weapons, and hydraulic works. The treatises are also a unique record of the intellectual development of a Renaissance architect. In the preface to his final treatise Francesco di Giorgio said that he had begun life practicing "many low, mechanical arts." Only later did he yield to his true inclinations toward the intellectual arts of design. This assessment of his career is confirmed by a comparison of his two treatises. The first, written in 1475–1476, displays a wealth of ingenious plans for buildings, cities, and machines, but it is badly written and it contains

Francesco di Giorgio Martini. Church of Santa Maria delle Grazie al Calcinaio. Cortona, Italy. 1484–1490

many incompletely translated passages from Vitruvius. Francesco di Giorgio's final treatise (1482?–1492) is a well-written masterpiece of architectural theory in which philosophical arguments on human nature are logically related to building programs and to designs according to an explicitly Aristotelian method. During his years in Urbino, Francesco di Giorgio acquired a good liberal education from the scholars who frequented the ducal library and who had helped him translate Vitruvius.

As a practicing architect and as a theorist, Francesco di Giorgio had to deal with the problems raised by Alberti's *De re aedificatoria,* which had become widely influential during the 1450s and 1460s. He undoubtedly knew about Alberti at that time and was thereby inspired to write a treatise, but he did not read *De re aedificatoria* until 1482. The question of Alberti's influence on Francesco di Giorgio is therefore complex. These two theorists were, in effect, complementary. Alberti's purpose was to argue for a change in architectural values, but his discussion of how those values might be realized was rudimentary. Francesco di Giorgio was obliged to build for patrons whom Alberti had persuaded. He assumed Alberti's values, restated them in different terms, and concentrated upon the task of defining systematic methods for designing functionally satisfactory modern buildings in the manner of the ancients. Francesco di Giorgio based his treatise on programs for the existing building types of his own time. Insofar as he could, he stated the programs, and argued for their validity, in the terms of ancient philosophy. He then translated the programs into forms in various ways, applying rules of symmetry, ideal geometry, proportions, and ornament derived from Vitruvius and from his studies of ancient ruins. He also created his own version of the human analogy, asserting that the ancients had always based all kinds of architectural forms on the human form. This allowed him to claim the sanction of antiquity for buildings that were not and could not be ancient in form or function. He did not follow Alberti's prescriptions for musical and arithmetic proportions. Instead, Franceso di Giorgio used geometrical procedures that led more directly to the forms of buildings. He validated these procedures by appealing to Vitruvian and human proportions. The designs in Francesco di Giorgio's treatises are highly original. In some cases they anticipated ideas that would not be realized for many decades.

Because of the clarity of his arguments and the originality and practicality of his designs, Francesco di Giorgio's treatises had a large influence. Leonardo da Vinci and Bramante knew them and used them. BALDASSARE PERUZZI, probably one of Francesco di Giorgio's last pupils, carried on the theoretical tradition when he began the treatise that was finished and published by SEBASTIANO SERLIO. Serlio's treatise was based in part on the treatises of Francesco di Giorgio, although it deals with a narrower range of architectural problems and it lacks all of Francesco di Giorgio's philosophical arguments. By the 1530s, these arguments were regarded as being unnecessary since the problems they were intended to solve had long been solved. Later in the sixteenth century, Francesco di Giorgio's treatises were studied and used by Daniele Barbaro, ANDREA PALLADIO, VINCENZO SCAMOZZI, and PHILIBERT DELORME.

Francesco di Giorgio's style is characterized by clarity of planning within carefully proportioned forms. He customarily used heavy planar walls and either columns or square piers as his load-bearing elements. He used cloister vaults in his earlier churches and later preferred barrel vaults and hemispherical domes, following the example of Alberti. The dominant visual characteristics of Francesco di Giorgio's buildings are unadorned walls and vaults and strong, horizontal stringcourses which he believed would tie a building together. He used orders sparingly as supporting elements for arches and vaults or as flat pilasters at the principal division points of walls. Following Brunelleschi, he set gray architectural elements against white plaster walls. Francesco di Giorgio's other ornaments were concentrated around doors and windows. His cornices, stringcourses, and frames of doors and windows were usually simple classical moldings, while friezes, capitals, consoles, and the like were richly detailed, free interpretations of ancient Roman ornament. By the early 1480s, Francesco di Giorgio's style was being imitated in Rome, and from there it spread to other parts of Italy, as far north as Turin and as far south as Naples. After 1510 his style was gradually supplanted by the mature Roman style of Bramante.

Francesco di Giorgio's most important contemporaries in architecture were Giuliano da Sangallo (see SANGALLO FAMILY) in Florence and Bramante in Milan, but their styles before 1500 had only local and limited influence. Francesco di Giorgio's style was the first Renaissance architectural style to be used in many parts of Italy. More than any other architect of his time, he realized Alberti's dream for a universal architecture in the manner of the ancients.

RICHARD J. BETTS

WORKS

1474–1484, Church of San Bernardino all'Osservanza, Siena, Italy. 1476–1482, Palazzo Ducale (additions), Gubbio, Italy. 1476–1482, Palazzo Ducale (Piazza del Duca Federico [façade], Giardino Pensile, Terazzo and Loggia del Gallo, Cortile del Pasquino, Stables, Studiolo of Federico da Montefeltro); 1476?–1482, Monastery of San Bernardino degli Zoccolanti; *1476–1494, Cathedral; Urbino, Italy. 1476?–1499?, Castle of San Leo; Castle of Mondavio; Castle of Sassocorvaro; Castle of Cagli; Italy. *1482?–1489, Convent of Santa Chiara; 1482?–1498, Church of San Bernardino degli Zoccolanti; Urbino, Italy. 1484–1490, Church of Santa Maria delle Grazie al Calcinaio Cortona, Italy. *1484–1493, Palazzo degli Anziani, Ancona, Italy. 1484–1503, Palazzo del Comune, Iesi, Italy. *1492–1497, Castel Nuovo, Naples. 1493–1501, Church of San Sebastiano in Valle Piata (not completed until 1504); 1498–1501, Church of Santo Spirito (not completed until 1509). Siena, Italy.

BIBLIOGRAPHY

Fragments of Francesco di Giorgio Martini's sketchbooks (1460s–1490s) are in the Galleria degli Uffizi, Florence.

BETTS, RICHARD J. 1977 "On the Chronology of Francesco di Giorgio's Treatises: New Evidence from an Unpublished Manuscript." *Journal of the Society of Architectural Historians* 36:3–14.

BURNS, HOWARD 1974 · "Progetti di Francesco di

Giorgio per i conventi di San Bernardino e Santa Chiara di Urbino." Pages 293–311 in *Studi Bramanteschi*. Rome: De Luca Editore.

DE LA CROIX, HORST 1960 "Military Architecture and the Radial City Plan in Sixteenth Century Italy." *Art Bulletin* 42:263–290.

DEZZI-BARDESCHI, MARCO 1968 "Le rocche di Francesco di Giorgio nel Ducato di Urbino." *Castellum* 8:97–140.

FIORE, FRANCESCO PAOLO 1978 *Città e macchine del '400 nei disegni di Francesco di Giorgio Martini*. Florence: Olschki.

FRANCESCO DI GIORGIO MARTINI 1474–1475 "Book of Machines and Castles." Unpublished manuscript. Available in the Department of Prints and Drawings, British Museum, London.

FRANCESCO DI GIORGIO MARTINI 1475–1476 *Trattato di architettura, ingegneria ed arte militare*. Unpublished manuscript available in Biblioteca Reale, Turin, Italy.

FRANCESCO DI GIORGIO MARTINI 1476?–1482? "Translation of Vitruvius." Unpublished manuscript. Available in the Biblioteca Nazionale Centrale, Florence.

FRANCESCO DI GIORGIO MARTINI 1482?–1492 "Trattato di architettura, ingegneria ed arte militare." Unpublished manuscript. Available in the Biblioteca Nazionale Centrale, Florence.

FRANCESCO DI GIORGIO MARTINI 1967 *Trattato di architettura, ingegneria ed arte militare*. Edited by Corrado Maltese. Milan: Edizioni Il Polifilo.

HERSEY, GEORGE L. 1969 *Alfonso II and the Artistic Renewal of Naples: 1485–1495*. New Haven: Yale University Press.

MILLON, HENRY A. 1958 "The Architectural Theory of Francesco di Giorgio." *Art Bulletin* 40:257–261.

PAPINI, ROBERTO 1946 *Francesco di Giorgio: Architetto*. Florence: Electa Editrice.

RETI, LADISLAO 1963 "Francesco di Giorgio Martini's Treatise on Engineering and its Plagiarists." *Technology and Culture* 4:287–298.

ROTONDI, PASQUALE 1970 *Francesco di Giorgio nel Palazzo Ducale di Urbino*. Milan: Provinciali Spotorno.

SCAGLIA, GUSTINA and PRAGER, FRANK D. 1972 *Mariano Taccola and His Book "De Ingeneis."* Cambridge, Mass.: M.I.T. Press.

WELLER, ALLEN S. 1943 *Francesco di Giorgio: 1439–1501*. University of Chicago Press.

FRANCIONE

Francione (1428–1495) was a cabinetmaker and a civil and military architect who took part in the rebuilding of Rome upon the return of the papacy. Giuliano da Sangallo (see SANGALLO FAMILY) worked under him in Rome from 1467–1472 and again in the 1480s building fortifications near Florence. In 1488, Francione was elected engineer of the Florentine Republic along with Francesco d'Angelo.

HOWARD SHUBERT

BIBLIOGRAPHY

HEYDENREICH, LUDWIG H., and LOTZ, WOLFGANG 1974 *Architecture in Italy 1400–1600*. Translated by Mary Hottinger. Harmondsworth, England, and Baltimore: Penguin.

FRANCKE, PAUL

Paul Francke (c.1538–1615), born in Weimar, Germany, became the leading architect in the duchy of Brunswick-Wolfenbüttel and one of the most important north German architects of the late Renaissance. His fame rests chiefly on two works for Duke Julius of Wolfenbüttel, the Juleum (University) at Helmstedt (1592–1597) and the medievalizing hall church of Beatae Mariae Virginis at Wolfenbüttel (1604–1615), one of the first Protestant churches.

ALISON LUCHS

WORKS

1574–1575, Fortress (expansion), Wolfenbüttel, Germany. 1592–1597, Juleum (University), Helmstedt, Germany. 1604–1615, Church of Beatae Mariae Virginis (not completed until 1626); (A)n.d., Arsenal; Wolfenbüttel, Germany. n.d., Church, Hornburg, Germany.

BIBLIOGRAPHY

APPUHN, HORST 1970 "Die Marienkirche in Wolfenbüttel: Zu ihrem ikonographischen Programm." *Niederdeutsche Beiträge zur Kunstgeschichte* 9:137–142.

FINK, AUGUST, and APPUHN, HORST 1965 *Die Marienkirche . . . in Wolfenbüttel*. 4th ed. Wolfenbüttel, Germany: Landeskirchenamt.

GRUNSKY, E. 1973 "Die evangelische Hauptkirche Beatae Mariae Virginis in Wolfenbüttel: Bemerkungen zum ikonographischen Programm." *Niederdeutsche Beiträge zur Kunstgeschichte* 12:204–228.

HEMPEL, EBERHARD 1965–1977 *Baroque Art and Architecture in Central Europe*. 2d ed., rev. Baltimore: Penguin.

FRANCQUART, JACQUES

Nourished by the baroque style of his native Brabant (now Belgium), Jacques Francquart (1582?–1651) appeared as one of the great proponents of Italian art, along with his brother-in-law WENZEL COBERGHER. He trained in Rome until 1613 and was later appointed engineer to the king (1621) in Brussels and ennobled. Throughout his multifaceted career—architect, landscape gardener, theoretician, designer—he elaborated the principles of a well-conceived style, combining Roman plasticity with the ornamental dynamism characteristic of the art of Brabant of the seventeenth century. He is the author of the first treatise (1616) on this hybrid style known as the Italo-Flemish.

PIERRE LENAIN
*Translated from French by
Shara Wasserman*

WORKS

*1615–1621, Church of the Jesuits; *1615–1648, Church of the Augustins (façade transferred to the Church of the Trinity); Brussels. 1628–1638, Church of the Great Beguinage (completed by LUCAS FAYDHERBE), Malines, Belgium.

BIBLIOGRAPHY

ACKERE, JULES EMILE VAN 1972 *Baroque and Classic Art in Belgium.* Brussels: Vokaer.
FRANCQUART, JACQUES 1616 *Premier Livre d'Architecture.* Brussels: Antoine.
FRANCQUART, JACQUES 1622 *Cent Tablettes et Ecussons d'Armes.* Brussels.
FRANCQUART, JACQUES 1626 *Portraits des Hommes illustres de l'Ordre de Saint Augustin.* Antwerp, Belgium.
PARENT, PAUL 1926 *L'Architecture des Pays-Bas meridionaux aux XVIᵉ, XVIIᵉ, XVIIIᵉ siècles.* Paris: Van Oest.
SCHOY, AUGUSTE 1879 *Histoire de l'influence italienne dans les Pays-Bas.* Brussels and Antwerp, Belgium: Hayez.

FRANK, JOSEF

Josef Frank (1885–1967) was born in Baden, Austria, and received his education at the Technical University in Vienna. Frank's primary architectural activity was residential design and his first private houses (villas) were designed in collaboration with Oskar Strnad and Oskar Wlach in 1913 and 1914 in a highly modern style. The single family was the central concern for Frank throughout his lifetime.

Frank taught building construction at the Kunstgewerbeschule in Vienna (1919–1925) and in 1925, founded with Wlach, a shop in Vienna named "House and Garden." Through this interior decorating firm, he produced and sold high quality furnishings for his commissions, developing a furnishing style of great popularity in Vienna. Arts and crafts was one of Frank's strongest interests.

In 1927, he was invited by the German Werkbund to contribute to its Stuttgart Exhibition, the famous Weissenhofsiedlung. The general director was LUDWIG MIES VAN DER ROHE and Frank was in excellent international company among the architects selected, LE CORBUSIER and WALTER GROPIUS among them. He represented his country at the first meeting of the International Congress for Modern Architecture (CIAM) in 1928 at La Sarraz, Switzerland, and played a leading role in the Austrian Werkbund, counterpart of the German organization. In 1929, Frank supervised the Austrian Werkbund Exhibition in Vienna, selecting the best of the Viennese architects. During this time, dissension in the organization developed and a split occurred, resulting in the emergence of the "Neuer Werkbund" under the leadership of JOSEF HOFFMANN. A combination of this controversy and the worsening political climate led Frank to emigrate to Sweden in 1934. There he worked for "Svenst Tenn," a furnishing design shop in Stockholm, designing textiles, furnishings, and objects of fine quality that became recognizable as part of the national Swedish style of design.

After the disheartening experience with the Austrian Werkbund, Frank's architectural production lessened considerably, although his influential design work in Sweden attested to his continued dedication to Arts and Crafts. In addition, he lectured at universities in Europe and the United States, stressing his uncompromising philosophy that modern architecture developed out of the "home."

JO ANNE PASCHALL

WORKS

1920, Workers Settlement, Pernitz, Austria. c.1926, Residence, Salzburg, Austria. c.1927, A. R. G. Residence, Pasadena, Calif. 1927, Weissenhofsiedlung; German Werkbund Exhibition, Stuttgart, Germany. 1929–1932, Austrian Werkbund Exhibition, Vienna, Austria. 1930, Country Home, Los Angeles. 1937, Cläeson House, Falsterbo, Sweden.

BIBLIOGRAPHY

ACHLEITNER, FRIEDRICH 1980 "Viennese Architecture Between the Wars: First Split Between Form and Content of Modernity." *Lotus International* 29:117–127.
CZECH, HERMANN 1980 "Joseph Frank: The Accidental House. The Thirteen Designs in Letters to Dagmar Grill." *Lotus International* 29:109–110.
FRANK, JOSEF 1931 *Architektur als Symbol: Elemente deutschen neuen Bauens.* Vienna: Schroll.
FRANK, JOSEF (editor) 1932 *Werkbundsiedlung: Internationale Ausstellung. 1932.* Vienna: Schroll.
HOCHSCHULE FÜR ANGEWANDTE KUNST WIEN 1981 *Josef Frank: 1885–1967.* Vienna: Löcker. Exhibition catalogue.
"Un ricordo di Josef Frank." 1967 *Domus* 449, Apr.:6.
SPALT, JOHANNES 1980 "The Form of Dwelling: Drawings of Josef Frank before 1934." *Lotus International* 29:111–116.

FRANQUE, FRANÇOIS

A French architect born in Avignon, François Franque (1710–c.1792) was trained by his father, JEAN BAPTISTE FRANQUE, before moving to Paris in the early 1750s. In time, he became general controller for the buildings of the Invalides, architect to the king, and a member of the Royal Academy of Architecture. His most significant designs were for religious buildings: the Logis Abbatial at the Saint Bénoit-sur-Loire monastery (1746), the Church at Port Royal Abbey (1760s; started by PIERRE CONTANT D'IVRY), and Notre Dame in Soisson (1740). The Seminary in Bourges (1780s) and his project for a residential rental building are typical of the neoclassicism of the period and were highly praised by JEAN FRANÇOIS BLONDEL in his *Cours d'Architecture.* In 1765, Franque redesigned the Peyrou Promenade in Montpellier using earlier proposals, and in 1793 he coordinated a master plan for the city of Marseille.

MARC DILET

WORKS

1740, Notre-Dame, Soisson, France. 1740, Seminary (main entrance), Bourges, France. 1746, Logis Abbatial, Saint Benoit-sur-Loire, France. 1750s, Grand Hospital, Avignon, France. 1750s, Maison de Voyer d'Argenson (entrance gate), Neuilly, France. 1750s, Maison Rue du Coq Saint Honere, Paris. 1760s, Church, Port Royal Abbey, France. 1770, Logis Abbatial de Premontres, Villers-Cotterets, France. 1770, Rental Building Celestins, Paris.

BIBLIOGRAPHY

FRANQUE, FRANÇOIS 1773 "Eloge de J. F. Blondel." *Journal des Beaux Arts et des Sciences.*

FRANQUE, JEAN-BAPTISTE

A French architect of the eighteenth century, Jean-Baptiste Franque (1683–1758) was born in 1683 in Villeneuve-les-Avignon and established a lifetime practice in Avignon, where his social and professional position brought him clients from the nobility of the Comtat and the whole southeast of France.

Franque was knowledgeable in the science of masonry construction which he applied in original ways to vaults and suspended stairs. He participated in the improvements made to the Pope's Petit Palais in Avignon, including the design of a remarkable stairway. In both his private and his public architectural realizations, his trademark was his vigorous and picturesque ornamentation, especially for private *hôtels.* Franque was in charge of the reconstruction of the Abbey of Montmajour near Arles, which burned in 1730 and for which he followed the original drawings of Pierre Mignard. After the flood of the Rhône in 1755, he oversaw the restoration of a number of houses in Avignon and made a proposal for a new bridge.

MARC DILET

WORKS

1708, Church of the Grand Seminaire Saint Charles; 1708, Hôtel Salvador; 1708, Petit Palais (stairway); 1708, Rue Sextier (façade); Avignon, France. 1730, Abbey of Montmajour (reconstruction), near Arles, France. 1741, Hôtel de Cambis (façade); 1741, Hôtel de Forbin (stairway); 1741, Hôtel de Villeneuve; 1754, Hôtel de Caumont; Avignon, France.

FRANZEN, ULRICH

Born in Germany, Ulrich Franzen (1921–) emigrated to the United States in 1936 and was educated at Williams College and Harvard University. Throughout his thirty years of practice, first in the offices of I. M. PEI (1950–1955) and then in his own firm, Ulrich Franzen and Associates, Franzen can best be described as an architect with a commitment to context and to the use of powerful forms. At first glance, what might appear to be a disparate grouping of elements and shapes becomes, under Franzen's careful architectural orchestration, a synthesis of materials and programs that come together in a unified whole to provide the user with a finely tuned machine for living or working. This concern for context can be seen in many of Franzen's educational buildings, including the Agronomy Building at Cornell University (1966–1969), Ithaca, New York; Residence (1966–1969) and Dining Halls (1969–1970), University of New Hampshire, Durham; the Harlem School of the Arts (1974–1979), New York, and the Hunter College buildings (1975–1982), New York.

Since 1958, Franzen has enjoyed a continuing relationship with the Phillip Morris Corporation and has designed their Research Center (1959–1961), Operations Center (1963–1966), and the Research Center II (1969–1971), Richmond, Virginia. Currently under construction is the Philip Morris Headquarters Building (1972–1982), New York.

Franzen has also designed a number of residences in the suburban New York City area including two for himself, one in Rye, New York (1955–1956), and one in Bridgehampton, New York (1977–1978).

JANE CAROLAN

WORKS

1955–1956, Ulrich Franzen Residence, Rye, N.Y. 1959–1961, Research Center; 1963–1966, Operations Center; Phillip Morris Corporation, Richmond, Va. 1966–1968, Agronomy Building, Cornell University, Ithaca, N.Y. 1966–1969, Residence Hall; 1969–1970, Dining Halls; University of New Hampshire, Durham, N.H. 1969–1971, Research Center II, Phillip Morris Corporation, Richmond, Va. 1972–1982, Phillip Morris Corporate Headquarters; 1974–1979, Harlem School of the Arts; 1975–1982, Hunter College Buildings; New York. 1977–1978, Ulrich Franzen Residence, Bridgehampton, N.Y. 1978–1980, Boyce Thompson Institute for Plant Research, Cornell University, Ithaca, N.Y.

BIBLIOGRAPHY

"Franzen: Four Current Projects." 1971 *Architectural Record* 150, July:107–116.
"Franzen High-rise Slated for Fifth Avenue." 1976 *Architectural Record* 159, June:39.
"Franzen Residence." 1979 *Architectural Record* 165, May:54–57.
"The Harlem School of the Arts." 1979 *Architectural Record* 165, May:97–104.
Hoyt, Charles 1975 "Ulrich Franzen: Changing Design Solutions for a Changing Era." *Architectural Record* 158, Sept.:81–88.
Nairn, Janet 1980 "Machine for Scientific Research Balances Internal Functions and External Esthetics." *Architectural Record* 168, Aug.:80–85.
"A Non-box for the Elderly." 1973 *Progressive Architecture* 54, May:72–75.
"Paraphernalia." 1969 *Progressive Architecture* 50, Apr.:118–121.
Ryder, Sharon Lee 1974 "Bravado with Brick." *Progressive Architecture* 55, Sept.:76–77.
"The Search for Appropriate Form." 1966 *Architectural Record* 139, May:127–140.
Smith, Herbert L., Jr. 1969 "Franzen Unifies an Architecture of Fragments into Good Places for People." *Architectural Record* 145, Feb.:113–132.
Stephens, Suzanne 1979 "Corporate Form-givers." *Progressive Architecture* 60, July:55–59.

FRAZEE, JOHN

John Frazee (1790–1852) was apprenticed at age seventeen to William Lawrence, a bricklayer and mason in New Jersey. In 1810, he worked as a stonecarver on the New Brunswick Bank in New Brunswick, New Jersey, with Ward Baldwin, and as a stonecutter on the City Hall for New York City. In 1818, he opened a marble shop in New York City with his brother William to carve mantles, tombstones, and church memorials. He carved many busts of public figures such as John Jay, Daniel Webster, and Andrew Jackson. Frazee's major work is the U.S. Custom House (now Federal Hall National Memorial) in New York City (1834–

1842). As supervising architect, he supplied working drawings and detailing for designs of Ithiel Town, Alexander Jackson Davis, and William Ross.

Donald Martin Reynolds

BIBLIOGRAPHY

"Autobiography of Frazee, the Sculptor." 1835 *North American Quarterly Magazine* 5, Apr.; 6, July.
Brown, Milton W. 1977 *American Art to 1900.* New York: Abrams.
Dunlap, William (1834)1969 *History of the Rise and Progress of the Arts of Design in the United States.* New York:Dover.
Larkin, Oliver 1949 "Early American Sculpture: A Craft Becomes an Art." *Antiques* 56, no. 3:176–178.
Taft, Lorado (1903)1924 *The History of American Sculpture.* Rev. ed. New York: Macmillan.
Tuckerman, Henry Theodore (1867)1967 *Book of the Artists.* Reprint. New York: Carr.

FREEDLANDER, JOSEPH HENRY

Born in New York City, Joseph Henry Freedlander (1870–1943) graduated from the Massachusetts Institute of Technology in 1889. After receiving his *diplôme* from the Ecole des Beaux-Arts in Paris in 1895, he returned to New York. He was a successful entrant to many competitions. He won commissions for the St. Louis Club House (1897), St. Louis, Missouri; the National Home for Disabled Volunteer Soldiers (1904), Tennessee; the Portland, Oregon, Auditorium (1911); and the Museum of the City of New York (1928).

Steven McLeod Bedford

WORKS

1897, St. Louis Club House, Mo. 1904, National Home for Disabled Volunteer Soldiers, Johnson City, Tenn. 1911, Auditorium, Portland, Ore. 1912, Perry Memorial, Put-in-Bay, Ohio. 1928, Museum of the City of New York. 1929, The Spa, Saratoga, New York. 1934, Bronx County Courthouse, New York.

BIBLIOGRAPHY

Bedford, Steven, and Nevins, Deborah 1980 *Between Tradition and Modernism.* New York: National Academy of Design.

FREYSSINET, EUGENE

Eugène Freyssinet (1879–1962) was born in the town of Objat near Perigueux, France. When he was six years old, his family moved to Paris, a city he did not like; he preferred the artisan world of his ancestors whose extreme concern for "the simplification of forms and economy of means" always appealed to him.

He entered the Ecole Polytechnique in 1899 and after graduating was accepted at the Ecole des Ponts et Chaussées where for the first time his artisan love of building coincided with that of his teachers. It was there, during the lectures of Charles Rabut in 1903–1904 that the idea of prestressing first came to him.

On July 1, 1905, he began his career as an engineer for local roads at Moulins, where between 1906 and 1913 he designed and often directly supervised the construction of numerous small bridges of reinforced concrete along with three major works: the 50 meter test arch with a prestressed tie (1907–1908) at Moulins, and the two three-hinged trussed arch bridges with spans of 68, 72.5, and 68 meters, one at Le Veurdre, designed in 1907 and completed in 1910, and one at Boutiron, completed in 1912. Each was fitted at midspan with horizontal jacks which raised the arches for decentering and prevented concrete creep from causing excessive downward deflections in the flat arch structures. These Freyssinet jacks have been widely used since then and they laid the essential basis for prestressing.

In 1914, Freyssinet left the highway department and joined the building firm of C. Limousin where, from 1914 to 1929, he designed and built a series of spectacular works which gained him international fame. First came the 96.25 meter span, two-ribbed arch bridge at Villeneuve-sur-Lot, begun in 1914 but not completed until 1919. The hingeless concrete arch supports an arcaded viaduct faced in brick. During World War I, he designed a number of industrial structures with barrel-shell-like roofs, and between 1921 and 1923 he built two immense parabolic-arched dirigible hangars at Orly with spans of 86 meters and a clear height of 50 meters at midspan. The arches were thin hollow sections connected laterally by thin slabs giving a corrugated over-all appearance.

In 1921, he completed the 64 meter span, two-hinged arch railroad bridge over the Sambre, the Candelier Bridge, in which he introduced concrete hinges at the supports and in which he jacked apart the arch at the crown to lift it off the centering.

In 1919, he won the competition for the crossing of the River Seine at Saint-Pierre du Vauvray. The 131.8 meter span hollow arches, completed in 1923, were the longest spanning concrete arches in the world. They rose 25 meters at midspan, and the deck was suspended below. Destroyed in 1940, it was rebuilt in 1946 in the same form. In 1926, he built a small suspension bridge at Laon, and in 1927 he completed the conoidal thin-shell-roof

sheds for railway repair shops at Bagneux.

Between 1924 and 1928, Freyssinet worked on his largest arch bridge, the three-span crossing of the Elorn estuary near Brest by the town of Plougastel. Completed in 1930 each arch is a hollow box, 180 meters in span, 27.5 meters in rise with a midspan section 4.5 meters high and 9.5 meters wide. Because of the great scale, he studied in detail the creep of concrete, out of which directly came his idea for prestressing that he patented on 2 October 1928 with his friend J. C. Seailles. In 1929, he left Limousin and set up a business at Montargis to produce factory-made prestressed concrete electrification poles. The business did not succeed but Freyssinet was able to demonstrate the potential for prestressing by saving the sinking Marine terminal at Le Havre in 1935. That year he joined the building firm of Campenon-Bernard where he designed and built numerous prestressed structures before, during, and after World War II.

His major prestressing works after 1945 were the 1946 Marne River Bridge of 55 meters span at Luzancy begun in 1941, five other Marne bridges completed between 1947 and 1951, three 150 meter span arch bridges near Caracas, Venezuela, between 1951 and 1953, the Basilica at Lourdes of 1956–1958, the Orly Bridge of 1958 and the Saint-Michel Bridge in Toulouse completed in 1962 just three months before Freyssinet's death.

Freyssinet's work has three fundamental bases: a directing idea about concrete as a material, an inventiveness in construction, and a sense of form.

All of Freyssinet's major new ideas sprang from his clear understanding of the creep behavior of concrete under high compression. To overcome this as well as to ease construction in his early arch bridges, he introduced jacks at the crown. This introduction of artificial forces to correct creep led directly to his basic idea of prestressing, a process in which high-strength steel, stressed to high initial tensions against high quality concrete, could for the first time make prestressing practical. In earlier efforts by others, low-strength steel lost most of its prestress because of concrete creep.

Before 1914, he invented a flat jack for arch decentering, in 1921 he invented the Freyssinet hinge of concrete, and in 1939 he designed the conical wedge anchorage for prestressing. His novel construction technique for Plougastel consisted of floating the completed arch scaffold into place for concrete casting. Thus, his major ideas sprang from the inseparable connection in his mind between design and construction.

Freyssinet created a series of forms that rank him among the greatest structural artists in history. Especially striking are his flat trussed arches before 1914, his thin-arched industrial roofs, the profiles of his record long-span arches of the 1920s, the thin-girder Marne bridges of 1946–1951, and the unique forms of his Orly and Toulouse bridges at the end of his life. All of these forms came from his intensive studies of concrete and of competitive construction. He set the forms himself without collaboration with architects or other designers.

DAVID P. BILLINGTON

WORKS

1910, Allier River Bridge, Le Veurdre, France. 1912, Allier River Bridge, Boutiron, France. 1914–1918, Industrial Roofs, France. 1919, Arch Roof Hangars, Villacoublay, France. 1919, Allier River Bridge, Chatel-de-Neuvre, France. 1919, Garonne River Bridge, Tonneins, France. 1919, Slab Roofs, Saint-Etienne, France. 1921, Sambre River Bridge, Erquelines (Candelier), France. 1921, Two Hangars, Orly, France. 1923, Seine River Bridge, Saint-Pierre-du-Vauvray, France. 1924, Two Hangars, Villacoublay, France. 1926, Railway Bridge, Laon, France. 1927, Railway Repair Shops (roof sheds), Bagneux, France. 1930, Elorn River Bridge, Plougastel, France. 1930, Railway Station, Reims, France. 1942–1949, Eleven Roadway Bridges, France. 1946, Marne River Bridge, Luzancy, France. 1947–1951, Five Bridges over Marne River, Annet; Trilbardon; Esbly; Ussy; Changis-Saint-Jean; France. 1951–1953, Three Bridges, La Guaira-Caracas Highway, Venezuela. 1958, Airport Highway Bridge, Orley, France. 1958, Saint Pius (basilica; with Pierre Vajo), Lourdes, France. 1962, Saint-Michel Bridge, Toulouse, France.

BIBLIOGRAPHY

BADOVICI, JEAN 1931 "E. Freyssinet." *L'Architecture Vivante* Spring–Summer:5–7.

BILLINGTON, DAVID P. 1976 "Historical Perspective on Prestressed Concrete." *Journal of the Prestressed Concrete Institute* 21, no. 5:48–71.

FREYSSINET, EUGÈNE 1921 "Le pont de Villeneuve-sur-Lot." *Génie Civil* 79, July 30:98–102, Aug. 6:124–128, Aug. 13:146–150.

FREYSSINET, EUGÈNE 1923a "Les Hangars à dirigeables en ciment armé en construction à l'aéroport de Villeneuve-Orly." *Génie Civil* 83, Sept. 22:265–273, Sept. 29:291–297, Oct. 6:313–319.

FREYSSINET, EUGÈNE 1923b "Le Pont Candelier." *Annales des Ponts et Chaussées* no. 2:165–197.

FREYSSINET, EUGÈNE 1928 "L'Amélioration des Constructions en béton armé." *Génie Civil* 93, Sept. 15:254–257.

FREYSSINET, EUGÈNE 1930 "Les Ponts en béton armé de très grande portée." *Mémoires et compte rendu des travaux de la Société des Ingénieurs Civiles de France.* 83, July–Aug.:622–658.

FREYSSINET, EUGÈNE (1933)1966 "New Ideas and Methods." *Travaux* April–May:607–622.

FREYSSINET, EUGÈNE 1935 "Une Révolution dans les Techniques du béton." *Mémoires et compte rendu des travaux de la Société des Ingénieurs Civiles de France.* 88, Sept.–Oct.:643–674.

FREYSSINET, EUGÈNE 1949 "A General Introduction to the Idea of Prestressing." *Travaux* April–May:19–49.

FREYSSINET, EUGÈNE 1954 "Naissance du Béton preconstraint et vues d'avenir." *Travaux* June:463–474.

GEMENY, ALBIN L. 1929 "The Freyssinet Method of Concrete–Arch Construction." *Public Roads* 10, Oct.:148–150.

GIEDION, SIGFRIED 1929 "Lumière et Construction: Reflexions à propos des ateliers de chemins de fer de Freyssinet." *Cahiers d'Art* 4, no. 6:275–284.

"A Half Century of French Prestressing Technology." 1966 *Travaux* April–May:entire issue.

ORDONEZ-FERNANDEZ, JOSÉ A. 1978 *Eugene Freyssinet.* Madrid: Xarait.

FREZIER, AMEDEE FRANÇOIS

Born in Chambéry, of Scottish descent, Amédée François Frézier (1682–1773) studied theology and mathematics in Paris with Philippe de Lahire and Pierre Varignon and traveled then to Italy. In 1707 he joined the Ingénieurs du Roi, for which he worked until he retired in 1764. He was posted first to Saint Malo in Brittany then, from 1711 to 1714, to South America, where he was to assess the strength of Spanish fortifications. In 1719 he was sent to Santo Domingo to build fortifications and lay out the town of Saint Louis, returning to France in 1727. He was for a short time in Phalsbourg then, as Ingénieur en chef, in Landau, where he spent ten years. In 1740 he became Directeur des fortifications in Brittany, established at Brest. His impact on architecture was made as the critic and opponent of JEAN-LOUIS DE CORDEMOY and his successors such as H. Leblanc, MARC ANTOINE LAUGIER, and JACQUES GERMAIN SOUFFLOT, all of whom upheld a theory of architecture relating to lightness of construction based on the model of Gothic architecture.

R. D. MIDDLETON

WORKS

1732–1737, Military Hospital, Landau, Germany. *1742–1758, Saint Louis (high altar and baldachin), Brest; 1755, Notre Dame, Lesneven; Brittany, France.

BIBLIOGRAPHY

COLOMBIER, PIERRE DU 1954 "Amédée François Frézier; Ingénieur Ordinaire en Chef du Roy à Landau." Pages 159–166 in Karl Schwingel (editor), *Festschrift für Karl Lohmeyer.* Saarbrücken, Germany: West Ost Verlag.

DALISSOT DE MONTENOY, CHARLES 1775 "Eloge historique de M. Frézier." Pages 143–159 in *La nécrologie des hommes célèbres de France.* Paris: Desprez.

FRÉZIER, AMÉDÉE FRANÇOIS (1706)1747 *Traité des*

feux d'artifice pour le spectacle. 2d ed, rev. Paris: Quai des Augustins.

FRÉZIER, AMÉDÉE FRANÇOIS 1716 *Relation du voyage de la mer du sud, aux côtes du Chily et du Pérou fait pendant les années 1712, 1713 et 1714.* Paris: Nyon.

FRÉZIER, AMÉDÉE FRANÇOIS 1737–1739 *La théorie et la pratique de la coupe pierres et des bois pour la construction des voûtes . . . ou, Traité de stéréotomie, à l'usage de l'architecture.* 3 vols. Strasbourg, France: Doullsseker. The above title was published in a revised and simplified edition as *Elémens de Stéréotomie, à l'usage de l'architecture, pour la coupe des pierres.* 2 vols. Paris: Jombert, 1759–1760.

FRÉZIER, AMÉDÉE FRANÇOIS 1738 *Dissertation sur les ordres d'architecture.* Strasbourg, France: Doullsseker.

HOEFER, JOHANN CHRISTIAN FERDINAND (editor) 1857 Volume 18, pages 859–865 in *Nouvelle biographie générale.* Paris: Firmin-Didot.

MIDDLETON, ROBIN DAVID 1962–1963 "The Abbé de Cordemoy and the Graeco-Gothic Ideal: A Prelude to Romantic Classicism." *Journal of the Warburg and Courtauld Institutes* 25:278–320, 26:90–123.

FRIEDMAN, YONA

Born in Budapest, Yona Friedman (1923–) was educated at the Budapest Institute of Technology and at the Technological Institute in Haifa, Israel, at which he later taught. He has worked in Paris since 1957. Friedman, who is more involved with architectural theory than with actual building (supporting his theoretical pursuits by his accomplishments in the sphere of film animation), is perhaps the best known of the French group of megastructuralists—the "Urban Spatialists"—to have emerged in the 1960s.

Following the Tenth Congrès International d'Architecture Moderne in 1956 and in response to the changed state of architecture and urbanism in the contemporary, highly mobile world, Friedman, PAUL MAYMONT, FREI OTTO, ECKHARD SCHULTZE-FIELITZ, Werner Ruhnau, and D. G. Emmerich in 1957 founded the Groupe d'Etude d'Architecture Mobile (GEAM, presently Groupe International d'Architecture Prospective or GIAP). According to GEAM, the world is in a state of crisis proceeding from a disjunction between the existing social order based on stability and permanence and the necessity for a social order responding to accelerated technological and scientific discovery and increased population growth. This crisis is reflected in architecture: Friedman contends that in preserving the concept of the static city and thereby reinforcing the idea of architect as artificer, architects have effectively negated mobility as a means by which architecture might adjust to changes in technology. For Friedman,

"mobility" entails functional planning, transportability, flexibility.

Friedman's spatial cities—so named because a third, vertical dimension added to the usual two of the surface plan creates a three-dimensional planning grid and multiplies the original usable surface area—contact the earth's surface only minimally. The infrastructure (a concept developed between 1957 and 1962) is completely separate from but supports a number of individualized living units. The space-defining elements are mobile and therefore can be manipulated by the individual. Between 1962 and 1963, Friedman explored the combinatory possibilities of this flexibility, and his first projects were published in the 1960s in Japan with the encouragement of KENZO TANGE. After 1966, he began to present his ideas to architects and finally to laymen by means of "manuals" in which he used cartoons for explanations. United Nations agencies distributed the manuals (1972) in numerous countries. The CDC Project (Ivry, France, 1976) represented Friedman's first real opportunity to test the possibility of mobile architecture. Unfortunately, the building, which had been conceived by the future users in accordance with the principles outlined in Friedman's manuals, was not executed.

Central to Friedman's theories, which he articulated in *L'Architecture Mobile* (1970), *Pour une Architecture Scientifique* (1971), *Où va l'Architecture* (1973), and in numerous journal articles, is the idea that the individual must assume responsibility for determining his own environment. Friedman has designed almost identical systems constituted of space frames supported on pilotis for Paris, London, Tunis, and New York.

SUSAN STRAUSS

WORKS

1953–1958, Cylindrical Shelters. 1958–1959, Spatial City (including spatial cities for Tunis and Paris). 1963, Bridge, English Channel. 1964, Business Center, Gare Saint Lazarre, Paris. 1976, CDC Headquarters, Ivry, France.

BIBLIOGRAPHY

"Aventure de la cité future." 1966 *Urbanisme: Revue français* 35, no. 92:12–81.

FRIEDMAN, YONA 1964a "Patterns of Town Planning." *Arts and Architecture* 81:30–31.

FRIEDMAN, YONA 1964b "La théorie des systèmes compréhensibles et son application à l'urbanisme." *L'Architecture d'Aujourd'hui* 34, no. 115:28–29.

FRIEDMAN, YONA 1966 "Teoria generale della mobilità." *Casabella* 30, no. 305:10–15; no. 306:10–13.

FRIEDMAN, YONA 1967 "A Research Programme for a Scientific Method of Planning." *Architectural Design* 37, no. 7:379–381.

FRIEDMAN, YONA 1968a "La Città come Meccanismo." *Casabella* 32, no. 326:14–25.

FRIEDMAN, YONA 1968*b* "Recherche d'une méthode." *Techniques et Architecture* 29, no. 2:76–82.

FRIEDMAN, YONA 1968*c* "Méthode des Mécanismes Urbains: Exemples." *Techniques et Architecture* 29, no. 4:70–71.

FRIEDMAN, YONA 1968*d* "Towards a Coherent System of Planning." *Architects' Yearbook* 12:53–63.

FRIEDMAN, YONA 1970 "Vers la démocratisation de l'environnement (ou comment sortir d'une impasse)." *Techniques et Architecture* 32, no. 3:82–87.

FRIEDMAN, YONA 1971*a* "The Flatwriter: Choice by Computer." *Progressive Architecture* 52:98–101.

FRIEDMAN, YONA 1971*b* "Individual Expression: Its Role and Its Possibilities in the Architecture of the Future." *Architecture, Formes et Fonctions* 16:77–80.

FRIEDMAN, YONA (1971*c*)1975 *Towards a Scientific Architecture.* Translated by Cynthia Lang. Cambridge, Mass.: M.I.T. Press.

HILL, ANTHONY 1976 "Yona Friedman: An Appreciation." *Journal of the Royal Institute of British Architects* 83:105.

MÜHLL, H. R. VON DER 1964–1965 "L'Architecture Mobile de Yona Friedman." *Architecture, Formes et Fonctions* 11:89–91.

RAGON, MICHEL 1964 "Mobile Architecture: Prerequisite for a New Urbanism." *Landscape* 13, no. 3:20–23.

RAGON, MICHEL 1974 "Yona Friedman: de l'habitat évolutif à l'autoplanification." *Urbanisme* 43, no. 143:75–77.

"L'Urbanisme Spatial." 1965–1966 *Architecture, Formes et Fonctions* 12:66–69.

Frigmelica, Padua (begun 1696), and was responsible for a number of unbuilt projects, among them a university library, Padua (1718), and the Duomo, Padua (1721–1722). Frigmelica's most impressive work was the Villa Pisani, Strà, which was begun in 1720. It includes a vast Palladian-style villa and a variety of out-buildings in the park, including an armory and a belvedere. The work was completed by Francesco Maria Preti.

Frigmelica's combination of Palladian and baroque elements exemplifies a kind of Italian equivalent to the English Palladian movement—with the proviso that in Frigmelica's case this Palladian influence can be seen as a traditional leaning rather than the result of foreign study. Nonetheless, the peculiar combination of Palladian and baroque recalls other European precursors to neoclassicism in the early eighteenth century such as JOHN VANBRUGH. Frigmelica's eclectic talents recall the rounded skills of the Renaissance architectural humanists.

NICHOLAS ADAMS

WORKS

Begun 1696, Palazzo Frigmelica, Padua, Italy. 1718–1728, Santa Maria del Pianto, near Padua, Italy. 1720, Villa Pisani (completed by F. M. Preti), Strà, Italy. 1730, San Gaetano, Vicenza, Italy.

BIBLIOGRAPHY

ZACCARIA, M. 1939–1940 "Giovanni Frigmelica." *Bollettino del Museo Civico di Padova* 29–30.

FRIGMELICA, GIOVANNI

Giovanni Frigmelica (1653–1732) was a north Italian baroque architect and humanist of modest talent. Born in Padua, he was largely self-educated in architecture and was employed, initially, as a librarian in the University of Padua. His first works date only from the 1690s and show a mixture of Palladian (see ANDREA PALLADIO) elements from his native Veneto and reflections of the great masters of the Roman baroque, FRANCESCO BORROMINI, GIANLORENZO BERNINI, and CARLO MADERNO. In 1721 or thereabouts, Frigmelica left Padua for Modena where he worked in the court of Ercole III as a poet writing under the pseudonym of Cesareo. Frigmelica also worked as an engineer and in Padua was responsible for the maintenance of the canals.

Among Frigmelica's works is the Church of Santa Maria del Pianto in Torresino, near Padua (begun 1718). The stiff Palladian façade is typical of his regional traditionalism while the cupola and the dramatic quality of the interior recall central Italian baroque. He also built the Palazzo

FRISONI, DONATO GIUSEPPE

Born in Laino, Lombardy, Donato Frisoni (1683–1735) worked as an ornamental plasterer and later as an architect in Central Europe. His earliest known works, the decorated ceilings of Strahov Palace (1705) and Sternberg Palace in Prague (1705, 1707) show the innovative combinations of Viennese and North Italian stucco motifs which made him in demand as a decorator.

He was called to Ludwigsburg in 1709 for stucco work in the palace of Duke Eberhard Ludwig of Württemberg. In 1715, he replaced the chief architect, Johann Friedrich Nette, and his three designs for the rebuilding of the palace were successive expansions of Nette's U-shaped plan. Frisoni's contemporary plans for the new town of Ludwigsburg show enlightened attitudes in the separation of the town from the palace and in the equal prominence given to Protestant and Catholic churches.

Frisoni also designed some decorative elements of Weingarten Abbey Church, notably the façade gable and the altars of the apse and transepts (1715–1724).

DOROTHY LIMOUZE

WORKS

1705, Strahov Palace (stucco decoration); 1707, Sternberg Palace (stucco decoration); Prague. 1709–1735, Ducal Palace (stucco decoration), Ludwigsburg, Germany. 1715–1724, Benedictine Abbey (façade gable, dome, upper stories of towers, altars), Weingarten, Germany. 1715–1735, Town of Ludwigsburg; 1717–1719, Banqueting House (Favortia); Ludwigsburg, Germany.

BIBLIOGRAPHY

BLAŽÍČEK, OLDŘICH J. 1962 "Dílo komských štukatéru 18. století u nas." *Umění* 10 no. 4:351–368.

DORY, LUDWIG 1967 "Donato Giuseppe Frisoni und Leopoldo Maria Retti." *Arte Lombarda* 12 no. 2:127–138.

HEMPEL, EBERHARD 1965 *Baroque Art and Architecture in Central Europe.* Harmondsworth, England: Penguin.

LIEB, NORBERT 1953 *Barockkirchen zwischen Donau und Alpen.* Munich: Hirmer.

SCHMIDT, RICHARD 1954 *Schloss Ludwigsburg.* Munich: Hirmer.

SPERLING, IVAN 1964 "Obnova štukové výzoby Paláce Straků z Nedabylic v Praze." *Památková Péče* 24:175–178.

FRONTINUS, SEXTUS JULIUS

A ranking Roman civil servant and military commander, three times consul, Sextus Julius Frontinus (c.35–105) is important in the history of architecture and urbanism because of his book on the water supply of Rome. He wrote it toward the end of his life, having been appointed *curator aquarum,* or water commissioner, in 97. Finding the vast system exploited by illegal means and to a degree in disrepair, he put it right and then set down what he had learned from his energetic renovation and from a careful study of the considerable legal and archival sources on file. The result, *On the Waters of the City of Rome* (*De aquis urbis Romae*), is the major document of the practical side of ancient urbanism that has come down to us, prime evidence for the existence of effective, honest civil servants who kept cities both large and small functioning, in his case by ensuring "that the water may flow without interruption, day and night" (2.103). He also wrote on military science—one manual survives— and on surveying, but only excerpts from the latter exist.

Half of the book on the aqueducts is technical, for Frontinus mastered every detail of a complicated, many-sided profession. He checked the office records against the actual summer flow of all nine great channels; he observed and understood the practical details of the watermen's daily work; he exposed and quashed dishonest access major and minor; and he instituted a methodical, revolving program of cleaning and maintenance without which the system could not have continued to function effectively. He describes each aqueduct and gives its history, quoting pertinent legal documents. The various specialists and work gangs of the *statio aquarum* or Water Office are carefully recorded. The list is long, beginning with assistant directors and staff architects and engineers, and ending with the men who crushed discarded terra cotta to gain the hydraulic cement used to line the conduits. The amount of record-keeping is impressive; even the preparation of daily work schedules for the labor force is mentioned. But Frontinus never loses sight of the main purpose of his office, to bring pure, palatable water to more than seven hundred public fountains, basins, and other public structures (such as baths), as well as to innumerable private parties (whose payment of water rates financed the system), in lawful and equitable distribution. He is quietly proud of his accomplishment, claiming that "not even the waste water is lost [being used to flush the sewers and public toilets]; the appearance of the City is clean and altered; the air is purer; and the causes of the [former] unwholesome atmosphere are now removed" (2.88). And he is very aware of the importance of the system historically, declaring, in a famous aside, that one ought to compare "the idle Pyramids, or the useless, though famous, works of the Greeks" with his "array of indispensable structures carrying so many waters" (1.16).

WILLIAM L. MACDONALD

BIBLIOGRAPHY

An English translation of the ancient text can be found in the Frontinus volume of the Loeb Classical Library series, published by Harvard University Press and Heinemann.

HERSCHEL, CLEMENS 1913 *The Two Books of the Water Supply of the City of Rome by Sextus Julius Frontinus.* New York: Longmans. Includes a useful commentary.

LANCIANI, RODOLFO (1880)1975 *Le acque e gli acquedotti di Roma antica.* Rome: Quasar. Originally published with the title *Topografia di Roma antica: I commentarii di Frontino intorno le acqve e gli acqvedotti.*

MATTHEWS, KENNETH D. 1970 "Roman Aqueducts: Technical Aspects of Their Construction." *Expedition* 13:2–16.

FROST, CHARLES S.

Charles Sumner Frost (1856–1932) first worked for his father, a builder, mill owner, and lumber merchant in Lewiston, Maine. After graduating from the Massachusetts Institute of Technology in 1876, he worked for several Boston firms, including PEABODY AND STEARNS from 1879 to 1881. In 1882, he joined HENRY IVES COBB in Chicago, where he stayed until 1889. On his own from 1889, he built small railway stations in Wisconsin, Illinois, and Iowa in a Richardsonian (see H. H. RICHARDSON) style. In practice with Alfred H. Granger from 1898 to 1910, he built the Smith Memorial Building and Saint Luke's Hospital (1907), both in Chicago, and the Northwestern Trust and Bank Building (1908), also in Chicago.

DONALD MARTIN REYNOLDS

BIBLIOGRAPHY

JENKINS, CHARLES E. (editor) 1897 "Charles S. Frost." *Architectural Reviewer* 1, no. 3: special issue.

FROST, HARRY T.

Harry Talfourd Frost (1887–1943), who was born in Hanley, England, emigrated to the United States in 1892. After acquiring a degree in architecture from Washington University in St. Louis, Missouri, in 1910, he worked in New York City as a draftsman for the United States Office of Immigration and in Washington in the office of the Supervising Architect. In 1912, he moved to Chicago and joined the office of EDWARD H. BENNETT. In 1923, he became a partner in the firm of Bennett, Parsons, and Frost. A specialist in city planning and civic improvement, he was chief of staff of the Chicago Zoning Commission from 1920 to 1921. He worked on similar projects for other cities, including Phoenix, Arizona, Pasadena, California, and Saint Paul, Minnesota. His last major commission in the 1930s was designing Quezon City in the Philippines.

DONALD MARTIN REYNOLDS

BIBLIOGRAPHY

"Obituary." 1943 *New York Times*. Dec. 30, p. 18, col. 2.

FRY, EDWIN MAXWELL

Edwin Maxwell Fry (1899–), a leading figure of the Modern movement in Britain, was born in Wallasey, Cheshire. He was educated at the Liverpool Institute (1910–1917) and from 1917 spent two years in the British army. In 1920, he attended the school of architecture at Liverpool University, whose principal was CHARLES H. REILLY; also on the faculty was PATRICK ABERCROMBIE. Fry said of those days that the students "aped the Americans in style but followed the Beaux-Arts tradition." He spent his university vacation of 1922 in the office of New York architects CARRÈRE AND HASTINGS.

In 1924, Fry left Liverpool for London and started working for the architectural and planning firm of Adams and Thompson. He remained there until 1934 except for a long interval between 1927–1930 when he worked in the architects department of Southern Railway. During the Adams and Thompson period, Fry changed from a neo-Georgian to a Modern movement architect, and the shift can be seen by comparing neo-Georgian Ridge End, Virginia Water, Surrey (1930) with his elegant modern showrooms for the Westminster Electricity Corporation, Victoria Street, London (1933), or with the Sassoon House, Peckham, London (1933–1934), a block of workers apartments close to the then new Owen Williams Peckham Health Centre.

In 1934, Fry founded his own practice and was to design the Sun House, Hampstead, London (1935), with its acknowledged indebtedness to LUDWIG MIES VAN DER ROHE's Tugendhat House, and later the generically similar Miramonte House, Coombe, Surrey (1937). Concurrently, Fry was designing with traditional materials as in the brick-and-boarding residence *Little Winch* at Chipperfield, Hertfordshire (1935).

WALTER GROPIUS joined Fry from 1934 to 1936, and together they produced a series of projects and designs, including the Levy House, Chelsea, London (1936), and the house at Shipbourne, Sevenoaks, Kent (1936), but their most important built design was the Impington Village College, Cambridgeshire (1936), a school for Henry Morris's progressive educational and community program. Shortage of work in Britain and an offer from Harvard University persuaded Gropius to establish himself in the United States, and from 1937 until World War II, Fry was again working without partners. Fry's work in this independent phase included Kensal House, Ladbroke Grove, London (1936–1937); working class apartments sponsored by the Gas, Light and Coke Company, with a nursery school and social amenities; apartments at 65 Ladbroke Grove, London (1938); and Electricity Showrooms, Regent Street, London (1938).

In 1934, WELLS W. COATES founded the MARS group as the British branch of the Congrès Internationaux d'Architecture Moderne. Fry was largely responsible for the MARS exhibition at the Burlington Gallery in 1937, aided by LÁSZLÓ MOHOLY-NAGY, and was deeply involved in the

MARS plan for London. Fry was to discuss this plan in his book *Fine Building*.

In 1939, Fry rejoined the army and in 1942 married his second wife, JANE DREW. Fry was sent to West Africa, and in 1944 he and Jane Drew were jointly appointed Town Planning Advisers to the British Resident Minister. The war years involved much research and writing for Fry and Drew. His study on the Thirties, *Fine Building* (1944) was published, as well as *Architecture for Children* (1944). Their tropical experience produced the jointly authored *Village Housing in the Tropics* (1947), mostly from Jane Drew's research, a forerunner of their more comprehensive and widely successful *Tropical Architecture in the Humid Zone* (1956).

A Fry and Drew architectural partnership was set up in 1945, joined by Lindsay Drake and DENYS LASDUN from 1951 to 1958, and from 1960 by Frank Knight and Norman Creamer.

In 1951, Prime Minister Nehru appointed Fry and Drew as senior architects to the Capital Project in Chandigarh, India, and Fry invited LE CORBUSIER to join the project. Fry was involved in the plan for the city and in much of the detailed design of the living and amenity areas.

In the postwar years, the Fry-Drew office grew both from British commissions and, conspicuously, from work in tropical countries, largely in Africa. Fry's design responsibilities were to be spread over numerous projects, but two projects on which he was to commit a great amount of time and energy were the Pilkington Glass Head Office Building, St. Helen's, Lancashire (1963) and University College, Ibadan, Nigeria (1953–1959). He retired from practice in 1973.

ROYSTON LANDAU

WORKS

1930, Ridge End House, Wentworth, Surrey, England. *1933, Westminster Electricity Supply Corporation Showrooms, Victoria Street; 1933–1934, Sasson House, Peckham; London. 1935, Little Winch House, Chipperfield, Hertfordshire, England. 1935, Sun House, Hampstead, London. 1936, Impington Village College (with Walter Gropius), Cambridgeshire, England. 1936, Levy House (with Gropius), Chelsea, London. 1936, Wood House (with Gropius), Shipbourne, Kent, England. 1936–1937, Kensal House, Ladbroke Grove, London. 1937, Miramonte House, Coombe, Surrey, England. *1938, Electricity Showrooms, Regent Street; 1938, Flats, 65 Ladbroke Grove; 1940, Cecil House, Gower Street; London. 1946, Aburi School and College, Ghana. 1946, Adisadel College, Cape Coast, Ghana. 1946, Amedzoffe School, Togoland. 1946, Prempeh College (with Jane Drew), Kumasi, Ghana. 1948, Nigerian Broadcasting Company House, Kaduna. 1950, Ashanti Secondary School (with Drew), Kumasi, Ghana. 1950, Passfield Estate, Lewisham, London. 1951–1956, Capital (with Le Corbusier and Drew), Chandigarh, India. 1953, Flats, Bromley Road, Lewisham, London. 1953–1959, University College (with Drew), Ibadan, Nigeria. 1958, Woman's Teacher Training College (with Drew), Kano, Nigeria. 1958, Wudil Teacher Training College (with Drew), Nigeria. 1959, Cooperative Bank, Ibadan, Lagos. 1960, Dow Agro Chemicals Offices, King's Lynn, Norfolk, England. 1960, Holy Cross School, Lagos, Nigeria. 1960, Liverpool University College of Engineering and Veterinary Science Building (with Drew), England. 1960, Saint Matthias School; 1960, Saint Patrick's School; 1961, British Petroleum Company Offices; Lagos, Nigeria. 1963, Pilkington Glass Head Office Building, St. Helen's, Lancashire, England. 1963, Rolls-Royce Engineering Centre and Computer Centre, Derbyshire, England. 1963, Wates Head Office, Norbury; 1964, Chelwood House, Gloucester Square; London. 1964, Isle of Thorns College, Chelwood Gate, Sussex, England. 1966, Lesislative Assembly and Government Centre, Port Louis, Mauritius. 1967, Woodsford Square, London. 1969, Mid-Glamorgan Crematorium, Wales. 1974, Porchester Terrace; 1975, Breadspear Crematorium, Northwood, London.

BIBLIOGRAPHY

BROCKMAN, H. A. N. 1978 *Fry, Drew, Knight, Creamer: Architecture*. London: Lund Humphries.

FRY, E. MAXWELL 1944 *Fine Building*. London: Faber.

FRY, E. MAXWELL 1969 *Art in a Machine Age*. London: Methuen.

FRY, E. MAXWELL 1975 *Autobiographical Sketches*. London: Elek.

FRY, E. MAXWELL, and DREW, JANE B. (1944)1976 *Architecture and the Environment*. Rev. ed. London: Allen & Unwin. Originally published with the title *Architecture for Children*.

FRY, E. MAXWELL, and DREW, JANE B. 1947 *Village Housing in the Tropics*. In collaboration with Harry L. Ford. London: Lund Humphries.

FRY, E. MAXWELL, and DREW, JANE B. 1956 *Tropical Architecture in the Humid Zone*. London: Batsford.

FRY, E. MAXWELL, and DREW, JANE B. 1964 *Tropical Architecture in the Dry and Humid Zones*. London: Batsford.

FUCHS, BOHUSLAV

Bohuslav Fuchs (1895–1972) lived and worked in Brno, Czechoslovakia. He was one of the most gifted disciples of JAN KOTĚRA. In the initial stage of his professional career, Fuchs was influenced by Czech cubism and by the Dutch red brick architecture. In 1923, he became one of the leaders of the Brno Avant-Garde Group. Soon afterward, Fuchs developed a specific functionalistic style characterized by the *von Innen nach Aussen* concept, stressing the emotionally interior volumes by a dynamic external expression of them. He admired the space-shaping role of staircases which, in his opinion, were the hearts of structures from which the space effects of other functions derived. This manifested itself in his own residence and particularly in the Avion Hotel in Brno (both completed in 1927–1928), where he succeeded, by means of ingeniously conceived staircases and galleries, in creating a wonderful play of volumes with four transparent stories in a structure situated on a narrow and deep lot.

In the late 1930s, Fuchs enriched his architecture by using more and more natural materials to blend a structure with its environment. Fuchs made a great contribution to all fields of architecture, including landscaping and town planning and such specific branches as furniture design. He realized about 200 buildings. From 1945 to 1958, he was professor of architecture at the Brno Technical University.

VLADIMÍR ŠLAPETA

WORKS

1920, Masaryk Hut, Šerlich Mount, Orlické Mountains, Czechoslovakia. 1921, House with Power Plant (with Josef Štěpánek), Háj, near Mohelnice, Czechoslovakia. 1925, Cemetery Funeral Hall; 1925, Zeman Café; Brno, Czechoslovakia. 1926–1927, Boarding Houses (Avion, Viola, and Radun), Luhačovice, Czechoslovakia. 1927–1928, Avion Hotel; 1927–1928, Brno Town Pavilion, Brno Exhibition Ground; 1927–1928, Bohuslav Fuchs Residence; 1927–1928, Triple House, Czechoslovak Werkbund Exhibition; 1928–1930, Masaryk Students' Hostel; 1929–1930, Eliška Machová Hostel; 1929–1930, Moravian Bank (with Arnošt Wiesner); 1929–1930, Spa House, Zábrdovice; 1929–1930, VESNA (women's special school; with Joseph Polášek); Brno, Czechoslovakia. 1931, Morava Recreation Home, Tatranská Lomnica, Czechoslovakia. 1931, Savings Bank (with Jindřich Kumpošt), Tišnov, Czechoslovakia. 1931, Savings Bank, Třebíč, Czechoslovakia. 1934, Sokol Gymnasium and Cinema, Jihlava, Czechoslovakia. 1935–1936, Green Frog Thermal Swimming Pool, Trenčianske Teplice, Czechoslovakia. 1936–1937, Provincial Military Command Building; 1938, Railway Station Post Office; Brno, Czechoslovakia. 1940, Vlčina Hotel, Frenštát, Czechoslovakia. 1968–1972, Department Store (with Kamil Fuchs), Znojmo, Czechoslovakia.

BIBLIOGRAPHY

FUCHS, BOHUSLAV 1967 Nové zónování: Urbanistická tvorba životního prostředí z hlediska sídelního a krajinného. Prague: The academy.
KUBINSZKY, MIHÁLY 1977 Bohuslav Fuchs. Budapest: Akadémiai Kladó.
KUDĔKKA, ZDENĔK 1966 Bohuslav Fuchs. Prague: Nakladatelství československých výtvarných umelců.
ROSSMANN, ZDENĔK (compiler) 1930 Architekt Bohuslav Fuchs: 1919–1929. Basel: Service des pays.
ŠLAPETA, VLADIMÍR 1972 "Bohuslav Fuchs 24.3.1895–18.9.1972." Bauwelt 63, no. 46:1760–1761.
ŠLAPETA, VLADIMÍR (compiler) 1981 "Bohuslav Fuchs-Josef Štěpánek, Korespendence." Zprávy Krajskeho vlastivědneho muzea v Olomovci.

FUGA, FERDINANDO

Ferdinando Fuga (1699–1781) was born in Florence, where he studied with the sculptor and architect Giovanni Battista Foggini until his departure for Rome in 1717. From this point onward Fuga's long and productive professional career was centered in Rome and Naples, which, along with Turin, constituted the three principal centers of architectural patronage in eighteenth-century Italy. Fuga's first Roman sojourn, between 1717 and 1726, was a period of intense study and assimilation of the city's architectural heritage. A characteristic example of Fuga's synthesis of earlier baroque design is an unexecuted project of 1722 for the Lateran façade, which imaginatively alludes to works by PIETRO BERRETTINI DA CORTONA, Carlo Rainaldi, and ANDREA POZZO, among others.

In 1726 Fuga was called to Naples by Cardinal Nicola Del Giudice, thus initiating the first of his two extended periods of activity in southern Italy. While there, he executed his first independent design, a chapel (1726–1727) undertaken along with other additions to the Cellamare Palace in Naples. The Cellamare Chapel, while continuing to draw on Roman precedent, is nonetheless a highly original design, particularly in the brilliant use of mural transparency and directed light. By 1728 Fuga was evidently in the service of the King of Naples, because in that year he was sent to Sicily to design a bridge over the River Milicia. The bridge was not executed according to Fuga's design, however, due to his return to Rome in 1730.

Fuga's appointment to the position of architect of the papal palaces in 1730 marks the beginning of his artistic maturity. Under the pontificates of Clement XII Corsini and Benedict XIV Lambertini, Fuga was awarded numerous commissions which, both in scale and importance, were remarkable in Rome during this period. It is likely that Fuga's Florentine origins played a part in securing him his papal appointment, for Clement XII openly favored Florentines, one of whom, ALESSANDRO GALILEI, won the competition for the Lateran façade for which Fuga had prepared a project ten years earlier. A drawing by Fuga suggests that he may have competed unsuccessfully in the second great competition organized by the Corsini Pope, that for the Trevi Fountain.

In the early years of Clement's pontificate, Fuga was concerned almost exclusively with enlarging the papal palace on the Quirinal (1732–1737) and with the construction of new buildings in its vicinity. Between 1730 and 1732 he extended the Manica Lunga further along the Via Venti Settembre and added the Palazzina del Segretario delle Cifre as its terminus. Of far greater interest is the Palazzo della Consulta (1732–1737) flanking the main entrance to the Quirinal Palace, which provided accommodations for the secretaries of the Consulta and the Brevi as well as lodgings for two small corps of papal guards.

The most remarkable features of the Palazzo della Consulta are its scenographic façade, its unusual plan and original arrangements for circulation. The ample extension of the façade, composed of thirteen bays of equal width, is animated by Fuga's subtle use of color and surface texture, as well as by his deft placement of sculpture. As a result, the palace effectively anchors the eastern side of the Piazza di Montecavallo and provides a scenic backdrop to the imposing mass of the Quirinal. Fuga's trapezoidal plan, unusual in Rome, efficiently organizes the multiple functions it was intended to serve, while keeping them physically separate. The grand staircase placed over the main entrance is at once a rationalization and an inversion of the more exuberant stair systems designed by Ferdinando Sanfelice which must have impressed Fuga during his stay in Naples.

Between 1733 and 1737, at the same time Fuga was occupied with the Palazzo della Consulta, he also was building the church of Santa Maria dell'Orazione e Morte (1733–1737) on the Via Giulia. In its longitudinal oval plan Fuga brilliantly integrated the sinuous continuity of mural structure in FRANCESCO BORROMINI's San Carlo alle Quattro Fontane with the muted axis of GIOVANNI LORENZO BERNINI's Sant'Andrea al Quirinale. The rich relief of the façade and the paired columns set into recessed compartments recall the highly sculptural designs of earlier Tuscan architects, notably MICHELANGELO, BARTOLOMEO AMMANNATI, and Pietro da Cortona.

In 1736 Fuga was elected to membership in the Roman Academy of Saint Luke, over which he would preside as *principe* from 1752 to 1754. The last major building Fuga undertook during the pontificate of Clement XII was the family palace on the Via della Lungara. In building the Palazzo Corsini (1736–1754) Fuga was obliged to incorporate an earlier structure, the Riario Palace, into his design. Fuga achieved a highly successful solution to his extremely difficult problem by using a block containing a monumental atrium and stairway as a central pivot linking the preexisting L-shaped wing with another identical to it. In marked contrast to the almost unrelieved flatness of the long street façade, the rear elevation boldly projects toward the extensive gardens which extend to the summit of the Janiculum Hill, embracing the landscape and drawing light into its interior in a way few Roman palaces can rival. Fuga's manipulation of light is particularly successful in the grand stairway, where it is used dramatically to punctuate the assent. The multiple vistas—both interior and exterior—which are revealed as the visitor climbs, together with the sloping entablatures and ramping vaults, call to mind baroque set designs by FILIPPO JUVARRA and the BIBIENA FAMILY.

Benedict XIV commissioned Fuga to erect a new façade for the Basilica of Santa Maria Maggiore (1741–1743), perhaps the architect's most spirited and overtly baroque design. Here again Fuga was constrained by the need to preserve and maintain visible the medieval mosaics on the preexisting façade, while also accommodating the late mannerist forms of FLAMINIO PONZIO's adjacent sacristy. Fuga's solution was to design a two-story *scaenae frons* with a portico at the ground level and an open benediction loggia above providing a view of the old façade decoration. More successfully than in any other of his buildings, Fuga establishes a rhythmic play of *chiaroscuro* effects and contrasting relationships of mass and void. On both levels the pediments carried by his two superimposed systems of orders project upward into attic levels, thus introducing vertical accents which culminate in Giuseppe Lironi's statue of the Madonna and Child. The tension between vertical and horizontal elements, and between curving and prismatic forms, as well as the superb rhythmic scansion of Fuga's façade of Santa Maria Maggiore clearly distinguish it from the restraint of Galilei's more severe and monumental façade of the Lateran.

In 1741 Fuga was also commissioned to build a small pavilion, or *Caffehaus,* in the gardens of the papal palace on the Quirinal. The U-shaped plan, with two projecting wings framing a recessed triple-arched loggia, continues a long Roman tradition of villa design going back to the Farnesina. The severe classicism of Fuga's exterior, which asserts the planar surface of the wall and respects the proprieties of the Doric order, stands in marked contrast to the rococo stucco ornament of the interior. Nonetheless, this interior decoration is subordinate to the supporting classical structure in a way that is emphatically Roman; comparison with the nearly contemporary Amalienburg pavilion at Nymphenburg points out the gulf which separates Fuga's austere synthesis of Roman classicism and true rococo design. The *Caffehaus* has been interpreted as an anticipation of neoclassical architec-

Fuga.
Church of Sant'Apollinare.
Rome.
1742–1748

Fuga.
Santa Maria Maggiore.
Rome.
1741–1743

ture, but such a viewpoint misconstrues Fuga's historical position. There is no evidence to suggest that he was theoretically disposed to emulate the architectural principles of ancient Greece, any more than he was familiar with specific Greek monuments. Rather, Fuga stands as a transitional figure, whose synthesis of earlier baroque architecture led him, especially in secular buildings, to designs of increasing austerity and reductive simplicity.

The third major building project in which Fuga was engaged under Benedict XIV is the church of Sant'Apollinare, which was begun in 1742 and dedicated in 1748, just three years before his departure for Naples. This substantial edifice was built to serve the German and Hungarian College, in which it is incorporated. Fuga's design reflects the functional requirements of the collegiate community, assuring easy access from the adjacent *palazzo* and providing numerous altars so that Mass may be said at more than one place at once. Both in plan and in elevation Sant'Apollinare is divided into three clearly distinguishable parts: a transitional space at the entrance, followed by a high barrel vaulted nave off of which open six lateral chapels, and culminating in a domed sanctuary. Fuga took special care to underscore the distinct functions of these spaces, employing vaults of different structure and elevation, contrasting bay rhythms, and, most importantly, special effects of lighting and ornament. Framed by the triumphal arch closing the nave, the gilded coffers of the sanctuary glow and shimmer in the radiant light which streams in from above. The right ornament and illumination of the sanctuary distinguishes the place where the Eucharist is enshrined, while the more austere area of the nave is appropriate for the religious congregation. The resulting contrast be-

tween these two areas, far from being inconsistent, as has been suggested, was intentional and brilliantly effected. Throughout Sant'Apollinare, but especially in the sanctuary, Fuga utilized the full repertoire of baroque ornament, but subordinated it to clear and distinct structural divisions, a mark of his growing classical restraint in the years following the façade of Santa Maria Maggiore.

In 1750 FERDINANDO SANFELICE and Domenico Antonio Vaccaro, the two most distinguished Neapolitan architects of the first half of the eighteenth century, both died. In the following year Charles III, king of Naples, prevailed upon Ferdinando Fuga and LUIGI VANVITELLI to leave Rome and enter his service. At the king's request Fuga had previously furnished designs for temporary festival architecture in Rome. While Vanvitelli was given the commission to build the royal palace at Caserta, Fuga was called upon to design the Albergo dei Poveri (1751–1781), an enormous poorhouse intended to provide for some eight thousand needy persons. Thus began the final period of Fuga's professional career. This vast undertaking was to occupy him for the last thirty years of his life, and even though work continued long after his death, only a fraction of the building was completed. Fuga's final design, which went through several preliminary stages, consists of an elongated quadrilateral structure with a central-plan church at the center flanked by a square court on each side. The façade dominating Piazza Carlo III, some one thousand feet long, is even more spare and unrelieved than are those of the Manica Lunga and the Palazzo Corsini, and, it must be admitted, is rather monotonous. Even in its incomplete state, however, the Albergo dei Poveri must be counted among the most ambitious architectural projects of the eighteenth century, surpassing in scale even the utopian fantasies of ETIENNE LOUIS BOULLÉE.

Fuga was responsible for other important buildings in Naples, among which were the Villa Favorita at Resina (c.1768), and the great public granary (1779), undertaken in his last years, the scale and spareness of which rivaled even the Albergo dei Poveri. Together with Vanvitelli, Fuga contributed to the formulation of an imported, classicizing court style in Naples, reflecting contemporary developments not only in Rome, but in France as well. Parallels between Fuga's designs and French architecture around 1750 suggest that there may have been a reciprocal exchange of ideas in this period. At the end of his career, stimulated at once by the utilitarian nature of his major commissions and the taste prevailing at court, Fuga's style became increasingly simple and classical, a process which had already begun before his departure from Rome. Nonetheless, as is evident in the oval atrium of the Villa Favorita, Fuga's work continued to embody baroque features. Ferdinando Fuga may be characterized historically as a transitional figure whose early work represents a creative synthesis of late baroque forms which, after midcentury, give way to an ever more rigorous and academic classicism.

JOHN PINTO

WORKS

1726–1727, Palazzo Cellamare (chapel), Naples. 1730–1732, Quirinal Palace (expansion); 1732–1737, Palazzo della Consulta; 1733–1737, Santa Maria dell'Orazione e Morte; 1734–1735, Casa di corezione feminile in the Capizio di San Michele a Ripa; *1736–1737, Quirinal Palace (carriage house); 1736–1754, Palazzo Corsini; 1741, Santa Cecilia in Trastevere (atrium); 1741–1743, Lateran Triclimium (restoration); 1741–1743, Quirinal Gardens (*Caffehaus*); 1741–1743, Santa Maria Maggiore (façade); 1742–1744, Ospedale di Santo Spirito (expansion); 1742–1748, Church of Sant'Apollinare; 1744, Ospedale di Santo Spirito (cemetery); Rome. 1744, San Paolo, Calvi d'Umbria, Italy. 1745, Palazzo Cenci-Bolognetti, Rome. 1751–1781, Albergo dei Poveri (not completed until 1819); 1763, Cemitero dei Tredici; Naples. c.1768, Villa Favorita, Resena, Italy. *1779, Granary; c.1780, Chiesa dei Gerolomini (façade); c.1780, Palazzo Caramanico; c.1780, Palazzo Giordano; Naples.

BIBLIOGRAPHY

BIANCHI, LIDIA 1955 *Disegni di Ferdinando Fuga e di altri architetti del settecento.* Rome: Cabinetto nationale della stampe.
BLUNT, ANTHONY 1975 *Neapolitan Baroque and Rococo Architecture.* London: Zwemmer.
BORSI, FRANCO 1975 *Il Palazzo della Consulta.* Rome. Editalia.
HAGER, HELLMUT 1964 *S. Maria dell'Orazione e Morte.* Rome: Marietti.
MATTHIAE, GUGLIELMO 1952 *Ferdinando Fuga e la sua opera romana.* Rome: Fratelli Palombi.
MILIZIA, FRANCESCO 1781 *Memorie degli architetti antichi e moderni.* 3d ed. Parma, Italy: Stamperia reale.
PANE, ROBERTO 1956 *Ferdinando Fuga.* Naples: Edizione Scientifiche Italiane.
PORTOGHESI, PAOLO (1966)1970 *Roma Barocca: The History of an Architectonic Culture.* Translated by Barbara Luigia La Penta. Cambridge, Mass.: M.I.T. Press.
STRAZZULLO, LUIGI (editor) 1976–1977 *Le lettere di Luigi Vanvitelli.* Galatine: Congedo.

FULLER, R. BUCKMINSTER

Although Richard Buckminster Fuller (1895–) is one of the great architectural innovators of the twentieth century, he conceived of the architectural profession—and his role in it—not as an end in itself, but as incidental to his broader purpose of advancing a long-range economic and technological program, a comprehensive global strategy, designed "to make man a success in the universe." He calls his program "design science" and it embraces solutions to the problems of shelter, but only as inseparable from the other survival tasks of transportation, food gathering, and energy harvesting.

Born in Milton, Massachusetts, he was the grandnephew of Margaret Fuller and the spiritual heir to the other New England transcendentalists, who inspired him to create his own universal values by applying a pragmatic American philosophy. He spent a brief time at Harvard University, but had no sustained interest in academic education. During World War I, he served in the U.S. Navy, where his assignments involved applied engineering and the formation of global strategies. These demonstrated and confirmed the practical applications of his later design philosophy.

After the war, he worked on the development of a new type of fibrous block for building lightweight structures. Frustrated because of wasteful and outdated practices in the building trades and by his dislike of commercial enterprises, Fuller was jobless and on the brink of suicide in the midst of the Depression. After a two-year period of seclusion, he concluded that although human nature could not practicably be reformed, human evolution could be advanced through reform of man's environment—a strategy that became the key to his architectural philosophy. It emphasized every increasing performance with ever less investment of materials—a notion of ephemeralization with which the word Dymaxion has become his cachet.

Fuller invented the Dymaxion House and the hexagonal air-liftable, 4-D (fourth-dimension) dwelling machine in 1927. He developed his prefabricated modular bathroom in 1929 (patented in 1936). He built the three-wheeled, rear engine Dymaxion car in 1932, and brought out the new polyhedral cartographic projection map—the Airocean World—in 1943. In Wichita House (1946), he applied aircraft tool and assembly techniques to the engineering and mass production of a transportable shelter with fewer than two hundred separate parts.

During this outburst of invention, Fuller did not regard himself primarily as an inventor or an architect. He was not entering the transportation or housing business. Rather, he was creating artifacts—practical applications of radical technology—as illustrations of how to accomplish ever more with ever less. After Wichita, he refined his philosophy of synergetics (a system of radial and spherical coordination that abandons Cartesian mensuration) and its inseparable counterpart of applied geodesic engineering. His engineering strategy is epitomized in the word he coined, "tensegrity," a contraction of tensional integrity. In tensegrity systems the structural integrity is guaranteed by the continuous tension elements of the system rather than by the discontinuous local compression members. In geodesic spheres Fuller insists dogmatically on the application of an icosahedral model to the surface of a sphere in which all of the projected vertices provide for the symmetrical subdivision of the icosahedral faces to arrive at the three-way great circles of the geodesic structure.

Fuller initiated large-scale applications of his geodesic domes with the DEW Line radar shelters of 1954, the Union Tank Car dome of 1958, and eventually the Montreal Expo Dome of 1967—his masterpiece, burned in 1976 when an acetylene torch ignited and burnt out the acrylic fabric; the skeleton of the basic structure survives. By the early 1960s his dome was recognized as a uniquely American contribution to world architecture: the only large dome that can be set directly on the ground with simple anchors rather than a foundation, and the only practical clear-span structure with no limiting dimension.

From 1959 to 1972 Fuller was based chiefly at Southern Illinois University in Carbondale, where he continued his explorations in design science. During this period he was also associated with CONSTANTINOS DOXIADIS and his World Society for Ekistics in Athens. Fuller was sympathetic with the objective of Doxiadis, who wanted to reorganize the study of architecture and structure into consideration of the entire city as a planning unit. But Fuller thought even that unit was too small for consideration. Only the whole big system works, said Fuller, systems do not function in isolation; the proper pattern of structural or economic study—the improvement of man's environment—must be nothing less than global. (This was an issue at which Fuller also parted company with the historian Lewis Mumford in the 1930s.)

In 1960 Fuller advanced his hypothetical plan to cover the midtown section of Manhattan with a dome two miles in diameter. For him this was an ultimate architectural artifact, conceived in terms of the inevitable trend toward the ephemeralization of environment controls. That is what shelter really is: environment control.

Since Buckminster Fuller is such a relentless comprehensivist, it is difficult to relate his work to the stylistic trends of his antecedents and contemporaries. He regarded the aesthetic formalism of the Bauhaus or the International school as irrelevant to truly functional design as the decorative preoccupations of the eclectics and the postmodernists. He regarded most of the tendency of the first half of the twentieth century that flourished as "industrial design" as a superficial and distorted application of functionalism. He received the Gold Medal of the American Institute of Architects in 1970, even though he had no professional degree or license. He was on friendly terms with fellow architects, but he never retracted his description of them as little more than "exterior decorators," whose work is irrelevant to the

R. Buckminster Fuller.
U. S. Pavilion, 1967
*   International Exposition.*
Montreal.
1967

proper application of engineering principles for the provision of universal shelter without regard to the notion of style or convention or tradition or "what looks good." He has been misunderstood for apparently rejecting the symbolic function of a home, but he admits the need of a fireplace as a source of more than heat; he feels that a dwelling machine can be as beautiful and as romantic as a jet airplane.

In the last analysis he has been admitted into the profession more by courtesy than by adherence to its tenets. Fuller does not believe in profession: people may call him an artist, but he does not profess to be one. In his generalized definition of architecture he resolves the concrete and the abstract without regard to aesthetics. Architecture, says Fuller, is the organizing of macrostructures from microstructures.

E. J. APPLEWHITE

WORKS

1937, Dymaxion Bathroom Unit (patented aluminum casting). 1940, Twin Dymaxion Deployment Units, Butler Manufacturing Company. 1946, Wichita House, Kans. 1950, Mini-Earth Sphere Geoscope, Cornell University, Ithaca, N.Y. 1953, Ford Rotunda dome, River Rouge Plant, Dearborn, Mich. 1954, U.S. Air Force DEW (Distant Early Warning) Line domes along the Arctic Circle from Scandinavia and Iceland through Canada to Alaska and the Aleutian Islands. 1954, Restaurant dome, Woods Hole, Mass. 1954, U.S. Marine Corps, portable shelter, Quantico, Va. 1958, Union Tank Car Company (384-foot diameter dome), Baton Rouge, La. 1958, Union Tank Car Company (354-foot diameter dome), Wood River, Ill. 1959, U.S. Pavilion, Sokolniki Park, Moscow. 1959, Palais de Sports, Paris. 1960, Botanical Garden Climatron, St. Louis, Mo. 1966, Placer County administration headquarters, Calif. *1967, U.S. Pavilion, 1967 International Exposition, Montreal. 1969, Airplane Museum, Schiphol Airport, Amsterdam. 1973, Weather radome, Mount Fuji, Tokyo.

BIBLIOGRAPHY

APPLEWHITE, E. J. 1978 *Cosmic Fishing: An Account of Writing Synergetics with Buckminster Fuller.* New York: Macmillan.
FULLER, R. BUCKMINSTER (1938)1971 *Nine Chains to the Moon.* Reprint. Garden City, N.Y.: Doubleday.
FULLER, R. BUCKMINSTER (in collaboration with E. J. Applewhite) 1975 *Synergetics: Explorations on the Geometry of Thinking.* New York: Macmillan.
FULLER, R. BUCKMINSTER (in collaboration with E. J. Applewhite) 1979 *Synergetics 2: Further Explorations in the Geometry of Thinking.* New York: Macmillan.
FULLER, R. BUCKMINSTER 1981 *Critical Path.* New York: St. Martin's.
HATCH, ALDEN 1974 *Buckminster Fuller: At Home in the Universe.* New York: Crown.
KENNER, HUGH 1973 *Bucky: A Guided Tour of Buckminster Fuller.* New York: Morrow.
MCHALE, JOHN 1962 *R. Buckminster Fuller.* New York: Braziller.
MARKS, ROBERT W., and FULLER, R. BUCKMINSTER (1960)1973 *The Dymaxion World of Buckminster Fuller.* Reprint. Garden City, N.Y.: Anchor.
ROBERTSON, DONALD W. 1974 *Mind's Eye of Richard Buckminster Fuller.* New York: Vantage.

FULLER, THOMAS

Thomas Fuller (1822–1898), an Ottawa architect, born in England, practiced in London before arriving in Canada in 1857. His work includes the Centre Block and Library of the Parliament Buildings, Ottawa (1859–1867). He moved to Albany, New York, in 1867 to supervise the erection of his winning design for the New York State Capitol, later modified by H. H. RICHARDSON and LEOPOLD EIDLITZ. With his partner Augustus Laver, he was awarded first prize for the 1871 design for the San Francisco City Hall and Law Courts. Fuller returned to Canada in 1881 to serve as chief architect of the Department of Public Works in Ottawa until 1898.

ROBERT HILL

BIBLIOGRAPHY

"Obituary." 1898 *American Architect and Building News* 62, Oct. 29:37.
"Obituary." 1898 *Canadian Architect and Builder* 11, Oct.:168.
THOMAS, C. 1979 "The Parliament Builder." *Canadian Heritage* Dec.:18.
ROSEBERRY, CECIL 1964 *Capitol Story.* Albany: State of New York.

FURNESS, FRANK

In the architecture of Frank Furness (1839–1912), the major design influences of his day were drawn together and seasoned with his own strong personality to produce buildings that were genuinely unforgettable in their creativity and power. Furness was the dominant force in the innovative and eccentric architectural development of Philadelphia in the late nineteenth century and received frequent national attention for the singularity of his products. In his forty-five years of practice he had the opportunity to design almost 400 buildings, almost all of them in the Philadelphia area. They included the majority of the city's civic buildings: banks, hospitals, university buildings, art academies, libraries, and railroad stations as well as factories, churches, major residences, and even ship and railroad car interiors and the zoo.

Furness's family background was conducive to achievement. He was born in Philadelphia, the youngest child of the Rev. William Henry Furness. Dr. Furness was an extraordinarily literate and broadly talented man. He was pastor of the First Congregational Unitarian Church, founded in 1796 by Joseph Priestly, whose great-grandson, H. H. RICHARDSON, was to become one of Frank Furness's leading architectural contemporaries. In addition, the elder Furness was a copious writer and a nationally recognized lecturer who spoke with equal eloquence for the cause of abolition as for the promotion of the arts. The intellectual home atmosphere was brightened by his friendships with such luminaries as Walt Whitman, William Ellery Channing, William Lloyd Garrison, and Ralph Waldo Emerson. Of the sons, William Henry Furness, Jr., became a prominent portrait painter and Horace Howard Furness was a renowned Shakespearean editor and scholar. Frank picked up his father's strong, but undeveloped, talent for drawing and his long-standing love of architecture.

Frank Furness never attended college. During his school years he learned draftsmanship in the Philadelphia architectural office of John Fraser. Through his brother William, he came to know RICHARD MORRIS HUNT, who had just returned from his study in Paris and had set up a working and teaching studio in New York City. Among Hunt's students were Charles D. Gambrill, HENRY VAN BRUNT, and GEORGE BROWNE POST. The former two were good friends of brother Horace Howard Furness and, partially as a result of the family friendships, Frank Furness, in 1859, became part of the Hunt atelier.

His stay in New York was interrupted, in 1861, by service with the Union Army, where he rose in rank from private to captain. For valor he became eligible for, and later received, the Congressional Medal of Honor. In 1864, he returned to Hunt's office, but within a year or two went back to Philadelphia to marry and to begin his own architectural practice.

American architecture in the 1860s was picturesque and eclectic. It drew its forms and details from all periods of world architectural history and was considered by its practitioners to be the culmination of all that had gone before. Principal design influences came from England and France. The English view was presented in the writings of JOHN RUSKIN, the famed medievalist, who advocated the picturesque silhouette, the realistic use of natural forms in ornament, and rich polychromy derived from natural material colors. Ruskin's precepts were visible to the students in New York in the work of such men as PETER B. WIGHT, LEOPOLD EIDLITZ, and JACOB WREY MOULD. The French tradition, a variant of Renaissance classicism marked by florid decoration and the distinctive mansard roof, was espoused by many, including JAMES RENWICK, ALFRED B. MULLETT, who, as supervising architect of the Treasury, spread Second Empire public buildings from coast to coast, and, of course, Hunt, the first American to have been trained at the Ecole des Beaux-Arts in Paris.

The literate Furness was well familiar with the writings of Ruskin as well as those of EUGÈNE EMMANUEL VIOLLET-LE-DUC, whose inventive use of exposed iron structural elements was echoed often in Furness's later work. Although he never visited Europe, Furness had the benefit of Hunt's Parisian experience. The students were nurtured in the classical design principles of the Beaux-Arts. Hunt demanded fine draftsmanship, a thorough knowledge of the orders, and a unified and disciplined approach to building design.

During the years in Hunt's atelier, two sidelights of Furness's personality came to the fore. One was his capacity for imaginative use of those parts of the English vocabulary that are at once colorful and pointed. At this, he emulated and even outshone Hunt, who considered himself to be a master of invective, gaining for himself a lifelong reputation for irascibility. The second was Furness's natural gift for caricature, the artistic ability to distort and exaggerate while maintaining the likeness of the subject. The capability carried itself into Furness's architecture as well as his own demeanor, as with jutting jaw and massive red mustache and wearing the loudest and largest of plaids he strode through life and work swearing and drawing at once, himself a living caricature. In many ways, he resembled his often fierce and always colorful buildings.

Through almost all of his career, Furness worked in partnership with others. His first work, the Unitarian Church of Germantown, Philadelphia (1866–1867), was done on his own, but by the time of its completion he had entered into partnership with his former employer, John Fraser, and with George W. Hewitt. The firm lasted until 1871, when Fraser left to become supervising architect of the Treasury. Furness and Hewitt continued their partnership until 1875.

It was during those years that a cocky young man by the name of LOUIS H. SULLIVAN walked into the office unannounced and declared his intent to work with the firm. After lacing him with a string of oaths, Furness hired him for one day, a time period that stretched into a number of months until economic hard times forced his layoff. The relationship, and especially Furness's colorful personality, remained memorable to Sullivan, whose writings give us our most graphic portrayal of his employer. Furness's inventiveness, as well as his style of architectural ornament, was decisively influential upon Sullivan's own significant contribution to American architecture.

The first masterwork of Furness's career was the Pennsylvania Academy of the Fine Arts (1871–1876), a two-storied structure housing an art school with a series of skylit galleries above. In the Academy, one sees Furness as the melder of the major Victorian influences. The general form of the building is French. Its tripartite composition with projecting central pavilion and mansard roof is strikingly similar to the Pavillon de la Bibliothèque of the Louvre, a building on which Hunt had worked while in Paris. The detailing of the Academy is thoroughly eclectic but primarily Gothic in derivation, centering on a great traceried window. The coloration is richly Ruskinian, red brick set against beige and brown sandstone, highlighted with polished granite, polychromatic glass, and painted bronze. Ornament ranges from patterning of glazed header bricks to bold panels of rock-faced stone, from Gothic tracery to a Greek statue, from realistically figurative panels to boldly stylized floral ornament, disparate elements that are brought into union with and by Furness's own personality. About the building there is a sense of playful caricature that mixes and modifies sources in a way that derives as much from Furness's own ability to distort artfully as it does from prototypes in Ruskin and Ruprich-Robert.

During the six years after 1875, when George Hewitt left the firm, Furness practiced alone. These were the years when his style matured and blossomed. They encompassed the Centennial Exhibition, for which he designed the Brazilian exhibition area (1876). More important was a related building outside of the exhibition grounds, the Centennial National Bank (1876). This, together with the Kensington National Bank (1877) and the Provident Life and Trust Company (1876–1879), firmly established Furness as a designer of major buildings and marked the height if not the maturity of his creative strength. The Provident, whose façade was a development and refinement of the Centennial Bank, may have been the most powerful architectural composition ever created in America. In it, certain elements of the Academy may be seen, notably the tripartite massing and the great pointed central window, but here architectural caricature is carried to its limit. The observer is less inclined to analyze stylistic influences than to be awed by the force of its pure formal creativity. Columns, reveals, corbels, and simulated roof tiles are gargantuan in size, stretched by the caricaturist's pen. They culminate in leafy ornaments that are at once elephantine and as delicate as a Victorian lady's white-gloved hand. The Provident interior was a single great skylit space lined on walls and floor with brilliantly colored glazed tiles set in vibrating geometric patterns. The deeply coved ceiling was supported by exposed iron trusses, their webs pierced in the stylized floral patterns that were becoming a Furness characteristic. The entire creation was mighty, arresting, even shocking.

In 1871, Furness hired Allen Evans as a draftsman. By 1881, he was a full partner, the firm becoming known as Furness and Evans, later Furness, Evans, and Company. Evans was much more the social businessman than the iconoclastic designer, and the two personalities meshed well by noninterference. Due largely to Evans's presence, the firm enjoyed an increased acceptance in the corporate business community and a greatly increased output. Banks continued to issue from the drawing boards. Though none would match the sheer power of the Provident, one, the tiny but vigorous National Bank of the Republic (1883–1884), was apparently so widely admired that literal copies have been found in such diverse places as Salem, Oregon, and Port Huron, Michigan. There were additional church commissions, including an artistically notable new First Unitarian Church (1883–1886). Dr. William Henry Furness, who had overseen the construction of the congregation's previous building (by WILLIAM STRICKLAND, 1828), as pastor emeritus saw his son design the replacement made necessary by his own successful pastorate. Notable among the many corporate clients were the railroads. For the Philadelphia and Reading, Furness, between 1879 and 1884, designed some 125 buildings, many of them commuter stations. In addition, there were six stations for the Baltimore and Ohio, including their masterful Philadelphia Passenger Station (1886–1888), and fourteen commissions for the Pennsylvania, reflecting a variety of building types including several commuter stations, a YMCA, a hotel, and a major enlargement and renovation of the massive Broad Street Station (1892–1893). Corporate work often led to personal work for company officers. The Furness and Evans years included a series of notable residences in Philadelphia and its growing suburbs. The houses, like the nearby commuter stations, were playful accretions of architectural elements usually displaying a multiplicity of materials, brick, wood, slate, stained glass, stone, often in a personal variant of the Stick style earlier developed by Hunt.

A late major commission of Furness's career was the Library of the University of Pennsylvania (1888–1891), constructed under the direction of a building committee chaired by his brother Horace Furness. The library was widely recognized in its time. Particularly praised was its functional layout, based upon a four-story central reading room flanked to one side by a large apsidal study ringed with small book-lined alcoves and to the other side by a glass-roofed bookstack. The concept of storing books in stacks rather than lining the walls of the reading rooms was relatively new at the time. It was a bold stroke by Furness to provide not only a large initial stack unit, but one that could be infinitely expanded by relocation of the end wall as extensions were made necessary by the growth of the collections. The library was the culmination of Furness's career. The element of caricature remained in the unorthodox overscaled crockets of the tower parapet and in the gigantic stairhall window, but the building did not glower and shock as did the Provident. The designer's bold hand had been calmed and mellowed by years of maturing experience. Color and originality were present in force, but the building as a whole possessed a more quiet strength than had been seen in the earlier work.

As the firm grew larger, Furness was less able to take a personal part in the design of each project. The firm began to embrace the new classicism, a style for which Furness had never displayed any particular affinity despite the knowledge of it that he had gained from Hunt. His design philosophy rapidly became an anachronism in the changing taste of the day. When the firm associated with MCKIM, MEAD, AND WHITE in the design of the Girard Bank (1905–1907), Allen Evans received the credit. The client, perhaps fearing another Provident, had stipulated that Furness was to have no hand in the work.

For several decades after his death in 1912, the work of Frank Furness was considered aberrant and disreputable. There was no room for his mannerism in the discipline of the American Renaissance, no room for his wit in the sobriety of the Modern. Only recently have those very few of his buildings that survive been accorded the respect that they deserve. The University of Pennsylvania Library, renamed the Furness Building, stands as his monument.

In the perspective of history, Frank Furness may be seen as the great final salvo in the pyrotechnics of the Victorian period, the person who tied together its varied sources into a cohesive and singular style. As an individual, he merits the ultimate praise that can be given to any artist, that he was able to create forms of power, integrity, and meaning sufficient to transcend the stylism of his own time and to speak eloquently to succeeding generations.

ANDREW CRAIG MORRISON

WORKS

*1866–1867, Unitarian Church, Germantown; 1868–1870, Church of the Holy Apostles; *1869–1871, Rodef Shalom Synagogue; *1871–1873, Jewish Hospital; 1871–1876, Pennsylvania Academy of the Fine Arts; *1872–1873, Philadelphia Warehouse Company; *1873–1875, Guarantee Trust and Safe Deposit Company; *1874, Armory for the First Troop (addition), Philadelphia City Cavalry; 1874–1875, Pennsylvania Institution for the Deaf and Dumb (addition); 1875?–1876, Thomas Hockley House; *1875–1876, Philadelphia Zoological Gardens Elephant House, Restaurant, and Gatehouses (the Gatehouses remain standing); *1876, Brazilian Pavilion, Centennial Exhibition; 1876, Centennial National Bank; *1876–1879, Provident Life and Trust Company; 1877, Kensington National Bank; *1878–1879, Church of the Redeemer for Seamen and Their Families; *1879–1880, Library Company of Philadelphia; Philadelphia. 1879–1881, William H. Rhawn House (Knowlton), Fox Chase, Pa. 1881, Clement Griscom House, *Dolobran,* Haverford, Pa. *1882–1884, Penn National Bank, Philadelphia. 1882, Samuel Shipley House, *Winden,* West Chester, Pa. *1883–1884, National Bank of The Republic; 1883–1886, First Unitarian Church and Parish House; Philadelphia. c.1884, Philadelphia and Reading Railroad Depot, Graver's Lane, Chestnut Hill, Pa. *1886–1888, Baltimore and Ohio Passenger Station, Philadelphia. *1886, Baltimore and Ohio Railroad Depot, Chester, Pa. 1887, William Winsor House (*Hedgley*), Ardmore, Pa. 1888–1891, Library, University of Pennsylvania, Philadelphia. 1889–1891, Williamson Free School of Mechanical Trades, Elwyn, Pa. 1891–1892, Chapel, Mount Sinai Cemetery, Frankford, Pa. *1892–1893, Pennsylvania Railroad Station at Broad Street (enlargement and renovation), Philadelphia. 1896–1911, Merion Cricket Club, Haverford, Pa. 1897–1898, Philadelphia Saving Fund Society (addition); *1898, West End Trust Building; 1905–1907, Girard Trust Company (with McKim, Mead, and White); Philadelphia.

BIBLIOGRAPHY

MASSEY, JAMES C. 1963a "Frank Furness in the 1870's." *Charette* 43, Jan.: 13–16.

MASSEY, JAMES C. 1963b "Frank Furness in the 1880's." *Charette* 43, Oct.: 25–29.

MASSEY, JAMES C. 1966 "Frank Furness: The Declining Years, 1890–1912." *Charette* 46, Feb.: 8–13.

MYERS, HYMAN 1976 *The Architect and the Building.* Philadelphia: Pennsylvania Academy of the Fine Arts.

O'GORMAN, JAMES F. 1973 *The Architecture of Frank Furness.* Philadelphia Museum of Art.

FURTTENBACH, JOSEPH

Joseph Furttenbach (1591–1667) became involved in architecture by default. Born in Leutkirch, Germany, as son of a senior member of the City Council, he was destined to become a merchant. At about age twenty, he embarked on a ten-year trip to Italy, described in detail in his *Newes Itinerarium* (1626), which in later years became the standard guidebook for travelers to Italy. The years spent in Italy became the basis for his numerous writings on architecture and also for his own limited and less significant career as an architect. In or about 1621, he returned to Germany and settled in Ulm. In subsequent years, he was engaged in writing a series of architectural treatises, published in Ulm between 1626 and 1630. *Newes Itinerarium* was followed by *Architectura Civilis, Architectura Navalis,* and *Architectura Martialis.* In 1631, Furttenbach was placed in charge of the *Stadtbauamt,* the agency responsible for construction activities in Ulm. While holding this office, Furttenbach designed the Brechhaus (1634), a hospital whose plan followed Italian models. He also continued his theoretical writings and published his most influential treatise, *Architectura Universalis* (1635). In 1640, he designed his own house which contained a famous collection of art works and models, described by W. Reinold in his *Inventarium* (1660). One year later he built the Kommödienhaus, a theater which seated one thousand spectators. During the remaining years of his life he continued his writing: the *Architectura Recreationis* (1640), containing engravings of the curtains for the Ulm theater, was printed in Augsburg, where also the *Architectura Privata* and the *Mannhafter Kunstspiegel* appeared in print.

Of Furttenbach's architectural works hardly a trace survives. His buildings were sober and distinguished themselves mainly through the addition of some decorative elements in the Italian style. His writings, however, contain elements which became important during the baroque period, especially the *enfilade,* "the arrangement in line of all doors of a Suite of State Rooms" and ample staircases (Hempel, 1965; p. 38). Most influential were those parts of his writings that dealt with the theater. Furttenbach was especially interested in the functioning of the machinery needed for performances and the arrangement of the stage. The influence of Sebastiano Serlio and Niccolo Sabbatini is as obvious as that of Giulio Parigi, whom he had met in Florence and of whose designs for Florentine festivities Furttenbach had obtained prints. The numerous engravings contained in Furttenbach's writings secured the success of his writings on the stage, since the precise information allowed the use of the various treatises as handbooks.

Egon Verheyen

WORKS

*1634, Brechhaus; *1640, Joseph Furttenbach Residence; *1641, Kommödienhaus; Ulm, Germany.

BIBLIOGRAPHY

Furttenbach, Joseph (1626)1971 *Newes Itinerarium Italiae.* Reprint. Hildesheim, Germany, and New York: Olms.

Furttenbach, Joseph 1628 *Architectura Civilis.* Ulm, Germany: Saur.

Furttenbach, Joseph (1629)1975 *Architectura Navalis.* Reprint. Hildesheim, Germany, and New York: Olms.

Furttenbach, Joseph (1630)1975 *Architectura Martialis.* Reprint. Hildesheim, Germany, and New York: Olms.

Furttenbach, Joseph (1635)1975 *Architectura Universalis.* Reprint. Hildesheim, Germany, and New York: Olms.

Furttenbach, Joseph (1640)1971 *Architectura Recreationis.* Reprint. Hildesheim, Germany, and New York: Olms.

Furttenbach, Joseph (1641)1971 *Architectura Privata.* Reprint. Hildesheim, Germany, and New York: Olms.

Furttenbach, Joseph 1663 *Mannhafter Kunstspiegel.* Augsburg, Germany: Schultes.

Hempel, Eberhard 1965 *Baroque Art and Architecture in Central Europe.* Harmondsworth, England: Penguin.

Hewitt, Barnard (editor) 1958 *The Renaissance Stage: Documents of Serlio, Sabbattini and Furttenbach.* Translated by Allardyce Nicoll, John H. McDowell, and George R. Kernodle. Coral Gables, Fla: University of Miami Press.

Mittenbühler, Robert L. 1969 *Aesthetic Currents in German Baroque Architecture.* Unpublished Ph.D. dissertation, Syracuse University, New York.

Nagler, A. M. 1953 "The Furttenbach Theatre in Ulm." *Theatre Annual* 11:45–69.

Reinbold, W. 1660 *Inventarium.* Augsburg, Germany.

GABRIEL, ANGE JACQUES

No doubt educated by his father, JACQUES GA-
BRIEL, Ange Jacques Gabriel (1698–1782) first
appears on entry to the Royal Academy of Architecture in 1728 and as a collaborator with his father
on the Place Royale in Bordeaux in 1729. Thereafter employed under his father on royal buildings,
he does not seem to have had a private career. He
does seem to have enjoyed special favor with
Louis XV, who was personally interested in architecture, and he succeeded his father as *contrôleur* of
Versailles in 1735, and as *premier architecte* and director of the Academy in 1742. He retired from the
position of *premier architecte* in March 1775, less
than a year after the death of Louis XV, but retained the honorary title and the directorship of
the Academy until his death in 1782.

From 1742 on, there was a rapid growth in the
scope of the king's requirements of his architect.
The royal apartments were constantly rearranged
or redecorated to satisfy the king's craving for privacy and his sophisticated conception of convenience and comfort. A comprehensive project
evolved for each of the major châteaux: Versailles,
Fontainebleau, Compiègne; the Château of La
Muette was transformed, and the newly acquired
Châteaux of Choisy and Bellevue were greatly extended. All the important royal residences were
provided with theaters; garden pavilions and
hermitages were built at Trianon, Fontainebleau,
Compiègne, and Choisy; hunting lodges were
built in the major royal forests of which one was
developed into the extensive Château of Saint
Hubert; a new parish church was built at Choisy
and another ordered for Saint Hubert. In addition,
Gabriel was entrusted with the vast project for an
Ecole Militaire, the completion of the Louvre to
accommodate the Royal Academies and the Grand
Conseil, and, following inconclusive competitions, the Place Louis XV, which ultimately included a new building for the Garde-meuble de la
Courenne behind one of its monumental façades.
Moreover, there was work to be done at the king's
behest for the members of his circle and the king
of Denmark.

In analyzing Gabriel's works, it is possible to
trace a precedent for each of them in the works of
the founding members of the Academy and to relate the differences to the doctrine elaborated in
academic circles in the intervening years; indeed,
in accordance with the fundamental principles of
the Academy, under whose influence Gabriel developed and over which he was to preside for his
entire independent career, it is essential to do so. If
Gabriel's transformation of his models may generally be related to JACQUES FRANÇOIS BLONDEL's

criticism of them it is not because there was any special connection between the two men but because it was Blondel, of all Gabriel's contemporaries, who wrote the fullest elaboration of the academic approach to architecture.

Starting from the fundamental classical standpoint of adherence to the rules bequeathed by antiquity and reliance on the authority of the masters, the Academicians invoked VITRUVIUS, ANDREA PALLADIO, and GIACOMO BAROZZI DA VIGNOLA, and studied the monuments of Rome. In addition, Blondel and his colleagues accorded similar status to CLAUDE PERRAULT and the Mansarts (see FRANÇOIS MANSART and JULES HARDOUIN MANSART), and they were particularly proud of their own achievement in the development of convenient plans and comfortable rooms. But neither the greatest ancients nor the moderns were considered beyond reproach, and no servile imitation or blind submission was called for: the perfection of architecture had still to be achieved and the only road to it was through emulation. Generous scope was accorded to individual genius, regulated by good taste. Difficult as good taste was to define, it did not free the architect's imagination from the discipline of classical principles—propriety and integrity above all.

By the 1740s, Blondel and other academic critics were concerned with the extent to which the more extreme exponents of the rococo had departed from these principles: they called on architects to renounce the illogical and the bizarre, to respect the architectonic principles of the seventeenth century as the only defense against the degenerate influence of fashion. Couched in general terms for maximum effect, though in practice mainly relevant to interior design, their criticism of the rococo was fully in accordance with the rationalism of their age—indeed with its love of physics—and if it is read in the light of the contemporary idea of "perfection" it will be seen to be the expression of a continually developing tradition. Moreover the contrary view—that the rococo was progressive, the critics retrogressive, and the tradition moribund—ignores the complexity

which the principle of propriety promoted, overlooks the monumental works projected or actually erected by the successors of Jules Hardouin Mansart in the decades dominated by Parisian domestic work, underestimates the significance of the revival of royal building activity in the later 1730s, and fails to account for the response of Ange Jacques Gabriel to the enlightened patronage of Louis XV.

When Gabriel's career as *premier architecte* began in 1742, the need for extensive reconstruction on the north side of the Cour Royale at Versailles was the principal concern. The first important project which may be attributed to him was the expansion of his father's limited scheme to replace the insecure building housing the Escalier des Ambassadeurs with a grand project for the reconstruction of the château on all three sides of the Cour Royale. Gabriel's task began with provision for the separation of the public and private lives of the monarchs in keeping with the standards of the time: he kept the old state apartments on the garden sides of the central block but doubled them with smaller comfortable rooms; at right angles, across the head of the Cour Royale, he placed new bedroom suites, also doubled, on either side of a great central *salon* which later came to be designated as the Council Chamber. Correcting the results of ad hoc evolution, he placed the principal staircase at the head of the king's apartments where, unlike the Escalier des Ambassadeurs, it would provide an appropriate introduction: it was balanced by a similar staircase for the queen, and both were provided with covered porticos as the eighteenth century required. The project was modified in 1749, by which time a scheme for building an opera house, under way in 1748, also had to be considered.

In both phases of the project, Gabriel experimented with attics and high roofs culminating in a great domed central pavilion: these provided for the more intimate, and more easily heated rooms required for the *petits appartements* together with accommodation for servants; in accordance with academic classical ideas of propriety they also expressed the hierarchical distinction between the principal blocks, containing the personal rooms of the king and queen, and those flanking it, containing the more public state rooms. The elevations of the early project are clearly derived from the garden façade of the château: the Ionic of LOUIS LE VAU and Jules Hardouin Mansart is translated into Doric—which Blondel considered the most appropriate order for the entrance front of a royal palace—and then, in 1749, into the Corinthian of the chapel. Unlike the ordonnance which Jules Hardouin inherited from Le Vau—in which there is no developed relationship between variation in plane and the plasticity of the order—Gabriel's progresses from pilaster to column in response to the projection of the hierarchically disposed masses to introduce variety while sustaining unity. The most immediate precedents for this work were, above all, François Mansart's Maisons and ROBERT DE COTTE's major projects for Spain and Germany.

The influence of François Mansart is also apparent in Gabriel's work at Fontainebleau (1749). To house the court in the degree of comfort to which it had become accustomed in the early eighteenth century, Jacques Gabriel had begun an immense new four-story wing in 1738. Somewhat less than half had been completed by 1742, but it was not until the end of the decade that Ange-Jacques undertook the great pavilion which was to join the new work with the old. In transforming his father's four-square project, from which pedimented frontispieces emerged to little effect, Ange Jacques referred to Mansart's Maisons: the basic plane of the walls with its sequence of pilasters is interrupted on each front by a second plane with its own sequence of pilasters; this is itself eclipsed by a peristyle of freestanding columns, and the frontispieces seem to grow out of the mass expressing innate vitality.

Between these monumental exercises, Gabriel had produced several schemes in the light, elegant mode developed largely in the domestic field by Jules Hardouin and his followers: a framework of quoins in light relief emphasizes the verticals, and large windows emphasize the voids; sculptural detail plays an important part but the orders are used sparingly for emphasis. The Bourse in Bordeaux (1744) extended the scheme of his father's Place Royale. The transformation of the Château of La Muette into a particularly elegant building with high and elaborate roofs was completed in 1746. The expansion of the accommodation for the king's entourage at Choisy into a large rectilinear block with concealed roofs was begun in 1746. After a decade of effort, a comprehensive scheme was produced in 1747 for the transformation of the undistinguished agglomeration of feudal and Ren-

Gabriel.
Le Butard.
Near Versailles, France.
1749–1750

aissance buildings which the king had inherited at Compiègne. A new church for the expanding village at Choisy, first planned in 1746, was built to a revised scheme between 1748 and 1756. A small retreat for the king and the marquise de Pompadour was built at Fontainebleau in 1749, and a *ménagerie* with a tiny formal garden centering on a pavilion was being built at Trianon at the same time. Several hunting pavilions were built in the forests around Versailles, notably Le Butard at Vaucresson (1749–1750).

Drawn there to hunt in its great forests, Louis XV was to make Compiègne one of the court's three principal residences: that the scheme for its transformation was, at the outset, consistent in style with contemporary smaller-scale work rather than with the more monumental scheme for upgrading Fontainebleau well demonstrates the degree to which an academic classical architect's scope for stylistic development was constrained by the circumstances of a commission. Versailles was the chief seat of Europe's greatest monarch, Fontainebleau his principal ancestral domain in the country, and Compiègne a provincial outpost upon which it was occasionally necessary for him to base himself when reviewing troop maneuvers in the north of France. It would certainly not have been appropriate to project a more monumental Cour Royale for Compiègne than the Cour de Marbre at Versailles, for which no grand project of transformation had yet been adopted, or the Cour Ovale at Fontainebleau. Given the interest shown by Louis XV in ameliorating the condition of Compiègne, it was perfectly appropriate, however, for Gabriel to follow the stylistic examples set by his father in the new wing at Fontainebleau, which began the transformation of the Cour du Cheval Blanc.

The small projects of the last two years of the decade dictated a duality of conception: the church at Choisy had to provide for a village parish but also for the king's public worship; the hermitages and hunting pavilions had to accord with the king's dignity but also provide an environment in which he could relax. In the garden pavilion at

Trianon—the Pavillon Français—and the hermitage at Fontainebleau, a rigorous formalism was complemented by the light, elegant articulation of the Parisian domestic mode. To temper the monumentality appropriate to a royal commission for the Choisy church, Gabriel referred again to François Mansart: as on the flanking pavilions of the Hôtel Carnavalet, the rustication of their façades must be supposed to continue behind the panels applied to frame the central openings, implying greater strength than is visually apparent: the ornamental tempers the monumental, playing across it in counterpoint.

At the same time, Gabriel's conception of the ornamental was changing. The acanthus consoles which were to support the cornice over the door at Le Butard were replaced in execution by the architectonic triglyph motif so popular with MICHEL-ANGELO. The next year, in a rejected alternative project for a second garden pavilion at Trianon, the triglyph consoles have swags threaded through them as in PHILIBERT DELORME's attic at the Tuileries; the weight of additional swags above the windows and the squat proportion of the urns recall JACQUES GERMAIN SOUFFLOT's work on the Hôtel Dieu in Lyons. Moreover, in contrast to his early interiors at Versailles and Fontainebleau—apartments for the Dauphin on his two marriages; intimate withdrawing rooms for the king, the queen, and other members of the royal family—which usually had to accord with the existing moderate rococo work of his predecessors,

Gabriel's earliest unconstrained essays in interior decoration for the hermitages and hunting pavilions were essentially tectonic. Recalling mid-seventeenth-century practice, this approach became more and more popular with Gabriel when free to adopt it. Most significant, however, is the *salon* of the Pavillon Français: doubtless inspired by the *salon* of the Pavillon de l'Aurore at Sceaux, but with free-standing Corinthian columns to mask the transition from octagon to circle, this is certainly one of the earliest interiors in which the orders reassert control after their eclipse in the period of the rococo, and it was fully in line with the progressive view that in interior decoration, as on façades, architecture is always superior to chimerical ornament.

The architectonic approach to decorative detail, developed by 1750, was complemented by strictness of line and firmness of form, notable particularly in lower and simpler roofs, continuous horizontals, drastic reduction in curved elements and carved ornament. This was the *noble simplicité* demanded by mid-century by critics in correction of prevailing eighteenth-century practice. Such measures were brought to bear in 1751 on the correction of plans for the Place de Bourgogne in Bordeaux prepared by a local architect, and in the transformation of the 1747 project for Compiègne.

At Compiègne, the entrance wing was suppressed in favor of a low colonnade between pavilions terminating the court's side wings: central frontispieces on these wings, matching those on the new pavilions, were based on the counterpoint principle developed at Le Butard, and the arcades of the ground floor were replaced by a rusticated basement, with the rustication violating the integrity of the rectangular window frames as it had rarely been allowed to do in France since the generation following the Italian late Renaissance masters. The king, the queen, and the Dauphin were given a new two-story range on the raised terrace addressing the park at an oblique angle to the entrance axis, the awkward junction being skillfully masked in the hemicyclical plan of the antechamber terminating the entry sequence in the wing at the head of the Cour Royale. The king's block, in the center of the elongated composition, is set well forward of the wings for the queen and Dauphin. Each section is flanked by rusticated pavilions. Another pavilion, with an applied temple-front motif, marks the center of the king's block; the sides of the central block, unlike the front, are treated in the same way as the pavilions flanking the side wings. Throughout, the windows of the principal floor are linked with those of the attic by panels suspended from the stringcourse but while those on the side wings are flat, like banners, on

Gabriel.
Pavillon Français, Palais de Versailles.
France.
1749

the king's façade they bear the motif of a cornice supported on triglyph consoles with threaded swags. Thus, each part of the building prepares for the next from the sides to the center where the whole composition culminates in the temple-front motif. The complex and subtle system with which Gabriel integrated this façade and relieved its protracted horizontals was disrupted by his pupil Louis Le Dreux in execution.

In plan, the project for the Ecole Militaire, upon which work began late in 1751, is clearly an expansion of Les Invalides to satisfy the basic requirements of the brief; in elevation it is a revision of the south façade of the Louvre, in terms of *noble simplicité*. Anticipating Blondel's criticism, Gabriel did not actually suppress Perrault's attic but demoted it to the status of a mezzanine with rectangular windows and raised new attics to stress the pavilions; above all, he introduced movement to the façade by establishing a progression from pilasters, on the main body of the building, to freestanding columns for the frontispieces. As for the rest of the vast scheme, the subsidiary buildings are quite as austere as those of Les Invalides and Saint Cyr.

In connection with the articulation of the two major buildings in the executed project for the Place Louis XV, approved in mid-1753 but modified in 1755 after work had begun, the colonnade of the Louvre must certainly be borne in mind. It is, however, an oversimplification to see this as the origin of Gabriel's scheme: the idea of a colonnade had been incorporated in several of the entries to the first competition for the design of the square; also, the system of articulation adopted here—a rusticated basement supporting a colossal order— was that evolved for royal squares by Jules Hardouin Mansart and Robert de Cotte. Blondel endorsed this in general but criticized the engaged columns of the Place Vendôme pavilions on the ground that column and wall were incompatible alternative modes of support. Unlike his predecessors, Gabriel had an extended range of view to

cope with and, instead of the familiar progression from pilaster to column, used a three-dimensional order throughout. His colonnades fill the central recessions of his twin buildings with a vitality which all the weight of their side pavilions was needed to contain; like the side peristyles, they are related to the wall by pilaster responds but no such premise links the partially engaged frontispieces to the mass. Instead, their outer columns are partially engaged. The former articulate forces implicit in the mass while the latter—in the light of the incompatibility of column and wall implicit in academic classical strictures against the engagement of columns—suggest an extraneous element imposed on the mass. The apparent continuity of the former between and beyond the pavilions binds each building into a tight unit, the intrusion of the latter as tetrastyle temple-front motif, echoed on the façade of the resited Eglise de la Madeleine beyond, assimilates all three buildings into a greater whole.

The decorative details of the two façades were drawn from the architectonic repertory developed in 1750. The window frames, which had to be visible in the half-light of the colonnade, are strong compositions in which the architrave pushes up to penetrate the zone of the frieze. The sentry boxes, defining the square in association with moats, rise like great pedestals from which the frontispieces thrust out, with curved pediments on triglyph consoles, in an utterly Michelangelesque context of interpenetrating masses.

The third major composition of the 1750s with the impress of Gabriel's Louvre experience clearly stamped upon it was the 1759 project for Versailles. As we have seen, the satisfaction of the complex compositional requirements at Versailles involved distinguishing the principal block containing the royal apartments and, ideally, further differentiating the principal entrances, though this had not been attempted in the earlier schemes, together with the integration of all the masses, including the chapel, into a coherent whole. Gabriel

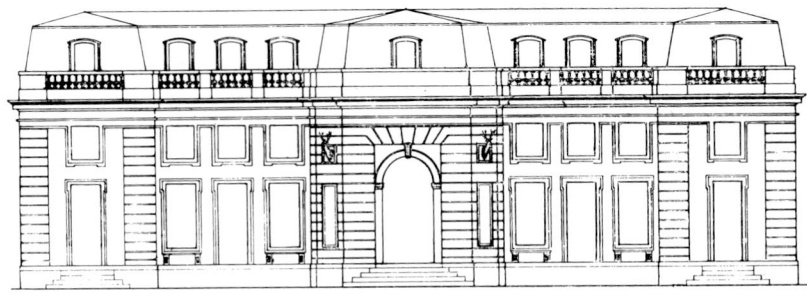

Gabriel.
Saint Hubert
(reconstruction).
Near Rambouillet, France.
1755–1774

rejected not only the high French roofs of the Cour de Marbre as he had rejected those of the Cour Carrée du Louvre in his 1754 projects for its completion, but also the traditional French approach to massing and articulation and the academically correct regular order. Instead, he adopted the Corinthian order of the chapel and worked almost entirely in the Roman idiom with homogeneous blocks and a selectively applied order, conceived of as an independent agent, as in GIOVANNI LORENZO BERNINI's third project for the Louvre.

Powerful half-columns like those in the central section of Bernini's façade were used by Gabriel to distinguish the main block containing the principal royal apartments; similar colonnades provided strong accents on the end façades of these wings without closing the composition to the chapel on the right. Only in the domed center can one speak of a pavilion in the traditional French sense; full columns were placed before the projecting mass here as a focal point. Full columns were also placed before the central three bays of the wings to distinguish the principal entrances: as these were in the same plane as the half-columns of the bays at either end of the wings they not only provided for the continuity of the ordonnance but, assimilated to the central pavilion, established a compositional pyramid. Beyond this, the coherence of the whole vast scheme depended upon the uniform entablature, the relatively simple contour, and the regular rhythm of the window frames.

Apart from these great projects—and authoritative revisions of a project by the Danish King Frederick V's architect Eigtwedt for a great church in Copenhagen, 1754—Gabriel worked on several more hunting pavilions and hermitages for Louis XV in the 1750s. Of the former, Saint Hubert near Rambouillet was the most significant. An expansion of Le Butard, Saint Hubert was to be Gabriel's only unconstrained exercise in the genre of the *maison de plaisance*. As at Champs, the principal reception rooms occupied the center where, dominated by the great high *salon,* they were flanked by subsidiary reception rooms and the main apartment on the ground floor while small comfortable rooms occupied the second floor; the servants were installed in the mansards. Although

the extraction of the *salon* from the main body of the building went as far as possible toward the integration of house and garden, the pavilion containing it—though rusticated in strong contrast to the main walls—was tightly bound to the main mass by a continuous entablature below a uniform roofline. When one considers that the basic approach here was evolved for Le Butard in 1750, the contrast between Gabriel's work at Saint Hubert (1755) and at the Château of La Muette (1746) is another startling indication of the effect of the measures he formulated in 1750–1751 in accordance with progressive principles.

Of the later hermitages, the projects for Choisy (1753) and Trianon (1761–1762) are essentially antithetical: the first, attached to an elegant country house, was vigorous in contour but symmetrical in plan and articulated in accordance with the simplest principles of the regular repetition of a single motif; the second is a clear cubic independent entity, informally arranged inside and articulated in accordance with the principle of progression to impose a hierarchical development on its four sides. Each derives from one of the two immediately relevant precedents, the retreats built for Louis XIV by Jules Hardouin Mansart at Trianon and Marly.

The Grand Trianon's low elevation, flat balustrated roof, and diversified plan integrated with its garden setting, was well suited to the requirements of Choisy; its sumptuousness was not. Although the form of the Choisy building recalls that of the new type of royal villa, in plan and articulation it recalls the new type of Parisian private house. As in many Parisian *hôtels,* the central *salon de parade*—the largest and therefore the highest room—projecting into the garden was flanked by two symmetrical apartments with rooms of *commodité* associated with rooms of *société,* all opening onto the garden thanks to the vigorous indentation of the façade. This diversified contour, expressing the internal divisions, was complemented by an articulation of the utmost simplicity: integration was achieved through the uniform treatment of the frames of the windows and doors, which formed a continuous series uninterrupted even by the quoins at the corners, and the Ionic order was used only to stress the projection of the octagonal principal salon into the garden.

At Marly, with a regular site at the perpendicular intersection of two extended axes, Jules Hardouin produced four identical façades centralized by pedimented avant-corps and integrated with a continuous order of Corinthian pilasters coupled only about the four main portals. Gabriel, at Trianon, also had to cope with a situation in which the principal axes of garden and entrance court were at right angles, but here the already established garden was at a higher level than the access road, and its axis was terminated close to the site of the pavilion by a botanical garden that did not provide a suitable view. Leaving the side bays without an order, Gabriel at first retained Mansart's expression of the triumphal arch motif to frame the larger central bay of three bay façades, but the executed project was expanded to five bays with an equally spaced order. Pilasters are used above the rusticated basement of the three-story south façade, containing the entrance, where it would enhance the already pronounced height. The same motif, used on the two-story façades facing the king's formal garden to the west and subsidiary gardens to the north, countered the dominant horizontals. On the west façade, moreover, the motif became a partially engaged colonnade forming a portico that breached the wall, breaking down the barrier between house and garden. No order was used on the east side above the botanical garden. Thus each façade was treated in a way utterly in accordance with the principles of propriety, and with the consequent hierarchical progression from east to west, Gabriel resolved the problems created by the axes and infused the inert cubic mass with vitality.

On the strength of the almost endless changes to the royal apartments at Versailles and at Fontainebleau in the 1750s, Gabriel's approach to interior decoration and that of Louis XV has generally been considered conservative, that is, unwilling to depart from the style of his youth. Such a judgment fails to notice his preferences elsewhere and to take into account the strongly felt need to preserve the unity of context. As we know from a contemporary discussion of the ceiling of the Council Chamber at Fontainebleau in 1751 and from later correspondence over the restoration of the ceiling of the queen's bedroom at Versailles, Gabriel placed no less importance on this latter principle than did academic critics such as Blondel. Apart from evidence drawn from the interiors of wholly new buildings, even at Versailles it is as clear as the context permitted that the attitude of the king and his *premier architecte* was progressive, that is, accepting the logic and discipline of classical architecture, rather than the fantasy and licence of the latest rococo, as the only true means of progress.

Among the most sumptuous examples of the modern taste subjected to the control of the antique were the king's bedroom and Council Chamber at Fontainebleau refurbished by Gabriel after their enlargement (1751–1754). The new work had to accord with the elements from the old but, given the character of the château, outright antique grandeur would not have been appropriate.

Gabriel. *Council Chamber. Versailles, France. 1755*

The Council Chamber at Versailles (1755) certainly is not a work in which architectonic elements dominate those of the rococo. Perhaps the most splendid royal exercise in the modern taste, it has little antique about it but the strength and symmetry of its moldings and the cornice and dado inherited from an earlier campaign: it had to effect the transition from the state bedroom of Louis XIV to the more agreeable apartment in which Louis XV actually slept. At the other end of that suite, in the apartment installed for the king's daughter, Madame Adelaïde, the rococo at its most ravishing was unopposed. In contrast to the work within this range, the dining room (1753–1754) on the first floor between the interior courts was given the purely tectonic paneling which Gabriel had long preferred for intimate rooms when free to do so. The main staircase and principal rooms of the 1759 project for Versailles are almost purely architectonic, and this approach, insofar as the staircases are concerned at least, dates back to the 1754 project for the Louvre.

The main rooms of the Choisy retreat and the Petit Trianon mark important stages in Gabriel's development of a tectonic approach to interior

Gabriel. Petit Trianon, Palais de Versailles. France. 1761–1768

decoration. In almost exclusively rectilinear rooms, ovoid forms still play an important part in the earlier work, but in the later one the frames of the paneling are strictly geometrical throughout, with classical moldings. The basic decorative motifs are the acanthus, the laurel, the swag, and the floral trophy. The great circular salon at Saint Hubert must have been as advanced for its date (1756–1757) as that of the Pavillon Français at Trianon was for 1749, for in it the rococo seems to have given way entirely before the classical. Apart from the order of Corinthian pilasters and the relief panels, which were the principal elements of the decoration, such motifs as the laurel wreath and the Vitruvian scroll—both already familiar on Gabriel's exteriors—play the parts which had formerly been given to *coquilles, roseaux, palmiers,* and so on.

The great projects of the last eleven years of the reign, after the reopening of the royal construction sites on the conclusion of the Seven Years War, were all revisions of earlier projects, at first in a spirit of optimism, then with a degree of realism as the truth of the financial situation became apparent. The approach to articulation which Gabriel had derived from Bernini in 1759 for Versailles proved invaluable not only for the introduction of selective emphasis but also for the localization of change in the context of existing work.

The first of these projects was for the Opéra at Versailles (1763). On the façade above the street the rustication was extended across the side bays, suppressing the verticals and leaving the horizontals unopposed. On the central projection, however, the verticals were strengthened by the substitution of engaged columns in antis for the pilasters, and the windows were linked. Unlike the revision of the great pavilion at Fontainebleau of thirteen years earlier, the forces displayed here are not extracted from within the mass and developed in a progression from pilaster to column from the sides to the center in scrupulously preserved horizontal layers, but confronted with one another in a contrast between the horizontal layers of rustication and the imposed verticals of the order. On the main façade, the central projection was suppressed and a colonnade substituted for the pilaster order supporting the pediment. The problem here had been to integrate the façade of the Opéra, itself necessarily centralized, with the end of the north wing with its colonnade and arcade, in a decentralized whole. Unlike those of Jules Hardouin, Gabriel's columns were not backed by pilasters and therefore neither connected to the wall nor, logically, to the existing system. The distinction between an approach to articulation based on pilasters expressing the forces in the wall and one based

on the conception of the column as self-assertive displayed here to give added power to the Opéra façade without disrupting integration with the rest of the wing, is a measure of Gabriel's subtle logic.

Revising the Opéra auditorium, Gabriel ultimately adopted the truncated ellipse of GASPARE VIGARANI's plan for Versailles and of the most modern theaters of Italy and France. At the same time Vigarani's Tuileries theater, then being reconstructed by Gabriel and Soufflot, inspired an essentially architectonic decorative scheme which led to the introduction of a colonnade in 1765: avoiding the clifflike appearance of the traditional opera house, this provided a strong vertical accent to complement the horizontals of the galleries and support for two recessed upper levels. A colonnade had been a feature of Vigarani's plans for both the Versailles and Tuileries theaters, but the form Gabriel gave it for his own project in 1765 recalls, rather, Palladio. The colonnade was finally recessed around a great central niche, defining the area where propriety forbade seating if the king was using his private box below. At first, Gabriel devised a sumptuous antique decoration based upon a form of arabesque popular with François Mansart but rarely seen in France since the progenitors of the rococo had transformed it; in the final project, both in the auditorium and the superb foyer this motif ceded to the type of relief panel that played an increasingly important role in Gabriel's late approach to interior decoration.

Pending the long delayed comprehensive rebuilding of Versailles—which was, in fact, never to go beyond the replacement of the right wing—there was continuous costly change to the royal apartments. As always, Gabriel had to conform to the spirit of existing work and he took as much care to do so whether that work was in the modern taste, as in the case of most of the rooms redecorated for the king's daughters in the late 1760s, or in the antique, as in the case of the ceiling of the queen's bedroom, where he drew upon the tradition of Charles Le Brun but classicized it by preserving the integrity of the frames with their antique moldings and where he replaced the more baroque elements with arabesques or allegories of greater *gravitas* and purer antique lineage. Arabesques played an important part in the Raphaelesque (see RAPHAEL) stucco work in the library of Madam Sophie (1769). In rooms off the main enfilades, above all the baths (1770) and library (1774) of the king, and in the salon of the comtesse du Barry at Fontainebleau (1772), Gabriel found himself less constrained: none of these rooms warranted the full éclat of an order—though the comtesse du Barry was given one at

Gabriel.
Opera House, Palais de
*   Versailles.*
France.
1761–1768

Fontainebleau—but each was treated in an essentially tectonic way.

There is no direct evidence that the 1759 project for Versailles was even provisionally adopted by the king pending the availability of funds, but it was the undisputed alternative to the mere rebuilding of the right wing when this could no longer be postponed in 1771. Further indirect evidence is provided by the fact that it was considered appropriate to raise the dignity of Fontainebleau and Compiègne after the Seven Years War. At Compiègne, revision took its departure from the existing work, but resulted in a radical transformation in keeping with the ideas embodied in the project for Versailles—which Le Dreux again failed to comprehend in execution. Greatly increasing the majesty of the Cour Royale and the fully integrated Place d'Armes before it, a colossal Ionic order was set over the basement of the pavilions, and the mansards were replaced by a balustraded attic broken only by the pediments. The colonnaded entrance screen was ultimately suppressed in favor of a wrought-iron grill in the interests of the complete integration of the Place d'Armes, with its surrounding arcades and assertive portals.

From the juxtaposition forms—the key to Gabriel's experiments since his first contrapuntal exercises of the late 1740s—it was but a short step to the juxtaposition of autonomous units. This was the solution adopted to salvage the overambitious and only partially executed project for the Ecole Militaire. In taking that step Gabriel referred to Bernini's Palazzo Chigi: three rectilinear masses are juxtaposed, the rusticated side blocks being sharply distinguished from the central one with its smooth wall and colossal order of pilasters. Precisely the same approach, but on a much smaller scale and without the sumptuous order, was adopted by Gabriel for a presbytery at Choisy in late 1763. In compositional technique as well as in the austerity of the completely unadorned side blocks, this building anticipated many of the products of the so-called Revolutionary architects.

The revision of the Ecole Militaire project embodied the idea that the major elements of the establishment—including a public chapel, library, large room for exercises and examinations, council chamber, and apartment for the governor—might all be housed in one principal building providing a suitable backdrop to the Champ de Mars. Twin buildings on the Champ de Mars, already completed, had temple-front motifs without pilaster responds rising through two stories. As there was no possibility of a consistently applied order, Gabriel chose to amplify their basic scheme on a monumental scale for the façade of the new block, at

Gabriel.
Ecole Militaire.
Paris.
1750–1768

first set back, ultimately inserted between them. The new composition, in fact, recalled Le Vau's south front at the Louvre, and referring to Blondel's criticism of the latter, once again it may be seen that Gabriel's work is in large measure determined by the application of academic principles to a suitable model: unlike Le Vau, Gabriel continued the entablature of his colossal Corinthian frontispiece right around the building, and the order itself is extended beyond the pedimented temple-front motif of the central three bays—where it provided apparent support for a great dome—to the first bay on each side, making it the key to the integration of the verticals and horizontals of the whole composition. The severe walls and regularly repeated window frames of the rest of the front continue around projections on the court side; juxtaposed between these projections and the central pavilion are superimposed arcades, changed to colonnades in execution, the lower range continuing beyond to frame the court. Thus, two contrasting systems of articulation were interlocked, and one of the last exercises in the traditional French

Gabriel.
Château de Fontainebleau
    (entrance front with
    alternatives for portal).
France.
1772–1773

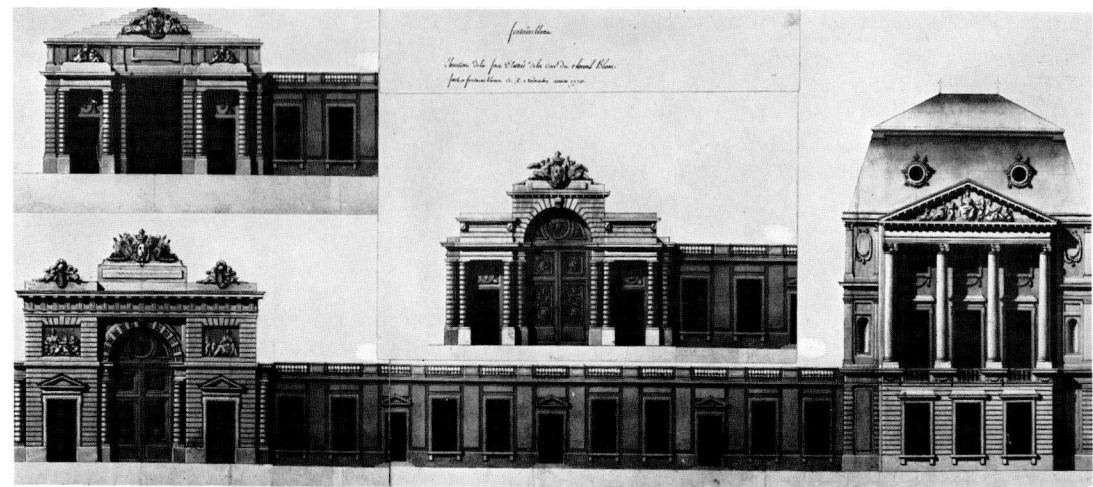

château form, still fully pyramidal in composition, was one of the first major buildings to combine the principal compositional techniques—juxtaposition, interpenetration, and confrontation—of the neoclassicists.

The staircase of the Ecole Militaire is the only one of Gabriel's *grands degrés* to have been executed. Without orders but divided by simple tectonic panels, as often with François Mansart, the walls are of the utmost austerity, relying for relief only on the frames of the doors, the niches, and the sumptuous Corinthian entablature. Apart from the coffering below the landing of the first floor, the dominant impression is made by the *rampe* with its rich arabesque scrolls. In compensation for the enforced self-effacement of the chapel without, the interior—modeled on the Vitruvian Corinthian Hall—gives the most persuasive impression of a pseudo-peripteral temple turned outside-in. The main rooms belong to the same school as those of the Petit Trianon, but on a monumental scale. The Council Chamber, for instance, features a great coffered cove and cornice with ingenious helmeted brackets, trophies of war instead of trophies of peace.

At Fontainebleau the grand project was initially based on the repetition of the original great pavilion and the development in Gabriel's style which took place in the 1750s affected it only in detail until repetition of the earlier work was no longer feasible. One new element was a triumphal entrance pavilion, but as in Jules Hardouin Mansart's work of regularization at the Palais des Etats at Dijon—the most immediately relevant precedent—its ordonnance derives from that of the side pavilions. In his revision of 1773, Gabriel adopted a colossal order of freestanding columns, as Jules Hardouin had done at Dijon, but the most significant change was in the designs for the entrance portal, three powerful alternative variations on the theme of Philibert de l'Orme's monumen-

tal entrance at Anet, rusticated to match the basement of the new pavilions. These projects have justifiably been considered typical of neoclassicism, yet one could hardly find a clearer demonstration of what the Academy meant by emulation of the works of the masters.

The 1759 project for Versailles was only slightly modified after the final decision in 1771 to execute it. As there was no mass corresponding to the chapel on the other side of the Cour Royale, the completely integrated scheme of 1759 tended to seem unbalanced. The central pavilion was given a hexastyle temple-front motif and the six-column peristyles of the end pavilions were replaced by projecting tetrastyle temple-front motifs which closed the composition at the sides to the formal exclusion of the chapel. Inside, exceptional richness was introduced to the great staircase by the relief panels and antique elements in the cove of the great vault, subjected to a framework of ribs with classical moldings following structural lines. The Council Chamber in the center of the scheme was perhaps the most purely architectonic room ever devised by Gabriel. Clearly derived from the existing bedroom of Louis XIV but without its baroque elements, it relies only on a most sumptuous expression of the Corinthian order complemented with rectangular or semicircular relief panels containing allegories and crowned by a highly classical ceiling in the antique taste.

In another mode, the dining room of the new wing at Bellevue (1773) was no less an architectural composition, the absence of an order notwithstanding. Gabriel took his departure from tradition in proposing a stone revetment and relied entirely on sculpture and rich classical cornice, niche, and architrave moldings for his decoration. Although the program for the sculpture here— Apollo and the Muses—recalls that of the foyer of the Opéra at Versailles, Gabriel's treatment of the portico on the end of the side wings in a late rejected version of the comprehensive project for Versailles provides the most persuasive analogy to his treatment of the walls of the dining room at Bellevue.

Gabriel served a connoisseur king who continually supplied him with new commissions, which it was his responsibility to see through with dispatch, in the age par excellence of evolved classicism with its clearly defined laws of propriety and its unfaltering belief that the ideal of architecture was not to be found in novelty but in the adaptation of traditional forms to modern requirements. Gabriel's was the ability of the great classicist to assimilate the lessons learned from others, and his work, viewed as a whole, provides a consummate example of the academic ideal of emulation. Like his greatest predecessors, he was inspired by constraint, and reason was his guide as much in his ordered, yet convenient, distribution as in his essentially architectonic articulation.

His concern to establish rapport between exterior and interior was fundamental to his approach to composition, though in the great projects the requirements of unity often inhibited a development in the articulation of that intimate relationship between plan and façade recommended by academic critics like Blondel. Though flexible, he always accepted the discipline of the axis, and the symmetry and regularity of individual rooms became increasingly important to him. He consistently sought to reconcile these formal aims with the practical requirements of comfort and convenience to which the eighteenth century's advanced standard of living had given rise—especially in the separation of public and private life.

As propriety dictated, he based his ordonnance on the most relevant models provided by his predecessors as premier architecte—in particular the garden façade of Versailles, Marly, the Place Vendôme, and the seventeenth-century projects for the completion of the Louvre. All of them were transformed in accordance with compositional principles deduced from the greatest masters of modern architecture—in particular François Mansart, Michelangelo, Bernini.

From Mansart, Gabriel learned how to express the innate vitality of his masses by varying the plasticity of the order in concert with the advance and recession of the plane of the wall. In response to specific compositional requirements, rather than expressionistic impulse, Gabriel experimented with other techniques to supplement this basic approach: the superposition of contrasting planes with specific reference to François Mansart; the interpenetration of forms with general reference to Michelangelo; the confrontation of column and wall for selective emphasis in the context of homo-geneous masses; and the juxtaposition of autonomous blocks, with specific reference to Bernini.

The decorative motifs with which Gabriel complemented these compositional principles were not new either, although after 1750 they constituted a rather more extensive repertory of essentially architectonic detail than he had inherited from his immediate predecessors. Principally derived from sixteenth-century French and Italian sources, especially Michelangelo, this repertory reflected the attitude of progressive critics who, rejecting the fantasy and license of the rococo, proclaimed the fundamental academic belief that progress depends upon reason and discipline. The introduction of this repertory, together with the measures he had adopted after 1750 to achieve the strictness of line, firmness of form, and simplicity of contour demanded by the mid-century critics in correction of prevailing practice, marked a watershed in the development of Gabriel's style. The sumptuousness which characterized his work in the 1740s gave way to the concept of *noble simplicité* founded on the premise that ornament should be provided by the architectural members of a building—above all, the orders and the frames of doors and windows. Moreover, in reverse of the process by which the rococo approach to ornament had tentatively spread from the interior to the exterior, during the years in which domestic architecture eclipsed public, this essentially architectonic approach to ornament was now to be translated from the exterior to the interior. Though he continued the rococo tradition well into the 1760s in his work on the royal apartments at the major châteaux, when not constrained by existing work Gabriel showed himself to be a leader.

Important as *noble simplicité* was to him, Gabriel always went to great lengths to avoid disparity in what he added to existing work. As so many of his designs were for great buildings of the past, no one approach can be said to characterize his style at a specific time as distinct from a specific project. Yet the clarity, indeed rectangularity, of mass which he preferred when free to do so—inherited from Jules Hardouin Mansart—and the compositional techniques which he assimilated from earlier masters to transform it—in particular the juxtaposition and confrontation of contrasting forms—together with the architectonic repertory of decorative detail, were the essential ingredients of the first phase of neoclassicism, the so-called style Louis XVI which might, far more reasonably, be labeled the style Gabriel.

CHRISTOPHER TADGELL

WORKS

1742–1775, Palais de Versailles (renovations and additions, including completion of right wing), France. 1744, Place Royale (Bourse; completion of work by Jacques Gabriel), Bordeaux, France. 1746, Château de La Muette (renovations), near Saint Germain, France. 1747-1782, Château de Compiègne (renovations and additions; completed posthumously by others), France. 1748-1756, Church, Choisy, France. 1749, Château de Fontainebleau (renovations, additions, and Great Pavilion), France. 1749, Palais de Versailles (Pavillon Français), France. 1749-1750, Le Butard (hunting lodge), near Versailles, France. 1750-1768, Ecole Militaire, Paris. 1751-1754, Château de Fontainebleau (additions, renovation of the King's Bedroom and the Council Chamber), France. 1753, Hermitage, Choisy, France. 1753-1754, Palais de Versailles (dining room renovations), France. 1754, Louvre (additions), Paris. 1755, Council Chamber, Versailles, France. 1755, Place Louis XV (two buildings), Paris. 1755-1774, Saint Hubert (additions to hunting lodge, including Great Circular Salon), near Rambouillet, France. 1761-1768, Palais de Versailles (Petit Trianon, Opera House, and Hermitage for the Trianon), France. 1764, Tuileries (reconstruction of theater; with Germain Soufflot), Paris. 1766, Château de la Muette (hunting lodge), near Saint Germain, France. 1772-1773, Château de Fontainebleau (renovations and additions, including comtesse du Barry's salon), France. *1773, Château de Bellevue (dining room), near Paris.

BIBLIOGRAPHY

BLONDEL, JACQUES FRANÇOIS (1752-1756)1904-1905 *Architecture française.* 4 vols. Reprint. Paris: Lévy.

BLONDEL, JACQUES FRANÇOIS 1771-1777 *Cours d'architecture.* 6 vols. Paris: Desaint.

BOTTINEAU, YVES 1962 *L'Art d'Ange-Jacques Gabriel à Fontainebleau (1735-1774).* Paris: Boccard.

FELS, EDMOND (1912)1924 *Ange-Jacques Gabriel.* Paris: Laurens.

GRANET, SOLANGE 1963 *Images de Paris: La Place de la Concorde.* Paris: Revue géographique et industrielle de France.

GROMORT, GEORGES 1933 *Jacques-Ange Gabriel.* Paris: Vincent, Fréal.

HAUTECOEUR, LOUIS 1943-1957 *Histoire de l'architecture classique en France.* 7 vols. Paris: Picard.

LAULAN, ROBERT 1950 *L'Ecole Militaire de Paris: Le Monument, 1751-1788.* Paris: Picard.

RACINAIS, HENRY 1950 *Un Versailles Inconnu: Les Petits Appartements des Rois Louis XV et Louis XVI au château de Versailles.* Paris: Lefèbvre.

TADGELL, CHRISTOPHER 1978 *Ange-Jacques Gabriel.* London: Zwemmer.

GABRIEL, JACQUES

One of several members of a French architectural dynasty to bear the same name, Jacques Gabriel (1667-1742) became JULES HARDOUIN MANSART's principal assistant, together with ROBERT DE COTTE, and was admitted to the Royal Academy of Architecture in 1699. *Premier ingénieur des ponts et chaussées* in 1716, he succeeded de Cotte as *premier architecte* and director of the Academy of Architecture in 1734 and 1735 respectively. Extensively employed by private patrons and on public works in the provinces, he was responsible in particular for the bridge at Blois, the Place du Palais des Etats and the Place d'Armes at Rennes, the Place Royale in Bordeaux, considerable work on the Palais des Etats at Dijon, the Cathedral of La Rochelle and the west front of the Cathedral of Orleans, the Louis XV wing at Fontainebleau, the transformation of the royal château of La Muette, and the early phase of Louis XV's extended campaign of work on the redecoration and extension of the royal apartments at Versailles.

CHRISTOPHER TADGELL

GADDI, TADDEO

Except for his activity as consultant to the Cathedral of Florence project (1355-1366), Taddeo Gaddi (14th century) is known from the documents only as a painter. His most important contribution to architecture is, therefore, his approval of Francesco Talenti's (see TALENTI FAMILY) pier design for the Cathedral (1357). Other attributions rest mainly on GIORGIO VASARI's account in the *Lives.*

CHRISTINE SMITH

WORKS

(A)1330-1340, Or San Michele (execution of a design by ARNOLFO DI CAMBIO); (A)after 1333, Ponte Santa Trinita (foundations); (A)after 1333, Ponte Vecchio (rebuilding); (A)after 1337, Bell Tower (completion of design by AMBROGIO GIOTTO DI BONDONE); Florence.

BIBLIOGRAPHY

LADIS, ANDREW 1978 "Taddeo Gaddi: Style and Chronology." Unpublished Ph.D. dissertation, University of Virginia, Charlottesville.

GAGLIARDI, ROSARIO

Rosario Gagliardi (1698?-1762?) was the most important architect working in southeastern Sicily and one of the finest architects Sicily has produced. Born in the city of Syracuse, Gagliardi moved to nearby Noto in the second decade of the eighteenth century. There he established citizenship and in the 1730s developed a thriving architectural practice which included not only the design of buildings in Noto but also the design and construction of buildings in Comiso, Caltagirone, Ragusa, and Syracuse. The extent of his activity is still unknown, but from the evidence available he had a formative influence on the urban environment and architecture of eighteenth-century Sicily. From his drawings it is clear that he was cognizant of Roman baroque experiments in spatial complexity and massing. These lessons he applied and incorporated into a Sicilian baroque style. Interior spaces were simplified but exterior façades were celebrated with a refined use of superimposed tiers, volutes, and free-standing columns. He perfected the design of the Sicilian belfry façade which can be best seen in his Church of San Giorgio (1744–1775) in Ragusa.

STEPHEN TOBRINER

WORKS

1713–1754, Monastery of Santa Maria dell'Arco; 1728–1750, Santa Maria La Rotunda; 1728, Santissimo Crocifisso; c.1729–c.1755, San Carlo Borromeo and the Jesuit College (portions); 1731, Casa del Refugio; 1732, Convent of Santa Maria del Carmine; 1733, Palazzo Battaglia; *1736, San Calogero; 1738–1750, Monastery of Santissimo Salvatore (portions); c.1739–1758, Santa Maria Assunta, Monastery of Santa Chiara; Noto, Italy. c.1740, Chiesa Madre, Comiso, Italy. c.1740–c.1760, Santissima Annunziata, Convent of San Domenico, Noto, Italy. c.1744–c.1775, San Giorgio, Ragusa, Italy. c.1744–1751, San Giuseppe; 1744–1751, Sant'Agata; Caltagirone, Italy.

BIBLIOGRAPHY

BLUNT, ANTHONY 1968 *Sicilian Baroque.* London: Weidenfeld & Nicolson.

BOTTARI, STEFANO 1958 "Contributi alla conoscenza dell'architettura del Settecento in Sicilia." *Palladio* New Series 8:69–77.

TOBRINER, STEPHEN 1982 *The Genesis of Noto: An Eighteenth Century Sicilian City.* London: Zwemmer; Berkeley: University of California Press.

GALILEI, ALESSANDRO

As a representative of the generation that led the transition from baroque to classicism, Alessandro Maria Gaetano Galilei (1691–1737), together with FERDINANDO FUGA, NICOLA SALVI, and LUIGI VANVITELLI, belongs to the most prominent architects of the first half of the eighteenth century in Italy.

Galilei was born in Florence. His father, the notary Giuseppe Maria Galilei, was descended from an old patrician Florentine family and was remotely related to Galileo Galilei. His mother, Margherita Merlini, was the daughter of the medalist Marc'Antonio Merlini, who was in charge of

the grand-ducal mint; her brother, Lorenzo, was a sculptor and architect. Galilei studied mathematics at the Florentine academy and architecture with Antonio Ferri and Giovanni Battista Foggini. His architectural training seems to have been concentrated mainly on the Florentine Cinquencento, as his sketches of buildings by BARTOLOMMEO AMMANNATI and BERNARDO BUONTALENTI attest. Also, his great veneration for MICHELANGELO, which he shared with the young Fuga, seems to have been implanted in those years.

Apparently, Galilei could find no employment in Florence and initially devoted himself to the study of mathematics. In June 1714, he left Florence, John Molesworth (later second Viscount Molesworth), the English minister to the court of Florence, having invited him to England to expand his architectural and technical knowledge. He arrived in London and was installed in Molesworth's house. Though his return to Florence had been planned for the following year, this became impracticable for financial reasons. From 1715, on, helped by his host, Galilei tried to obtain private commissions and, when that failed, turned to public projects. Designs for seven London churches (1715–1716) and projects for two royal palaces, in Saint James's Park and Hyde Park respectively (1716–1718), are known from this period. Nothing went beyond the planning stage. Only in 1718 did he finally succeed in establishing himself in England. In May of that year he concluded a five-year contract with Nicholas Dubois, the translator of GIACOMO LEONI's first English Palladio edition (see ANDREA PALLADIO) (1715). Together, they shared in the development of the Burlington (see LORD BURLINGTON) estates in the West End of London. The first three houses were built in Brewer and Cork Streets; these remained standing until the beginning of the twentieth century. In the same year (1718), the duke of Manchester entrusted Galilei with the erection of the east façade of Kimbolton Castle in Huntingtonshire. That summer, during a stay in Ireland, he drew up plans for Castletown near Dublin, the country seat of William Conolly, speaker of the Irish parliament. In addition, for another Irish acquaintance of the Molesworth family, Marmaduke Coghill, he designed a garden temple for his house, Drumcondra, in Dublin. Castletown was executed only from 1722 on, under the supervision of EDWARD L. PEARCE, whose role in the completed building cannot be clearly distinguished from that of Galilei. The overall plan is probably the latter's, as is presumably also the articulation of the façade, since during Pearce's stay in Florence (1723) Galilei gave him two façade designs. It was also in 1718 that a reproduction of an orangerie

Galilei.
Kimbolton Castle (east
portico).
Huntingtonshire, England.
1718–1719

designed by Galilei appeared in the standard botanical work of Robert Bradley, *The Gentleman and Gardener's Calendar.* Through these commissions, Galilei achieved independence, and in the autumn of 1718 he married an Englishwoman, Letizia Martin.

Through the Tuscan ambassador to Paris, Neri Corsini, who in 1718–1719 was in London for negotiation, Galilei received an offer to return to Florence as architect to the court. After some initial hesitation he accepted, dissolved his contract with Dubois at a financial loss, and in August 1718 left England for Florence. During his five-year stay in England, Galilei maintained a critical distance from the contemporary architecture of CHRISTOPHER WREN, JOHN VANBRUGH, and NICHOLAS HAWKSMOOR; the neo-Palladianism of Burlington developed only after he had left England. In his villa designs he did accept the Palladian layout—a main block connected to side wings by colonnades—which had become the hallmark of English country house design—but he remained faithful to Florentine models of façade design, above all to the villa designs of Ferri. Striving for planarity, he imposed upon the façades a grid of verticals (strips or pilasters) and horizontals (stringcourses) and attempted to achieve three-dimensional effects through the use of large-scale stairways in front of the façade. The body of the building remained static. Only with the portico of Kimbolton Castle did he dare to move from walls structured by relief to the use of columnar orders; here, the elegance of the Doric order contrasts with the "castle air" of the Vanbrugh façades. Galilei preferred to express monumentality by means of a harmonious arrangement of the massings of the building itself and by a clear definition of the contours. This rather static feeling is also reflected in the design for the royal palace. Preserved only in a summary sketch, it relies for its inspiration on the Palazzo Pitti in Florence.

In his London church designs, also preserved only in sketches, Galilei appears largely unimpressed by the English longitudinal buildings with towers. Instead, he attempted to harmonize central domed buildings with the needs of the Anglican rite (galleries are included). Deriving theoretically from LEON BATTISTA ALBERTI and SEBASTIANO SERLIO, his seven designs constitute an eclectic selection of Renaissance and moderately baroque forms. Most noteworthy is the design of a Doric temple ringed by columns on three sides, an almost archeological reconstruction. Even in the ornamentation, this ambivalence becomes apparent. In general, he confines himself to canonical forms; all the more ornamental details can be traced back to Florentine forms. As yet there can be discovered no originality of style, but beneath the academic influences a talent is recognizable. With the portico of Kimbolton, however, Galilei found his own expression.

More important for Galilei than his reaction to English contemporary architecture was the artistic philosophy of Lord Shaftesbury, with its demand for a return to Greek art, that is, to the revival of a strictly antibaroque approach in architecture. He learned of this philosophy from Molesworth who was a friend of Shaftesbury's. Apparently, Galilei was also in contact with other reform groups, but of these little is known.

For Galilei, the time spent as Florentine court architect (1720–1731) was not very productive artistically: aside from the great obsequies (1721 for Margherita Louise d'Orleans; 1724 for Louis I of Spain; 1725 for Cosimo III) there were only engineering commissions from the court. However, as the Corsini family's private architect, he planned an unexecuted expansion of their Florentine town palace and a series of smaller works for various of their estates. Among these is the simply shaped high altar of the Monastery of San Gaggio (1730–1731). In 1722–1724, he remodeled the *galleria* of the Palazzo Cerretani. Here, the spare, severely rectangular ornamentation is in sharp contrast to the usual heavy decoration of the Florentine late baroque. In 1725–1730, he remodeled an existing house near Cortona as a villa for the brothers Venuti; a planned expansion of this was never carried out. The rebuilding of the cathedral choir of Cortona (1729) involved only the addition of a triumphal arch and the arrangement of the choir. Here, his very sparing use of decorative motifs fitted well into the older structure. A Madonna-oratory in Scarperia, started in 1724 but unfinished, is most interesting: a domed structure over a circular plan, the interior almost totally without decoration and of a cool elegance, with a Michelangelesque layering of the walls. The tomb which Sir Edward Gascoigne commissioned for his parents in 1726, was destroyed in 1854 when the church in

Berwick-en-Elmett where it had been erected was rebuilt. Designed as an aedicula in pantheon form, it was decorated only by the great coat-of-arms.

In spite of the small number of commissions, the period was decisive for the development of Galilei's style. The stimulus to renew architecture by returning to antiquity which Galilei had derived from his English sojourn found theoretical support in his Florentine circle of friends, a group of philologists, historians, and theologians around Antonio Maria Salvini, Antonio Francesco Gori and Giovanni Bottari, who belonged to Ludovico Antonio Muratori's "republic of scholars." In 1727, in Cortona, the brothers Venuti founded the Accademia Etrusca, of which Galilei was one of the earliest members. The rediscovery of Giotto and Dante and the new appreciation of FILIPPO BRUNELLESCHI as the founder of the Florentine Renaissance can be traced back to this circle of scholars. For one of them, sometime around 1729, Galilei reconstructed a late Roman martyr-memorial after a letter of Saint Gregory of Nyssa (Giovanni Battista Caracciolo, *Sancti Patri Gregorii Nysseni Epistolae septae,* Florence, 1731). Characteristic for this group of scholars is a new, epistemological view of history and art as a continuous process which also takes in the Middle Ages and tries to re-evaluate them. This attitude is manifested in Galilei's report (1724) on the condition of the Cistercian Abbey of San Galgano near Siena, in which he demands that the Gothic structures be preserved, as well as in his brief against the erection of a baroque high altar in the baptistery of Florence, in which he argues for the maintenance of the unity of the building out of respect for the achievement of earlier times. In this same report, Galilei takes occasion to launch a basic attack on the baroque as such: the principle of the straight line, the right angle, and the unconditional subordination of ornament becomes an absolute law of "true and good" architecture which rests exclusively on symmetry, proportion, and functionality.

With the election of Clement XII to the papacy in July 1730, Galilei was given the opportunity to put his theory into practice. His patron, Neri Corsini, became Cardinal Secretary of State. Neri Corsini, closely connected with the "republic," initiated a reform program in economics and the arts. The greatness and pre-eminence of Italian art were to be revived. An energetic building policy served the same purpose. Disregarding the Roman architects, above all FILIPPO JUVARRA, all major papal commissions were given to the virtually unknown Florentines Galilei and Fuga, with the exception of the Fontana di Trevi, which was designed by NICOLA SALVI.

In December 1731, Galilei was called to Rome

Galilei.
Corsini Chapel, San
  Giovanni in Laterano.
Rome.
1732–1735

by Neri Corsini to build the family funeral chapel in San Giovanni in Laterano, for which he was granted a leave of absence from the Florentine court. The Cappella Corsini (1732–1735) provides the key to Galilei's style as well as to the intentions of Neri Corsini. In accordance with the wishes of the pope, typologically it follows the Cappella Paolina in Santa Maria Maggiore. But now the cupola, drum, and transepts form units, each of which is sharply set apart from the other. Nothing is blurred. The spatial compartments strike harshly against each other, and the inner structure is made clearly visible. Statues and reliefs are subordinated to the architecture, the sculptors having had to agree to this by contract. The baroque harmony of architecture, sculpture, and painting is abolished in favor of the autonomy of architecture. Painterly effects are achieved through the material itself, through very subtle gradations in color of the different marbles. The Cappella Corsini is a model of structural clarity and elegance of forms, to which nothing else in the Rome of that era is comparable.

In 1732, Galilei won the great competition for the design of the façade of San Giovanni in Laterano. The spokesman for the jury was the French architect ANTOINE DERISET, a friend of Galilei. Supported by Pier Leone Ghezzi, he carried Galilei's model to victory over the bitter resistance of the Accademia di San Luca which favored Vanvitelli. Galilei's design—a two-story façade, both stories opening to loggias, the whole articulated only by colossal pilasters, a barely protruding central bay, and a scarcely elevated pediment—had to be made more "Roman" to placate the Accademia. The central bay was accentuated by columns and the top balustrade made steeper, changes which had a negative effect on the total proportions. The entrance hall is again encrusted with carefully harmonized colors of marble. All frames for portals and niches are derived from the entablature of the Corinthian order, and no ornament is without a demonstrable ancient example. The entire apparatus of forms is canonized. The plain, flat, almost skeletonlike building with its spare ornamentation deeply shocked the Roman art world. No such uncompromising rationality and functionality had yet been expressed in architecture. It is a work that provides an exact demarcation between two styles: for the baroque it was too severe, for the later classicism, lacking freestanding columnar porticos, it was not sufficiently doctrinaire.

A project to redesign the piazza in front of the new façade with surrounding colonnades, planned in 1735–1737, was left unexecuted after the death of Galilei. In connection with the building of the façade, Galilei also completed the east wing of the Lateran Basilica.

Galilei.
San Giovanni in Laterano
(façade).
Rome.
1732–1736

Galilei.
San Giovanni dei Fiorentini
(façade).
Rome.
1733–1735

In 1733–1735, on a commission from the pope, Galilei erected the façade of San Giovanni dei Fiorentini, the Florentine national church in Rome. The rather traditional front, consciously taking up motifs of the Cinquecento when the church was built, is generally considered Galilei's weakest Roman work. Designed in a great hurry, the plan appears not to have been quite thought through. However, inconsistencies such as the superposition of two Corinthian orders as well as the organization of the lower story go back to Michelangelo's wooden model for the façade of San Lorenzo in Florence which at the suggestion of Bottari was originally considered for San Giovanni. The much criticized steepening of the upper story also had to take into account surroundings that were urbanistically more compact than those that exist today.

Among smaller works from that period, the designs of 1731 for a villa Neri Corsini in Anzio should be mentioned. This was a simple building whose main feature was a grand outside staircase. It was executed in 1732–1735 under the supervision of NICOLA MICHETTI, who made changes in Galilei's design.

Sometime around 1736, Galilei seems to have remodeled the Villa Feroni on the Gianicolo in Rome, which was destroyed in 1849. Apparently, Galilei organized the building with pilasters and built a stairway over an oval ground plan. In his own time, with few exceptions, Galilei met with rejection. His buildings irritated but were not without influence on the development of both Salvi and Vanvitelli, as well as on the young architects of the French Academy in Rome: JACQUES GERMAIN SOUFFLOT, JEAN LAURENT LEGEAY, and LOUIS LE LORRAIN. Through Galilei, in the 1830s, Rome engaged in a discussion of the basic principles of architecture which in turn set in motion a swift disengagement from the baroque. Galilei did not create a new style with his buildings, but he made Rome's voice heard once more as the promoter of a new development and thus opened the way to classicism. His concern with a pure, functional architecture, with what might perhaps be termed Vitruvian architecture (see VITRUVIUS), is the immediate starting point for the classicism that was created in Rome by the members of the French Academy.

ELISABETH KIEVEN
Translated from German by
Beverley R. Placzek

WORKS

1718–1719, Castletown (built in 1722–1725 by Edward L. Pearce), Celbridge, County Kildare, Ireland. 1718, Garden Temple, All Hallows College, Drumcondra, Dublin. 1718–1719, Kimbolton Castle (east portico),

Huntingdonshire, England. *1718–1719, Houses, Cork and Brewer Streets, London. 1722–1724, Galleria degli stucchi, Palazzo Cerretani, Florence. 1724, Madonna del Vivaio (oratorio), Scarperia, Italy. *1726–1728, Gascoigne Monument, Berwick-in-Elmet, Yorkshire, England. 1725–1730, Villa (remodeled); 1729, Santa Maria (choir); Cortona, Italy. 1730–1731, San Gaggio (altar), Florence. 1731–1735, Villa Corsini (executed by Nicola Michetti), Anzio (Lazio), Italy. 1732–1735, Corsini Chapel, San Giovanni in Laterano; 1732–1736, San Giovanni in Laterano (east portico); 1733–1735, Palazzo Lateranense (west façade); 1733–1735, San Giovanni dei Fiorentini (façade); 1733–1735, San Giovanni in Laterano (penitenzieria); *c.1736, Villa Ferroni (remodeled); Rome.

BIBLIOGRAPHY

CARAFFA, FILIPPO 1974 "La Cappella Corsini nella Basilica Lateranense (1731–1799)." *Carmelus* 21:281–338.

CRAIG, MAURICE; GLIN, KNIGHT OF (DESMOND FITZ-GERALD); and CORNFORTH, JOHN 1969 "Castletown, Co. Kildare." *Country Life* 145:722–726, 798–802, 882–885.

GOLZIO, VINCENZIO 1961 "La facciata di S. Giovanni in Laterano e l'architettura del Settecento." Pages 450–463 in Leo Bruhns (editor), *Miscellanea Bibliothecae Hertzianae*. Munich: Schroll.

KIEVAN, ELISABETH 1973 "Galilei in England." *Country Life* 153:210–212.

KIEVAN, ELISABETH 1975 "The Gasçoigne Monument by Alessandro Galilei." *Leeds Arts Calendar* 77:13–23.

KIEVAN, ELISABETH 1982 "Alessandro Galilei (1691–1737), Architekt in England, Florenz und Rom." London: Zwemmer. Forthcoming publication.

NAVA, ANTONIO 1936 "La storia della chiesa di S. Giovanni dei Fiorentini nei documenti del suo archivio." *Archivio della Reale Deputazione romana di storia patria* 59:337–362.

OSWALD, ARTHUR 1968 "Kimbolton Castle, Huntingdonshire." *Country Life* 144:1474–1478, 1584–1587, 1644–1648, 1696–1699.

ROSSEN, SUSAN F. (editor) 1974 *The Twilight of the Medici*. Detroit, Mich.: Wayne State University Press.

SANPAOLESI, PIERO 1956 "L'Oratorio del Vivaio a Scarperia: Architettura di Alessandro Galilei." Pages 193–198 in *Atti del VIII. congresso nazionale di storia dell'architettura*. Rome: Centro di studi per la storia dell'architettura.

TOESCA, ILARIA 1952 "Alessandro Galilei in Inghilterra." *English Miscellany* 3:189–221.

TOESCA, ILARIA 1953 "Un parere di Alessandro Galilei." *Paragone* 4, no. 39:53–55.

WITTKOWER, RUDOLF (1958)1980 *Art and Architecture in Italy: 1600–1750*. Rev. ed. Harmondsworth, England: Penguin.

ZANGHERI, LUIGI 1975 "Apparti di Alessandro Galilei alla corte Medicea." *Antichità viva* 14, no. 1:32–36.

GALLEN-KALLELA, AKSELI

Akseli Gallen-Kallela (1865–1931), a Finnish architect, trained first in Helsinki and then in Paris. Although best known as a painter and graphic artist, he shared the interest of Finnish *Jugendstil* designers in indigenous architecture and crafts. Like them, Gallen-Kallela saw Karelian loghouses as one of the most significant indigenous architectural forms; this attitude is evident in his own log villa on Lake Ruovesi (1894–1895). Here, as in the house at Tarvaspää (1911–1913), he designed both house and furnishings. Gallen-Kallela often collaborated with contemporary Finnish designers, most notably in the furnishings for the Iris Room and the Kalevale frescoes of the Finnish Pavilion, Paris (1900). Other such collaborations made the Finnish *Jugendstil* a unique but true *Gesamtkunst*.

JUDITH S. HULL

WORKS

1894–1895, Villa Kallela, Lake Ruovesi, Finland. 1900, Kalevale Frescoes and Furnishings, Iris Room, Finish Pavilion, World Exhibition, Paris. 1911–1913, Villa at Tarvaspää, Espoo, Finland.

BIBLIOGRAPHY

NIILONEN, KERTTU (editor) 1966 *Kalela: Wilderness Studio and Home*. Helsinki: Otava.

GALLI BIBIENA FAMILY

The introduction, especially of accidental points, or rather the invention of viewing scenes by the angle, produces the finest effects imaginable. . . . Ferdinando Bibiena was the inventor of those scenes, which by the novelty of their manner, drew the eyes of all the curious upon him. They soon began to look upon as unpleasing objects for a stage, those streets and narrow passages, those galleries that were always made to tend to its center, there at once to limit the spectator's imagination and sight [Nagler, 1959, pp. 314–315].

Thus did Count Francesco Algarotti, a distinguished collector of drawings and connoisseur of opera and theater, praise the accomplishments of the most influential figure in the history of the baroque theater. Ferdinando Galli (da) Bibiena (1657–1743) and his brother Francesco (1659–1739) were the cofounders of an artistic dynasty that flourished for over a century. Three generations of Bibienas traveled from their headquarters in Bologna to the courts of Barcelona, Lisbon, Vienna, Bayreuth, Stockholm, and St. Petersburg. In addition to constructing or renovating theaters and decorating palaces and churches, they con-

Ferdinando Galli Bibiena. Veduta per angolo (an etching from L' Architttura civile). 1711

ceived the grandiose ephemeral architecture and orchestrated the elaborate spectacles that proclaimed royal births, marriages, and deaths. No major court was without their services, and their presence stimulated native artists to imitate their sophisticated and justly acclaimed techniques resulting in a proliferation of *bibieneschi* and a blurring of artistic identities that has persisted to the present.

Algarotti's enthusiastic endorsement of Ferdinando Galli Bibiena was published some twelve years after the latter's death when his numerous sons, nephews, and grandsons were adding further luster to the family reputation. The more ample and dynamic space of his *scena* or *veduta per angolo* (angle view) had long since replaced the static symmetry of the seventeenth-century stage with its dependence on a central perspective inherited from Renaissance painting. Articulating the more complex spatial dialogue of the *per angolo* was an architecture whose structure and scale were not subject to troublesome restrictions of time or cost. It thus remains among the freest expressions of baroque imagination, still utopian in its objective of creating a world more perfect than the real world, yet differing significantly from the mirrorlike character of the older aristocratic stage. The seemingly limitless depth and the multiplicity of spatial intervals produced by the swift, oblique movement of the angle view ruptured the continuity between stage and auditorium, between illusion and reality, which was an essential component of the aristocratic theater world of the baroque. The central perspective employed in that stage had operated only for the benefit of the privileged spectator seated in the center of the theater, whereas the asymmetry of the angle view projected a space whose pictorial logic was independent of favored viewpoint and thus offered its audience a more generous, "democratized" visual experience.

Because the theater is a supremely collaborative enterprise, the success of the family firm rested on the ease with which one member might assume the duties of another in the event that he was unable to complete a project; thus the Bibienas cultivated a group manner. Documentation of the family is still relatively scarce. However, it is possible to distinguish between the contributions of certain members. Originally from Tuscany, the Gallis appended the name of their native town, Bibiena, when Ferdinando's father, Giovanni Maria (1618?–1665) sought to distinguish himself from another assistant of the same name in the workshop of the Bolognese painter, Francesco Albani. Ferdinando and Francesco initially studied painting and subsequently learned the complex art of *quadratura* (illusionistic ceiling painting) from

Mauro Aldrovandini and Giacomo Antonio Mannini. Their skill as *quadraturisti* served them throughout their careers, but it was especially useful during the early years when they frescoed palaces, country villas, and theaters in Emilia and Romagna. It was as fresco painters that the two brothers entered the service of Ranuccio Farnese, duke of Parma, before collaborating as stage designers for the festivities that marked the wedding of the duke's son with a German princess in 1690. Surviving drawings and prints testify to the splendor and the relative conservatism of the spatial concepts employed in the ballets, *L'eta dell'oro* and *L'idea di tutte le perfezioni,* suggesting that the revolutionary *veduta per angolo* was not fully or consistently implemented at that time.

Ferdinando continued to work for the Farnese for another twenty years, eventually as first ducal architect. He frequently left Parma to produce stage designs and renovate theaters in Modena, Genoa, Turin, Venice, Rome, and Milan. Meanwhile, Francesco was building a reputation as a stage designer, fresco painter, and architect of projects that, for the most part, have not survived. In 1702, he journeyed to Naples to supervise the celebration mounted to honor the visit of King Philip V of Spain. His labors were so successful that Emperor Leopold I invited him to Vienna to reconstruct the Grosseshoftheater or court theater (1704).

Francesco's peripatetic ways set the pattern for the rest of the family. While he was in Nancy supervising the construction of the opera house (1707–1709), Ferdinando was borrowed from the Farnese by Charles III of Spain to take charge of his wedding. Only after three years (1711) did he return to Parma, and then for a very brief stay, for within months he was called to Vienna. He became the first imperial theater architect in 1717. In preparing the sumptuous entertainments for the Hapsburg court, Ferdinando was assisted by his gifted sons Alessandro (1686–1748), Giuseppe (1695–1747), Antonio (1697–1774?), and Giovanni Maria the younger (1693–1777?).

Before assuming his new post in Vienna, Ferdinando hastily published *L'Architettura civile preparata su la Geometria, e ridotte alle Prospettive* (1711), the treatise that was to enhance his reputation further and to publicize his claim to be the inventor of a new type of perspective. It is clear that he conceived the text as a manual for instruction in the technical refinements of the new perspective, and, indeed it was reprinted twice, in 1725 and 1731, when it appeared in an economical pocket-sized format that was designed for the architectural students at the Accademia Clementina in Bologna—an institution dominated by various members of the Bibiena family from its inception (1710) until mid-century.

L'Architettura civile reflects the knowledge and experience of the seasoned craftsman. Its five-part text contained references to VITRUVIUS, LEON BATTISTA ALBERTI, SEBASTIANO SERLIO, ANDREA PALLADIO, VINCENZO SCAMOZZI, and GIACOMO BAROZZI DA VIGNOLA among architectural theorists, and LEONARDO DA VINCI, GIULIO ROMANO, and Albrecht Dürer, among masters of perspective. In the third part, Ferdinando discusses the various ways of creating spatial illusion, yet his lengthy consideration of *sotto in su* or worm's eye views does not acknowledge the achievements of the great fresco painter ANDREA POZZO, whose own classic on perspective, *Tractatus perspective pictorum et architectorum,* had appeared between 1693 and 1702, and whose painted *oeuvre* in Italy and Vienna certainly would have been known to Ferdinando.

If Ferdinando's text provided a theoretical and technical basis for *quadratura,* the entire family offered countless practical demonstrations of its superiority over older models. Illusionistic walls and ceilings in such surviving structures as the ballroom of the Palazzo Fantuzzi in Bologna (1678–1684) by Francesco, the Oratory of Santa Maria del Seraglio in San Secondo (1685–1687) by Ferdinando, the choir of the Peterskirche in Vienna (1730–1732), the cupola of the Holy Trinity Church in Bratislava (1744–1745), and the sacristy of the Cathedral of Cremona (1763–1765) by Antonio, testify to the brilliant implementation and amplification of Ferdinando's principles and confirm his belief that *quadratura* and stage design were important areas of architectural experimentation.

The ephemeral nature of the majority of the architectural works produced by the Bibiena family has rendered especially useful the testimony of drawings and prints. Extant albums of sketches not only establish individual differences in approach between one personality and another, but they also occasionally allow us to follow the evolution of an architectural type or complex spatial ensemble from first tentative expression to elaborate resolution. Among these albums, one in the theater collection of the Nationalbibliothek in Vienna, two in the *Accademia di San Luca* in Rome, and one in the Houghton Library of Harvard University have been attributed, with varying degrees of certainty, to Ferdinando, Giuseppe, and Antonio. An album in the Theatermuseum of Munich has recently been attributed to Alessandro and another in the collection of the late Donald Oenslager in New York is most likely the work of Antonio. The etchings of Pietro Abati and Carlo Antonio Buffagnotti for the *Varie opere di Prospet-*

tive (1703–1708) reproduced drawings by Ferdinando and Francesco, and the engravings of Andreas Pfeffel published between 1740 and 1747 under the title *Architettura e prospettive* document some of Giuseppe's major theater work from his earliest years as his father's assistant until the publication of the volume when he had succeeded Ferdinando as first imperial theater architect and was at the height of his career.

The enormity of the Bibienas' contribution to the history of the theater has overshadowed their achievement in other areas. Justly celebrated as the most innovative and prolific theater architects of the eighteenth century, little of their output has survived. Francesco is the unluckiest in this respect. His magnificent Grosseshoftheater (1704) was dismantled in 1747 to make way for a Redoutensaal designed by his nephew, Antonio; his Salle des Machines, the court theater in the ducal palace at Nancy (1708), was transformed into a military warehouse during the War of the Austrian Succession and completely destroyed in 1818; and the splendid Teatro Filarmonico of Verona (1715–1731), so auspiciously inaugurated with the premiere of Antonio Vivaldi's *La fida ninfa,* fell victim to a fire just seventeen years later. Giuseppe and Antonio were more fortunate: the former's Markgräfliches Opernhaus (1745–1748), commissioned by Frederick the Great's sister for her court in Bayreuth, is perhaps the best preserved theater of Bibiena conception. Its glittering interior, whose construction was supervised by Giuseppe's son Carlo Ignazio (1728–1787), is one of the major examples of central European rococo, contrasting vividly with the sober classicizing exterior built by Joseph St.-Pierre, the court architect.

Whereas the Bayreuth opera house represents a culmination of the ornate aristocratic theater pro-

Giuseppe Galli Bibiena. Markgräfliches Opernhaus. Bayreuth, Germany. 1745–1748

totype originated by Francesco, the structures conceived by Antonio are already marked by a compactness of design and sobriety of ornament that represents a departure. Having worked in Austria, Hungary, and Czechoslovakia for over thirty years, Antonio returned to Bologna where the senate charged him with the task of building a new public theater. The Teatro Pubblico (1755–1763) was a municipal theater not requiring a royal or princely box, and thus the bell-shaped plan adapted by Antonio from such earlier family models as the Grosseshoftheater or Filarmonico achieved a striking fluidity of movement and a greater degree of ornamental coherence than was previously obtainable. During the nineteenth and twentieth centuries, both the exterior and interior of the theater underwent substantial changes.

Antonio's Teatro Scientifico (1767–1769), built for a learned society in Mantua, is intimate in scale and generally conforms to the "scholarly" prototype whose most distinguished predecessor and apparent inspiration was Palladio's Teatro Olimpico. Heavily damaged during World War II, it was restored in 1972. Using a modified bell plan and employing four rows of boxes that feature Tuscan, Doric, Ionic and Corinthian orders, it more pointedly expresses the antiquarian interests of its patrons. Since the academy met only during the day, the interior originally was illuminated by natural light. Indeed, the character of the theater is curiously hybrid as it seems located between the Palladian tradition of the ancient theater and the more recent Bibiena models. Antonio's last building, the Teatro dei Quattro Cavalieri Associati in Pavia (1771–1777), has undergone so many mutations and "restorations" (1845, 1909, 1925, 1931, 1934, 1975) that one must compare the extant structure with surviving prints published on the occasion of its opening. While the plan and general decorative scheme follow that of the Nuovo Teatro Pubblico, there is a more emphatic separation between the stage and the audience and a more effective unity between the

gravely classical exterior and the interior.

In domestic and ecclesiastical architecture, the Bibienas were scarcely innovators; however, their experience as stage designers informed their sense of space and their handling of ornamentation. Ferdinando's plans for the church of San Antonio Abate in Parma date from that brief period when he returned from Spain. Construction was begun in 1712 and not completed until long after his death in 1760. The high façade of the church has much in common with the elaborate temporary triumphal arches that Ferdinando was called upon to create in the streets of Parma on the occasion of royal celebrations, but it is in the interior, and especially in the ceiling vaults that the scenographer's delight in illusionism expresses itself. The real ceiling is frescoed to resemble a sky while a second ceiling of trellised wood covering it effects a lively play of light and shade.

Recently, knowledge of Ferdinando's activity as an architect was broadened by the addition of the Villa Paveri Fontana at Caramello di Piacenza (1739) to the list of his works. Ferdinando made a particular effort to address the structure, with its rectangular plan and central cortile, to the vast park surrounding it. He introduced loggias, open staircases, and other types of "infiltrated spaces" that derived from the prototypes he employed in his stage sets.

Antonio Bibiena's parish church at Villa Pasquali near Sabbioneta (1765–1774) was not completed until after the architect's death, and the original plan, calling for two high bell towers, was never followed by the architect who succeeded him. In contrast to the somewhat heavy exterior, the interior of the longitudinal plan offers an impression of lightness due to the ample transept and vast presbytery. The solidity of the lower part of the church is complemented by the delicacy of the upper part with its seemingly floating cupola and the familiar double ceiling and trellis effect so characteristically Bibiena.

Alessandro, the eldest of Ferdinando's sons,

worked for most of his life as court architect to the illustrious electors of the Palatinate in Mannheim. He built an opera house (1737–1742) that was destroyed by fire in 1795, but his activities as architect for the Jesuits (College, [1730–1731]; Church [1738–1748]) earned him fame throughout central Europe. The church, greatly damaged during World War II, has been described by Georg Dehio as the most important baroque church in southwest Germany. Completed by Franz Wilhelm Raballiatti, a student of Alessandro's, it compares in ornamental gravity with the Gesù in Rome, though the addition of characteristically German bell towers further emphasizes the height at the expense of the width of the structure. As in most Bibiena churches, the cupola is quite high, and although the interior is strongly lit, it lacks the illusionistic frescoes characteristic of other Bibiena churches.

By 1787, the year the last Bibiena died, the reformist aestheticians who promoted neoclassicism were assailing the baroque illusionism with which this name was synonymous. In particular, they indicted the debased and rhetorical spatial language still employed in stage design by the *bibieneschi*. Yet in the midst of hostile criticism, even the sternest of the reformers, FRANCESCO MILIZIA, still praised Ferdinando as "gran maestro . . . alla pittura e alla prospettiva della scena" (Muraro Povoledo, 1970, p. xiv).

DIANE M. KELDER

WORKS

FRANCESCO BIBIENA

1678–1684, Palazzo Fantuzzo, Bologna, Italy. *1704, Grosseshoftheater, Vienna. *1708, Salle des Machines, Ducal Palace, Nancy, France. *1715–1731, Teatro Filarmonico, Verona, Italy.

FERDINANDO BIBIENA

1685–1687, Santa Maria del Seraglio (oratory), San Secondo, Italy. 1712–1743, Church of Sant'Antonio Abate (not completed until 1760), Parma, Italy. 1739, Villa Paveri Fontana, Caramello di Piacenza, Italy.

ALESSANDRO BIBIENA

*1730–1731, Jesuit College; *1737–1742, Opera House; 1738–1748, Jesuit Church (not completed until 1760); Mannheim, Germany.

GIUSEPPE BIBIENA

1745–1748, Markgräfliches Opernhaus (interiors), Bayreuth, Germany.

ANTONIO BIBIENA

1730–1732, Peterskirche, Vienna. 1744–1745, Holy Trinity Church (cupola), Bratislava, Czechoslovakia. 1755–1763, Nuovo Teatro Pubblico (now the Teatro Communale), Bologna, Italy. 1763–1765, Cathedral of Cremona (sacristy), Italy. 1765–1774, Parish Church (not completed until 1784), Villa Pasquali, near Sabbioneta, Italy. 1767–1769, Teatro Scientifico, Mantua, Italy. 1771–1777, Teatro dei Quattro Cavalieri Associati, Pavia, Italy.

BIBLIOGRAPHY

ALGAROTTI, FRANCESCO (1755)1924 *Saggio sopra l'opera in musica.* In G. F. Malipiero, *I profeti di Babilonia.* Reprint of 1762 ed. Milan: Bottega di poesia.

GALLI BIBIENA, FERDINANDO 1703–1708 *Varie opere di prospettive.* Bologna, Italy: Camillo.

GALLI BIBIENA, FERDINANDO 1711 *L'Architettura civile preparata su la geometria, e ridotta alle prospettive.* Parma, Italy: Monti.

HADAMOWSKY, FRANZ 1962 *Die Familie Galli-Bibiena in Wien.* Vienna: Pracher.

KELDER, DIANE M. 1968 *Drawings by the Bibiena Family.* Philadelphia Museum of Art.

MATTEUCCI, ANNA MARIA; LENZI, DEANNA; ET AL. 1979 *Architettura, Scenografia, Pittura di paesaggio: L'Arte del settecento emiliano.* Bologna, Italy: Museo Civico.

MAYOR, A. HYATT 1945 *The Bibiena Family.* New York: Bittner.

MILIZIA, FRANCESCO (1771)1794 *Trattato completo, formale e materiale del teatro.* Venice, Italy: Pasquali. Originally published with the title *Del Teatro.*

MURARO, MARIA TERESA, and POVOLEDO, ELENA (editors) 1970 *Disegni teatrali dei Bibiena: Catalogo della mostra.* Venice, Italy: Fondazione Giorgi Cini.

MYERS, MARY L. 1975 *Architectural and Ornament Drawings: Juvarra, Vanvitelli, the Bibiena Family and other Italian Draughtsmen.* New York: Metropolitan Museum of Art.

NAGLER, ALOIS M. (1952)1959 *A Source Book in Theatrical History.* New York: Dover. Originally published with the title *Sources of Theatrical History.*

OECHSLIN, WERNER 1975 "Il contributo dei Bibiena, Nuove attività architettoniche." *Bolletino del Centro Internazionale di Studi di Architettura Andrea Palladio* 17:131–159.

GALLIER, JAMES SR.

James Gallier, Sr. (1798–1866), one of the best known and most successful architects of New Orleans in the mid-nineteenth century, was born in the village of Ravensdale, County Louth, Ireland. After a rudimentary education Gallier studied architecture at the School of Fine Arts in Dublin, while also working as a builder. He studied there for only a few months, the only formal architectural education he ever had.

In the summer of 1822, he left Ireland for London, working for various architects and builders. He married Elizabeth Tyler, and served for a time

James Gallier, Sr.
City Hall (Gallier Hall).
New Orleans, Louisiana.
1845–1850

as clerk of the works for an architect named Wilkins in building a prison at Huntingdon, where his son JAMES GALLIER, JR., was born. Returning to London in 1828, he superintended the building of a row of houses for John Deering, architect, and furnished plans for several new buildings and alterations to old ones.

Recognizing that his best opportunity for success was in America, he left London for New York in February 1832. He worked and studied for a time with JAMES H. DAKIN who had been a partner in the noted architectural firm of TOWN AND DAVIS. He later formed a partnership with MINARD LAFEVER. During this time, he wrote and published the *American Builders Price Book* and wrote and delivered a course of lectures on architecture. Having heard of greater opportunities in New Orleans, he left for the south in October 1834, accompanied by Dakin's brother, Charles B. Dakin.

After spending a few weeks in Mobile, Alabama, Gallier and Dakin arrived in New Orleans and began practicing architecture together. They immediately became popular with the growing Anglo-American segment of the city, and in their first year they designed many of the most important buildings, including the great Saint Charles Hotel (1835–1836), the Merchants Exchange (1835), the Arcade Baths (1835–1836), and Christ Church (1835), besides several fine houses. All were in the Greek Revival style.

In 1835, James Dakin came to New Orleans to join his brother Charles. The brothers then formed a partnership and Gallier withdrew to continue on

his own. In 1837 Dakin and Dakin designed Saint Patrick's Church in the Gothic style, but a disagreement with the church trustees caused them to withdraw from the project and Gallier was called in to complete it (1839–1840). Most of Saint Patrick's interior design as well as many of its exterior details are Gallier's work.

Gallier carried on a successful practice that included important residential and commercial commissions in almost all of which he was both architect and builder. Occasionally, however, he built from the plans of other architects. Among his last and best known works was the classic City Hall (1845–1850) which, after the construction of a new city hall in the 1950s, was called Gallier Hall in his honor.

Around 1850, Gallier's eyesight began to fail and he retired, turning the business over to his son and to his former bookkeeper, John Turpin. The new firm name was Gallier, Turpin and Co. In his retirement years, Gallier and his second wife traveled extensively in the United States, Europe, North Africa, and Egypt. In 1866, Gallier and his wife were lost off Cape Hatteras in the wreck of the steamer *Evening Star*.

Although many of Gallier's most significant buildings no longer exist, his reputation was so firmly established that for the century following his retirement almost all Greek Revival buildings in Louisiana were attributed to him. His identified buildings, numerous extant drawings, and his published autobiography (1864) assure him of an important position in the architectural and social history of the United States.

SAMUEL WILSON, JR.

WORKS

1835, Barton Academy, Mobile, Ala. *1835, Christ Church, New Orleans, La. 1835, Government Street Presbyterian Church, Mobile, Ala. *1835, Merchant's Exchange; *1835–1836, Arcade Baths; 1835–1836, William Nott House; *1835–1836, Saint Charles Hotel; *1838, Thomas Hale House; 1838, Paloc and Dufour Houses; 1839–1840, Saint Patrick's Church (completion); 1843, Commercial Exchange; 1844, W. N. Mercer House (Boston Club); 1845–1850, City Hall (Gallier Hall); New Orleans, La.

BIBLIOGRAPHY

CHRISTOVICH, MARY LOUISE (editor) 1972 *The American Sector (Faubourg St. Mary)*. Volume 2 in *New Orleans Architecture*. Gretna, La.: Pelican Publishing.

CHRISTOVICH, MARY LOUISE; EVANS, SALLY KITTREDGE; and TOLEDANO, ROULHAC 1977 *The Esplanade Ridge*. Volume 5 in *New Orleans Architecture*. Gretna, La.: Pelican Publishing.

GALLIER, JAMES (1864)1973 *Autobiography of James Gallier, Architect*. Reprint. New York: Da Capo.

HAMLIN, TALBOT (1944)1964 *Greek Revival Architecture in America.* Reprint. New York: Dover.

HUBER, LEONARD V. 1971 *New Orleans: A Pictorial History.* New York: Crown.

HUBER, LEONARD V.; McDOWELL, PEGGY; and CHRISTOVICH, MARY LOUISE 1974 *The Cemeteries.* Volume 3 in *New Orleans Architecture.* Gretna, La.: Pelican Publishing.

SCULLY, ARTHUR, JR. 1973 *James Dakin Architect: His Career in New York and the South.* Baton Rouge; Louisiana State University Press.

TOLEDANO, ROULHAC, and CHRISTOVICH, MARY LOUISE 1980 *Faubourg Tremé and the Bayou Road.* Volume 6 in *New Orleans Architecture.* Gretna, La.: Pelican Publishing.

WILSON, SAMUEL, JR., and LEMANN, BERNARD 1971 *The Lower Garden District.* Volume 1 in *New Orleans Architecture.* Gretna, La.: Pelican Publishing.

GALLIER, JAMES JR.

Born in Huntingdon, England, educated by Dr. Hawkes in New York and Mississippi before attending the University of North Carolina at Chapel Hill, James Gallier, Junior (1827–1868) practiced in New Orleans, Louisiana, from 1850 to 1868 first with John Turpin, then with Richard Esterbrook. His residence is today a house museum.

Designing generally in restrained versions of Italianate and Modern French styles, he did dwellings and many commercial buildings, notably the French Opera (1859), Luling Mansion (1865), and the Bank of America (1866), all in New Orleans.

HENRY W. KROTZER, JR.

WORKS

*1850, Armand and Michael Heine Stores; *1850, James Robb Banking House; *1851, Horace Commack and Thomas Dixon Stores; 1852, Leeds Iron Foundry; 1855, Robert Heath Stores; *1856, Bank of New Orleans; 1856, Lavinia Dabney House; *1856, Michael Heine House; c.1857, E. J. Forstall House; 1857–1859, Gallier House; *1859, French Opera; 1865, Florence Luling House; 1866, Bank of America; 1866, Gallier Family Tomb; *1867, James Gallier Stores; New Orleans, La.

BIBLIOGRAPHY

CABLE, MARY 1980 *Lost New Orleans.* Boston: Houghton Mifflin.

CHRISTOVICH, MARY LOUISE ET AL. 1972 *The American Sector.* Volume 2 in *New Orleans Architecture.* Gretna, La.: Pelican.

CHRISTOVICH, MARY LOUISE; EVANS, SALLY KITTREDGE; and TOLEDANO, ROULHAC 1977 *The Esplanade Ridge.* Volume 5 in *New Orleans Architecture.* Gretna, La.: Pelican.

GALLIER, JAMES (1864)1973 *Autobiography of James Gallier, Architect.* Reprint. New York: Da Capo.

HUBER, LEONARD V. 1971 *New Orleans: A Pictorial History.* New York: Crown.

HUBER, LEONARD V.; McDOWELL, PEGGY; and CHRISTOVICH, MARY LOUISE 1974 *The Cemeteries.* Volume 3 in *New Orleans Architecture.* Gretna, La.: Pelican.

SCULLY, ARTHUR JR. 1973 *James Dakin, Architect: His Career in New York and the South.* Baton Rouge: Louisiana State University Press.

WILSON, SAMUEL JR., and LEMANN, BERNARD 1971 *The Lower Garden District.* Volume 1 in *New Orleans Architecture.* Gretna, La. Pelican.

GALLISSÀ SOQUÉ, ANTONIO

Antonio Gallissà Soqué (1861–1903) was a Spanish Art Nouveau architect and Gothic Revivalist active in Barcelona. A follower of LLUÍS DOMÈNECH I MONTANER, he belongs to the second period of Catalan *Modernismo.* He studied under Elias Rogent y Amat and received his architectural degree in 1885. In 1890, he won a competition for the La Riva Pantheon (1891). He built a number of other funerary monuments but is principally known for his work in wrought-iron detailing and ceramic decoration. Gallissà Soqué served as president of the Unió Catalanista and as vice-president of the Ateneo Barcelonés. He was also a professor at the School of Architecture in Barcelona.

ELIZABETH A. T. SMITH

WORKS

1891, Santa María de Cervelló; 1891, La Riva Pantheon, New Cemetery; 1902, Casa Llopis i Bofill, calle Valencia; n.d., Church of Santa María del Mar (Altar de la Concepcíon), Barcelona, Spain. n.d., Arús Pantheon, Vilaser de Mar, Spain. n.d., Guardiola Pantheon, Lloret de Mar, Spain. n.d., Federico de Gomis House, El Papiol, Spain. n.d., José Pujol Houses, Esplugues de Llobregat, Spain.

BIBLIOGRAPHY

BASSEGODA NONELL, JUAN 1976 "Arquitectura." In *Modernismo en Cataluña.* Barcelona, Spain: Ediciones de Nuevo Arte Thor.

BOHIGAS, ORIOL 1973 *Reseña y catálogo de la arquitectura modernista.* Barcelona, Spain: Lumen.

CIRICI PELLICER, A. 1951 *El arte modernista catalan.* Barcelona, Spain: Aymá.

GALLO, FRANCESCO

Francesco Gallo (1672–1750) was born and died in Mondovi, in the Piedmont region of Italy, the center of his architectural practice which included

Gallo.
Vicoforte (drum and
*   dome.)*
Mondovi, Italy
1728–1733

over a hundred known works. He was also active as a hydraulic, topographic, and military engineer and was noted for his command of structural design. Gallo abandoned an early military career after being wounded, and he turned to architecture. Throughout his career, he avoided complexities of space and structure, although his late work, in the 1730s, while exhibiting a continuing awareness of the work of FILIPPO JUVARRA, shows an increasing interest in the late-seventeenth-century forms of GUARINO GUARINI, perhaps as a result of seeing the early work of BERNARDO ANTONIO VITTONE. A trip to Rome (in 1726, according to Nino Carboneri) precedes his work of greatest interest.

The Church of the Assunta at Carrù (1702–1725) conveniently displays Gallo's early adherence to undistinguished, traditional longitudinal plans in which nave chapels between widely spaced piers defined by Palladian (see ANDREA PALLADIO) motifs (as in many late-sixteenth-century churches in north Italy), led to a narrower choir and apse. His centrally planned San Ambrogio at Cuneo (begun 1703, interrupted work 1710, not completed until 1743) with splayed corner piers, three-quarter round columns, curving walls, and tall, ribbed hemicycle vault is more dynamic spatially and structurally perhaps because of the late date of completion. The central-plan Santa Chiara at Mondovi (1712) with an unusual two-story concave façade (which strangely prefigures that of LUIGI VANVITELLI done in 1749 for Santa Maria degli Angeli in Rome), however, also contains three-quarter round columns, here leading to the apses and a yet taller attic below the vault.

San Giovanini Battista at Racconigi is Gallo's major work of the early 1700s. Begun in 1719 (completed 1730), the plan is a lengthened Greek cross, extended by a one bay for the choir and apse with fully round columns supporting salient arches differentiating chapels from the central space. Oval windows punctuate the base of the dome and the vaults of the arms. Carboneri sees San Giovanini as marking a concern for new ample

rhythms and solemn spatial themes.

The most significant monument of Gallo's career is the large oval dome of the Vicoforte at Mondovi. The sanctuary had been begun early in the seventeenth century but was left incomplete at the height of the base of the drum. Gallo's eight heavy piers alternating with Palladian motifs (oval windows above in the attic) for the drum contrast painfully with the early portion, but they are harmoniously integrated in the interior where the lower and upper windows piercing the drum and vault belie the immense structural effort. Below, after the completion of the dome (1728–1733), Gallo redesigned the pedestal for the miraculous image on the sacred site and encased it in a baldachin (1749) that owes much to CARLO FONTANA's altar baldachin in Santa Maria in Traspontina in Rome.

Among Gallo's later works, Santa Trinità, Fossano (1723–1728), with its imposing concave façade derived from Juvarra's Santa Cristina in Turin, and Santa Croce, Cavallermaggiore (1737–1743), with an uncharacteristic structural emphasis and activity, stand out.

HENRY A. MILLON

WORKS

1702–1725, Assunta, Carrù, Italy. 1703, 1710–1743, Sant'Ambrogio, Cuneo, Italy. 1712, San Chiari, Mondovi, Italy. 1719–1730, San Giovanini Battista, Racconigi, Italy. 1723–1728, San Trinità, Fossano, Italy. 1727, San Pietro, Casale Monferrato, Italy. 1728, Annunziata, Busca, Italy. 1728–1733, Vicoforte (drum and dome); 1749, Vicoforte (pedestal and baldachin); Mondovi, Italy. 1737–1743, San Croce, and San Bernardino, Cavallermaggiore, Italy.

BIBLIOGRAPHY

AMEDEO, R. 1972 "Notizie inedite sulla Chiesa del Gallo nel Borgo Maggiore de Garessio." *Bollettino Società Studi Storici Archeologici ed artistici nella provincia di Cuneo* no. 67:143–145.

BELLINI, A. 1976–1977 "Vicende architettoniche del Palazzo Cavour di Santena, opera inedita di Francesco Gallo." *Bollettino della Società Piemontese d'Archeologia e Belle Arti* 30–31:48–61.

BONINO, ATTILO 1928 "Francesco Gallo—Architetto." *Bollettino della Società Piemontese di Archeologia e Belle Arti* 12, nos. 1–2:20–45.

BRINCKMANN, ALBERT E. 1931 *Theatrum Novum Pedemontii.* Düsseldorf, Germany: Schwann.

CARBONERI, NINO 1954 *L'architetto Francesco Gallo.* Turin, Italy: Società Piemontese d'archeologia e di belle arti.

CARBONERI, NINO 1963 Volume 1, pages 41–43 in *Architettura, Mostra del Barocco Piemontese.* Turin, Italy.

CARBONERI, NINO 1972 "I progetti di Francesco Gallo per il Santuario di Oropa." *Bollettino Società Storici Archeologici ed artistici nella provincia di Cuneo* no. 67:5–11.

GANCHEQUI, LUIS PEÑA

Luis Peña Ganchequi (1926–), born in Oñate, Spain, is one of those rare architects who is dedicated to both the Modern movement and national identity without ever falling into the trap of vernacular folklore. His works respond to the same feeling for place that the local people have, but his intellectual discipline has allowed him to rise above what might have degenerated into mere advocacy architecture. Both poles, the modern and the national architecture, temper each other to produce buildings that always seem to have been there but that contain a cultural interest far beyond the boundaries of the Basque country. Most of his work is to be found in Motrico, Oyarzun, and Ataun. In San Sebastian, the public squares El Trinidad and El Tenis (the latter in collaboration with Eduardo Chillida) are his best, together with his Euskadi Monument in Oyarzun Cemetery to those who died defending Basque liberties against Franco.

DAVID MACKAY

GANDON, JAMES

James Gandon (1742–1823), the major resident exponent of neoclassicism in Irish architecture, was born in London. He was the first and greatest pupil of WILLIAM CHAMBERS to whom he was apprenticed from around 1757 to around 1763: his drawing style, his preference for Roman rather than Greek architecture, and his Francophile inclinations are Chambersian. It was Paul Sandby, however, to whom he was indebted for introductions to many of his most important patrons, and for enduring friendship.

He never traveled beyond Britain or Ireland. During his career in England, he published a number of slight decorative designs and—with John Woolfe—a continuation in two volumes of *Vitruvius Britannicus* by COLEN CAMPBELL. In 1769, he was awarded the Royal Academy's first gold medal in architecture and entered a number of architectural competitions (Royal Exchange, Dublin, 1768–1769, second place; Saint Luke's Hospital, London, 1776, first place; the building as erected is the work of GEORGE DANCE THE YOUNGER). He secured only one major commission in England, that for the Shire Hall, Nottingham (c.1769–1772). Princess Dashkova promised him employment in Saint Petersburg, but, attracted by the offers of a number of powerful Irish connoisseurs, friends of Sandby, he traveled to Dublin in 1781 to build the Custom House (1781–1791).

The Custom House shows his dependence on Chambers and on a wide range of earlier English architects, particularly CHRISTOPHER WREN. After the uncertainties of his English work, it shows an assured style based on an intellectual control of three-dimensional composition, a critical study of Roman antiquity, and a management of architectural sculpture in which he was brilliantly served, as in other major works, by the sculptor Edward Smyth.

Much of his most important work dates from the 1780s: the extensions to the Parliament House (House of Lords extensions [1784–c.1789]), Carlisle Bridge (begun in 1791), and other work in collaboration with the Wide Streets Commissioners, then replanning Dublin as a consequence of the building of the Custom House on a new site. Also in the 1780s, he began work on the Four Courts (1786–1802); begun in 1776 by THOMAS COOLEY), a tribute to Wren, to the "movement" of ROBERT ADAM, and to the compositional geometry of the French neoclassicists.

Gandon's domestic practice was of less consequence and did not challenge the dominance in this field of JAMES WYATT. His greatest country house is Emo Court, County Leix (begun c.1790). A number of his ingenious and elegant villas survive.

Gandon consolidated the neoclassical tradition in Irish architecture. His style was conservative and academic, his decoration austere, his taste fastidious, eclectic, heavily dependent on English precedent, and informed by French practice. He established new standards of professional conduct in

Gandon.
Custom House.
Dublin.
1781–1791

Gandon.
Four Courts (completion).
Dublin.
1786–1802

Ireland and much influenced the early nineteenth-century architects Henry Aaron Baker (his assistant and only pupil, apart from James Malton), RICHARD MORRISON and FRANCIS JOHNSTON. He served a small clique of connoisseurs who exercised immense political power in Dublin in the most brilliant decades of the eighteenth century. He retired around 1808.

EDWARD MCPARLAND

WORKS

c.1769–1772, Shire Hall, Nottingham, England. 1781–1791, Custom House, Dublin. c.1781–1785, Coolbanagher Church, County Leix, Ireland. *1784–1787, Courthouse and Jail, Waterford, Ireland. 1784–c.1789, Parliament House (extensions to House of Lords); 1786–1802, Four Courts (completion); Dublin. c.1788, William Ashford House, Sandymount, County Dublin. c.1790–c.1793, Houses, Beresford Place, Dublin. Begun c.1790, Emo Court, County Leix, Ireland. Begun 1791, Carlisle Bridge, Dublin. 1794, Emsworth, County Dublin. Begun 1800, King's Inns, Dublin.

BIBLIOGRAPHY

CRAIG, MAURICE (1952)1980 *Dublin 1660–1860.* Reprint. Dublin: Allen Figgis.
CURRAN, CONSTANTINE 1949a "The Architecture of the Bank of Ireland." In Frederick G. Hall, *The Bank of Ireland 1783–1946.* Dublin: Hodges Figgis; Oxford: Blackwell.
CURRAN, CONSTANTINE 1949b "Cooley Gandon and the Four Courts." *Journal of the Royal Society of Antiquaries of Ireland* 79:20–25.
GANDON, JAMES, JR., and MULVANY, THOMAS (editors) (1846)1969 *The Life of James Gandon.* With an introduction by Maurice Craig. Reprint. London: Cornmarket.
MCPARLAND, EDWARD 1974 "Emo Court, Co. Leix. . . ." *Country Life* 155:1274–1277, 1346–1349.
MCPARLAND, EDWARD 1980a "The Early History of James Gandon's Four Courts." *Burlington Magazine* 122:727–735.

GANDY, J. M.

Joseph Michael Gandy (1771–1843), apprenticed to JAMES WYATT in 1787, studied at the Royal Academy School and traveled to Italy between 1789 and 1797. Upon return to England, he was employed as a draftsman by Sir JOHN SOANE, Gandy's sole professional friend and ally. He published two pattern books of rural architecture (1805), but failed to establish his own practice. Gandy's elaborate architectural fantasies were exhibited at the Royal Academy and the British Institution.

BRIAN LUKACHER

WORKS

1804, Storrs Hall, Windemere, England. 1805, Phoenix Fire and Pelican Life Insurance Offices, London. 1810, Assembly Room, Liverpool, England. 1818, Doric House, Bath, England.

BIBLIOGRAPHY

SUMMERSON, JOHN 1963 "The Vision of J. M. Gandy." In *Heavenly Mansions, and Other Essays on Architecture.* New York: Norton.
TSELOS, DIMITRIS 1941 "Joseph Gandy: Prophet of Modern Architecture." *Magazine of Art.* 34:251–253, 281.

GANDY-DEERING, JOHN PETER

John Peter Gandy-Deering (1787–1850), younger brother of JOSEPH GANDY, was trained by JAMES WYATT before entering the Royal Academy in 1805. Awarded the Silver Medal in 1806, he exhibited at the Academy from 1805 to 1833. After working for Wyatt, he joined the Barrack Office, winning the 1810 competition for the Bethlehem Hospital, London (unexecuted), and serving from 1811 to 1813 as draftsman to the Society of Dilettanti's Ionian Expedition, led by Sir William Gell. His drawings were published in *Unedited Antiquities of Attica* (1817) and *Antiquities of Ionia,* III (1840), edited by WILLIAM WILKINS, chief inspirer of Gandy-Deering's Greek Revival style and his single neo-Tudor work, Stamford Infirmary (1826–1828). Gandy-Deering relinquished architecture and became high sheriff of Buckinghamshire in 1840 and Member of Parliament for Aylesbury in 1847.

R. WINDSOR LISCOMBE

WORKS

*1822–1826, United University Club (with William Wilkins), Pall Mall East; 1825–1826, Saint Mark's Church (interior remodeled by A. W. Blomfield in 1878), North Audley Street; London. 1826–1828, Stamford Infirmary, England. 1830, Pimlico Literary Institution, Ebury Street; *1830–1837, Exeter Hall, Strand; London.

BIBLIOGRAPHY

GELL, WILLIAM (1817–1819)1875 *Pompeiana.* London: Chatto.
LISCOMBE, R. WINDSOR 1980 Pages 95, 96, 111–112, 161–162, 164–165 in *William Wilkins: 1778–1839.* London: Cambridge University Press.
SOCIETY OF DILETTANTI (1817)1833 *Unedited Antiquities of Attica.* 2d ed. London: Priest.
WILKINS, WILLIAM (editor) 1840 *Antiquities of Ionia.* London: Society of Dilettanti.

8

GANGHOFER, JÖRG

Born near Moosburg, Germany, Jörg Ganghofer (?–1488) was also known as Jörg von Halspach and Jörg, der Maurer von Polling. From 1468, he was city architect in Munich where he began his most important work, the Frauenkirche. Upon Ganghofer's death in 1488, the building was complete with the exception of the tower. The vaulting of the choir, which continues unbroken into the ambulatory, shows the influence of the cathedral at Augsburg which the parish council sent Ganghofer to study in 1470. Ganghofer also worked on the completion of the old town hall in Munich.

JOANNE E. SOWELL

WORKS

1468–1488, Frauenkirche; n.d. Townhall (plans for completion and vaulting); Munich.

BIBLIOGRAPHY

FRANKL, PAUL 1962 *Gothic Architecture.* Harmondsworth, England: Penguin.

GARBETT, EDWARD LACY

Edward Lacy Garbett (?–1898) is known only through his writings. His most successful work, *Rudimentary Architecture* (1850), urged architects to design buildings fit for their functions that also appeared "polite, refined, expressive and exhaulting." He criticized the imitation of architecture from other eras as a method antithetic to thoughtful design. He linked architectural style with constructional systems and predicted that the truss system would be the origin of a new style.

ALICE H. R. HAUCK

BIBLIOGRAPHY

DE ZURKO, EDWARD ROBERT 1957 *Origins of Functionalist Theory.* New York: Columbia University Press.
DOBSON, EDWARD 1852–1853 *The Student's Guide to the Practice of Measuring and Valuing Artificer's Works.* London. Includes notes on design by Edward Lacy Garbett.
EMERSON, RALPH WALDO 1939 Volume 4 in *The Letters of Ralph Waldo Emerson.* Edited by Ralph L. Rusk. New York: Columbia University Press.
GARBETT, EDWARD LACY (1850)1906 *Rudimentary Architecture for the Use of Beginners and Students, the Principles of Design in Architecture as Deducible From Nature and Exemplified in the Works of the Greek and Gothic Architects.* 9th ed. London: Crosby Lockwood.
GARBETT, EDWARD LACY 1856 "Preliminaries to Good Building." Pages 95–104 in *Papers and Practical Illustrations of Public Works of Recent Construction.* London.
GARBETT, EDWARD LACY 1877 *Finite Avarice: A Socialism Drawn from the Genesis Trade-Union Law.* London.
GREENOUGH, HORATIO (1853)1966 *Form and Function.* Reprint. Berkeley: University of California Press.
PARSONS, WILLIAM 1892 *The Late Earl of Rosse's Argument to Prove the Truth of the Christian Revelation.* Edited by Edward Lacy Garbett. London: Reeves.
PEVSNER, NIKOLAUS 1972 "Bartholomew and Garbett." *Architectural Review* 152:239–241.
RUSKIN, JOHN 1903 *Stones of Venice.* Volume 9 in *The Complete Works of John Ruskin.* Edited by E. T. Cook and Alexander Wedderburn. London: Allen.
WINTER, ROBERT W. 1958 "Fergusson and Garbett and American Architectural Theory." *Journal of the Society of Architectural Historians* 17:25–30.

GARCIA DE PAREDES, JOSÉ MARIA

José Maria Garcia de Paredes (1924–) was born in Sevilla, Spain. He received his architectural degree in Madrid in 1950. He is considered one of the outstanding members of the so-called second generation of postwar Spain. His architecture is the result of meticulous work in which the diverse factors that condition each project intervene in a balanced manner. His work is characterized by an expressive moderation atypical of Spanish architecture and could be considered eclectic if it were not for the extreme coherence of his solutions.

Among his major works are the Major Aquinas School and the Church of Almendrales in Madrid (1961), the School of Arts and Crafts in Teruel (1963), the Church and Convent for the Carmelites in Córdoba (1961), housing in Plaza de los Campos, Granada (1967), and the Manuel de Falla Center in Granada (1975).

In all of them the originality of the planning and the economy of means achieve stylistically related results of great internal coherency which place his work among those of the greatest quality in present-day Spain. Particularly significant is the Manuel de Falla Center which can be considered one of the best works of its kind on an international level and is probably his most complete work.

The architecture of Garcia de Paredes lies in the periphery of contemporary currents in style, marking its own strong trajectory.

MIGUEL ANGEL BALDELLOU
Translated from Spanish by Tomlyn Barns

WORKS

1951, Chamber of Commerce (with R. de la Hoz), Córdoba, Spain. 1953, Major Aquinas School (with R. de la Hoz), Madrid. *1957, Spanish Pavilion, Eleventh Triennial, Milan. 1958, Church of Our Lady of the Angels (with J. Carvajal), Vitoria, Spain. 1960, School of Engineers of Telecommunications (with Carvajal), Madrid. 1961, Church and Convent of the Carmelites, Córdoba, Spain. 1961, Parish Center of Almendrales, Madrid. *1962, Mañuel de Falla Exhibition, Granada, Spain. 1963, School of Arts and Crafts, Teruel, Spain. 1964, Middle School Teaching Center John XXIII, Granada, Spain. 1965, Office Building, Calle Orense, Madrid. 1967, Housing, Plaza de los Campos; 1968, Hotel Luz Granada; Granada, Spain. 1973, Bank of Granada, Bilbao, Spain. 1973, Hotel Los Galgos, Sevilla, Spain. 1975, Bank of Granada, La Coruña, Spain. 1975, Mañuel de Falla Center, Granada, Spain.

BIBLIOGRAPHY

DOMENECH GIRBAU, LLUIS 1968 *Arquitectura española Contemporánea.* Barcelona, Spain: Blume.
FLORES LOPEZ, CARLOS 1961 *Arquitectura española Contemporánea.* Madrid: Aguilar.
"La Obra de José Maria Garcia Paredes." 1965 *Hogar y Arquitectura* 61:17–64.

GARCÍA MERCADAL, FERNANDO

Fernando García Mercadal (1896–) was born in Saragossa, Spain, and received his architectural degree in Madrid in 1921. Awarded the prize "Pensión de Roma" shortly after completing his studies, he resided in several European countries between 1923 and 1927. He worked in Rome, Berlin, Vienna, and Paris and was an assistant in the studios of PETER BEHRENS, HANS POELZIG, and LE CORBUSIER. By means of articles which he published in the Spanish magazine *Arquitectura* during this time, García Mercadal informed his Spanish colleagues of the decisive transformations which the avant-garde movements were on the verge of introducing to European architecture. During these years, he also carried out his studies on the Mediterranean house, seeking a compromise between popular Spanish architecture and the contemporary Cubist forms. Returning to Spain, he built the so-called Rincón de Goya (literally "corner of Goya") in Saragossa, a commemorative building along the lines of the new avant-garde architecture. In 1928, he attended the first Congrès International d'Architecture Moderne in La Sarraz, Switzerland. With a group of young architects, he founded the Grupo de Arquitectos y Técnicos Españoles para el Progreso de la Arquitectura in 1930. His work as an avant-garde architect ended with the Spanish civil war in 1936. After this date, he carried out extensive projects in the field of hospital architecture.

CARLOS FLORES LOPEZ
Translated from Spanish by
Tomlyn Barns

WORKS

1927–1928, Rincón de Goya, Saragossa, Spain. 1933–1934, One-family housing, Parque-Residencia, Madrid.

BIBLIOGRAPHY

FLORES, CARLOS 1961 *Arquitectura española contemporánea.* Madrid: Aguilar.
GARCÍA MERCADEL, FERNANDO 1930 *La Casa Popular en España.* Madrid: Espasa-Calpe.

GARCIA NUÑEZ, JULIÁN

Argentina's first native born pioneer of modern architecture, Julián Garcia Nuñez (1875–1944) studied in Barcelona, Spain, with ANTONIO GAUDÍ and LLUÍS DOMÈNECH I MONTANER. Returning to Buenos Aires in 1903, he created a unique style of Art Nouveau by combining the sensuous forms of the Catalan school with the linear detailing of German *Jugendstil*.

Bankrupt in the Depression, he abandoned architecture and destroyed all of his awards and sketches.

ELIZABETH D. HARRIS

WORKS

1908, Spanish Hospital; *1903–1930, residences, offices, churches, and a cinema; Buenos Aires.

BIBLIOGRAPHY

BULLRICH, FRANCISCO 1969 *New Directions in Latin American Architecture.* New York: Braziller.
ROSSELOT, HERNÁNDEZ 1975 "Art Nouveau in Buenos Aires." *Connoisseur* 189, May:54–61.

GARLING, HENRY B.

Henry Bayly Garling (1822–1904), the son of a builder by the same name, was an able eclectic architect. Born in England, he is remembered primarily for three unexecuted competition designs: the War Offices (1856) and the Foreign Offices (1857), both in the Second Empire mode, and the New Law Courts, The Strand (1866).

LISA B. REITZES

BIBLIOGRAPHY

COLE, DAVID 1980 *The Work of Sir Gilbert Scott.* London: Architectural Press.
PORT, M. H. 1968 "The New Law Courts Competition: 1866–67." *Architectural History* 11:75–93.

GARNER, THOMAS

A reticent but able exponent of the refined church architecture of the late Gothic Revival in England, Thomas Garner (1839–1906) was a pupil of GEORGE GILBERT SCOTT. From 1869 to about 1897, he worked in association with GEORGE F. BODLEY. The importance of his contribution to the partnership has often been underrated.

ANDREW SAINT

WORKS

1876–1881, Saint Michael's Church, Camden Town; 1878–1879, River House, Chelsea Embankment; London. 1880–1884, Saint Swithun's Quadrangle, Magdalen College, Oxford. 1884–1891, Hewell Grange, Worcestershire, England. 1886–1888, President's Lodgings, Magdalen College, Oxford. 1896, Moreton, Hampstead, London.

BIBLIOGRAPHY

GARNER, THOMAS, and STRATTON, ARTHUR 1908–1911 *The Domestic Architecture of England during the Tudor Period.* 2 vols. London: Batsford.
"Obituary" 1906 *The Builder* 90, May 12:523, 531.
"Obituary" 1906 *Building News* 90, May 11:666.
VEREY, DAVID (1976)1977 "George Frederick Bodley." In Jane Fawcett (editor), *Seven Victorian Architects.* University Park: Pennsylvania State University Press.
WARREN, E. P. 1910 "The Life and Work of George Frederick Bodley." *Journal of the Royal Institute of British Architects* 17:305–340.

GARNIER, CHARLES

Jean-Louis-Charles Garnier (1825–1898) was the architect of the Paris Opera House (1860–1875), one of the most sumptuous and widely celebrated buildings erected in France during the nineteenth century.

He insisted upon his humble origins. His widow recorded in a biographical manuscript that Garnier, the son of a blacksmith from the notorious rue Mouffetard, was apprenticed at thirteen as an *architecte-vérificateur* only because he proved too frail to work the bellows in his father's shop. After several unprofitable weeks, Garnier was placed in a primary school and studied evenings at the Ecole gratuite de Dessin. There he met the sculptor Jean-Baptiste Carpeaux, later the most famous contributor to the decoration of the Opera House. In 1840 he entered the somnolent architectural atelier of Jean-Arnould Léveil and, when it closed three months later, passed on to that of LOUIS HIPPOLYTE LEBAS, no less conservative, but very busy, and successful in the competitions at the Ecole des

Beaux-Arts, to which Garnier was admitted in 1842. During his years with Lebas he claimed to have gotten no advice from his master beyond "C'est très bien, très bien, continuez," but he learned a great deal from his fellow student Jules André. To support himself Garnier worked as a draftsman for EUGÈNE EMMANUEL VIOLLET-LE-DUC and one Galimard.

He was *en loge* for the Grand Prix de Rome in 1846 and again in 1848, winning the second time with a stern design for a *conservatoire des arts et métiers.* During his five years as a *pensionnaire* in Rome (1848–1854), he became friends with students with whom he worked henceforth—Gustave-Rudolphe Boulanger, Paul Baudry, Jules-Eugène Lenepveu and at least six others—and got to know the brilliant Roman balls and festivals, which fascinated him for their pageantry. He was hired by the duc de Luynes to draw the funerary monuments of the House of Anjou for publication. Although this book was never issued, the project led to Garnier's Gothic funerary chapel for the duke's family in the parish church at Dampierre (1855–1861), soon after his return to Paris.

In 1852 Garnier visited Greece and Turkey with the writer Edmond About, executing a reconstruction of the temple at Aegina with brilliant polychrome decoration. On the boat to Constantinople he met Théophile Gautier, later to be an important supporter in the pages of the *Moniteur universel.*

The first years back in Paris were discouraging after the pleasures of the Villa Médicis. Garnier held a series of trivial governmental posts: *inspecteur* for THÉODORE BALLU restoring the Tour Saint Jacques (1854–1856); *inspecteur* under Vallez for the construction of the Ecole des Mines (1856–1857); *sous-inspecteur* for the maintenance of the customs houses of Paris under Jäy (1859–). A private commission in 1859 to design an apartment building on the recently-created Boulevard de Sebastapol (63, later changed to 75) provided three thousand francs with which he took his bride to Italy. Finally in 1860 he was named architect of the fifth and sixth *arrondissements* with a good salary but menial duties and an interdiction to accept private work.

In December 1860, a competition for a great new opera house in Paris was announced. Among the 171 projects submitted, Garnier's placed fifth, entitling him to compete in a second round. On May 29, 1861, he was awarded the commission to erect the most grandiose and expensive monument of the Second Empire.

While continuing to study and refine his design, Garnier supervised the ground-breaking on

August 27, 1861 and the setting of the first stone on July 21, 1862. On August 15, 1867, the exterior was complete and the scaffolding removed to great public acclaim, F. L. J. DUBAN writing Garnier, "Je ne puis que dire, c'est beau, c'est beau, c'est beau!" (August 17, 1867, Bibliothèque de l'Opéra). The interior, however, was not yet complete and the end of the Second Empire drawing near. Work was suspended by the war of 1870; the building was used as a hospital warehouse, barracks, and fort during the Commune of 1871; and only on January 5, 1875 was it actually inaugurated—the Emperor's Pavilion remaining incomplete to this day.

Garnier's Opera House immediately established the new standard for its type: efficiently providing for the comfort of the actors and spectators alike, and magnificently composed in volume, space, and decoration. Much of his success was owed to his understanding of architectural *mise en scène*. For all the sumptuousness of its detailing, the Opera House is extraordinarily clear and simple in basic layout, immediately graspable to the professional and layman alike.

The profession admired the composition of characteristic volumes and its tightly controlled plan. Volumetrically, the building consists of a severe, gabled flytower enframing the elegantly molded dome of the auditorium which rests on the solid block of foyers below and picks up the theme of the lateral domes of the Emperor's Pavilion and the Refreshment Pavilion to either side. This exterior composition of volumes was the direct expression of the interior composition of spaces—its "repoussée." Furthermore, since the flytower is the one feature of an opera house that distinguishes it from a concert hall or a public auditorium, Garnier's emphasis on it enabled his composition to proclaim the building's function. Internally, the Opera House was divided into a series of simple spatial units, from front to back: the grand foyer, the stairhall, the auditorium, the stage, and the dressing rooms—tied firmly together on each side by two broad halls running from one end of the building to the other. These halls link the spaces and bind the composition together to form the background mass from which emerge the characteristic volumes, the flytower, auditorium, and lateral pavilions.

The composition of volumes and spaces, however, works also in four dimensions, as one approaches and passes through the building. From the far end of the specially-created Avenue de l'Opéra, stretching a mile to the Place Royale in front (opened in 1877), the building presents a simple, legible image: the triangular flytower embracing the copper auditorium dome with the giant colonnade beneath. As one mounts the ave-

nue this silhouette dissolves as the dome and flytower sink in perspective, but upon entering the Place de l'Opéra the lateral pavilions and domes come into view, repeating the initial theme and drawing the eye around the structure into the square flanking it. Were one a subscriber coming by carriage, one then would drive around beneath the Refreshment Pavilion and alight under cover to enter the low, mirrored rotunda of the *Vestibule des Abonnés* under the auditorium itself. Having readied one's self there, one then would have mounted the grand staircase, first up a pair of flights from the *vestibule* to the main floor onto which open the arcades of the main façade, then on up the second single flight to the caryatid-flanked door to the orchestra and from there either to the right or left to reach the piano nobile upon which spread out the foyers, *fumoirs,* and refreshment rooms as well as the *premières loges* of the auditorium. This was the promenade of the subscribers, the wealthiest and oldest members of Parisian society. The humbler ticket holders, occupying the *seconde, troisième, quatrième,* and *cinquième loges,* took a different route: through the arcades across the façade and up to their seats by means of two extensive banks of stairways on either side of the stairhall. Their high perches had balconies so that these poorer cousins could view the comings and goings of the *haut monde* and constitute an audience for their social drama. Thus Garnier laid out two routes for the two types of operagoers, the movement of both capacious and smooth, combined at the stairhall to compose a single socially-graded tableau.

For all his neatness in composing his volumes and spaces, Garnier's greatest success perhaps was in the visual content of the tableaux he created. No one before had handled decoration, detail, and style quite the way he did here. The spaces looked their parts: the rococo *Vestibule des Abonnés* where servants gathered apart from the general public; the Sansovinesque stairhall for the ceremonial processions of arrival and departure; the palatial foyer for conversation between acts; the gilded auditorium, a careful reproduction of the old opera auditorium which had become such a part of the subscriber's memories and social geography. Garnier found convincing analogies and rendered them with brilliant vividness.

The stairhall was surely his most striking invention. In 1863, as soon as his design was complete, critics understood that although Venetian sixteenth-century architecture was the source of its form vocabulary, Paolo Veronese's paintings of crowded scenes of noble entertainment were the source of the tableau. Garnier saw his space decorated with flowers and hanging banners, illumi-

nated by candelabras and chandeliers, and crowded with richly dressed and bejeweled subscribers, "Recalling in real life the resplendant tableaux that Veronese fixed upon his canvases" (Garnier, 1871, p. 59). Garnier sought to recall the social theater of Renaissance Venice, not by reproducing JACOPO SANSOVINO's architecture, but by fantasizing upon Veronese's painterly vision of that architecture.

The effort to catch the social spirit of the past transformed the detailing of the Opera House into personal elaborations of historical forms. Conventional moldings gain more emphatic, elastic curves; foliage now writhes and twirls as if burgeoning after a rain in the jungle; masks grimace humanly; caryatids adjust their positions and reach out to grasp lanterns or palms. PAUL SÉDILLE wrote, "While his flora proceeds from well-known ancient fragments, it has become, under his pencil, an intense vegetation producing at once all the strangest flowers and fruits, convulsing with amazing pulsations of sap" (Sédille, 1898, p. 341). No one had drawn ornament so freely and expressively before.

Garnier's sense of detailing went hand in hand with one more talent important for the success of his design: his handling of color, both in painted decoration and materials. Parisians, used to buildings going up in the monochrome yellow local limestone, were delighted to see colored marble columns positioned across Garnier's façade, marble inlays in the friezes and the green copper domes touched with gilding. (Gautier wanted the domes entirely gilded, perhaps expressing Garnier's wishes.) Inside the Opera House there were polished, veined marbles of all kinds as well as masses of gilding, vast illusionistic ceilings by Baudry (in the foyer) and Lenepveu (in the auditorium), and

the first monumental mosaic ceiling in nineteenth century Paris covering part of the stairhall.

Garnier's technique was academically impeccable, as his conventional training would lead one to expect. The volumes respond to the internal spaces as any rationalist would wish in order to communicate the building's nature; the details all have respectable (if sometimes distant) sources. Yet Garnier was the declared enemy of rationalism in architecture, announcing in 1878: "Sometimes when I take up my pencil to compose, I feel invaded by those theoretical ideas that rise before me like a schoolteacher confronting a child who has made a mistake; but I assure you that instead of trying to reason at such times, I chase these visions from me as best I can, until feelings alone, and nothing else, guide my eyes, my hand, and my thoughts" (Garnier, 1878–1881, vol. 1, p. 122). This intuitiveness, however, was one of tactics, for he had earlier explained, "Exactly that which makes the hand sure and the eye decisive is the very introduction into the brain of all the indispensable doctrines and their existence there, embodied, set in place, and ready to manifest themselves when they are needed" (Garnier, 1871, p. 413). Indeed, this is just how Garnier's design works. It builds upon academic paradigms and models, but by intuitive inflection and amalgamation, it animates them—as in the boudoirlike *Vestibule des Abonnés* or the Veroneselike stairhall—and produces a specific form that is immediately meaningful for the general public. Garnier discovered where popular taste and conservative art overlapped, and made something of it. This was not done again with such success until the Columbian Exposition of 1893.

The impact of the Opera House was immense.

Charles Garnier.
Opera.
Paris.
1860–1875

Charles Garnier.
Opera (grand staircase).
Paris.
1860–1875

The public loved it, both for its aura of monumental classicism and for its actual brashness and obviousness. Among the younger generation of architects, the Opera House tipped the scale in favor of an intuitive academicism, winning over many of the older rationalists like Duban and LOUIS DUC, and leaving the doctrinaire rationalists a small circle around HENRI LABROUSTE and Viollet-le-Duc. There followed upon the inauguration of the Opera House the last great, baroque flourish of Beaux-Arts academicism during the Third Republic until World War I.

With the completion of the Opera House, as far as the history of architectural form, Garnier's career was at an end. Others took up where he left off. He built nothing comparable during the remaining twenty-three years of his life; his first was also his last great work. Indeed his fifteen-year effort seemed self-contained and necessarily played out by the time of its inauguration, a critic wrote in 1875, "The Opera . . . is one of the most characteristic manifestations of the nineteenth century; all by itself it constitutes a period of evolution during which one witnesses a style originate in the first courses of stone, assert itself in all its maturity in the exterior forms, and die of exuberance in the *foyer de la danse;* thus once the Early Gothic evolved into the Flamboyant" (Lavezzari, 1875, col. 32). Yet this is only a somewhat exaggerated example of the typical career of a French government architect. His great moment is like his winning Grand Prix design, a single magisterial demonstration of imaginative *virtu* that admitted him to an intellectual and professional elite.

Garnier was active in teaching, in government commissions, and in professional organizations, but less active than many. He never conducted an atelier for architecture students at the Ecole des Beaux-Arts, but nonetheless in the drafting room at the Opera he brought together a brilliant group of young men who called him their master, including the Grand Prix winners JULIEN GUADET, Louis Noguet, JEAN-LOUIS PASCAL, Emile Bénard, Georges Scellier de Gisors (see GISORS FAMILY), and PAUL NÉNOT—virtually the whole first rank of the next generation. In fact, if not technically, Garnier was the premier *maître d'atelier* of the epoch.

He was elected to the Institut de France in 1874; was inspecteur général des bâtiments civils (1877–1896); was president of the Société centrale des Architectes twice (1889–1891, 1895–1897); and served on the Conseil des Bâtiments Civils and the Commission des Monuments Historiques (1895–1898). He spoke out loudly on the reform of the Ecole des Beaux-Arts in 1863, and remained a popular speaker, chiefly due to his

sharp wit. In 1886 he was awarded the Gold Medal of the Royal Institute of British Architects. But mostly he wrote and his short pieces for the *Moniteur universel* were published in *A travers les Arts* (1869); in 1871 his theory of opera design in *Le Théâtre* (1871); in 1878–1881 the four volumes of his *Nouvel Opéra de Paris* followed in 1892 by his *Monographie de l'Obsérvatoire de Nice;* in 1884 his 1852 reconstruction of the temple at Aegina, *Le Temple de Jupiter panhellenique à Egine;* and finally in 1890 and 1892 his figurative history of domestic architecture erected at the Exposition universelle of 1889, *Constructions élevées aux Champs de Mars,* and *L'Habitation humaine* (with A. Ammann).

Garnier's architectural works aside from the Opera House fall almost entirely into four categories: tombs; places of public amusement (casino at Monte Carlo [1878–1881], the panoramas Valentino [1882–1883], and Marigny [1883–1884], and the casino at Vittel [1883–1885], together with the baths and hotel at the latter town); private establishments in Paris (Maison Hachette [1878–1880], Cercle de la Librairie [1878–1879]); and buildings related to his Mediterranean retreat at Bordighera (Villa Garnier [1872–1873], Villa Bischofsheim [1878–1880], parish church [1879–1885], school [1874], there and Bischofsheim's observatory at Nice [1880–1888]). Outside these categories fall the functional Dépot des Décors for the Paris Opera (1863–1869) and the medievalizing parish church of Sainte-Grimonie at La-Capelle-en-Thiérache, Aisne (1883–1887). None of these were major government monuments, serious subjects of architectural effort like the Opera House, producing profound and general precedents for official architects and Grand Prix competitors. The Parisian establishments are bits of educated background architecture; the tombs small private decorative gestures (although ones of originality and richness in colored marbles and bronze); the Bordighera buildings relaxed fantasies; the amusement places works of commercial vulgarity all too convincingly derived from more serious sources; the observatory a private scientific establishment on a mountaintop scattered with engines made wierd and wondrous by their exaggerated detailing. All of them are off-hand works, and it is extraordinary how relaxed they seem. Garnier knew how to be architecturally idle with great cleverness and charm. He amused himself. He did odd things that interested him and, when his mind was engaged, did them very well.

Garnier transformed and revitalized the nineteenth-century Beaux-Arts tradition: he created a brilliant, intuitive architecture which nonetheless drew upon the academic sources and paradigms. He showed the style's more careful practitioners what could be made of it. They gratefully accepted his demonstration and worked for two generations in the glow of his magnificent Opera House. He was French on a vaster plane in the same sense as Charles de Gaulle: a man who convinced his countrymen—and indeed his profession internationally—that their enterprise had some sort of grandure which they had been too myopic to glimpse, giving it henceforth purpose, worth, and self-respect.

DAVID T. VAN ZANTEN AND
CHRISTOPHER MEAD

WORKS

Christopher Mead, who has spent two years in Paris documenting Garnier's career, has contributed the dates of Garnier's works other than the Opera.

1855–1861, Family Chapel, Dampierre, France. 1859, House, 63 (later 75) Boulevard de Sebastopol; 1860–1875, Opera House; 1863–1869, Dépôt des Décors, Opera House; Paris. 1872–1873, Villa Garnier; 1874, School; Bordighera, Italy. 1878–1879, Cercle de la Librairie; 1878–1880, Maison Hachette; Paris. 1878–1880, Villa Bischofsheim, Bordighera, Italy. 1878–1881, Casino, Monte Carlo. 1879–1885, Parish Church, Bordighera, Italy. 1880–1888, Bischofsheim's Observatory, Nice, France. 1882–1883, Panorama Valentino; 1883–1884, Panorama Marigny; Paris. 1883–1885, Casino, Vittel, France. 1883–1887, Church of Sainte-Grimonie, La-Capelle-en-Thiérache, France.

BIBLIOGRAPHY

GARNIER, CHARLES 1869 *A travers les Arts.* Paris: Hachette.
GARNIER, CHARLES 1871 *Le Théâtre.* Paris: Hachette.
GARNIER, CHARLES 1878–1881 *Le nouvel Opéra de Paris.* 4 vols. Paris: Ducher.
GARNIER, LOUISE 1925 "Charles Garnier par Mme Garnier." *L'Architecture* 38:377–390.
GAUTIER, THÉOPHILE 1861–1867 *Moniteur universel* Feb. 11, 1861; May 13, 1863; May 20, 1863; Aug. 5, 1867.
LAVEZZARI, E. 1875 "Le Nouvel Opéra." *Revue générale de l'architecture* 32:30–33.
SÉDILLE, PAUL 1898 "Charles Garnier." *Gazette des Beaux-Arts* 20:341–346.
STEINHAUSER, MONIKA 1969 *Die Architektur der Pariser Oper.* Munich: Prestel.

GARNIER, TONY

Tony Garnier (1869–1948) belongs to the first generation of architects of the Modern movement. His urban planning reflected a wide range of concepts related to politics, social reform, and even geography. His architectural design was based on a recognition of modern technology and new materials—especially reinforced concrete—and new functional requirements. His style thus expressed his conception of the principles of classical architecture. Garnier is best known today for the project for an ideal city—the cité industrielle—and his later work, which had considerable impact on architects of the second generation of the Modern movement, is a reflection and a development of this early project.

Born in Lyons, Garnier remained faithful to the socialist ideals of his youth, reflected in his cité industrielle, along with such progressive interests as modern urbanism, manufacturing, electric power, the building of worker's housing, and public education.

Garnier received his early training at the Ecole des Beaux-Arts in Lyons, where he studied with Antoine-Georges Louvier. In 1889, he began his studies in architecture at the Ecole Nationale Supérieure des Beaux-Arts in Paris, first in the atelier of Paul Blondel and then in that of Scellier de Gisors (see GISORS FAMILY). Despite Garnier's radical and innovative tendencies, he was sympathetic to the training that he received from these traditionally oriented architects. Later he designed the main hall of his art school for the cité industrielle as a close reproduction of the main hall of the Ecole des Beaux-Arts in Paris. Garnier was also influenced by JULIEN GUADET and by the radical students at the Ecole des Beaux-Arts, who were concerned with large-scale civic projects and their relation to social values.

During this period Garnier was also interested in the construction for the International Exposition held in Paris in 1889, particularly the Eiffel Tower, and he may well have studied the work of FRANÇOIS HENNEBIQUE, who promoted reinforced concrete construction.

While at the Ecole des Beaux-Arts, Garnier competed for the Grand Prix de Rome six times, finally succeeding in 1899 with a project for a national bank, which is considered a high point of the Beaux-Arts system of planning. In Rome, Garnier worked mainly on his ideal city project, but he also sketched ancient ruins in the vicinity of Rome and studied ancient Greek buildings on a trip to Athens. His later designs demonstrated his keen observation of both ancient and modern architecture of the Mediterranean area.

Garnier's cité industrielle can be associated with the socialist–utopian doctrines of Charles Fourier and with the philosophy of Emile Zola. His first study for the cité industrielle was sent to Paris in 1901. The Ecole refused to exhibit it but included an enlarged version of the original study in the final exhibition (1904) of Garnier's work.

Land in the cité was owned in common and the administration of the city was responsible for all the basic needs of the citizens. In planning the city, Garnier was influenced by current regionalist thought which was concerned with the development of the potentials of specific regions, including geographic, agricultural, industrial, and cultural characteristics. Finally, the cité industrielle reflects contemporary urban designs that stressed the purely aesthetic development of urban form.

In the cité Garnier successfully integrated the theoretical and formal approaches. He chose a specific industrial character for the cité because most new cities were created as industrial centers. The cité was also designed for a specific area in the southeast of France, similar to that of Lyons, where it could use the raw materials, electric power, and transportation of neighboring towns. Garnier thus considered all the elements of a real city: residential and public areas, consisting of administration, assembly, museum and sports centers; the station area, with multistory structures and shops; factories; the silk manufacturing center; the old town; the hospital area; the hydroelectric station and dam; the cemetery; and the farms. These elements were separated from each other and the result is the most characteristic element of the formal design—its parklike character—in which all sections are surrounded by green belts that would permit future expansion of the city. This parklike character was reinforced by the control and separation of vehicular and pedestrian traffic. Another characteristic of the city—the linear shape of the residential sector—was the result of Garnier's concern with the orientation of the houses toward the south light.

Garnier considered the buildings of the cité within a modern urban and social context. The functions located in the administration center, the concentration on designs for several types of multistoried buildings, and the large, pavilion-type

hospital, hydroelectric dam, and modern railroad station with its two-way cantilever, are examples. He also saw these designs as a product of the new economical material of reinforced concrete (with which he chose to build his cité), and he developed a wide spectrum of design possibilities for his material. These included its expression as massive Roman concrete structures, as an imitation of the thin supports of cast iron, as Mediterranean vernacular wall architecture. In addition, the special design characteristics of reinforced concrete led Garnier to omit detail and to emphasize simple geometric volumes, rhythmic patterns inherent in the massing of the buildings and in the arrangement of solids and voids in the wall surfaces, and the relation of the architecture to the site and to the underlying harmony found in nature.

Although Garnier's designs recognized the academic architectural tradition, the cité industrielle was the source for later developments in modern architectural design. LE CORBUSIER responded to Garnier's work, particularly in his first designs for worker's housing based on the Maison Domino, and the planning concepts of the cité were eventually codified in the 1933 Athens Charter.

Not all of the work on the cité industrielle was completed by 1904. Several of the drawings for buildings, such as the railroad station, are dated 1917, the year before Garnier published the first edition of *Une Cité Industrielle*. In this publication Garnier revised some of the designs to accord with buildings he had built since 1904, including the civic projects on which he was engaged at Lyons. However, the essential concept of the cité, its well developed architectural solutions, and all of their implications for future developments in urban planning and in architectural design were achieved by 1904.

Garnier's later work should be seen as an extension of this earlier achievement. Two more projects, forming sections of urban planning projects, followed Garnier's return to France in 1904. The first was a competition projected by the Fondation Rothschild in 1905 for the improvement of housing conditions for workers, which included new types of habitations with common services. In his solution, Garnier placed his apartment block across the site (an irregular city block) in a zigzag, avoiding air wells, providing maximum amount of light and air, and permitting maximum public space. The second project was a competition for a new commercial center for Marseilles, in which the area around the Bourse was to be redesigned. Garnier won second place with an impressive urban center, which, however, with its high closely spaced fourteen-story buildings, was a departure

*Tony Garnier.
Plate from* Cité Industrielle.

from his urban principles, and may have been influenced by current European concepts of the skyscraper.

Garnier's work after his return to France, however, was devoted almost entirely to projects for Lyons. In 1904, Mayor Augagneur commissioned Garnier to design a municipal dairy, built in 1905. Then, Augagneur was replaced by Edouard Herriot, a socialist interested in urban reform, who became Garnier's enthusiastic supporter. His sympathy with Garnier's concerns and his interest in the young architect's ideal city ensured a permanent collaboration and a friendship between the two men. From 1908 to 1912, Garnier worked on studies and proposals for the future planning of Lyons, and was a member of a planning committee, created in 1912, to determine zoning regulations, new circulation patterns, and the creation of parks and industrial areas.

In 1960, Garnier became architect for the new slaughterhouses (Abattoirs de la Mouche, 1909–1913) in Lyons, for which he designed one of the first modern buildings of this type. Like the designs for the cité industrielle, the Lyons design adapted the principles of the Ecole des Beaux-Arts. There is a clear division of functions and a logical circulation pattern including a covered street, the "spine" of the design, and subsidiary passageways. The Lyons abattoir was intended to have been constructed of reinforced concrete, but the material was too expensive, and Garnier turned to the more traditional iron. With this material, the design reappeared as the structure for the factory in his published version of the cité industrielle.

Garnier's last work prior to World War I was the Lyons Stadium (1913–1918), designed in connection with the 1914 international planning exposition in Lyons. Garnier was chief architect of the exposition, which was planned along lines similar to those of the cité industrielle. Specialists from many different disciplines collaborated on the enterprise, which included examples of urban development throughout Europe.

During World War I, Garnier suspended his architectural work and devoted himself to the publication of *Une Cité Industrielle* (1918) and *Les grands travaux de la ville de Lyons* (1920). Garnier's Lyons work included, in addition to the projects mentioned above, some which were never realized—a central postal, telephone, and telegraph building, which was a remodeling of FRANÇOIS SOUFFLOT LE ROMAIN's Hôtel-Dieu, an Ecole des Beaux-Arts, a hospital for five thousand patients, and a Bourse du Travail. All were closely related to projects in the published version of the cité industrielle. Another group of designs in the Lyon volume were projects that Garnier completed after

Tony Garnier. Plate from Cité Industrielle.

publication, including a central telephone building (1927), a weaving school (1930–1933), and the Quartier des Etats-Unis (1920–1935), a very large housing project that included shops, a nursery, a primary school, a library, a stadium, and a swimming pool. It marks an important stage in the evolution of housing projects in France: it was the first of this scale to have been designed in a homogeneous manner, around an over-all plan.

These municipal projects demonstrated Garnier's ability to design large and complex projects rationally, comprehending modern functions and utilizing modern technology. But there is another side to Garnier's artistic expression—one in which he develops modern technology and design for their emotional qualities. This is reflected in his few residential designs and in memorial projects. Garnier's domestic architecture included his villas (1909–1911)—two at Saint Rambert and one at Saint Didier-au-Mont-d'Or—and several later villas recorded in his *travaux de Lyon*. The earlier villas included in *Une Cité Industrielle,* form part of the Mediterranean vernacular style of the cité industrielle residences. Reinforced concrete is conceived as unadorned, solid wall, punctured by simple openings.

Garnier's most important late work, the Hôtel de Ville at Boulogne-Billancourt (1931–1935), designed in association with the architect J. H. E. Debat-Ponsan, is Garnier's last major work. It demonstrates a sophisticated knowledge of the design possibilities of reinforced concrete, based on the conception of architectural design that Garnier had formulated and mastered by 1912.

Garnier was first noted by Le Corbusier, who visited him in Lyons in 1908, and he was first publicly recognized in Le Corbusier's art magazine *L'Esprit Nouveau* in 1920. In 1925 Garnier merited an exhibition of his work in the Musée des Arts

Décoratifs in Paris. He was a member of the Institut de France, the Royal Institute of British Architects, the Academy of Architecture of the Soviet Union, the Society of Architects of Uruguay, the Academy of Lyons, and the Société Académique of Lyons. He received the Conseil Supérieur de l'Ordre des Architectes and an honorary degree from Princeton University. When he died in 1948 at Bedoule, he left behind him a solid body of architectural and urban design work and a major contribution to the forming of twentieth-century architectural and urban planning concepts.

DORA WIEBENSON

WORKS

1904–1905, Vacherie du Park de la Tête-d'Or, Lyons, France. 1909–1911, Villa, Saint-Didier-au-Mont-d'Or, France. 1909–1911, Two villas, Saint-Rambert, France. 1909–1913, Abbattoirs de la Mouche; 1911–1927, Hôpital Grange-Blanche; 1913–1918, Stade de Gerland; 1920–1935, Quartier des Etats Unis; 1922–1925, Monument aux morts; Lyons, France. 1925, Pavillon de Lyon-Saint-Etienne, Exposition des Arts Décoratifs, Paris. 1927, Central Téléphonique, Moncey, France. 1930–1933, Ecole du Tissage à la Croix-Rousse, Lyons, France. 1931–1935, Hôtel de Ville (with J. H. E. Debat-Ponsan), Boulogne-Billancourt, France.

BIBLIOGRAPHY

GARNIER, TONY (1918)1932 Une Cité Industrielle: Etude pour la construction des villes. 2d ed. Paris: Vincent.
GARNIER, TONY 1920 Les grands travaux de la ville de Lyon. Paris: Massin.
GARNIER, TONY 1938 L'Oeuvre de Tony Garnier. Paris: Morancé.
GARNIER, TONY 1951 Tony Garnier 1869–1948. Lyons, France: Durand-Girard.
LYON, MUSÉE DES BEAUX-ARTS 1970 Tony Garnier. Lyons, France: The Museum. An exhibition catalogue.
PAWLOWSKI, CHRISTOPHE 1967 Tony Garnier et les débuts de l'urbanisme fonctionnel en France. Paris: Centre de recherche d'urbanisme.
VERONESI, GIULIA 1947 Tony Garnier. Milan: Il Balcone.
WIEBENSON, DORA 1969 Tony Garnier: The Cité Industrielle. New York: Braziller.

GAROVE, MICHELANGELO

Michelangelo Garove (1650–1713), who worked in Piedmont, Italy, was born in Bissone, Switzerland. He was the most creative architect in Piedmont between the deaths of GUARINO GUARINI and AMEDEO DI CASTELLAMONTE and the arrival of FILIPPO JUVARRA. Garove inherited the supervision of a number of buildings begun by Guarini and received commissions from Duke Vittorio Amedeo II and from the duke's mother, Maria Giovanna Battista, as well as from nobles of the court. Garove's architecture shows the influence of Guarini's structure, lighting, and decorative detail and of Castellamonte's simple, direct planning and spatial organization.

HENRY A. MILLON

WORKS

1682, Chapel of the Beato Amedeo of Savoy, Cathedral, Vercelli, Italy. 1684–1695, San Martino, La Morra, Italy. 1684–?, Palazzo Asinari di San Marzano, Turin, Italy. 1685, Sanctuary of the Madonna of San Giovanni, Sommariva Bosco, Italy. 1690s, Palazzo Morozzo della Rocca; 1696–?, San Filippo (main altar); Turin, Italy. Begun 1699, Grand Gallery (not completed), Venaria Reale (new wing), Italy. 1711, Castello (not completed), Rivoli, Italy.

BIBLIOGRAPHY

BAUDI DI VESME, ALESSANDRO 1966 "Garove, Michelangelo." Volume 2, pages 515–516 in Schede Vesme. Turin, Italy: Stamperia Artistica Nazionale.
BRAYDA, CARLO; COLI, LAURA; and SESIA, DARIO Pages 39–40 in Ingegneri e architetti del sei e settecento in piemonte. Turin, Italy: Società degli ingegneri e degli architti.
MILLON, HENRY A. 1960–1961 "L'Altare maggiore della chiesa di San Filippo Neri di Torino." Bollettino della Società Piemontese di Archeologia e di Belle Arti New Series 14–15:83–91.
MILLON, HENRY A. 1967 "Michelangelo Garove and the Chapel of the Beato Amedeo of Savoy in the Cathedral of Vercelli." Pages 134–142 in D. Fraser, H. Hibbard, and M. Lewine (editors), Essays in the History of Architecture Presented to Rudolf Wittkower. London.

GARRETT, DANIEL

Daniel Garrett (?–1753) acted as man of business to LORD BURLINGTON, supervising many of his building projects of the 1730s. In his own works, mainly in the north of England, he pioneered the use of rococo and Gothic forms. In 1747, he published a book of farmhouse designs which was the first of its kind.

PETER LEACH

WORKS

1735–1753, Wallington Hall (reconstruction), Northumberland, England. 1737–1742, Castle Howard (steps and boundary wall to Mausoleum), Yorkshire, England. 1738–1750, Raby Castle (alterations), County Durham, England. 1740, Forcett Park, Yorkshire, England. 1744–1748, Fenham Hall, Newcastle upon Tyne, England. 1744–1751, Gibside (stables, banqueting house, etc.), County Durham, England. 1746–1750, Nunwick Hall, Northumberland, England. 1748–1753, Northumberland House (reconstruction and extension), London. 1750, Kippax Park, Yorkshire, England.

BIBLIOGRAPHY

GARRETT, DANIEL 1747 *Designs and Estimates of Farm-houses, etc. for the County of York, Northumberland, Cumberland, Westmoreland and Bishoprick of Durham.* London.

LEACH, PETER 1974 "The Architecture of Daniel Garrett." *Country Life* 156:694–697, 766–769, 834–837.

GARSTIN, JOHN

Major-General John Garstin (1756–1820) of the Bengal Engineers was employed on map and survey work in Calcutta and Bengal, India, from 1778. While posted to Patna (1784–1793), he supervised the construction of and probably also designed a Granary (or Grain Gola) in the shape of a beehive at Bankipore (1784–1786). His only other known major work is the neoclassic Town Hall in Calcutta (1807–1813). He was acting chief engineer and took charge of the surveyor general's office in 1807, becoming surveyor general of Bengal the following year. In 1810, he became chief engineer, holding both appointments until 1813. He died in Calcutta.

PAULINE ROHATGI

WORKS

1784–1786, Granary (Grain Gola), Bankipore. 1807–1813, Town Hall, Calcutta.

BIBLIOGRAPHY

PHILLIMORE, REGINALD HENRY (1945)1950 *Historical Records of the Survey India.* 2 vols. Dehra Dun, India.

GÄRTNER, FRIEDRICH VON

Friedrich von Gärtner (1792–1847) stands next to LEO VON KLENZE as the most prominent architect of the first half of the nineteenth century in Munich. Over against the one-sided antique classicism of Klenze, his lifelong rival, Gärtner represented "romantic classicism"—a position that included a programmatic turn toward Christian medieval styles without, however, abandoning the rational design principles of French classicism. Unlike Klenze, Gärtner did not succeed immediately in gaining the favor of the client they shared, King Ludwig I of Bavaria. Only after a joint meeting with the king in Rome in 1827 did Gärtner receive

commissions that gave him a part in the most important architectural project of the time in Munich, the Ludwigstrasse; begun by Klenze, it was Gärtner who carried it to completion.

Gärtner was born in Koblenz, Germany, the son of Andreas Gärtner, who was later made Hofbaurat (court building counselor). Gärtner studied architecture in Munich (1808–1812), Karlsruhe and Paris (1814, with CHARLES PERCIER and PIERRE LEONARD FONTAINE). After the classic grand tour to Italy (1814–1817), a journey to England made him aware of the problems of advancing industrialization (1819). From 1819 until his death, Gärtner lived in Munich. At first, he taught at the Academy; it was ten years before he received his first commission from the king. A commission to build the Royal Residence in Athens provided him with the occasion for two trips to Greece (1835–1836, 1840). Unlike Klenze, Gärtner—through his activities as a teacher at the Academy—left a great number of pupils who disseminated his architectural principles, the Gärtnerstil, throughout Munich and other German cities.

Gärtner's very first building in Munich, the Ludwigskirche (1829–1844), showed a complete departure from Klenze's classicistic architectural ideal as it had taken shape in the buildings already existing on the Ludwigstrasse. The cubic compactness of Gärtner's basically organized structure corresponds to the sober emphasis on planes and planar framing for which the stylistic models are to be found in German and Italian Romanesque church building. The special features of the Ludwigskirche—the broadly extended façade, the wide set of the bulky flanking towers, the rounded arcades leading to side annexes—all take the urbanistic situation into account, namely the direction of the Ludwigstrasse from north to south. In his second building, the Bavarian Court and State Library (1832–1843), which he had succeeded to remove from the unfavorable vicinity of Klenze's Glyptothek on the Königsplatz, Gärtner again sought to adapt to the broad urbanistic concept of the street by an extreme longitudinal extension and planar organization of the façade of the building. Here, as in the later Saltworks Administration Building (1838–1843), Gärtner, who knew KARL FRIEDRICH SCHINKEL's work in Berlin, used facings of burnt brick, the contrasting red and yellow colors of which define the exterior appearance of the building. In these buildings the king's principle of utmost economy harmonizes with Gärtner's predilection for honesty of material and clear characterization of the building's purpose.

Apart from various other administrative buildings, Gärtner's main achievement is the monumental form he created for the beginning and end of the Ludwigstrasse. In analogy to the Odeonsplatz at its southern beginning, shortly before its northern end Gärtner devised a rectangular plaza which he set on the diagonal. The course of the street, which remains unimpeded throughout, then comes to a monumental conclusion with the Siegestor (victory gate; 1843–1852). The façades of the buildings on this northern square—university and educational buildings—are free variations of early Florentine Renaissance schemes and Romanesque-Gothic ornamental details. However, for the starting point and end of the street, Gärtner, at the behest of the king, copied specific historic structures: the Feldherrenhalle at the south end after the Loggia dei Lanzi in Florence, the *Siegestor* at the north end after the Arch of Constantine in Rome. Although these buildings show some proportional digressions from the originals, as the realization of an aesthetic attitude which evokes the historic model in an approximate copy, they reveal the problematic nature of Gärtner's historicism. Here, however, allowance must be made for the political and ideological aims of his royal client. The real significance of Gärtner's architecture lies in the way historical models were altered to meet the pragmatic and utilitarian criteria—administrative, cultural, and educational—of the new building needs and in the aesthetic effect of the resulting buildings on the era's sense of political and cultural representation.

EBERHARD DRÜEKE
Translated from German by
Beverley R. Placzek

WORKS

1829–1844, Ludwigskirche; 1832–1843, Bavarian Court and State Library; 1835–1840, Ludwig Maximilian University; Munich. 1836–1841, Royal Residence, Athens. 1838–1843, Saltworks Administration Building; 1841–1844, Feldherrenhalle; 1843–1852, Siegestor; Munich.

BIBLIOGRAPHY

EGGERT, KLAUS 1963 "Friedrich von Gärtner, der Baumeister König Ludwigs I." *Neue Schriftenreihe des Stadtarchivs München* 15:1–208.
HEDERER, OSWALD 1976 *Friedrich von Gärtner 1792–1847: Leben, Werk, Schüler.* Munich: Prestel.

GASPARI, ANTONIO

Antonio Gaspari (c.1658–1738) was born probably at Rovigo in northeastern Italy. His greatest legacy is a spectacular collection of some three hundred drawings at the Museo Correr in Venice, which prove him not only to have been a devoted and sensitive follower of BALDASSARE LONGHENA and Venice's great sixteenth-century architects but

also to have known the Roman baroque at first hand. His oval Cathedral at Este (1690–1708) and richly decorated Palazzo Zenobio in Venice (before 1700) mark appealing transitions from the robust images of the full baroque to the more refined delicacy of the Venetian rococo. GIORGIO MASSARI completed two of Gaspari's churches and integrated his motifs into the dominant style of the Venetian eighteenth century.

DOUGLAS LEWIS

WORKS

1670s?–1680s?, San Michele and Villa Widmann (with BALDASSARE LONGHENA?), Bagnoli di Sopra, Italy. 1682?–1710, Palazzo Pesaro (completion); 1682?–1712, Palazzo Rezzonica (completed c.1750 by GIORGIO MASSARI); 1683, San Marcuda (chancel, church completed 1728–1736 by GIORGIO MASSARI); (A)1683–1693, San Marziale; 1684, San Moisè (chancel projects); Venice, Italy. 1680s?–1710s?, Villa Pesaro (completion); 1690–1708, Santa Tecla, Este, Italy. 1691–1697, Palazzo Zane (court façades, stair, garden pavilion, and library; reworked by DOMENICO ROSSI); (A)1692?, Palazzo Albrizzi (remodeling), San Canciano; 1692–1695, Santa Maria degli Scalzi (Altar of Santa Teresa); Venice, Italy. 1693, Santa Maria del Carmine (work on façade), Padua, Italy. 1694–1696, Morosini Arch, Sala dello Scrutinio, Ducal Palace; (A)1694–1698, Palazzo Barbaro-Curtis at San Vidal; Venice, Italy. 1695–1697, Saints Maria and Donato (remodeling), Murano, Italy. Before 1696, Palazzo Zorzi at San Severo (remodeling); before 1697, Palazzo Michiel dalle Colonne, Grand Canal; before 1698, Santa Sofia (reconstruction); before 1698, Palazzo Gozzi-Seriman (stair), Santa Maria Mater Domini; before 1700, Palazzo Zenobio at the Carmine; 1700–1704, San Vidal; 1704, San Marziale (high altar); 1705–1706, San Canciano (façade); 1705–c.1712, Santa Maria della Consolazione della Fava (completed c.1714–1724 by GIORGIO MASSARI); Venice, Italy. 1706 and later, Villa Correr, Casale Scodosia, Padua, Italy. 1707–1708, Palazzo Giustinian del Vescovo (remodeling; now the Museo Vetrario), Murano, Italy. (A)1730s, San Bartolomeo (campanile), Venice, Italy.

BIBLIOGRAPHY

BASSI, ELENA 1963 "Episodi dell'architettura veneta nell'opera di Antonio Gaspari." *Saggi e Memorie di Storia dell'Arte* 3:55–108, 171–188.
LEWIS, DOUGLAS 1967 "Notes on XVIII Century Venetian Architecture." *Bollettino dei Musei Civici Veneziani* 12:1–51.
LEWIS, DOUGLAS 1979 *The Late Baroque Churches of Venice.* New York: Garland.

GAU, FRANZ CHRISTIAN

Franz Christian Gau (1790–1853), born in Cologne but established in Paris from 1810, was as much a scholar and teacher as a practical architect. He spent the years from 1815 to 1821 traveling in Italy and Egypt, becoming close to the philologist Barthold Niebuhr and gathering material for his *Antiquités de la Nubie* (1822–1827) and the third (1829) and fourth (1838) volumes of the *Ruines de Pompeii* (begun by François Mazois). In the 1820s, he conducted a private architectural school attended by GOTTLIEB BINDESBOLL and GOTTFRIED SEMPER. His ambition to design a Gothic cathedral like that in Cologne was partially realized when in 1839 he was appointed architect of the large Paris parish church of Sainte Clothilde which he began in 1846 but left for his assistant THÉODORE BALLU to complete after his death.

DAVID T. VAN ZANTEN

WORKS

1825–1827, Presbytery, Saint Severin; 1839–1853, Sainte Clothilde (not completed until 1857 by Théodore Ballu); 1841–1843, Eglise de la Rédemption (rebuilding); Paris.

BIBLIOGRAPHY

GAU, FRANZ CHRISTIAN 1822–1827 *Antiquités de la Nubie.* Stuttgart, Germany: Cotta.
GAU, FRANZ CHRISTIAN 1829–1838 Volumes 3 and 4 in *Ruines de Pompeii.* Paris: Didot. Volume 3 begun by François Mazois.

GAUCHER DE REIMS

See JEAN D'ORBAIS.

GAUDÍ Y CORNET, ANTONIO

Antonio Gaudí y Cornet (Antoni Gaudí i Cornet) (1852–1926) was born in or near Reus (there is a controversy as to his birthplace), a very proud small city south of Barcelona in Catalonia, Spain. He remained emphatically Reusian (also the birthplace of two other heroes of the day, General Juan Prim and the painter Mariano Fortuny) and patriotically Catalan, apparently insisting on speaking Catalan to his interviewers, even King Alfonso of Spain, whether or not they understood that Mediterranean tongue.

Unlike most architecturally schooled Spaniards of his day, Gaudí was of relatively humble origin—not of the middle or upper classes—and this may explain why upon his enthusiastic reception later by Barcelona patrons and before he became so isolatedly devout, he was said to have been a dandy. In this respect, Gaudí's career and attitudes went through a transformation comparable to the painter Francisco Goya, also relatively humble in origin but becoming a favorite at the royal court.

Gaudí himself later claimed that his family origin explained in a way some of the innovations of his architecture. His immediate family made copper tubing for the distilling of brandy, and he once commented, "I have that quality of spatial comprehension because I am the son, grandson, and great-grandson of coppersmiths. . . . On my mother's side of the family there were also smiths; her grandfather was a cooper (which is the same as a smith); my maternal grandfather was a sailor, and sailors also are people of space and circumstance. . . . The smith is a man who can make a volume from a sheet. . . . The metalsmith embraces all three dimensions, and thus unconsciously he achieves a dominion over space which not everybody possesses. . . ."

Gaudí had an extensive formal education. He first attended a school run by the father-to-be of his closest associate, FRANCESCO BERENGUER, then transferred to another such school, and in 1863 entered for five years a religious academy in Reus run by the Padres Escolapios. This Escuela Pía was also attended by two Catalans of later prominence, José Ribera and Eduardo Toda, with whom at age fifteen he published the magazine *El Arlequín* and with whom in 1867–1870 he composed a project for the restoration of the famous but abandoned monastery of Poblet near where Ribera grew up. In 1868, Gaudí's family was able to send him to the Instituto de Enseñanza Media and Facultad de Ciencia of the University of Barcelona where he passed two courses necessary for his secondary school diploma; by 1873, he had prepared to enter the new School of Architecture which then moved to Elias Rogent's new Barcelona University building where Gaudí was matriculated in 1874. He received his title of architect in March 1878.

Gaudí was apparently an eccentric student of strong likes and dislikes, reacting against the architectural conservatism of some of his teachers who would then fail him. He gathered much outside experience, however, working in the offices of important Catalan builders of the day, some of whom were his teachers at architectural school. This was, in part, to relieve his family of the considerable expense of his education. The work consisted largely of drafting and, in some cases, calculations that astounded his employers. The major work of this sort he did for José Fontseré who was involved in the creation of Barcelona's Parque de la Ciudadela, whose actual Castilian citadel had been razed in 1868 and where the famous International Exposition was to take place in 1888. He also did a good deal for his mentor, the neo-Gothic architect JUAN MARTORELL MONTELLS who in

1883 was to nominate Gaudí as architect of the Sagrada Familia church, a task that occupied him the rest of his life.

Our best evidence of the quality of Gaudí's schoolwork and of his draftsmanship comes from those of his school projects that escaped the destruction of what had been his atelier at the Sagrada Familia church when the Spanish Civil War broke out in the summer of 1936. He had apparently loaned these drawings for an exhibition at the School of Architecture at some time, and they had been stored there, by oversight, instead of being returned to him. They were found in the 1960s when the architectural school moved to the Technical University of Barcelona. We know approximately eighteen of these either as originals or from photographs made before the destruction, and they show him to have been a master of the Beaux-Arts system of *esquisse*, plan, sections, elevations, and details. They are rich in a number of styles, exhibiting tendencies ranging from Romantic Classicism to the neobaroque with, in the details, a great deal of incised *neo-grèc* and a fascination—perhaps derived from EUGÈNE EMMANUEL VIOLLET-LE-DUC—with the mechanistic attachments of cast-iron elements to solid or laminated masonry. Already here, as would be the case in his later executed works, each project is quite different and unique. This was presumably because he saw each one as a holistic architectural design rising out of problems that were, basically, distinct, and each project is charged with an intangible atmosphere of its own, as can also be said of any of his

later buildings. He ranges from precise, finite details to romantic, dreamy overall effects, sometimes in the same rendering.

Some sense of this we also gain from a diary kept during the late 1870s and virtually his only written "statement." The multitude of quotations from him were later "reported" and not written by himself. On the subject "Understanding the Object; Freehand Drawing," he wrote:

Given the matter, it is necessary to study it and understand it, purging it of all that is superfluous, and once it has been carefully set forth will all its difficulties and inconveniences, we will proceed to attempt to apply form to the idea, always tending toward a simplified form, but giving satisfaction to the artistic conception, and not letting go of it until all of the difficulties of structure, form, plan, facilities, etc. have been solved.

It should be understood that at this time architecture in Catalonia was developing an originality—short-lived, perhaps, but almost without parallel in world history. This movement—not really a style in any sense of uniformity, because it was almost outrageous in its originalities—is called the *Renaixensa* (renascence, not renaissance). This cultural resurgence largely came about from patronage by burgeoning industrialist families and from innate Catalan patriotism as the region was being allowed more of its former *fueros* (independent rights and privileges) that had been suppressed in the seventeenth century by the Castilians. It was also tinged with nostalgia for the later Middle Ages when Aragon had more or less controlled the northern Mediterranean as far as Turkey, and delight in certain of the crafts and the lifestyle of Spain's former Muslims (totally ejected from the peninsula in 1609–1614). Essentially, this new *haute bourgeoisie* ceased to imitate the older aristocracy of Spain and their wealthy counterparts in northern Europe and began to ask their architects—often members of their own clans—to design a wide variety of buildings symbolic of the new wealth and urbanism of their status, that is to say, their status in contrast to the rest of Spain. Several of their architects outdid themselves in their creativity, Gaudí in particular.

Early *Renaixensa* works are characterized by abrupt blocky effects, often in brick or in brick contrasting with the "nobler" ashlar stone. The bricks were deployed in a variety of ways expressing the character of terra cotta—sometimes as geometric modules, sometimes as arcades and corbeled arches, sometimes in terms of Muslim patterns as the Muslims had been masters of brick architecture in the peninsula. Gaudí, especially in his Casa Vicens, was responsible for introducing polychromatic terra cotta, particulary in the form of lusterware, evolved in part from the long famous Span-

Gaudí y Cornet.
Casa Vicens.
Barcelona, Spain.
1883–1885

ish lusterware of Manises near Valencia. Whatever palatial style the newly rich adopted for the exterior, for the interiors of their residences and apartments their most advanced ideas about domestic high life in the 1870s and early 1880s were based on the norms of the medieval Muslims—then their enemies—which Spain's own monarchs had adapted from Andalusia during the Reconquest. The core section, for instance, of Gaudí's Palacio Güell (1886–1889) was based on the Alhambra, probably from the Goury-Jones volume of renderings of it, which was in the library of the Barcelona School of Architecture.

For the first few years in active practice, Gaudí did not actually build anything very substantial. He continued to be involved in large projects with those whom he had been assisting. In fact, over a career of forty-eight years he erected only some fifteen whole structures; it is the uniqueness of each one and his solutions to radically different functional, structural, monumental, geometrical, and decorative programs that make them so architecturally exciting and even visionary in effect. As regards the sequentials, evolutionary character of this works, it is necessary to study his renderings and sketches, which often show that a building was more transformed as it was being erected than in his preliminary sketches and drawings for it. His basic structural concepts were sometimes worked out in miniature: in small sketches for chairs (i.e., in model form) in a network of hanging funicular cords, or in time-lapse photos of moving objects.

His largest projects in his first years were collaborative: an overall layout and possibly some built structures for a textile cooperative in Mataró north of Barcelona, and a vast electric-lighting system for the Barcelona waterfront. He also worked on a small theater, decorated a pharmacy, and designed three chapels (two of which were carried out). He designed furniture for himself and for a pantheon (1878) built by Juan Martorell at Comillas, a Catalan enclave near Santander. He also designed street fixtures, including lamp posts still used in Barcelona, and the costumes and vehicles for a celebratory cavalcade. Almost all of those carried out have long disappeared, and they survive only in exquisite drawings.

His first actual buildings, from the mid-1880s, represent the jostling geometrics, laminated surfaces, and contrasts of building material (ashlar masonry versus rubble, or brick and terracotta versus cast-iron elements) common to other *Renaixensa* architects such as Lluís Domènech i Montaner. The buildings concerned are the Casa Vicens (1883–1885, although the property was obtained in 1878 and some details were added as late as 1888); a summer villa, *El Capricho* (1883–

1885), for a member of the same Comillas family in the north; and work on the estate (*finca*) of his major patron, Eusebio Güell, of which the stable and rear gatehouse survive (c.1889–1887). Although organized and constructed quite differently, all three of these buildings are resplendent in textural and polychromatic contrasts. On two of them the ceramic tiles—in some cases identical—are laid in strips, surfaces, or polygons, and in the Finca Güell they are shattered into pieces in order to fit curved surfaces better and are actually embedded as tiny bits in the mortar channels, so enriching the effect.

The Palacio Güell (c.1886–1889), erected on a narrow street in the old quarter of Barcelona, is another matter. This is an impressive, ashlar, masonry palace with an almost Venetian façade and two great parabolic arched gates admitting carriages into its lobby, whence the vehicles move forward into a grade-level parking room; horses are led down a ramp to stables in the basement, from which their grooms walk up a spiral ramp

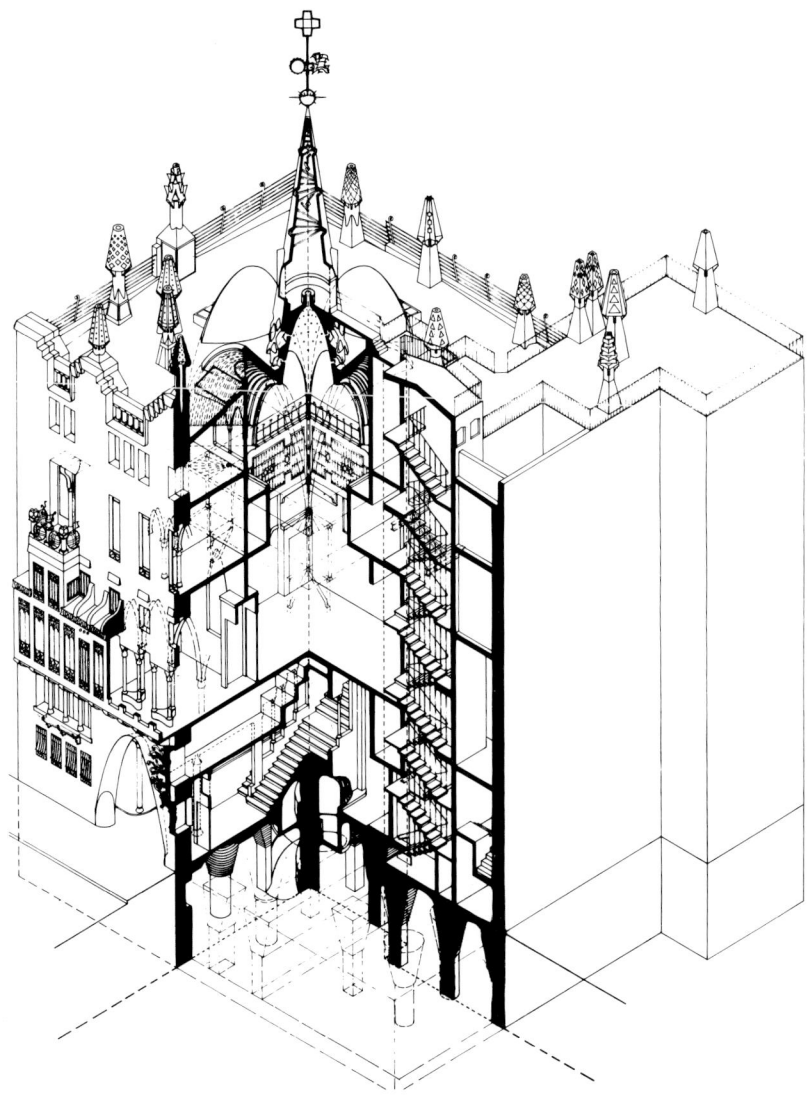

Gaudí y Cornet. Palacio Güell (isometric rendering of building as it stands today). Barcelona, Spain. 1886–1889

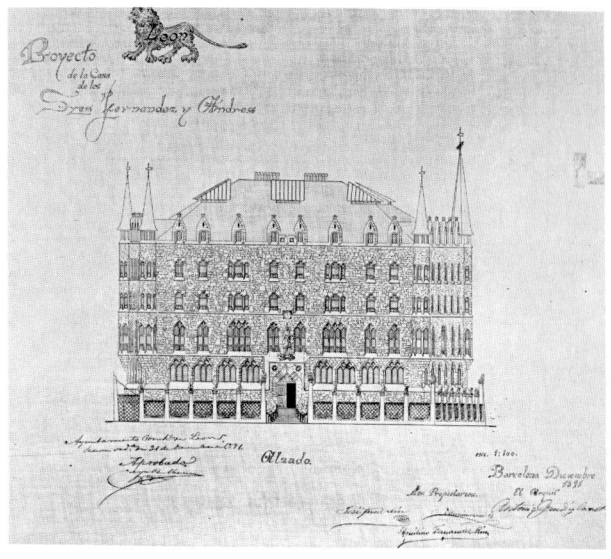

Gaudí y Cornet.
Casa Fernández y Andrés
(rendering of proposed
façade by Gaudí)
León, Spain.
1891–1894

Gaudí y Cornet.
Colegio de Santa Teresa de
Jesús.
Barcelona, Spain.
1888–1890

back to ground level. The passengers ascend a series of circumvallating stairways to the *piano nobile* where a central core is open to a domed, pierced, and pinnacled ceiling. The roof is attained by further galleried stairways past domestic quarters that give onto the three-storied central core via jalousies. The roof is a fairyland of broken-tile encrusted chimneys and ventilators looking for all the world as if Picasso (whose studio was once on the street) had made them twenty-five years later. The servant wing, incidentally, except for its portion of the street façade, is done in brick (for Spaniards an inferior material), while the "palace" is in superior stone masonry from the Güell quarry at Garraf south of Barcelona; the roof of the servants' wing has its chimneys and ventilators of simple brick while those on the palace are totally covered with polychrome tile mosaic.

Gaudí's next effort was the design of an Episcopal Palace at Astorga in the central Spanish province of León for the new Bishop Juan Bautista Grau Vallespinós who apparently commissioned Gaudí to do it because they were both from Reus. Like a modern environmentalist, Gaudí prepared himself for the project by consulting the León volume in a publication *España, sus monumentos y arte, su naturaleza e historia,* the recent update of an extensive romantic publication of the 1840s called *Recuerdos y bellezas de España;* he also carried on a lengthy correspondence with the bishop himself about the customs and countryside of León. The bishop was apparently delighted with the resultant plans of August 1887 for the building, but church officials in Madrid, who controlled such works, waited two years to give the go-ahead. In 1889, Gaudí went to Astorga to supervise construction himself with a crew of Catalan masons. The finished lower floors are quite unlike Gaudí's submitted plans—vastly more monumental because of

revisions in the project on actual arrival there and personal study of the countryside. When the bishop died unexpectedly in 1893, local masons, unable to carry out Gaudí's vaulting system, gave up. Construction was resumed in 1905 by a local architect who roofed the building two years later. It became the Museo de los Caminos in 1964.

Through another Catalan connection—textile merchants who were acquainted with Eusebio Güell—Gaudí was commissioned to do the Casa Fernandez y Andrés (1891–1894), a business and apartment block on a major plaza in the nearby city of León. This is a neo-Gothic palace, and in this case—exceptionally—very much like his actual drawings for it, which have been found where they were hidden under the façade statue of Saint George when it was restored in the 1950s. The sense of continuity of effect in the design of these two Gothic Revival structures in Astorga and León seems to be part of a general Catalan architectural reaction to the blocky masonry of competitive parts in the early *Renaixensa* style. With Gaudí, flow now substitutes, as in other Catalan designers, for the jostling of cubic forms, anticipating the linear whiplash effects that will be predominant at the turn of the century.

Gaudí in the late 1880s also went in another direction, echoing his prior Mudéjar tendencies, but rather more in a North African Berber mode. This is embodied in the Colegio (school) de Santa Teresa de Jesús (1888–1890) for a conventual order recently founded (1876) by Enrique de Ossó (beatified October 14, 1979). Its exposed, laminated brick and rubble and its cornice profile were, of course, developed by him for economic reasons, but they suggest a relationship with the Berber civilization of the Atlas mountain region of North Africa. Actually, Gaudí himself had direct contact with that area only a few years later when, with the second marqués of Comillas, he voyaged there and designed for the marqués a Spanish Franciscan mission in Tangier.

This mission was one of his major projects (although it was never even begun), and he had many renderings of it in his destroyed archive. We know visually about it only from an illustration in the Ráfols biography of him of 1928–1929 and from a postcard that he himself sent to the owners of his building in the city of León. The mission is interesting for the way in which it reflects the Colegio de Santa Teresa in its walls and window slits, but its towers anticipate the *flèches* of the Sagrada Familia church. Whatever the ultimate source, Gaudí's architectural forms always became highly personal in a creative way, and *Mudéjarismo* was a compound style into which they could fit.

The Casa Calvet, an apartment building of 1898–1904, was his last work of eclectic character, and it also conforms to the tendency of Catalan architects toward the end of the century to seek continuity instead of a competitive *Formspiel* in their architectural designs. In this case he adopted the dynamism of the historical baroque enhanced by the floral and sumptuous linearism of the Art Nouveau—especially in the internal elevator stairwell. For this project, Gaudí received the first annual prize (1900) given by the Ayuntamiento of Barcelona for structures completed during the previous year. It would appear that the prize was essentially for the exterior; some of its office furniture does not appear to have been designed until after the turn of the century, and the year 1904 is recognized as the date of completion of the building.

It was in the first years of the twentieth century that Gaudí achieved his "mature" manner of designing and building, just as Frank Lloyd Wright was doing with his Willetts and Heurtley "Prairie" houses of the identical years. For Gaudí one would say "manner" rather than "style" because he had no style as such but rather sought an architecture whose form was identical with its structure not simply as in engineering design but rather seeking an organicism of nature's structure and nature's quadratic geometry of curves and curving planes—no longer the Platonic solids or medieval quadratur and triangulatur. After 1900, no two of his buildings as finished, are in any way identical in any terms, whereas before 1900 some buildings had at least similar historical references.

What happened is most easily demonstrated by comparing surviving drawings of chairs that were sketched by Gaudí around 1878 and 1901–1902, respectively. The earlier chair has all the monumentality and mechanistic gadgetry that we associate with the early *Renaixensa,* bulgy and con-

Gaudí y Cornet.
Project for a Franciscan
Mission in Tangier.
1898

Gaudí y Cornet.
Casa Calvet.
Barcelona, Spain.
1898–1904

fronted parts such as we have seen in his early buildings. The later drawings, for chairs in the Casa Calvet and anticipating some for the Casa Batlló, are of essentially "free form" furniture. In his quick sketches, we can see him searching for the essential function of a chair as a support for the human body at rest—a palm, as it were, to support the seat of the person and another hand to retain the upper back. The animality of the result is not surprising, since we know it in a somewhat more obvious way in contemporary Art Nouveau furniture that imitates the antelope or an insect. The loose calligraphy that animates and decorates the earlier drawing has become the actual basis of the

Gaudí y Cornet.
Study for an armchair.

*Gaudí y Cornet.
Study for an armchair.*

*Gaudí y Cornet.
Studies for chairs in business
office of Casa Calvet.*

later sketches. The whole effect has become less constructional and more totally spatial, and so does all of Gaudí's architecture from about 1901 on.

The villa Bell Esguard (1900–1909), which he built in Barcelona on the slopes of Mount Tibidabo, on which presumably the temptation of Christ by the devil took place, ("all these things will I give Thee"), is very vertical in effect with a roof on which one can imagine oneself as on an "exceeding high mountain" (Matthew 4:8). The building is castellated because it was constructed beside the ruins of the ancient country residence of King Martin "el Humano," last of the great fourteenth-century Aragonese monarchs. Its rubble wall has now taken on a remarkable variegated texture. The slitlike vertical windows, which we have seen in the Theresan school and Tangier mission, are reminiscences of the Gothic, but they are transformed here into a proto-cubist masonry collage of vari-colored stones and bits quarried nearby. Inside, it is actually an anthology of the so-called board vaults for which Catalonia was famous: various highly inventive manners of covering a room and supporting the floor above by means of dia-

phragm arches and thin shells of laminated tiles, culminating in a parabolic shell vault that supports the roof to which one is invited to ascend.

Gaudí, like Domènech i Montaner and the RAFAEL GUASTAVINOS, delighted in exploiting the potentialities of these *bóvedas tabicadas* (board vaults). After 1900, Gaudí deployed them and other masonry in ways that would approximate forests, cliffs or escarpments, caves, waves, and pinnacles so that his architecture became poetic, musical, metaphoric, sculptural, and painterly (in the twentieth-century sense of that medium).

This is to be seen in all his twentieth-century designs. For instance, in the Park Güell (1900–1914), an English-garden housing development that Eusebio Güell commissioned him to do on the Montaña Pelada (Bald Mountain) in order to reforest it and to provide picturesque sites for upper middle class homes, the mere "urbanistic" layout required fantastic structural terracing of roads, platforms and galleries. The Greek Theater—now a playground because the housing did not prosper and the park was sold to the city after Güell's death in 1918—is supported on a quantity of Greek Doric columns that are actually hollow, allowing for drainage of the theater's (now playground's) gravel surface to sewers. Modern sections of the structure of the sometimes multilevel terrace-roads can be seen in César Martinell's English edition (pp. 361–370).

In these years, Gaudí carried out two projects that reflect his ideas about the identity of form, structure, nature, and geometry. From 1904 to 1906, he was engaged in remodeling an apartment house on the Paseo de Gracia, Barcelona, that had originally had a façade something like his own Casa Calvet of less than a decade earlier. The remarkable transformation that occurred in Gaudí's twentieth-century designing is here apparent. The façade was so thoroughly changed—even structurally—that its original condition can be detected only in the still rectangular windows of the upper four floors. The ground floor was totally opened up into a succession of fluid arching columns that step out on to the sidewalk and say, "Here we are, holding up the façade!" The *piano nobile* and two flanking windows of the third floor above are made with huge bonelike (its nickname is Casa de los Huesos) glazed openings of considerable depth and indeterminate façade plane. Most of the remaining façade windows have metal balconies looking for all the world like scuba masks. The façade was topped by a foliate tower (with spiral stair within) inscribed to the Holy Family and a ceramic hyperbolic paraboloid cresting with vari-colored tiles that change hue as they inch across the crest like snails. Above the *piano nobile,* the sur-

face is covered with iridescent tiles like the surface of shoal water. He also transformed the elevator-lightwell court into a funnel-shaped space that provides core parts of the edifice with an even, reflected illumination all day long.

The Casa Milá nearby on the Paseo de Gracia (1906–1910) is quite a different matter. About 1906, under the stimulus of the prominent Catalan critic Eugenio D'Ors, Art Nouveau Modernismo went "Mediterranean" in a rather neoclassical way that is called Noucentisme. In the Casa Milá, Gaudí also went Mediterranean but in a manner harmonious with nature, not the counternature effect of the white cubic piles of houses on Mediterranean islands—at that time stimulating TONY GARNIER, JOSEF HOFFMANN, LE CORBUSIER, and others toward a proto-International architecture. The Casa Milá's rocklike façade has been likened to the outcroppings of Montserrat (serrated cliffs), which Gaudí and all Catalans hold in pious and mountain-climbing respect, and has been called Pyrenean. But it is rather more like the rocky coast of the Mediterranean because of its eroding sine-curve pattern of balconies and their kelplike iron gratings, as well as certain of its interior decoration.

The Casa Milá is also a layer cake. It does not have an internal metal skeleton supporting its successive floor façades as most urban structures of the time did, echoing Chicago and New York. Rather, each floor has its own total structure of slightly inward inclined stone piers resting on the floor below. These piers support a pattern of I-beams between whose flanges leap *bovedillas*, low-rise tile

Gaudí y Cornet.
Casa Milá.
Barcelona, Spain.
1906–1910

vaults, that support the entire floor above. As we can see from the façade, piers do not have to be directly on top of each other, but can appear to rest on windows below, and one of the ground floor leaning piers was so far out on the sidewalk that the city considered it a violation. Gaudí offered to cut it off, but the city rescinded. The Casa Milá is nature all through, from the hexagonal *baldosas* (concrete tiles) of the floors with seaweed patterns to the Jujol-plastered ceilings that are rippled in the fashion of criss-crossing sea waves.

Although the bulk of the Casa Milá is rocky (it is nick-named" La Pedrera," the stone quarry), when one ascends to the roof one is in a mystical cosmic world of knight-helmeted chimneys and helicoidal lozenge-patterned ventilators and access stairways. That is to say, the sinusoids which, running horizontally, determine the balconies of the exterior of the buildings, here rise heavenward in more exact interlaced patterns. And through one of the arches (Collins, 1960, Fig. 6), one can see on the horizon the steeples of the Sagrada Familia church, a snapshot, as it were, of the Holy Jerusalem, whose towers also peek over the benches of the Park Güell.

The projects most important to Gaudí himself were his religious works. They began when in 1883 he was awarded the commission of the Expiatory Church of the Sagrada Familia to be built on the fringe of Barcelona in a set of blocks that the city planner ILDEFONSO CERDÁ had set aside for a hippodrome. The huge church and others contemporary with it were occasioned by the impact of intense urbanization on major world cities. The project for the Sagrada Familia had been started by a pious book dealer of Barcelona, José María Bocabella y Verdaguer, under the influence of his priest, the Mercedarian José María Rodriguez, and after a pilgrimage to the shrine of Loreto in Italy, (to which the angels in 1294 presumably flew a small brick house of the Holy Trinity in Nazareth). Señor Bocabella decided to campaign for a church dedicated to (1) the Holy Family as representative of the virtues of domestic life; (2) Saint Joseph as patron of the working class; and (3) the expiation of the sins of a materialistic age. Impressed by a French Marist publication in Dijon devoted to Saint Joseph, Bocabella established in Barcelona in 1866 the *Asociación de Devotos de S. José* and published a version of the Dijon magazine called *El Propagador de la Devoción a San José* (now *Templo*, since 1981 *Temple*). The worship of Saint Joseph had started in late medieval times and had flourished especially under Santa Teresa. He had briefly been the patron saint of Spain and was revived by the Vatican in the late nineteenth century in an effort to stress the craftsmanship and carpentry of Saint Joseph against socialist and communist trade unions. We can today see this as a parallel to the German development of the *Bauhütte*, that is, traditional and nationalistic, mason lodges clustered around a church building site. When he purchased the terrain, Bocabella said, "On this site will rise the sumptuous expiatory church of the Holy Family, surrounded by gardens for the recreation and enjoyment of children, and accompanied by Catholic schools and workshops with the object of uplifting those gangs of street urchins who wander about lost, and so to facilitate their moral and physical development" Gaudí later described to a French visitor the cluster of artisans about the church "from which will rise the noises of work, like the buzzing of bees, toward the sunlit church, a mystical hive."

The building itself went through a number of design modifications representing most of Gaudí's developing manners. Early, in 1875, it was thought that the church would replicate the shrine at Loreto in Italy, but no architect was selected. After buying the land, Bocabella in 1882 secured a neo-Gothic project from the diocesan architect Francisco de Paula del Villar y Lozano with whom

Gaudí had worked at the Abbey of Montserrat, and the cornerstone was laid on Saint Joseph's Day, 19 March 1882. The crypt was started and was excavated by August 1883. Because of an internal dispute, Gaudí took over from del Villar in November 1883 on the advice of his mentor, Juan Martorell. Gaudí completed the crypt in 1887, following del Villar's strict neo-Gothic except for the chapel of Saint Joseph which was somewhat more dynamic. From 1891 to 1893, the apse walls and finials were constructed, but not vaulted, in a rather free neo-Gothic. The first transept façade (Nativity) was constructed from 1893 to 1903 in an evolving *Modernista* character, and from 1892 to 1917, Gaudí made studies for the other transept (Passion), which has been constructed since 1954 according to his 1917 drawing. Construction of the towers and spires of the Nativity façade continued until after Gaudí's death (1903–1930). Structurally, the most important aspects of the church were his studies for the nave (1898–1925) in which Gaudí moved from essentially Gothic to more of a pier inclination, hyperbolic paraboloid vaults, and, around 1925, pierced hyperboloid vaults lit from clearstories under the church roof, treelike inclined piers, and flattened hyperboloid webbs for windows. All of this was to achieve "equilibration," that is, a masonry structure that is self-supporting within itself—no props, no buttresses (which Gaudí called crutches).

Some of these equilibrated structural ideas were worked out at the church for the Güells's textile factory workers' colony at Santa Coloma de Cervelló, south of Barcelona, where Gaudí was involved from 1898 to about 1915. Here he used his famous hanging catenary cord models with pellet weights hooked onto cords, proportional to the "loads" at these points on the inverted arches. The weights converted the hanging curves of the model into funicular poligons off which his masons could take measurements for the job, as if the whole network were a three-dimensional graphic-static working drawing. Gaudí had photographs made of these hung models, on which sheets had been draped to create exterior and interior effects. On such essentially linear photographs he then drew or painted the eventual building forms, inside and out. He appears to have spent a decade on this theoretical preparation because the first stone was laid only in 1908, and construction seems not to have started until 1912. Gaudí himself did not visit the site after late 1914, when he was abandoning all projects other than the Sagrada Familia church. Although he is said to have used the Colonia Güell Church as a "laboratory" for the structural calculations at the Sagrada Familia Church, the former, to judge from its built crypt,

Gaudí y Cornet. Expiatory Church of the Holy Family (Sagrada Familia). Barcelona, Spain. 1926 (work still in progress)

was to be a rather brusque and literal interpretation of the funicular model, executed in a variety of vernacular materials such as basalt and over-fired brick. The Sagrada Familia church, on the other hand, was to rise smoothly and symmetrically like a great cathedral, following the leaning treelike

Gaudí y Cornet. Church, Güell Workers' Colony. Santa Coloma de Cervelló, Spain. 1898–c.1915

piers up to the quadratically curved-surface vaults and quite pristine in overall form.

Structure alone, however, will not explain these churches. Gaudí was a deeply religious man, coached in part by Bishop Grau for whom he built the palace in Astorga. He worked out an *iconographic* program for the Sagrada Familia Church that would in its complexities outdo even Saint Thomas Aquinas and Emile Mâle. We have many sectional drawings, both vertical and horizontal, listing the major figures to whom parts are dedicated; and the Nativity façade was produced by Segal-like superrealistic techniques for which Gaudí employed all sorts of sketches, photographs, plaster casts, and clay and metal models of the persons and animals portrayed.

What is very interesting, ritually, are the reformations that Gaudí carried out for Bishop Pedro Campins in the interior of the Cathedral of Palma de Mallorca (1901–1915). The original Mediterranean nature of such a Catalan Gothic church, with its heavy walls and vast democratic space rising up to the vaults, had become cluttered in Renaissance and baroque times with a large choir in the nave and retables that subdivided, like screens, the flow of nave space to the sanctuary. Gaudí and the bishop cleared all that out. They gave the congregation a full view as far as the ultimate apsidal Lady Chapel and they hung a suspended baldachin over the altar so that the priests could get the entire congregation into an empathetic, direct involvement in the liturgy such as was generally not to occur in Catholicism until after Pope John XXIII's Second Vatican Council in 1962—sixty years later.

Antonio Gaudí was a genius out of time, stimulating artists and laymen in various ways, depending on their sympathy with his poetics. He can be enthused about, but not really categorized or catalogued stylistically.

GEORGE R. COLLINS

*Gaudí y Cornet.
Detail of a Patio
of a Provincial
Diputación.*

WORKS

1878, Furniture for Comillas Pantheon; 1883–1885, El Capricho Summer Villa; Comillas, Santander, Spain. 1883–1885, Casa Vicens, calle de San Gervasio; 1883–1926, Expiatory Church of the Holy Family (Sagrada Familia; work still in progress); c.1884–1887, Güell Estate (additions), Las Corts de Sarría; 1886–1889, Palacio Güell; Barcelona, Spain. 1887–1893, Episcopal Palace (not completed until 1907), Astorga, León, Spain. 1888–1890, Colegio de Santa Teresa de Jesús, Bonanova, Barcelona, Spain. 1891–1894, Casa Fernández y Andrés, León, Spain. 1898–1904, Casa Calvet, 48 calle Caspe, Barcelona, Spain. 1898–c.1915, Church, Güell Workers' Colony, Santa Coloma de Cervelló, Spain. 1900–1909, Villa Bell Esguard, Bonanova; 1900–1914, Park Güell, Montaña Pelada; 1901–1902, Hermenegildo Miralles

Estate, Las Corts de Sarriá; Barcelona, Spain. 1901–1915, Cathedral of Palma de Mallorca (interior), Spain. 1904–1906, Casa Batlló (remodeling); 1906–1910, Casa Milá; Barcelona, Spain.

BIBLIOGRAPHY

Bibliographic material on Gaudí and his times is enormous. For a descriptive listing of approximately 1,800 items down to the early 1970s, see Collins 1973.

BASSEGODA NONELL, JUAN 1977 *Antonio Gaudí; Vida y Arquitectura.* Tarragona, Spain: Caja de Ahorros Provincial.

BASSEGODA NONELL, JUAN 1979 *Obras Completas de Gaudí.* 2 vols. Tokyo: Rikuyosha.

BASSEGODA NONELL, JUAN, and GARRUT ROMA, JOSÉ M. 1970 *Guia de Gaudí.* Barcelona, Spain: Literarias Científicas.

BERGOS MASSÓ, JUAN (1954)1974 *Antoni Gaudí: L'home i l'obra.* Barcelona, Spain: Universidad Politécnica.

CASANELLES, ENRIC (1965)1968 *Nueva Visión de Gaudí.* English ed. Greenwich, Conn.: Graphic Society.

CIRICI-PELLICER, ALEJANDRO 1951 *El arte modernista catalán.* Barcelona, Spain: Aymá.

CIRLOT, JUAN EDUARDO (1950)1965 *El arte de Gaudí.* Rev. ed. Barcelona, Spain: Omega.

COLLINS, GEORGE R. 1960 *Antonio Gaudí.* New York: Braziller.

COLLINS, GEORGE R. (compiler) 1973 *A Bibliography of Antonio Gaudí and the Catalan Movement, 1870–1930.* With the assistance of Maurice E. Farinas. Volume 10 in *Papers of the American Association of Architectural Bibliographers.* Charlottesville: University of Virginia Press.

COLLINS, GEORGE R., and BASSEGODA NONELL, JUAN 1982 *The Designs and Drawings of Antonio Gaudí.* N.J.: Princeton University Press. Includes an up-to-date chronology of all of Gaudí's works.

DESCHARNES, ROBERT 1971 *Gaudí the Visionary.* Edited by George R. Collins. With photographs by Clovis Prévost. New York: Viking.

FLORES, CARLOS 1982 *Gaudí, Jujol y el Modernisimo Catalan.* 2 vols. Madrid: Aguilar.

MARTINELL BRUNET, CÉSAR (1951)1969 *Conversaciones con Gaudí.* Barcelona, Spain: Aymá. Originally published with the title *Gaudí i la Sagrada Familia, comentada por el mateix.*

MARTINELL BRUNET, CÉSAR (1967)1975 *Gaudí: Su vida, su teoria, su obra.* Edited by George R. Collins. Cambridge, Mass.: M.I.T. Press.

PANE, ROBERTO 1964 *Antoni Gaudí.* Milan: Comunità.

PUIG BOADA, ISIDRO (1929)1972 *El Templo de la Sagrada Familia.* Barcelona, Spain: Omega.

PUIG BOADA, ISIDRO 1981 *El pensament de Gaudí: Compilació de textos i comentaris.* Barcelona, Spain: Colegio de Arquitectos de Catalunya.

RÁFOLS FONTANALS, JOSÉ F., and FOLGUERA, FRANCESCO (1928)1960 *Gaudí.* Rev. ed. by Rafols Fontanals. Barcelona, Spain: Canosa.

SWEENEY, JAMES JOHNSON, and SERT, JOSEP LLUÍS

(1960)1970 *Antonio Gaudí*. New York: Praeger.
TARRAGÓ, SALVADOR 1974 *Gaudí*. Barcelona, Spain: Escudo de Oro.

GAUTHEY, EMILAND MARIE

Born in Chalon-sur Saône, Emiland Marie Gauthey (1732–1806) studied mathematics with his uncle at Versailles, then architecture with G. P. M. Dumont in Paris, before moving, in 1757, to the school of the Ponts et Chaussées, with which institution he was to be associated for the rest of his life, building bridges and canals in Burgundy, in particular the Canal du Centre (1783–1791). But he was intimately involved also with architecture, advising JACQUES GERMAIN SOUFFLOT on the construction of Sainte Geneviève (for which the church at Givry was said to be a test model) and evolving a theory of design based on the honest expression of efficient structure.

R. D. MIDDLETON

WORKS

1766–1770, Pont Gauthey (Pont de Pierre), over the Thalie, near Chalon-sur-Saône; 1770–?, Hôtel de Ville and Gateway, Givry-sur-Saône; 1770–1791, Church, Givry-sur-Saône; 1774–1777, Hôtel de Ville, Tournus; Saône et Loire, France. 1776–1780, Palais des Etats, Côte d'Or (north wing between the Cour de Flore and the rue des Forges; with Jean Thomas Dumorey), Dijon, France. 1777–1780, Pont de la Barque, over the Vallière, near Louhans; *1778–1780, Château de Chagny; 1778–1784, Theater (only facade survives), 34 rue aux Fèvres, Chalon-sur-Saône; Saône et Loire, France. 1781–1786, Pont de Pierre, over the rue de Baulches, near Auxerre, Yonne, France. 1781–1790, Pont des Echavannes, over the Saône, Chalon-sur-Saône; 1782–1785, Pont de Louhans, over the Seille; 1782–1785, Pont de Saint Yan, over the Arconce; *1782–1788, Pont de Louhans, over the Solnan; 1782–1790, Pont de Navilly, over the Doubs; *1782–1787, Pont de Cuisery, over the Seille; 1783–1787, Pont de Bellevesvres, over the Brenne; 1783–1787, Pont de Gueugnon, over the Arroux; 1784–1789, Pont Saint Laurent (enlargement of an earlier bridge), over the Saône, Chalon-sur-Saône; 1785–1789, Pont de Blanzy, over the Bourbince; 1786–1789, Pont de Navilly, over the Guyotte; Saône et Loire, France. 1786–1790, Pont de Cousin, Avallon, Yonne, France. n.d., Immeuble des Mines de Blanzy, 24 Quai des Messageries, Chalon-sur Saône, Saône et Loire, France.

BIBLIOGRAPHY

DARTEIN, FERNAND DE (1904)1909 "La vie et les travaux d'Emiland Gauthey." Pages 1–89 in *Etudes sur les ponts en pierre remarquables par leur décoration antérieurs au XIXᵉ siècle*. Paris: Béranger.
GAUTHEY, EMILAND MARIE 1809–1816 *Traité de la construction des ponts*. 3 vols. Paris: Firmin-Didot.
GAUTHEY, EMILAND MARIE n.d. "Mémoire sur les règles de l'architecture." Unpublished manuscript, Ecole des Ponts et Chaussées, Paris.
READ, JAMES J. 1974 "Emiland Marie Gauthey: 1732–1806." Unpublished B.A. dissertation, University of Cambridge.

GAYNOR, JOHN P.

John Plant Gaynor (c.1826–1889), of whom little personal is known, styled himself an architect-engineer. Born in Ireland, he came to the United States by 1849. Opening an office in 1851 in Brooklyn, he built the landmark iron Haughwout Building (1856) in Manhattan, and a similar iron office block in Brooklyn. In San Francisco after 1863, he is credited with many homes, three iron bridges, and the large iron-front Savings and Loan Society Building. He built the ornate Grand Hotel in 1870, and finally in 1873–1874 the world-acclaimed Palace Hotel, with its famous seven-story glass-roofed carriageway court. In the 1906 earthquake, the Palace was gutted by fire, but its innovative solid structure survived. Gaynor died in San Francisco.

MARGOT GAYLE

WORKS

*1856, Halsey Office Building (later the Arbuckle Building), Fulton Street, Brooklyn, N.Y. 1856, Haughwout Store, 490 Broadway, New York. 1864, W. C. Ralston House (Belmont; now Notre Dame College), near San Francisco. *1870, Grand Hotel, New Montgomery Street; 1870, Savings and Loan Society Building, Clay Street; *1873–1874, Old Palace Hotel, New Montgomery Street; San Francisco.

BIBLIOGRAPHY

GEBHARD, DAVID ET AL. 1973 *A Guide to Architecture in San Francisco and Northern California*. Santa Barbara, Calif.: Peregrine Smith.
GAYLE, MARGOT, and GILLON, EDMUND V., JR. 1974 *Cast-Iron Architecture in New York*. New York: Dover.
"The Haughwout Establishment." 1859 *Cosmopolitan Art Journal* 3, no. 3.
LEWIS, OSCAR, and HALL, CARROLL 1939 *Bonanza Inn*. New York: Knopf.
OLMSTED, ROGER, and WATKINS, T. H. 1968 *Here Today: San Francisco's Architectural Heritage*. San Francisco: Chronicle Books.

GEARY, STEPHEN

Stephen Geary (c.1797–1854) was an architect and civil engineer, inventor, and specialist in cemetery design. He entered the Royal Academy Schools in 1817, and in 1830 designed King's Cross in London. He is credited with the design of the first gin palace in London, but is best known for his pioneering work in laying out the first great cemeteries in the London area.

JAMES STEVENS CURL

WORKS

*1830–1836, King's Cross, Battle Bridge; 1837, Saint Pancras Collegiate School; 1837–1839, Cedar of Lebanon Catacombs at Highgate Cemetery; London.

BIBLIOGRAPHY

BOASE, FREDERIC 1965 Volume 1, column 1133 in *Modern English Biography, Containing Many Thousand Concise Memoirs of Persons Who have Died Between the Years 1851–1900*. London: Frank Cass.
CURL, JAMES STEVENS 1977 *Nunhead Cemetery, London: A History of the Planning, Architecture, Landscaping and Fortunes of a Great Nineteenth-Century Cemetery*. London: Ancient Monuments Society.
CURL, JAMES STEVENS 1980 *A Celebration of Death. An introduction to some of the buildings, monuments, and settings of funerary architecture in the Western European Tradition*. London: Constable.
GEARY, STEPHEN 1840 *Cemetery Designs for Tombs and Cenotaphs*. London: Tilt & Bogue.
LEIGH, PERCIVAL (1840)1930 *The Comic Latin Grammar*. New York: Dodd.
WHITTOCK, N. 1840 *On the Construction and Decoration of the Shop Fronts of London*. London: Sherwood, Gilbert and Piper.

GEDDES, NORMAN BEL

Norman Bel Geddes (1893–1958), one of America's most versatile and influential designers, displayed early the recalcitrant spirit that was an ingredient of his later success. Expelled from school at sixteen, he attended the Cleveland School of Art for three months and the Chicago Art Institute for only seven weeks. However, while still in his twenties, he won international recognition as a brilliant theater designer, particularly for innovations in lighting, the use of color to evoke moods, and his radically simple sets. Over his career but most actively from 1916 to 1936, he staged more than two hundred productions, including operas, dramas, and musicals.

In 1927, Geddes rechanneled his energies into the nascent profession of industrial design, establishing the first firm in the United States to specialize in this field. He designed an enormous range of products, from soap dispensers and stoves to commercial scales and vending machines. His seminal book, *Horizons* (1932), asserts his modernist credo.

Geddes's interest in transportation led him to restyle automobiles, airplanes, ships, and trains according to aerodynamic principles or "streamlin-

ing," a concept with which he became identified. In the mid-1930s, he began to study highway design and traffic problems; this research culminated in his book *Magic Motorways* (1940) and in the General Motors pavilion at the 1939 New York World's Fair. He designed every feature of this popular exhibit (visited by more than twenty-four million people), from the building and its ingenious circulation system to the famous Futurama, a miniature "city of tomorrow."

Though not a licensed architect, Geddes produced many architectural projects which, like his interests, were split between the theatrical and the practical. His dozens of interiors for restaurants, hotels, nightclubs and theaters exploited his dramatic flair, as did his many unexecuted designs for theaters or the aerial and aquarium restaurants planned for the 1933 Chicago Fair. His practicality surfaced in his prefabricated systems for housing, suburban developments, and a master plan for Toledo, Ohio.

Born Norman Geddes in Adrian, Michigan, he added the name of his first wife, Bel, to his as a joint *nom de plume* and later retained it. He died in New York in 1958, still active and at work on his autobiography, which was published posthumously.

CAROL WILLIS

WORKS

1929, Toledo Scale Company Building, Ohio. *1937–1939, General Motors Exhibition (Futurama), New York World's Fair. *1940, Prototypes for Prefabricated Houses for Housing Corporation of America.

BIBLIOGRAPHY

GEDDES, NORMAN BEL 1932 *Horizons*. Boston: Little, Brown.
GEDDES, NORMAN BEL 1940a *Current Biography: 1940*. Edited by Maxine Block. New York: Wilson.
GEDDES, NORMAN BEL 1940b *Magic Motorways*. New York: Random House.
KELLEY, WILLIAM (editor) 1960 *Miracle in the Evening: An Autobiography of Norman Bel Geddes*. Garden City, N.Y.: Doubleday.
PULOS, ARTHUR J. 1970 "The Restless Genius of Norman Bel Geddes." *Architectural Forum* 133:46–51.

GEDDES, PATRICK

Patrick Geddes (1854–1931) was born and educated in Perth, Scotland. He was London professor of botany at the University of Dundee (1889–1919) and professor of sociology, Bombay University (1921–1924). Geddes refused knighthood in 1912, but accepted it in 1931. He died in Montpellier, France.

Throughout his life Geddes was a compulsive builder. In addition to numerous dwellings—built or reconditioned—mainly for the poor, Geddes built the first Hall of Residence (1892) for students of Edinburgh University and the Outlook Tower (1895); he supervised the reconstruction in London of Crosby Hall (1910), and built the Scots College in Montpellier, France (1924).

However, Geddes's main contribution to architecture was in the field of ideas, most of which emerged in the ten years between Geddes's biological studies in London under Thomas Huxley (1874–1878) and his appointment as professor of botany at Dundee (1889).

His papers containing new insights derived from the interrelation of disciplines antagonized the academic world and gave Geddes the reputation of an unpredictable and unsound scholar, which dogged him throughout his life.

During the years between Geddes's appointment to Dundee (which required his attendance only three months a year) and the outbreak of World War I, he was very active in promoting the official recognition not only of sociology, but also of city planning. In 1903, Geddes prepared what Sir PATRICK ABERCROMBIE called "the first comprehensive town planning report ever undertaken." This was a study of Dunfermline, entitled *City Development,* which took "full note of places and things as they stand, of people as they are, of work, family, and institutions, of ideas and ideals; yet patiently plans out, then boldly suggests, new and practicable developments; and these not only for the immediate future but for the remoter and higher issues which a city's long life . . . involves." (Geddes, 1904, p. 19).

In the same year (1903), Geddes founded the Sociological Society with Victor Brandford, and the first chair of sociology in London University was endowed for him in 1907 by J. Martin White. However, academic antipathies were too strong and he lost it to a "safer" man, T. H. Hobhouse (Philip Boardman, *The World of Patrick Geddes,* 1978, p. 231).

John Burns, member of parliament and member of the cabinet, succeeded in getting the first Town Planning Act through parliament in 1909, and it was Geddes who stimulated his action. Geddes's truly magnificent "Cities and Town Planning Exhibition" (1910) filled an entire gallery of the Royal Academy in London. This coincided with the first town planning conference, which was attended by more than twelve hundred architects, municipal engineers, and city officials. The cities exhibition had an electrifying effect on all who saw it and who heard Geddes's exposition of architecture and town planning as the outcome of the local history of each city. As he said in *Cities in Evolution:*

On pain of economic waste, of practical failure no less than of artistic futility, and even worse, each true design, each valid scheme should and must embody the full utilisation of its local and regional conditions, and be the expression of local and of regional personality. "Local character" is attained only in course of adequate grasp and treatment of the whole environment, and in active sympathy with the essential and characteristic life of the place concerned. Each place has a true personality; and with this shows some unique elements—a personality too much asleep it may be, but which it is the task of the planner, as master-artist, to awaken. (1915, pp. 396–397).

World War I cut short Geddes's work on the replanning of Dublin and in 1915 he left to tour India with his huge exhibition. Unfortunately, the ship containing the exhibition cases was torpedoed and sank, but for the next four years Geddes visited city after city in India writing reports on how "conservative surgery" could achieve the desired goals of city improvement more efficiently, more cheaply, and with the goodwill rather than the desperate antagonism of the inhabitants.

Shortly after the war, Geddes—now almost seventy—paid his third visit to America, where he gave a series of lectures at the New School for Social Research in New York and came in contact with the pioneer group of American housing and regional planners: CLARENCE S. STEIN, ALBERT MAYER, CATHERINE BAUER, and—above all—Lewis Mumford, whose writings were very strongly influenced by Geddes's pioneering ideas.

JAQUELINE TYRWHITT

WORKS

1887–1899, Summer Schools; 1892, Ramsay Gardens; *1895, Outlook Tower; Edinburgh. 1910, Crosby Hall (reconstruction), London. *1913, Edinburgh Zoo. *1923, Lucknow Zoo, India. *1924, Scots College, Montpellier, France.

BIBLIOGRAPHY

BOARDMAN, PHILIP 1978 *The Worlds of Patrick Geddes.* London: Routledge.

GEDDES, PATRICK 1902 "Edinburgh and its Region: Geographic and Historical." *Scottish Geographical Magazine* 18:302–312.

GEDDES, PATRICK (1904)1973 *City Development: A Study of Parks, Gardens, and Culture Institutes.* Reprint. New Brunswick, N.J.: Rutgers University Press.

GEDDES, PATRICK 1905 "Civics: As Applied Sociology." *Sociological Papers* 1:103–138.

GEDDES, PATRICK 1906 "Civics: As Concrete and Applied Sociology." *Sociological Papers* 2:57–119.

GEDDES, PATRICK 1911 "The Civic Survey of Edinburgh." Pages 537–574 in *Transactions of the Town*

Planning Conference, 1910. Edinburgh: Outlook Tower.

GEDDES, PATRICK (1915)1972 "Cities in Evolution: An Introduction to the Town Planning Movement and to the Study of Civics." In Marshall Stalley (editor), *Patrick Geddes: Spokesman for Man and the Environment.* New Brunswick, N.J.: Rutgers University Press.

GEDDES, PATRICK (1918) *Town Planning Toward City Development: A Report to the Durbar of Indore.* 2 vols. Indore, India: Holkar State Press.

TYRWHITT, JAQUELINE (editor) 1947 *Patrick Geddes in India.* London: Lund Humphries.

GEDDES, ROBERT

Born in Philadelphia, Robert Geddes (1923–) graduated from the Harvard Graduate School of Design in 1950. He has been dean of Princeton University's School of Architecture since 1965. He was a co-founder in 1954 of the firm Geddes Brecher Qualls Cunningham in Princeton, New Jersey, and Philadelphia.

Geddes has embraced all aspects of architecture in the execution of small and large buildings, new and old developments, furniture, landscape, city planning, and the writing of theory. As exemplified in his designs for Princeton University and Southern Illinois University, Carbondale, Geddes's architecture represents a meaningful contribution to the modern architectural vocabulary. His designs have structural clarity and plasticity of forms with careful organization contrasting unique and serial functions. Currently working as planning coordinator for new developments for Miami, Philadelphia, and New York City, Geddes is known to "give form to all the possibilities of architecture." He believes that the task of architectural design includes ethical and aesthetic values at both individual and social levels, which the building then "communicates."

MARC DILET

WORKS

1954, Geddes House, Radnor, Pa. 1955, Lawncrest Center; 1957, Roosevelt Playground; 1957–1965, Tarkin Playground (stages I and II); Philadelphia. 1958, Dolphin Swim Club, Lower Bucks County, Pa. 1958, Pender Laboratory, Moore School of Electrical Engineering, University of Pennsylvania; 1962, Police Headquarters; 1963, Northeast Regional Library; Philadelphia. 1963, Temple Beth Sholom, Manchester, Conn. 1964, Master plan, University City Science Center; 1965, Pine Street Rowhouses; Philadelphia. 1966, Geddes House, Princeton, N.J. 1966, Unitarian Church of Delaware County, Springfield, Pa. 1966–1968, Theater and Fine Arts Complex, Beaver College, Glenside, Pa. 1967, Graduate Research Center, University of Pennsyl-

vania, Philadelphia. 1967, Residence and Dining Halls, University of Delaware, Newark. 1968–1972, Dining Hall and Academic Buildings, Institute for Advanced Study, Princeton University, N.J. 1971, Science/Academic Building, Beaver College, Glenside, Pa. 1972, IBM Branch Office Building, Bethlehem, Pa. 1972, Stauffer Dormitory and Dining Hall, University of Pennsylvania, Philadelphia. 1973, Coatesville Public Housing, Pa. 1974, Psychology Building, Rutgers University, New Brunswick, N.J. 1974, United States Mint (renovation), Philadelphia. 1975, Humanities and Social Sciences Center, Southern Illinois University, Carbondale. 1976, Dock Street Theaters and Shops, Philadelphia. 1978, United States Navy Recreation Facility, Sandy Hook Bay, N.J. 1979–?, Liberty State Park, Jersey City, N.J.

BIBLIOGRAPHY

"Architectural Principles in the Age of Uncertainty." 1979 *New Jersey Architect's Handbook* Aug.

"Making Connections: Architecture and Urban Design." 1980 *New Jersey Architect's Handbook* Oct.

"The Nature of the Built Environment." 1974 *Progressive Architecture* 55:72–81.

"Possibilities in Architecture." 1977 *Architectural Record* 7:103–108.

"Theory in Practice: This Architecture Reflects the Dual Values of Teacher and Practitioner." 1972 *Architectural Forum* 137, no. 2:34–41; no. 3:52–59.

GENDT, A. L. VAN

After having worked for the State Railroad, Adolf Leonard van Gendt (1835–1901), who was born in Alkmaar, Netherlands, established himself in Amsterdam as an independent architect in 1874. He appears to have been a successful businessman who exploited the economic prosperity of Amsterdam in that period and made his office into one of the largest in the city. He became famous for his technical capability and was often asked to assist as an engineer in constructing parts of large buildings, such as the Central Station in Amsterdam (designed by P. J. H. CUYPERS, 1881–1889) and the Stadsschouwburg in Amsterdam. After 1896, his sons Johan Godart and Adolf Daniel Nycolaas became partners in his office; after his death, the firm continued to contribute its engineering expertise to major structural projects.

WIM DE WIT

WORKS

1881, Hollandsche Manege, Vondelstraat; 1882–1884, Palace of People's Industry (arcade), Frederiksplein; 1885, Concert Hall, Van Baerlestraat; 1890, Heineken Villa, Tweede Weteringsplantsoen; 1897, Shopping Arcade, Raadhuisstraat; 1903–1921, Housing for Koninklijke Nederlandsche Stoomboot Maatschappij, Prins Hendrikkade and Koekoeksplein; 1913, Oranje

Nassau Veem, Realengracht; 1914, De Rijnstroom Shop and Offices, 92–96 Rokin; Amsterdam.

BIBLIOGRAPHY

A. D. N. van Gendt, Architect, Amsterdam. 1916 Bussum, Netherlands: Schueler.

EVERS, HENRI (1905–1911)1916–1918 *De architectuur in hare hoofdtijkperken.* 2 vols. 2d ed. Amsterdam: Veen.

FANELLI, GIOVANNI (1968)1978 *Moderne architectuur in Nederland: 1900–1940.* Translated from Italian by Wim de Wit. The Hague: Staatsuitgeverij.

GUGEL, EUGEN (1886)1916–1918 *Geschiedenis van de bouwstijlen in de hoofdtijdperken der architectuur.* 2d ed. Rotterdam, Netherlands: Bolle.

LANSINK, LYDIA 1979 "A. L. van Gendt, ingenieur-architect: 1835–1901." Unpublished thesis, University of Amsterdam.

ROY VAN ZUYDEWIJN, H. J. F. DE 1969 *Amsterdamse Bouwkunst: 1815–1940.* Amsterdam: De Bussy.

GENGA, GIROLAMO

Girolamo Genga (1476–1551) was born in Urbino, Italy, and also died there. Apart from a sojourn in Mantua around 1517 and a visit to Rome in the early 1520s, Genga spent his life in Urbino working for the delle Rovere dukes. Genga is known primarily as a painter for whom architecture was a secondary and later interest. His early training with Luca Signorelli in the 1490s and Pietro Perugino from 1502 to 1504 aligns his painting with the early sixteenth-century schools of Rome and central Italy. The same is true of his architectural projects which date to the middle of his career and derive from the works of DONATO BRAMANTE and RAPHAEL. Classical in nature, buildings such as the Villa Imperiale near Pesaro (begun 1530) stand as provincial reflections of trends initiated in the larger artistic centers of Renaissance Italy during the first decades of the sixteenth century.

SARAH E. BASSETT

WORKS

1523–1525?, Ducal Palace (renovations and additions), Urbino, Italy. 1530–1535?, Monte dei Imperiale Villa (renovations and additions), Pesaro, Italy. 1535, Santa Maria delle Grazie, Sinigalia, Italy. 1543, San Giovanni Battista, Pesaro, Italy.

BIBLIOGRAPHY

MÜNTZ, EUGÈNE 1889 *Histoire de l'art pendant la Renaissance.* 3 vols. Paris: Hachette.

SALMI, M. 1927–1928 "Intorno al Genga." *Rassegna marchigiana* 6:229ff.

THODE, HENRY 1888 "Ein fürstlicher Sommeraufenthalt in der Zeit der Hoch-Renaissance: Die Villa Monte Imperiale bei Pesaro." *Jahrbuch der königlich preussischen Kunstsammlungen* 9:161–184.

GENTZ, HEINRICH

Heinrich Gentz (1766–1811) was born in Breslau and educated in Berlin, where he studied architecture under KARL VON GONTARD. His robust neoclassical style was first formed when he was in Italy (1790–1795) on a royal stipend. Named *Hofbaumeister* in 1795, he first won acclaim for his entry in the 1797 competition for a monument to Frederick the Great. The influence of FRIEDRICH GILLY—his brother-in-law—is reflected in the pure geometric forms of these designs and especially in the sheer walls and abstract composition of his major building the New Mint at Berlin (1798–1800), which housed the Bauakademie, where both men taught. In the Schloss at Weimar (1800–1803), Gentz created some of the most refined yet chastely powerful interiors of German neoclassicism. After Prussia's defeat at Jena, Gentz executed two rare royal commissions: an extension to the Prinzessinnenpalais in Unter den Linden (1810) and the Mausoleum of Queen Louise at Charlottenburg (1810).

BARRY BERGDOLL

WORKS

*1798–1800, New Mint, Berlin. 1800–1803, Schloss (stairhall, Festsaal, gallery, and other interiors), Weimar, Germany. 1802, Theater, Bad Lauchstadt, Germany. 1803, Schloss (library); 1803–1804, Schloss (Reitbau); *1803–1804, Stadthaus and Festsaal; 1803–1805, Schloss (Schiesshaus); Weimar, Germany. 1810, Mausoleum of Queen Louise, Charlottenburg; 1810, Prinzessinnenpalais (new wing); Berlin.

BIBLIOGRAPHY

DOEBBER, ADOLPH 1911 *Das Schloss in Weimar.* Jena, Germany: Gustav Fischer.

DOEBBER, ADOLPH 1916 *Heinrich Gentz: Ein Berliner Baumeister um 1800.* Berlin: Heymann.

DOEBBER, ADOLPH 1918 "Heinrich Gentz: Ein Vorläufer Schinkels." *Wochenschrift des Architektenvereins zu Berlin* 13:17–22.

HENTZEN, ALFRED 1935 "Die Baugeschichte des Kopfbaus unter den Linden am ehemaligen Prinzessinnenpalais." *Jahrbuch der preussischen Kunstsammlungen* 56:100–116.

JERICKE, ALFRED, and DOLGNER, DIETER 1975 *Der Klassizismus in der Baugeschichte Weimars.* Weimar, Germany: Böhlhaus.

GENZMER, FELIX

German architect, educator, author, and city planner, Felix Genzmer (1856–?) is known primarily as one of the pioneers of the new art and science of city planning, in direct succession to CAMILLO SITTE and JOSEPH STÜBBEN. Born in Labes,

Pomerania (now Poland), Genzmer grew up in Halberstadt and studied architecture at the Technische Hochschulen in Hannover and Stuttgart, Germany (1875–1879).

His first position, with the building department of the national railroad (1880–1887), was followed by three years in the city building office of Cologne (1887–1890). It was in this period that Camillo Sitte published his revolutionary book on the principles of city planning and Joseph Stübben, as planner for Cologne, was applying his urban development plan for that city and writing the first edition of his influential book, *Der Städtebau*. Genzmer assisted in preparing drawings for Stübben's book.

From 1890 to 1894, Genzmer was municipal building director for Hagen in Westphalia; but an even greater opportunity came with his appointment in 1894 as building director for the city of Wiesbaden. A building boom in this major resort city and a large staff gave Genzmer the opportunity to have a major impact in designing urban spaces and a whole series of monumental structures in historical styles.

Genzmer's call in 1903 to become professor at the Technische Hochschule in Charlottenburg (Berlin) was coupled with the establishment of the first chair for city planning at a German university. He also became architect for the royal (later state) theaters at this time and retained that position until 1920, but Genzmer's greatest impact was in the development of the teaching of city planning and in the design of urban expansion plans, new communities, and housing developments for many locations in Germany. The principles Genzmer taught with his colleague JOSEPH BRIX in Berlin were published as *Städtebauliche Vorträge* from 1908 on.

Genzmer received many honors and played an influential role on competition juries and as critic. On the occasion of his seventieth birthday in 1926 he was described as still very active and in full health of body and mind.

RON WIEDENHOEFT

GEORGE, ERNEST

Ernest George (1839–1922) was articled to Samuel Hewitt of London and entered the Royal Academy Schools, where he gained the Gold Medal for Architecture in 1859. He practiced first with Thomas Vaughn (1861–1871), then with Harold Peto (1876–1890), and finally with Alfred Yates (1893–1919). The majority of his work is domestic in a lively mixed style, with turrets, gables, and much decoration in red brick and terra cotta, de-

rived from a free use of the late Gothic and early Renaissance of northern Europe. He published several volumes of topographical etchings. His pupils included HERBERT BAKER, Guy Dawber, Edwin Lutyens, and ROBERT WEIR SCHULTZ.

GODFREY RUBENS

WORKS

1873, 6–7 Saint Mary At Hill, London. c.1874 Saint Pancras Church, Rousdon, Devon, England. 1885–1890, 110–113 Mount Street; 1886, Saint Andrew's Church, Guildersfield Road; 1887, Albermarle Hotel, Piccadilly; 1894–1897, Claridges Hotel, Brook Street; London. 1894–1897, Motcombe Mansion, Dorsetshire, England. 1901–1910, Royal Exchange Buildings; 1901–1910, 77–78 South Audley Street; London.

BIBLIOGRAPHY

The Builder 1922 133:900–903.
Architect's Journal. 1922 56:855, 857–860.
Journal of the Royal Institute of British Architects. 1922–1923 30:106–107.

GEORGE, WALTER

Walter George (1881–1962), one of several British architects involved with EDWIN LUTYENS and HERBERT BAKER in the building of New Delhi, remained there after Indian independence in 1947. Articled to his father, he won the Soane Medallion. In 1915, he became Baker's representative in New Delhi, but began to practice independently in 1920. After independence, George twice was president of the Indian Institute of Architects and was instrumental in founding the Indian Institute of Town Planning.

GAVIN STAMP

WORKS

n.d., Council Chamber, Simla, India. n.d., Residences for the rulers of Jind, Mandi, and Bahawalpur; n.d., Saint Stephen's College; n.d., Saint Thomas's Church; New Delhi.

BIBLIOGRAPHY

GEORGE, WALTER 1912 *The Church of Saint Eirens at Constantinople.* London: Frowde.
"Obituary: Walter Sykes George." 1962 *Journal of the Royal Institute of British Architects* Series 3 69:102.

GERBIER, BALTHAZAR

Balthazar Gerbier (1592–1663), a Dutch-born Huguenot, was a courtier, diplomat, painter, promoter of an academy, and architect. He went to London in 1616 in the suite of the Dutch ambassador and entered the service of the duke of Buckingham for whom in 1624–1625 he carried out alterations at both York House, London, and New Hall, Essex. In 1629, he entered the service of King Charles I, was knighted in 1638, and appointed Master of Ceremonies in 1641.

Of uncertain political persuasion during the Interregnum, he was banished from court at the Restoration but probably (with PETER MILLS) designed the temporary triumphal arches erected in London to celebrate the coronation of Charles II (1661). He advertised his availability as an architect by publishing *A Brief Discourse Concerning the Three Chief Principles of Magnificent Building* (1662) and *Counsel and Advise to All Builders* (1663). In 1662 he was in charge of designing or remodeling Hampstead Marshall for Lord Craven, but as he died a year later most of the work remained to be completed by WILLIAM WINDE who possibly was his pupil.

Some of Gerbier's mannerist drawings survive, but the destruction of his buildings makes any assessment of his work difficult.

JOHN BOLD

WORKS

*1624–1625, New Hall (alterations), Essex, England.
*1624–1625, York House (alterations), The Strand;
*1661, Triumphal Arches (with Peter Mills); London.
*1662–1663, Hampstead Marshall (remodeling; not completed until 1688 by William Winde), Berkshire, England.

BIBLIOGRAPHY

CROFT-MURRAY, EDWARD, and HULTON, PAUL 1960 Pages 328–330 in *Catalogue of British Drawings.* London: Trustees of the British Museum.
GERBIER, BALTHAZAR (1662)1969 *A Brief Discourse Concerning the Three Chief Principles of Magnificent Building.* Reprinted in *The Art of Building.* Farnborough, England: Gregg.
GERBIER, BALTHAZAR (1663)1969 *Counsel and Advise to All Builders.* Reprinted in *The Art of Building.* Farnborough, England: Gregg.
HILL, OLIVER, and CORNFORTH, JOHN 1966 *English Country Houses: Caroline, 1625–1685.* London: Country Life.
"Sir Balthazar Gerbier." 1890 Volume 21, pages 227–229 in Leslie Stephen (editor), *Dictionary of National Biography.* London: Smith, Elder.
SUMMERSON, JOHN (1953)1977 *Architecture in Britain 1530–1830.* 6th rev. ed. Harmondsworth, England: Penguin.

GERLACH, PHILIPP

Philipp Gerlach (1679–1748) of Spandau (Germany) was the son of the Brandenburg-Prussian military architect whose main work was the House of the Commander (Komandantenhaus) in Berlin.

The son entered military service at an early age and was soon taken into the administration of buildings. He became a captain in 1702 and an engineer-major in 1711. He is generally considered to have been a pupil of JEAN BAPTISTE BROEBES from whom he also learned copper engraving. In 1707, he became chief of municipal building in Berlin, and in 1720 Frederick William I appointed him overall director of building. As head of the entire state building administration, he was in charge of building- and fire-police, surveying and land registry, and of approving all building development plans, fortifications and bridges, as well as all buildings belonging to the king himself. Under supervision of the king, from 1732 to 1736, he directed the expansion of the Berlin district of Friedrichstadt after his own plans by extending the sober main streets with their uniform two-story building lines to the west and south, ending them at the city gates in geometrical plazas (square, octagon, circle). From the circular plaza to the south, the streets radiated in three prongs into the city. This was an altogether excellent urbanistic achievement, brilliantly connecting French plaza form with the Roman solution of the Piazza del Popolo but of course lacking the latter's monumental execution. The westernmost of these streets was built up with representative palaces, thus becoming the main street of the new quarter. Among these palaces, Gerlach designed and built the Palais von Marschall (1735–1736) and the Royal Gold and Silver Manufactory (1735–1737). Gerlach's most important civic building is the former Kammergericht (Superior Court of Justice; 1733–1735). Like the palaces, it is a broad two-story building with a mansard roof. Articulation and ornament are restrained but dignified. Pilaster strips running up through the stories accentuate the flat side projection and the gabled central projection. High windows, delicate grooves and tessellation, and the balanced proportions and concentration of the sparse architectural sculpture into the center point to French training, but also to the norms of Goldmann and Sturm. Gerlach's plain church buildings, adapted to their function as Protestant preaching halls, are entirely in the latter tradition. Only the high and ostentatious towers give expression to the otherwise sober king's religiously prompted need for splendor. The pre-eminent example of this is Gerlach's tower for the Garnisonkirche (garrison church) in Potsdam (1731–1735). In its urbanistically dominant position, jutting as it did into the street that leads from the royal palace, it was considered the most magnificent and beautiful baroque tower of North Germany. A high substructure set into pilaster strips was surmounted by three monumental stories articulated by columnar orders. The ideas in GIOVANNI LORENZO BERNINI's towers of St. Peter's in Rome and the Münzturm (mint tower) of ANDREAS SCHLÜTER in Berlin were here skillfully carried forward and adjusted to the particular situation.

In 1737, because of illness, Gerlach resigned from the army and from all his offices.

FRITZ-EUGEN KELLER
Translated from German by
Beverley R. Placzek

WORKS

*1707–1727, Friedrichs Hospital with Church (completion); *1718, Palace of Montargues; *1721–1722, Garrison Church; Berlin. *1721–1724, Nicolaikirche, Potsdam, Germany. *1724, Town Hall and Guard House, Prenzlau, Brandenburg, Germany. *1726–1728, Jerusalem Church; *1727, Main Guard House; *1730–1731, Von Sydow Palace; *1731–1734, Petrikirche; Berlin. *1731–1735, Garrison Church, Potsdam, Germany. 1732, Crown Prince's Palace (remodeling); 1732–1736, Friedrichstadt Quarter (enlargement); 1733–1735, Superior Court of Justice (rebuilt 1965); *1734–1735, Splitgerber House; *1735–1736, Palais von Marschall; *1735–1737, Palais von Görne; *1735–1737, Royal Gold and Silver Manufactory; Berlin.

BIBLIOGRAPHY

BORRMANN, RICHARD 1893 *Die Bau- und Kunstdenkmäler von Berlin.* Berlin: Springer.
HAGER, WERNER 1942 Pages 165–166 in *Die Bauten des deutschen Barocks: 1690–1770.* Jena, Germany: Diederichs.
HEMPEL, EBERHARD 1965 Pages 218–219 in *Baroque Art and Architecture in Central Europe.* Harmondsworth, England: Penguin.
HERZ, RUDOLF 1928 *Berliner Barock: Bauten und Baumeister aus der ersten Hälfte des 18. Jahrhunderts.* Berlin: Deutsche Verlag für Politik und Geschichte.
MIELKE, FRIEDRICH 1968 *Die Garnisonkirche zu Potsdam.* Frankfurt: Lorch.
REUTHER, HANS 1969 *Barock in Berlin.* Berlin: Rembrandt.
ZUCKER, PAUL 1959 Pages 216–217 in *Town and Square.* New York: Columbia University Press.

GESELLIUS, HERMAN

Herman Gesellius (1874–1916) is the least known partner of the firm Gesellius-Lindgren-Saarinen because of his premature death. He was educated at the Polytechnic Institute in Helsinki together with ARMAS LINDGREN and ELIEL SAARINEN. The three formed a partnership even before they graduated, becoming the most prominent office in Finland. Although Gesellius played a practical role in the office, he was nevertheless a skillful interior designer and was especially interested in the Viennese *Jugendstil.* His work has a clean, harmonious refinement and constructive quality. After Lindgren's departure from the office, Gesellius worked with Saarinen on the designs for the Helsinki and Viipuri Railroad Stations (from 1904 on) and for Molchow Haus, a country estate in Germany (1905–1907). Gesellius left the office in 1907 and designed only a few buildings after that. The most notable is the Wuorio Office Building in Helsinki (1908–1910), where his early constructivism is clear and light and no longer bears National Romantic features.

PIRKKO-LIISA LOUHENJOKI

WORKS

HERMAN GESELLIUS, ARMAS LINDGREN AND ELIEL SAARINEN

1899–1900, Finnish Pavilion, World's Fair, Paris. 1900–1901, Pohjola Insurance Company, Helsinki. *1901–1902, Suur-Merijoki Manor House, Viipuri, Finland. 1902–1903, Architect's Studio and House (Hvitträsk), Kirkkonummi, Finland. 1902–1905, National Museum; *1903–1904, Northern Joint Stock Bank; Helsinki.

HERMAN GESELLIUS AND ELIEL SAARINEN

1905–1907, Molchow Haus, Mark Brandenburg, Germany.

HERMAN GESELLIUS

1908–1910, Wuorio Office Building; 1910, Apartment House, 11 Annankatu; Helsinki.

BIBLIOGRAPHY

CHRIST-JANER, ALBERT (1948)1980 *Eliel Saarinen.* With a Foreword by Alvar Aalto. 2d ed., rev. University of Chicago Press.
EATON, LEONARD K. 1972 *American Architecture Comes of Age.* Cambridge, Mass.: M.I.T. Press.
RICHARDS, J. M. 1978 *800 Years of Finnish Architecture.* Newton Abbot, England: David & Charles.
SALOKORPI, ASKO 1970 *Modern Architecture in Finland.* London: Weidenfeld & Nicolson.
SMITH, J. BOULTON 1975 *The Golden Age of Finnish Art.* Helsinki: Ministry of Foreign Affairs.
TUOMI, RITVA 1979 "Kansallisen tyylin etsimisestä; On the Search for a National Style." Pages 56–96 in *Abacus* (Yearbook of the Museum of Finnish Architecture). Helsinki: The museum.

GHAMBARELLI FAMILY

The Ghambarelli were a family of stone carvers, masons, sculptors, and architects from the region of Gamberaia near Settignano, Italy. The family produced two of the best known architect-sculptors of the Italian Renaissance, BERNARDO ROSSELLINO (1409–1464) and Antonio Rossellino (1425–1479).

Of the eldest of the Ghambarelli, Jacopo (1371–?) and his brother Matteo (1373–1453), little is known beyond their association with the Florentine stonemason's guild (Maestri di Pietra e Legname) in 1399. Matteo's sons formed a loose shop association in the mid-fifteenth century in Florence that dominated architectural and sculptural commissions in the city. The head of the shop was Bernardo Rossellino who is known mostly as an architect. His brothers Domenico (1401–1480), Giovanni (1412–?), Tomasso (1421–?), and Antonio (1425–1479) formed the nucleus of the shop. The group executed numerous buildings and architectural renovations in Florence using a subdued, well-ornamented reduction of Brunelleschian (see FILIPPO BRUNELLESCHI) style.

Apart from Bernardo, the most distinguished of the brothers was Antonio who was chiefly active on his own as a sculptor. He was noted particularly as the creator of large tombs that employed many architectural elements. The largest of the tombs built under his direction was the tomb for the Cardinal of Portugal and its chapel in the Church of San Miniato al Monte in Florence (1461–1466). The work unites sculpture, painting, and architecture in a vaulted airy space. The sculptured details are rich and precisely observed, and the architecture is strongly classical.

With the death of Bernardo and Antonio the shop lost its importance.

NICHOLAS ADAMS

WORKS

1436–1438, Aranci Cloister, Badia Fiorentina; 1448–1452, Spinelli Cloister, Santa Croce; 1459–1465, Palazzo Spinelli; 1461–1466, Tomb Chapel of the Cardinal of Portugal, San Miniato al Monte; Florence.

BIBLIOGRAPHY

CARLI, ENZO 1967 *Pienza: La città di Pio II*. Rome: Editalia.

FORSTER, KURT 1976 "The Palazzo Rucellai and Questions of Typology in the Development of Renaissance Buildings." *Art Bulletin* 58:109–113.

MACK, C. R. 1975 "The Palazzo Rucellai: Some New Proposals." *Art Bulletin* 56:517–529.

MAGNUSON, TORGIL 1958 *Studies in Roman Quattrocento Architecture*. Stockholm: Almqvist & Wiksell.

SAALMAN, HOWARD 1966 "Tommasso Spinelli, Michelozzo, Manetti and Rossellino." *Journal of the Society of Architectural Historians* 25:151–164.

SAALMAN, HOWARD 1980 *Filippo Brunelleschi: The Cupola of Santa Maria del Fiore*. London: Zwemmer.

GHERARDI, ANTONIO

Although our knowledge of Antonio Gherardi (1644–1702) is limited, he is nonetheless recognized as having had one of the more fertile minds of the late seventeenth century, a period dominated by the prodigious academic CARLO FONTANA.

Born in the town of Rieti, in Latium, Gherardi's early training was as a painter. He was an apprentice under Francesco Mola until Mola's death in 1666. By 1674, he had become a member of the Accademia di San Luca and had worked under Pietro da Cortona on the cartoons of the Story of Urban VIII, now in the Palazzo Barberini.

Of the time between Gherardi's work under Mola and Cortona we know very little. His later works indicate that he traveled north, to Venice and possibly to Turin. By 1675, he had begun to execute the chapel of San Francesco Solano in Santa Maria in Araceli, Rome. The chapel does not survive intact, but among its more interesting details is a pair of column capitals turned palm trees, with putti swinging from them, a motif perhaps inspired by the martyrdom of San Francesco in the New World.

Two of Gherardi's other Roman works, also chapels, show what Rudolf Wittkower (1958) and Paolo Portoghesi (1970) feel to be the influence of FRANCESCO BORROMINI, GIOVANNI LORENZO BERNINI, and GUARINO GUARINI. Commissioned by a family that for two generations held the posts of councillors of the city of Rome, the Avila Chapel in Santa Maria in Trastevere was remodeled by Gherardi around 1680 because it had fallen into disrepair. The constricted space of the chapel is visually expanded on every surface. The lateral tombs,

Gherardi.
Avila Chapel, Santa Maria in Trastevere.
Rome.
c.1686

in the shape of urns, are housed in pavilionlike structures. The tombs and pavilions are in fact only half the width they appear to be. Columns framing the altarpiece—a painting of San Gerolamo by Gherardi—diminish in height as they recede, making the altar seem to extend further into space, a motif used by Borromini in the garden passageway of the Palazzo Spada. Putti seem to float within the space encircled by a balustrade which frames the dome's opening. Light floods the dome through a light box; another light box is located above the altarpiece.

The Chapel of Santa Cecilia in San Carlo ai Catinari (1691–1702) was commissioned by La Congregazione dei Musici in honor of its patron, Saint Cecilia. Gherardi here uses painted stucco sculpture in a fashion both reminiscent of Bernini and quite distinct in its richness from the monochromatic Avila Chapel. But here too the complex dome and its light box are the focus of attention. Putti playing instruments are perched precariously atop the rim of the Guariniesque, truncated dome. We look through it into a dramatically lit space, culminating in a stucco relief image of the Holy Spirit.

Gherardi's diverse talents, expressed in numerous and little known works in Gubbio and Rieti, and his often lighthearted style, presaging the architecture of the eighteenth century, make him a figure worthy of further investigation.

M. Elizabeth Garza

WORKS

Begun 1675, Chapel of San Francesco Solano, Santa Maria in Araceli; c.1686, Avila Chapel, Santa Maria in Trastevere; 1691–1702, Santa Cecilia Chapel, San Carlo ai Catinari; Rome.

BIBLIOGRAPHY

Mezzetti, Amalia 1948 "La pittura di Antonio Gherardi." *Bollettino d'Arte* 33:157–179.

Pickrel, Thomas 1981 "Antonio Gherardi: Painter and Architect of the Late Baroque in Rome." Unpublished Ph.D. dissertation, University of Kansas, Lawrence.

Portoghesi, Paolo 1970 *Roma barocca.* Cambridge, Mass.: M.I.T. Press.

Wittkower, Rudolf (1958)1980 *Art and Architecture in Italy: 1600–1750.* Rev. ed. Harmondsworth, England: Penguin.

GHIBERTI, LORENZO

Few things of importance were made in our land that were not designed or devised by my hand. And especially in the building of the dome, Filippo and I, for eighteen years, were competitors at the same salary; thus we executed said dome. We shall write a treatise on architecture and treat this matter [Ghiberti, 1945, p. 47].

Thus ends the second autobiographical book of the *Commentaries* of Lorenzo Ghiberti (1378?–1455). This epitaph continues to puzzle the architectural historian. The city in question is Florence, the dome that of the Cathedral of Santa Maria del Fiore (1294?; redesigned 1357; new plans 1366), and the competitor none other than Filippo Brunelleschi, the most important Italian architect of the early Renaissance.

This cathedral provides the only solid example of Ghiberti's practical architectural activity, but the question of his specific contribution to the design and execution of the church is a thorny one. For a number of reasons, Ghiberti's architectural legacy remains, unfortunately, within the realm of architectural theory and design—known specifically through the architectural backgrounds of his reliefs and architectural settings for statuary. The precocious insight intimated in these examples, however tangential they may seem, are closely related theoretically to actual architectural work. They militate for a firm position for Ghiberti in the purview of Renaissance architecture, although through his multifaceted artistic career, he never actually attained the status of architect to which he had aspired and which he leads us to believe he had attained.

Ghiberti's actual paternity is still contested as it was in his day. Lorenzo was most probably born illegitimately to Mona Fiore, a farmer's daughter and her common-law husband Bartolo di Michele, called Bartoluccio. Bartoluccio later adopted Lorenzo after his marriage to Lorenzo's mother in 1406. They were wed only after the death of Mona's first legitimate husband, the man whose namesake Lorenzo guarded throughout his life, Cione Paltami di Ser Buonaccorso Ghiberti of Pelago, near Florence.

At Bartoluccio's knee, the young Lorenzo learned the goldsmith's trade—an orientation to material and technique that would mark his work for years to come. His style, rooted in the International Gothic—the prevailing style throughout western Europe between roughly 1400 and 1420—is witnessed in the first set of bronze doors Lorenzo cast for the Baptistery of Saint John the Baptist (1060?–1150) in Florence located across from the bell tower and cathedral with which it forms an ecclesiastical complex.

A careful look at the Sacrifice of Isaac panel (now in the Bargello Museum in Florence) presented in the competition sponsored by the wool guild of Florence in 1401 for the so-called North doors of the Baptistery, provides an example of how Lorenzo's early Gothicizing style is already mixed with a yearning for antique forms. The young goldsmith crafted a tensely muscled, nude youth of obvious antique inspiration, whose aging father Abraham, with arm suspended in mid-air brandishing a knife, pauses momentarily to ponder the piteous sight of his beloved son. At that pregnant moment, an angel, drapery awhirl, sweeps in obliquely from the upper right-hand corner of the panel and bids Abraham halt. The precious and mannered posture of Abraham counterpoises the powerfully naturalistic nude figure of Isaac.

Lorenzo was victorious in this commission over, among others, Brunelleschi, and Lorenzo worked on the doors from 1403 to April of 1424. The doors were influential and notorious monuments of this artistically driven city of Florence, being posited on a processional path from and facing the cathedral (and later moved to their present northern location). Later on in his architectural undertakings at the cathedral, Brunelleschi would be victorious over Ghiberti.

In 1412 or 1413, the same guild commissioned him to fashion a bronze statue of Saint John the Baptist to stand in the common guild sanctuary of the Church of Or San Michele (1285–late fourteenth century) in Florence. The year 1416 led him briefly out of Florence to Siena to build a baptismal font and to the altar to marry one Marsilia, daughter of the wool carder Bartolommeo. His successful and only marriage bore him two sons, Tomaso (born 1417) and Vittorio (born 1418).

The year 1419 provided ostensibly the first example of a quasi-architectural commission. Scantily documented, his services were procured for the design of a stairway for the papal apartment in the Convent of Santa Maria Novella then under preparation. His design was never implemented; that of a competitor was.

The second decade of the fifteenth century was a busy and notorious period for Lorenzo, heralding the fame and honor to follow. Beginning in January 1420, he headed work on the choir stall and other furnishings of the sacristy and Strozzi tomb chapel and its portal adjoining Santa Trinità. Some scholars have attributed the entire original design for the sacristy to Ghiberti on the basis of the similarity of motifs found in architectural reliefs and statuary niches such as the acanthus scroll. Scanty documentation again proves nothing in this matter except that at that time he was involved with the woodwork of the choir stalls and that he dealt with the bank of the Strozzi, a wealthy Florentine family.

Ghiberti's part in the supervision and preparation of the dome of the Florentine Cathedral comes into question at this juncture. Unfortunately, his precise donation to this capital monument defies final definition. Succinctly, events proceeded as follows. After an initial competition for the dome design in 1419, in which Ghiberti and Brunelleschi competed, both producing fundamentally diverging masonry models (Ghiberti's plan was to vault over centering, Brunelleschi's was without centering), Brunelleschi's model was accepted and Ghiberti's rejected.

They are found, however, in the documents, collaborating that same winter on a model for the dome. In the spring of 1420, the building of the dome began, to be completed only in 1436, and both were appointed supervisors of construction together with the master mason Battista d'Antonio. All drew the same salary, and hence it is surmised that they were of equivalent value to the project. Ghiberti maintained this exalted position until 1436 with two brief interruptions in 1425–1426 and in 1431.

His name is mentioned in the pertinent records only three times: in 1426, 1429, and 1432. In 1426, the *Opera* of the Cathedral retained Brunelleschi on a full-time basis and Ghiberti on only a part-time basis. During this time, he could draw pay only on the days he worked; Brunelleschi's salary was almost treble at that time. From 1426 on, it seems as if Brunelleschi's artistic personality and ideas assumed front stage. Ghiberti sank into the shadows of the great architect.

Judgments of Ghiberti's actual contribution to the architecture of the dome have ranged, throughout history, from his own proud claim cited above to ANTONIO MANETTI CUACCHERI's begrudging and parsimonious credits to Lorenzo in his *Life of Brunelleschi* to the label of sinecure by others. Sober and solid documentation suggests that Brunelleschi, as a more experienced, practical architect, bore the major responsibility for the dome's construction. It is unlikely, however, in light of Ghiberti's early and chronic mention in the records and of his singular artistic stature in Florence and association with other architects of his day, that Ghiberti was completely uninvolved. Further witness to his continuing interest and involvement in architectural projects is his submission again in the 1435 competition of a design for the choir of the cathedral allowing for an octagonal choir screen with an altar in the center under the dome of the crossing. The rejection of the design on the very practical basis that it did not provide sufficient space for singers and officiating clergy is proof enough that architectural viability was not in question but merely the mechanics of the circulation through the space designed.

His contribution thus remains inassessable. An

Ghiberti.
Bronze doors ("Gates of
Paradise"; detail of Story
of Jacob and Esau
panel), Baptistery of
Saint John the Baptist.
Florence.
1424–1452

Ghiberti.
Bronze doors ("Gates of
Paradise"; detail of Story
of Joseph panel),
Baptistery of Saint John
the Baptist.
Florence.
1424–1452

Ghiberti.
Bronze doors ("Gates of
Paradise"; detail of King
Solomon panel),
Baptistery of Saint John
the Baptist.
Florence.
1424–1452

analysis of his works must furnish the student of architecture with the only clues to Ghiberti's architectural vision.

Evidence of Lorenzo's architectural proclivity and acumen are found in the ideal architectural backgrounds of his second set of Baptistery doors christened (by MICHELANGELO, some surmise) the "Gates of Paradise." Commissioned on January 2, 1424, by the merchants' guild of Florence, the two bronze doors chased in gold with Old Testament panels were completed only in 1452. Ghiberti seems to have worked very slowly and carefully at everything he did, treating every medium with the painstaking and cautious hand of the goldsmith.

The character of Lorenzo's visionary architecture is immediately evident in the Jacob and Esau panel. Isaac and his son stand slightly off center to the left before a classically inspired Renaissance edifice, raised by steps and populated on its first and second stories by clusters of people actively engaged and unified through the continuous narrative technique of Italian Trecento origin. The building, an arcaded portico of sorts divided into three sections or bays by the round-headed arched openings, has an airy, spacious, and regular quality. The arches are all flanked by engaged pilasters with bases and sport exactly rendered Corinthian capitals. The capitals in turn support an entablature consisting of a cornice and plain frieze. The roof type is difficult to discern, and the building has a cardboard-thin quality.

In the Story of Joseph panel of the doors, Ghiberti had set himself the task of designing a centrally planned building, the architectural dream of Renaissance architects and theoreticians. Once again, the union of the arcuated and trabeated systems with, in addition, a second-story band of gabled aediculae flanked by Corinthian pilasters furnished the unifying structural language. Whereas the roofing type is once again indeterminate, the ambulatory around the central cylindrical core suggests precedents like the Temple of Vesta at Tivoli (early first century B.C.) and the domed Santa Costanza in Rome of early Christian (fifth century) origin. The building is raised on a podium and accessible from a stairway, hence, clearly oriented—both characteristically Roman or Etruscan features in temple architecture.

In the Solomon panel of the doors, Ghiberti created not isolated classicizing buildings but a unified piazza or group of buildings, all complementing one another within the cityscape. The Gothic, rib-vaulted church with an anomalous classical second story, the stage of the union of the two protagonists, is an architectural anachronism in this square—perhaps to represent the removal of the event in time and space. Thinking away this building, we are left with a screen wall in the foreground, a kind of scaled-down version of the screen wall of the Roman Sanctuary of Fortuna Primigenia at Praeneste (Palestrina) probably of the early first century B.C. Together with a stairway, it sets the building off from the street where crowds gather. Flanking this are trabeated and arcuated buildings on either side whose elements are the same as in the past two panels discussed. The whole complex suggests a theatrical backdrop due to the lack of a certain stability and monumentality of form, probably accreditable to the fact that Ghiberti was working in bronze and not in stone.

On the whole, Ghiberti's architectural fantasies are made up of consistent and homogeneous elements chosen carefully from the repertory of antique forms: pilasters, Corinthian capitals, gabled aediculae, trabeated and arcuated porticoes, and facades, all of an obvious Roman flavor. The syntax of this classical vocabulary is archeologically quite correct, with each element being carefully articulated *all'antica*.

Beneath the seemingly rigid and limited matrix of classical forms, we can discern a distinctly personal taste. Ghiberti's choices from this classical storehouse are narrow and refined, and his rendering of the forms is a rational, pure, and severe one. Ghiberti's pilasters and entablatures, for example, are slender and elongated; they lack fluting or other decoration and display a draftsmanlike precision and definition. They are, in fact, too perfect.

It has been noted that at this time in Italy no other architect employed the pristine and clear forms that Ghiberti has bequeathed. In fact, Ghiberti's architectural concoctions are so singularly precocious that one is left wondering how different the path of Renaissance architecture would have been had Ghiberti's dream to practice architecture been fulfilled.

It must be kept in mind, however, that although not a practicing architect on a grand scale, Ghiberti had to have been influential over architectural ideas of the day. The design of an ideal architecture is not so foreign to actual architectural planning. Also, the movement back and forth between media such as painting, sculpture, and architecture was characteristic of Renaissance and later periods: witness LEONE BATTISTA ALBERTI, RAPHAEL, and Michelangelo, painters who designed architecture, and DONATO BRAMANTE the architect who began painting, to name a few.

Lorenzo was born and buried a Florentine. After the second set of doors, he retired to his manor house at San Giuliano a Settimo to pursue serious writing. He had arrived financially at the position in life to which he had aspired and died very rich and famous. Before his death, he held a prominent place in the Florentine humanist coteries of his day, socializing with such literati as Ambrogio Traversani, Niccolo Niccoli, and Leonardo Bruni.

It is thought that Ghiberti trained Antonio Pollaiuolo and ANTONIO AVERLINO FILARETE. Paolo Uccello, Donatello, and MICHELOZZO DI BARTOLOMEO were active in his workshop. His influence can also be seen in the work of Lorenzo Monaco, Raphael, and LUCA DELLA ROBBIA.

In book two of his *Commentaries,* Ghiberti offers to posterity a new form of history of art written from a stylistic rather than an anecdotal point of view. The first artist to furnish an autobiography, Ghiberti aligns himself with both his past Italian Trecento heritage of forms and ideas and the contemporary scientific and academic approach to the arts. Ghiberti thereby secured a firm place for himself in even another realm, the historiography of art.

TINA WALDEIER BIZZARRO

WORKS

1403–1424, Saint John the Baptist (bronze doors of the baptistery; now in Bargello Museum); 1420–1426, Santa Maria del Fiore (dome; with Filippo Brunelleschi); 1424–1452, Bronze doors ("Gates of Paradise"), Baptistery of Saint John the Baptist; Florence.

BIBLIOGRAPHY

ACKERMAN, JAMES S. 1974 *A Bibliography of Italian Renaissance and Baroque Architecture.* Cambridge, Mass.: Harvard University Press.

ANDERSON, WILLIAM J. 1927 *The Architecture of the Renaissance in Italy.* London: Batsford.

BOTTARI, GIOVANNI G., and TICOZZI, STEFANO 1822–1825 *Raccolta di lettere sulla pittura, scultura et architettura scritte da piu celebri personaggi dei secoli XV, XVI e XVII.* Milan: Silvestri.

CLARK, KENNETH M. 1946–1947 "Architectural Backgrounds in Fifteenth Century Italian Painting." *The Arts* 1:131ff; 2:35ff.

GENGARO, M. L. 1938 "Precisazioni su Ghiberti architetto." *L'Arte* 41:280ff.

GHIBERTI, LORENZO 1947 *I Commentarii: A Cura di Ottavio Morisani.* 2 vols. Naples: Ricciardi.

GOLDSCHEIDER, LUDWIG 1949 *Ghiberti.* London: Phaidon.

HEYDENREICH, LUDWIG H., and LOTZ, WOLFGANG 1974 *Architecture in Italy: 1400 to 1600.* Harmondsworth, England: Penguin.

KRAUTHEIMER, RICHARD 1955 "Ghiberti-Architetto." *Bulletin of the Allen Memorial Art Museum* 12:484.

KRAUTHEIMER, RICHARD 1962 "Lorenzo Ghiberti." Volume 6, pages 312–332 in *Encyclopedia of World Art.* New York: McGraw-Hill.

KRAUTHEIMER, RICHARD, and KRAUTHEIMER-HESS, TRUDE 1956 *Lorenzo Ghiberti.* N.J.: Princeton University Press.

MANETTI, ANTONIO 1927 *Vita di Filippo di Ser Brunellesco.* Florence: Rinascimento del Libro.

MARQUAND, A. 1894 "A Terracotta Sketch by Lorenzo Ghiberti." *American Journal of Archeology* 9:207ff.

PICA, A. 1943 "La cupola di S. Maria del Fiore e la collaborazione Brunellesco-Ghiberti." *Emporium* 97:70ff.

POGGI, GIOVANNI 1909 *Il Duomo di Firenze: Documenti sulla decorazione della chiesa e del campanile tratti dall'archivio dell'Opera.* Berlin: Cassirer.

Santa Maria del Fiore: La costruzione della chiesa e del campanile secondo i documenti tratti dall'archivio dell'Opera secolare e da quello di stato per cura di Cesare Guasti. 1887 Florence: Ricci.

SCHLOSSER, JULIUS VON 1941 *Leben und Meinungen des Florentinischen Bildners Lorenzo Ghiberti.* Basel: Holbein.

VASARI, GIORGIO (1568)1973 *Le opere di Giorgio Vasari, con nuove annotazioni e commenti.* 9 vols. Edited by G. Milanesi. Reprint. Florence: Sansoni. Originally published in 1550 with the title *Le vite de più eccelenti architetti.* There are many English translations and selections from Vasari's *Lives;* the standard one by G. du C. de Vere was published in ten volumes in London by the Medici Society in 1912–1915.

GHICA-BUDESTI, NICOLAE

Nicolae Ghica-Budesti (1869–1943) graduated from the School of Engineering, Bridges, and Highways in Bucharest in 1893. In 1901, he finished his studies at the Ecole des Beaux-Arts in Paris, where he was the favorite student of Victor A. F. Laloux. He was a professor at the School of Architecture in Bucharest from 1908 to 1938.

Although Ghica-Budesti received his professional schooling in the nineteenth century, his architectural views belonged to the twentieth century. He was one of the outstanding and most active promoters of a national school of architecture, and his works are rendered in a neo-Rumanian style. He was the coordinator of the Commission of Historical Monuments in Rumania from 1921 to 1943 and wrote a historical study of religious architecture in Rumania.

CONSTANTIN MARIN MARINESCU

WORKS

1912, Museum of History (now Museum of the History of the Communist Party), Bucharest. 1912, Museum of Archeology, Tîrgoviste, Rumania. 1912, Lyceum, Rîmnicu-Vîlcea, Rumania. 1925, Greek Catholic Church, Polonă Street, Bucharest.

BIBLIOGRAPHY

CANTACUZÈNE, GEORGE 1927 "L'architecture roumaine d'aujourd' hui." *L'Architecture* 40, 10:351–357.

IONESCU, GRIGORE 1965 Volume 2 in *Istoria Arhitecturii in Romania.* Bucharest: Editura Academiei Republicii Romañe.

IONESCU, GRIGORE 1969a *Arhitectura in Romania: Perioda anilor 1944–1969.* Bucharest: Editura Academiei Republicii Socialiste Româñia.

IONESCU, GRIGORE 1969b "Nicolae Ghica-Budesti: 100 ans depuis sa naissance." *Revue Roumaine d'Histoire de l' Art* 6:31–33.

IONESCU, GRIGORE 1972 "Saptezeci si cinci de ani de la infiintarea invatamintului de arhitectura din Romania." *Arhitectura* 20:35–42.

MAMBRIANI, ALBERTO 1969 *L'Architettura Moderna nei Paesi Balcanici.* Bologna, Italy: Capelli.

PATRULIUS, RADU 1973–1974 "Contributii Romanesti in Arhitectura Anilor '30." *Arhitectura,* 21, no. 6:44–52; 22, no. 1:53–59.

SASARMAN, GHEORGHE 1972 "Incepturile gindirii teoretice in arhitectura româneasča (1860–1916)." *Arhitectura* 20, no. 6:44–46.

GHIYAS, MIRAK MIRZA

Apparently Persian by birth, the architect Mirak Mirza Ghiyas (?–1565?) is credited with the construction of one of the most important Islamic monuments in India, the vast garden tomb of the Mogul emperor Humayun at Delhi (probably 1556–1565). Built of red and beige sandstone, this imposing mausoleum combined lucid Persian design with traditional Indian materials and signaled the advent of the new and grandiose Mogul architectural style that came to full flowering, some seventy years later, with the creation of the Taj Mahal (see USTAD AHMAD LAHAWRI).

Until recently, almost nothing was known about Mirak Ghiyas beyond his name, but some new evidence now allows a tentative reconstruction of the architect's career. First of all, it seems plausible to identify him with a master stonecutter called Mirak Mir Ghiyas, mentioned in the memoirs of the first Mogul emperor Babur. In 1529, Babur charged this Mirak Ghiyas with the completion of some royal building projects at Agra and Dholpur. Following Babur's death in 1530, the architect apparently returned to his homeland and took up residence in Herat. From passing references in the recent edition of Khwaja Hasan Nithari's *Mudhakkir-i-Ahbab,* a collection of biographical notices compiled in 1566, we learn that Mirak Ghiyas (here called Mirak Sayyid Ghiyas) owned extensive property in Herat, where he enjoyed widespread fame as an outstanding architect and builder. Nithari also records that Mirak Ghiyas later shifted from Herat and settled in Bukhara where he constructed various architectural projects for the local ruler ꜣUbaid Allah Khan, including a large garden to the west of the city, possibly the large seminary known as Madrasa-i-Mir ꜣArab (1535–1536), and possibly also the bridge called Pul-i-Mihtar Qasim over the river Kohtak.

From around 1540 to 1556, the activities of Mirak Ghiyas cannot be traced, though we may assume that he continued to reside in Bukhara until his eventual return to India to undertake construction of Humayun's tomb. After a period of exile in Afghanistan, Humayun had begun his reconquest of northern India in 1554, and it is possible that the distinguished architect was one of those who accompanied him. Otherwise, he may have been summoned from Bukhara in 1556, when the emperor Humayun died suddenly at Delhi. Mirak Ghiyas's connection with the project is documented by the contemporary Mogul author ꜣAbd al-Qadir Badaoni, who also states that the tomb was completed in 1570 after eight or nine years of construction. However, an earlier completion date in 1565 seems more likely, since in that year, Humayun's devoted senior wife, Haji Begam, went on pilgrimage to Mecca, and it is doubtful that she would have absented herself while construction of the tomb was still in progress. Following her return to India in 1568, the faithful Haji Begam resided at the tomb complex until her own death in 1582 (according to later tradition, it was Haji Begam who provided funds for the enormous cost of the tomb).

Moreover, from the evidence of the *Mudhakkir-i-Ahbab,* we know that by 1566 Mirak Ghiyas was already dead and buried back in Bukhara. Hence, he must have left India at least several months before. This same literary source also informs us that Mirak Ghiyas had a son named Sayyid Muhammad Mirak, and it was he who had been entrusted with the task of supervising the final stages of the tomb's construction. Since Badaoni does not mention the son, we may conclude that his involvement was minor and that Mirak Ghiyas fully deserves his fame as the architect of the first great Mogul structure.

W. E. BEGLEY

WORKS

*1529–1530, Buildings commissioned by Babur, Agra and Dholpur, India. *c.1535, Garden, near Bukhara, Russia. *(A)1535–1536, Mir ꜣArab Seminary; (A)1535–1536, Mihtar Qasim Bridge over River Kohtak; Bukhara, Russia. 1556–1565, Tomb of Humayun, Delhi, India.

BIBLIOGRAPHY

BABUR 1970 *Babur-Nama (Memoirs of Babur).* Translated by A. S. Beveridge. Reprint. New Delhi: Oriental.

Ghiyas.
Tomb of Humayun.
Delhi, India.
1556–1565

BADAONI, ꜣABD AL-QADIR (1864–1869)1973 *Muntakhabu't-Tawarikh.* Translated by G. S. A. Ranking, W. H. Lowe, and T. W. Haig. 3 vols. Reprint. New Delhi.
NAQVI, S. A. A. 1947 *Humāyūn's Tomb.* New Delhi: Archeological Survey of India.
NITHARI, KHWAJA BAHAꜣ AL-DIN HASAN 1969 *Mudhakkir-i-Ahbab.* Edited by Syed Muhammad Fazlullah. Hyderabed, India: Daꜣiratuꜣl-MaꜣArif.
STEPHEN, CARR (1876)1967 *Archaeology and Monumental Remains of Delhi.* Reprint. Allahabad, India: Kitab Mahal.

GIBBERD, FREDERICK

One of Britain's most prolific architects, Frederick Gibberd (1908–) has made a sizable and varied contribution to the development of postwar architecture, town planning, and landscape design. Born in Coventry, of a middle class Warwickshire family, and educated at King Henry VIII School, Birmingham, Gibberd began his architectural career as an articled pupil in the Birmingham offices of Crouch, Butterfield, and Savage. A year later, in 1925, he enrolled at the Birmingham School of Architecture. An early friend and roommate at Birmingham was F. R. S. Yorke, with whom Gibberd toured Europe and who influenced his career as a prominent practitioner of the Modern movement in Britain. Greatly influenced by LE CORBUSIER and LUDWIG MIES VAN DER ROHE, Gibberd admired the work of WELLS W. COATES and BERTHOLD LUBETKIN in England.

Moving to London and establishing his private practice in 1930, Gibberd completed his first major project, Pullman Court, Streatham, in 1936. This housing project, consisting of 218 small flats of a strongly modernist design, reflects both Gibberd's interest in low-cost, functional housing and his concern for the creation of a more humane environment. Arousing international interest, Gibberd's work was exhibited by the Museum of Modern Art, New York, in 1937.

During the war years, unable to enlist due to illness, Gibberd taught at the Architectural Association School in London, where he was principal from 1942 to 1944. Among his students were Philip Powell and John Hidalgo Moya (see POWELL AND MOYA). Gibberd also became involved in the design and manufacture of prefabricated houses, working with the British Iron and Steel Federation.

The years of postwar reconstruction saw Gibberd's increasing involvement in town planning and public housing, most notably his appointment as chief architect for Harlow New Town, a position he held until 1972. Gibberd's town plans and numerous provincial civic centers are characterized by his concept of town design, where the town as a whole is viewed as "a landscape structure, not a town plan with landscape superimposed" (Aldous, 1978).

Major projects of the 1950s and 1960s include Gibberd's extensive work at Heathrow Airport (1950–1969), his famous Liverpool Roman Catholic Cathedral (1960–1967), Didcot Power Station (1964–1968), and Ulster Hospital, Belfast (1953–1961). All are stylistically consistent with the Modernist preoccupation with the principles of function and construction of his formative years. In 1965, Gibberd established the practice Frederick Gibberd and Partners with R. J. Double, J. W. Grimes, Jack Forrest, and George Dutton. More recently, Gibberd completed the widely acclaimed London Central Mosque (1977) and one of his personal favorites, the Inter-Continental Hotel, London (1975).

Gibberd was knighted in 1967.

NICHOLAS BOYARSKY

WORKS

1933–1936, Pullman Court, Streatham, London. 1937–1939, Macclesfield Nurses Home, Cheshire, England. 1945–1949, Somerfield Estate, Hackney, London. 1946–1963, Nuneation Town Centre, Warwickshire, England. 1949–1951, Lansbury Market, London. 1950–1969, Terminal Buildings, Heathrow Airport, near London. 1952, Market Square, Harlow, Essex, England. 1953–1961, Ulster Hospital, Belfast. 1956, Bath Technical College, Somerset, England. 1956–1968, Civic Center, Saint Albans, Hertfordshire, England. 1958, Derwent Reservoir, Durham and Northumberland, England. 1959–1969, Civic Centre, Donaster, Yorkshire, England. 1960–1967, Roman Catholic Cathedral, Liverpool, England. 1962–1966, Douai Abbey, Berkshire, England. 1964, Saint George's Chapel, Heathrow Airport, near London. 1964–1968, Didcot Power Station, Berkshire, England. 1966–1975, Arundel Great Court, The Strand; 1968–1975, Inter-Continental Hotel, Hyde Park Corner; London. 1970–1977, London Central Mosque.

BIBLIOGRAPHY

ALDOUS, TONY 1978 "The Gibberd Touch." *Architect's Journal* 167, no. 2:56.
GIBBERD, FREDERICK (1947)1952 *Harlow New Town.* 2d ed. Essex, England: Harlow Development Corporation.
GIBBERD, FREDERICK 1952 "Expression in Modern Architecture." *Journal of the Royal Institute of British Architects* 59, Jan.:79–87.
GIBBERD, FREDERICK (1953)1970 *Town Design.* 6th ed. London: Architectural Press.
GIBBERD, FREDERICK 1968 *Metropolitan Cathedral of Christ the King.* London: Architectural Press.
GIBBERD, FREDERICK 1980 *Harlow: The Story of a New Town.* Stevenage, England: Publications for Companies.
GIBBERD, FREDERICK, and YORKE, F. R. S. (1937)1961 *Modern Flats.* 2d ed. London: Architectural Press.
SHARP, DENNIS 1978 "Faith in Design." *Building* 235, no. 7040:64–69.

GIBBS, JAMES

James Gibbs (1682–1754) was one of the most successful architects working during the early eighteenth century and the first British architect to have received professional training abroad. Born in Fittysmire near Aberdeen in Scotland, the son of a prosperous Roman Catholic merchant, he was educated at Marischal College, and sometime around 1700 he traveled through Holland, Belgium, France, Germany, and Austria to Italy. Arriving in Rome in 1703, he began training for the priesthood at the Scots College but he left in the following year to become a pupil of CARLO FONTANA, then the leading Roman architect. Gibbs describes the architecture and sculpture of the Renaissance and baroque periods as well as of classical antiquity that he studied at this time in the manuscript *"A Few Short Cursory Remarks."*

Returning to Britain in 1708, he set up practice in London, and among his first patrons was the politician and amateur architect, John Erskine, eleventh earl of Mar, who commissioned a lodge (c.1710) at Alloa in Clackmannanshire, Scotland, which combined seventeenth-century Roman and Parisian features but may not have been built. The internationalism of Gibbs's early work is also reflected in his affiliation as a founder-member in 1711 of Kneller's Art Academy and later his membership in other cosmopolitan London art clubs.

In 1713, after considerable competition, Gibbs was appointed NICHOLAS HAWKSMOOR's cosurveyor to the Commission for Building Fifty New

Churches in London, for which he made several designs, including a large Ionic peripteral temple-like church (1713), probably the first in British architecture, which reached only the model stage, although he succeeded in building Saint Mary-le-Strand (1714–1723) in London. This and other early works—the Newcastle monument (c.1714–1723) in Westminster Abbey, James Johnston's octagonal pavilion (c.1720) at Twickenham, and partly or wholly unexecuted schemes for Wimpole Hall (c.1719–1730) in Cambridgeshire, the seat of his most distinguished patron, Edward Harley, second earl of Oxford, for Lowther Hall (c.1716–1728) in Westmorland, and for Cannons House (1716–1719) in Middlesex—show Gibbs's dependence on a wide variety of Roman baroque and rococo as well as current French ideas and may be compared to contemporary work by WILLIAM TALMAN, JOHN VANBRUGH, and Hawksmoor. Much of this work was for deposed Tories and Jacobites, men of conservative artistic taste but with a willingness to provide Gibbs with substantial commissions during the uncertain years from 1716, following his dismissal, on political grounds, as the new churches surveyor. A few formative works—the additions to Burlington House (c.1715) in London, for young Richard Boyle, third earl of Burlington, Witham Park (1717) in Somerset, unexecuted but published in *Vitruvius Britannicus* (1717) (a design that anticipated ROBERT ADAM's remodeling of Osterley Park, Middlesex, 1763), Sudbrook Park (c.1717–1728) in Surrey, and Down Hall (1720–1721) in Essex, abandoned because of the death of the client, the poet Matthew Prior—are examples of Gibbs's pioneer use of motifs from both ANDREA PALLADIO and classical antiquity, paralleling similar endeavors by COLEN CAMPBELL and LORD BURLINGTON.

In 1720, Gibbs was appointed architect for rebuilding Saint Martin-in-the-Fields (1720–1726) in London, where he presented an unusually ambitious and extrovert solution to the daunting problem of designing a church in the form of a classical pseudoperipteral temple while retaining the lofty steeple traditional to this building type. The result is one of the most original and influential achievements of English Protestant church architecture. The publication of the Saint Martin designs in Gibbs's *A Book of Architecture* (1728) assured its imitation throughout the English-speaking world, particularly in America. Some elements were reused by Gibbs in the Oxford Chapel (1721–1724) in London and at All Saints Cathedral in Derby (1723–1725), and the idea of a modern building clothed as a classical temple was also the basis of his scheme for the Cambridge Public Building, although because of disagreement with the University authorities concerning the site, only one-third, the Senate House (1722–1730), was realized.

The Fellows' Building (1724–1749) at King's College, Cambridge, Saint Bartholomew's Hospital (1728–1754) in London, and the majority of the designs for country houses, garden buildings, and decorative accessories published in *A Book of Architecture,* some of which were realized, are further evidence of this new approach to classicism, as are a handful of his church monuments, particularly to Matthew Prior (1721–1723) and James Craggs (1724–1727) in Westminster Abbey. Gibbs was the first British artist to regard designing tombs as the legitimate pursuit of the architect rather than exclusively that of the sculptor or mason, an idea inherited from Fontana, who had been a pupil of GIOVANNI LORENZO BERNINI.

A further dimension was added to Gibbs's now almost unrivaled country house practice when in 1726 he replaced Vanbrugh as architect at Stowe in Buckinghamshire, and during the next two decades, working with CHARLES BRIDGEMAN and then CAPABILITY BROWN, he designed various garden buildings for Viscount Cobham. One of the most remarkable is the pair of Boycott Pavilions (1726–1728), which were originally crowned by enormous hexagonal obelisks with concave bases, a motif derived from JOHANN BERNHARD FISCHER VON ERLACH's reconstruction of the Mausoleum of Artemisia at Halicarnassus (*Entwurf einer historischen Architektur,* 1721), which Gibbs again used on the Turner Mausoleum (1739–1741) at Kirkleatham, Yorkshire. Another is the Temple of Liberty (1741–1744) in a striking and grammatically convincing Gothic style, an interest which had been stimulated from the time Gibbs was elected a member of the Society of Antiquaries in London in 1726. He and Bridgeman collaborated on other occasions, at Tring Park (c.1724–1739) and Gubbins (c.1725) in Hertfordshire, both important early examples of the new landscape garden, but these were swept away in later "improvements."

Gibbs's national reputation lay partly in the attraction of his buildings. Writing in *Itinerarium Septentrionale* (1726) of the newly revived classicism, Alexander Gordon thought "if this fine Humour for Architecture subsist in the Nation, and such Buildings as the great Artist Mr. Gibbs has adorn'd London with, continues to be carried on, very few Cities in Europe (Rome excepted) will contend with it for Magnificence." His reputation also rested on some 380 different designs published in *A Book of Architecture* as sources for imitation. As he stated in the introduction, the book was intended for "such Gentlemen as might

Gibbs.
Saint Martin-in-the-Fields
(rebuilding).
London.
1720–1726

Gibbs.
Radcliffe Library.
Oxford.
1737–1754

be concerned in Building, especially in the remote parts of the Country" by providing "useful and convenient Buildings and proper Ornaments; which may be executed by any Workman who understands Lines." This was followed in 1732 by *Rules for Drawing the Several Parts of Architecture,* which immediately became the classic manual for builders. ROBERT MORRIS wrote in *The Art of Architecture* (1742, pp. 25–26):

> Learn of Palladio, how to deck a Space;
> Of [INIGO] JONES you'll learn Magnificence, and Grace:
> Campbell will teach, the Beauty they impart;
> And Gibbs, the Rules and Modus of the Art.

Meanwhile during the 1730s, Gibbs was intimately involved in a series of scandals in the London building world concerning corrupt practices by city officials and their architect "stooges," which contributed to his losing the most prestigious civic commission of the age, the new Mansion House (1728–1737), to a less talented rival, GEORGE DANCE THE ELDER.

Even so, in 1737 Gibbs succeeded Hawksmoor as architect of Dr. John Radcliffe's Library (1737–1754) at Oxford. In the building accounts and in a series of preparatory drawings the design can be charted as it evolved out of Hawksmoor's germinal idea toward an independent masterpiece: an enormous, free-standing, domed rotunda circumscribed by twenty-four giant engaged columns on a rusticated basement, like a classical pseudoperipteral temple, with a luxuriously fitted interior accommodating a vestibule surmounted by a circular, domed reading room, which Gibbs

described and illustrated in *Bibliotheca Radcliviana* (1747). At the opening of the library in 1749, he received an honorary M.A. degree from the University, followed immediately by a brief visit to Aix-la-Chapelle. Although he was afterward concerned with several important domestic commissions, notably Bank Hall (c.1750) at Warrington, Lancashire, a bold, undecorated Palladian essay, and some interiors at Ragley Hall (c.1750–1755) in Warwickshire, which confirms his ability to handle rococo ornament on a large scale, old age and continuing ill health brought Gibbs's career to an end. He died in London a wealthy man, leaving his Marylebone house and art collection to the Scottish painter Cosmo Alexander, while to the Radcliffe he bequeathed an impressive library, including many architectural books (some now in the Bodleian Library, Oxford) and hundreds of preparatory drawings (now in the Gibbs Collection, Ashmolean Museum, Oxford), some of which are undoubtedly by his draftsman, John Borlach, who subsequently became an architect. Other major collections of Gibbs drawings are in the Royal Institute of British Architects Drawings Collection and the Victoria and Albert Museum, London.

TERRY F. FRIEDMAN

WORKS

c.1710, Mar Lodge, Alloa, Clackmannanshire, Scotland. c.1714–1723, Newcastle Monument, Westminster Abbey; 1714–1723, Saint Mary-le-Strand; *c.1715, Burlington House (additions); London. *1716–1719, Cannons House, Middlesex, England. c.1716–1728, Lowther Hall, Westmorland, England. c.1717–1728, Sudbrook Park, Surrey, England. 1719–1720, Saint Clement Danes (steeple), London. c.1719–1730, Wimpole Hall, Cambridgeshire, England. c.1720, James Johnston's Octagonal Pavilion (Orleans House); c.1720, Alexander Pope's Villa; Twickenham, Middlesex, England. 1720–1721, Down Hall, Essex, England. 1720–1726, Saint Martin-in-the-Fields (rebuilding); 1721–1723, Matthew Prior Monument, Westminster Abbey; 1721–1724, Oxford Chapel (Saint Peter, Vere Street); London. 1722–1730, Senate House, Cambridge. 1723–1725, All Saints (cathedral), Derby, England. 1724–1727, James Craggs Monument, Westminster Abbey, London. c.1724–1739, Tring Park, Hertfordshire, England. 1724–1749, King's College Fellows Building, Cambridge. *c.1725, Gubbins, Hertfordshire, England. *c.1725–1726, Whitton Park, Middlesex, England. c.1726–1728, Gibbs Building and Boycott Pavilions, Stowe, Buckinghamshire, England. c.1728, Hackwood Park, Hampshire, England. c.1728–1732, Kelmarsh Hall, Northamptonshire, England. 1728–1737, The Mansion House; 1728–1754, Saint Bartholomew's Hospital; London. 1734–1735, Duchess of Norfolk's House, London. 1737–1754, Radcliffe Library, Oxford. 1739, Temple of Friendship, Stowe, Buckinghamshire, England. 1739–1741, Turner Mausoleum, Kirkleatham, Yorkshire, England. c.1740, Hartwell House; 1741–1744, Temple of Liberty, Stowe; Buckinghamshire, England. 1741–1755, Saint Nicholas Church West, Aberdeen, Scotland. 1743–1754, Patshull Hall and Church, Staffordshire, England. *c.1744–1748, Ladies' Temple; 1747–1748, Cobham Monument; Stowe, Buckinghamshire, England. c.1750, Bank Hall (Town Hall), Warrington, Lancashire, England. c.1750–1755, Ragley Hall, Warwickshire, England.

BIBLIOGRAPHY

James Gibbs's manuscript "A Few Short Cursory Remarks . . ." is in the collection of Sir John Soane's Museum, London.

BILL, E. G. W. (compiler) 1979 *The Queen Anne Churches: A Catalogue of the Papers in Lambeth Palace Library of the Commission for Building Fifty New Churches in London and Westminster 1711–1759.* Introduction by H. M. Colvin. London: Mansell.

CAMPBELL, COLEN (1715)1968 *Vitruvius Britannicus.* Reprint of 1728 ed. New York: Blom.

COLVIN, HOWARD; CROOK, J. MORDAUNT; and FRIEDMAN, TERRY 1980 *Architectural Drawings from Lowther Castle, Westmorland.* London: Society of Architectural Historians of Great Britain.

COX, J. C., and HOPE, WILLIAM H. ST. JOHN 1881 *The Chronicles of the Collegiate Church or Free Church of All Saints, Derby.* London: Bemrose.

FRIEDMAN, TERRY 1980*a* "Scheemakers's Monument to the Best of Sons." *Burlington Magazine* Jan.:61–65.

FRIEDMAN, TERRY 1980*b* "The Rebuilding of Bishopsgate: A Case of Architecture and Corruption in Eighteenth Century London." *Guildhall Studies in London History.* Apr.:75–90.

GIBBS, JAMES (1728)1968 *A Book of Architecture.* Reprint. New York: Blom.

GIBBS, JAMES (1732)1924 *Rules for Drawing the Several Parts of Architecture.* London: Hodder and Stoughton.

GIBBS, JAMES 1747 *Bibliotheca Radcliviana.* London: The author.

GILLIAM, S. G. 1958 *The Building Accounts of the Radcliffe Camera.* Oxford: Clarendon Press for the Oxford Historical Society.

GORDON, ALEXANDER 1726 *Itinerarium Septentrionale.* London: The author.

KERSLAKE, JOHN 1977 Volume 1, pages 96–98, volume 2, plates 262–268 in *Early Georgian Portraits.* London: Her Majesty's Stationery Office.

LITTLE, BRYAN 1955 *The Life and Works of James Gibbs, 1682–1754.* London: Batsford.

MORRIS, ROBERT 1742 *The Art of Architecture.* London: Dodsley.

PERKS, SYDNEY 1922 *The History of The Mansion House.* Cambridge University Press.

SUMMERSON, JOHN N. (1946)1977 *Architecture in Britain 1530 to 1830.* Harmondsworth, England: Penguin.

WHIFFEN, MARCUS 1946 "The Progeny of St. Martin in the Fields." *Architectural Review* 100:3–6.

WHINNEY, MARGARET 1964 *Sculpture in Britain 1530 to 1830.* Harmondsworth, England: Penguin.

WILLIS, PETER 1977 *Charles Bridgeman and the English Landscape Garden.* London: Zwemmer.

WILLIS, ROBERT, and CLARK, JOHN WILLIS 1886 Volume 1, pages 560–563, volume 3, chapter 3, in *The Architectural History of the University of Cambridge, and of the Colleges of Cambridge and Eton.* Cambridge University Press.

GIBSON, JOHN

John Gibson (1817–1892) was the most prolific of all Victorian bank architects, his fame being linked largely to one patron, the National Provincial Bank of England: He was employed in Sir CHARLES BARRY's office from 1835 to 1844. He applied, with taste and authority, Barry's Renaissance palazzo formula to commercial buildings from 1844 well into the 1880s.

MARGARET RICHARDSON

WORKS

1845–1848, Central Baptist Chapel, Bloomsbury Street, London. 1847–1867, Charlecote Park (remodeling), Warwickshire, England. 1848, Imperial Insurance Office, Threadneedle Street, London. 1855, Compton Verney (restoration), Warwickshire, England. 1860, Bodelwyddan Church, near Saint Asaph, Wales. 1860–1875, Town Hall, Todmorden, Yorkshire, England. 1864–1865, National Westminster Bank, 15 Bishopsgate; 1865, National Provincial Bank of England, Threadneedle Street; London. 1866, Church of Saint Mary and Saint Margaret, Combrook, Warwickshire, England. 1869, National Provincial Bank, Waterloo Street, Birmingham, England. 1869–1875 Dobroyd Castle, Todmorden, Yorkshire, England. 1872, National Provincial Bank of England, Newcastle-upon-Tyne. 1873, National Provincial Bank, Piccadilly, London. 1874, National Provincial Bank, Middlesborough, Yorkshire, England. 1876–1879, Society for Promoting Christian Knowledge (now Nigeria House), Northumberland Avenue; 1879, Child's Bank, 1 Fleet Street; London. 1879–1880, Church of Saint James, Milverton, Warwickshire, England.

BIBLIOGRAPHY

GIROUARD, MARK (1971)1979 *The Victorian Country House.* Rev. ed. New Haven: Yale University Press.

HITCHCOCK, H. R. (1954)1972 *Early Victorian Architecture in Britain.* Reprint. New York: Da Capo.

"Obituary." 1892 *The Builder* 63:524–525.

"Presentation of the Royal Gold Medal." 1890 *The Builder* 58:448–449.

GIBSON, ROBERT WILLIAMS

Robert Williams Gibson (1854–1927) was a versatile and talented architect born in Essex, England.

Following training at the Royal Academy in London and a Continental tour, Gibson won the competition to build the Episcopal Cathedral of Albany, New York. Gibson remained in Albany until 1888 when he moved downriver to New York City, where he lived for the rest of his life.

MOSETTE GLASER BRODERICK

WORKS

1881–1904, All Saints Cathedral; 1884, Albany Rural Cemetery Chapel; 1885, Craig House; 1887, National Commercial Bank; Albany, N.Y. 1888–1889, Christ Church, Rochester, N.Y. 1888–1889, Saint Stephen's, Olean, N.Y. 1889–1894, New York Eye and Ear Infirmary, Second Avenue, New York. 1892–1893, Seawanhaka Corinthian Yacht Club, Oyster Bay, N.Y. 1896–1897, New York Botanical Garden, Bronx, N.Y. 1903, Women's Hotel (now Martha Washington Hotel), East 29th Street, New York. 1904–1905, National Cathedral School, Washington. 1904–1905, Morton F. Plant House (now Cartier's), New York.

BIBLIOGRAPHY

GIBSON, ROBERT W. 1923 *The Morality of Nature: A Philosophy of Evolution.* New York: Putnam.
HISTORIC ALBANY FOUNDATION 1978 *Albany Architects.* Albany, N.Y.: The foundation.
A History of Real Estate, Building and Architecture in New York City. (1898)1967 Reprint. New York: Arno.
"Obituary." 1927 *The Builder* December 2:848.

GIEDION, SIEGFRIED

For several decades, Siegfried Giedion (1888–1968) was the historian–advocate par excellence of the modern movement in architecture. He also enjoyed close ties with modern artists, whose vision gave "the decisive impetus for my work."

The son of a Swiss industrialist, Giedion trained as an engineer in Vienna. In 1913, he became a student of art history, chiefly under Heinrich Wölfflin in Munich. In his dissertation, *Late Baroque and Romantic Classicism* (1922), he interpreted an age's "space conception," separating superficial, historicizing modes from deep "constituent" trends, and studied the past for guidance in the present.

From his home in Zurich, Giedion traveled widely, writing for periodicals. He was lifelong friends with WALTER GROPIUS and LE CORBUSIER. In 1925, Giedion undertook his ground-breaking study of the French engineering tradition, *Bauen in Frankreich* (1928). With Le Corbusier, Giedion played an important role in the founding (1928) of the Congrès Internationaux d'Architecture Moderne, for which he served as secretary general until their disbandment in 1956.

Giedion is most widely known as the author of *Space, Time and Architecture* (1941), which became the bible of architecture students the world over by virtue of its contemporary outlook, its telling illustrations, and its selective typological approach. Architecture and urbanism were related to their underlying spatial and artistic vision, and these to science and technology. The interpenetration of inner and outer space, the new structural potentialities, and the demand for morality were the book's leading themes. Its vivid close-ups based on firsthand information and ranging from Masaccio to Edgerton, Sixtus V to ALVAR AALTO, JOHN SMEATON to ROBERT MAILLART, offered a brilliant conspectus of the modern movement and its antecedents.

Three other books are also of importance. In *Mechanization Takes Command* (1948), Giedion followed the dominant process of the modern age into the "intimate spheres"—food production, domestic surroundings, the kitchen and bath—while studying the underlying principle of movement in its scientific and artistic expressions.

The creation of monumental art and architecture by the Egyptians and Sumerians and their discovery—prompted by ritual and cosmology—of the vertical axis, the plane surface, orthogonal relationships, and proportion, form the subject of *The Eternal Present: The Beginnings of Architecture* (1964). Finally, Giedion's *Architecture and the Phenomena of Transition* (1970) centers on Roman construction and ordering principles, in which architecture was virtually identified with interior space, extension to the outdoors coming to the fore only in the baroque. The industrial era vastly augmented the possibilities for openness, transparency, and interpenetration.

Giedion's bold generalizations as well as his strict modernist canon and rejection of stylistic historicism may be disputed, but one should not misinterpret his functionalist enthusiasm or his link to CIAM rationalism. A descendent of Alois Riegl and the great idealist systematizers, he was altogether antipositivist in outlook. His generous schemes accommodated the complex and irrational in man, the clairvoyance of the artist, and the flair of the historian.

MARTIN S. JAMES

BIBLIOGRAPHY

GIEDION, SIEGFRIED 1922 *Spätbarocker und romantischer Klassizismus.* Munich: Bruckman.
GIEDION, SIEGFRIED 1928 *Bauen in Frankreich: Eisen, Eisenbeton.* Leipzig and Berlin: Klinkhardt & Biermann.
GIEDION, SIEGFRIED (1941)1967 *Space, Time and Architecture: The Growth of a New Tradition.* 5th ed.

Cambridge, Mass.: Harvard University Press.

GIEDION, SIEGFRIED (1948)1969 *Mechanization Takes Command: A Contribution to Anonymous History.* Reprint. New York: Norton.

GIEDION, SIEGFRIED (1956)1958 *Architecture, You and Me: The Diary of a Development.* Cambridge, Mass: Harvard University Press. Originally published with the title *Architektur und Gemeinschaft, Tagebuch einer Entwicklung.*

GIEDION, SIEGFRIED 1962 *The Eternal Present: The Beginnings of Art.* New York: Pantheon for the Bollingen Foundation.

GIEDION, SIEGFRIED 1964 *The Eternal Present: The Beginnings of Architecture.* New York: Pantheon for the Bollingen Foundation.

GIEDION, SIEGFRIED (1970)1971 *Architecture and the Phenomena of Transition: The Three Space Conceptions in Architecture.* Cambridge, Mass: Harvard University Press. Originally published with the title *Architektur und das Phänomen des Wandels.*

Hommage à Giedion: Profile seiner Persönlichkeit. 1971 Basel and Stuttgart, Germany: Birkhäuser Verlag.

GIERGL, KÁLMÁN

Kálmán Giergl (1863–1954) was a renowned professor of architecture in Budapest, Hungary, when that city was developing rapidly at the turn of the century. After his studies in Berlin, he returned to Budapest. He designed several public and private buildings of the developing capital. He designed the building of the New York Insurance Company (1891–1896) and of the High Court of Justice (1891–1896), both in Budapest. Giergl's best known work is the Musical Academy (1907), Budapest, with its pioneering application of ferroconcrete.

JUDITH KOÓS

WORKS

1891–1896, High Court of Justice Palace (detail design); 1891–1896, New York Insurance Company Palace (detail design); 1900–1901, Clotilde Palaces (two); 1907, Musical Academy; Budapest.

BIBLIOGRAPHY

FÁBIÁN, GÁSPÁR 1936 *Nagy Magyar építőmüvészek* ("Great Hungarian Architects"). Budapest: Szerző.

KOÓS, JUDITH 1969 "The Effect and Works of L. C. Tiffany in Hungary." *Acta Historiae Artium* 15:199–216.

KOÓS, JUDITH 1979 *Style 1900: A szecesszó iparmüvészete Magyar-országon* ("Style 1900: Applied Arts of the Art Nouveau in Hungary"). Budapest: Képzömüy.

MERÉNYI, FERENC 1969 *Magyar építészet: 1867–1967* ("Hungarian Architecture: 1867–1967"). Budapest: Müsaki Könyvkiadó.

GILBERT, BRADFORD L.

Bradford Lee Gilbert (1853–1911), born in Watertown, New York, studied architecture in the office of J. CLEVELAND CADY. In 1882 he established a practice in New York City, specializing in the design of railroad structures and public buildings. His major stations included the Illinois Central Railroad Station (1892–1893) in Chicago and the remodeling and enlarging of New York's Grand Central Station (1898–1899), replaced just a few years later by WARREN AND WETMORE's Grand Central Terminal. The Tower Building (1888–1889), generally considered the first building in New York City to use skeleton construction, was Gilbert's most famous work.

MARJORIE PEARSON

WORKS

*1881–1882, General Railroad Office Building, Northern Pacific Railroad Co., Saint Paul, Minn. 1881–1882, Union Station, Saginaw, Mich. 1883–1884, Peninsular Club, Grand Rapids, Mich. 1884–1885, Union Station, Concord, N.H. *1885–1886, Riding Club; *1887–1888, Young Men's Christian Association Building, Harlem Branch; New York. *1888–1889, Newberry Memorial Chapel, Detroit. *1888–1889, Tower Building, New York. *1891–1893, Jefferson Avenue Presbyterian Church, Detroit. 1892–1893, Illinois Central Railroad Station, Chicago. 1895–1896, Mexican National Railroad Station and Offices, Colonia, Mexico City. 1895–1896, Railroad Station, Syracuse, N.Y. 1897, English-American Building, Atlanta, Ga. *1898–1899, Grand Central Station (remodeling and enlargement), New York. 1903, Engine Company 258, Ladder Co. 115 Firehouse, Queens, N.Y.

BIBLIOGRAPHY

CONDIT, CARL W. 1960 Pages 46–48 and 204–205 in *American Building Art: The Nineteenth Century.* New York: Oxford University Press.

GILBERT, BRADFORD L. 1895 *Sketch Portfolio of Railroad Stations and Kindred Structures.* New York: Railroad Gazette.

"Gilbert, Bradford Lee." (1910)1967 Volume 14, pages 298–299 in *National Cyclopedia of American Biography.* Reprint. Ann Arbor, Mich.: University Microfilms.

A History of Real Estate, Building and Architecture in New York City. (1898)1967 Reprint. New York: Arno. See especially pages 467–471.

MEEKS, CARROLL L. V. (1956)1978 Pages 89, 107–108 in *The Railroad Station: An Architectural History.* Reprint. Secaucus, N.J.: Castle.

SCHUYLER, MONTGOMERY (1909)1961 "The Evolution of the Skyscraper." Pages 419–436 in William H. Jordy and Ralph Coe (editors), *American Architecture and Other Writings.* Cambridge, Mass.: Belknap. This article originally appeared in *Scribner's Magazine* 46:257–271.

GILBERT, C. P. H.

Charles Pierrepont H. Gilbert (1863–1952) was born in New York. He attended Columbia University and the Ecole des Beaux-Arts in Paris, then went west to begin his architectural career in the mining towns springing up in Arizona and Colorado. Gilbert returned to New York and began his practice in the newly developing domestic quarter of the city, the West Side, about 1885. Gilbert specialized in domestic work. He did many houses in Brooklyn's Park Slope and in Manhattan as well as country houses, often for the same clients, in Long Island and Westchester County. Gilbert was a successful practitioner in many domestic modes but he is primarily known for his facility in the François I style. Later in his career, Gilbert designed apartment houses in Brooklyn and Manhattan.

DENNIS STEADMAN FRANCIS and
MOSETTE GLASER BRODERICK

WORKS

1887, 838–846 Carroll Street, Park Slope; 1888, Thomas Adams, Jr., House, Park Slope; 1888–1904, Harvey Murdock Houses, Montgomery Place; Brooklyn, N.Y. *1890–1891, Hotel Castleton, Staten Island, N.Y. 1894–1895, House, 330 West 76 Street; 1898–1900, E. C. Converse House, 3 East 78 Street; 1899, I. D. Fletcher House, 2 East 79 Street; New York. *1900, Mortimer Schiff House, Oyster Bay, N.Y. 1900, Henry Seligman House, 30 West 56 Street; 1901, Lydia S. Prentiss House, 1 Riverside Drive; 1903, J. R. DeLamar House, 233 Madison Avenue; 1905, Morton I. Plant House (extension; now Cartier Building), 4 East 52 Street; 1909, 11 East 70 Street; 1917, Otto Kahn House, 1 East 91 Street; 1923, 23 West 71 Street; New York.

BIBLIOGRAPHY
LANDAU, SARAH B.   1975   "The Row Houses of New York's West Side." *Journal of the Society of Architectural Historians* 34:19–36.

LANDMARKS PRESERVATION COMMISSION   1973   *Park Slope Historic District Designation Report*. New York: Landmarks Preservation Commission.

"Obituary."   1952   *New York Times* Oct. 27, p. 27.

"Some Designs of C. P. H. Gilbert."   1899   *Architectural Record* 9:165–172.

GILBERT, CASS

The place of Cass Gilbert (1859–1934) in American architectural history is based primarily on his design of the Woolworth Building in New York (1911–1913), where he dealt successfully with the many aesthetic and financial details involved in the planning of a gigantic skyscraper.

Born in Zanesville, Ohio, he worked as a carpenter's helper and draftsman for Abraham Radcliff in Saint Paul in 1876. Two years later, he enrolled in the Massachusetts Institute of Technology, where he studied with WILLIAM R. WARE and became familiar with the works of H. H. RICHARDSON, WILLIAM R. EMERSON, WILLIAM BURGES, PEABODY AND STEARNS, Cabot and Chandler, and CUMMINGS AND SEARS. Early in 1880, he traveled to England, France, and Italy, thus gaining a better understanding of the Gothic, Roman, and Renaissance styles of architecture.

On his return in 1880 he joined McKIM, MEAD, AND WHITE, but he returned to Saint Paul in 1882 to establish his own practice. A partnership formed with James Knox Taylor lasted from 1884 until 1892. During this decade they built residences, churches, municipal and commercial buildings, railway stations, and bridges. The most famous was the Minnesota Capitol in Saint Paul (1895–1903). As with the other structures Gilbert built at this time, the Minnesota Capitol—a variant of the National Capitol—showed no great originality.

Nevertheless, the composition catapulted Gilbert onto the national scene. He built the multi-storied Brazer Building in Boston (1896) and the Broadway–Chambers Building in New York (1899–1900), for which he permanently moved his office to New York. He also received commissions for the United States Custom House (1901–1907) and the Union Club (1902), both in New York City. The first was a pompous composition monumentally scaled and richly decorated, reflecting the growing wealth and power of the nation. The second, based on the Florentine palazzi of the fifteenth century, was much more restrained in keeping with the requirements of his clients for an unostentatious but aristocratic and handsome structure.

Gilbert's next major job was a twenty-four-story office building on West Street, New York (1905–1907). Gothic in design, it displayed for the first time the clustered columns, late medieval niches, flamboyant arches, and other fourteenth-century terra-cotta details later admired in the Woolworth Building.

The high praise won by Gilbert brought him the commission for the headquarters of the Woolworth business empire which upon completion was the tallest building in the world. The site on Broadway facing City Hall Park allowed a broad façade and a soaring tower 760 feet in height with two rear wings for added space. Gilbert thus avoided the financial problems that had plagued earlier towers, while retaining the highly desirable symbolic character. But the most admired aspect was the lightweight, fire-resistant, and glistening terra-cotta cladding which enhanced the form of

Gilbert.
United States Custom
House.
New York.
1901–1907

Gilbert.
Rotunda Room, United
States Custom House.
New York.
1901–1907

the tower and called to mind the glorious cathedrals of medieval Europe.

The last of this Gothic set was the New York Life Insurance Building (1925–1928), a modest forty-story tower rising out of a three-tiered setback system which provided fifteen floors of company space in the lower two sections and high-priced revenue space above. Thus, the shape of the structure was determined by its function.

The buildings that followed were classically correct and competent but cold and unoriginal. Considering the revolutionary developments in America and Europe by men like FRANK LLOYD WRIGHT, WALTER GROPIUS, LUDWIG MIES VAN DER ROHE, and LE CORBUSIER, Gilbert's late works made little contribution to the history of architecture.

WINSTON WEISMAN

WORKS

1888, Dayton Avenue Presbyterian Church; 1889, Charles P. Noyes House; 1895, Boston Clothing House Block; 1895–1903, Minnesota State Capitol; Saint Paul, Minn. 1896, Brazer Building, Boston. 1899–1900, Broadway-Chambers Building; 1901–1907, United States Custom House; 1902, Union Club; New York. 1902–1904, Saint Louis Art Museum, Louisiana Purchase Exposition Art Building, Mo. 1905–1907, West Street Building; 1911–1913, Woolworth Building; New York. 1924–1925, Chamber of Commerce Building, Washington. 1925–1928, New York Life Insurance Building.

BIBLIOGRAPHY

"The Brazer Building, Boston, Mass." 1897 *American Architect and Building News* 56:64.

"The Broadway Chambers." 1900 *Architects' and Builders' Magazine* 33, Nov.: 45–52.

JONES, ROBERT ALLEN 1976 "Cass Gilbert, Midwestern Architect in New York." Unpublished Ph.D. dissertation, Case Western Reserve University, Cleveland, Ohio.

JORDY, WILLIAM H. 1976 Volume 3 in *American Buildings and Their Architects.* Garden City, N.Y.: Anchor.

KIRKHAM, GUY 1934 "Cass Gilbert, Master of Style." *Pencil Points* 15:541–556.

MURPHY, PATRICIA ANNE 1976 "The Early Career of Cass Gilbert: 1878 to 1895." Unpublished M.A. thesis, University of Virginia, Charlottesville.

"New York Life Insurance Company Building, New York." 1929 *American Architect* 135:351–414.

SCHUYLER, MONTGOMERY 1906 "The New Custom

Gilbert.
Woolworth Building.
New York.
1911–1913

Gilbert.
New York Life Insurance
Building.
1925–1928

House at New York." *Architectural Record* 20, July:1–14.

SCHUYLER, MONTGOMERY 1913 "The Towers of Manhattan; and Notes on the Woolworth Building." *Architectural Record* 33, Feb.:99–122.

SWALES, F. 1912 "The Work of Cass Gilbert." *Architectural Review* 31:3–16.

TORBERT, DONALD 1958 *A Century of Art and Architecture in Minnesota.* Minneapolis: University of Minnesota Press.

WEBER, P. J. 1897 "A Review of the Works of Cass Gilbert." *Architectural Reviewer* 1, 30 June:42–65.

WEISMAN, WINSTON 1970 "A New View of Skyscraper History." Pages 115–160 in Edgar Kaufman, jr. (editor), *The Rise of an American Architecture.* New York: Praeger.

"The West Street Building." 1907 *Architectural Record* 22, Aug.:102–109.

GILDEMEISTER, CHARLES

See CARSTENSEN, GEORG.

GILES, ALFRED

London-born Alfred Giles (1853–1920) was an apprentice in the firm of Giles and Bivens while taking night courses at the University of London. In 1873, Giles emigrated to Texas for health reasons and settled in San Antonio just in time for the coming of the railroad and the building boom that followed. He soon became a leading architect in central Texas, and in the first decade of the twentieth century, a period of growth in northern Mexico, Giles opened a branch office in Monterrey. Between 1900 and 1910, he designed major buildings throughout that area and was active in Texas and Mexico until his death.

MARY HOLLERS JUTSON GEORGE

WORKS

1876, Edward Steves House; 1880, Fort Sam Houston (Officers' Quarters, Staff Post); San Antonio, Tex. 1881, Gillespie County Courthouse, Fredericksburg, Tex. 1884, Wilson County Courthouse, Floresville, Tex. 1893, William Maverick House; 1894, Edwin Terrell House; 1896, Daniel Sullivan Stable and Coach House; 1900, Incarnate Word (Mother House, Convent); San Antonio, Tex. 1901, Banco Mercantil; 1901, La Reinera; Monterrey, Mexico. 1906, Penitentiary; 1906, Palacio Municipal; Chihuahua, Mexico. 1910, Arco de la Independicia, Monterrey, Mexico.

BIBLIOGRAPHY

JUTSON, MARY HOLLERS 1972 *Alfred Giles: An English Architect in Texas and Mexico.* San Antonio, Tex.: Trinity University Press.

GILL, IRVING

Irving John Gill (1870–1936) originated a style of architecture which grew out of his experiments in reinforced concrete. He reduced forms to cubic masses, and the sheer walls were without ornament. Interior detailing was simplified, and rooms were well lighted through sharply incised openings.

When reinforced concrete was in its infancy, Gill not only developed a body of details for its use but experimented with its structure. He perfected a tilt-up system for concrete walls in 1912, and by 1915 had lifted 60-foot walls into place. He brought various refinements to the material: a membrane at the core of walls to eliminate condensation; color rubbed into floors to give the appearance of old leather; exterior and interior walls were made sensitive to color by applying paint in which all primary colors were mixed with white.

His preoccupation with "the sanitary house" prompted him to cove walls into floors to eliminate joints, and to install drains in bathroom and kitchen floors so the walls could be washed down. Among his numerous inventions was a garbage disposal which carried waste to a basement incinerator (1907).

Gill himself planned the gardens around his buildings, selecting trees for the shadows they cast on sheer walls; his unroofed "green rooms" extend into open gardens by trellised walks. His housing for low-income families showed the same fine gradation between private and shared outdoor space as his large houses, and the amenities of plan were in both. His favorite design was for Lewis Courts (1910), low-income housing in Sierra Madre, California.

Born of Quaker parents on a farm near Syracuse, N.Y., his father and brother were builders. Gill's skill at drawing turned him to architecture and after a year's apprenticeship with E. G. Hall, he was drawn to Chicago by the reputation of Louis H. Sullivan. He worked in J. LYMAN SILSBEE's office before joining the ADLER AND SULLIVAN firm in 1890 as a draftsman on the Transportation Building for the 1893 Columbian Exposition.

The liberating influence of Sullivan was vital to Gill's development, and the respect Sullivan instilled in his draftsmen for the sheer walls of indigenous African architecture proved important. When he moved to San Diego, California in 1893, he recognized the appropriateness to the semiarid climate of the mud forms of the California missions, and they suggested concrete as a modern equivalent. The mission arch was always present in his style.

He formed a partnership in 1898 with William

S. Hebbard, which lasted nine years. Gill's personal style appeared early in the interiors: smooth slab doors, elimination of moldings, flush detailing of unfinished wood. Their residential work was in English country house, Craftsman, and Prairie styles. Before the partnership was dissolved Gill's austere cubic forms were emerging.

His 1907 Laughlin House in Los Angeles approached the problem of form for concrete, and three California buildings established his direction: in La Jolla, the Wilson Acton Hotel (1908) and the first laboratory for the Scripps Institution of Oceanography (1908–1910), a pure cubic form with well-lighted work spaces; and the Holly Sefton Memorial Hospital (1908–1909) in San Diego, which was domestic in scale; the setbacks of the plan allowed for a play of volumes. Gill explored this play more timidly in 1911 in the Miltimore House in South Pasadena, and the Timken House in San Diego, but returned to it in two of his most famous houses, the Scripps House, San Diego (1915), and the Dodge House, Los Angeles (1914–1916). In the Dodge House, the floor plan was looser, with social rooms oriented to a recessed raised patio and porches off all bedrooms.

His most characteristic concrete buildings were commissioned by Ellen Scripps for a tract overlooking the bay in La Jolla. Three buildings for Bishop's School for Girls (1909, 1910, 1916) are connected by arcades, a scheme typical of his low-income housing. The finest of the Scripps group is the 1913 Women's Club of tilt-up construction; in the symmetrical plan the landscaping reinforces the serenity of the building. A recreation building (1914) and the Scripps House complete the group.

Eclectic styles gained favor after 1915, and Gill's commissions declined. He designed a number of buildings for the new industrial town of Torrance (1913), the Horatio West Court (1919) in Santa Monica, and, with John Siebert, several buildings in Oceanside, all in California. One was a kindergarten (1931) with glass walls opening to outdoor classrooms. His last work, touching in its simplicity, was a chapel and cottages (1933) for an Indian resettlement development in Lakeside, California.

ESTHER MCCOY

WORKS

1904–1906, George Marston House (with William S. Hebbard); 1906, Burnham House (with Hebbard); San Diego, Calif. 1907, Bailey House (with Hebbard), La Jolla, Calif. 1907, Laughlin House, Los Angeles. *1907, Melville Klauber House, San Diego, Calif. 1908, Wilson Acton Hotel, La Jolla, Calif. *1908–1909, Holly Sefton Memorial Hospital for Children, San Diego, Calif. 1908–1910, Scripps Institution of Oceanography; 1909, Bentham Hall, Bishop's School; La Jolla, Calif. 1910,

Gill.
Dodge House.
Los Angeles.
1914–1916

Lewis Courts, Sierra Madre, Calif. 1910, Scripps Hall, Bishop's School, La Jolla, Calif. 1911, Miltimore House, South Pasadena, Calif. *1911, Timken House, San Diego, Calif. 1912, Banning House, Los Angeles. 1913, Twelve workmen's cottages, Torrance, Calif. 1913, Women's Club; 1914, Recreation Building; La Jolla, Calif. *1914–1916, Dodge House, Los Angeles. 1915, Scripps House; 1916, Gilman Hall, Bishop's School (with Louis J. Gill); La Jolla, Calif. 1919, Horatio West Court, Santa Monica, Calif. 1927, First Church of Christ Scientist, Coronado, Calif. 1929, City Hall, Fire and Police Station (with John Siebert); 1931, Kindergarten (with Siebert); Oceanside, Calif. 1933, Rancho Barona Resettlement Development for Indians, Assumption Church, and twelve cottages, Lakeside, Calif.

BIBLIOGRAPHY

ANDREWS, WAYNE (1947)1978 *Architecture, Ambition, and Americans: A Social History of American Architecture.* Rev. ed. New York: Free Press.
GEBHARD, DAVID 1974 "Irving Gill." Pages 112–118 in *California Design 1910.* Pasadena: California Design Publications.
GILL, IRVING 1916 "The Home of the Future: The New Architecture of the West: Small Homes for a Great Country." *The Craftsman* 30, May:140–151.
JORDY, WILLIAM H. 1972 Volumes 3 and 4 in *American Buildings and Their Architects.* New York: Doubleday. Volume 3: *Progressive and Academic Ideals at the Turn of the Twentieth Century.* Volume 4: *The Impact of the European Modernism in the Mid-twentieth Century.*
KAMERLING, BRUCE 1979 *Irving Gill: The Artist as Architect.* California: San Diego Historical Society.
MCCOY, ESTHER 1960 *Five California Architects.* New York: Reinhold.
STARR, KEVIN 1973 *Americans and the California Dream.* New York: Oxford.

GILLY, FRIEDRICH

Although he built only a handful of country and city houses in his short career, Friedrich Gilly

Gilly.
Interior sketch.
1794

(1772–1800) inspired an entire generation of German architects through his visionary renderings. With the single image of a Doric temple to the memory of Frederick the Great (1797), Gilly was acclaimed by younger architects and the literary Romantics in Berlin as the prophet of a new architecture based on a profound insight into the essence of antiquity. This single design determined KARL FRIEDRICH SCHINKEL's choice of an architectural career.

Gilly's talent was early recognized and nurtured by his architect father David Gilly. Descended from a French Huguenot family who had settled in Pomerania in 1689, David Gilly had been the first to pass the newly established state architectural examination in 1770 and rose rapidly in the civil service to the position of director of building in Pomerania. The younger Gilly was introduced to architectural practice and theory in his father's private architectural school, founded at Stettin in 1783. There, the practical nature of David Gilly's rural commissions and the tradition of French rational theory combined to engender a style of chaste simplicity relying solely on harmonious proportions and balance of solids and voids which was to have continued influence on the analytical abstraction of Friedrich Gilly's designs.

In 1788 Friedrich Gilly accompanied his father who, like FRIEDRICH WILHELM ERDMANNSDORFF, CARL GOTTHARD LANGHANS and Schadow, had been summoned to Berlin by Friedrich Wilhelm II, who was eager to break with the francophile taste of Frederick the Great. At the Academy under these masters of Prussian neoclassicism and the artists Becherer and Chodowiecki, Friedrich Gilly's linear rendering style and sense of bold, simple composition was further developed. Also in 1788, he was named inspector in the Royal Buildings Department, serving under Erdmannsdorff at Schloss Charlottenburg and under Langhans on the neo-Gothic Marienkirche tower. Gilly's official career followed the model of his father's. He served as a surveyor in the Schwedt region and in 1790 made a tour of inspection of canals and waterworks in Westphalia and Holland. Although Langhans's Palladian (see ANDREA PALLADIO) classicism is the basis of Gilly's first design,

the house at 14 Jägerstrasse, Berlin, an impassioned study of antique literature, history, and archeological publications and a reading of the aesthetic theories of Johann Joachim Winckelmann and Goethe were the determining factors in his quest for the purity of earliest classical design. Influenced by the circle of Romantics around the poets Tieck and Wackenroder, Gilly saw his own architectural rebirth as the inspired search of a lonely artist, a self-image evoked in such sketches as a Temple to Loneliness, a private library set in a Campo Santo, and the disquieting interior sketch of 1794 in which the elemental, primitivist architectural elements are rendered as stereometric forms in a crisp linear style. As he was unable to visit Italy because of the French invasion, antiquity remained for him a literary and pictorial ideal to be sought in all architecture.

In his views of the medieval Marienburg Castle, drawn on a 1794 tour of inspection in East Prussia with his father, Gilly exploited the dramatic vantage points, sharp light contrasts, and integration of architecture and nature of GIOVANNI BATTISTA PIRANESI's style to convey the aesthetic power of north German brick architecture. Exhibited in 1795 and later published as lithographs, these views led to the royal restoration of the Prussian monument and mark the beginning of a concern with the brick tradition that was given its mature theoretical statement in the late work of Schinkel.

The competition for a monument to Frederick the Great announced by the Academy in 1796 revived a notion already debated during the monarch's reign and repeatedly thwarted by disputes over the appropriate form and cost. With the exception of the winner Carl Gotthard Langhans, the younger contestants all conceived of the competition as a forum for ideal statements. Gilly even relocated his project to a reorganized Leipziger Platz on Berlin's periphery, incorporating a new Potsdamer Gate leading to Frederick the Great's beloved Sanssouci. The gate, a synthesis of the Greek propylaeum with a Roman triumphal arch, is a conscious reinterpretation of Langhans's epoch-making Brandenburg Gate into the stereometric solids of revolutionary classicism. Already in 1787, the archeologist Hans Christian Genelli had proposed a Doric temple for the monument. Gilly set this temple in an architecturally controlled precinct defining a dramatic processional through the gate and monument. Atop a massive substructure enclosing the royal sarcophagus, the temple, bathed in light and housing the cult statue of the king, rises as the crystalline embodiment of the ideal. A compelling image of German cultural achievement and unity, it was to have resounding

Gilly.
Design for a monument to
Frederick the Great.
1797

echoes in later German architecture from LEO VON KLENZE's Walhalla to FRIEDRICH AUGUST STÜLER and JOHANN HEINRICH STRACK's National Gallery.

The sensitivity to pictorial qualities and symbolic program reliant on metaphors of pure geometry revealed in light seem closer to ETIENNE LOUIS BOULLÉE's Newton Monument (1784) than to the Palladian classicism of Prussia; but Gilly could scarcely have known such designs. His axial *parti* remains more traditional, his forms are more historical in their associations. Supported by a royal stipend, Gilly traveled in 1798–1799 to France, England, Southern Germany, and Vienna. In Paris, he was especially attracted by the works of FRANÇOIS JOSEPH BÉLANGER, whose Bagatelle is both the basis of Gilly's own Villa Molter in the Berlin Tiergarten section (1798) and the subject of one of his eloquent articles for the first German architectural periodical, David Gilly's *Sammlung Aufsätze und Nachrichten die Baukunst betreffend.* Gilly also carefully studied the spherical dome of Jacques-Guillain Legrand and JACQUES MOLINOS's Halle au Blé and their Théâtre Feyedeau, one of many theaters he studied in Paris and London. His last year in Berlin was especially devoted to projects for a new Berlin theater. In Gilly's designs, the circular auditorium of Peyre (see PEYRE FAMILY) and CHARLES DE WAILLY's Odéon and the antique prototypes recalled in CLAUDE NICOLAS LEDOUX's Besançon theater are subject to further abstraction and analytic reduction. His boldly massed exterior, with its clear expression of the interior volumes, was to recur in such theater designs as GEORG MOLLER's at Darmstadt and GOTTFRIED SEMPER's at Dresden.

Upon his return to Berlin, Gilly assumed the position of professor of optics and perspective at the newly founded Bauakademie and began a closer association with his brother-in-law, HEINRICH GENTZ. Gilly's influence is especially strong in Gentz's Mint (1798–1800) for which he de-

signed the sculptural frieze. His own late designs, such as the Hündebrücke and a sketch of a mausoleum, are far more severe in their abstraction and definition of space within a grid than either the work of his contemporaries or his own work of only two years earlier.

Although confined to paper, Gilly's designs were copied by Schinkel, von Klenze, and others and continued to challenge German architects in the early nineteenth century. After Gilly's death in Karlsbad in 1800, Schinkel faithfully completed his few unfinished projects and continued to mine the rich legacy of the drawings. Schinkel always considered Gilly his only master.

BARRY BERGDOLL

WORKS

*1792–1794, House, 14 Jägerstrasse, Berlin. 1795, Schloss (remodeling of five rooms), Schwedt, Pomerania, Germany. 1797, Church, Paretz, Germany. 1797, Grave of Duchess Maltzahn, Dyherrnfuhrt, Germany. 1799, House, 30 Bruderstrasse, Berlin. 1799, Theater, Königsberg, Germany. *1799, Villa Molter, Tiergarten, Berlin. *1800, Farm Buildings and Tahitian Hut, Schloss Bellevue, Berlin.

BIBLIOGRAPHY

ADLER, FRIEDRICH 1881 "Friedrich Gilly, Schinkel's Lehrer." *Centralblatt der Bauverwaltung* 1:8–10, 17–19, 22–24.

DOEBBER, ADOLF 1916 *Heinrich Gentz: Ein Berliner Baumeister um 1800.* Berlin: Heymann.

FLESCHE, HERMAN 1947 "Friedrich Gilly." Pages 65–76 in *Fünf Deutsche Baumeister.* Braunschweig: Westerman.

GILLY, DAVID 1797 *Über Erfindung: Construction und Vortheile der Bohlen-Dächer.* Berlin.

GILLY, DAVID 1797–1798 *Handbuch der Landbaukunst.* 2 vols. Berlin: The author.

GILLY, DAVID (editor) 1797–1805 *Sammlung nützlicher Aufsätze und Nachrichten die Baukunst betreffend.*

GILLY, DAVID 1809–1818 *Praktische Anweisung zur Wasserbaukunst. . . .* Berlin.

GILLY, FRIEDRICH 1799a "Beschreibung des Landsitzes Rincy unweit Paris." *Sammlung nützlicher Aufsätze und Nachrichten die Baukunst betreffend* 1:116–122.

GILLY, FRIEDRICH 1799b "Beschreibung des Landhauses Bagatelle bey Paris." *Sammlung nützlicher Aufsätze und Nachrichten die Baukunst betreffend* 2:106–115.

GILLY, FRIEDRICH, and FRICK, FRIEDRICH (1799–1803)1965 *Schloss Marienburg in Preussen.* Düsseldorf, Germany: Galtgarben.

HEDERER, OSWALD 1976 *Klassizismus.* Munich: Heyne.

HERRMANN, WOLFGANG (1932)1977 Volume 1 in *Deutsche Baukunst des 19. und 20. Jahrhunderts.* Basel: Burkhaüser.

JOHANNES, HEINRICH 1942 "Das Denkmal Friedrichs des Grossen von Gilly." *Kunst im Deutschen Reich* 6:156–164.

KAUFMANN, EMIL 1933 *Von Ledoux bis Le Corbusier: Ursprung und Entwicklung der autonomen Architektur.* Vienna: Passer.

KLINKOTT, MANFRED 1977 "Friedrich Gilly, 1772–1800." In "Fünf Architekten des Klassizismus in Deutschland." *Dortmunder Architekturheft* 4:11–41.

LAMMERT, MARLIES 1964 *David Gilly: Ein Baumeister des deutschen Klassizismus.* Berlin (east): Akademie-Verlag.

LEVEZOW, KONRAD 1801 *Denkschrift auf Friedrich Gilly.* Berlin: Realsch.

NEUMEYER, ALFRED 1938 "Monuments to 'Genius' in German Classicism." *Journal of the Warburg and Courtauld Institutes* 2:159–163.

ONCKEN, ALSTE 1935 *Friedrich Gilly: 1772–1800.* Berlin: Deutscher Verein für Kunstwissenschaft.

PEVSNER, NIKOLAUS 1968 "Karl Friedrich Schinkel." *Studies in Art, Architecture and Design* 1:174–195.

REITDORF, ALFRED 1940 *Gilly; Wiedergeburt der Architektur.* Berlin: Hugo.

RIEMER, H. 1931 "Friedrich Gillys Verhältnis zum Theaterbau." Unpublished Ph.D. dissertation, University of Berlin.

SCHMITZ, HERMANN (1914)1925 *Berliner Baumeister vom Ausgang des Achtzehnten Jahrhunderts.* 2d ed. Berlin: Verlag für Kunstwissenschaft.

SCHMITZ, HERMANN 1909 "Friedrich Gilly." *Kunst und Künstler* 7:201–206.

SCHMITZ, HERMANN 1910 "Schloss Paretz." *Kunst und Künstler* 8:506–512.

SIMSON, JUTTA VON 1976 *Das Berliner Denkmal für Friedrich den Grossen.* Frankfurt: Propylaen.

WEDEPOHEL, EDGAR 1965 "Description de Bagatelle." *L'Oeil* June:16–23, 46.

GILMAN, ARTHUR DELAVAN

Arthur Gilman (1821–1882), author, lecturer, architect, and planner, was a prime intellectual force in Boston architectural circles between 1843 and 1866. Eschewing both the work of CHARLES BULFINCH and the powerful yet provincial heritage of the engineer architects of the Greek Revival (ALEXANDER PARRIS, SOLOMON WILLARD, and ISAIAH ROGERS), he favored a contemporary, international frame of reference, first English, then French.

Born in Newburyport, Massachusetts, Gilman sought the ministry, attending Dummer Academy and Trinity College, Hartford, which he left in 1840. He surfaced dramatically in 1843 with a series of brilliant articles in the *North American Review,* given twice by demand to rapt audiences as the Lowell Lectures of 1844. Widely read and intimately familiar with English architectural theory and building, he lauded the work of CHARLES BARRY and AUGUSTUS W. N. PUGIN, both at their apogee in London. Puginian tenets supported his vigorous defense of the Gothic Revival as manifested in recent work of RICHARD UPJOHN and JAMES RENWICK, and A. J. DOWNING's conception of the unity of landscape and building. With Boston's colonial architecture he aligned the contemporaneous, Italianate designs of his friend Charles Barry, likewise based on Renaissance models.

Following a professional trip abroad and study in England, he is known to have practiced in part with EDWARD C. CABOT through 1857. Gilman's early work consistently reflects the massing and scale of Barry, which is also evident in Cabot's designs for the Boston Athenaeum (1846–1849). Churches were the bulk of Gilman's early practice. All are of English derivation, but of differing style, notably the Gothic Saint Paul's, Dedham (1857), the Italo-Romanesque Sears Chapel, Brookline (1858–1863), and his famous Arlington Street Church, Boston (1859–1861), based on JAMES GIBBS's Saint Martin-in-the-Fields, London (1726), a source for colonial designs. He promoted this style again in 1863 with his defense of the threatened Hancock House (1737) on Beacon Hill, lending new status to Boston's eighteenth-century remains. The measured drawings of the building by his young colleague JOHN HUBBARD STURGIS were the first to be made of an American house.

Gilman's maturity was characterized by a new interest in the French academic design theories of Second Empire Paris, which produced his plan for Boston's Back Bay (1856), where his spacious mansions set new standards of style. In 1859, he married Frances Juliet Raynor of Syracuse, New York, and may well have traveled abroad. From 1859 until 1866, when he moved to New York, he practiced with GRIDLEY J. F. BRYANT of the largest architectural office in Boston. The firm's Boston City Hall (1862–1865), Boston City Hospital

(1861–1864), and Horticultural Hall (1865) set new French standards for American public building.

His late work is structurally innovative and important. His role was central in the New York State Capitol competition, first with Edward Kendall as partner (1867), then working with THOMAS C. FULLER on revised designs. His Equitable building (1867), New York, holds the title of one of the first skyscrapers. Ultimately, as a consultant to ALFRED B. MULLETT on the State, War, and Navy Building (1871–1875), Washington, he extended to gargantuan scale the French, mansardic design concepts he initiated in the Boston City Hall.

MARGARET HENDERSON FLOYD

WORKS

*1845, Saint Paul's Episcopal Church, Dedham, Mass. *1845–1850, W. P. Winchester House, Watertown, Mass. 1852, Hollis Hunnewell House, Wellesley, Mass. 1855, Town Hall, Exeter, N.H. *1857, Hotel Pelham (with Alfred Stone), Boston. 1857, Saint Paul's Episcopal Church (second building), Dedham, Mass. 1858, Church of the Immaculate Conception (with Patrick Keely); *1858, Statehouse (extension; with Gridley J. F. Bryant); Boston. 1858–1863, Christ Church (Sears Chapel), Brookline, Mass. 1859–1861, Arlington Street Church; 1860, John Bates House; *1860, Gardner Brewer House; 1861, Block of Houses (with Bryant); 1861, S. Hooper House; 1861, J. L. Simmons Houses; 1861, Samuel Ward House; 1861–1864, Boston City Hospital (with Bryant); Boston. 1862, George W. Drowne House, Providence, R.I. 1862–1865, City Hall (with Bryant), Boston. 1864–1866, State Capitol (extension), Concord, N.H. 1865, Horticultural Hall (with Bryant), Boston. 1866, B. Stark House, New London, Conn. 1867, Equitable Life Assurance Company Building, New York. *1869–1871, Saint John's Episcopal Church, Staten Island, N.Y. 1869–1872, United States Post Office (with Alfred B. Mullett), Boston. 1871–1875, State, War, and Navy Building (with Mullett), Washington. 1872, Drexel Building; 1872–1873, Bennett Building; New York. 1873, Butler Exchange Building, Providence, R.I. *1873, Equitable Life Assurance Company Building, Boston. *1873–1877, Paran Stevens Building, New York.

BIBLIOGRAPHY

BUNTING, BAINBRIDGE 1967 *Houses of Boston's Back Bay.* Cambridge, Mass.: Harvard University Press.

FLOYD, MARGARET HENDERSON 1973 "A Terra-Cotta Cornerstone for Copley Square: Museum of Fine Arts, Boston 1870–1876 by Sturgis and Brigham." *Journal of the Society of Architectural Historians* 32:83–103.

FLOYD, MARGARET HENDERSON 1979 "Measured Drawings of the Hancock House by John Hubbard Sturgis: A Legacy to the Colonial Revival." *Architecture in Colonial Massachusetts* 51:87–111.

FLOYD, MARGARET HENDERSON n.d. "John Hubbard Sturgis of Boston and the English Architectural Image." Unpublished manuscript.

FOLLETT, JEAN 1979 "Alfred Stone and the Hotel Pelham." Unpublished paper presented at the Student Symposium of the New England Chapter of the Society of Architectural Historians, 1980.

GILMAN, ARTHUR DELAVAN 1843 "Downing on Rural Architecture." *North American Review* 56, Jan.:1–17.

GILMAN, ARTHUR DELAVAN 1844a "Architecture in the United States." *North American Review* 58, Apr.:436–480.

GILMAN, ARTHUR DELAVAN 1844b "Landscape Gardening." *North American Review* 59, Oct.:302–329.

GILMAN, ARTHUR DELAVAN 1863 "The Hancock House and its Founder." *Atlantic Monthly* 11:692–707.

HAMLIN, TALBOT F. (1931)1943 "Arthur Delavan Gilman." Pages 297–298, in *Dictionary of American Biography.* New York: Scribner.

HITCHCOCK, H. R., and SEALE, WILLIAM 1976 *Temples of Democracy: The State Capitols of the U.S.A.* New York: Harcourt.

LANGSAM, WALTER E. 1968 "The New York Capitol 1863–1876." Unpublished M.A. thesis, Yale University, New Haven.

MACKAY, ROBERT B. 1980 "The Charles Street Jail: Hegemony of a Design." Unpublished Ph.D. dissertation, Boston University.

PEABODY, ROBERT SWAIN n.d. "Reminiscences of R. S. Peabody." Unpublished manuscript in the Peabody Papers, Boston Public Library.

STANTON, PHOEBE B. 1968 *The Gothic Revival and American Church Architecture.* Baltimore: Johns Hopkins University Press.

TUCCI, DOUGLASS SHAND 1978 *Built in Boston.* Boston: New York Graphic Society.

WEISMAN, WINSTON 1970 "A New View of Sky-

Gilman.
Arlington Street Church.
Boston.
1859–1861

scraper History." Pages 113–160 in Edgar Kaufman, Jr. (editor), *The Rise of an American Architecture.* New York: Praeger.

WHITEHILL, WALTER M. 1968 *Boston: A Topographical History.* 2d rev. ed. Cambridge, Mass.: Harvard University Press.

WRENN, GEORGE 1962 "The Boston City Hall, Bryant and Gilman Architects, 1862–1865." *Journal of the Society of Architectural Historians* 21, Dec.:188–192.

GINGELL, WILLIAM BRUCE

William Bruce Gingell (1819–1900) was the chief commercial architect of Bristol, England, and pioneered a massive High Victorian style for warehouses. He was articled to a Bath architect in 1844 and went into partnership with THOMAS FULLER in 1848. His own first major and influential work was Bristol General Hospital (1852–1857).

MARGARET RICHARDSON

WORKS

1852–1857, Bristol General Hospital, Guinea Street; 1854–1858, West of England and South Wales Bank (now Lloyds Bank; with T. R. Lysaght), Corn Street; *1860, Warehouse, 12 Temple Street; c.1860, Christopher Thomas Soap Factory, Straight Street; c.1865, W. J. Roger's Jacob Street Brewery; 1876, E. S. and A. Robinson Limited, Victoria Street; c.1881, Christopher Thomas Soap Factory, Broad Plain; Bristol, England.

BIBLIOGRAPHY

CRICK, CLARE 1975 *Victorian Buildings in Bristol.* England: Bristol and West Building Society.

HITCHCOCK, H. R. (1954)1972 *Early Victorian Architecture in Britain.* Reprint. New York: Da Capo.

"Obituary; Mr. W. Bruce Gingell." 1900 *The Builder* 78, no. 2991:548.

GINSBURG, MOISEI YAKOVLEVICH

Moisei Yakovlevich Ginsburg (1892–1946) was born in Minsk, Russia. The son of a provincial architect, he was perhaps one of the most broadly educated members of the pioneer generation of Constructivists. After graduating as an architect in 1914 from the Academy of Fine Arts in Milan, Ginsburg returned to Russia and began to study engineering at the Rizhsky Polytechnic from which he qualified as an engineer in 1917. In 1921, after three years of private practice in the Crimea, Ginsburg moved to Moscow where he began to teach in a junior capacity. In 1923, on the publication of his first theoretical work, *Rhythm in Architecture,* and two important articles setting forth the credo of Constructivism, Ginsburg became professor of history and theory at the Vkhutemas (the State Higher Art and Technical Studios) in Moscow. At the same time, he began teaching at the Moscow Institute of Higher Technology.

In the following year, he gave a series of lectures at the Russian Academy of Artistic Studies, and these lectures formed the basis of his definitive elaboration of Constructivist architectural theory; his book *Style and Epoch* was published in 1924. The following year he founded the OSA group (Association of Contemporary Architects) in collaboration with a number of prominent Constructivist architects, among them A. Vesnin (see VESNIN FAMILY).

In 1926, Ginsburg and Vesnin founded the seminal Soviet architectural journal *Sovremenia Arkhitektura* (Contemporary Architecture) which continued to appear regularly in six issues a year, until OSA was obliged to merge with VANO, the state-sponsored Scientific All-Union Association of Architecture. Unlike the compositional preoccupations of his principal theoretical treatise, Ginsburg's contributions to *Sovremenia Arkhitektura* focused on the evolution of a sound functionalist method and on the problems of determining the relationships that obtain between architectural form and social order.

After a period of intense activity during which he designed one major public institution after another—from his Textile Building projected for Moscow in 1925 to his Courts of Justice, under construction in Alma-Ata from 1927—Ginsburg began to concern himself almost exclusively with the invention of a collective housing form that would be appropriate to the new social order. From 1928, he served as the chief architect on a Vkhutemas faculty team charged with the evolution of new residential prototypes, the so-called Dom Kommuna. Of the three prototypes finally evolved for Stroikom, the Building Committee of the Economic Council of the Soviet Union, only the split-level, one-and-a-half-story Stroikom type F apartment was actually realized, first in Moscow with the Narkomfin block completed on Novinsky Boulevard in 1929, and then in Sverdlovsk, in a slightly more complex block built over approximately the same period. It was typical of Ginsburg that in each instance he would collaborate with a different architect; in Moscow with I. F. Milinis and in Sverdlovsk with A. PASTERNAK.

This turned out to be the high point of Ginsburg's career as a building architect. From the early 1930s on, he was either involved in avant-gardist planning proposals such as his linear Green City for the outer suburbs of Moscow (1930) in collaboration with M. BARSHCH, or he entered one competition after another without success (Sverdlovsk Theater, 1931; Palace of the Soviets, 1932). However, unlike other members of the Constructivist generation, he was to remain active until the mid-1940s even if the Ordjonikidze Sanatorium in Kislovodsk (under construction 1935–1937) was not finally finished to his liking.

KENNETH FRAMPTON

WORKS

1928–1929, Narkomfin Block (with I. . Milinis), Moscow. 1928–1929, Type F. Residential Block (with A. Pasternak), Sverdlovsk, Russia. 1928–1931, Courts of Justice (with Milinis); 1929–1934, Administration Building, Turkestan-Siberia Railway; Alma-Ata, Russia. 1932, Low-rise Housing, Chernigov Industrial Area (with M. Barshch), Russia. 1935–1937, Ordjonikidze Sanatorium, Kislovodsk, Russia.

BIBLIOGRAPHY

KHAN-MAGOMEDOV, S.O. (1972)1975 *M. J. Ginzburg.* Milan: Angeli.
KOPP, ANATOLE 1970 *Town and Revolution.* New York: Braziller.
LISSITZKY, ELEAZAR (1930)1970 *Russia: An Architecture for World Revolution.* Translated by Eric Dluhasch. Cambridge, Mass.: M.I.T. Press.
SHVIDKOVSKY, O. A. 1971 *Building in the USSR: 1917–1932.* London: Studio Vista; New York: Praeger.

GIOCONDO, GIOVANNI

Fra Giovanni Giocondo (1433–1515) was one of the most unusual architect–humanists of the Italian Renaissance. Although his fame rests on an important early edition of VITRUVIUS's *Ten Books on Architecture* (1511), during his lifetime he was one of the most respected Italian architectural engineers.

Born in Verona, he became a Franciscan monk, and according to GIORGIO VASARI, studied the ancient monuments in Rome. His collection of Latin inscriptions was much admired, and he seems to have been an expert in Greek as well as something of a theologian.

Precisely when Fra Giocondo's architectural career began is not known. In 1487, however, he completed the construction of Poggioreale in Naples. Thereafter (1495–1505), he was employed by the kings of France, Charles VIII and Louis IX, as an architect. Although no works from this period survive, he was responsible for the construction of a bridge over the River Seine (c.1500), Paris. On his return to Italy, he was employed in some hydraulic works and in the planning of the Rialto area of Venice (not executed). As a military architect, he planned and superintended the construction of defenses at Treviso (1509–1511). These defense works, involving the complete encirclement of the town, are an example of a transitional form of bastioned defense; the gun platforms are rounded rather than angled as in later works by Antonio da Sangallo (see SANGALLO FAMILY) and others.

It is a measure of Fra Giocondo's reputation as a structural expert that on the death of DONATO BRAMANTE, though almost eighty years old, he was invited to Rome by Pope Leo X to oversee the difficult structural problems at St. Peter's. With Giuliano da Sangallo and RAPHAEL, Fra Giocondo helped in the revisions and improvement of Bramante's plans.

Fra Giocondo's edition of Vitruvius was enormously influential. Although the text had been printed before (c.1486), Fra Giocondo's edition was illustrated, and thus interpreted, by his woodcuts. It was on Fra Giocondo's edition that Raphael based his own version of Vitruvius.

NICHOLAS ADAMS

WORKS

*c.1500, Bridge, River Seine, Paris. *1509, Fortifications, Padua, Italy. 1509–1511, Fortifications, Treviso, Italy. *1514, St. Peter's (structural additions), Rome.

BIBLIOGRAPHY

DE LA CROIX, HORST 1972 *Military Considerations in City Planning: Fortifications.* New York: Braziller.
VAGNETTI, LUIGI (editor) 1978 *2000 anni di Vitruvio.* Florence: Edizione della Cattedra di Composizione Architettonica la della Facoltà di Architettura di Firenze.

GIORGIO DA SEBENICO

During the fifteenth century, the towns along the eastern coast of the Adriatic—present-day Yugoslavia—were a part of the territory belonging to Venice. Italian artists not only moved freely in this zone but many found important commissions there. MICHELOZZO DI BARTOLOMEO, for example, worked extensively in Ragusa. In return, a number of Slav artists and architects migrated into Italy. The most distinguished of these émigrés during the Renaissance was probably LUCIANO LAURANA who worked on the Ducal Palace at Urbino. Another one was Giorgio da Sebenico or Sebenik (?–1475), a sculptor and architect. As a sculptor he worked in a style that recalls that of GIOVANNI and BARTOLOMEO BON in Venice; as an architect, he tended to follow his more distinguished compatriot Laurana.

The first reference to Giorgio da Sebenico (his

family name was Orsini) appears around 1441 in Sebenik where he is noted as the *capomaestro* of the cathedral; there he may have been born around 1410. Thereafter, he is recorded as a sculptor working on an altar in Spalato (now Split) in 1448. It is not known precisely when he first came to Italy but in 1452 he probably built or carved the window frames of the Loggia dei Mercanti, Ancona, and shortly thereafter, in 1458, he built the Portal of San Agostino in the same city. In 1464, he was appointed state engineer to the republic of Ragusa, but he left after only a year. In 1465, he probably went to Urbino where he worked on the Ducal Palace under the direction of Laurana. In 1470, we find him in Rome. He died in Ancona in 1475.

The full extent of Giorgio da Sebenico's work and career has not yet been clarified. He was, most certainly, a remarkably versatile artist. His architectural style combines a highly ornamental sculptural manner with classical motifs in the manner of Urbino. For that reason, a number of otherwise undocumented works have tended to be associated with his name. For example, the Palazzo Communale, Pesaro (1470), was attributed to Giorgio da Sebenico largely on the basis of its Urbinate windows.

Giorgio da Sebenico's sculptural style, related to that of Bartolomeo Bon, is in the tradition of the Venetian High Gothic.

NICHOLAS ADAMS

WORKS

1448, Duomo (Anastasius Altar), Split, Yugoslavia. 1452–1458, Loggia dei Mercanti; 1458, Sant'Agostino (portal); Ancona, Italy. 1465–1470, Ducal Palace (with Luciano Laurana), Urbino, Italy.

GIOTTO DI BONDONE

The fame of Giotto di Bondone (1267?–1337) is associated primarily with accomplishments in the field of painting. Architecture, however, was an important consideration throughout his career. In his paintings, Giotto depicted illusionistic architectural structures with a solidity and realism remarkable for their time, and he took architectural surrounds into close account when he planned his fresco cycles. Nevertheless, it appears that Giotto came to design an actual building only toward the end of his life and that his work as an architect was limited to a single project.

Giotto was born in the village of Colle di Vespignano near Florence, Italy, and he died in Florence. Although little is known about the details of his life, contemporary and later sources indicate that Giotto's work as a painter took him to

important centers of artistic activity in Italy and possibly to Avignon in France. These travels acquainted him with key local and international artistic movements including the classicizing styles in Rome and Florence and the most modern Gothic forms in Naples and Avignon.

A document of 1334 tells that in that year Giotto was appointed architect of the cathedral in Florence and supervisor of its workshop. He does not seem to have worked on the unfinished cathedral itself (begun 1294–1296 by ARNOLFO DI CAMBIO). Instead, he initiated within the cathedral group a new project, the campanile or bell tower adjacent to the cathedral. A symbol of civic pride, the campanile was the most important architectural undertaking in Florence for two decades. Giotto, however, died long before the tower was complete, and his plan was not followed in the two successive campaigns led by Andrea Pisano (see PISANO FAMILY) and Francesco Talenti (see TALENTI FAMILY) that finally brought construction to an end.

Giotto's tenure of less than three years as *capomaestro* saw the completion of the foundations and the first story of the socle. (The bench around the base and the portal are later additions.) His overall plan seems to be represented in a drawing preserved in the Museo dell'Opera del Duomo in Siena, Italy. Although certain details of the design and decoration of the tower in the drawing have led some scholars to consider the drawing a work dating from around 1340 by an architect from Siena for an unexecuted project there, the identification of the drawing with Giotto's project is well supported. Not only is the first story of the campanile socle in Florence reproduced almost exactly in the drawing, but the drawing is also closely related to the paintings of Giotto; the clarity of style and the conservatism of the tower design are more in accord with architecture in Florence than with the intricately decorated Gothic style favored in architecture in Siena around this time and the influence of the drawing is traceable in Florence. Indeed, the drawing may be a near contemporary copy, perhaps by a Sienese artist, of a lost original by Giotto.

Both the drawing and the campanile socle show that Giotto responded both to the reverence for local tradition in architecture and to the ambition that characterized major projects in Florence in the fourteenth century. Thus, although the basic form of Giotto's campanile shaft adhered to established patterns for tower design in Florence, Giotto modernized and elaborated the type by incorporating ideas from disparate sources, and he conceived of the bell tower on a colossal scale. The classicizing decoration of the earlier buildings in the cathedral group—the baptistery (c.1060–1150) and the cathedral—was a major source for the campanile shaft. Giotto's design is particularly close to the work of Arnolfo di Cambio, yet Giotto transformed the strict classicism of Arnolfo's cathedral into a richer, more overtly Gothic style that seems partly dependent on his knowledge of another project of several decades earlier, the façade of the cathedral in Siena (begun 1284), designed by Giovanni Pisano. Giotto's interest in the latest Gothic developments is demonstrated in the striking form of the belfry in the Siena drawing. Its arrangement of octagon, spire, and pinnacles is closely related to contemporary French and German structures, whose designs may have been transmitted through works in the minor arts. Nevertheless, the drawing shows these forms well integrated with the design of the shaft.

Although a synthesis of Gothic and classical forms was typical of fourteenth-century architecture in Tuscany, the pictorial character and arrangement of these elements in Giotto's campanile project are striking. Giotto's ideas as an architect were shaped by long experience in his primary occupation as a painter. Various details of the socle and the Siena drawing are prefigured in his paintings and in those of his contemporaries, and a painter's interest in color is demonstrated by the lively tricolor decoration achieved by the introduction of a generous amount of pink into the stark green and white marble incrustation which characterizes the earlier buildings in the cathedral group. In addition, the overall organization, based on enframing elements that establish a grid system, is closely analogous to that of his fresco cycles.

Even though only a small part of Giotto's project was actually built, both that part and his design as represented in the Siena drawing had some influence in Florence after his death. The later campanile projects by Andrea Pisano and Francesco Talenti show this most clearly, but even the quasi-architectural tabernacle at Or San Michele designed in the early 1350s by ANDREA DI CIONE ORCAGNA reflects Giotto's plan for the bell tower.

Giotto is sometimes associated with the design of buildings other than the campanile, but all such attributions seem controversial at best. Although the same document that names Giotto architect of the cathedral group in Florence also appoints him city architect, no existing structures apart from the campanile can be connected with him there. Indeed, Giotto would have had little time to devote to other architectural projects, since during his brief term of office, in addition to his responsibilities for the bell tower, he worked for a time at the behest of the government of Florence on an unspecified project at the court of Milan. Giotto's role as city architect may in fact have been merely

Giotto Di Bondone. Campanile of the Cathedral. Florence. c.1334

advisory or even honorary. It is significant that no contemporary reference to Giotto, including the document that gives him architectural authority in Florence, refers to work on earlier architectural projects. The proud city of Florence had no architect of international stature in the early 1330s, and it seems likely that Giotto's assignment to the most important architectural project there was largely due to his acknowledged pre-eminence among Florentine artists.

KAREN CHRISTIAN

BIBLIOGRAPHY

GIOSEFFI, DECIO 1963 *Giotto architetto.* Milan: Edizioni di Comunità.
KREYTENBERG, GERT 1978 "Der Campanile von Giotto." *Mitteilungen des kunsthistorischen Institutes in Florenz* 22:147–184.
PAATZ, WALTER 1937 *Werden und Wesen der Trecento-Architektur in Toskana.* Burg, Germany: Hopfer.
TRACHTENBERG, MARVIN 1971 *The Campanile of Florence Cathedral: Giotto's Tower.* New York University Press.

GIOVANNONI, GUSTAVO

Gustavo Giovannoni (1873–1947), architect, teacher, and historian of architecture, pursued a long career as one of the principal figures in the cultural life of Rome in the first half of the twentieth century. Soon after taking his degree in civil engineering in 1895, he became assistant to GUGLIELMO CALDERINI at the Engineering School in the course of general architecture, a material he taught as professor beginning in 1905. His own activity as architect is of minor importance; much more significant are his contributions to the major Italian periodicals of art and architecture, in which he published studies in ancient Roman construction techniques and in medieval, Renaissance, and modern architecture. He also published numerous books on these subjects. Giovannoni's initiatives in the cultural field are also noteworthy. He was one of the founders of the Roman Association of the Cultivators of Architecture, founder in 1921 with MARCELLO PIACENTINI of the magazine *Architettura e Arti Decorative,* and founder of the magazine *Palladio* in 1937. He was also president of the Accademia di San Luca and was a member of the Accademia d'Italia. In 1935, he founded the Center for the Study of the History of Architecture, and for almost thirty years he was a member of the Higher Council of the General Direction of Antiquities and Fine Arts.

In 1931, he founded the School of Architecture of the University of Rome and he was dean of the school from 1931 to 1935. During that time, he banned all magazines on modern architecture from the school library and determined the general reactionary outlook of the school. Giovannoni taught restoration of monuments there until his death in 1947. His antiromantic theory of restoration, as opposed to that of EUGÈNE EMMANUEL VIOLLET-LE-DUC, permitted no new interpretive interventions by the restorer, but insisted rather on the careful preservation of the original intentions of the architect.

Giovannoni adamantly opposed the gutting of the Spina del Borgo quarter in Rome in the 1930s to make way for the present Via della Conciliazione; he reported that he had risked exile by the Fascist government for his views. Yet, in spite of his theoretical pretensions regarding the preservation of the environment, Giovannoni was involved in some of the most devastating destruction of Rome's urban fabric. A member of most of the government building commissions, he approved destruction of large parts of the capital during the 1920s and 1930s. One of his own proposals for redesigning the city was the plan of Rome he presented with the *La Burbera* group in 1929 at the exhibition of master plans. Giovannoni's project would have destroyed a large segment of baroque Rome to make way for two monumental avenues and a major piazza, all dotted with Babylonia-inspired buildings.

Giovannoni's illustrious career as critic, historian, and teacher was unfortunately marred by his support of the monumentalist architectural initiatives of both Hitler and Mussolini and by a violent opposition to the Modern movement.

ELLEN R. SHAPIRO

WORKS

1907–1911, Piazza Caprera Quarter; 1909, Peroni Beer Factory; 1913, Peroni Beer Company Buildings; 1920, Aniene Garden City Master Plan (with others); 1920, Garbatella Quarter, Piazza B. Brin, Via Guglielmotti (with others); 1924, Church of the Guardian Angels; Rome.

BIBLIOGRAPHY

CEDERNA, ANTONIO 1979 *Mussolini Urbanista: Lo sventramento di Roma negli anni del consenso.* Bari, Italy: Laterza.
CURUNI, ALESSANDRO 1979 *Riordino delle Carte di Gustavo Giovannoni.* Rome: Multigrafica.
DE ANGELIS D'OSSAT, GUGLIELMO 1949 *Gustavo Giovannoni: Storico e Critico dell'Architettura.* Rome: Istituto di Studi Romani.
MARINO, ROBERTO 1948 "Giovannoni." *Bassegna Critica di Architettura* 1, no. 1:4.
ZEVI, BRUNO (1950)1975 *Storia dell'architettura moderna.* 5th ed., rev. Turin, Italy: Einaudi.

GIRAL FAMILY

Etienne Giral (1665–1740s?). Born in Montpellier, France, Etienne began the construction of the famous Peyrou Promenade (1717–1718) for the installation of the Louis XIV statue.

Jean Giral (1679–1753). Younger brother of Etienne, Jean designed the Chapel of the Royal College of Jesuits (1707) and the Chapel of the General Hospital (1751), both in Montpellier. In the two chapels, he combined Doric and Ionic pilasters in one and Ionic and Corinthian details in the other. His design for the Market of the Poissonnerie (1748) is reminiscent of a Greek temple of the Tuscan order.

His work took a less monumental quality in private hôtels. For both of his major commissions, the Château de la Mosson (1723–1729) and the Palais Episcopal (1723), also in Montpellier, he animated the main façades in a departure from the neoclassicism of the period, developing a style with flat arcades, pleasant sculptures, broken flight stairways (*escaliers brisés*), and vernacular elements.

Jean-Antoine Giral (1720–1787). Etienne Giral's son, Jean-Antoine continued the embellishment of the Peyrou Promenade which became known throughout Europe. From 1767 to 1774, he modified the arcades of the Peyrou aqueduct and integrated terraces to the lower gardens. During this period, he designed the famous Peyrou Water Tower ornamented with sculpted fishing nets. The Peyrou Water Tower belongs to the major monuments of the Louis XVI style.

Named official architect of the Languedoc States, Jean-Antoine became influential in the south of France.

Jacques Donnat (1742–1824). Son-in-law of and taught by Jean-Antoine Giral, Jacques Donnat continued the family's practice and became city architect. He is best known for his design of the Halles aux Colonnes in Montpellier.

MARC DILET

WORKS
ETIENNE GIRAL
1717–1718, Peyrou Promenade; 1744, Halles aux Herbes et aux Poissons; Montpellier, France.

JEAN GIRAL
1707–1748, Chapel, Collège des Jesuites; 1723, Palais Episcopal; 1723–1729, Château du la Mosson; 1741–1753, Chapel of the General Hospital (not completed until 1756 by Jacques Nogaret); 1748, Hôtel Cambacéres-Murales (now Guerre); 1748, Hôtel du Trésorier de la Bourse; 1748, Marché de la Poissonnerie; Montpellier, France.

JEAN-ANTOINE GIRAL
1752–1757, Hôtel Saint Come (now Collège du Chirurgie); 1767–1774, Peyrou Promenade, Aqueduct, and Water Tower; 1773, Hôtel Granier (now Grasset-Morel); 1773, Villa Haguenot (now Azais); Montpellier, France.

BIBLIOGRAPHY
GIRAL, ETIENNE, and GIRAL, JEAN-ANTOINE 1767 *Mémoires pour la Ville et Port de Cette.* Montpellier, France: Picot.

GIRARDIN, RENE LOUIS

An aristocrat and an amateur and patron of the arts, the Marquis de Girardin (1735–1808) attended the court of Stanislaus Leszcynski in the late 1750s, where he saw the exiled Polish king's fantastic gardens, and was in England, Italy, and Germany in the early 1760s. Inheriting the estate of Ermenonville in France in 1762, he redesigned it as a Rousseauesque model of conditions reflecting economic prosperity and social order. His design for the estate is a major example of the early French picturesque garden. Here Girardin blended pictorial "scenes" with nature. Despite the influence of Jean-Jacques Rousseau and of CLAUDE-HENRI WATELET, his treatise on gardening (1777) is con-

cerned mainly with a description of the technical means by which aesthetic effects could be achieved.

DORA WIEBENSON

WORK
1762–c.1778, Ermenonville Estate, France.

BIBLIOGRAPHY
GIRARDIN, RENÉ LOUIS (1777)1979 *De la composition des paysages.* Edited by M. H. Conan. Paris: An English translation by D. Molthus, *An Essay on Landscape,* was published in London in 1783.
GIRARDIN, STANISLAS 1788 *Promenade, ou Itinéraire des Jardins d'Ermenonville.* Paris: Mérigot.
MARTIN-DECAEN, ANDRÉ 1912 *Le dernier ami de J.-J. Rousseau: Le Marquis René de Girardin (1735–1808).* Paris: Perrin.
WIEBENSON, DORA 1978 Pages 70–75, 81–88 in *The Picturesque Garden in France.* N.J.: Princeton University Press.

GIRAULT, CHARLES-LOUIS

Charles-Louis Girault (1851–1932) was born in Cosne, France, and studied under M. Daumet. He received the Prix Jay in 1875, the Prix Jean Leclère and Rougevin in 1888, and the coveted Grand Prix de Rome in 1880. His work is typical of the grand and decorative classicism popular at the end of the nineteenth century and the beginning of the twentieth. Among Girault's most monumental structures, his Tomb of Louis Pasteur at the Pasteur Institute in Paris (1896) is built with huge slabs of colored marble and adorned with elaborate early Christian mosaics. Girault's Petit Palais built for the 1900 Paris exhibition is also heroic as it

Girault.
Arc du Cinquantenaire.
Brussels.
1905

Girault.
Musée du Congo Belge.
Tervueren, Belgium.
1904–1911

evokes the traditional grand manner of French seventeenth-century classicism on the outside combined with a less austere decorative interior. He also designed the Arc du Cinquantenaire in Brussels (1905) and the Musée du Congo Belge at Tervueren near Brussels (1904–1911).

PETER L. DONHAUSER

WORKS

*1889, Palais d'Hygiène; *1889, Palais de la Chambre de Commerce; International Exhibition, Paris. 1896, Tomb of Louis Pasteur, Pasteur Institute; 1900, Petit Palais, International Exhibition; Paris. 1904, Royal Palace of Laeken (additions), Brussels. 1904–1911, Musée du Congo Belge, Tervueren, Belgium. 1905, Arc du Cinquantenaire, Brussels.

BIBLIOGRAPHY

GIRAULT, CHARLES-LOUIS 1921 "The Franco-British Union of Architects." *Architectural Review* 50:113–117.
LOUVET, A. 1933 "Charles Girault." *L'Architecture* 46:253–262.
WORDSDALE, DERRICK 1978 "The Petit Palais des Champs-Elysées; Architecture and Decoration." *Apollo* 106:207–211.

GISORS FAMILY

The Gisors family of Parisian architects included Jacques Pierre Gisors (1755–1818); his cousin Alexandre Jean Baptiste Guy de Gisors (1762–1835); Guy's nephew, Alphonse Henry de Gisors (1796–1866); and Alphonse's grandson, Louis Henry Georges Scellier de Gisors (1844–1905). They all studied architecture in the schools of the French Academy and served in the national buildings service. Their work continued the French classical tradition. Jacques, Guy, and Alphonse distinguished themselves by providing assembly rooms for legislative bodies in the Palais des Tuileries, the Palais Bourbon, and the Palais du Luxembourg in Paris. Guy and Alphonse also designed many public buildings in the provinces.

RICHARD CLEARY

WORKS

JACQUES PIERRE GISORS
*1793, Assembly Hall, Convention Nationale, Palais des Tuileries; 1795–1797, Assembly Hall, Conseil des Cinq-Cents (now the Chambre des Deputes), Palais Bourbon; Paris.

GUY DE GISORS
1810, Church of Saint Vincent, Mâcon, France.

ALPHONSE DE GISORS
c.1828, Hôtel de la Prefecture; c.1828, Hôtel de Ville; Ajaccio, Corsica. 1836–1840, Palais du Luxembourg (remodeling); 1838–1843, Ecole de Médecine (clinics); 1841–1847, Ecole Normale Supérieure; Paris.

LOUIS SCELLIER DE GISORS
1882, Postal Warehouse, Paris.

BIBLIOGRAPHY

FOUCART, BRUNO, and NOËL-BOUTON, VÉRONIQUE 1971 "Les projets d'église pour Napoléonville (1802–1809) de Guy de Chabol à Guy de Gisors." *Bulletin de la Société de l'Histoire de l'Art Français.* 1971:235–252.
GISORS, ALPHONSE HENRY DE 1847 *Le palais du Luxembourg, fondé par Marie de Médicis regents, considérablement agrandi sous le règne de Louis Philippe I*ᵉʳ. Paris: Plon.
HAUTECOEUR, LOUIS 1953–1955 Volumes 5 and 6 in *Histoire de l'architecture classique en France.* Paris: Picard.
JOYANT, EDOUARD 1937 "Les Gisors: Architectes." *Bulletin de la Société de l'Histoire de l'Art Français* 1937:270–293.

GIULIO ROMANO

Giulio Pippi, known as Giulio Romano (¿1499–1546), was the most gifted of RAPHAEL's assistants and a major figure in Italian art and architecture during the late Renaissance. A painter as well as an architect, like Raphael, Giulio was raised in the architectural traditions of the High Renaissance with its sophisticated knowledge of classical antiquity and its balanced interdependence of structure and ornament. Giulio chose not to imitate High Renaissance style, but rather to embellish and elaborate its themes. With BALDASSARE PERUZZI and MICHELE SANMICHELI, Giulio formed a group of architects, sometimes called Mannerists, who violated the classical norms derived from antiquity and perfected by Raphael and DONATO BRAMANTE. Although Giulio's major work was done in Mantua in northern Italy, he was the first Renaissance artist of note born in Rome.

Giulio was probably apprenticed to Raphael when quite young; by 1514 he is recorded as Raphael's assistant in the Vatican, working on the Stanza dell'Incendio frescoes. As a painter Giulio took progressively a more prominent role in Raphael's shop and on his master's death in April 1520, he inherited his major commissions. The beginning of Giulio's independent career as an artist and an architect may be dated from the death of Raphael.

The Villa Lante al Gianicolo in Rome, completed by Giulio in 1523, was begun by Raphael in 1518. The most imposing of his buildings in Rome, however, is the Palazzo Maccarani in Piazza

Sant'Eustachio (c.1520–1524). The combination of the classical orders with the rusticated base is typical of the Roman High Renaissance and recalls buildings like Bramante's Palazzo Caprini or Raphael's Palazzo Alberini, but the forms are expressed in quite a different way. The windows of the second story, for instance, rest precariously on the string course, not over the rusticated piers as would be classically correct. On the third story, the "pilasters" have no capitals. Are they true pilasters, and thus apparently load-bearing, or are they merely decorative strips or panels? Giulio's skill at weaving together these ambiguities without entirely disrupting the Renaissance character of the façade suggests a degree of playfulness that marks his distance from the more sober balance between structure and ornament of the High Renaissance.

In 1524, Giulio Romano was invited to Mantua by Duke Federico Gonzaga. Giulio built his masterpiece, the Palazzo del Tè (1525–1532). On the Isola del Tè, in the low-lying lake country outside Mantua, it seems to have been the duke's original intention to provide a hideaway for himself and his mistress, but the project grew so that on two occasions Giulio had to change and expand the plans.

What stands today is a low four-sided structure enclosing an open courtyard. The exterior appears to be a pilaster façade of a conventional High Renaissance type, much like Bramante's Belvedere Courtyard in the Vatican in Rome. On closer inspection, however, it is apparent that the symmetry of the orders conflicts with the body of the palace and that the orders have been laid on, leaving a margin of the building at the edge. Although this conflict has been interpreted by Nikolaus Pevsner (1946), Ernst Gombrich (1934–1935), and Frederick Hartt (1958) as an example of Giulio's rejection of the classical tradition, recent evidence by Egon Verheyen (1977) and Kurt Forster and Richard J. Tuttle (1974) strongly suggests that Giulio was required to incorporate the window

openings of the pre-existing villa and did so with as little irregularity as he could manage. Rather than demonstrating Giulio's rejection of the classical style, these new arguments seek to prove that Giulio did all that he could to adhere to classical principles.

Where Giulio seems to have in fact played with the classical rules is in the vestibule of the main entry. There one finds a sophisticated blending of classical sources, the coffers from the Basilica of Maxentius in Rome, and the plan from Fra Giocondo's edition of Vitruvius of 1511 (Lotz & Heydenreich, 1974). Yet despite this erudition, note that Giulio has left the columns in their roughened state, as if awaiting the mason's chisel. The contrast of refined elegance and rude unfinished form continues in the courtyard. There Giulio alternates rusticated surfaces and fine ashlars in a haphazard design. This kind of play is carried even further on two of the sides of the courtyard where triglyphs appear to be falling out from the entablature.

Giulio Romano.
Giulio Romano House.
Mantua, Italy.
1538–1544

Giulio Romano.
Palazzo del Tè.
Mantua, Italy.
1525–1532

Giulio Romano.
Palazzo del Tè.
Mantua, Italy.
1525–1532

Some scholars have seen this too as a deliberate attack on the classical conventions and thus call it troubling, perplexing, and disturbing (Pevsner, Gombrich, Hartt). More recent scholarship (notably Verheyen) has tended to see these motifs as witty, possibly intended to evoke humorously the rushed nature of construction. It is probable that this kind of allusive architectural humor for the initiates is intended to correspond to the iconographic complexity of Giulio's fresco decoration in the rooms of the palace.

Federico's pleasure at the Palazzo del Tè was demonstrated by the many honors he bestowed on Giulio. In June 1526 Giulio was named a citizen of Mantua and given a house. In August of the same year he was made a nobleman. He was also made responsible for all Gonzaga buildings in Mantuan territory and many simple structures in the area, such as the Peschiara or Fish Market (1530) in Mantua, bear the mark of Giulio's hand.

Giulio made a number of additions to the Gonzaga city residence, the Palazzo Ducale in Mantua. A small palace was built there for Federico's wife (1531), as well as a backdrop for theatrical performances and tournaments, the Estivale in the Cortile della Cavallerizza (1538–1539). The Estivale's elevation is based, once again, on Bramante's Palazzo Caprini, but the twisted columns recalling the Solomonic columns at Saint Peter's in Rome and the segmental arches on the third story suggest a kind of dynamic series of pressures forced one against the other. Once again, the stable harmony of the High Renaissance has been turbulently disturbed.

With the death of Federico Gonzaga in 1540, the regent Cardinal Enrico Gonzaga continued the patronage of Giulio Romano. Giulio was put to work largely on ecclesiastical projects, notably restorations of the cathedral in Mantua (1544–1546) and the abbey of Saint Benedetto al Polirone (1540–1546).

Giulio was frequently called to neighboring towns or to Ferrara and Bologna for architectural consultations. In Bologna he proposed a façade for the Gothic Church of San Petronio (1546) which was not built. He was also invited to Vicenza to propose a resystematization of the market square (1542) later completed by ANDREA PALLADIO. While in Vicenza he may have left drawings for the Palazzo Thiene; its Roman manner suggests Giulio more than the youthful Palladio to whom it has traditionally been attributed.

It is true that Giulio Romano was better known as a painter than as an architect; engravings of his Mantuan frescoes in the Palazzo del Tè and elsewhere spread his fame quickly to northern Europe. He is the only artist of the Italian Renaissance mentioned in the works of William Shakespeare ("Winter's Tale," V, ii). If anything, Giulio's fame has increased in the modern age. His nonconformity has been perceived as a symbol of protest by modern architects as well as a source of inspiration to contemporary architects like ROBERT VENTURI who value what they perceive, sometimes incorrectly, as his ambiguities of form.

NICHOLAS ADAMS

WORKS

c.1520–1524, Palazzo Maccarani; *1521, Giulio Romano House; completed 1523, Villa Lante al Gianicolo; Rome. *1524–1538, Castle at Marmirolo (additions); 1525–1532, Palazzo del Tè; c.1530, Pescheria; c.1530, 12–13 Piazza Broletto; c.1530, 22 Via Carlo Poma; c.1530, 2 Via Solferino; *1531, Palazzina della Paleologa; 1533–1549, Porta della Cittadella; 1538–1539, Estivale, Palazzo Ducale; 1538–1544, Giulio Romano House; Mantua, Italy. 1540–1546, Abbey of San Benedetto al Polirone (restoration), near Mantua, Italy. 1542, Palazzo Thiene (completed by Andrea Palladio), Vicenza, Italy. 1544–1546, Cathedral (restoration), Mantua, Italy.

BIBLIOGRAPHY

FORSTER, KURT, and TUTTLE, RICHARD J.   1974   "The Palazzo del Tè." *Journal of the Society of Architectural Historians* 30:267–293.

GOMBRICH, ERNST   1934–1935   "Zum Werk Giulio Romanos." *Jahrbuch der Kunstsammlungen Wien* 8:79; 9:121.

HARTT, FREDERICK   1958   *Giulio Romano.* 2 vols. Northford, Conn.: Elliots Books.

LOTZ, WOLFGANG, and HEYDENREICH, LUDWIG   1974   *Architecture in Italy 1400–1600.* Harmondsworth, England: Pelican.

PEVSNER, NIKOLAUS   1946   "The Architecture of Mannerism." Pages 116–137 in Cecil Grayson (editor), *The Mint.* London: Routledge.

Giulio Romano.
Estivale, Palazzo Ducale.
Mantua, Italy.
1538–1539

VERHEYEN, EGON 1977 *The Palazzo del Tè in Mantua: Images of Love and Politics.* Baltimore: Johns Hopkins University Press.

GIURGOLA, ROMALDO

See MITCHELL and GIURGOLA.

GOČÁR, JOSEF

Josef Gočár (1880–1945) was an outstanding representative of the avant-garde generation of cubists in Czechoslovakia. From 1923 until his death, he taught architecture at the Academy of Fine Arts in Prague. A follower of JAN KOTĚRA's Modern school, he prepared and propagated the program of cubism in architecture. Together with PAVEL JANÁK and OTAKAR NOVOTNÝ, he formed a trio of the most important architects and pedagogues of the post-Kotěra generation who, through their work and personal example, prepared the soil for the brilliant period of Czech functionalism between the two world wars.

VLADIMÍR ŠLAPETA

WORKS

1909–1910, Wenke Department Store, Jaroměř, Czechoslovakia. 1911–1912, Black Virgin Mary House, Prague. 1911–1912, Sanatorium, Bohdaneč, Czechoslovakia. 1921–1923, Czechoslovak Legion Bank, Prague. 1923–1924, Tannery School, Hradec Králové, Czechoslovakia. 1924–1925, Czechoslovak State Pavilion, Paris. 1924–1927, School Complex, Hradec Králové, Czechoslovakia. 1925–1926, Agricultural Education House, Prague. 1926–1927, Ambrož Choir House; 1927–1932, Czechoslovak Railways Administration; Hradec Králové Czechoslovakia. 1927–1933, Saint Venceslas Church, Vršovice District; 1932–1933, Czechoslovak Werkbund Housing Estate (three villas), Baba District; Prague.

BIBLIOGRAPHY

BENEŠOVÁ, MARIE 1958 *Josef Gočár.* Prague: Nakladatelství československých výtvarných umělců.

BENEŠOVÁ, MARIE 1971 *Josef Gočár.* Prague. Exhibition catalogue.

GOČÁR, JOSEF 1930 *Josef Gočár.* With an introduction by Zdeněk Wirth. Geneva: Meister der Baukunst.

GODDE, ETIENNE HYPPOLITE

A French architect born in Breteuil (Oise), France, Etienne Hyppolite Godde (1781–1869) studied at the Ecole des Beaux-Arts in Paris. Awarded the second Grand Prix of architecture in 1800, he worked in the Seine district and was chief architect of the city of Paris from 1813 to 1848. From 1806, Godde was mostly involved with restorations and extensions of religious buildings. He designed several new churches using basilical plans, as for Notre Dame de Bonne Nouvelle (1823–1830) and Saint Pierre du Gros Caillou (1822), both in Paris. His most important work is the Seminary of Saint Sulpice (1820–1838) for which he used only traditional arched windows. He collaborated with J. B. C. LESUEUR on the extension of the Paris City Hall between 1840 and 1845.

MARC DILET

WORKS

1820–1838, Chapel and Seminary, Saint Sulpice; 1820–1838, Private Residence, Rue de Londres; 1822, Saint Pierre du Gros Caillou; 1823–1830, Notre Dame de Bonne Nouvelle; 1823–1835, Saint Denis du Saint Sacrement; 1823–1835, Saint Pierre de Chaillot Church and Presbytery; 1840–1845, City Hall (extension); 1840–1845, Père Lachaise and Montparnasse Cemeteries (entrance doors); Paris. n.d., Church in Boves, Picardie, France.

GODEFROY, MAXIMILIAN

Maximilian Godefroy (1765–1840?), who spent fourteen years in the United States as an exile from the Napoleonic regime, was one of several foreign-born architects who helped introduce modern European ideas to the young nation. During his stay (1805–1819) through the later Federal period, he was connected with much of the advanced monumental building undertaken in the city of Baltimore. Of his projects for other American cities, only those for Richmond, Virginia, where he resided briefly in 1816, and Bardstown, Kentucky, were carried out.

Born in Paris of middle-class parents, Godefroy received a good education, including some instruction in drawing and perhaps in engineering. He began a self-education in architecture shortly before he left France, a process he continued in America. JACQUES FRANÇOIS BLONDEL's *Cours d'architecture* (1771–1777) supplied Godefroy with much of his theory; from personal observation and from other books, especially JEAN-NICOLAS-LOUIS DURAND's *Précis des leçons d'architecture* (1802–1805), he acquired the compositional methods and forms recently developed in France.

In America, Godefroy's relationship with the English trained BENJAMIN HENRY LATROBE reinforced his neoclassical taste and facilitated his adaptation to American practices. Working largely for Baltimore's influential upper class, Godefroy advanced the cause of professional architects in

Godefroy.
Saint Mary's Chapel.
Baltimore.
1806–1808

Godefroy.
Unitarian Church.
Baltimore.
1817–1818

America, joining his efforts with those of Latrobe to overcome the xenophobia of local mechanics and native-born builder-architects. His works included several building types: commercial, ecclesiastical, governmental, commemorative. Usually with some simplification, he adopted the compositional principles of French neoclassicism, using such favored motifs as the light, open entrance void and the solid, rectilinear, essentially horizontal block. Because of their self-sufficiency and isolation, several of his buildings might have been constructed in France a generation earlier.

In addition, Godefroy's structures were imbued with specific symbolic meanings derived from Blondellian theories, a characteristic which is confirmed and clarified by comparison with his allegorical sculpture and engravings. In Baltimore, the thin, curvilinear Gothicism of Saint Mary's Chapel (1806–1808) gave it a femininity appropriate for a building dedicated to the Virgin; the simple, bold forms and Tuscan order of the Unitarian Church (1817–1818) endowed it with a masculinity; the commemorative nature of the Battle Monument (1815–1825) resided in its Egyptian elements. Godefroy's eclecticism was thus linked closely to eighteenth-century ideas on the expression of architectural character, and can be seen as preceding the major nineteenth-century revivals in America.

Living beyond his means and exercising a witty, but caustic tongue, Godefroy, in the end, exhausted his credit and his friendships, and in 1819 he and his wife left America for England, where she expected a legacy. After several years of limited activity there, he was back in France by 1827, where he received a small Royalist pension and architectural appointments in Brittany and Normandy. Extant buildings demonstrate his ability to work in an acceptable Durandesque manner. Nothing is known of him after a letter dated at Laval, France, on August 25, 1840.

ROBERT L. ALEXANDER

WORKS

1806–1808, Saint Mary's Chapel; *1812–1813, Commercial and Farmers Bank; Baltimore. 1812–1813, Saint Thomas' Church, Bardstown, Ky. *1812–1822, Masonic Hall; 1813–1815, First Presbyterian Churchyard (gates and vaults); 1814, Fort McHenry (sallyport); 1815–1825, Battle Monument; Baltimore. *1816–?, Courthouse; *1816–1830, Capitol Square; Richmond, Va. 1817–1818, Unitarian Church, Baltimore. *1825–1826, Catholic Charities School, London. 1829–1833, Palais de Justice (restoration and new wing), Laval, France. 1829–1836, Hospice des Aliénés, Nayenne, France. 1831–1840, Préfecture (entrance, auxiliary buildings, and restoration), Laval, France.

BIBLIOGRAPHY

ALEXANDER, ROBERT L. 1958a "The Drawings and Allegories of Maximilian Godefroy." *Maryland Historical Magazine* 53:17–33.
ALEXANDER, ROBERT L. 1958b "The Public Memorial and Godefroy's Battle Monument." *Journal of the Society of Architectural Historians* 17:19–24.
ALEXANDER, ROBERT L. 1974 *The Architecture of Maximilian Godefroy.* Baltimore: Johns Hopkins University Press.
BLONDEL, JACQUES FRANÇOIS 1771–1777 *Cours d'architecture, ou Traité de la décoration, distribution et construction des bâtiments.* 12 vols. in 6 vols. Paris: Desaint.
DAVISON, CAROLINA V. 1934 "Maximilian and Eliza Godefroy." *Maryland Historical Magazine* 29:1–20.
DURAND, JEAN-NICOLAS-LOUIS 1802–1805 *Précis des leçons d'architecture données à l'Ecole Polytechnique.* 2 vols. Paris: Barnard and the author.
QUYNN, DOROTHY M. 1957 "Maximilian and Eliza Godefroy." *Maryland Historical Magazine* 52:1–34.

GODWIN, EDWARD WILLIAM

Son of a Bristol currier turned painter–decorator, Edward William Godwin (1833–1886) began his career under William Armstrong, city engineer of Bristol. He established his own practice in 1853, but his works were unimportant until he won the Northampton Town Hall Competition in 1861. Godwin left Bristol in 1865 to set up practice in London and soon after began to design domestic furniture. Later he also became deeply involved in stage design and production, although never quite giving up architecture. In his early career he admired GEORGE GILBERT SCOTT and was very friendly with WILLIAM BURGES; some of his Gothic architecture reveals their influence. Later he moved in Whistler's Bohemian circle and designed many novel studio houses.

JOHN O'CALLAGHAN

WORKS

1857, Warehouse, Merchant Street, Bristol, England. 1857–1860, Saint Baithin's Roman Catholic Church, Saint Johnston, County Donegal, Ireland. 1860, Perry's Carriage Manufactory (later Anderson's Warehouse), Stokes Croft, Bristol, England. 1861–1864, Northampton Town Hall, England. 1864–1866, Congleton Town Hall, England. 1865, Saint Martin's Villas, 43–44 Billing Road; Northampton, England. 1867–1868, Castle Ashby (entrance lodges and garden wall), Northamptonshire, England. 1867–1868, Rheinfelden, Billing Road, Northampton, England. 1867–1870, Dromore Castle, County Limerick, Ireland. 1867–1870, Glenbeigh Towers, County Kerry, Ireland. 1871, House, Fallows Green, Harpenden, England. 1871–1874, Beauvale House (gate lodge and farmhouses); 1873–1874, Cottages and Rectory, Moor Green; Nottinghamshire, England. 1876, Corner Houses and Semidetached Pairs, Bedford Park, Chiswick; 1877–1878, Whistler Studio, Chelsea; 1878, Frank Miles Studio House, Chelsea; 1878, Princess Louise Studio, Kensington Palace; 1881, Fine Art Society's Gallery (new front and entrance); 1881–1885, Tower House, Chelsea; London. 1882, Shuttleworth House, Dallington Park, Northampton, England. 1884, McLean's Fine Art Gallery (new front and entrance), 7 Haymarket; 1884, Oscar Wilde House (decoration), 16 Tite Street; London.

BIBLIOGRAPHY

ASLIN, ELIZABETH 1969 *The Aesthetic Movement: Prelude to Art Nouveau*. New York: Praeger.
BENCE-JONES, MARK 1964 "An Aesthete's Irish Castle: Dromore Castle, Co. Limerick." *Country Life* 136:1274–1277.
GIROUARD, MARK (1971)1979 "Beauvale Lodge, Nottinghamshire." Pages 147–149 in *The Victorian Country House*. Rev. ed. New Haven: Yale University Press.
GIROUARD, MARK 1972 "Chelsea's Bohemian Studio Houses: The Victorian Artist at Home—Part 2." *Country Life* 152:1370–1374.
GODWIN, E. W. 1878 "On Some Buildings I have Designed." *The British Architect and Northern Engineer* 10:210–212.
GREEVES, T. AFFLECK 1967 "London's First Garden Suburb: Bedford Park, Chiswick—Part 1." *Country Life* 142:1524–1529.
HARBRON, DUDLEY 1949 *The Conscious Stone: The Life of Edward William Godwin*. London: Latimer House.
O'CALLAGHAN, JOHN 1976 "The Fine Art Society and E. W. Godwin." *Fine Art Society Centenary Catalogue* 1976:5–9.

GODWIN, GEORGE

George Godwin (1813–1888) was an English architect, archeologist, and journalist, but he was best known as the influential editor of *The Builder* from 1844–1883. He was articled to his father George Godwin from 1826 to 1835, worked on his own, and later practiced in partnership with his brother Henry. He wrote many books and was an effective antislum crusader.

MARGARET RICHARDSON

WORKS

*1840–1841, Brompton National School, Kensington, London. 1847, Church of Saint Mary (restoration), Ware, Hertfordshire, England. 1849, Church of Saint Mary Boltons, Kensington, London. 1849–1867, Church of Saint Mary Redcliffe (restoration); 1853, Redcliffe Infants' School and Residence, Pile Street; 1855, Walls Court Farm, Stoke Gifford; 1860, Stanley Farm; Bristol, England. 1867, Rockhurst (with Henry Godwin), West Hoathly, Sussex, England. 1867, Elmdale (with Godwin), Clifton Downs, Bristol, England. 1868–1869, Church of All Saints (with Godwin), Little Munden, Hertfordshire, England. 1870, Church of Saint Jude, Collingham Road; 1871, Redcliffe Mansions, Kensington; 1874, Church of Saint Luke, Redcliffe Square; London.

BIBLIOGRAPHY

GODWIN, GEORGE 1835 "The Nature and Properties of Concrete." *Transactions of the Royal Institute of British Architects* 1, part 1:3–37.
GODWIN, GEORGE 1838–1839 *The Churches of London*. 2 vols. London: C.TiH.
GODWIN, GEORGE 1851 *London Shadows*. London.
GODWIN, GEORGE 1853 *History in Ruins*. London: Chapman & Hall.
KING, ANTHONY 1976 "Architectural Journalism and the Profession: The Early Years of George Godwin." *Architectural History* 19:32–53.
"Obituary." 1888 *The Builder* 54:75–77, 101.

GOFF, BRUCE

Bruce Alonzo Goff (1904–1982) is one of the most inventive architects in the history of American architecture. His work is intrinsically significant for its spatial creativity and historically significant as a link between that of A. J. DOWNING and

FRANK LLOYD WRIGHT on one hand and the circle led by ROBERT VENTURI and CHARLES W. MOORE on the other.

Born in Alton, Kansas, Goff received no formal architectural education. Instead, he was apprenticed to the Tulsa, Oklahoma, firm of Rush, Endacott and Rush when he was twelve years old. He was designing buildings for the firm by 1919, when he was fifteen and was made a full partner in 1929, having elected to remain with the firm rather than to attend college. From the beginning he was strongly influenced by Frank Lloyd Wright, his mentor and later close friend. This is apparent in the Graves Summer House (1919) near Los Angeles, his first design to be built and one that closely resembles Wright's summer cottages of the early 1900s. It also initiates Goff's frequent use of a symmetrical, centrally focused plan.

Beginning in the 1920s, while still in his late teens, Goff sought other visual models from a variety of books and periodicals. A wide range of influences is consequently reflected in his Tulsa work of this period, including the Austrian Secession in the Robinson Studio (1923–1926), LOUIS H. SULLIVAN and the Prairie school in the Boston Avenue Methodist–Episcopal Church (1926–1929), the Dutch Expressionists in the Page Warehouse (1927–1928), and even the International style in the Riverside Studio (1928–1929). In most instances, he skillfully assimilated these influences so that specific sources rarely exist, a remarkable achievement for so young a practitioner. And throughout this period as throughout his career he remained faithful to Wright's basic philosophy of design, in particular the emphasis on highly personal designs for individual clients.

Goff's Tulsa office closed in 1934 as a result of the Depression, and Goff accepted Alfonso Iannelli's invitation to join his Chicago firm. Iannelli had met Goff while on a business visit to Tulsa, had been impressed by Goff's work, and had taken him to Taliesin to meet Wright around 1927. The association with Iannelli lasted less than a year, but it enabled Goff to establish a practice in the Chicago suburb of Park Ridge in 1935. He also began teaching at the Chicago Academy of Fine Arts, and from 1936 to 1937 he served as director of architectural design for the Vitrolite division of the Libbey–Owens–Ford Glass Company. In this capacity he lived briefly in Detroit.

At first Goff's formative phase continued. Thus his Elin House (1938–1939), Northfield, Illinois, partly resembles Wright's Usonian houses of the period and partly recalls work by such Chicago contemporaries as George Fred Keck (see KECK & KECK). But by 1940, the majority of his designs show a personal character without close parallels,

as in the sharply angular Unseth House (1940), Park Ridge, Illinois. More distinctive is the Bartman House (Triaero) of the following year, near Fern Creek, Kentucky. A humanized and fully transformed version of R. BUCKMINSTER FULLER's Dymaxion House (1927), it is Wrightian in spirit only. In the Spencer House Project (1941), Chicago, Goff designed the first in a series of freely shaped interiors that contrast with the precise geometry of the Bartman house. It relates to PAUL NELSON's *Maison Suspendue* project (1936–1938), among others, but the personal vocabulary and the ultimate realization of the concept in later years is entirely Goff's.

With the outbreak of World War II, Goff enlisted in the United States Navy and was stationed in the Aleutians from 1942 to 1944, and in California from 1944 to 1945. Following his release from service, he remained briefly in California, opening an office in Berkeley where he stayed until joining the faculty of the department of architecture at the University of Oklahoma in January 1947.

As a member of the navy's construction division during the war years, Goff had limited opportunities to design. Several of the military facilities that he remodeled drew attention because of their distinctive appearance, but his most publicized design of the period was a military chapel (1945) in Camp Parks, California, a convincing demonstration of Goff's skill in working with prefabricated building systems (Quonset huts) and of his clever adaptations of found materials. Material shortages of the immediate postwar period hampered Goff's California career but they could not impede his steady production of unusual designs. They ranged from essays in precise geometry to explorations of freely formed space. Among the more innovatively structured are the Gillis House Project (1945) for Bend, Oregon, Goff's first design to incorporate a spiral motif; and the Leidig House Project (1946) for Hayward, California, in which circular platforms were loosely arranged on the surface of a vast interior pool.

After one semester of teaching at the University of Oklahoma in Norman, Goff was appointed chairman of the department of architecture in June 1947 and held that position until his resignation from the university in December 1955. Under his direction the school received widespread attention and attracted students from many parts of the country as well as some from abroad; Herb Greene is perhaps the most prominent of architects who studied with Goff in this period. Goff also received numerous commissions from sympathetic clients, and his designs began to be published regularly. Many of the innovative concepts that he had been developing since the early 1940s were at last realized. For the Ford House (1948–1950), Aurora, Illinois, Goff devised a composition of interlocking spherical volumes made from parts of Quonset huts. A penchant for unusual materials found expression in walls made of coal, ceilings covered with coiled rope, and skylights fashioned from surplus airplane parts. For the Wilson House (1951–1952), Pensacola, Florida, designed for his navy commander, Goff created a house of sharply defined cubes with beveled edges. In the Bavinger House (1950–1955), near Norman, Oklahoma, Goff produced one of his most famous designs: a logarithmically spiraled stone wall, its edges made imprecise by an irregular parapet, encloses a general volume. It is lit by a continuous skylight that separates this wall from the suspended roof. Inside, discs suspended from a central mast take the place of conventional rooms, each hovering above a pool that covers most of the lower level of the house. It is a space of revolutionary potential.

In January 1956, Goff moved to Bartlesville, Oklahoma, where he maintained his home and office in Wright's Price Tower. Commissions and devoted student assistants soon followed. For Joe Price, a client who became one of Goff's major supporters, he designed an angular retreat with carpeted floors that turn up to form integral seating areas beneath a ceiling covered with feathers. The Price House (1956–1958), Bartlesville, has twice been expanded by Goff: a hexagonal pavilion with a glass-walled pool (1966–1968) was added to serve as a gallery for Price's collection of Japanese art, and a tower with onyx cabinets (1974–1978) was added to provide a private study high above the Oklahoma prairie. Other designs of the late 1950s and early 1960s show Goff's continuing fascination with unusual, complex geometries and reflect his determination to achieve an architecture expressive of each particular client. All incorporate geometric ornament that amplifies some theme of architectural composition. Most use materials in unexpected ways. Many explore variations of centrally focused plans composed of interlocking figures that include squares, triangles, and circles in various combinations. Others are freer in form, as the second project for the Rudd House (1959–1960), near San Francisco. In this design, a linear element to contain corridor and informal living space was made to curve freely through an existing grove of trees; individual, podlike elements attached by bridges to the curved spine were to serve as places of private retreat. Goff's designs were not limited to houses in these years: his project for the Viva Hotel (1961), Las Vegas, Nevada, anticipated several features that JOHN PORTMAN would later popularize.

In 1964, Goff accepted an offer to move to Kansas City, Missouri, and design a series of prefabricated houses as part of a speculative venture. These prototypes for Briar Associates (1964) remained projects; they lack the energy of his designs for individual clients. In other commissions of his Kansas City period, Goff's characteristic ornament is often suppressed and forms are expressed more starkly than in his usual designs of the postwar period. Among the most striking examples is a linear house of intersecting cylinders for sociologist Hugh Duncan (1965–1967) near Cobden, Illinois.

In 1970, Goff moved to Tyler, Texas, again in response to commissions for speculative work. Several designs that resulted for the planned vacation community of Lake Village (1970–1973), near Tyler, were built and proved Goff's work commercially viable. Bruce Plunkett, the Lake Village developer who had studied with Goff at the University of Oklahoma, became the second of Goff's major clients. The Plunkett House that Goff designed in 1970 as a feature of the Lake Village community—a romantic essay planned to include an onion-shaped dome—showed a renewed interest in decorative values. Later designs of the 1970s continued this emphasis, incorporating such elements as extended eaves, sculpturally shaped chimneys, richly colored glass mosaics, and stenciled patterns. More significantly, these later designs include such spatial features as ramped floors and room-sized movable elements.

In his seven decades of practice, Goff has designed nearly 500 buildings of which some 140 have been built. Most are houses for suburban or small-town sites in midwestern America. His cli-

Goff.
Bavinger House.
Near Norman, Oklahoma.
1950–1955

ents are usually professionals without inherited wealth or strong social ties who enthusiastically support Goff's architectural interpretations of their particular needs. The resulting diversity is astonishing and frustrates any attempt at orderly categorization.

Because of his midwestern origins and his philosophical dependence on Wright, it is fair to regard Goff as a late manifestation of the Prairie school. Certainly his work reflects a concern with particular conditions of site, materials, and individual clients common to Prairie school architects. But Goff's work surpasses theirs in terms of spatial and modal variety. In this aspect, his work recalls that of late eighteenth- and early nineteenth-century architects influenced by the picturesque point of view. Like those architects, he seeks in each design to express the individual character of the client. And like Downing and Wright, who championed similar ideals, Goff believes such architecture to be positively expressive of a democratic society. Few innovative architects have sublimated their personal preferences as effectively as Goff in achieving these ends.

Beginning in the 1970s, the idea of an architecture based on personal choice has received widespread attention. Goff's long-established support of this view makes his work seem premonitory of certain examples by such architects as Robert Venturi and Charles W. Moore. Goff's work has proved more popular with a broad segment of the population and partly as a consequence is thought vulgar by critics sensitive to higher design fashions. Yet underlying the sometimes odd shapes and unusual colors is a spatial quality of more easily recognized worth that also interprets various client demands. In this, Goff shows, as Downing foresaw, that one source of a new architecture lies with the client as well as with the architect.

DAVID G. DE LONG

WORKS

1919, Graves Summer House, near Los Angeles. 1923–1926, Robinson Studio; 1925–1927, Tulsa Club; 1926–1929, Boston Avenue Methodist-Episcopal Church; *1927–1928, Page Warehouse; 1928–1929, Riverside Studio; Tulsa, Okla. *1937, Libbey–Owens–Ford Showroom, The Merchandise Mart, Chicago. 1938–1939, Elin House, Northfield, Ill. 1939–1940, Cole House; 1940, Unseth House; Park Ridge, Ill. 1940–1941, Colmorgan House, Glenview, Ill. 1941, Bartman House (Triaero), near Fern Creek, Ky. 1944–1945, Camp Park Military Facilities; 1945, Military Chapel (moved to San Lorenzo, Calif. in 1947); Camp Parks, Calif. 1947–1948, Ledbetter House, Norman, Okla. 1948–1950, Ford House, Aurora, Ill. 1949–1950, Cox House, Boise City, Okla. 1949–1950, Hopewell Baptist Church, near Edmond, Okla. 1950–1955, Bavinger House, near Norman, Okla. 1951–1952, Wilson House, Pensacola, Fla.

1956–1958, Price House, Bartlesville, Okla. 1957–1958, Pollock House, Oklahoma City. 1958–1959, Jones House, Bartlesville, Okla. 1958–1960, Gutman House, Gulfport, Miss. 1960–1961, Redeemer Lutheran Church and Education Building, Bartlesville, Okla. 1964–1965, Dace House, Beaver, Okla. 1965, Hyde House, Kansas City, Kans. 1965–1967, Duncan House, near Cobden, Ill. 1965–1967, Nicol House, Kansas City, Mo. 1966–1968, Price House (addition), Bartlesville, Okla. 1970–1972, Glen Harder House, near Mountain Lake, Minn. 1970–1972, Second Plunkett House, Lake Village, near Tyler, Tex. 1970–1973, Jacob Harder House, Mountain Lake, Minn. 1974–1976, Second Barby House, Tucson, Ariz. 1974–1978, Price House (addition), Bartlesville, Okla. 1975–1980, Taylor House (alterations), Seattle, Wash.

BIBLIOGRAPHY

COOK, JEFFREY 1978 *The Architecture of Bruce Goff.* New York: Harper.
DE LONG, DAVID G. 1977 *The Architecture of Bruce Goff: Buildings and Projects, 1916–1974.* 2 vols. New York: Garland.
FUTAGAWA, YUKIO (editor) 1975 *Global Architecture 33: Bruce Goff, Bavinger House and Price House.* Tokyo: A. D. A. Edita.
MOHRI, TAKENOBU 1970 *Bruce Goff in Architecture.* Tokyo: Kenchiku Planning Center.
MURPHY, WILLIAM, and MULLER, LOUIS 1970 *Bruce Goff: A Portfolio of the Work of Bruce Goff.* The Architectural League of New York.
PARK, BEN ALLAN 1957 "The Architecture of Bruce Goff." *Architectural Design* 27:151–174.
SERGEANT, JOHN and MOORING, STEPHEN (editors) 1978 "A. D. Profiles 16: Bruce Goff." *Architectural Design* 48, no. 10: entire issue.

GOLDBERG, BERTRAND

Bertrand Goldberg (1913–) established his own office in Chicago in 1937. He attended Harvard University (1930–1932) and the Armour Institute of Technology, and studied under LUDWIG MIES VAN DER ROHE at the Berlin Bauhaus (1932–1933). Goldberg's projects reveal a strong relationship between form, contemporary industrial techniques, and sociological needs. In particular, he harmonizes modern structure with multiple uses and needs in high-rise buildings. Although apprenticed in Chicago, his work is a clear departure from the ideas of the Chicago school and of Mies.

PATRICIA C. PHILLIPS

WORKS

1937–1944, Town of Suitland (design and construction), Maryland. 1960, Marina City Towers; 1963, Raymond Hilliard Center, Chicago. 1968, Saint Joseph Hospital, Tacoma, Wash. 1970, Health Sciences Center, State University of New York, Stony Brook.

BIBLIOGRAPHY

COOK, JOHN W., and KLOTZ, HEINRICH 1973 *Conversations with Architects.* New York: Praeger.
SKY, ALISON, and STONE, MICHELLE 1976 *Unbuilt America.* New York: McGraw-Hill.

GOLDINGHAM, JOHN

John Goldingham (1767–1844), a mathematician and astronomer of Danish origin, first served as a midshipman with the British Royal Navy. He settled in Madras in 1786 and assisted William Petrie at his private observatory. In 1794, he was appointed astronomer and first superintendent of the East India Company's Surveying School, Madras. He was appointed civil engineer to supervise all government buildings in 1800, beginning with renovations to Old Government House in the Fort. The Company's Garden House was enlarged and the surrounding park laid out between 1800 and 1801, while his most distinguished building, the Grecian Banqueting House next door, was opened in 1803. Goldingham became a fellow of many learned societies and published a number of papers.

PAULINE ROHATGI

WORKS

1799–1800, Kerr's Chapel; 1800–1801, Garden House and Park; 1800–1803, Banqueting House; Madras, India.

BIBLIOGRAPHY

ARCHER, MILDRED 1964 "Georgian Splendour in South India." *Country Life* 135, no. 3499:728–731.
ARCHER, MILDRED 1969 *British Drawings in the India Office Library.* London: H.M. Stationery Office.

GOLLINS, MELVIN, WARD

Frank Gollins, James Melvin, and Edmund Ward established the office of Gollins, Melvin, Ward in London in 1947. The partnership now has, in addition to six partners, nine associates and an average total staff of about 150. Initially, work was confined to rebuilding bomb-destroyed dwellings in London. But as the economy picked up, so their work and its scale increased: primary schools, secondary schools, technical colleges, universities. Construction and extension of buildings for the National Health Service burgeoned. Parallel with this work in the public sector, the partnership became involved with the private sector—offices, high-rise developments, headquarters for major companies.

The partners' design preferences were formulated by 1957 in the office buildings on New Cavendish Street, London. This was one of the earliest uses of curtain-wall glazing in London, and it was certainly the most confident handling of its day. Within three years, they had developed the curtain-wall medium as foregrounding at Castrol House, 174–204 Marylebone Road, London. Their Library and Arts Tower, University of Sheffield (1959), was being constructed at the same time and it was to weave a network of glass and steel into a sharply rising verticality. It was a happy accident that the top floor was to house the University's architecture department.

CHRISTOPHER FAWCETT

WORKS

1950, Infant and Junior High School, Oxhey, Hertfordshire, England. 1956, Secondary School, Southborough, Kent, England. 1957, Office Buildings, 93–97, 118–126 New Cavendish Street, London. 1959, Library and Arts Tower, University of Sheffield, Yorkshire, England. 1960, Castrol House Office Building, 174–204 Marylebone Road, London. 1961, Technical College, Scarborough; 1962, University House, University of Sheffield; Yorkshire, England. 1964, Regional Hospital Administration Offices, Headington, Oxford. 1964, Residential Development, Hermitage Lane, Hampstead, London. 1965, College of Education, Loughborough, Leicestershire, England. 1965, Women's Royal Army Corps College, Camberley, Surrey, England. 1966, District General Hospital, Hillingdon, Middlesex, England. 1966, Equitable Life Assurance Society Headquarters Offices, Coleman Street, London. 1967, Holophane Limited Factory and Offices, Bletchley, Buckinghamshire, England. 1968, Royal Military College of Science, Shrivenham, Wiltshire, England. 1969, Commercial Union Tower Offices, Leadenhall Street, London. 1970, The Polytechnic, Sheffield, Yorkshire, England. 1970, Royal Military Academy, Sandhurst, Camberley, Surrey, England. 1971, Biological Sciences Building, University of Sheffield, Yorkshire, England. 1972, District General Hospital, Harold Wood, Essex, England. 1973, Manufacturers Life Insurance Company Headquarters Offices, Stevenage, Hertfordshire, England. 1975, Equitable Life House, Walton Street, Aylesbury, Buckinghamshire, England. 1975, New Covent Garden Market, Nine Elms; 1975, Royal Opera House (additions), Covent Garden; 1975, Westminster City School, Nine Elms; London. 1978, Mombasa Airport Development, Kenya. 1978, American Express International Banking Corporation Headquarters (with Peter Wood and Associates), Brighton, Sussex, England.

BIBLIOGRAPHY

COOPER, MAURICE 1975 "Good Gollins." *Building Design* 237, Feb. 14:2.
CRAWFORD, DAVID 1975 "A 30-Years-Old Practice Looking at Architecture." *Building* 228, Feb. 28:39.
Architecture of the Gollins Melvin Ward Partnership. 1974 With an introduction by Tony Aldous. London: Humphries.

GOLOSOV, ILYA, and GOLOSOV, PANTELEMON

Ilya Golosov (1883–1945) and Pantelemon Golosov (1882–1945) lived and worked in Moscow throughout their lives. They were educated together at the Stroganov College and graduated as architects in 1912 from the Moscow College of Painting, Sculpture, and Architecture. Of the two, Ilya Golosov was clearly the more creative. Whereas Pantelemon was an accomplished professional as a neoclassic and Constructivist architect, Ilya was independently inventive, above all in his well-known design for the Zuyev Workers' Club (1926–1928) on Lesnaya Street, Moscow. A distinguishing attribute of the younger Golosov's work was the bold plasticity of his larger Constructivist compositions as in the Zuyev Club or in his equally remarkable projects for a Palace of Culture (1926) and a Dom Kommuna (1928), both designed for Stalingrad. Like his unbuilt 1923 Palace of Labor and his Electrobank project of 1927, each of these larger works comprised boldly contrasting cylindrical and orthogonal forms.

With the official instigation of Social Realism, Ilya Golosov reverted to an architecture of historical pastiche. As a member of the pro-Constructivist OSA group (Association of Contemporary Architects), he found himself opposed to the strictly functionalist position then still being advanced by MOISEI YAKOVLEVICH GINSBURG and by his brother Pantelemon. This schism deepened with Ilya Golosov's historist project for the Palace of the Soviets competition of 1931. That his brother was loath to relinquish Constructivism is borne out by his own functionalist design for the Pravda Building, Moscow (1930–1934), and it would be another decade before the elder Golosov would produce a Social Realist work. This transformation appears finally in his neoclassical artist's hostel built in 1940 on the Dragomikov Embankment, Moscow. Of the two, only Ilya Golosov built extensively, above all during the Stalinist era, when he realized some seven major government commissions between 1934 and 1940, including a large sector of workers' housing, the Yausky Building, Moscow (1934). The war years saw Ilya Golosov engaged in the design of battle monuments, and his very last design was a memorial museum to the Red Army.

Although neither of the Golosovs was a brilliant teacher, both were involved in teaching throughout the best part of their lives, Pantelemon at the Moscow Institute of Architecture and Ilya at the Vkhutemas, the Moscow Polytechnic, and the Moscow Institute of Architecture.

KENNETH FRAMPTON

WORKS

1925–1926, Central Telegraph Building Competition; 1926, Textile Building; 1926–1928, Zuyev Workers' Club; 1934, Collective Housing, Yausky Boulevard; Moscow. 1936–1940, Hydro-Electric Station, Gorky, Russia.

BIBLIOGRAPHY

BARKHIN, MIKHAIL GRIGOR'EVICH 1974 Volume 1 in *Mastera Sovetskoĭ arkhitektury ob arkhitekture.* Moscow.
KOPP, ANATOLE 1970 *Town and Revolution.* New York: Braziller.
KROHA, J., and HRŮZA, J. 1973 *Sovetska architektonika avant garda.* Prague: Odeon.
SHVIDOVSKY, O. A. 1971 *Building in the USSR: 1917–1932.* London: Studio Vista; New York: Praeger.

GONDOUIN, JACQUES

After studying with JACQUES FRANÇOIS BLONDEL, Jacques Gondouin (1737–1818) gained royal favor to become a resident of the French Academy in Rome from 1759 to 1763.

In 1770, he was assigned the construction of a new college of surgery in Paris, for which he employed the greater portion of the site occupied by the Collège de Bourgogne to erect an ensemble at once monumental and functional. The much admired new school of surgery was inaugurated in 1775.

During a second trip to Italy, he made a series of drawings of Hadrian's villa at Tivoli which he presented to his friend, GIOVANNI BATTISTA PIRANESI. On returning to France, he built for himself on the banks of the Seine a villa, *Les eaux vives,* in the style of ANDREA PALLADIO.

In 1802, the destruction of the church of the Franciscans in Paris allowed him to build a new square decorated with a monumental fountain opposite the school of surgery.

At the end of his career, he realized works which he had proposed since 1769. He also built the six pavilions of the Ecole Pratique, Paris, and planned the ensemble of monastic buildings for the Franciscans.

In 1807, he prepared a project for the renovation of the Château of Versailles, and from 1806 to 1812 he was in charge of the construction of the Vendôme Column.

GÉRARD ROUSSET-CHARNY
Translated from French by Richard Cleary

BIBLIOGRAPHY

ADHÉMAR, JEAN 1934 "L'Ecole de Médecine." *L'Architecture* 47, no. 3:105–108.

HUARD, PIERRE, and IMBAULT-HUART, MARIE J.
1972–1973   "La Médicalisation du quartier des
Cordeliers aux 18° et 19°s." *Bulletin de la Société de
l'Histoire et de l'Île de France.*

GONTARD, KARL VON

Born in Mannheim, Germany, to a ballet master at
the Opera house of the margrave of Bayreuth, Karl
Philipp Christian von Gontard (1731–1791) followed his father's profession until, in 1749, he entered the Court Building Office (*Hofbauamt*) of
the Bayreuth court. The margrave sent him to
Paris in 1750, where he studied at JACQUES
FRANÇOIS BLONDEL's private Academy of Architecture. In 1752, he returned to Bayreuth via Holland. In 1754–1755, he accompanied Margrave
Frederick and Margravine Wilhelmine to the
south of France and Italy, where they spent some
time in Rome and in Naples. After the death of
Joseph Saint-Pierre (1754), Gontard became building inspector, taking over Saint-Pierre's position as
head of the Court Building Office, which he directed jointly with Rudolf Heinrich Richter. In
1756, he became engineer-captain and in 1761
teacher of architecture and perspective at the Bayreuth Academy of Art. After the death of the
margrave (1763), Gontard was called to Potsdam
by Frederick the Great. There, he took over the
direction of the Building Office (*Baukontor*)
which put him in charge of all royal building. In
1767, he was ennobled. However, in 1768, in spite
of continuing appreciation of his art, he fell into
disfavor with the king, so that his pupil, Georg
Christian Unger, was called in to carry on communication. In 1779, Gontard was transferred to the
same position in Berlin. He was promoted to engineer-major only by Frederick William II, in 1786.
That same year, he was made a member of the
Royal Prussian Academy of Arts and Mechanical
Sciences. From that time until his death, he was
able once again to exercise his architectural talents
under royal protection.

Gontard's early private buildings in Bayreuth—modest and with restrained decoration
adapted to local conditions—reveal the influence
of the Parisian school of classicist architecture as
imparted by Blondel. Larger-scale palaces came
into being after the Italian tour, for instance, the
Palais Reitzenstein (1761). In his most important
early work, the expanded southern section of the
New Castle in Bayreuth (1757–1764), the early
classicist influence on the Rococo forms is noticeable both in the interior decoration and in the architecture. This stylistic tendency was continued in
the completion of the New Palace in Potsdam

(1765–1769), although the king had prescribed
the use of the older motifs of "Friderician rococo";
the building did conform to the king's historicizing
understanding of the classicist aspects of seventeenth-century architecture. Through a greater use
of decoration in the antique mode, Gontard here
emphasized the ornamental factor in such a way as
to render the tectonic form more comprehensible.
The Communs, which he placed in front of the
palace, and their connecting colonnaded exedra
built after an altered plan of JEAN LAURENT
LEGEAY, still show the influence of the baroque
theatrical stage effects of his Bayreuth beginnings,
as do the King's Colonnades (1777–1780) in Berlin. However, in the Temple of Friendship and the
Temple of Antiquity in the park of the New Palace
in Potsdam (1768–1770), the sentimental streak in
this type of classicism is simply expressed. In his
numerous middle class houses which left an enduring mark on the urban picture of Berlin and Potsdam, the influence of English early classicism is
more and more noticeable. The two domed towers
of the churches on the Gendarmenmarkt in Berlin
(1780–1785) are urbanistically of the greatest significance; in them, Gontard, using monumental
Palladian (see ANDREA PALLADIO) motifs, continued the traditional representative tower architecture of the Prussian kings.

The Marmorpalais (Marble Palace) which he
built for Friedrich Wilhelm II in Potsdam (1786–
1789) signified a shift away from this declamatory
style and a decisive turn toward English neoclassicism. Gontard's late decorative style, seen in the
King's Chambers in the Berlin Palace (1786–1789),
combined elements of the late Friderician rococo
with motifs of the mature style of ROBERT ADAM.
By the time of his death in 1791, Gontard prepared
the way for the full flowering of classicism in Berlin. His most notable pupils were Friedrich Wilhelm Tittel and HEINRICH GENTZ.

INA MARIA KELLER and FRITZ-EUGEN KELLER
Translated from German by
Beverley R. Placzek

WORKS

*1753–1754, Layritz House; 1753–1754, Liebhardt
House (with Joseph Saint-Pierre); 1756–1757, Court
Pharmacy; 1757–1764, New Palace (new wing, in part
with Rudolf Heinrich Richter); 1758, Spindler House;
1759–1761, Adhémar Palace; 1759–1761, Gontard
House; 1760–1761, Künssberg Palace; *1761, Hunting
Lodge; 1761, Reitzenstein Palace; 1762, Ellrodt Palace;
Bayreuth, Germany. 1765–1776, Houses, Nauensche
Plantage (1765–1768); Burgstrasse (1770); Alter Markt
(1770–1772); Berlinerstrasse (1772); Am Bassin
(1773–1776); Am Kanal (1776); 1765–1769, New Palace (stairway and interior design); 1768–1770, Temple
of Friendship and Temple of Antiquity, near the New

Palace; Potsdam, Germany. 1776, Spittel Colonnades; 1777–1780, King's Colonnades; *1780–1781, Döblitz House (later General Lottery Building, High Court of Administration); 1780–1781, Towers of the German and French churches on the Gendarmenmarkt (destroyed but rebuilding begun); *1786–1789, Berlin Palace (royal chambers); Berlin. 1787–1789, Marble Palace, Potsdam, Germany. *1787–1789, Oranienburg Gate, Berlin.

BIBLIOGRAPHY

BORRMAN, RICHARD 1893 *Die Bau- und Kunstdenkmäler von Berlin.* Berlin: Springer.
DRESCHER, HORST 1975 "Das Neue Palais in Potsdam und der Spätstil der friderizianischen Architektur." Pages 217–236 in *Festschrift für Margarete Kühn.* Munich: Deutscher Kunstverlag.
HEMPEL, EBERHARD 1965 Pages 251, 272 in *Baroque Art and Architecture in Central Europe.* Harmondsworth, England: Penguin.
KELLER, FRITZ-EUGEN 1982 "Die Königskammern Friedrich Wilhelms II." In Klünner, Werner, Peschken, and Goerd (editors), *Das Berliner Stadtschloss* Berlin: Propyläen.
SCHMITZ, HERMANN (1925)1980 Pages 22–28 in *Berliner Baumeister vom Ausgang des 18. Jahrhunderts.* Reprint. Berlin: Mann.
SITZMANN, KARL 1952 "Die Frühzeit des Architekten Carl Gontard in Bayreuth." *Archiv für Kunstgeschichte und Altertumskunde von Oberfranken* 36:140–185.
ZIELER, OTTO 1913 *Potsdam: Ein Stadtbild des 18. Jahrhunderts.* Berlin: Weide.

GONZALEZ Y ALVARE-OSSORIO, ANIBAL

Anibal Gonzalez y Alvare-Ossorio, (1876–1929), Andalusian architect, was born in Seville, Spain. He studied at the School of Architecture in Madrid, obtaining the title of architect in 1902.

Gonzales was formed in the eclectic atmosphere at the turn of the century, although very soon, in a series of urban buildings, he developed his own version of the north European Art Nouveau. However, Gonzalez became convinced that a truly new architecture for the twentieth century must be based on the Spanish vernacular tradition, and this is what gave his works their strength.

The work that best characterizes his style was that for the association of the Spanish-American Exposition of Seville. From 1911, the year in which he won the project competition, until the final inauguration of the Exposition in the same year as his death (1929), Anibal Gonzales studied in great detail the mudejar tradition and that of the local Gothic and baroque, which he united in the grand academic composition which constituted the general scheme of the Exposition. The

plan for an area of growth in the city of Seville to function as the grounds for the future Exposition constitutes the most important aspect of his proposal, of which a system of gardens that connect the southwest of the historical city with the borders of the Guadalquivir River and the highway to Cadiz are the basic elements. In the plan are shown the great representative spaces of the Plaza of America, with the Mudejar Pavilion (1916), and the large circular Plaza of Spain, with an ordered exedra enclosed by a porticoed building and a ground system of descending planes in which are combined colored pavements, waterlines, and green spaces. Other buildings, such as the Luca de Tena House (1926), the house at 41 Cuna Street, the Chapel of the Luises (1926), the Miguel Noguera House (1909), all in Seville, and the Chapel of the Virgin of Carmen (1928) in Triana, also clearly demonstrate his search for a new expression of the indigenous tradition, resulting in work of polychrome richness and composite clarity that shows the exceptional flexibility of the eclectic tradition in its latest manifestations.

IGNASI DE SOLÀ-MORALES
*Translated from Spanish by
Judith E. Meighan*

WORKS

1909, Miguel Noguera House; 1916, Mudejar Pavilion; 1926, Luca de Tena House; 1926, Chapel of the Luises; Seville, Spain. 1928, Chapel of the Virgin of Carmen, Triana, Spain.

BIBLIOGRAPHY

BASSEGODA NONELL, JUAN (editor) 1969 *El modernismo en España.* Madrid: Comisaria de Exposiciones. Exhibition catalogue.
GINER DE LOS RIOS, BERNARDO 1952 *Cinquenta años de arquitectura española, 1900–1950.* Mexico City: Patria.
PÉREZ ESCOLANO, VÍCTOR 1973 *Anibal González, arquitecto.* Seville, Spain: Diputación Provincial.
VILLAR MOVELLÁN, ALBERTO 1973 *Arquitectura del Modernismo en Sevilla.* Seville, Spain: Diputación Provincial.

GOODHART-RENDEL, H. S.

Harry Stuart Goodhart-Rendel (1887–1959) as an architect has been partially eclipsed by his fame as a historian of Victorian architecture. His buildings, varying stylistically from neo-Georgian (of a late character) to his own brand of Victorian revival and sometimes a personal modern, show his historical knowledge and his incisive and original mind. He believed in rational eclecticism, and he admired

French architecture as well as the High Victorian Gothic Revivalists.

ALAN POWERS

WORKS

1907, Clive Buildings (façades), Calcutta. 1911, The Pantiles, Englefield Green, Surrey, England. 1922–1927, Saint Mary (additions), Bourne Street, London. 1924, Tetton House (alterations), Somerset, England. 1929–1931, Hay's Wharf, Tooley Street, London. 1932, Saint Wilfrid, Brighton, England. 1946–1951, Saint Leonard-on-the-Sea. 1953–1957, Westminster Technical College, Vincent Square, London. 1957, Franciscan Church, Crawley, England. 1957–1959, Holy Trinity Dockhead, Bermondsey, England. 1958, Our Lady of the Rosary, Marylebone Road, London.

BIBLIOGRAPHY

FERRIDAY, PETER 1955 "A Great Critic: A Study of Mr. Goodhart-Rendel." *Builder* 138:4–5.
GOODHART-RENDEL, HARRY STUART 1924 *Nicholas Hawksmoor.* London: Benn.
GOODHART-RENDEL, HARRY STUART 1932 *Vitruvian Nights.* London: Methuen.
GOODHART-RENDEL, HARRY STUART 1953 *English Architecture since the Regency.* London: Constable.
PEVSNER, NIKLAUS 1965 "Goodhart-Rendel's Roll-Call." *Architectural Review* 138:259–264.
POWERS, ALAN 1979 "H. S. Goodhart-Rendel: The Appropriateness of Style." *Architectural Design* 49, nos. 10–11:44–51.

GOODHUE, BERTRAM GROSVENOR

The career of Bertram Grosvenor Goodhue (1869–1924) spanned from the late nineteenth century through the early twentieth century. Strikingly romantic and individualistic in his attitudes, and standing outside the mainstream of Beaux-Arts classicism, with a strong attachment to medieval and Hispanic traditions, Goodhue nevertheless searched for an architecture that embraced modern materials, inventions, and ideas.

Goodhue was raised in the rural town of Pomfret, Connecticut. At fifteen, he moved to New York City to work in the office of Renwick, Aspinwall, and Russell, under JAMES RENWICK, architect of Grace Church and Saint Patrick's Cathedral.

In 1891, Goodhue won a competition for a church in Dallas, Texas. To carry out the work he associated with RALPH ADAMS CRAM and Charles Francis Wentworth of Boston, becoming a partner in the firm of Cram, Wentworth, and Goodhue in 1892. Upon Wentworth's death in 1897, the firm changed to Cram, Goodhue, and Ferguson in 1898. Goodhue and Cram together produced a

magazine of criticism, *The Knight-Errant,* and were at the center of a local bohemian intelligentsia with ties to Charles Eliot Norton and Charles Herbert Moore at Harvard University. Goodhue pursued an interest in the art of typography and book design. He designed the Cheltenham typeface, and *The Altar Book* (1896) printed by Daniel Berkeley Updike's Merrymount Press, the American counterpart to WILLIAM MORRIS's Kelmscott Press.

All Saints' Church, Ashmont (1892–1913) was the first major building which Cram and Goodhue completed. The building's simple but rugged forms of dark granite recalled those by H. H. RICHARDSON, although the church and especially its interior revealed an erudite knowledge of Anglo-Catholic ritual, medieval English precedents, and work by contemporary English architects like JOHN DANDO SEDDING. Although this commission established the firm's reputation as Gothic church architects and linked them with such American contemporaries as COPE AND STEWARDSON, it was only part of an oeuvre that included a series of impressive libraries and designs for houses, apartment houses, and schools in varied styles.

Goodhue was an avid traveler. The journey that influenced him most was to Persia and on around the world in 1902. Several Persian gardens he visited had a strong effect on his subsequent designs. Emanating from these trips and other journeys of the mind came a series of drawings and descriptions of imaginary places like Traumburg (1896), Monteventoso (1899), and the Villa Fosca (1897). Although enchanting for their romantic effect, they also confirm that Goodhue had a deft command of site planning, massing, structure, and ornamental detail.

Cram, Goodhue, and Ferguson won the competition to design major additions to the United States Military Academy at West Point (1903–1910), and this secured their national reputation. Organized around major east–west and north–south axes, the winning entry integrated the existing mid-nineteenth century castellated Gothic buildings with several large new buildings. The tremendous scale and rugged forms of the new buildings, especially the splendidly grim Cadet Chapel (1903–1910), set in the picturesque site along the Hudson River, seemed to recall the stepped masses at Mont Saint-Michel—an image that recurred in Goodhue's designs. This monumental effect was not created *tabula rasa* by rejecting the traditions of the campus, but by encompassing old and new construction in a complex and subtle composition. Required to establish a local field office, Goodhue moved back to New

York. From 1903 to 1913, the two offices—in Boston headed by Cram and Ferguson and in New York headed by Goodhue—functioned with increasing artistic independence.

Saint Thomas Church (1906–1913) in New York was the last collaborative effort between Goodhue and Cram, and it is an extremely distinguished work in which innovative vaulting techniques and contemporary iconography received as much consideration as Gothic forms and ecclesiastical ritual. The chunky, almost brutal exterior forms and especially the bold squatty corner tower were designed to give the church a great presence among the tall skyscrapers that were anticipated to surround the building. On the interior, the expressive use of freshly conceived ornament heightens the effect of the sublimely elegant nave and chancel. The unusually large and dramatic reredos was completed in close collaboration with the sculptor Lee Lawrie.

A series of churches subsequently was designed solely by Goodhue, all with a style, structure, and use of material and craft that seemed especially his own. Of these, the First Baptist Church (1909–1912) in Pittsburgh was the most strikingly modernistic, especially its ornament and the composition of its plan. His very success as a church architect, however, made it more difficult to secure other types of commissions, especially for the skyscraper he yearned to design.

For the newly created Panama Canal Zone, he designed a spare concrete hotel, and at San Diego for the Panama-California Exposition (1911–1915) he designed a grouping of theatrical buildings in a Hispanic idiom in which voluptuous ornament was densely massed in counterpoint to broad blank walls forming a backdrop for the green and floral landscape. The imagery of this fair gave impetus to the Spanish Colonial Revival in California in the 1920s.

In 1913, after designing his first scheme for the Cathedral of the Incarnation in Baltimore (1911–1924), Goodhue visited the modern Gothic cathedral under construction in Liverpool to the designs of GILES GILBERT SCOTT. It was a daunting and cathartic experience, and caused Goodhue not only to redesign the Baltimore cathedral with a bolder, simpler effect, but to reassess his attitudes about architectural form.

On December 31, 1913, the firm of Cram, Goodhue, and Ferguson was dissolved and Goodhue set up his own practice in New York. In his design for the new Saint Bartholomew's Church (1914–1918), Goodhue moved away from Gothic to a Romanesque-Byzantine idiom to incorporate the triple portal from the old church, designed by STANFORD WHITE. Saint Vincent Ferrer (1914–1919) was a transitional building, at once a brilliant summary of his Gothic designs and an intimation of the striking designs he was about to create. Several houses provided opportunities to explore an architectural expression using a minimum of ornament. Of these, he favored the Philip Henry House (1918–1920) at Scarborough, New York, for its spare, laconic forms and its simple walls constructed of rough, random local stone.

Four large projects reflect Goodhue's attempts to move away from conventional styles and uses of ornament: the Marine Corps Base and Naval Air Station at San Diego (1916–1918), composed of austere stucco buildings linked by arcades; the Rockefeller Chapel (1918–1927) at the University of Chicago, still Gothic in style but Roman in scale; the National Academy of Sciences Building (1919–1924) in Washington, in which freshly conceived stripped classical forms on the exterior were balanced by a richly tiled central rotunda; and the evocative winning scheme in the competition for the new Nebraska State Capitol at Lincoln (1920–1932), in which the striking and enigmatic design, admired as a daring departure from the typical classical precedent, fused elements of many styles into one vigorous composition of freely styled stepped masses culminating in a central tower that embodied the romantic image of a skyscraper.

Subsequently, he designed a series of buildings which were unusually free in style, exotic in aura, and composed of stripped forms adorned only with integrally composed sculpture and symbolic inscriptions. Goodhue's passion for the skyscraper found expression in a distinguished entry in the Chicago Tribune competition (1922), and in a proposed eighty-story ecclesiastical office building for New York (1923) which would have been the tallest building in the world at that time.

Goodhue's death in 1924 came at an awkward moment. His position as an American modernist was not yet confirmed by completed buildings, only by his ideas. Nevertheless, his influence on a younger generation of architects, such as RAYMOND HOOD, RALPH WALKER, WALLACE HARRISON, and PAUL CRET had been substantial, and with his last designs he had helped to establish both the broad stylistic characteristics and the philosophical intentions of American modernism in the 1920s and 1930s.

RICHARD OLIVER

WORKS

1892–1913, All Saints' Church (with Ralph Adams Cram and Frank W. Ferguson; not completed until 1941), Ashmont, Mass. 1899, Deborah Cook Sayles Public Library, Pawtucket, R.I. 1901, Public Library, Nashua, N.H. 1902, Gillespie House, Montecito, Calif. 1903–1910, United States Military Academy (with

Cram and Ferguson), West Point, N.Y. 1905, La Santissima Trinidad Church (with Cram and Ferguson), Havana. 1906–1913, Saint Thomas Church (with Cram and Ferguson), New York. 1909–1912, First Baptist Church (with Cram and Ferguson), Pittsburgh. 1911–1915, Panama-California Exposition Buildings, San Diego, Calif. 1914–1916, Town Plan and Buildings, Tyrone, N.M. 1914–1918, Saint Bartholomew's Church; 1914–1919, Church of Saint Vincent Ferrer; New York. 1916–1918, Marine Corps Base and Naval Air Station, San Diego, Calif. 1918–1920, Philip Henry House, Scarborough, N.Y. 1918–1927, Rockefeller Chapel, University of Chicago. 1919–1924, National Academy of Sciences Building, Washington. 1920–1924, Sterling Memorial Library, Yale University, New Haven. 1920–1932, Lincoln State Capitol, Nebraska. 1922–1926, Central Public Library, Los Angeles.

BIBLIOGRAPHY

BAKER, JAMES MCFARLAN 1915 *American Churches, Volume II.* New York: American Architect.
GOODHUE, BERTRAM GROSVENOR 1914 *A Book of Architectural and Decorative Drawings.* New York: Architectural Book Publishing.
HOAK, E. W., and CHURCH, W. H. 1930 *Masterpieces of Architecture in the United States.* New York: Scribner.
The International Competition for a New Administration Building for The Chicago Tribune. 1923 Chicago: The Tribune Company.
"The Nebraska State Capitol." 1934 *American Architect* 145: Entire issue.
OLIVER, RICHARD 1982 *Bertram Grosvenor Goodhue.* New York: Architectural History Foundation.
SCHUYLER, MONTGOMERY 1911 "The Works of Cram, Goodhue and Ferguson, 1892–1910." *Architectural Record* 29, Jan.:1–112.
WHITAKER, C. H. (editor) 1925 *Bertram Grosvenor Goodhue—Architect and Master of Many Arts.* New York: American Institute of Architects Press.

GOODMAN, PERCIVAL

Percival Goodman (1904–) was born in New York and educated in Paris at the Ecole des Beaux-Arts. Returning to the United States, he began his own firm, Whitman and Goodman, and specialized in religious and institutional design. Currently a professor emeritus of Columbia University, he is the author of the classic planning text, *Communitas* (1947; with Paul Goodman).

EUGENIE L. BIRCH

WORKS

1950, Temple Beth El, Providence, R.I. 1955, Fairmount Temple, Fairmount Village, Ohio. 1960, Congregation Saarey Zedek, Southfield, Mich. 1970, Center for American Studies, Taiwan. 1975, Queensborough Community College, Queens, N.Y.

BIBLIOGRAPHY

GOODMAN, PERCIVAL, and GOODMAN, PAUL 1947 *Communitas.* University of Chicago Press.

GOODWIN, FRANCIS

Francis Goodwin (1784–1835), through his high-pressure salesmanship, obtained many commissions for English provincial public buildings, particularly churches, in the 1820s. Working principally in a showy Perpendicular, he also used effectively a [JOHN] SOANE-inspired neoclassical style. His commissioned House of Commons design (1833) employed both. Overwork on his 1835 Parliament Houses competition entry killed him.

M. H. PORT

WORKS

1809, Trinity Chapel, Saint Margaret's Church, King's Lynn, Norfolk, England. 1821–1824, Saint Peter's Church, Ashton-under-Lyne, Lancashire, England. *1821–1828, Christ Church, West Bromwich, Staffordshire, England. *1822–1825, Town Hall, Manchester, England. 1823–1824, Town Hall, Macclesfield, England. 1823–1827, County Gaol, Derbyshire, England. 1824–1827, Central Market, Leeds, England. 1828, Public Rooms, Bradford, Yorkshire, England. c.1830, Parsonage, Bilston, Staffordshire, England. 1830–1835, Lissadell Court, County Sligo, Ireland. c.1834, Row of Cottages, Curraghmore, County Waterford, Ireland. 1835, Gate Lodge, Teddesley Hall, Staffordshire, England.

BIBLIOGRAPHY

GOODWIN, FRANCIS (1833a)1835 *Rural Architecture.* 2d ed. London. Originally published with the title *Domestic Architecture.* The second edition includes additional designs for cottages.
GOODWIN, FRANCIS 1833b *Plans, etc., of the New House of Commons.* London.
"Obituary." 1835 *Architectural Magazine* 2:476.
"Obituary." 1835 *Gentleman's Magazine* 2:659–660.
PORT, MICHAEL 1958 "Francis Goodwin: An Architect of the 1820's." *Architectural History* 1:60–72.

GOODWIN, PHILIP L.

Philip Lippincott Goodwin (1885–1958) is known, with EDWARD DURELL STONE, as the designer of the original Museum of Modern Art (MOMA) on West 53rd Street in New York. This building, done in the International style and constructed of concrete and steel faced with marble and glass, was completed in 1939. Thereafter, Goodwin served as director of the department of architecture and vice-chairman of the Board of Directors at MOMA.

A native of New York, Goodwin received his bachelor's degree from Yale University in 1907. He studied architecture at Columbia University from 1908 to 1911, and in Paris from 1914 to 1915. He began his architectural career as a draftsman with the New York firm of DELANO AND ALDRICH (1914–1916), then was a partner in Goodwin, Bullard, and Woolsey. In 1921, he went into practice on his own.

Goodwin designed the Essex Building in Hartford, Connecticut (1924), and collaborated on numerous private homes. He was also an avid collector of modern art and donated many works of art to the Wadsworth Atheneum in Hartford.

ANNA LEE SPIRO

BIBLIOGRAPHY

GOODWIN, PHILIP L. 1933 *Rooftrees: The Architectural History of an American Family.* Philadelphia: Lippincott.
GOODWIN, PHILIP L. 1943 *Brazil Builds.* With photographs by G. E. Kidder Smith. New York: Museum of Modern Art.
GOODWIN, PHILIP L., and MILLIKEN, HENRY O. 1924 *French Provincial Architecture.* New York.
PATTERSON, AUGUSTA OWEN 1941 "An Architect on the Skyline." *Town and Country* 96, no. 4231:78–79.

GORDON, J. RIELY

Competition winner and successful salesman, Virginia born James Riely Gordon (1863–1937) designed the capitol of Arizona (1899–1900) in Phoenix and, by frequently modifying exterior materials on similar plans, seventy-two Texas and Midwestern courthouses. Gordon served thirteen terms as president of the New York Society of Architects.

ROXANNE WILLIAMSON

WORKS

1890–1891, Fayette County Courthouse, La Grange, Tex. 1891–1982, Victoria County Courthouse, Victoria, Tex. 1892–1896, Bexar County Courthouse, San Antonio, Tex. 1893, Texas Pavilion, World's Columbian Exposition, Chicago. 1894–1897, Ellis County Courthouse, Waxahachie, Tex. 1895–1896, Wise County Courthouse, Decatur, Tex. 1899–1900, Arizona Capitol, Phoenix.

BIBLIOGRAPHY

Gordon's drawings of more than two hundred buildings, plus plans, photographs, and specifications, are in the Architectural Drawings Collection of the University of Texas at Austin.
GOELDNER, PAUL KENNETH 1970 "Temples of Justice: Nineteenth Century County Courthouses in the Midwest and Texas." Unpublished Ph.D. dissertation, Columbia University, New York.
HITCHCOCK, H. R., and SEARLE, WILLIAM 1976 *Temples of Democracy: The State Capitols of the USA.* New York: Harcourt.
ROBINSON, WILLARD B. 1974 *Texas Public Buildings of the Nineteenth Century.* Austin: University of Texas Press.

GORES, LANDES

Born in Cincinatti, Ohio, Landes Gores (1919–) graduated from Princeton, and from Harvard University (1942) where he studied with WALTER GROPIUS and MARCEL BREUER. At Harvard, he met PHILIP C. JOHNSON with whom he was associated from 1945 to 1951. Since 1952, he has practiced alone in New Canaan. Works from this period include Strathmoor Village (1967), the Van Doren Hospital (1974), both in Fairfield, Connecticut. Stricken with polio in 1954, Gores nevertheless continued his career, albeit on a limited scale.

NICHOLAS PECKHAM

WORKS

1951, Gores Residence, New Canaan, Conn. 1954–1962, Offices and Laboratories, York Research Corporation, Stamford, Conn. 1957, W. G. Harris Residence, Richmond, Va. 1961, Middle School and Science Building, New Canaan Country Day School, Conn. 1963, F. Alex Close Residence, New Preston, Conn. 1967, Strathmoor Village; 1974, Van Doren Hospital; Fairfield, Conn. 1978, House for All Seasons, New Canaan, Conn.

BIBLIOGRAPHY

GORES, LANDES 1958 "One More Round in the School Cost Battle." *Journal of the American Institute of Architects* 29, no. 5:255–260.
GORES, LANDES 1959 "In Memorium E. L. W." *Journal of the American Institute of Architects* 32, no. 3:28.
GORES, LANDES (NEOSCOPOS) 1960–1961 "Tracings from an Oaken Table." *Journal of the American Institute of Architects* 33, no. 2:63–65; no. 3:60–62, no. 5:41–42; 34, no. 3:61–62; 35, no. 2:48–49.

GORIO, FEDERICO

Born in Milan, Federico Gorio (1915–) worked within the circle of the neorealistic *Scuola romana*, collaborating with LUDOVICO QUARONI, MARIO RIDOLFI, Michele Valori, and others on postwar reconstruction. Concentrating on planning problems of housing developments, Gorio distinguished himself with such works as the experimental apartment house in Salerno, Italy (1956–1961).

At present, Gorio teaches town planning at the University of Rome.

ANTONINO TERRANOVA

WORKS

1949-1951, INA-Casa Tiburtino Housing (with others), Rome. 1954, Primary School, Siderno Marina, Italy. 1955-1959, Spine Bianche Housing (with others), Matera, Italy. 1955-1962, INA-Casa and INCIS Housing (with others), Via Cavedone, Bologna, Italy. 1956-1961, Experimental Apartment House, Salerno, Italy. 1963-1964, CECA-Italsider Housing, Piombino, Italy. 1974, Corviale IACP Housing (with others), Rome. 1974-1977, Pescara Master Plan, Italy. 1976, Città Sant'Angelo Master Plan, Italy.

BIBLIOGRAPHY

CONFORTO, GINA ET AL. 1977 *Il dibattito architettonico in Italia: 1945-1975*. Rome: Bulzoni.
GIRARD, F.; SPAGNESI, G.; and GORIO, FEDERICO 1974 *L'Esquilino e la Piazza Vittorio: Una Struttura urbana dell'Ottocento*. Rome: Editalia.
GORIO, FEDERICO 1968a *Il mestiere di architetta*. Rome: Edizione dell'Ateneo.
GORIO, FEDERICO 1968b *Per una ricerca edilizia*. Rome: Edizione dell'Ateneo.
GORIO, FEDERICO 1978 *L'Urbanistica dell'empirismo alla Teoria*. Milan: Angeli.
GREGOTTI, VITTORIO 1968 *New Directions in Italian Architecture*. New York: Braziller.
ISITUTO NAZIONALE DI URBANISTICA, ROME (1952)1954 *Urbanisti italiana*. 2d ed. Rome: The institute.
TAFURI, MANFREDO, and DAL CO, FRANCESCO (1976)1979 *Modern Architecture*. New York: Abrahms. Originally published in Italian.

GOUJON, JEAN

Although more renowned as a sculptor, Jean Goujon (c.1510-c.1568) was also an important architect who contributed greatly to the design and execution of France's most heroic Renaissance buildings. Believed to have been born either in Paris or Normandy, Goujon was probably trained in the traditional classical manner, although no documentation exists of his early life. It is known, however, that in 1540 he began work at the church of Saint-Maclou in Rouen for which he designed and decorated two marble columns supporting the organ, the gates of the church, and a large fountain. Of less certainty is whether Goujon worked here on the tomb of Dreux-Bréze, governor of Normandy.

Goujon's arrival in Paris marked the beginning of his most productive period. For twenty years he worked on and off with both PIERRE LESCOT and PHILIBERT DELORME and, in fact, is believed to have been responsible for the entire façade decoration of the Henri II addition to the Louvre between 1548 and 1562, which is usually attributed solely to Lescot. Goujon supervised the sculptural scheme of this addition and helped integrate it with an appropriate structural design conceived by both him and his friend Lescot.

With Delorme—whom Goujon found less appreciative and less compatible than Lescot—a similar decoration-design partnership existed in the building of the Château d'Anet where, among other decorative programs, Goujon designed the bedroom ceiling of Diane de Poitiers in 1550. Goujon also executed a bust of Diane at this time which, it is said, she found flattering. In 1557, not coincidentally, Goujon was named official court architect by King Henri II, probably at the behest of the king's mistress, Diane. Goujon also worked on the Hôtel de Carnavalet (c.1550) and the Hôtel de Guise (Soubise, c.1558).

Goujon combined his talents as architect and sculptor unlike any artist at the time. His sculpture has a unique quality of scale and proportion that matches the building which it adorns to the extent that—in the case of the Louvre particularly—neither sculpture nor building is complete one without the other.

PETER L. DONHAUSER

WORKS

1540-1542, Saint-Maclou (additions), Rouen, France. 1544, Saint-Germain l'Auxerrois (interior decoration), Paris. 1544-1556, Château d'Ecouen (additions), France. c.1550, Fontaine des Innocents; c.1550, Hôtel Carnavalet (additions); 1553-1559, Château d'Anet (with Philibert Delorme); 1555-1562, Henri II Addition, Louvre (with Pierre Lescot); c.1558. Hôtel de Guise (Soubise; additions); Paris.

BIBLIOGRAPHY

BERTY, ADOLPHE 1860 *Les Grands Architectes Français de la Renaissance*. Paris: Aubry.
BLOMFIELD, REGINALD 1911 "Pierre Lescot and Jean Goujon." *Journal of the Royal Institute of British Architects* 18:109-128.
DU COLOMBIER, PIERRE 1949 *Jean Goujon*. Paris: Michel.
HAUTECOEUR, LOUIS (1948)1965 Volume 1 in *Histoire de l'Architecture Classique en France*. Paris: Picard.
LISTER, REGINALD 1903 *Jean Goujon: His Life and Work*. London: Duckworth.
VITRY, PAUL (1908)1927 *Jean Goujon*. Paris: Laurens.

GOULD, CARL F.

Carl Freylinghuysen Gould (1877-1939) was born in New York and graduated from Harvard University in 1898, after which he studied at the Ecole des Beaux-Arts in Paris for four years. Upon his return to New York, he worked briefly in the offices of McKim, Mead, and White and George B. Post and became a junior partner in the firm of Carpenter, Blair, and Gould. His association with Daniel H. Burnham of Chicago in the preparation of municipal plans for San Francisco furthered his special interest in city planning. Gould arrived in Seattle, Washington, about 1909 and entered practice independently. In 1914, he joined Charles H. Bebb in partnership and, over the years, produced notable work in both traditional and modernistic styles.

Bebb and Gould served as consulting architects on the State Capitol Group in Olympia, Washington, which was constructed from designs by the New York firm of Wilder and White between 1912 and 1926. They were named architects of the campus plans for the University of Washington in Seattle in 1915, and Western Washington State College in Bellingham in 1925. The firm collaborated with George B. Post and Company on one of its major projects, the Olympic Hotel in Seattle (1924–1929). Gould helped establish the University of Washington department of architecture, which he headed as first chairman from 1914 to 1926.

ELISABETH WALTON POTTER

WORKS

1910, Brownell-Bloedel House; 1914–1915, Administration Building, United States Government Locks (with Charles Bebb); Seattle, Wash. 1914–1915, Charles X. Larrabee House; 1914–1915, Young Women's Christian Association Building; Bellingham, Wash. 1915, Seattle Times Building (with Bebb); 1915–1937, University of Washington Campus Plan (with Bebb); 1924–1929, Olympic Hotel (with George B. Post and Company); 1925, Montlake Bridge (with Blaine and Associates), Montlake Boulevard, University of Washington; 1926, Suzzallo Library (with Bebb), University of Washington; 1927, Henry Art Gallery (with Bebb), University of Washington; Seattle, Wash. 1928, Library, Western Washington State College, Bellingham. 1932, Seattle Art Museum (with Bebb), Volunteer Park, Wash. 1934, Everett Public Library, Wash. 1934, United States Marine Hospital (United States Public Health Service Hospital; with Gould and John Graham, Sr.), Seattle, Wash.

BIBLIOGRAPHY

"Carl F. Gould." 1912 *Pacific Builder and Engineer* 14, no. 2:41.

"Carl F. Gould, Dean of Seattle Architects, Passes." 1939 *Pacific Builder and Engineer* 45, no. 3:1.

WOODBRIDGE, SALLY BRYNE, and MONTGOMERY, ROGER 1980 *A Guide to Architecture in Washington.* Seattle: University of Washington Press.

GRAHAM, BRUCE JOHN

A general partner in the Chicago office of SKIDMORE, OWINGS, AND MERRILL (SOM) since 1960, Bruce John Graham (1925–) is a leading American designer of large-scale buildings. Born in Bogota, Colombia, Graham received a Bachelor of Architecture degree from the University of Pennsylvania in 1948. Before joining SOM as chief of design in 1951, he worked in the offices of HOLABIRD, ROCHE, and Burgee in Chicago.

According to Graham, architecture illuminates an age by concretizing its characteristic values and ideas. Graham concentrates on the creation and refinement of an approach. His design for the Inland Steel Company (1958) in Chicago represents the development of a Miesian (see LUDWIG MIES VAN DER ROHE) curtain wall idiom. Other major buildings, in whose design Graham has played a significant role, are the Brunswick Building (1965), the Equitable Building (1965), and the Civic Center (1965), all in Chicago. The evolution of type is nowhere more evident than in the tubular frame construction buildings developed with engineer Fazlur Khan.

The Sears Tower (1974) in Chicago, with its nine bundled tubes, may be seen as the logical development of the John Hancock type. The Hancock Building (1970) also set the stage for Graham's latest multi-use buildings such as those in Hong Kong and in Cairo. In addition, Graham has worked on the designs for the Hyatt International Hotels in Cairo and in Kuwait City.

SUSAN STRAUSS

WORKS

1957, United States Navy Service School, Great Lakes, Ill. 1958, Inland Steel Headquarters; 1965, Brunswick Office Building; 1965, Civic Center; 1965, Equitable Life Assurance Society of the United States Office Building; Chicago. 1968, Boots Pure Drug Corporate Headquarters, Nottingham, England. 1969, One Marine Midland Plaza Bank and Offices, Rochester, N.Y. 1970, John Hancock Center; 1971, Hartford Fire Insurance Company; Chicago. 1971, One Shell Plaza; 1972, Two Shell Plaza; Houston. 1974, First Wisconsin Plaza Bank and Offices, Madison, Wisc. 1974, Sears Tower; 1975, Harrison Trust and Savings; Chicago. 1977, Khaneh Center Multi-use Complex, Tehran. 1977, Office Building, 60 State Street, Boston. 1978, New World Center Multi-use Complex, Hong Kong. 1980, Arab International Bank Multi-use Complex; 1980, Hyatt International Hotel; Cairo. 1981, Hyatt International Hotel and Cultural Center, Kuwait City.

BIBLIOGRAPHY

SCHULZE, FRANZ 1980 "Bruce John Graham." Pages 303–304 in Muriel Emanuel (editor), *Contemporary Architects.* New York: St. Martin's.

GRAHAM, JAMES GILLESPIE

James Gillespie (1776–1855) was born in Dunblane, Perthshire, Scotland. On the death of his father-in-law in 1825, he assumed the additional surname of Graham. Nothing is known of his early life or architectural training.

In 1800, he became the architect for the Macdonald estates in Skye and North Uist which brought significant commissions in the Highlands including Achnacarry, Inverness-shire (1802–1805), and Armadale Castle, Skye (1814–1822). Other Gothic work included the richly detailed Duns Castle, Berwickshire (1817–1821), and Dunninald, Angus (1819), with a *trompe l'oeil* Gothic dining room. After 1829, A. W. N. PUGIN was employed to produce drawings for the Houses of Parliament competition, London (1835), for new Murthly Castle, Perthshire (1827–1832), and for other buildings such as Saint John's Tolbooth Church, Edinburgh (1839–1842).

Gillespie Graham built Gray's Hospital, Elgin, Morayshire (1812–1815) and Blythswood House, Renfrewshire (1818–1821) in a severe and dry classical style which he used with panache in the layout and design of the Moray estate, Edinburgh (1821–1828), culminating in the duodecagonal Moray Place. He laid out the town of Birkenhead, Cheshire, England (1825–1828), but only Hamilton Square seems to have been built to his design.

JAMES MACAULAY

WORKS

1802–1805, Achnacarry, Inverness-shire, Scotland. *1802–1805, Culdees Castle, Perthshire, Scotland. *1810–1813, Crawford Priory (with David Hamilton), Fife, Scotland. 1813, Saint Mary's Roman Catholic Cathedral, Edinburgh. 1814, Saint Andrew's Roman Catholic Cathedral, Glasgow, Scotland. *1814–1822, Armadale Castle, Inverness-shire, Scotland. 1812–1815, Gray's Hospital, Elgin, Morayshire, Scotland. 1817–1821, Duns Castle, Berwickshire, Scotland. *1818–1821, Blythswood House, Renfrewshire, Scotland. 1819, Dunninald, Angus, Scotland. 1821–1828, Moray Estate, Edinburgh. 1825–1828, Hamilton Square, Birkenhead, Cheshire, England. *1827–1832, (New) Murthly Castle (with A. W. N. Pugin), Perthshire, Scotland. 1833–1839, George Heriot's Hospital Chapel (with Pugin), Edinburgh. 1838–1842, Taymouth Castle (with Pugin), Perthshire, Scotland. 1839–1842, Saint John's Tolbooth Church (with Pugin), Edinburgh.

BIBLIOGRAPHY

DUNBAR, JOHN G. (1966)1978 *Architecture of Scotland.* Rev. ed. London: Batsford.
LINDSAY, IAN G. (1948)1973 *Georgian Edinburgh.* 2d ed. Revised by David Walker. Edinburgh: Scottish Academic Press.
MACAULAY, JAMES 1974–1975 "James Gillespie Graham in Skye." *Bulletin of the Scottish Georgian Society* 3:1–4.
MACAULAY, JAMES 1975 *The Gothic Revival, 1745–1845.* Glasgow, Scotland: Blackie.
STANTON, PHOEBE 1971 *Pugin.* London: Thames & Hudson.
YOUNGSON, A. J. 1966 *The Making of Classical Edinburgh, 1705–1840.* Edinburgh University Press.

GRAHAM, ANDERSON, PROBST, and WHITE

The firm of Burnham and Root, founded by DANIEL H. BURNHAM, underwent several changes. When Root died in 1891, it was renamed D. H. Burnham and Company. When Burnham died in 1912, the firm was reorganized as Graham, Burnham and Company. In 1917, this firm was dissolved and the present partnership, Graham, Anderson, Probst, and White was formed. Although both this firm and Burnham Brothers (formed by Burnham's sons) may be regarded as successors, the larger portion of the practice went to Graham, Anderson, Probst, and White. This was due to the experience, expertise, and entrepreneurship of the oldest man in the group, Ernest R. Graham (1866–1936), who joined the firm in 1894 and directed its social, political, and business interests after Burnham's death eighteen years later.

Peirce Anderson (1870–1924), the chief designer during the firm's golden age (1912 to 1929), had the broadest education, including an A.B. from Harvard University and a postgraduate degree in engineering from Johns Hopkins University, and a *diplôme* from the Ecole des Beaux-Arts. He joined D. H. Burnham and Company in 1900.

Edward Probst (1870–1942) joined the firm in 1893 after working for, among others, PETER B. WIGHT. In 1908, he was given the responsibility for the supervision of working plans. His son, Marvin G. Probst, was president of the firm until his death, at which time he was succeeded by William R. Surman.

Howard Judson White (1870–1936) joined the firm in 1898 as a draftsman. In 1905, he became Graham's assistant, assuming responsibility for letting contracts and supervising construction.

The firm has designed a wide variety of building types, including public buildings, office buildings, railway stations, museums, concert halls, memorials, educational institutions, libraries, hospitals, department stores, hotels, banks, warehouses, parking facilities, industrial and power plants, and military projects.

During the course of its long and varied practice, it has produced buildings in every style of the period from 1912 to the present, including Beaux-Arts, Art Deco, Art Moderne, the International style, and others. The firm consistently has constructed high-quality buildings that have been fully used over long periods of time.

SALLY CHAPPELL

WORKS

1909–1928, Selfridge and Company Building, London. 1911–1914, United States Post Office, Washington. 1911–1919, Field Museum of Natural History, Chicago. 1912, Columbus Memorial, Washington. 1912, Continental National Bank Building (now the Central Trust Company of Illinois), Chicago. 1914, Equitable Building, New York. 1914, Mount Wilson Observatory, Pasadena, Calif. 1924, Chicago Union Station. 1924, Strauss Building, Chicago. 1924, Union Trust Building, Cleveland, Ohio. 1926, Gimbel Brothers, Philadelphia. 1926–1931, Cleveland Union Terminal Group, Ohio. 1927, Heyburn Building, Louisville, Ky. 1928, Chase National Bank Building, New York. 1929, Broad Street Station, Philadelphia. 1929, Civic Opera House; 1929, Merchandise Mart; 1929, John G. Shedd Aquarium; Chicago. 1930, Burlington Station, Omaha, Nebr. 1930, Stewart Memorial Library, Coe College, Cedar Rapids, Iowa. 1931, Chicago Historical Society. 1932, Pennsylvania Station, Philadelphia. 1932, United States Post Office, Chicago. 1933, Northerly Island, Chicago Exposition Authority. 1933, Union Station, Los Angeles. 1933, Wrigley Aquarium and Planetarium, Catalina Island, Calif. 1945–1959, Buildings, University of Illinois, Champagne-Urbana. 1945–1959, Kraft Factory and Office Building, Minneapolis, Minn. 1945–1959, Scott Edens Plaza Shopping Center, Wilmette, Ill. 1961, Department of State Building, Washington. 1961–1969, Baxter Travenol Laboratories, Deerfield, Ill. 1971, Honeywell Building, Arlington Heights, Ill. 1973, DuPage County Administrative Center, Wheaton, Ill. 1980, Loyola School of Law, Chicago.

BIBLIOGRAPHY

The correspondence, drawings, commissions log, papers, photographs, and unpublished documents of Graham, Anderson, Probst, and White, are in the archives of the firm in Chicago.

The Architectural Work of Graham, Anderson, Probst and White. 1933 2 vols. London: Batsford. Contains plates only.

CONDIT, CARL W. 1964 *The Chicago School of Architecture: A History of Commercial and Public Building in the Chicago Area, 1875–1925.* University of Chicago Press.

CONDIT, CARL W. 1973 *Chicago, 1910–1929: Building, Planning and Urban Technology.* University of Chicago Press.

GRANDJEAN DE MONTIGNY, AUGUSTE-HENRI-VICTOR

Auguste-Henri-Victor Grandjean de Montigny (1776–1850) arrived in Rio de Janeiro with the artistic mission brought from France by Dom João IV in 1816. Winner of the Grand Prix de Rome in 1799 after studying in the workshops of Charles PERCIER AND Pierre Leonard FONTAINE, Grandjean de Montigny initiated the Ecole des Beaux-Arts curriculum at the Imperial Academy of Fine Arts in Rio, which he designed, becoming its first titled professor of architecture.

Architect, painter, and urban planner, Grandjean de Montigny maintained prestige within the court until his death, gaining commissions for public structures and private homes which ranged eclectically from Greco-Roman to neo-Tuscan.

ELIZABETH D. HARRIS

WORKS

1816, Roman Arch; 1819–1826, Customs House; 1830s, Grandjean de Montigny House; 1834–1836, Customs House II; 1834–1841, Market; 1838, Pedro II High School (converted from São Joaquim Seminary); Rio de Janeiro, Brazil.

BIBLIOGRAPHY

CASTEDO, LEOPOLDO 1969 *A History of Latin American Art and Architecture.* New York: Praeger.

RIOS FILHO, ADOLFO MORALES DE LOS 1942 *Grandjean de Montigny e a evolução da arte brazileira.* Rio de Janeiro: Empresa a Noite.

GRANPRE MOLIERE, M. J.

M. J. Grandpré Molière (1883–) had a considerable influence in Holland through his ideas and designs as a professor at the Technical University in Delft.

Starting in the 1920s, he practiced as a qualified architect and formed a philosophical aesthetic as a teacher. His theories were based on the philosophy of Thomas Aquinas, and his buildings recalled early Christian and early Romanesque architecture. His buildings nevertheless had a smoothness and simplicity of wall surfaces. Molière built very few buildings, but his students, called the Delft school, spread his ideas widely. It is ironic that Molière's ideas—so etherial—stem from the Technical University, as it is widely known for its pragmatic engineering ideas.

SUZANNE FRANK

WORK

1916–1919, Vreewijk (housing complex), Rotterdam, Netherlands.

BIBLIOGRAPHY

BERLAGE, H. P. 1925 *De ontwikkeling der moderne bouwkunst in Holland.* Amsterdam: Maatschappij voor goede en goedkoppe lectuur.

FANELLI, GIOVANNI (1968)1978 *Moderne architectuur in Nederlands: 1900–1940.* Translated from the Italian and edited by Wim de Wit. The Hague: Staatsuitgeverij.

FEENSTRA, C. 1920 *Tuinsteden en Volkshuisvesting in Nederland en buitenland.* Amsterdam: Van Mantgen & de Doe.

"De Hedendaagse menbelstijl door ingenieur M. J. Granpré Molière." 1919 Pages 59–61 in *Jaarboek van Nederlandsche ambachts—en nijverheidskunst.* Rotterdam, Netherlands:

VRIEND, J. J. 1974 *Links Bouwen, Rechts Bouwen.* Amsterdam: Uitgeverij Contact.

WATTJES, J. G. 1931 *Moderne Nederlandsche Villa's en landhuizen.* Amsterdam: Kosmos.

WILS, JAN 1921 *Volkswoningbouw.* The Hague: Haagache Kunstring.

GRANVILLE, WALTER

Walter Long B. Granville (c.1819–1874) was the most important mid-Victorian architect to work in Calcutta. With the exception of his Gothic High Court (1864–1872), Granville's public buildings were distinguished additions to the classical architectural tradition of the capital of British India. Little is recorded about Granville's career. In 1858, he went out to India as architect to the Eastern Bengal Railway; in 1864, he became consulting architect to the Government of Bengal with the express purpose of designing public buildings in Calcutta. Granville's appointment terminated in 1869, and several of his buildings were finished by others.

GAVIN STAMP

WORKS

1849–1854, Saint James's Church, Hatcham, London. 1862–1874, All Souls' Church (not completed until 1875), Cawnpore, India. 1864–1868, Post Office; 1864–1872, High Court (tower completed by Barnfather); *1866–1872, Senate House and University; 1866–1874, Imperial (Indian) Museum (not completed until 1875; altered); Calcutta.

BIBLIOGRAPHY

STAMP, GAVIN 1981 "British Architecture in India: 1857–1947." *Journal of the Royal Society of Arts* 129:357–377.

GRAPPIN FAMILY

The Grappin were a family of master masons active in the workshop of Saint-Gervais-Saint-Protais, Gisors, France, throughout the sixteenth century. The north façade, nave, and north tower were executed under the direction of Robert Grappin (c.1485–1543) from 1521 until his death. The west façade, begun by Robert, was completed by his son Jean I Grappin (c.1510–?), sculptor and *maistre d'oeuvre* after 1558. Jean II Grappin (?–c.1598), either brother or son of Jean I, continued as master of Saint-Gervais until 1598. Attributed to the Grappin are parts of Notre-Dame, Magny; the west façade of Saint-Gervais, near Magny (1549–1550); Vétheuil (1551); Genainville (1551); Montjavoult (c.1565); and the towers of Nucourt and Chaumont-en-Vexin.

HILARY BALLON

WORK

1521–1598, Saint-Gervais-Saint-Protais, Gisors, France.

BIBLIOGRAPHY

BLOMFIELD, REGINALD (1921)1974 Volume 2 in *A History of French Architecture from the Reign of Charles VIII till the Death of Mazarin, 1494–1661.* Reprint. New York: Hacker.

HAUTECOEUR, LOUIS (1943)1965 "La Renaissance des humanistes." Volume 1, part 2 in *Histoire de l'Architecture classique en France.* Rev. ed. Paris: Picard.

PÉPIN, EUGÈNE (1939)1963 *Gisors et la Vallée de l'Epte.* Paris: Laurens.

REGNIER, LOUIS 1905 "Eglise de Gisors." *Congrès archéologique de France* 72:64–73.

GRAY, EILEEN

Born in Ireland and educated at the Slade School in London, Eileen Gray (1879–1976) spent her adult life in Paris. Early in her career, she designed and executed screens and small pieces of furniture in lacquer and by the 1920s, she produced total interiors. In the late 1920s, she began her work in architecture, being one of very few women in the field at the time. Her architectural oeuvre includes two houses, one designed for JEAN BADOVICI, editor of the influential journal *L'Architecture Vivante,* interiors, and many projects. Although Gray employed the mainstream stylistic vocabulary of the International style, her work is distinguished for its high degree of functional flexibility and sensitivity.

DEBORAH F. NEVINS

WORKS

1926–1929, "E-1027" House, Roquebrune, France. 1930–1931, Jean Badovici Apartment, Paris. 1932–1934, Tempe a Pailla House, Castellar, France.

BIBLIOGRAPHY

JOHNSON, STEWART 1979 *Eileen Gray: Designer 1879–1976.* London: Debrett.

NEVINS, DEBORAH 1980 "Maison en Bord de Mer."

Residential Interiors 5, Sept.:114–118.

RYKWERT, JOSEPH 1971 "Eileen Gray: Two Houses and an Interior." *Perspecta* 13–14:66–73.

GREBER, JACQUES

Jacques Gréber (20th century), architect-urbanist, began his career landscaping military cemeteries. More attracted to the natural than to the built environment, he landscaped country houses in France and America. His major planning schemes for Philadelphia and Ottawa separated economic and residential activities by parkways and excluded railways from city centers.

ELIZABETH MCLANE

WORKS

Begun 1917, American military cemeteries, Bois Belleau, Suresnes, La Fère en Tardenois, Romagne sous Montfacon, France. n.d., Fairmont Parkway; n.d., Robin Museum (with PAUL CRET); Philadelphia. n.d., Vanderlip Village, Palos Verdes, Calif. n.d., Villa Altana, Antibes, France. n.d., Villa Espalmador, Villefranche, France. n.d., Villa Marlia, Lucca, Italy.

BIBLIOGRAPHY

"Le Fairmont Parkway à Philadelphie." 1962 *La Vie Urbaine* New Series Jan.–Mar.:1–18.

"L'Exposition Internationale de Paris, 1937: Jacques Gréber Architecte-en-Chef." 1937 *Architecture et Urbanisme* 57, no. 1:3–11; no. 2:21–27.

LAPRADE, ALBERT 1934 "Les Jardins de Jacques Gréber." *L'Architecture* 47, July:241–254.

"National Capitol Plan for Ottawa, Canada. Edward Fiset, Joint Architect and John M. Kitchen, Joint Architect." 1967 *Journal of the Royal Architectural Institute of Canada* 44, Apr.:31–42.

"New Plans for Paris." 1921 *Architectural Record* 49, Jan.:71–78.

"Ottawa: Un example d'aménagement urbain et régional donné par une capitale etrangère." 1958 *La Vie Urbaine* July–Sept.:223–235.

"The Paris International Exposition of 1937, M. Jacques Gréber, Chief Architect." 1936 *Architecture* 73, Apr.:197–200.

"Paris 1937: Jacques Gréber Architect-in-Chief." 1936 *Pencil Points* 17, Mar.:123–127.

"Plan d'Aménagement de la Capitale Nationale du Canada." 1950 *La Vie Urbaine* no. 55:23–69.

GREEN, E. B.

Edward B. Green (1855–1950), born in Utica, New York, graduated from Cornell University in 1878. He established partnerships with William S. Wicks (1884–1917), his son (1917–1933), and R. Maxwell James (1936–1950). Green employed a broad range of styles—often with the highest competency—during the more than sixty years that he monopolized Buffalo architecture.

JACK QUINAN

WORKS

1890, First Presbyterian Church; 1895, Dun Building; 1900, Albright–Knox Art Gallery; 1900, Buffalo Savings Bank; 1901, Buffalo Central Y.M.C.A.; 1905, Chamber of Commerce Building; Buffalo, N.Y. 1909–1912, 1926, 1933, Toledo Museum of Art, Ohio. 1913, Marine Trust Building; 1922, Buffalo Athletic Club; 1923, Genesee Building; Buffalo, N.Y. 1927–1930, Dayton Art Institute, Ohio. 1928, New York State Office Building; 1930–1937, State University of New York at Buffalo (master plan and Crosby Hall, Norton Union [now Squire Hall], Lockwood Library [now Abbott Library], Parker Hall, Clark Gymnasium); 1935, U.S. Courthouse; 1939, War Memorial Auditorium; Buffalo, N.Y.

BIBLIOGRAPHY

FOX, AUSTIN M. 1980 "The Greening of Buffalo: How Architect E. B. Green Shaped the Profile of the City." *Buffalo Spree* 14:66–68.

"Funeral of Edward B. Green, Noted Architect, Tomorrow." 1950 *Buffalo Evening News* Feb 13.

McCONNELL, OVIATT 1935 "Tomorrow—What? Architect Expects Future City to Be for Convenience, Beauty." *The Buffalo Times* June 15.

GREEN, WILLIAM CURTIS

William Curtis Green (1875–1960) was articled to JOHN BELCHER and from 1898 contributed topographical drawings to *The Builder*. He set up on his own in 1899, and in 1910 went into partnership with the firm of Dunn and Watson. Later, he developed a practice noted both for its craftsmanship and for its elegant use of "Manhattan" classicism. The Dorchester Hotel (1930) in London was his major work.

MARGARET RICHARDSON

WORKS

1899, Bristol Tramways Generating Station, Bristol, England. 1904, Power Station, Chiswick, London. 1904, Power Station, Hitchin, Hertsfordshire, England. 1904, Tucketts Farm Estate, Netherton, Devonshire, England. 1905, Quaker Meeting Hall, Croydon, London. 1913, Rystwood House, Forest Row, Sussex, England. 1922, Barclays Bank, 160 Piccadilly, London. 1924, Old Stanmore Estate, Winchester, England. 1925, Ashmore Manor, Dorsetshire, England. 1926, Westminster Bank, 63 Piccadilly; 1927, London Life Assurance Building, King William Street; 1928, Offices, 9 Duke Street; London. 1929–1932, Stockgrove Park, Leighton Buzzard, Buckinghamshire, England. 1929, Stratton House, Piccadilly; 1930, Dorchester Hotel, Park Lane;

1932, Barclays Bank, Knightsbridge; London. 1932, Goodmans Furze, Headly, Surrey, England. 1934, Saint Christopher's Church, Cove, Hampshire, England. 1934, Queen's Hotel, Leeds, Yorkshire, England. 1935, Barclays Bank, Bond Street; 1936, Equity Law Building, Lincolns Inn Fields; London. 1937, Robinswood House, Fairware, Sussex, England.

BIBLIOGRAPHY

LLOYD, J. S. (editor) 1978 *W. Curtis Green RA: Architect and Draughtsman, 1875–1960*. London: Green, Lloyd & Adams. Exhibition catalogue.
"Obituary." 1960 *The Builder* 198, no. 6098:642.
REILLY, CHARLES HERBERT 1931 *Representative British Architects of the Present Day*. London: Batsford.
RICHARDSON, A. E. 1949 Foreword in *The Drawings of W. Curtis Green RA*. London: Batsford.

GREENE, CHARLES SUMNER, and GREENE, HENRY MATHER

Charles Sumner Greene (1868–1957) and Henry Mather Greene (1870–1954) pioneered the California bungalow and thus changed the way in which many Americans live. Their artistic philosophy, stimulated by the Arts and Crafts movement, and their early training, which emphasized a logical approach to design and superb craftsmanship, encouraged their break with tradition and prompted them to use the most modest of materials to bring dignity to the smallest of homes and elegance to their larger residences.

Charles was born in Brighton, now a suburb of Cincinnati, Ohio, in 1868, followed by his brother, Henry, fifteen months later. Their family had participated in the origins of the United States; among their forebears were such distinguished Americans as Generals Christopher and Nathanael Greene, Benjamin Franklin, Cotton Mather, Reverend Richard Mather, and Senator Charles Sumner.

The brothers' early lives were spent on the Mather family farm in Virginia while their father was attending medical school. In this rural atmosphere they were exposed to the beauties of nature, and their appreciation of natural materials was further enhanced by their schooling in St. Louis, Missouri. Their father, determined that his sons follow in the footsteps of their great-great-grandfather, a Boston architect, enrolled them in the first manual training school in the United States opened by Calvin Milton Woodward under the direction of Washington University. Woodward had spent some time in England studying the principles of WILLIAM MORRIS and upon his return to the United States had based his school curriculum upon the Morris doctrines. Throughout their high school careers, Charles and Henry Greene spent each afternoon in the shops learning the properties of wood, metals, and other materials and the tools with which to work them. They developed their talents, quickly becoming fine craftsmen. These skills, combined with their knowledge of the characteristics of differing materials and their adherence to the direct and simple philosophy of William Morris, provided them with a fundamental attitude about the determinants of design.

When he finished high school, Charles postponed further academic study for one year at the request of his father in order that he and Henry could begin their architectural training together. During this period he devoted himself to painting, photography, and the writing of poetry and grew more and more resistant to the prospect of continuing formal academic studies and to the field of architecture. Eventually, however, he and his father reached a compromise, and both he and Henry enrolled in a special two-year course in architecture at the Massachusetts Institute of Technology, which provided for two additional years of apprenticeship in architectural offices. However, the Beaux-Arts curriculum at M.I.T. was in dramatic contrast to their experience on the Mather farm and the influence of the William Morris philosophy in the Woodward Manual Training Program. Charles, with his romantic, almost mystical nature, found the M.I.T. program strange and burdensome at first, but Henry found the experience interesting though contrary to his basic beliefs. During the course of the next two years, however, both brothers became fascinated by Greek history and the classic forms of architecture which encouraged their careful study of scale, proportion, and composition. In 1891, they began their apprenticeships in the Boston area, Charles, with the firm of Winslow and Wetherell, and Henry, with SHEPLEY, RUTAN, AND COOLIDGE, successors to the firm of H. H. RICHARDSON, and later with Chamberlin and Austin. It was while working with Shepley, Rutan, and Coolidge that Henry worked on drawings for the famed arched quad at Stanford University.

During this period of apprenticeship, Charles and Henry were exposed to the Shingle style concepts fostered by Richardson, and they spent a good deal of their free time in the Boston Museum of Fine Arts, where they were first introduced to the arts of the Orient. In later years, both the Shingle style and Oriental art forms were to influence their designs of the California bungalows. On weekends, they visited an aunt in East Braintree where they took part in musical quartets, played the piano and violin, and developed social graces and cultural interests which were to be advantageous in future dealings with their distinguished clientele.

In 1893, Charles and Henry visited their parents who had moved to Pasadena, California, for their health. En route, they stopped in Chicago to attend the World's Columbian Exposition of 1893 and were drawn immediately to the simple integrity they found in the Japanese pavilion. Here was a structure that embodied the straightforward principles they had learned in the manual training school, and it inspired a lifelong interest in all aspects of the Oriental culture. When they arrived in California, they were entranced with the citrus groves, poppy fields, and foothills of the San Gabriel Valley. They admired the California Mission structures and were excited by the freedom and the vitality of a community which was then on the brink of one of the largest building booms in history. They extended their visit in order to build a residence for a friend of their father's, and by opening a temporary one-room office for this purpose, they formed the architectural firm of Greene and Greene.

They never returned to work in the Boston area but built their careers in Pasadena. For nearly ten years, they searched for ways to break from the traditional architectural vocabularies of the day. As their reputations as young, creative architects grew and their ability to communicate their own developing philosophies to clients developed, their work radically changed. During this period, the 1896 design for the Kinney–Kendall Building in the heart of downtown Pasadena drew considerable acclaim for its straightforward design; it was also one of the largest structures in town when built. The youthful architects aptly reduced remnants of historicism to thin spandrels and cornice,

composing these ornate textures to work for them in establishing the strong horizontal lines of the building. The remainder of the exterior was comprised of broad expanses of glass, allowing for light into the heart of the interior offices. By preference, however, this was one of the very few commercial structures designed by the brothers. They refused several opportunities for commercial work, preferring to do residences where they could relate to the personalities of their clients.

By the turn of the century, Charles and Henry had rid their designs of nearly all eclectic tradition and reflected more and more the directness of geometry, the influence of the California climate, and the freedom of the lifestyle in California.

In 1899, Henry married Emeline Augusta Dart, and two years later, Charles married Alice Gordon White, soon sailing to England, his bride's birthplace, for their honeymoon. At that time, the Arts and Crafts movement was flourishing in England and through such publications as *The International Studio,* Charles must have been aware of the movement's proponents and their activities. Although there is no record of the people with whom he associated, he undoubtedly did come in direct contact with those creative individuals whose works were changing the course of design.

In the two years immediately after Charles's return to California, an extraordinary period of growth occurred in the development and crystallization of the two brothers' creative energies and ideas. In addition, the first two issues of Gustav Stickley's *Craftsman Magazine* appeared in 1902, followed later by Will Bradley's articles in the *Ladies' Home Journal.* The Stickley influence was immediately seen in the furnishings and interiors of the Greenes' James A. Culbertson House in Pasadena (1902) which was almost completely furnished with the same pieces of furniture illustrated in those first two issues of the *Craftsman Magazine.*

Between 1902 and 1904, the Greene and Greene architectural vocabulary reached back to the fundamentals of the manual training school to burst forth in new and exciting directions. Charles and Henry responded to climate, orientation, site, and budget, and developed an extraordinary rapport with their clients. Their designs were symphonies in wood and the articulated details of their houses were almost like furniture. Their total involvement with design encompassed landscape, furnishings, carpets, lighting, hardware, fabrics, silver, pottery, and such personal effects as book plates. The owners' wives, daughters, or nieces were often called upon to carry out stitchery patterns for curtains, draperies, and pillows.

In 1902, Charles completed what was to be the

Greene and Greene. Kinney–Kendall Building. Pasadena, California. 1896

first phase of his own house, and in 1904, Henry built a unique home designed for two generations, providing complete privacy for his own family and equal privacy for his mother-in-law. Both plans exhibited the tight central hall with cellular spaces along each side.

In 1903, when Arturo Bandini requested a simple wooden house based upon the courtyard principles of his Southern California ancestors, the Greenes broke away from the tight English plan and responded freely to the random movement of the site and to the casual lifestyle of the area. Their plan forms relaxed, opened up, embraced the out-of-doors, created exterior gardens and vistas, and eliminated walks as barriers to the exterior. From this time on, they designed spaces inside and out—porch, terrace, garden, vista, sometimes enclosed structurally, sometimes by landscape, sometimes by scale, proportion, change of level or material, but always with the awareness of human response to space and environment.

The early designs between 1902 and 1904 revealed the Greenes' enthusiasm for the integrity and directness of Stickley's Mission Oak furniture. This is demonstrated by the furniture for Jennie A. Reeve in 1904, where the design for the house pulled together all of the individual facets of their unfolding architectural expression. That same year, Greene and Greene were given an opportunity to demonstrate their talents on a grander scale in their design of a residence for an extraordinary client, Adelaide M. Tichenor. She shared their interest in the Orient and was willing to explore new modes of expression while maintaining her own cultured taste and standards. Before the unfortunate and untimely remodelings, this house testified to the Greenes' total control of the systems, philosophies, and principles of the style they had created. Although the vocabulary is the same, the location by the sea, the different climate from that of the San Gabriel Valley, and the personal interests of the client added new dimensions to the Greenes' work. Furniture softened; harsh lines were sculpted yet remained logical; applied decoration disappeared; the purity of form, composition, grace of line, scale, and proportion dominated. Necessary elements of joinery and structure became the focus of enrichment.

Both Charles and Henry were small in stature, modest and genteel in manner, but their mild appearance masked a determination, confidence, and conviction that continually spurred them and their craftsmen to seek artistic perfection. As individuals they were very different. Henry was a family man who devoted a great deal of time to his four children and shared with his family his belief in the union of life and environment. Charles, on the other hand, was a true visionary. Although quiet in temperament, he exhibited an artistic drama that sometimes made him seem unapproachable, and his creative imagination left him impatient with the mundane aspects of daily chores. Although no less devoted than Henry to his wife and children, his work consumed the major portion of his time.

Between 1904 and 1907, the Greene and Greene practice, with offices in both Los Angeles and Pasadena, grew at an amazing rate. Their association with two master craftsmen, Peter and John Hall, and master glass artisan Emile Lange, formerly with the LOUIS C. TIFFANY Studios in New York, established a team enterprise which developed and produced extraordinary achievements in a relatively short time. The Greenes' bungalow designs had a tremendous influence on other architects, builders, and owners in southern California, the United States, and even such distant places as Australia. There were also major houses during this period—in particular, the Henry M. Robinson Estate (1905), using brick, frame, and gunite, an unusual departure from their Shingle style. Nevertheless, it was the one- and two-story single-family dwellings that brought the brothers such high acclaim. Their works were quickly publicized and their influence changed the face of neighborhoods, towns, and cities. Their dominance in Pasadena, California, has been compared to the impact of FRANK LLOYD WRIGHT's work in Oak Park, Illinois, and BERNARD R. MAYBECK's in Berkeley, California.

As the Greenes' articulated architectural vocabulary refined rapidly between 1904 and 1907, numerous earlier clients or new owners came to them to update, add to, or imbue their earlier designs with their later detailing. Of particular interest were the additions and alterations in 1906 to the 1903 Van Rossem House for James W. Neill, the 1900 Katherine Duncan House for Theodore Irwin (1906), as well as the substantial expansion of Charles Greene's own home.

In 1907, the Greenes' practice abruptly changed. For some time, Pasadena had been attracting wealthy Easterners who vacationed in the

Greene and Greene. John C. Bentz House. Pasadena, California. 1906

Greene and Greene.
James W. Neill House
(additions and
alterations).
Pasadena, California.
1906

Greene and Greene.
Robert R. Blacker House.
Pasadena, California.
1907

Greene and Greene.
David B. Gamble House.
Pasadena, California.
1908

Greene and Greene.
S.S. Crow (Edward S.
Crocker) House.
Pasadena, California.
1909

many elaborate winter hotels in the area. One by one, they began to build private homes along the grand avenues of Pasadena. Between 1907 and 1911, the charm and regional appropriateness of the Greene and Greene designs caught the imagination of Easterners with taste, culture, and unlimited budgets. In this five-year period, the brothers designed seven or eight elaborate houses which have come to be regarded as their ultimate bungalows. No aspect of design of house, furnishings, or landscaping was left untouched. In the quest for excellence, contracts included overages which permitted work to be torn out and done over whenever the craftsmen failed to come up to the brothers' high standards.

These masterworks include the Pasadena courtyard residence for Freeman A. Ford (1907), the grand estate for Robert R. Blacker (1907), the tasteful elegance and restraint in the design of the home for David B. Gamble (1908), the rambling ranch house quality of the residence for Charles M. Pratt in the foothills of Ojai, California (1909), the sensitive adaptations of the southern California vocabulary to the climate of Berkeley, California, in the home of William R. Thorsen (1909), and the disciplined restraint and subtle grace of Henry Greene's independent design for S. S. Crow of Pasadena (1909). The reputation of Greene and Greene rests primarily upon these masterworks which have been the focus of attention and have received the highest critical acclaim. However appropriate this acclaim may be, the real impact of the Greenes' influence upon other architects and upon the way Americans live was derived from the dozens of small bungalows for persons of more modest means.

By 1909, Charles Greene was so exhausted by the opportunities and demands of the firm and his self-imposed total preoccupation with his work that he took his family to England for a year. During his absence, Henry continued the work, saw to the construction of designs completed before Charles's departure and carried on independent projects which illustrate the differences between the two brothers and the excellence of his own independent designs.

By 1911, Charles and Henry had become so accustomed to the artistic freedom and pursuit of excellence which their later clients had allowed that their personal standards priced their designs out of the market, and the demand for their work rapidly declined. Furthermore, the widespread poor imitations of their wooden bungalows by those who neither understood nor shared their commitment to the Arts and Crafts philosophy led to a general disenchantment with any kind of wooden building identified as a bungalow.

When Charles returned from England in 1910, the firm engaged in several grand and elaborate designs for various clients in Pasadena, Los Angeles, and other parts of the country. Of these, only one ever got past the drawing stage due to the extravagant costs of scale and craftsmanship. This one design, the gunite-and-tile courtyard residence (1911) for Cordelia Culbertson and her two maiden sisters, represented an interesting exploration of new materials. Natural woods were nowhere to be seen; the changing nature and plasticity of gunite and plaster brought about soft, sometimes curved forms as opposed to the linear composition of their expressed wooden construction. The Victorian personalities of the three Culbertson sisters were a challenge to the Greenes but, as always, they were best when dealing with clients of strong and unique personalities. The extraordinary qualities of the design were to attract the second owner, Francis F. Prentiss who acquired the house in 1917, to become as significant a client for the continued development of the interior and furnishings as had been the Culbertson sisters.

Meanwhile between 1911 and 1917, the firm worked on a variety of designs, some built and some not, in many different expressions, but never with the vitality and impact of their vocabulary for the California bungalows.

In 1917, Charles moved to Carmel, California, where his interests in philosophy, photography, painting, and poetry could be shared with new friends in that artistic community. The brothers continued the Pasadena offices of Greene and Greene until reorganization of the firm in 1922, after which Charles practiced as C. Sumner Greene in Carmel and Henry assumed full responsibility for the former firm in Pasadena. In spite of this professional reorganization, however, the two brothers maintained a close personal relationship and continued to work together on the frequent modifications for former clients, particularly for the owners of their ultimate bungalows.

In 1918, however, Charles, as C. Sumner Greene, designed and began construction of a stone house for D. L. James at Carmel Highlands. Construction took five years and at times Henry was consulted on soil conditions as well as structural and foundation design. The James House remains a timeless, unique, and original architectural achievement.

The 1920s provided both Charles and Henry with a variety of works, both large and small, which provide a basis for analyzing their independent talents. In addition to the James House, Charles Greene's own studio (1923) and his library addition and alterations to the Martin Flavin House (1928) attest to his interest in carving and his own personal craftsmanship.

In the early 1920s, Charles Greene built a small bungalow in Carmel for himself and his family, but it was his brick studio on the front of the site which provided an insight into Charles's inquisitive and imaginative mind. The materials, taken from a demolished hotel, were primarily brick, with a tile roof that was never quite completed. He selected special sands to mix with the plaster for the interiors so that he could leave the walls natural and unpainted. Throughout the plastering, the screed was never used and the straight line was avoided in order to express the nature of the hand application done by him and his son. Wooden carvings, which his family referred to as cookie cutters, were created, and abstract patterns were pressed into the wet plaster, creating a rhythmic textural design which picked up the different light qualities in the room and emphasized the shadow changes throughout the day. In 1923, a similar treatment was used for a client with the addition of soft watercolors in the wet plaster imprints of the cookie cutters, and a light glaze over the final finish created soft pastel nuances dancing around parts of the frieze.

The most important independent works of both brothers came toward the end of the 1920s with the addition of the vast water gardens for the Mortimer Fleishhacker Estate (1927) by Charles Greene in Woodside, California, and the Walter L. Richardson Ranch House (1929) by Henry in Porterville, California. The Richardson House was designed by Henry but was to be built by the family and ranch hands of the Porterville Ranch. Henry turned to the soil for the material of the building which today is as appropriate to its sur-

Greene and Greene. Cordelia A. Culbertson House. Pasadena, California. 1911

Greene and Greene. Walter L. Richardson House. Porterville, California. 1929

roundings and purpose as when it was built. Foundations were of stone from the site, and because of the extraordinary heat of the valley, the walls were constructed of an adobe made from the muds of the ranch. Wrought-iron hardware was created by the blacksmith. The most important factor in the design is the boldness of the compositional forms and straightforward detailing which took into account the construction by unskilled hands.

The difference in the vocabulary of the Greenes during their early, middle, and late years, is evidence of their ability to recognize and adapt to change and their capacity to explore new materials, forms and technology. The common thread weaving through all their work is the appropriateness of material, the form given to buildings, the skills composing each new vocabulary, and the demand for quality and craftsmanship. The manual training program had given them the skills to work with their hands. It had also given them a philosophy which enabled them to select the determinants which gave form to their architecture.

Although the Greenes' archievements were overlooked between World Wars I and II, they were rediscovered by the young architects who were searching for roots and direction in the postwar years. They were honored by the local and the national chapters of the American Institute of Architects, and books and articles on their work appeared. In 1966, the heirs of Cecil and Louise Gamble gave the David B. Gamble House of 1908 to the City of Pasadena in a joint agreement with the University of Southern California. The Gamble House is now open to the public. In 1968, the Greene and Greene Library and Archives were established at the Gamble House to encourage scholarly research on the architects and their work.

Seventy-five years after the construction of their ultimate bungalows, the influence of Charles and Henry Greene continues. The dignity they gave to the small house, as well as the elegance of their masterworks, has emphasized to the public the union of building and site, of home and environment. This has encouraged ordinances to protect the quality of neighborhoods and the value of communities and has prompted public forums to air the great issues of redevelopment and change in a growing, complex society.

RANDELL L. MAKINSON

WORKS

1896, Kinney–Kendall Building; 1901, Charles S. Greene House; 1902, James A. Culbertson House; 1903, Arturo Bandini House; Pasadena, Calif. 1903, Mrs. Mary R. Darling House, Claremont, Calif. 1903, Josephine Van Rossem House; 1903, Martha, Violet, and Jane White House; 1904, Mrs. James A. Garfield House; 1904, Henry M. Greene House; Pasadena, Calif.

1904, Jennie A. Reeve House; 1904, Adelaide M. Tichenor House; Long Beach, Calif. 1905, Henry M. Robinson House; 1905, South Pasadena Realty and Improvement Company Bridge; 1906, John C. Bentz House; 1906, John A. Cole House; 1906, Caroline S. DeForest House; 1906, F. W. Hawks House; 1906, Theodore M. Irwin House; 1906, James W. Neill House (additions and alterations); 1906, Robert Pitcairn, Jr., House; 1907, Robert R. Blacker House; 1907, Freeman A. Ford House; 1908, David B. Gamble House; Pasadena, Calif. 1909, Earle C. Anthony House, Beverly Hills, Calif. 1909, S. S. Crow (Edward S. Crocker) House, Pasadena, Calif. 1909, Charles M. Pratt House, Ojai, Calif. 1909, William R. Thorsen House, Berkeley. 1911, Nathan Bentz House, Santa Barbara, Calif. 1911, Cordelia A. Culbertson House, Pasadena, Calif. 1913, William M. Ladd House, Ojai, Calif. 1915, Nathan H. Williams House, Altadena, Calif. 1918–1923, D. L. James House, Carmel Highlands, Calif. 1920s, Charles S. Greene House; 1923, Charles S. Greene Studio; Carmel, Calif. 1924, Thomas Gould, Jr., House, Ventura, Calif. 1927, Mortimer Fleishhacker Estate (water garden), Woodside, Calif. 1928, Martin Flavin House (library addition and alterations), Carmel Highlands, Calif. 1929, Walter L. Richardson House, Porterville, Calif.

BIBLIOGRAPHY

BANHAM, REYNER 1977 "Introduction." Volume 1 in Randell L. Makinson, *Greene and Greene*. Salt Lake City, Utah: Peregrine Smith.
CURRENT, WILLIAM 1974 *Greene and Greene: Architects in the Residential Style*. Dobbs Ferry, N.Y.: Morgan.
MAKINSON, RANDELL L. 1968 "The Gamble House by Greene and Greene." *Prairie School Review* 4:1–31.
MAKINSON, RANDELL L. 1974 *A Guide to the Works of Greene and Greene*. Salt Lake City, Utah: Peregrine Smith.
MAKINSON, RANDELL L. 1975 "Greene and Greene." *Approach* 1975:10–29.
MAKINSON, RANDELL L. 1976 "Greene and Greene." Pages 274–282 in Frank Russel (editor), *Art Nouveau Architecture*. New York: Rizzoli.
MAKINSON, RANDELL L. 1977–1979 *Greene and Greene*. 2 vols. Salt Lake City, Utah: Peregrine Smith.
McCOY, ESTHER (1960)1977 *Five California Architects*. New York: Praeger.

GREENE, JOHN HOLDEN

John Holden Greene (1777–1850), a distinguished local builder-architect working chiefly from 1806 to 1830, began his career in Providence, Rhode Island, during a major period of city growth; his fifty or more public, commercial, religious, and residential buildings (twenty-two are still standing) altered the city's character. Born in Warwick, Rhode Island, in 1777, he arrived in Providence in 1794 where he worked on Caleb Ormbee's First

Congregational Church then under construction. By 1806, he had established what became an extensive shop.

Greene's work was rooted in traditional sources. He owned a copy of JAMES GIBBS's *Book of Architecture* and used BATTY LANGLEY's and other mid-eighteenth century works for inspiration. CHARLES BULFINCH and ASHER BENJAMIN supplied Federal motifs, including elliptical fanlight doorways and windows, and Greene added a mixed Gothic, Adamesque (see ROBERT ADAM), and classical decorative vocabulary. So many of the handsome residential buildings, both brick and wood, which formed the bulk of his work were designed on a square, two-story scheme with monitor roof and double balustrades that the type became identified with his name.

The elegant wooden Sullivan-Dorr House (1809–1810) is built on the skillful L-plan which Greene frequently employed; it is also light in scale; its Gothic detailing and the scheme with raised central section flanked by lower wings introduced a Federal character new to Providence. Also Federal was the three-story Benjamin Hoppin House (1817) with double-curved bays fronted by a slender columniated two-story porch that followed the bay curves. However, the Grant-Tylor (c.1825) and the Orray-Taft (c.1827) houses, both lavishly embellished, were Georgian in form. The Kingsbury and the Benjamin Harris Houses built in 1834 were somewhat rudimentary essays in the Greek Revival style.

Of Greene's five churches, three, all of stone, still stand. Saint John's (1810), with its Battey Langley Gothic detailing, reflects Bulfinch's Boston Federal Street Church. The interior scheme, a shallow saucer dome set on four colossal corner supports, follows that of Bulfinch's Hollis Street Church; Greene used this form again for his First Congregational Church (1814–1816) in Providence and for the Independent Presbyterian Church of Savannah, Georgia (1819). Both buildings, inspired by Bulfinch's new South Church in Boston, derive from Gibbs's Saint Martin's-in-the-Fields, but in the Providence church, considered by Greene his masterpiece, the portico columns are compacted against the vestibule wall and the pediment is cut by a colossal Gothic mullioned arched window, resulting in a bold vertical thrust that is reinforced in the spire by entablature sections which break out at an angle around the columns.

Of Greene's public buildings, the brick Friend's School (1819) and the Dexter Asylum (1826–1830), both in Providence, follow the classic format of a raised central gabled pavilion with lower wings. For the Roger Williams Bank Building (1824) and the Bristol Hotel (1824) in Provi-

*John Holden Greene
Saint John's Cathedral.
Providence, Rhode Island.
1810*

dence, Greene employed a timber-framed construction sheathed with granite similar to ALEXANDER PARRIS's Quincy Market, both forerunners in the metal skeleton development. Mill construction techniques were incorporated in many of his brick blocks.

ANTOINETTE F. DOWNING

WORKS

1794–1798, Allen House; 1806, Greene House; 1809–1810, Sullivan-Dorr House; *c.1810, Harding House; 1810, Saint John's Cathedral; 1814–1816, First Congregational Church; *1816, Hoppin House; *1818, Watson House; 1818–1820, Larcher House; 1818–1822, Candace Allen House; 1819, Friend's School (altered); Providence, R.I. 1819, Independent Presbyterian Church, Savannah, Ga. *1819, Peck House; *1820, Whipple House; 1821–1824, Whitaker House; 1822, Burroughs House (enlarged); 1822, Franklin House (altered); 1822, Greene–Dyer House (altered); *1822, Universalist Church; c.1823, Adams House; *before 1824, Chafee House; *before 1824, Peck House; *before 1824, Waterman House; 1824, Bristol Hotel; 1824, Roger Williams Bank Building; 1824, George Bucklin House; 1824, William Bucklin House; c.1825, Smith House; c.1825, Woordward House; *1825, Grant–Tyler House; 1825–1826, Cooke and *Greene Houses; 1825–1828, Hall House; 1826, Arnold–Palmer House; *1826–1830, Dexter Asylum; *c.1827, Orray–Taft House; 1827–1828, Beckwith House; c.1828–1830, Dyer Block; *1830–1831, Hallet House; *1834–1835, Benjamin Cooke Harris House; *1834–1835, Kingsley House; Providence, R.I.

BIBLIOGRAPHY

BENJAMIN, ASHER, and RAYNERD, DANIEL (1806)1972 *The American Builder's Companion.* Reprint. New York: Da Capo. Introduction by William Morgan.
BINNEY, MARCUS 1981 "All in Easy Circumstances." *Country Life* 169, no. 4363:900–903.

BINNEY, MARCUS 1981 "Thriving Entrepôt of Dissent, Providence, Rhode Island." *Country Life* 169, no. 4362:782–784.

CADY, JOHN HUTCHINS 1957 *The Civic and Architectural Development of Providence, Rhode Island.* Providence, R.I.: The Book Shop.

DOWNING, ANTOINETTE F. 1937 *Early Homes of Rhode Island.* Richmond, Va.: Garrett & Massie.

DOWNING, ANTOINETTE F. 1957 "New Light on the Sullivan-Dorr House." *Rhode Island History* 16, no. 2:33–40.

HITCHCOCK, H. R. (1939)1968 *Rhode Island Architecture.* Reprint. New York: Da Capo.

HURDIS, FRANK DeVOE 1972 *John Holden Greene.* Providence, R.I.: Preservation Society.

HURDIS, FRANK DeVOE 1973 "The Architecture of John Holden Greene." Unpublished M.A. thesis, Cornell University, Ithaca, N.Y.

KELSEY, RAYNER WICKERSHAM 1919 *Centennial History of Moses Brown School.* Providence, R.I.: Moses Brown School.

LORD, AUGUSTUS MENDON 1916 *An Old New England Meeting House.* Providence, R.I.: Privately printed.

MECHANIC'S FESTIVAL 1860 *An Account of the Seventy-First Anniversary of the Providence Association of Mechanics and Manufacturers.* Prepared by Edwin M. Stone. Providence, R.I.: Knowles Anthony.

PAIN, WILLIAM 1774 *The Practical Builder, or Workman's General Assistant.* London: I. Taylor.

PIERSON, WILLIAM H., JR. (1970)1980 *American Buildings and their Architects: The Colonial and Neo-Classical Styles.* New York: Anchor.

PLACE, CHARLES A. (1925)1968 *Charles Bulfinch; Architect and Citizen.* Reprint. New York: Da Capo.

SWAN, MABEL M. 1947 "John Holden Greene, Architect." *Antiques* 52, no. 1:24–27.

GREENE, WILLIAM H.

Born in Liverpool, William Howe Greene (1865–1937) received his architectural education at the Liverpool Architectural Society. When he passed his Royal Institute of British Architects exams in 1892, he set out for St. John's, Newfoundland where a major fire had devastated that city and where a cousin was a principal merchant.

His education and his connections enabled him to form a partnership with JOHN A. PEARSON of Toronto and to obtain a number of substantial commissions. Apart from providing designs for some of the more important commercial buildings on Water Street he was also asked to design a number of institutional buildings. He worked in what can best be described as the free classic idiom of the Queen Anne movement. After serving in World War I, he appears to have spent his time between England and France and not practiced architecture again.

SHANE O'DEA

WORKS

1892–1893, Ayre and Sons Limited; 1893, Marshall Building; 1893–1894, Church of England College; 1897–1900, Cabot Tower; 1906, Pitt's Building; St. John's, Newfoundland.

GREENWAY, FRANCIS

Arriving in 1814 as a convict, Francis (Howard) Greenway (c.1777–1837), a Bristol-trained architect, became Australia's first and, some believe, pre-eminent architect. When he arrived, architecture was yet to begin. From the outset, and after his freedom, his designs in New South Wales were characteristic of his provincial training and vitally simple, a sophisticated beginning to Australian colonial architecture. Appearing relatively plain, the majority of his works, both as colonial civil architect and privately, were severely chaste, suggesting that more pretense might be possible but unnecessary. He believed that fine proportion, a proper use of materials, and appropriate plans were sufficient in the hands of a gifted architect.

DONALD LESLIE JOHNSON

WORKS

1817–1820, Saint Matthew's Church of England, Windsor; 1818, Saint Luke's Church, Liverpool; 1819, Court House, Windsor; New South Wales, Australia. 1819, Hyde Park Barracks; *1822, Campbell House; Sydney. 1823–1825, Hospital, Liverpool, New South Wales, Australia.

BIBLIOGRAPHY

ELLIS, MALCOLM H. (1949)1966 *Francis Greenway: His Life and Times.* Reprint of 2d ed. Sydney: Angus & Robertson; San Francisco: Tri-ocean Books.

HERMAN, MORTON (1954)1970 *The Early Australian Architects and Their Work.* 2d ed. Sydney: Angus & Robertson.

GREGORINI, DOMENICO

Domenico Gregorini (c.1690/1695–1777), son of the architect Ludovico Gregorini, was born in Rome in the early 1690s. He studied in the Accademia di San Luca, where he won first prize in the Concorso Clementino of 1713. He was elected a member of the Congregazione de' Virtuosi al Pantheon in 1722 and, also in the early 1720s, became architect of Cardinal Pietro Ottoboni, vice-cancelliere.

Gregorini's first important work was the Oratory of the Confraternity of the Santissimo Sacramento in Santa Maria in Via, Rome. The oratory itself and the annexed building on its left date from 1727–1731; a matching wing on the right was built in 1734, but it was eventually demolished with the opening of the Via del Tritone. The façade of this oratory reflects the high baroque architecture of FRANCESCO BORROMINI and PIETRO DA CORTONA in several major elements of its design and in some decorative motifs. But for all its derivative features, it is a work of distinctive character, animated by the bold, clear movement of the wall masses and the crispness of the decorative details. The interior is the first instance of Gregorini's use of the oval plan, albeit in modified form.

The large *confessione* in front of the high altar of San Lorenzo in Damaso, Rome, was commissioned and consecrated by Cardinal Ottoboni in 1737. Its appearance is partially recorded by a contemporary painting and complemented by written descriptions. The large oval opening in the church floor leading to the subterranean chapel, supported by a ring of piers and columns, points to the design of the porch of Gregorini's major work, the restoration of the basilica of Santa Croce in Gerusalemme (1741–1744), Rome. In this papal commission, Pietro Passalacqua served as Gregorini's assistant.

The organization of the façade of Santa Croce, disregarding the use of curves and the rococo decorative features, is very similar to that of San Giovanni in Laterano, ALESSANDRO GALILEI's newly raised classicizing structure. Gregorini had participated in the 1732 competition for the Lateran façade, and not only the formal similarities but also the very monumentality and clarity of Santa Croce's architecture seem a result of the experience and outcome of that competition. The curving façade covers an oval vestibule consisting of a spacious and lofty inner core, demarcated by a ring of columns and piers that support a cupola with lantern, and a lower, darker aisle surrounding it. This design, with its stress on spatial values, its devaluation of the outer wall as the space-creating element, and the importance given to the isolated structural supports, is almost unprecedented in eighteenth-century Rome, and singles out Gregorini for the originality of his vision.

Gregorini's known activity does not extend beyond 1750. He was made a member of the Accademia di San Luca in 1748, but only a few projects by him are recorded in the second half of the 1740s, most of them outside of Rome. He remained in this city steadily for the following three decades, however, until his death in 1777.

NINA A. MALLORY

WORKS

1727–1731, Oratory of the Confraternity of the Santissimo Sacramento in Santa Maria in Via (and adjoining

Gregorini. Santa Croce in Gerusalemme (restoration of the basilica). Rome. 1741–1744

buildings); *1734, Oratory of the Confraternity of the Santissimo Sacramento in Santa Maria in Via (right wing); *1734, Theater of Tor di Nona; *1737, *Confessione,* San Lorenzo in Damaso; 1741–1744, Santa Croce in Gerusalemme (restoration of the basilica); Rome. 1743–1746, Aldrovandi Chapel, San Petronio, Bologna, Italy. 1744, City Gate; 1745–1747, Bishop's Palace (additions); Montefiascone, Italy. 1748, Tomb of Antonio Buoncompagni Ludovisi, Madonna delle Forme, Isola dei Liri, Italy. 1749, Tomb of Maria Eleonora Buoncompagni Ludovisi, Santa Maria del Popolo, Rome.

BIBLIOGRAPHY

MALLORY, NINA A. 1977 *Roman Rococo Architecture from Clement XI to Benedict XIV (1700–1758).* New York and London: Garland.

PORTOGHESI, PAOLO (1966)1970 *Roman Barocca: The History of an Architectonic Culture.* Translated by Barbara Luigia La Penta. Cambridge, Mass.: M.I.T. Press.

GREY, WILLIAM

When Bishop Field arrived in Newfoundland in 1844 he found a land ecclesiologically impure but it was not until 1849 when he appointed the Reverend William Grey (1819–1872) diocesan architect that any improvements were effected. During Grey's stay in Newfoundland (1849–1853, 1857) he designed numerous churches and lectured on church architecture to his theological students. It is reasonable to assume that Grey, actively supported by Field, redesigned or encouraged use of the proper style in many churches there.

SHANE O'DEA

WORKS

1851, Parsonage; 1851–1853, Saint Peter's Church; Portugal Cove, Newfoundland. 1851–1854, Saint Saviour's Church, Hermitage, Newfoundland. 1853, Saint Francis's Harbour Church; 1857, Battle Harbour Parsonage and Church; 1857, Forteau Church; Labrador, Newfoundland. 1857, Tilt Cove Church, Newfoundland. 1857–1859, Church of Saint Mary the Virgin, St. John's, Newfoundland.

GRIFFIN, MARION MAHONY

A native Chicagoan, Marion Lucy Mahony (1871–1962) was the second woman to receive an architectural degree from the Massachusetts Institute of Technology. She returned to Chicago where she became an active participant in the momentous architectural developments of those years. Working initially for her cousin Dwight Perkins, she soon joined the Oak Park Studio of FRANK LLOYD WRIGHT. From 1895 to 1910, she drafted key works for Wright. Many of the designs for the famous portfolio *Ausgeführte Bauten* (1910) are by her hand. Plates 14 and 15 actually bear her monogram, MLM (Marion Lucy Mahony), later changed to MMG (Marion Mahony Griffin). From the same period, many of Wright's interior furnishings, mosaics, stained glass, and murals may be properly attributed to her. She probably did even more, but the Wrightian oeuvre of those years has yet to be completely published.

In 1911, she married her Oak Park Studio colleague WALTER BURLEY GRIFFIN and her career as one of an artistic union was launched. The winning in 1912 of the international competition for Canberra by Griffin was assisted if not assured by Mahony's dramatic presentation drawings. She and her husband settled in Australia and soon became prominent and influential members of that country's architectural movement. Although her specific contribution to the husband–wife teamwork is not adequately documented, it can be considered major. The brilliant ceiling of the Capitol Theatre, Melbourne (1924), is certainly her design, and much of the total concept of the Castlecrag Community, Sydney (1921), with its emphasis on an ideal balance between nature and man owes much to her anthroposophical ideas.

After her husband's death in 1937, she returned to Chicago and devoted her time to writing and several community projects which, however, remained unexecuted. Her unpublished memoirs, "Magic of America," are deposited in the Burnham Library of the Art Institute of Chicago and at the New York Historical Society. Establishing the extent of Marion Mahony Griffin's collaboration with Wright and others presents difficult problems, and virtually nothing solely attributable to her has been left standing.

MARK LYONS PEISCH

BIBLIOGRAPHY

BROOKS, H. ALLEN 1966 "Frank Lloyd Wright and the Wasmuth Drawings." *Art Bulletin* 48: 193–202.
TORRE, SUSANA (editor) 1977 *Women in American Architecture: A Historic and Contemporary Perspective.* New York: Whitney Library of Design.

GRIFFIN, WALTER BURLEY

The career of Walter Burley Griffin (1876–1937)—architect, landscape designer, and city planner, who worked in the United States, Australia, and India—was unusually rich and diverse. Born near Chicago, Griffin visited the World's Columbian Exposition of 1893, where he studied firsthand the triumph of classical eclecticism, and simultaneously, in LOUIS H. SULLIVAN's Transportation Building, the beginning of the countermovement. In the surrounding area, he found rich examples of FRANK LLOYD WRIGHT's first prairie homes. As a student in the department of architecture, University of Illinois, Champaign, NATHAN C. RICKER directed his studies, providing a curriculum that included the basics of design and structure but, quite remarkably for the time, also the contemporary architectural ideas from Europe.

After receiving his B.S. in architecture (1899), Griffin assisted Wright in his Oak Park Studio. Griffin's first major independent commission was the W. H. Emery House, Elmhurst, Illinois, 1901–1902. His choice of materials contrasting plaster and stained wood, banks of casement windows, and heavy eaves all point to Wright. The interior arrangement, however, involving partial floors of living space connected by flights of stairs, indicates a spatial concept not in Wright's work of that period and shows a most "unprairielike" interest in the vertical rather than a horizontal extension of space. The precise relationship of Griffin to Wright—whether disciple, follower, apprentice, or associate—will never be clearly understood. In the Emery House we can see the debt owed by a beginner to the acknowledged master, but also the evidence of an emerging, original talent.

Griffin then continued to work on his own as well as at the Oak Park Studio, where he frequently collaborated with Wright's talented design assistant, the architect–renderer MARION MAHONY (GRIFFIN). Their marriage in 1911 was a complete merging of personalities and ideals, an artistic union so perfect that to distinguish or separate their later careers becomes virtually impossible.

The J. G. Melson House (1912), in the Rock Crest–Rock Glen Community, Mason City, Iowa, shows Griffin's mature and varied talents, and is an example of his interest in and original use of landscape architecture. This community plan for twenty houses had remained undeveloped because of the uninviting character of the rocky and uneven ground. The site necessitated a skillful invention of individual house plans, the most successful of which was the Melson House. Built of rough-hewn limestone quarried on the spot, this design demonstrates the power and beauty of native material, to which the row of cast concrete capstones over the vertical mullions of the windows form an effective contrast. In fact, the scheme at Mason City may be the high point of Griffin's American career. The informal, but skillful arrangement of houses with a communal park in the middle, the avoidance of monotony, the collaboration of a number of professional colleagues (BARRY BYRNE and others), and the social nature of the plan were examples of Griffin's clearsightedness.

A final American work was the Stinson Memorial Library, Anna, Illinois, built in 1914 on a plan developed in 1912. Griffin's use of local fieldstone for the main part of the building shows his predilection for rough-surfaced, indigenous materials, and although this is a modest-sized building, the external effect is one of massive, almost cyclopean character. The library also includes a small auditorium in the basement that serves as a community center. Instead of filling in the uneven levels of the sloping site, Griffin adapted his plan to the unpromising location—one can enter the library directly from the street, and the auditorium from its own door in the rear. Here again are the hallmarks of Griffin's architectural philosophy: respect for materials, the function of the building itself, the building site and its natural surroundings, and most of all, an intense awareness of the needs of the community. In 1912 Griffin won an international competition with a plan for Australia's capital city of Canberra. To plan *ab initio* a large city on a virgin site in the foothills of the Australian Alps was an exciting prospect for an architect and planner barely thirty-six years of age. This plan marked the end of Griffin's American career, and although he retained Barry Byrne as partner, Australia became his major base of operations. While the imprint of Griffin's plan can be seen today only in the center of Canberra, his intention to use the location as, in his words, "a large natural amphitheatre" for the administrative and government buildings, has proven basically sound. The exquisite

presentation renderings by Marion Griffin succeeded in showing the visual beauty of Griffin's plan. By using as an axis a line connecting the proposed capitol with the nearby Mount Ainslie, he emphasized the natural beauty and setting of the plan, which merged academic city plan concepts with the more socially advanced community concept of the English "Garden City." Dwelling areas were clearly separated from industrial and commercial sections. Highways were screened from residential areas by parks. There is a strongly classical emphasis on formal geometry and a constant attempt at impressive vistas. Although placed nominally in charge of the capital project, Griffin encountered insurmountable opposition from Australian governmental leaders. In addition, World War I and the Great Depression prevented most construction of his original plan. Even so, one sees today the wisdom and vision of Griffin's plan. The Molonglo River (now Lake Burley Griffin) has been effectively dammed for striking effects, and water, the leitmotif of earlier plans, is also found as a key to Griffin's plan for Canberra. The beauty and practicality of Griffin's plan was fully taken into account by the prize-winning scheme (1980) for the completion of Canberra's parliamentary complex by another American firm, MITCHELL AND GIURGOLA.

Undeterred by the delays and frustrations at Canberra, Griffin soon had a busy practice in his adopted homeland. He designed the Capitol Theatre (1921–1924), Melbourne, along European rather than American lines. A handsome lounge, a boldly cantilevered balcony, but most of all the exotic ornament of the theater ceiling with its varicolored and changing lights are still remembered, although the theater has been crudely and thoughtlessly remodeled. The Castlecrag Community (1921–1935) in Sydney, where Griffin lived, was an ambitious experiment in suburban development that carried Walter and Marion Griffin's social, religious, and educational ideas to a new height. There was a school based on the anthroposophical theories of Rudolf Steiner, an outdoor theater for dramatic events, and a community center. Newman College, University of Melbourne (1915–1917), was an unconvincing effort by Griffin to design in the Gothic spirit, but the large refectory with its reinforced concrete dome was a dramatic use of a material not yet well-known in Australia. During the Depression, Griffin designed a number of municipal incinerators, the most successful being the Pyrmont Incinerator, Sydney (1934–1935). There, Griffin gave powerful form and remarkable beauty to a structure whose purpose was neither inviting nor aesthetically challenging.

In 1935 Griffin traveled to India on the strength of several promising projects. His most interesting plans, sadly, remained on paper. In actuality, he constructed only an office and plant for the Pioneer Press (1936–1937), Lucknow. The plain wall surfaces are relieved by banded windows with similar accents in massive wings at each end of the building. Griffin died less than two years after reaching India.

Griffin was a small, well-knit man with a handsome and reflective countenance. Time meant nothing to him and his lack of punctuality led some to accuse him of a lack of practicality and dependability. For the record he opposed officialdom almost as a matter of principle; was genuinely concerned about contemporary problems and their solution through peaceful means; and his kinship and love of nature merged understandably with an interest in anthroposophy and later theosophy, probably first encountered at Wright's Oak Park Studio. Griffin's career in Australia and, to a lesser degree in India, saw the introduction of planning as a science and art, something of ultimate importance for the orderly and healthy growth of towns and cities. His domestic design introduced Australia to the basic concepts of Louis Henry Sullivan, Frank Lloyd Wright, and the Chicago school (or Prairie school) of which he was a distinguished representative.

MARK LYONS PEISCH

WORKS

1901–1902, W. H. Emery House, Elmhurst, Ill. 1908, W. S. Orth Twin House, Kenilworth, Ill. 1912, J. G. Melson House, Mason City, Iowa. 1912–1914, Stinson Memorial Library, Anna, Ill. 1915–1917, Newman College; 1921–1924, Capitol Theatre; Melbourne. 1921–1935, Castlecrag (community plan); 1934–1935, Pyrmont Incinerator; Sydney. 1936–1937, Pioneer Press Building, Lucknow, India.

BIBLIOGRAPHY

BIRRELL, JAMES 1964 *Walter Burley Griffin.* Brisbane, Australia: University of Queensland Press.

BROOKS, H. ALLEN 1972 *The Prairie School: Frank Lloyd Wright and His Midwest Contemporaries.* University of Toronto Press.

JOHNSON, DONALD LESLIE 1977 *The Architecture of Walter Burley Griffin.* South Melbourne, Australia: MacMillan.

PEISCH, MARK L. 1964 *The Chicago School of Architecture: Early Followers of Sullivan and Wright.* New York: Random House.

Prairie School Review. 1964 Chicago: Prairie School Press.

VAN ZANTEN, DAVID T. (editor) 1970 *Walter Burley Griffin: Selected Designs.* Palos Park, Ill.: Prairie School Press.

GRIFFINI, ENRICO AGOSTINO

Enrico Agostino Griffini (1887–1952) received his degree in engineering from the Milan Politècnico in 1910. Griffini worked best collaboratively. His most important associates included Piero Portaluppi and Paolo Mezzanotte beginning in 1910, Giuseppe Manfredi beginning in 1925, and Piero Bottoni and EUGENIO FALUDI beginning in 1928. Griffini was a member of the Movimento Italiano per l'Architettura Razionale. He participated in numerous Italian and international exhibitions. In 1932, he published *Costruzione Razionale della Casa,* an important Italian architectural manual that drew heavily on the publications of the Congrès Internationaux d'Architecture Moderne (CIAM) and the work of ALEXANDER KLEIN.

DENNIS DOORDAN

WORKS

1929, Bissoncello Workers Housing (with G. Manfredi); *1933, Model Houses (with P. Bottoni and E. Faludi), Fifth Triennale; 1937, Palazzo delle Assicurazione Generali; Milan.

BIBLIOGRAPHY

CENNAMO, MICHELE 1976 *Il Movimento Italiano per l'Architettura Razionale.* Naples: Societa Editrice Napoletana.

GRIFFINI, ENRICO AGOSTINO (1932)1946 *Costruzione Razionale della Casa.* 2 vols. 4th ed. Milan: Hoepli.

GRIFFINI, ENRICO AGOSTINO 1950 *Progetti e Realizzazione MCMXX–MCML.* Milan: Stucchi.

GRIMALDI, GIOVANNI FRANCESCO

Born in Oppido Lucano in southern Italy, Giovanni Francesco Grimaldi (1543–c.1613) was an early baroque painter-architect. Active in Naples where he was responsible for the Church of San Paolo Maggiore (1590–1603), he transferred to Rome in 1591. There, he was active along with GIACOMO DELLA PORTA in the first designs for the church of the Theatine order, of which he was a member, Sant'Andrea della Valle, Rome (1591–1665).

NICHOLAS ADAMS

WORKS

1590–1603, San Paolo Maggiore, Naples. 1591–1616, Sant'Andrea della Valle (with Giacoma della Porta; not completed until 1665 by CARLO MADERNO and Carlo Rainaldi), Rome.

GROPIUS, MARTIN

Martin Gropius (1824–1880) was an influential architect and educator in Prussia during the second half of the nineteenth century. Born in Berlin, he was the son of a silk manufacturer, in whose house KARL FRIEDRICH SCHINKEL, Gottfried Schadow, and Carl Bötticher were frequent guests. As a pupil of Bötticher at the Bauakademie in Berlin, Martin Gropius became a direct follower of the architectural philosophy of Hellenic Renaissance initiated by Schinkel.

Gropius in turn became professor at the Bauakademie, director of the Kunstschule in Berlin, and supervisor of all the art schools in Prussia. His first major commission was the Insane Asylum at Neustadt-Eberswalde (East Germany, still extant), and two other hospitals of his still exist in Berlin. From 1866, he developed an extensive practice with Heino Schmieden, building many villas and executing important public commissions, including the provisional Reichstag in Berlin (1871). His style, which was considered a modern alternative to unimaginative eclecticism, is best characterized as tectonic clarity and honest expression of materials. Through extensive use of terra cotta and red and yellow brick, Gropius developed a rich polychromy that was widely admired in the latter decades of the century.

RON WIEDENHOEFT

WORKS

1862–1863, Insane Asylum, Eberswalde, Neustadt, Germany. 1867–1871, Municipal General Hospital, Friedrichshain, Berlin, Germany. 1875–1878, Garrison Hospital, Tempelhof, Berlin, Germany. 1877–1879, Library and Zoological Institute, University of Kiel, Germany.

BIBLIOGRAPHY

KLINKOTT, MANFRED 1971 *Martin Gropius und die Berliner Schule.* Unpublished Ph.D. dissertation, Technische Universität, Berlin.
SCHLIEPMANN, HANS 1892 *Martin Gropius.* Berlin.

GROPIUS, WALTER

Born in Berlin, Georg Walter Adolf Gropius (1883–1969) was one of four children of Walther and Manon (Scharnweber) Gropius. In addition to serving their country in every generation, Gropius's forebears were teachers, parsons, civil servants, bakers, jewelers, artists, and architects. Among the latter was grand-uncle MARTIN GROPIUS, himself influenced by the work of the great Prussian architect KARL FRIEDRICH SCHINKEL. Walther Gropius, father of Walter, also an architect, was a city building councilor and devoted, as previous generations of the family had been, to veneration of Schinkel, Schinkel's master, David Gilly, and FRIEDRICH GILLY.

These were bourgeois families, members of the growing middle class of Prussia and initially influenced by the liberalism of the early nineteenth century, the social revolution of 1848, the *Gründerzeit* which followed the Franco-Prussian War, and by the Wilhelminian periods.

As any child of an upper middle class family, Walter attended an elementary school and the Gymnasium—in fact, four of the latter to complete his *Abiturium.* Long since destined for a career in architecture, he enrolled in the Munich Technische Hochschule but remained there only a single term, returning to Berlin during the terminal illness of his younger brother Georg. Walter became an office boy and field clerk in the architectural office of Solf and Wichards who had designed his uncle Erich Gropius's house in Janikow, Pomerania. This experience was followed by his voluntary service for a year as a cadet in the famed Wandsbeck Hussar regiment.

He delighted his family with the decision to continue his architectural studies at the Technische Hochschule of Berlin-Charlottenburg. He was already in advance of his fellow students, having been tutored by his father in the Schinkel–Gilly principles and in the study of proportion, by the Solf and Wichards experience, and by actual architectural and building commissions for his uncle Erich and Erich's neighbors in Pomerania. He endured two years of the traditional program, gaining little from its method of learning by rote, memory, and emulation.

In 1907, enabled by a bequest from a grand-aunt, he spent a study year in Spain. There, he was impressed by the historic monumental buildings, the paintings by the masters, the ceramics and tile work of the Moors and Spaniards, and, according to letters to his mother, the beauty of the women. In Madrid, he met the famed museum director Karl Ernst Osthaus who, impressed, sent him to PETER BEHRENS, the architect-designer of buildings, interiors, furnishings, factories and power plants, and products for the *Allgemeine Elektrizitäts–Gesellschaft* (AEG). His favored position as Behrens's lieutenant provided him with wide opportunities to work and learn, yet in no more than twenty months, Gropius felt that he was prepared to begin his own practice. This he did, establishing it not far from Behrens's own office in Neu Babelsburg, and engaging as his principal associate ADOLF MEYER, an architect of experience and common sense.

Gropius.
Fagus Factory (with
Meyer).
Alfeld, Germany.
1911–1912

Gropius.
Werkbund Exhibition (with
Meyer).
Cologne, Germany.
1913–1914

Gropius.
Werkbund Exhibition (with
Meyer).
Cologne, Germany.
1913–1914

Early practice. Gropius spent much time in the preparation of an exposé describing the social needs and economic benefits to result from mass-produced housing. This document he presented to Walther Rathenau, managing director, and his father, Emil Rathenau, chairman of the board of the AEG. Little came of this effort, although the organized ideas of the proposal served Gropius himself as a guide for his own work in housing.

Gropius wrote numerous letters to every possible prospective client, particularly to industrialists who were considering expansion or replacement of their factories. He also lectured and wrote about achieving improvement of industrial production through the design of better environments for workers within factories. One of those who heard Gropius and who also had received his letter was

Carl Benscheidt, owner of the Fagus-Werk, manufacturer of shoe-lasts. Gropius's ideas struck a responsive chord in this already social-minded industrialist, and Gropius was commissioned to redesign the façade for a Fagus building then in the stages of preliminary sketches being prepared by architect-engineer Eduard Werner. The result was a building which in 1911–1912 was several decades ahead of ordinary industrial design and which established Gropius's reputation. Most notable is its great expanse of glass and its pioneering use of curtain wall construction.

Other commissions came slowly to the new office and most of those he did receive resulted from the loyal support of his family; few of these, if any, showed further promise beyond that of the Fagus factory. In 1913–1914, however, through his activities in the recently formed (1907) *Deutscher Werkbund,* Gropius was enabled to design major structures for that organization's Cologne Exhibition. His designs for these buildings continued the line he had begun with the Fagus factory.

At the Werkbund meeting in Cologne that year, HERMANN MUTHESIUS postulated the need for a standardized approach to architecture and other design which he insisted would redound to German industry's and the profession's benefit. His doctrinaire viewpoint had already been published and HENRY VAN DE VELDE took exception to it, putting forward the right and responsibility of the designer to be individually creative. Though Gropius was sympathetic to Muthesius's ideas and personally critical of van de Velde's teaching methods, he found Muthesius's manner crude and offensive and rose to support van de Velde. The argument went unresolved, but van de Velde never forgot his unexpected ally. This clash, the meeting, and the exhibition would be forgotten within weeks by the advent of war.

The war years. Gropius's cadet year had prepared him little for war. Thus, when the Wandsbeck Hussar Regiment was mobilized in August 1914, Sergeant Gropius and his fellows thought that the event would be no more than a bivouac or a saber-rattling excursion that would surely bring the French to their senses. But within hours Gropius would lead a mounted patrol reconnoitering enemy lines and encampments. During the following four years, Gropius rarely would be away from the German front lines within France, Belgium, and Italy, and then only for reasons of wounds received in battle, for special training assignments, or for hard-won brief furloughs with his family.

There were other fateful events in these years. One of them was the reappearance in his life of Alma Schindler Mahler—the widow of Gustav Mahler—whom he married in 1915. They had first met early in 1910, and were drawn together in a passionate love affair. Rarely together during the war years, her restlessness and resulting dalliance led to their divorce after the war.

Demobilized in November 1918, Gropius was immediately caught up in the spirit of revolution of the postwar period. He took active roles in the many organizations of architects and artists that had spontaneously come into existence at that time. Prominent among these was the Arbeitsrat für Kunst, the Novembergruppe, and Die gläserne Kette. The first two had formed in reaction to the already established Deutscher Werkbund and to the Bund Deutscher Architekten which had only continued their past conservative directions. There was a constant ferment of ideas as to the roles of artists and architects in the new era, and changes in existing institutions were sought. Gropius believed that the Arbeitsrat für Kunst would provide the opportunity to revive the medieval ideal of the building lodges of builders and artists which had produced a cultural unity based on co-operation between the various crafts. Before Christmas 1918, Gropius and BRUNO TAUT had prepared a manifesto which called for great community centers located in the open countryside between cities which would contain hotels, theaters, other cultural facilities, and well-planned housing developments. The manifesto prescribed advisory councils of architects and landscape architects. Gropius also demanded housing for families in high structures, widely separated to provide green open space, light, and air.

Weimar. Late in 1918, the Novembergruppe was founded calling for the organization of "revolutionary" artists and for their collaboration in architectural projects. A year later, the Novembergruppe and the Arbeitsrat für Kunst combined bringing art and architecture together, but within eighteen months the partnership would dissolve. Out of this effort, however, grew the utopian correspondence of Bruno Taut's friends from both organizations. The correspondents as a group would be known as Die gläserne Kette (Glass Chain) and each member would be provided a pseudonym to give a sense of separation between ideas propounded and temporal man. Intended by Gropius to be a contribution to the utopian thinking of the Glass Chain, but not completed for submittal, was his Mountains for Living (*Wohnberge*) project. Appearing at a distance as huge mounds of great height and length, the structures consist of regular and pyramidal sections of many levels of housing for families of every size and stage of life. Each mountain is connected by moving sidewalks, rapid transit, highways, and roadways at several levels. The terraces are planted, giving the appear-

ance of a green "mountain." The orderly structures, organized economically and rationally, anticipated by several decades a plethora of similar projects.

Gropius had not forgotten the opportunity held out to him four years earlier by Henry van de Velde to direct the Kunstgewerbeschule in Weimar. He saw it as a means to attain the social goals he had expressed in his first public address in 1911, and, in the winter of 1918–1919, he sought out those still in authority who could fulfill the offer made to him. The opportunity would become greater by his appointment as director not only of the Kunstgewerbeschule but also of the art academy in Weimar. These Gropius brought together under the name Staatliches Bauhaus Weimar.

From April 1919 on, Gropius had a real and effective instrument, the Bauhaus, for putting into action those ideals for which he had joined the Arbeitsrat für Kunst. The leaflet announcing the opening of the Bauhaus was lyrical and romantic:

The ultimate aim of all visual arts is the complete building. . . . Together let us desire, conceive and create the new structure of the future which will embrace architecture and sculpture and painting in one unity and which will one day rise toward heaven from the hands of a million workers like the crystal symbol of a new faith (Gropius, Bauhaus Manifesto, 1919).

The manifesto did give hope to the young; its words served to rally them, though the training program would be different from the proclamation. It was a new kind of school, very different from the schools for artists and craftsmen and from those for industrial workers; in the Bauhaus, Gropius sought comprehensiveness and integration of all those artistic, craft, and industrial skills. To do so, he had to develop a very special kind of curriculum and train a special kind of teacher, one who would combine the artistic abilities with the craft skills. Among the faculty were Paul Klee, Wassily Kandinsky, Gerhard Marcks, JOHANNES ITTEN, and LÁSZLÓ MOHOLY-NAGY. JOSEF ALBERS, HERBERT BAYER, and MARCEL BREUER, initially students, later became masters.

Though the workshops and studios slowly built up to a full complement for crafts and art, there would not be an architectural curriculum as such, Gropius firmly believing that the completion of workshop studies, at least to the journeyman level, had to precede a program in architecture. To the students and young masters who had come to the Bauhaus for such study, the delay seemed onerous even though the workshops included those for construction, metal work, carpentry, interior design (painting), and furniture. A few students became draftsmen in Gropius's pri-

vate office. Despite a multifaceted life as director and teacher, lecturer and fund-raiser, and political buffer, further complicated by a confusing private life involving his mother, his wife, and his mistress, he had reopened his practice in the first year of the Weimar Bauhaus with Adolf Meyer, entering architectural competitions and carrying out commissions.

Perhaps best known among their works of that period was their entry in the Chicago Tribune Building competition which had little chance against RAYMOND M. HOOD's Gothic tower. Gropius's design for the monument to the workers who fell in defeating the Kapp Putsch (1922) was realized. Better known is the timber house (1921) for Adolf Sommerfeld in Berlin, the lumber merchant and builder; though sometimes criticized as being outside of Gropius's own principles, the design is more easily understood when it is known that the teak lumber of which the house was built was salvaged from a dismantled German warship and then assembled in a simple method of construction. Gropius's first opportunity to design a theater came as a commission to remodel an old music hall in Jena (State Theatre, 1923–1924): its straight, clean lines inside and out focused all attention on the stage offerings, unlike the usual ornate theaters of that day. Within the Bauhaus, Gropius conceived the idea of *Baukasten im Grossen,* "large building blocks," rooms of standard sizes which could be combined in such numbers as would meet the varying needs of families and in such manner as to provide variety in their street façades.

Still another interesting project which was one of the highpoints in Gropius's career was the Philosophy Academy (1924) for Erlangen, Germany. The concept of the center for study, research, and contemplation by philosophers from all over the world who were concerned with a great diversity of subjects and who were related mainly by their intellectual qualities was that of Professor Hoffmann of Erlangen University. But it was Gropius who developed the comprehensive, integrated program as well as the initial sketches for the building. Unfortunately, the proposal did not attract the support it deserved, and it went unbuilt.

To answer charges of lack of accomplishment in the Bauhaus's first years and to publicize the school, a great exhibition of the work of the students and masters was held in August 1923. The event was a great cultural festival with music, ballet, lectures, demonstrations, and displays; it featured a model house largely designed by Georg Muche and completely furnished by the workshops and studios. Gropius had hoped that the Bauhaus community development of which the model house, the Haus am Horn, was its only evidence, would win financial support but, given the inflationary period, it did not. Proposed as a cooperative venture, its utopian aspects were not received well by possible investers. The exhibition, however, did win great numbers of friends and materially increased the industrial contracts for the Bauhaus workshops.

Midyear 1923 was uniquely eventful in that Gropius met and married Ilse Frank. Though some fifteen years younger than he, she soon became a dedicated partner in the Bauhaus enterprise.

The exhibition did not, however, ameliorate the attacks made on it by politicians who saw its social ideals as a threat to their own ends, by the crafts unions which believed the workshops to be competitive, and by the Weimar bourgeoisie who found the students, so many of them veterans, impoverished, bohemian, revolutionary, idealistic and searching, to be foreign in attitude and behavior. JOHANNES ITTEN's students, particularly those who followed him to Weimar from Vienna, permeated the Bauhaus with their fantasy. Gropius had no quarrel with Itten's technique of teaching but disagreed with his "masdasnan" leanings which had brought a cultist atmosphere to the school and offended those already antagonistic to the school.

Although it would seem that the Bauhaus was appropriately idealistic for Weimar with its heritage of intellectual thought and cultural attainment and now the seat of Germany's government, the bourgeoisie had become smug and ultraconservative and eschewed new ideas. The environment of Weimar by the mid-1920s had very little of the spirit of Goethe, and an invitation in 1925 from the city of Dessau to move the Bauhaus there was eagerly accepted by Gropius and the masters.

Dessau. The invitation from Dessau included commissions for Gropius to design a building for the school and houses for the masters. By working day and night to complete the plans and by efficiently organizing the work on the site, Gropius and the staff were able to move out of their temporary quarters in Dessau into the new building within a year. The design satisfied the complex program requirements of the curriculum involving workshops, studios, offices, cafeteria, auditorium, student housing, Gropius's private architectural office, and other spaces in a bridge across an intervening street, and a second school, not under his direction. Its simple blocks, great glass walls and other fenestration, and walls free of any kind of ornamentation would make it one of the best known landmarks of modern design. The row of masters' houses, attached except that for Gropius, placed in a wooded area a short walk away and apart from the older traditional buildings of Dessau, were of simple design, flat-roofed and starkly utilitarian, exciting less attention. Housing at low cost for the students was a greater problem, alleviated only in part by a 28-room dormitory attached to the Bauhaus building itself.

Most of the masters accompanied Gropius to Dessau, and the places of those who did not were filled by graduates who had completed their work in the workshops and design studios and were prepared to take their places as "young masters."

These were augmented by new appointments and by visiting lecturers who offered a greater variety of subjects than previously given. The reputation of the school was now international, and the number of students multiplied, many of them penniless refugees from the East. Their financial problems and those of the faculty and school persisted despite the best efforts of The Circle of Friends of the Bauhaus to obtain grants and contributions and those of Gropius to obtain contracts for the workshops. There were also administrative problems and a succession of business managers vainly attempted to satisfy the opinionated committees of city and state inquiring as to the disposition of the funds.

Gropius continued to direct; to teach; to involve the *Meisterrat* (faculty council) and the students' representatives; to fend for the school politically; to travel for lectures, workshop contracts, and commissions; and yet he maintained some semblance of a personal life. His private office produced plans for the extensive Toerten housing project (1926–1927) commissioned by the city. Designed for occupancy of low-income families,

*Gropius.
Bauhaus.
Dessau, Germany.
1925–1926*

*Gropius.
Bauhaus.
Dessau, Germany.
1925–1926*

its first stages were built, comprising rowhouses, a number of apartments, and a cooperative shopping facility. Gropius designed an Arbeitsamt (1927–1928), also commissioned by the city. Functional and attractive, it is, in the 1980s, still providing orderly entrance, interview facilities, and egress for the lines of people seeking answers to employment-related questions. Perhaps as well known as Gropius's two houses designed and built for the Werkbund's 1927 housing exhibition, the Weissenhof at Stuttgart; these gave Gropius the opportunity to experiment with both dry and semidry construction methods; both houses were simple, box-like structures located between the buildings of LE CORBUSIER, LUDWIG MIES VAN DER ROHE, and other European architects. Still another distinguished project of this time is the Total Theater for Erwin Piscator, a prominent Berlin theatrical producer. Here, Gropius sought to solve all the problems of sight lines, audience participation, acoustics, a variety of stage elevations, and access and egress; to provide for ballet, symphony, concerts, opera, intimate theater, and theater on a grand scale; all with a sense of drama, grandeur, involvement, totality, and focus. Though the building as designed by Gropius was not built, the concept does contain prototypical solutions to problems of theater design; Gropius subsequently further developed many of its ideas in other projects.

The students continued the efforts made in Weimar to interest the community in the Bauhaus and to improve "town–gown" relationships by mutual involvement in festival days and other activities. Unfortunately, these overt actions were sometimes misunderstood or even deliberately misinterpreted, for many of the political problems which had arisen in Weimar were carried to Dessau. The crafts unions were apprehensive; the art academies, openly critical; and the far right, the members of the growing National Socialist Party, aggressive against the Bauhaus. The condemnation of the Bauhaus was paralleled by the personal vilification of Gropius. Indeed, these attacks became so vehement and so pointed that he believed the solution lay in his resignation as director. Publicly, he voiced a desire to return to a full-time practice of architecture, and privately, both he and his wife (now renamed Ise) sought a more peaceful family life. Gropius recommended as his successor HANNES MEYER, a Swiss architect who recently had become a member of the faculty; Meyer had carried out interesting work in his private practice and appeared to be a sound choice for the directorship. It was with obvious relief that Gropius vacated his offices and house and departed for Berlin. He appeared to have few regrets, for the removal of the Bauhaus from Weimar to Dessau

for political reasons had only served to accelerate the development and spread of his influential ideas; the works of his private office, particularly the Bauhaus building itself, would augment the Fagus-Werk and the Cologne Exhibition buildings as examples of a new approach to architectural design.

Berlin. Even before leaving Dessau, Gropius had begun plans and arrangements for a long-desired study tour of the United States—a reconnaissance trip of several weeks, across the United States, inspecting buildings, completed or in progress; interviewing architects, construction company officials, and bankers; and visiting national parks, night-clubs, hospitals, and museums. Though Gropius found no one of the stature of Henry Ford in the housing industry and was disappointed in the quality of the houses and apartment buildings they observed, the organization and rapid construction of high buildings amazed him.

Returning to Berlin, Gropius was quickly occupied with his practice, his lectures throughout Europe, his research projects, and the activities of professional associations to which would soon be added the Congrès Internationaux d'Architecture Moderne (CIAM). His lectures and articles were well-publicized and well-received; his call for a "hundred-year plan for Berlin" and his proposal for *Wohnhochhäuser im Grüen* (highrise housing in green areas) drew attention. He was quickly recognized for his contributions by an honorary doctorate awarded by the Technische Hochschule of Hannover, the first of almost thirty he would receive in his lifetime. His office entered many competitions, winning more second-place awards than first prizes. Some of Gropius's entries, such as those for housing developments and sanatoria, provided alternative plans carefully defined as to their relative merits and undoubtedly confusing to the judges. Projects of importance did proceed; among these, was the Spandau-Haselhorst Housing Development (1929) for which he served as coordinator of the several architects involved; Siemensstadt (1929–1930), in which he was one of several architects whose individual work was successfully related; and am Lindenbaum (1929) in Frankfurt am Main for which he was the sole architect. There were designs for a housing development for upper-income families to be built on the Wannsee shores of Berlin's Havel Lake (1931), for houses fabricated from copper (1931), standardized houses for Argentina, and for his model *Wachsendes Haus* (growing house). Among other projects requiring great effort which did not progress, second-place awards being no compensation or recognition of their real architectural worth, were the Aschrott Welfare Center and the

Aschrott Home for the Aged (1929) in Kassel. The Mendelssohn Sanatorium which benefited from the previous studies also failed to progress, a victim of hard times. Benefiting from his Total Theater studies were Gropius's proposals for the State Theater of Kharkov (1930) and the Palace of the Soviets in Moscow (1931), their auditoriums and congress halls reflecting the variety and flexibility of the prototype. There was other work in the six-year period in Berlin: an engineering school in Hagen (1929), automobiles for the Adler Motor Werk (1929–1933), a Werkbund exhibition for Paris (1930), furniture designs for mass production (1929), and other industrial products.

Neither Gropius's preoccupation with work, his travels, nor the distance away from Dessau could prevent echoes of the problems of the Bauhaus from reaching him. Hannes Meyer, upon assuming that directorship, soon changed the Bauhaus's apolitical stance and reputation, which Gropius had insisted on, to one of condoning if not fostering communist doctrine within and without the school. Less to be criticized was Meyer's emphasis on a greater social orientation for the work of the Bauhaus, city planning as context for architecture, a new concentration on architectural education at the expense of art, and his introduction of a greater variety of teachers and visiting lecturers. The resulting controversy within the school became public, and the mayor of Dessau had little choice but to dismiss Meyer. On Gropius's recommendation, the mayor engaged Mies van der Rohe to redirect the Bauhaus along safer lines. It was a situation made to order for the enemies of the Bauhaus; not even Mies could withstand the harassment and was forced by the overwhelming strength of the National Socialist Party in the *Landtag* (legislature) to close the Dessau Bauhaus. Reopening the school in a vacant factory in Berlin–Steglitz, Mies persisted until 1933, when the threat of seizure and worse forced the permanent closing of the Bauhaus.

There was nothing at all that Gropius, himself under criticism by the Nazis, could do to aid the Bauhaus in its trauma. He had not joined the Party; he had resigned from the Werkbund board in protest against the interference of the government, and he had openly welcomed Russian officials interested in his work. In fact, he had visited Leningrad to lecture in 1931, and had engaged in controversial discussion and correspondence with Nazi officials. Though he had reluctantly continued his professional registration with the Nazi-created *Reichskulturkammer,* he received no commissions from the government, then the principal source of work. Gropius did try to obtain work through the government's architectural competitions, submitting entries for the proposed central building of the Reichsbank and for a great recreation and cultural center for the *Kraft durch Freude* movement, a prototype to be built in the Tiergarten in Berlin. His Reichsbank design is for a massive building block, unrelieved by anything except its jutting wings, unadorned, and with monotonous fenestration. The Tiergarten center is of greater interest, involving site design on a great scale and invoking visions of massive party demonstrations as much as those of recreation. Though Gropius developed his entries with great care, they must have been done with some sense that the efforts would be fruitless; there could not have been the least possibility that Gropius would be rewarded. A few other projects were completed by Gropius; residences and an exhibit for the manufacturers of nonferrous metal products (1934).

Invitations to speak, teach, or practice elsewhere on the Continent, in England, and in the United States had multiplied. In the spring of 1934, he addressed audiences in London and Liverpool. So impressive were those appearances and the accompanying exhibit of his work that he received an offer to return to England for the design of a housing project for Manchester. He also agreed to participate in a great theater congress in Rome in October 1934. It was an unparalleled opportunity to present his Total Theater concept to Europe's most outstanding theater designers and producers. Gropius applied and received official permission to travel to Rome and to work for a brief period in London. Walter and Ise attended the congress where his Total Theater evoked interest as well as criticism. Departing Rome, they went to Zurich for a lecture and immediately thereafter to London, closing a chapter of their lives and opening a new one.

England. Gropius's arrival in England was unheralded. He was met by Jack Pritchard, head of Isokon, Limited. Having heard Gropius speak earlier that year, he was convinced that here was an architect-designer who could contribute something new and fresh to his organization. Pritchard had prepared well for the introduction and transition to England of Walter and Ise Gropius. He provided them with an apartment in his Lawn Road Flats in Hampstead, recently completed by WELLS W. COATES. The locale was the center of the intellectual and artistic life of London; Gropius's neighbors included avant-garde poets, artists, and writers and many of the elite of British society; some were, like themselves, expatriates from the Continent. It is true that they encountered an introspective and austere economic environment, but it was also a socially conscious and searching intellectual one, and despite his lan-

Gropius.
Adler Automobile Bodies.
1933

guage handicap he was made to feel at home.

Pritchard had arranged for a partnership with EDWIN MAXWELL FRY, already well-known for his effort toward contemporary design. Their first project would be a river-front apartment building for A. P. Simon in Manchester. A similar project followed, this time an apartment building to be built on the Philip Sargent Florence estate in Birmingham. The most interesting housing scheme that Gropius and Fry developed featured three high-rise apartment blocks to be built on Saint Leonard's Hill (1935) overlooking Windsor Park and Castle and notable for the manner in which the architects preserved the open spaces and wooded areas of the estate. Unfortunately, none of these projects would procede for reason of funding, and Gropius's discouragement was matched only by that of Pritchard.

Gropius remained in communication with his family, *Bauhäusler,* and other friends in Germany by correspondence and through the many refugees who increasingly came to England. His activities in CIAM hardly lagged and he participated in the Modern Architecture Research Group of England. Gropius was drawn into the activities of Dartington Hall, an English counterpart of the Bauhaus as envisioned by Mr. and Mrs. Leonard Elmhirst, its patrons. There, Gropius was an honored guest, a heeded adviser, and an architect.

Still another project of note which went un-

built was Gropius's and Fry's proposal for a new residence hall for Christ's College (1936) in Cambridge. Their design departed from the traditional architecture of the College buildings on the site, though not so radically as to be an affront. Despite the best arguments of their supporters among the masters, the design was rejected, and safer, more traditional architects were engaged.

Through Jack Pritchard's friendship with Henry Morris, the energetic and innovative education officer of Cambridgeshire, Gropius and Fry were commissioned to design a community school and activities center for Impington (1936). Though their original scheme was very much altered to fit the stringent budget, in subsequent years additions and alterations have almost effaced the coherent Gropius-Fry design; yet, it remains a landmark in education facilities and the principal artifact of Gropius in England.

The efforts to bring Gropius to the United States which had begun in the 1920s had continued, and in 1935–1936 they intensified. He was now frequently queried as to his interest in university lecture tours, in heading a new school of architecture to be located in New York State, in a housing research position, and in an appointment at Harvard University in the Graduate School of Design. From Harvard, an alumnus, a teacher, the dean, and the president came at intervals to talk with Gropius and ultimately to convince him. Once his mind was made up to accept, he began to arrange his departure from England and, more completely than before, from Germany. There was unfinished work in the office which would be left in Fry's capable hands. The family properties in Germany would be the concern of his brother-in-law, and Gropius returned there to close out his apartment and to arrange for shipment of his personal effects to the United States. During this period, he sought formal approval by the Nazi government of his move to the United States; perhaps this became less difficult when the government learned that Gropius would supplant a Beaux-Arts-trained architect at Harvard. Gropius was believed to be a loyal German, by his own statement and actions, though at odds with the Nazis over their requirements placed on the professions; furthermore, he was out of their grasp. It was for the well-being of family and friends, he later explained, that he followed the course of formalities.

In retrospect, Gropius felt that his stay in England had been an enriching one; he was particularly impressed by English restraint and understatement. The friendships he made became lifelong. The sympathy extended to him at the time of his daughter's death and the assistance provided during the severe illness suffered by Ise, the unsolicited

Gropius.
Impington Village College
   (with Fry).
Cambridgeshire, England.
1936

financial aid from the Elmhirsts, the constant concern of Jack Pritchard for their comfort, Max Fry's endless patience, and the welcome and continuing hospitality of the professional associations were unforgettable and very much alive in his memory ever after.

Harvard University. Within a month of Gropius's arrival in Cambridge in April 1937, the *Architectural Record* published his views on architectural education. In this article, Gropius expressed his desire to develop within each young architect the ability to approach a problem according to its technical, economic, and social conditions. At Harvard, Gropius found a strange dichotomy of established custom and yet a fierce independence of thought. Beaux-Arts attitudes remained little changed in the recently reorganized Graduate School of Design. Gropius brought to Harvard an articulate statement of the new movement in architecture with its focus on social values and its emphasis on rational means of construction. Rapidly, it permeated the classes, and when he was appointed chairman of the department of architecture in 1938, the Beaux-Arts approach to architecture was truly of the past. Subsequently, virtually all the schools in the United States would turn away from the traditional systems and adopt curricula based on the new attitudes and principles.

At Harvard, Gropius faithfully appeared twice each week at each student's drafting table. His words were few and his sketches still fewer, Gropius nevertheless elicited response from every student. A gesture, a line, or a few questions were sufficient to give a new direction. His attention was a complete one. On many occasions, he appealed to his class to concern itself with the realities of the housing problem and the requirements of the then emerging legislation, to examine the earlier experience, and to experiment in construction methods. He emphasized the need to seek and to try to understand the responsibilities of the architect toward the complex problems of society; he would reiterate constantly his view of the relatedness of ideas and actions to the totality of the environment. He challenged each student to find within himself his own expression, his own interpretation within the collaborative efforts of architects, city planners, and landscape architects. Always, Gropius called for unity within diversity. At Harvard, he was able to complete the changes in education in architecture and related design fields which he had begun in the Bauhaus. Despite the constant trend toward specialization, Gropius remained firm in his view that comprehensive education must precede the narrower or specialized training. Gropius was determined that there would be no mold, no imitation.

His appointment at Harvard, under the custom prevailing in some of the professional graduate schools, permitted and encouraged private practice. Deterred by the Depression as much as by the fact that Gropius and Marcel Breuer, whom he had recently brought over, were unknown, commissions for work came slowly to their small office. Among the earliest of the several houses upon which they collaborated were Gropius's (1937) and Breuer's own homes. That for Gropius, particularly, was to win attention as one of the first truly modern houses in New England. Built on a knoll in an apple orchard in Lincoln, Massachusetts, it did not appear out of place next to the neighbor-

Gropius.
Gropius House (with
  Breuer).
Lincoln, Massachusetts.
1937

ing Colonial structures—this despite its flat roofs, terraces, and fenestration. Other houses for venturesome clients followed, capped by the great mansion for the Frank family (1939) near Pittsburgh, Pennsylvania, and in 1941, when Breuer resigned from the partnership, by an innovative housing development at New Kensington, also near Pittsburgh. This was a low-cost project built for defense workers; it comprised wood structures seemingly scattered at random over a difficult hillside terrain. It would elicit much criticism but would establish a new high level of design for the Federal agency involved.

Several years later, Gropius entered a competition for Smith College, without result. Not a competition entry, but a proposal which also failed to mature, was Gropius's and Breuer's scheme for Black Mountain College (1939) in North Carolina. With Jorgé Gonzalez Reyna, Gropius proposed a large cathedral for Torreon, Mexico, the first church that he had ever designed. In 1942, Gropius and KONRAD WACHSMANN developed plans for a recreation center in Key West, Florida. That year, Gropius, with the experience of his copper house and other dry-panel buildings and Wachsmann's innovative ideas for construction, promoted the General Panel Corporation, a prefab organization. Their product was recognized for its ingenuity and innovative design, and their production method was an example for industry; unfortunately, financing systems were far too slow to meet marketing, sales, and cash-flow requirements.

Soon after his arrival in the United States, Gropius again had concerned himself with the problems of lowering housing costs. He called for a reorganization of the construction industry to meet the problems through improvement in production and site methods. His teachings and writings were directed toward the role and responsibilities of the architect in such a program. His General Panel Corporation house was intended to fulfill these needs, at least in part. Gropius became consultant to the Container Corporation of America which opened for him new vistas, for this work involved factories in Illinois, North Carolina, and in Colombia, and conferences in Colorado. Gropius managed all these projects, proposed or completed, while scrupulously maintaining his teaching and administrative responsibilities at Harvard.

Despite his newly won competence in the English language, his well-known democratic principles and actions, and his acceptance by neighbors and colleagues, the prewar years and the period of the war itself made Gropius conscious of the fact that he was an alien—a citizen of an aggressor nation with which his host country was at war, though he would become a citizen of the United

States in 1944. His wartime efforts were confined to sending countless packages of food and other necessities to his family, *Bauhäusler,* and other friends; to aiding individuals to leave war-torn Europe; and to re-establish them elsewhere. He was frequently called on to assist other professionals, academics, artists, and musicians; beseeched by Marcel Breuer, he had first brought him to England and then to the United States. Among the many others whom he aided were Herbert Bayer, MARTIN WAGNER, Konrad Wachsmann, and Nikolaus Pevsner. From its inception in 1937, Gropius was involved in László Moholy-Nagy's New Bauhaus in Chicago and in its successor schools. Harvard University's Graduate School of Design was in its own lean period; the classes eked out with students from neutral countries, returning veterans, and, for the first time beginning in 1942, with women, a wartime condition which would become a permanent and felicitous one. There was little respite for Gropius; with stringent budgets and reduced faculty, there was greater demand on his time. His practice struggled and survived, a place for students to gain experience with at least part of their academic expense subsidized by Gropius himself.

Postwar period.   Immediately after the war, Gropius renewed his Chicago ventures which he had begun in 1922 when he and Adolf Meyer entered the Chicago Tribune competition; his first postwar activity was his involvement in Michael Reese Hospital's and the Chicago South Side's pioneering efforts in planning, redevelopment, and conservation. His alumnus, Reginald Isaacs, had conceived of his assignment to salvage the Hospital situated in a slum area in Gropius's own comprehensive terms: the institution, its community, the city, the metro area and the region considered in a total approach of social, economic, political and physical concerns for their people. It would be Gropius's first major experience in planning and the first full test of his city planning ideas. He remained as an active consultant for more than a decade in this successful demonstration.

A major change in his life and practice came with the formation of The Architects Collaborative (TAC) early in 1946. His experience, wisdom, and renown, coupled with the vigor and fresh ideas of young associates, established the bases for a practice that would become world encircling and world famous. The first years of the new firm were not easy ones; always, there were more projects that failed than those that were built. Again, there were many residences to design and build among these, prototypes for an entire generation of architects everywhere. Among the projects which did not procede was the Hua Tung University of

Shanghai (1948), and among those that did was the Junior High School for Attleboro, Massachusetts (1948), both of which also became models. In 1947, Gropius was adviser to General Lucius Clay on the reconstruction of Germany. In 1949, TAC and he were given their initial opportunity to build for Harvard: the Graduate Center (1949–1950). It was also a challenge to create buildings that would relate to the traditional environment of Harvard and yet be an honest contemporary solution to the 24-hour needs of the students, one that would be stimulating and satisfying and yet remain within the stringent construction budget. This the architects did very well, though many students over the years would have preferred better sound insulation rather than the aesthetics of the contemporary art which was underwritten by an alumnus.

In the School of Design, the friendship between Dean Hudnut and Gropius had long since cooled and indeed there was scarcely veiled enmity. Hudnut was almost hidden in the background and Gropius was increasingly in the fore; his fame was world-wide, and he in fact headed the faculty (some of them his associates in TAC). Hudnut controlled the budget and the appointment process; the handling of these was not to Gropius's liking, and he resigned in mid-1952, a full term before his age under Harvard's rules would have required him to retire.

Emeritus career. At an age when most men retire, Gropius began his emeritus career in full vitality and with enthusiasm. Unfortunately, architectural commissions did not immediately match that enthusiasm. Again, there was residential work, a school, and a housing project for the Navy at Quonset, Rhode Island (1953). There were noteworthy proposals, designs for buildings which would not be built, among them an office building for the American Association for the Advancement of Science to be located on a restricted site in Washington (1952). Gropius, TAC, and other architects, organized together as the Boston Center Architects, proposed a re-use of railroad yards near central Boston. Unfortunately, there was too little cooperation from the city, and their Back Bay Center could not be realized.

There were rewards, however, few so extraordinary as his seventieth birthday celebration in 1953 with Mies van der Rohe and several hundred others paying tribute to him in a "Gropius Fest" in Chicago. There were also other honors accorded him. Perhaps none of these pleased him so much as the honorary degree awarded by Harvard.

In 1954, Gropius was able to visit Japan; its culture and architecture had a profound effect on him when he discovered that Zen and his own philosophy were in accord and that the Japanese traditional modular construction was fundamentally similar to what he had strived to establish. In 1954 also, he received the Matarazzo Prize at the São Paulo Biennale, enabling him to visit South America.

Returning to Cambridge, he found studies well advanced for the campus and buildings of Springfield College in Springfield, Massachusetts, by a collaborative group which included TAC and himself, HIDEO SASAKI as landscape architect, and Reginald Isaacs as planner. Soon thereafter, with the same group, there was an ill-fated project for a civic center at Tallahassee, Florida—ill-fated in that racial bigotry prevented the construction of what would be one of Gropius's most emulated designs. However, architectural satisfaction and profitability were achieved with the now rapidly growing reputation of TAC.

Gropius and PIETRO BELLUSCHI were selected as design consultants for a major office building to be built in New York City by Pan-Am Airlines (1957). Its Grand Central Station site heading Park Avenue was a strategic but difficult one. The original proposal by the developers and their architects called for a typical vertical boxlike structure. Gropius's principal recommendation was to reduce the bulk of the building by cutting the four corners, resulting in a prismatic effect that gave some sense of continuity and flow around and beyond the building. Additionally, he accelerated pedestrian movement through the building in several directions by means of escalators and stairs. Persuading the developers that art was a requirement of architecture, he brought in artists to create works for the building. Despite his efforts, the building, as any building would have done, evoked criticism for its size by architects who failed to note the already changed scale of Park Avenue buildings.

The United States Embassy (1956) in Athens is another work in which Gropius gave particular attention to the surrounding traditional architecture. The resulting building is a classic one in its proportions, colonnade, portico, atrium, and its marble and stone. Inevitably, it would draw criticism as well as praise as one of few United States embassies designed to recognize the culture of the host country. The loyalty of an alumnus led to the large commission for a university in Baghdad, Iraq (1957), and with this and other worldwide work in the offing, TAC International was established in Rome. It was a glorious time in Gropius's life: he was practicing architecture.

His return to Germany in 1956 was a triumphant one. Gropius and TAC designed an apartment building in the Hansaviertel of Berlin lo-

Gropius.
University (with TAC).
Baghdad.
1957

Gropius.
Interbau Apartment (with
TAC).
Berlin.
1955

cated among the works of other architects. The largest commission of all was a great housing development for some 50,000 families in the Britz-Buckow-Rudow area of Berlin, which project subsequently would be named officially *Gropiusstadt*. Gropius served as coordinator as well as overall planner, and architect with TAC of portions of it. In addition, he designed the major school in the development. Naturally, he and TAC would be commissioned to design the Bauhaus-Archiv which would house the growing collection of Bauhaus artifacts, originally to be built on the Rosenhöhe in Darmstadt, but ultimately erected in Berlin. For the Rosenthal Ceramics industry, Gropius designed a new factory in Selb, Germany (1963); in his lifelong effort to improve the environment of workers, he created an internal glazed central court with flowers and birds and natural light which can be seen from everywhere within the enclosed factory walls. Gropius's most extraordinary building at this time was the Thomas Glass Factory in Amberg, Germany (1967). This cathedrallike structure took its high gabled roof form from the functional requirement to take the heat away from the glassblowers below. From the project for Rosenthal came the opportunity to plan for the expansion of the town of Selb itself. This was done according to Gropius's belief that a well-located town should be the center of growth of a planned larger city with precautions to preserve the good qualities of the original town or village center.

Gropius's welcome in Germany was almost matched by that in England. The Gold Medal of the Royal Institute of British Architects and the Gold Albert Medal of the Royal Society of Arts were awarded to him. Of greater consequence to Gropius were the prospects of commissions. However, few materialized. The Monico building on

Piccadilly Circus appeared to have promise only to be delayed too long for the developers by disputes regarding solutions for the problem of Circus traffic. Gropius's office–apartment building was built at 45 Park Lane, London (1960).

Gropius's ventures in architectural design in Canada also stopped short of construction. The first of these was a great complex of apartments, hotels, shops, offices, and public buildings for the Toronto waterfront. Shortsightedly, the Ontario Association insisted that Gropius's and TAC's consultation would not be in accord with the Ontario Architects' Act. In 1964, a proposed development for Place Sainte Cyrille in Quebec offered Gropius a challenge to design within the traditionalist feelings of Quebec citizens; in response, he drafted the strongest kind of urban design principles to meet the character of the city. With the rivalry between city and provincial governments, changes in the project, and division among the developers, Gropius asked that his name be disassociated from the project.

In the United States, there were mounting opportunities. The John F. Kennedy Federal Office Building in Boston (1968) was one of these, and Gropius found it appropriate that the building he designed would be built within an urban setting created by his alumnus I. M. PEI. In Cleveland, the Tower East Office Building (1967), like the Kennedy Building, allowed Gropius to fulfill his desire for art integrated with architecture.

An addition to the Huntington Galleries in Huntington, West Virginia (1968), and an extraordinary residence for the German ambassador in Buenos Aires (1968) designed with AMANCIO WILLIAMS of that city, were highpoints of Gropius's late years. The latter design, unfortunately not built, would have permitted its park setting to be visually almost unimpaired, with the first story being depressed below and the second story elevated above eye level.

The great Bauhaus Exhibit in 1969 had been a huge success, and several sets of it were touring the world. International honors and recognition had come in a steady stream, among them, ultimately, more than three score honorary degrees, memberships, prizes, medals, and other tributes. His charisma was great, and the regard in which Gropius was held by former students, friends, and colleagues had been a lasting one. Despite his age, his death on July 5, 1969, seemed premature.

REGINALD R. ISAACS

WORKS

1911–1912, Fagus Factory (with Adolf Meyer), Alfeld, Germany. 1913, Diesel Railway Car, Königsberg, Germany. 1913, World's Fair (interiors), Ghent, Belgium. 1913–1914, Furniture Designs. 1913–1914, German Railroad Sleeping Car. 1913–1914, Werkbund Exhibition (with Meyer), Cologne, Germany. 1921, Adolf Sommerfeld House, Dahlem, Berlin. 1922, Memorial Sculpture, Weimar, Germany. 1923–1924, State Theater (renovation; with Meyer), Jena, Germany. 1925–1926, Bauhaus Building; 1926, Master's Housing; 1926–1927, Toerten Housing; Dessau, Germany. 1926–1927, Weissenhof Houses (two), Stuttgart, Germany. 1927–1928, City Labor Office (Arbeitsamt), Dessau, Germany. 1929, Feder Furniture Stores, Berlin. 1929, Am Lindenbaum Housing Development, Frankfurt. 1929, Spandel-Haselhorst Housing Development; 1929–1930, Siemensstadt Housing Development; Berlin. 1929–1933, Adler Automobile Bodies. 1930, Werkbund Exhibition, Paris. 1931, Copper Houses, Finow, Germany. 1931, Tomb, Dresden, Germany. 1931–1933, Stoves, Frank Ironworks, Hannover, Germany. 1934, Nonferrous Metals Exhibition (with Joost Schmidt), Berlin. 1936, Donaldson House (with Fry), Kent, England. 1936, Levy House (with Fry), Chelsea, London. 1936, Impington Village College (with Fry), Cambridgeshire, England. 1937, Gropius House (with Marcel Breuer), Lincoln, Mass. 1939, Frank Mansion, Pittsburgh. 1941, Housing Development (with Breuer), New Kensington, Penn. 1948, Junior High School (with The Architects Collaborative), Attleboro, Mass. 1949–1950, Harvard University Graduate Center (with TAC), Cambridge, Mass. 1953, Wherry District Housing, Quonset, R.I. 1955, Interbau Apartment (with TAC), Berlin. 1956, United States Embassy (with TAC), Athens. 1957, Pan American Building (with Pietro Belluschi), New York. 1957, University (with TAC), Baghdad. 1958, Temple Oheb Shalom (with TAC), Baltimore. 1960, Office and Apartment Building (with TAC), London. 1962, School (with TAC), Gropiusstadt; 1964, Bauhaus-Archiv (with TAC), Berlin. 1963, Rosenthal Ceramics Factory (with TAC), Selb, Germany. 1967, Thomas Glass Factory (with TAC), Amberg, Germany. 1967, Tower East Office Building, Cleveland, Ohio. 1968, Huntington Gallery (with TAC), Huntington, W. Va. 1968, John F. Kennedy Federal Office Building, Boston. 1968, Rosenthal Ceramic Tea Set.

BIBLIOGRAPHY

ARGAN, GIULIO CARLO (1951)1975 *Walter Gropius e la Bauhaus.* Turin, Italy: Einaudi.

BAYER, HERBERT 1938 *Bauhaus: 1919–1929.* Edited by Walter and Ise Gropius. New York: Museum of Modern Art.

FITCH, JAMES MARSTON 1960 *Walter Gropius.* New York: Braziller.

FRANCISCONO, MARCEL 1971 *Walter Gropius and the Creation of the Bauhaus.* Urbana: University of Illinois Press.

GIEDION, SIEGFRIED 1954 *Walter Gropius: Work and Teamwork.* New York: Reinhold.

GROPIUS, WALTER (1936)1965 *The New Architecture and the Bauhaus.* Translated by P. Morton Shand. Cambridge, Mass.: M.I.T. Press.

GROPIUS, WALTER 1945 *Rebuilding Our Communities.* Chicago: Theobald.

GROPIUS, WALTER 1952a *Architecture and Design in the Age of Science.* New York: Spiral.

GROPIUS, WALTER (1952b)1962 *Scope of Total Architecture.* Edited by Ise Gropius. New York: Collier.

GROPIUS, WALTER (1967)1968 *Apollo in the Democracy.* Translated by Ise Gropius. New York: McGraw-Hill.

GROPIUS, WALTER, and HARKNESS, SARAH P. (editors) 1966 *Architects Collaborative: 1945–1965.* Tenfen, Switzerland: Niggli.

HERBERT, GILBERT 1959 *The Synthetic Vision of Walter Gropius.* Johannesburg: Witwatersrand University Press.

HESSE, FRITZ 1964 *Erinnerungen an Dessau.* 2 volumes. Hannover, Germany: Schmorl & von Seefeld Buchhandlung.

HÜTER, KARL HEINZ 1976 *Das Bauhaus in Weimar.* Berlin: Akademia Verlag.

LANE, BARBARA MILLER 1968 *Architecture and Politics in Germany: 1918–1945.* Cambridge, Mass.: Harvard University Press.

O'NEAL, WILLIAM B. (editor) 1966 Volume 3 in *Walter Gropius, Papers.* Charlottesville, Va.: The American Association of Architectural Bibliographers.

SCHEIDIG, WALTHER (1966)1967 *Crafts of the Weimar Bauhaus: 1919–1924.* Translated by Ruth Michaelis-Jena. New York: Reinhold. Originally published in German.

WEBER, HELMUT 1961 *Walter Gropius und das Faguswerk.* Munich: Callwey.

WINGLER, HANS MARIA (1962)1979 *The Bauhaus: Weimar, Dessau, Berlin, Chicago.* Translated by Wolfgang Jabs and Basil Gilbert. Cambridge, Mass.: M.I.T. Press.

GRUEN, VICTOR

Victor Gruen (1903–1980) was educated at the Architectural School and the Academy of Arts in

Vienna. He maintained a private practice there until the advance of Hitler. In 1938, he emigrated to New York where he worked for the Ivels Corporation and in the office of NORMAN BEL GEDDES. He later formed a design partnership with Elsie Krummeck (1940–1948) and eventually settled in Los Angeles where he established the firm of Victor Gruen Associates (1951).

Gruen aspired to create environmental architecture rather than stylish buildings, with the conviction that it was of paramount importance to provide the public with comfort and convenience wherever they shopped, worked, and lived.

Troubled by the alienation of the suburban dweller who had fled the city in chaotic numbers and also aware of the difficulties of the merchants who had followed to cater to them, Gruen strove to reconnect them by translating the ideal of the Greek agora into modern terms through the proliferation of shopping malls across America.

Of the many shopping centers Gruen built, Northland Center in Detroit, Michigan (1954), and Southdale Center in Minneapolis, Minnesota (1956), stand out as striking examples of his imaginative approach to shopping malls. Northland exhibits the initial ingenious solution for traffic circulation and parking problems, and Southdale exemplifies his theory that malls should be "festive and colorful" with a multistoried interior, sculptures, gardens, and an open-air café.

Feeling passionately that the city core nurtured the most essential aspects of urban life, he created innovative plans for its revitalization and blueprints for future cities. His plan for Fort Worth, Texas (1955), never implemented due primarily to its seemingly radical exclusion of cars and its promotion of mass transit, later served as the model for city planners all over the world. Gruen also had the opportunity to couple his interest in urban renewal with his vast experience with shopping centers to complete such projects as The Mall, Fresno, California (1968), and Midtown Plaza, Rochester, New York (1962), the first inner-city enclosed mall.

LYNDA GREENBERG

WORKS

*1939, Lederer Shop, Fifth Avenue, New York. 1954, Northland Center, Detroit, Mich. 1956, Southdale Shopping Center, Minneapolis, Minn. 1960, Museum of Arts and Sciences, Evansville, Ind. 1960, Cherry Hill Center, Camden, N.J. 1962, Midtown Plaza, Rochester, N.Y. 1962, Randhurst Shopping Center, Mount Prospect, Chicago. 1966, Sea World, San Diego, Calif. 1968, The Mall, Fresno, Calif.

BIBLIOGRAPHY

BAKER, GEOFFREY, and FUNARO, BRUNO 1951 *Shopping Centers.* New York: Reinhold.

BUCHANAN, COLIN 1958 *Mixed Blessings: The Motor in Britain.* London: Hill.

ECKBO, GARRETT 1964 *Urban Landscape Design.* New York: McGraw-Hill.

FITCH, JAMES MARSTON 1961 *Architecture and the Esthetics of Plenty.* New York: Columbia University Press.

GIEDION, SIEGFRIED 1958 *Architecture: You and Me.* Cambridge, Mass.: Harvard University Press.

GRUEN, VICTOR 1952 "Shopping Centers: The New Building Type." *Progressive Architecture* 33, June.

GRUEN, VICTOR 1956 "Transformation of Typical Downtown (Ft. Worth)." *Architectural Forum* 104, May:146–155.

GRUEN, VICTOR 1962 "Approaches to Urban Revitalization in the United States." *Journal of the Architectural Association* 78, Dec.:178–194.

GRUEN, VICTOR 1964 *The Heart of Our Cities.* New York: Simon & Schuster.

GRUEN, VICTOR 1973 *Centers for the Urban Environment.* New York: Van Nostrand.

GRUEN, VICTOR, and SMITH, LARRY 1960 *Shopping Towns U.S.A.* New York: Reinhold.

HAMLIN, TALBOT F. 1952 *Forms and Function of 20th Century Architectures.* New York: Columbia University Press.

JACOBS, ANNE 1961 *Death and Life of Great American Cities.* New York: Random House.

KETCHUM, MORRIS (1948)1957 *Shops and Stores.* Rev. ed. New York: Reinhold.

TUNNARD, CHRISTOPHER 1963 *Man-Made America: Chaos or Control?* New Haven: Yale University Press.

GUADET, JULIEN

Julien Guadet (1834–1908) was born in Paris where he entered the Ecole des Beaux-Arts in 1854 as a student of PIERRE FRANÇOIS HENRI LABROUSTE; in 1856, he transferred to the atelier of Jules André. Guadet also worked under CHARLES GARNIER at the Paris Opera from 1861 until 1864 when he won the Prix de Rome. Guadet's importance lies in his career as a teacher: professor of an official architectural atelier at the Ecole from 1872 to 1894, he was the Ecole's professor of architectural theory from 1894 until 1908. His lectures, (1901–1904), codified Beaux-Arts composition and sought to resolve the split between the Romantic and classical factions of French architecture.

CHRISTOPHER MEAD

WORKS

1880–1884, Hôtel des Postes; 1891, Tomb of Eugene Delaplanche, Père-Lachaise Cemetery; After 1900, Théâtre Français (restoration); n.d., Tomb of Charles Bigot, Père-Lachaise Cemetery; Paris.

BIBLIOGRAPHY

GUADET, JULIEN 1886 *Conférence sur le Nouvel Hôtel*

des Postes (*Extrait des Mémoires de la Société des Ingénieurs Civils*). Paris: Chaix.

GUADET, JULIEN (1901–1904)1909 *Eléments et Théorie de l'Architecture.* 3d ed. Paris: Librairie de la Construction Moderne.

HAUTECOEUR, LOUIS 1957 *La fin de l'architecture classique.* Volume 7 in *Histoire de l'architecture classique en France.* Paris: Picard.

PASCAL, JEAN-LOUIS 1909 "Notice sur la vie et les oeuvres de Julien Guadet." In Julien Guadet, *Eléments et Théorie de l'Architecture.* 3d ed. Paris: Librairie de la Construction Moderne.

VAN ZANTEN, DAVID 1977 "Architectural Composition at the Ecole des Beaux-Arts from Charles Percier to Charles Garnier." In Arthur Drexler (editor), *The Architecture of the Ecole des Beaux-Arts.* New York: Museum of Modern Art.

GUARINI, GUARINO

Guarino Guarini (1624–1683), Theatine priest and one of the most original architects of the last half of the seventeenth century in Europe, was born in Modena, Italy, in the Este duchy, and died in Milan. He was active as an architect in Modena, Messina, Paris, Vicenza, Verona, and Turin. Five of the seven churches that he built survive, as well as one palace, one college, two castles, and an altar; he prepared unexecuted designs for four churches for the Theatine Order in Vicenza, Lisbon, Nice, and Prague, as well as projects for four other churches in Messina and Piedmont.

Guarini was also a mathematician and prolific author. In addition to treatises on architecture, quantity surveying, and fortifications, he wrote philosophical and theological tracts, including geocentric, geometrical explanations for the motion of the planets, a treatise on geometry, and, in his youth, a play for the stage. His *Euclides Adauctus* (Turin, 1676) made him a forerunner in the development of projective and descriptive geometry.

Although Guarini's importance to the history of geometry is still to be assessed fully, there is little doubt he was the only architect among the many inspired by FRANCESCO BORROMINI who was able to produce works both personal and provocative that approach the level of Borromini's achievement. His work also shows study of GIOVANNI LORENZO BERNINI who, with Borromini and PIETRO BERRETTINI DA CORTONA, was active in Rome during the years Guarini studied for the priesthood (1639–1647) in the Theatine House at San Silvestro on the Quirinal Hill.

Guarini's concern with geometry may have contributed to his interest in Borromini's buildings, but in contrast to Borromini's designs in which the underlying geometrical construction is seldom apparent, the generating figure in Guarini's constructions is celebrated, emphasized, and multiplied. Yet, even though Guarini's buildings openly reflect geometric conceptions, his treatise on architecture (largely mathematical) warned against ill-considered application of mathematics and architectural theory: "Even though architecture proceeds from mathematics, it is nonetheless a pleasing art, that does not wish, for the sake of reason, to offend the senses: wherefore, though many of the rules of architecture follow the precepts of mathematics, whenever adherence to these rules offends sight, change them, drop them, or finally, contradict them." Geometry was useful for Guarini in theory and development of a design until, in practice, visual judgment superseded.

Inasmuch as Guarini's architecture was, in some of its aspects, more accessible than Borromini's, he had a significant effect on succeeding generations, of greater consequence in Germany and Austria than in France and Italy. Knowledge of his publications and of his buildings in Piedmont may be seen in the work of many major German and Austrian architects of the eighteenth century, including LUCAS VON HILDEBRANDT, the DIENTZENHOFER BROTHERS, JOHANN BERNHARD FISCHER VON ERLACH, JOHANN BALTHASAR NEUMANN, and JOHANN MICHAEL FISCHER.

Early years to 1662

Guarino (baptized Camillo) Guarini was one of five sons, all of whom entered the Theatine Order. In 1639, at age fifteen, Guarini became a novitiate and was sent to Rome for education. Ordained in 1648 in Modena, he began his vocation in the Theatine House attached to San Vincenzo. He assisted in the construction of the church and was nominated professor of philosophy in 1650. Guarini's alternative design for a dome in wood at the crossing of San Vincenzo was approved in 1653, but was not executed. In 1655, Prince Alfonso d'Este for obscure reasons vetoed Guarini's election to leadership of the Order in Modena. Guarini was exiled and forbidden to return (other than short visits to his family) for sixteen years.

Except for a letter from Guastalla in 1656, nothing is known of Guarini's whereabouts between 1655 and 1660, when his presence is documented again in a Theatine House in Messina, Sicily. While teaching philosophy and mathematics there, he accomplished his first known design for the church and house of the Order. The church, Santissima Annunziata, was damaged in the earthquake of 1783 and destroyed in the one of 1908. The appearance of the monastery is preserved, however, in an engraving by Francesco Sicuro,

Guarini.
Engraving of Santissima
*   Annunziata (façade).*
Messina, Italy.
1660

published in 1768, and the church façade in an engraving in Guarini's *Architettura Civile* and in a photograph taken before 1908.

The church façade owes much not only to Borromini's façade for the Oratorio dei Filippini (in that its shallow, concave central section holds a convex entrance bay) and to church façades with volutes connecting the lower to a narrow upper level, but also to Sicilian three-tiered façades. Guarini demonstrated considerable ability and sophistication in using the campanile to effect a transition between the plane of the façade and the skewed axis of the nave, and in the unusual pairing, throughout the lower level, of column and pilaster which he reversed at the second level in the central bay.

Guarini is next recorded back in Modena, where he designed a tomb in San Vincenzo during the summer of 1662. He may have returned earlier in the year, at the death of his mother, from either Paris or Messina. In September or October of 1662, he was surely in Paris. From this moment his activities become better known.

Paris, 1662–1666

On 28 November 1662, the Prince de Conti laid the cornerstone of the new Theatine Church in Paris, Sainte Anne-la-Royale. The site on the left bank of the Seine had been purchased, and excavations for the foundations of an oval church, designed by MAURIZIO VALPERGA, were begun in the summer of 1661 with funds left to the Order in Cardinal Mazzarin's will. Valperga's design was replaced by Guarini's in the fall of 1662. Construction on the building was interrupted in 1666 due to lack of funds with no more than crossing and transept completed; only provisionally finished between 1714 and 1720, it was destroyed in the early 1820s. However, as Guarini's earliest recorded complete design (plan, section, and elevation appear in the *Architettura Civile* and, in addition, a preparatory drawing for the section has been preserved), Sainte Anne merits attention.

The plan, a Greek cross with extended choir and two-tiered central dome, is unusual in that due to the shape of the crossing piers, the chapels (transverse elongated octagons) are wider than the domed crossing, and the drum is larger or wider than the crossing.

The octagonal chapels are vaulted with pairs of rib-bands (reminiscent of those in Borromini's church in the Collegio di Propaganda Fide) which rise to unusual extended hexagonal lanterns. Larger spatial units than the crossing in plan and section (with oval subchapels further extending their longitudinal direction), the chapels are emphatically separate from the crossing. At the same time, they are decisively linked to the central space by diagonally placed main piers which through their surfaces as well imply a continuity of space from crossing to the chapels. The continuity is emphasized by the arches, diagonal in plane, that span between crossing and arms to join in the same thin edge, or arris, as the corners of the piers.

Guarini developed an equal tension between parts in his treatment of the drum and dome. The drum was designed as two concentric drums with the smaller, or inner supporting the dome. The inner drum consisted of eight paired columns and arches quite open to the outer. The outer drum on its interior surface had paired pilasters joined by arches to the corresponding paired columns of the inner drum. The annular barrel vault between the two drums was pierced at the crown (in line with the arches of the inner drum) by circular openings with small lanterns. A viewer would have looked up through the cornice ring, through the paired columns of the inner drum to the sixteen windows of the outer drum and above them into the lighted domelets and lanterns between the drums.

Above the drum, the inner surface of the lower dome, pierced by eight windows in the lower half (corresponding to the arches of the inner drum), contained applied pairs of rib-bands, springing from low pedestals, that arched across two of the windows to the pedestal next but one. Being joined in this manner where they intersected, the ribs left a large opening for the second dome (a ribbed star in plan also pierced by windows at its base) over 60 percent of the diameter of the lower dome. An octagonal lantern capped the second dome. The layered openness of the drum and dome would have been unusual in Italy and France except for the analogous expansion of space at upper levels in some of the earlier designs of FRANÇOIS MANSART (Château at Blois) which Guarini may have known. (Mansart's designs after 1662 may show an awareness of the design for Sainte Anne.)

The exterior at the lower level was to have been curvilinear with a broad convex central section the width of the entrance bay (and its two oval chapels) intersecting with disjunctive flanking concave bays marked by salient entablature and columns at both levels of the façade. The exterior of the drum also contained interrupted concave entablatures over the sixteen pairs of columns (which were more widely spaced flanking the axes and diagonals) returning to intersect above the eight windows on the minor axes.

Bernini visited the site on 14 June 1665 and said he thought the church would turn out well. Sebastiano Locatelli, a Bolognese priest, is reported to have said in 1664 that it would surpass the Val-de-Grâce in beauty.

When work was begun again, the direction of the church was changed. The completed transept bays became the initial bay of the nave and the choir, while a low, closed dome was built over the crossing. In the other direction, nonconforming semicircular apses were added to the crossing to enclose the central space. The whole was covered by a steep gallic roof.

While in Paris, in addition to publishing *Coelestis Mathematicae,* Guarini prepared another architectural design, a project for a large palace. The scale, in Parisian units, indicates it to be sizable, about 130 by 88 meters. The palace project was, perhaps, prompted by a request to Italian architects in 1664 for designs for the Louvre. Guarini, who was not invited to participate, may have prepared plans in a parallel effort (they do not, however, include the pre-existing Louvre structure). Guarini's plan included a two-story arcaded courtyard with four oval stairs in the corners. The elevations (a *piano nobile* with mezzanine and attic resting on a one-story base) were devoid of pilasters or vertical articulation and did not reflect the curvilinear interior courtyard. The austerity of the elevations suggest that when Guarini prepared the designs he had not seen the proposals submitted by Cortona, Carlo Rainaldi, and Borromini nor had he yet formulated the six modes of decoration found in the *Architettura Civile.* The contrast of exterior austerity with richness in the courtyard was probably an intentional Guarinian juxtaposition.

Perhaps due to a dispute over excessive expenditures for Sainte Anne, Guarini left Paris for Italy in the early fall of 1666. He may have been in Turin as early as November 1666, again attached to the Theatine House.

Turin, 1666–1683

Ecclesiastical buildings. When Guarini arrived in Turin, San Lorenzo, the church of the Order, had been under construction for some time. Foundations for the church (designer unknown) had been begun in 1643, but even though construction was well along by 1661 it was not sufficiently advanced to preclude the adoption of a new design by AMEDEO DI CASTELLAMONTE in 1664. Evidently, though, Guarini was able once again to transform the preceding work into a structure wholly his own. Since documents for work done on San Lorenzo before Guarini's arrival include payments for work on the façade, some demolition as well as rebuilding, restructuring, and conversion must have taken place.

Twelve years later, in 1678, the dome was completed; in the fall of 1679 a cross was placed on top of the lantern. Although still lacking a main altar, the church was inaugurated on 12 May 1680 with Guarini celebrating the first mass. The altar (begun in September 1680) was still not finished at the time of Guarini's death and was consecrated only in 1696.

Some of the rich, multicolored marble encrustation of the lower level of the church was installed during Guarini's lifetime. Further decoration of the church and chapels continued well into the eighteenth century. The entrance façade on Piazza Castello was never executed, as the crown preferred to extend a uniform façade across the entire side of the square. The campanile (placed to the right of the annular vaulted retrochoir) was left unfinished.

The central plan of San Lorenzo includes a narthex with rib-band arches reminiscent of those in Sainte Anne-la-Royale, a main domed central space with convex-shaped chapels in all four corners, shallower convex chapels on the lateral axis, an oval domed choir, and an annular vaulted retrochoir.

Broad-footed pendentives rest on the convex corner chapels and rise to a cornice ring interrupted by eight horizontal oval openings. The broken cornice ring supports the ribbed drum/dome and lantern. The drum/dome is also opened by large vertical oval windows at its lower level. Above, where the pairs of arches intersect, the web has been removed so that the arches alone intersect to form a light-encircled octagonal base ring for the lantern. Further above, on the inner surface of the lower dome of the lantern, pairs of rib-band arches, remarkably like the applied arches of the lower main dome of Sainte Anne-la-Royale, spring in both directions, intersecting to form an opening for the ultimate dome of the lantern which has eight vertical oval windows near its base.

Whereas the ribs and lower dome of the lantern resemble those at Sainte Anne, the principal ribs of the drum/dome at San Lorenzo, free of web from the point of intersection, are assertively structural (supporting the lantern as they do) and differ significantly from those at Sainte Anne. The eight great parabolic arches shape a drum/dome that is increasingly open, increasingly filled with light as it ascends. Rather than the depiction of a light-filled celestial scene on the inner dome surface, Guarini opened the dome to skylight, an analogue for celestial illumination.

But the spectators' wonderment at this structural, intellectual, and theological tour de force did not end with the drum/dome and lantern. The upper structure rests on a fractured cornice ring. Where keystones would appear to be structurally essential, oval openings are placed at the crest of each of the four main arches. In addition, the mas-

Guarini.
San Lorenzo (view up into
the dome).
Turin, Italy.
1667–1679

Guarini.
San Lorenzo (view up into
the dome).
Turin, Italy.
1667–1679

Guarini.
San Lorenzo.
Turin, Italy.
1667–1679

sive pendentives and thick main arches rest, at the lower level, on the vaulting of convex corner chapels which are supported in turn only by a pair of widely spaced marble columns. Yet further, above the corner chapel, at the center of the vault, an oculus discloses only empty space above, precisely where the great pendentive should bring its weight to bear. At the crest of the arch leading to the chapel, to emphasize that it does not carry the weight of the pendentive, arches, and drum/dome, Guarini perforated the wall with yet another strategically placed opening.

A structure such as that of the drum/dome cannot be held up by a cornice ring that is discontinuous, by pendentives and arches that are only minimally supported; the secret remains hidden. Only when examined from inside, behind the pendentives, is the actual structure revealed: four large arches that spring from the corners of the main central space above and behind the wall of the corner chapels rise to support the drum/dome, arching above the oval windows of the cornice ring; four smaller arches that spring from the haunches of the four main arches span (on the diagonal between the main arches) to form, together with the main arches, an octagonal base for the arches of the drum/dome.

At Sainte Anne-la-Royale, Guarini did not disclose any support for the weight of the exterior drum. There, too, arches hidden above the level of the vault of the chapel transmitted the load to four diagonal piers. In Turin, the wish to astonish, confound, or tease has grown to engage the entire structure, yet the structural manipulation is not without purpose. The richly surfaced lower level, with its multiple unresolved directional emphases and structure patently inadequate to its task finds in contrast, in an upper level bathed in a revealing celestial light, a resolution in which arches intersect unambiguously to support the superimposed lantern. The profusion of ornament and complexity of form at the lower level is replaced by openness, austerity, and celestial simplicity.

Shortly after his arrival in Turin, Guarini was also asked to complete the chapel to house the principal relic of the Savoy dynasty, the Holy Shroud, believed to have enveloped the body of Christ. In April 1667, a wood model of his design was begun. (The plan and section published in the *Theatrum Sabaudiae . . .* in 1682 may depict the model.) In June 1668, Guarini was appointed engineer for the chapel, a post he held until his death.

The chapel for the Santissima Sindone had a history. When the Shroud was brought to Turin from Chambery in 1578, it was housed temporarily in a round oratory or tempietto (attributed to both ASCANIO VITOZZI and ANDREA PALLADIO) before being placed in a ciborium in the main chapel of the cathedral in 1587.

In 1611, work was begun on an oval chapel to be placed between the main apse of the cathedral and a new west wing to be built for the Palazzo Reale. The chapel design was prepared by Vitozzi and CARLO CASTELLAMONTE. Work stopped, however, before completion. In 1655/1656, a new design raised the main level of the chapel to that of the *piano nobile* of the royal palace. Flanking stairs, to either side of the apse, were planned from the cathedral to the chapel which was to be open and visible from the cathedral.

By 1657, an entirely new design by Bernardino Quadri and Amedeo di Castellamonte was approved and Quadri was retained as engineer. The earlier structure was demolished and the new, elevated chapel, circular rather than oval, was begun the same year. By the time Guarini received the commission ten years later, rough construction and sheathing in black marble had reached the level of the entablature of the main order.

Guarini's new design and transformation of the chapel had reached the level of the entablature of the drum by 1680. The dome was completed and roofed in 1682. Before Guarini's death, a contract had been signed for the removal of interior scaffolding. The design he left for the altar was replaced by a design of ANTONIO BERTOLA in 1692. Decorative sculpture on the stairs, bronze capitals, and other work continued under Bertola's direction into the early eighteenth century. Bertola also substituted inlaid marble and brass for the plain terra-cotta tile pavement specified by Guarini.

The plan of the chapel inherited by Guarini was itself unusual and perhaps suggested to him that an equilateral triangle could be successfully inscribed within it. Castellamonte's circular plan was divided into nine bays by the nine pier/pilasters of the main order. One pier was, however, omitted at the junction of cathedral apse and Sindone chapel, producing an opening two bays wide. A pair of entrances to the Sindone chapel from the cathedral were placed at the top of flights of stairs in the two bays flanking the larger central opening. Opposite the larger opening a third entrance, on axis, led to the ducal palace.

The omitted pier and the three entrances, each separated from the others by two bays, may have suggested to Guarini the imposition of a triangular vaulting plan with large arches spanning the two-bay open space to the cathedral and the two bays between the entrances. (Guarini may also have noted the circular plan with inscribed hexagon by Vitozzi at Santissima Trinità in Turin.) He capped the superfluous pilasters under the arches, which no longer served in the new triangular/hexagonal scheme, with decorative, broken segmental pediments.

The main arches of the Sindone form large broad-footed pendentives above the three entrances reducing, above the cornice ring, the opening or span of the dome by one quarter. In the drum, maintaining the conversion of nine bays to six (that is, three main arches and three pendentives), Guarini placed six arched windows, one above each of the main arches and pendentives. A second level of broad-footed pendentives between the arches of the drum established the base for the perforated dome.

In plan, the dome consists of six inscribed hexagons. Each smaller hexagon is at a higher level and is formed by arches that span from the center point of the arches of the preceding level (providing space under the arches for windows). At the top of the dome an oculus above the sixth level is partially veiled by an open, dome-shaped, slender, twelve-pointed star. A hemispherical lantern dome reveals the dove of the Holy Spirit within a glory, brightly lighted from below by twelve oval windows hidden at the base of the dome.

As at Sainte Anne-la-Royale and San Lorenzo, at the Sindone actual structure and appearance are diverse. The pendentives of the lower level are pierced by circular windows equal in size and shape to those under the main arches, indicating that the pendentives cannot support the whole of the drum and dome, and suggesting that, at their level, form and structure may be given alternative readings. At the next level the drum is nearly double thickness with a passageway between the inner and outer drums. The major weight of the dome is supported by the outer drum and, therefore, by the outer walls at the lower level, with correspondingly less real (but more apparent) weight supported by the cornice ring, main arches, and pendentives. While the arches of each hexagon of the dome spring from the crest of the next lower arch, there is also at that point a supporting console. The consoles mark the inner surface of twelve buttresses which, on the exterior, rise from the top of the drum (aligned with the twelve-pointed star) to join at the oculus where they support the lantern dome. The distinctive triple-level pinnacle, resting on the

Guarini.
Santissima Sindone Chapel.
Turin, Italy.
1667–1682

stepped outer surface of the lantern dome, cannot be seen from the interior.

The black marble decided upon before Guarini's arrival was intended to reinforce the sepulchral character of the chapel as the locus of the Holy Shroud. Although he retained the somber gloom of the chapel at the lower levels, Guarini spoke of the Resurrection, of a triumphant transformation, in the diaphanous dome with its radiant celestial glory.

Early in 1672, Guarini was commissioned, probably by Carlo Emanuele II, to design a church for the recently arrived (1655) Order of the Missionaries of Saint Vincent de Paul. With an initial gift from the duke, the cornerstone for the Immacolata Concezione was laid in June 1673, but work began in earnest only in 1675. Two years after the death of the duke in 1675, funds ran out and construction was halted at the level of the main cornice. Legacies made it possible to continue in 1694 and the church was consecrated in 1697. The main altar, in black marble, and the choir stalls were completed by 1698. The church was paved in stone and marble in 1718. Decoration of the side altars extended well into the eighteenth century as did the vault painting, partially executed in 1730 and completed in 1738 to celebrate the canonization of Saint Vincent de Paul. The façade was completed, perhaps not to Guarini's design, in 1730.

The plan, one of three double-ended longitudinal plans by Guarini (San Filippo Neri, Turin, and Santa Maria Ettinga, Prague, neither executed), consists of two circular bays with ribbed domes separated by a narrower "transept" with vault and diagonal rib-bands that meet in the center of the nave. Each of the circular bays contain lateral chapels; the transept, hexagonal chapels. A small domed retrochoir was placed behind the massive altar. The façade, with a convex curve in the center that reversed on either side, reflected the initial circular bay. (The plan of the façade belongs to the group of his churches that includes Sainte Anne-la-Royale, Paris; Santa Maria della Divina

Providenza, Lisbon; Santa Maria Ettinga, Prague.) None of the three spaces is dominant. The paired pilasters with ressants continue in the ribs that join at what would most likely have been oculi with lanterns (as in the designs for Lisbon and Prague)—lighted areas in contrast to the unlighted vault of the transept. But the open ends of the circular bays remain unresolved. The pilasters of the transept, placed diagonally as at Paris, support diagonal rib-bands that form a vault lower than the circular bays. An uninterrupted vault surface extends from the oculus to the rib-band of the transept, fusing the spaces.

At the upper level above the chapels, Guarini once again employed a thick or double wall. As in Borromini's chapel in the Collegio di Propaganda Fide, Guarini's church includes a continuous gallery above the chapels of the circular bays and transept. Light flows across the gallery to enter the church through arched windows at the gallery level above the chapels, entrance, and main altar. But the vaults of the hexagonal chapels in the transept were to be open to the lighted gallery, allowing light to plunge vertically into the chapel space. The open vaults were closed when the building was completed in 1694–1697.

The dynamic spatial sequence, with its circular, intersecting spaces, diagonal ribs in the vault, borrowed gallery lighting, and dramatic plunging lighting made the church of the Immaculate Conception one of Guarini's most important achievements, the most transmittable.

When Guarini designed the church and sanctuary of the Consolata in Turin in 1678, he once again dealt with pre-existing construction. Probably shortly after 1675, the abbot had begun a new longitudinal-plan church to replace a crumbling Romanesque structure. The plan was later judged to be inadequate and when Guarini was called in to redo the scheme, at least four of the main nave piers had already been constructed. An engraving of Guarini's scheme (in plan and section) for the Church of Sant' Andrea and its attached sanctuary of the Consolata indicates the inclusion of portions of the pre-existing structure. By 1701, most of the construction was complete except for the east hemicycle which still retained the main altar and crypt of the Romanesque church. The cupola above the hexagonal sanctuary was finished in 1703. In 1729, FILIPPO JUVARRA added a new sanctuary and altar to the sanctuary. In 1899–1904, CARLO CEPPI encircled the sanctuary with additional oval and hexagonal chapels in an accomplished neobaroque.

Guarini's plan converted the partially built longitudinal plan of the Church of Sant' Andrea into an oval by placing two hemicycles (of three

Guarini.

Plan of the Immacolata Concezione.

Turin, Italy.

1673–1677 (not completed until 1697)

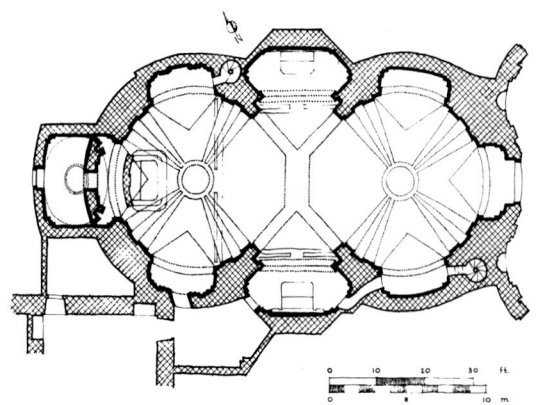

radiating chapels each) at the entrance and apse, on either side of a single, central rectangular bay. The entrance was shifted from the west to the south, in the rectangular bay between the hemicycles, on axis with a hexagonal sanctuary chapel, in area half the size of Sant' Andrea, but about equal in height, across the nave to the north side of Sant' Andrea.

Lighting in the two structures was different. In Sant' Andrea there were lunette windows above each of the chapels, clearstory windows in the ribbed half-domes of the hemicycles and in the barrel vault of the central bay, while in the sanctuary chapel there was a third level of almost square windows below those in the two upper levels.

The vaulting in Sant' Andrea consists of traditional, ribbed half-domes with penetrations and a ribbed barrel vault. Both in plan and in vaulting, Sant' Andrea is reminiscent of the much earlier Church of the Annunziata in Parma (which lacks, however, the penetrations for clearstory lighting). The attached sanctuary, however, was to have had as its dome a hexagonal star-shaped paneled vault with penetrations rising above an encircling polygonal ambulatory vaulted with alternating circular and oval domes.

The scheme as engraved was modified in execution. The piers with single pilasters in the hemicycles on the engraved plan were enlarged and given paired pilasters matching those of the main piers of the nave. The central piers of the sanctuary chapel were also strengthened (lozenge-shaped columns were replaced by robust piers with pilasters). Pairs of columns flanking the piers gave greater central focus to the new, much higher, central domed space of the sanctuary. Much of the contrast between church and sanctuary was eliminated.

It has been argued (Lange, 1970) that the alterations must have been made by Guarini since the enlargements would have required additional foundations, more plausible at the initiation of work than later. But the strengthening and regularizing of church and sanctuary appears to have eliminated much that was characteristically Guarini. At Guarini's death, Bertola was charged with the completion of the structure, as he had been for the Sindone Chapel. The changes more likely are due to Bertola, but the popularity of the sanctuary and the zealousness of the stewards of the Consolata have so "enriched" the building that only with great difficulty can the late seventeenth/early eighteenth century structure be divined.

In Guarini's engraved scheme, there would have been an elevated tension between the two emphasized directions: the longitudinal oval (entered on the side) with at the east end its ancient and venerable crypt, perhaps dating from the fourth century, and, on the cross axis, opposite the entrance, the sanctuary with the image of the Consolata. The contrast of vaulting and lighting would have reinforced the distinction between the two and heightened the tension. Much of the counterpoint was lost in the stolid, constructed design.

The façade of the engraved design consisted of free-standing columns flanking an entrance with pairs of pilasters. Additional free-standing columns with pilaster responds marked chapels on the curving flank of the hemicycles. As constructed in 1703, the entrance façade (known from an engraved view of 1841) consisted of a planal, trabeated portico intermediate in height between the lower level of the chapels and the upper level of the vaulted central space of Sant' Andrea, composed of pilasters on high socles (much higher than those shown in the engraved section) flanking a low doorway with a window above. (The view from 1841 also shows an entrance in the center of the west hemicycle opened subsequent to the completion of the building in 1703.)

Before turning to Guarini's major achievements in secular architecture—the Castello at Racconigi, the Palazzo Carignano, and the Collegio dei Nobili in Turin—note must be taken of the other churches and unrealized projects.

The church Guarini designed in 1675 for the Theatines in Vicenza (San Gaetano) was not realized, but he is credited with the design of Santa Maria d'Araceli in the same city. That church, in plan a rectangle containing a concentric oval central space and enclosing ambulatory and prepared the same year as the design for San Gaetano, is unlike other designs of Guarini's except, perhaps, the oval plan of Sant' Andrea at the Consolata.

Santa Maria d'Araceli was built from 1675 to 1680 without the supervision of Guarini by the architect Carlo Borrella presumably following Guarini's designs. Drawings of the church done in 1695 by Gaetano Farine (discovered and published by P. Portoghesi), perhaps faithful copies of lost drawings by Guarini, reveal changes made in execution.

The drawings indicate that in addition to an entrance on the long axis of the oval opposite the main altar there were to be lateral entrances as well, where today there are chapels. A tension between the direction of the axes, planned also at the Consolata, is absent in the building as constructed.

Four piers with salient columns define the central space, while four high spaces on the axes and four low spaces behind the piers form a Greek cross set within the oval. Columns to either side of the four column/piers define the entrance to each of the high, cross-vaulted ancillary spaces. The four salient columns placed in front of the piers define a circular center in the oval central space—a ribbed dome with lantern resting on a cornice ring without a drum. This plan, both longitudinal and central, fuses the directionality of the oval and the ancillary space of an aisled longitudinal plan with the centrality of the circle and the Greek cross.

The antecedent to the main altar of San Lorenzo, Guarini's most important altar design, was probably the altar for San Nicolò in Verona, completed in 1683, the year of Guarini's death. The three-tiered altar, concave in plan, virtually fills the entrance to the choir and apse. Several concentric rows of free-standing rich marble columns (smooth shafts at the first and third level, spiral at the second) frame the most salient, and more decisively concave, groups at the lower level, which flank a convex portico that contains a cross and tabernacle. Putti, angels, and a seated figure of Saint Nicholas giving a benediction complete the embellishment of the most compelling monument in the church.

Guarini is known to have finished the plans for the Madonna di Loreto in the village of Montanaro near Turin in 1680. The church, also built without Guarini's supervision, was complete by 1684. Aside from a plan that emphasized both the cross axis and the longitudinal direction (a rectangular central space with an inscribed longitudinal octagonal dome, an emphasized rectilinear transept, and a curiously large hexagonal sanctuary reminiscent in plan of the sanctuary at the Consolata), the church displays little of Guarini's usual ingenuity.

Of greater interest are his unrealized designs. Two of the churches, San Gaetano in Vicenza and San Filippo Neri at Casale Monferrato (built by Sebastiano Guala who ignored Guarini's design) are "nine-spot" central churches (in plan a modified Greek cross with satellite chapels in the four corners), two variations on a theme. San Gaetano has a central space invaded by the expanding oval of the arms, with a contrasting expansion of the central space in the double-layered dome lighted from hidden sources, while at San Filippo, the circular central space extends into the space of the arms to aggregate them. In both churches, the four central piers appear to be only columns. At San Gaetano, a small pier is encased in columns; at San Filippo, there are only four columns that do triple duty to define the central space, portions of both the arms, and the satellite chapels.

Two other designs were for central plan (octagonal and hexagonal) structures; one for the four-tiered curvilinear Church of Oropa (1680) and one, rectilinear, for the Somaschi Fathers in Messina (probably designed after Guarini arrived in Turin). In the plan for Messina, a hexagonal ribbed dome (in structure similar to San Lorenzo in Turin) is cavalierly supported on triple columns enclosing small triangular piers. The triangular piers, widest toward the subsidiary encircling spaces, define the ambulatory and divide it into six cross-vaulted oval chapels separated by six smaller spaces with circular domed lanterns. On the exterior, twelve pairs of massive Corinthian columns mark the extent of the planes of the hexagon separated from each other by niches containing figures of monumental proportions.

At Oropa, large triangular piers support the tiered central octagon and shape the lower eight ancillary oval chapels which bay outward to form the undulating convexities of the lower level. Three levels of inscribed octagons supported on squinches, each with its own set of windows, rise to form an octagonal cloister dome with oval windows in its base, a conclusion recalling both Sainte Anne-la-Royale in Paris and San Lorenzo in Turin. The number and size of openings in both of these churches would have made them even more light-filled than San Lorenzo.

Guarini's design for the three-tiered San Gaetano in Nice, France (designed, perhaps, in the late 1660s), was also a central plan, but based on a pentagon inscribed in a circle. Five semicircular chapels open off the spaces of the inscribed pentagon, one containing the main altar with a columnar screen behind as at San Lorenzo. As they bay outward the apsidal chapels form an undulating façade. The entrance was placed in a narrow bay, also convex, between the flanking chapels. The drum was made of intersecting arches that formed a second inscribed pentagon. The dome, a five-pointed star open in the center, supported a pentagonal lantern. The church was built in the eighteenth century on the new design of BERNARDO ANTONIO VITTONE on another site in Nice.

Guarini's designs for longitudinal churches, San Filippo Neri in Turin, Santa Maria della Divina Providenza in Lisbon, and Santa Maria Ettinga in Prague, are grouped in that order in this *Architettura Civile*. San Filippo, designed in 1679, has three octagonal bays with lateral chapels (formed by diagonally oriented piers reminiscent of Sainte Anne-la-Royale) and an apsidal main chapel and entry bay of identical shape, forming a double-ended plan. The nave, entrance bay, and apse were to be vaulted with ribbed panels while transverse arches marked the individual bays. All the vaults were to rise to the same height without a dominant spatial focus.

At Prague, also designed in 1679 and also double-ended, an oval entrance chapel and bay preceding the choir flanked a larger octagonal central space. Lanterns were placed in the center of the vault of each bay at the juncture of the rib-bands of the domed vaults. The separateness of each of the bays and the dominance of the central one were emphasized.

In the church at Lisbon, a Latin-cross plan, the nave consists of two nearly circular bays with oval chapels. Oval chapels form the transept, the apse is circular, and the crossing, spatially, is an eroded square. Lanterns cap the nave bays, the nave chapels, the sanctuary, the transepts, and the crossing. The vaulting is more fluid and undulating and punctuated more decisively than at San Filippo or Santa Maria Ettinga. It may well be the latest of the group, designed, perhaps, in 1681.

The designs for three of the buildings realized (the Consolata, Santa Maria d'Araceli, and the Church at Montanaro) were low-cost constructions compared to Sainte Anne-la-Royale, San Lorenzo, and the Santissima Sindone. Guarini's low-budget buildings are less ambitious, less audacious, perhaps less imaginative. In contrast to Borromini, who seemed able to convert a humble project into a major architectural achievement, Guarini appears to have achieved the grand and monumental when stimulated by a liberal budget.

Secular buildings. The publication in 1686 of a number of plates from Guarini's treatises included the Paris Palace, the Castello at Govone, the Palazzo Carignano in Turin, and the city gate of Turin to the east toward the Po River, the Porta del Po. Omitted were the Villa Maggiordomo at Gerbido near Turin and the Carignano Castello at Racconigi (even though two finished drawings for Racconigi were prepared by Guarini before his death, perhaps as early as 1676/1677).

The Villa Maggiordomo, attributed to Guarini because of the resemblance of the garden elevation of the villa to the courtyard elevation of the Palazzo Carignano in Turin, can also be shown to contain, on the ground floor, windows that conform to a drawing by Guarini prepared for the Palazzo Carignano in 1679, but not used there. The seven-bay garden façade of the two-story building (ground floor with mezzanine and a single level above), contains a three-story, centrally placed oval pavilion of three bays, rising and protruding from the main block. The walls of the main portion of the villa, and the setback bays that flank the salient seven bays, are framed by simple, flat pilaster strips and stringcourses. With restrained means Guarini achieved a building of considerable breadth and boldness.

At Govone, where the site included a significant slope, Guarini placed a U-shaped castello on the crest of the slope to form a courtyard that opened to an elevated terrace with ramps and fountain at a lower level. The main vaulted *salone* of the *castello* was placed on the courtyard at the main level which was reached by twin flights of stairs from the terrace. Here, too, the bays were formed by pilaster strips and stringcourses (except for the bays at the center of the courtyard façade flanking the main *salone*) where Serlian (see SEBASTIANO SERLIO) or Palladian openings gave contrast and emphasis to the *salone*. The building was altered and impoverished somewhat in execution. Guarini may not have supervised construction.

Guarini's involvement with the design of the Porta del Po (the responsibility of the Communal Council) probably dates from 1674. Construction of the gate was underway in 1675 and was completed late in 1679. Somewhat earlier, in May 1679, Guarini had become a citizen of Turin.

The gate, now destroyed, is seen to best advantage in a print from *La Sontuosa Illuminazione della città di Torino* published in 1737. The design went through at least two stages, the first seen in the engravings prepared in 1674 for the *Theatrum Sabaudiae. . .* probably before construction was initiated. In the executed design the gate was made to appear more robust and martial by banding of the Doric columns, pilasters, and piers, and more rhetorical by replacing the standing figures on the entablature (Minerva, Hermes, and Mars?) and flanking seated *Taurini* with an enlarged attic containing historical reliefs. The attic was topped by obelisks, escutcheons, and a central standing figure. The central convex bay, set between two V-shaped receding rectilinear walls, contained the entry arch with an inscribed tablet above. The publication of Guarini's *Trattato di Fortificazione* in 1676 may have been related to work on the gateway.

Although the only recorded payment by Emanuele Filiberto of Carignano to Guarini for his work on the design of the prison and *castello* at Racconigi is dated 1677, it seems likely that design preceded demolition and that construction was begun in 1676. The remodeling of the building (a medieval castle with four square corner towers and open courtyard) was unfinished at Guarini's death and work may have languished from 1679 when available funds were probably diverted to build the Palazzo Carignano in Turin, begun in that year. In any case, only the north side of the Castello and the tall central pavilion (replacing the earlier courtyard) were completed by 1712 (the date of a print by Bartolomeo Giuseppe Tasnière, showing the *castello* and garden from an elevated position to the south).

The main stairs to the garden (symmetrical S curves partially encircling a pond with fountain) were completed by MICHELANGELO GAROVE following Guarini's designs. Until the replacement of the stair in 1755 by GIAMBATTISTA BORRA, the south elevation was much as Guarini left it, a four-story, seven-bay central section with a terrace flanked by semi-salient single bays joined to fully salient, three-bay corner pavilions with hipped roofs, topped by small arched roof pavilions. In the center of the building, the tall pavilion that lighted the *salone* (three bays on the façade, five on the flanks) was covered by a bell-shaped roof.

The south side, the east and west flanks, the *salone,* and the chapel were remodeled and rebuilt by Borra between 1756 to 1760 in nascent neoclassic with Anglo-Saxon overtones. At the top of a straight flight of steps, flanked by classical cheek walls, a pedimented, tetrastyle portico announced the main *salone.* In the 1830s and 1840s, two-story wings, designed by Ernesto Melano, were added to the east and west.

When Guarini received the commission, several architects had previously prepared plans for the *castello,* outbuildings, gardens, and park, among them Carlo Morello and CARLO LANFRANCHI. A plan of the park, whose terrain was enlarged through purchases from 1644 to 1682, was sent to France for criticism in 1670. A large drawing of both the garden and park, prepared before Guarini's intervention, has been attributed to ANDRÉ LE NOSTRE. Portions of the garden and park were executed following this drawing.

Guarini appears to have accepted much of the garden plan, and concentrated his attention on the *castello,* its outbuildings, and its forecourt. Where previous architects had linked the square block of the *castello* to lower wings to the east and west that turned north to enclose the initially large symmetrical *parterre de broderie,* Guarini from the outset (there are at least three stages of his designs)

treated the main block as a free-standing structure with four large corner pavilions with different grand stairs on the entry court and garden façade. The symmetrical entrance façade stairs were changed, but the disposition of the remainder, including interior spaces, remained firm as Guarini studied the relation between *castello,* outbuildings, and forecourt.

As at Govone and Gerbido, the bays are formed by flat pilaster strips and stringcourses with pronounced rusticated quoins, using the simplest of the six systems of surface articulation outlined by Guarini in his Treatise. His plan eliminated the earlier wings to the east and west but retained and reinforced the north–south galleries flanking the parterres by adding colonnades to either side. A secondary lateral axis, focused on the tri-lobed pool and fountain of the garden stair, was emphasized by pairs of open, columnar, square pavilions aligned both with the north–south galleries and the secondary lateral axis.

To the east and west of the *castello,* Guarini developed symmetrical respondent hemicycles (with niches) that enclosed semicircular fountains. Outbuildings formed an open courtyard behind the hemicycles. These hemicycles may have suggested to Guarini that the earlier half-octagonal forecourt be replaced by a larger colonnaded hemicycle with service buildings and stables behind. Had forecourt, outbuildings, terraces (curiously lacking in most of the drawings by Guarini), *castello,* fountains, pools, garden, and park been achieved, Racconigi would have been the first full realization in Italy of the new French standards for integration of primary structures with outbuildings, garden, and park. None of the enframing, announcing, and directing outbuildings of Guarini was built. Replacement of the formal French gardens with an English park began in 1788 under Giacomo Pregliasio. In 1820–1821, Saverio Kurten eliminated what remained.

Construction of a Jesuit Collegio dei Nobili was encouraged by the Madama Reale, Maria Giovanna Battista, widow of Carlo Emanuele II, as a part of a larger plan to promote the development of the second enlargement of Turin toward the Po to the east. A site for the Collegio on the main piazza on the second enlargement was given to the Jesuits by the Madama Reale in 1678. Early in 1679, that site was exchanged for a larger one (three full blocks) extending north from the Piazza Reale (San Carlo) along the old moat all the way to Piazza Madama. The center block was to contain a large church, dedicated to San Giovanni Battista, facing east. To the north was the house of the Order and on the block to the south, the Collegio dei Nobili.

Guarini.
Castello.
Racconigi, Italy.
1676–1683 (left unfinished)

Guarini received the commission early in 1679, and construction was begun in April. In May, work began on the Palazzo Carignano diagonally opposite the northeast corner of the site of the Collegio dei Nobili; also in 1679, Guarini was asked to design San Filippo Neri to the east across the street from the Collegio dei Nobili. Had San Filippo been built, a significant grouping of structures in the new enlargement would have been designed by Guarini.

Even though construction of the Collegio dei Nobili was aided by a grant from the Madama Reale, funds ran out with no more than half the structure complete. Only the ground floor of the north wing and a bit more of the north half of the east wing were built. On the south and east, the ground floor and the two above were completed. The main stair at the south end was finished. It is one of Guarini's finest small stairs. The west wing (if one was included in the design) did not reach ground level.

Construction was supervised by Michelangelo Garove who, in 1685, submitted an estimate and proposal to stop the north wing at the first floor. In 1688, a portion of the building was occupied. After the suppression of the Jesuits in 1784, a project was undertaken in 1788 to complete the building and adapt it to other uses. Construction, including a new entrance portal, was completed in 1824 by GIUSEPPE TALUCCHI.

In plan the structure was a broad U with the east wing longer than the north and south. Stairs were placed at both ends of the east range. A corridor ran along the courtyard face of the east wing. Rooms of double height looked out on the street while between these rooms and the corridor there were two levels of rooms, an original and inventive arrangement.

On the exterior, three floor levels were decisively indicated by unbroken entablatures and by pilasters (Doric, Ionic and Corinthian) made in specially designed exposed brick. Mezzanine windows were integrated with the larger windows of each level.

In contrast to the modest statements made by the *Castello* at Govone, the Villa del Maggiordomo, and the Castello at Racconigi, major ordering elements (pilasters, entablatures), openings, and decorative embellishments (window surrounds, panels, consoles, brackets, pediments) project substantially from the wall surface, casting deep shadows. Their dimensions are such that even though the wall remains legible it is subordinate to the ubiquitous, vigorous large- and small-scale relief elements that cover it.

With a major church opposite and the palace of a member of the ruling family of Piedmont on

Guarini. Collegio dei Nobili. Turin, Italy. 1679–1683 (left unfinished)

an adjacent site, Guarini may have chosen to maintain the street edge rather than compete. Even so, within the limits of supportive rectilinearity, the surface of the structure has been invested with a sense of potential strength and vigor.

Emanuele Filiberto of Savoy who commissioned the Palazzo Carignano, Guarini's most important palace, knew something of Guarini firsthand from his work at Racconigi and from San Lorenzo and the Sindone Chapel nearing completion in 1679. The Prince of Carignano had been born a deaf-mute. Although he learned to talk and read lips, he remained celibate until 1684 when he was pressed by his mother, Marie de Bourbon-Soissons, to marry and produce heirs. The children of his younger brother, Eugenio Maurizio, who had been expected to insure the collateral Carignano-Soissons line, failed in 1680 and the task fell to the fifty-six-year-old Emanuele Filiberto. From 1684 until 1699, when Vittorio Amedeo II and Anne d'Orleans produced a male child, Emanuele Filiberto was heir presumptive.

Even though in 1679 when Emanuele Filiberto commissioned Guarini to design the Palazzo Carignano he could not have known of the role he was to play in the dynastic ambitions of his mother, he could have expected that the palace would pass either to the Soissons branch or to the duke. Perhaps with Emanuele Filiberto's knowledge, Guarini conceived a palace with regal airs, drawing on Bernini's three designs for the Louvre in Paris.

The palace was built on land that Emanuele Filiberto's father, Tommaso of Savoy-Carignano, had owned since the 1640s outside the walls of

Turin toward the Po River. Guarini was paid for the design of the palace on 6 August 1679. Excavations for the foundations were begun in January 1680. By October 1680, the vault of the entry was completed and the walls and roof were finished by late 1681 or early 1682. The vaulting of the oval atrium and grand *salone* occurred between July 1682 and the end of 1683. At some point, plans to complete the rear wing enclosing the courtyard were abandoned.

Decoration of the palace, begun in December 1683, was sufficiently complete to have its rooms blessed in the summer of 1683, but it was not finished until the early years of the eighteenth century. Work on the garden and stables, begun in March 1680, was ended in 1686. Further work on the carriage house and stable was carried out in 1697–1698.

In the early 1880s, Carlo Ceppi was commissioned by the city to design and erect a bronze tablet on the façade to commemorate the birthplace of Vittorio Emanuele II. (Vittorio Emanuele's father, Carlo Alberto of Savoy-Carignano, became king of Savoy at the death of Carlo Felice, the last of the direct Savoy line.) In the central bay of the palace at the upper level, Ceppi introduced a pediment pierced by an oval opening, a segmental arch spanning between the two separated portions of the façade, and a baroquish crowning element to which the bronze tablet was applied.

A new wing to house the Chamber of Deputies (to the rear enclosing the courtyard) was begun in 1861 on the designs of Domenico Ferri, a scene designer, and completed in 1871. The original stables were replaced in 1790 on the designs of Giovanni Battista Feroggio, and today, after devastation in an air raid in 1943, the façade announces the new location of the Biblioteca Nazionale.

Guarini's preparatory drawings for the Palazzo Carignano survive and chronicle the development of the design through four stages from a rectilinear structure with a square courtyard (which recalls Bernini's third design for the Louvre) to the grand curvilinear scheme that was constructed (which recalls Bernini's first design for the Louvre). Guarini apparently knew Bernini's designs which had been on view in Paris in 1665 while Guarini was at work on the construction of Sainte Anne-la-Royale. The drawings offer a rare insight into the development of Guarini's thought.

Guarini's first plan divided the façade into three parts; two four-bay corner pavilions and a set-back central section of eleven bays containing a three-bay salient entrance. In the second plan, Guarini included curved forms, introducing an oval central atrium and *salone*, with a pair of symmetrical main stairs baying into the courtyard as

they followed the curve of the oval. The third design retained the oval but flipped the symmetrical stairs to the outside, to the façade, using a complex series of jagged flights and landings that were reflected in deep angular flexions of the façade wall. In the final scheme, a revolutionary plan, the stairs followed a gentle, continuous curve from the stair vestibules (on the courtyard) to the vestibule before the grand *salone* at the *piano nobile,* on axis above the entrance portal.

The façade reveals the presence of the oval atrium and grand *salone* (behind the curving stair) in the baying forward of the central section with its separation (or split) in the center for the ground level entrance and declamatory balcony at the *piano nobile.* Reverse concave curves join the seven bays of the convex central section to the four bays of the corner pavilions, uniting and stabilizing the whole.

In elevation, two main levels divide the whole, a rusticated ground floor (with mezzanine) and a *piano nobile* (also with mezzanine and an attic). The rusticated Doric pilasters of the ground level are changed to a giant order of Corinthian pilasters above. Between the pavilions and the entrance, in the curved central section, pilasters were doubled and the rhythm quickened by a progressive reduction of the width of the bays. The center was further emphasized by the progressive salencies of pilasters and entablature approaching the open central bay.

The oval grand *salone,* the generator of the plan for the central section, was vaulted by a spectacular ribbed dome with large oval oculus. Through the oculus, an apparently suspended domical surface, mysteriously lighted, contained a painted scene, the climax of the sequence of entry, stair, and vestibule. Here again, Guarini's design did not disclose the verity of structure. The painted surface was the underside of a suspended plaster dome supported from above by wood trusses (in the space of the oval clearstory) and illuminated by light from the oval windows of the clearstory that was reflected from the top of the masonry vault.

The Palazzo Carignano was the most important palace design in Italy of the last quarter of the seventeenth century and the only palace in Italy in that period with pronounced regal, rhetorical, and representational character.

At Guarini's death, his buildings were continued by Michelangelo Garove (Collegio dei Nobili, Castello at Racconigi, San Filippo, Palazzo Carignano), Antonio Bertola (Santa Sindone, San Filippo Neri, Palazzo Carignano), and GIOVANNI FRANCESCO BARONCELLO (Palazzo Carignano, Castello at Racconigi). Other structures designed and built by them exhibit an intimate knowledge

Guarini.
Palazzo Carignano (main
stair).
Turin, Italy.
1679–1683

Guarini.
Palazzo Carignano
(atrium).
Turin, Italy.
1679–1683

of Guarini's work. Publication of some of Guarini's plates as *Dissegni di Architettura* in 1686 may have sustained an interest in the master. With the death of Baroncello (1694), Garove (1713), and Bertola (1719), Guarini's direct influence waned. The major architects of the succeeding generation in Piedmont, FRANCESCO GALLO and GIAN GIACOMO PLANTERY, though occasionally showing knowledge of Guarini's buildings, drew more heavily on the sober manner of Amedeo di Castellamonte in Piedmont and the Bernini/Carlo Fontana tradition beyond.

It was not until the third and fourth decade of the eighteenth century that interest in Guarini became a decisive formative force in Piedmont due, perhaps, to the presence of Filippo Juvarra, whose acknowledged appreciation of Borromini and emulation of his decorative manner may have rekindled an interest in Guarini. In any case, the early work of the young Bernardo Vittone, a nephew of Plantery, shows study of Guarini. Vittone's later conflation of the two unfinished manuscripts of Guarini (preserved by the Theatines), *Architettura Civile* and *Architettura Ecclesiastica,* into the single treatise published in 1737, exerted a profound influence on his own development most evident in his works from 1737 to 1742. The dissemination of Guarini's treatise (perhaps reinforced by the publication in 1720 and 1725 of the plates and text of Borromini's *Chiesa e la Fabbrica della Sapienza . . .* and *Opus architectonicum . . . S. Philippi Nerii . . .*) drew the attention of a number of architects in Piedmont to

Guarini. Among them, in addition to Vittone, are Ignazio Michela, FILIPPO NICOLIS DI ROBILANT, and PIETRO BONVICINI.

Outside Piedmont, in Germany, Austria, and Central Europe, interest in Guarini seems to have been continuous, stimulated partly by direct contact with Guarini's architecture by individuals such as Lucas von Hildebrandt and partly by the dissemination of *Dissegni* after 1686. Gerhard Franz, A. M. Renner, and Christian Norberg-Schulz have chronicled this aspect of interest in Guarini. The duke of Bavaria's request in 1682 for drawings of Guarini's work at Racconigi documents additional dissemination. Although the influence of Guarini on Italian architecture is admittedly limited, the exuberant character of German, Austrian, and Czechoslovakian baroque owes as much to Guarini as to Borromini.

HENRY A. MILLON

WORKS

*1660, Santissima Annunziata (façade), Messina, Italy. *1662–1667, Sainte-Anne-la-Royale (left unfinished), Paris. 1667–1679, San Lorenzo; 1667–1682, Santissima Sindone Chapel; 1673–1677, Immacolata Concezione (not completed until 1697); *1674–1679, Porta del Po; Turin, Italy. 1675–1680, Santa Maria d'Araceli (design altered in execution), Vicenza, Italy. 1676–1683, Castello (left unfinished), Racconigi, Italy. 1679–1683, Collegio dei Nobili (left unfinished); 1679–1683, La Consolata; 1679–1683, Palazzo Carignano; Turin, Italy. 1681–1683, Madonna di Loreto, Montanaro, near Turin, Italy. n.d., Castello, Govone, Italy. (A)n.d., Villa del Maggiordomo, Gerbido, near Turin, Italy.

BIBLIOGRAPHY

ANDEREGG-TILLE, MARIA 1962 *Die Schule Guarinis.* Winterthur, Switzerland: Keller.

ARGAN, GIULIO CARLO 1933 "Per una storia dell'architettura piemontese." *L'Arte* 36:391–397.

BATTISTI, EUGENIO 1959 "Note sul significato della Cappella della Santa Sindone nel Duomo di Torino." *Atti del X Congresso di Storia dell'Architettura.* Rome: Centro di Studi per la Storia dell'architettura.

BUSCALIONI, PIETRO 1938 *La Consolata nella storia di Torino del Piemonte.* Turin, Italy: Bonis.

BRINCKMANN, ALBERT E. 1931 *The Theatrum Novum Pedemontii.* Dusseldorf, Germany: Schwann.

BRINCKMANN, ALBERT E. 1933 "La grandezza di Guarino Guarini e la sua influenza sull'Architettura in Germania nel '700." *Atti della Società Piemontese di Archeologia e Bella Arte* 15:348–374.

CARBONERI, NINO 1963 "Guarini." Volume 1 in Vittorio Viale (editor), *Mostra del Barocco Piemontese.* Turin, Italy: Città di Torino.

CARBONERI, NINO 1964 "Vicende delle cappelle per la Santa Sindone." *Bollettino della Società Piemontese di Archeologia a Belle Arte* 18:95–109.

CHEVALLEY, GIOVANNI 1921 "Il Palazzo Carignano a Torino." *Bollettino della Società Piemontese di Archeologia e Belle Arte* 5:4–14.

CHEVALLEY, GIOVANNI 1942 "Vicende costrutive della Chiesa di S. Filippo Neri in Torino." *Bollettino del Centro di Studi Archeologici ed artistici del Piemontese* 2:63–99.

COFFIN, DAVID 1956 "Padre Guarino Guarini in Paris." *Journal of the Society of Architectural Historians* 15, no. 2:3–11.

CREPALDI, GIUSEPPE M. 1963 *La real chiesa di San Lorenzo in Torino.* Turin, Italy: Rotocalco Dagnino.

FRANZ, HEINRICH GEBHARD 1972 "Guarini und die barocke Baukunst in Böhmen: Ein Beitrag zur Frage nach dem Verhältnis der regionalen zu den universalen Europäischen Kunstströmungen." Volume 2, pages 121–129 in *Actes du 22e Congrès International d'histoire de l'Art.* Budapest: Akadémiai Kiadó.

GABRIELLI, NOEMI 1972 *Racconigi.* Turin, Italy: Istituto bancario San Paolo.

GUARINI, GUARINO 1660 *La Pieta Trionfante.* Messina, Italy.

GUARINI, GUARINO 1665 *Placita Philosophica.* Paris: Thierry.

GUARINI, GUARINO 1671 *Euclides Adauctus.* Turin, Italy: Zapatae.

GUARINI, GUARINO 1674 *Modo di Misurare le fabriche.* Turin, Italy: Gianelli.

GUARINI, GUARINO 1675 *Compendio della sfera celeste.* Turin, Italy.

GUARINI, GUARINO 1676 *Trattato di Fortificazione, che hora si usa in Fiandra, Francia et italia.* Turin, Italy: Gianelli.

GUARINI, GUARINO 1678 *Leges Temporum et Planetarum.* Turin, Italy: Ianelli.

GUARINI, GUARINO 1683 *Coelestis Mathematicae.* Milan: Montiae.

GUARINI, GUARINO (1686)1966 *Desegni d'Architettura Civile e ecclesiastica" di Guarino Guarini e l'arte del maestro.* Critical edition with facsimile plates by Daria De Bernardi Ferrero. Turin, Italy: Albra.

GUARINI, GUARINO (1737)1968 *Guarino Guarini, Architettura Civile.* With an introduction by Nino Carboneri and critical notes by Bianca Tavassi la Greca. Milan: Il Polifilo.

Guarino Guarini e l'internazionalità del Barocco. 1970 2 vols. Turin, Italy: Accademia delle Scienze. With articles by Giulio Carlo Argan, Eugenio Battisti, Sandro Benedetti, Aldo Bertini, Franco Borsi, Nino Carboneri, Georges Cattaui, Augusto Cavallari Murat, Umberto Chierici, Vera Comolli Mandracci, Daria De Bernardi Ferraro, Marcello Fagiolo, Heinrich Gerhard Franz, Andreina Griseri, Enrico Guidoni, Augusta Lange, Carrado Maltese, Paolo Marconi, Henry A. Millon, Werner Mueller, Christian Norberg-Schulz, Werner Oechslin, Mario Passanti, Paolo Portoghesi, Gianni Sciolla, Manfredo Tafuri, Luciano Tamburini, Francesco G. Tricomi, Paolo Verzone, and Rudolf Wittkower.

HAGER, WERNER 1954 "Guarini." *Kunstchronik* 7:266.

HAGER, WERNER 1957 "Zum Verhaltnis Fischer-Guarini." Kunstchronik 10:206–208.

HAGER, WERNER 1960 "Guarinis Theaterkassinade in Messina." *Das Werk des Künstlers Hubert Schrade zum 60. Geburstag.* Stuttgart, Germany: Kohlhammer.

HAGER, WERNER 1961 "Guarini: Zur Kennzeichnung seiner Architektur." Volume 16, pages 418–428 in *Miscellanea Bibliothecae Hertzianae.* Munich: Schroll.

MARCONI, PAOLO 1976 "'Vortuti fortuna comes', Guarino Guarini e il caduceo ermetico." *Ricerche di storia dell'arte* 1–2:29–44.

MIDANA, ANTONIO 1929 "Il duomo di Torino e la real Cappella della SS. Sindone." *Italia Sacra* 1929:50.

MILLON, HENRY A. 1964 Guarino Guarini and the Palazzo Carignano in Turin." Unpublished Ph.D. dissertation, Harvard University, Cambridge, Mass.

MILLON, HENRY A. 1965 *Art Bulletin* 47:531–532.

MORGANSTERN, J. 1964 "Guarino Guarini: The Church of the Padre Somaschi for Messina." Unpublished M.A. thesis, New York University.

OLIVERO, EUGENIO 1928a "La vita e l'arte del P. Guarino Guarini." *Il duomo di Torino* 2, May.

OLIVERO, EUGENIO 1928b "Gli scritti del P. Guarino Guarini." *Il duomo di Torino* 2, June.

OLIVERO, EUGENIO 1940 "La Madonna di Loreto in Montanaro." *Bollettino del di Studi Archeologici ed Artistici del Piemonte* 1:5–11.

PASSANTI, MARIO 1941 "La Real Cappella della Santa Sindone." *Torino* nos. 10–12.

PASSANTI, MARIO 1963 *Nel Mondo Magico di Guarino Guarini.* Turin, Italy: Toso.

POMMER, RICHARD 1967 *Eighteenth Century Architecture in Piedmont: The Open Structures of Juvarra, Alfieri, and Vittone.* New York University Press.

PORTOGHESI, PAOLO 1956a "L'architetto Guarini." *Civiltà delle machine* 4:57–61.

PORTOGHESI, PAOLO 1956b *Guarino Guarini.* Milan: Electa.

PORTOGHESI, PAOLO 1956c "Il tabernaco Guariniano dell'altare Maggiore della chiesa di San Nicoloa Verona." *Quaderni dell'Istituto di Storia dell'Architettura* 17:16–20.

RAMIREZ, JUAN ANTONIO 1981 "Guarino Guarini, Fray Juan Ricci and the 'Complete Salmonic Order'." *Art History* 4:175–185.

RIGOTTI, GIORGIO 1932 "La chiesa dell'Immacolata Concezione." *Bollettino della Società Piemontese di Acheologia e Belle Arte* 16:56–73.

SANDONINI, TOMASO 1890 "Del Padre Guarini Guarino." *Atti e Memorie della Deputazione di Storia Patria per Modena e Parma* Series 3 2, no. 5:488–533.

SCHMERBER, HUGO 1902 "Einige Nachrichten über Guarino Guarini." *Monatsberichte für Kunstwissenschaft und Kunsthandel* 2:286–287.

TAMBURINI, LUCIANO 1968 *Le Chiese di Torino dal Rinascimento al* barocco. Turin, Italy: Bouquiniste.

TERZAGHI, ANTONIO 1959 "Origini e sviluppo delle cupola ad arconi intrecciati nell'architettura barocca del Piemonte." *Atti del X Congresso di Storia dell'Architettura.* Rome: Centro di studi per la storia dell'architettura.

WITTKOWER, RUDOLF (1958)1980 *Art and Architecture in Italy: 1600–1750.* 4th ed., rev. Harmondsworth, England: Penguin.

GUAS, JUAN

Juan Guas (c.1433–1496) was one of the most distinguished architects of late Gothic Spain. He worked in a style which, although it derived from Flanders, he made uniquely his own by including elements of Islamic origin derived from the mudejar architecture indigenous to Toledo where he had passed most of his formative years. Furthermore, his later works did much to establish the so-called Isabelline Gothic style practiced in Spain and even in the New World well into the sixteenth century.

Guas was born probably about 1433 in the Breton town of Saint Pol de Leon. His father, Pedro, presumably accompanied by Juan, was in Toledo employed on the cathedral by 1448 if not before under the Flemish master of the works, Hanequin de Bruselas. Both Pedro and Juan are listed as *pedreros* working on the Portal of the Lions (1452–1466) under the direction of Hanequin. The term *pedrero* defines an experienced stonemason capable of executing the intricate ornamental tracery characteristic of this portal but not the figural or decorative sculpture. Since Pedro's name no longer appears anywhere after 1458 it is probable that Juan learned more from Hanequin, to whom he might even have been apprenticed, than from his father. Nevertheless, when Juan Guas married in 1459 the list of his assets suggests he was already of considerable status. His earliest surviving work is the cloister of the old cathedral of Segovia begun in 1472 and moved with its later

portal to the site of the new cathedral in 1524. The style of the windows is closely related to the flamboyant Flemish tracery of the Santiago Chapel at Toledo (1432–1439), almost certainly from the hand of Hanequin de Bruselas.

In 1476, with the victory of Toro, the rule of Ferdinand and Isabella over a united Spain was assured. As a memorial to that victory and as a tomb for herself and her husband, Isabella founded in Toledo the Franciscan monastery of San Juan de los Reyes. Very probably when work began in 1477 Juan Guas was the architect. His epitaph of 1496 stated clearly that he built San Juan de los Reyes. The famous drawing on parchment preserved in the Prado shows in perspective and section the choir of the church; it can be attributed to Guas and probably can be dated 1477 or 1478. The lower walls, substantially as shown in the drawing, were completed before 1492 when the conquest of Granada added a pomegranate to the royal arms. The most important difference between the building and the drawing is the introduction just below the springing of the vaults of a cornice adapted from the Islamic *muqarnas* or honeycomb vault. Juan Guas, formed in Toledo, was here reacting to the local mudejar tradition, though he translated into stone what would normally have been executed in wood, brick, or stucco.

The upper parts of the chapel cannot be securely dated but are probably quite late. However, as early as 1475, Juan Guas was at work on the Castle of El Real de Manzanares for the first duke of Infantado. The boldly projecting *muqarnas* cor-

Guas.
Franciscan Monastery of
*   San Juan de los Reyes.*
Toledo, Spain.
1477–1496 and later

Guas.
Palace of El Infantado.
Guadalajara, Spain.
1480–1483

nice of this extraordinary building, its richly sculptured gallery or *azotea,* and the hemispherical rustication of the upper towers all prefigure the Infantado Palace at Guadalajara (1480–1483). The latter, according to an inscription in the patio, was designed by Juan Guas and built with the help of Egas Cueman, son of Hanequin de Bruselas, as *entallador* or decorative carver. The patron was the second duke of Infantado. The palace has suffered much mutilation. The fifth duke in 1569 opened pedimented classical windows into the entrance façade, some of which penetrated the *azotea,* displaced upward the crowning member of the portal, and raised the level of the patio about 150 centimeters, replacing in the process the original spiral piers of the lower arcade with Tuscan columns. In 1936, the palace was gutted by fire, destroying the elaborate mudejar interiors, the most famous in all of Spain. Repairs to the façade in 1961 restored the *azotea* and replaced the arms above the portal in their original position. The façade is studded with diamond-shaped rustication, while smaller-scale diapering enriches the portal piers and the *azotea.* Here mudejar style coincides with late Gothic, just as contemporary miniatures often have diapered grounds. Cornices employ *muqarnas* and *bolas,* ubiquitous in later Isabelline Gothic design. Above all, both façade and patio are a celebration of heraldry. Densely fashioned escutcheons and supporters, wild men, and lions and griffins encrust the surface in the manner of the choir of San Juan de los Reyes. Such heraldic emphasis was a symptom of this style's conscious period as expressed by other architects, but none surpassed Guas in sheer inventiveness.

Mudejar design did not dominate all Guas's later works. A series of purely Flemish portals, all ecclesiastical, are quite free of it. Arranged in order of probable stylistic progression, they are the

church portal of the Monastery of el Paular (1484), province of Segovia; the cloister portal of the old Cathedral of Segovia (1483–1485); the sacristy portal of the Church of the Parral, Segovia, perhaps as late as 1494; and the west portal of the Church of Santa Cruz, Segovia, of 1485 or later. The latter two use heavy mouldings fringed with dense tracery in lenticular shapes like the traceries of the Segovia cloister and the lower windows of that of San Juan de los Reyes. It was these eccentric forms, further developed under ENRIQUE EGAS, son of Egas Cueman, a frequent collaborator of Juan Guas, that were to characterize the so-called Isabelline Gothic style of the late fifteenth and early sixteenth centuries.

JOHN DOUGLAS HOAG

WORKS

1472, Old Cathedral of Segovia (cloister); 1472–1475, Geronimite Monastery of El Parral; Segovia, Spain. 1475–1479, Castle of El Real de Manzanares, Province of Madrid. 1477–1496 and later, Franciscan Monastery of San Juan de los Reyes, Toledo, Spain. 1478–1485, Dominican Monastery of Santa Cruz, Segovia, Spain. 1480–1483, Palace of El Infantado, Guadalajara, Spain. 1483–1485, Cathedral of Segovia (cloister portal); 1484, Monastery of El Paular (porch and portal of chapel); c.1485, Church of Santa Cruz (west portal); Segovia, Spain. 1487–1489, Dominican College of San Gregorio (chapel), Valladolid, Spain. c.1494, Church of the Parral (sacristy portal), Segovia, Spain.

BIBLIOGRAPHY

AZCÁRATE, JOSÉ MARÍA de 1956 "La Obra Toledana de Juan Guas." *Archivo Español de Arte* 29:9–42.
CHUECA GOITIA, FERNANDO 1965 *Historia de la Arquitectura Española, Edad Antiqua y Edad Media.* Madrid: Editorial Dossat.
HERRERA CASADO, ANTONIO 1975 *El Palacio del Infantado en Guadalajara.* Guadalajara, Spain: Institución Provincial de Cultura Marqués de Santillara.
LAYNA SERRANO, FRANCISCO 1941 *El Palacio del Infantado en Guadalajara.* Madrid: Hauser and Menet.

GUASTAVINO Y MORENO, RAFAEL, and GUASTAVINO Y ESPOSITO, RAFAEL

Rafael Guastavino y Moreno (1842–1908) and his son, Rafael Guastavino y Esposito (1872–1950) are often thought to be one person. They specialized in vaulting, roofing, and stairways constructed according to the Catalan thin-shell, laminated tile-vaulting system. The father was born in Valencia, Spain, and died in Asheville, North Carolina; the son was born in Barcelona, where his father worked as a *maestro de obras* and untitled architect, and died in Bay Shore, Long Island. In part by introducing high-quality Portland cement mortar in addition to the usual water-soluble Plaster of Paris, the father perfected the age-old Mediterranean, and especially Catalan, system of laminated *bóvedas tabicadas* (board vaults). He went to the United States in the 1880s where his Guastavino Fireproof Construction Company flourished in an era of great urban conflagration. The Guastavino terra-cotta masonry resisted flames as well as intense heat which would have shattered stone masonry because of the latter's exploding water of crystallization. The Guastavino system also for the first time provided "masonry" vaulting for wide spans in churches and public buildings that previously had simply been plastered metal mesh (as in St. Patrick's Cathedral, New York) or had wooden hammer-beamed vaults. As the Catalan laminated tile shell owes its rigidity to its edge-maintained curvature instead of the buttressing necessary for voussoir "gravity" vaulting and as it is essentially a cohesive beam extended into space, the Guastavinos were able to provide the unique spacial effects of many of the new landmark buildings executed by important American architects between the 1880s and 1940s. The son actually outdid his father technically, as for example in the crossing dome of Saint John the Divine in New York—the largest dome ever erected without scaffolding. When the Guastavino Company decided in the 1960s to retire from the field, it had installed Catalan-type vaulting in more than a thousand buildings in the United States, Canada, and nine other countries. The firm held twenty-four patents, including five for acoustical tile together with WALLACE CLEMENT SABINE. One of the most interesting aspects of the Guastavino system was the research, with Sabine, into the matter of acoustical tiles for vault soffits and wall surfaces. First patented was the Rumford Tile, in 1914, a kilned tile that absorbed sounds by virtue of its spongelike air chambers produced from clay that had been mixed with small particles of peat that burned out. They then devised a molded tile containing minute pumice particles that would not "pack" but left small air spaces, this masonry tile proved to be 60 percent effective in absorbing sounds in three octaves above middle C. Called Akoustolith, it was patented in 1916 and was used in many churches and public buildings.

GEORGE R. COLLINS

WORKS

For a complete listing of Guastavino works, see George R. Collins's Guastavino Archive, Columbia University, New York. This list includes buildings in the accompanying illustrations.

Guastavino and Guastavino. Domes constructed by R. Guastavino Co.

1897, New York University Library, Bronx, N.Y. 1897, University of Virginia Library (rebuilding of dome), Charlottesville, Va. 1901, Institute of Arts and Sciences, Brooklyn, N.Y. 1903–1904, Bank of Montreal. 1904, Madison Square Presbyterian Church; 1905–1906, Columbia University Chapel; New York. 1905–1906, McKinley National Memorial, Canton, Ohio. 1905–1908, Rodelf Sholem Synagogue, Pittsburgh. 1906–1910, Elephant House, Bronx Zoo, New York. 1906–1910, Smithsonian Museum, Washington. 1907, Girard Trust Company, Philadelphia. 1908–1909, Saint John the Divine, New York. 1908–1911, Saint Francis de Sales Church, Philadelphia. 1909, Saint Barbara's, Brooklyn, N.Y. 1909, J. J. Jermain Memorial Library, Sag Harbor, N.Y.

BIBLIOGRAPHY

COLLINS, GEORGE R.   1968   "The Transfer of Thin Masonry Vaulting from Spain to America." *Journal of the Society of Architectural Historians* 37: no. 3:200–201. Includes a bibliography of books and articles on the bóveda tabicada from the 17th century to the 1960s, and writings by Rafael Guastavino y Moreno.

GUEDES, AMANCIO

Amancio d'Alpoim Miranda Guedes (1925–) was born in Lisbon and studied architecture under Donald Pilcher at the University of Witwatersrand, South Africa. Guedes had a prolific and creative private practice in Mozambique, South Africa, and Angola from 1949 to 1975, working from his home in Lourenço Marques. He has been teaching architecture at the University of Witwatersrand since 1975.

His style was influenced by the Iberian tradition, especially as manifested in the exuberance of Spanish-Portuguese rococo, Art Nouveau, and the work of ANTONIO GAUDÍ Y CORNET, but transformed by intimate contact with African art and his particular fascination with Dada (Tristan Tzara was a close friend). Underlying many aspects of his work is a profound sympathy with FRANK LLOYD WRIGHT and LE CORBUSIER, inspiration from ANDREA PALLADIO, CHARLES RENNIE MACINTOSH, ADOLF LOOS, and LOUIS I. KAHN, and a desire to explore further their intellectual ideas.

RONALD LEWCOCK

WORKS

1951, Prometheus Apartments; 1954, Tonelli Condominiums; 1956, Smiling Lion Apartments; 1962–1964, Sagrada Familia Church, Machava; Lourenço Marques. 1963, Mayers House, Piet Retief, South Africa. 1963–1972, Waterford School, Swaziland. 1966, Church of Santa Ana de Munhuana, Lourenço Marques. 1967–1968, Desirello House, Illovo, Johannesburg, South Africa. 1973–1975, Totta Standard Building, Port Alexandre, Angola.

BIBLIOGRAPHY

L'Architecture d'Aujourd'hui 1962 6, no. 37:58–62.
BEINHART, JULIAN 1961 "Amancio Guedes." *Architectural Review* 129:240–251.
BERMAN, ALAN 1978 "Down There on a Visit." *Architecture + Urbanism* 6:3–52.
GUEDES, AMANCIO 1977 *Fragments from an Ironic Autobiography.* Johannesburg.

GUERRA FAMILY

Giovanni Guerra (1540–1618) and his two brothers, Gaspare (1560–1622) and Giovanni Battista (dates unknown), were architects and painters from Modena, Italy. Giovanni also practiced as an engraver. From 1575, he was a member of the Accademia di San Luca in Rome.

Giovanni worked with DOMENICO FONTANA during the pontificate of Sixtus V and participated in the competition for the moving of the Vatican obelisk. Immersed in the flash of Zuccari's art, Giovanni was not original but his abundant graphic production has a large range of themes. Giovanni drew extensively the gardens that he visited, and since the architecture of his drawings is very precise, these drawings are a valuable documentation of the original landscaping and layout of, among others, the Villa Lante at Bagnaia and the villa at Pratolino.

MARTHA POLLAK

WORKS

1579, Cappela Gregoriana, St. Peter's; 1587–1589, Biblioteca Apostolica; 1587–1589, Lateran Palace; 1587–1589, Salone Sistino; 1587–1589, Scala Santa; Rome. 1596, San Filippo Neri, Modena, Italy. 1598–1599, Cathedral, Ripatransone, Italy. 1606–1607, Chiesa Nuova, Rome. 1609–1610, Villa d'Este, Tivoli, Italy.

BIBLIOGRAPHY

CECCHI GATTOLIN, ENRICHETTA 1979 "Precisioni e aggiunte per Giovanni Guerra." *Antichita viva* 18, no. 4:16–27.
HEIKAMP, DETLEF 1969 "Pratolino nei suoi giorni splendidi." *Antichita viva* 8, no. 2:14–34.
HESS, J. 1969 "Entwürfe von Giovanni Guerra für Villa Lante in Bagnaia, 1598." *Römisches Jahrbuch für Kunstgeschichte* 12:195–202.
Libri di immagini, disegni, e incisioni di Giovanni Guerra. 1978 Modena, Italy. Exhibition catalogue.
MONBEIG GOGUEL, CATHERINE 1974 "Giovanni Guerra da Modena, disegnatore e illustratore della fine del Rinascimento." *Arte illustrata* 58:164–178.
PARMA ARMANI, E. 1973 "La storia di Ester in un libro di skizzi di Giovanni Guerra." *Bollettino ligustico per la storia e la cultura regionale* 4:82–100.

GUGLER, ERIC

Most of the work of Eric Gugler (1889–1974) consists of monuments and public buildings. Gugler, who was also a sculptor and mural painter, spent three years (1911–1914) at the American Academy in Rome as a McKim fellow. Two of Gugler's unrealized projects, the Hall of Our History for Pine Mountain, Georgia, and the Battery Park Project for New York, suggest the inspirational, commemorative, and patriotic themes which Gugler addressed in most of his work.

PATRICIA C. PHILLIPS

WORKS

1930, Chicago War Memorial (with Roger Bailey). 1934, White House (enlargement and reconstruction of the executive wing), Washington. 1939–1940, Business Administration Building, World's Fair, New York.

BIBLIOGRAPHY

GUGLER, ERIC 1953 "The Hall of our History." *National Sculpture Review* 2:9–11.
"Obituary." 1974 *The New York Times* May 17.
SKY, ALISON, and STONE, MICHELLE 1976 *Unbuilt America.* New York: McGraw-Hill.

GUIDO, ANGEL

Angel Guido (1896–1960) studied architecture at Cordoba University in Argentina. When he returned to his native city of Rosario, he began to

iron elements, iron the like of which had never been cast before—robust, organic structures in a bizarre new style juxtaposed against overwhelmingly *beaux-arts* Paris. Opinion on the controversial entrances would be divided for years: the architect's self-proclaimed *style Guimard* was transformed by his detractors into *le style Métro,* a name that stuck although first coined as a pejorative.

Guimard has been called an architect-designer. Adhering to the unitary tenets of Art Nouveau, he designed and supervised installation of many of his interiors, including fireplaces, wallpaper, vases, and furniture. His imaginative chairs and sofas are of wood wrought into an unmistakable whiplash configuration, baroque in detail but with a complete absence of symmetry or repeats. Guimard's design philosophy owed much to WILLIAM MORRIS's Arts and Crafts Movement, heralding an elegant rapport between art and trade. In 1907, Guimard published a stunning catalogue of castings for architectural details.

Two years later, Guimard married the American painter Adeline Oppenheim, and their residence on the Avenue Mozart was a fitting monument to "the master of the soft line," a completely integrated dwelling and office where façade, décor, and furnishings embraced naturalistic arabesques.

Guimard's obsession with Art Nouveau stifled him in later life; a style rather than a movement, it expired before World War I, long before Guimard abandoned it. As a result, his postwar buildings were undistinguished, with only a pale imprint of his former inventive exuberance. In the late thirties, he and his wife moved to New York, and he died relatively unknown in a hotel suite in 1942.

JOHN MAXTONE-GRAHAM

WORKS

1888, Restaurant du Quai d'Autueil; 1889, Pavilion de l'Electricité, Exposition Universel; 1893, Maison Jassedé; 1893, Maison Roszél; 1895, Ecole du Sacré-Coeur; 1894–1895, Castel Béranger; 1896–1899, Castel Béranger (decoration); *1897–1901, Salle Humbert de Romans; Paris. 1898–1900, Maison Coilliot, Lille, France. 1899–1900, Castel Henriette, Sèvres, France. 1900–1913, Métropolitain (entrances); 1902–1905, Maison Nozal; *1909–1910, Hôtel Guimard; 1910–1911, Maison Mezzara; 1911–1913, Synagogue Rue Pavée; 1912, Hôtel Guimard (decoration); Paris. *1930, La Guimardière (incomplete), Vaucresson, France.

BIBLIOGRAPHY
BARILLI, RENATO 1969 *Art Nouveau.* Translated by Raymond Rudorff. London: Hamlyn.
CULPEPPER, RALPH 1971 "Les Premières Oeuvres d'Héctor Guimard." *L'Architecture d'Aujourd'hui* 43, no. 154:8–9.
GRAHAM, F. LANIER 1970 *Héctor Guimard.* New York: Museum of Modern Art.
GUIMARD, HÉCTOR 1902 "An Architect's Opinion of 'l'Art Nouveau'." *Architectural Record* 12:127–133.
GUIMARD, HÉCTOR 1907 *Fontes Artistiques pour Constructions, Fumisterie, Articles de Jardins et Sepultures, Style Guimard.* Paris: Fonderies de Saint Dizier.
MADSEN, STEPHAN TSCHUDI (1956)1975 *Sources of Art Nouveau.* Translated by Ragnar Christophersen. Reprint. New York: Da Capo.
"Master of the Soft Line." 1969 *Architectural Design* 39:296–297.
MIOTTO-MURET, LUCIANNA, and PALLUCCHINI-PELZEL, VITTORIA 1969 "Une Maison de Guimard." *Revue de l'Art* no. 3:75–79.
PLANTIN, YVES, and BLONDEL, ALAIN 1971 "Hector Guimard—La Salle Humbert de Romans." *L'Architecture d'Aujourd'hui* 43, no. 155:17–18.
POUPÉE, HENRI 1970 "Actualité de Guimard." *La Construction Moderne* no. 4:41–57.

GUMMER, W. H.

William Henry Gummer (1885–1966) designed many fine public buildings throughout New Zealand. A New Zealander by birth, he worked as a young man with EDWIN LUTYENS in London and DANIEL H. BURNHAM in Chicago, after study at the Royal Academy School of Architecture. From 1923 to 1961 he was partnered in Auckland, New Zealand, by C. R. Ford.

JOHN STACPOOLE

WORKS

1914, Champtaloup House; 1917 Young Women's Christian Association Hostel; 1918, New Zealand Insurance Building; Auckland, New Zealand. 1919, Craggy Range House; 1920, Tauroa House; Havelock North, New Zealand. *1923, Bryant and May Factory, Wellington. 1924, Bridge of Remembrance, Christchurch, New Zealand. 1924, Grey Lynn Public Library, Auckland, New Zealand. 1926, Arden House, Havelock North, New Zealand. 1926, Remuera Public Library; 1926, Dilworth Building; 1927, Gummer House; 1928, Domain Wintergarden; Auckland, New Zealand. 1928, Massey Memorial, Wellington. 1929, Mayfair Flats; 1930, Railway Station; 1935, Dingwall Building; Auckland, New Zealand. 1936, National Art Gallery and Museum; 1938, State Insurance Building; 1938, Public Library; 1964, National War Memorial; Wellington.

BIBLIOGRAPHY
"William Henry Gummer." 1967 *NZIA Journal* 34, no. 3:86–90.

GUMPP FAMILY

The descendants of the Innsbruck carpenter Christoph Gumpp the Elder (?–1623) formed a dynasty of artists, architects, and engineers. Pioneers of the baroque style in Tyrol, they were active chiefly in Innsbruck and Munich.

Christoph Gumpp the Younger (1600–1672), court architect to the Tyrolean Hapsburgs, designed the domed circular votive church of Mariahilf (1647–1649) in Innsbruck as well as the Comödienhaus (1628–1630) and Hoftheater there. His five artist sons included the cartographer, printmaker, and engineer Johann Baptist (1651–1728); the painter Johann Anton (1654–1719), active at the Munich Residenz and Nymphenburg; and Johann Martin the Elder (1643–1729), architect of the Fugger-Taxis (1679–1680) and Ferrari palaces (1683–1691) in Innsbruck.

Johann Martin's son Georg Anton (1682–1754) is regarded as the most important member of the family. His work reflects his study of high baroque architecture in Rome but introduces original features. He designed the Gumpps' acknowledged masterpiece, the Landhaus of the Tyrolean estates (1724–1728), an administrative palace representing Tyrolean identity and self-government. His brother Johann Martin the Younger (1686–1765) was primarily a military engineer, but he also built the south wing of the Innsbruck Hofburg (1754–1756).

As court architects in Innsbruck, the Gumpps were prolific designers of temporary structures for festivals and funerals, many recorded in prints. Christoph the Younger, Johann Martin the Elder, and Georg Anton contributed to the design of a family masterpiece, the Cistercian Abbey (1692–1699, 1719–1725) at Stamms.

Krapf (1979, p. 240) says of the Gumpps: "In a land too small for the development of a regional style, their chief importance lay in their activity as mediators."

ALISON LUCHS

WORKS

CHRISTOPH GUMPP THE YOUNGER

1627–?, Jesuit Church; *1628–1630, Comödienhaus; 1647–1649, Church of Mariahilf; Innsbruck, Austria. 1649–1660, Church and Convent (renovation), Sankt Georgenberg, Austria. 1649–1660, Stiftskirche of Wilten (renovation), near Innsbruck, Austria. Before 1653–1655, Hoftheater, Innsbruck, Austria.

JOHANN MARTIN GUMPP THE ELDER

1672–1680, Jesuit College; 1679–1680, Fugger-Taxis Palace; 1683–1691, Ferrari Palace; 1690–1692, Government House (remodeling); Innsbruck, Austria. 1692–1699, Cistercian Abbey, Stams, Austria. 1700–1705, Spitalskirche, Innsbruck, Austria.

JOHANN ANTON GUMPP

*1675, Holy Sepulcher in Theatine Church, Munich.

1684–1689, Schloss Lustheim (ceiling frescoes), Schleissheim, Germany. 1690–1695, Abbey Church of Sankt Florian (ceiling frescoes; with Melchior Steidl), Austria. 1716–1719, Schloss Dachau (frescoes), Germany. 1718–1719, Pagodenburg (ceiling paintings), Nymphenburg, Munich.

GEORGE ANTON GUMPP

1713–1719, Stiftskirche (portico), Wilten, near Innsbruck, Austria. 1715–1717, Chapel of the Holy Blood, Cistercian Abbey, Stams, Austria. 1718–1719, Franciscan Convent (now the Volkskunstmuseum), Innsbruck, Austria. 1719–1725, Cistercian Abbey (continuation and completion), Stams, Austria. 1721–1723, Pfeiffersberg Palace; 1724–1728, Landhaus; 1729–1732, Johanneskirche; Innsbruck, Austria. 1729–1732, Abbey Church (rebuilding), Stams, Austria.

JOHANN MARTIN GUMPP THE YOUNGER

*1708, Stiftskirche (Holy Sepulcher; with Johann Ferdinand Schor), Wilten, near Innsbruck, Austria. 1754–1756, Hofburg (south wing), Innsbruck, Austria.

BIBLIOGRAPHY

BOURKE, JOHN 1978 *Baroque Churches of Central Europe.* London: Faber.
HEMPEL, EBERHARD (1965)1977 *Baroque Art and Architecture in Central Europe.* 2d ed., rev. Baltimore: Penguin.
KRAPF, MICHAEL 1979 *Die Baumeister Gumpp.* Vienna and Munich: Herold.
KRAPF, MICHAEL 1980 *Die Baumeister Gumpp: Eine Künstlerdynastie des Barock in Tirol.* Vienna: Österreichische Galerie. Exhibition catalogue.
STERNATH, HERMANN 1980 "Eine Künstlerdynastie des Barock in Tirol." *Weltkunst* 10:1414–1415.

GÜNTHER, IGNAZ

Ignaz Günther (1725–1775), sculptor and altar architect, was born in Altmannstein, Germany. His work was well known in southern Germany. The baroque influence was evident in his sculpture, but he developed a loose and free rococo style and was receptive to the upcoming neoclassical style between 1766 and 1770.

First trained by his father, who was a sculptor and carpenter, Günther went to Munich in 1743. Through the efforts of Johann Baptist Straub, he apprenticed there for seven years. From 1750, Günther lived in Salzburg, Austria, where he worked with Paul Egell. His primary work included designing altars, columns, and sculptures. In 1753, Günther became a member of the Academy of Art in Vienna where he designed Saint Borromäus Church, which included several altars and sculptures. He graduated with highest honor from the Academy and received many recommendations.

Returning to Munich in 1754, he continued to design altars and sculptures for churches in the area; in 1756, he was appointed "sculptor of the court." Günther's masterpiece of the rococo period was the Church of Rott designed in 1761–1762. Günther's use of fantasy and free style distinguished him from other artists of this period. His transition to the neoclassical style included such works as the altars at Starnberg (1766–1768) and Neustift (1765–1766). After the death of Karl de Groff in 1773, Günther became the master sculptor of the Royal Bavarian Court. Despite his short life, Günther had a prosperous and productive career.

THOMAS ALEXANDER BOCK

WORKS

1761–1762, Church, Rott am Inn, Germany. 1763, Weyarn Church (altar), Germany. 1765–1766, Neustiff Church (altar), Germany. 1766–1768, Church at Starnberg (altar), Germany.

BIBLIOGRAPHY

BIERMANN, GEORG 1914 *Deutsches Barock und Rokoko.* 2 vols. Leipzig: Schwabach.
FEULNER, ADOLF 1947 *Ignaz Günther.* Munich: Bruckmann.

GÜNTHER, MATTHÄUS

Born in Unterpeissenberg, Bavaria, Germany, Matthäus Günther (1705–1788) was best known for his numerous rococo paintings. His work was renowned especially in southern Germany. He received his training from COSMAS DAMIAN ASAM. From 1762 to 1784, Günther was director of the Augsburg Academy of Art. Because of his popularity, he was commissioned to build several churches in Austria and Bavaria.

Günther vacillated between baroque and rococo styles. The churches of Welden (1754), Druisheim, and Steerzing were examples of combined baroque composition and rococo elements. Between 1740 and 1760, one of Günther's accomplishments that won critical praise was the interior of the Church of Amorbach (1745–1747). The composition of his paintings became lighter and the colors more pronounced. The transition to the rococo style was clearly evident in the light composition, sensitive forms, reduction of illusions and a sense of open space. Other examples of this transitional style were the churches of Witten (1754), Indersdorf (1755), Aldersbach (1760), Sünching (1761) and Rott am Inn (1763). His later works did not show any new tendencies. Günther did not compromise with the upcoming neoclassical style. The light and free character of the rococo style blended well with the heavy and traditional Bavarian baroque, at least in his early works.

THOMAS ALEXANDER BOCK

WORKS

1745–1747, Amorbach Church (interior), Germany. 1754, Welden Church, Austria. 1760, Aldersbach Church, Germany. 1760, Sünching Church, Bavaria, Germany. 1763, Church, Rott am Inn, Germany.

BIBLIOGRAPHY

HAMMER, HEINRICH 1912 *Entwicklung der barocken Deckenmalerei in Tirol.* Strassburg, Austria: Heitz.
SCHRÖDER, A. 1883–1929 In *Archiv für Christliche Kunst.* 44 vols. Stuttgart, Germany: Rottenburger.

GURLITT, CORNELIUS

Born in Nischwitz, Saxony, Cornelius Gurlitt (1850–1938) left school early and started an apprenticeship as a carpenter. However, he soon returned to his studies, reading architecture in Berlin and Stuttgart and entering practice in 1871. From 1879, he was employed as an assistant at the Dresden Museum for the Applied Arts, and here he wrote his three-volume study, *Geschichte des Barockstiles, des Rococo und des Klassicismus* (1887–1889). The success of the book led to his appointment to a chair in architecture at the Technische Hochschule in Dresden, where he remained until his retirement in 1920.

Gurlitt's output was prodigious. In ninety-seven books and over 400 articles he wrote on a range of topics from the history of architecture, painting, sculpture, and town planning to issues of current debate and even politics. He is best remembered, however, for his championing of the baroque, winning for this period the same recognition that Jakob Burckhardt had already won for the civilization of the early Renaissance. In architecture, his enthusiasm for the baroque led him to reject the ideas of KARL FRIEDRICH SCHINKEL and his followers as formally and intellectually barren; instead, he looked first to GOTTFRIED SEMPER and then to members of the younger generation such as PAUL WALLOT and Alfred Messel for a rejuvenation of architecture; by 1900, he was already applauding the work of HENRI VAN DE VELDE. During the 1920s and 1930s, he received many honors, but he wrote little between the early 1920s and his death in 1938.

N. O. A. BULLOCK

GUTBROD, ROLF

Konrad Rolf Dietrich Gutbrod (1910–), working from his native Stuttgart, Germany, has developed an architecture of irregular elements forming organic urban ensembles. His designs done in collaboration with FREI OTTO have incorporated tensile roofs as further associative forms. Recent Middle Eastern works, beginning with the Mecca Conference Center (1974), have adapted these humanistic principles to an Arab context.

THOMAS G. BEDDALL

WORKS

1954–1956, Concert Hall "Liederhalle" (with Adolf Abel and Blasius Spreng); 1957–1965, SDR Broadcasting and Television Studios, Villa Berg (with Helmut Weber and Hertha-Maria Witzemann); Stuttgart, Germany. 1960–1962, IBM Administration Building (with Bernhard Binder), Berlin. 1963–1965, German Embassy, Vienna. 1963–1968, Library and Auditoriums, University of Cologne, Germany. 1965–1968, Württembergische Bank (with Hermann Kiess), Stuttgart, Germany. 1966–1967, German Pavilion, Expo '67 (with Frei Otto), Montreal. 1966–1968, Gropiusstadt Housing, Berlin. 1966–1973, Freie Waldorfschule Teachers' College and Classroom Building (with Wolfgang Henning), Uhlandshoehe, Stuttgart, Germany. 1967–1970, Max-Planck-Institut Laboratories for Biology and Chemistry, Berlin. 1969–1974, Conference Center and Hotel (with Frei Otto), Mecca, Saudi Arabia. 1970–1976, SDR Radio Station Building, Neckarstrasse, Stuttgart, Germany. 1979–?, Museums of European Art, Tiergarten, Berlin. 1981–?, Government Center, Riyadh, Saudi Arabia.

BIBLIOGRAPHY

BOYD, ROBIN 1967 "Expo '67—Germany." *Architectural Review* 142, no. 846:129–135.
DREW, PHILIP 1976 *Frei Otto: Form and Structure.* London: Crosby Lockwood Staples.
"Freie Waldorfschule Stuttgart." 1974 *Bauwelt* 65, no. 28:969–971.
GUTBROD, ROLF A. 1967 "Funk- und Fernsehstudios des Süddeutschen Rundfunks." *Deutsche Bauzeitung* 101, no. 10:785–791.
GUTBROD, ROLF A. 1975–1976 "Hôtel et Centre de conférence de la Mecque." *L'Architecture Française* 390, Apr.:74–83; 400, Dec.:56–63.
"IBM Building, Berlin." 1963 *Architect and Building News* 224, no. 42:613–616.
"Württembergische Bank in Stuttgart." 1970 *Werk* 57, no. 8:517–519.

GUTT, ROMUALD

Romuald Gutt (1888–1974), a Polish architect, studied architecture in Winterthur, Switzerland, and graduated in 1908. He is the designer of numerous buildings in Poland.

His style developed from historically inspired forms to the Modern style, yet each work always bore individual characteristics. Gutt's particular concern for integration of the natural environment with the built-up surroundings can be noted in many of his works.

LECH KŁOSIEWICZ

WORKS

1919–1926, Girls' Vocational Training School; 1926–1933, Academy of Political Science; Warsaw. 1946, Patriots' Cemetery, Palmiry, near Warsaw. 1948–1954, Main Statistics Office Building; 1956, Chinese Embassy (with others); Warsaw.

BIBLIOGRAPHY

The Polish Avant-Garde: 1918–1939. 1981 Paris: Moniteur; Warsaw: Interpress. Exhibition catalogue.
Warszawska Szkoła Architektury: 1915–1965. 1967 Warsaw: P.W.N.
WISŁOCKA, IZABELLA 1968 *Awangordowa Architecktura Polska: 1918–1939.* Warsaw: Arkady.

GUTTON, HENRI B.

Henri B. Gutton (1851–1933) worked primarily in Nancy, Lorraine, France, after 1900, where he built commercial structures and fanciful Art Nouveau residences, including villas in the Parc de Saurupt which he and EMILE ANDRÉ planned in 1901.

Other members of the Ecole de Nancy with whom he collaborated include Joseph Hornecker and his nephew Henri-Barthelemi Gutton. In Paris in 1906, Gutton designed the Grand Bazar de la rue de Rennes, an airy construction of iron and glass in a restrained Art Nouveau style.

CHRISTOPHER RIOPELLE

WORKS

1900–1901, Graineterie Job (now the Graineterie Genin-Louis; with Henri-Barthelemi Gutton); 1901, Parc de Saurupt (with Emile André); 1905, Villa Marguerite (with Joseph Hornecker), Parc de Saurupt; Nancy, France. 1906, Grand Bazar de la rue de Rennes (now the Magasins Réunies), Paris.

BIBLIOGRAPHY

FORD, GEORGE BURDETT 1908 "Rational Ironwork for Store and Loft Building." *American Architect and Building News* 94, no. 1708:89–91.
FORTUNY, PASCHAL 1910 "Dix Années d'Architecture." *Gazette des Beaux-Arts* 1:191–210, 426–440.
Nancy, Architecture 1900. 1977 Paris: Caisse nationale des monuments historiques et des sites.

GWILT, JOSEPH

Joseph Gwilt (1784–1863) was born in South-wark, London, and trained in his father's office before entering the Royal Academy Schools in 1801. He designed in the neoclassical, Tudor, and Renaissance styles, though Saint Thomas's Church, Charlton (1847–1850), was Byzantine. Between 1814 and 1818, he studied in France, Flanders, and especially Italy, as recorded in his *Notitia Architectonicae Italiana* (1818). He succeeded his father as surveyor to the Commissioners of Sewers for Surrey (1807–1846) and was architect to various companies. His more celebrated career as an architectural theorist and critic began in 1811 with a treatise on arches and included a translation of VITRUVIUS (1826), which became the standard English text; a volume on architectural criticism (1837) denigrating the Greek Revival and favoring the Renaissance style; and editions of WILLIAM CHAMBERS (1825) and PETER NICHOLSON (1848). Gwilt's major publication, the popular *Encyclopaedia of Architecture* (1845), a much expanded version of his *Rudiments of Architecture* (1826), was compiled with the assistance of his architect son, John Sebastian Gwilt (1811–1890).

R. WINDSOR LISCOMBE

WORKS

1804, Saint Ives Vicarage, Huntingdonshire, England. *1813–1814, Saint Margaret's Church, Lee, Kent, England. 1828–1829, Stamford Hill Chapel (additions, including tower; now Saint Thomas's Church), Clapham Common, Surrey, England. *1838, Grocer's Hall (remodeling), Poultry, London. 1842–1843, Markree Castle (with J. S. Gwilt), County Sligo, Ireland. 1847–1850, Saint Thomas's Church, Charlton, Kent, England.

BIBLIOGRAPHY

GRANGER, FRANK S. (1931)1962 Page xxxiv in *Vitruvius on Architecture*. Cambridge, Mass.: Harvard University Press.

GWILT, JOSEPH 1811 *Treatise on the Equilibrium of Arches*. London: Priestley & Weale.

GWILT, JOSEPH 1818 *Notitia Architectonicae Italiana, or Concise Notes on the Buildings and Architecture of Italy*. London: Egerton.

GWILT, JOSEPH 1822 *Sciography, or Examples of Shadows, with Rules for Their Projection Intended for the Use of Architectural Draughtsmen and Other Artists*. London: Bohn.

GWILT, JOSEPH (1823)1825 "Historical, Descriptive, and Critical Account of the Catholic Church of Saint Paul's, London." Volume 1, pages 1–40 in J. Britton and A. C. Pugin, *Illustrations of the Public Buildings of London*. London: J. Taylor.

GWILT, JOSEPH (editor) 1825 *A Treatise on the Decorative Part of Civil Architecture* by William Chambers. London: Priestley & Weale. Including Chambers's essay, "An Examination of the Elements of Beauty in Grecian Architecture."

GWILT, JOSEPH 1826 *The Architecture of Marius Vitruvius Pollio in Ten Books*. London: Priestley & Weale.

GWILT, JOSEPH 1826 *Rudiments of Architecture: Practical and Theoretical*. London: J. Taylor.

GWILT, JOSEPH 1837 *Elements of Architectural Criticism for the Use of Students, Amateurs and Reviewers*. London: Williams.

GWILT, JOSEPH 1842 *An Encyclopaedia of Architecture, Historical, Theoretical and Practical*. London: Longman.

GWILT, JOSEPH (editor) 1848 *Principles of Architecture* by Peter Nicholson. London: Bohn.

LISCOMBE, R. WINDSOR 1980 Pages 70, 194, 256, 258 in *William Wilkins: 1778–1839*. Cambridge University Press.

"Obituary." 1863 *Gentleman's Magazine* 215:647–652.

PEVSNER, NIKOLAUS 1972 pages 77, 249 in *Some Architectural Writers of the Nineteenth Century*. Oxford University Press.

GWYNN, JOHN

John Gwynn (1713–1786) was responsible for several fine bridges, including Shrewsbury, Shropshire (1769), Atcham, Shropshire (1769), Worcester (1771), and Magdalen, Oxford (1772). A "fine, lively, rattling fellow," in James Boswell's words, he must be commemorated in architectural annals as the author of *London and Westminster Improved* (1766), a pioneering report of the comprehensive replanning of London and a seminal for JOHN NASH's later town improvements.

JOHN HARRIS

WORKS

1769, Atcham Bridge; 1769, Shrewsbury Bridge; Shropshire, England. 1771, Worcester Bridge, England. 1772, Magdalen Bridge, Oxford.

BIBLIOGRAPHY

GWYNN, JOHN 1766 *London and Westminster Improved*. London: The author.

HABLIK, WENZEL

Not a trained architect, Wenzel August Hablik (1881–1934) was a painter, graphic artist, and designer active in the German Arts and Crafts movement. His work reveals an expansive imagination and invites one to enter a personal world of fantasy inspired by nature's diversity and wonder. Various of Hablik's oil paintings were exhibited at the Berlin Sezession, 1909, the Deutscher Künstlerbund in Weimar, 1910, and the Hagenbund Vereinigung in Vienna, 1911. What he considered the most significant work of his career was completed in 1909, a portfolio of twenty etchings entitled *Schaffende Kräfte* (Creative Forces) which involves a journey through an imaginary universe of crystalline structures, each leaf of the folio conceived to spark latent forces that bind the viewer with a cosmic spirit. The etchings were shown at the third annual Sturm Graphic Exhibition, 1912, along with works by Gauguin, Gris, Kandinsky, Kokoschka, and Picasso. Hablik is best known for the architectural fantasies which he composed after 1918, largely in association with the utopian-Expressionist groups of the *Arbeitsrat für Kunst* and *Die gläserne Kette.*

Hablik recalled spending many hours of his youth exploring the surrounding mountains of his native Brüx, Bohemia (now Most, Czechoslovakia). It was on one of his mountain walks that his imagination was first kindled by the discovery of a quartz crystal, an occasion which he was to regard as the beginning of his ever deepening interest in natural phenomena and most especially in geological formations with their expressive qualities and cosmic meanings.

Having completed an apprenticeship in cabinet making in his father's shop, Hablik left home in 1896 to pursue painting and drawing. After a brief period of apprenticeship in an architects' and surveyors' office and attendance at the local *Gewerbeschule,* he enrolled in 1897 at the art academy in Teplitz. The critical years of artistic study were spent at the Kunstgewerbeschule des Österreichischen Museums in Vienna (1902–1905), where he was a member of the painting studio headed by the school's director, Felcian von Myrbach. Hablik continued his studies at the Akademie für Bildende Künste in Prague (1905–1906). His artistic talents were recognized in 1907 by Ferdinand Avenarius, the influential art patron, publisher of the periodical *Kunstwart,* and founder of the cultural organization *Dürerbund.* Hablik was invited to become a member of Avenarius's art colony on the North Frisian island of Sylt. Among the products of this period with Avenarius are the

Schaffende Kräfte, and a small sketch of 1908 for an airborne explorer colony.

Hablik settled in Itzehoe, Schleswig-Holstein (northwest of Hamburg), upon the invitation of Richard Biel, a wealthy timber merchant and one of his early patrons. In 1917, Hablik married Lisbeth Lindemann, a textile designer and weaver. Together, they set up the Werkstatt für Handweberei (Atelier for Hand-Weaving) to which Hablik contributed designs while pursuing his private visions and delvings into the natural sciences, world religions, and the occult.

Representative of Hablik's diverse interests are two later portfolios of etchings, *Das Meer* (1918) and *Cyklus Architektur* (1925), the latter being a written manifesto and a compendium of the architectural images that most fascinated him: the airborne colony, the exhibition temple, the domed building, and the tower. Through his architectural fantasies Hablik explored ideals of emotive and symbolic expression at the center of which was the pursuit of empathetic formal means and of the Romantic ideal of the *Gesamtkunstwerk.* These ideals had motivated various artists in Germany before World War I and were part of the background for architectural Expressionism after the war. Hablik's earliest sketches and his later utopian-Expressionist projects highlight important continuities between the arts of *Jugendstil* and Symbolism and those of Expressionism.

EUGENE A. SANTOMASSO

WORKS

1911, Richard Biel Villa (interior redesign); 1918, Hotel Central Restaurant (interior redesign); c.1918, Wenzel Hablik House (interiors); 1918, Town Hall (interior redesign); c.1925, Wenzel Hablik House (redesign of façade); Itzehoe, Germany.

BIBLIOGRAPHY

AVENARIUS, FERDINAND 1909 "Unsere Bilder und Notel." *Der Kunstwart* 22, Aug.:231–232.

BENDER, EWALD 1910 "Radierungen von Wenzel Hablik." *Deutsche Kunst und Dekoration* 26:165–170.

BORSI, FRANCO, and KÖNIG, G. K. 1967 Pages 111–114, 297–308 in *Architettura dell' Espressionismo.* Genoa, Italy: Vitali & Ghianda; Paris: Vincent, Fréal.

HABLIK, WENZEL A. 1922 "Die freitragende Kuppel und ihre Variabilität, unter Berücksichtigung verschiedener Materialien und Verwendungsmöglichkeiten." *Frühlicht* 3, Spring:94:98.

MARTIUS, LILLI 1960 "Wenzel Hablik." *Kunst in Schleswig-Holstein* 1960:35–52.

ROSSOW, WALTER ET AL. 1980 *Arbeitsrat für Kunst: Berlin, 1918–1921.* Berlin: Akademie der Künste. Exhibition catalogue.

SANTOMASSO, EUGENE A. 1979 "Wenzel A. Hablik." Pages 22–26 in George R. Collins (editor), *Visionary Drawings of Architecture and Planning: 20th Century Through the 1960's.* Cambridge, Mass.: M.I.T. Press. Exhibition catalogue, Drawing Center, New York.

SANTOMASSO, EUGENE A. 1980 "Wenzel A. Hablik: The 'Schaffende Kräfte' Folio and Its Relationship to Expressionist Aims and Ideals." *Architectural Association Quarterly* 12, no. 3:18–24.

TRAUTWEIN, MARTHA 1968 "Erinnerungen an Wenz und Lisbet Hablik." *Die Heimat* 8, Aug.:237–239.

UNGERS, O. M. (editor) 1963 Pages 14–19, 57–58, 104–110 in *Die gläserne Kette: Visionäre Architekturen aus dem Kreis um Bruno Taut, 1919–1920.* Berlin.

URBAN, MARTIN 1960 *Wenzel Hablik.* Kiel, Germany: Schleswig-Holstein Landesmuseum. Exhibition catalogue.

HABRAKEN, N. J.

Nikolaas Johannes Habraken (1928–) is the most influential Dutch critic of the mass housing of the 1950s and a theoretician of a new design strategy.

Habraken grew up in the Dutch Indies and spent the war years in a Japanese internment camp. After the war, his family returned to the Netherlands, and Habraken became a constructional engineer (Technical University, Delft, 1955). From 1955 to 1964, he worked in the architects' office of Lucas and Niemeijer in Voorburg. In 1961, in his essay *De dragers en de mensen* (English translation, *Supports,* London, 1972), he demanded a total revision of the thinking about building and living. The creation of a new relationship between the human being, matter, and machine was needed; design ought to be disconnected from the existing aesthetics and connected with the biological strategy of building as a natural process. On the one hand, he recognized the right of the individual to full development; on the other, he saw it as the individual's duty to take on the responsibility for his own housing. The designer, Habraken argued, can provide only the conditions for this participation in the process of shaping the environment. In this technological utopia, according to Habraken, the city planner designs supporting structures while the architect designs the dwellings to fill the spaces.

From 1964, Habraken tried to realize his utopia on three levels: culture, research, and education. From 1964 to 1969, he was editor of the Dutch *Forum* which aimed at the development of a common language so that the disciplines involved in the shaping of the total environment could communicate again. In the same year, he became director of the Stichting Architecten Research (SAR, Foundation of Architects' Research) to explore the industrial possibilities of his scheme and to study the coordination problems between technical and planning aspects. When a new constructional department was created at the Technical University at Eindhoven, Netherlands, he was appointed chairman. Since 1975, he has been chairman of the department of architecture at the Massachusetts Institute of Technology.

CEES L. BOEKRAAD

HADFIELD, GEORGE

George Hadfield (1763–1826), born in Livorno, Italy, of British parentage, returned to England in 1779 and studied architecture at the Royal Academy. After working under JAMES WYATT, for approximately six years, he went to Italy in 1790 on the Royal Academy's first Travelling Scholarship in architecture. Two of his reconstruction drawings of ancient architecture were exhibited in London in 1795. His failure to be voted into the Architects' Club on January 2, 1795, despite endorsement by HENRY HOLLAND and Wyatt, was probably decisive in his acceptance of the superintendence of construction of the Capitol building in Washington. By October 1, he was in America at his new position, but controversy over William Thornton's plan and a number of other matters led to his resignation on November 18. Soon reinstated, however, he continued work until discharged in June 1798.

For the next twenty-eight years, Hadfield designed government and private buildings in and near Washington. His earliest design was for the Treasury Department Building (1796–1797). Fifteen bays long, it had a four column Ionic portico with parapet entablature (not pedimented) based on the order of the Erechtheion. Had it been built as designed, it would have predated BENJAMIN HENRY LATROBE's similar order on the Bank of Pennsylvania. As erected, however, the building had a central pedimented bay in the vernacular tradition common in America since the 1750s.

While many Regency style features, such as recessed round-headed windows and stucco finishes, are in his work, Greek orders were used frequently and with originality. For the central portion of the Custis–Lee Mansion (1817), he designed a monumental pedimented portico of six massive unfluted Doric columns, modeled on Paestum. Completed by 1817, it antedates WILLIAM STRICKLAND's Second Bank of the United States. His Washington City Hall (1820–1826, 1849–1850) was a particularly felicitous blend of Regency detailing, bold simple massing, and an Ionic order.

DANIEL D. REIFF

Hadfield.
Washington City Hall.
Washington.
1820–1826, 1849–1850

WORKS

*1796–1797, Treasury Department Building; *1798–1800, War Department Building; *1801–1802, Washington Jail; *1801–1803, Marine Barracks; 1801–1803, Marine Commandant's House; Washington. 1802–1804, 1817, Custis–Lee Mansion (wings and center), Arlington, Va. *1803, The Arsenal; 1816–1819, Commodore David Porter House; 1820–1826, 1849–1850, Washington City Hall (wings and center); *1822, Assembly Rooms; *1824, Second Bank of the United States (branch office); 1826, John Peter Van Ness Mausoleum, Oak Hill Cemetery; Washington.

BIBLIOGRAPHY

Two ink and wash drawings by George Hadfield, signed and dated September 1798, are in the Avery Architectural Library, Columbia University. One drawing is reproduced in Deborah Nevins and Robert A. M. Stern, The Architect's Eye: American Architectural Drawings from 1799–1978. *New York: Pantheon, 1979.*

CUNNINGHAM, H. F. 1915 "The Old City Hall, Washington, D.C." *Architectural Record* 37:268–273.

GOODE, JAMES M. 1979 *Capital Losses: A Cultural History of Washington's Destroyed Buildings.* Washington: Smithsonian Institution.

GOODFELLOW, G. L. M. 1965 "George Hadfield." *Architectural Review* 138:35–36.

HUNSBERGER, GEORGE S. 1955 "The Architectural Career of George Hadfield." Columbia Historical Society, *Records* 51–52:46–65.

KIMBALL, FISKE 1943 "George Hadfield." Volume 8, pages 76–77 in *Dictionary of American Biography.* New York: Scribner.

MADDEX, DIANE 1973 *Historic Buildings of Washington, D.C.* Pittsburgh: Ober Park Associates.

NELLIGAN, MURRAY HOMER 1962 *Custis-Lee Mansion, the Robert E. Lee Memorial, Virginia.* Washington: U.S. Government Printing Office.

REIFF, DANIEL D. 1971 *Washington Architecture, 1791–1861: Problems in Development.* Washington: U.S. Commission of Fine Arts.

RICHMAN, MICHAEL 1974 "George Hadfield (1763–1826): His Contribution to the Greek Revival in America." *Journal of the Society of Architectural Historians* 33:234–235.

HADRIAN

An artist and intellectual as well as a tireless administrator, Hadrian (76–138) was deeply involved in architecture, a commitment given full play after he succeeded the Emperor Trajan in 117. His unceasing activity as a builder is recorded in ancient writings, numerous inscriptions, and hundreds of dated buildings and fragments of buildings throughout the widespread Roman world. He founded cities and enlarged and embellished existing ones almost routinely. He designed the Temple of Venus and Rome (121–136) across from the Colosseum; other projects are mentioned in the ancient texts. The forms of celebrated works of his day whose architects are unknown, such as the Pantheon in Rome and the vast villa near Tivoli, surely owe as much (or more) to his quick, encompassing mind as to the abilities of his architectural staff. His influence on architecture was abiding not only because of his talent and tastes, but also because of the human and material resources he could summon up in quantity in any corner of the Roman empire in order to raise the monumental works future ages would study.

The double temple of Venus and Rome, larger than the Parthenon, sits on a high concrete terrace. A fairly traditional colonnade once enclosed a two-part cella of discrete chambers set back-to-back; the whole was surrounded by a second, free-standing colonnade some distance from the temple proper. Hadrian sent the plans to APOLLODORUS, the leading professional of the age and once Trajan's architect in chief, who criticized them; the two men fell out. Hadrian seems however to have taken Apollodorus's advice, and he sought the aid of another architect, DECRIANUS, in moving a colossal statue of Nero away from the site where he was to place his temple (120s).

His architectural sympathies are best studied at the Pantheon, with its novel yet compelling combination of the old and the new and its rich, multiple symbolism of earth, empire, and the heavens, and at his sprawling villa. The latter, a kind of private architectural laboratory where experiments could be carried out full scale, is unique. Stylistically, it exhibits nearly every phase of Greco-Roman design as well as numerous original concepts. Asymmetrical in plan, it consists of groups of pavilions of variegated shapes strung out along eccentrically disposed axes. There are temples, baths, theaters, studios, pools, dining halls, belvederes, underground porticoes, shops, grand fountains, shrines, and buildings whose use even now is uncertain. There are centralized vaulted spaces incipiently baroque in character, some with gored, pumpkinlike interior surfaces. The orders are there but they are made to march around curves and countercurves, to help support vaults, and to lend purely scenic accents to richly modulated spaces; several of the buildings have plans unrelated to anything in Western architecture for centuries to come. The villa was closely studied by Italian masters, beginning in the sixteenth century.

WILLIAM L. MacDONALD

WORKS

120s, Colossus of Nero (moved); 121–136, Temple of Venus and Rome; Rome.

BIBLIOGRAPHY

BARATTOLO, ANDREA 1973 "Nuove ricerche sull'architettura del Tempio di Venere e di Roma in età adrianea." *Deutsches Archäologisches Institut, Römische Abteilung, Mitteilungen* 80:243–269.
MacDONALD, WILLIAM L. (1965)1982 Chapter 6 of *The Architecture of the Roman Empire.* Rev. ed. New Haven: Yale University Press.
MacDONALD, WILLIAM L., and BOYLE, BERNARD M. 1980 "The Small Baths at Hadrian's Villa." *Journal of the Society of Architectural Historians* 39:5–27.

HAEFELI, MAX ERNST

Max Ernst Haefeli (1901–1976) studied architecture in Zurich with KARL MOSER. After working in Berlin and in Zurich with his father, he opened his own office in Zurich. In connection with an exhibition in 1928, he built model houses which manifested a new "liberated" form of dwelling. In 1937, he formed an office with WERNER MOSER and RUDOLF STEIGER, in which each of them also worked independently. Haefeli had a great part in the building of the Cantonal Hospital in Zurich (1942–1951). His later works are marked by a cultivated empiricism.

MARTIN STEINMANN

WORKS

1925, Ritter House, Erlenbach, Switzerland. 1928,

Hadrian.
Temple of Venus and Rome
(Reconstruction).
Rome.
c.305

Model Houses; 1929–1932, Neubühl Estate (with CARL HUBACHER and Rudolf Steiger, Werner Moser and Emil Roth, PAUL ARTARIA and HANS SCHMIDT); Zurich. 1931–1932, Krollreuter House, Küsnacht, Switzerland. 1938–1939, Allenmoos Swimming Pool (with Moser); 1938–1939, Congress Building (with Moser and Steiger); Zurich. 1941, Heberlein House, Wattwil, Switzerland. 1942–1951, Cantonal Hospital (with Architektengemeinschaft für das Kontonsspital), Zurich. 1947–1948, Haefeli House, Herrliberg, Switzerland. 1948, Moos Swimming Pool (with Moser and Steiger), Schlieren, Switzerland. 1951–1953, Hohenbühl Apartment Buildings (with Moser and Steiger), Zurich. 1953–1954, Eternit Administration Building (with Moser), Niederurnen, Switzerland. 1956–1957, Farbhof Apartment Buildings (with Moser); 1960–1964, Palme Commercial Building (with Moser and Steiger); Zurich.

BIBLIOGRAPHY

VON MOOS, STANISLAUS, and STEINMANN, MARTIN (editors) 1980 "Haefeli, Moser, Steiger." *Archithese* 2:3–74.

HAESLER, OTTO

Born to a poor Munich house painter, Otto Haesler (1880–?) was never formally trained in architecture. Instead, he trained as a stonemason and then worked briefly for Ludwig Bernouilly and HERMANN BILLING. He received his first independent commissions in Celle, northeast of Hannover, and remained in Celle as municipal architect until 1934, when he was driven into hiding by Nazi persecution. In 1946, he moved to East Berlin, and resumed his practice in East Germany.

Haesler was one of the most innovative housing designers in Germany. He was one of the first to introduce flat-roofed cubic forms in housing, to include major community facilities in public housing developments, and to experiment with steel frame construction in mass housing. He was also one of the first to turn to *Zeilenbau*, the arrangement of housing in carefully regulated north-south rows in order to obtain maximum light and air for each apartment. Although Haesler collaborated with Karl Völker, LEBERECHT MIGGE, and WALTER GROPIUS and although he was a member of the Executive Council of the German Werkbund, he nevertheless led an isolated existence in Celle in the 1920s, and his work was not as well-known as that of the other leaders of the modern movement in Germany.

BARBARA MILLER LANE

WORKS

1906–1914, Farm Buildings and Rural Schools, near Celle, Germany. 1906–1914, Houses; 1920–1924, Siedlung Maria Glück (miners' housing; with Karl Völker); 1924, Siedlung Italienischer Garten (with Völker); 1924–1926, Siedlung Georgsgarten (with Leberecht Migge); Celle, Germany. 1928–1929, Friedrich-Ebert-Ring Siedlung, Rathenow, Germany. 1929, Kurzag Offices, Braunschweig, Germany. 1929, Siedlung Dammerstock (with Völker and Walter Gropius), Karlsruhe, Germany. 1929, Volksschule (with Rektorhaus); 1929, Waach Housing Group; Celle, Germany. 1929–1931, Siedlung Rothenburg, Kassel, Germany. 1930, Houses, Celle, Germany. 1930, Youth Hostel, Müden near Celle, Germany. 1930–1931, Home for the Aged (with Völker); 1930–1931, Siedlung Blumenlägerfeld; Celle, Germany. 1931, Houses, Misburg, Germany. 1946–19?, Rathenow (reconstruction of old town with Völker), Germany.

BIBLIOGRAPHY

HAESLER, OTTO 1929 "Volksschule in Celle. 6 Abbildungen." *Wasmuths Monatshefte für Baukunst und Städtebau* 12:168–170.
HAESLER, OTTO 1930a "A German Public School at Celle." *American Architect* 138, no. 2586:24–27.
HAESLER, OTTO 1930b *Zum Problem des Wohnungsbaues.* Berlin: Reckendorf.
HAESLER, OTTO 1957 *Mein Lebenswerk als Architekt.* Berlin: Henschelverlag.
HAESLER, OTTO 1960 "Die gute Wohnung für alle." *Deutsche Architektur* 9, no. 7:393.
HAESLER, OTTO, and VÖLKER, KARL 1931 "Haus auf der Bauausstellung Berlin 1931. 3 Abbildungen." *Wasmuths Monatshefte für Baukunst und Städtebau* 15:242–243.
LANE, BARBARA MILLER 1968 *Architecture and Politics in Germany: 1918–1945.* Cambridge, Mass.: Harvard University Press.

HAGEN, G. B.

Gustav Bartholin Hagen (1873–1941) entered the Royal Academy in Copenhagen in 1897. He studied under HACK KAMPMANN and MARTIN NYROP and graduated in 1906. Hagen made the transition from National Romanticism, Old English inspirations, and neoclassicism to the Danish "functional tradition." His elaborate planning and fertile fantasy made him a sure winner in competitions. For the Halsskov School, designed in neoclassic revival, he introduced the glass-covered central hall as multipurpose room, which idea he developed further for the Øregård School, where the interior was almost free from decoration. In the Dyssegård School, he was a functionalist. From 1937, he was in partnership with his son, Ole Hagen.

LISBET BALSLEV JØRGENSEN

WORKS

1909–1913, Electricity Services Office (with Rolf

Schroeder), Copenhagen. 1913, Savings Bank, Køge, Denmark. 1921, Halsskov School, Korsør, Denmark. 1922–1924, Øregård School (with Edvard Thomsen); 1929–1930, Skovshoved School (with Alfred Brandt); 1929–1933, Dyssegård School; Copenhagen.

BIBLIOGRAPHY

JØRGENSEN, LISBET BALSLEV 1980 Pages, 140, 141 in *Danmarks arkitektur, Magtens bolig*. Copenhagen: Gyldendal.

HAGUE, THOMAS

The career of Thomas Hague which flourished from 1840–c.1855 is obscure. H. R. Hitchcock noted his early use of minimally clad, cast-iron structural members in a warehouse (c.1855) at Finch Lane, London. Another warehouse (1852) shows the same pioneering use of large windows on two floors visually united by a setback horizontal spandrel. Hague was a Fellow of the Royal Institute of British Architects (1840–1852).

JILL LEVER

WORKS

*1852, Warehouse, 31–33 Bush Lane; c.1855, Warehouse, 22 Finch Lane; London.

HAIGHT, CHARLES C.

Much of the work of Charles Coolidge Haight (1841–1917) was an unpretentious variation of Victorian Gothic. Born in New York City, Haight was to obtain commissions through his father's association with Trinity Church and his Episcopalian associates throughout his architectural career.

Haight grew up in New York City and began to study law at Columbia College after he received his bachelor's degree there in 1861. In 1862, he enlisted in the Union Army. Haight attained the rank of captain before sustaining a severe wound in the Battle of the Wilderness. Following his release from the army, Haight spent time in the architectural office of a friend from the Seventh Regiment, Emlyn T. Littel, before opening his own architectural office in 1867. Haight, Littel, RICHARD UPJOHN, and his son, RICHARD M. UPJOHN, HENRY M. CONGDON, and Henry Hudson Holly all were located in the old Trinity Building in New York City which had been designed by the senior Upjohn.

Haight's early work, largely undocumented, consisted of country churches and country houses in Victorian Gothic and English Tudor. The churches, such as Saint Luke's (1868–1877) in Portland, Maine, whose final version was much changed from the original plan for financial reasons, show the influence of Richard Upjohn. During the 1870s, Haight was appointed architect for the Trinity Corporation, in which capacity he designed a number of warehouses and tenements in New York.

Although Haight's work encompassed a full range of building types, his most important work is in Collegiate Gothic. Anticipating the popularity of Collegiate Gothic in the 1890s, Haight designed several buildings for Columbia College's now demolished mid-town campus in New York between 1874 and 1884. The most notable of these was Hamilton Hall with its double-gabled ends which did not match because one of the gables expressed an interior staircase. The building made an excellent transition between busy Madison Avenue and the quiet interior of the college quadrangle. With the commission for the General Theological Seminary, New York, Haight was able to plan a whole complex in the English Collegiate Gothic mode. The buildings of the seminary, begun in 1883 with Sherred Hall, are arranged in a U-shape around a double quadrangle, creating a cloistered effect, with the chapel as the central building.

In a departure from the style of his earlier buildings, Haight's 1887 New York Cancer Hospital resembles a French château. Since it was believed that square corners harbored more germs, the wards were built in three large round towers. Later, two more circular towers and a chapel were added. The rough stone façade of the 1890 H. O. Havemeyer House, also in New York City, suggests Richardsonian (see H. H. RICHARDSON) Romanesque.

Haight's 1894 Collegiate Gothic Vanderbilt Dormitory in New Haven, Connecticut, was the first of several buildings which Haight executed for Yale University. The U-shaped dormitory enclosed a quadrangle and moderated effectively between two disparate neighboring buildings. Shortly after the turn of the century, Haight formed an association with Alfred M. Githens, who collaborated on later buildings at Yale, such as Leet-Oliver Hall (1908).

Although Haight never lost his preference for Victorian Gothic architecture, his work remained restrained and unpretentious. Frequently dealing with inexpensive building materials, he kept his designs uncomplicated, allowing the exterior to reflect the usage of the interior. His brick 105th National Guard Artillery Armory, in the Bronx, New York (1910), is a late example which embodies these qualities.

CAROLINE M. MACK

WORKS

1868–1877, Saint Luke's Cathedral, Portland, Maine. *1880, Hamilton Hall, Columbia College; 1880–?, General Theological Seminary (partially demolished); 1883, Sherred Hall, General Theological Seminary; 1887, Downtown Association Building; 1887, New York Cancer Hospital; *1890, H. O. Havemeyer Residence; *1894, Lawyer's Title Insurance Co.; New York. 1894, Vanderbilt Dormitory; 1895, Phelps Hall and Archway; 1908, Leet-Oliver Hall; Yale University, New Haven. 1910, 105th National Guard Artillery Armory, Bronx, N.Y.

BIBLIOGRAPHY

SCHUYLER, MONTGOMERY 1899 "A Review of the Work of Chas. C. Haight." *Supplement to the Architectural Record,* July.

SCHUYLER, MONTGOMERY 1909 "The Architecture of American Colleges—Yale." *Architectural Record* 26:393–416.

ḤĀJJĪ B. AL-ḤUSAYN AL-DĀMAGHĀNĪ

See MUḤAMMAD B. AL-ḤUSAYN, and ḤĀJJĪ B. AL-ḤUSAYN AL-DĀMGHĀNĪ.

HAKEWILL FAMILY

The Hakewill brothers, Henry (1771–1830), architect, James (1778–1843), architect and antiquarian, and John (fl.1806–1810), architect, were the sons of John (1742–1791), painter and decorator. Henry's two sons, John Henry (1811–1880) and Edward Charles (1812–1872), both practiced as architects. James had four sons of whom the eldest, Arthur William (1808–1856), was an architect.

JILL LEVER

WORKS

1804, Cave Castle, Yorkshire, England. 1809–1815, 1818–1821, Rugby School (buildings and chapel), Warwickshire, England. 1810–1815, Wolverton Church, Buckinghamshire, England. 1822–1824, The Middle Temple (parliament chambers), London. 1823–1825, Stisted Hall, Essex, England. 1824–1827, Saint Peter's Church, Eaton Square, London. c.1825, Shrubland Hall, Leamington Priors, Warwickshire, England.

HALFPENNY, WILLIAM

William Halfpenny (?–1755) is described by BATTY LANGLEY in his *Ancient Masonry* (1736) as "Mr William Halfpenny, alias Hoare, lately of Richmond in Surry, carpenter." As an architect, Halfpenny is of little consequence, and as such would have found no fame. He may have come from Yorkshire, as he submitted designs in 1723 for Holy Trinity Church, Leeds. In 1726, he submitted designs for a timber bridge across the Thames at Fulham. He soon moved to Bristol, where he published *Perspective Made Easy* (1731), and from where he must have designed the Horse Barracks at Hillsborough, County Down, Ireland, in 1732. The conventionality of his practice is typified by Cooper's Hall, Bristol (1743), and the Redland Chapel, Bristol (c.1740–1743). He never conformed to the Palladian idiom and, in fact, many of his designs are marked by a feeling for the baroque. There is some evidence in his *A New and Compleat System of Architecture* (1749) that he was acquainted with the founder of Irish neo-Palladianism, Sir EDWARD LOVETT PEARCE, a relation of Sir JOHN VANBRUGH, and these twin experiences flavor Halfpenny's work. He entered the field of architectural publishing as a compiler of pattern books with *Practical Architecture* (1724), a cheaply produced, clearly expounded guide to the orders and to such elements as doors and windows. By these means, builders and architects everywhere could find the exact proportions for elements in a "correct" taste, in the case of this book taken from COLEN CAMPBELL's *Vitruvius Britannicus* (1715 and 1717), as well as from existing buildings by, or believed to be by, INIGO JONES. From 1725, with *The Art of Sound Building,* to 1754, with *Improvements in Architecture and Carpentry,* Halfpenny cap-

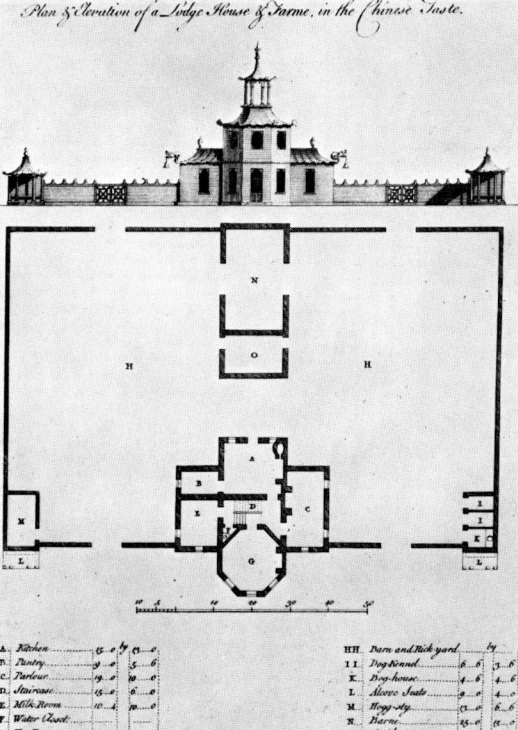

Halfpenny.
Plan for a Chinese
Farmhouse.
From Chinese and Gothic Architecture.
1752

tured, between himself and Langley, the pattern book market. A survey of the contents of Halfpenny's books demonstrates that he is a propagandist for British, that is, national, architecture, espousing the cause of Inigo Jones rather than a "foreigner" like ANDREA PALLADIO. It can be stated that the look of Georgian architecture in the cathedral and market towns of Britain owed a huge debt to this pattern book boom, one that was unique. Halfpenny did not confine himself to the orders or elements, but also provided models for farmhouses (*Twelve Beautiful Designs for Farm Houses* [1750]), for exotic architecture (*Rural Architecture in the Gothic Taste* [1752] and *Rural Architecture in the Chinese Taste* [1750-1752]). Halfpenny's models were never chic or fashionable; indeed, they were old-fashioned, and they never achieved the academic correctness of Colen Campbell's work or the suavity of LORD BURLINGTON's.

JOHN HARRIS

WORKS

c.1740-1743, Redland Chapel; 1743, Cooper's Hall; Bristol, England.

BIBLIOGRAPHY

HALFPENNY, WILLIAM (1724)1968 *Practical Architecture.* Reprint of 1730 ed. New York: Blom.

HALFPENNY, WILLIAM (1725)1968 *The Art of Sound Building.* Reprint. New York: Blom.

HALFPENNY, WILLIAM [Michael Hoare] (1728*a*)1747 *The Builders Pocket Companion.* 3d ed. London: R. Ware.

HALFPENNY, WILLIAM (1728*b*)1968 *Magnum in Parvo, Or, The Marrow of Architecture.* Reprint of 1928 ed. New York: Blom.

HALFPENNY, WILLIAM 1731 *Perspective Made Easy.* London: John Oswald.

HALFPENNY, WILLIAM 1748 *Arithmetick and Measurement.* London: R. Ware.

HALFPENNY, WILLIAM 1749 *A New and Compleat System of Architecture.* London: Brindley.

HALFPENNY, WILLIAM (1750*a*)1774 *Twelve Beautiful Designs for Farm Houses.* 3d ed. London: Sayer.

HALFPENNY, WILLIAM 1750*b* *Twenty New Designs of Chinese Lattice.* London: Sayer.

HALFPENNY, WILLIAM (1750-1752)1968 *Rural Architecture in the Chinese Taste.* Reprint. New York: Blom.

HALFPENNY, WILLIAM 1751 *Andrea Palladio's First Book of Architecture.* London.

HALFPENNY, WILLIAM (1752*a*)1968 *Chinese and Gothic Architecture Properly Ornamented.* Reprint. New York: Blom.

HALFPENNY, WILLIAM 1752*b* *Geometry Theoretical and Practical.* London: Sayer.

HALFPENNY, WILLIAM 1752*c* *Rural Architecture in the Gothic Taste.* London: Sayer.

HALFPENNY, WILLIAM 1752*d* *Useful Architecture in Twenty-One New Designs for Erecting Parsonage-Houses, Farm-Houses, and Inns.* London: Sayer.

HALFPENNY, WILLIAM 1753 *The Country Gentleman's Pocket Companion.* London: Sayer.

HALFPENNY, WILLIAM 1754 *Improvements in Architecture and Carpentry.* London.

HALFPENNY, WILLIAM; MORRIS, ROBERT; AND LIGHTOLER, TIMOTHY 1757 *The Modern Builder's Assistant.* London: Sayer.

HALLET, ETIENNE SULPICE

Trained in France, Etienne Sulpice Hallet (c.1760-1825) settled in New York (where he was called Stephen Hallet) about 1786. He moved to Philadelphia by 1790, and in 1792 he entered the Capitol competition. Though all initial submissions were rejected, Hallet was paid to develop his further, and three additional designs were submitted; a fourth was completed after WILLIAM THORNTON's design was accepted. Hallet was never the less awarded the same prize as Thornton and in September 1793, he was hired to develop workable plans and supervise construction; in November 1794 he was dismissed. He left Washington in August 1796, was in Havana in 1800, and in New York City in 1812, where he died.

Although Hallet seems to have built nothing, his competition drawings in French eighteenth-century classical style, certainly influenced Thornton's capitol designs.

DANIEL D. REIFF

BIBLIOGRAPHY

BENNETT, WELLS 1916 "Stephen Hallet and His Designs for the National Capitol, 1791-94." *Journal of the American Institute of Architects* 4:290-295; 324-330; 376-383; 411-418.

BUTLER, JEANNE FOLLEY 1976 "Competition 1792: Designing a Nation's Capitol." *Capitol Studies* 4:31-36.

KIMBALL, FISKE 1932 "Etienne Sulpice Hallet." Volume 8, pages 152-154 in *Dictionary of American Biography.* New York: Scribner.

KIMBALL, FISKE, and BENNETT, WELLS 1923 "William Thornton and the Design of the United States Capitol." *Art Studies* 1:76-92.

PADOVER, SAUL K. (editor) 1946 *Thomas Jefferson and the National Capitol.* Washington: U.S. Government Printing Office.

HALPRIN, LAWRENCE

Born in New York, Lawrence Halprin (1916-) studied plant science at Cornell University and the

University of Wisconsin and landscape architecture at Harvard University under WALTER GROPIUS, MARCEL BREUER, and Christopher Tunnard. Following service in the U.S. Navy and a four-year associateship with THOMAS D. CHURCH, Halprin opened his own office in San Francisco in 1949. In subsequent years, through practice, writing, and teaching, he became a leading figure in the Bay Area School of Landscape Architecture, acquiring an international reputation.

Halprin's philosophy and approach to landscape design includes an interest in interpersonal relations, theater, and dance, developed through contact with the work of his wife, Anna Halprin, choreographer and dancer. His book, *RSVP Cycles* (1970), explores the creative process and the role of group participation in design. A second important influence on his work is his respect for the forms of nature, which represent process. The two can be seen integrated in the Lovejoy Fountain (Portland, Oregon; 1961) and the Auditorium Forecourt Plaza (Portland, Oregon; 1968) where the design forms are based on observation of nature but are not fulfilled until occupied by people.

Halprin's completed professional work ranges from ecological land use planning to private gardens, but perhaps his most important contribution is his innovative urban renewal and design.

MICHAEL LAURIE

WORKS

1955, Old Orchard Shopping Center, Skokie, Ill. 1957, Sproul Plaza and Student Union, University of California, Berkeley. 1961, Lovejoy Plaza, Portland, Ore. 1962, Ghiradelli Square, San Francisco. 1962, Nicollet Mall, Minneapolis, Minn. 1966, Ida Crown Museum Garden, Jerusalem. 1968, Auditorium Forecourt Plaza, Portland, Ore. 1968, Sea Ranch, Mendocino County, California. 1969, Market Street, San Francisco. 1971, Israel National Park, Mount Carmel, Jerusalem. 1976, Freeway Park, Seattle, Wash. 1976, Transit Mall, Portland, Ore. 1978, Levi Strauss Headquarters, San Francisco.

BIBLIOGRAPHY

HALPRIN, LAWRENCE (1963)1972 *Cities,* New York. Rev. ed. Cambridge, Mass.: M.I.T. Press.
HALPRIN, LAWRENCE 1968 *New York, New York.* New York: The author.
HALPRIN, LAWRENCE 1970 *RSVP Cycles: Creative Processes in the Human Environment.* New York: Braziller.
HALPRIN, LAWRENCE 1972 *Notebooks of Lawrence Halprin: 1959–1971.* Cambridge, Mass.: M.I.T. Press.
LAURIE, MICHAEL 1971 "Lawrence Halprin: A Profile." *Landscape Design* Feb.: 12–13.
LINDGREN, NILO 1974a "A Radical Experiment in Reorganization." *Landscape Architecture* 64, no. 3:133–139.
LINDGREN, NILO "Halprin Revisited in 1973: Still

Changing to Stay Alive." *Landscape Architecture* 64, no. 3:140–147.
Process Architecture 1978 Feb., no. 4:special issue.

HAMILTON, ANDREW

In 1732, Andrew Hamilton (c.1676–1741), eminent Philadelphia lawyer, presented to the Pennsylvania Assembly a plan, elevation, and site proposal for the Pennsylvania State House (now Independence Hall), and subsequently closely supervised its construction. Traditionally, therefore, Hamilton has been called its architect, though Edmund Woolley, a master carpenter, prepared the working drawings.

GWEN W. STEEGE

WORKS

1732–1740, Pennsylvania State House (now Independence Hall), Philadelphia.

BIBLIOGRAPHY

PETERSON, CHARLES E. 1952 "American Notes: Early Architects of Independence Hall." *Journal of the Society of Architectural Historians* 11:23–26.
RILEY, EDWARD 1953 "The Independence Hall Group." *Transactions of the American Philosophical Society* 43, part 1:7–42.

HAMILTON, DAVID

David Hamilton (1768–1843) practiced in Glasgow, Scotland, from 1800, first in the late Adam manner with French and Soanic details. By 1809 he was in Gothic and neo-Greek, moving into a strong Greco-Roman from 1822. With his son James he experimented resourcefully with Scots Jacobean and neo-Norman in the 1830s, and with Italian Baroque in the 1840s.

DAVID M. WALKER

WORKS

1802–1805, Hutcheson's Hospital; *1803–1805, Theatre Royal; Glasgow, Scotland. 1813, Erskine Church; 1815–1816, Town House, Port Glasgow; Renfrewshire, Scotland. 1820–1821, Castle Toward, Rothesay, Argyllshire, Scotland. *1822–1825, Hamilton Palace (new north front developed from a design by Francesco Saponieri), Lanarkshire, Scotland. 1827–1829, The Royal Exchange (now Stirling's Library), Glasgow, Scotland. 1831–1834, Dunlop House, Ayrshire, Scotland. *1841, Glasgow and Ship (later Union) Bank, Ingram Street, Scotland.

BIBLIOGRAPHY

GILDARD, THOMAS 1895 *An Old Glasgow Architect on*

some Older Ones in Transactions of the Philosophical Society of Glasgow. Glasgow, Scotland: The Society.

GOMME, ANDOR, and WALKER, DAVID 1968 Architecture of Glasgow. London: Lund Humphries.

HAMILTON, THOMAS

A leading Scottish architect of the early nineteenth century working mainly in the classical style, Thomas Hamilton (1784–1858) was born in Glasgow. He was educated at Edinburgh High School in the same class as WILLIAM BURN. Hamilton worked in the family business as a mason-carpenter for sixteen years. He entered several architectural competitions from 1815, winning the Robert Burns Memorial, Alloway (1818), and a gold medal at the Paris International Exhibition (1855). He was a founder member of the Royal Scottish Academy. He is buried in the Calton Cemetery close to his masterpiece, the Royal High School.

BRUCE WALKER

WORKS

1818–1823, Robert Burns Monument, Alloway, Ayr, Scotland. 1825–1829, Royal High School, Calton Hill; (A)1827–1830, Arthur Lodge (formerly Salisbury Cottage), Dalkeith Road; Edinburgh. 1827–1830, Assembly Rooms and Steeple, Ayr, Scotland. 1827–1831, King's Bridge; 1827–1834, George IV Bridge; 1830–1832, Robert Burns Monument, Calton Hill; 1831–1833, Dean Orphanage, Belford Road; *1834, Earl Gray Pavilion, Royal High School Playground; 1844–1846, Royal College of Physicians, Queen Street; Edinburgh.

BIBLIOGRAPHY

BURN, WILLIAM, and HAMILTON, THOMAS 1824 A Report Relative to Proposed Approaches from the South and West of the Old Town of Edinburgh. Edinburgh.

FISHER, IAN 1965 "Thomas Hamilton of Edinburgh: Architect and Town Planner (1784–1858)." Unpublished thesis, Christ Church, Oxford.

HAMILTON, THOMAS 1816 Observations Explanatory of the Two Designs for Completing the College of Edinburgh. Edinburgh.

HAMILTON, THOMAS 1817 "Proposal for Forming a Communication Between the North and South Sides of the City of Edinburgh, by Means of a Bridge Entering the Lawn Market, Nearly Opposite Bank Street. Illustrated by a Plan." Scots Magazine Mar:163–165.

HAMILTON, THOMAS 1819 Attestations Referred to in Letter to the Lord Provost of Edinburgh from Thomas Hamilton Junior, Relative to His Qualifications for Filling the Office of Superintendent of Public Works in the City of Edinburgh. Edinburgh.

HAMILTON, THOMAS 1830 A Report Relative to the Proposed Improvements on the Earthen Mound. Edinburgh.

HAMILTON, THOMAS 1850 A Letter to Lord John Russell on the Present Crisis Relative to the Fine Arts in Scotland, with Plans and Perspective Views of the Proposed Galleries on the Mound. Edinburgh.

HUGHES, T. HAROLD 1926 "Great Scottish Architects of the Past. No. 7: Thomas Hamilton." Quarterly Illustrated of the Royal Incorporation of Architects in Scotland 20:97–115.

YOUNGSON, A. J. 1966 The Making of Classical Edinburgh: 1750–1840. Edinburgh University Press.

HAMLIN, A. D. F.

Born in Istanbul, Turkey, of American parents, Alfred Dwight Foster Hamlin (1855–1926) graduated from Amherst College in 1875, studied architecture at the Massachusetts Institute of Technology, and attended the Ecole des Beaux-Arts (1879–1881) as a student in JULIEN GUADET's atelier. Returning to the United States, Hamlin worked briefly for McKIM, MEAD, AND WHITE. Then, in 1883, he became WILLIAM ROBERT WARE's assistant at the new architecture department of Columbia College's School of Mines, where he taught until his death. Following Ware's retirement in 1903, he was director of the architecture program. While he designed several buildings with C. P. Warren for Robert College in Istanbul (1909–1912), he is best known as a scholar and teacher. His publications include A Textbook on the History of Architecture (1928). Active in civic improvement efforts in New York City, Hamlin was architectural adviser for several public buildings.

DENNIS McFADDEN

WORKS

1896, Blair Academy, Blairstown, N.J. 1909–1912, Robert College, Istanbul, Turkey (with C. P. Warren).

BIBLIOGRAPHY

HAMLIN, A. D. F. (1916)1973 A History of Ornament. 2 vols. Reprint. New York: Cooper Square.

HAMLIN, A. D. F. (1928)1954 A Textbook on the History of Architecture. Rev. ed. New York: Longmans.

ROHDENBURG, THEODOR K. 1954 A History of the School of Architecture Columbia University. New York: Columbia University Press.

HAMLIN, TALBOT F.

Talbot Faulkner Hamlin (1889–1956), born in New York City, graduated from Amherst College in 1910 and in 1914 received a bachelor of architecture degree from Columbia University. Hamlin was then employed as a draftsman by the firm of Dana and Murphy In 1920 he was made a partner and the firm became Murphy, McGill, and Hamlin. Hamlin opened his own office in 1930 and practiced until 1934. Like his father A. D. F. HAMLIN, he was an author and educator as well as an architect. He first taught in the Columbia University Extension Program in 1916. He joined Columbia's regular faculty in 1926 and taught there until 1954. From 1934 to 1945 he was librarian of the Avery Architectural Library. Hamlin wrote numerous articles, reviews, and books including *Greek Revival Architecture in America* (1944) and *Benjamin Henry Latrobe* (1955), for which he was awarded the Pulitzer Prize.

DENNIS McFADDEN

WORKS

1920?, Ginling College, Nanking, China. 1925?, Brescia Hall, College of New Rochelle, N.Y.

BIBLIOGRAPHY

HAMLIN, TALBOT F. (1944)1964 *Greek Revival Architecture in America.* Reprint. New York: Dover.
HAMLIN, TALBOT F. (editor) 1952 *Forms and Functions of Twentieth-century Architecture.* 4 vols. New York: Columbia University Press.
HAMLIN, TALBOT F. 1955 *Benjamin Henry Latrobe.* New York: Oxford University Press.
"Hamlin, Talbot (Faulkner)." 1954 Volume 15, pages 318–319 in Marjorie Dent Caridee (editor), *Current Biography.* New York: H. W. Wilson.

HANKAR, PAUL

Paul Hankar (1859–1901) was one of the most brilliant creators of Belgian Art Nouveau. His work differs from that of VICTOR HORTA and others through its rationalism shaped by the French Gothic Revival and the English Domestic Revival.

Son of a stonecutter, Hankar was born in Frameries, Hainaut, Belgium. He received a traditional education, first learning the art of stonecutting and later moving to Brussels to continue his training with an ornamental sculptor. At age twenty he entered the studio of an architect to study architecture. Apprentice, draftsman, and eventually chief of the atelier, he remained for fifteen years with his master, HENRI BEYAERT, the great creator of Flemish historicism in Belgium.

Hankar's independent career was short, lasting only seven years, but it was exceptionally concentrated. He realized about ten townhouses in the residential quarters of Brussels, two large villas, and several interior decorations for stores. For these commissions he also designed the furnishings. In large part destroyed by modern speculative building, his oeuvre is now represented primarily by drawings and furniture dispersed in museums,

revealing an innovative artist ranking with Horta, HENRY VAN DE VELDE, and GUSTAVE SERRURIER-BOVY in Belgium, and HECTOR GUIMARD and HENRI SAUVAGE in France.

Fascinated by the rationalism of EUGÈNE EMMANUEL VIOLLET-LE-DUC, a friend of his master Beyaert, he denied himself the graphic and sculptural exuberances of his contemporaries. The only decoration of his glass and brick façades were wooden tracery of Japanese inspiration and stylized forms superbly executed in wrought iron. This restrained but perfectly mastered art had a decisive influence on OTTO WAGNER, who visited Hankar's installations for the Museum of the Congo in Tervueren in 1897, and on CHARLES RENNIE MACKINTOSH. Although he died young, by the end of the nineteenth century Hankar had already opened the way for the stripped aesthetic of modernism through his refusal to compromise his ideals and through the elegant restraint of his style.

FRANÇOIS LOYER
*Translated from French by
Richard Cleary*

WORKS

1888, Hotel Zegers-Regnard; 1888–1891, Tomb of Charles Rogier; 1893, Hotel Paul Hankar; *1894–1895, Zegers-Regnard Hotel and House; *1896, Clasens Store; Brussels. 1896–1897, Museum of the Congo (interior), Tervueren, Belgium. 1896–1899, Buysse Cottage, Wondelgem, Belgium. 1897, Hotel Ciamberlani; 1897–1898, Hotel Janssens; *1897–1898, Hotel Renkin; *1899–1900, Chocolate Store Senez-Sturbelle; Brussels. 1900, Chocolate Store Senez, Antwerp, Belgium.

BIBLIOGRAPHY

BORSI, FRANCO, and WIESER, HANS 1971 *Bruxelles: Capitale de l'Art Nouveau.* Brussels: Vokaer.
CONRARDY, CHARLES, and THIBAUT, RAYMOND 1923 "Paul Hankar (1859–1901)." *La Cité* 4, no.2:21–25; no. 3:37–42.
DE MAEYER, CHARLES 1963 *Paul Hankar.* Brussels: Meddens.
MAUS, OCTAVE 1900 "Habitations modernes. M. Paul Hankar." *L'Art Moderne* July:229–231.
MAUS, OCTAVE, and SOULIER, GUSTAVE 1897 "L'Art décoratif en Belgique. MM. Paul Hankar et Adolphe Crespin." *Art et Décoration* Sept.:89–96.

HANSEN, CHRISTIAN FREDERIK

Christian Frederik Hansen, (1746–1845) ranks as the most important Danish architect of his age. He created a usable formula of romantic classicism, which for many generations was to dominate Danish architecture and which to some extent had significance to architecture in the rest of Europe as well. Born in Copenhagen, he was admitted to the Royal Academy of Fine Arts at the age of ten and later on trained by Caspar Frederik Harsdorff. The French character of Harsdorff's classicism inevitably left its marks on the young architect, soon employed by Harsdorff as his assistant at the building of Frederik V's chapel at Roskilde Cathedral.

In 1779, Hansen won the Gold Medal of the Academy. In 1782, he obtained the scholarship connected to the prize and left his native town for further studies abroad, which exerted a distinct influence on his artistic development. Particularly, his long stay in Italy seemed to have left indelible impressions of the classical and Renaissance monuments. In Rome, he probably got an excellent view of international currents in contemporary architecture.

In 1784, he was compelled to break off the stay in Rome and return to Denmark in order to take up the post as surveyor in Holstein, a post he held for more than twenty years. His official activities in these years never included substantial enterprises, except for the Orphanage at Altona (1792–1794), which offered him an occasion to design a large number of private buildings. He was responsible for the long row of fashionable buildings on the Altona Pall-Maille (1801–1805) as well as for a large number of country houses built for the rich Hamburg merchants in the little towns on the bank of the Elbe such as Ottense, Othmarschen, Nienstedten, and Blankenese. His works in those years show a broad scope of stylistic ideas and show above all his profound acquaintance with new French theories modified by the classic models, in particular those of ANDREA PALLADIO. He seems to have experimented with a number of architectural motifs in a rather undogmatic and romantic treatment of borrowed and original forms. His first building, Cesar Godeffroy's country house at Nienstedten (1789–1792), is more traditional, continuing motifs and designs by Harsdorff, but already the general character shows the impact of Palladian architecture. This becomes even more evident in the country house of Peter Godeffroy at Blankenese (1790–1796), where the Harsdorff motifs are replaced by strong impressions of modern French theories. The country house of Thornton has a rather oblong plan, in all probability due to the special wishes of the owner, as Hansen at the time tended to blocklike solutions.

During the years as surveyor in Altona, he demonstrated his undisputed gifts as architect, but it probably was his administrative ability that finally led him to the more significant sphere of action in the capital. A skillful architect was strongly needed in Copenhagen. Within relatively few years, a large number of the most outstanding monumental buildings of the Danish capital were to be re-erected. In 1794, the royal palace Christiansborg was destroyed by fire; in 1795, a considerable part of the city, including several distinguished public buildings, was ravaged by fire; and in 1807, another part of the city was destroyed by the English bombardment. After Harsdorff died in 1799, Hansen was entrusted with the planning of the rebuilding of the royal palace, the combined city hall and law courts, and later also the cathedral and the gymnasium. In 1808, Hansen was also appointed director of buildings with extensive authority in all building matters. That same year, he was also appointed professor at the Royal Academy of Fine Arts, where his influence was equally unchallenged. The somewhat sturdy and conservative influence he exercised on Danish architecture was furthermore magnified by a long career; he held both posts until he was eighty-eight years old.

It was his lot to transform the baroque appearance of medieval Copenhagen into a classical one, a project which succeeded to such a degree that the phrase "the Athens of the North" commonly was attached to the city. Taking over the great building enterprises in Copenhagen, he started a new, significant phase in his work. Common for most of his Copenhagen buildings were the restricted conditions of work. The planning usually was bound by existing foundations and walls or extremely irregular plots as, for instance, for the city hall and law courts, a complex of buildings started in 1803 and finished in 1816. For the main façade toward the square, Hansen chose a somewhat enlarged replica of one of Palladio's villas, with a huge portico to dominate the square, but the masterly exploitation of the irregular plot and the elaborate handling of the buildings fully demonstrate his genuinely romantic attitude toward dramatic effects such as the two great arcades framing the little by-street Slutteristræde, with its somber entrance to the town prison. In 1803, he also began the re-erection of the huge royal palace, Christiansborg, inaugurated in 1828 but never fully completed, and finally destroyed by fire in 1884. The existing walls of the old rococo palace as well as the stories were to be reused. Hansen turned the former decorative elegance of the palace into a solemn and severe simplification stressing the block. The main façade was provided with an enormous portico; the western wing to the riding ground with the former tower was demolished and replaced with a lower, simple colonnade, in contrast to the preserved rococo buildings around the riding ground. The interiors showed the influence of French Empire decoration as well as that of the interior decoration of KARL FRIEDRICH SCHINKEL, probably due to Hansen's son-in-law, the German architect GUSTAV FRIEDRICH HETSCH, to whom part of the interiors must be ascribed. The only building preserved of Hansen's Christiansborg is the chapel (1810–1829), one of his most original and significant works. Here, too, he was dependent on existing walls, but he broke conclusively with the previous arrangement. In this building, the Roman influence is most clearly felt even though the interior bears a close relationship to Frederik V's chapel at Roskilde Cathedral by Harsdorff. The exterior is formed as a clear paraphrase on GIACOMO BAROZZI DA VIGNOLA's Sant' Andrea in Rome. In spite of its pure classicism, the whole building group of the palace is restrained by a sort of unacademic spirit with its strongest effect seen in oblique perspective from the newly formed square diagonally across the palace, where the chapel's clear-cut form dominates the stage.

Hansen designed several other churches, the most important one being the Cathedral of Copenhagen, Our Lady. This was originally a medieval church, but it was rebuilt in the eighteenth century and finally destroyed by English artillery in 1807. In this case, too, he was limited by the existing walls. Hansen re-erected the church in clear stereometric forms, dominated by the high, massive tower; a Doric portico was mounted on the main façade. The single-naved interior with coffered ceiling supported by colonnades depends essentially on French models. With the close proximity of the University of Copenhagen, also destroyed by the bombs of 1807, Hansen probably thought of rearranging the surroundings of the church as an academic-ecclesiastical forum, including the rather long square between the church and the university. In the years 1810–1816, he rebuilt the Metropolitanskolen, the old gymnasium, as the shorter wall in the square in a classicism corresponding to the church. The square was finally completed in 1836 with the main building of the university by Hansen's pupil, Peter Malling.

VILLADS VILLADSEN

WORKS

1789–1792, Cesar Godeffroy House, Nienstedten, Germany. 1790–1796, Peter Godeffroy House, Blankenese, Germany. 1792–1794, Orphanage, Altona, Germany. *1798, Manor House Perdol, Holstein, Germany. 1792–1803, City Hall, Oldesloe, Denmark. 1801–1805, Baurs House, 49 Pall Maille, Altona, Germany. 1802, Søholm House; 1803–1816, City Hall and Law Courts; *1803–1828, Christiansborg Palace (re-erected); 1810–1816, Gymnasium, Metropolitanskolen; 1810–1826, Our Lady Cathedral; 1810–1829, Chapel, Christiansborg Palace; Copenhagen. 1818–1820, Hospital, Schleswig, Germany. 1820–1823, Church, Hørsholm, Denmark. 1828–1833, Church, Husum, Germany. 1828–1834, Church, Neumünster, Germany.

BIBLIOGRAPHY

HANSEN, CHRISTIAN FREDERIK   (1825–c.1840)1921 *Sampling af forskjellige offertlige og private Bygninger.* Kjöberbaun, Denmark: Asmassen.

JACKSTEIN, WERNER   1937   *Landesbaumeister C. F. Hansen.* Neumünster, Germany.

LANGBERG, HARALD   1950   *Omkring C. F. Hansen.* Copenhagen: Prior.

LUND, HAKON   1975a   *Christiansborg Slot.* Copenhagen.

LUND, HAKON   1975b   *Nogle tegninger af C. F. Hanse.* Copenhagen: Kunstakademiets Arkitektskole.

LUND, HAKON, and KÜSTER, CHRISTIAN L.   1968 *Architekt C. F. Hansen: 1756–1845.* Hamburg, Germany: Altonaer Museum.

RUBOW, JORN   1935   *Artes* 3:127–165.

RUBOW, JORN   1936   *C. F. Hansens arkitektur.* Copenhagen: Gad.

HANSEN, HANS CHRISTIAN

Hans Christian Hansen (1803–1883) played a prominent role in Danish and Greek Revival architecture in the mid-eighteenth century. Born in Copenhagen, he attended the Royal Academy of Fine Arts, becoming an architect in 1826. The Academy and Danish architecture as a whole then was entirely dominated by the powerful character of CHRISTIAN FREDERIK HANSEN, whose romantic classicism was deeply rooted in the Italian renaissance of ANDREA PALLADIO as well as the theories and models of French revolutionary architects. For some time, Hansen worked for this influential architect. More important however was his close connection to GUSTAV FRIEDRICH HETSCH, an architect more familiar with contemporary German currents. In 1829, Hansen won the Gold Medal of the Academy, and 1831 he left Denmark with a scholarship for three years of further studies abroad. After a long stay in Munich, he went on to Rome, at that time the meeting place of the most outstanding younger Danish architects and artists. He stayed in Rome until 1833, determined to continue his studies in Greece, an attractive goal for his generation of architects, to whom the classical Greek forms had gained momentum. After the wars of freedom, the young nation moreover offered rather safe conditions for traveling, and Hansen was one of many who took the opportunity to go to Greece in order to study the classic architecture.

In Athens, he got in touch with the director of buildings, the Schinkel-trained (see KARL FRIEDRICH SCHINKEL) German architect Edouard Schaubert, who in 1834 was instrumental in obtaining Hansen's appointment as royal Greek architect. An immense rebuilding program was to be planned and trained architects were needed and sought for. Hansen stayed in Greece for about eighteen years active in building activities, archeological studies, and restorations as well as the teaching of a new generation of artisans and architects. He was soon involved in the newly started excavations at the Acropolis, which had been turned into a Turkish fortification during the war. Together with Schaubert and the Holsteiner Ludwig Ross, he reconstructed the Nike Apteros temple, demolished by the Turks and used as fortification material. Hansen continued excavations of painted fragments on the Acropolis, a valuable study which he, however, never accomplished and published. An extensive collection of measurements and sketches gives evidence of his profound knowledge of the classic monuments and shows that the archeological experience included the Greek Byzantine architecture as well, an interest he shared with his architect brother, THEOPHILUS HANSEN, who in 1838 also came to Athens.

In his building practice, Christian Hansen obtained a great number of private and public commissions, as for instance The Mint at the Klaftomonos Square in Athens (1834–1836), originally conceived as a theater. His principal work in Athens is the University (1839–1850) in Ionian style, influenced by Copenhagen classicism as well as Schinkel's classicism and the nearby classic monuments, but handled in an original and distinct idea around the Ionian templum in antis. He furthermore took part in the building of some churches, the Roman Catholic Saint Paul's in Piraeus (1838) and the Anglican Saint Paul's in Athens (1841). In 1850, he left Greece to build the arsenal and dockyards in Trieste for the Austrian Lloyds Steamship Company. These he formed as a group of somewhat severe buildings in the widespread *Rundbogenstil* of the time.

His many prominent buildings abroad had given him a good reputation in his own country, and having concluded the building in Trieste, he in 1856 was appointed professor at the Royal Academy of Fine Arts in Copenhagen, a post he held until 1881. The great things expected from him were, however, never quite fulfilled. The buildings begun shortly after his return to Copenhagen are his best. The City Hospital (1856–1863), a large coherent building, was spacious and was conceived such that it was able to serve the increasing demands of later times. Influenced by his own experience and by his brother's Vienna buildings, he chose an elaborate Byzantine style for the hospital wth strips of red and yellow bricks and distinct Byzantine motifs, which had a certain style-forming effect on Danish architecture. The monotony of the long main façade is broken up by a telling central part explicitly formed as a Greek-cross church. For the University of Copenhagen, he designed a great number of buildings of which the Observatory (1859–1861) and the Zoological Museum (1863–1870) are the most outstanding. As to the museum, he did not fully succeed in adjusting the building to its surroundings. Certainly, it was without the grandeur seen in his earlier buildings. The same could be said about some of his later works such as the church in Holbaek (1869–1872), Saint Joseph's Hospital in Copenhagen (1873–1875), and the Christiansdal Convent (1870–1871). In his architectural practice, he industriously took part in many different historical currents, whereas as a teacher he firmly maintained the classic Greek architecture as the ideal.

VILLADS VILLADSEN

WORKS

1834–1836, Mint, Athens. 1838, Saint Paul's, Piraeus, Greece. 1839–1850, University of Athens. 1841, Anglican Church (with Charles R. Cockerell and others), Athens. 1852–1856, Austrian Lloyd Steamship Company Arsenal, Trieste, Italy. 1856–1863, City Hospital; 1859–1861, Observatory; 1863–1870, Zoological Museum; Copenhagen. 1869–1872, Church, Holbaek, Denmark. 1870–1871, Christiansdal Convent, Denmark. 1873–1875, Saint Josef's Hospital, Copenhagen.

BIBLIOGRAPHY

ÅKERSTROM-HOUGEN, G. 1972 "Den nyklassiska Arkitekturen i Grekland." *Konsthistorisk Tidskrift* 1972:16–42.
HAUGSTED, IDA 1980 "The Architect Christian Hansen and the Greek Neo-classicism." *Scandinavian Studies in Modern Greek* 1980:63–91.
LINDHØLM, SVEN 1955 "Brodrene Christian og Theophilus Hansens vaerker i Athen." *Arkitekten Manedshaefte* 57, nos. 4–5:69–74.
MPIRÊS, KŌSTOS E. 1966 *Ai Athēnai apo tou 19ou eis ton 20oun aiona.* Athens.
STRØMSTAD, P. 1963 "Kommunehospitalets opførelse." Pages 22–38 in *Københavns hospitalsvæsen 1863–1963.* Copenhagen.
VILLADSEN, VILLADS 1978 "Studien über den byzantinischen Einfluss auf die europäische Architektur des 19. Jahrhunderts." *Hafnia* 1978:43–77.
VILLADSEN, VILLADS "Københavns Universitets bygninger." Volume 4, pages 240–260 in Sv. Ellehøj and L. Grane (editors), *Københavns Universitet.* Copenhagen.

HANSEN, THEOPHILUS

Theophilus Hansen (1813–1891) is generally considered the last great academic classicist in European architecture. Through his many works and his various original solutions to traditional models, he exerted a great influence on the fashionable and monumental buildings in several large cities of Europe.

Born in Copenhagen, he grew up in the lower stratum of the Biedermeier bourgeoisie. The father, an immigrated Norwegian, died when Theophilus was only eleven, but endowed with obvious talents for drawing, he attended the Royal Academy of Fine Arts a few years later to become an architect, probably inspired by his architect brother HANS CHRISTIAN HANSEN. The Royal Academy and Danish architecture in general had for some decades been dominated by the unyielding personality of CHRISTIAN FREDERIK HANSEN (not related to the brothers) and his somewhat sturdy romantic classicism. Around 1830, his influence began to wane as his son-in-law and fellow professor at the Academy, GUSTAV FRIEDRICH HETSCH, more attentive to the new signals of the time, succeeded in transposing the architecture of KARL FRIEDRICH SCHINKEL to Danish soil. The formative years of Theophilus Hansen coincided with that evolution and he bound himself to Hetsch, who in return considered the young pupil exceedingly talented. In the mid-1830s, Theophilus Hansen finished his training as an architect; by that time, he had already been assistant teacher at the Academy for several years. Apart from the stylistic influence, Hansen inherited from Hetsch a distinct rationalistic attitude toward architecture that stressed the importance of structure rather than surface.

Affected by Hetsch's great interest in medieval brick-building and urged by the art historian N. L. Høyen, who was deeply concerned with the preservation of medieval monuments, Hansen in 1837 drew up a project for the restoration of the beautiful but ramshackle Romanesque Cathedral of Ribe. However spectacular, the project was a romantic fancy and was never carried out, but it held some significance as the first of its kind in Denmark.

In the spring of 1838, Hansen left Denmark on a voyage that was to be of great importance to his future career. About that time, the situation seemed rather hopeless to the young ambitious architect, whose work consisted largely of designs for artisans and industry. Public and private building had reached a halt, and having been offended by not being awarded the Academy's prize, he decided to go abroad. He received financial support for a tour of Germany but he intended to go as far as Greece, where his older brother had been living for some years. En route to Greece, Hansen visited Schinkel's famous buildings in Berlin, and with even greater interest he thereafter studied the medieval architecture of Meissen, Prague and Nurem-

Theophilus Hansen.
The Parliaments.
Vienna.
1874–1884

berg. Not very pleased with the architecture of LEO VON KLENZE and FRIEDRICH VON GÄRTNER in Munich, he continued through northern Italy via Venice and Trieste and finally reached Athens in the autumn of 1838. In Athens, the main concern in those years was the reconstruction of the town as the young nation's capital after the Turkish occupation. Christian Hansen was deeply involved in that process and Theophilus too was immediately caught up in the numerous chances of archeological studies and architectural practice.

Theophilus stayed abroad and paid only short visits to his native country. He stayed in Athens until 1846, when he moved to Vienna. During these years, he achieved a profound knowledge of ancient Greek architecture, classic as well as Byzantine, a fact that became of considerable significance for his later buildings. During the years in Athens, he collaborated with his brother and with Edouard Schaubert, director of buildings in Greece, who exerted a great influence on the architectonic planning and administration of the young nation.

In 1842–1843, Theophilus erected the stately house for the merchant Demetrios across from the new royal palace. The building was later to become the Hotel Grande Bretagne, and it was completely rebuilt in 1958. Originally, it was a well-composed house of three stories in an Italianate villa style accomplished with a rich Schinkelesque classicism. That same year, he was entrusted with the building of the observatory (1842–1846) in Athens on Nymphaion Hill presented to the university by the Greek banker Georg von Sina, who lived in Vienna. Hansen chose an arrangement related to Schinkel's observatory in Berlin, but he carried it out in an original and lucid handling of the cross form, and the façade was a reduced replica of the university's main façade. There is strong evidence that Theophilus in the early 1840s was also involved with the planning of the new Metropolis-church in Athens and that the final designs were by him. The building's history is rather intricate. In 1843, as the foundation was laid, Theophilus Hansen and Schaubert were dismissed from state service as were other foreigners employed by the state, and the building of the church was entrusted to a number of different architects.

In 1846, Theophilus was invited to go to Vienna by the architect LUDWIG VON FÖRSTER, the founder and editor of *Allgemeine Bauzeitung*. Hansen soon became Förster's partner in building matters and stayed with him until 1852 when they dramatically broke off relations and Hansen started his own establishment in Vienna. During the years with Förster, Hansen left his marks on most of the buildings they designed together, such as the Hotel National (c.1846–c.1852), Taborstrasse, Vienna, and the Protestant Gustaf Adolf Church (1849–1850) in Gumpendorff, Vienna. In 1849, the two architects were entrusted with the building of the army museum in Vienna, a part of the huge arsenal constructed after the revolution of 1848. Presumably, it was Hansen's design, and after the break with Förster, the erection of the museum at least was laid in the hands of Hansen. It became a decisive breakthrough, which gave him recognition and valuable connections to the army and state administration. From the mid-1850s on, he was commissioned with a disproportionate part of the enormous public and private building activity of the double monarchy.

In these works, Hansen turned away from the classicism of Schinkel, which was his acknowledged ideal, and formed instead an original neo-Byzantine style, which he considered an entirely new international formula, introduced on a grand scale in the Army Museum (1849–1856). He obviously felt attracted by the rational accordance between structure and form in Byzantine architecture, most evidently demonstrated in the chapels at the Invalidenhaus in Lwow (1854–1859) and the Protestant Cemetery at Matzleinsdorf near Vienna (1859). Hansen won an undisputed international reputation with a considerable number of monumental buildings on the fashionable Vienna Ringstrasse, which about 1860 was laid out on the former ramparts surrounding the inner town.

Probably influenced by a visit to Italy in 1856, Hansen turned to a more conventional Italian Renaissance architecture, first used in the buiding of the Protestant School at Karlsplatz (1859) and shortly thereafter in the magnificent housing block Heinrichshof (1861) on the Ringstrasse opposite the Opera—a building which became the model for a large part of the private housing blocks in the Ringstrasse area. It was characterized by a maximum exploration of floorspace and an overwhelming outer splendor. The style was mainly Italian Cinquecento mixed with classic Greek details.

For two decades Hansen assumed the position as the master builder par excellence of rich and fashionable Vienna, insuring the consistent artistic accomplishment of his buildings by designing interior arrangements and furniture as well. Parallel to the Renaissance style, he reassumed the pure, cultivated classicism, culminating in the Parliament in Vienna (1874–1884). During the 1860s, he had worked out plans for the two houses of the Austrian parliament, which in the final designs were joined into a single but extremely articulated structure, with the two meeting halls placed on either side of the pompous central hall. Details were handled with convincing accordance to the classic models.

In the late 1850s, Hansen had reassumed relations with Greece, designing the Academy of Science (1859–1887), Athens, with the idea to form a homogeneous group of classicistic buildings round the university, the so-called Athenian trilog, concluded in 1885–1921 by the National Library. The Academy of Science was designed in a distinct Ionian style with convincing quotes from the nearby Erechtheion and Propylaea in a disorganization of mass symmetrically displayed around the main portico. He used basically the same form in the Doric National Library (1885–1892) conceived as a templelike main building flanked by parallel wings.

VILLADS VILLADSEN

WORKS

1842–1843, Demetrios House (Hotel Grande Bretagne); 1842–1846, Observatory; 1843, Cathedral (foundations); Athens. c.1846–c.1852, Hotel National (with Ludwig von Förster), Taborstrasse; 1849–1850, Gustaf Adolf Kirche (with Förster), Gumpendorf; 1849–1856, Army Museum (with Förster); Vienna. 1854–1859, Invalidenhaus, Lwow, Poland. 1856, Schloss Hernstein, near Baden, Austria. 1856–1858, Greek Church; 1858, Protestant Cemetery and Chapel, Matzleindorf; 1859, Palais Sina, Hoher Markt; 1859, Protestant School, Karlsplatz; Vienna. 1859–1887, Academy of Science, Athens. 1861, Heinrichshof; 1864–1869, Musikverin; 1868, Palais Archduke Wilhelm; 1869, Rudolfhof; 1869–1877, Exchange; 1870–1873, Epstein Palais; 1872–1873, Ephrussi Palais; 1872–1879, Academy of Fine Arts; 1874–1884, The Parliaments; Vienna. 1885–1891, National Library (not completed until 1892), Athens.

BIBLIOGRAPHY

ÅKERSTRÖM-HOUGEN, G. 1972 "Den nyklassiska Arkitektruen i Grekland." *Konsthistorisk Tidskrift* 1972:16–42.

GANS, JÜRG 1972 "Theophil Hansens 'Hellenische' Bauten in Athen und Wien." *Österreichische Zeitschrift für Kunst und Denkmalpflege* 24, nos. 1–2:67–81.

LAIOS, G. S. 1972 *Simon Sinas*. Athens: Grapheion Demosieumatontes Akademias Athenon.

LHOTSKY, ALPHONS 1941 *Die Baugeschichte der Museen und der neuen Burg.* Vienna: Kunsthistorisches Museum.

NIEMANN, G., and FELDEGG, F. VON 1893 *Theophilos Hansen und seine Werke.* Vienna: Schroll.

RUSSACK, HANS H. 1942 *Deutsches Bauen in Athen.* Berlin: Limpert.

STROBL, ALICE 1961 *Das k. k. Waffenmuseum im Arsenal.* Graz, Austria: Böhlaus Wachf.

VILLADSEN, VILLADS 1974 *Ribe domkirke. Et gulaldermotiv.* Ribe, Denmark.

VILLADSEN, VILLADS 1978 "Studien über den byzantinischen Einfluss auf die europäische Architektur des 19. Jahrhunderts." *Hafnia* 1978:43–77.

VILLADSEN, VILLADS 1979 "Eng ung arkitekts rejsedagbog." *Architectura* 1979:88–108.

HANSOM, JOSEPH A.

Inventor of the Patent Safety Cab (Hansom cab) and founder of *The Builder* (1842), Joseph Aloysius Hansom (1803–1882) designed a great number of ecclesiastical buildings for the Roman Catholic Church in a conventional Gothic Revival style in which the details were too often commonplace and undistinguished.

JILL LEVER

WORKS

1832–1834, Birmingham Town Hall (with Edward Welch; completed by Charles Edge), England. Opened 1866, Saint Benedict's Church, Hindley near Wigan; Opened 1866, Saint Walburge's Church, Preston; Lancashire, England. Opened 1873, Saint Philip Neri's Church (never completed), Arundel, Sussex, England.

BIBLIOGRAPHY

Additional information on Joseph Hansom can be found in the Stephen Welsh Manuscripts, Royal Institute of British Architects, British Architectural Library, WeS /1/13, 83pp, compiled 1974.

"The Late Mr. J. A. Hansom, Architect." 1882 *The Builder* 63, July 8:43–44.

HANSSON, OLOF

Olof Hansson (1919–) first became known in Finland because of his restoration projects, which demanded knowledge about architectural history and structure of form, an eye sensitive to details, and skill in combining the new with the old—the basic qualities in all of his work. Another important source of influence was the work of ERIK BRYGGMAN, from whom Hansson learned the importance of proportions and the façade. His annex for the State Archives in Helsinki (1961–1972) shows the sensitive approach to the site and neighborhood, not by imitating the old, but by adapting the new to the existing building. Hansson has also served as a professor of architecture at Tampere University in Finland since 1975.

PIRKKO-LIISA LOUHENJOKI

WORKS

1959–1961, German Church (renovation); 1961–1972, State Archives (annex), Helsinki. 1962–1969, Institute of Nuclear Physics, Helsinki University. 1964–1972, Oy Philips Ab, Storage and Industrial Building, Espoo, Finland. 1974–1977, Library and Workers' Institute, Tammisaari, Finland. 1974–, Espoo Church (renovation), Espoo, Finland. 1976–, Helsinki University Library (renovation). Begun 1980, Library, Kirkkonummi, Finland.

BIBLIOGRAPHY

Finnish Architecture. 1975 The Hague: Museum of Finnish Architecture and the Netherlands Congress Center. Exhibition catalogue.

HARDENBERGH, HENRY JANEWAY

Henry Janeway Hardenbergh (1847–1918) was a New Jersey-born, New York-based architect best remembered for two gracious, still thriving New York City landmarks: the German-Renaissance Revival *Dakota* Apartment House (1880) and the Plaza Hotel (1905).

The *Dakota,* America's first luxury apartment house, pioneered the stacking of the rich. At the time, well-to-do urban Americans lived in free-

Hardenbergh.
Plaza Hotel.
New York.
1905

standing or rowhouses, scorning any multiple dwelling as a type of tenement, a set of "mere shelves under a common roof." But the *Dakota* inaugurated a new lavishness of square-footage, décor, and amenities and an abundance of light and air, offering not just architectural gentility, as had earlier apartment houses, but splendor.

JEAN-LOUIS BOURGEOIS

WORKS

1880, Dakota Apartment House; 1891, American Fine Arts Society (Art Students' League); 1892, Waldorf Hotel; 1896, Astor Hotel; New York. 1901, Willard Hotel, Washington. 1905, Plaza Hotel, New York. 1912, Copley Plaza Hotel, Boston.

BIBLIOGRAPHY

BACH, RICHARD F. 1918 "Henry Janeway Hardenbergh." *Architectural Record* 44, July:91–93.
GOLDSTONE, HARMON H., and DALRYMPLE, MARTHA 1974 *History Preserved: A Guide to New York City Landmarks and Historic Districts.* New York: Simon & Schuster.
A History of Real Estate, Building, and Architecture in New York City During the Last Quarter of a Century. (1898)1967 Reprint. New York: Arno.
LANDAU, SARAH BRADFORD 1975 "The Row Houses of New York's West Side." *Journal of the Society of Architectural Historians* 34, no. 1:19–36.
SCHUYLER, MONTGOMERY 1897 "The Works of Henry Janeway Hardenbergh." *Architectural Record* 6, no. 3:335–375.

HARDOUIN MANSART, JULES

Jules Hardouin (1646–1708) grew up in the household of his great-uncle, FRANÇOIS MANSART, who helped to train him, whose name he took, and many of whose papers and drawings he inherited. In the past, the two men have sometimes been confused, but a recent thorough study of the elder Mansart's life and work has separated them once and for all. Hardouin Mansart's buildings, however, are probably more familiar to many because of his vast works at Versailles, and his Place Vendôme and Church of the Invalides in Paris. But he has not yet been the subject of a detailed scholarly biography, and a number of questions of date, attribution, and the degree of his involvement in certain projects with complicated histories remains to be answered. He was marked for architecture from the start, as an autobiographical statement about his early years makes clear (Braham and Smith, 1973, vol. 1, pp. 163–166). In due time, he made use of some of his great-uncle's ideas, but at first he seems to have been influenced more by LOUIS LE VAU and by LIBÉRAL BRUANT, for whom

he worked on the Hôtel des Invalides as early as 1670. By that time, he had already designed several buildings, and at twenty-five he was working at Versailles, albeit in a subordinate position.

The next year, however, he gained commissions from Louis XIV himself, for the king's Château du Val in the forest of Saint-Germain, and for Madame de Montespan's Château at Clagny. In 1678, he was put in charge at Versailles, and from then on, until his death thirty years later, he was the leading architect of the kingdom. He was appointed to ever more important state offices concerned with public architecture and construction, was ennobled in 1683 (the same time as ANDRÉ LE NÔTRE), made Comte de Sagonne in 1693, and achieved, in 1699, the exalted post of *Superintendant des Bâtiments du Roi.* His career was a hectic one, and he produced so many buildings that some, such as Saint-Simon, who detested him, thought he took the designs of his employees and passed them off as his own. Whatever the truth of this, the demands made upon him required close collaboration with others; he was good at this as, for example, his work with ROBERT DE COTTE and with Charles Lebrun shows. He understood the king's needs and provided for them effectively, excelling at the architecture of ceremony and display, while at the same time he helped to make the Parisian townhouse more benign and informal. He designed some buildings that belong in or close to the first rank, such as the Invalides church, and created one of the most harmonious, and famous, public squares in Europe, the Place Vendôme; both remain quintessential symbols of the *siècle d'or.*

Although Hardouin Mansart worked in the provinces, from Saint-Omer in the north to Arles in the south (where the Hôtel de Ville is his), by far the greater part of his buildings is found in and near Paris. Some of his structures, such as triumphal arches for fêtes and similar temporary works, are known only through drawings and engravings, and the same is true of many of the fairly large number of his buildings that have been demolished. Some, such as the Place des Victoires in Paris, are now so changed—one can say mutilated—that it is difficult to get a sense of the original effect. On the other hand, the amount of archival material, especially that relating to the royal works, is huge; as Bourget says, "La variété des ordres [from the king] est stupéfiante." And because Hardouin Mansart was a considerable public figure, he appears in various publications of the time. Several sculptured portraits of him exist, among them two by Coysevox and another by Lemoine; in these he appears as a ranking grandee.

The broad and general tendencies observable in

his nonroyal domestic architecture are an increased horizontality (François Mansart's remarkable high roofs appear much less often) and, more important for the evolution of housing, a discernible relaxation of formality. This is not to say that the rococo prettiness and gaiety, the mirrored linearity, of the eighteenth century appears in his work, for it does not. But the grand formality of his great-uncle's and Le Vau's houses is softened, and the décor found in those of Hardouin Mansart and his contemporaries prefigures to a considerable degree the style that appeared after the death of Louis XIV in 1715. A new, wider variety of room shapes is found, as, for example, in the king's Château du Val (1674), where one section of square plan was divided evenly into four rooms each of different plan and shape. Both the setting and the furnishings of hôtel and château life became more intimate, a tendency clearly recorded in the royal retreats as well, those places where the king and those closest to him could relax, to a degree, after the ceremonial rigor of Versailles or the Louvre. In these retreats also, some characteristics of the rococo appear: an increased use of mirrors and an elegant lightness of decorative line.

The new horizontality was seen as early as the late 1660s, when Hardouin Mansart built the Hôtel de Noailles at Saint-Germain. There, the roof, though pitched and visible, was quite low by previous standards. The main block had two stories, but the upper one was only half the height of the rez-de-chaussée, and this, together with the low roof, formed a nine-bay composition emphatically horizontal (the wings, each almost as long as the main block and aligned on its axis, were only one story high). The upper story windows were nearly square and gave it the appearance of an attic; there, and on the story below, there seem to have been raised panels of the kind François Mansart often used, for example, at the Hôtel Carnavalet in Paris. Clagny, near Versailles, though of two stories rising from the three sides of a traditional court, was given a strong horizontal accent by the addition of lengthy single-story elements attached to the ends of the courtyard wings, on the transverse axis of the open, entrance side of the court. This tendency continued in the sweeping horizontality of such structures as the Grand Trianon, about which more below.

Some of Hardouin Mansart's châteaux were of more or less traditional design. That at Dampierre, for example, built for the duc de Luynes, is two stories high, with great roofs of the kind that bear the Mansart name. The wings flanking the court, however, do not join the main block, whose courtyard-side corners, unusually, turn into projecting, domed turrets. At the royal Château of Marly

(1679), no longer standing, his originality in planning and design was strikingly evident, as a number of drawings and engravings make clear. The king's building proper was a two-storied, freestanding square block, elevated on a low terrace reached by broad staircases placed on both the cardinal and diagonal axes. Centered within this was a large, two-story octagonal salon from which grand salons radiated along the cardinal axes to the four façades. The remaining, large corner areas were each ingeniously divided to form the apartments of king and others, while upstairs smaller apartments were placed around an octagonal gallery.

The result seems to have been a unique exercise in centralized planning, perhaps bearing a distant relationship to the Villa Rotonda of ANDREA PALLADIO but unlike it in its blockiness and lack of any roofs or vaults above the line of the crowning balustrade. The nine-bay exterior façades were quoined at the corners but otherwise divided by shallow Corinthian pilasters raised on high pedestals, creating an overall appearance somewhat like that of the central part of the main façade of JOHN VANBRUGH's Castle Howard. But the royal block was only one element in an extraordinary plan that included some fifteen additional buildings. Twelve of these, freestanding pavilions for courtiers, were arranged in two symmetrical files, facing each other across a broad, terraced, slightly sunken parterre; the balance contained a chapel, offices, and the like. The dominance of the main block, the rigid symmetry of the open-ended plan, the independence of the small pavilions, and the communal situation of the parterre are all reflected in THOMAS JEFFERSON's plan for the University of Virginia at Charlottesville.

Of Hardouin Mansart's work in Paris, three grand conceptions stand out. The Place des Victoires, of which only a fraction exists today, was circular in plan, with a statue of the king, by Desjardins, at the center; four extravagant, columniated lantern supports stood guard over the royal effigy. Between the several streets giving on to the circle (some more or less radial and one tangent), he placed blocks of houses whose concave and flanking façades have largely disappeared; those that remain are mostly disfigured. These were supported on an arcuated basement; above rose two stories whose bays were divided by Ionic pilasters, the whole crowned by dormered, mansard roofs.

The Place Vendôme, though not free from change, is far better preserved. It stems from the purchase of the land in 1685 by the king, who planned to build an open square around which the royal library and academies could be placed. But it was not until 1698 that the work actually was

taken up, with Hardouin Mansart in charge. By then, the concept had changed: the king gave the site to the City of Paris, stipulating that although Hardouin Mansart's façades were to be finished, the areas behind them could be sold to individuals; the library and academies were abandoned. Still, a royal statue, by Girardon, was placed in the middle where Napoleon's Column now stands.

The Place is a rectangle with two openings placed opposite each other. The interior corners are cut off diagonally and they, together with the axial centerpieces of the unbroken sides, are faced with shallow Corinthian temple fronts placed above the arcaded rez-de-chaussée that runs around the entire enclosure (except for the north–south axial openings). The two-storied bays of the balance of the work are divided by Corinthian pilasters, and the roof is studded with round-headed dormers that rise directly from the eaves' line. Even though the scale was changed by the addition of the column, the baroque tension between the long, bordering façades and the axial openings remains, as does the sense of dignity evoked by the iteration of the well-proportioned bays and temple fronts. Perhaps the most impressive thing about the design of the Place Vendôme is the way in which the interior angles are cut off: not much space is taken up in doing this—just enough to underline the effect of enclosure, but not so much as either to emphasize the diagonals or detract from the force of the controlling, invisible central axis. The result is a success, a baroque concept, as Anthony Blunt (1957) has said, with classical details; in spite of differences, the long sides remind one of the façade of LUIGI VANVITELLI's Bourbon palace at Caserta.

The history of the Invalides is complicated, but the essential facts are as follows. The Hôtel proper, a home for wounded veterans, was begun by Bruant in 1670; he and Hardouin Mansart were on good terms and the younger man was employed here by Bruant. A somber but effective design of gridiron plan with many enclosed courts, arcaded throughout at ground level, it is similar in some respects to the Escorial (1562–1583), especially as both have churches centered on the main axis (in Paris, the Church of Saint-Louis). By 1676, the king was interested in adding a second church, also on axis and connected with the first, that may have been proposed as a burial place for the Bourbon dynasts. This scheme never came to anything, but shortly thereafter (before 1679), the present building, the Dôme des Invalides, was begun by Hardouin Mansart. Construction was completed in 1691, but the interior decoration was still unfinished at the time of the architect's death. The insertion of Napoleon's tomb by LUDOVICO VISCONTI in the early 1840s radically altered the intended architectural effect of Hardouin Mansart's interior.

The Dôme has a square plan from which a block rises up through two stories; above that is the famous dome, with its two drums, carrying the gilded and beribbed cupola topped by a needlelike flèche. At ground level, inside below the dome, is the central rotunda; this connects by low passageways to circular chapels set on the diagonals, and expands, on the cardinal axes, into high, broad, barrel-vaulted tribunes, forming a Greek-cross composition. The main façade, away from the Hôtel proper, faces south on the Place Vauban; on the opposite side of the building a vaulted, spacious transitional chamber, containing a baroque baldachin reminiscent of GIOVANNI LORENZO BERNINI's in St. Peter's, connects with the earlier Church of Saint Louis. In section, the design can be described only as extraordinary. The external width of the main drum is equal to only a third of the total height (about a hundred meters) of the building, and this 1:3 proportion, together with the fact that the drum and dome together are more than twice as tall as the two-storied, square block from which they rise, produces an emphatic vertical declaration. The long, horizontal roofs of the Hôtel and the basilica of Saint-Louis help to make the domed tower stand out, and the design succeeds as a result of a sureness in massing and in composing the relationships among major elements worthy of Hardouin Mansart's great-uncle.

In section, the building is equally remarkable. The dome proper consists of three parts, one superimposed above another. The lowest is in effect a huge, circular ribbed cove. In elevation it lies in the zone of the second, upper drum and culminates in a very wide circular opening, or internal oculus; that is, it is cut off horizontally below the height where its crown would be if a full hemisphere had been constructed. The next dome is complete, a thin masonry canopy above the first; it rises to a height equivalent to a point a little above the entablature of the second drum. Neither of these first two vaults is hinted at on the exterior, where what one sees is the third structure, a covered framework that gives the building its curving silhouette and supports the lantern with its flèche. From the interior, the paintings on the undersurface of the second dome are seen through the wide, ringed opening of the first. The windows of the lower drum light the building's main volume proper, those of the second the paintings on the second dome. The origin of this system is hard to trace, though it may be an invention of François Mansart's. Timber domical superstructures over masonry domes were not uncommon; the structure of those at Saint Mark's in Venice is a case in point. But the triple system, which CHRISTOPHER WREN was to use at Saint Paul's in London (begun in 1675), seems not to have existed in monumental form before the Dôme des Invalides. However, drawings by François Mansart for the projected (but never built) Bourbon dynastic chapel at Saint-Denis (made about 1662–1663) suggest this kind of structure, and scholars agree that Hardouin Mansart used these drawings in preparing the designs of his great church.

The nature of the plan affects the appearance of the superstructure as well. In order to load the main supporting piers (those that divide the diagonally placed circular chapels from the adjacent, broad tribunes) with the weight of the domical superstructure in an efficient manner, the external buttresses of the first drum are placed directly over those piers. This means that they too are on the diagonals of the drum, facing the corners of the square block below. Like those at St. Peter's, they are vertical masses of solid masonry projecting from the drum's cylindrical surface that terminate

Hardouin Mansart.
Dome des Invalides.
Paris.
Begun c.1677

Hardouin Mansart and
*   Bruant*
Invalides, Church of St.
*   Louis.*
Paris.
early 1670s

in three-quarters-round columns; this diagonal emphasis is accentuated by the scroll buttresses that connect them to the second drum above. To animate the design further, Hardouin Mansart set the lantern on a circular base that projects well out from the cap of the dome, making a deep cut into the silhouette of the uppermost part of the superstructure. Finally, he turned the corners of his square lantern out on to the diagonals.

The net result is thoroughly baroque and at the same time somewhat medieval. The emphatic height of the composition is medieval in the sense that the rounded exterior dome form is not seen so much as a spreading, encompassing width, as is the case with most domed monumental buildings, but more as the final feature of a stable and powerful multistaged tower; this effect is emphasized by the proportions of the block and by the lack of any projecting nave; the basic conception brings to mind MICHELANGELO's centralized design for St. Peter's. The entranceway from the Place Vauban is splendid, an exercise in right-angled baroque design that both emphasizes the vertical axis of the building (the plinth of the second story, for example, is missing from the center bay) and presents, from ground level, an imposing, sober monumentality. Not only do centerpieces in certain projects of François Mansart come to mind, such as those for the Château at Blois and for the Louvre, but, with respect to the Dôme's upper story, the Arch of Hadrian in Athens and the façade of Bernini's Santa Bibiana in Rome as well. The interior is dignified and sober, with a classically correct order of the kind found in the Pantheon in Rome. The sculptural decoration, though dramatic enough, is subordinated to the architectural lines of the whole, the net effect prefiguring somewhat that of JACQUES GERMAIN SOUFFLOT's Panthéon in Paris, with which the plan and elevation of the Dôme have other affinities as well.

It was in 1669 that Louis XIV commissioned Le Vau to alter radically the existing château at Versailles. Le Vau produced a refined example of French classicism, a building with courts open to both garden and city sides, the latter, deeper one incorporating remnants of the original building built for Louis XIII in 1624. Le Vau died in 1670, and Hardouin Mansart was working at Versailles as early as 1673, though in a minor capacity. In 1678, when the Peace of Nijmegen made it possible for the king to put his schemes for the extension of the building into practice, he was put in charge. He worked there, following the king's directives and working closely with major artists such as Lebrun and Le Nostre, from then almost until his death—the same period during which he produced Marly, Saint-Cloud (1685), and his grand Parisian structures. His first objective was to fill in Le Vau's garden court or terrace; this became the Hall of Mirrors. Le Vau's projecting wings, which became the Salons of Peace and of War and whose appearance can be traced in the later work, thus became part of a single garden façade; on the opposite side, in the Marble Court, changes were also made but not such drastic ones. Louis then required his architect to add immense north and south wings set back from the garden façade, joined to the flanks of the Marble Court and its extension almost at eastern extremities. Each wing is longer than the central block, and the whole, in its completed state, forms an almost overwhelming building some 430 meters long from end to end. The literal center of this, overlooking the Marble Court and back-to-back with the Hall of Mirrors, was the king's bedroom, the focus of the entire composition.

Hardouin Mansart has been criticized for mutilating Le Vau's handsome building and for creating an almost unassimilable ensemble. But although it is true that the architecture is in some ways rather undistinguished, it is also true that he created what the Sun King demanded, giving him a ceremonial structure, a place where the extravagant court ceremonies could be acted out according to the king's wishes and where visitors would be all but overwhelmed by what Nietzsche called "an oratory of power by means of forms." The exterior elevation of this most famous of all palaces, much of which Hardouin Mansart took over from Le Vau, consists of a rusticated, arcaded rez-de-chaussée above which the main floor of round-headed windows is divided into bays by shallow pilasters and is punctuated by slight projections

Hardouin Mansart.
Palais de Versailles (Hall of Mirrors).
France.
1678–1689

three to five bays wide separated by freestanding columns. Above that there is a third story, about half the height of the one below, a kind of attic. The low roofs are not visible, and the long, unwavering progress of the skyline is punctuated only by sculptured trophies and fire-vases set upon a continuous balustrade.

Some of the satellite buildings that Hardouin Mansart added to the palace are of considerable interest. To the garden side of the south wing, just to the southwest of it, he replaced Le Vau's Orangery with another one well below the level of the terrace of the garden façade of the main structures. The vaulted storage areas under that terrace display the kind of stereometry for which French stonemasons are famous (other fine vaults were executed for Hardouin Mansart in, for example, the Versailles Stables and the ground floor of the Hôtel de Ville at Arles). The façade of this storage area, facing the unroofed citrus garden, is a sober composition of rusticated arcades, with robust, unfluted Tuscan columns embellishing the centerpieces. The corners of the retaining walls of the upper terrace are turned by unusual convex transitional forms, and the terrace above is gained by two impressive, broad staircases flanking the sides of the garden proper.

To the southeast of the central building, and on axis with the sequence of ever wider courts leading away from the king's bedchamber, the Avenue de Paris forms the central line of an arrowhead plan of three streets that spread out from the courts. Between the two acute angles thus formed, but well away (some 300 meters) from the main buildings, Hardouin Mansart inserted two vast stables. These are horseshoe-shaped, with their open ends facing toward the courts and the palace; the northern building was for riding horses, the southern for draft and coach animals. Behind each, where the buildings broaden as the avenues diverge, he placed service wings and exercise yards. The planning is of interest because of the efficient solutions achieved for complex functional arrangements, and the design of the exteriors is, together

with that of the Grand Trianon, perhaps as good as anything Hardouin Mansart did at Versailles. Almost all of the vertical surfaces are rusticated; no orders appear. Horizontality is emphasized by the lines of the rustication, a proportionately low, two-story elevation, and continuous systems of mansard roofs of very moderate but uniform elevation. The centerpieces are excellent, perhaps unique. Those on the axes of the inner curves of the horseshoe-shaped courts consist of simplified, almost abstract temple fronts framing large arches flanked by broad panels of trophies in relief. Above the doorways, just under the deep soffits of the arches, Girardon's triads of splendid horses charge out of the shadows.

On the other side of the main buildings, in the vast park, Hardouin Mansart had built several small pavilions over the years. In 1687, the king required that he replace Le Vau's Trianon de Porcelaine, one of several retreats in the vicinity, with a new building, known as the Grand Trianon. This is a one-story, almost rambling structure of somewhat eccentric plan, a series of wings connected at right angles but not composed into a symmetrical group overall. With its large arcades and door-windows, profusion of color, and lack of a rez-de-chaussée, it is an informal place in contrast to the huge main palace to the south. It has a rather exuberant flavor, with its exterior columns, pilasters, and paneling carried out in veined and mottled marbles that range from green-black to pinkish-red. The overall effect is somewhat Mediterranean, and the directness of the relationship between the living quarters and the gardens is exceptional. This liveliness is accentuated by the baroque freestanding Ionic order used for the open porticoes: the paired columns, similar in design to those the architect used on the façade of his own house in the Rue de Tournelles in Paris, swell slightly as they rise, before diminishing in diameter in traditional entasis. Out in the gardens, Hardouin Mansart built beautiful fountains. One of them, the Buffet d'Eau, is an entertaining piece, smaller than the grand cascade and pools he and

Hardouin Mansart.
Grand Trianon, Palais de
*   Versailles.*
France.
1678–1689

PIERRE LEPAUTRE built at Saint-Cloud but equally successful.

The last of his major buildings at Versailles is the chapel. Earlier chapels had existed there, but in 1688 the king called for a new one. A domed building (based once again on François Mansart's Saint-Denis project) was proposed and then abandoned, but in 1689 the design for the present structure was approved and work on it begun. Not much was done, however, until 1698, and the interior was not completed until after the architect's death. The chapel lies at the base of the north wing, hard by the original, core building. Its curving sanctuary is at the east, and the entrance is embedded in the structure of the north wing; much of the building, however, is free-standing. Because of its simple, U-shaped basilican plan and its steeply pitched, unclassical roof, the chapel contrasts strongly with the neighboring forms. The exterior design elements are classical—pilasters, balustrades, fire-vases, and the like—but the overall effect is that of an essentially medieval building gotten up in fancy dress. The interior is equally remarkable, but mostly for different reasons. In order for the king to make his way from his suite to the chapel without changing levels, his box is on the main floor; below, on the rez-de-chaussée, is the nave proper, an arcaded zone of uncluttered and effective design. The proportions of this interior, like those of the exterior superstructure, are essentially Gothic: tall and proportionately quite narrow. Above the arcades, at the royal level, there is a colonnaded gallery; both levels follow the hair-pin, basilican plan, with the king elevated at the entrance end, and the altar, below, in the curve of the other. Except for the paintings on the ceilings and vaults, the interior architecture is chiefly white and off-white; colored marbles, in the Italian manner, had been proposed but the idea was abandoned.

It is probably too early to make confident judgments about Hardouin Mansart's ability or his contribution to architecture. The surviving drawings and many other original documents have not yet been thoroughly sifted and studied, and the roles of his assistants (Lepautre and PIERRE LASSURANCE, chiefly), and of collaborators such as Lebrun and De Cotte need careful attention. But it can safely be said that the accusation that some of his best work was produced by his employees and assistants is unlikely to be true, for the drawings and documents already published (by Bourget and Cattaui and by the Maries, among others), make it clear that he was the certain author of enough first-class designs to show that his professional ability cannot be seriously questioned. However, the possibility of an inspiration from the papers of his great-uncle should be kept in mind when the building in question can be firmly connected with the style and detailing of the elder man's work.

Hardouin Mansart had numerous talents. Like so many architects of the past, he was a good engineer; the aqueduct at Marly and the Pont Royal in Paris (done with JACQUES GABRIEL) attest to this. Probably he designed more gardens than he is usually given credit for. He excelled at planning, both from the point of view of the use of sites and in the preparation of plan solutions for various functions; he was to a degree a city planner as well. If the planning at Versailles has, in the central buildings at least, a certain monotony, it can be argued that in the last analysis he was as little responsible for this as CARLO MADERNO was for giving St. Peter's in Rome an extended nave. He understood the power of horizontality as well as or better than his great-uncle did, using it tellingly to suggest continuity and reliability. His elevations tend on the whole to be typical of their period, with arcades below and the orders, usually in the form of pilasters, above, but he was capable of striking originality, as in the major centerpieces of the Versailles stables. He was not at all wedded to the handbooks' prescriptions for the orders, as is shown by details such as the spread-out, very broad pilaster-panels at the Grand Trianon, with their garlandlike extended capitals.

When he had a free hand, he was in his own way as good at massing as François Mansart had been. The free-standing Dôme des Invalides is a case in point. Each successive major horizontal zone of the building rises logically and satisfyingly from the one below, the whole being firmly based on the great block which, because it is not overarticulated, appears capable of supporting the superstructure. The baroque energies of these forms, culminating in a rush of ascending lines up along the gilded surfaces of the dome proper to the pointed tip of the flèche, generate one of the chief monumental symbols of seventeenth-century architecture. Along with his abilities at composition went the corollary ability to handle, and control, scale; he could never have succeeded as Louis's chief architect without it. Like his great-uncle, he was rarely in doubt about what ought to be large and what small and what the relationship between the two should be. This helped him to focus his architecture confidently, and it helped him to create that dramatic sense of grandeur one so readily associates with his name. If in all this he was not as particular, as discriminating, about details as some, it may be that he simply could not spend the time on them. In a less hectic world, with less demanding patrons, he might have avoided criticism on this score. In any event, the abilities of his craftsmen, and of the major artists with whom he worked, must often have saved him from worse failings.

He was an architect of very considerable artistic resources, as the wide variety of his plans and forms show. He did not have a single, clearly characterized style, partly because he responded to such a broad spectrum of commissions. He involved himself in the training of architects and in the reorganization, in 1699, of the Royal Academy of Architecture. He does not seem to have been particularly intellectual, and it is certain that he was envied and, in some quarters, thoroughly disliked. He may well have earned the dislike, but it is hard to imagine that anyone who met frequently with the king, who was so close to the source of all power, could have avoided envy. Today, it appears that he tried to do too much; if this is so, his best work is all the more impressive.

WILLIAM L. MacDONALD

WORKS

*1666?, Petit Hôtel de Conti; *before 1670, Hôtel de Lorge; Paris. *Before 1670, Hôtel de Noailles, Saint-Germain, France. 1670, Hôtel des Invalides (with Libéral Bruant); 1673?, J. Hardouin Mansart House, Rue de Tournelles; Paris. *1674, Château of Clagny, France. *1674, Château du Val, Saint-Germain, France. 1675, Château of Dampierre, France. 1675, Hôtel de Ville, Arles, France. 1678-1689, Palais de Versailles, France. ?-1679, Dôme des Invalides, Paris. *1679, Château of Marly, France. 1684, Notre Dame, Versailles, France. 1685, Château at Saint-Cloud, France. 1685, Place des Victoires; 1685, Pont Royal (with Jacques Gabriel); 1698, Place Vendôme; Paris.

BIBLIOGRAPHY

BLUNT, ANTHONY (1957)1973 Pages 338-345; 362-371 in Art and Architecture in France: 1500-1700. 2d ed., rev. Harmondsworth, England: Penguin.
BOURGET, PIERRE, and CATTAUI, GEORGES 1960 Jules Hardouin Mansart. Paris: Vincent, Fréal. Well illustrated.
BRAHAM, ALLAN, and SMITH, PETER 1973 François Mansart. 2 vols. London: Zwemmer. See especially volume 1, pages 163-166 (the Hardouin manuscript), 181-182, and references on page 286. On pages 89 and 163, the authors refer to a dissertation and a forthcoming book on Hardouin Mansart by M. Bertrand Jestaz.
HAUTECOEUR, LOUIS 1948 Pages 527-688 in Le règne de Louis XIV. Volume 2 in Histoire de l'architecture classique en France. Paris: Picard.
MARIE, ALFRED, and MARIE, JEANNE 1972 Mansart à Versailles. 2 vols. Paris: Fréal. Includes documents and drawings.

HARDOY, JORGE FERRARI

Jorge Ferrari Hardoy (1914-1976), after studying architecture in Buenos Aires, Argentina (1932-1937), worked with his partner Juan Kurchan in LE CORBUSIER's studio in Paris. Together with ANTONIO BONET, they designed the Hardoy Chair based on a continuous steel rod supporting a saddle leather or canvas sling at four points. In Buenos Aires, with Kurchan, he designed an apartment house (1940) that shows the marked influence of Le Corbusier. Alone, he developed the master plan for a community of 50,000 people within a sector of Buenos Aires known as Bajo Belgrano (1950). He was professor of architecture in Rosario, Argentina, and was a delegate to the Interamerican Congress of Modern Architecture.

EDUARDO CATALANO

WORKS

*1940, Apartment House, Virrey del Pino; 1950, Urbanización del Bajo de Belgrano; Buenos Aires.

BIBLIOGRAPHY

"Architettura spontanea." 1956 Domus 292, Mar.:6.
HARLING, ROBERT (editor) 1973 Studio Dictionary of Design and Decoration. New York: Viking.
"Urbanización del Bajo de Balgrano." 1953 Revista de Arquitectura 38:17-75.

HARDWICK, PHILIP

The son of THOMAS HARDWICK, Philip Hardwick (1792-1870) attended the Royal Academy Schools from 1808 while also a pupil in his father's office, entering into partnership in 1819. Philip Hardwick's stylistic range, which included Greek Doric, Tudor Gothic, Jacobean, and English baroque, were both varied and successful.

JILL LEVER

WORKS

1827–1829, Saint Katherine's Docks (warehouses and offices); 1829–1835, Goldsmiths' Hall; *1836–1840, Euston and Victoria Hotels (Doric gateway and lodges, Euston station); 1843–1845, Lincoln's Inn (hall and library; with PHILIP C. HARDWICK); London.

HARDWICK, THOMAS

Thomas Hardwick (1752–1829) entered the office of WILLIAM CHAMBERS in 1767 and the Royal Academy Schools two years later. His travels in Italy from 1776 to 1779 are well documented by drawings which show gifted draftsmanship and reveal collaborations with GIACOMO QUARENGHI and JOHN SOANE. Returning to London, Hardwick won first prize for a women's penitentiary, defeating GEORGE RICHARDSON. Once established, Hardwick concentrated largely on ecclesiastical and public buildings. His exquisite detailing, in the manner of Chambers, could not redeem a basic lack of imagination.

PIERRE DE LA RUFFINIÈRE DU PREY

WORKS

1787–1790, Wanstead Church, Essex, England. *1791–1792, Saint James's Chapel, London. 1796–1797, Shire Hall, Dorchester, England. 1806–1809, Nelson Column, Hereford, England. *1812–1813, Millbank Penitentiary; 1813–1817, Saint Marylebone Parish Church; 1814, Saint John's Chapel, London. 1822–1823, Saint John's Church, Workington, England. 1822–1826, Saint Barnabas Church, London. 1823–1825, Holy Trinity Church, Bolton, England. 1824–1825, Saint John's Church, Farnworth, England.

BIBLIOGRAPHY

DUNBAR, J. G. 1968 "An English Architect at Naples." *Burlington Magazine* 110:265–266.
DU PREY, PIERRE DE LA RUFFINIÈRE 1972 "Soane and Hardwick in Rome: A Neo-Classical Partnership." *Architectural History* 15:51–67.
DU PREY, PIERRE DE LA RUFFINIÈRE 1974 Review of John Harris, *A Catalogue of British Drawings for Architecture, Decoration, Sculpture and Landscape Gardening 1500–1900 in American Collections. Studies in Burke and His Time* 15:305–309.
FOWLER, LAURENCE HALL and BAER, ELIZABETH 1961 *The Fowler Architectural Collection of The Johns Hopkins University.* Baltimore: Evergreen House Foundation.
HARDWICK, THOMAS 1786 "Observations on the Remains of the Amphitheater of Flavius Vespasian at Rome." *Archaeologia* 7:369–373.
JONES, THOMAS 1946–1948 "Memoirs of Thomas Jones." *Walpole Society* 32:40–45, 58–65, 68, 79, 89.

HÄRING, HUGO

Born in Biberach, Germany, son of a cabinetmaker, Hugo Häring (1882–1958) entered the Technical University at Stuttgart in 1899 as an architectural student. Not satisfied with the dry and academic historicism favored at the time, he moved to Dresden in 1901 to take courses with PAUL WALLOT and FRITZ SCHUMACHER. When THEODOR FISCHER got a chair at his former school in 1903, Häring returned to Stuttgart where he graduated the same year. Both Schumacher and Fischer belonged to the modestly progressive group of architects who preceded the generation of WALTER GROPIUS and LUDWIG MIES VAN DER ROHE. Their influence is still prevalent in some of Häring's earlier commissions, such as the Römer House in Neu-Ulm (1916–1919).

From 1903 on, Häring practiced in Ulm, Hamburg, and Allenburg, Eastern Prussia, before he moved to Berlin around 1921. For a while he shared an office with Mies van der Rohe, whose few theoretical statements had some impact on Häring's own ideas on architecture. As secretary of the architects' association *Der Ring,* he participated in several Congrès Internationaux des Architectes Modernes meetings before he resigned over a controversy with Gropius. When the Nazis took over, he withdrew from all public activities, restricting himself to teaching at the Reimann Schule, which he headed until 1943. He then moved back to Stuttgart, where he spent the last years of his life in seclusion.

Häring's work as an architect amounts to a rather limited number of projects, even fewer of which were actually built. Among his more interesting commissions only the farm complex at Garkau (1924–1925) gained a wider reputation. His real importance is based on his theoretical contribution to the Modern movement, in which he temporarily assumed a leading role within the German avant-garde. Often misunderstood as formalism, his organic, curvilinear forms sought to adjust to the various working and living conditions of the inhabitants. He actually proceeded from a functional point of view, thereby taking a strong position against what he believed to be the geometrical approach of LE CORBUSIER.

WOLF TEGETHOFF

WORKS

1916–1919, Römer House, Neu-Ulm, Germany. 1924–1925, Farm Complex, Garkau, Germany. 1926, Fischtal-grund Housing Estates, Zehlendorf; 1929–1931, Siemensstadt Colony, Charlottenburg; 1931, House, Berlin Building Exposition; 1936, Ziegler House, Steglitz; Berlin. 1949–1950, Werner Schmitz House; 1949–1952, Guido Schmitz House; Biberach, Germany.

BIBLIOGRAPHY

HÄRING, HUGO 1968 *Die Ausbildung des Geistes zur Arbeit an der Gestalt: Fragmente.* Berlin: Mann.
JOEDICKE, JÜRGEN 1960 "Haering at Garkau." *Architectural Review* 127:313–318.
JOEDICKE, JÜRGEN 1966 "Hugo Häring." *Arts and Architecture* 83:8–12.
LAUTERBACH, HEINRICH, and JOEDICKE, JÜRGEN (editors) 1965 *Hugo Häring: Schriften, Entwürfe, Bauten.* Stuttgart, Germany: Krämer. Includes a fairly complete list of Häring's writings.
LOTZ, WILHELM 1931 "Architektur-Reportage." *Kunstblatt* 15:55–58.
PEHNT, W. 1973 *Expressionist Architecture.* New York: Praeger. Originally published in German.

HÅRLEMAN FAMILY

The Hårleman Family came to Sweden around 1660, called in from Holland by the Swedish Queen Hedvig Eleonora, who could use skillful architects, painters, sculptors, stucco workers, and gardeners for the construction or rebuilding of her different palaces, castles, and gardens. Christian Hårleman (1631–1687) was born in Oldenburg, Germany, and received a gardener's training in Holland, which qualified him for the employment at the Swedish court. In 1666, he was appointed gardener of the Royal Garden (kungsträdgården) in Stockholm. His son Johan (1662–1707) apparently learned from his father who also sent him abroad for five years to study the art of gardening in England, Holland, Germany, France, Spain, and Italy. Back in Sweden in 1685, he immediately was given the position of royal gardener. In the 1690s, he was promoted to inspector of the royal gardens and knighted. Mostly, he cooperated with the royal architect Nicodemus Tessin the Younger (see TESSIN FAMILY) whose drawings for the gardens of the royal palaces of Stockholm, Drottningholm, Ulriksdal, and Karlberg in French baroque of latest fashion he had to follow and accomplish.

Carl Hårleman (1700–1752), the most renowned member of the family, was only seven when his father died and left the mother with six small children. Nevertheless, she succeeded in arranging for him an education which in due time brought him into the field of architecture. On the recommendation of Tessin the Younger, Carl Hårleman in 1721 received financial support from the Swedish state that made it possible for him to travel and study art and architecture abroad. On this really Grand Tour, he visited Holland, Belgium, France, and Italy. After four years in Paris, he spent the year 1726 in Italy, mostly in Rome. In the spring of 1727, when staying in Venice, he received a message from Tessin the Younger that he was wanted in Stockholm for assistance in building the Royal Palace in Stockholm which was about to start up again after a break of nearly twenty years. It was here that Hårleman was to spend his main activity as fulfiller of Tessin's intentions (Tessin died in 1728) and as an enthusiastic introducer of the French rococo style in all branches of architecture, interior decoration, and applied arts. Some of his best works of interior decoration are to be found in the Royal Palace of Stockholm and at Drottningholm. At the latter palace, he also enlarged the old Tessin building, and at Svartsjö, he designed a new small provincial palace for the royal family.

Along with his commissions for the royal family, Hårleman created a national variation of JACQUES FRANÇOIS BLONDEL's manor houses which became a model for later architects such as J. E. Rehn and C. F. Adelcrantz (see ADELCRANTZ FAMILY). He combined them with a garden in which he replaced the traditional baroque central path by a grass parterre and also introduced a motif of his own with intersecting diagonal paths. He abandoned fountains and cascades and tended to reduce the waterworks to a single big reflecting pool.

In 1732, Hårleman had the opportunity to go to France once more. He had the explicit mission to find distinguished craftsmen and artists for the completion of the Royal Palace in Stockholm and succeeded in making contracts with several sculptors and painters among whom were Guillaume Taraval, Antoine Bellette, J. Ph. Bouchardson, and C. G. Cousin. In 1744–1745, he visited Paris for the last time, and there is no doubt that these close and regularly renewed contacts with the French arts and crafts brought the Swedish rococo period to a level rivaling the best in France. Supported by Hårleman LOUIS TARAVAL during the 1730s made his most important contribution as the leader of an art school for Swedish students involved in the works at the Royal Palace, a school which eventually became the Swedish Royal Academy of Fine Arts, officially established in 1768. At that time, Hårleman had been dead for sixteen years, but what he had started was now carried on by a number of Swedish artists who owed the high standards of their basic education to him.

Carl Hårleman should also be remembered as a collector of architectural drawings. When taking over from Tessin the Younger as royal architect and high commissioner of public buildings, he also inherited Tessin's collection of drawings which he increased considerably. This famous Tessin-Hårleman Collection is now in the National Museum in Stockholm, comprising around 10,000 items and containing drawings mainly of Italian, French, and Swedish architecture from the sixteenth to the eighteenth centuries as well as designs for dramatic performances and festivals.

ULF G. JOHNSSON

WORKS
CHRISTIAN HÅRLEMAN

1685–1709, Drottningholm, Ulriksdal, and Karlberg, Sweden. 1700, Royal Garden, Stockholm.

CARL HÅRLEMAN

1728–1753, Royal Palace (interior decoration), Stockholm. 1740, East India Company, Göteborg, Sweden. 1740s, Caroline Mausoleum, Riddarsholms Church, Sweden. 1745–1753, Royal Palaces, Drottningholm, Svartsjö, Sweden.

BIBLIOGRAPHY
STAVENOW, ÅKE 1927 *Carl Hårleman; en studie i frihetstidens arkitekturhistoria.* Uppsala, Sweden: Almqvist & Wiksell.

HARMON, ARTHUR L.

See SHREVE, LAMB, and HARMON.

HARRIS, CYRIL M.

Born in Detroit, Michigan, Cyril M. Harris (1917–) obtained a doctorate in physics from the Massachusetts Institute of Technology in 1945. A highly acclaimed acoustical consultant and winner of numerous awards, Harris is best known for his work on the John F. Kennedy Center for the Performing Arts (Washington, 1965–1971), Orchestra Hall (Minneapolis, Minnesota, 1974), and Avery Fisher Hall (New York, 1976). He has published extensively on architectural acoustics and noise control. Since 1952, he has taught at Columbia University.

NICOLAS B. COLLINS

WORKS
1962–1968, Metropolitan Opera House (with WALLACE HARRISON), New York. 1965–1971, John F. Kennedy Center for the Performing Arts (with EDWARD DURELL STONE), Washington. 1969, Krannert Center for the Performing Arts (with MAX ABRAMOVITZ), Urbana, Ill. 1974, Orchestra Hall (with Hammel, Green and Abrahamson), Minneapolis, Minn. 1976, Avery Fisher Hall (with PHILIP JOHNSON and John Burgee), New York. 1979, Orchestra Hall (with Fowler, Ferguson, Kingston, and Ruben), Salt Lake City, Utah. 1980, National Centre for the Performing Arts (with Johnson and Burgee), Bombay. n.d., Powell Symphony Hall, St. Louis, Mo.

BIBLIOGRAPHY
BLIVEN, BRUCE, JR. 1972 "Quiet Man." *New Yorker* June 17:39–42.
HARRIS, CYRIL M. (editor) (1957)1979 *Handbook of Noise Control.* 2d ed. New York: McGraw-Hill.
HARRIS, CYRIL M. (editor) 1975 *Dictionary of Architecture and Construction.* New York: McGraw-Hill.
HARRIS, CYRIL M. (editor) 1977 *Historic Architecture Sourcebook.* New York: McGraw-Hill.
HARRIS, CYRIL M., and CREDE, CHARLES E. (editors) 1963 *Shock and Vibration Handbook.* 3 vols. New York: McGraw-Hill.
HARRIS, CYRIL M., and KNUDSEN, VERN O. (1950) 1968 *Acoustical Designing in Architecture.* 2d ed., rev. New York: Wiley.

HARRIS, E. VINCENT

Emmanuel Vincent Harris (1876–1971), born in Devonport, England, was articled to James Harvey and then entered the Royal Academy Schools. An assistant to LEONARD A. S. STOKES and to Sir WILLIAM EMERSON, Harris later worked for the London County Council for seven years, leaving when he won the competition for Glamorgan County Hall (1908–1911). His style was a monumental neo-Georgian, and he was a persistent and successful entrant in competitions.

JILL ALLIBONE

WORKS
1905–1906, Electricity Transformer Station, Upper Street, Islington, London. 1908–1911, County Hall, Swansea, West Glamorgan, Wales. 1910–1912, 2 Duke Street, Westminster, London. *1912, Headquarters Fire Station, Cardiff, Wales. 1920–1932, War Memorial Halls, Sheffield, England. 1926, 24 Old Bond Street, London. 1926–1928, Town Hall, Braintree, Essex, England. 1927–1934, Public Reference Library; 1927–1938, Town Hall (extension); Manchester, England. 1929–1930, 1935–1938, County Hall (and additions), Kingston-upon-Thames, Surrey, England. 1930–1933, Civic Hall, Leeds, West Yorkshire, England. 1930–1936, County Council Offices, Tuanton, England. 1930–1954, Exeter University (laboratories, library, and administrative blocks), Devon, England. 1935–1950, County Hall, Trent Bridge, Nottinghamshire, England. 1937–1958, Council House, Bristol, England. 1947–1953, Saint Mary's College, Durham University, County Durham,

England. 1951–1959, Government Offices, Whitehall; 1958–1960, Central Library, Kensington; London.

BIBLIOGRAPHY

"Obituary." 1971 *Building* 221, no. 6690:66.
"Obituary." 1971 *The (London) Times* August 2:12b.
"The Royal Gold Medallist 1951." 1950–1951 *Journal of the Royal Institute of British Architects* Series 3 58:149–152.
"Tribute." 1971 *The (London) Times* August 12:14h.

HARRIS, HARWELL HAMILTON

Harwell Hamilton Harris (1903–) was one of the principal exponents of a regional architecture for California in the 1940s and 1950s. Born in Redlands, California, the son of an architect, his first ambition was to be a sculptor, but the day he caught sight of FRANK LLOYD WRIGHT's Barnsdall House in Los Angeles, he determined to be an architect. Ever the enemy of what he called the "regionalism of restriction," typified by New Orleans's Old French Quarter, he admired the "regionalism of liberation . . . in tune with the emerging thought of the time." His heroes were the Californians BERNARD MAYBECK and the brothers CHARLES S. GREENE and HENRY M. GREENE. His wife, the former Jean Murray Bangs, turned scholar to honor their achievements.

After serving a three-year apprenticeship to RICHARD JOSEF NEUTRA in Los Angeles, he went into private practice in 1933, escaping from Neutra's impersonal discipline into a world that honored the sensuous quality of redwood and other woods. He practiced in Texas and North Carolina. He was also director of the architectural school at the University of Texas and professor at North Carolina State.

WAYNE ANDREWS

WORKS

1935, Harwell Hamilton Harris House, Los Angeles. 1941, Weston Havens House, Berkeley. 1948, Clarence Wyle House, Ojai, Calif. 1949, Ralph Johnson House, Los Angeles. 1949, G. M. Loeb House, Redding, Conn. 1951, Harold English House, Los Angeles.

BIBLIOGRAPHY

ANDREWS, WAYNE (1947)1978 *Architecture, Ambition, and Americans: A Social History of American Architecture.* Rev. ed. New York: Free Press.
HARWELL, HAMILTON HARRIS 1965 *A Collection of His Writings and Buildings.* Raleigh, N.C.: School of Design.
"How a House Can Enrich the Life Within." 1953 *House Beautiful* 95, no. 5:157, 208–209, 230–231.

HARRIS, THOMAS

The first to describe mid-nineteenth century English architecture as "Victorian," Thomas Harris (1830–1900) was an outspoken proponent of iron as a building material. His designs and buildings often display polychromed and chamfered bricks but are just as often unambitious. Contemporary critics considered his writings revolutionary. Forgotten upon his death, Harris was rediscovered by critics in the 1940s.

JOHN H. WILSON

WORKS

*1873, Milner Field, Yorkshire, England. 1873–1874, Foster Warehouse, Lisson Grove, London. 1876, British Executive Commissioner and Delegate Residence, Centennial International Exhibition, Philadelphia. 1889, 58–60 Shaftsbury Avenue–45 Wardour Street, London. 1889, Stokesay Court, Shropshire, England.

BIBLIOGRAPHY

DONNER, PETER F. R. 1943 "A Harris Florilegium." *Architectural Review* 93:51–52.
GOODHART-RENDEL, H. S. 1949 "Rogue Architects of the Victorian Era." *Journal of the Royal Institute of British Architects* Series 3 56:251–259.
HARBRON, DUDLEY 1942 "Thomas Harris." *Architectural Review* 92:63–66.
HARRIS, THOMAS 1860 *Victorian Architects.* London: Bell and Daldy.
HARRIS, THOMAS 1894 *Three Periods of English Architecture.* London: Batsford.

HARRIS, WILLIAM CRITCHLOW

William Critchlow Harris (1854–1913) was born at Bootle, Lancashire, England, but emigrated with his family to Charlottetown, Prince Edward Island, in 1856. He apprenticed with the Halifax, Nova Scotia, architect DAVID STIRLING (1870–1875), after which he began his own practice in Charlottetown. In 1877, Stirling joined him in a partnership. From 1880 to 1882, Harris was in Winnipeg, Manitoba, where he narrowly lost a controversial competition for the design of the city hall. He returned to Prince Edward Island, but after 1899 he based himself in Halifax, with William Horton as partner.

Harris's best work was done as a church architect working in a High Victorian Gothic idiom. His early churches, such as Saint James's, Mahone Bay, Nova Scotia (1886), followed English Gothic precedents, but the acoustical benefits inherent in apses, shallow transepts, and unified interior volumes led him to shift his interest to the French

Gothic style, beginning with Saint Paul's Church, Charlottetown, in 1895. Rib-vaulted timber ceilings, resonating panels in chancel walls, and juniperwood sounding-posts under choir floors also give his later churches excellent acoustical qualities. In 1906, the Anglican Diocese of Nova Scotia rejected his plan for its new cathedral in favor of a Perpendicular Gothic design by BERTRAM GROSVENOR GOODHUE. Although entirely lacking in acoustical sophistication, Goodhue's church boasted a central tower and therefore looked more like a cathedral to churchmen influenced by the canons of the English Ecclesiologists. Harris, who had sung in the procathedral choir in his apprentice days and always dreamed of building the cathedral, never fully recovered from the disappointment. Ironically, the tower of Goodhue's cathedral was never built.

Harris also designed courthouses, business blocks, and dwelling houses, initially in Second Empire and Queen Anne styles, but later in a Romanesque Revival style which owed much to H. H. RICHARDSON. He was not an innovator, but neither was he an imitator. Within the context of his time, he developed as a stylist of individuality and character. He did not travel, and his formal training was limited to his time with Stirling in Halifax; yet, his achievements, especially as a church architect, were considerable. He believed he could design a church as well as any of his contemporaries, and he was probably right. Most of his churches were built in little visited rural places in the Canadian "lower provinces," and in consequence they were, and are, little known.

A fascinating episode in Harris's career was his retention by the Cape Breton Coal, Iron, and Railway Company to design all the buildings in its planned town of Broughton, Nova Scotia (1904–1906). After fifty buildings had been erected, the company failed, and the forest reclaimed the site.

Harris died in Halifax. Close to a hundred of his buildings survive, sixty of them in Prince Edward Island.

ROBERT C. TUCK

WORKS

1881, MacLennan House, Charlottetown, Prince Edward Island. 1884, All Saints, Clifton Royal, New Brunswick. 1886, Saint James's, Mahone Bay, Nova Scotia. 1887, Saint Paul's, Sturgeon, Prince Edward Island. 1887, King's County Courthouse, Georgetown, Prince Edward Island. 1888, All Souls Chapel; 1889, Connally Building; 1889, Saint Paul's Rectory; Charlottetown, Prince Edward Island. 1892, All Saints, Springhill, Nova Scotia. 1895, Saint Paul's, Charlottetown, Prince Edward Island. 1898, Saint Patrick's, Fort Augustus, Prince Edward Island. 1898, Saint John's; 1898, Lawson House; Windsor, Nova Scotia. 1898,

King's Playhouse, Georgetown, Prince Edward Island. 1898, Saint John's, Milton, Prince Edward Island. 1899, Saint Malachy's, Kinkora, Prince Edward Island. 1902, Saint Mary's, Indian River, Prince Edward Island. 1903, Trinity Church, Sydney Mines, Nova Scotia. 1903, Saint Andrew's, Mulgrave, Nova Scotia. 1911, Saint Cuthbert's, St. Theresa, Prince Edward Island.

BIBLIOGRAPHY

TUCK, ROBERT C. 1978 *Gothic Dreams, The Life and Times of a Canadian Architect.* Toronto: Dundurn.

HARRISON, HENRY G.

Henry G. Harrison (1813–1895), an Englishman by birth and training, started a practice in New York City in 1853. Although he was competent in several styles, his background, founded on the theories of A. W. N. PUGIN and the English Ecclesiologists, made him most fluent in the Gothic Revival style. He soon became a favorite architect of the Episcopal Church and built several widely acclaimed parish churches in the New York City area. His finest ecclesiastical work, the Cathedral of the Incarnation in Garden City, New York (1877–1883), is a superb Perpendicular Gothic Revival structure. Harrison also designed several blocks of rowhouses, the North Pavilion of Women's Hospital in New York (1862–1869), and a fine Gothic Revival estate called The Cliffs in Oyster Bay, New York (1863–1865), for James W. Beekman.

ANNE H. VAN INGEN

WORKS

1854–1857, Christ Episcopal Church, Hudson, N.Y. *1860–1862, Beekman Hill Methodist Church, New York. 1863–1865, The Cliffs, Oyster Bay, N.Y. *1862–1869, Women's Hospital (north pavilion); *1869, Manhattan Market; New York. 1877–1883, Cathedral of the Incarnation, Garden City, N.Y. 1880–1883, Trinity Cathedral, Omaha, Neb.

BIBLIOGRAPHY

Material on Henry G. Harrison can be found in the Archives of the Episcopal Diocese of Long Island, Garden City, N.Y., and the Print and Manuscript Collections, New-York Historical Society.

"Death of Henry G. Harrison, Architect." 1895 *American Architect and Building News* 49, Sept. 7:97–98.

HUNTINGTON, DAVID C. 1972 *Art and the Excited Spirit: America in the Romantic Period.* Ann Arbor: University of Michigan Museum of Art. Exhibition catalogue.

WHITE, JAMES F. 1962 *The Cambridge Movement: The Ecclesiologists and the Gothic Revival.* Cambridge University Press.

YOUNGS, MARY 1951 *History of the Cathedral of the Incarnation.* Garden City, N.Y.: Privately printed.

HARRISON, PETER

Peter Harrison (1716–1775), one of the most gifted designers in the American Colonial period, was born in York, England, and came to Newport, Rhode Island in 1740. In his fine public buildings in Newport, Boston, and Cambridge—all designed between 1748 and 1761—he exhibited an outstanding ability to weld architectural elements drawn from literary sources in use by the architectural practitioners of the day into a powerful and vital unity. He was also one of the first colonial architects to reflect the puristic and academic eighteenth-century Palladianism (see ANDREA PALLADIO) espoused by LORD BURLINGTON and his group. In Harrison's work, as pointed out by Fiske Kimball (1926), the broken and scrolled pediments and the buildings in the vernacular style of CHRISTOPHER WREN's followers disappeared to give way to "self-contained unbroken forms" and "the large and ordered dignity of the temple and the basilica."

Harrison was the fourth and youngest child of Yorkshire Quakers, Thomas and Elizabeth (Dennyson) Harrison, who lived near the shipping center of Hull, where Peter and his brother Joseph learned the arts of seamanship and made personal contacts with merchants from London and the colonies that set their future course. Peter also developed skills in cartography, drafting, and surveying and soon was to demonstrate both his architectural ability and a thorough grasp of the current academic and puristic ideals promulgated by Lord Burlington. In 1734–1736 Harrison had a firsthand opportunity to watch a major Palladian work—the Assembly Rooms in the cathedral city of York—go up under the aegis of Burlington himself, who was lord lieutenant of the shire. Harrison was probably also already acquiring what was to be the best privately owned architectural library in the colonies. Listed in the inventory of his estate taken in 1775 and first published by Carl Bridenbaugh, this library included the most important of the works sponsored by Burlington, among them COLEN CAMPBELL's *Vitruvius Britannicus* (1716–1725); ISAAC WARE's *Designs of Inigo Jones and Others* (1733); Edward Hoppus's *Palladio* (1735–1736); and WILLIAM KENT's *Designs of Inigo Jones* (1727) and *Designs for Houghton Hall, Holkham* (1736). Harrison also owned and used JAMES GIBBS's two popular volumes, *A Book of Architecture* (1728) and the *Rules for Drawing* (1732); these, more allied to the baroque of Wren's time, supplied much of Harrison's architectural vocabulary.

Harrison's first years in the colonies were devoted, with his brother Joseph, to commercial pursuits and he was by 1740 in command of a ship owned by the Newport merchant John Banister; by 1746, when he married Elizabeth Pelham, daughter of Edward Pelham, a wealthy and socially prominent Newport resident, he was already making public-spirited use of his talents, drafting a plan for Louisburg and Cape Breton and serving on a committee to draw plans and to design and build Fort George on Goat Island, a project that continued past 1755 and was never completed. He also built Beavertail Lighthouse in Jamestown (1753). All his services and the designs for his five major buildings were, except for Christ Church in Cambridge (1760–1761), rendered gratis.

Harrison's selection of a design for his first building, the Redwood Library (1748–1750), clearly established his alliance with Burlington's academic school. A small wooden rusticated Roman Doric pedimented temple with portico and side wings, it was an almost literal adaptation of a classical scheme that had appeared in Hoppus, in Ware, and in Kent. It was probably the first time that this scheme was used in the American colonies. THOMAS JEFFERSON later used it.

For King's Chapel in Boston (1749–1758), a hip-roofed rough-cut stone structure with a strong porticoed foretower, Harrison made full working drawings (now lost). The steeple, which according to Harrison was to be "fully Decorated" to counterbalance the severely plain exterior, was never built. For the handsomely articulated and classically scaled interior, the vocabulary came chiefly from Gibbs's *Rules* as did the detailing for Christ Church in Cambridge, built some ten years later. Both buildings exemplified Harrison's free use of

Peter Harrison. King's Chapel. Boston. 1749–1758

Peter Harrison.
Brick Market.
Newport, Rhode Island
1761–1773

the classical vocabulary of the day in developing an organic unity of form.

To meet the requirements of Sephardic ritual for Touro Synagogue (1759–1763), a square, severely plain, brick hip-roofed structure with a one-story Ionic porch, Harrison followed the plan and interior arrangement of the Portuguese Synagogue in London (1701) closely enough to indicate a personal acquaintance with this structure. The model for the interior architectural treatment, however, derives from such English sources as the plate in Kent's *Designs* showing a two-story galleried hall in Whitehall Palace, with details for the colossal colonnades drawn from Gibbs's *Rules.* Except for a change in the upper part of the Ark of the Covenant, the building has survived almost unaltered, with its cool clarity intact.

The scheme Harrison selected as suitable for the Brick Market (1761–1773) in Newport was taken from INIGO JONES's Old Somerset House published in the first volume of Campbell's *Vitruvius Britannicus.* In this two-story hip-roofed building decorated with a colossal order embracing both stories, set over a high arcaded basement, Harrison simplified and reinterpreted the design in brick used for the windows and the Ionic pilasters.

Among domestic buildings in Rhode Island, only one, the Matthew Cozzens House in Middletown (1750, now demolished), has been attributed specifically to Harrison. Stylistically advanced, it was a square hip-roofed house with belvedere, and a façade embellished with two-story pilasters set above a one-story open Ionic porch that extended around the house. In scale and design approach it relates to Harrison's public buildings as does the somewhat similar Shirley–Eustis House (after 1746) in Roxbury, Massachusetts; recent research by Frederic C. Detwiller tends to verify a tradition

that Harrison worked on the latter house. In Newport, the Francis Malbone House (1760) resembles Touro Synagogue while the Vernon House (1758) and the Peter Buliod House (1755) are also classically scaled and rusticated like the Redwood Library.

A little summer house built for Abraham Redwood in 1766 from a design in Gibbs's *Book of Architecture* is the only extant building attributed to Harrison after 1761–1762, but in 1768–1769 he worked on a house and designed other buildings for John Wentworth in Portsmouth, New Hampshire.

Harrison was a devoted Loyalist; he left Newport in 1766 to become collector of customs in New Haven. He died there a year after a rioting mob attacked his house, destroying furniture, his beautiful library, and his drawings.

ANTOINETTE F. DOWNING

WORKS

(A) After 1746, Shirley–Eustis House, Roxbury, Mass. 1748–1750, Redwood Library, Newport, R.I. 1749–1758, King's Chapel, Boston. *1750, Matthew Cozzens House, Middletown, R.I. *1753, Beavertail Lighthouse, Jamestown, R.I. (A)1755, Peter Buliod House, Newport, R.I. *1755, Fort George, Goat Island; (A)1758, Vernon House; 1759–1763, Touro Synagogue; (A)1760, Francis Malbone House; Newport, R.I. 1760–1761, Christ Church, Cambridge, Mass. 1761–1773, Brick Market, Newport, R.I. 1766, Abraham Redwood Summer House (now on grounds of Redwood Library); *1768–1769, John Wentworth House; Portsmouth, N.H.

BIBLIOGRAPHY

BRIDENBAUGH, CARL 1949 *Peter Harrison, First American Architect.* Chapel Hill: University of North Carolina Press.
BRIDENBAUGH, CARL 1959 "Peter Harrison, Addendum." *Journal of the Society of Architectural Historians* 18, Dec.:158–159.
CAMPBELL, COLEN (1715–1725)1967 *Vitruvius Britannicus or The British Architect.* Reprint. New York: Blom.
CORDINGLY, WILLIAM WADE 1921 "Shirley Place, Roxbury, Massachusetts, and its Builder, Governor William Shirley." *Old-Time New England* 12:51–63.
DOWNING, ANTOINETTE F. 1937 *Early Homes of Rhode Island.* Richmond, Va.: Garrett.
DOWNING, ANTOINETTE F., and SCULLY, VINCENT, J., JR. (1952)1967 *The Architectural Heritage of Newport, Rhode Island, 1640–1915.* 2d ed., rev. New York: Bramhill.
FRIEDMAN, LEE M. 1946 "The Newport Synagogue." *Old-Time New England.* 36:49–57.
GIBBS, JAMES (1728)1968 *A Book of Architecture.* Reprint. New York: Blom.
GIBBS, JAMES (1732)1924 *Rules for Drawing.* London: Hodder and Stoughton.

HOPPUS, EDWARD 1736 *Andrea Palladio: Architecture in Four Books.* London: Cole & Wilcox.

ISHAM, NORMAN MORRISON 1916 "The Brick Market." *Bulletin of the Society for the Preservation of New England Antiquities.* 6, no.2:3–11, 20–23.

KENT, WILLIAM (1727)1967 *Designs of Inigo Jones.* Farnborough, England: Gregg.

KIMBALL, SIDNEY FISKE 1926 "The Colonial Amateurs and Their Models: Peter Harrison." *Architecture* 53, no. 6:155–160; 54, no. 1:185–190, 209.

KIMBALL, SIDNEY FISKE (1932)1943 "Peter Harrison." Volume 8, page 347 in *Dictionary of American Biography.* New York: Scribner.

MASON, GEORGE C. 1891 *Annals of Redwood Library and Athenaeum.* Newport, R.I.: Redwood Library.

METCALF, PRISCILLA 1954 "Boston Before Bulfinch: Harrison's King's Chapel." *Journal of the Society of Architectural Historians* 13, Mar.:11–14.

"Obituary of Peter Harrison." 1775 *The Connecticut Journal* May 3.

SCHLESS, NANCY HALVERSON 1971 "Peter Harrison, The Touro Synagogue and the Wren City Church." *Journal of the Society of Architectural Historians* 30, Oct:242.

SCHWARTZ, ESTHER I. 1958 "Touro Synagogue Restored, 1827–29." *Journal of the Society of Architectural Historians* 17, no.2: 23–26.

TATUM, GEORGE B. 1975 "1776—How America Really Looked: Architecture." *American Art Journal* 7, May:4–22.

Touro Synagogue of Congregation Jeshuat Israel. 1948 Newport, R.I.: Society of Friends of Touro Synagogue National Historic Shrine.

WARE, WILLIAM ROTCH (1898–1900)1923 *The Georgian Period.* 3 vols. Rev. ed. New York: U.P.C. Book Co.

HARRISON, THOMAS

Thomas Harrison (1744–1829), of Lancaster and Chester, was a provincial architect with a national reputation among architectural *cognoscenti,* such as C. R. COCKERELL, Lord Elgin, Canon Blomfield, and Joseph Farington. Until recently, however, Harrison's reputation remained obscure. During his own lifetime, two factors contributed to this obscurity: his unworldly temperament and his geographical isolation in the northwest of England. Modern scholarship has gone some way toward rescuing Harrison's work from neglect.

Harrison was the son of a joiner from Richmond, Yorkshire. Thanks to Sir Lawrence Dundas of Aske, he traveled in Italy in 1769–1776. In Rome he so impressed Pope Clement XIV that he was admitted—through direct papal intervention—to the Academy of Saint Luke. From this period date his unexecuted designs for the Cortile del Belvedere in the Vatican; for the sacristy of St. Peter's; and for the Piazza del Popolo. In Rome he

had shown himself an able exponent of Continental neoclassicism. After his return to England he developed a Greek Revival style as pure—and as doctrinaire—as that of any of his contemporaries.

Harrison designed a number of neoclassical houses, notably Broomhall, Fife (1796–1799) for Lord Elgin. And it was his relationship with Elgin which ensured him a special place in the history of the Greek Revival. Harrison first suggested that Elgin make use of the embassy at Constantinople to collect casts and specimens of Greek antiquities. So we owe the Elgin Marbles, at least partly, to Harrison.

But domestic architecture formed only a minor part of his practice. His major concern was with monumental public buildings, as his architectural talents were not domestic but heroic. In Lancaster, Chester, Liverpool, and Manchester, he produced a series of neoclassical public buildings, all of characteristic simplicity and strength. Outstanding among these are the Lyceum, Liverpool (1800–1803); the Portico Library, Manchester (1802–1806); and Chester Castle (1788–1822).

Harrison never visited Greece. He was a Greek Revivalist only at secondhand, working laboriously from engravings by PETER NICHOLSON, JAMES STUART and NICHOLAS REVETT, and the Society of the Dilettanti volumes. Nevertheless it was at Chester Castle—Harrison's masterpiece—that the Greek Revival in Britain came of age. Certainly, with no less than eighty-four columns, the Chester Castle complex is a veritable mason's paradise. And the sweeping curve of its Shire Hall, columned and coffered, cast in a classic amphitheatrical mould, is a triumph of neoclassical design. As the whole project developed—over a period of nearly forty years—its details became increasingly archeological. In that respect it epitomized architectural tendencies in England as a whole between the 1780s and the 1820s: a move away from neoclassical abstraction toward the precision of pure Greek Revivalism.

Thomas Harrison. Chester Castle. Cheshire, England. 1788–1822

Harrison was only a reluctant Goth. He was interested in the structure rather than the details of medieval Gothic. His open-crowned steeple for the church of Our Lady and Saint Nicholas, Liverpool (1811–1815) is an able piece of engineering. His Hawkstone Citadel, Shropshire (1824–1825), exploits to the full the Picturesque principle of multiplied viewpoints. And his Lancaster Castle (1788–1799) is a remarkable essay in rationalized medieval forms: its polygonal Shire Hall, in particular, displays the mind of a classicist and a mathematician; the mind of an engineer.

As a monumental designer Harrison possessed an innate sense of scale; an instinct for the sublime. His Lord Hill Column at Shrewsbury (1814–1816) was the largest Doric column in the world. His Doric Anglesey Column at Plas Newydd (1816–1817) was very nearly as large. And his George III Jubilee Monument on Moel Fammau in Wales (1810)—a sublime monument to a mad King—must have been a prodigious example of neoclassical megalomania. But Harrison's sense of scale was more than a mere obsession with the gigantic. He had an instinct for the majesty of primitive forms. His massive Manchester Exchange (1806–1809) has long since disappeared. But the North Gate at Chester (1808–1810) still stands. This is a wonderfully powerful example of Harrison's monumental style, with primitivistic columns, broad-based dentils and shallow segmental arches.

Certainly at this point architecture and engineering are still marching in the same direction. For Harrison was not only a remarkable architect. He was also a great engineer. He combined both functions with rare success. In fact, his public career began and ended with remarkable feats of engineering: the Skerton Bridge at Lancaster (1783–1788) and the Grosvenor Bridge at Chester (1827–1829). Skerton Bridge was the first large-scale masonry bridge in Britain with a level road surface from bank to bank. And its combination of five elliptical arches, bold balustrade and dividing aedicules anticipates the compositional vocabulary of three more famous bridges— Kelso Bridge, Waterloo Bridge and London Bridge—all designed by Harrison's friend JOHN RENNIE. As for Grosvenor Bridge, it defies all comparison. Soaring like a rainbow across the river Dee, it marks the culmination of Harrison's career. At the time of its construction it was the largest single-span stone arch in the world—no less than two hundred feet. Harrison designed this great bridge during the early 1820s, but he did not live to see its completion in 1831.

Harrison's executed works are remarkable enough. But his unexecuted works were more remarkable still. Many of these survive in Chester City Archives; in the Cheshire Museum, North-wick; in the County Record Office, Chester; in the R.I.B.A. Drawings Collection; and in the Mollon Collection. As a young man he might have redesigned the Belvedere in the Vatican; he might have rebuilt the sacristy of St. Peter's; he might have created the Piazza del Popolo. As a middle-aged man he might have designed part of Edinburgh New Town; Lowther Castle, Westmorland; and the Woronzow Palace in the Ukraine. In old age he might have designed Waterloo Bridge, the Thames Embankment and even perhaps Trafalgar Square. All these are instances of lost commissions, designs which were outmanoeuvred rather than defeated. And this can perhaps be explained in terms of temperament. Harrison was a shy, solitary scholar, not an architectural politician. He was a committed architect, not a committee man.

J. MORDAUNT CROOK

WORKS

1783–1788, Skerton Bridge, Lancaster, England. 1788–1799, Lancaster Castle (completed by J. M. GANDY in 1802–1823), England. 1788–1822, Chester Castle, Cheshire, England. 1796–1799, Broomhall, Fife, Scotland. 1800–1803, Lyceum, Liverpool, England. 1802–1806, Portico Library (altered 1922), Manchester, England. *1806–1809, Manchester Exchange, England. 1808–1810, North Gate, Cheshire, England. *1810, Moel Fammau Monument, Denbighshire, Wales. 1811–1815, Church of Our Lady and Saint Nicholas (steeple), Liverpool, England. 1814–1816, Lord Hill Column (original design by Edward Haycock), Shrewsbury, England. 1816–1817, Anglesey Column, Plas Newydd, Wales. 1824–1825, Hawkstone Citadel, Shropshire, England. 1827–1829, Grosvenor Bridge (not completed until 1831), Cheshire, England.

BIBLIOGRAPHY

CROOK, J. MORDAUNT 1971 "The Architecture of Thomas Harrison." *Country Life* 149:876–879, 944–947, 1088–1091, 1539.

PIROTTA, L. 1960 "Thomas Harrison architetto inglese accademico di San Luca per sovrana motu proprio." *Strenna dei Romanisti* 21:257–263.

STILLMAN, DAMIE 1973 "British Architects and Italian Architectural Competitions, 1758–1780." *Journal of the Society of Architectural Historians* 32:43–66.

HARRISON and ABRAMOVITZ

The firm of Harrison and Abramovitz is known for some of the major commissions of our time: the United Nations Buildings (1947–1953) and the Lincoln Center for the Performing Arts (1959–1966), both in New York City, and the Albany Mall (1963–1978), Albany, New York. It has contributed to the team effort and technological innovation connected with large public edifices, urban plans, and office buildings characteristic of institutional and corporate commissions since World War II. In addition, Harrison has designed a number of highly original smaller structures, such as the so-called fish church in Stamford, Connecticut (1953–1958), and the Museum of Science and Technology in Flushing, New York (1963–1964).

Wallace K. Harrison (1895–1981) was born in Worcester, Massachusetts. In 1916, he came to New York City, where he worked for a year for McKim, Mead, and White while attending night classes at the atelier of William Wiley Corbett. In 1919, he went to Paris, where he passed the Beaux-Arts examination and enrolled in the atelier of Colonel Gustave Umbdenstock. Harrison returned to McKim, Mead, and White in New York for a year and then won a Rotch Traveling Scholarship that allowed him to visit Egypt, Syria, Greece, and France, and to spend a year at the American Academy in Rome.

Upon his return to New York City in 1922, Harrison worked as a draftsman for Bertram G. Goodhue and for Raymond M. Hood. In 1926, he married Ellen Milton, a sister-in-law of Abby Rockefeller, and the following year he became a partner of Helmle and Corbett. By 1929, Corbett was serving as one of several advisers to Rockefeller Center (1929–1933); Harrison participated in this project from its inception through the eventual expansion to Sixth Avenue (1941–1974). Although the initial buildings received mixed reviews, they are now acclaimed as a pioneering urban center created through the ingenious use of multilevel, superblock planning. The Center's Art Deco office skyscrapers in Indiana limestone are embellished with landscaped terraces, walkways, fountains, ornamental sculpture, and frescoes. They are grouped around a sunken plaza and include an underground shopping concourse and the famous Radio City Music Hall.

Max Abramovitz (1908–) was born in Chicago. In 1929, he received a B.S. from the University of Illinois, and two years later a master's degree from Columbia University. In 1932, a Columbia University fellowship enabled him to spend two years at the Ecole des Beaux-Arts. In 1934, Abramovitz joined Corbett, Harrison, and William H. McMurray as a designer; he became a partner of Harrison, André Fouilhoux, and Abramovitz in 1941. The firm became Harrison and Abramovitz in 1945 after Fouilhoux's death.

The two architects taught briefly at the Columbia School of Architecture: Harrison in 1925 and Abramovitz in 1931. Morris Lapidus studied with Harrison. From 1939 to 1942, Harrison and Abramovitz taught at the Yale School of Architec-

ture, transforming the school's program from Beaux-Arts to Modern.

The choice of Harrison and Abramovitz to design the Perisphere and Trylon theme buildings for the 1939/1940 World of Tomorrow Fair in New York City forecast the role they were to play in the city for the next two decades. In 1947, responsibility for the design and building of the United Nations Headquarters was given to Harrison, assisted by Abramovitz. The slender, thirty-nine-floor Secretariat (1949–1950) was one of New York's first glazed, curtain-wall skyscrapers.

It was in the early 1960s that one of the firm's most important commissions was executed: Lin-

Harrison and Abramovitz. Rockefeller Center (with Hood, Reinhard and Hofmeister, Corbett, McMurray, and Fouilhoux). New York. 1929–1933, 1941–1974

Harrison and Abramovitz. RCA Building, Rockefeller Center New York. 1929–1933, 1941–1974

Harrison and Abramovitz. United Nations Buildings (with Le Corbusier, Niemeyer, and Markelius). New York. 1947–1953

Harrison and Abramovitz.
Metropolitan Opera House.
New York.
1962–1966

Harrison and Abramovitz.
Philharmonic (now Avery
Fisher) Hall.
New York.
1959–1962

Harrison and Abramovitz.
Phoenix Mutual Life
Insurance Building.
Hartford, Connecticut.
1960–1964

Lhasa, contributed to the Capitol's overblown design and costs ($2 billion).

Harrison became increasingly absorbed by his work in Albany while Abramovitz worked independently in France and the American Midwest. By 1978, Abramovitz formed a new partnership with Michael Harris and James Kingsland; Harrison and Abramovitz are associated only for supervision of the United Nations Buildings; otherwise, Harrison works independently. Both architects have received numerous awards. In 1957, Harrison received the highest honor for an American architect, the Gold Medal of the American Institute of Architects.

VICTORIA NEWHOUSE

WORKS

1929–1933, 1941–1974, Rockefeller Center (with Raymond M. Hood, L. A. Reinhard and Henry Hofmeister, Harvey Wiley Corbett, William H. McMurray, and André Fouilhoux); *1939–1940, Perisphere and Trylon, World's Fair; 1947–1953, United Nations Buildings (with Le Corbusier, Oscar Niemeyer, and Sven Markelius); New York. 1950–1951, 1955–1956, Corning Glass Center and Administrative Building, N.Y. 1950–1953, Alcoa Building, Pittsburgh. 1952?–1967, Educational Buildings and Chapels, Brandeis University, Waltham, Mass. 1953–1958, First Presbyterian Church, Stamford, Conn. 1954?–1958, Residence and Auditorium, Rockefeller Institute; 1959–1960, Time-Life Building; 1959–1962, Philharmonic (now Avery Fisher) Hall; New York. 1960–1964, Phoenix Mutual Life Insurance Building, Hartford, Conn. 1962–1966, Metropolitan Opera House; 1963–1964, Museum of Science and Technology, Flushing; New York. 1963–1978, South Mall, Albany, N.Y. 1967–1971, United States Steel Building, Pittsburgh. 1968?–1970, Banque Rothschild Building, Paris.

BIBLIOGRAPHY

"A Brilliant Canopy for Worship." 1958 *Architectural Forum* 108, Apr.:104–107.
"Alcoa Complete: Pittsburgh's 30-Story Aluminum Waffle is America's Most Daring Experiment in Modern Office Building." 1953 *Architectural Forum* 99, Nov.:124–131.
HARRISON, HELEN A. 1980 *Dawn of a New Day: The New York World's Fair, 1939/40.* New York: Queens Museum. Exhibition catalogue.
KOOLHAAS, REM 1978 *Delirious New York.* New York: Oxford University Press.
KRINSKY, CAROL HERSELLE 1978 *Rockefeller Center.* New York: Oxford University Press.
KRINSKY, CAROL HERSELLE 1981 "St. Petersburg-on-the-Hudson: The Albany Mall." *Art the Ape of Nature.* New York: Harry N. Abrams, Inc.
"The Secretariat a Campanile, a Cliff of Glass, a Great Debate." 1950 *Architectural Forum* 93, Nov.:93–113.
WIND, HERBERT WARREN 1954 "Architect." *New Yorker* Nov. 20:51–79; Nov. 27:51–85; Dec. 4:55–85.

coln Center for the Performing Arts. Eighteen blocks of slums were cleared largely through the efforts of Robert Moses to make way for a municipal art center, in large part conceptualized in 1935–1938 as an extension of Rockefeller Center. Harrison acted as coordinator for the Center and architect for the Metropolitan Opera House (1962–1966); Abramovitz was responsible for Philharmonic Hall (now Avery Fisher Hall; 1959–1962). Clad uniformly in travertine, and neoclassical in style, the buildings are grouped around a large, well-frequented plaza. Lincoln Center has become a prototype for cultural centers throughout the United States.

Harrison's most recent commission was the Albany South Mall. Constructed in concrete and marble, four twenty-three-story Agency buildings, a forty-four-story office tower, a Legislature and a Justice building, a library and an egg-shaped Performing Arts Center are grouped on a platform consisting of promenades, garages, and storage spaces. Governor Rockefeller's monumental concept, inspired in part by the Dalai Lama's Palace in

YOUNG, EDGAR B. 1980 *Lincoln Center: The Building of an Institution.* New York University Press.

HARTUNG, HUGO

Born in Jena, Germany, trained at the Technische Hochschulen in Dresden and Berlin-Charlottenburg, and eventually a teacher at the Technische Hochschule in Dresden, Hugo Hartung (1855–1932) was principally a builder of houses. In these houses, Hartung employed strongly medievalizing forms—steeply pitched roofs and turrets—and combined them with relatively open plans and plain wood and plaster surfacing materials. Like OTTO MARCH, therefore, Hartung contributed to the development of domestic architecture in Germany in the late nineteenth and early twentieth centuries.

Hartung was also influential as an architectural historian and publicist. His *Motive der mittelalterlichen Baukunst in Deutschland* (Berlin, 1896–1902) and *Ziele und Ergebnisse der italienischen Gotik* (Berlin, 1912) did much to suggest, at the beginning of the twentieth century, that medieval architecture could be a source for a simple and even primitive geometry. A similar affection for simple geometry was prominent in Hartung's other writings, including his accounts of his travels in the Near East, which he published in the *Zentralblatt der Bauverwaltung* in 1907, and which he illustrated with sketches of essentially cubic buildings in Egypt and the Levant.

BARBARA MILLER LANE

WORKS

1888?, Buildings, Applied Arts Exhibition, Munich. 1891?, Charlottenau Estate (with K. Schäfer), Zehlendorf; 1900?, Hartung House, Villencolonie Grünewald; Berlin. n.d., Bank, Mainz, Germany. n.d., District Administrative Offices; n.d., Evangelical Church; Thorn, Germany. n.d., Kaiser Wilhelm Monument, Arnstadt, Germany. n.d., Schloss Eichhof, Lauterbach, Germany.

BIBLIOGRAPHY

Berlin und seine Bauten. 1896 2 vols. Berlin: Ernst & Son.
"Der Entwurf für den Kaiserthurm auf der Alteburg bei Arnstadt." 1901 *Zentralblatt der Bauverwaltung* 21:260.
HARTUNG, HUGO 1888 "Die Bauten der Kunstgewerbe-Ausstellung in München." *Zentralblatt der Bauverwaltung* 8:385–387.
HARTUNG, HUGO 1896–1902 *Motive der mittelalterlichen Baukunst in Deutschland in photographischen Originalaufnahmen.* 3 vols. Berlin: Wasmuth.
HARTUNG, HUGO 1902 *Studienentwürfe, Aufnahmen und Ausführungen.* Berlin: Wasmuth.
HARTUNG, HUGO 1907 "Wanderungen im Orient." *Zentralblatt der Bauverwaltung* 27:566–569, 578–580.
HARTUNG, HUGO 1912 *Ziele und Ergebnisse der italienischen Gotik.* Berlin: Ernst & Son.
"Landhaus Charlottenau bei Zehlendorf." 1891 *Zentralblatt der Bauverwaltung* 11:461–462.
"Die Villencolonie Grünewald bei Berlin." 1900 *Zentralblatt der Bauverwaltung* 20:4–6, 16–17.

HARTWELL and RICHARDSON

Boston-born Henry Walker Hartwell (1833–1919) began his architectural practice in Boston in 1856 after a five-year apprenticeship with Joseph and HAMMATT BILLINGS. For twenty-five years, he practiced either alone (1856–1869 and 1879–1881) or in partnership with the little-known Boston architects Albert Swasey, Jr., and George Tilden, producing a variety of polychromatic Victorian Gothic and Queen Anne style public buildings and churches. In 1881, during the construction of his exuberant Queen Anne town hall for Belmont, Massachusetts, Hartwell formed a permanent partnership with William Cummings Richardson (1854–1935) who had collaborated on the building's design. Although Richardson was twenty years Hartwell's junior, this marked the beginning of the most successful period in both architects' careers. Hartwell was primarily responsible for construction, Richardson, who had been trained at the Massachusetts Institute of Technology, for design. While not innovative in style, the architects enjoyed great popularity in the 1880s and 1890s as they provided clients with well-designed, comfortably up-to-date buildings in the accepted styles of the day. Throughout the 1880s, their nonresidential work was influenced more and more by H. H. RICHARDSON (for example, First Spiritual Temple, Boston, 1884), while their best residential work, a series of suburban houses near Boston, showed their skillful handling of the Shingle style and their careful attention to interior detail (Henry Yerxa House, Cambridge, Massachusetts, 1887–1888). In 1895, the English architect James Driver joined the firm, and their work turned toward classical-style public schools and Colonial Revival houses, more staid and conventional than their buildings in the 1880s and early 1890s. After Hartwell's death (1919) and Driver's departure from the firm (1921), Richardson continued to practice in Boston under the original firm name Hartwell and Richardson until his own death in 1935.

SUSAN E. MAYCOCK

WORKS

1874–1875, Central Congregational Church (Hartwell,

Swasey, and Co.), Fall River, Mass. 1878–1879, Town Hall (Hartwell and Tilden), Milton, Mass. 1881–1882, First Baptist Church, Cambridge, Mass. 1881–1882, Town Hall, Belmont, Mass. 1883–1884, Odd Fellows Hall, Cambridge, Mass. 1884, First Spiritual Temple, Boston. 1884, Moses Stevens House, North Andover, Mass. 1885, H. O. Underwood House, Belmont, Mass. 1886–1887, Christ Church; 1887–1888, Stillman Kelley House; 1887–1888, Henry Yerxa House; Cambridge Mass. 1889–1890, Memorial Library, Acton, Mass. 1889–1890, David Ritchie House, Cambridge, Mass. 1891, Youth's Companion Building, Boston. 1893, Central Congregational Church, Newtonville, Mass.

BIBLIOGRAPHY

HARTWELL, HENRY W. 1896 "School Architecture." Unpublished manuscript. Lecture delivered to the American Institute of Instruction, Bethlehem, N.H., July 10, 1896.
VOGEL, SUSAN MAYCOCK 1973 "Hartwell and Richardson: An Introduction to Their Work." *Journal of the Society of Architectural Historians* 32, no. 2:132–146.

HARVEY, JOHN

John Harvey was an assistant of SAMUEL WYATT from 1785 onward, later working on his own with indifferent success until around 1819. His only known surviving building is the Shire Hall at Stafford (1794) to a plan by Wyatt—a bold, yet exquisitely detailed design in a manner transitional between Adamesque (see ROBERT ADAM) and a more austere neoclassicism.

ANDOR GOMME

WORKS

1794, Shire Hall, Stafford, England. *1813, Millbank Penitentiary (superseded by ROBERT SMIRKE), London.

BIBLIOGRAPHY

PEVSNER, NIKOLAUS 1974 *The Buildings of England: Staffordshire.* Harmondsworth, England: Penguin.
RICHARDSON, GEORGE (1802–1808)1970 Volume 2, plates 7–10 in *The New Vitruvius Britannicus.* Reprint. New York: Blom.

ḤASAN B. ḤUSAYN AṬ-ṬŪLŪNĪ

Born in Cairo, Egypt, Ḥasan b. Ḥusayn aṭ-Ṭūlūnī (c.1432–1517), scion of the aṭ-Ṭūlūnī family (see AḤMAD B. AḤMAD B. MUHAMMAD AṬ-ṬŪLŪNĪ AND FAMILY), had a long career as architect-engineer to several of the Mamlūk sultans of Egypt. He was given the title of chief architect in 1453 by Sultan Inal and held it off and on for the next

sixty-four years. The earliest known construction associated with him appears to be that of the mausoleum of Sultan Khūshqadam (which has not survived) in the northern cemetery of Cairo. During the reign of Sultan Qaytbay, 1468–1496, one of the greatest of Mamlūk builders, he restored numerous monuments and structures. He directed the work on Qaytbay's *madrasah* (theological school) on Rauḍa Island (completed 1482 and still extant but with extensive modern restorations) as well as the work on the famed donkey-driven waterwheels and mills of Cairo.

AMY W. NEWHALL

BIBLIOGRAPHY

IBN IYĀS (1893–1895)1921 *An Account of the Ottoman Conquest of Egypt in the Year A.H. 922 (A.D.1516).* Translated by W. H. Salmon. London: Royal Asiatic Society.
IBN TAGHRIBIRDI 1909–1950 *An-nujûm az-Zâhirâ.* Edited by William Popper. Berkeley: University of California Press.
MAYER, LEO A. 1956 *Islamic Architects and Their Works.* Geneva: Kundig.

HASE, CONRAD WILHELM

Trained as a master mason in Hannover, Germany, Conrad Wilhelm Hase (1818–1902) continued technical studies in Munich where he also studied architecture under FRIEDRICH VON GÄRTNER. Gärtner's brick *Rundbogenstil* is the basis of Hase's early designs for the Hannover Railways and his first major building, the Provincial Museum, won in an 1853 competition. The exploration of brick as a building material dominated Hase's designs to the last, but beginning with the Christuskirche (1859–1863)—the largest of one hundred churches he designed—he employed North German Brick Gothic as models. These he studied in numerous restorations and study trips through Lower Saxony with his students, but he always allowed structural and material considerations to take first place in his own design. An influential teacher from 1849, Hase founded the Hannover School of Gothic Revivalists who carried his brick style throughout Northern Germany and Scandinavia in the 1870s and 1880s.

BARRY BERGDOLL

WORKS

1853–1855, Provincial Museum (now Künstlerhaus), Hannover, Germany. 1857–1864, Schloss Marienburg (restoration, completed by Edwin Oppler), near Nordstemmen, Germany. 1859–1860, Hase House; 1859–1863, Christuskirche, Hannover, Germany. 1865, Saint Spiritus Hospital Chapel, Einbeck, Germany. 1867–

1870, Church, Langenhagen, Germany. 1867–1869, Saint Martin, Dassel, Germany. 1869–1871, Protestant Church, Hagenburg, Germany. 1872–1873, Cathedral High School, Verden, Germany. 1877–1879, Railroad Station, Oldenburg, Germany. 1884–1886, Martinskirche, Bernburg, Germany. 1885–1886, Church, Rhüden, near Seesen, Germany. 1886, House, 24 Wilhelm-Busch-Strasse, Hannover, Germany. 1900, Cemetery Chapel, Hameln, Germany.

BIBLIOGRAPHY

DEHIO, GEORG 1977 Handbuch der deutschen Kunstdenkmäler: Bremen/Niedersachsen. Berlin: Deutsche Kunstverlag.

HASE, CONRAD WILHELM 1855–1883 Die mittelalterlichen Baudenkmäler Niedersachsens. 3 vols. Hannover, Germany: Architekten und Ingenieure Verein.

HASE, CONRAD WILHELM c.1875 Reise Aufnahmen aus Lippoldsberg, Hoexter (Oberweger) und Wimpfen. . . . Hannover, Germany: Coehn & Risch.

KOKKELINK, GÜNTHER 1968 "Die Neugotik Conrad Wilhelm Hases." Hannoverische Geschichtsblätter 28, nos. 1-3.

MOHRMANN, KARL 1902 "Aus dem Leben eines deutschen Künstlers." Zentralblatt der Bauverwaltung 22:166–168.

MUTHESIUS, STEFAN 1974 Das englische Vorbild. Munich: Prestel.

SCHÖNERMARK, GUSTAV 1889–1895 Die Architektur der Hannoverischen Schule. 7 vols. Hannover, Germany: Manz.

HASENAUER, CARL

Carl (von) Hasenauer (1833–1894) was born in Vienna as the son of a carpenter at court. From 1850 to 1855 he studied at the Academy of Fine Arts in Vienna where he became well acquainted with the work of his teachers Eduard van der Nüll (see SICCARDSBURGH AND VAN DER NÜLL) and August Siccardsburgh. After his studies he traveled through Europe and until 1865 built some villas for upper class clients. In 1861, he won third prize in the competition for the Vienna Opera House.

In 1867, he, together with THEOPHILUS HANSEN, HEINRICH VON FERSTEL, and Moritz Löhr, took part in the competition for the Museums of Art and Natural History in Vienna. As none of the projects was satisfactory, the competition was repeated—without any better result. The problem was solved at last by GOTTFRIED SEMPER, who, having been asked for advice, proposed the Imperial Forum, consisting of the U-shaped New Imperial Palace, two triumphal arches crossing the Ringstrasse and two museums. Semper chose Hasenauer as a partner for these works, but the partnership was not successful. From 1871 to 1873,

Hasenauer was intensely occupied with the design and construction of the buildings for the World's Fair in Vienna (1873). Afterward, he tried to pass Semper's work off for his own.

After Semper's death in 1879, the design and construction of the Ringstrasse complex, including the Court Theater, were carried out under Hasenauer's direction. The Forum, one wing of the palace, and the triumphal arches were never built.

From 1884 to 1894, Hasenauer was professor at the Academy of Fine Arts in Vienna, the last two years as rector.

Hasenauer became famous for the Ringstrasse buildings, but his particular talents were most effective in upper class residential buildings. The monumental projects he directed or took part in were either influenced by predecessors or dominated by Semper. His buildings for the Worlds Fair were derived—but further developed—from an 1845 exhibition project by van der Nüll. Without a doubt, the grand idea of the Imperial Forum and the basic design of the Court Theater have to be ascribed to Semper. But in some way Hasenauer was more modern than his greater predecessors as the architect of the interior.

Toward the end of the century, the baroque, extrovert demonstration of wealth and power became obsolete and the stratification of society was now more hidden by architecture than it was exposed. This process was accompanied by a growing complexity of upper class private life. Hasenauer met these demands by emphasizing the interior organization and decoration of a building and separating it from the outside by solid walls. He even covered with walls the bold, transparent iron-and-steel construction of the "Rotunde" by Scott Russel for the 1873 fair.

His villas, the Lützow Palace (1870) and Hermesvilla (1882–1886), have very complex floor plans, with a rich and elegant interior decoration. They are designed in German or French Renaissance Revival, allowing an irregular layout and a dominating effect of walls. In Aziendahof (1867–1868), he concentrated all his efforts on the interior by designing a glass-covered interior passage, serving as a bazaar.

RENATE BANIK-SCHWEITZER

WORKS
c.1860, Villa, Mödling, near Vienna. c.1860, Villa Gerold, Neuwaldegg (now Vienna). 1861, Villa Ranzoni, Gmunden, Austria. 1864, Villa Zang, Neidling (now Vienna). *1867–1868, Aziendahof (shops and apartments); 1870, Lützow Palace; *1871–1873, World's Fair (chief architect); 1872–1881, Museums of Art and Natural History (with Gottfried Semper); 1874–1888, Court Theater (with Semper);

1881–1894, New Imperial Palace (with Semper; not completed until 1913); Vienna. 1882–1886, Hermesvilla, Lainz (now Vienna). 1883–1884, Hospital of Barmherzige Brüder (with Otto Hofer and Anton Schönmann); 1886, Tegetthoff Monument; 1888, Maria-Theresa Monument; 1889, Grillparzer Monument; Vienna.

BIBLIOGRAPHY

BEETZ, WILHELM 1929 *Die Hermes-Villa in Lainz.* Vienna: Gerlach & Wiedling.
CZEIKE, FELIX 1963–1964 "Carl Freiherr von Hasenauer: Der persönliche Nachlass im Archiv der Stadt Wien." *Jahrbuch des Vereins für Geschichte der Stadt Wien* 19–20:251–276.
EGGERT, KLAUS 1963 "Die Hermesvilla im Lainzer Tiergarten bei Wien." *Alte und moderne Kunst* 8, no. 66:2–10.
EGGERT, KLAUS 1976 *Der Wohnbau der Wiener Ringstrasse im Historismus 1855–1896.* Volume 7 in *Die Wiener Ringstrasse—Bild einer Epoche.* Wiesbaden, Germany: Steiner.
EGGERT, KLAUS 1978 "Gottfried Semper, Carl von Hasenauer." Volume 8, pages 79–231, in *Die Wiener Ringstrasse—Bild einer Epoche.* Wiesbaden, Germany: Steiner.
LHOTSKY, ALPHONS 1941 *Die Baugeschichte der Museen und der Neuen Burg.* Vienna: Berger.
WAETZOLDT, STEPHAN (editor) 1977 *Bibliographie zur Architektur im 19. Jahrhundert: Die Aufsätze in den deutschsprachigen Architekturzeitschriften, 1789–1918.* Nendeln, Germany: KTO Press.

HASTINGS, THOMAS

See CARRÈRE and HASTINGS.

HATCH, STEPHEN D.

Stephen Decatur Hatch (1839–1894) was born in Swanton, Vermont, and received his architectural training in the New York office of JOHN B. SNOOK. In 1864, he established his own practice in New York and maintained an active career designing many important commercial buildings and hotels. He also had a thriving business in upper class residences in New York City. Hatch's commercial buildings of the late 1860s and the 1870s were in the popular Second Empire style. In his later commercial buildings, he adopted a loose, late Victorian mode. His residences were usually in the Italianate brownstone manner favored in the post-Civil War years.

DENNIS STEADMAN FRANCIS,
JOY M. KESTENBAUM,
and MOSETTE GLASER BRODERICK

WORKS

1868, Gilsey Hotel; *1868, Jay Gould House; 1870, Robbins and Appleton Building; *1873, Windsor Hotel; *1875–1877, Union Dime Savings Bank; New York. 1876, Jubilee Hall, Fisk University, Nashville, Tenn; *1876–1877, William Rockefeller House; *1878–1879, Boreel Building; *1880, London, Liverpool, and Globe Insurance Company Building; *1881, Murray Hill Hotel; c.1886, United States Army Building, Whitehall Street; 1889–1890, Manhattan Savings Institute Building, 664 Broadway; 1893–1894, Roosevelt Building, Broadway at 13th Street; New York.

BIBLIOGRAPHY

New York's Great Industries. 1885 New York Historical Publishing Company.
"Obituary." 1894 *American Architect and Building News* 45, Aug. 25:69.
"Obituary." 1894 *Architecture and Building* 21, Aug.: 78.
"Obituary." 1894 *Real Estate Record and Builders Guide* 54, Aug. 18:228.

HAUBERRISSER, GEORG VON

Descended from a Rhenish family of architects, Georg Joseph, Ritter von Hauberrisser (1841–1922), designed the neo-Gothic City Hall for Munich (1867–1872, extended 1899–1909) and many other municipal buildings in Germany. Also active in historic preservation and restoration, Hauberrisser was honored by several German cities and academies, and became an honorary member of the Royal Institute of British Architects.

BARBARA MILLER LANE

WORKS

1867–1874, City Hall (extended 1899–1909), Munich. 1879–1887, City Hall, Kaufbeuren, Germany. 1881–1891, Herz Jesukirche, Graz, Austria-Hungary. 1882?, Santa Fé Estate, Rio de Janeiro. 1884, Defresser House, Munich. 1884–1890, City Hall, Wiesbaden, 1888–1903, Church of Saint Sebald (restoration), Nuremberg, Germany. 1890–?, Deutschordensburg Busau (reconstruction), Moravia, Austria-Hungary. 1892–1906, Saint Paul's Church, Munich. 1897–1900, City Hall, Landshut, Germany. 1897–1900, City Hall, Saarbrücken, Germany. 1902–1904, House (Georg Hauberrisser Residence); 1902–1904, Kaulbach Museum; Munich.

BIBLIOGRAPHY

DÖRING, OSKAR 1924 *Zwei Münchener Baukünstler: Gabriel von Seidl, Georg von Hauberrisser.* Munich: Allgemeine Vereinigung für christliche Kunst.
HAUBERRISSER, GEORG 1883 *Das neue Rathaus in München.* Munich: Autotypie.
MEGELE, MAX 1951 *Baugeschichtlicher Atlas der Landeshauptstadt München.* Munich: Megele.
München und seine Bauten. 1912 Munich: Bruckmann.
SCHMITZ, J. 1921 "Professor Dr. Georg Hauberrisser." *Zentralblatt der Bauverwaltung* 41:141–142.

Zeitschrift für Baukunde. 1882–1884 5, no. 3:24, plates 19–33; 7, no. 1:1–4, plates 1–2, no. 4:203, plate 12.
ZILS, WILHELM 1913 *Geistiges und Künstlerisches; München in Selbstbiographie.* Munich: Kellerer.

HAUGAARD, WILLIAM E.

William E. Haugaard (1889–1949), director of the New York State Department of Architecture from 1928 to 1949, was born in Brooklyn, New York, and received architectural training at the Pratt Institute, the Massachusetts Institute of Technology, and the Atelier Duquesne in Paris. Between 1911 and 1917, he served as a draftsman with the Istmusian Canal Commission in Panama. Haugaard's work before his state appointment included military, ecclesiastical, and residential projects. State facilities constructed under his supervision included Brentwood State Hospital and Attica State Prison. Upon retirement, Haugaard served as chief of planning for the New York City Housing Authority.

WESLEY HAYNES

WORKS

1926, Parmley Apartment House, Summit, N.J. 1935, Long Island Park Commission Buildings, Queens, N.Y. n.d., Attica State Prison, New York. n.d., Pilgrim State Hospital, Brentwood, N.Y. n.d., Union Congregational Church, Richmond Hill, Staten Island, N.Y.

BIBLIOGRAPHY

Architectural Record 1935 77:353.
"The Parmley Apartment House, Summit, New Jersey." 1926 *Architectural Record* 59:244–249.
"W. E. Haugaard, 59, Long an Architect." 1948 *New York Times,* Sept. 18, p. 17.

HAUSSMANN, GEORGES-EUGENE

Georges-Eugène Haussmann (1809–1891) was the dynamic and audacious prefect of the Department of the Seine who directed the rebuilding of Paris in the 1850s and 1860s. The Emperor Napoleon III originally conceived the great project, but his charge to Haussmann left the prefect wide discretion. Thus, Haussmann's ideas were indelibly imprinted on the city, and by example, on urban planning around the world.

Haussmann was born in Paris, the son of a Protestant bourgeois family with strong Bonapartist connections. His maternal grandfather was a Napoleonic general, and Prince Eugène de Beauharnais, Napoleon I's stepson, was his godfather. Haussmann grew up in Paris and was educated at the Lycée Henri IV, the Collège Bourbon, and the Law School of the University of Paris. In 1831 he exploited his minor role in the Revolution of 1830 and his friendship with a son of the new king, Louis-Philippe, to win appointment as secretary-general of the prefecture of the Department of the Vienne in western France, beginning a career in the prefectoral corps that continued without interruption until 1870. In Bordeaux after the Revolution of 1848 he openly supported the candidacy of Louis-Napoleon Bonaparte for the presidency of the newly established republic and was rewarded by appointment early in 1849 as prefect of the politically volatile Department of the Var. The next year he was moved to another trouble spot, the Department of the Yonne, and in late 1851 he was named prefect of the Gironde to assure the adherence of Bordeaux to the new Bonapartist regime established after Louis-Napoleon's *coup d'état* of December 1851. In 1853, the emperor, impressed by Haussmann's abilities and his political loyalty, called him to Paris to direct his planned renovation of the capital.

The emperor had three principal objectives in his plan for Paris, which Haussmann adopted as his own: to make Paris a fittingly magnificent capital for a great imperial power; to adapt the city to the need of a rapidly growing population and of the new age of industry, expanding trade, and railroads; to establish a secure seat of government by facilitating the suppression of collective violence in the streets.

In seventeen years of massive demolitions, matching construction, and heavy expenditure, Haussmann fulfilled the emperor's unprecedented assignment. Under his administration Paris acquired 90 miles of new streets, hundreds of new public and private buildings, 4400 acres of parks, including the spacious Bois de Boulogne and the Bois de Vincennes, a daily inflow of 33 million gallons of fresh spring water for domestic use, and 354 miles of underground sewers including the huge collector sewers that virtually ended the discharge of waste water into the Seine within Paris.

Financial difficulties and political changes in the empire at the end of the 1860s led to Haussmann's dismissal early in 1870. In succeeding decades he engaged in several business ventures, served a term in the Chamber of Deputies as a deputy from Corsica, and wrote his memoirs (1890–1893), an indispensable source on his work in Paris. He died in Paris on January 9, 1891.

In planning new streets Haussmann was guided by classical principles of urban design associated with the Ecole des Beaux Arts—the straight line, perspectives, and uniform façades. His long, straight avenues, such as the Boulevard de

Sébastopol and the Boulevard Voltaire, put a characteristic and lasting mark on the city's face. Perspectives were always a consideration when he planned a new street, and the new Opera House closing the perspective of the Avenue de l'Opéra, and the Arc de Triomphe terminating those of the eight new avenues radiating from the Place de l'Etoile testify to that interest. To him, too, Paris owes its last *ordonnances,* exemplified by the four-story buildings, topped by rounded roofs, and decorated with Corinthian pilasters on the Place de l'Opéra, the Place du Théâtre-Français, and the Place Saint-Michel.

Haussmann's classical taste in architecture was reflected in buildings—designed by architects in his administration—such as the Tribunal de Commerce (1860–1865) by ANTOINE-NICOLAS BAILLY and the west façade of the Palais de Justice (1857–1868) by LOUIS-JOSEPH DUC as well as in most of the *mairies,* barracks, theaters, schools, and hospitals built in Paris during the Second Empire. Haussmann did, however, energetically second Napoleon III's interest in the use of new industrial building materials and in the innovative design that they made possible. According to his own account, Haussmann induced his old schoolmate VICTOR BALTARD to design the iron and glass pavilions (1854–1866) for the central markets that served the city until the markets were moved to outlying sites in the 1970s.

In judging Haussman's work antiquarians and preservationists deplore his destruction of historic buildings and quarters. Marxist critics see it as the beginning of the conquest of Paris by the bourgeoisie, a calculated effort to expel the working class from the capital. Some city planners blame him for failing to relieve overcrowding of people and buildings, others for creating traffic congestion by converging streets on a single point and by locating monuments in the lines of major avenues. Nonetheless, his parks and planted squares provided open space throughout the city and made it more livable, and they continue to do so a century later. His streets served the needs of traffic reasonably well until they were overwhelmed by automobiles in the 1960s.

Although he is properly credited with rebuilding much of the city, even more impressive perhaps was his accomplishment of superimposing a new city on the old without destroying the old. The harmonious blending of styles of architecture from the thirteenth century to the twentieth in the central quarters of Paris is owing in no small part to Haussmann.

His influence on urban planners and builders of his own time and later may be seen in copies of his monumental avenues in a number of French cities—Lyon, Toulouse, Avignon, for example— and in Brussels, in Rome, in the Paseo de la Reforma in Mexico City, in the Benjamin Franklin Parkway in Philadelphia. Moreover, the record of his audacity in Paris and its results have inspired city planners everywhere who, like DANIEL H. BURNHAM, would "make no little plans."

DAVID H. PINKNEY

BIBLIOGRAPHY

CHAPMAN, J. M., and CHAPMAN, BRIAN 1957 *The Life and Times of Baron Haussmann: Paris in the Second Empire.* London: Weidenfeld.

GAILLARD, JEANNE 1977 *Paris la ville: L'Urbanisme parisien à l'heure d'Haussmann: Des provinciaux aux parisiens; La Vocation ou les vocations parisiennes.* Paris: Editions Honore Champion.

HAUSSMANN, GEORGES-EUGÈNE 1890–1893 *Memoires du Baron Haussmann.* 3 vols. Paris: Victor-Havard.

LAVEDAN, PIERRE 1975 *Histoire de l'urbanisme à Paris.* Paris: Hachette.

MALET, HENRI 1973 *Le Baron Haussmann et a Rénovation de Paris.* Paris: Les Editions municipales.

PINKNEY, DAVID H. 1958 *Napoleon III and the Rebuilding of Paris.* Princeton University Press.

REAU, LOUIS; LAVEDAN, PIERRE et al. 1954 *L'Oeuvre du Baron Haussmann: Préfet de la Seine, 1853–1870.* Paris: Presses universitaires de France.

SAALMAN, HOWARD 1971 *Haussmann: Paris Transformed.* New York: Braziller.

HAVILAND, JOHN

John Haviland (1792–1852) was born near Taunton in Somerset, England, but his professional career is so closely tied to Philadelphia that he is usually grouped with the most innovative and versatile American architects active during the second quarter of the nineteenth century.

When he was nineteen, Haviland was bound to James Elmes, (1782–1862), a London architect remembered more for his writing on architectural subjects than for the distinction of his buildings. The Chapel of Saint John the Evangelist (1812–1813) in Chichester is the only structure associated with Haviland's apprenticeship in England. Clearly the chapel's polygonal form owes something to the Tower of the Winds (110–35 B.C.), as pictured in the first volume of JAMES STUART and NICHOLAS REVETT's *Antiquities of Athens* (1762), while the Choragic Monument of Lysikrates (334 B.C.), another Athenian building from the same publication, provided a model for the cupola that perches so awkwardly on the pediment above the entrance. We shall probably never be able to prove the hypothesis that this last was a feature added by the youthful apprentice while supervising the erection of the chapel during his master's illness, but there can be no doubt that the initial impetus for Haviland's later predilection for Greek forms came from his three years in Elmes's office.

Both the adverse effect of the Napoleonic wars on building activity in England and the receipt of a small legacy doubtless contributed to Haviland's decision to go to Russia in 1815, where he hoped for an appointment to the Corps of Imperial Engineers. Before this ambition could be realized, however, Haviland's attention was directed toward the United States, and in the fall of 1816 he took up residence in Philadelphia. There the following year he married a young widow, and though his two sons and two stepsons later assisted him on occasions, only Edward is credited with having designed a few buildings in his own right.

Young, relatively unknown in his adopted country, and trained in a profession that would not become fully recognized or firmly established for another generation, Haviland proposed to support his family by augmenting his occasional architectural fees with more regular earnings from books and lectures. The first volume of his *Builder's Assistant* (1818) appeared about the same time he opened a drawing academy in partnership with Hugh Bridport, a London-born artist who had recently immigrated to Philadelphia. The academy closed in 1822, but two years later Haviland accepted the post of professor of drawing at the newly established Franklin Institute, a position he held for the remainder of the decade. The final two volumes of *The Builder's Assistant* appeared in 1819 and 1821, respectively, and though now numbered among the rarest architectural books, Haviland's builders' guide is nonetheless important as the first American publication to illustrate the Greek orders. Unfortunately, whatever income Haviland derived from his initial efforts as an author was not sufficient to prevent his bankruptcy in 1820.

In many ways the buildings Haviland designed for Philadelphia during the 1820s marked the high point of his career. The First Presbyterian Church (1820–1822) on Washington Square was demolished for a parking lot in the late 1930s, but its designer's handling of the Greek orders may still be observed at Saint Andrew's Episcopal Church (1822–1824; since 1921 Saint George's Greek Orthodox Church), nearby. The latter was Haviland's own church and its crypt his place of burial. Nor can there be any doubt of the debt owed Greek sources by the building erected for the Franklin Institute (1825–1826) and now occupied by the Atwater Kent Museum. In this case Haviland took the design of the façade directly from the Choragic Monument of Thrasyllus, an atypical structure de-

*Haviland.
Franklin Institute.
Philadelphia.
1825–1826*

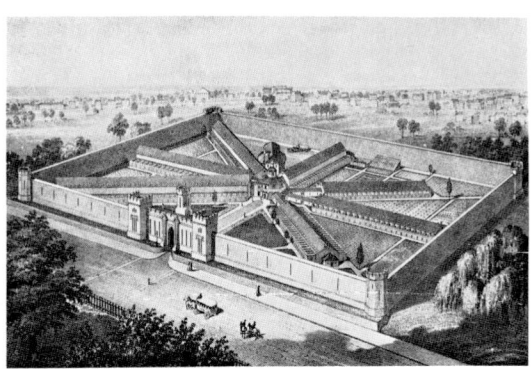

*Haviland.
Eastern State Penitentiary.
Philadelphia.
1821–1837*

stroyed by the Turks but known from a plate in the second volume of Stuart and Revett's *Antiquities of Athens* (1787). On the whole, time and urban redevelopment proved kinder to Haviland's buildings than to those of many of his contemporaries. Though considerably altered and restored (most recently in 1971), the theater on Walnut Street that in '828 he remodeled from a structure built in 1809 is said with some justice to be the oldest theater in continuous existence in the English-speaking world.

But the Philadelphia building that brought Haviland international attention made use of Gothic details instead of his favorite Greek ones. The principal elements that went into the design of the Eastern State Penitentiary (1821–1837) had all been used before, but Haviland was the first to give every prisoner a separate cell, with its own exercise yard, arranged along corridors radiating from a central core—a scheme that offered maximum surveillance with a minimum of supervisory

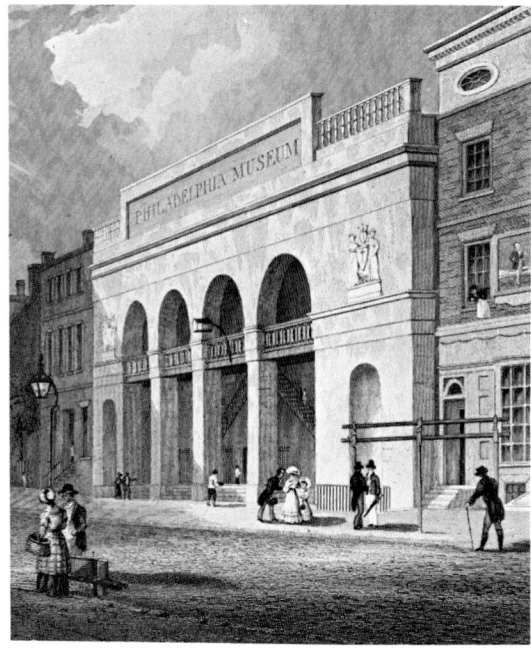

Haviland.
Philadelphia Arcade.
1825–1828

personnel. As the culmination of a generation of experiments in penal reform, the Philadelphia prison was among the most famous American buildings of its day and the first to exert wide influence abroad.

The better to provide for his large and growing family, during the 1820s Haviland was led to add the roles of promoter and speculator to that of architect. Doubtless with Samuel Ware's Burlington Arcade (1815–1819) in London as their model, he and the attorney Peter A. Browne headed a group that financed and built similar arcades in Philadelphia (1825–1828) and New York (1826–1827). Neither venture was a success financially, but the structures Haviland designed are usually considered among the first built in America specifically for commercial purposes. The profits its promoters anticipated also failed to materialize at the amusement park (1828) Haviland and Browne built on the outskirts of Philadelphia. Called the Labyrinthine Garden, its principal feature was a Chinese pagoda more than a hundred feet high. Pressed to meet financial obligations connected with these projects, Haviland diverted funds entrusted to him for the construction of the Naval Hospital (1826–1833) at Port Nelson, Virginia, and when even this drastic measure failed to stem the tide, in 1829 he was again obliged to go through bankruptcy for a second time.

Plagued by financial losses and with his professional reputation under a cloud, by 1830 Haviland was again viewing literary pursuits as a possible source of income. A second edition of *The Builder's Assistant* was brought out in Baltimore in that year—this time in four volumes and with the word "practical" added to the title—and from his personal papers, now on indefinite loan to the University of Pennsylvania, it appears that about this time Haviland considered publishing a periodical devoted specifically to architecture, a novel idea for the place and time. Nothing came of this project, however; instead, Haviland contented himself with a new edition of Owen Biddle's *Young Carpenter's Assistant,* first published in Philadelphia in 1805. Among the twenty plates he contributed to the 1830 edition is that illustrating the Miner's Bank, one of more than half a dozen buildings he had designed for Pottsville, Pennsylvania, in 1830–1831. The bank was demolished in 1926, but it is remembered as the first building in America to have its façade faced with iron plates, in this case cast to resemble ashlar masonry.

Although his architectural practice never fully recovered from the reverses of the 1820s, the Miner's Bank was by no means the only one of Haviland's later commissions worthy of note. In Philadelphia the colonnade that fronted the row of houses he designed for the Blight family in 1830 must have given the block of Chestnut Street between Fifteenth and Sixteenth something of the air of Regency London, and until its removal in the 1960s, the paneling he installed in the Assembly Room of Independence Hall provided generations of Americans with their concept of the classical setting in which took place the major political events of the American Revolution. But these were also the years when Haviland saw his designs passed over in favor of those submitted by others as he competed unsuccessfully for commissions to design the most important Philadelphia buildings.

Outside his adopted city, the fame of the Eastern Penitentiary still made Haviland someone to

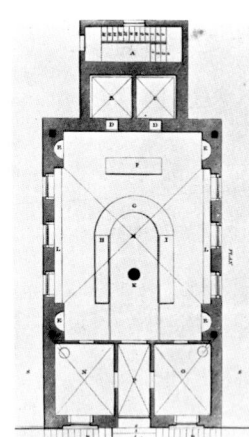

Haviland.
Plan of Miner's Bank.
Pottsville, Pennsylvania.
1830–1831

Haviland.
Miner's Bank.
Pottsville, Pennsylvania.
1830–1831

be considered when a new prison was called for. The schemes he provided for Missouri (1833–1836) and Rhode Island (1834–c.1837) may have offered little of interest, but the New Jersey Penitentiary (1833–1836), near Trenton, not only continued the radial plan used earlier in Philadelphia, but also first employed Egyptian details for an American prison. Like the castellated Gothic, the Egyptian was well calculated to impress on the observer what one of the commissioners of the Eastern Penitentiary referred to as "a cheerless blank indicative of the misery which awaits the unhappy being who enters within its walls." Associations of this kind, combined with economy—Egyptian details proved cheaper than Gothic ones—also led to the use of Egyptian motifs for the New York City Halls of Justice and House of Detention (the "Tombs"), erected between 1835 and 1838 under Haviland's supervision and apparently in great part from his designs. In fact, the quality of buildings like the New York prison or the Essex County Court House in Newark, New Jersey, begun a year later, have led historians to consider their designer the most important of the Egyptian Revival architects working in America. And though none achieved the fame of the Eastern Penitentiary, during the late 1830s and 1840s prisons continued to be erected from Haviland's designs as far wast as Arkansas as well as at such Pennsylvania sites as Harrisburg, Reading, and Lancaster.

Despite his financial problems, Haviland seems to have retained the respect of other members of his profession: he was elected a Corresponding Member of the Royal Institute of British Architects and was one of a small group that in 1835 founded the American Institution of Architects, the forerunner of the American Institute of Architects.

GEORGE B. TATUM

WORKS

1812–1813, Chapel of Saint John the Evangelist, Chichester, England. 1819–1820, Moses Moody Villa, Haverhill, Mass. *1820–1822, First Presbyterian Church; 1821–1837, Eastern State Penitentiary; 1822–1824, Saint Andrew's Episcopal Church (now Saint George's Greek Orthodox Church); 1824–1826, Pennsylvania Institution for the Education of the Deaf and Dumb (now Philadelphia College of Art); 1825–1826, Franklin Institute (now Atwater Kent Museum); *1825–1828, Philadelphia Arcade; Philadelphia. *1826–1827, New York Arcade. 1826–1833, United States Naval Hospital, Port Nelson, Va. 1827–1828, Walnut Street Theater (remodeling); *1828, Chinese Pagoda and Labyrinthine Garden; *1830, Colonnade Row; Philadelphia. *1830–1831, Miner's Bank, Pottsville, Pa. *1831–c.1833, Independence Hall (restoration of Assembly Room), Philadelphia. 1833–1836, Missouri Penitentiary, Jefferson City. 1833–1836, New Jersey Penitentiary, near Trenton. 1834–c.1837, Rhode Island Penitentiary, Providence. 1835–1838, New York City Halls of Justice and House of Detention. *1836, Essex County Court House and Jail, Newark, N.J. *1837–1838, Whig and Cliosophic Society Buildings, Princeton University, N.J. *1838, Arkansas Penitentiary, Little Rock. 1838, Pennsylvania Fire Insurance Company; *1838–1841, Philip Syng Physick (Roberts) House; Philadelphia. *1846–1848, Berks County Prison, Reading, Pa. 1848–1851, Lancaster County Prison, Pa. *1848–1851, Pennsylvania State Insane Asylum, Harrisburg, Pa. *1850, Metropolitan (Brown's) Hotel, Washington.

Haviland.
New York City Halls of
Justice and House of
Detention.
1835–1838

BIBLIOGRAPHY

BAIGELL, MATTHEW ELI 1965 "John Haviland." Unpublished Ph.D. dissertation, University of Pennsylvania, Philadelphia.

BAIGELL, MATTHEW ELI 1966 "John Haviland in Philadelphia, 1818–1826." *Journal of the Society of Architectural Historians* 25:197–208.

BAIGELL, MATTHEW ELI 1967 "John Haviland in Pottsville." *Journal of the Society of Architectural Historians* 26:307–309.

CARROTT, RICHARD 1978 *The Egyptian Revival: Its Sources, Monuments, and Meaning, 1808–1858.* Berkeley: University of California Press.

HAMLIN, TALBOT (1944)1964 *Greek Revival Architecture in America.* Reprint. New York: Dover.

HAVILAND, JOHN (1818–1821)1830 *The Builder's Assistant.* 4 vols. 2d ed. Baltimore. The first edition, in three volumes, was published in Philadelphia.

HAVILAND, JOHN (editor) 1830 *Young Carpenter's Assistant* by Owen Biddle. Philadelphia. First published in 1805; Haviland added twenty new plates.

HITCHCOCK, H. R. (1962)1976 *American Architectural Books.* 3d rev. ed. Reprint. New York: Da Capo.

JOHNSTON, NORMAN B. 1964 "John Haviland: Jailor to the World." *Journal of the Society of Architectural Historians* 23:101–105.

STUART, JAMES and REVETT, NICHOLAS (1762)1968 Volume 1 in *Antiquities of Athens.* Reprint. New York: Arno.

TEETERS, NEGLEY K. and SHEARER, JOHN D. 1957 *The Prison at Philadelphia.* New York: Columbia University Press.

HAVILLAND, T. F. DE

Thomas Fiott De Havilland (1775–1866), eldest son of Sir Peter De Havilland, was born in Guernsey and joined the Madras Engineers in 1792. After serving at Pondicherry, in Ceylon, and in operations against Tipu Sultan, he became civil engineer and architect of the Madras presidency in 1814 and acting chief engineer in 1821. His most important work was Saint Andrew's Church (1814–1821) based upon a proposed design by JAMES GIBBS for Saint Martin's-in-the-Fields. The other church in Madras (1814–1816) associated with him was constructed under his supervision to the designs of James Caldwell. Renovations to Fort Saint George, Madras, in 1819 included the conversion by De Havilland of the Old Banqueting Hall into offices. De Havilland retired to the family estate in Guernsey in 1825.

PAULINE ROHATGI

WORKS

1812, Jeybourg Barracks, Guernsey, England. 1814–1816, Saint George's Cathedral; 1816–1821, Saint Andrew's Church; 1817, Saint Andrews Bridge; 1819, Fort Saint George (conversion of Banqueting Hall to general offices); Madras, India. n.d. Military Buildings and Havilland Arch, Seringpatam, India.

BIBLIOGRAPHY

HAVILLAND, THOMAS FIOTT DE 1822 *Report on Indian Limestones.* Madras, India.
HAVILLAND, THOMAS FIOTT DE c.1825 *Public Edifices of Madras.* Madras, India.

HAVLÍČEK, JOSEF

Josef Havlíček (1899–1961) was one of the most outstanding avant-garde architects in Czechoslovakia. Havlíček strove for a practical realization of the doctrines of the Congrès Internationaux d'Architecture Moderne (CIAM) and of LE CORBUSIER's theses. In 1928–1936, he worked together with KAREL HONZÍK. His best known building, the General Pension House (1929–1933) in the Žižkov District of Prague, was one of the achievements of the couple. The structure is a lapidary block of cruciform plan with strip windows, and exhibits a uniform modular system. Although Havlíček is usually regarded as a prominent representative of the functionalistic architecture of Czechoslovakia, his works display an ever deeper tendency toward a fixed, dominating elementary form. He strove for a unification of architectural volumes in geometric shapes such as cubes, cruciform blocks, or—in the postwar period—pyramids. This idea culminated in an unrealized plan of the late 1950s suggesting to clear the New Town of Prague and to create there a new scenery by building a system of pyramidal skyscrapers.

VLADIMÍR ŠLAPETA

WORKS

1927, Habich House; 1928, Villa (with Karel Honzík), Smíchov District; 1929–1930, Houses (with Honzík), Pankrác District; 1929–1933, General Pension House (with Honzík), Žižkov District; Prague, 1936–1940, Sanatorium, Poděbrady, Czechoslovakia. 1937, Block of Flats; 1938, Apartment House; Letná, Prague. 1945–1950, Housing Development, Hradec Králové, Czechoslovakia. 1946–1958, Housing Development, Kladno Rozdělov, Czechoslovakia. 1950, Dairy Factory (with Josef Hrubý and František Kerhart), Strakonice, Czechoslovakia. 1950, Dairy Factory (with Hrubý and Kerhart), Zábřeh, Czechoslovakia.

BIBLIOGRAPHY

HAVLÍČEK, JOSEF 1964 *Návrhy a stavby: 1925–1960.* Prague: STWL.
HAVLÍČEK, JOSEF, and HONZÍK, KAREL 1931 *Stavby a plány.* With an epilogue by Karel Teige. Prague: Odeon.
PICA, AGNOLDOMENICO 1938 *Nuova architettura nel mondo.* Milan: Hoepli.
ROTH, ALFRED (1940)1946 *La Nouvelle Architecture.* 2d ed. Zurich and Erlenbach, Switzerland: Éditions d'architecture.
SARTORIS, ALBERTO (1932)1941 *Gli elementi dell'architettura funzionale.* 3d ed. Milan: Hoepli.

HAWKS, JOHN

John Hawks (1731?–1790) was one of the first professional architects in America. He trained in England under "Mr. [Stiff?] Leadbeater" and came to North Carolina in 1764. He designed and supervised construction of Tryon's Palace in New Bern; his plans and elevations for the tripartite Gibbsian (see JAMES GIBBS) building compose perhaps the fullest surviving set of colonial architectural drawings. He also designed other public and private buildings during a prosperous and politically active life in New Bern, for which drawings survive.

CATHERINE W. BISHIR

WORKS

*(A)1766, Church, Hillsborough, N.C. *1766, Courthouse (alterations); 1767–1770, Tryon's Palace (reconstructed in 1950s); New Bern, N.C. (A)1767–1773, Chowan County Courthouse, Edenton, N.C. (A)1770s–1780s, John Wright Stanly House, New Bern, N.C.

BIBLIOGRAPHY

The papers of John Hawks are in the Southern Historical

Collection, *Wilson Library, University of North Carolina, Chapel Hill.*

DILL, ALONZO T., JR. 1942 "Tryon's Palace: A Neglected Niche of North Carolina History." *North Carolina Historical Review* 19:119–167.

DILL, ALONZO T., JR. 1955 *Governor Tryon and His Palace.* Chapel Hill: University of North Carolina Press.

HERZOG, LYNDA VESTAL 1977 "The Early Architecture of New Bern, North Carolina." Unpublished Ph.D. dissertation, University of California, Los Angeles.

HAWKSMOOR, NICHOLAS

Nicholas Hawksmoor (1661–1736) was the most inventive architect of the English baroque period and indeed one of the most original British architects of any period. In spite of references to his life and work in architectural literature, his reputation until the middle of the twentieth century was eclipsed by that of his contemporary and colleague JOHN VANBRUGH. In private life Hawksmoor was a modest man who chose (in an age of rhetoric) to be buried in a country churchyard (Shenley, Hertfordshire) with a simple gravestone. He never succeeded his great master, CHRISTOPHER WREN, as Surveyor of the King's Works, but he was nevertheless jealously and proudly aware both of his experience as the best trained English architect of his generation and of the power of his fertile imagination.

Hawksmoor was born in 1661 at or near East Drayton, a remote Nottinghamshire village; when about eighteen he was taken by the decorative plasterer Edward Gouge to London and became clerk to Wren. Recognizing his talents, Wren during the 1680s trained him, since there was no organized architectural instruction, and found work for him, first administrative and executive (at Winchester Palace 1683–1685), but including (before 1690) the making of designs. Hawksmoor's travel sketch book of 1680–1683 contains naïve but observant drawings of English provincial towns and buildings; by 1688 he could produce an expert and imaginative, though never executed, plan for a "villa" at Ingestre, Staffordshire, which shows a liking for giant orders and great ingenuity in shaping spaces.

In the following decade these qualities were realized in a country house, Easton Neston in Northamptonshire (c.1695–1710), the commission for which he obtained through Wren; drawings survive from his by now accomplished hand for other assignments received in the same way. The Writing School of Christ's Hospital, London (1692–1695) revealed Hawksmoor as the master of monumental, arcaded architecture, although the executed building was stylistically less impressive than the preliminary design. An unexecuted design for rebuilding Saint Mary's Church, Warwick, after a fire in 1694 already exemplifies the delight, sympathy, and skill in Gothic revivalism to match surviving medieval work that recurred in later, executed designs.

It was impossible for an English architect at this time to make his living solely by designing, and during the 1690s Hawksmoor's official employment continued in posts controlled by Wren. He became clerk of works at Kensington Palace in 1689 and (on stylistic evidence) probably designed the King's Gallery there (1695–1696), a massive brick-built range in which broad vertical bands substitute for pilasters. He was also principal draftsman at Saint Paul's Cathedral from 1691 to 1710, while from 1696 personally and from 1698 officially he assisted Wren in designing Greenwich Hospital (now the Royal Naval College). A study of draftsmanship shows that, while Wren retained authority and responsibility for the most public aspects of Greenwich, Hawksmoor was working closely with him and was allowed free rein in King William Court (1699–1707) and the back of Queen Anne Block (1700–1703).

The early history of Easton Neston is obscure: the center block was roofed and its stone façades were completed in 1702 according to inscriptions, and an early writer's account that the kitchen and stable wings (of which one survives) were built about twenty years earlier by Wren is credible. The hypothesis recently advanced, that Hawksmoor's center block (which he later called one of his "own children") is a stone casing of a brick house designed by Wren, cannot be sustained on reexamination of the evidence. The laying of a water supply from over a mile away in 1694 most probably anticipates construction of the main house, which far from a recasing shows many marks of an integrally designed and intricate complex of spaces.

Easton Neston is impressive outside and both exciting and economical inside. The interior has

Hawksmoor. Easton Neston (later altered). Northamptonshire, England. c.1695–1710

Hawksmoor.
Easton Neston
(later altered).
Northamptonshire,
England.
c.1695–1710

been altered, but the staircase and the upper gallery across the middle of the house survive to give some idea of the original effect. The entrance was at the single-story end of the hall, the center part of which extended up through two full stories. The visitor thus met in the state rooms a series of changes of volume and direction as he passed through spaces half the height and, in the hall and staircase, the whole height of the house. The main elevations of Easton Neston, only 120-feet wide, comprise nine bays of a giant order whose close spacing gives a vertical emphasis unusual in English houses of the time. The north end elevation mixes with two-story fenestration of the main fronts an arrangement of mezzanines making four floors. This patterning confirms by analogy Hawksmoor's authorship of the King William Court at Greenwich. It reflects but is not entirely necessitated by the interior disposition of the house with four floors of small private apartments in the corners of the plan between the state rooms. Clearly, Hawksmoor did not consider that all fronts of a building need conform to one scheme.

Easton Neston depends on the high quality of its stone detailing and other craftsmanship as well as on Hawksmoor's practicality in combining state and private rooms in a small space. The house follows in time WILLIAM TALMAN's Chatsworth and Wren's Tring, but anticipates Castle Howard, Yorkshire, the first designs for which were made in 1699 by Hawksmoor jointly with Vanbrugh. In a remarkable partnership, which was continued in the design of Blenheim Palace (begun 1705), Hawksmoor acted as draftsman, detail designer, and business negotiator with the building tradesmen; upon his skill and insight in interpretation and his experience in practical matters depended the realization of Vanbrugh's first work in architecture. The patron, the third earl of Carlisle, paid Hawksmoor an annual fee and the expenses of a supervisory trip from London to Yorkshire. Hawksmoor accepted the situation in which Vanbrugh was acknowledgedly the architect, but each found cause for respect in the other. Thus, while many details both of design and building procedure at Castle Howard are due to Hawksmoor, it was undoubtedly Vanbrugh who conceived the great series of south-facing rooms and the dome which opens out of the ceiling of the entrance hall.

Vanbrugh, who was dedicated to the principle of success—in doing better than others—undoubtedly learned in architecture more from Hawksmoor than from any other single source. Ultimately, the stylistic difference between their later independent work may be that Hawksmoor was the inventor and Vanbrugh an exponent. But Castle Howard and Blenheim, which were works of collaboration, show a joint style which is not identical with the independent works of either partner. When work on Blenheim began, with Hawksmoor officially salaried as assistant to Vanbrugh, the latter had six years' experience, and even though he still profited from Hawksmoor's practice and relied on his draftsmanship, there were now many respects in which Vanbrugh used his assistant by choice rather than by necessity. We are better informed about Hawksmoor's role in this second joint work because of the abundance of documents including a book of letters between him and Henry Joynes, clerk of works at Blenheim. In this correspondence are found not only many details about the building works but also personal sidelights and practical advice from the older man to the younger. Joynes became a capable architect and, while the style of his independent work is scarcely exciting, it was he who came closest to finding in Hawksmoor the kind of teacher the latter had received in Wren.

The initial years of the building history of Blenheim are part of the biography of Vanbrugh, but Hawksmoor was certainly responsible for the details (though not the concept) of the extraordinary roof line there, and surviving drawings show that the design of the arcaded entrance hall, which prefigures his church of Saint George, Bloomsbury, was worked out by Hawksmoor.

According to a Treasury document, the Orangery (1704–1705) in the gardens of Kensington Palace was to be "according to the alteration of the Draft proposed by Mr. Vanbrugh," and this sole mention of an architect's name has been taken to indicate Vanbrugh's responsibility for the design. However, this evidence is at best ambiguous, as often happens with committee minutes, and the exterior of the Orangery shows the same sophisticated patterning use of windows and niches as the north end of Easton Neston. It is this character, rather than the use of Doric columns rusticated in rings—a motif common to both architects from Blenheim onward—or the elegant detailing of the two circular rooms at the ends of the Orangery, that suggests Hawksmoor, still clerk of works at Kensington, as the author of both the preliminary design and the final one.

In 1707–1710, Hawksmoor was engaged in executive rather than design work for Vanbrugh in connection with Kimbolton, the last project on which they are known to have collaborated. At this time, the completion of the dome and towers of Wren's Saint Paul's and the many problems of the work at Greenwich and then at Blenheim occupied much of Hawksmoor's mind. It was either at Greenwich Hospital or through the proximity of Blenheim to Oxford that Hawksmoor came into contact with GEORGE CLARKE, who as one-time secretary to the Admiralty had an interest in the sailor's hospital but who as a Fellow of All Souls, collector of drawings, and amateur architect was a party to most building projects in the University of Oxford. Clarke sought opinions and sketches from anyone who would give them, and Hawksmoor was as likely to offer seven designs (as he did for the Queen's College, Oxford, in 1708–1709) as one.

Hawksmoor designed, as another Oxford don of the time observed, "grandly for a college"; although he was eminently practical in the smallest of commissions and in problems like smoking chimneys, Oxford and Cambridge figured largely in that world of dreams on paper on which an architect relies to recharge his creative imagination. The Queen's College designs are full of baroque rhetoric, with Latin orders as well as plain or rusticated masonry: in one, a giant hexastyle chapel portico; in another, an oval chapel with giant pilasters; in yet another, a lofty tower to face the High Street and rival Oxford's medieval towers. Their impracticality lay neither in their visionary character nor in their planning, which included convenient features such as covered cloister walks and innovative ones such as the division of lodgings horizontally, by corridors, instead of vertically in the college tradition, by staircases. Sometimes donations and funds for building were of very finite size and colleges neither could anticipate funds by large-scale borrowing nor would gladly wait another generation for money to accumulate. In other cases, however, colleges seem to have preferred to build piecemeal.

None of the Queen's College schemes was followed, although there is a family resemblance between them and the design adopted in 1710, whose authors appear to have been Clarke himself and the Oxford mason William Townesend. The regularity of the front quadrangle at Queen's is not unique—a recent symmetrical example was the Peckwater Quadrangle at Christ Church (1707–1714) designed by another Oxford amateur, HENRY ALDRICH—but its achievement over a period of half a century perhaps owed as much to Clarke's personal influence as to that of Hawksmoor's rejected proposals.

Hawksmoor made equally grandiose designs for enlarging All Souls College. This effort would later bear fruit in the building of the north quadrangle, begun in 1716. The first practical result of his connection with Clarke, however, was the commission, gained in unofficial competition with others, for the Clarendon Building (1712–1713) to house the University Press then accommodated inconveniently in the basement of Wren's Sheldonian Theatre. The brief included the provision

*Hawksmoor.
Old Clarendon Building.
Oxford.
1712–1713*

*Hawksmoor.
Old Clarendon
  Building (detail).
Oxford.
1712–1713*

of space for two separate printing businesses, placed on either side of a central vestibule on the axis of the existing Schools Quadrangle. Hawksmoor marked this axis by correct Roman Doric porticoes, full on the north (entrance) front and applied toward the quadrangle: the giant columns four feet in diameter set the scale for the whole building, the rest of whose elevations imply but do not use the order.

The massive scale of the order is paralleled by the monumental treatment of the wall surface, which is cut back in layers in such a way as to give lively movement to the elevation and an impression of immensely sculptural solidity to the mass of the building. Hawksmoor's design, made at the beginning of his fifties, certainly sums up his feelings thus far about architecture in general and that of the antique in particular; it may also embody some of the exaggerated respect for learned institutions entertained by the outsider: the factory appears as a temple of learning.

The surface plainness and restriction of detail in the Clarendon Building may be appropriate to the industrial side of its character, but they are no less relevant to the development of an aspect of Hawksmoor's style that first appeared in the

Christ's Hospital Writing School—a plain style in which relief is a matter of thickness and not of enrichment. The sparsely and carefully placed detail of the Clarendon, too, is architectural in the specific sense that it is derived not from ideas of pattern or natural forms such as garlands but from the elements of architecture itself: the decorative use, sanctioned by MICHELANGELO, of particulars of the Doric order out of context (the guttae from under a triglyph) or the triplicated oversize keystone, a motif commonly supposed to have come from sixteenth-century Italian Mannerism but found nowhere in so pronounced a form before Hawksmoor.

The division of a life into phases and the discernment of turning points are artificial and to some extent arbitrary devices; they are nevertheless common not only to biographers but to all mankind. Hawksmoor himself would have recognized that the need to consider the Clarendon Building in relation to its neighbors and to the space between them arose at about the same time as several other projects involving the planning of spaces as well as buildings. It was in about 1710, with the completion of Saint Paul's Cathedral, that he made designs, no doubt in consultation with Wren, for a circular domed baptistery to stand on Ludgate Hill west of the cathedral, and for a wedge-shaped precinct of four-story buildings with ground-floor arcades surrounding the cathedral.

The finishing of Saint Paul's also suggested the possibility of public money becoming available thereafter for Greenwich Hospital, where work was badly behind schedule. Some money was indeed provided, but nothing remotely on the scale Hawksmoor had in mind. His first project for a great chapel may date from 1699, but most of the extant drawings were made after 1705 and the only dated scheme (the third) is of 1711. All included a further court south of the four blocks proposed by Wren and closed by a chapel on the central axis; since neither the land of the axis nor INIGO JONES's Queen's House further south belonged to the hospital, the projects were all hopeless of execution. Nevertheless as late as 1728, perhaps with an eye to George II who had recently come to the throne, Hawksmoor published a pamphlet in support of his ideas. The second scheme included an oval arcaded forecourt whose shape was certainly a deliberate reminiscence of GIOVANNI LORENZO BERNINI's St. Peter's Piazza in Rome. The third one, of 1711, centered on a Greek-cross church on a square base which combined in a homogeneous whole a surprising range of derivations from DONATO BRAMANTE (in the hemispherical stepped-back dome) to FRANCESCO BORROMINI (in the concave curves of the substructure of the dome).

All the projects were attempts to provide the architectural center Greenwich lacked: a monumental building for Wren's domes and colonnades to frame instead of the sky above the distant Queen's House. All seem to have belonged to the category of dreams, put on paper independently of Wren, or of Vanbrugh who became deputy surveyor (architect) to the hospital in 1705 and surveyor in 1716.

In the university towns of Oxford and Cambridge Hawksmoor's imagination soon extended beyond individual buildings. In about 1712 he made designs for King's College, Cambridge, and also proposed a plan for the "reform" of the town of Cambridge. This was to retain but adapt the existing street pattern to make squares and other enclosed spaces, including a long one like the Piazza Navona in Rome; the element of spatial surprise and mobility evident in the interior of Easton Neston was at Cambridge to be found in the diversity of these spaces, the way they were separated by narrower passages, and the siting in relation to them of public and college buildings as well as obelisks and similar eye-catching monuments. Hawksmoor developed an obsession with obelisks, and a note on his plan for Cambridge refers, in justification of his ideas, to the replanning of Rome under Pope Sixtus V by DOMENICO FONTANA, in which the reinstatement of the ancient obelisks of Rome visually played an important part.

The only fruit of the Cambridge plans was some influence on the form and siting of JAMES GIBBS's Fellows' Building at King's College. Hawksmoor's plans to make Oxford a Roman city (1712–1713), starting from the Clarendon Building and including several colleges, bore little more fruit, although again there was a small legacy in the work of Gibbs. From about 1712 until the 1730s Hawksmoor was concerned with a succession of designs for the Radcliffe Camera, the library named after its donor John Radcliffe, Queen Anne's physician. The commission for the camera was ultimately to go to Gibbs after Hawksmoor's death, but the selection of the site, the impetus toward its purchase and clearance, and the choice of a circular form (more appropriate both iconographically and functionally for the commemoration of the donor than for the accommodation of his books and their readers) were due to Hawksmoor. Historically, the Oxford and Cambridge plans are of great interest for their range of spatial ideas and antique references, including at Oxford a dodecastyle peripteral temple as a new university church, as well as for their imaginative placing of rigidly symmetrical buildings in settings whose shape and orientation were determined by the existing features of the site.

Hawksmoor's greatest contribution to a city's architecture, and the body of work on which his fame ultimately rests, resulted from the unique combination of circumstances which led to the "Fifty New Churches" scheme. In 1710 the parishioners of Greenwich asked Parliament for financial aid to rebuild their church from the coal tax that had been imposed on London to pay for the rebuilding, now completed, of Saint Paul's and the London City churches destroyed in the Great Fire of 1666. The majority in Parliament, Tory in politics and High Church (ritualist Episcopalian) in religion, introduced a bill to prolong the tax so as to build fifty churches, mostly in the new suburbs of London and Westminster. Of this optimistic number only a dozen were realized; of those, Hawksmoor designed six and shared two more with JOHN JAMES. He owed this opportunity to his appointment, from 1711 until the termination of the scheme in 1733, as one of the two surveyors or executive architects to the Fifty Churches Commission. While the stated function of the buildings was the provision of facilities for Anglican worship in new neighborhoods, the 1711 Act mentioned specifically towers and steeples, and it is clear that they were to be monuments both to High Church piety and to Tory political ideals of conformity and order, altogether more impressive than the approximately fifty churches built by Wren after the Great Fire.

Hawksmoor's experience and the recommendation of Wren and Vanbrugh (both members of the commission) gained him both the executive position and the selection of particular churches. The commission's preference for open sites, porticoes, and steeples, for the use of Portland stone instead of brick, and for the celebration of the concept then referred to as "the Queen's greatness" (as head of both the nation and the Church of England) provided Hawksmoor with a brief whose range has seldom been equaled in either public or private architecture. His six churches survive, though all have suffered at times from decay, neglect, or fire. Since they are neither fashionable places of worship nor centers of mass tourism, their maintenance is a serious problem and their visitors, although enthusiastic, are relatively few in number. Their steeples follow in invention from those of Wren, developing further the formula of LEON BATTISTA ALBERTI in which the classical vocabulary is adapted to the steeple's inherent Gothic verticality by building up a sequence of foursquare templelike forms; the results may be considered bizarre but their contribution to the London skyline is significant and unforgettable.

The first church to be built, Saint Alfege, Greenwich (1712–1718), is contemporary with the Clarendon Building in Oxford and shares its use of a giant Doric order, its exploration of the depth of the wall in rectangular strips and panels, and the use of exaggerated keystones. In this church the portico *in antis* is at the east end facing the main street; since the commission required correct orientation in the churches, Hawksmoor ingeniously arranged entrances from the portico on either side of the altar recess. He seems to have liked an unusually large number of entrances, partly for convenience and for easy access to the side galleries but partly also for the use of such entrances to establish symmetry in plan and elevation about the transverse axis. Indeed his six churches are all set out in some way on an intersection of axes at right angles, allowing him to imply the centrality which was so popular among late Renaissance and seventeenth-century European architects, without stating it with the definiteness of European baroque churches. Roman Catholic churches of the time were in the last analysis stage settings for the Mass and the presence of the Eucharist, and their symmetry, however important aesthetically, must liturgically be reconciled to this function. The High Anglicans gave reverence to the altar—the new churches were specifically to have altar recesses raised on three steps from the church floor—but the pulpit and baptismal font shared the emphasis of the interior. There is a vagueness about Hawksmoor's church interiors, even where the seating has not been rearranged, which is achieved with a varying degree of subtlety and which seems to have been intended to convey the sense of solemnity and awe which Vanbrugh recommended in a memorandum to his fellow commissioners. At Greenwich, the ceiling, without internal supports, floats over floor and galleries in a single expanse, an oval set in a rectangle.

Greenwich church may be entered not only at the east and from the sides but also through the western tower, for whose recasing Hawksmoor made a design, known from an engraving. It culminated in an open octagonal lantern with projecting piers at the angles, of a boldness and girth better suited to the monumentality of the pilastered walls below than is the elegant domed turret executed by John James (1730–1732). By that time the commission had met serious financial difficulty, not least through the great expense of Hawksmoor's and THOMAS ARCHER's churches; its constitution had also changed after the accession of George I in 1714 and the return of a Whig Parliament, and even James's turret was only built after the new commissioners had tried to deny responsibility for building steeples as well as churches. Hawksmoor meanwhile had removed a design he considered too good to abandon to a

Hawksmoor.
Saint George-in-the-East.
Wapping, London.
1714–1729

Hawksmoor.
Saint Anne.
Limehouse, London.
1714–1729

church across the Thames, Saint George-in-the-East, Wapping.

Saint George-in-the-East was one of three churches begun by him in 1714 in the fast growing parish of Stepney, the other two being Saint Anne, Limehouse, and Christ Church, Spitalfields; all were finished in 1729–1730. The numerous preliminary and working drawings that survive for all three throw considerable light on Hawksmoor's working methods. He made a general practice of allowing his buildings to evolve gradually during the course of execution: thus, as in the case of his master Wren's treatment of Saint Paul's, successive drawings show a rise in the level below which the design is fixed and above which it is still capable of change. At Saint George's, the steeple and also the turrets over the spiral staircases to the galleries grew in height and complexity. One drawing also bears a note indicating in the architect's mind a degree of transferability of ideas—in this case an unspecified but major feature of the roof—between this church and Saint Anne, Limehouse. Both churches were planned (Saint George was gutted in 1941 and only its shell restored) as a square—or nearly square rectangle—within a larger one, implying rather than stating the arms of a Greek cross between the two. The centrality thus adumbrated is not reinforced by entrances on the transverse axis; there are instead doors at the ends of the side elevations. Hawksmoor did not repeat the giant pilaster articulation of the Greenwich church; the others in the group developed instead the astylar massing and relief cutting of the Clarendon Building.

The steeple of Saint Anne, Limehouse, which has often been compared to Gothic towers, shows both Hawksmoor's structural ingenuity and the relationship between the conscious and unconscious in his formal invention. The tower rests on two huge niches placed back to back so that one niche looks into the church and the other forms

half of a baptisterylike domed cylindrical entrance vestibule projecting from the west front. The lantern above the belfry developed from a square tower to an octagon resembling the ancient Tower of the Winds in Athens; to this classically inspired nucleus were finally added the piers, buttresses, and pyramidal pinnacles that produce a silhouette evocative of Gothic steeples.

In Christ Church, the third Stepney church, Hawksmoor came closest to the Gothic, with a broach spire as a steeple. Until it was rebuilt in the nineteenth century after lightning damage, the spire was embellished with small dormer windows and other ornaments which gave it a less "Hawksmoorian" bareness than it now displays! The spire was a late addition to the design, which until 1722 was intended to end at the stage over the belfry in a flat top. Only then was the portico designed, tetrastyle with a central arch and flat side roofs. It is in fact a colossal *serliana* or Venetian window which echoes the same shape on the belfry front and the orthodox Venetian window on a smaller scale at the east end of the church. The use of arches, portholes, and other window shapes is another example of the patterned fenestration first observed at Easton Neston.

Christ Church is the narrowest and ostensibly the most basilican of Hawksmoor's churches, but the transverse axis is nonetheless clearly marked and plays an important part in the interior organization. The columniation of the nave is not uniform; instead the middle three bays form a separate group, a rectangle within a rectangle, distinguished by the substitution for columns of piers and half-columns; in addition the middle arch is slightly wider than the others. The transverse axis was originally marked also by a cross aisle in the pews between north and south central doorways; these were subsequently blocked and their outside steps removed, but it is planned to reinstate them as part of the present (1980) restoration. The fronts at least of the side galleries may also be restored, to make better sense of the very tall pedestals of the internal columns.

The other two churches, Saint Mary Woolnoth in the City of London (1716–1724), and Saint George (1716–1730), Bloomsbury, are more obvious variations on the square plan. Saint Mary, a rebuilding of a church patched up after the Great Fire, is indeed a square within a square with a central clearstory lantern resting on a triplet of columns at each corner. The west front rises into a single broad rectangular peristyle containing the belfry, with two elegant square turrets above. As in all three Stepney churches, this tower is broader than it is deep, presenting a very definite façade to the beholder.

Saint George, Bloomsbury has a basically square interior. The site was a difficult one, limited by existing buildings on the west and east and streets on the north and south. Hawksmoor contrived an eastern apse for the altar with north and south side galleries, a full hexastyle portico on the south and an extra bay on the north to exploit the lateral extent of the site. It cannot be established which of three similar porticoes, Saint George, Bloomsbury, Saint George, Hanover Square (by James); and Saint Martin-in-the-Fields (by Gibbs)—was designed first, but their simultaneity is not surprising in view of the 1711 Commission's interest in porticoes. Originally, the tower at Bloomsbury had a western entrance facing the apse; the ambiguity between the two axes was complete, with the dominance of either prevented by a complex series of shapes in ceiling and wall articulation. After many vicissitudes the north gallery was removed and the large wooden altar niche was transferred from the apse to the north side; the ambiguities, however, remain.

The steeple at Bloomsbury has been much misunderstood. It is a free version rather than an archeological reconstruction of the Tomb of Mausolus at Halicarnassus described by Pliny, a pteron carrying a stepped pyramid. Hawksmoor liked, and exploited the associative powers of, objects elevated prominently out of context: here the formal and historical references were compounded by placing on the top a statue of King George I as head of the Church of England, originally accompanied at the base of the pyramid by the heraldic supporters, lion and unicorn, of the royal arms as in the painted hatchments commonly installed in churches in the eighteenth century.

Hawksmoor designed two churches in collaboration with John James; in these, the commission evidently held its permanent architects to a tight budget and forbade alterations during execution. Both Saint John, Horselydown (1727–1733), and Saint Luke, Old Street (1727–1733; only the steeple survives), were orthodox aisled churches, and both had extraordinary steeples that show Hawksmoor's liking for evocative incongruity to extremes that, to judge from works carried out with more latitude and better documentation, he would surely have wished to temper. Saint John had a tapered, fluted Ionic column, Saint Luke a fluted obelisk: second thoughts mattered to Hawksmoor.

In 1716, Hawksmoor's efforts in the direction of All Souls, Oxford, were finally, though partially, rewarded with the commencement of the north quadrangle. This contains the Codrington Library, built from a bequest, and, from other donations, a range of lodgings, a common room with two towers, a cloister walk on the street side (begun 1728), and a new hall and buttery (begun 1730). In 1714, he had written a long and often quoted "explanation" of his designs, which is often interpreted as a plea for the preservation of the medieval buildings of the college. But though he indeed says "something in favour of the Old Quadrangle" his preferred solution is at least to add to it "much conveniency and beauty" if not to rebuild it altogether. He also offered the college a choice between a Gothic or "monastic" design and a "Greek" one, an odd stylistic label which may mean antique but not specifically Roman, rather as Gothic meant for him medieval including Romanesque. The college chose the medievalizing design

Hawksmoor.
Christ Church.
Spitalfields, London.
1714–1729

Hawksmoor.
Saint Mary Woolnoth.
City of London.
1716–1724

Hawksmoor.
All Souls College (north
  quadrangle).
Oxford.
1716–1735

Hawksmoor.
Saint Michael (tower).
Cornhill, London.
1718–1724

in harmony with the old chapel, with the interiors in a simple classical style. In offering an almost arbitrary choice of alternatives, Hawksmoor anticipated the historicism of the early nineteenth century in which a far more informed and more specific Greek Revival was included.

Especially in the towers—which are ornamental rather than useful—Hawksmoor captured much of the spirit as opposed to the letter of Gothic architecture, giving a practical demonstration of the observation already apparent two decades earlier in his project for Warwick church: he was aware that medieval buildings are designed on principles different from classical ones and cast shadows in a different way. In the same year, 1716, he published an engraved west elevation of the Gothic church at Beverley, Yorkshire, in connection with an appeal for funds to repair it; this is the date also of the final steeple design for Saint Anne, Limehouse, which like the towers of Beverley has an affinity with those at All Souls. Hawksmoor persuaded the college to commission six engravings of his designs "to be shown to future benefactors," and in 1734 a contracting mason had to agree to follow "the printed drawing."

The London coal tax was used to complete the towers of some of Wren's City churches; on Hawksmoor's own word, he was the designer of the pseudo-Perpendicular tower of Saint Michael, Cornhill (1718–1724). In this thick-set tower with four very large corner pinnacles, he contrived to produce a Gothic effect with hardly any Gothic details: the arches are roundheaded and there are almost pure Romanesque corbel tables.

In 1715, Hawksmoor was succeeded as clerk at Kensington by Henry Joynes, receiving instead the senior clerkship to the palaces of Whitehall, Westminster, and Saint James's. This appointment, in the first stage of a reorganization of the Royal Works, was rescinded three years later in the second stage. At the accession of George I in 1714, Wren, aged eighty-two, was still Surveyor. Discontent with his French taste and his easy but personal control of the Works, fostered by the third earl of Shaftesbury's pamphlet *Letter Concerning Design* (1712), coincided with a declining royal interest in architecture and the self-advertisement of COLEN CAMPBELL, the first volume of whose *Vitruvius Britannicus* appeared in 1715 to launch the Palladian (and Inigo Jones) Revival. In the Royal Works, political and personal advantage went under the guise of reform, and the shabby conduct by which in 1718 Hawksmoor and Wren were replaced by nonentities rankled in Hawksmoor's mind for the rest of his life. The stylistic "reform," by which neo-Palladian taste ousted that for the baroque, was aided but not initiated by Campbell's advo-

cacy and Shaftesbury's patent attack on Blenheim, Hampton Court, and Saint Paul's. The plainer style of Hawksmoor's and also Vanbrugh's designs after about 1710 belongs to a larger change in English taste of which neo-Palladianism was the most successful manifestation. Hawksmoor's use of the Venetian window motif at Christ Church, Spitalfields, contains an element of parody though not of insincerity, and a number of other designs after about 1714 show growing interest in Italian cinquecento details, though it must be remembered that Hawksmoor's eclecticism, if selective on particular occasions, remained wide in general. The result of this interest can be seen in his designs for Worcester College, Oxford, of about 1717, and through the designs' influence in the executed library range of that college designed by Clarke and Townesend. The Worcester College designs are remarkable nonetheless for Hawksmoor's annotations giving detailed sources in Imperial Roman buildings.

A major shift in taste combined with loss of office could mean financial disaster to an architect; although in his letters he grumbled more about money than about the gout which racked him and which at times prevented him from writing or drawing, Hawksmoor's practical sense and experience ensured him an adequate practice. When the Duchess of Marlborough found in 1722 that the completion of Blenheim (from which Vanbrugh had resigned in 1716) was beyond the capacity of herself and a cabinetmaker, she reengaged Hawksmoor, who was happy to design the Woodstock Gate and some of the interiors (1722–1725). In the southeast rooms he designed heavy fret ceilings of a type associated with Jones. In the Long Library (gallery) he not only designed wood- and plasterwork but also exploited the shape inherent in the plan to make a sequence of five spaces of differing heights and widths. The Woodstock Gate is a Roman triumphal arch in spirit though by no means literal in design. Its inscription still directs the visitor to the column where he "will know more" of the Duke of Marlborough's great deeds; Hawksmoor intended a column or obelisk placed betwen the gate and the house to control the visitor's progress kinetically as well as indoctrinate him historically. He left Blenheim, which he viewed "like a loving nurse that almost thinks the child her own," about 1725, as quietly as he had come back three years earlier. In 1731, he saw the column, ultimately designed by Lord Herbert and placed by the Duchess more conventionally on the main axis of the house but so far away that its inscription is seldom read. On that occasion, Hawksmoor asked unsuccessfully for an interview with the Duchess "only to try what she would do," as he told his most constant patron, Lord Carlisle.

In the 1720s and 1730s, many letters passed between the architect in London and Lord Carlisle at Castle Howard; Hawksmoor urged his patron to keep his letters "not for their good language but because there are sundry instructions useful for the workmen," and the letters at Castle Howard are full of information not only about the later buildings there but also about Hawksmoor's opinions in the years when he traveled to Yorkshire and the earl to London infrequently. Carlisle had moved into Castle Howard in 1712 without building the northwest wing; several years later, after much work on the gardens as well as practical forestry and agriculture, he turned to the garden buildings. A long poem, "Castle Howard," by one of his daughters and published in 1732, mentions no architects and ascribes by implication the entire work to Carlisle himself. Common sense as much as documents would show this to be impossible. But the aesthetic exploitation of the gently rolling hilly terrain of Carlisle's estate does seem to be the result of cooperation between himself, Vanbrugh, and Hawksmoor. Buildings fit into their surroundings with an inevitability that enhances the dramatic manner in which they appear and disappear as the visitor traverses the estate.

The execution of Vanbrugh's Temple at Castle Howard, begun shortly before Vanbrugh's death in 1726, was Hawksmoor's responsibility; one of his letters describes the design as Vanbrugh's in contradistinction to alternatives of his own. Other outlying buildings, however, were begun in the decade between Vanbrugh's death in 1726 and Hawksmoor's and are due to the latter's invention. The Pyramid on a hilltop south of the house (1728) was conceived as a memorial to the sixteenth-century founder of the estate. It is one of the first of many eighteenth-century skyline "eye-catchers"; it also had the virtue, according to the poem, of representing, with Vanbrugh's obelisk and Temple and Hawksmoor's Mausoleum, the "Grecian, Roman and Egyptian form."

The Mausoleum, begun in 1729 and finished only about 1742 after the death of both architect and patron, is one of Hawksmoor's major works, some would say his greatest. Its design is unusually well-documented by letters, from the choice of site through those of form and style to many details of the work; they show, too, his ability to feed his patron with ideas in a manner so casual that vital decisions sometimes seem to have been accidental. The Mausoleum, a peripteral circular temple enclosing a domed cell, is a large building, no mere garden ornament or toy chapel; its Doric columns equal in scale those of the Clarendon Building and

Hawksmoor. Mausoleum, Castle Howard. Yorkshire, England. 1729–1736 (not completed until 1742)

are set closely together with a disregard for the letter of antiquity duly criticized by Lord Burlington.

Hawksmoor defended his design variously on grounds of precedent, structural necessity, and aesthetic self-confidence; he would not change it "tho' I should be hired to do it." Whatever the letter, it recreated the spirit of antiquity exactly and cogently. In proportions it is utterly different from Bramante's Tempietto, its formal archetype. Its simplicity of outline and geometry foreshadows the great monuments of neoclassicism, but its unorthodoxy has both an assurance that is personal to Hawksmoor and an evocative quality that places it in the baroque tradition. The whole Castle Howard landscape is Virgilian, as the poem emphasizes, and seems to us today to recall the mythological landscapes of Claude Lorrain; of the buildings, Hawksmoor's somber house of the dead is the most noble.

The Mausoleum's close ring of columns suggests a fence to exclude the living; whereas Carlisle's son bowed to Palladian taste and provided a grand exterior staircase, Hawksmoor's intention was to conceal the approach steps in the base so that no entrance was apparent. The implications are repeated inside, where only one small door was left and where the evenly bright light gives an air of finality uncannily like that of Michelangelo's Medici Chapel in Florence. Hawksmoor did not know that building and the resemblance must come from a similarity of intention and means.

For Castle Howard Hawksmoor also designed a small open circular Temple of Venus (1731–1735; destroyed), a small rusticated pyramid and the monument called the Four Faces. Of these woodland objects the last is the simplest in origin but

*Hawksmoor.
Carrmire Gate, Castle
Howard.
Yorkshire, England.
c.1730*

the most complex in association: a square urn left from the roof line of the mansion, perhaps the first architectural "ready-made," elevated on a base like some esoteric quotation from a forgotten source. The Carrmire Gate (c.1730), on the long straight drive from the York road, mixes associations: the many pyramids of the mythical Tomb of Porsenna, medieval fortifications, the rustic gateways of Serlio, and one of Hawksmoor's favorite motifs, a triangular pediment with the lower member broken.

Hawksmoor's last years saw the execution of the street front screen to the Queen's College, Oxford, to a new design of his (1733–1736), with a light and elegant domed open temple over the gateway. Then also was begun his best known but least recognized work, the west towers of Westminster Abbey, on which he worked from 1734 until his death. The creative mind embraces both novelty and constancy: the Westminster towers continue his theme of Gothic as a style of lines and shadows, and make it clear that for him the exactness of detail mattered not for its historical correctness but so that it should fit the idea in his mind. Here he used classical moldings for a High Gothic effect, and the sensitive conclusion of a historic building is as unassuming as the man himself.

He died on March 25, 1736, at his house on Millbank, Westminster, of "gout in the stomach." Hawksmoor once defined "following the Ancients" as "strong reason and good fancy, joined with experience and trials, so that we are assured of the good effect of it." So personal and unliteral a summation of the Renaissance tradition could not appeal to eighteenth-century rationalism. His obituarist praised his stoic equanimity no less than his "learned and ingenious" architecture and his remarkable knowledge of architectural history. As he never left England, that knowledge was entirely from books, but it was omnivorous. He left an extensive architectural library and some two thou-

sand drawings, very few of which can be among the nearly six hundred now known from his hand or his office. His historical knowledge was essential to the eclecticism out of which his genius fashioned a style richly evocative, personal, and coherent, and of the essence and not the trappings of architecture.

Hawksmoor's seriousness, temper, and wit appear in his letters, his face in the unflattering but fascinating portrait bust at All Souls, Oxford, made at the end of his life by Henry Cheere, possibly assisted by Roubiliac. It shows a wise, not to say disillusioned man, inclined to stoutness, but not a pretentious or arrogant one. Through the sculptor's skill it is possible to feel that we have met him; yet ultimately we meet him in his buildings and in details like the gallery entrances at Saint George-in-the-East. Their most obvious element, the triple keystone, is nowhere displayed with more incongruity or overemphasis. Incongruous because a monolithic lintel does not need one, the keystone has to be there as part of a statement about the greatness of God and the goodness of the church and its sovereign head, and also about the nature of stone and the truth of geometry (which for a believer are also about God). The keystone is overemphatic because, once seen, it becomes the archetypal example. Hawksmoor seems to have taken literally, as Wren never did, the latter's claim that geometry was the basis of everything. Here he pared down the eared doorcases of Michelangelo and Borromini to prismatic stones, yet he superimposed three doorcases one upon another. The range of his sources was known and understood in his own time. The eloquence of what he made from them has perhaps had to wait for modern concepts of empathy, metaphor, and the subconscious to be appreciated.

KERRY DOWNES

WORKS

*1692–1695, Christ's Hospital Writing School, City of London; 1695–1696, King's Gallery, Kensington Palace; London. c.1695–1710, Easton Neston (later altered), Northamptonshire, England. 1699–1707, King William Court (south and west ranges), Greenwich Hospital; 1700–1703, Queen Anne Block (east range), Greenwich Hospital; (A)1704–1705, Orangery, Kensington Palace; *1711–1712, Kensington Charity School; London. 1712–1713, Old Clarendon Building, Oxford. 1712–1718, Saint Alfege, Greenwich; 1714–1729, Christ Church, Spitalfields; 1714–1729, Saint Anne, Limehouse; 1714–1729, Saint George-in-the-East, Wapping; 1716–1717, Queen Anne Block (court loggias), Greenwich Hospital; 1716–1717, Saint James's Palace (stable yard arcade); 1716–1724, Saint Mary Woolnoth, City of London; 1716–1730, Saint George, Bloomsbury; London. 1716–1735, All Souls College (north quadrangle), Oxford. 1718–1724, Saint Michael (tower), Cornhill. London. 1722–1725, Blenheim Palace (Long Library, southeast rooms, Woodstock Gate), Oxfordshire, England. *1727–1733, Saint John (with John James), Horselydown, Bermondsey; *1727–1733, Saint Luke (with James), Old Street, Finsbury; London. 1728, Pyramid; 1729–1736, Mausoleum (not completed until 1742); c.1730, Carrmire Gate; *1731–1735, Temple of Venus; Castle Howard, Yorkshire, England. 1733–1736, The Queen's College (screen and gateway), Oxford. 1734–1736, Westminster Abbey (west towers and gable; not completed until 1745), London.

BIBLIOGRAPHY

BILL, E. G. W. (compiler) 1979 *The Queen Anne Churches: A Catalogue of the Papers in Lambeth Palace Library of the Commission for Building Fifty New Churches in London and Westminster, 1711–1759.* Introduction by H. M. Colvin. London: Mansell.

COLVIN, H. M. (compiler) 1964 *A Catalogue of Architectural Drawings of the 18th and 19th Centuries in the Library of Worcester College, Oxford.* Oxford: Clarendon Press.

COLVIN, H. M. (editor) 1976 *The History of the King's Works, 1660–1782.* London: Her Majesty's Stationery Office.

DOWNES, KERRY (1959)1979 *Hawksmoor.* London: Zwemmer.

DOWNES, KERRY 1966 *English Baroque Architecture.* London: Zwemmer.

GOODHART-RENDEL, H. S. 1924 *Hawksmoor.* London: Benn.

GREEN, DAVID (1951)1967 *Blenheim Palace.* London: Country Life.

LONDON COUNTY COUNCIL 1957 *Survey of London. XVIII: Spitalfields.* London: Athlone Press.

WATKIN, DAVID 1972 *Sale Catalogues of Libraries of Eminent Persons. 4: Architects.* London: Sotheby Parke-Bernet.

WEBB, GEOFFREY 1931 "The Letters and Drawings of Nicholas Hawksmoor Relating to the Building of the Mausoleum at Castle Howard." *Walpole Society* 19:111–164.

WHITECHAPEL ART GALLERY 1977 *Hawksmoor Exhibition.* London: The Gallery.

WREN SOCIETY 1924–1943 *Volumes 1–20.*

HAY, WILLIAM

Born and trained in Aberdeenshire, Scotland, William Hay (1818–1888) went to Edinburgh in 1844 to assist John Henderson. In 1846–1850, he was GEORGE GILBERT SCOTT's clerk of the works for the cathedral at Saint John's, Newfoundland, Canada. After 1853, Hay established a considerable practice in Toronto and southern Ontario. This passed to his pupil, Henry Langley, and to Thomas Gundry in 1860 when Hay moved to Halifax in partnership with David Stirling. Hay returned to Edinburgh in 1863. In partnership with George Henderson he restored the interior of Saint Giles, Edinburgh, and designed the Bermuda Cathedral (1886–1888) at Hamilton. Affable, with Episcopalian and Masonic connections, Hay favored Scott's Gothic for churches and Mansard for institutions.

FREDERICK H. ARMSTRONG

WORKS

1842, Cruden Episcopal Church, Aberdeenshire, Scotland. 1853, Commercial Bank (now Empire Life Building), Kingston, Ontario. *1854, Toronto General Hospital. 1854–1858, Catholic House of Providence; 1855–1856, Saint Basil's Church; Toronto. 1855–1856, Saint Michael's College (much altered), University of Toronto. 1857, Saint George's Anglican Church, Newcastle, Ontario. *1859–1860, Yorkville Town Hall, Toronto. 1863, Keith Hall, Halifax, Nova Scotia. 1872–1883, Saint Giles (restoration of interior), Edinburgh. 1886–1888, Cathedral of the Most Holy Trinity (not completed until 1905), Hamilton, Bermuda.

BIBLIOGRAPHY

ARMSTRONG, FREDERICK H. 1981 "William Hay." Volume 11 in *Dictionary of Canadian Biography.* University of Toronto Press.

ARTHUR, ERIC 1964 *Toronto: No Mean City.* University of Toronto Press.

"Obituary." 1888 *The Builder* 54:414.

"Obituary." 1888 *Canadian Architect and Builder* 1, no. 7:11.

WALLACE, WILLIAM STEWART (1926)1963 "William Hay." Page 307 in *Macmillan Dictionary of Canadian Biography.* 3d ed., rev. & enl. Toronto: Macmillan.

HAYASHI, SHŌJI

Born in Tokyo, Japan, Shōji Hayashi (1928–) studied at the Tokyo Institute of Technology. Since graduation in 1953, he has been working at the Nikken Architects' Office in Tokyo, the biggest architects' office in the world. He has designed a number of office buildings. His technical design approach is notable; around 1970 he replaced the popular central core system for large office buildings by the double-core system with a central space. The Pola Gotanda Building (1971) in Tokyo which was designed in his double-core system won a prize from the Architectural Institute of Japan.

SAKA-E OHMI

WORKS

1960, San-ai Dream Center; 1964, Palace (side building); 1971, Pola Gotanda Building; 1971, International Business Machines Headquarters; 1976, Mitsui-bussan Building; Tokyo.

Hayashi.
Pola Gotanda Building.
Tokyo.
1971

BIBLIOGRAPHY

HAYASHI, SHŌJI   1980   *Kenchiku Ronshū*. Tokyo.
HAYASHI, SHŌJI   1981   *Watashino Jūkyoron*. Tokyo.
MIYAWAKI, M.   1976   *Tsukuru Jutsuni tsuite Gonino Dezaināto Katatta*. Tokyo.
TAIRA, KEIICHI   1972   *Nikken Architects' Office*. Tokyo.

HEBEBRAND, WERNER

Werner Hebebrand (1899–1966) was a leading German city planner. He worked under ERNST MAY in Frankfurt from 1925 to 1929. Planner in Frankfurt from 1946 and professor in Hanover from 1950, he became head city planner of Hamburg in 1952 and later contributed to the preservation of Regensburg.

RON WIEDENHOEFT

WORKS

1930s, Hospital in Wolgograd, Russia. 1930–1931, Tuberculosis Sanitorium Sonnenblick, Marburg, Germany. 1949, Westend Synagogue (reconstruction), Frankfurt. 1951, Labor Union School, Lohr on the Main, Germany. 1964–1967, Group of Atrium Houses, Hamburg-Klein Flottbek, Germany.

BIBLIOGRAPHY

CONRADS, ULRICH ET AL. (editors)   1964   *Hommage à Werner Hebebrand*. Essen, Germany: Druck.
HEBEBRAND, WERNER   1955   *Probleme der Gross-Stadt*. n.p.
"Werner Hebebrand."   1969   *Neue deutsche Biographie* 8:164–165.

HEBRARD, ERNEST

Ernest Michel Hébrard (1866–1933), born in Paris, a distinguished graduate of the Ecole des Beaux-Arts, won the Grand Pris de Rome in 1904. While in Rome, he became associated with Hendrik Andersen, Norwegian-born sculptor and internationalist, who conceived the idea for a "World Center of Communications," an ideal extraterritorial city for which Hébrard produced highly detailed plans (c.1906–1912). The city was never built, but the plans received wide notice in the press.

Hébrard's scheme for the reconstruction of earthquake-damaged Salonika, Greece (1918–1933), consolidated his reputation as an urbanist. He planned a new town at Dalat, Indochina (1921–1923), and in 1923 he was appointed head architect to the French Indochinese colonial government. Hébrard returned to Europe in 1926 and became active as a consultant to archeological and planning authorities in Athens.

For his architectural works in southern Europe and southeast Asia Hébrard developed styles combining features of local traditional architecture and the compositional systems of French academic planning.

ALFRED WILLIS

WORKS

1918–1933, Master Plan for Salonika (partially executed), Greece. 1921–1923, New Town at Dalat, Indochina. 1923, Government Center, Hanoi, Indochina.

BIBLIOGRAPHY

ANDERSON, HENDRIK   1913   *Creation of a World Centre of Communication*. 2 vols. Paris: Privately printed.
DREYFUS, R.   1923   "Le nouveau plan de Salonique." *L'Architecture* 36:101–110.
LAVEDAN, PIERRE   1933   "Ernest Hébrard." *L'Architecture* 46:109–112.
POTTIER, E., and PICARD, C.   1933   "Ernest Hébrard." *Revue archéologique* Series 6 2:148–150.
SMETS, MARCEL   1977   *L'avènement de la Cité-jardin en Belgique*. Brussels: Mardaga.
UNION OF INTERNATIONAL ASSOCIATIONS   1914   *The Union of International Associations: A World Center*. Brussels: Office Centrale des Associations Internationales.
L'Urbanisme   1933   May. Special issue on Ernest Hébrard.

HEGEMANN, WERNER

Influential in the development of city planning as an interdisciplinary concern, Werner Hegemann (1881–1936) was born in Mannheim, Germany, and traveled extensively. Encouraged by his uncle OTTO MARCH, he studied architecture and city planning. From Charlottenburg, where he came under the influence of CAMILLO SITTE's ideas, he attended the Sorbonne and the universities of Pennsylvania, Berlin, Strassburg, and Munich, where he received his Ph.D. (1908) in political science and economics.

From Philadelphia and Boston, he was called back to direct the pioneering city planning exhibition of 1910 in Berlin and Düsseldorf (Hegemann, 1911–1913). In 1913, the People's Institute of New York invited him to give a nationwide lecture tour that led to consultantships in Oakland and Berkeley, California. After visiting Japan, China, and Australia, World War I prevented his return to Germany. In the United States, he established offices in Milwaukee, Wisconsin, in association with Elbert Peets, and in New York with JOSEPH HUDNUT, planning the layouts of several garden suburbs and estates. Hegemann and Peets published *The American Vitruvius: An Architects'*

Handbook of Civic Art (1922), considered a landmark in city-planning literature.

Hegemann left the United States in 1921 for Berlin where he designed his home in a somewhat Muthesian style. In 1922 he became the editor of *Wasmuths Monatshefte für Baukunst und Städtebau* (Berlin). He wrote countless articles and several books concerning his almost worldwide personal acquaintance with contemporary architecture and planning.

He also wrote a number of books on historical subjects, all sharply critical of accepted heroes such as Frederick the Great and Napoleon. *Das steinerne Berlin* (1930) exposes the Prussian state as villain behind the deplorable housing conditions in that city. Deeply committed to fighting Nazism, he published an outspoken attack on Hitler, *Entlarvte Geschichte: Aus Nacht zum Licht: Von Arminius bis Hitler* (1933). While the book was publicly burned in Berlin, he became part of the intellectual diaspora, and settled with his family in New York. He taught at The New School for Social Research and at Columbia University's School of Architecture, and was working on a three-volume housing survey when he died on April 12, 1936. Friends and colleagues prepared the last two volumes for publication.

CHRISTIANE C. COLLINS

BIBLIOGRAPHY

CALABI, DONATELLA 1977 "Werner Hegemann, o dell'ambiguità borghese dell'urbanistica." *Casabella* 428:54–60.

HEGEMANN, WERNER 1911 *Amerikanische Parkanlagen: Zierparks, Nutzparks, Aussen- und Innenparks, Nationalparks, Park-Zweckverbände. Ein Parkbuch zur Wanderausstellung von Bildern und Plänen amerikanischer Parkanlagen.* Berlin: Wasmuth.

HEGEMANN, WERNER 1911–1913 *Der Städtebau nach den Ergebnissen der allgemeinen Städtebau-Ausstellung in Berlin, nebst einem Anhang: Die Internationale Städtebau-Ausstellung in Düsseldorf.* 2 vols. Berlin: Wasmuth.

HEGEMANN, WERNER 1915 *Report on a City Plan for the Municipalities of Oakland & Berkeley.* Oakland, Calif.: Kelley-Davis.

HEGEMANN, WERNER 1923 *Gothenburg 1923: International Cities and Town Planning Exhibition.* Gothenburg, Germany: Zachrissons.

HEGEMANN, WERNER 1929 *Reihen- und Geschäftshaus-Fassaden.* Berlin: Wasmuth.

HEGEMANN, WERNER (1930)1976 *Das steinerne Berlin: Geschichte der grössten Mietskasernstadt der Welt.* Braunschweig: Vieweg.

HEGEMANN, WERNER 1931 *Problemas urbanos de Rosario.* Rosario, Argentina: The Municipality of the City.

HEGEMANN, WERNER 1936–1938 *City Planning: Housing.* 3 vols. New York: Architectural Book Publishing.

HEGEMANN, WERNER, and PEETS, ELBERT (1922)1972 *The American Vitruvius: An Architects' Handbook of Civic Art.* Reprint. New York: Blom.

HEIDE, AUGUST F.

August Franklin Heide (1862–1943), born in Alton, Illinois and trained as an apprentice, was the leading architect in Everett, Washington, from the time of his engagement by the Everett Land Company in 1892 on. Earlier, he studied and practiced in Chicago, Los Angeles, and Tacoma, Washington. In Everett, he collaborated briefly with Charles Hove and later worked in association with Emil De Neuf and Carl Siebrand.

ELISABETH WALTON POTTER

WORKS

1891, Harstad Hall, Pacific Lutheran University, Tacoma, Wash. *1892, Hewitt Block (with Charles Hove); 1892, Swalwell Block (with Hove); *1897–1898, Snohomish County Courthouse; Everett, Wash. *1904, Washington State Building, Louisiana Purchase Exposition, St. Louis, Mo. 1904–1905, Everett Public Library (with Emil De Neuf), Wash. *1905, Washington State Building, Lewis and Clark Centennial Exposition, Portland, Ore. 1910–1911, Snohomish County Courthouse (with Carl Siebrand), Everett, Wash.

BIBLIOGRAPHY

An Illustrated History of Skagit and Snohomish Counties; Their People, Their Commerce and Their Resources. 1906 Chicago: Interstate Publishing.

DILGARD, DAVID, and BIDDLE, MARGARET 1974 "Survey of Everett Buildings, 1890–1905." Unpublished manuscript prepared for the City of Everett, Department of Community Development, Wash.

HUME, M. (compiler) 1902 *Seattle Architecturally.* Seattle, Washington: Bebb & Mendel, Saunders & Lawton, De Neuf & Heide.

WOODBRIDGE, SALLY BRYNE, and MONTGOMERY, ROGER 1980 *A Guide to Architecture in Washington State.* Seattle: University of Washington Press.

HEIDELOFF, KARL ALEXANDER VON

Born in Stuttgart, Karl Alexander von Heideloff (1789–1865) began collecting examples of medieval architecture on travels in southern Germany as early as 1808. In 1816, Duke Ernst von Sachsen-Coburg-Gotha commissioned him to restore Coburg Castle. Heideloff settled in Nuremberg in 1820 where, as Conservator of City Art Treasures (from 1824) and later Royal Bavarian Conservator (from 1837), he restored many of the city's medieval monuments in the area. His numerous illustrated books and the Polytechnical School of Nuremberg, which he helped found in 1823, were aimed at design reform by emulating medieval practices. Treatises on the geometrical composition methods of late Gothic architects as well as collections of details such as his influential *Ornamentik des Mittelalters* (1838–1855) provided the tools, while the *Bauhütte* (1844) or medieval crafts ateliers were the means to reintegrate architecture and crafts. Heideloff's own churches, based on late Gothic styles, reflect his conception of architecture in terms of decoration and a neoclassically trained bias for geometrical principles and symmetry.

BARRY BERGDOLL

WORKS

1820, Dürer-Pirckheimer Fountain, Maxplatz; *1820, Laufer Gate Guard Houses; Nuremberg, Germany. 1823–1825, Monument to Uz, Amsbach, Germany. *1826, House, 26 Hauptmarkt, Nuremberg, Germany. 1831–1834, Bamberg Cathedral (restoration), Germany. *1834, Nuremberg Castle (restoration), Germany. *1838–?, Coburg Castle (restoration), Germany. 1839–1842, Schloss Lichtenstein, Württemberg, Germany. *1840–1841, Stifftskirche (restoration), Stuttgart, Germany. 1843–1844, Church (rebuilding), Neustadt vor der Halde, Germany. 1843–1844, Saint Peter, Sonneberg, Germany. *1843–1846, Pfarrhof, Saint Lorenz, Nuremberg, Germany. *1845–1847, Saint Trinitatus, Leipzig. 1853–1859, Mariensäule, Wiesentheid, Germany. 1854–1857, Saint Jakob (restoration), Rottenburg ob der Tauber, Germany.

BIBLIOGRAPHY

BOECK, URS 1958 "Karl Alexander Heideloff." *Mitteilungen des Vereins für Geschichte der Stadt Nürnberg* 48:314–390.

HEIDELOFF, KARL A. (1838–1843)1855 *Nürnbergs Baudenkmale der Vorzeit, oder Musterbuch der altdeutschen Baukunst.* Nuremberg, Germany: Lotzbeck.

HEIDELOFF, KARL A. 1838–1855 *Die Ornamentik des Mittelalters.* Nuremberg, Germany: Geiger.

HEIDELOFF, KARL A. 1844 *Die Bauhütte des Mittelalters in Deutschland.* Nuremberg, Germany: Stein.

HEIDELOFF, KARL A. 1855 *Die Kunst des Mittelalters in Schwaben.* Stuttgart, Germany: Ebner & Seubert.

HENSOLDT, H. C. 1845 *Die neue Stadt-Pfarr-Kirche in Sonneberg im Herzogthum Sachsen-Meiningen.* Nuremberg, Germany: Stein.

MENDE, MATTHIAS 1972 "Das Dürer-Denkmal in Nürnberg." Pages 163–181 in Hans E. Mittig and Volker Plagemann (editors), *Denkmäler im neunzehnten Jahrhundert.* Munich: Prestel.

MÜLLER, WERNER 1978 "Friedrich Hoffstadts und Carl Alexander Heideloffs Turmkonstruktionen vor dem Hintergrund der oberdeutschen Steinmetzlehre des 16. bis 18. Jahrhunderts." *Zeitschrift für Kunstgeschichte* 41:41–56.

ROTHBART, GEORG 1845 *Das Luther Zimmer.* Nuremberg, Germany: Stein.

HEINS and LA FARGE

George Louis Heins (1860–1907) and Christopher Grant La Farge (1862–1938), who had met as students of architecture at the Massachusetts Institute of Technology and subsequently trained in H. H. RICHARDSON's Boston office, formed a partnership in New York in 1886. Heins, the son of John and Maris Vaughn Heins, born in Philadelphia, had transferred to M.I.T. after two years at the University of Pennsylvania. C. Grant La Farge, eldest son of the distinguished artist John La Farge, and Margaret Perry La Farge, born in Newport, Rhode Island, grew up steeped in the art world of his father's studio. This young partnership proved felicitous and complementary: La Farge was essentially the designer, Heins essentially the builder and administrator. When, in 1891, Heins married Aimée Thérèse La Farge, his partner's aunt, these bonds were strengthened.

In 1888, after years of deliberation, the Episcopal authorities in New York City decided to implement Bishop Horatio Potter's dream of a cathedral open to all people, and organized a contest for the plan of the Cathedral of Saint John the Divine. Heins and La Farge, both students of ecclesiastical architecture, entered the contest competing with some sixty others, and were the winners. They envisaged a cruciform building (520 feet long), using Richardson Romanesque and Byzantine elements freely, crowned with an immense tower and conical spire over a wide round-arched crossing, with massive marble monoliths surrounding the high altar. Their plan was accepted, contracts signed to last until the death of either partner. The ground was broken in 1890, and building begun with an opening service on the Feast of St. John the Divine on December 27, 1892.

As the cathedral grew, so did the firm, handling other ecclesiastical buildings such as Saint Matthew's in Washington (1893), civic and institutional buildings such as the original subway stations for the New York Rapid Transit Commission (1904), and all buildings for the New York Zoological Park (1899).

La Farge, a fellow of the American Institute of Architects, served, at intervals, on the advisory committees for the schools of architecture at Columbia University, M.I.T. and Princeton University, and also as trustee and secretary for the American Academy in Rome. Heins, in 1899 appointed New York State Architect by Governor Theodore Roosevelt, designed state buildings until his untimely death in 1907.

With the partnership dissolved and the original cathedral contract ended, La Farge continued in charge of the cathedral in increasingly adverse circumstances due to the growing appreciation of Gothic forms and their association with church building. Despite earlier modifications in the plan to meet this trend, of which RALPH ADAMS CRAM was the personable and able protagonist, the trustees, finally convinced that Saint John the Divine should be Gothic in idiom, were at odds with La Farge. Confusion and misunderstandings resulted and Cram was called in as a consultant. Hence, in 1911, with the choir completed, the agreement with La Farge came to a close and the future of the cathedral was assigned to Cram, BERTRAM G. GOODHUE, and Frank W. Ferguson, as Cram desired.

For La Farge, this was a profound tragedy, but he remained undefeated and active for another twenty-five years, whether in partnership or alone. During World War I he was involved in housing in Washington and the building of the Naval Hospital in Brooklyn, New York. In 1921 Princeton awarded him an honorary M.F.A. In later years, he was associated with his son Christopher G. La Farge.

FRANCES S. CHILDS AND
JAMES P. MORTON

WORKS

HEINS AND LA FARGE

1892–1911, Cathedral of Saint John the Divine, New York. 1893, Saint Matthew's Roman Catholic Cathedral, Washington. 1894, Fourth Presbyterian Church and Parsonage; 1899, New York Zoological Park buildings; New York. 1899–1900, Roman Catholic Chapel, West Point, N.Y. 1902, Grace Church Clergy House; New York. 1904, New York Subway Stations.

LA FARGE AND BENJAMIN MORRIS

1915, Saint James Cathedral, Seattle, Wash. 1915, Saint Patrick's Church, Philadelphia.

BIBLIOGRAPHY

HALL, EDWARD H. (editor) (1920)1965 A Guide to the Cathedral of St. John the Divine in the City of New York. 17th ed. New York: Dean and Chapter of the Cathedral Church.

KERVICK, FRANCIS W. 1962 Architects in America of Catholic Tradition. Rutland, Vt.: Tuttle.

LA FARGE, CHRISTOPHER GRANT 1907 "The Cathedral of Saint John the Divine." Scribners Magazine 41:385–401.

LA FARGE, JOHN (1954)1957 The Manner is Ordinary. Garden City, N.Y.: Image.

MUCHIGROSSO, ROBERT 1980 American Gothic: The Mind and Art of Ralph Adams Cram. Washington: University Press of America.

WICKERSHAM, GEORGE W. II 1977 The Cathedral Church of St. John the Divine. New York: Conroy.

WODEHOUSE, LAWRENCE 1976 American Architects from the Civil War to the First World War. Detroit, Mich.: Gale.

HEINZELMANN, KONRAD

Konrad Heinzelmann (1390?–1454) was a member of a generation of late Gothic German architects whose works Paul Frankl has termed "classic" (Frankl, pp. 185–187). Heinzelmann worked on the Church of Saint George at Nördlingen from 1427 to 1438. In 1438, he spent a short period in Rothenberg-an-der-Tauber as city architect and supervised work on the Church of Saint Jacob. By April of 1439, he had left for Nuremberg to add a choir to the Church of Sankt Lorenz. After Heinzelmann's death in 1454, the choir was completed by Konrad Roriczer (see RORICZER FAMILY).

JOANNE E. SOWELL

WORKS

1427–1438, Church of Saint George, Nördlingen, Germany. 1439–1454, Church of Saint Lorenz (choir), Nuremberg, Germany.

BIBLIOGRAPHY

FRANKL, PAUL 1962 Gothic Architecture. Baltimore: Penguin.

GÜMBEL, ALBERT 1909 "Rechnungen und Aktenstücke zur Geschichte des Chorbaus von St. Lorenz in Nürnberg unter der Leitung Konrad Heinzelmanns." Repertorium für Kunstwissenschaft 32:1–30, 132–159.

HEJDUK, JOHN

John Hejduk (1929–) was educated at Cooper Union School of Art and Architecture in New York (1947–1950), the University of Cincinnati (1952), and the Harvard Graduate School of Design (1953). In 1954, he won a Fulbright Fellowship enabling him to study in Rome. Hejduk established a private practice in New York City in 1965 and has been professor of architecture and dean of the School of Architecture, Cooper Union, since 1964. His concerns are largely conceptual: his work entails a continual search for and exploration of generating principles of form and space. As such, his work was included in a 1972 publication with that of Michael Graves, Peter Eisenman, Richard Meier, and Charles Gwathmey, who perhaps misleadingly came to be known as the New York Five. The restoration of the Foundation Building at Cooper Union constitutes Hejduk's one major executed building (1975).

SUSAN STRAUSS

WORKS

1960, Demlin House, Locus Valley, N.Y. 1969, Hommel Apartment Building; 1975, Cooper Union Foundation Building (restoration); New York.

BIBLIOGRAPHY

"Art: Architectural Drawings, the Grace of Fine Delineation." *Architectural Digest* 35, no. 2:78–83.

BALFOUR, ALAN 1980 "John Hejduk." Pages 352–354 in Muriel Emanuel (editor), *Contemporary Architects*. New York: St. Martin's.

BLETTER, ROSEMARIE HAAG 1979 "Five Architects and 'Five on Five'." *Journal of the Society of Architectural Historians* 38, no. 2:205–207.

"Deux Projets," 1972 *L'Architecture d'Aujourd'hui* 44, no. 163:43–45.

Five Architects—Eisenman, Graves, Gwathmey, Hejduk, Meier. (1972)1975 New York: Oxford University Press.

"Five on Five." 1973 *Architectural Forum* 138, no. 4:46–57.

GOLDBERGER, PAUL 1974 "Should Anyone Care About the 'New York Five' or Their Critics the 'Five on Five'." *Architectural Record* 155:113–116.

HEJDUK, JOHN 1965 "Hors du Temps Dans l'Espace." *L'Architecture d'Aujourd'hui* 35, no. 122:xxi–xxiii.

HEJDUK, JOHN, and ROWE, COLIN 1957 "Lockhart, Texas." *Architectural Record* 121:201–206.

"John Hejduk." 1975 *Architecture and Urbanism* 53:73–154.

"John Hejduk et la Cooper Union." 1976 *L'Architecture d'Aujourd'hui* 186:47–52.

Projects/John Hejduk. 1972 Paris: Le Corbusier Foundation. Exhibition catalogue.

HELIN, PIERRE LOUIS

Pierre Louis Hélin (1734–1791) was born in Versailles, France, and won the Prix de Rome in 1754. Returning to France in 1759, he made his reputation designing monasteries. Roman baroque models strongly influenced his early work, but by the late 1770s, he had conformed to the prevailing taste for neoclassicism.

RICHARD CLEARY

WORKS

*1768–1776, Carthusian Church of Bourbon-lez-Gaillon, France. *1775–1782, Church of the Visitation, Paris. *1779–1781, Abbey of Notre-Dame of Soissons, France. *1778–1780, Church of the Priory of Hautes-Bruyères, near Rambouillet, France.

BIBLIOGRAPHY

GALLET, MICHEL 1963 "Un baroque attardé, Pierre-Louis Hélin." *Art de France* 3:187–194.

GALLET, MICHEL 1972 *Paris Domestic Architecture of the Eighteenth Century.* Translated by James Palmes. London: Barrie & Jenkins.

HÉLIN, PIERRE n.d. *Compositions divers d'architecture.* Paris: Chéreau.

HÉLIN, PIERRE n.d. *Iᵉ, IIᵉ, IIIᵉ cahiers d'études de croisées faites d'après les plus beaux édifices de Rome et d'Italie.* Paris: Chéreau.

HELLMUTH, OBATA, and KASSABAUM

One of the largest post-World War II American architectural firms, Hellmuth, Obata, and Kassabaum (HOK) was established in 1955 following the reorganization of the St. Louis firm of Hellmuth, Yamasaki, and Leinweber. Specializing in large-scale projects for corporate and institutional clients, the firm has regional offices in New York, Washington, Texas, and San Francisco as well as international branches in Cairo and Saudi Arabia. The son of a St. Louis architect, George Hellmuth (1907–) organized HOK on a tripartite system in which he assumed responsibility for administration and client relations and George Kassabaum 1920–1982) supervised construction. Gyo Obata (1923–), who studied with ELIEL SAARINEN at the Cranbrook Academy of Art, is the partner in charge of design.

Noted for a capacity to work with complex and large-scale building programs, HOK has designed many office buildings, schools, health-care facilities, libraries, shopping centers, and airports. The firm has often relied on a modular system of design with a clear and flexible plan. The Dallas-Ft. Worth Regional Airport (completed in 1973) facilitates connection between airlines by transporting passengers along a central spine with terminals branching off this linear artery, and it was proposed that it serve as the core of a linear city that has never developed.

The modular system also permits future expansion and has an open plan adaptable to different functions, two concepts fundamental to the master plan for the new campus of Southern Illinois University at Edwardsville (1963–1966). Although most of the firm's clients have been corporations and institutions, the design and choice of materials are sensitive to the individual user. In the International Business Machines Advanced Systems Development Laboratory, Los Gatos, California (1963?), the redwood used in construction harmonizes with the surrounding forests while the design takes advantage of the natural beauty of the site by giving each office a view of either the internal gardens or the landscape.

JANET PARKS

WORKS

1956, Bristol Primary School, Webster Groves, Mo. 1963, Berkeley Junior High School, St. Louis, Mo. 1963, Congregational Temple Israel, Creve Coeur, Mo. 1963?, International Business Machines Advanced System Development & Laboratory, Los Gatos, Calif. 1963–1966, Southern Illinois University, Edwardsville. 1964, Lindell Terrace Apartments, St. Louis, Mo. 1968, The

Galleria, Houston, Tex. 1969, Ralston Purina Corporate Headquarters, St. Louis, Mo. 1972, E. R. Squibb World Headquarters, Laurenceville, N.J. 1973, Dallas–Fort Worth Regional Airport, Texas. 1973, John S. Legman Building, Missouri Botanical Garden, St. Louis. 1974, Central Laundry Facility, Hospital Linen Services, Incorporated, Kansas City, Mo. 1975, Easton Center for Equitable Life Assurance Company, Easton, Pa. Begun 1975 Riyadh International Airport, Saudi Arabia. 1976, Smithsonian Institution National Air and Space Museum, Washington. 1978, Community Federal Center, St. Louis, Mo. 1978, Helen D. Lockwood Library (addition), Vassar College, Poughkeepsie, N.Y. 1980, Olympic Fieldhouse, Lake Placid, N.Y.

BIBLIOGRAPHY

COLUMBIA UNIVERSITY 1973–1979 *Avery Index to Architectural Periodicals.* 15 vols. and 3 supps. 2d ed., rev. & enl. Boston: Hall.

HELLMUTH, GEORGE F. 1980 "Hellmuth, George F(rancis)." Page 354 in Muriel Emanuel (editor), *Contemporary Architects.* New York: St. Martin's.

LEGNER, LINDA 1980 "Hellmuth, Obata and Kassabaum." Pages 354–356 in Muriel Emanuel (editor), *Contemporary Architects.* New York: St. Martin's.

HENARD, EUGENE

Eugène Alfred Hénard (1849–1923), born in Paris, studied in his father Antoine-Julien Hénard's atelier at the Ecole des Beaux-Arts. Hénard graduated in 1880 and subsequently became a respected member of the Société Centrale des Architectes Français, the most prestigious French architectural society. In 1905, he was awarded its highest honor, the *Prix Dejean,* for excellence of professional work and study.

In 1882, Hénard secured an appointment to the *Travaux de Paris,* the office in charge of municipal architecture. He continued to rise through its ranks until the end of his active career. As an architect in the *Travaux de Paris* Hénard was principally concerned with the remodeling and design of school buildings.

It was, however, through his other work that Hénard made lasting contributions to the city of Paris and to the development of urbanism in France. Between 1887 and 1900, Hénard made major contributions through his work at and suggestions for the *Expositions Universelles* of 1889 and 1900. In 1900, he was awarded the Gold Medal for his architectural work at that year's exposition, as well as the Grand Prix for his efforts in its planning. He was also made a *Chevalier de la Légion d'Honneur* and was decorated by Russia, Norway, Spain, Belgium, and other countries for his contributions to the expositions. In his official capacity in the 1889 exposition Hénard recorded and subsequently published all details relative to CHARLES L. F. DUTERT and Coutamin's Palais des Machines. For the 1900 *Exposition Universelle,* Hénard exerted a significant influence over the over-all plan for the Invalides area; in addition, he designed several structures, including the Palais de l'Electricité and the Salle des Illusions.

After 1900, Hénard evidenced a steadily growing and increasingly informed concern with larger city problems in Paris. Between 1903 and 1909, Hénard made independent studies of many of the major current city planning problems in Paris. He published these studies in eight serially released *fascicules* which he called *Etudes sur les transformations de Paris* (1903–1909). These *fascicules* provided detailed background information and histories of the problem studied as well as information about solutions to similar problems attempted in other cities. And running throughout them, in a variety of proposed solutions to specific problems, was a coordinated, coherent, large-scale, long-term (75–100 years) program for the amelioration of inadequacies of park space, housing, and surface circulation in Paris.

Throughout his career, Hénard also worked to assure the preservation of Paris as a great and beautiful historic city. He became president by 1910 of the newly formed and government sponsored *sous-commission des perspectives monumentales de la ville de Paris.* This subcommittee replaced several committees that had formerly been involved only in the preservation of single buildings and had proven ineffective even in that role. Under Hénard, the new subcommittee became effective in establishing in Paris the idea of preserving entire urban perspectives. Under Hénard, the most important historical areas of Paris were catalogued, fully described, and ranked by order of importance and urgency for preservation. In part as a result of Hénard's efforts, new legislation was passed in France that guaranteed the preservation of entire urban perspectives. Thus, such imposing vistas as the banks of the Seine, the Vert Galant-Pont Neuf, the numerous *places* throughout the city, many of which were threatened in Hénard's day, were preserved.

Hénard became internationally known among planners and his advice was respected especially on problems of circulation and parks. Besides giving many speeches in Paris, he was asked to address the American Institute of Architects at their thirty-ninth convention in 1905; he delivered a paper in London in 1906 to the Seventh International Congress of Architects; he was one of the principal speakers at the large and very important Town Planning Conference held in London in 1910. His work appeared at numerous other international meetings and expositions between 1910–1914.

Between 1908 and 1912, Hénard was in charge of the commission within the *Musée Social* under which the first modern plans for the extension and improvement of the city of Paris were prepared. Just before he retired, and largely because of his efforts, a new society of professionals devoted to the study of urban questions was formed in Paris. Hénard was asked to be the first president of the *Société Française des Architectes Urbanistes* (1913); but the same year he suffered a cerebral hemorrhage, retired, and remained inactive until his death.

PETER WOLF

BIBLIOGRAPHY

BARDET, GASTON 1939 "Un précurseur: Eug. Hénard." *L'Architecture d'aujourd'hui* 10, Mar.:18.
BARDET, GASTON (1945)1978 *L'Urbanisme.* 8th ed. Paris: Presses universitaires de France.
CHOAY, FRANÇOISE 1965 *L'Urbanisme: Utopies et réalitiés, une anthologie.* Paris: du Seuil.
COLLINS, GEORGE R., and COLLINS, CHRISTIANE C. 1965 *Camillo Sitte and the Birth of Modern City Planning.* New York: Random House.
HÉNARD, EUGÈNE 1887 *Un projet de train continu pour l'Exposition Universelle.* Paris: Chaix.
HÉNARD, EUGÈNE 1896 *L'Exposition Universelle de 1900 devant le Parlement: Pourquoi il est nécessaire d'exécuter le projet issu du concours public de 1894 et des travaux du jury.* Paris: Delarue.
HÉNARD, EUGÈNE 1903–1909 *Etudes sur les transformations de Paris.* 8 parts in 1. Paris: Librairies imprimeries réunies.
HÉNARD, EUGÈNE 1911 *Rapports à la commission des perspectives monumentales de la ville de Paris.* Paris: Marétheux.
ROTIVAL, MAURICE E. H. 1960 "Homage à Eugène Hénard: Urbaniste de Paris, 1900–1909. *L'Architecture d'aujourd'hui* 31, no. 88:131–133.
WOLF, PETER M. 1969 *Eugène Hénard and the Beginning of Urbanism in Paris: 1900–1917.* The Hague: International Federation for Housing and Planning and Centre de Recherche d'Urbanisme.

HENNEBIQUE, FRANÇOIS

François Hennebique (1842–1921) was born in Neuville-St-Vaast near Arras in northern France. At eighteen, he apprenticed himself to a stonemason, becoming so skilled at building and organization that he had established himself as an independent contractor when only twenty-five years old. In 1879, while planning an iron-framed villa in Lombardzeyde on the Belgian coast, a neighboring villa similarly designed was destroyed by fire. Hennebique proposed a redesign which replaced the iron beams by iron bars embedded in concrete.

For the next twelve years, he did research on this new material while continuing his construction business. In 1892, he took out patents in France and Belgium, retired from contracting, and established offices in Brussels and Paris as a consulting engineer. He built up a vast network of concessioneers throughout Europe and elsewhere. Initially, the designs were done in Paris and local builders were then licensed to construct works in the "Système Hennebique." Soon there were many branch design offices as well. By 1918, over 31,000 Hennebique designs had been constructed of which about 3,600 were bridges, 17,700 buildings, and 7,600 reservoirs, baths, and tanks. When Hennebique died in 1921, the total had risen to 40,000.

In 1898, Hennebique began to publish a monthly magazine, *Le Béton Armé,* which chronicled the major structures and events of the firm. In 1899, he moved into a large office at Rue Danton in Paris.

From 1892 on, Hennebique had talented engineers on his staff, and it is difficult to know which of the Hennebique structures he himself designed. Three of his best known bridges, for example, are too different visually and technically to be called of one style. Each of the spans for the Vienne River Bridge at Châtellerault, France (1899), is formed by four slender arch ribs that support thin vertical members carrying the light horizontal roadway desk. The spans are 40 m, 50 m, and 40 m. The Meuse River Bridge at Liège, Belgium (1905), is a solid sculpted continuous three-span beam slightly arched in the middle 55-meter span and anchored at the ends of the two much shorter side spans. The Risorgimento Bridge in Rome of 100 m span, the longest arch in reinforced concrete when completed in 1910, is a hollow box girder deeply haunched at the supports. A series of bridges built between 1902 and 1907 were similar in appearance to the Châtellerault Bridge which could be called the clearest expression of a Hennebique bridge style.

Many of the Hennebique buildings show a slender framing, often left exposed on industrial buildings such as the early spinning mill at Lille, France, of 1896. The framing is by one-way slabs, beams, girders, and columns all made monolithic.

Hennebique based his designs on calculations derived from numerous tests. Some of his early formulas were found to be incorrect in principle but almost never dangerous in practice. Some of his nineteenth-century ideas such as the rectangular stress block for concrete compression in beams and the use of full steel stress in concrete compression zones, although discredited early in the century, have recently been reinstated with modifications as the accepted method for analysis.

The most complete impartial discussion of Hennebique's work up to 1902 is found in P. Christophe's *Le Béton Armé,* which summarizes all major systems in the new material. Although describing only a small percentage of the over 7,000 structures built by 1902, Christophe gives a picture of great variety and ingenuity. More than anyone else, Hennebique had shown by 1902 that reinforced concrete would be competitive for almost every problem in structural engineering.

Joseph Monier (1823–1906) had patented systems of reinforced concrete by 1867 but he did not have Hennebique's organizational skill. Also, Hennebique's construction background favored him over Monier, who had been a gardener and had gotten his ideas initially from reinforcing potterylike vessels.

DAVID P. BILLINGTON

WORKS

It is impossible to list even the major works in the System Hennebique. They were documented yearly in the Relevé. *The following list includes some of the most important works up to 1902 and a few major ones thereafter.*

1894, Refinery of Saint-Ouen, Paris. 1895, Large Mills, Nantes, France. 1895, Spinning Mill, Tourcoing, France. 1896, Barrois Spinning Mill, Lille, France. 1896, Justice Building, Verviers, Belgium. 1897, Bank, Basel. 1897, Canal Bridge, Evilard, France. 1897, Flon River Bridge, Lausanne, Switzerland. 1897, Frings Spinning Mill, Hellemmes, Lille, France. 1898, Coal Silo, Aniche Mines, France. 1898, Echez River Bridge, Tarbes, France. 1898, Fontaine Workshops, Boulogne-sur-Seine, France. 1899, Lys River Bridge, Ghent, Belgium. 1899, Vienne River Bridge, Châtellerault, France. 1900, Grand Palais; 1900, Palais des Lettres, Sciences et Arts; 1900, Petit Palais; Paris. 1902, Bormida River Bridge, Millesimo, Italy. 1904, Hennebique House, Bourg-la-Reine, France. 1905, Meuse River Bridge, Liège, Belgium. 1906, Ill River Bridge, Feldkirch, Austria. 1906, Loire River Bridge, Decize, France. 1907, Rhone River Bridge, Pyrimont, France. 1907, Loire River Bridge, D'Imphy, France. 1907, Viaduct, Dewine-Merxem, France. 1910, Tiber River Bridge, Rome.

BIBLIOGRAPHY

Le Béton Armé. 1898–1921. Monthly journal published by the Hennebique Company in Paris.

CHRISTOPHE, PAUL 1902 *Le Béton Armé.* Paris: Béranger.

COLLINS, PETER 1959 *Concrete: The Vision of a New Architecture; A Study of Auguste Perret and His Predecessors.* London: Faber.

Ferro-Concrete. 1909 Monthly review of Mouchel-Hennebique construction.

The Hennebique Armored Concrete System. 1908 New York: Hennebique.

MARSH, CHARLES F. (1904)1907 *Reinforced Concrete.* 3d., rev. & enl. New York: Van Nostrand.

HENRICI, KARL

Karl Henrici (1842–1927), prominent German city planner, was a proponent of the principles of CAMILLO SITTE. Born near Göttingen, he was a professor in Aachen for forty-five years (1875–1920). His many urban extension plans, especially those for Dessau, Hanover, and Munich, were widely influential.

RON WIEDENHOEFT

BIBLIOGRAPHY

HENRICI, KARL 1893 *Preisgekrönter Konkurrenz-Entwurf zu der Stadterweiterung Münchens.* Munich: Werner.

HENRICI, KARL 1894 *Von welchen Gedanken sollen wir uns beim Ausbau unserer deutschen Städte leiten lassen?* Trier, Germany: Lintz.

HENRICI, KARL 1904 *Beiträge zur praktischen Aesthetik im Städtebau: Eine Sammlung von Vorträgen und Aufsätzen.* Munich: Callwey.

JUSGEN 1927 "Tote." *Deutsche Bau-Zeitung* 61:816.

"Zum achtzigsten Geburtstag von Karl Henrici." 1922 *Stadtbaukunst alter und neuer Zeit* 3:49–50.

HENTRICH, HELMUT

Helmut Hentrich (1905–), principal (with Hubert Petschingg) of Hentrich-Petschnigg and Partners of Düsseldorf, represents International style giganticism in German corporate architecture of the 1960s and beyond. His high-rise office towers, but especially the gaudy, standardized Horten store façades, have had a leveling influence in German cities.

RON WIEDENHOEFT

WORKS

1952, Drahthaus, Düsseldorf, Germany. 1957, BASF Office Tower, Ludwigshafen, Germany. 1960, Thyssen Office Buiding, Düsseldorf, Germany. 1962, Kaiserhof Office Building, Hamburg, Germany. 1963, Bayer Office Building, Leverkusen, Germany. 1964, Europa Center, Berlin. 1964, Unilever Office Building; 1966, Finnlandhaus Office Building; Hamburg, Germany. 1968, Hoechst Calculating Center, Frankfurt. 1969, Finance Management Building, Münster, Germany. 1970, Procter and Gamble Administration Building, Schwalbach, Germany. 1970, Rank Xerox Administration Building, Düsseldorf, Germany. 1970, Ruhr University, Bochum, Germany. 1974, VEBA Office Building, Düsseldorf, Germany. 1976, South German Iron and Steel Administration Building, Mainz, Germany. 1978, Klockner Haus Office Building, Düsseldorf, Germany.

BIBLIOGRAPHY

HENTRICH-PETSCHNIGG and PARTNERS 1969 *Bauten: 1953–1969.* Düsseldorf, Germany.

HENTRICH-PETSCHNIGG and PARTNERS 1970 *Standard Bank, Johannesburg.* Johannesburg.

HENTRICH-PETSCHNIGG and PARTNERS 1971 *Bauten: 1970–71.* Düsseldorf, Germany.

HENTRICH-PETSCHNIGG and PARTNERS 1972 *Denkmalpflege: 1947–1972.* Düsseldorf, Germany.

HENTRICH-PETSCHNIGG and PARTNERS 1975 *Bauten: 1972–75.* Düsseldorf, Germany.

HERBE, PAUL

Paul Herbé (1903–1963) was born in Reims, France, the son of an architect. His first major project was in 1933 when, with R. Camelot, he won the design competition for a girls' school in Beaune, France. The two went on to design the French pavilion at the 1935 World's Fair in Zagreb, Yugoslavia, and the ceramics and pottery pavilion for the 1937 World's Fair in Paris, and participated as consultants in the 1939 World's Fair in New York.

Herbé ended his association with Camelot at the outbreak of World War II but resumed his practice in 1945 with two other French architects, J. Marmey and M. Patout. During this time, Herbé was named official consulting architect to the Tunisian government. In Tunis particularly, he contributed to the city's modernization with designs for a number of schools and villas whose forms reflected the essentially white vernacular structures of the old town. In 1948, Herbé was named urban consultant for the Sudan and the Niger where he presented various urban development schemes that were never realized. Also in 1948, Herbé began his association with Jean Le Couteur with whom he designed such ambitious projects as the Basilique du Sacré Coeur de Jésus (1961) in Algiers, and the University of Madagascar (1962–1964) in Tananarive. He succeeded AUGUSTE PERRET as *chef d'atelier* at the Ecole des Beaux-Arts and continued to design with Le Couteur until his death in 1963.

PETER L. DONHAUSER

WORKS

1933, Girls' School (with R. Camelot), Beaune, France. *1935, French Pavilion (with Camelot), World's Fair, Zagreb, Yugoslavia. *1937, Ceramics and Pottery Pavilion (with Camelot), World's Fair, Paris. 1939, Fish Research and Breeding Facility (with Camelot), Beaune, France. 1945–1948, Hôpital de Bizerte (with J. Marmey and M. Patout), Zarzouna, Tunisia. 1945–1948, Villa (with J. Marmey and M. Patout), Hammamet, Tunisia. 1948–1951, Ecole de Porto Farina, Bizerte, Tunisia. 1950, Palais de la Foire, Lille, France. 1958, Apartment House and Operation S.C.I.C. (with Jean Le Couteur), Louveciennes, France. 1959–1962, Hospital (with Le Couteur), Fort Lamy, Chad. 1961, Basilique du Sacré Coeur de Jésus (with Le Couteur), Algiers. 1962, Eglise Saint-Paul (with Le Couteur), Aulnay-sous-Bois, France. 1962–1964, University of Madagascar (with Le Couteur), Tananarive.

BIBLIOGRAPHY

ARROU, PIERRE 1956 "Un Immeuble moderne dans un quartier ancien." *Construction Moderne* 72, no. 1:13–16.

HERBÉ, PAUL 1962 "La Basilique du Sacré Coeur de Jesus—Algiers." *Construction Moderne* 78, no. 1:36–45.

HERBERT, HENRY

See PEMBROKE, EARL OF.

HERE DE CORNY, EMMANUEL

Emmanuel Héré de Corny (1705–1763) was the chief architect to Stanislaus Lezcyznski, ex-king of Poland, duke of Lorraine, and father-in-law of Louis XV. Architect and patron enjoyed an unusually close relationship that produced inventive designs for châteaux and garden pavilions in Lorraine and one of the outstanding achievements of eighteenth-century town planning in Nancy.

Héré was born in Nancy, near Metz. His father was a builder from Tyrol who had come to Lorraine in the service of Duke Leopold. Héré probably received his architectural training from his father and from the court architect Jean Nicolas Jennesson. His name first appears in the records of the ducal buildings department as a clerk when he was fifteen. As the official responsible for the buildings and grounds of the ducal château at Lunéville, Héré came to the attention of Stanislaus, who, arriving in Lorraine as duke in 1737, wished to make improvements to the property. Stanislaus found Héré more sympathetic than Jennesson to his own strong ideas about architecture, and he named Héré first architect in 1738. Under Stanislaus's patronage, Héré gained both financial remuneration and public recognition. Acting on his father-in-law's recommendations, Louis XV ennobled Héré in 1752, granted him the Seigneurie Corny on the Mosel River in 1753, and made him a member of the prestigious Ordre de Saint Michel in 1757. Héré had the honor in 1753 of presenting his plans for the embellishment of Nancy to the French court in person. Plagued by illness from 1757, Héré was incapacitated in 1760 and died in Lunéville three years later.

During Héré's childhood years, the presence of leading French architects such as JULES HARDOUIN

MANSART and GERMAIN BOFFRAND in the employ of Duke Leopold had invigorated architecture in Lorraine. Their work turned the attention of local patrons and architects from Italian sources of inspiration to Paris, and, particularly through Boffrand's example, to Bavaria and Austria. The well-traveled Stanislaus broadened these architectural horizons with his taste for the exotic, and Héré's buildings reflect this polyphaletic environment.

Héré's first major commission was Notre Dame de Bon-Secours built in Nancy as a funerary church for Stanislaus and his family (1738–1741). The attenuated proportions of the façade result from Héré's use of columns salvaged from the portico of the unfinished château of Malgrange begun by Boffrand in 1712 combined with the tall, single tower common in French parish churches. The interior consisted of a simple nave and apse (the present apse built c.1850), but it displays a profusion of ornament recalling southern German churches rather than French models. Héré brought this exuberance to the exterior of the Church of Saint Jacques in Lunéville in his highly sculptural tower tops and clock cartouche (1743–1747). He also completed the interior and designed the magnificent baroque organ case.

Stanislaus chose not to reside in Nancy, preferring country houses as settings for his elegant court. Héré remodeled the châteaux of Lunéville (c.1737) and Commercy (c.1745–1747), but rather than finishing the château of Malgrange, he demolished it and built a sprawling complex of his own design noteworthy for its principal building covered with faïence tiles and flanked by long colonnades (1739–1740).

Life at the court of Lorraine resembled the French court as it relaxed at Trianon or Marly rather than the rigid ceremony of Versailles. Politically powerless, Stanislaus felt no need to project an aura of grandeur, and he cultivated an image of refinement as a patron and *amateur* of arts and letters. The buildings closest to his affections were the many small, ornate garden pavilions built by Héré between 1737 and 1750 on the ducal estates of Einville, Chanteheux, Commercy, Malgrange, and Lunéville. These served as retreats, concert halls, dining rooms, and baths, and they were at the vanguard of the fashion for exotic garden structures that swept Europe in the mid-eighteenth century. Two examples of this genre were the Kiosk, or *Bâtiment à la Turque,* and the Trèfle, or *Bâtiment chinois,* built by Héré at Lunéville in 1737 and 1740, respectively. Both derived their exotic character from their broad, tiered roofs, which made only the most casual reference to oriental architecture. In plan and elevation they followed European precedents. The general conception of these little buildings likely came from Stanislaus, who left their specific appearance to Héré.

Water was an integral part of the setting and decoration of the pavilions. Besides jets, cascades, and pools, Héré's repertory included such unusual effects as the Colonnade Hydraulique at Commercy, where water flowed from the column capitals and down the shafts, and the Kiosk at Commercy with its windows curtained by a fine stream of water. Water also served as the motive power for the miniature village in the gardens of Lunéville known as *Le Rocher* (1742–1752) designed by Héré and populated by mechanical figures created by François Richard.

Stanislaus's châteaux were frequently visited by persons traveling from Paris to Germany. Voltaire and Montesquieu were among those providing first-hand accounts of them. The publication of Héré's works in 1753 made them available to a broader audience. The Trèfle apparently was the model for the Japanese Tea House built by Frederick II at Sanssouci near Potsdam, and certain aspects of the gardens, such as the rustic setting of *Le Rocher,* may have contributed to the development of the picturesque garden. RICHARD MIQUE, best known as the architect of Marie Antoinette at the Trianon, worked under Héré and later succeeded him as first architect before entering the service of the French court.

With the death of Stanislaus in 1766, Lorraine officially came under direct French rule. Louis XV saw no need to maintain the costly ducal estates and allowed them to decay or had them demolished. The best surviving examples of Héré's work are to be found in Nancy. Between 1740 and 1750, Stanislaus commissioned Héré to build the Mission Royale of the Jesuits (1741–1743), a new wing to the Hôpital Saint Julien (1747), and the Hôpital des Frères Saint Jean de Dieu (1750). In the following decade he undertook a more ambitious program of improvements in his capital city with the construction of a public square dedicated to Louis XV.

Begun by Héré in 1752 and inaugurated four years later, the Place Royale (now Place Stanislaus) and its attendant streets and squares addressed the two principal concerns of French architects engaged in town planning in the mid-eighteenth century: utility and embellishment. Héré placed the pedestrian statue of Louis XV at the intersection of two axes; one formed by a broad road traversing Nancy and the other consisting of three squares that linked two parts of the city separated by fortifications. The sequence and proportions of the squares, the Place Royale with its statue, the

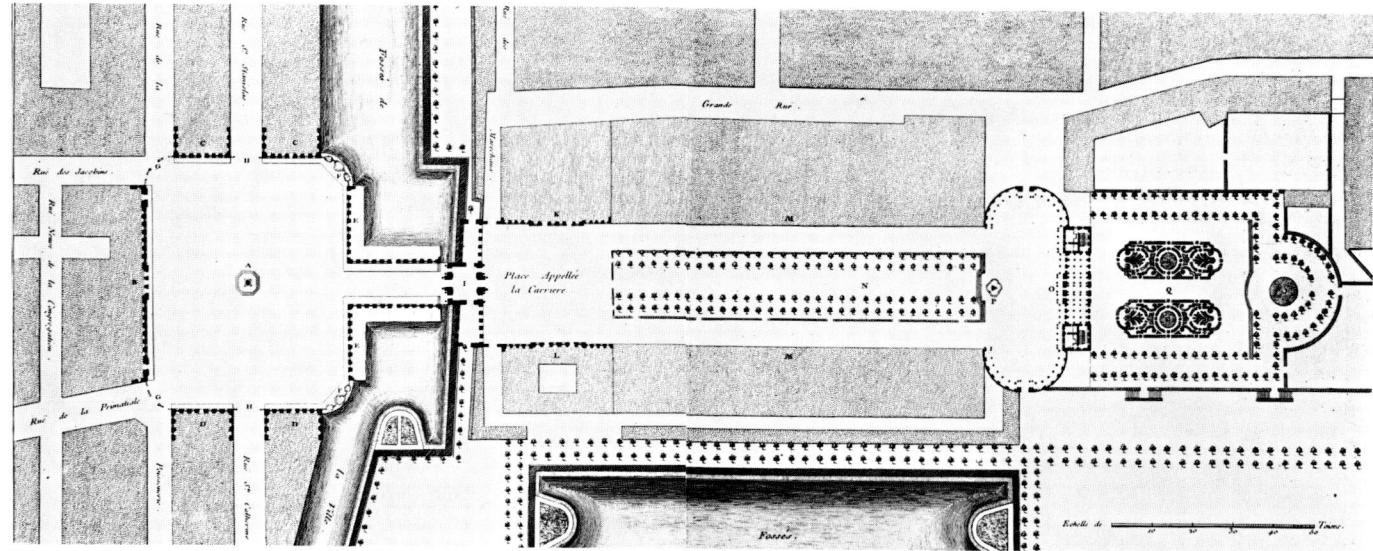

Héré de Corny.
Place Royale (now Place
Stanislaus).
Nancy, France.
1752–1756

promenade of the Carrière, and the Hemicycle serving as the forecourt of the Intendance were determined by the site. Rather than attempting to minimize their differences, Héré gave each square a distinct appearance fitting to its use and lending variety to the overall composition. The façades of the Place Royale recall those of two great Parisian *places royales,* the Place Vendome and the Place des Victoires, distilled from the more immediate example of Boffrand's ducal palace in Nancy, demolished after 1739. More modest elevations face the residences lining the Place de la Carrière, and long colonnades similar to those at Malgrange distinguish the Intendance.

The new road and squares improved traffic circulation, provided a spine for orderly future development, and created urban vistas along the axes. Stanislaus and Héré believed the open spaces would contribute to public health by admitting plenty of fresh air to the city. Particularly striking is Héré's use of greenery and water. The corners of one side of the Place Royale have elaborate fountains framed by rococo ironwork by Jean Lamour. Rows of trees embellish the Place de la Carrière, which has a number of smaller fountains, and shade additional promenades along the old fortifications. Such an integration of greenery into a town plan occurred in other, contemporary projects for royal squares, including the Place Louis XV (now the Place de la Concorde) built in Paris by JACQUES ANGES GABRIEL and the unbuilt Place Louis XV planned for Rouen by ANTOINE MATHIEU LE CARPENTIER.

Héré's buildings, squares, and promenades in Nancy established a new town center bringing together public services such as governmental agencies, a theater, cafés, a reading room, and a medical school. These activities as much as their settings celebrated the benevolent rule of Louis XV,

to whom they were dedicated, and of Stanislaus Lezcyznski, by whose will they were realized.

Héré was a talented designer and an effective administrator, but he never formed a distinct, personal style, and he had no reputation as a teacher or theoretician. Nevertheless, his works captured the idyllic spirit of the court of Lorraine and made tangible contemporary thought about garden design and town planning.

RICHARD CLEARY

WORKS

c.1737, Château of Lunéville (remodeling); *1737, Kiosk; Lunéville, France. 1738–1741, Notre Dame de Bon-Secours, Nancy, France. *1739–1740, Château of Malgrange, near Nancy, France. *1740, Pavilion of Chanteheux, near Lunéville, France. *1740, Trèfle, Lunéville, France. 1741–1743, Mission Royale des Jesuits, Nancy, France. *1742–1752, Le Rocher; 1743–1747, Saint Jacques (completion); Lunéville, France. c.1745–1747, Château of Commercy (remodeling); c.1745–1750, Garden Pavilions; Commercy, France. *1747, Pavilion de l'Hôpital Saint Julien; 1750, Hôpital des Frères Saint Jean de Dieu; 1752–1756, Place Royale (now Place Stanislaus); Nancy, France.

BIBLIOGRAPHY

BOYÉ, PIERRE 1910 *Les châteaux du Roi Stanislaus en Lorraine.* Paris: Berger-Levrault.

HÉRÉ DE CORNY, EMMANUEL 1753 *Plans et élévations de la place royale de Nancy & des autres edifices à l'environnement bâtis par les ordres du Roy de Pologne duc de Lorraine.* Paris: François.

HÉRÉ DE CORNY, EMMANUEL 1753–1756 *Recueil des plans, élévations et coupes, tant géométrales qu'en perspective, des châteaux, jardins, et dépendances que le Roy de Pologne occupe en Lorraine y compris les bâtimens qu'il a fait éléver.* 2 vols. Paris: François.

MAROT, PIERRE 1954 *Emmanuel Héré (1705–1763): Biographie du premier architecte du roi Stanislas d'après les notes de Pierre Bové.* Nancy, France: Berger-Levrault.

MAROT, PIERRE 1966 *La Place royale de Nancy: Image*

de la réunion de la Lorraine à la France, du monument du Bien-Aimé à la statue du Bienfaisant. Paris: Berger-Levrault.

OSTROWSKI, JAN 1972*a* "Nurt egzotyczny w architekturze Stanislawa Loeszcyzńskiego w Lotaryngii." *Kwartalnik Architektury i Urbanistyki* 17:161–176.

OSTROWSKI, JAN 1972*b* "Le Rocher: Théâtre d'automates du roi Stanislas à Lunéville." *Le Pays lorrain* 53:175–184.

OSTROWSKI, JAN 1974 "Temple de Plaisir: Niezwykły Pałac Stanislawa Leszczyńskiego w Chanteheux." *Kwartalnika Architektury i Urbanistyki* 19:293–316.

OSTROWSKI, JAN 1975 "L'église Notre-Dame de Bonsecours à Nancy." *Le Pays lorrain* 56:26–37.

RAU-GRÄFIN v.d. SCHULENBURG, JULIA 1973 *Emmanuel Héré: Premier architecte von Stanislas Leszczynski in Lotharingen (1705–1763).* Berlin: Mann.

SCOTT, BARBARA 1968 "King Stanislas of Poland at Lunéville." *Apollo* 87:100–107.

WIEBENSON, DORA 1978 *The Picturesque Garden in France.* N.J.: Princeton University Press.

HERHOLDT, J. D.

Johan David Herholdt (1818–1902) was one of the most influential figures in the Danish architecture of the latter half of the nineteenth century. In 1857, he was commissioned with the building of the university library in Copenhagen. Featuring elaborate brickstone façades, the building became of lasting importance to Danish architectonic tradition, stressing a certain national romantic origin.

VILLADS VILLADSEN

HERMOGENES

Hermogenes (active c.220–190 B.C.) is known to us primarily because the Roman architect VITRUVIUS knew his writings and cited them with approval. Hermogenes wrote books on two temples he built: for Dionysos at Teos (c.220–205 B.C.) and for Artemis at Magnesia on the Meander (c.205–190 B.C.) (both in Ionia, western Turkey). Both were excavated in the nineteenth century but now require re-excavation and further study. There has been considerable and continuing argument about the dates of the two temples and of Hermogenes's career. The most reasonable interpretation of the relevant inscriptions puts the temple of Dionysos in the years before 205 B.C. and the temple of Artemis in the years before 190 B.C.

The name Hermogenes occurs in an inscription of appropriate date from Priene (also in Ionia), which seems to deal with some form of architectural design, and since the plans of Hermogenes's two known temples relate closely to the fourth-century temple of Athena at Priene, it is likely that this Hermogenes is the architect praised by Vitruvius. If so, he was a citizen of Priene, for otherwise his origin would have been specified in the inscription. An alternative theory that he came from Alabanda (in Caria, southwest Turkey) seems based on a mispunctuation of Vitruvius's text; in any case he apparently came from western Asia Minor.

Like some other Ionian architects, Hermogenes was a strong proponent of the Ionic order, as opposed to the Doric. He regarded Doric as unsuitable for temples because of the inherent difficulty of combining a uniformly spaced colonnade with a regular triglyph frieze at the corners of a building, and he even went so far as to convert from Doric to Ionic a temple (probably that at Teos) on which work had already begun. This story and the wording of the Priene inscription suggest that Hermogenes may also have been a contractor.

In addition to these general views, Vitruvius also attributes to Hermogenes two specific innovations in temple design, the pseudodipteral plan and eustyle column spacing. Large temples in Ionia had previously been built with two rows of columns surrounding the cella building—the dipteral plan. In a pseudodipteral temple the same relation of outer colonnade to cella building was maintained, but the inner colonnade was omitted, providing an unusually deep unobstructed portico round about. This not only saved expense and provided useful shelter for visitors to the sanctuary, as Vitruvius tells us, but it also was thought to have an aesthetic advantage in giving a sharper contrast between the white marble columns and the dark shadow between them. The temple of Artemis at Magnesia is indeed pseudodipteral (with eight columns on the fronts and fifteen on the sides), but it is doubtful if Hermogenes invented the scheme. Much earlier Doric temples approximating it are probably irrelevant, but two Ionic temples, at Chryse in the Troad (northwest Turkey) and at Messa on the nearby island of Lesbos, are also pseudodipteral and may well be a generation or two earlier than those of Hermogenes. The scheme was certainly a popular one in Asia Minor thereafter, however, and Hermogenes may well have been influential in effecting that.

The eustyle column spacing seems to have been less influential. In his general account of temple design (which assumes the temple to be Ionic), Vitruvius presents a system of classifying colonnades by the ratio of column diameter to space between columns. The eustyle colonnade, with the space between columns equal to two and a quarter

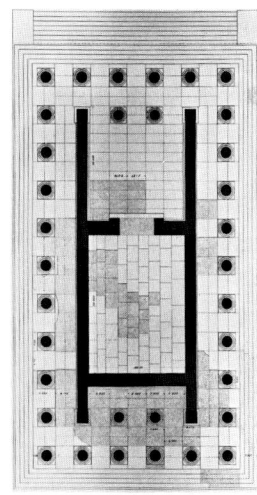

Hermogenes.
Plan of Temple of Dionysos.
Teos (now Siǧacik), Turkey.
c.220–205 B.C.

Hermogenes.
Order of Temple of
*   Dionysos.*
Teos (now Siǧacik), Turkey.
c.220–205 B.C.

diameters, is given as the ideal, devised by Hermogenes for his temple at Teos. The Greek terminology used suggests a Greek origin for the system, and the way in which Vitruvius presents it suggests that Hermogenes, if not its inventor, was at least Vitruvius's immediate source. The eustyle column spacing does occur in the small temple of Zeus (c.200 B.C.) at Magnesia, which has therefore also been attributed to Hermogenes, but it is not embodied exactly in Hermogenes's temple at Teos, appears still less in the temple of Artemis at Magnesia, and seldom occurs elsewhere.

The Temple of Dionysos at Teos is very close in size and plan to the temple of Athena at Priene; it has six columns by eleven columns, with wall and column axes falling on a uniform square grid, a very deep pronaos (deeper even than at Priene), and a shallow opisthodomos or false porch behind the cella. The elevation is less similar, however. In place of the Ephesian column bases of Priene, Hermogenes chose Attic ones (see KALLIKRATES) but set them on Asiatic plinths; and in the entablature he put a continuous sculptured frieze as well as dentils, whereas there were dentils alone, in the Asiatic manner, at Priene.

The same two features of the elevation are also found in the temple of Artemis at Magnesia and have been regarded as special characteristics of Hermogenes. They are not restricted to him, however, and occur earlier even in Ionia. As at Teos,

the walls and columns of the temple of Artemis are set out on a grid, but here the central interval is widened by one-third along the whole length of the temple, so regularizing the less systematic variation in column spacing found in Ionian temples of the sixth century B.C. With eight columns on the fronts, the temple of Artemis is of course much bigger than that of Dionysos, and the pseudodipteral porticoes around the cella and the deep pronaos suggest that Hermogenes had a keen awareness of space.

Other buildings have also been associated with Hermogenes on grounds of style. The temple of Zeus at Magnesia has already been mentioned. It was too small to have a surrounding colonnade, but in addition to the eustyle spacing of its porches, it had a deep pronaos, a continuous frieze with dentils, an Attic profile for the wall base (but not for the columns), and other elements similar in style to the temple of Artemis; therefore, the attribution is reasonable. Monumental altars at Priene and Magnesia (both probably second century B.C.) have also been attributed to Hermogenes because of their Attic column bases and combination of frieze and dentils. The type consists of a wall articulated by columns, either attached or barely free-standing, which runs around three sides of a raised platform so as to frame the broad stairway leading up to the altar proper on the platform top. If by Hermogenes, these altars would presumably be earlier than the famous Altar of Zeus at Pergamon and might well have influenced that, the most elaborate version of the type. But the evidence for the attribution is insufficient, and the altars are not closely datable on their own. The south stoa on the agora at Magnesia (late third century B.C.) could also be by Hermogenes for its Ionic capitals are of the same type as those of the two temples at Magnesia, and there is independent evidence dating some parts of the agora to the late third century B.C. However, this capital type does not seem to be exclusive to Hermogenes, who may in any case have been busy at Teos at this time.

In assessing the importance of Hermogenes, two crucial questions arise, neither of them easy to answer: did Vitruvius's work depend closely on Hermogenes, so that through him Hermogenes influenced the architects of the Renaissance and later, and to what extent was Hermogenes an innovator rather than an articulate follower and adapter of current ideas? Vitruvius praises Hermogenes as a rich source of information for posterity and we have seen that his classification of colonnades according to their spacing probably derives from Hermogenes. Vitruvius's specifications for a normal temple were presumably also based on Hermogenes, for they produce a pseudodipteral building with eight columns by fifteen columns and eustyle column spacing, combining precisely those features from the temples at Teos and Magnesia that Hermogenes was most proud of. It has been argued that Hermogenes was also the source for Vitruvius's more detailed rules for the Ionic order and a careful study of the Ionic capitals from Magnesia has shown that they come close to conforming to the rules given by him. But the capitals definitely associated with Hermogenes do not conform exactly and the entablature in Hermogenes's temples is not particularly similar to the Vitruvian version. The detailed rules may thus have come from one of the other Greek sources known to Vitruvius, and Hermogenes's influence through Vitruvius on later architecture cannot be readily defined.

We have already noticed that the pseudo-dipteral plan, the Attic column base on a plinth, and the combination of continuous frieze with dentils all had precedents in Ionia. The Ionic capital type adopted by Hermogenes is widespread in Asia Minor and represents a development rather than a marked break with earlier tradition (the volute eyes are set lower on the capital, and the canalis joining the volutes has a straight rather than a curved lower edge). Given the vague dating of so many specimens, it is hard to say how far Hermogenes was himself responsible for the development. As so often in the classical world, "invented" may really mean "was the first to write about," but the great popularity of some of Hermogenes's "inventions" suggests that his writings were widely read. Although others besides Vitruvius were impressed by the beauty of his temple of Artemis at Magnesia, the evidence tends to suggest that Hermogenes's place in the history of architecture depends more on his books than on his buildings.

J. J. COULTON

WORKS

*c.220–205 B.C., Temple of Dionysos, Teos (now Siğacik), Turkey. *c.205–190 B.C., Temple of Artemis; *(A)c.200 B.C., Temple of Zeus; Magnesia on the Meander (now Ortaklar), Turkey.

BIBLIOGRAPHY

DINSMOOR, W. B., SR. (1950)1975 *The Architecture of Ancient Greece: An Account of its Historic Development.* Reprint. London: Batsford. Originally published as a third edition of W. J. Anderson and R. P. Spiers, *The Architecture of Ancient Greece and Rome.* London: Batsford, 1902.
DRERUP, HEINRICH 1964 "Zum Artemistempel von Magnesia." *Marburger Winckelmann-programm* 1964:13–22.
GERKAN, ARMIN VON 1929 *Der Altar des Artemis-Tempels in Magnesia am Mäander.* Berlin: Schoetz.
GROS, PIERRE 1978 "Le dossier vitruvien d'Hermogénès." *Mélanges de l'Ecole Française de Rome, Antiquité* 90:687–703.
HOEPFNER, WOLFRAM 1968 "Zum ionischen Kapitell bei Hermogenes und Vitruv." *Mitteilungen des Deutschen Archäologischen Instituts, Athenische Abteilung* 83:213–234.
HUMANN, KARL 1904 *Magnesia am Mäander.* Berlin: Reimer.
SOCIETY OF THE DILETTANTI 1881–1915 Volumes 4 and 5 in *Antiquities of Ionia.* London: The society.

HERON

Heron of Alexandria (1st century) was a famous geometer and writer on mathematics and mechanics, as well as the author of treatises on machines with application to building. In the tradition of Hellenistic mathematics, Heron's works emphasized a geometrical approach to the solution of mathematical, and especially, mechanical and statical problems. Heron contributed thereby to the dominance of logical theory over experimental practice that extended through the rest of antiquity and the Middle Ages.

B. M. BOYLE

BIBLIOGRAPHY

DRACHMANN, AAGE G. 1963 *The Mechanical Technology of Greek and Roman Antiquity.* Copenhagen: Munksgaard; London: Hafner; Madison: University of Wisconsin Press.

HERRERA, JUAN DE

Juan de Herrera (1530–1597), the architect of Philip II, is the most famous Spanish architect of the sixteenth century. He was the founder and first great master of classicism in Spain. His austere and monumental style marks the complete assimilation of the Italian humanist tradition into a new and peculiarly Spanish architectural idiom whose key qualities were simplicity and geometric clarity. Herrera's style had few direct imitators but his buildings set a standard of classical purity and they remained a fruitful source for architects until the end of the eighteenth century. Herrera was also a key figure in the development of the architectural profession in Spain. As a courtier and an intellectual involved in all the royal architectural projects, Herrera established a new image of the architect as primarily a designer rather than a builder.

Juan de Herrera was born in the village of Maliaño near Santander, the son of an impoverished but honorable *hidalgo* family. Very little is known of his life before he became an architect. He is thought to have attended the University at

Valladolid. He entered the army in 1548, leaving Spain for the Italian campaigns. In a brief account of himself written in 1584, Herrera claimed to have returned to Spain with Emperor Charles V. It is assumed that he moved with the emperor's small retinue to the royal retreat at Yuste in 1556 but he does not appear in accounts of the emperor's household. At the death of Charles V in 1558, Herrera seems to have moved to Madrid and entered the service of Philip II, where he remained the rest of his working life.

Little is known about Herrera's private life. He was always concerned to establish his family on a sound financial footing but he never became a wealthy man. In 1571, he married María de Alvaro, a widow with a modest fortune. She died in 1576. In 1582, Herrera married his niece, Iñes de Herrera. Two children from this marriage died in infancy. In 1586, the king named Herrera *corregidor* of Santander and Herrera was able to take possession of the family seat at Maliaño which he had inherited through Iñes. During the last years of his life, however, Herrera remained in Madrid where he continued to be active in the royal projects. In 1587, Philip II released him from his formal duties at court and gave him a rental income of 1000 ducats per year.

Herrera never had the practical training which was considered necessary for an architect in Spain in the sixteenth century. He may have studied architecture on his own in Italy and in Flanders. He may also have known the Italian engineer and clockmaker Juanello Turriano who was in the emperor's suite at Yuste. If so, Herrera's later interest in engineering and technology might date from that time. Herrera must have acquired some training as a draftsman since, in 1562, he prepared the illustrations for a manuscript of a medieval astronomical treatise for Honorato Juan, the tutor to the royal children. As far as is known, Herrera's formal training as an architect began in 1563 when Philip II appointed him to be one of several assistants to the royal architect, JUAN BAUTISTA DE TOLEDO.

Herrera worked closely with Juan Bautista de Toledo for more than four years. In February 1567, when Juan Bautista died, the king raised Herrera's salary from 100 ducats to 250 ducats per year. In the margin of his appointment, the king wrote "Herrera arquitecto," the first recorded reference to Herrera as an architect. The exact nature of Herrera's duties is not known. His initial appointment was as a draftsman but his salary in 1567 indicates that he occupied an important position (the architects supervising construction on royal buildings were making only slightly more than a quarter of this sum).

Herrera learned the principles and techniques of classical architectural style in the office of Juan Bautista de Toledo. As a draftsman, he was in charge of preparing drawings for the royal projects from Juan Bautista's designs. Herrera was also exposed to the Italian theoretical tradition. Juan Bautista was an Italian-trained classicist whose learned approach to architecture was unique in Spain at the time. With such a mentor, Herrera was well placed to learn the more intellectual aspects of classicism; the orders, geometry, and the Renaissance theory of proportions which were later important in his own work. Herrera was probably personally close to Juan Bautista as well; he appeared as one of the witnesses to the latter's will in 1567.

Herrera's career as an architect is inseparable from Philip II, his patron and supporter throughout the reign. It may have been the king who first noticed Herrera's talent. Certainly, by 1567, Herrera had established a close relationship with the king which he enjoyed the rest of his life.

Philip II was himself passionately interested in architecture and he involved himself in every phase of his royal projects. It was unusual for a monarch to take such an active interest in architecture, at least in Spain. In fact, Philip II restructured the royal building organization in order to gain complete control over the design process. In 1569 and again in 1572, the king authorized the revision of the statutes governing the building of the Escorial, and the regulations were later extended to all the royal projects. The position of "master of the works," the traditional Spanish title for an architect, was left vacant or diminished in authority. The architects on the site were transformed into executants of plans which were handed down to them from the king and they were strictly forbidden to introduce any changes of their own.

Juan de Herrera was the immediate beneficiary of this system and it is usually thought that he himself wrote the regulations of 1572. Herrera was responsible only to the king who authorized the plans of the royal buildings, and the king and Herrera could work together without interference from other architects. From 1567 onward, the king's dependence upon Herrera steadily increased until he was, in effect, the royal architect. Herrera's position, however, remained unofficial until 1579 when Philip II finally confirmed his status by appointing him "architect to the king," a position which had not been filled since the death of Juan Bautista de Toledo.

Herrera's career as an architect can be set within the frame of one great building program: the royal monastery of San Lorenzo et El Escorial outside Madrid. The Escorial was Philip II's greatest project. He had vowed its construction after his victory at the battle of San Quentin on 10 August 1557. The program, established in 1561, was for a Jeronymite monastery, a dynastic mausoleum, and a royal palace. Construction began in 1563 under the direction of Juan Bautista de Toledo who had been called back from Italy to design the complex.

Although Herrera was in Juan Bautista's office at this time, he probably did not have a major share in the master plan of the Escorial. Other architects—FRANCESCO PACIOTTO and Giovanni Castello il Bergamasco—were called in to criticize and made revisions in Juan Bautista's plans for the church and the main staircase. However, by 1567, only the foundations of the complex and part of the Cloister of the Evangelists were well advanced. Many projects for the rest of the building existed but it was Herrera who took charge of the design of the Escorial from 1568 to its completion in 1584.

Herrera prepared the final drawings for the Escorial as it was being built. His changes in the designs were substantial and large portions of the building can be attributed to him. Like sixteenth-century buildings in Italy, the Escorial was built from measured architectural drawings which were prepared piece-meal as each section of the building was readied for construction. Herrera reworked the designs of his predecessors and cast them into his own style. It is not always possible to determine how much he depended upon earlier projects but the design of the southern façade (1568), the roof system (1569), the infirmary (1570), the monastic section (from 1571), and the royal palace (from 1579) are considered his. Herrera's most original contributions to the Escorial are the main façade on the west (begun in 1572, the central section built 1579–1584), the gallery of the infirmary, and the church with its Courtyard of the Kings in front. The church was begun in 1574 and completed in 1582. In September 1584, the monks celebrated the laying of the final stone of the Escorial. Herrera designed the architecture of the monumental cenotaphs of Charles V and his family and of Philip II and his family which flank the main altar in the sanctuary. Pompeo Leoni was responsible for the sculpture. The main altarpiece with statues by Leoni and paintings by FEDERICO ZUCCARI and PELLEGRINO TIBALDI was also designed by Herrera. This decoration was completed only in the 1590s.

Herrera's use of architectural sources was highly self-conscious and eclectic. His composition of the main façade was based upon earlier designs by Juan Bautista de Toledo. Herrera kept the major elements: repeated windows, continuous cornices, temple front, and towers; but he moved

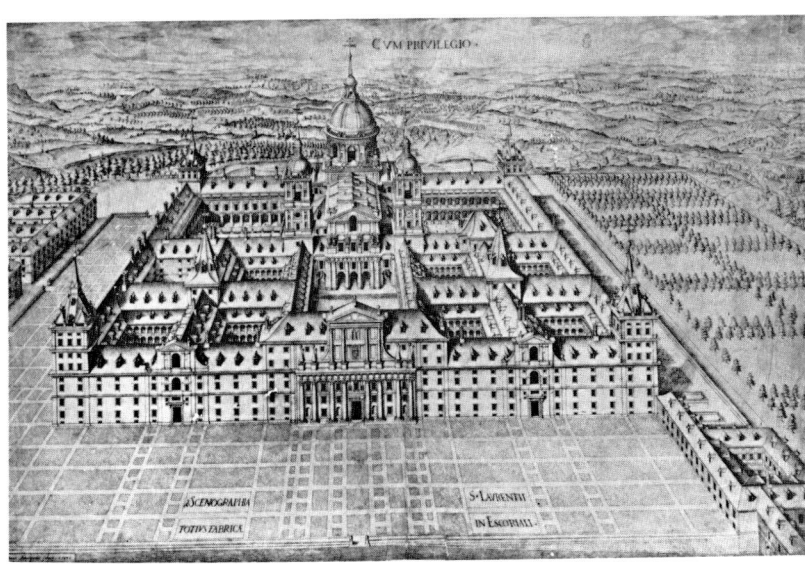

Herrera.
Drawing of El Escorial.
Madrid.
1568–1584

the towers to the corners of the building, stressed them with high pitched roofs, and he simplified the temple frontispiece and added a massive central pavilion (the royal library) as a backdrop. His sources were Italian and French as well as Spanish. The temple front recalls GIACOMO BAROZZI DA VIGNOLA's design for Santa Maria del Orto in Rome (1565–1566); the pavilion resembles the avant-corps of French châteaux; and the corner towers are drawn from the Spanish royal fortresses which were the residences of the Spanish kings. None of these features was evident in Juan Bautista's straightforward Italianate composition although he had also stressed the combination of religious and palatial motifs in his designs. The controlling idea behind Herrera's use of these sources was his desire to symbolize, in architectural terms, the fusion of religious and dynastic functions in the program.

The gallery of the infirmary on the southwest side is one of Herrera's most graceful compositions. Delicately scaled Doric and Ionic columns are used for a two-story gallery overlooking the gardens. On the lower level, paired Doric columns and a section of straight entablature alternate with a single column supporting a pair of arches in a rhythm more informal than Herrera used elsewhere at the Escorial.

The design of the royal basilica of the Escorial was the subject of prolonged debate. Philip II did not like Juan Bautista's design and sought advice from Francesco Paciotto (1567) and from the Florentine Academy of Design which submitted criticisms and a series of designs which arrived in Spain in 1572. The final synthesis of these ideas fell to Herrera. The church is square in plan with four great piers supporting a central dome. On the west, beyond the narthex, is an ante-church on a central plan with a low vault. Above is the monks'

choir which overlooks the space of the basilica. On the east, the deep sanctuary extends the longitudinal axis of the building into the area of the royal palace which enfolds it. With remarkable clarity, Herrera defined the ceremonial functions of the church, dividing it into public church, monastic choir, and royal basilica (which was visible but inaccessible to the public). The royal burials were in a special chamber beneath the altar. In the reign of Philip III, this was remodeled into the present royal Pantheon.

The sources of Herrera's design are in the earlier plans of Juan Bautista de Toledo which were based upon Saint Peter's in Rome and in GALEAZZO ALESSI's Church of Santa Maria in Carignano in Genoa. Herrera was perhaps also influenced by ANDREA PALLADIO in the design of the public ante-church.

The interior of the church is monumental and severe. A single order of fluted Doric pilasters and entablature is used throughout with a secondary order of unfluted Doric pilasters on the arches in the piers. Splendor of color is reserved for the sanctuary where the rich gilt bronze and colored marbles provide a lavish setting for the royal cenotaphs and the main altar. On the exterior, the church dominates the entire complex, its dome rising on a high drum which is opened in great windows flanked by paired engaged Doric columns. Between the columns are empty niches, a theme stated on the main façade and repeated in the enormous bell towers which flank the entrance to the church. The dome is capped by a domed lantern which is also used on the towers. The main façade of the church forms the eastern end of the Courtyard of the Kings. Its elements are simple: two arches leading into the palatial and monastic sections of the Escorial and three arches opening into the narthex of the church, a colossal order of six Doric columns engaged to the wall. Above them are six statues of Old Testament kings standing on pedestals against the simple pediment broken by a large central window. The rhythm of arches and windows against that of the columns and statues creates one of Herrera's most subtle harmonies.

Herrera's style at the Escorial is homogeneous in spite of the diversity of sources that often lie behind his compositions. His classicism conveys what the sixteenth century called "authority": a simple, monumental grandeur that rejects any ornamental display as trivial. Herrera preferred the simple forms of the orders—Tuscan Doric above all—and he did not use the fanciful capitals, terms, balusters, or grotesque decoration in favor with Italian architects. He avoided figural and sculptural relief decoration on his buildings. When sculpture was used, as on the main façade or on the façade of the Church of the Escorial, it was confined to figures in niches or standing on pedestals. More frequently, the niches are empty. Instead, Herrera favored simple geometric panels, cut in relief, and pilaster strips applied to the wall; he retained only the most abstract classical motifs, such as the obelisk, as decoration. His restrained architectural vocabulary never directly evoked the art of antiquity. His austere classicism was assertively modern, a Christian classicism purged of any pagan references.

Herrera's style most closely resembles the Italian classicism of Vignola, and a number of Herrera's favorite motifs such as thermal windows and obelisks and the forms of the classical orders probably derive from Vignola's architecture or his treatise, *Le Regole.* But Herrera's style is far more abstract. Herrera most often used the classical elements to emphasize an underlying geometry. On the main façade, he flattened the temple front against the wall of the pavilion so that the columns lack any rhythm or independence from the wall. The orders become part of the wall which is divided into a series of geometric units marked by the corner towers, secondary portals, and the pilaster strips, windows, and cornices.

The Escorial was intended to be, and still is, the quintessential symbol of the reign of Philip II but its meaning has been variously interpreted depending upon the view of that monarch. In the sixteenth century, Fray José de Sigüenza saw the Escorial as the triumphant expression of Christian piety; later writers have often criticized its severe style as an expression of the king's austere personality. Philip II was certainly the major figure in the project, contributing his own ideas, which Herrera molded into a distinctive style.

In 1584, Herrera commissioned a complete set of copperplate engravings of the Escorial from the Flemish engraver Pedro Perret. These were published in 1589 with an explanatory summary by Herrera. The plates were prepared from Herrera's drawings and those of his assistants on the model of such sets as Antonio Labacco's engravings of

Antonio da Sangallo's (see SANGALLO FAMILY) designs for Saint Peter's or Etienne Dupérac's etchings of MICHELANGELO's projects in Rome. The Escorial is completely illustrated in perspective, plans, elevations, and sections as well as in detailed elevations of the sanctuary, main altar, and fountain in the Courtyard of the Evangelists. Herrera's *Estampas* is the most ambitious publication of any single building in the sixteenth century and it helped to spread the fame of the Escorial throughout Europe.

Herrera was involved in other royal building projects during the building of the Escorial. In 1571, Philip II again turned his attention to the building of the Alcázar in Toledo, begun in 1537 by ALONSO DE COVARRUBIAS. Geronimo Gilli, the Italian architect who had worked for Juan Bautista de Toledo, was put in charge at the site and Herrera provided the plans for improvements to the main staircase (1574–1575) and the designs for the southern façade. The staircase had been designed as a symmetrical, open-well staircase of five ramps by Covarrubias in 1553 but Herrera enlarged it, making the staircase the monumental focus of the building. The southern façade is a stylar composition of ten bays, four stories tall. The basement level is of rusticated arches and there are rusticated Doric pilasters on the first floor. The second-story pilasters are plain and there is an open gallery on the upper floor. The paired pilasters at the corners and the rustication recall sixteenth-century Italian palace design but the upper gallery is a traditional Spanish feature. The façade was completed in 1585. It was destroyed in 1936 but has since been rebuilt.

In 1571, Herrera also assumed control of the design of Philip II's palace at Aranjuez, south of Madrid, another of the royal projects begun by Juan Bautista de Toledo. Herrera was responsible for building the chapel and the design of the main façade and atrium behind it and for the laying out of the extensive gardens which were an important feature of the site. His designs for the façade in brick and stone used many of the motifs which appeared on the façade of the Escorial: corner towers and a central temple frontispiece. Construction continued until 1586 when the palace was still incomplete. It was finished in a different style in the eighteenth century.

In 1582, Philip II authorized the building of the Exchange (Lonja), now the Archives of the Indies, on a site near the Cathedral in Seville. Construction was begun according to Herrera's plans in 1584 and was completed in 1598. The Lonja is Herrera's most important secular building. It is square in plan, halls enclosing a central courtyard on two sides with two secondary courtyards on

Herrera.
Alcázar.
Toledo, Spain.
1571–1575

Herrera.
Exchange (Lonja).
Seville, Spain.
1582–1598

opposite sides. On the exterior, the Lonja is a square two-storied block of eleven bays on a side, each bay articulated by Doric pilasters on pedestals which are set against flat stone framing which surrounds the walls (of stone on the lower story, of brick above). Herrera used paired pilasters at the corners and again at the second bays in from the corners, suggesting residual towers; but the cornice is topped by a continuous balustrade marked only by tall obelisks at the corners. The exterior architecture of the Lonja is a crisp, layered skin which looks foward to the modulated surfaces of seventeenth-century architecture rather than backward to the clear membering of the sixteenth-century Italian style.

Earlier Spanish exchanges were open halls. Herrera departed from this tradition by introducing a magnificent open-well staircase and a central courtyard inside the Lonja. The courtyard is modeled on the design of the Courtyard of the Evangelists at the Escorial. There is no evidence that Herrera traveled to Seville to inspect the building during construction, which may account for a certain coarseness in detail as noted by Chueca (1953).

Herrera's most personal design is his last great project for the Cathedral of Valladolid, on the site of an earlier collegiate church in the center of the city. Construction of a late Gothic church had been underway since 1527 according to the designs of Diego de Riaño and RODRIGO GIL DE HON-

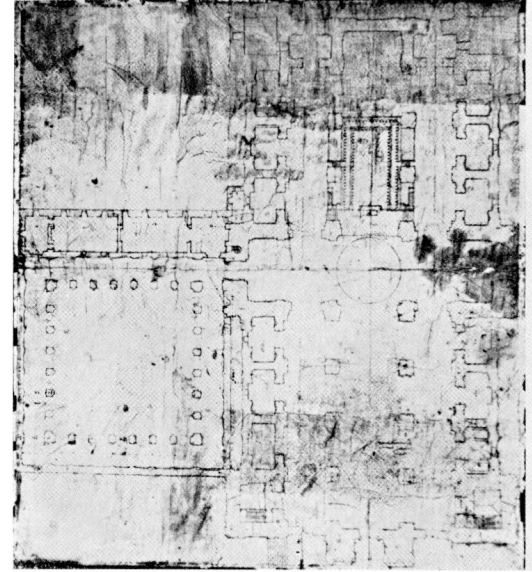

TANÓN but little was built. Herrera's designs, which were probably prepared about 1585, called for the destruction of this church and its replacement by a vast cathedral which would be a worthy monument to the birthplace of Philip II. The Cathedral of Valladolid was to be a symmetrical double square in plan with four corner towers and a central dome supported on four piers.

By 1589, construction was ready to begin but it proceeded very slowly. In 1596, Philip II finally raised the church to cathedral status but, by 1597, when Herrera died in Madrid, only part of the foundations and a portion of the main piers had been built. The main vaults were not closed until 1655. Herrera's design for the main façade was used only in the lower story, and in 1730 new designs were provided by ALBERTO DE CHURRI-GUERA. The cathedral remained a fragment but it was nevertheless one of Herrera's most influential buildings. Kubler (1959, p. 15) has stressed the influence of Herrera's rectangular sanctuary on the design of Salamanca Cathedral and on the New World cathedrals of Mexico, Puebla, and Lima. The Pilar in Saragossa, designed in 1675 by Felipe Sanchez and reworked by Francisco de Herrera the Younger in 1680, was based upon Herrera's plan for Valladolid.

Enough of Herrera's original drawings as well as later shop drawings for the cathedral survive to form an idea of his intentions. The exterior of the church was Doric; but a sober Composite capital, based on SEBASTIANO SERLIO, was used for the pilasters on the interior of the nave. Later elevation and section drawings suggest that Herrera's church would have resembled the architecture of the Escorial but the massing was bolder, both in scale and in relief. Herrera used the same vocabulary of geometric ornament, and his composition for the façade was based upon the church at the Escorial; but Valladolid Cathedral was planned as a massive, free-standing block of colossal proportions; even as a fragment, the effect of its huge piers and columns is extraordinary.

Herrera's responsibilities were broad but he was primarily a designer. The execution of his buildings was handled by assistants. This was necessary because the projects were too numerous and too far-flung for Herrera to supervise them all directly but also because Herrera was not trained in the Spanish building profession. It is doubtful if he could have functioned at all as an architect without the support of Philip II; but, even with the king's authority, it would have been difficult for him to supervise construction. As a result, Herrera depended upon loyal assistants, who prepared drawings and who headed the building programs. Several of these assistants are mentioned in Herrera's will of 6 December 1584. Among the most important are Juan de Valencia, who served Herrera as he had served Juan Bautista de Toledo as a draftsman. FRANCISCO DE MORA also prepared working drawings from Herrera's designs. He was Herrera's closest assistant and follower and, on Herrera's recommendation, succeeded him as royal architect. Diego de Alcántara was Herrera's architect in Toledo after Geronimo Gilli and Bartolomé Ruiz and Juan de Minjares filled similar positions at Aranjuez. Not mentioned in the will is Juan de Minjares who moved to the Escorial in 1576 where he supervised construction until the Escorial was finished. He then went to Seville to direct the building of the Lonja and to the works at Granada.

At Valladolid, Herrera's designs were carried out by Diego de Praves who was succeeded by his son, Francisco, in 1620. These architects were all trained in the Spanish building profession but they were also followers of Herrera's style and men whom he could trust to execute his designs faithfully. These subordinates made it possible for Herrera to play the role of the cultivated, intellectual architect and to raise the status of architecture from a craft to an independent discipline. Herrera himself insisted that the architect was not a craftsman and not an amateur, but an independent professional. Herrera became the Spanish model of a great architect but, curiously, none of his followers was able to imitate his style or his role successfully. In spite of his reputation and his numerous assistants, Herrera founded no school.

Herrera's style has often been considered inimitable (see Kubler, 1959). It depends upon its geometric clarity rather than upon any elaboration of decorative motifs. Underlying Herrera's architecture was his belief in the Renaissance system of harmonic proportions which he had learned from Juan Bautista de Toledo and from Italian authors like LEON BATTISTA ALBERTI. Herrera's abstract and intellectual interpretation of the Renaissance style is especially clear in his drawings. Many drawings for the Escorial and the Cathedral of Valladolid survive. Like those made for such Italian buildings as Saint Peter's in Rome, they are exact, measured, and to scale. Most are plans, elevations, and sections. But contrary to Italian practice, there is no shading, no indication of relief, except in the measurements. Such drawings conveyed exact instructions to the builders and they were followed with precision, but they do not reveal the steps in Herrera's creative process. We have no sketches, perspective views, or studies of decoration such as one finds among the drawings of Italian architects. Herrera's drawings for architectural details show that he was concerned above all to express geometric relationships in the surfaces of the wall. An individual motif of decoration, such as a thermal window or a balustrade, simply had no meaning outside the mural composition. Such an abstract style is difficult to imitate and, in the seventeenth century, Spanish taste shifted to favor freer, more decorated architecture.

Herrera was a courtier and an intellectual as well as an architect and he was an important figure in the royal bureaucracy. From 1579, he earned 400 ducats per year as royal architect and he earned an equal amount as *aposentador de palacio*, the courtier in charge of palace furnishings, an important post which was held later by the painter Velazquez under Philip IV. Herrera's relations with Philip II were close and multifaceted. From 1581 to 1584,

he was in Portugal preparing the royal lodgings for Philip II and studying building projects for the king. He also kept the king informed of events at court. Kubler (1981) has published an interesting exchange of notes between the king and Herrera concerning alchemists at court in 1572. Herrera may have been interested in occult science. He was certainly deeply interested in mathematics. In 1582, Philip II established an Academy of Mathematics in Madrid which opened for instruction and discussion in 1584, bringing together mathematicians, geographers, fortification experts, and men interested in mechanics and technology. Herrera was in charge of organizing the new Academy and he was probably largely responsible for choosing its subjects.

Herrera's own interests in technology were of long standing. In 1568, he had invented a new type of crane which was installed at the Escorial; in 1574, he had ordered that all the stone for the construction of the church of the Escorial be cut and finished at the quarry. This action was resisted by the architects at the site but Herrera claimed that it, together with his other inventions, had made it possible to build more rapidly and at less cost. In 1573, Herrera was granted permission to market a new type of astrolabe for navigation, and in 1579, he became involved in the king's great project to map the Spanish Empire. He owned the papers of the geographer Pedro Esquivel. In 1580, he was working with the military architect Felipe Tercio in Portugal and he frequently advised on fortification designs or on engineering and hydraulic projects. In 1587, Herrera invested in an iron mine in Asturias which was to be operated by machines of his own design but this was sold in 1591.

The extent of Herrera's interests can be documented from the contents of his excellent library. Herrera collected architectural books and prints but also treatises on mathematics and mechanics. He was particularly interested in the mechanics of Aristotle and Archimedes, and in 1584, he requested a copy of the recent Italian translation of Guido Ubaldo del Monte's *Mechanicorum Liber* from the secretary to the Spanish Embassy in Venice.

Herrera also collected the writings of the Spanish philosopher and mystic Raymond Lull. He wrote a short treatise of his own—the *Tratato del cuerpo cúbico*—which was based on Lull's doctrine and which attempted to illustrate it with geometric relationships derived from the cube. The relation between this treatise and Herrera's architecture is difficult to fathom; but it suggests that geometry was the guiding principle not only of his architecture but also of his philosophical outlook.

CATHERINE WILKINSON

WORKS

1563–1584, San Lorenzo El Escorial Royal Monastery (after general plans by Juan Bautista de Toledo and others), Madrid. 1571–1585, Alcázar (reworking of the main staircase design; southern façade design; with Geronimo Gilli), Toledo, Spain. 1571–1586, Royal Palace (main façade and the atrium), Aranjuez, Spain. 1582–1598, Exchange, Seville, Spain. 1585–1597, Valladolid Cathedral (not completed), Spain. 1590–1597, El Escorial (sanctuary of the basilica), Madrid.

BIBLIOGRAPHY

CERVERA VERA, LUIS 1945 *Las Estampas y el Sumario de El Escorial por Juan de Herrera.* Madrid: Tecnos.

CERVERA VERA, LUIS 1972 *El "Ingenio" creado por Juan de Herrera para cortar hierro.* Madrid: Castalia.

CERVERA VERA, LUIS 1977 *Inventario de los Bienes de Juan de Herrera.* Valencia, Spain: Albatros.

CHUECA GOITIA, FERNANDO 1953 *Arquitectura del Siglo XVI.* In *Hispaniae XI.* Madrid: Plus-Ultra.

CHUECA GOITIA, FERDINANDO 1947 *La Catedral de Valladolid.* Madrid: Consejo Superior de Investigaciones Científicas.

El Escorial 1563–1963. 1963 2 vols. Madrid: Patronomio Nacional.

HERRERA, JUAN DE 1935 *Tratado del Cuerpo Cúbico, conforme a los principios y opiniones del "Arte" de Raimundo Lulio.* Madrid: Plutarco.

HERRERA, JUAN DE 1954 *Sumario y Breve Declaracion de los Diseños y estampas de la fabrica de San Lorenço el Real del Escurial, Madrid, 1589.* Madrid: Tipografis Artistica.

IÑIGUEZ ALMECH, FRANCISCO 1963 "Los Ingenios de Juan de Herrera." Volume 2, pages 181–214 in *El Escorial 1563–1963.* Madrid: Patrimonio Nacional.

IÑIGUEZ ALMECH, FRANCISCO 1965 *Las Trazas del Monasterio de S. Lorenzo de El Escorial.* Madrid: Real Academia de Bellas Artes de San Fernando.

KUBLER, GEORGE 1975 "Galeazzo Alessi e l'Escuriale." Pages 599–603 in *Galeazzo Alessi e l'Architettura del Cinquecento.* Genoa, Italy: Sagep.

KUBLER, GEORGE 1981 *Building the Escorial.* N.J.: Princeton University Press.

KUBLER, GEORGE, and SORIA, MARTIN 1959 *Art and Architecture in Spain and Portugal and Their American Dominions, 1500–1800.* Baltimore: Penguin.

LLAGUNO Y AMÍROLA, EUGENIO, and CEÁN BERMÚDEZ, JUAN AGUSTÍN 1977 Volume 2 in *Noticias de los arquitectos y arquitectura de Espana desde su restauración.* Reprint. Genoa, Italy, and Madrid: Turner.

LÓPEZ SERRANO, MATILDE 1944 *Trazas de Juan de Herrera y sus seguidores para el Monasterio del Escorial.* Madrid: Patrimonio Nacional.

RODRIGUEZ Y GUTIÉRREZ DE CEBALLOS, ALFONSO 1966 "Juan de Herrera y los Jesuitas." *Archivum Historicum Societatis Iesu* 35, no. 25:285–321.

RUIZ DE ARCAUTE, AGUSTIN 1936 *Juan de Herrera.* Madrid: Espasa-Calpe.

SÁNCHEZ CANTÓN, FRANCISCO JAVIER 1941 *La Librería de Juan de Herrera.* Madrid: Consejo Superior de Investigaciones Científicas.

SIGÜENZA, FRAY JOSE DE 1907–1909 *Historia de la Orden de San Jerónimo, Madrid, 1600.* Madrid: Balliére e Hijos.

TAYLOR, RENE 1967 "Architecture and Magic: Considerations on the Idea of the Escorial." Pages 81–109 in Howard Hibbard (editor), *Essays in the History of Architecture Presented to Rudolf Wittkower.* London: Phaidon.

HERRON, RON

Ronald James Herron (1930–) is best known for his association with Archigram, the loosely knit group of young English architects who met in the early 1960s and began publishing *Archigrams,* a series of broadsheet manifestoes designed to stir things up on the London architectural scene. Herron had received his diploma from the Regent Street Polytechnic and was working under Hubert Benett at the London County Council when Peter Cook invited him to contribute to *Archigram 1.* Herron shared with the Archigram group (never a precisely defined quantity) a fascination with change and flexibility, or metamorphosis, as well as a playful, irreverent attitude toward architecture and drawing. Throughout the early 1960s, the Archigram people, including Herron, wrote and drew and talked and worked for Theo Crosby on the redevelopment project for Euston Station and eventually formed their own firm, Archigram Architects.

The typical product of the firm was a drawing or an exhibition, both natural fields of endeavor for a group that believed in flexibility, ephemerality, and change as the only constant. Herron was the group's leading image-maker, as Cook was the leading spokesman. Herron is a witty and talented draftsman; his Walking City creations have become, with Cook's Plug-in Cities, the standard Archigram illustrations in texts and journals.

Archigram Architects dissolved in 1974, and Herron joined Theo Crosby again, this time as a partner in the design firm Pentagram. In 1980, he moved to Derek Walker Associates, where he is currently a partner. He teaches at the Architectural Association School of Architecture and is a visiting lecturer at the University of Southern California in Los Angeles.

JANET R. WHITE

WORKS

1954–1957, Prospect County College for Girls (with Hubert Benett); 1960–1962, South Bank Arts Centre (with Benett); *1963, Living City Exhibition, Institute of Contemporary Art; *1965, Archigram Exhibition, Architectural Association; *1969, Archigram Exhibition, Camden Arts Centre; 1973, Malaysia Exhibition, Commonwealth Institute; 1973–1974, Rod Stewart

House (addition; with Dennis Crompton and Diana Jowsey); 1975–1978, Saint Christopher's Place (rehabilitation of shops, apartments, and an office); 1977, Director's Studio (studios); 1977–1980, Reuters (office interiors), Fleet Street; London. *1978, Cape Building Products Exhibit, Building Exhibition, Birmingham, England. 1980, Blackrod Offices; 1981, L'Oreal Headquarters; London.

BIBLIOGRAPHY

COOK, PETER 1965 "Archigram." *Architectural Design* 35:559–572.
COOK, PETER 1975 "Passi lunghi passicorti: Archigram 1974–75." *Casabella* 398:20–31.
COOK, PETER 1980a "The Architecture of Optimism." *Journal of the Royal Institute of British Architects* 87:41–44.
COOK, PETER 1980b "Preview of the Exhibition—Forum Design, Linz, Austria." *Architectural Design* 50, no. 3–4:62–65.
COOK, PETER ET AL. (1972)1973 *Archigram.* New York: Praeger.
SCOTT, FRED 1976 "It's Architecture Again." *Architectural Design* 46:670–675.

HERTS and TALLANT

Although short-lived, the partnership of Herts and Tallant produced what are, as a group, New York's most accomplished theaters in the short span of eleven years. Both former students at the Ecole des Beaux-Arts in the 1890s, Henry Beaumont Herts (1871–1933) and Hugh Tallant (1869–1952) formed the partnership of Herts and Tallant in 1900. Some of their work was executed in a variety of revival styles, although always with great individuality. The Renaissance Brooklyn Academy of Music (1906–1908), the classical Aguilar branch of the New York Public Library (1903–1905), the Rice Residence (1901–1903), and the baroque Lyceum Theater (1902–1903) are works from this group. But in all their work there was a consistent undercurrent of Art Nouveau and other nonclassical styling, which was fully expressed in the New Amsterdam Theater (1902–1903). That building's interior, one of the great works of Art Nouveau in the northeastern region, contained almost exclusively the "realistic" ornament and floral forms of the American Art Nouveau, executed in glazed polychrome terra cotta, plasterwork, and wood. Much of their work emphasized the lavish use of glazed terra cotta, both for interior decoration and for exterior cladding, and the old Folies Bergère Theater (1910–1911) is probably the most accomplished work of the latter category. Herts was an expert in cantilevered balconies in theaters (of which he designed more than thirty

before his death), and both men practiced architecture independently after 1911.

CHRISTOPHER S. GRAY

WORKS

1899–1900, Aguilar Free Library; 1901–1903, Rice Residence; 1902–1903, Lyceum Theater; 1902–1903, New Amsterdam Theater; 1903–1904, Liberty Theater; 1903–1905, Aguilar Branch, New York Public Library; 1906–1908, Brooklyn Academy of Music; 1910–1911, Folies Bergère; New York.

HESSE, LUDWIG FERDINAND

Born in Belgrade, Serbia, Ludwig Ferdinand Hesse (1795–1876) entered the Berlin Academy in 1819 where he trained as both a painter and an architect. Under KARL FRIEDRICH SCHINKEL, he designed decoration for and directed construction of the neo-Gothic Werdesche Church (1821–1831); but Schinkel's neoclassical buildings of the mid-1820s most influenced Hesse's early buildings, especially the Veterinary School (1839–1840) in Berlin. Named *Hofbaumeister* at Potsdam in 1831, Hesse worked under LUDWIG PERSIUS whose villa style formed the basis for his own domestic style.

In collaboration with FRIEDRICH AUGUST STÜLER—whom Hesse succeeded as *Oberhofbaurat* in 1859—he developed King Friedrich Wilhelm IV's ideas for the Orangery (1851–1860) and the Belvedere on the Pfingstenberg (1847–1852) at Sanssouci, both drawing upon such sixteenth-century Roman villas as the Villa Madama and the Villa Pamphilj.

BARRY BERGDOLL

WORKS

*1830, British Hotel and Houses, Luisenstrasse; 1836, Scheckler Sugar Refinery Warehouse; 1839–1840, Veterinary Medicine School; 1841, Mausoleum of Queen Luise (extension), Charlottenburg Park; Berlin. 1846, Friedrich Wilhelm Koch House, 28 Jägerallee; 1847, Bayerisches Haus am Wildpark, Sanssouci; 1847, Müllerwohnhaus, Sanssouci; 1847, Teehaus, Sanssouci; 1847, Weinberghaus, Sanssouci; 1847–1852, Belvedere, Pfingstenberg, Sanssouci; 1849, Winzerhaus, Sanssouci; 1851–1860, Orangery and Terraces, Sanssouci; Potsdam, Germany. 1852, Charité Hospital (summer pavilion), Berlin. 1852, Dreikönigstor, Obeliskenstrasse, Potsdam, Germany. 1865–1867, Elisabeth Hospital, Berlin.

BIBLIOGRAPHY

BÖRSCH-SUPAN, EVA 1977 *Berliner Baukunst nach Schinkel, 1840–1870.* Munich: Prestel.
DEHIO, LUDWIG 1961 *Friedrich Wilhelm IV. von Preussen, ein Baukünstler der Romantik.* Berlin: Deutscher Kunstverlag.

HESSE, LUDWIG F. 1854–1855 *Ländliche Wohngebäude in der Umgegend von Sanssouci und Potsdam.* Berlin: Riegel.

HESSE, LUDWIG F. 1854–1856 *Sanssouci in seinen Architecturen unter der Regierung Seiner Majestät Friedrich Wilhelm IV. von Preussen.* Berlin: Riegel.

HETSCH, G. F.

Gustav Friedrich Hetsch (1788–1864) was born in Stuttgart and trained in Germany and France. In 1815, he went to Copenhagen, where he remained. He assumed an important position in Danish architecture and applied arts, adding a sound rationalism to the Danish tradition. Among his rather few but significant buildings are to be mentioned the Synagogue (1833) and the Roman Catholic Church of Saint Ansgar, both in Copenhagen.

VILLADS VILLADSEN

HIGGINS, DANIEL P.

See EGGERS and HIGGINS.

HIGGINSON, AUGUSTUS BARKER

Augustus B. Higginson (1866–1915) studied with the Boston firm of Andrews and Jacques (1889–1891) and at the Ecole des Beaux-Arts (1892–1894) in Paris. He practiced first in Chicago (1895–1900), where he was active in the Arts and Crafts movement, and then in Santa Barbara, California.

GWEN W. STEEGE

WORKS

c.1900, Edwin S. Fetcher House, Winnetka, Ill. c.1905–1910, Higginson House, 1000 Channel Drive, Montecito, Calif. 1909, Coe House, Santa Barbara, Calif.

BIBLIOGRAPHY

ROBIE, VIRGINIA 1905 "A Bachelor's Cottage in the Country." *House Beautiful* 5:30–31.

HIGUERAS DIAZ, FERNANDO

Born in Madrid, Fernando Higueras Diaz (1930–) graduated from the Superior Technical School of Architecture there in 1959.

Higueras is very much a loner in his field. His designs are restless and defiant and run counter to current styles yet possess an absolute internal consistency. His work consists of private houses as well as multi-family units, offices, colleges, and hotels. From 1963 to 1970, all his projects were built in collaboration with Antonio Miró.

MIGUEL ANGEL BALDELLOU
Translated from Spanish by
Judith E. Meighan

WORKS

1968, Nuria Espert House, Alcoceber, Castellon, Spain. 1973, Hotel (with Ricardo Novara), Fuerteventura, Canary Islands, Spain. 1974, Church (with others), Onil, Spain. 1977, Apartments, Isla Margarita, Venezuela.

BIBLIOGRAPHY

BENEVOLO, LEONARDO (1963)1971 *History of Modern Architecture.* 2 vols. Cambridge, Mass.: M.I.T.

FLORES LOPEZ, CARLOS 1961 *Arquitectura española contemporánea.* Madrid: Aguilar.

HIGUERAS, FERNANDO 1977 *José de Castro Arines.* Madrid: Ministerio de Educación y Ciencia.

HILBERSEIMER, LUDWIG KARL

Born in Karlsruhe, Germany, of German-French ancestry, Ludwig Karl Hilberseimer (1885–1967) was educated privately and later studied architecture at the Technische Hochschule in Karlsruhe under J. W. Durm, whose interpretation of the history of architecture as the history of the art of building (Baukunst) was a major influence. Other influences were WILLIAM MORRIS, Peter Kropotkin, HEINRICH TESSENOW, TONY GARNIER, and HERMANN MUTHESIUS, and, among his contemporaries, the industrial architecture of HANS POELZIG and the architectural ideas of his long-time friend and colleague LUDWIG MIES VAN DER ROHE. Mies was instrumental in bringing Hilberseimer to the Illinois Institute of Technology after his departure from Nazi Germany.

After World War I he joined the November Group and was active in the Berlin Dada movement; for a time he was a Dada architect, as can be seen in the austere, anti-art, machinelike cityscapes of his early projects which are reflected in the paintings of George Grosz of the same period.

In the 1920s he became an art critic while practicing as an architect, and was a European correspondent for the *Chicago Tribune* on the new architecture in Germany and Central Europe; in addition, he played a major role as critic, writer, and teacher in clarifying the theoretical basis of modern architecture and as a spokesman for "the new objectivity" (*die neue Sachlichkeit*).

Hilberseimer was one of the major theoreticians of modern city planning. His first study of the city in 1924, *Hochhaustadt* (High-rise City), was layered on two levels: the lower stories for workshops, light industry, markets, and garages, and the upper stories for apartment houses for city workers. Traffic serviced the lower levels, and pedestrian walks on the upper levels were connected by footbridges. Standardization of interiors, furniture, and equipment would allow city dwellers to move from one area to another with only a suitcase. Later, in 1932, as the result of intensive studies of housing, the orientation of buildings for sunlight, and other social and hygienic factors, he was to reject the vertical centralized city in favor of horizontally planned decentralization. His first decentralized city project was made at the Bauhaus for the city of Dessau where he had been appointed master of housing and city planning in 1928. In this study, industry was related to wind directions to prevent pollution of residential areas by toxic gases, while housing and industry were to be within walking distance, that is, one mile maximum; at the same time, industry was related in a linear pattern to road and rail transportation.

This dramatic change in his concept of the city did not alter the close connection he sought between dwelling and workplace, which was a characteristic of both vertical and horizontal city projects. In the process he had rejected a dependence on technology for the solution to urban problems of the twentieth century in favor of a city based on the human scale. This altered viewpoint, the result of a profound philosophical conviction, was to become the basis of his ideas and teaching at the I.T.T. in Chicago from 1938 to 1967.

If his fame in Germany rested on his projects and creative ideas, it has been as a unique and gifted teacher, as a master of the Socratic method, that Hilberseimer's influence has been greatest in the United States. He believed that the solution to problems in contemporary architecture and city planning was to be found in an analytical study of the object, logical thinking, and interested disinterestedness.

He was the recipient of numerous awards and distinctions in this country and abroad.

REGINALD MALCOLMSON

WORKS

1925–1927, Housing Estates, Adlergestellstrasse, Adlershofstrasse, Dörpfeldstrasse; 1926, Rheinlandhaus (shops, offices, and a theater), Belleallianceplatz; 1927, Shops, Kreuzbergstrasse, Mehringdammstrasse, Obentrautstrasse; Berlin. 1927, Town House, Werkbundsiedlung, Stuttgart, Germany. 1932, Blumenthal House, Zehlendorf Wilski Strasse; 1935, Fuchs House, 19 Steglitz Dietrich-Schäfer-Weg; 1935, Town House, 9 Charlottenburg am Rupenhorn; Berlin.

BIBLIOGRAPHY

HILBERSEIMER, LUDWIG KARL 1925 *Grossstadtbauten.* Hannover, Germany: Apos.

HILBERSEIMER, LUDWIG KARL 1927a *Grossstadt-Architektur.* Stuttgart, Germany: J. Hoffmann.

HILBERSEIMER, LUDWIG KARL 1927b *Internationale Neue Baukunst.* Stuttgart, Germany: J. Hoffmann.

HILBERSEIMER, LUDWIG KARL 1929 *Beton als Gestalter.* Stuttgart, Germany: J. Hoffmann.

HILBERSEIMER, LUDWIG KARL 1930 "Hallenbauten." In *Handbuch der Architektur.* Leipzig: Gerlach.

HILBERSEIMER, LUDWIG KARL 1944 *The New City.* Chicago: Theobald.

HILBERSEIMER, LUDWIG KARL 1949 *The New Regional Pattern.* Chicago: Theobald.

HILBERSEIMER, LUDWIG KARL 1955 *The Nature of Cities.* Chicago: Theobald.

HILBERSEIMER, LUDWIG KARL 1963a *Contemporary Architecture: Its Roots and Trends.* Chicago: Theobald.

HILBERSEIMER, LUDWIG KARL 1963b *Einfaltung einer Planungsidee.* Berlin: Ullstein.

HILDEBRANDT, JOHANN LUCAS VON

An innovator in Austrian architecture and interior and landscape design of the eighteenth century, Johann Lucas von Hildebrandt (1668–1745) was born in Genoa, Italy, and spent the first twenty-eight years of his life in that country. His German father was a captain in the Genoese army who later joined the imperial army; his mother was probably Italian. Hildebrandt moved to Vienna in 1696 and spent the following forty-nine years working in that capital city of the Austro-Hungarian Empire. Hildebrandt's architecture, along with that of his great rival JOHANN BERNARD FISCHER VON ERLACH, defines the broad spectrum of the Austrian baroque.

Hildebrandt's architectural education was begun in Genoa and continued in Rome where he went around the year 1690. According to a letter to the Emperor Leopold I of June 19, 1699, in which he petitioned for an appointment as court architect, he studied the fundamentals of military and civil engineering and architecture with CARLO FONTANA and Ceruti. Hildebrandt stated that his architectural career began around 1693, but no buildings have been documented to him until after he reached Vienna.

He had been an imperial military engineer since 1695, and in this capacity he met one of his important patrons, Prince Eugen of Savoy, under whom he made three field campaigns in Piedmont in 1695–1696. Immediately following these campaigns, probably at Prince Eugen's suggestion,

Hildebrandt left Italy to begin an architectural career in Vienna.

By 1698, Hildebrandt was employed in court service in Vienna as a councillor; in 1700, his petition was granted and he became a court architect. Despite Hildebrandt's many years of association with the Hapsburg Court, that patronage was to yield little, as through the years he lost most major court projects to Fischer von Erlach. Hildebrandt was ennobled in 1720 for his service to the court, and in 1723, at the death of Fischer von Erlach, he became first architect. This position again turned out to be more honorary than real, as Hildebrandt continued to lose commissions, this time to Fischer the Elder's son, Johann Emanuel Fischer von Erlach. His request of 1724 to become first court engineer remained unfulfilled because of the intrigues of the younger Fischer von Erlach.

Hildebrandt's primary sources of patronage came from the aristocracy, beginning with Prince Eugen and including many of the great Austro-Hungarian families such as the Harrachs, Starhembergs, Dauns, and especially the Schönborns. Count Friedrich Carl von Schönborn, imperial vice-chancellor and later prince-bishop of Würzburg and Bamberg, one of the greatest architectural patrons of the eighteenth century, chose Hildebrandt as his architect before 1705. Over 200 letters from Hildebrandt's hand are extant and many of these are to Friedrich Carl von Schönborn concerning his many building projects.

In 1706, Hildebrandt married Francisca Johanna Perpetua Geist, and they had eight children. Hildebrandt's life was periodically marred by attacks of epilepsy from which he suffered since childhood. In the later years of his life, he complained of weakness of the eyes, a condition which did not keep him from continual work. Hildebrandt had a court salary and a pension from the Spanish court, and he received individual payment for his commissions. He purchased a house on the Schösselgasse in 1719, and in 1741 also had a house in rural Matzleinsdorf.

In marked contrast to the elder Fischer von Erlach, Hildebrandt left no theoretical writings and his letters deal only with the practical matters of his commissions. His working method was to make plans and drawings for his projects—ninety are still extant—, to check sites when possible, and to oversee the progress of construction. He left much of the actual day-to-day supervision to Franz Jänggle who was associated with him since soon after his arrival in Vienna. Wooden models were constructed under Hildebrandt's supervision for some of his larger commissions such as the revisions for the Hofburg Palace and the Church of Saint Lawrence at Gabel.

Hildebrandt's patrons report that he had a strong and vehement temper, especially when objections were raised as to his artistic decisions. Field Marshall Johann Joseph Count Harrach reported that at an interview with the architect about errors in a building project Hildebrandt had "cried like a baby," disclaiming all fault. Despite such occasional outbursts of temperament, Hildebrandt managed to stay on congenial terms with many of his patrons over decades and likewise managed to work amiably with several contemporary architects and artists on joint projects. Although he was associated with most of the eminent painters of his time, including Paul Troger, Daniel Gran, and Johann Michael Rottmayr, there are no known portraits of the architect.

Although Hildebrandt was occasionally called upon to build churches it is clear that his contemporaries particularly esteemed him for the dwellings he designed and for the interiors and gardens that accompanied them. These dwellings were of

Hildebrandt.
Daun-Kinsky City Palace.
Vienna.
1713–1716

Hildebrandt.
Daun-Kinsky City Palace.
Vienna.
1713–1716

several types and posed varying architectural problems. The garden palace was a type particularly suited to his genius and is the one to which he made the most original contributions. A structure of modest size and used mainly in the summer, the garden palace was characteristically set outside of the city walls and had a garden setting.

The city palace type, like those clustered in the narrow streets around the Imperial Hofburg, were used during the other seasons. Boasting richly ornamented principal façades, these palaces are usually flanked by contiguous structures. Hildebrandt's brilliant solution to the façade and the interior stairway of the Daun-Kinsky Palace (1713–1716) constitutes his major contribution to this genre.

Yet another, even larger, palace type upon which Hildebrandt worked were the royal and ecclesiastical residences set within cities; they included the Würzburg Residence (1719–1738), the Bishop's Residence (1709–1710) at Salzburg, and the Imperial Hofburg (1723) in Vienna. These structures, which combined characteristics of city and garden palaces, had other prerequisites dictated by scale and the necessity of enlarged ceremonial spaces.

In addition, Hildebrandt was asked to design landed estates for the aristocratic families he served, among others the Harrach Estates at Bruck-an-der-Leitha (1707–1711) and at Halbthurn (1711–1722); the Schönborn Estate (1712–1717) near Göllersdorf; and Schlosshof (1725–1729) in the Marchfeld for Prince Eugen. These projects involved the alteration of existing structures, new additions, and the unification of the entire estate through gardens.

Hildebrandt also built many houses with richly decorated street façades for the wealthy merchant class, including the Schreyvogel House (1705) in Breslau, Silesia, and the Bartolotti (1720) and Merklein (1730) Houses in Vienna.

Although Hildebrandt's architectural activities in Italy between 1693 and the time he entered the army in 1695 remain obscure, seven drawings existing in the Archive of the Church of Santa Maria di Carignano in Genoa are signed Gio. Luc Ildebrandt, archi[to], and may be assigned to this period. They show two unexecuted projects for monastic buildings for the church. Italianate in plan and elevation, these drawings evidence Hildebrandt's thorough grounding in Renaissance and baroque palace design, and they also indicate his early interest in the interrelationship of separate buildings through space, which had also intensely interested his teacher Carlo Fontana.

Almost immediately after his arrival in Vienna, Hildebrandt became involved, in 1697, with the building of a garden palace for Count Heinrich Franz Mansfeld-Fondi, a field marshall and councillor of Emperor Leopold I. The defeat of the Turks under their powerful leader Kara Mustafa before the gates of Vienna in 1683 had released a euphoria among the populace which evidenced itself, among the aristocracy, in a desire to move beyond the confines of the narrow streets and fortifications of the city.

The Mansfeld-Fondi Palace (later Schwarzenberg), one of Hildebrandt's most brilliant and influential early creations, is one of the few buildings for which early preparatory drawings exist (Schwarzenberg Central Archive, Krumau, Austria). Hildebrandt placed the palace at the bottom of the rising terrain and spread the garden out behind it through a series of ramps and terraces in a triangulated composition. Originally, the garden was to have been punctuated mid-way by a Borrominesque (see FRANCESCO BORROMINI) garden house with external undulating walls and an interior whose horizontally placed central room was flanked by longitudinal oval spaces.

The *cour d'honneur* was originally entered from the Rennweg via undulating ramps. The principal palace building, a long rectangular block, has low connecting structures which link it to lateral service wings to create a U-shaped plan, in the manner of French palace design. The *cour d'honneur* is completely cut off from the garden which must be entered through the square vestibule and the garden salon of the palace's dominant *corps de logis*. A semicircular ramp passes through the open arcaded vestibule which strongly projects from the lateral wings. Giant Ionic pilasters define the palace's *piano nobile,* and the wall surfaces on all façades are drafted.

On the garden façade, the three central bays swing forward, enclosing the main salon which

Hildebrandt. Mansfeld-Fondi Garden Palace (court façade). Vienna. 1697–1715

rises through two stories. The external crown enclosure of the vault of this room may be seen above the vestibule. Drawings show that Hildebrandt's intention was to decorate the rooflines of the vestibule and garden salon with balustrades and figural sculpture, giving the palace a festive appearance and one more in keeping with the concept of the garden palace as a *maison de plaisance*.

The type of axial composition Hildebrandt used in the Mansfeld-Fondi Palace, with its alterations of direction, was often seen in Italian garden designs of the sixteenth century, for example, in the garden at the Villa d'Este, Tivoli (c.1555). In these gardens, circular stairs, ramps, and terraces were used with the same intention as in Hildebrandt's design, namely, to draw one through the composition revealing all of its parts. Particularly important for Hildebrandt was the mannerist Villa Giulia, Rome (1552), for which GIACOMO BAROZZI DA VIGNOLA had designed the casino with its semicircular stairs (Nymphaeum side) which stands in the garden's center. Hildebrandt copied this façade, almost exactly, for the vestibule of the Mansfeld-Fondi Palace.

The Mansfeld-Fondi Palace evidences that rich synthesis of Italian, French, and German sources characteristic of Hildebrandt's style of the first decade of the eighteenth century. Aspects of LOUIS LE VAU's Vaux-le-Vicomte Garden Palace (the oval salon), of Guarino Guarini's Palazzo Carignano (the oval salon), and of GIOVANNI LORENZO BERNINI's first Louvre's east façade project (the crown enclosure of the vault) suggest themselves as possible sources of inspiration for the architect at this time. Hildebrandt knew personally the work of baroque architects such as Bernini, Guarini, and Borromini from his travels in Italy. He could have known Bernini's projects from his own teacher, Carlo Fontana, who had been that architect's assistant for ten years.

In 1715, Count Mansfeld-Fondi died, and in 1716, his uncompleted garden palace—only the chapel and rooms on the west side were decorated—was sold to Count Adam Franz von Schwarzenberg. Hildebrandt was removed from the project and replaced by Johann Bernard Fischer von Erlach, assisted by his son, who completed the interiors, including the garden salon. The appointment of Fischer von Erlach must have been a blow to Hildebrandt, especially as that architect proceeded to alter his intentions for the garden façade and interiors. In 1723, Fischer raised the height of the windows of the projecting central section of the garden façade, pushing those on the second register through the attic story. This gave greater weight to the central section, altering the flowing quality of Hildebrandt's façade. Judging from the

completed chapel, Hildebrandt's interiors would have been lighter in tonality and more delicately articulated than the dark, more classicizing ones put in place.

Intending to build a summer retreat, Prince Eugen of Savoy acquired the island of Czepel on the Danube in the vicinity of Budapest. Hildebrandt's plans for it, in the style of a garden palace, were ready in 1701. Building on the Ráckeve Palace began in 1702 with a visit to the site by the architect who completed designs for the interiors in 1703. A one-story, three-winged, U-plan structure, it is dominated by a *corps de logis* comprised of a vestibule and a two-story octagonal garden salon vaulted with a cupola. This salon has convex corners on the cross-axes and projects outward into the garden. The wings of the broad *cour d'honneur* terminate in pavilions and the court originally closed on the fourth side with an elaborate iron fence and gate of Hildebrandt's design. A Palladian (see ANDREA PALLADIO) motif defines the vestibule exterior, and its roof is an open terrace affording a view of the river. The cupola rising behind the vestibule is faced with an aedicular motif and originally carried a distinctive mansard roof.

Hildebrandt reduced the garden palace to a single story so that there is a direct flow through the center of the building on the ground floor from entry to garden salon and into the garden itself. This feature distinguished many of his later designs, including the Starhemberg-Schönburg Garden Palace. The articulation of the court façade with tall rectangular windows filling almost the entire wall area between Ionic pilasters suggests a direction that will culminate in the Lower Belvedere.

Prince Eugen lost interest in Ráckeve, presumably because of the continuing Hungarian rebellions against the imperial government. Despite having spent enormous sums on the palace, he seems to have visited it only once after its completion, in 1717, following the siege of Belgrade.

One of Hildebrandt's finest garden palaces, the Starhemberg-Schönburg (1705–1706), exists today in a much altered state and is best understood through six engravings by Salomon Kleiner. In its original state, the palace was cut off from the city by a garden wall which swung backward in a great curve at the center. Behind the wall, a linden arbor and fountains lined the approach to the *cour d'honneur* and created a fore-garden. The main palace block, with only a subterranean and principal story, stood detached from lower lateral service wings, in the manner of some of Palladio's villas. The main garden, behind the palace, was seen from the *cour d'honneur* through open iron gates that stretched between the main block and the service wings. In contrast to most of Hildebrandt's garden palaces, the Starhemberg-Schönburg Palace stood within a garden rather than as the starting point for one.

The *corps de logis,* articulated by giant Composite pilasters, was the dominant decorative and vertical element on the court façade, as at the Ráckeve and Mansfeld-Fondi palaces. Composed of a projecting oval vestibule behind which an octagonal garden salon with convex corners was placed, the *corps de logis* was entered at ground level. The central three bays of the garden salon formed a *ressaut,* and on the interior the room was carried through two stories. A crown enclosure for the vault on the exterior included an exuberant balustrade and statuary.

The principal sightline of the complex passed through the transparent core of the open vestibule and garden salon into the garden and up to the belvedere. The magnificent, and unexpectedly classical, garden belvedere was opened in the middle by a Palladian motif. In the Starhemberg-Schönburg Palace, as at Ráckeve Palace, Hildebrandt abandoned mannerist oppositions of direction for a clear and flowing design along the longitudinal axis.

Today, this delightful palace is scarcely recognizable; among the most ruinous changes, the open vestibule has been enclosed and made into a stair hall; a mezzanine story has been added; and the garden with its belvedere no longer exists.

Built for his great patron Friedrich Carl von Schönborn in the Viennese suburb of Alser, the Schönborn Garden Palace was to be filled with the vice-chancellor's extensive collections of paintings and sculpture. The project involved additions and alterations to an older country house. Hildebrandt's drawings of 1705 were executed by his associate Franz Jänggle in the years 1706–1711; his opulent interior decor was not completed until 1721. To the original rectangular two-story building block, which ran along a street, Hildebrandt added two perpendicular wings at the rear to create a three-sided court. This court was separated from the garden behind it by an outward-curving wall. At the center of the court façade, a projecting rectangular stair pavilion with convex outside corners was added. The juncture of the wings with the main block was punctuated by small circular stair towers, reminiscent of those found in medieval German castles.

The two-story palace originally had an eleven-bay street façade; it is much altered today. A Salomon Kleiner engraving shows that the central *ressaut* of five bays was articulated by giant Corinthian pilasters and had a separate mansard roof and roofline balustrade carrying statues. Imaginative carved window surrounds, a distinctive Hildebrandt touch, marked the *piano nobile* of the *ressaut.* The side portions of the façade bore simple, sloping roofs and had drafted wall surfaces with lisens defining each window bay. Both side and central elevations of this street façade were carried in detail to the court façade and its lateral wings.

On the interior, a vestibule leads from the decorative entry portal on the street to the exquisite two-storied stair pavilion on the court side. The pavilion is a small room, on whose outside walls, in either direction, a staircase winds upward to a landing which forms a bridge back over the lower portion of the room. Light streams into both levels of the pavilion illuminating one of Hildebrandt's most beautiful carved stone balustrades carrying sculptural putti and vases.

Hildebrandt's garden for the palace was one of his most extravagant creations. It began with a large embroidered floral parterre and continued upward in stepped parterres through basket-arcaded paths dressed with over a hundred statues. The garden culminated in a circular "comedy parterre" where seven carved figures depicting characters from the theater were displayed before the garden belvedere.

The belvedere merged an open two-story central pavilion of undulating outline with lateral one-story open arcades. For the central section, Hildebrandt's imaginative genius transformed such dull double-storied Roman baroque fountain prototypes as the Acqua Paola (1610–1614) into a witty and joyous garden ornament. The lower level, a grotto, had a fountain cascade; the upper level, a transparent superstructure, held a playfully growling carved lion, an emblem from the Schönborn family crest. At the Schönborn Garden Palace, Hildebrandt's indulgent patron Friedrich Carl von Schönborn allowed the architect to give free play to his rich Germanic sense of fantasy.

In the years at the turn of the century, Hildebrandt designed three important churches. The most influential was the Dominican Church of Saint Lawrence at Gabel in Bohemia (1699–1711), which was to affect the development of Bohemian baroque architecture, particularly that of KILIAN IGNAZ DIENTZENHOFER. The Saint Peter's Church, Vienna (1703–1717)), and the Piaristen Church of Maria Treu, Vienna, probably planned in 1698 but built in 1716–1746, are similiar to Saint Lawrence and may be attributed to Hildebrandt on stylistic grounds.

The Church of Saint Lawrence was built adjacent to and connected on its north wall with the newly completed (1697) monastery of the Dominicans. The original patron of the church, Count Franz Anton von Berka, died in the course

Hildebrandt.
Saint Peter's.
Vienna.
1703–1717

of building and the new patrons hired Domenico Petrini to finish the church which had been completed to the top of the galleries of the piers. Petrini followed a wooden model made by Hildebrandt and completed the pendentives, the high drum with its eight windows, and the cupola and lantern. The roof of the church and the original, richly colored interior decor were destroyed by fire in 1788 and were not accurately restored. Today, the majestic interior space is articulated in monochromatic tones of grey and white.

Hildebrandt signed a contract to provide the plans for Saint Lawrence in 1699, and in that year he visited the site. He probably checked on the building's progress in 1702 and 1704 when he visited near-by Rumburg to inspect his Santa Maria Loretto Chapel (1715) which was going up contemporaneously.

Hildebrandt's plan for Saint Lawrence shows a composite of longitudinal and centralizing elements. The four massive principal piers of the domed central space flare outward and create an octagonal core. Semicircular niche chapels are cut into the piers with columns placed before them to carry galleries. On the longitudinal axis, horizontal ovals create the narthex and choir, and the latter closes with a semicircular apse. Narrow, lozenge-shaped spaces attached at the cross-axis hold altars and give the implication of a Greek cross to the plan. The entire body of the church is placed within a rectangle, and around the perimeter a service corridor encircles the structure.

The interior is a sequence of separate spaces with separate vaulting systems which are interconnected by torsion arches (arches whose thrust is divided directionally at the center) at their points of juncture. Movement through the church is one of expanding and contracting sequential spaces, dominated by the domed center. Above the convex piers, huge concave pendentives carry the Latin dome to a great height. The counter rhythm in the piers and pendentives is a familiar motif in Guarini's architecture, and the Gabel church resembles that architect's church of the same dedication, San Lorenzo in Turin. The plan and elevation of Hildebrandt's church also suggests the rich complexity of those by Borromini, particularly his Sant' Agnese in Piazza Navona with its octagonal core, high dome, and niche chapels.

The two-tower façade at Gabel has a three-bay central projection expressive of the interior narthex. Although the entry bay steps backward, no single section of the façade is heavily emphasized so that a flowing quality and a balance between horizontal and vertical elements are achieved.

Emperor Leopold I laid the cornerstone for the Saint Peter's Church in Vienna on April 22, 1702.

It was begun under the direction of the Italian engineer Gabriele Montani who made an early plan for it. By 1703, Montani was off the project and Hildebrandt appears to have reworked his ideas. The structure was completed enough by the spring of 1707 for contracts for the interior decorations to be negotiated. Franz Jänggle, Hildebrandt's building supervisor, continued construction on the building which because of monetary difficulties of the Trinity Brotherhood, its patron, was not completed until 1713–1717 when the cupola fresco was painted by Johann Michael Rottmayr and the high altar was completed by Antonio Galli-Bibiena (see GALLI DA BIBIENA FAMILY).

Saint Peter's façade resembles that of Saint Lawrence at Gabel, but, possibly because of site restrictions, the two towers splay outward and the central section is not so broad, and therefore a more vertical façade is achieved. The plan of Saint Peter's has a longitudinally placed oval at its center with six rectangular chapels along the sides. The chapels on the cross-axis are large and open; the other four chapels show similarities with the niche chapels at Gabel: they are smaller, have galleries and pendentives above them, but are without the counterrhythm between sections. The pendentives emphasize a cross shape in the interior and are punctuated by large oval windows; this may also have been Hildebrandt's original intention for Saint Lawrence where today these are suggested through oval paintings. The pendentive zone is structurally superfluous, like Borromini's at San Carlo alle quattro Fontane, as an oval cupola on a drum covers the oval congregational area. The rectangular narthex is flanked by the towers, while the choir, two separately vaulted rectangles, is flanked by sacristies. Reveted in bundled Composite pilasters and decorated in dark tones of red, grey, ochre, and gold, Saint Peter's interior remains one of the most splendid baroque church interiors of Vienna.

The teaching Order of the Piarists had been established since 1701 in the newly created suburb of Vienna, the Josefstadt, and in 1716, their large church, Maria Treu, was reported as being under construction. Built with the patronage of Emperor Leopold I, it was presumably designed by an imperial architect; this must have been Hildebrandt as the church so strongly resembles Saint Lawrence at Gabel. The emperor had admired the model for that church, and Hildebrandt's designs for Maria Treu were probably done around the same time, in 1698–1699.

Because of financial difficulties, construction on Maria Treu continued over several decades with Franz Jänggle supervising the work in the years 1716–1731. The last building phase, after Hildebrandt's death, was in 1750-1752, and was directed by Mathias Geri. At that time, a low domical vault, devoid of drum and windows as Hildebrandt had probably intended, was completed over the central space. An additional room was added to the choir and changes were made in its vaulting. The façade and towers were erected, but without the completion of their decoration.

The plan of Maria Treu is close to that of Saint Lawrence at Gabel except in the choir. Kilian Ignaz Dientzenhofer, while working in Vienna in 1725, drew the plans of both the Saint Peter's Church and Maria Treu, then under construction. Dientzenhofer's plan of Maria Treu, a variant of what exists today, suggests that Hildebrandt may himself have chosen the rectangular shape for the choir and that a vaulting scheme closer to his other churches was probably intended.

In the interior, the niche chapels are taller than at Saint Peter's and do not have the accompanying galleries and clear definition of the pendentive zone found in both earlier churches.

The outline of the Maria Treu façade, swelling forward at the center between two towers, appears to be by Hildebrandt, but the attribution of the decorative detailing is much debated. Today's dry and academic façade was not finished until 1858-1860 and was modeled on an engraving of 1724 by Salomon Kleiner.

In 1715, Hildebrandt participated in the imperial competition held for the design of the votive Karlskirche in Vienna, along with Johann Bernhard Fischer von Erlach and Ferdinando Galli da Bibiena (see GALLI DA BIBIENA FAMILY). As with most major court commissions, the elder Fischer won out over Hildebrandt, who had prepared plans and a wooden model for the church.

Among Hildebrandt's later churches are the Loretto Church (1715) at Göllersdorf, the Seminary Church of the German Order of Knights (1717) in Linz, and the plan for the large church and monastery (1719) at Göttweig. The Loretto Church at Göllersdorf was built on the Schönborn family estate to house a family burial chapel. Dedicated in 1715, the complex is comprised of a simple, rectangular, monastic tract connected to an octagonal church, a shape often associated with mortuary architecture. A rectangular choir is attached to the octagon on the side opposite the monastery. The austere exterior is articulated with lisens with only the choir carrying more decorative paired pilasters. The equally simple interior is also defined by pilasters and has a low cupola rising above it. Hildebrandt's four richly textured altars, placed on the diagonal walls, seem most representative of his design ideals in this subdued complex.

Called upon throughout his career to build parish churches by his aristocratic clients, including one at Pottendorf (1714-1717) for the Starhembergs, and at Stranzendorf (1733) and Göllersdorf (1740-1741) for the Schönborns, Hildebrandt chose in these churches to use simple plans, respecting the tradition of rectangular spatial envelopes with apsial closings that was familiar in parish church architecture in Austria and Germany. As Hildebrandt did not visit the sites of these smaller projects, the simplicity of his designs may also indicate a deference to provincial building habits and techniques.

On the façades at Pottendorf and Stranzendorf, Hildebrandt achieved a sense of monumentality seldom seen in parish churches by using the traditional element of the single tower. A large tower was set upon a square projecting narthex which, in turn, was amalgamated to the lower side portions of the façade with concave wall segments. The tremendous vertical thrust given the façade by the tower is thus tied to the building as a whole.

Twenty-five years after the Loretto Church, Hildebrandt was again working on a church for Göllersdorf. In 1740-1741, he renovated the Gothic parish church: reveting the interior with pilasters, changing the vaulting, and altering two chapels. The swelling cylindrical façade is the church's most striking exterior feature and imparts a baroque intensity to an otherwise classicizing renovation. A late work, the Göllersdorf Parish Church represents the duality apparent in Hildebrandt's late style, which tends to be dominated by cooler, more sedate treatments of space and decoration, but in which the architect could also revert to the spatial and decorative vocabulary used by him earlier.

Hildebrandt closely supervised the building of the small Seminary Church of the German Order of Knights (Deutsche Ritterorden) in Linz, Austria, commissioned by Count Franz Anton Harrach. Construction began in May 1717 under the direction of the Linz architect Johann Michael Prunner, and was concluded in 1725. The plan is a longitudinal oval, like his earlier Saint Peter's Church; there is a shallow high-altar niche and slight wall stepbacks on the other three sides. The rectangular narthex has an organ loft in its second story, and both rooms may be entered from the seminary to which the church is connected along one side. The church carries one of Hildebrandt's most elegant exterior designs. The curving front façade is tied to a single tower through large volutes, while pilasters, oval windows, and sculptural detailing play over all of the undulating exterior walls.

Had Hildebrandt's grand plan for the rebuilding of the Benedictine Monastery at Göttweig

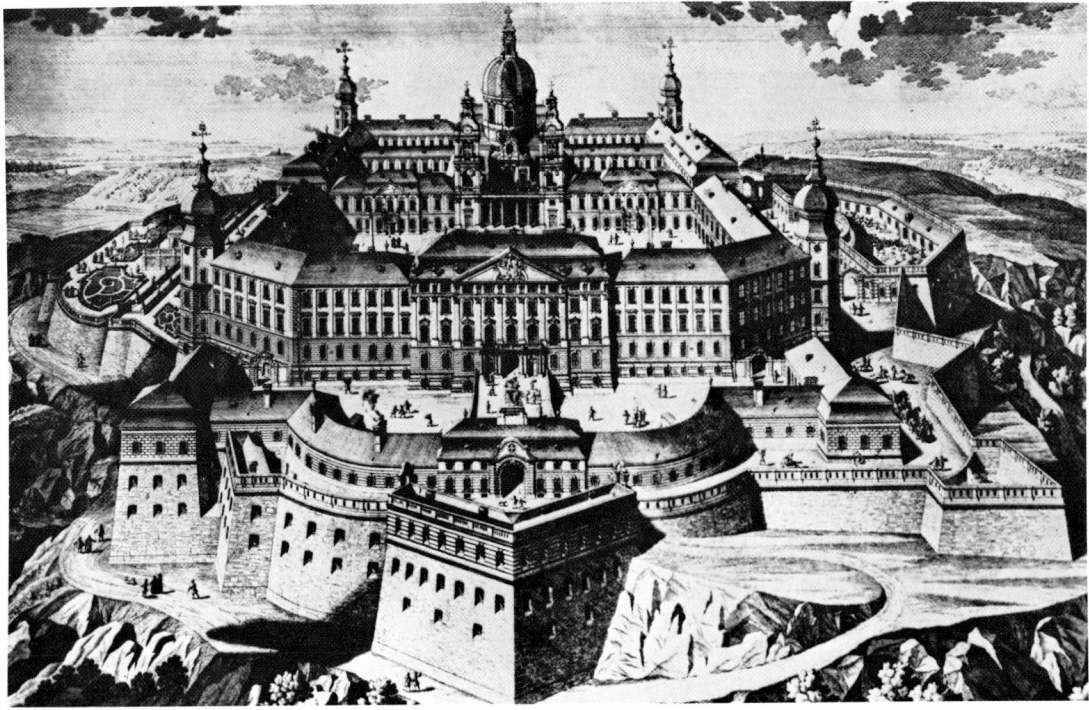

been completed, it would have rivaled JAKOB PRANDTAUER's monastery at Melk in scale and magnificence. The earlier monastery at Göttweig had been badly damaged by fire in 1718, and through Friedrich Carl von Schönborn, Hildebrandt was put in contact with the monastery's abbot, Dr. Gottfried Bessel. The architect presented drawings to him for new buildings in February 1719, and on the basis of these a contract was signed for an entirely new monastic complex on May 4, 1719; in July, building began.

Hildebrandt's ideas for the plan and exterior may be reconstructed through his drawings and an engraving by Salomon Kleiner. The complex, consisting of a large rectangular monastic block, had the church embedded within its center, reminiscent of the Escorial Monastery in Spain. It was to have dominated its hilltop site by being raised on a massive, fortresslike stone substructure. Entry to the main block would have been on the west through two outer forecourts placed on the longitudinal axis with the church. Across a broad inner court, the church would have been seen in the center of the monastic buildings and connected to them through horizontally placed wings flanking the façade.

Only the east and north monastic wings were ever completed, and a portion of the south wing and a fragment of the west wing also went up in the period of 1724–1739. Without the west wing, the church is not contained within the monastery as Hildebrandt intended, and it is today approached laterally from the south.

The choir and nave of the monastery's Gothic church, whose interior had been redone in the baroque style in the seventeenth century, were retained by Hildebrandt who planned to place a tall dome with a drum at the crossing and who redesigned the façade. A much simplified version of Hildebrandt's ideas for the façade and towers was erected in 1750–1765, with the classicizing five-bay central colonnade a part of the original conception. However, the accompanying towers are without their caps and no dome was ever built.

Only one of the major interior spaces Hildebrandt planned was ever built at Göttweig, a magnificent stairhall (1739), one of a pair originally projected to fill each of the beveled corners of the west building tract. From the inner court, the stairhall is entered through a loggia defined by Tuscan columns with a broad flight of stairs running along the wall at either side of the room. These flights turn toward the room's center at landings on the back wall where two short flights lead to the final single flight which runs back through the space of the room to reach the upper floor on the court side over the loggia. The entire stairhall is not perceived until the second landing when the broad expanse of the overhead vault covering the room and carrying an illusionistic fresco by Paul Troger (1738) is seen. Windows on three levels light the stairhall, illuminating the blind arches, terms, sculpture, and vases in niches which adorn the white walls of the room. The sheer size and financial magnitude of the Göttweig project precluded its completion, but artistic difficulties also arose between architect and client and played a part in the slow progress of construction and the eventual abandonment of Hildebrandt's scheme.

The Schreyvogel House, Breslau, Silesia, built in 1705, is the first large city house documented to Hildebrandt, although it was probably not the first one he built. His patron was a wealthy businessman, like many other clients for whom Hildebrandt later built houses in Vienna. These commissions constituted an avenue of bourgeois patronage for the architect that complemented that of the aristocracy and the imperial establishment. In scale and lavishness of exterior adornment, these houses imitate the city palaces of the aristocracy, but they did not vie with them in interior magnificence.

The Schreyvogel House stood on a corner lot, its four wings wrapped around an inner court. On the principal street façade, three main stories were divided into seven bays with the central three projecting slightly and defined by giant Composite pilasters above a banded lower story. Long attributed to Fischer von Erlach and related to his earlier Viennese palace façades, the Schreyvogel House is closer to Roman sources known to both architects, particularly Gianlorenzo Bernini's Chigi Palace, Rome (1664).

Hildebrandt was entrusted by 1702 with the interior decoration of the City Palace of Prince Eugen of Savoy, which had been built by Fischer von Erlach in 1696–1697. In 1708–1709, he was busy widening the palace to twelve bays on the street façade, apparently following Fischer's original conception, and in 1723–1724 he added another five bays.

In 1713–1716, with the construction of the splendid Daun-Kinsky City Palace, Hildebrandt was able to add something of his own invention to the rich fabric of city palaces in Vienna. Asked by Count Wirich Philipp Daun to design a palace for a narrow long tract of land, he accommodated a rectangular plan with two inner courts to the site. The structure has three stories plus a mezzanine story, but has only seven bays on the street façade. Hildebrandt, covered these with a sparkling array of decorative elements which stress the unification of the parts rather then their separation. The ground story is energetically defined by facets which serve as bases and appear to blend into the giant pilasters above them. These in turn flow upward toward the crowning balustrade, statues, and trophies. A slight *ressaut* occurs at the three central bays where tapered ornamented pilasters are used, but there is no real break in the flow across the wall surface.

The stairhall, fit into an oblong space in a wing, flows upward through two stories along an outside wall. The opposite stair wall, introduced by an atlante, is opened by arches and a fantastic scroll balustrade. A corridor on the court side leads to the second flight above which the stairhall opens overhead through another two stories where an encircling balcony on the mezzanine level frames an illusionistic ceiling fresco by Marcantonio Chiarinis. From the top corridor, lighted by large windows, the brilliant decorative program of the upper stairhall may be viewed.

The Austrian State Chancellery, which went up rather rapidly in the years 1717 to 1719, is one of Hildebrandt's few large commissions for the Hapsburg court. The brittle articulation of the exterior shows none of the brilliant manipulation of decorative devices characteristic of his other Viennese city palaces; it is probably reflective of court taste rather than Hildebrandt's own preferences.

In June 1723, a few months after Fischer von Erlach's death, Hildebrandt presented his extensive plans for renovations and additions to the deteriorating Hofburg Palace in Vienna to the imperial court (drawings, Albertina, Vienna). Again, he received a rebuff when his plans were turned down in preference to those of the Fischer von Erlachs—construction took place under the younger Fischer from 1726. As early as 1702, Hildebrandt had been paid for a model of the Hofburg, and contracts of 1709–1711 indicate that drawings by the architect were accepted. Hildebrandt's monumental Triumphal Arch Gateway was erected in 1699 between the Kohlmarkt and the inner Burghof section of the Hofburg. The younger Fischer, whom Hildebrandt despised, managed to include its demolition in his efforts of 1728; Hildebrandt's plans would have retained the Gateway.

Of the court projects that came regularly to Hildebrandt, many had to do with funerary arrangements and were largely sculptural, including several imperial sarcophagi. These works combined architectonic elements with emblemata, statues, and illuminations by dozens of candles.

The double garden palace, the Lower and Upper Belvedere built for Prince Eugen of Savoy on the Rennweg in Vienna, is Hildebrandt's largest, most opulent garden palace and remains, unlike most of his other work in this genre, reasonably well preserved. The palaces were constructed by Prince Eugen as a summer residence (Lower Belvedere) and to display his art collections and provide lavish entertainment (Upper Belvedere). Over 200 of his collection of 400 paintings came to be housed in two galleries in the Upper Belvedere, along with sculpture, both antique and contemporary, and part of his enormous library.

Brought up in the shadow of Versailles court life, Prince Eugen remained a Francophile in terms

Hildebrandt.
*The Belvederes (engraving
by Salomon Kleiner).
Vienna.*

property and the Mansfeld-Fondi Palace, and a separate garden was developed for it running parallel to the main garden.

Between 1731 and 1740, Salomon Kleiner prepared a set of engravings, *Wunderwürdiges Kriegs- und Siegslager oder Abbildungen der Hoff- Lust- und Gartengebäude Eugenii Francisci,* which set forth Prince Eugen's many building projects and in particular the Belvedere Palaces as they originally appeared. Judging from them, the exterior of the Lower Belvedere remains unchanged; however, on the interior, alterations occurred in the eighteenth century so that today the principal rooms remaining intact are the marble salon, the marble cabinet, the frescoed salon, and the marble gallery.

Several areas on the exterior of the Upper Belvedere that were originally open have been enclosed. On the garden side, the five entries of the middle *ressaut* and the doors on the corner pavilion have been covered with glass and decorative iron work. Four open round-arched entries on the ground floor wings, seen in a drawing, were changed into windows. On the court side, the five entries on the vestibule were glazed and given decorative iron work in the nineteenth century, and because of this Hildebrandt's entry ramp was pushed forward to a position in front of the vestibule rather than passing directly through it, in the manner of the ramp on the Mansfeld-Fondi Palace. Still in their original state among the principal rooms of the Upper Belvedere are the *sala terrena,* the stairhall, the marble salon, the chapel, and two of the cabinets of the corner towers.

The garden remains unaltered in outline, but important sculpture has been removed. The menagerie, formerly on the east side of the Upper Belvedere, has been destroyed, while the orangerie with its separate garden is greatly altered.

The principal entrance to the Lower Belvedere Palace is from the Rennweg. The palace runs the width of the garden as the site was regularized and defined as an oblong to accomplish the symmetry and axiality customary to a baroque garden. The garden lies completely enclosed between the Lower Belvedere and the Upper Belvedere which stands at the top of the sloping terrain. A triangular court to the south of the Upper Belvedere is the formal entrance to that palace from a road which runs along the far side of the Mansfeld-Fondi Garden Palace. This entrance, used principally on the occasion of festive gatherings, has a huge reflecting pool in its center. Optically, one's first perception of the Upper Belvedere, from the upper court side, is across a *miroir d'eau.* The projecting entry vestibule, defined by arched openings, horizontal oval windows, terms, decorative sculpture, and a free-standing gable, was originally a *porte cochère,* so

of architectural taste. Louis XIV refused Prince Eugen's request to enter the king's military service because of enmity toward his mother, so that at age twenty he went to the Hapsburg Emperor Leopold I from whom he received a military commission. Before his fortieth birthday, Prince Eugen became president of the Imperial War Council and, together with the duke of Marlborough, resoundingly defeated the troops of Louis XIV at Blenheim. The Belvedere Palaces incorporate into their iconography many episodes from his eventful life.

Prince Eugen purchased land along the Rennweg east of the Mansfeld-Fondi Garden Palace in 1693 and began terracing for a garden. In 1704, the outline of the Lower Belvedere appeared on a city map which Hildebrandt had helped prepare. The palace was constructed on the architect's plans in the years 1713–1715 with the interiors completed by 1716. In 1717, the landscape specialist Dominique Girard, a pupil of ANDRÉ LE NOSTRE, was called from service in Munich to develop the gardens. The Upper Belvedere Palace was begun in 1721 and completed in 1725. The map of 1704 makes clear that the Upper Belvedere Palace was not envisaged in the first building phase and that the garden was to have been closed with a simple belvedere, not a palace. An orangerie (1716) was placed along the north side of the awkwardly shaped triangular section between Prince Eugen's

that the entire stairhall would have been the visitor's introduction to the Upper Belvedere's interior spaces.

At the Lower Belvedere entrance along the Rennweg, a magnificent three-portal gate carrying the cross of Savoy in its transparent gable, is set into a generous concave curve of wall. Because of the exigencies of site, Hildebrandt created a closed pentagonal courtyard by bending the arms of his usual U-shaped garden palace plan.

The wings and main court façade, except for a central *ressaut* of seven bays, are two-storied structures simply defined by lisens and drafted surfaces. Their simplicity is in contrast to the lavishly articulated seven-bay *ressaut* whose three central bays also carry a second story. On the *ressaut's* ground floor, tall rectangular windows fill the space between paired pilasters. The decorative detailing is carried out in carved stone adding a coloristic interest to the pale ivory of the building's painted plaster surfaces. The architect's idiosyncratic decorative vocabulary enlivens the second-story pilasters and the roofline before the three separate mansard roofs. Hildebrandt subtly graded all of the court roofs for height and complexity to culminate in the roof of the central *ressaut,* an idea repeated in the Upper Belvedere and characteristic of his garden palace designs. The courtyard is a subdued prelude to the wealth of decoration and flowing interconnected spaces to be encountered along the sightline which begins with the entry gate and continues through the single door of the central *ressaut* into the garden and upper palace at its end.

The main orientation of the Lower Belvedere's interiors is toward the garden, with three of the original principal rooms—the square marble salon and the two rectangular lateral galleries—extending through the entire width of the building. The two-story marble salon is reveted with dusky red marbles on the floor, the pilasters, and the ornate fireplace chimneys. On the walls, illusionistic architectural paintings by Gaetao Fanis combine with plastic stucco military trophies alluding to

Prince Eugen's triumphs in that field. The ceiling fresco by Martin Altomonte, "The Allegory of the Investiture of Prince Eugen by Pope Clement XI" (1716), expands the personal aspects of the iconographic program, which is analogous to programs usually reserved for monarchs in the baroque period.

Hildebrandt's rich decorative schemes continue in the other rooms of the palace. The marble gallery combines delicate red and white stucco patterns and large niches containing marble statues of the Olympian deities. Mirrors fill the end walls of the room, illusionistically extending its space, as they also do in the mirror room where they reflect Prince Eugen's porcelain collection.

The garden façade of the Lower Belvedere is intimate in character, despite its great length. A luminous clarity, variety, elegance, and rapport with nature make it one of Hildebrandt's finest exteriors. It is divided centrally by a seven-bay *ressaut* identical to that on the court side. Low wings terminating in pavilions flow outward from this center and are separately roofed. The building appears to hug the ground with the flowing quality of the elevation achieved through large rectangular windows. Only a thin tissue of wall exists between each window so that Hildebrandt essentially dissolved the barrier between interior and garden.

The garden leading uphill to the Upper Belvedere has two principal fountains along its main axis. At the first of these, there is a steep upward step in the terrain and a directional change occurs leading to broad paths at the sides which are lined with sculpture. A return to the main axis leads into a sunken parterre, enclosed on three sides with grassy slopes. From this parterre the two palaces are subtly connected through optical devices which provide a unique moment in the experience of the total design of the palaces and gardens. The Upper Belvedere appears above a stepped, cascaded fountain which optically forms a pedestal upon which the palace seems to float. The Upper Belvedere is transformed at this point into a lower palace type, closer to the Lower Belvedere, by the visual elimination of the ground story, an illusionistic device stemming from Andre Le Nostre's garden designs.

Entering the garden from the Lower Belvedere, one passes through low floral parterres, succeeded by high basket gardens, and thus views the Upper Belvedere in its entire length, a high, massive structure. In the sunken parterre, a more intimate view of the palace, seen now in detail, is achieved. The green patina of the palace's many copper-sheathed roof sections, its roof sculpture, and filials all play, like a fantastic mirage, against the sky. As one reverses direction to exit the sunken parterre, the central *ressaut* of the Lower Belvedere comes into view, but with its wings hidden by the basket gardens. It too has undergone a transformation — to a garden pavilion.

The intricate iconographic program of the garden and palaces was expanded in the fountain sculpture of the sunken parterre. Around the cascade, sculptures of Hercules and Apollo appeared as dual symbolic aspects of Prince Eugen's personality — the powerful conqueror of foes and the great protector of the arts and sciences. On the upper terrace of the garden, statues of Jupiter and Juno stand before the gleaming modern Olympus, the Upper Belvedere, which crowns the slope and looks down upon the Viennese capital.

The central ceremonial rooms of the Upper Belvedere are entered directly from the garden. In plan a long rectangular block, the two-story palace rises to three stories at the center. Projecting from the garden façade is a pavilion with beveled corners, and from the court side, a rectangular vestibule protrudes, while octagonal tower pavilions close all four corners of the building. The *sala terrena,* stairhall, and monumental marble salon are at the building's core with the wings, in the enfilade system, composed of rectangular rooms of varying sizes in two rows.

On the exterior, the ground story is horizontally drafted and has rusticated stone window and door surrounds with dropped keystones. Such mannerist decorative devices recur frequently as part of Hildebrandt's vocabulary of ornament. On the garden façade, the five-bay pavilion is richly encrusted with the architect's eccentric surface ornamentation.

From the garden, the principal rooms of the Upper Belvedere are entered through the *sala terrena* which, with its four giant atlantes at the room's center, is a kind of sculptural gallery preceding the unfolding of the painting and sculpture collections in the rooms above. Subdued in color, it is white as is the stairhall, but it is exuberant in decorative detail. The walls are covered with stucco designs which open in the center of the low sail vaults into narrative scenes.

From the broad expanse of the *sala terrena,* a single, contracted, and dimly lighted staircase in the center of the back wall leads to the vestibule and stairhall on the court side of the palace. This brilliantly lighted, sumptuously decorated room is fully perceived only with a reversal of direction at the first landing where the stair divides and continues up the outside walls. In the stairhall, giant terms support the springing of the vault, and marble putti cavort about the huge lanterns of the stair balustrade. The marble salon, reveted with giant paired pilasters, has an illusionistic fresco with an allegory of victory on its ceiling vault. The marble salon of the Upper Belvedere completes the imagined Olympian climb, which has revealed, through the conquest of space, the beauties of art and combined them with the glorious deeds of the patron to yield an eternal paradisical image.

The Belvedere Palaces passed into the hands of Prince Eugen's sole heir, a niece, at his death. She sold them, along with great portions of the prince's art collections and library, to the imperial family in 1752. As part of the patrimony of Austria's illustrious baroque period in art, the Belvedere Palaces are preserved today as museums.

In 1725, Prince Eugen bought the Estate of Hoff with its seventeenth-century palace on the River March and provided Hildebrandt with an opportunity to create his most grandiose garden scheme (1725–1732). Hildebrandt added two wings to the older Schlosshof Palace to create a *cour d'honneur,* embellished the interiors, and built a chapel. In a highly original way, he then tied the palace in the center of the plan to the landscape through an ingenious system of stone terraces, curving stairways, balustrades, fountains, and gates. Only architectural remnants remain of the Schlosshof garden which, like so much of Hildebrandt's work, must be studied through engravings.

At about the same time (c.1725–1730), Hildebrandt designed the exquisite small Garden House for the Palace at Siebenbrunn in Lower Austria for Prince Eugen. A horizontal oval in plan with free-flowing walls, the centralized space has a domical covering and an oval mansard roof. The exterior doors, one on all four sides, and the round-headed windows between them are separated by Ionic pilasters. The doors and window surrounds are adorned with a tracery of stucco decorations.

Hildebrandt's work at the Mirabell Palace in Salzburg (1721–1727) has been much altered and portions were destroyed in a fire in 1818. However, enough fragments — the garden façade, the stair, and the marble hall — remain to suggest the beauty of the original conceptions which may be reconstructed from Hildebrandt's drawings and the engravings by Johann August Corvinus. Hildebrandt had already designed the interiors of the Residence of the Archbishop Franz Anton Harrach in Salzburg (1709–1710), when he was again called upon by that patron in 1721 to provide drawings for renovations and additions to the Mirabell Palace. These included designs for the garden and court façades, a marble hall, a chapel, a stairway, and the garden. In 1722, the old stair was destroyed, and the new one, with an open central cone, was erected and provided with one of Hildebrandt's most brilliant carved balustrades with sculpted putti by Raphael Donner. Hildebrandt was commissioned to enlarge, modernize in the baroque style, and add gardens to many of the landed estates of his aristocratic clients. Schlosshof for Prince Eugen, the Harrach Estates in Bruck-an-der-Leitha and Halbthurn in Burgenland, and the Schönborn Estate near Göllersdorf were such projects. In all cases, Hildebrandt began from a core of older structures and sought to embellish them and to integrate them through gardens with the surrounding landscape. Successful in all cases, Hildebrandt's conceptions were destroyed when subsequent changes in taste dictated new arrangements. Engravings by the busy Salomon Kleiner again help in partial reconstructions of the original compositions.

The Harrach Estate at Halbthurn in Burgenland had been destroyed by the Turks and was rebuilt from designs by Hildebrandt in 1701–1711. The main palace is a long rectangular block with pavilions on either end. The garden façade has a central *ressaut* of three accented bays crowned by a gable, in a treatment close to the later garden façade at Werneck Palace (c.1735). The *cour d'honneur* was originally entered from the side, and ancillary structures detached from the main block formed two large courts on the longitudinal axis with it.

At the Harrach Estate in Bruck-an-der-Leitha (1707–1711), as seen in an engraved bird's-eye-view, only the garden façade could be made symmetrical due to the sprawling array of older buildings. Yet, Hildebrandt's addition of decorative detailing in the *cour d'honneur* helped to balance and harmonize all parts of the main structure.

Over several decades, Hildebrandt poured much effort into designs for the estate of Friedrich Carl von Schönborn near Göllersdorf after his purchase of the property in 1710. In 1712, the older palace was restored, and by 1713, twelve rooms had been redecorated following elegant designs by Hildebrandt. Two pavilions were added to the U-plan palace in 1713 and the garden was under construction. In that year, MAXIMILIAN VON WELSCH was consulted on the garden water works and the projected orangerie, which he suggested be put in the center of the garden. Instead, Hildebrandt's orangerie, composed of two courts, one with convex wings, was built at the end of the garden.

The palace has been greatly altered with only the chapel remaining of the interior decor. Hildebrandt's rich central gable on the garden façade still stands, but his huge garden layout was destroyed. Through its baroque radial plan, the house and garden were spatially interrelated to one another and to adjacent landscaped gardens. The layout proceeded from a huge forecourt through palace, garden, and orangerie to a back-court, in a manner analogous to the solution at the Belvedere Palaces.

With the beautiful Shrine of Saint John of Nepomuk (1733) Hildebrandt brought to a close his long association with the construction of the Schönborn estate at Göllersdorf. He placed the shrine, an open ciborium, in the landscape on the chief axis with the *cour d'honneur* of the palace. A statue of the saint stands beneath the canopy on a stone altar. Again, as so often in his past work, Hildebrandt achieved an interrelationship between architectural works through landscape, with each element maintaining its distinct character but also fulfilling part of the grand plan.

Hildebrandt's name is associated with many projects for the Franconian branch of the Schönborn family, among them the Würzburg Residence, the Schönborn Chapel of Würzburg Cathedral, a project for the Würzburg Cathedral façade, and Werneck Palace, but the only work to be built entirely from his designs is the great stair pavilion in the Weissenstein Palace at Pommersfelden (1711–1713). The palace, built on a family estate by Elector Lothar Franz von Schönborn, archbishop of Mainz and bishop of Bamberg, whose nephew, Friedrich Carl von Schönborn, was an active participant in the planning process. Lothar Franz's architect was Johann Dientzenhofer (see DIENTZENHOFER BROTHERS) and the rest of the palace is attributed to him. However, Friedrich Carl seems to have insisted from the beginning that his architect, Hildebrandt, design the central stairhall because Dientzenhofer's contract specifically excluded that portion of the structure.

Hildebrandt's major activity for Pommersfelden occurred in 1713 when he presented his ideas for the monumental central pavilion housing the stair on the court side, and on the garden side, the *sala terrena* on ground level and the Imperial Hall on the *piano nobile*. A major achievement in eighteenth-century staircase design, it was carried out in 1714–1715 with the decoration of the ceil-

Hildebrandt.
Weissenstein Palace
(stairhall).
Pommersfelden, Germany.
1711–1715

ing frescoes of the Imperial Hall by Johann Michael Rottmayr; the stairhall by Rudolf Byss followed in 1717.

In 1713, Maximilian von Welsch was also brought into the planning activity at Pommersfelden to work mainly on the gardens and stables. This collective planning strategy in which the patrons were active participants typifies the Schönborn family's approach to building. Unfortunately, the contributions of individual architects have often been obscured by this process. Hildebrandt's name disappears from the building correspondence in 1714, nonetheless the attribution of the central pavilion to him is secure. Hildebrandt's many drawings for the project have not survived, but an engraved series on Pommersfelden done in 1728 by Salomon Kleiner indicates the structure's original appearance.

The monumental rectangular central pavilion has concave corners and boldly projects on the garden and court side of the U-plan palace. The stairhall rises the entire three stories of the structure with a double stairway running in three separate flights around its center. A corridor on the ground floor and balconies on the upper stories encircle the room on all four sides. A coved vault decorated with an illusionistic fresco covers the generous expanse over the stair. Upon entry from the *cour d'honneur,* the entire room immediately opens to the viewer in a manner which is exceptional in Hildebrandt's oeuvre. A *sala terrena,*

called the "grotto," and the garden are entered by passing directly through the center of the stairhall. The complicated iconography of the decorative program, which celebrates the election of Charles VI to be Holy Roman Emperor, and the role that the Schönborn family, particularly Lothar Franz, played in this event, gradually unfolds as the main rooms and garden are experienced.

The central stairway climbs to a landing that serves as a podium from which the ceiling fresco and stairhall may again be viewed. The balconies which are strikingly lighted on three sides, give an airy, skeletal quality to the upper reaches of the room. Behind the upper landing, a centralized vestibule serves as an interlude before the Imperial Hall is entered. The vestibule is created by the convex curve of the wall and by a richly decorated oval cove vault through whose open oculus a fresco and sculpture on the third level may be seen.

The outline of the Imperial Hall, with eight freestanding columns on podia and pilasters defining the walls, remains unchanged, but the gallery of Schönborn family portraits together with those of Emperor Charles VI and his wife Elisabeth Christina have been removed.

The monumental stairhall, the disposition of the rooms, and the bold projection of the pavilion at Pommersfelden affected the architecture of JOHANN BALTHASAR NEUMANN, particularly in the Würzburg Residence and Werneck Palace in whose creation Hildebrandt was an active participant.

Hildebrandt's contributions to projects for the Residence at Würzburg, on which he worked from its inception, are difficult to define and have been variously appraised by historians. The newly elected bishop of Würzburg, Johann Philipp Franz von Schönborn, began in 1719 to plan alterations on a palace on the outskirts of the town. In the same year, Hildebrandt was in Würzburg presenting plans for this structure which eventually became the entirely new palace and garden, the Residence (1720–1753). This great project was run from the Schönborn power centers in Vienna, Mainz, and Würzburg. The matter of individual artists' contributions is clouded by the rivalry that seems to have begun immediately between Balthasar Neumann and Hildebrandt. Nineteen years Neumann's senior, Hildebrandt was highly respected as the builder of one great stairhall for the Schönborns, at Pommersfelden, and he seems to have been occupied with that aspect of the planning. When Friedrich Carl von Schönborn was named prince-bishop of Würzburg in 1719, at the death of his brother, Hildebrandt's design activities were intensified until 1738 when a break occurred between him and Neumann over the stairhall. Hildebrandt's ground plan is not extant and so his ideas on the interior spatial disposition are hard to determine. Hildebrandt visited Würzburg several times, but Neumann, continually at the site, appears to have had the final word on many important questions involving the plan and its dimensions. Other architects, including Johann Dientzenhofer, Maximilian von Welsch, ROBERT DE COTTE, and GERMAIN BOFFRAND, were consulted and made contributions to the project, so that the Würzburg Residence emerges as one of the great collective works of the eighteenth century. Elements of the building's decoration, both interior and exterior, bear the stamp of Hildebrandt's individualistic style, as seen in the chapel and the cour d'honneur. The handling of forms, in the garden pavilion, the stairhall, and elsewhere, also suggest the influence of Hildebrandt.

Hildebrandt was again teamed with Balthasar Neumann in the planning of a Schönborn project, the Werneck Palace in Franconia for Prince-Bishop Friedrich Carl von Schönborn. In 1731 and again in 1733, Neumann was required to send plans for the palace to Hildebrandt in Vienna for inspection. Neumann's plans of 1733 were accepted in all essentials except for the palace's central pavilion which held the stair. Neumann was called to a building conference in Vienna in 1734 and construction was begun in the same year. Hildebrandt's influence pertained primarily to the enlargement of the stair, a tighter grouping of the principal rooms and to the decoration of the interiors. The two towers in the corners of the cour d'honneur, similar to those at the Schönborn Garden Palace in Vienna and to those at Göllersdorf, indicate Hildebrandt's participation while the projection of the pavilion on the garden façade also stems from his conceptions.

Hildebrandt's architectural achievements represent that remarkable synthesis of elements from several architectural vocabularies, the Italian, French, and Austrian, that was uniquely possible in the late baroque period. His earliest efforts on reaching Vienna, e.g. the Mansfeld-Fondi Garden Palace and Saint Lawrence at Gabel in particular are full of references to Italian architecture and landscape design, particularly of the mannerist and baroque periods, and these are never totally lost. The architecture of Palladio, Vignola, Borromini, Guarini, Fontana, and others had obviously been influential in his education.

Soon after the turn of the century, Hildebrandt began to move to a mature style which was deliberately nonclassicizing, perhaps spurred by his rivalry with Fischer von Erlach whose architecture represented that position and was the official language chosen by the imperial court, which habitually neglected him. Hildebrandt's architecture of this period seems moved by non-Italian sources in a decisive way, particularly from France, but also from Austrian architecture which he was coming to know quite intimately from his travels to the landed estates of his aristocratic clients.

Such clients as Prince Eugen, desired a less formal, more intimate approach to architecture for the palaces they built for their own pleasure. For these clients, Hildebrandt developed the garden palace type along original lines, stressing the rich definition of the corps de logis with its focus on the stairhall and grand salon. His diverse solutions to the problem of the stairhall, one of the great preoccupations of eighteenth-century architecture, drew upon his knowledge of the great Genoese palaces of the sixteenth century with their elaborate stairways. But at Pommersfelden, the Daun-Kinsky Palace, the Upper Belvedere, and the monastery stairhall at Göttweig, Hildebrandt added his own brillant insights into questions of scale, lighting, and the combination of architectonic elements with decorative elements of sculpture and painting. As a landscape architect, Hildebrandt sought the interrelationship of garden and house through a flowing longitudinal design in which boundaries between the parts are subtly dissolved, but never completely.

Hildebrandt's designs for decorative ornamentation of a rich, elegant, and often eccentric type were well-suited to the refined taste of his age and led him to original solutions both for the articulation of interiors and for exteriors, as in his beguiling and witty city palace façade for the Daun-Kinsky Palace. Born in Italy, Hildebrandt has come to be perceived as the most Viennese of architects of the eighteenth century.

BEVERLY HEISNER

WORKS

1697–1715, Mansfeld-Fondi Garden Palace (later Schwarzenberg Palace; later completed by Johann Bernard Fischer von Erlach and Johann Emanuel Fischer von Erlach); 1698–1699/1716–1746, Church of Maria Treu (not completed until 1751 by Mathias Gerl) 1699, Triumphal Arch Gateway, Kohlmarkt; Vienna. 1699–1711, Dominican Church of Saint Lawrence, Gabel, Bohemia. 1701–1711, 1722, Harrach Estate, Halbthurn, Burgenland, Austria. 1701–1717, Ráckeve Palace, Czepel, Hungary. 1702, 1708–1709, 1723–1724, City Palace of Prince Eugen of Savoy (interiors and additions); 1703, Sarcophagus for the Archduchess Maria Josefa, Capucine Church; (A)1703–1717, Saint Peter's Church; Vienna. 1704–1709, Loretto Chapel, Rumburg, Bohemia. 1705, Castrum doloris for Leopold I, Augustine Church, Vienna. *1705, Schreyvogel House, Breslau, Silesia. 1705–1706, Starhemberg-Schönburg Garden Palace (not completed until 1711 by Franz Jänggle; interior not completed until 1721 by others);

1705–1711, Schönborn Garden Palace; Vienna. 1707–1711, Harrach Estate, Bruck-an-der-Leitha, Austria. 1709–1710, Archbishop's Residence, Salzburg, Austria. *1709–1711, Harrach Estate, Aschach-an-der-Donau, Austria. *1711, Liechtenstein Estate, Guntramsdorf, Austria. (A)1711–1715, Weissenstein Palace (stair pavilion and central pavilion), Pommersfelden, Germany. 1712, Sarcophagus of Joseph I, Capucine Church, Vienna. 1712–1717, Schönborn Estate, Göllersdorf, Austria. 1713–1716, Daun-Kinsky City Palace; 1713–1716, Garden Palace, Lower Belvedere; Vienna. 1714–1717, Parish Church, Pottendorf, Austria. 1715, Church of Maria Loretto, Göllersdorf, Austria. c.1715–1725, Schönborn Chapel, Würzburg, Germany. 1717, Seminary Church of the German Order of Knights, Linz, Austria. 1717–1719, Austrian State Chancellery, Vienna. 1719, 1724–1739, Monastery of Göttweig (east and north wings and stairhall), Austria. 1719–1738, Prince-Bishop's Residence, Würzburg, Germany. 1720, Bartolotti von Partenfeld House, Vienna. 1720–1725, Poor House and Soldier's Hospital, Alser, Austria. 1721–1725, Garden Palace, Upper Belvedere, Vienna. 1721–1727, Mirabell Palace (later altered), Salzburg, Austria, 1724, Parish Church, Georgswalde, Bohemia. *1725, Saint John of Nepomuk Shrine, Augarten Bridge, Vienna. c.1725–1730, Garden House, Siebenbrunn Palace, Austria. 1725–1732, Schlosshof Estate, Marchfeld, Austria. 1727, Parish Church, Seelowitz, Moravia. 1727–1730, 1734–1735, Harrach Garden Palace; 1730, House, 3 Tiefer Graben; 1730, Merklein House; 1730, Teubelhof House; Vienna. 1731, Marian Column, Göllersdorf, Austria. 1732–1745, Werneck Palace (with Johann Balthasar Neumann), Germany. 1733, Parish Church, Aspersdorf, Austria. 1733, Parish Church, Stratzendorf, Austria. 1733, Saint John of Nepomuk Shrine, Schönborn Estate, Göllersdorf, Austria. 1736, Castrum doloris for Prince Eugen of Savoy. 1740–1741, Parish Church, Göllersdorf, Austria. Before 1746, Monastery of Klosterbruck, near Znaim, Austria.

BIBLIOGRAPHY

AURENHAMMER, HANS 1955 "Ikonographie und Ikonologie des Wiener Belvederegartens." *Wiener Jahrbuch für Kunstgeschichte* 17:86–108.

AURENHAMMER, HANS 1973 *J. B. Fischer von Erlach.* London: Allen Lane.

BRINCKMANN, ALBERT E. 1932 *Von Guarino Guarini bis Balthasar Neumann.* Berlin: Deutscher Verein für Kunstwissenschaft.

FRANZ, HEINRICH GERHARD 1943 *Studien zur Barockarchitektur in Böhmen und Mähren.* Brno, Czechoslovakia: Rohrer.

FRANZ, HEINRICH GERHARD 1962 *Bauten und Baumeister der Barockzeit in Böhmen.* Leipzig: Seeman.

FREEDEN, MAX HERMAN VON 1952 *Residenz Würzburg.* Munich: Deutscher Kunstverlag.

FREEDEN, MAX HERMAN VON (1953)1963 *Balthasar Neumann, Leben und Werk.* 2d ed., rev. Munich: Deutscher Kunstverlag.

GRIMSCHITZ, BRUNO 1924 *Johann Lucas von Hildebrandts Kirchenbauten.* Vienna: Wiener Jahrbuch für Kunstgeschichte Sonderdruck.

GRIMSCHITZ, BRUNO 1944 *Wiener Barockpäläste.* Vienna: Wiener.

GRIMSCHITZ, BRUNO 1946 *Das Belvedere in Wien.* Vienna: Wolfrum.

GRIMSCHITZ, BRUNO 1959 *Johann Lucas von Hildebrandt.* Vienna: Herold.

HAGER, WERNER 1942 *Die Bauten des deutschen Barocks: 1690–1770.* Jena, Germany: Diederichs.

HAUTTMANN, MAX 1921 *Geschichte der kirchlichen Baukunst in Bayern, Schwaben und Franken: 1550–1780.* Munich: Schmidt.

HEGEMANN, HANS W. 1943 *Die deutsche Barockbaukunst Böhmens.* Munich: Bruckmann.

HEMPEL, EBERHARD 1965 *Baroque Art and Architecture in Central Europe.* Baltimore: Penguin.

HOFMANN, WALTER 1968 *Schloss Pommersfelden.* Nuremberg, Germany: Carl.

KELLER, HARALD 1936 "Das Treppenhaus im deutschen Schloss- und Klosterbau des Barock." Unpublished Ph.D. dissertation, University of Munich.

KERBER, OTTMAR 1947 *Von Bramante zu Lucas von Hildebrandt.* Stuttgart, Germany: Kohlhammer.

KNOPP, NORBERT 1966 *Das Garten-Belvedere.* Munich: Deutscher Kunstverlag.

McKAY, DEREK 1977 *Prince Eugene of Savoy.* London: Thames & Hudson.

SEDLMAIER, RICHARD, and PFISTER, RUDOLF 1923 *Die Fürstbischöfliche Residenz zu Würzburg.* Munich: Müller.

SEDLMAYR, HANS 1930 *Österreichische Barockarchitektur: 1690–1740.* Vienna: Filser.

SEDLMAYR, HANS (1956)1976 *Johann Bernhard Fischer von Erlach.* 2d ed., rev. Vienna: Herold.

WAGNER-RIEGER, RENATE 1955 "Die Piaristenkirche in Wien." *Wiener Jahrbuch für Kunstgeschichte* 17:49–62.

WENZEL, WERNER 1970 *Die Gärten des Lothar Franz von Schönborn.* Berlin: Mann.

HILDRITH, ISSAC

Issac Hildrith (c.1741–1807) was born in Ellerton, Yorkshire, England. His education included training in carpentry and construction. In 1770, he emigrated to Norfolk, Virginia, joined the Loyalist cause, and finally settled in Shelburne, Nova Scotia, in 1783. There, he designed and built Christ Church (1788–1789). In 1798, he became architect and master builder of the new Government House, a ROBERT ADAM inspired dwelling, taken from G. RICHARDSON, *A Series of Original Designs.*

GARRY D. SHUTLAK

WORKS

1788–1789, Christ Church, Shelburne, Nova Scotia. 1798–1807, Government House, Halifax, Nova Scotia.

BIBLIOGRAPHY

FERGUSSON, CHARLES B. 1970–1971 "Issac Hildrith

(c.1741–1807): Architect of Government House, Halifax." *Dalhousie Review* 51:510–516.

MARTELL, JAMES 1965 *The Romance of Government House.* Reprint. Halifax, Nova Scotia: Queen's Printer.

RICHARDSON, G. 1795 *A Series of Original Designs.* London.

ROBERTSON, MARION 1970 "Issac Hildrith—a Shelburne Loyalist." *Nova Scotia Museums Quarterly* 1:18–21.

HIORNE, FRANCIS

Francis Hiorne (1744–1789) was the eldest son of the architect–builder WILLIAM HIORNE. He was notable as a Gothic architect although he did produce two classical churches, Saint Anne's, Belfast, Ireland (completed 1776), and Saint Bartholomew's, Tardebigge, Worcestershire (1777).

Apart from the triangular Hiorne's Tower (c.1787) in the park of Arundel Castle, Sussex, Hiorne's Gothic works are churches, the most notable ones being his rebuilding of Saint Giles', Stony Stratford, Buckinghamshire (1776–1777), and Saint Mary's, Tetbury, Gloucestershire (1777–1781). Both are hall churches with wooden clustered piers supporting plaster ribbed vaults. They epitomize the light, elegant sophistication of late eighteenth-century Gothic before the advent of scholarship and correctness.

JAMES MACAULAY

WORKS

*Completed 1776, Saint Anne's Church, Belfast. 1776–1777, Saint Giles' Church (rebuildilng), Stony Stratford, Buckinghamshire, England. 1777, Saint Bartholomew's Church, Tardebigge, Worcestershire, England. 1777–1781, Saint Mary's Church, Tetbury, Gloucestershire, England. c.1787, Hiorne's Tower, Arundel Castle, Sussex, England. c.1787, Saint Peter's Chapel, East Gate, Warwick, England.

BIBLIOGRAPHY

CLARK, KENNETH (1928)1974 *The Gothic Revival.* Rev. ed. New York: Harper.

DAVIS, TERENCE 1974 *The Gothick Taste.* Newton Abbot, England: David & Charles.

EASTLAKE, CHARLES L. (1872)1970 *A History of the Gothic Revival.* Edited with an introduction by J. Mordaunt Crook. England: Leicester University Press.

PEVSNER, NIKOLAUS (1960)1973 *The Buildings of England: Buckinghamshire.* Reprint. Harmondsworth, England: Penguin.

PEVSNER, NIKOLAUS 1968 *The Buildings of England: Worcestershire.* Harmondsworth, England: Penguin.

PEVSNER, NIKOLAUS, and WEDGWOOD, ALEXANDRA 1966 *The Buildings of England: Warwickshire.* Harmondsworth, England: Penguin.

VEREY, DAVID (1970)1974 *The Cotswolds.* Volume 1 in *The Buildings of England: Gloucestershire.* Reprint. Harmondsworth, England: Penguin.

WHIFFEN, MARCUS 1944 "In the Modern Gothic Manner." *Architectural Review* 96, July: 2–4.

HIORNE, WILLIAM, and HIORNE, DAVID

William Hiorne (c.1712–1776) and David Hiorne (?–1758) were probably assistants of FRANCIS SMITH and William Smith and took over their Warwick practice on William Smith's death in 1747, acting throughout Midland England as both masons and architects. Most of their known work is Palladian (see ANDREA PALLADIO) and sometimes strongly derivative (the swagger Foremark Hall [1759–1761], for example, is based on ISAAC WARE's Wrotham Park). Arbury Hall (1748–1755) is a notably early and competent essay in Gothick, influenced doubtless by SANDERSON MILLER and completed by HENRY KEENE. In church design they leaned heavily on JAMES GIBBS, but the steeple at Great Houghton (1754) suggests a provincial THOMAS ARCHER. William's son Francis continued the practice.

ANDOR GOMME

WORKS

1748–1755, Arbury Hall; *1749–1750, Saint Batholomew's Church, Birmingham; Warwickshire, England. 1752–1758, Holy Cross Church, Daventry, Northamptonshire, England. 1753–1756, Kyre Park, Worcestershire, England. 1754, Saint Mary's Church, Great Houghton, Northamptonshire, England. 1755–1756, County Jail, Derby; 1759–1761, Foremark Hall; Derbyshire, England.

BIBLIOGRAPHY

HUSSEY, CHRISTOPHER 1956 *English Country Houses: Mid Georgian, 1760–1800.* London: Country Life.

WHIFFEN, MARCUS 1948 *Stuart and Georgian Churches: The Architecture of the Church of England Outside London, 1603–1837.* London: Batsford.

WOOLFE, JOHN, and GANDON, JAMES (1767–1771)1970 Volume 5, plates 31–35 in *Vitruvius Britannicus.* Reprint. New York: Blom.

HIPPODAMOS

Hippodamos (c.500–440 B.C.) architect and city planner, was born most probably in or near the city of Miletos in Asia Minor, with which his name was later associated. In fact, neither his birthdate nor his birthplace are absolutely certain; his name was associated also, in antiquity, with Samos and with Thourioi. However, the attribution of his birth to Samos is not well supported and seems to have no significance with respect to his later career; Thourioi was founded only in 443 B.C., which would place Hippodamos's birth after that date were he born there, impossible in terms of other facts of his life. Furthermore, Hippodamos was supposed to have been responsible for the plan of Thourioi, which makes it hard to see how he could have been born there as well.

Of Hippodamos's upbringing, education, and early career nothing is known. His earliest activity was said to have been in connection with the new plan for the city of Miletos, which had been destroyed in 479 B.C. and whose rebuilding was begun immediately afterward. Hippodamos was credited with laying out the plan for the rebuilt city, apparently according to a new system, and from this surely stemmed the linking of his name with that of his native (or adopted) city, which persisted throughout antiquity.

Following his experience at Miletos, Hippodamos appeared shortly afterward in Athens, where he was entrusted with laying out the plan of Peiraios, the port city of Athens, founded under Themistokles about 470 B.C. To Hippodamos was attributed the plan of the entire project, laid out in whole or in part during his lifetime; he lived there for much of the remainder of his life. Finally, Hippodamos is said to have provided the plan for the new city of Thourioi in southern Italy, founded as a pan-Hellenic colony in 443 B.C., although it is not clear that he ever lived there.

It has been suggested as well that Hippodamos was involved with the plan for Rhodes, laid out in 408 B.C., but this is not well attested, and it seems impossible to square with the other, better established elements of his history. For if it is correct, as all modern authorities agree, that Hippodamos was born around 500 B.C., any direct connection with the plan for Rhodes would have required him to have a lifespan of almost a hundred years, which is improbable in the extreme. On the other hand, a shorter and more plausible lifespan which includes the plan for Rhodes would negate any meaningful connection between Hippodamos and the new plan for Miletos. Since Miletos was probably his birthplace and was certainly the place from which he drew his name and his reputation as a city planner, this second possibility seems equally unlikely.

Although there are many gaps in the story of Hippodamos's life as it has come down to us, there is some quite detailed information about his ideas. The most important report was given by Aristotle (*Politics*, II.8) who wrote that Hippodamos, who "contrived the art of laying out towns," aspired also to a reputation as a philosopher and was the first without experience of public office to speculate about the constitution of the ideal community. By this account, Hippodamos was also desirous of personal notoriety and affected somewhat eccentric manners and style of life.

Aristotle followed these remarks with an outline of Hippodamos's prescriptions for the ideal community. It was to have 10,000 citizens, divided into three groups: artisans, soldiers, and husbandmen; and sectors of the city plan were to be assigned to each group. Similarly, the city's territory was to be divided into three sections: sacred, public, and private; the first section for the support of religion, the second for the support of the common defense, and the third allocated to the husbandmen, or individual farmers. A tripartite division of the law paralleled this system of land division.

Aristotle was not uncritical of Hippodamos's notions, although it is clear that his interest was confined essentially to their relation to contemporary political theory and that he was largely unmindful of their physical planning implications. Nonetheless, Aristotle's testimony is valuable in more than one way. First, his detailed criticisms prove that Hippodamos was the author of a written treatise, rather than being known simply for his contributions to planning practice. Second, Aristotle's description of Hippodamos's ideal *polis* suggests strongly that Hippodamos's ideas were formed within the frame of the philosophical idealism characteristic of his day, which is to say that here as elsewhere in the fifth century B.C. practice was dominated by principle. For support of this conclusion, however, we should look less to the testimony of Aristotle than to the evidence on the ground, since it is in the physical remains that we should expect to see Hippodamos's reputation ultimately confirmed.

The plan of Miletos, as we know it today, was laid out on a peninsula with two bays near the center of one long side. Each bay became a harbor, while the land between the bays was dedicatd to the major public functions of the city. Next to the harbors were found markets, and in the center of the site lay the major agora and buildings housing religious and governmental functions. The remainder of the site was laid out in grids of streets, two smaller grids and one larger, dividing the land for residential use. The city was not to be completely developed for several centuries, yet it continued to follow the dispositions of the plan of the fifth century B.C., attesting to the plan's continuing utility. Hippodamos may or may not have been responsible for this plan himself, but he cannot have failed to be aware of its lessons. When his own turn came shortly after, at Peiraios, he demonstrated his grasp of the principles enunciated at Miletos.

The plan of Peiraios, like Miletos laid out on a peninsula, incorporated one larger and two smaller bays, each to be developed as a harbor. Around and between the harbor sites were specific areas for public functions: commercial, religious, and military. The adjoining areas were provided with grids of streets suitable for smaller-scale commercial and residential functions. So effective was this plan that it was respected through many centuries of later development, and one of its several agoras was named after Hippodamos, its deviser.

At Thourioi in southern Italy, with whose plan Hippodamos may have been connected only indirectly, that is, through the adoption there of his precepts rather than through the influence of his actual presence, archeological evidence suggests that the plan for the new colony was laid out as a grid of three major streets in one direction, intersected at right angles by four other streets. The allocation of specific functions within the grid of streets is not known, but if Hippodamian principles were applied there would have been the appropriate divisions by function that are known from the earlier sites of Miletos and Peiraios.

However, the fifth-century B.C. sites associated specifically with Hippodamos's name do not preserve sufficient indications to give unequivocal testimony to the nature of his practice. In addition, there is the possibility at Miletos that Hippodamos may not have been responsible entirely or at all for the new plan after 479 B.C., although he surely knew it; much of the public building activity there was undertaken only centuries later and may reflect later ideas. At Peiraios, the modern city lies over the ancient site, and many uncertainties remain about the details of the original plan. At Thourioi, the archeological evidence, while solid, is still no more than a skeleton of the whole as it once must have been. We must look beyond the fifth-century B.C. evidence if we are to account for Hippodamos's reputation as the father of city planning in antiquity. It may be that the most fruitful approach is a comparison between planned cities as they were before and after the time of Hippodamos.

For an example of pre-Hippodamian planning in the Greek world, we may take the evidence from Megara Hyblaea in Sicily, a small colonial settlement founded around 750 B.C. In the second half of the seventh century B.C., the town plan was formalized with the laying out of streets of uniform width, running roughly north–south. Excavation has revealed two distinct districts, side by side, each with a site of parallel streets, but with the streets of the one district at an angle to those of the other. The blocks of land thus described were rhomboids rather than rectangles, and the agora that lay at the juncture of the two districts was a trapezoid in plan. We see regularity, even a rudimentary order, but the overall impression is still of a tentative approach to formal planning. Even after buildings were placed in the space of the agora, its basic irregularity persisted. The artful and sophisticated spatial arrangements which characterized the city centers of later ages are scarcely even implied here. Furthermore, although Megara Hyblaea was never to reach any great size, it is clear in any case that expansion of civic functions within the original city plan would have been very difficult. Future needs were not represented in the relatively primitive planning of the seventh century B.C.

By contrast, when we turn to the post-Hippodamian era, we find a marked contrast with the evidence from earlier centuries. Cities of the fourth century B.C. in particular show clear evidence of the presence of a new style in planning. Perhaps the outstanding example of city design in this period appears in the plan of the city Priene in Asia Minor, laid out about the middle of the fourth century B.C. Not only are the remains well preserved on this site but also, more important, there were no later periods of major rebuilding in the city's history which might have obscured the fourth-century plan.

In the plan of Priene, the agora was located, from the start, at the center of the city, and around it were arranged stoas and commercial and public buildings. Uphill and nearby was the Temple of Athena, and not far away was the theater, taking advantage of the rising ground. Further inland and a thousand feet higher up lay the acropolis. Downhill from the agora, carried on a terrace at the lowest part of the site, lay the gymnasium and the stadium. The grid of streets led away from the agora, the major streets running along the contours of the site, the minor ones across them. Sacred, public, and private areas were delimited carefully, with a regard for future as much as for present convenience. In many cases, individual areas were not filled in, nor projected functions housed, until long after the original plan was first laid down. Yet, allowing for changes over time, this plan functioned successfully for centuries, and the original formal organization continued to be the determinant of the entire urban ensemble.

Surely it is here that we see the "art" of laying out towns to which Aristotle referred: the allocation of specific areas and locations within the city plan to specific urban functions according to contemporary ideas about the nature of the city, expressing thereby the concept of the city as a product of culture and art, simultaneously democratic, dignified, and graceful. Equally, it is surely here that we see the evidence for the real contribution of Hippodamos. He was on this proof not merely a geometer, laying out lines upon the ground, nor yet a philosopher, responsible for a new definition of the *polis*. He was essentially an artist, creating an urban aesthetic that gave reality not only to the aspirations of his own time but was to maintain its force and its meaning throughout the succeeding centuries of Greek culture.

As for Hippodamos's work as an architect, the record is not at all clear. At Peiraios, there was the Hippodamian agora, which has led some to believe that Hippodamos designed whatever buildings stood around it. But an agora is a space, independent of any buildings that may flank it, and there is no evidence to suggest that Hippodamos designed any building for that location. Indeed, there is firm evidence on the site itself that buildings were erected there long after Hippodamos's day, and in some cases these were the first buildings on the ground.

No actual building was attributed positively to Hippodamos's hand in antiquity nor has archeological evidence been found more recently to support the conclusion that he designed or supervised the construction of any building anywhere. Rather, and on the contrary, it is perhaps precisely because Hippodamos was so well known for his activities as a city planner that we should not seek to make him an architect in the modern sense of the word. For it should not be overlooked that in ancient Greece the term "architect" was applied in a general way to the supervisor of any project, not just to the designer of a building. Many an artist who would not be recognized as such today, for example, PHEIDIAS the master sculptor, was called "architect" in antiquity. Hippodamos would have merited the title of architect from his work in designing and supervising the layout of city plans alone, without being a designer of buildings as well.

Early scholars suggested that Hippodamos was named the father of city planning becuse he was the inventor of the orthogonal grid of streets which appears in most ancient cities, especially those newly founded or refounded. Excavation has shown that this cannot be so. Numerous Greek city plans that have come to light in recent decades had orthogonal street grids that antedate Hippodamos by a century or more. Plans with parallel files of streets were known in the Nile valley, to name only one area outside the Greek world, at least a millennium earlier. It is inconceivable that Aristotle, among others, was ignorant of these facts.

It was asserted in turn that if Hippodamos did not invent the orthogonal street grid—as he clearly did not—then he was responsible for the dissemination of a particular kind of grid. The orthogonal grid advanced as particularly Hippodamian is distinguished by narrow blocks of land, usually four or five times as long as they are wide. The difficulty with this claim is that it simply ignores the evidence of important sites, for instance, Miletos and Priene, that do not fit the scheme because the blocks of land are almost square there.

A third position was that Hippodamian planning is characterized not only by the orthogonal street grid and long, narrow blocks of land, but most of all by the presence in the city plan of several major streets that are wider than the others. Sometimes, the major streets intersect at the center of the plan; sometimes, they do not. It is undeniable that Greek city plans from the fifth century B.C. onward almost invariably have a few major streets, along with many minor ones. The difficulty is to see how so simple a functional device can be held out as the principal achievement of the father of city planning.

From today's remote viewpoint, it would seem most likely that Hippodamos was acknowledged the father of city planning in the Greek world not for his association with the orthogonal grid, whatever its proportions, but for his advocacy of rational planning per se, of which the orthogonal grid was only one manifestation. Two considerations may support this conclusion. The first of these is the influence of geometry on Greek thought from the sixth century B.C. onward.

The achievements of Greek mathematics, originating in the metaphysical speculations of the Pythagorean school, first culminated in systematic logic and, later, in the perfect geometrical formulations of Euclid. The relationships between metaphysical speculation on the divine order of the universe and the discovered order of the world of mathematics, specifically geometry, was obvious to the ancients. Similarly obvious was the connection between logic as a system of explication and proof in philosophy and geometry as a system of explication and proof in mathematics. The orthogonal grid could be seen as an example of the practical application of systematic logic and philosophical thinking to the real world, perhaps even to some degree as a validation of the importance attached to logic by Greek philosophy.

The second consideration is the coordination of the parts with respect to the whole in a city plan, which first appeared in the fifth century B.C. It has been noted that orthogonal plans appeared outside the Mediterranean long before their use in the Greek world. It has also been noted that orthogonal plans appeared in the Greek world at least a century before the time of Hippodamos. However, it seems to be true that the pre-Hippodamian plans were ordered only up to a certain point, as though the principles and purposes of regular planning were acknowledged, but the problem of making a city from these principles had yet to be solved.

By contrast, in the fourth century B.C., complete and sophisticated plans, such as that for Priene, became the rule. It is not too difficult to conclude that Hippodamos was the leading figure who, in the fifth century B.C., drew the earlier ideas together and provided them with a functional and aesthetic framework, as distinct from simple gridded land division, in the city plan as a whole.

Hippodamos thus assumes his historical position neither as philosopher nor surveyor but as the one who first demonstrated the application of geometry, that is, logic, to a major area of human concern.

B. M. BOYLE

WORKS

c.475 B.C., Town Plan, Miletos, Turkey. c.470 B.C., Town Plan, Peiraios, Greece. c.443 B.C., Town Plan, Thourioi, Italy.

BIBLIOGRAPHY

English translations of the ancient texts can be found in the volumes of the Loeb Classical Library series, published by Harvard University and Heinemann.

ARISTOTLE, *Politics*, 2.8.

CASTAGNOLI, FERDINANDO 1971 *Orthogonal Town Planning in Antiquity.* Translated by V. Caliandro. Cambridge, Mass., and London: M.I.T. Press.

GIULIANO, ANTONIO 1966 *Urbanistica delle citta greche.* Milan: Saggiatore.

MARTIN, ROLAND 1956 *L'urbanisme dans la Grèce antique.* Paris: Picard.

McCREDIE, J. R. 1971 "Hippodamos of Miletus." In P. G. Mitten, J. G. Pedley, and J. Ascott (editors), *Studies Presented to George M. A. Hanfmann.* Mainz, Germany: Von Zabern.

WARD-PERKINS, JOHN B. 1974 *Cities of Ancient Greece and Italy: Planning in Classical Antiquity.* New York: Braziller.

HITTORFF, JACQUES IGNACE

Jacques Ignace Hittorff (1792–1867), born Jakob Ignaz Hittorff, designer of the Gare du Nord in Paris, was an architect who belonged to no recognized group but who through persistence and intuitive brilliance made his own position. Although he worked in France all his career, he was German by birth, keeping in touch with Germany and often producing Germanic designs. Although a student of CHARLES PERCIER, in his writings he tried to further progressive ideas—but he was never accepted as one of the younger "romantic" designers of the circle of F. L. J. DUBAN and HENRI LABROUSTE. Although a number of his buildings were structurally advanced, especially in the use of iron, his manner of design remained conventional. Yet he made himself a considerable force in French architecture during an extraordinarily long period from the Empire and Restoration through the Monarchy of July to the end of the Second Empire by sheer personal persistence—German accent and all. Those who called him "le Prussien" had in mind his manner of working as much as his place of birth. He participated in the "Polychromy Controversy" during the 1830s and 1840s, and although he did not have the most extraordinary things to say, he made himself the center of the conflict by the sheer mass of his contribution. At the end of his career, in the design of the Gare du Nord (1858–1866), after repeated attempts to settle upon a design in the neobaroque manner of the time, he threw it all over and returned to the Greek Ionic colonnades of neoclassicism to produce one of the most succinct and powerful designs of the Second Empire—as opaque theoretically as it is lucid visually.

Hittorff was the only son of a successful tinsmith on the Heumarkt in Cologne. The city was occupied by the French revolutionary armies soon afterward in 1794 and, lying on the west bank of the Rhine, incorporated into France itelf by the Treaty of Lunéville of 1801 (the Congress of Vienna in 1815 reassigned the city to Prussia). Like his friend Heinrich Heine, contemporaneously brought up in francophied Düsseldorf, Hittorff grew up as a Frenchman, no less enthusiastically so for the prosperity his father experienced under the Gallic regime.

Hittorff's father raised him to be an architect, arranging lessons for him with the painter Caspar Arnold Grein and the local architects Christian Löwenstein and Michael Leidl. At the age of fifteen, he entered the employ of the contractor Franz Leister, evidently working not only as a mason but also as a designer.

In 1810, Hittorff went to Paris, as did many Rhenish artists of his time—FRANZ CHRISTIAN GAU from Cologne among them. In 1811, he was admitted to the Ecole des Beaux-Arts as a student of Charles Percier, the most respected designer and teacher of the age. There he did well as a student, although not brilliantly; he won the affection of Percier and earned the position of assistant to the elderly FRANÇOIS JOSEPH BÉLANGER for the construction of the celebrated iron dome of the Halle au Blés (1811–1813). On that project he became close friends with JOSEPH LECOINTE, Belanger's favorite pupil brought up in his own house. This association was fortuitous: before the revolution,

Belanger had been the architect of the Comte d'Artois, the future Charles X, and upon the Bourbon restoration in 1814 he was appointed *architecte des Menus-Plaisirs* with, in 1815, Lecointe as *inspecteur* and Hittorff as *sous-inspecteur*. They designed the decorations of Paris for the entry of Louis XVIII (May 3, 1814)—including a pair of temples on the Point Neuf—and subsequently the settings for the translation of the remains of Louis XVI to Saint-Denis (January 21, 1815) and the marriage of the Duc de Berry to Princess Caroline of Naples (June 1816).

On May 1, 1818, Belanger died, and Lecointe and Hittorff were appointed together to replace him as *architectes pour les fêtes et cérémonies* (Hittorff having been promoted to full *inspecteur* in 1817). A series of impressive decorations followed: those for the funerals of the Prince de Condé (1818), the Duc de Berry (1820) and Louis XVIII (1824); that for the baptism of the Duc de Bordeaux (May 1, 1821; published by Hittorff and Lecointe in 1827); and finally that for the coronation of Charles X at Rheims (May 29, 1825)—the last coronation in that great cathedral in the history of France. Their style of decoration was Empire, in the most elegant Percieresque mode, but could also be pseudo-Gothic, as was the case of the temporary portico erected on the façade of Notre Dame for the baptism of the Duc de Bordeaux (Percier, when similarly decorating Notre Dame for the marriage of Napoleon and Marie Louise of Austria in 1810, had also used the Gothic style). Hittorff and Lecointe set the tone for fashionable taste in Restoration Paris and were asked to decorate a number of interiors (in the hotels Osmand, Nervo, Gause, Boradin, Borda, and Jacqueminot-Poulic, as well as in the Tuileries for Charles X, 1825–1830) and to erect two theaters, the Salle Favart (1825) and the Théâtre de l'Ambigu-Comique (1827–1828).

All this represented amazing success, especially for a partnership half German; it was accompanied by an effort on Hittorff's part to cut a social and intellectual figure as well as a professional one. He went out in society, especially to the *salon* of Baron Gérard, frequented by Alexander von Humboldt and the philologist Jean-Antoine Letronne who became a close friend. He traveled to England in 1820 and around Germany for three months in 1821. But most important, Hittorff went to Italy for twenty-two months from September 1822 to June 1824 to make good the gap in his education resulting from his not having won the five-year *pension* at the French Academy in Rome.

Hittorff's Italian trip occasioned a crisis in his career—his involvement in the "Polychromy Controversy"—when his observations of traces of painted decoration on the Greek temples in Sicily were attacked by the scholar Désiré Raoul-Rochette. The conflict broke out when on July 3, 1830, Raoul-Rochette addressed the Académie des Beaux-Arts questioning Hittorff's ideal reconstruction of the painted treatment of the so-called Temple of Empedocles which Hittorff had excavated at Selinus in December 1823 and published in his book with Ludwig Zanth, *Architecture antique de la Sicile* (1827). A lengthy controversy followed in journals and in books, Letronne in particular coming to Hittorff's defense. This must have been confusing for Hittorff because the evidence for such painted decoration was widely admitted by 1830—especially after the excavation of the temple at Aegina in 1811, a painted reconstruction of which LEO VON KLENZE had just completed in his Glyptothek in Munich—and furthermore because Antoine Chrysostum Quatremère de Quincy, Raoul-Rochette's patron, had published the definitive study of polychromy in Greek sculpture, his *Jupiter olympien,* in 1814–1815. Nothing, one might think, would have been safer to explore, and indeed for the first seven years of Hittorff's work no criticisms were voiced. Things were happening in 1830, however, that made Hittorff's ideas suddenly objectionable. The issue of ancient Greek polychromy had been taken up as the instrument to attack academicism by radical students at the end of the 1820s, particularly in connection with Henri Labrouste's reconstruction of the temples at Paestum sent to Paris from the French Academy at Rome in 1829. By the early 1830s, it was a craze among French architecture students as well as among their English, German and Scandinavian contemporaries, OWEN JONES, GOTTFRIED SEMPER, and GOTTLIEB BINDESBØLL all producing extraordinary visions of Greek architectural color. By the end of the decade a number of public buildings were being erected in this style: the Dumont d'Urville tomb in the Cimitière Montparnasse (1842–1844) by Simon Claude Constant-Dufeux, the "Pompeiian House" (1842–1843) at Aschaffenburg by FRIEDRICH VON GÄRTNER, the Monopteros (1837) and Central Post Office (1836) in Munich by von Klenze, and—most particularly—the Thorwaldsen Museum (1834–1848) in Copenhagen by Bindesbøll. These younger, self-proclaimed "romantic" architects' intentions were quite different from Hittorff's. Labrouste, Constant-Dufeux, and their friends saw polychromy as proof that Greek architectural decoration was accumulative and thus free from academic rules. Semper and Jones believed it proof of elemental laws of decorative art. Hittorff, on the contrary, presented Greek architectural polychromy as a tightly systematized part of the orders serving to articulate the forms and enrich the expression of character. Nonetheless he was damned by association—and perhaps also by his nationality and a peculiar Liberalism that manifested itself upon the Revolution of July 1830.

On August 22, 1830, just three weeks after the overthrow of the Bourbon dynasty Hittorff had served so well, the Assemblée Générale des Artistes convened to sketch ideas for the reorganization of state art education and patronage. Out of this grew the Société Libre des Beaux-Arts, intended as an independent liberal force in French art politics, with Hittorff among its leaders (and, upon occasion, its president). He displayed theoretical architectural projects at the society's meetings, published in its journal, and by this and other means garnered important commissions from the new government. First came the commission to redesign the Place de la Concorde (1832–1835), then that in 1833 to complete the church of Saint-Vincent-de-Paul (on which he had been working since 1831), and finally that in 1834 to develop the Champs-Elysées. For the last project he produced a series of brilliantly painted Pompeiian restaurant and entertainment pavilions (1834–1840), which he erected in much toned-down form, but with the adventurous use of iron in their structure. For the church, begun in 1824 as a conventional basilica by Hittorff's father in law, JEAN-BAPTISTE LEPÈRE, he proposed a two-towered façade, a broadened apse embracing the inner aisles as well as the nave, and an extensive polychromatic decorative program. This decoration was carried out internally during the 1840s with Hippolyte Flandrin's friezes and François Edouard Picot's God the Father in the apse, but not externally—Hittorff's suggestions of enameled pediments, friezes, and murals being rejected by Baron Haussmann after a trial piece was set in place by the painter Jules Jollivet. For the execution of this external polychromy Hittorff intended a product called *lave emaillée*—painted and fired pumice in thin sheets—developed in 1827 by the chemist Mortelèque and, from 1833 to 1841, produced by Hittorff himself as a business enterprise, Hachette et Cie. The firm executed fireplace surrounds, altar frontals, and a tabletop for Prince Friedrich Wilhelm of Prussia, all to Hittorff's designs.

In its medievalizing towers, Byzantine decoration, and early Christian colonnades, Hittorff's Saint-Vincent-de-Paul marked the beginning of the eclectic combining of architectural elements from distant historical sources that was to characterize mid-nineteenth century French design. But with its square, modular plan and Greek details it remains distinct from such arcuated, volumetric designs as CHARLES AUGUSTE QUESTEL's Saint-Pierre at Nîmes (1838–1848) or LÉON VAUDOYER's

Hittorff.
Church of Saint-Vincent-de-Paul.
Paris.
1833–1848

Hittorff.
Church of Saint-Vincent-de-Paul.
Paris.
1833–1848

Marseilles Cathedral (1845–1893). Instead, it seems part of a series of German church projects studying eclectic combinations of elements and polychromatic decoration: the unbuilt Apostelkirche in Munich of 1818–1826 by von Klenze and others, the Bonifaziusbasilika there of 1833–1850 by GEORG FRIEDRICH ZIEBLAND, the Residenzkapelle there of 1827–1837 by von Klenze, and the cathedral projects for Potsdam and Berlin by Prince Friedrich Wilhelm begun in 1823. Indeed, in 1845, Friedrich Wilhelm, now king of Prussia, requested of Hittorff a set of drawings of Saint-Vincent-de-Paul rendered with all its polychromatic decoration.

On February 25, 1848, as Hittorff—now fifty-six years old—was finishing the decoration of Saint-Vincent-de-Paul, another revolution installed yet another government in France, that which on December 2, 1852 was proclaimed Louis Napoleon's Second Empire. It was the fourth Hittorff had served, and he did so with greater success than ever. As before, he obtained major commissions in very different professional fields—as architect to members of the imperial family, as a government architect, and as a private designer for great business enterprises.

Hittorff's contact with the imperial family grew out of the renewed interest in Greek polychromy that was part of the exotic *néo-grec* fashion of the 1850s. In 1851, he had published his compendious *Architecture polychrome chez les Grecs,* finally silencing Raoul-Rochette, which at once caught the eye of Napoleon III. In 1853–1855, the Empress Eugénie employed him to erect the Institut Eugénie-Napoleon, a palatial orphanage endowed by her. In 1855, the emperor's uncle, the prince Jérome Napoleon, commissioned Hittorff together with his friend Ingres to create a painted model of an ideal "Temple of the Muses" for his mistress, Rachel. This was followed in 1856 by the request for a project for the Maison Pompeiienne the prince was preparing to build on the Avenue Montaigne (it was actually erected to the brilliantly polychrome *néo-grec* designs of Alfred Normand in 1856–1860).

At the same time, Hittorff's government post of *architecte du Bois de Boulogne et des Champs-Elysées* became far more than a sinecure when these areas and the spaces in between were redeveloped by Haussman. Hittorff produced a number of impressive projects (especially for the Avenue de l'Impératrice) and erected a ring of large, uniform houses around the Place de l'Etoile (1852–1855). Elsewhere in Paris, he was commissioned to complete the *mairie* of the Fifth Arrondissement (1847–1850; begun by P. S. B. Guénepin) and to

design and erect that of the first (1855–1861).

Hittorff's greatest accomplishments during the Second Empire, however, were as a private architect. In 1851–1852, he built yet another theater, the Cirque Napoleon," polychromed and covered with a daring iron roof. Then in 1856–1859, together with Charles Rohault de Fleury (see ROHAULT DE FLEURY FAMILY), Auguste Pellechet, and Alfred Armand, he erected the elegant Hôtel du Louvre on the Place du Théâtre Français, still functioning today as a palace hotel. Finally, in 1858–1866, he designed and erected the huge Gare du Nord, still the most dramatic of Paris's terminals.

The station was Hittorff's last as well as his most memorable monument, and it sums up his dilemma as well as the powers he brought to bear to overcome it. A body of preliminary studies among his papers at Cologne show him attempting arched schemes with broad lunettes revealing the train shed in the rationalist spirit of the Gare de l'Est nearby. These, however, he rejected for the mere clothing of the iron volume in an openwork of stone Greek columns and lintels, incongruously combined with five wide arches. The industrial artifact thus is neither concealed nor transformed by its architectural dress; its forms instead are integrated with those of the historical styles just as the walking beam and the Doric column are made part of the same organism in contemporaneous steam engines. Second Empire critics found the station neither one thing nor another and could not "read" it, yet it has been intuitively recognized since its inauguration as an immensely simple and powerful expression of nineteenth-century corporate architecture.

Hittorff's social and intellectual activities continued during the Second Empire, but now in the calm sphere of recognized success. He was a friend of Heine, Dumas, Mérimée, and Ingres, with the last of whom he conducted musical *salons*. He traveled repeatedly to London and to Germany and knew the old classicists CHARLES R. COCKERELL, CHARLES BARRY, GOTTFRIED SEMPER, and FRIEDRICH HITZIG. He addressed Friedrich Wilhelm IV of Prussia as "mon royal confrère." In 1853, he was elected to the Académie des Beaux-Arts and, upon the death of his old enemy Raoul-Rochette in 1854, had the boldness to campaign to be elected his successor as *secrétaire perpétuel* of that body—losing, however, to another scholar, Ernest Beulé. Hittorff had produced a number of historical studies aside from his polychromy researches—*Architecture moderne de la Sicile* (Hittorff & Zanth, 1835); *Parallèle entre les arabesques peintes des anciens et celles de Raphael* (1844)—and now in two conceptual papers he stated his theory of architecture: "Notice

Hittorff.
Gare du Nord.
Paris.
1858–1866

Hittorff.
Gare du Nord.
Paris.
1858–1866

sur les ruines d'Agrigente" read at the annual public meeting of the five academies in 1859, and "Mémoire sur Pompeii et Pétra" (1866). Here he demonstrated that the vocabulary of ancient architecture was essentially structurally irrational and ideal, a series of symbols that might be combined in a wide variety of ways to express subtle nuances of architectural character.

On March 25, 1867, Hittorff died in Paris after a short illness.

DAVID T. VAN ZANTEN

WORKS

*1818, Decorations for the funeral of the Prince de Condé; *1820, Decorations for the funeral of the duc de Berry; *1821, Decoration for the baptism of the duc de Bordeaux, Notre Dame; Paris. *1824, Decorations for the funeral of Louis XVIII, Basilica of Saint Denis, France. *1825, Decoration for coronation of Charles X, Cathedral at Rheims, France. *1825, Salle Favart; *1825–1830 Tuileries Palace (interior decorations); 1827–1828, Théâtre de l'Ambigu-Comique; 1832–1835, Place de la Concorde (plan); 1833–1848, Church of Saint-Vincent-de-Paul (completion); 1834–1840, Restaurant Pavilions, Panorama, and Circus on the Champs-Elysées; 1847–1850, Mairie of the Fifth Arrondissement (completion); 1851–1852, Cirque Napoleon (Cirque d'Hiver); 1852–1855, Houses (with Charles Rohault de Fleury), Place de l'Etoile; 1853–1855, Institut Eugénie-Napoleon; 1854–1855, Temple of the Muses (with J. A. D. Ingres); 1855–1861, Mairie of the First Arrondissement; 1856–1859, Hôtel du Louvre (with Charles Rohault de Fleury, Auguste Pellechet, and Alfred Armand); 1858–1866, Gare du Nord; Paris.

BIBLIOGRAPHY

BEULÉ, CHARLES ERNEST 1868 Eloge de Hittorff. Paris: Didot.
GROMORT, GEORGES 1922 "Architecture." Volume 2 in Histoire générale de l'art français de la Révolution jusqu'à nos jours. Paris: Librairie de France.
HAMMER, KARL 1968 Jakob Ignaz Hittorf: Ein Pariser Baumeister, 1792–1867. Stuttgart, Germany: Hierjehann.
HITTORFF, J. I. 1851 Architecture polychrome chez les Grecs. Paris: Firmin-Didot.
HITTORFF, J. I. 1866 "Mémoire sur Pompeii et Pétra." Volume 25, part 2, pages 377–416 in Mémoires de l'Academie des inscriptions et belles-lettres. Paris: The academy.
HITTORFF, J. I., AND LECOINTE, JEAN 1827 Description des cérémonies et des fêtes qui ont eu lieu pour le baptême de son altesse royale Monseigneur Henry-Charles-Ferdinand-Marie-Dieudonné d'Artois, duc de Bordeaux. Paris: Renouard.
HITTORFF, J. I., AND ZANTH, LUDWIG 1827 Architecture antique de la Sicile. Paris: Donnard.
HITTORFF, J. I., AND ZANTH, LUDWIG 1835 Architecture moderne de la Sicile. Paris: Renouard.
LABROUSTE, LÉON 1868 Notice sur Hittorff. Paris: Firmin-Didot.
NORMAND, ALFRED 1867 "Notice sur la vie et les oeuvres de J. I. Hittorff, artiste français." Moniteur des architectes Series 2 2:113–121, 145–148.
SCHNEIDER, DONALD 1977 The Works and Doctrine of Jacques Ignace Hittorff (1792–1867). New York: Garland.

HITZIG, FRIEDRICH

A pupil of both the Architecture and the Applied Crafts Academies in Berlin, Georg Heinrich Friedrich Hitzig (1811–1881) was trained under KARL FRIEDRICH SCHINKEL and in 1835 in Paris, where he was much influenced by the works of Charles PERCIER AND Pierre Leonard FONTAINE. Hitzig's efforts to integrate Italian, and later French, Renaissance elements into the neoclassical framework of Schinkel's style were also found in the domestic work of Johannes Strack, EDUARD KNOBLAUCH, and other Schinkel pupils; together, they defined Berlin's domestic architectural types. In his influential villa designs of the 1840s and 1850s, Hitzig adapted the courtly villas of Schinkel and LUDWIG PERSIUS to urban sites and the requirements of middle-class patrons.

From the late 1850s, Hitzig's designs favor greater plastic elaboration played off against sheer wall surfaces and draw on a broader historical range; he introduced mansard roofs and certain baroque motifs as in the Kronenberg Palace, Warsaw (1866–1870). His Gothic-style country houses, largely variations on Schinkel's Schloss Babelsberg at Potsdam, reflect the development of a brick architecture for more utilitarian building types. Hitzig's later career saw several important public commissions and his appointment in 1875 as president of the Art Academy.

BARRY BERGDOLL

WORKS

*1845, House, 8 Lennestrasse; 1847, Hitzig House; 1847, Krause House, 45 Leipzigerstrasse; Berlin. *c.1850, Drake House, 3 Königgrätzer Strasse, Berlin. c.1850, Schloss Kittendorf, Germany. c.1850, Schloss Tornow, Pomerania, Germany. *1852, Palais Pourtales, Königsplatz; *1853, Double House, 12–12a Bellevuestrasse; *1853, Villa Gerson, 29 Tiergartenstrasse; c.1855, House, 37 Tiergartenstrasse; *1855, Ottoscher Zirkus; Berlin. 1855, Schloss, Graf Schwerin in Göhren, Germany. 1858, House, 16 Margaretenstrasse; *1859–1864, Börse; 1860, House, 35 Tiergartenstrasse; Berlin. *1866–1870, Palais Kronenberg, Warsaw, Poland. c.1867–1868, House, 5 Wilhelmplatz; *1869–1876, Reichsbank; 1870–1871, House of the Reichenheimstiftung; 1871, Provisional Reichstag Building (with MARTIN GROPIUS and Heinrich Schmieden); 1877–1880, Zeughaus (rebuilding inner court to a museum); Berlin.

BIBLIOGRAPHY
BÖRSCH-SUPAN, EVA 1977 *Berliner Baukunst nach Schinkel, 1840–1870.* Munich: Prestel.
HITZIG, FRIEDRICH 1855–1862 *Ausgeführte Bauwerke.* 2 vols. Berlin: Ernst & Korn.
HITZIG, FRIEDRICH 1867 *Die Börse in Berlin.* Berlin: Ernst & Korn.
HITZIG, FRIEDRICH 1875 *Das Palais des Herrn von Kronenberg in Warschau.* Berlin: Ernst & Korn.

HOADLEY, DAVID

Not much is known about David Hoadley (1774–c.1840), a Connecticut builder. The victim of excessive local adulation in the 1920s and 1930s (chiefly by the lawyer-antiquarian George Dudley Seymour and the architect J. Frederick Kelly), Hoadley's role as an architect is now hard to assess. Bronson's history of Waterbury and Atwater's history of New Haven, our only sources, speak of him strictly as a builder. They give his biography: born in Naugatuck he began as a carpenter, was employed in 1795 in the construction of the Waterbury Meeting House, soon made a regional reputation as a builder. In 1813, he won the contract for building the United Church (1813–1815) in New Haven by underbidding ITHIEL TOWN, lived in New Haven until around 1830 when he retired to Waterbury. This account has been greatly inflated by modern writers, who have elevated Hoadley from builder to designer and have claimed many undocumented buildings as his (e.g., the Bristol, Timothy Bishop [Huggins], and Pinto [Bowditch] houses in New Haven; the Collins Hotel [Straitsville Tavern], Naugatuck; the Darius Beecher house, Bethany; and churches in Milford, Cheshire, Southington, and Litchfield); but in fact the only recorded works are those listed below, and Hoadley's part in their design is unknown. Nevertheless the group as a whole suggests the presence of a dominant artistic personality in west-central Connecticut at this time who stimulated the flowering of a regional style of considerable distinction, and Hoadley's name is associated, one way or another, with many of its principal works.

ELIZABETH MILLS BROWN

WORKS

Hoadley is known to have been engaged in the contruction of the buildings listed below; no information about design exists unless specified.

*1805, John Kingsbury House, Waterbury, Conn. 1809, Christ Church (joinery), Bethany, Conn. 1810, Congregational Church (joinery), North Milford (now Orange), Conn. 1813, Congregational Church (joinery and plastering), Norfolk, Conn. 1813–1815, United Church (contractor; designs by Peter Banner, Ithiel Town, Ebenezer Johnson); *c.1815, Dexter House (Law Chambers; later Staples House); *c.1815, Nathan Smith House; New Haven. 1818, Congregational Church (contractor), Avon, Conn. *c.1819, DeForest House; *1819, Philosophical Building (plan and construction); Yale College; New Haven. *1823, Hartford Turnpike Bridge (design by Ithiel Town), Whitneyville, Conn. *c.1825, Eli Whitney House (design by Town); *1827, Tontine Hotel (design by Town); New Haven. 1829, Samuel Russell House (design by Town and Davis), Middletown, Conn.

BIBLIOGRAPHY
See also the Arnold Guyott Dana Scrapbooks, on file at the New Haven Colony Historical Society.
ATWATER, EDWARD E. (editor) 1887 *History of the City of New Haven.* New York: Munsell.
BRONSON, HENRY 1858 *The History of Waterbury, Connecticut.* Waterbury, Conn.: Bronson Bros.
BROWN, ELIZABETH MILLS 1965 *The United Church on the Green, New Haven, Connecticut: An Architectural History.* New Haven: The United Church.
BROWN, ELIZABETH MILLS 1976 *New Haven: A Guide to Architecture and Urban Design.* New Haven: Yale University Press.
HOLDEN, REUBEN A. 1967 *Yale: A Pictorial History.* New Haven: Yale University Press.
KELLY, J. FREDERICK 1948 *Early Connecticut Meetinghouses.* New York: Columbia University Press.
SEYMOUR, GEORGE DUDLEY (1932)1943 "David Hoadley." Volume 9 in *Dictionary of American Biography.* New ed. New York: Scribner.

HOBAN, JAMES

Born in Ireland, James Hoban (c.1762–1831) received his early training as "an artisan" on several Dublin buildings before he emigrated to America in 1785. He was in Charleston, South Carolina, by 1790, but he did not design the Statehouse at Columbia, as is often assumed. In 1792, he returned to Philadelphia before moving to Washington, D.C.

Hoban's 1792 entry in the Capitol competition was unsuccessful, but his proposal for the President's House was awarded the $500 first prize and a gold medal. The original elevation was based on Leinster House, Dublin (1745–1747), but changes made at the behest of THOMAS JEFFERSON and then of George Washington, resulted in the well-known design which was carried out. It was based on Plate 41 of JAMES GIBBS's *A Book of Architecture* (1728) and permitted the future expansion of the building Washington had requested.

Superintendent architect of the Capitol between 1793 and 1802, he was also captain of the Washington artillery in 1799 and a member of the City Council from 1802 until his death in 1831.

DANIEL D. REIFF

WORKS

1792–1801, President's House (White House); *1793–1794, Blodgett's Hotel; (A)*c.1793–1796, John Mason House; *1794–1795, Little Hotel; *1818–1819, State Department Building; *1818–1820?, War Department Building; Washington.

BIBLIOGRAPHY

BAIGELL, MATTHEW 1969 "James Hoban and the First Bank of the United States." *Journal of the Society of Architectural Historians* 28, May:135–136.

GIBBS, JAMES (1728)1968 *A Book of Architecture.* Reprint. New York: Blom.

GOODE, JAMES M. 1979 *Capital Losses: A Cultural History of Washington's Destroyed Buildings.* Washington: Smithsonian Institution.

HALL, LOUISE 1950 "First Architectural School? No! But. . . ." *American Institute of Architects Journal* 14, Aug.:79–82.

"James Hoban: The Architect and Builder of the White House." 1907 *American Catholic Historical Researches* 24:35–52.

KIMBALL, FISKE 1917–1918 "The Genesis of the White House." *Century Magazine* 95:523–528.

KIMBALL, FISKE 1932 "James Hoban." Volume 9, pages 91–92 in *Dictionary of American Biography.* New York: Scribner.

MADDEX, DIANE 1973 *Historic Buildings of Washington, D.C.* Pittsburgh: Ober Park Associates.

OWEN, FREDERICK D. 1901 "The First Government Architect: James Hoban, of Charleston, S.C." *Architectural Record* 11:581–589.

REIFF, DANIEL D. (1971)1977 *Washington Architecture, 1791–1861: Problems in Development.* 2d ed. Washington: U.S. Commission of Fine Arts.

RYAN, WILLIAM, and GUINNESS, DESMOND 1980 *The White House: An Architectural History.* New York: McGraw.

VERHEYEN, EGON 1978 " 'The Splendor of its Empire': Reconsidering Jefferson's Role in the Planning of Washington." Pages 183–206 in Erich Hubala and Gunter Schweikhart (editors), *Festschrift Herbert Siebenhüner.* Würzburg, Germany: Kommissionsverlag Ferdinand Schoningh.

VERHEYEN, EGON 1981 "James Hoban's Design for the White House in the Context of the Planning of the Federal City." *Architecture* 11:66–82.

HOCHEDER, KARL

Karl Hocheder (1854–1917) was one of the chief representatives of South German architectural historicism; like GABRIEL VON SEIDL, THEODOR FISCHER, and Hans Grässel, he sought to revive the Renaissance and the baroque. Born in Weiherhammer near Weiden (Oberpfalz), he studied at the Technische Hochschule in Munich. He started on a career in the State Building Office (*Bauamt*), but from 1898 on, he taught at the Technische Hochschule in Munich. Despite the constrictions imposed by their style, his buildings fulfilled every practical requirement with an economy of means. The Müllersche Volksbad (1896–1901) long remained a model for the technique of bathhouse building. The Bavarian Ministry of Transportation (1905–1913) was a monumental building encompassing picturesque squares and streets; the drum-cupola which crowned it was one of the earliest reinforced concrete constructions in Germany.

HANS REUTHER
*Translated from German by
Beverley R. Placzek*

WORKS

1896–1901, Karl Müllersches Volksbad; 1902–1904, Fire Station, Blumenstrasse; 1904, Evangelische Kirche, Neu Pasing; *1905–1913, Bavarian Ministry of Transportation; Munich. 1907, Town Hall, Bolzano, Italy. 1908, Hocheder Residence, Renatastrasse, Munich.

BIBLIOGRAPHY

GMELIN, L. 1901–1902 "Das Karl Müllersche Volksbad in München." *Kunst und Handwerk* 52:85–198.

HOCHEDER, KARL 1916 *Der Neubau K. B. Verkehrsministeriums in München.* Berlin.

HOFFMANN, JOSEF

Josef Franz Maria Hoffmann (1870–1956) belongs to the very small group of Austrian architects who influenced the course of architectural history beyond the borders of their own country; in this he is comparable to his teacher OTTO WAGNER and his exact contemporary and later antagonist ADOLF LOOS. Like Loos, Hoffmann came from Moravia, then a province of the Austro-Hungarian monarchy, where he was born as the son of the well-to-do mayor of Pirnitz (Brtnice), now in Czechoslovakia. He grew up close to the land and its peasants whose arts and crafts he cherished throughout his life.

As a student of architecture at the Vienna Academy of Fine Art, Hoffmann was a pupil first of CARL HASENAUER and later of Otto Wagner, and in 1895 he graduated with such distinction that he was awarded the Rome Prize. He returned from Italy with many travel sketches and studies of both historical and vernacular buildings, gardens and sculptures. He began working for Otto Wagner but at the same time started to make a name for himself by entering competitions and by designing successful exhibition arrangements for the newly founded Vienna Secession. He also attracted attention with his boldly innovative interiors, commissioned by clients who were either artists or supporters of the Secession.

Only four years after his graduation, he was appointed professor at the Kunstgewerbeschule in Vienna, a position he held until 1936. Several of his students or assistants later made important contributions to both the practice and teaching of design, among them Eduard H. Ascherman, who practiced in New York City before World War I.

Hoffmann was always eager to promote young talent; he helped Egon Schiele and Oskar Kokoschka when they were unknown beginners and in 1907 offered a position to the equally unknown Charles Edouard Jeanneret (LE CORBUSIER) who had come to show him a portfolio of watercolors. Le Corbusier, though he did not accept the offer, for the rest of his life remained grateful for this early encouragement and for additional support he received later when Hoffmann voted in favor of Le Corbusier's entry in the 1927 international competition for a League of Nations Building.

Hoffmann always counted artists such as Gustav Klimt, Kolo Moser, Franz Metzner, and Anton Hanak among his most intimate friends, and many of his works testify to his special concern for the advantageous positioning of works of art in an architectural framework. At the same time, under the sway of JOHN RUSKIN, WILLIAM MORRIS, and the British Arts and Crafts movement, he strove for a total harmony between environment, architecture, furniture, and all objects of daily use. He never lost his love for fine craftsmanship and decoration as an integral part of architecture though the nature of his decorative treatment changed considerably over time. He admired CHARLES R. ASHBEE's Guild of Handicraft and, with the financial support of Frits Wärndorfer, a well-to-do industrialist in Vienna, he and Kolo Moser in 1903 founded the Wiener Werkstätte for the production of well-designed products of fine craftsmanship; it lasted thirty years and was a great success artistically but not financially. It consumed a great deal of Hoffmann's energy that otherwise might have been expended on architecture. He designed for the Werkstätte furniture, metalwork, tableware, glass, china, jewelry, fabrics, wallpaper, bookbindings, objects in leather, and much else.

Hoffmann's architecture always shows him as a master of great natural facility in the pleasing arrangement of forms and spaces, with a love for strong contrasts, color effects, and frequently rich decoration. In his best works, he manages to fuse successfully the great tendencies he absorbed in his youth: the classicist rationalism of Otto Wagner and the free, picturesque mode of the British Arts and Crafts movement together with the special personal contribution of CHARLES RENNIE MACKINTOSH. At the same time, his work mirrors faithfully the major changes of style in the world of architecture around him and at times also the influence of admired young collaborators, who seem to have affected him in the same way that he and his friend JOSEPH MARIA OLBRICH had affected their teacher Otto Wagner.

At the outset of his career, Hoffmann displayed complete mastery of the kind of grandiloquent use of the classical vocabulary and Beaux-Arts methods of composition that one would expect from a student of Hasenauer and Wagner at the end of the Ringstrasse era: his Rome Prize project (1895) for an international congress palace, 1.5 km long with a central dome 160 m high, well exemplifies this mode, and there are some early competition projects and sketch designs for utopian buildings that belong in the same category. A brief but intensive love affair with the curvilinear international Art Nouveau followed, best illustrated by the Apollo Candle Shop (1899), Vienna; the interior of the Bergerhöhe (1899), Hohenberg, Austria; and a number of early exhibition designs for the Vienna Secession (1898–1899).

By the turn of the century, a process of simplification and formal purification had set in; it found an early climactic expression at the fourteenth exhibition of the Secession (1902), dedicated to the display of Max Klinger's Beethoven sculpture. On this occasion, Hoffmann created two remarkable abstract reliefs in stucco. Two years later, the white cubic forms of the flat-roofed, severely plain Purkersdorf Sanatorium (1904) demonstrated the same attitude in a major piece of architecture. A number of factors seem to have triggered this turning away from the youthful exuberence of the Art Nouveau phase, among them the rationalism and inherent classicism of Otto Wagner which tended toward planarity and rectangularity, the formal reticence or sophistication of some British work (Ashbee, M. H. BAILLIE-SCOTT, CHARLES F. A. VOYSEY, and Mackintosh), and the theoretical arguments for simplicity and truthfulness by such writers as Alfred Lichtwark and HERMANN MUTHESIUS. In Hoffmann's practice, this meant a restriction to a few preferred geometric forms, chief among them the square, and to color schemes dominated by white, or white and black. A series of interiors and houses in Vienna, above all on the Hohe Warte, illustrated various stages in this process and, at the same time, the beginning of a next phase in Hoffmann's creative exploration: a turning to ever richer decorative treatment and to an ever more explicit classicism, as is clearly manifest in his exhibition pavilions for the Vienna Kunstschau (1908), the international art exhibition in Rome (1911), and the Cologne Werkbund exhibition (1914).

In these buildings and in Hoffmann's last two great houses to be done in Vienna before World War I—the Ast House (1909–1911) and the Skywa-Primavesi House (1913–1915)—Hoffman was part of that general reorientation along neoclassicist lines that characterized the decade. At the same time, he wholeheartedly joined the movement toward a preservation or revival of forms from the folkloristic vernacular, typified by his design for the Primavesi House in Winkelsdorf (1913–1914), a timber building in block construction with a thatched roof.

There is one building, however, that does not fit easily into any of the well-known and generally accepted stylistic subcategories of the early twentieth century, a building that looks unlike any of its contemporaries and that alone would have sufficed to secure a place in the history of world architecture for Hoffmann: the Stoclet House and its garden in Brussels, which was designed in 1905 and finished in 1911, complete with furniture, glass, china, and tableware all specially designed for the purpose and carried out by the Wiener Werkstätte. Client and architect were ideally matched in this project, and the resulting building is completely controlled by the congruity of their intentions, from the palatial scale and disciplined multi-axial layout to the most minute detail, such as a door handle or flower vase. Though classicism remains the ordering matrix, it rarely becomes explicit and its very essence is denied by a continuous recourse to atectonic uses of the building's elements: bridgelike segments that seem to hover, windows that are cut into the wall as if it were insubstantial, and, above all, a persistent framing by decorative moldings of all planes of the façades and of most surfaces in important rooms of the interior. Everything is controlled in carefully composed sequences of contrasting yet coordinated rooms arranged around a high central hall. If on the outside

of the building such features as a tower and an apselike half-cylindrical projection recall the iconography of ecclesiastical buildings, the analogy is equally inviting when one is confronted with the hierarchical spatial organization of the great dining room that houses the shimmering splendor of Gustav Klimt's mosaics. A similar richness of decorative effect had been anticipated in the small but exquisite hunting lodge at Hochreith (1906) near Hohenberg, Austria, for the Austrian industrialist Karl Wittgenstein. In these works as in even earlier sumptuous yet controlled interiors for Max Biach (1902) and Sonja Knips (1903) one can discern very clearly the anticipation of forms and juxtapositions of materials and colors, such as black and gold, that in the mid-1920s became typical of the international Art Deco.

When the new artistic movements of Expressionism, Cubism, and De Stijl began to make themselves felt in Vienna, Hoffmann, beginning a new phase in his oeuvre, did not fail to respond, in each case translating the achievements from the realm of painting into decorative devices for the purposes of his designs.

The sharply angled battlements of Hoffmann's city hall for Ortelsburg, East Prussia (1916–1918), recall Expressionism; angular forms, translated into a playful mode, occur equally in many interior and furniture designs of the early 1920s where they become fused, however, with uses of transparency and abstraction that would be unthinkable without an awareness of Cubism. At the same time, the artistic personality of Dagobert Peche, who had joined the Wiener Werkstätte, indubitably made a considerable impression on Hoffmann, who greatly admired the decorative facility of the younger man. More important for his architecture was the impact of De Stijl and of the early houses by Le Corbusier, with whom Hoffman remained in touch. He visited some of Le Corbusier's buildings

Hoffmann.
Adolphe Stoclet House.
Brussels.
1905–1911

Hoffmann.
Adolphe Stoclet House
Dining Room.
Brussels.
1905–1911

Hoffmann.
Austrian Pavilion,
*   Exposition Internationale*
*   des Arts Décoratifs.*
Paris.
1924–1925

with his students when they went to Paris in connection with the 1925 Exhibition of Decorative Arts.

Hoffmann's Austrian Pavilion for the exhibition of 1925 had an asymmetrical layout of loosely arranged elements that was more akin to the typical "free plan" of Modern movement buildings than to any of Hoffmann's own earlier exhibition pavilions with their strict symmetry and classicist rigor. But the most unexpected feature of the Paris pavilion was the treatment of its façades; these were articulated by a series of large superimposed horizontal moldings made up from elongated S-shapes divided by V-shaped arrises which together produced a striking overall impression. The motif of horizontal striation, essentially an atectonic feature, for a number of years played an important role in Hoffmann's façade designs: it occurred at the Ast Country House near Velden, Austria (1923–1924), and at the Austrian pavilion for the Venice Biennale (1934–1935).

The late 1920s and early 1930s—years of economic crisis in many parts of the world—were difficult years for Hoffmann, not only because of personal problems including severe illness, but also because of the decline and final demise of the Wiener Werkstätte and increasing hostility toward the concept of decorative arts and decorated architecture on the part of younger architects whose ideological orientation came from Adolf Loos, JOSEF FRANK, and the Modern movement. Hoffmann's attitude in this phase of his architectural activity was pluralistic; on the one hand, he continued to produce richly decorated designs as in the interior for Ernst Bauer (1927) or in the bar of the remodeled Graben Coffeehouse (1928–1929); on the other hand he was also responsible for designs that eschewed decoration in favor of geometric simplicity, transparency, and lightness, as in his houses for the Werkbund estate (1932) and other housing

schemes such as that for Neustrassäcker (1924) which remained on paper. Oswald Haerdtl, his young collaborator on many of these projects and eventually, from 1930 to 1939, his partner, may well have been instrumental in keeping Hoffmann abreast of the latest trends, and in directing design developments in the corresponding direction.

A great retrospective exhibition, arranged by Haerdtl on the occasion of Hoffmann's sixtieth birthday in 1930, certainly conveyed the impression not only of an impressive past achievement but also of a strong openness toward the future with a clear connection to the mainstream of the Modern movement.

In that same year, the Austrian Werkbund mounted a large and successful exhibition of members' work under the general direction of Josef Hoffmann, who designed the main hall and a coffeehouse with garden terrace. But three years later, Hoffmann left the Werkbund in protest against intrigues and polemics directed against him and his attitude toward architecture and the decorative arts. Together with CLEMENS HOLZMEISTER, he founded a New Austrian Werkbund, and in 1934, again in an exhibition, he gave a polemical demonstration of his ideals under the telling motto "Das befreite Handwerk" (Liberated Craftsmanship)—as if to prove that it was still possible to follow the same ideals of artistic craftsmanship that had motivated him since the beginning of his career. On this and similar occasions, he exhibited highly decorative, richly molded, and often brightly colored and gilt pieces of furniture, including carved mirror-frames.

The annexation of Austria by Germany in 1938 at first seemed to promise new commissions, since Hoffmann, though himself not politically implicated, had good connections to those newly in power and was in fact appointed to reorganize the decorative arts and crafts in Austria. He arranged a House of Fashion (1938) in the historic Lobkowitz palace in Vienna and remodeled the former German embassy for the purposes of an officers' club, *Haus der Wehrmacht* (1940) in neoclassicist forms. But soon the war brought an end to all non-war-oriented building activity. Projects for a guest-house of the City of Vienna (1938–1939) and a mausoleum of Skanderbeg (1944) as a gift to Albania remained on paper, as did most projects—including a city hall for Addis Ababa (1954–1955)—which the aged architect drew during the postwar years, though the City of Vienna built a number of public housing schemes from his designs which were done partly in collaboration with Josef Kalbac. Being strictly regimented and economically controlled, they gave little scope to architectural imagination.

As a human being, Hoffmann defies any attempt to describe and comprehend the full complexity of his personality. Under the mask of the easy-going, somewhat taciturn Austrian bourgeois of settled habits lay hidden a highly sensitive and sensuous artist who was directed by a powerful will and uncompromising reliance on intuition. But he also appears beset by inhibitions, hidebound by convention, shy and vulnerable to the extreme. Averse to any intellectual formulation of artistic principles, he was nevertheless guided by certain moral convictions acquired during his early years and by a set of compositional devices that can be discerned once one penetrates beneath the surface of the almost bewildering richness and variety of his forms and spaces. One will often find not only straightforward symmetry but also the kind of ambiguity that results from making the same element in a composition part of two interlocking schemes of symmetry just as one will observe how his atectonic handling of detail often introduces ambiguity. One will also, time and again, meet unequivocal attempts to impart commonly understandable readability to architecture, to make it a vehicle of signification. Above all, one will sense in Hoffmann a simple joy of being able to invent and manipulate forms so easily, a joy that did not leave him even in the very last years of his long career.

Critics at the beginning of the twentieth century were unanimous in their praise of Hoffmann, and in 1924 PETER BEHRENS designated him as "one of the strongest personalities . . . not only among our Austrian architects but among the totality of our generation" (unpublished typescript, translated by the author). In 1928, the American critic Shepard Vogelgesang even wrote: "No recent architect has influenced Europe more comprehensively than Hoffmann" (*Architectural Forum* 49 (1928), p. 697). But this period of initial recognition was soon followed by an almost total eclipse, partly due to the fact that Hoffmann's oeuvre did not easily fit into a historiography inspired by Modern movement doctrine. It is only in recent years that his true stature has begun to reemerge and his creations are valued again; there are replicas of Hoffmann furniture in many recent interiors and his designs fetch high prices on the international art market. In the meantime, unfortunately, many of his buildings and interiors have been lost or disfigured—which makes the few that remain intact all the more precious.

During his lifetime, Hoffmann was the recipient of many honors: he held honorary doctorates from the Technical Universities in Dresden, Berlin, and Vienna, and received numerous Austrian and foreign decorations.

EDUARD F. SEKLER

WORKS

*1898, Ver Sacrum Room, First Exhibition of the Vienna Secession; *1899, Apollo Candle Shop, Am Hof; *1899, Exhibition Designs for the Third, Fourth, and Fifth Exhibition of the Vienna Secession; 1900–1901, Carl Moll House, Hohe Warte; 1901–1902, Friedrich Spitzer House, Hohe Warte; *1902, Max Biach House (interiors); Vienna. *1903, Knips Summer House, Seeboden, Carinthia, Austria. *1903, Wiener Werkstätte (workshop, office, and showrooms; with Karl Moser), Vienna. 1904, Purkersdorf Sanitorium, Austria. *1904, Vienna School of Applied Arts Room, St. Louis World's Fair, Mo. *1905–1906, Alexander Brauner House, Hohe Warte, Vienna. 1905–1911, Adolphe Stoclet House, Brussels. 1906, Wittgenstein Hunting Lodge, Hochreith near Hohenberg, Austria. *1907, Fledermaus Cabaret-Theater (interiors); *1908, Kunstschau Exhibition Building and Arrangement; 1909–1911, Eduart Ast House, Hohe Warte; Vienna. *1910–1911, Gustav Mahler Tomb, Vienna. 1911, Pavilion, International Art Exhibition, Rome. 1912, Austrian Section for Monumental Art, Dresden Art Exhibition, Germany. 1912–1913, Edmund Bernatzik House; 1912–1913, Kaasgraben Estate (four double houses); Vienna. 1912–1914, Hugo Koller House (remodeling and interior design), Oberwaltersdorf, Austria. 1913, Hospital, Jajce, Yugoslavia. *1913–1914, Primavesi House, Winkelsdorf, Czechoslovakia. 1913–1915, Josefine Skywa House (Primavesi House), Vienna. 1914, Pavilion, Cologne Werkbund Exhibition, Germany. 1916–1918, City Hall, Ortelsburg, Germany. 1919–1922, Sigmund Berl House, Fredenthal, Czechoslovakia. 1920–1921, Fritz Grohmann House, Würbenthal, Czechoslovakia. 1922–1923, Karl Dunckel House, Budapest. 1923, Boudoir, Exhibition of Austrian Decorative Arts, Vienna. 1924, Eduard Ast House, Aue near Velden, Carinthia, Austria. *1924–1925, Austrian Pavilion, Exposition Internationale des Arts Décoratifs, Paris. 1924–1925, Sonja Knips House; 1924–1925, Winarsky Hof Public Housing; *1927, Ernst Bauer Apartment (interior); 1928, Vogel and Noot Prefabricated Steel House (with O. Haerdtl); 1928–1929, Graben Coffeehouse (remodeling); Vienna. 1928–1929, Isidor Diamant House, Cluj, Rumania. 1929, Lengyel House (interior), Bratislava, Czechoslovakia. *1929, Doblinger Gramophone Shop (with Haerdtl); 1929–1930, Otto Wagner Monument; 1930–1932, Werkbund Estate (four houses), Lainz; 1932, Altmann and Kühne Shop (with Haerdtl), Graben; Vienna. 1934–1935, Austrian Pavilion (with Robert Kramreiter), Venice Biennale, Italy. *1937, Boudoir d'une grand vedette Exhibition Room, Paris World's Fair. *1938, Lobkowitz Palace (remodeling and interior of House of Fashion; with Josef Kalbac); *1940, Meissen Porcelain Factory (sales room), Kärtnerring; *1940, Haus der Wehrmacht (remodeling of former German Legation); 1953–1954, Public Housing (with Kalbac), Heiligenstädterstrasse; Vienna.

BIBLIOGRAPHY

ANKWICZ-KLEEHOVEN, HANS 1957 "Josef Hoffmann." Volume 10, pages 171–179 in *Grosse Öster-*

reicher, *Neue Österreichische Biographie.* Vienna and Zurich: Amalthea.

EISLER, MAX 1920 "Josef Hoffmann: 1870–1920." *Wendingen* Series 3 nos. 8–9:special issue.

FREY, DAGOBERT 1920 "Josef Hoffmann zu seinem 50. Geburtstage." *Der Architekt* 23:65–72.

KLEINER, LEOPOLD 1927 *Josef Hoffmann.* Berlin, Leipzig, and Vienna: Hubsch.

ÖSTERREICHISCHER WERKBUND (editor) 1930 *Josef Hoffmann zum 60. Geburtstage.* Vienna: Almanach der Dame.

ROCHOWANSKI, LEOPOLD 1950 *Josef Hoffmann.* Vienna: Österreichische Staatsdruckerei.

SEKLER, EDUARD F. 1967 "The Stocklet House by Josef Hoffmann." Volume 1 in Douglas Fraser et al. (editors), *Essays in the History of Architecture Presented to Rudolf Wittkower.* London: Phaidon.

SEKLER, EDUARD F. 1972 "Gli schizzi el viaggio in Italia di Josef Hoffmann e Josef Olbrich." In *Artisti Austriaci a Roma.* Rome: Istituto Austriaco di Cultura in Roma. Exhibition catalogue.

SEKLER, EDUARD F. 1982 *Josef Hoffmann: Das architektonische Werk.* Salzburg, Austria: Residenz Verlag. Forthcoming publication.

VERONESI, GIULIA 1956 *Josef Hoffmann.* Milan: Il Balcone.

VOGELGESANG, SHEPARD 1928 "The Work of Josef Hoffmann." *Architectural Forum* 49, no. 4:697–712.

WEISER, ARMAND 1930 *Josef Hoffmann.* Geneva: Meister der Baukunst.

HOFMEISTER, HENRY

See REINHARDT and HOFMEISTER.

HÖGER, FRITZ

Johannes Friedrich (Fritz) Höger (1877–1949), one of the representatives of German Expressionist architecture, was born in Beckenreihe, Germany. He can be considered a northern German in birth and upbringing; his Holstein heritage with its roots deeply planted in north German Gothic traditions influenced his work throughout his productive career as an architect. He passionately loved *Backstein* (clinker brick), native to northern Germany, and consistently used brick in his designs. The decorative surface treatment of his buildings was often the end result of his studio research into the various effects that light plays upon the many variations of brick color and surfaces available, such as glazed, unglazed, or vitrified. To view a Höger building properly, one must be aware of the light factor and its relationship to the time of day and the surface and pattern of the bricks.

Höger studied at the Hamburg School of Architecture (1897–1899), and in 1901–1905, he worked in the architectural firm of Lund and Kallmorgen in Hamburg. By 1907, he was working independently, designing in the early years residences, school buildings, and small businesses. Around 1910, the first evidence of his involvement with the Hamburg *Kontorhaus* (office building) style was evident with his design for the Klostertorhof Kontorhaus (1910–1911) in Hamburg. Following World War I, his continued involvement with the *Kontorhaus* design, a postwar Expressionistic attitude, and his beloved *Backstein* culminated in the Chilehaus (1923), Hamburg, perhaps the most important example of *Kontorhaus* design and German Expressionist architecture outside of Berlin. The twelve-story building clearly exhibits the potentialities of decorative brickwork and the play of light as it curves and molds itself to the natural contours of the street, which forms the shape of an enormous bow of a ship. From an Expressionistic point of view, the building as a symbol boldly represents both the shipping offices it contains and the harbor city of Hamburg, where it seems to be moored. In 1927, another *Kontorhaus* named the Springenhof was begun nearby the Chilehaus. It was built over a series of phases and was completed in 1943. Both buildings weathered World War II and without doubt are Höger's most important works.

Höger continued to design until his death in 1949. He was considered by many to be one of Germany's most popular architects, whereas others reduced him to cliché and criticized his obsession with *Backstein*.

JO ANNE PASCHALL

Höger. Chilehaus. Hamburg, Germany. 1923

WORKS

1910–1911, Klostertorhof Kontorhaus; 1923, Chilehaus; Hamburg, Germany. 1927, Hanover Advertising Offices, Germany. 1927–1928, Scherk Perfume Factory, Berlin. 1927–1943, Sprinkenhof Kontorhaus, Hamburg, Germany. 1928, Flughafen Estate, Fuhlsbüttel, Hamburg, Germany. 1928–1929, Town Hall, Rüstringen, Germany. 1929–1930, Church at Hohenzollernplatz, Wilmersdorf, Berlin. 1930, City Hospital, Delmenhorst, Germany.

BIBLIOGRAPHY

BERKENHAGEN, EKHART (editor) 1977 *Fritz Höger: Baumeister-Zeichnungen.* Berlin: Kunstbibliothek.

"Chile House, Hamburg." 1925 *Architectural Review* 58, Nov.:192–194.

PEHNT, WOLFGANG 1973 *Expressionist Architecture.* New York: Praeger.

"The Rathaus at Rüstringen, Germany. 1931 *Architectural Review* 69, Feb.:plate 5.

WESTPHAL, CARL J. (editor) 1938 *Fritz Höger der niederdeutsche Backsteinbaumeister.* Lübeck, Germany: Wolfshagen-Scharbeutz.

HÖGG, EMIL

Emil Högg (1867–1954) was a leading German architectural educator of the conservative school, 1911–1933. Born in Heilbronn, he studied in Stuttgart, Germany, and was a follower of FRITZ SCHUMACHER in Bremen before becoming a professor in Dresden in 1911. He remained in East Germany after World War II and died in Dresden.

RON WIEDENHOEFT

WORKS

1911–1933, City Hall (reconstruction), Jena, Germany. 1911–1933, Hospital, Annaberg, Germany. 1911–1933, Zeiss-Ikon Optical Works, Jena, Germany.

BIBLIOGRAPHY

SCHUBERT, O. 1955 "Obituary." *Deutsche Architektur* 4:139.

HOLABIRD and ROCHE

Holabird and Roche established one of the most creative and influential architectural offices to flourish during the great age of Chicago building. William Holabird was born in American Union, New York (a place no longer listed in atlases), on September 11, 1854, the son of Samuel Beckley Holabird, a general in the United States Army. He was accepted as a cadet in the United States Military Academy in 1873, but left two years later over a dispute with the authorities. With little more than two beginning years of an engineering education behind him, he moved to Chicago, where he entered the office of WILLIAM LE BARON JENNEY as a draftsman. From this association with the older architect he derived a strongly functional approach to design, with the emphasis on economy, durability, maximum openness of unencumbered interior space, and generous window areas for maximum light and ventilation. The formal treatment of the visible elevations was to grow directly from the functional requirements and the structural solutions by means of which they might be realized.

Martin Roche, who was born in Cleveland, Ohio, on August 1, 1853, moved to Chicago with his family in 1857. His education was limited to elementary school and the school of the Chicago Art Institute, which he left in 1867 to begin his career as an apprentice to a cabinetmaker. Like Holabird, he also received his practical education as an architect in Jenney's office, which he entered in 1872.

William Holabird formed a partnership with Ossian C. Simonds in 1880, and expanded it to include Roche in 1881. Simonds left two years later, when the immensely productive association of Holabird and Roche was established. The firm was offered so little business in its first two years that Roche was compelled to design furniture for manufacturers to supplement the partners' meager income. The first commission for a newly constructed building came in 1885, but it could hardly have seemed very promising, since it was a little two-story shop and apartment block in Chicago. The union of Holabird's engineering and planning skills and Roche's artistic talents, however, virtually guaranteed success, and it came suddenly in 1886 with a commission for a Chicago skyscraper that was eventually to attract worldwide attention. Subsequent commissions were offered in a steadily rising flood, and the partners were soon regarded as the leading architects in the Middle West. The original partnership flourished for forty-four years, until the death of Holabird in Evanston, Illinois, on July 19, 1923. The promotion of Holabird's son to the status of partner allowed the firm to retain the name until the death of Martin Roche on June 6, 1927, at which date the office assumed the present title of Holabird and Root.

The first commission that offered the possibility of an enviable future success was for the Tacoma Building in 1886. The permit for the construction of this important pioneer skyscraper was issued on April 10, 1888, and the twelve-story building was opened late in the following year. The structural system, which was primarily the work of the engineer Carl Seiffert, embodied all the techniques and materials regularly used at the time. The cast-iron columns rested on a grillage of wrought-iron beams carried in turn by reinforced concrete rafts. The spandrel and floor girders were wrought-iron, the floor beams steel, and the mullions and lintel beams cast iron. All connections between the elements of the frame were riveted, which marked the most extensive use of this technique up to the time. The Tacoma Building exemplifies the typical skyscraper construction of the late 1880s. All floor, roof, and wind loads

Holabird and Roche.
Pontiac Building.
Chicago.
1891

Holabird and Roche.
Old Colony Building.
Chicago.
1893–1894

were divided between the iron and steel skeleton and brick bearing walls. The street elevations were true curtain walls carried entirely by the iron framing members. On the interior, however, the frame was supplemented by two brick walls that rose through the entire height of the building. The fact that these walls were reinforced with diagonal and rectangular wrought-iron bracing suggests that they were precursors of the later wind-resisting shear wall of reinforced concrete. The rear elevations, contiguous to adjacent buildings, were traditional bearing walls of brick. The street elevations of the Tacoma were opened to an extraordinary degree by means of generous, closely spaced windows and oriel bays distributed over the full width of both elevations and rising from the second-floor level to the top of the parapet. The strongly unified treatment of the wall, the repetitive pattern of windows set at several light-reflecting angles, the delicate terra cotta ornament, and the general quality of lightness and openness made the Tacoma a prize work. Its demolition on its fiftieth anniversary was a serious loss to American architecture.

The architects never exactly duplicated the formal design of the Tacoma. The hallmark of their numerous office buildings in Chicago is the strongly articulated or cellular wall distinguished by bay-wide openings of Chicago windows (a broad fixed sash flanked at the edges by narrow movable sashes), continuous and slightly projecting piers, recessed spandrels, and skillfully handled ornament in terra cotta designed to frame window areas and to delineate and accent the narrow bands

of piers and spandrels. The full aesthetic and functional realization of this program came to maturity in the Marquette Building (1894–1895), designed in collaboration with the engineer Corydon T. Purdy. Purdy previously collaborated with the architects in the commission for the Old Colony Building (1893–1894), for which the engineer introduced portal-arch bracing in the steel frame. The more traditional column-and-girder cage of the Marquette is clearly expressed in the two street elevations, but this simple rectangular geometry is enhanced by a terra-cotta ornament that offers a particularly eloquent demonstration of how skilled architects transform functionally correct building into compelling visual art.

With the exception of the Chicago Building (1904), which marked a return to the oriels or projecting bays of the Tacoma, Holabird and Roche adhered steadfastly to the flat cellular wall of the Marquette in a long series of store and office blocks erected in Chicago through 1910. The fundamental program in all cases could be reduced to a few abstract concepts, yet the architects were able to develop a rich diversity of architectonic expressions out of this simple functional approach. Of the many buildings placed under construction around the turn of the century, three can be singled out by the historian as particularly handsome examples of the genre. In the McClurg Building (1899–1900), the Annex of the Mandel Brothers Store (1900,1905), and the Brooks Building (1909–1910), the distinctions of the designs arose from variations on mouldings, ornamental details, and clustered shafts, combined with subtle differences in the proportions of bays and in the depths of window reveals. Each building clearly belongs to a unified body of work—a local school of architecture—yet each possesses its own individualized features.

Around 1910 Holabird and Roche struck out in a new direction, away from the sobriety of the commercial style toward greater extravagance of form and a freer use of historical details. The new departure was most strongly marked by the La Salle Hotel (1908–1909), an opulent work in the influential Beaux-Arts mode usually known as the Second Empire Style. The handsome and well-planned building placed the architects on the road to becoming the leading hotel designers in the Middle West, with such enviable commissions to their credit as the huge Palmer House (the third of that name, 1923–1925, 1927) and the even grander Stevens Hotel (1925–1927), successively the largest of their kind in the world. In addition, they designed comparable though more modest hotels in other cities, most notably in Columbus, Ohio; Grand Rapids, Michigan; Kansas City, Missouri;

Milwaukee, Wisconsin; and Minneapolis, Minnesota.

On an equal scale in both size and complexity is the City–County Building of Chicago (1910-1911), which fills an entire block and originally provided space for the city hall, the municipal offices, and the county court house. The massive colonnades of the exterior walls are impressive examples of an orthodox classical tradition, but the elliptical vaults covering the extremely broad main corridors, their soffits finished in polychromatic mosaic, spring from a more innovative spirit. Another building covering an entire city block is the former administrative center and printing plant of Rand McNally and Company (1911-1912), in which the articulated walls with their subdued Gothic details belong more clearly to the earlier Chicago style. The last work placed under construction as well as designed by Holabird and Roche belongs to the creative tradition of the Tacoma and the Marquette. The commission was awarded shortly before Martin Roche died in 1927. The 333 North Michigan Building (1927-1928), based on ELIEL SAARINEN's second-prize entry in the competition (1922) for the Tribune Building (1923-1925), marked the introduction of the Art Deco style to Chicago. The prolific office thus ended its history where it had begun more than forty years earlier, giving to commercial building a new form that served to inaugurate a new architectural style.

CARL W. CONDIT

WORKS

*1888-1889, Tacoma Building; 1891, Pontiac Building; 1893-1894, Old Colony Building; 1894-1895, Marquette Building; 1898, Gage Group; 1898, Williams Building; *1898-1899, Cable Building; 1899-1900, McClurg Building; 1900, 1905, Mandel Brothers Store Annex; 1903, Champlain Building; 1904, Chicago Building; *1904-1905, 1909, Republic Building; *1908-1909, La Salle Hotel; 1909-1910, Brooks Building; 1910-1911, City–County Building; 1911-1912, Rand McNally Building; 1920, Crerar Library; 1923-1925, 1927, Palmer House; 1924-1926, Roanoke Tower; 1925-1927, Stevens Hotel; 1927-1928, 333 North Michigan Building; Chicago.

BIBLIOGRAPHY

CONDIT, CARL W. 1964 *The Chicago School of Architecture: A History of Commercial and Public Building in the Chicago Area, 1875-1925.* University of Chicago Press.

CONDIT, CARL W. 1973 *Chicago, 1910-29: Building, Planning, and Urban Technology.* University of Chicago Press.

"Holabird, William." 1943 Volume 9, pages 127-128 in *Dictionary of American Biography.* New York: Scribner.

HOLCOMB, PAUL 1929 *Depreciation and Obsolescence in the Tacoma Building.* Chicago: National Association of Building Owners and Managers.

MUJICA, FRANCISCO 1929 *History of the Skyscraper.* Paris: Archaeology and Architecture Press.

RANDALL, FRANK A. 1949 *History of the Development of Building Construction in Chicago.* Urbana: University of Illinois Press.

WEBSTER, J. CARSON 1959 "The Skyscraper: Logical and Historical Considerations." *Journal of the Society of Architectural Historians* 18:126-139.

WINKLER, FRANZ 1912 "Some Chicago Buildings Represented by the Work of Holabird and Roche." *Architectural Record* 31:313-387.

HOLDEN, CHARLES

Charles Holden (1875-1960) was one of the greatest English architects of his generation and a designer who was anxious to use modern methods and a modern idiom without ever forgetting the lessons of tradition. Holden was born in Bolton, Lancashire, and was apprenticed to E. W. Leeson of Manchester while studying at the Manchester Technical School. He moved to London and worked for CHARLES R. ASHBEE whose Arts and Crafts ideals were complemented by Holden's own admiration for the poetry of Walt Whitman. However, Holden found Ashbee's practice too rarefied, and in 1899 he became chief assistant to H. Percy Adams (see ADAMS, HOLDEN, AND PEARSON), an efficient designer of hospitals. Holden rapidly became indispensable in designing the massing and elevations suitable for Adam's plans and designed several buildings of distinction before becoming Adams's partner in 1907. These included the Belgrave Hospital for Children, London, whose stylized Tudor in brick shows the influence of Ashbee and of HENRY WILSON, and the Extension to the Law Society, London, which was Holden's first essay in an austere mannerist classicism. Holden's design for the Bristol Central Reference Library won independently in competition, was deferential to the adjacent Bristol Cathedral but had a powerful massing which may have influenced CHARLES RENNIE MACKINTOSH's design for the Glasgow School of Art.

Holden's design for the British Medical Association, London, was remarkable both for its inventive mannerist architecture and for its integrated sculpture by Jacob Epstein. Holden was a member of the Art-Workers' Guild and friendly with many artists; throughout his career, he was determined to employ modern sculptors on his buildings, often despite the opposition of clients. A visit to the United States in 1913 encouraged Holden to develop beyond historical styles to a simplified and monumental modern architecture; his simplification of classicism in the years before 1914 is, in some ways, analogous to the contemporary work of ADOLF LOOS.

Holden worked for the Imperial War Graves Commission in 1918 and from 1920 until 1926 was its fourth principal architect (along with EDWIN LUTYENS, HERBERT BAKER, and REGINALD BLOMFIELD). Many of the sixty-seven war cemeteries he designed are remarkable for their austere, almost brutal geometry. A similar concentration on pure geometry, disciplined by a classical sense of form, distinguishes Holden's famous work for the London Underground Railways. In 1915, Holden met Frank Pick, the inspired administrator of Underground Electric Railways and, later, the London Passenger Transport Board. Both Holden and Pick were interested in industrial design and were founder members of the Design and Industries Association. Pick, who commissioned Edward Johnson to design the sans-serif London Transport lettering and other artists to design posters, asked Holden to design the new Underground headquarters above Saint James's Park station. This monumental stripped-classical building, with sculpture by Eric Gill, Henry Moore, and others, clearly reflects Holden's knowledge of American skyscraper design.

After 1924, Holden redesigned several existing Underground stations and designed new ones on the extensions to the system. Those on the Modern extension of the Northern Line are in Holden's monumental stripped classical manner, faced in Portland stone. In 1930, Holden and Pick toured Holland, Germany, and Scandinavia, and this experience of modern architecture strongly influenced Holden's designs for the new stations on the Piccadilly Line. The most famous of these is at Arnos Grove, a structure of brick and reinforced concrete and metal windows, whose pure geometry with a drum above a rectilinear base is reminiscent of the Stockholm City Library by ERIK GUNNAR ASPLUND. Holden and his assistants designed every detail of these stations, often in association with S. A. Heaps, the London Passenger Transport Board chief architect.

In 1931, Holden was commissioned to design his most monumental executed building, the new University of London. As the Senate House was not a utilitarian structure but an important public building in central London, Holden adopted a monumental treatment in Portland stone, a material Holden loved and understood. Although superficially in a stripped classical manner, this is a design of great subtlety, with a rhythm of fenestration and an attention to detail and to weathering that were a legacy of the Gothic Revival combined with a central tower which is reminiscent of an American skyscraper. As Holden mistrusted the longevity of structural steel, the building is of self-supporting masonry construction. It was designed for gradual extension, which has not always proceeded to Holden's designs.

Holden's last years were largely spent as an adviser on town planning in London. He collaborated with WILLIAM GRAHAM HOLFORD on the City of London and prepared a plan for the South Bank of the Thames. A man of peculiar modesty who believed that architecture is a collaborative effort, Holden twice declined a knighthood.

GAVIN STAMP and ALAN POWERS

WORKS

1900–1903, Belgrave Hospital for Children, Kensington; 1902–1904, Law Society (extension), Chancery Lane; 1903, British Seamen's Hospital, Istanbul. 1903–1904, Norwich House, High Holborn, London. 1903–1906, King Edward VII Sanatorium, Midhurst, Sussex, England. 1904, Tunbridge Wells General Hospital, Kent, England. 1905–1906, Central Reference Library; 1906–1912, Bristol Royal Infirmary, Bristol, England. 1907–1908, British Medical Association (later Rhodesia House; now Zimbabwe House), Strand; 1908, Women's Hospital, Soho Square; London. c.1911–1912, Tomb of Oscar Wilde (with Jacob Epstein), Père Lachaise Cemetery, Paris. 1911–1929, Sutton Valence Public School, Kent, England. 1914–1923, King's College for Women, Kensington, London. 1918–1926, War cemeteries in France and Belgium. 1922, War Memorial Gateway, Clifton College, Bristol, England. 1924–1929, Underground Stations (including Piccadilly Circus and Leicester Square; rebuilding); 1925–1926, Underground Stations, Northern Line; 1927–1930, London Transport Headquarters, 55 Broadway; 1931–1933, Underground Stations, Piccadilly Line; 1931–1937, Senate House and buildings for London University, Bloomsbury; London. 1933, National Library of Wales, Aberstwyth. 1952–1958, London University (Birbeck College, Students' Union, and the Warburg Institute), Bloomsbury, London.

BIBLIOGRAPHY

HANSON, BRIAN 1975 "Singing the Body Electric with Charles Holden." *Architectural Review* 158:349–356.

HUTTON, CHARLES 1969 "Dr. Charles Holden." *Artifex* 3:35–53.

"Obituary." 1960 *Journal of the Royal Institute of British Architects* 17:383–384.

PEVSNER, NICKLAUS 1942 "Patient Progress—The Life Work of Frank Pick." Volume 2, pages 190–209 in *Studies in Art, Architecture and Design*. London: Thames & Hudson. Originally appeared as an article in *Architectural Review* 42:31–48.

REILLY, C. H. 1931 "Charles Holden." *Building* September:396–401.

STAMP, GAVIN, and HARRIS, JOHN 1977 *Silent Cities*. London: Royal Institute of British Architects.

HOLL, ELIAS

Elias Holl (1573–1646) was born in Augsburg, Germany. His father, Hans Holl, under whom Elias obtained his training, as well as his grandfather Sebastian Holl and great-grandfather Jakob Hall had been masons working in the city of Augsburg. Elias's training encompassed first of all technical aspects of construction and to a lesser degree the designing of buildings. Local building traditions dominated, but to a certain extent other influences can be documented as well. In 1587, Holl worked with his father on the house for Max Rehlinger which had been designed in the "Welsh manner" (Italian style) by Wendel Dietrich. Holl participated in the construction and decoration of the house for Hans Mehrer and was also involved in the construction and rebuilding of houses for the merchant Anton Garb. The architectural activities of these early years which Elias executed under his father's responsibility are mentioned in Holl's family chronicle. At the time of his father's death in 1594, Elias had not yet established himself as a *Meister* (master) and therefore was not allowed to accept commissions on his own. Only on May 25, 1596, did Elias present proof of his mastership.

In 1590, Jakob Fugger had suggested a study trip to Italy but this proposal was rejected by Elias's father. Finally, in 1600, Elias was given an opportunity to visit Italy. Anton Garb, for whom Holl had worked earlier, took Elias with him on a trip to Venice which lasted from November 18, 1600, to January 31, 1601. This was probably the only encounter with Italian architecture. The exposure to the buildings of Jacopo Sansovino and Andrea Palladio must have made a strong impression on Elias, yet his own architectural activity in subsequent years does not give any indication that he wanted to adopt their styles for his works. His own recollections in the family chronicle are very brief and surprisingly unspecific. What did establish Holl after his return as the leading master in Augsburg was his technical ability, the mastery of the craft of the mason.

After his return from Italy, Holl was involved in the construction of two major buildings, the Giesshaus or foundry (1601) and the Beckenhaus or baker's house (1602). Holl was also consulted with regard to the construction of the Zeughaus (armory) which originally had been entrusted to the city's official mason, Jakob Erschey. Holl's criticism of the design and especially the structural features of the building under construction led to the retirement of Erschey and Holl's appointment as Erschey's successor in 1602. This appointment meant that Holl was responsible for all official building activity in the city. During the following years, major new buildings were erected with Holl's participation: The Zeughaus (1602–1607), the Siegelhaus (1605; destroyed 1809), the Metz(i)g or slaughterhouse (1609), the Kaufhaus or shop building and the Barfüsserbrücke (1611), the Gymnasium (school building) next to Saint Anna's (1613) and the Neue Bau (1614). In the same year, construction began on Holl's most important building, the City Hall (1614–1620). Two of the city gates, the Klinkertor (destroyed) and the Rote Tor were built in 1622, followed by Holl's last work for Augsburg, the Heilig Geist Spital (Holy Ghost Hospital), constructed between 1625 and 1630. Holl's activities as the official city mason came to an end in 1631, when he was dismissed for religious reasons as a consequence of the Edict of Nantes. Holl, a Protestant, refused to return to the church. Reinstated in his office in 1632, when King Gustav Adolf took the city, he was dismissed again in 1635 after the departure of the Swedes. Devoting the last years of his life on writing the family chronicle (our main source for Holl's activity together with the acts of the city's construction office). Holl died in Augsburg. He was married twice, first in 1595 to Maria Burckhart with whom he had eight children and in 1610, three years after his first wife's death, to Rosina Reischlen who bore him thirteen children and died in 1635.

The events of Holl's life, his rise from obscurity to the highest office the city of Augsburg could bestow upon a mason, and his fall as a consequence of the religious strife of seventeenth-century Europe, have early on led to a mystification of his personality. This tendency has continued up to the present century. The existence of a great number of architectural models, believed to have been done in connection with the building of the City Hall and therefore attributed to Holl, has furthermore confused the image of Holl the architect since it had to combine a great variety of styles in the work of one individual. Only the thorough analysis of the models and drawings undertaken by Rudolf Pfister and Ingebors Albrecht has established Holl's share in each of the works originally attributed to him. Jürgen Zimmer's investigation into the sources for the City Hall has further prepared the framework into which this building has to be placed.

The construction of many new public buildings in Augsburg at the beginning of the seventeenth century must be seen in connection with a tendency toward urban monumentalization which began in the late sixteenth century with the erection of elaborate fountains along Augsburg's north–south axis, which might have been identical with the Roman Via Claudia Augusta. Markus

Welser's *History of Augsburg* (1594 and 1595), his archeological interest in the former Roman colony, his belief in Augsburg as an image of Rome, and his profound interest in VITRUVIUS must be seen as major factors in the architectural projects in which Holl was involved.

To be able to evaluate Holl's role properly, one must keep in mind that his position as city mason did not provide him with an absolute authority to design buildings according to his own ideas. On the contrary, Holl was first of all charged with the execution of plans by others which had been approved by his superiors, the *Bauherren* Matthäus Welser and Bernhard Rehlinger. As the circumstances of Holl's appointment indicate, he was first of all hired as engineer.

The Zeughaus (armory) was the first structure erected by Holl after his criticism of Erschey had led to his official appointment. Although he changed the groundplan through the addition of a second wing (thus creating the L-shaped structure), the façade which is characterized by a sculptural quality culminating in Reichel's Saint Michael over the entrance follows the design of Joseph Heinz. The basic design features of the Zeughaus also determine the appearance of the Siegelhaus in which Matthäus Welser and Joseph Heinz collaborated and the façade of the Stadtmetz(i)g which was delineated by Heinz. Matthias Kager is responsible for the façades of the Kaufhaus and of the Neue Bau. Heinz's as well as Kager's proposals emphasize sculptural elements in doors and window frames and the horizontal and vertical articulation of the buildings. These features contrast strongly with Holl's authentic designs for the Willibaldsburg near Eichstätt. A residential wing is bracketed by two corner towers. Both the wing and the towers were altered in later years. The original state is rendered in an engraving by Merian of 1627. Ornamentation is almost absent from the façade and limited to the arcades of the courtyard. Thus, Holl created a massive and blocklike appearance stressing the basic character of the building as fortress. Holl's city gates in Augsburg are marked by the same severity in appearance.

The designs for the Gymnasium near Saint Anna's follow the style of the Willibaldsburg. The cubic quality of the structure dominates the few ornamental elements (limited to window frames, a small gable over the center of the façade, and the ashlar at its corners). The external symmetry is also maintained in the interior where the staircase occupies the center of the building. This was a new feature which would be fully explored in the staircases of baroque palaces.

The Heilig Geist Spital (Holy Ghost Hospital) is Holl's last work for the city of Augsburg and is claimed as his own in the family chronicle. Originally, only an addition to an existing structure was planned; after its collapse, however, the entire hospital project was redesigned, stressing the simplicity which had become the hallmark of Holl's authentic structures. The courtyard whose asymmetrical form is the result of the topography of the site is marked by a two-story arcade. The openings of the second story were walled in at a later time.

The most important of Holl's structures is the City Hall. Its architecture and decoration (the latter destroyed during World War II) were engraved by Salomon Kleiner in 1733. A wooden City Hall erected in the middle of the thirteenth century had been replaced in 1385 by a stone building which in turn had been altered in subsequent centuries. In 1609–1610, Holl prepared drawings and a model of this structure in connection with his proposal to modernize City Hall. The placement of windows and portals would have been systematized and the former three front gables of unequal height were to be replaced by a common roofline and one large roof. Some elements of the old building, such as the tower and the corner balcony, would have remained part of the new structure, stressing the continuity of the old in the new. This early project was not executed, and plans for the rebuilding of City Hall were resumed only in 1614 when Holl proposed new plans. A series of plans and wooden models reflects the various proposals under consideration at this time. At an early planning stage, the "old" elements (tower, corner balcony) disappeared and the initially planned U-shaped structure was turned into a rectangular one, first with three gables which had characterized the appearance of the medieval City Hall, then with one large center gable over the front and back façades and two smaller and lower ones over the sides. This latter feature was eventually replaced by two towers. Work on the fabric was carried out between August 1615 when the cornerstone for the north wing was laid and May 1620 when the main portal was erected. Holl was not involved in the interior decoration of the building. Holl's design stresses the center part of the building where the Golden Hall is located. This room occupied two stories and reaches through the entire depth of the building. The wings with their towers (which house the staircases) are clearly subordinated to the center and this relation is expressed in the different treatment of the windows and the portal and also in the fact that the center and the wings are set off against each other.

Holl's building departs from the features traditionally found in city halls. Instead, it resumes elements which can be linked with sixteenth-century reconstructions of Vitruvius's Basilica at Fano (at that time believed to have been located in Rome). There, all the elements that characterize Holl's model before the addition of the towers are found. The relation to this model is unique as is the building itself, which has never been imitated in any other city hall.

Holl's achievement as architect has to be seen primarily on the basis of those works he himself designed and executed. From the Willibaldsburg to the Heilig Geist Spital, these elements remain constant: the emphasis on cubic forms, clear separation of individual elements within a building, subordination of decorative elements. In these elements, Holl's works can be distinguished from those of Heinz or Kager.

EGON VERHEYEN

WORKS

*1601, Foundry; 1602, Baker's House; 1602, Saint Anna's Tower; 1602–1607, Armory; *1605, Siegelhaus; 1605, Wertachorugger Tor; 1609, Slaughterhouse; Augsburg, Germany. 1609, Willibaldsburg, Eienstädt, Germany. 1611, Barfüsserbrücke (substructure preserved); 1613, Saint Anna Gymnasium; *1614, Neue Bau; 1614–1620, City Hall; *1622, Klinkertor; 1622, Rotes Tor; 1625–1630, Heilig Geist Spital; Augsburg, Germany.

BIBLIOGRAPHY

ALBRECHT, INGEBORG 1937 "Elias Holl, Stil und Werk des 'Maurmaisters' und der Augsburger Malerarchitekten Heinz und Kager." *Münchner Jahrbuch der Bildenen Kunst* 12:101–136.

BAUM, JULIUS 1908 *Die Bauwerke des Elias Holl.* Strasbourg, France: Heitz & Mündel.

HAGER, WERNER 1971 "Vergleichendes zu Elias Holl." *Aachener Kunstblätter* 41:231–236.

HIEBER, HERMANN 1923 *Elias Holl: Der Meister der deutschen Renaissance.* Munich: Piper.

LIEB, NORBERT 1955 "Augsburger Baukunst der Renaissancezeit." Pages 229–247 in Hermann Rinn (editor), *Augusta 955–1955: Forschungen und Studien zur Kultur- und Wirtschaftsgeschichte Augsburgs.* Munich: The editor.

MEYER, CHRISTIAN 1910 *Die Hauschronik der Familie Holl.* Munich: Nahr & Funk.

PFISTER, RUDOLF 1937 "Die Augsburger Rathausmodelle des Elias Holl." *Münchner Jahrbuch der Bildenen Kunst* 12:85–100.

SCHÜRER, OSKAR 1938 *Elias Holl: Der Augsburger Stadt Werkmeister.* Berlin: VDI.

STANGE, ALFRED 1927 "Zur Bibliographie des Elias Holl." *Münchner Jahrbuch der Bildenden Kunst* 4:20–22.

WALTER, RENATE VON 1972 *Das Augsburger Rathaus: Architektur und Bildgehalt.* Augsburg, Germany: Mühlberger.

ZWIMMER, JÜRGEN 1977 "Das Augsburger Rathaus und die Tradition." *Münchner Jahrbuch der Bildenden Kunst* 28:191–218. Includes a catalogue of Holl's architectural drawings and models.

HOLLAND, HENRY

The reputation of Henry Holland (1745–1806) among the leading architects of his generation rested on his ability to produce designs that were distinguished by a subtlety of plan and restraint in decoration and that even in his work for princely clients lost nothing by a scaling down of proportion and avoidance of the grandiose. The eldest son of a successful builder and occasional architect whose firm had long been established at Fulham, on the outskirts of London, young Holland trained under his father and assumed responsibility for the execution of several of the firm's commissions during the 1760s. This led to his being taken on in 1770 as an assistant to CAPABILITY BROWN, the architect and landscape gardener, who had for some time been a friend and business associate of the elder Holland. As Brown's own sons showed no interest in their father's profession, he came increasingly to rely on Holland's collaboration for the architectural side of his practice, and in 1773 the ties were strengthened by Holland's marriage to Capability's elder daughter, Bridget.

Thus established, Holland came to the notice of many potential clients. Even before Brown's death in 1783, he was giving independent designs, notably for Brooks's Club (1776) and the early development scheme for Hans Town (1777 and later) on land belonging to Lord Cadogan. He continued, however, to collaborate with his father-in-law in such undertakings as the restoration of Cardiff Castle (1777), Trentham Hall (1775–1778), and Nuneham Courtenay (1781–1782). From 1783, Holland became the favorite architect of the Whig hierarchy whose Gallic sympathies had an undoubted influence on him. Although most of his external designs remained basically Palladian (see ANDREA PALLADIO), his schemes for internal arrangement and decoration show his interest in current French taste. Although he did not himself visit Paris until 1785, the published works of J. M. Peyre (see PEYRE FAMILY), PIERRE PATTE, and JACQUES GONDOIN were available for study in the early stages of his most important work, the rehabilitation of Carlton House (1783–1796) for the Prince of Wales. It was for this commission that Holland took on a French émigré assistant, J. P. Trécourt, and subsequently employed several French artisans.

Carlton House was, of course, an exceptional commission demanding a degree of magnificence

Holland.
Carlton House
(rehabilitation).
London.
1783–1796

Holland.
Marine Pavilion.
Brighton, Sussex, England.
1786–1787

for royal functions, although even here Holland was able to achieve what HORACE WALPOLE described as an "August simplicity." In less exalted but still important houses, his arrangement of rooms as an *enfilade,* leading into each other, and the replacement of elaborate plasterwork with vertical strips of painted design, as at Althorp and Southill, became hallmarks of his later style.

As a result of declining health Holland carried out little work after 1803. He died in 1806, at Sloane Place (1777), the elegant house which he had built for himself, and where was displayed the fine collection of antique fragments which he had commissioned his one-time draftsman, CHARLES HEATHCOTE TATHAM, to collect for him in Italy. His office drawings and other papers passed to an uncaring nephew, Henry Rowles, who destroyed them.

DOROTHY STROUD

WORKS

1769–1774, Claremont House (with "Capability" Brown), Esher, Surrey, England. 1774–1775, Benham Place (with Brown), Newbury, England. *1775–1778, 1782, Cadland (with Brown), Hampshire, England. *1775–1778, Trentham Hall (remodeling, with Brown), Staffordshire, England. 1776–1778, Brook's Club, London. *1777, Cardiff Castle (restoration, with Brown), South Wales, England. 1777 and later, Hans Town (including the development of Sloane Street, Hans Place, Cadogan Place, Holland's House), London. 1778–1781, Berrington Hall, Herefordshire, England. 1781–1782, Nuneham Park (alterations, with Brown), Oxfordshire, England. *1783–1796, Carlton House (re-

habilitation), London. 1786–1787, Marine Pavilion, Brighton, Sussex, England. 1787, York House (additions; now Dover House), Whitehall, London. 1787–1789, Althorp (remodeling), Northamptonshire, England. 1787–1802, Woburn Abbey (alterations), Bedfordshire, England. 1788–1792, Broadlands, Hampshire, England. *1791–1794, Drury Lane Theater, *1792, Covent Garden Theater (remodeling); London. 1792, Swan Hotel, Bedford, England. *1795, Debden Hall, Essex, England. 1796–1800, Southill House, Bedfordshire, England. *1800, Wimbledon Park House, Surrey, England. 1803–1804, Albany Chambers, London.

BIBLIOGRAPHY

HODSON, H. B. 1855 "Holland the Architect." *The Builder* 13:437.
STROUD, DOROTHY 1966 *Henry Holland: His Life and Architecture.* London: Country Life.

HOLM, HANS JØRGEN

Hans Jørgen Holm (1835–1916) received his education at the Royal Academy in Copenhagen and was the favorite pupil of JOHAN DANIEL HERHOLDT, one of the innovators of Danish historicism. Holm followed in the footsteps of his master in the search for a national style suitable for his time. To him, neoclassicism was the cause for loss of tradition. Out of his many travel sketches of European medieval and Renaissance architecture he managed to create a personal free style distinguished by simplicity. As a traditional revivalist he focused on local building materials and construction methods, but he did not neglect modern technical achievements. He organized a comprehensive measuring of old Danish architecture, the result of which was published from 1872–1913 and turned out to be most influential on architectural education in Denmark. His most important student was MARTIN NYROP.

LISBET BALSLEV JØRGENSEN

WORKS

1869, Sundby Church, Copenhagen. 1870–1872, Sanderumgård Manor, Denmark. 1875, Christianshavn Secondary School; 1879–1906, Royal Library; 1884, Villa Schwartz; 1888–1893, Mineralogical Museum, Nørrevold; 1892, Funeral Chapel, Vestre Kirkegård; 1893–1894, Overformynderiet, Stormgade; Copenhagen.

BIBLIOGRAPHY

JØRGENSEN, LISBET BALSLEV 1979 Pages 56, 93–196 in *Danmarks arkitektur, Enfamiliehuset.* Copenhagen: Gyldendal.
JØRGENSEN, LISBET BALSLEV 1980 Pages 133–136, 173 in *Danmarks arkitektur, Magtens bolig.* Copenhagen: Gyldendal.

HOLZMEISTER, CLEMENS

Clemens Holzmeister (1886–) was born in Fulpmes, Austria. He first practiced architecture in 1914, but his most important contributions were in the field of teaching. Holzmeister was educated at the Technische Hochschule in Vienna where he was professor of architecture for one year in 1919. From 1919 to 1924, he was professor at the Staatsgewerbeschule in Innsbruck and from 1924 to 1938 he was professor and head of the architectural master class at the Academy of Fine Arts in Vienna. In Düsseldorf, Germany, Holzmeister held a professorship at the Kunstakademie from 1928 to 1932. He left Austria in 1938 to live in Turkey where he was professor of architecture at the Technical School in Istanbul (1940–1949). Holzmeister again assumed his professorial duties at the Academy of Fine Arts in Vienna upon his return from Turkey in 1954. Since 1957, he has taught his own master class near Salzburg, where he lives.

Trained with an essentially historical viewpoint toward architecture, Holzmeister used his background of tradition as a reference point from which to transform and expand both his design and his theory of building. An important aspect of his architectural ideas lies in a potentiality to "perform" in a theatrical and emotional way. Thus, a more rational design choice is sacrificed for the immediately impressive façade.

PETER L. DONHAUSER

WORKS

1922–1923, City Crematorium, Vienna. 1923, Parish Church, Batschuns, Voralberg, Austria. 1924, Heroes' Church of Mary, Vorkloster, Austria. 1924–1925, Public Housing Development, 128 Linzerstrasse, Vienna. 1926–1928, Women's School, Linz, Austria. 1930, Parish Church of Judas Thaddeus; School, 6 Grinzingerstrasse; Vienna. 1931, Government and Bank Buildings, Istanbul, Turkey. 1931–1932, Presidential Palace, Ankara. 1933, Parish Church of Saint Albert, Berlin. 1933–1934, Seipel-Dollfuss Church, Vienna. 1953–1960, Festival Theater (additions and development), Salzburg, Austria. 1960, Evangelical Church, Kitzbühl, Austria. 1965, German Embassy (with ROLF GUTBROD), Vienna.

BIBLIOGRAPHY

ACHLEITNER, FRIEDRICH 1966 "Clemens Holzmeister." *BAU* 21, nos. 1–2:11–23.
BECKER, PAUL 1966 *Clemens Holzmeister und Salzburg.* Salzburg, Austria: Residenz Verlag.
FAUSTENHAMMER, ROBERT 1971 "Clemens Holzmeister." *Planen, Bauen, Wohnen* nos. 39–40:9–18.
GREGOR, JOSEPH 1953 *Clemens Holzmeister: Das Architektonische Werk.* Vienna: Österreichische Staatsdruckerei.
HOLZMEISTER, CLEMENS 1934 *Casabella* 7:4–16.
HOLZMEISTER, CLEMENS 1937 *Bauten, Entwürfe und Handzeichnungen.* Salzburg, Austria: Pustet.
HOLZMEISTER, CLEMENS 1967 "Recent Church Architecture in America." *Planen Bauen, Wohnen* Dec.:11–21.
HOLZMEISTER, CLEMENS 1976 *Architekt in der Zeitenwende.* Salzburg, Austria: Bergland.
WEISER, ARMAND 1927 *Clemens Holzmeister.* Berlin, Leipzig and Vienna: Hubsch.

HONEYMAN and KEPPIE

John Honeyman (1831–1914) was born in Glasgow and was educated at Merchiston Castle School, Edinburgh, and Glasgow University for the Ministry, which he left before his final examinations. He trained as architect with Alexander Munro, Glasgow, and worked for McVicar Anderson, London, before establishing a practice in Glasgow in 1854. An authority on medieval architecture and an innovator with considerable artistic talent, he designed buildings that were always refined and positive. He was joined by John Keppie (1863–1945), former chief draftsman with Campbell, Douglas, and Sellers in 1889, the same year that CHARLES RENNIE MACKINTOSH joined as a draftsman. Mackintosh exerted considerable influence from the outset and was a partner from 1904 to 1913 when he left Glasgow for London. The firm became Keppie and Henderson in 1945 and still exists as Keppie Henderson and Partners.

BRUCE WALKER

WORKS

1863, Lansdowne United Presbyterian Church, Great Western Road; 1872, F. and J. Smith's Warehouse (since altered, now Ca d'Oro), Gordon and Union Streets; Glasgow, Scotland. 1877, Scots Church, Genoa, Italy. 1878, Cathedral Square (now Barony North); 1881, Westbourne Church, Westbourne Gardens; Glasgow, Scotland. 1891, Loretto School Chapel (with John Keppie), Musselburgh, East Lothian, Scotland. 1893, Glasgow Herald (with Charles Rennie Mackintosh and Keppie), Mitchell Street; 1895, Northpark House, Queen Margaret Drive (with Mackintosh and Keppie), Belmont; 1896–1898, Martyr's Public School (with Mackintosh and Keppie), Barony Street, Townhead; 1908, Savings Bank (with Keppie), Gallowsgate, Camlachie; Glasgow, Scotland.

BIBLIOGRAPHY

HONEYMAN, JOHN 1877 *Trades-Unionism: The Blight on British Industries and Commerce.* Glasgow, Scotland: Maclehose.
HONEYMAN, JOHN 1883 *Open Spaces in Towns.* Glasgow, Scotland: Machals.
HONEYMAN, JOHN 1888 "Glasgow Cathedral." *The Architect* 40:113–114.

HONEYMAN, JOHN 1897 *"Betterment" in Relation to Municipal Improvements.* Glasgow, Scotland: Maclehose.

HONEYMAN, JOHN 1900 "Working Class Dwellings: Effects of Injudicious Legislation." *Journal of the Royal Institute of British Architects* Series 3 7:249–253.

HONEYMAN, JOHN 1907 "Our National Galleries." *The Builder* 92:416–418.

"John Honeyman, R.S.A." 1914 *Journal of the Royal Institute of British Architects* Series 3 21:238.

"John Keppie, R.S.A." 1945 *Journal of the Royal Institute of British Architects* Series 3 52:242.

HONTAÑON, JUAN GIL DE

Juan Gil de Hontañon (?–1526) of Rasines, near the Cantabrian coast of Spain, was a professional builder of some standing by 1500 when he was consulted on the works of Siguenza Cathedral. In 1503, he began a funerary chapel as the square apse of the hall church of San Antolin, Medina del Campo (Valladolid). Santa Clara at Briviesca (Burgos), another funerary chapel which reflects the Constable's Chapel at Burgos, can be attributed to Juan Gil and was probably begun about the same time. In 1512, he was made master of the works of the new cathedral at Salamanca designed by a committee two years earlier. Construction was begun from the west and by 1520 had risen to the vaults of the side chapels. The elaborate west portals suggest the late Gothic school of Burgos. In 1513, Juan Gil designed a new crossing lantern and adjacent vaults for Seville Cathedral whose original crossing designed by Simon de Colonia had col-

Juan Gil de Hontañon. Cathedral of Segovia. Spain. 1524–1526

lapsed two years earlier. Juan Gil's complex rib vaults have cusping similar to the apse of the Cartuja of Miraflores at Burgos.

In 1524, he gave the drawings for and was made master of the new cathedral of Segovia. The construction, obviously posthumous, was in the hands of his son Rodrigo Gil on and off until 1540 when the last nave vault west of the crossing was closed. The spare simplicity of the west façade and tower contrasts sharply with the Isabelline exuberance of Salamanca. This has led some authorities to suggest that at the end of the evolutionary history of Spanish Gothic there was a return to unadorned simplicity equivalent to the later transformation of Renaissance forms by JUAN DE HERRERA.

JOHN DOUGLAS HOAG

WORKS

1503–c.1521, Chapel, Church of San Antolin, Medina del Campo (Valladolid), Spain. (A)1503?–1523, Chapel, Church of Santa Clara, Briviesca (Burgos), Spain. 1505–1516, Cloister and Chapter House of Palencia Cathedral, Spain. 1509–1519?, Church of San Cristobal, Almorox (Toledo), Spain. 1512–1526, Cathedral of Salamanca, Spain. 1513–1517, Cathedral of Seville (crossing lantern and adjacent vaults), Spain. 1524–1526, Cathedral of Segovia, Spain.

BIBLIOGRAPHY

CASASECA CASASECA, ANTONIO 1978 "Trazas para la Catedral de Segovia." *Archivo Español de Arte* 201:29–51.

CHUECA-GOITIA, FERNANDO 1951 *La Catedral nueva de Salamanca: Historia documental de su construcción.* Spain: University of Salamanca.

HOAG, JOHN D. 1958 "Rodrigo Gil de Hontañon: His Work and Writings." Unpublished Ph.D. dissertation, Yale University, New Haven.

ORTIZ DE LA TORRE, ELIAS 1923 *Juan y Rodrigo Gil de Hontañon.* Santander, Spain.

ORTIZ DE LA TORRE, ELIAS 1940–1941 "Sobre los arquitectos Juan y Rodrigo Gil de Hontañon y Juan de Rasines." *Archivo Español de Arte*, 14:315–317.

TORRES BALBÁS, LEOPOLDO 1952 *Arquitectura Gótica.* Madrid: Editional Plus Ultra.

HONTAÑON, RODRIGO GIL DE

Rodrigo Gil de Hontañon's (c.1500–1577) style is difficult to characterize. In many major projects he continued the work of other architects and a number of his own designs, left incomplete at his death, were altered by his successors. His importance derives from two quite separate aspects of his work. First, as no other Spanish architect of his time, he perfected a truly national Renaissance style. His second legacy is a manuscript surviving in a late seventeenth-century copy in which he recorded much of the late medieval architectural practices of design and construction inherited from his father.

Rodrigo Gil was the son, perhaps illegitimate, of Juan Gil de Hontañon of Rasines in the province of Santander near the Cantabrian coast. This region, like the district around Lake Como in Italy, had for generations supplied most of Spain's stone masons and builder–architects. Juan Gil espoused a purist late medieval style derived from Burgos; a reaction against the highly ornamented Isabelline Gothic of JUAN GUAS and Simon de COLONIA (see COLONIA FAMILY). By 1512 Juan Gil was master of the works of Salamanca Cathedral and in 1524 he designed and became master of Segovia Cathedral. Both buildings, somewhat larger than the church at Amiens, attest to the reputation of Juan Gil to whom Rodrigo had been apprenticed at least since 1519. Rodrigo Gil must have already been a master mason at his father's death in 1526 as he succeeded to the mastership of Segovia which he held intermittently until 1540 when work stopped with the completion of the structure west of the transepts.

Rodrigo Gil respected his father's design for Segovia but when in 1538 he became master of Salamanca Cathedral his Bramantesque innovations for the nave clerestory resulted in a lawsuit by the contractors. The year before he had contracted to build from his own design a stone façade for the College of San Ildefonso (1537–1553) in the famous university town of Alcala de Henares near Madrid. The composition evolves from a series of interlocking squares increasing in density toward the portal. A similar method, suggested by parts of his manuscript, may have been used to set out the transverse section of Salamanca Cathedral. This process, very different from LEON BATTISTA ALBERTI's use of squares in the façade of Santa Maria Novella, may give the design its extraordinary liveliness. The accounts reveal that a number of highly paid decorative sculptors contracted for various parts of the façade, finished in 1553, transforming the architect's role almost into that of the conductor of an orchestra. The three windows of the piano nobile suggest early sixteenth-century French dormers and some of the carvers indeed had French names. Here, however, the frames contrast in typically Spanish fashion against a smooth wall rather than open sky. Late medieval elements blend harmoniously; notably the enormous knotted cord of the college's founder, Cardinal Ximenes de Cisneros, which frames the center block. At the third level both corner pilasters and the four piers of the portal section are canted forty-five degrees. Originally all six elements terminated in pinnacles or *candeleros*. Those of the

center four were suppressed when about December 1552 a gable was substituted for the rectangular attic of the original design. Perhaps about the same time a balustrade replaced the rich late Gothic cresting punctuated by *candeleros* designed by Rodrigo for the Monterey Palace, Salamanca, in 1539 and for the east exterior façade of the cloister at Santiago de Compostela of 1540.

Rodrigo Gil returned to Segovia Cathedral in 1560 or 1561. There he provided a new design for the chevet with seven rather than five radiating chapels. A drawing, probably his, shows a late, purely medieval structure except for a coffered dome and lantern over the crossing in the manner of SEBASTIANO SERLIO. (Rodrigo's drawings were still being followed by the builders as late as 1591.) It seems he had returned to his youthful status as a late medieval builder–architect on a grand scale. It was surely in this capacity that he visited the works of the Escorial near Madrid in 1564 and 1566 where he gave purely technical advice.

Rodrigo's manuscript, probably begun no earlier than 1560, is concerned exclusively with the problems of design and structure of a late medieval builder. The text was badly distorted by Simon Garcia, the copyist of 1681, but the numerous plans, diagrams, and elevations in the first six chapters must have been copied fairly accurately as they do not reflect the current Baroque idiom. All the methods given for setting out a plan establish only interior space, excluding walls and buttresses whose design is treated elsewhere. Two plans concern a five-aisled church twice as long as wide whose transepts do not project. Instructions for generating the plan are garbled but the result much resembles Salamanca and Segovia Cathedrals where the outer aisles have become side chapels. A method is also given for proportioning the members of a complex late Gothic rib vault according

Rodrigo Gil de Hontañon.
College of San Ildefonso
(façade).
Alcala de Henares, Spain.
1537–1553

to function. From the instructions for erecting such a vault we find it is domical with semicircular diagonal ribs, a typical Spanish form. Throughout the manuscript the solutions and formulae produce fundamentally Spanish late medieval structures. Rodrigo Gil's contribution to the history of architecture is thus as an essentially Spanish master of both late medieval and Renaissance styles.

JOHN DOUGLAS HOAG

WORKS

1533–?, Church of Santiago, Medina de Rioseco, Spain. 1537–1553, College of San Ildefonso (façade), Alcala de Henares, Spain. 1539–1541, Monterey Palace; 1552–?, Convent of Las Bernardas de Jesus; Salamanca, Spain. 1566–1572, Church of La Magdalena, Valladolid, Spain.

BIBLIOGRAPHY

CAMON AZNAR, JOSÉ (editor) 1941 *Compendio de Architectura y Simetria de los templos por Simon Garcia. año de 1681.* Salamanca, Spain: Hijos de Francisco Nuñez.
CASASECA CASASECA, ANTONIO 1978 "Trazas para la Catedral de Segovia." *Archivo Español de Arte.* 201:29–51.
CHUECA GOITIA, FERNANDO 1951 *La Catedral de Salamanca: Historia decumental de su construcción.* Universidad de Salamanca.
GONZÁLEZ NAVARRO, RAMÓN 1971 *Universidad de Alcalá, Esculturas de la Fachada.* Madrid: Ediciones Castilla.
HOAG, JOHN D. 1958 "Rodrigo Gil de Hontañon, his Work and Writings." Unpublished Ph.D. dissertation, Yale University.
KUBLER, GEORGE 1944 "A Late Gothic Computation of Rib Vault Thrusts." *Gazette des Beaux-Arts* Series 6 26:135–148.
MARIETEGUI, EDUARDO 1868 "Compendio de Arquitectura y Simetria de los templos . . . por Simon Garcia . . ." *El Arte en España* 7:113–127,154–184,193–215.
NAVASCUÉS PALACIO, PEDRO 1972 "Rodrigo Gil y los Entalladores de la Fachada de la Universidad de Alcalá." *Archivo Español de Arte.* 177:103–117
PEREDA DE LA REGUERA, MANUEL (editor) 1951 *Rodrigo Gil de Hontañón.* Santander, Spain: Imp. y Enc. de la Libreria Moderna.

HONZÍK, KAREL

Karel Honzík (1900–1966) received his architectural education at the Technical University in Prague, Czechoslovakia, where he became a professor in 1945. His most important architectural works, particularly the General Pension House in Prague, were done in cooperation with JOSEF HAVLÍČEK. Since the mid-1930s, he was ever more engaged in literary and theoretical activity. He worked out a theory of environment and lifestyle whose main features corresponded to the ideas of RICHARD JOSEPH NEUTRA's biorealism.

VLADIMÍR ŠLAPETA

WORKS

1928, Villa (with Josef Havlíček), Smíchov District; 1929–1930, Houses (with Havlíček), Pankrác District; 1929–1933, General Pension House (with Havlíček), Žižkov District; Prague. 1938–1941, Cottage Houses, near Prague.

BIBLIOGRAPHY

HONZÍK, KAREL 1946 *Tvorba životního slohu.* Prague: Petr.
HONZÍK, KAREL 1956 *Architektura všem.* Prague: Státní nakadatelství krásné literatury, hudby a umění.
HONZÍK, KAREL 1960 *Cestou k socialistické architektuře.* Prague: Státní nakladatelství technické literatury.
HONZÍK, KAREL 1963 *Ze zivota avantgardy.* Prague: Československý spisovatel.
PECHAR, JOSEF 1969 *Životní dílo Karla Honzíka.* Prague. Exhibition catalogue.

HOOD, RAYMOND M.

In the period between the end of World War I and the Great Depression, the meteoric career of Raymond Mathewson Hood (1881–1934) epitomized the age of the skyscraper as the developing form of an American architecture.

Born in Pawtucket, Rhode Island, on March 21, 1881, Hood studied at Brown University (1898–1899), before transferring to the architectural department at the Massachusetts Institute of Technology. Upon receiving his B.S. degree in 1903, he became a draftsman for the Boston firm of RALPH A. CRAM, BERTRAM G. GOODHUE and Frank W. Ferguson. Goodhue, a creative and inspiring genius with an individual approach to Gothic design, unquestionably made a deep impression. In 1905, Hood began the course in architecture at the Ecole des Beaux Arts in Paris.

He returned in 1906, worked briefly with Cram, Goodhue and Ferguson, and soon joined the Pittsburgh firm of HENRY HORNBOSTEL. In 1908 he went back to Paris, completing his studies for the degree of Architecte Diplomé par le Gouvernement Française in 1910. Before returning to Hornbostel's office in 1911, Hood traveled in Europe for a year.

In 1914 Hood left for New York City to start out on his own. For the next eight years clients were few and their jobs small. Then, on June 10, 1922, the Chicago Tribune announced a worldwide competition for the design of the "world's most beautiful office building." JOHN MEAD HOWELLS invited Hood to enter with him. They won first place. Although a traditional Gothic style, the design distinguished itself by the clarity and logic of its plan and the mass of the tower.

The Tribune Tower (1924) was followed by the American Radiator Building (1924). The program called for a relatively small structure, however, to achieve the effect of a tower, Hood pinched the building in from the lot lines to free the walls all the way around. To convey a feeling of massiveness, Hood used black brick so the external fabric would not appear to be punched full of holes by the windows. Although fundamentally a Gothic design, Hood took it a step further. The building terminated with a romantic silhouette. The upper details of the tower were gilded, a striking emphasis by daylight. At night, however, with the effective use of floodlights, the top of the tower literally glowed in the dark.

Hood's office now had plenty of work. Through his future partner, J. André Fouilhoux, came the contract for the Saint Vincent de Paul Asylum (1924) in Tarrytown, New York, quite French in feeling. Still in the Gothic idiom was the Masonic Temple and Scottish Rite Cathedral (1929) in Scranton, Pennsylvania. In London, with J. Gordon Reeves, Hood designed the National Radiator Building (1928) which also featured a black exterior.

The New York Zoning Ordinance of 1916 required setbacks from the street (and yard) but permitted 25 percent of the lot to go to unlimited heights as a tower. Hood's interpretation may be seen in the New York Daily News Building, completed in 1930. The L-shaped lot ran through the block. To free one side of the building for windows, valuable land was sacrificed to create a private way from street to street. A series of setbacks from the main streets up to the tower gave the building a modern, cubistic form. Verticality was emphasized by piers of white brick of equal width between vertical strips of windows. The top of the building was cut off squarely, which influenced the next generation of tall New York City buildings.

Free from traces of Gothic detail at last, each of Hood's later buildings essayed a new approach to design. The Beaux Arts Apartments (1930), designed with Kenneth Murchison, emphasized the horizontal with a band of white brick running below each tier of windows. The piers between the windows were in alternate courses of red and black brick. Frankly modern in form and materials were the two General Electric Showrooms (1931), in Flushing, and in Bay Ridge, New York. For Joseph M. Patterson, owner of the Daily News, Hood designed a somewhat cubistic house in Ossining, New York (1930).

Hood was one of eight architects on the Board of Design for the Chicago World's Fair of 1933. The unusual asymmetrical scheme for the layout of the grounds was Hood's proposal. Hood also designed the General Electric Pavilion at the fair (1933).

In 1930 three firms of architects, L. A. REINHARD AND Henry HOFMEISTER; HARVEY WILEY CORBETT, WALLACE K. HARRISON and William H. McMurray; and Hood and JACQUES ANDRÉ FOUILHOUX; associated for the Rockefeller Center project on which Hood had been working as a consultant. As a pioneering example of multiblock planning of a commercial development in New York City, it paved the way for the superblock projects of the future. Since interruption of the street pattern was not permitted at the time, the project was tied together by a pedestrian concourse below the street level. Most of the office space was concentrated in the seventy-story skyscraper in the center. Smaller towers located schematically on the diagonals of the central tower permitted the windows to open up over lower buildings. A great contribution to the quality of life in the city was made by the donation of open space for public use, particularly the "Channel Gardens" leading in from Fifth Avenue to the plaza beyond with its impressive fountain. Low roofs were landscaped with gardens. Although Hood was one of eight architects who collaborated on the plan, his guiding hand is evident throughout, most especially in the dramatic form of the central RCA Building which, in many ways, recalls the New York Daily News Building. The initial phase of the Rockefeller Center project was completed in 1933.

Hood's last skyscraper, designed as the Great Depression closed in, was the McGraw-Hill Building (1931). To secure maximum light in this loft-

Hood.
Daily News Building (with Howells).
New York.
1930

Hood.
McGraw-Hill Building (with Godley and Fouilhoux).
New York.
1931

type structure, the windows were arranged in horizontal bands. No longer was the skyscraper to be designed as a solid form with a vertical emphasis, but rather as a light shell structure whose exterior fabric was hung on a steel frame. This new form was distinguished by the innovative use of color: the enclosing shell between the bands of windows was of glazed, bluish-green terracotta blocks, graded in hue from the bottom to the top. This building marked the end of the skyscraper era of the twenties. Different in feeling from anything Hood had designed before, it clearly pointed the way to the International style.

Hood is remembered as a small, shy man, bristling with energy and ideas, who through use of a humorous story or parable swayed many intractable clients. His philosophy of design may seem inconsistent, but, as he once said, "I could never build the same building twice."

WALTER H. KILHAM, JR.

WORKS

1924, American Radiator Building, New York. 1924, Chicago Tribune Tower (with John Mead Howells). 1924, Saint Vincent de Paul Asylum (with J. André Fouilhoux), Tarrytown, N.Y. 1926, Bethany Union Church, Chicago. 1927, National Broadcasting Company (studios); 1928, Apartment House, 3 East 84 Street (with Howells); New York. 1928, National Radiator Building (with J. Gordon Reeves), London. 1929, Masonic Temple and Scottish Rite Cathedral (with Frederick Godley, Fouilhoux, and H. V. K. Henderson), Scranton, Pa. 1930, Beaux Arts Apartments (with Kenneth M. Murchison, Godley, and Fouilhoux); 1930, Daily News Building (with Howells); New York. 1930, Joseph M. Patterson House (with Howells), Ossining, N.Y. 1930–1933, Rockefeller Center (with L. A. Reinhard and Henry Hofmeister, Harvey Wiley Corbett, Wallace K. Harrison and William H. McMurray, and Fouilhoux); 1931, McGraw-Hill Building (with Godley and Fouilhoux); New York. 1931, Rex Cole Showroom, Bay Ridge, N.Y. 1931, Rex Cole Showroom, Flushing, N.Y. 1933, Electricity Building, Chicago World's Fair.

BIBLIOGRAPHY

HOOD, RAYMOND M. 1931 *Raymond M. Hood.* New York: McGraw.

KILHAM, WALTER H., JR. 1973 *Raymond Hood, Architect: Form Through Function in the American Skyscraper.* New York: Architectural Book Publishing Company.

HOOKE, ROBERT

Robert Hooke (1635–1703) was a scientist of remarkably diverse accomplishments whose career, like that of his friend CHRISTOPHER WREN, branched out into architecture. Hooke's architectural career began in 1666 when he produced a plan (lost) for rebuilding the city after the Great Fire of London. With EDWARD JERMAN and PETER MILLS, he was appointed one of the city surveyors for rebuilding London and became closely involved with Wren, who, with HUGH MAY and ROGER PRATT, was one of the King's Commissioners for the rebuilding. Both Hooke and Wren worked on the monument commemorating the fire, and their respective shares in its design are uncertain. Hooke also worked with Wren on the rebuilding of the city churches. Again, it is not clear what role Hooke played as a designer, but he was very active as an administrator. Indeed, in spite of continual ill health, Hooke had enormous energy, and although architecture never became his main interest, as it did for Wren, he had several important independent architectural commissions, particularly in the 1670s. His main works do not survive, but they are recorded adequately enough to show that as a designer he was competent but dull. "French planning and Dutch detailing" (Colvin) are the most obvious characteristics of his style. Although he was wholly without Wren's genius as an architect, the speed at which Hooke built such huge edifices as Bethlehem Hospital (1674–1676) demonstrates that he must have matched him in organizational ability.

IAN CHILVERS

WORKS

1671–1676, The Monument (with Christopher Wren); *1672–1678, Royal College of Physicians, Warwick Lane; *1674–1676, Bethlehem (Bedlam) Hospital, Moorfields; *1675–1679, Montagu House, Bloomsbury; London. 1678–1680, Willen Church, Buckinghamshire, England. (A)early 1680s, Ramsbury Manor, Wiltshire, England. *1688–1693, Aske's Almshouses, Hoxton, London.

BIBLIOGRAPHY

In addition to the items listed below, Robert Hooke also figures in much of the literature on Christopher Wren, especially the volumes of the Wren Society.

BATTEN, M. I. 1936–1937 "The Architecture of Dr Robert Hooke." *Walpole Society* 25: entire issue.

DOWNES, KERRY 1966 *English Baroque Architecture.* London: Zwemmer.

DUTTON, RALPH 1951 *The Age of Wren.* London: Batsford.

'ESPINASSE, MARGARET (1956)1962 *Robert Hooke.* London: Heinemann.

GUNTHER, R. T. 1930–1937 Volumes 6, 7, 8, and 10 in *Early Science in Oxford.* Oxford: The author.

HOOKE, ROBERT (1935)1968 *The Diary of Robert Hooke:1672–1680.* Edited by Henry W. Robinson and Walter Adams. London: Wykeham.

KEYNES, GEOFFREY 1960 *A Bibliography of Dr Robert*

Hooke. Oxford: Clarendon.

REDDAWAY, R. F. (1940)1951 *The Rebuilding of London after the Great Fire.* London: Arnold.

SUMMERSON, JOHN (1953)1977 *Architecture in Britain: 1530 to 1830.* 6th ed., rev. Harmondsworth, England: Penguin.

HOOKER, PHILIP

Philip Hooker (1766–1836) was the leading architect of the Albany, New York, region during that town's transition from a small Dutch village to a flourishing state capital. He designed a majority of the new public buildings and held several civic offices, notably city surveyor from 1819 to 1832 and city superintendent from 1821 to 1827.

His buildings, more derivative than original, characterized by conservative design, skilled massing, and refined elegance of decoration and detail, reveal his familiarity with a broad range of neoclassic styles.

Apart from his 1815 statement that he had "an experience of twenty-five years in building and a close application in the research of ancient and modern architecture" (Root, 1929, p. 134), nothing definite is known of his training. However, his father, Samuel, was a carpenter and builder in Albany from 1772, when he arrived from Rutland, Massachusetts (where Philip had been born), until 1797 when he removed to Utica, New York. Philip surely was apprenticed to him, as was his younger brother, John. He knew Boston and New York, for he was clearly influenced by CHARLES BULFINCH, JOSEPH F. MANGIN, JOHN MCCOMB, and Thomas McBean.

In 1801, he was an organizer of the Albany Mechanics' Society and in 1814 he was elected to the Committee of Fine Arts of The Society for the Promotion of Useful Arts.

Generally he worked alone, though between 1797 and 1803 he had a partner, Elisha Putnam, a builder. Later he was required to adapt Thomas E. Taylor's plans for the Albany Academy (1815–1817) and to incorporate in his Albany City Hall (1829–1831) a cupola designed by John Kutts. He collaborated with the Anglo-American landowner George Clarke, delineating the latter's designs for an extraordinary, never built, Albany residence (1816) and for the Clarkes' country seat, Hyde Hall, in Otsego County (1817–1835). Otherwise, his designs were solely his.

He left no descendants, no followers, no writings, and no lasting influence. So much of his work has been destroyed by fire or urban progress that his importance is now largely historical.

DOUGLAS R. KENT

WORKS

1797–1798, North Dutch Church, Albany, N.Y. *1797–1804, Union College, Schenectady, N.Y. *1802–1803, Saint Peter's Church; *1803, New York State National Bank; Albany, N.Y. *1803–1810, Trinity Church, Utica, N.Y. 1804–1806, First Presbyterian Church, Cazenovia, N.Y. *1805–1809, First New York State Capitol; *1805–1811, South Dutch Church; *1810, Bank of Albany; Albany, N.Y. *1813–1815, Second Presbyterian Church; *1814, Mechanics and Farmers Bank; 1815–1817, Albany Academy; *1815–1817, Lancaster School; 1816–1817, First Lutheran Church; Albany, N.Y. 1817–1835, Hyde Hall, Springfield, Otsego County, N.Y. *1822, Saint Peter's Church (steeple); *1824–1825, Pearl Street Theater; Albany, N.Y. 1825–1827, Hamilton College Chapel Front, Clinton, N.Y. *1826–1827, First Presbyterian Church, Utica, N.Y. 1827, Richard P. Hart House, Troy, N.Y. *1828–1830, Fourth Presbyterian Church; *1829, Clinton Market; *1829, Washington Market; *1829–1830, North Market (additions); *1829–1830, Saint Mary's Church; *1829–1831, City Hall; Albany, N.Y. 1830, Rutger B. Miller House, Utica, N.Y.

BIBLIOGRAPHY

Additional information concerning Philip Hooker is in the George Hyde Clarke Family Papers, Department of Manuscripts and University Archives, Cornell University, Ithaca, N.Y.

BAGG, M. W. 1877 *The Pioneers of Utica.* Utica, N.Y.: Curtiss & Childs.

BEACH, ALLEN C. 1879 *The Centennial Celebrations of the State of New York.* Albany, N.Y.: Weed.

FOERSTER, BERND 1965 *Architecture Worth Saving in Rensselaer County, New York.* Troy, N.Y.: Rensselaer Polytechnic Institute.

GERBER, MORRIS 1970 Volume 1 in "Old Albany." Albany: Albany Institute.

HOOPER, JOSEPH (1898)1900 *A History of Saint Peter's Church in the City of Albany.* Albany, N.Y.: Fort Orange Press.

KENT, DOUGLAS R. 1967 "History in Houses: Hyde Hall, Otsego County, New York." *Antiques* 92:187–193.

KIRKER, HAROLD 1969 *The Architecture of Charles Bulfinch.* Cambridge, Mass.: Harvard University Press.

ROOT, EDWARD W. 1929 *Philip Hooker: A Contribution to the Study of the Renaissance in America.* New York: Scribners.

Transactions of the Society for the Promotion of Useful Arts in the State of New York. 1814 3:entire issue.

SPAFFORD, HORATIO GATES 1813 *A Gazetteer of the State of New York.* Albany, N.Y.: Southwick.

HOPE, THOMAS

Born in Amsterdam, Thomas Hope (1769–1831) used the wealth he derived from the family bank, Hope and Company, to influence the development of classical taste in England by patronizing contemporary designers and artists rather as Lord Burlington had before him. He displayed his collections, which also included antique sculpture and vases and old masters, in his house on Duchess Street, London, originally designed by ROBERT ADAM but extravagantly remodeled by Hope (1799–1804, 1819). He opened this to the public by ticket and also illustrated its interiors in a volume of outline engravings (1807). His designs were closely related to the Empire style of PERCIER AND FONTAINE, but his remarkable country house, Deepdene in Surrey, which he rebuilt (1818–1819, 1823), was an essay in asymmetrical picturesque planning on a sloping site with a subtle interlocking of house and garden.

DAVID WATKIN

WORKS

*1799–1804, 1819, Remodeled House, Duchess Street, London. *1818–1819, 1923, Remodeled House, Deepdene (with the assistance of WILLIAM ATKINSON; remodeled by Hope's son in 1836), Surrey, England.

BIBLIOGRAPHY

HOPE, THOMAS 1804 *Observations on the Plans and Elevations Designed by James Wyatt, Architect, for Downing College, Cambridge.* London: Shuny.
HOPE, THOMAS (1807)1971 *Household Furniture and Interior Decoration: Classic Style Book of the Regency Period.* Reprint. New York: Dover.
HOPE, THOMAS (1809)1962 *Costumes of the Greeks and Romans.* 2 vols. Reprint. New York: Dover. Originally published with the title *Costumes of the Ancients.*
HOPE, THOMAS 1812 *Designs of Modern Costume.* London.
HOPE, THOMAS 1835 *An Historical Essay on Architecture.* 2 vols. London: John Murray.
WATKIN, DAVID 1968 *Thomas Hope (1769–1831) and the Neo-classical Idea.* London: John Murray.

HOPKINS, JOHN HENRY

John Henry Hopkins (1792–1868), an Episcopal churchman, influenced that denomination's preference for Gothic architecture in the mid-nineteenth century. Particularly important were his Gothic design for the large new Trinity Church, Pittsburgh (1825), and his *Essay on Gothic Architecture* (1836), the first publication in this country specifically on that subject.

GWEN W. STEEGE

WORKS

*1825, Trinity Church, Pittsburgh, Pa. *1832, Trinity Church, Rutland, Vt. 1860, Vermont Episcopal Institute, Burlington, Vt. 1860–1863, Saint Thomas's Church, Brandon, Vt. 1863–1865, Trinity Church, Rutland, Vt.

BIBLIOGRAPHY

HOPKINS, JOHN HENRY 1836 *Essay on Gothic Architecture.* Burlington, Vt.: Smith & Harrington.
HOPKINS, JOHN HENRY, JR. 1873 *The Life of the Late Right Reverend John Henry Hopkins.* New York: Huntington.
KUNITZ, STANLEY J., and HAYCRAFT, HOWARD (editors) 1938 *American Authors.* New York: Wilson.
PIERSON, WILLIAM H., JR. 1978 *American Buildings and Their Architects: Technology and the Picturesque, The Corporate and the Early Gothic Styles.* Garden City, N.Y.: Doubleday.
WODEHOUSE, LAWRENCE 1973 "John Henry Hopkins and the Gothic Revival." *Antiques* 103:776–783.

HOPPER, THOMAS

Thomas Hopper (1776–1856), the most eclectic Regency architect, was born in Kent, England, and trained by his surveyor father. His interpretive use of sources and spatial ingenuity were apparent in the enlargement of Craven Cottage, Fulham (1806?), which combined Egyptian, Gothic and neoclassical motifs. Consequently the Prince Regent employed him at Carlton House, London (1807), where Hopper's celebrated cast-iron and stained glass conservatory was inspired by Henry VII's Chapel, Westminster. A country house architect, adapting many styles, from the neo-Greek Leigh Court, Somerset (1814) to the neo-Norman Penrhyn Castle, Caernarvonshire (1825?–1844?), he designed public buildings, including the neo-Palladian Arthur's (Carlton) Club, London (1826–1827). He was surveyor for Essex from 1816 until his death.

R. WINDSOR LISCOMBE

WORKS

*1806?, Craven Cottage (enlargement), Fulham, England. *1807, Carlton House; *1808–1809, The Royal Society of Musicians Building; London. 1814, Leigh Court, Somerset, England. *1818, North Stoneham Park, Hampshire, England. 1820?, Gosford Castle, County Armagh, Ireland. 1822–1826, Essex County Jail, Springfield, England. 1825?–1844?, Penrhyn Castle, Caernarvonshire, Wales. 1826–1827, Arthur's (now the Carlton) Club, London. *1828–1839, Llanover House, Gwent, Wales. 1832, Danbury Place, Essex, England. *1840?–1850, Butterton Hall, Staffordshire, England. *1842–1843, Kinmel Park, Denbighshire, Wales. *1843–1847, Birch Hall, Essex, England. 1845–1851, Saint Mary's Hospital, Paddington, London. 1846–1849, Wivenhoe Park, Essex, England. *1847–?, Easton Lodge, near Dunmow, England.

BIBLIOGRAPHY

BAYLEY, STEPHEN, and HUGHES, QUENTIN 1976 "The Hall of the Mountain King." *Architectural As-*

sociation Quarterly 8, no. 4:39–43.

CROOK, J. MORDAUNT, and PORT, MICHAEL H.   1973
Volume 6, pages 312–314 in *The History of the King's Works*. London: Her Majesty's Stationery Office.

HUSSEY, CHRISTOPHER   1958   "Penrhyn Castle, Caernarvonshire." Pages 181–192 in *English Country Houses. Late Georgian 1800–1840*. London: Country Life.

SEARLE, ARTHUR   1970   "Thomas Hopper." *Essex Journal* 5:132–140.

HOPPIN, FRANCIS L. V.

Francis Laurens Vinton Hoppin (1867–1941) was born in Providence, Rhode Island, and attended the School of Architecture of the Massachusetts Institute of Technology from 1884 to 1886. After a brief period in France, he returned to the United States, and joined his brother's Providence firm (Hoppin, Reader and Hoppin). He then served an apprenticeship with McKIM, MEAD, AND WHITE. In 1894, along with Terrence Koen, another Mckim, Mead, and White alumnus, Hoppin established his own New York City practice. Hoppin and Koen were joined by Robert Palmer Huntington in 1904. The firm specialized in designing opulent country and city residences along with grand public buildings.

STUART N. SIEGEL

WORKS

*1896, Mrs. Susanne B. Minturn House; 1897–1899, Engine Company Number 65 Station House; New York. 1899–1900, Charles W. Cooper House, Tuxedo Park, N.Y. 1900–1901, Blithewood, Andrew C. Zabriskie House, Barrytown, N.Y. 1901–1902, The Mount, Edith Wharton House, Lenox, Mass. 1901–1903, James P. Lanier House, New York. 1905–1906, Honorable George B. McClellan House, Princeton, N.J. 1905–1906, R. T. Wilson House (alteration); 1905–1907, E. D. Baylies House; 1905–1909, Police Headquarters; New York. 1907–1909, Newbold Morris House, Lenox, Mass. 1909–1911, Ashintully, Robb de Peyster Tytus House, Tyringham, Mass. 1909–1912, Hopeland House, Robert P. Huntington House, Staatsburgh, N.Y. 1913–1916, Albany County Courthouse, N.Y. 1921, West Side Meeting House, New York.

BIBLIOGRAPHY

FEREE, BARR   1903   "Talks with Architects: Mr. F. L. V. Hoppin on the House and Garden." *Scientific American Building Monthly* 35, no. 3:47, 61.

"Some Country and City Residences by Hoppin & Koen Architects."   1911   *New York Architect* 5, July:149–156.

SWARTWOUT, EGERTON   n.d.   "An Architectural Decade." Unpublished manuscript.

WILSON, RICHARD G.   1979   *The American Renaissance: 1876–1917*. New York: Pantheon.

HOREAU, HECTOR

Born at Versailles, Hector Horeau (1801–1872) studied at the Ecole des Beaux-Arts in the ateliers of Eugène Charles Frédéric Nepveu and François Debret. In 1826, he embarked on a grand tour through Italy, Greece, and Egypt. A maverick architect, who built little, he exhibited and published many imaginative schemes for urban improvements, mainly of iron and glass, including proposals for Les Halles in Paris (1844) and the Crystal Palace in London (1849). He was acclaimed architect of the Commune in 1870 and was imprisoned thereafter.

R. D. MIDDLETON

WORKS

*1829–1830, Posthouse, 2 rue Pigalle; *1832–1835, Apartment Block, 102–104 rue de Bac; *1835, Château des Fleurs, corner of rue Vernet and rue Galilée; Paris. *1847, Jardin d'été et d'hiver, Quai d'Albret, Lyon, Rhône, France. *1848, Chalet des Champs Elysées, 101–115 Champs Elysées, Paris. 1854, Britannia Farm, Ghistelles (Gistel), near Ostende, Belgium. *1855–1856, The Poplars, 18 or 20 Avenue Road, Primrose Hill, London. 1857–1858, Pippingford Park, Nutley, Sussex, England.

BIBLIOGRAPHY

BOSC, ERNEST   1872   "Notice nécrologique sur Hector Horeau." *Moniteur des Architectes* 1872:225–227, 241–247.

BOUDON, FRANÇOISE; LOYER, FRANÇOIS; and DUFOURNET, PAUL   1979   *Hector Horeau: 1801–1872*. Paris: Centre d'Etudes et de Recherches Architecturales.

DUFOURNET, PAUL   1981   *Horeau précurseur, idées, techniques, architectures*. Paris: Académie d'Architecture.

HOREAU, HECTOR   1841–1846   *Panorama d'Egypte et de Nubie avec un portrait de Méhémet Ali*. Paris: The author.

HORIGUCHI, SUTEMI

Sutemi Horiguchi (1895–) was one of Japan's leading architects of the twentieth century. Graduating from Tokyo University in 1920, he became a member of a group of Japanese architects called the Secessionists or *Bunriha,* the first society of modern architecture in Japan. Bunriha felt that styles, as such, were harmful and that architecture should be an honest expression of structure, and it had exhibits in January and July of 1920 at Tokyo University that stirred public interest in architecture and art. These architects were from privileged classes and their architectural movement, therefore, lacked social consciousness. The new architecture was influenced by European Expressionism; Horiguchi, in particular, was sympathetic to Western architectural ideas.

In 1922, the Secessionists presented Japan's modern architecture at the Peace Memorial Exposition in Tokyo, for which Horiguchi designed several buildings. In 1923 and 1924, Horiguchi traveled in Europe; Holland, Germany, and Austria particularly had a profound impact on him, though he was stimulated by ancient Greek architecture to study Japan's own traditions. He visited the Weimar Bauhaus on that trip and was impressed by its works and its fresh energy. With the Depression, social action began to take precedence and the Secession's influence faded.

In 1936 the Kosaku Bunka Renmai, patterned on the Werkbund, was founded; Horiguchi was a leading member. The group issued a publication, *Kosaku Bunka,* which described their ideas, proposals, and experiments.

Horiguchi expressed traditional Japanese reverence for nature in his landscaping as in his autumn plants garden of the Okada House (1934), Tokyo, which he composed with few materials in a restricted space.

During the pre-World War II period, Horiguchi became the leading contemporary architect of works in the more traditional building style of post-and-beam construction, the Shoin and Sukiya styles of logical structure. Horiguchi became an expert on the classical teahouse and adapted parts of it to modern residential architecure. He built a number of residential buildings for which he received wide acclaim. The Wakasa House, Tokyo (1939), is one of the most progressive in pre-World War II Japan. It is reminiscent of WALTER GROPIUS's work in its asymmetric cubic volumes.

The Hotel Hasshokan in Nagoya (1950–1953), for which Horiguchi completed a number of buildings, possesses a striking modernity both aesthetically and technically while employing the traditional Sukiya style—logical construction at the peak of perfection. The integrated relationship of the garden to the house is outstanding.

In 1954, Horiguchi designed the Japanese Pavilion for São Paulo's Quadricentennial exposition in Brazil. The building stands on pillars placed on natural stones within the surrounding pond, with corridors jutting over the water and deep eaves.

Horiguchi became a professor at the Teikoku Bijutsu Gakkō (Imperial Fine Arts Academy) in 1932, a lecturer at Tokyo University in 1946, and from 1949 to 1955 was professor at Meiji University, where he built several ferroconcrete buildings. From 1965 to 1970, he was professor at Kanagawa University He is the recipient of many awards.

REGINALD R. ISAACS

WORKS

1922, Peace Memorial Exposition Buildings; 1930, Kakkawa House (courtyard), Meguro; Tokyo. 1930, Yoshikawa House, Hyogo Prefecture, Japan. 1934, Okada House, Omori; 1936, Nakanishi House; Tokyo. 1936, Torida Racecourse, Ibarghi Prefecture, Japan. 1938, Oshima Weather Observatory, Oshima Island; 1939, Wakasa House, Shibuya; Tokyo. *1950–1953, Hasshokan Hotel (buildings and gardens; later rebuilt), Nagoya, Japan. 1954, Japanese Pavilion, Quadricentennial Exposition, São Paulo, Brazil. 1957, Villa, Tokyo.

BIBLIOGRAPHY

HORIGUCHI, SUTEMI (1941)1970 *The Tea Ceremony of Rikyū.* Reprint. Tokyo: Publishing Association.
HORIGUCHI, SUTEMI (1949)1968 *Teahouses by Rikyū.* Tokyo: Shoten.
HORIGUCHI, SUTEMI 1955 *Architectural Beauty in Japan.* Tokyo: Shinkokai.
HORIGUCHI, SUTEMI 1969 *A Study of Teahouses.* Tokyo: Publishing Association.
HORIGUCHI, SUTEMI (editor) 1970 *A General History of Architecture.* Tokyo: Ōmusha.

HORNBOSTEL, HENRY

Henry Hornbostel (1867–1961), born in Brooklyn, New York, in 1891 graduated at the head of his class from the School of Mines at Columbia University. After working in the office of Palmer and Wood, he left for Paris to study in the atelier of Ginain at the Ecole des Beaux-Arts. At the Ecole, he was known for his brilliant drawing skills and was called *l'homme perspectif* because he often submitted perspective sketches in *esquisse* competitions. While still a student at the Ecole, Hornbostel worked for the architects C. L. GIRAULT and Blavette on their plans for pavilions for the World Exposition of 1900. In 1897, he returned to New York where he found work as a free-lance delineator, providing drawings for several well-known firms, including McKIM, MEAD, AND WHITE and CARRÈRE AND HASTINGS. His abilities also attracted the attention of his former teacher, WILLIAM ROBERT WARE, who employed him to teach design to the fourth-year architecture students at Columbia, a position he held until 1903.

Able to distill the components of building programs as well as render them in a bold and forceful style, Hornbostel was extremely successful in open competitions. Associated with Howells and Stokes, he won second prize in the Hearst competition for the plan of the University of California (1899). In 1904, while associated with William Palmer, he won the competition for the Carnegie Institute of Technology in Pittsburgh, Pennsylvania. While in Pittsburgh for the construction of that campus, Hornbostel founded the school of architecture at the Institute and served as its first director. The firm of Palmer and Hornbostel continued to flourish until World War I. They designed city halls in Oakland, California (1910), Pittsburgh, Pennsylvania (1910), Wilmington, Delaware (1910), and Hartford, Connecticut (1911), and the Soldiers and Sailors Memorial in Pittsburgh (1907).

Hornbostel was best known for his designs for several East River crossings in New York City, including the Manhattan side of the Brooklyn Bridge (1903), the Williamsburg Bridge (1905), the Queensboro Bridge (1905), and the Hell Gate (1917).

In World War I, Hornbostel served in the United States Expeditionary Force, attaining the rank of major. After the war, he returned to practice, designing the Oakland, California, Technical High School (1917), the Oakland Auditorium (1920), Emory University, Atlanta, Georgia (1920), the Harding Memorial Tomb (1924), and the Seward Monument, East Seward, Alaska (1929).

STEVEN MCLEOD BEDFORD

WORKS

1903, Manhattan Terminal Building, Brooklyn Bridge, New York. 1904, Carnegie Institute of Technology, Pittsburgh. 1905, Williamsburg and Queensboro Bridges, New York. 1907, Soldiers and Sailors Memorial, Pittsburgh. 1910, City Hall, Oakland, Calif. 1910, City Hall, Pittsburgh. 1910, City Hall, Wilmington, Del. 1911, City Hall, Hartford, Conn. 1917, Hell Gate Railroad Bridge, New York. 1920, Emory University, Atlanta, Ga. 1924, Harding Memorial Tomb, Warren, Ohio. 1929, Seward Memorial, East Seward, Alaska.

BIBLIOGRAPHY

"As He Is Known." 1915 *Brickbuilder* 26:26.
"New Brooklyn Bridge Terminal." *Architects and Builders Magazine* 526–527.
"The New East River Bridges." 1903 *Architecture* 8:103–105.
NORTH, A. T. 1920 "Emory University." *American Architect* 118:429–432.
SWALES, F. S. 1926 "Master Draftsman XVII: Henry Hornbostel." *Pencil Points* 7:72–92.

HORTA, VICTOR

Baron Victor Horta (1861–1947) is recognized as the brilliant originator of the Art Nouveau, an influential style in late nineteenth-century architecture and decorative arts. Unfortunately, many of his best works have been demolished or altered.

His career is partly unknown because records were destroyed by the architect himself; even Horta's memoirs, written late in life, are unpublished, but excerpts have been quoted in several critical texts. From these and from remaining buildings, drawings, and photographs it is possible to estimate the scope and value of Horta's achievement and to trace an outline of his development.

Victor Horta was born in Ghent, Belgium, to elderly parents. His father, Pierre, was a master shoemaker of Spanish descent, his mother was Flemish. At first interested in music, the young boy turned toward architecture and design while his family favored textile production as a promising career. By the time he was seventeen, Horta knew his own mind. A friend of the parents persuaded them to let him take the tall, handsome lad to Paris, where employment was found for Horta in a display and decorating studio. He worked there some eighteen months until his father's death recalled him to Ghent.

Horta's command of various crafts serving architecture and interior design stemmed from this training in Paris, but he remembered France in other terms. He was powerfully attracted by monumental Paris, by the grandeur and consistency of French architecture under official patronage from Louis XIV to Napoleon III. When Horta arrived in Paris, the boulevards of Baron GEORGES-EUGÈNE HAUSSMANN looked fresh and CHARLES GARNIER's Opéra was just being finished. To mark France's resurgence from the defeat of 1871, Paris held a world's fair in 1878. The overall plan was due to EUGENE-EMMANUEL VIOLLET-LE-DUC, the great architectural theorist who died the year following. Viollet and GUSTAVE EIFFEL together designed the twin iron and glass Grandes Galeries for the fair. Horta was impressed by them and by Eiffel's and LOUIS-CHARLES BOILEAU's Bon Marché department store built of the same materials. In Paris, young Horta discovered the full power of the academically controlled design of the past and the great potential of modern technology. Furthermore, in the rationalist writings of Viollet-le-Duc he found a comprehensive philosophy for modern architecture.

Horta read the message of Paris, he tells us, to mean that a bold, rigorously logical and well-schooled architect could give form to his age and nation; eternal fame would be his reward. Horta felt that he was the man to do this. He added a second goal: he would serve the tastes and sentiments of his times with designs so individual that his work would be acclaimed as the embodiment of modern Western architecture. With these interlocking ambitions the nineteen-year-old apprentice returned to Belgium.

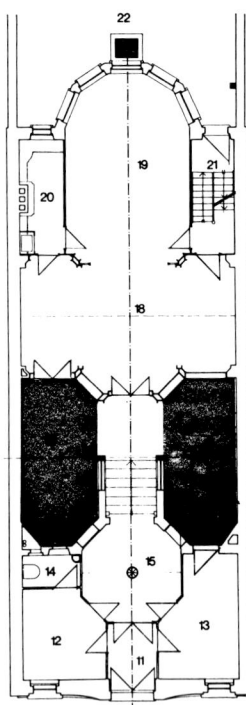

Horta.
Tassel House (*plan of main
floor*).
Brussels.
1892–1893

Horta was admitted to the Academy of Fine Arts in Brussels in 1881 as a student of architecture, and there he came to the notice of Professor ALPHONSE BALAT, Royal Architect to King Leopold II. Balat was then building the Royal Museum of Fine Arts, splendid and restrained, especially when compared to JOSEPH POELAERT's huge Palais de Justice, just being completed. Balat was furthermore a specialist in iron and glass construction, building some forty such structures over a lifetime. Horta must have learned considerably from him after being accepted in Balat's office in 1884; at the same time, Horta independently entered various competitions, winning prizes. The following year Horta returned to Ghent to build three brick houses, neat and conventional. Horta came back to Balat's office where he stayed nearly four years, preparing to achieve the goals he had set himself in Paris. Balat gave him increasing responsibility, culminating in the design of a permanent exhibition pavilion for sculptures by Joseph-Marie-Thomas (Jef) Lambeaux. The commission was complicated and the neoclassical architecture was overdetailed, but the pavilion was more coherent and thoughtful than the houses in Ghent. Horta stayed in Balat's good graces, and when the master died Horta was given the responsibility of completing his work in progress.

The Lambeaux Pavilion of 1889 was a conspicuous example of Horta's frequent collaboration with sculptors in designing monuments, either public or private, often funerary. Horta began this work in 1884, and for half a century it provided him with useful contacts.

In 1890, Horta opened his own office. Over the next two years he designed and built two houses in Brussels; the second, the Maison Autrique, was a prelude to his personal style. Derived mainly from Viollet-le-Duc's street fronts, Horta's design was more lyrical. He used thin cast-iron posts at the window openings; beneath these openings the stonework was perforated by small ventilating apertures which appeared on some of his façades over the years. Horta was interested in several such ingenious conveniences and took trouble integrating them into his designs. During this period, Horta began to teach (at the Free University of Brussels), an activity which played an increasing role in his career.

In 1892, Horta designed his first really accomplished house which quickly became famous. The client was Professor Tassel of the University of Brussels, a mathematician also associated with the Solvays, the great industrial chemists. He had bought a small lot on a newly opened city street and seems to have given his architect a free hand within the limits of the building code. Horta built just such a work as he had foreseen in his ideal program—modern and individual yet respectful of tradition.

The Tassel street-front made a firm statement, with its smooth stone wall, horizontally banded in warmer and cooler tones, and crowned by a strong double cornice. A broad bow of windows, widening toward the top, was held in the masonry like a jewel in its setting; the wall curved gently forward to clasp the iron framework of the glazing. Lateral window openings balanced the upward motion, being wider at the ground floor and narrow at the top. Above the entrance, a low mezzanine window was framed in stone but the main floors made a feature of wrought and cast iron, rivets included, in the center bay. The parti, a narrow front with projecting bay, was traditional in such city houses yet the clarity, the suavity, and the freely exposed metal of the Tassel façade had no precedents.

The Tassel front door was centered and led immediately to stair halls and accessory areas ingeniously lit by skylights on either side. Straight ahead, benefiting from this indirect light, lay a surprisingly ample T-shaped reception zone. The stem of the T, used for dining, extended to a bay window overlooking a garden; portieres could close the dining from the living area. From the hallway, curving stairs led to the mezzanine with easy grace; the balustrade, the colored glass, the central iron post, the mosaic floor, and the painted walls and ceiling were all involved in a symphony of linear excitement. This ornamentation, so emphasized, was neither vegetal nor classicizing yet recalled both themes while creating an entirely novel sensation. Nothing upstairs was equally extraordinary and as in all Horta's work, the exterior back wall was unapologetically plain, angular brickwork. The Tassel interiors have been altered.

The Tassel House made Horta famous and launched the Art Nouveau on the Continent. It was more a challenge to routine architecture than a new concept, excepting only the ingenious handling of daylight. Why was it published and imitated? Not because of the lighting but because of the smooth juncture of parts and the ornamental use of reflexive, sinuous line. These features were modulated to suggest a variety of emotional intensities; Horta demonstrated an effective vocabulary of ornament. The "whiplash line" and related devices were no novelties, especially in graphic design; in 1895, an anonymous editor of the new art periodical, *The Studio,* already suggested that this vogue had been launched a decade earlier by Elihu Vedder's widely admired, illustrated *Rubáiyát* of Omar Khayyám. Yet, no single source would suffice, the taste for vibrant, freely deployed decoration had been growing in the West for some time, stimulated by Oriental precedent on occasion. It was not an imitative, eclectic trend but an evocative one, and with this reliance on feeling rather than learning, Western designers and their clients were liberated from the revival styles and put in touch with their real world. Horta brought this mode to fulfillment in a major art. His contribution was soon disputed and emulated to the point of parody but Horta was busy with new commissions; however irritating the competition, he could expect to outdistance it.

The year 1894 brought an influx of commissions to Horta, beginning with two regular townhouses and several collaborations with sculptors. One of these was with Constantin Meunier for a great Monument to Labor which remained unfinished. Meunier, whose statues usually depicted workers, and the project for the monument serve to emphasize the importance of the Belgian labor movement. At that time, it was fighting for decent working conditions, living wages, and political suffrage. A few capitalists supported the movement, notably the Solvay brothers whose independent discoveries and business acumen had brought them wealth and influence. The Solvays now employed Horta to design two monuments, one a family tomb, and asked his help in redecorating parts of their country house. Before the year was out, a second-generation Solvay, Armand, and his enterprising wife asked Horta to design and furnish a new residence on the most sought-after new boulevard, the Avenue Louise. The site allowed a house twice as wide as normal.

Horta designed a magnificent structure for them, tall bays projected on either side of a recessed center; the windowed bays were metallic and the walls were of two-toned stone. As usual, the top story was set back and this allowed the undulating façade to demonstrate a crisp skyline to advantage. The dignified symmetry of the exterior and its superb ornamental details made a great show. The carriage entrance lay to the left, leading into the house so that one alit indoors in a perspective of paired iron piers. The carriage drove on to stables at the back of the garden while visitors entered the house facing a broad flight of skylit stairs leading to a wide landing with a full mural in oils by Théo van Rysselberghe, Belgium's chief pointillist painter. At either end of the landing, the stairs turned and continued to the main floor. Below lay coatrooms and a reception room with trophies of the chase. Flanking the stairs at the main level were hinged panels of rich wood with ornamented glass inserts, shielding on the one hand a large dining room overlooking the garden and on the other a suite of living rooms overlooking the avenue. First came the ladies' salon, a music room with a grand

piano elaborately designed, like all the furniture and fittings, by Horta. This area was separated by a small, vitrine-enclosed lobby from the gentlemen's salon with a billiard table as its largest feature. The glassed screens allowed vistas across the whole depth of the main floor; space seemed indefinable amid the shifting perspectives. Everywhere one saw warm colors, on the carpeted floors, the damasked walls, and on the ceilings of shallow metal coffers all stenciled. The specially carved wood furniture and embroidered, built-in sofas, the intricate marble and metal mantelpieces holding sculpture, the masterfully modeled bronze hardware, and airy, rhythmic chandeliers, united to create an atmosphere of fairyland. The main bedrooms were carried out more simply but in the

Horta.
Solvay House.
Brussels.
1894–1900

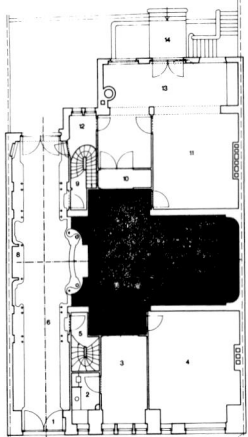

Horta.
Solvay House (plan of main
*   floor).*
Brussels.
1894–1900

Horta.
Solvay House (dining room
*   chandelier).*
Brussels.
1894–1900

Horta.
Maison du Peuple.
Brussels.
1895–1899

Horta.
Maison du Peuple (plan of
    street floor).
Brussels.
1895–1899

Horta.
Maison du Peuple
    (auditorium).
Brussels.
1895–1899

Thus, Horta became involved with both the most liberal and the most oppressive elements of his society. That same year, he undertook to complete the unfinished works of the royal architect when his old master, Balat, died. Horta was already President of the Central Society of Architecture in Belgium. Fifteen years after leaving Paris with high ambitions and no training, he was starting to reach his goals.

Through the Solvays, Horta was approached to design a new Maison du Peuple for Brussels (1895–1899). Such *maisons* had sprung up in many Belgian communities: they were housing workers' cooperatives for food and clothing and for health and emergency insurance, and offices of the Belgian Workers' Party which had newly succeeded in winning increased suffrage and a larger presence in Parliament. The *maisons* also provided centers for formal and informal meetings, from celebrations to demonstrations. The Brussels *maison* had been operating in a disused synagogue for years, but with increasing success and membership a new facility was needed; the Solvays backed this enterprise. The plot bought for this was just over a quarter of an acre, irregular in plan, and subject to restrictions of building height and of land use; 20 percent was to be unbuilt. Although the cost had to be held down (and was), the building had to present the character and success of the labor movement. Horta soon discovered that he had undertaken to work for not one client but "a hundred," not always in agreement and ready to change requirements. Other obstacles arose, including a major error in the design of the steel frame, engineered in his own office, discovered after construction was advanced. Horta held his course and adapted his design over four and a half years until in 1899 the new Maison du Peuple was inaugurated to general satisfaction. It was Horta's most important work, and a masterpiece of modern European architecture. Opened with pride, it was demolished with hardly a murmur (but for a few enthusiasts) in 1964. This, with the earlier razing of FRANK LLOYD WRIGHT's Larkin Building, signaled the low point in the recognition of mod-

same spirit. So much artistry meant that the Solvay House was not completed until 1900.

Horta found himself busier than ever in 1895. He accepted two major commissions, one for headquarters to house the various activities of the fast-growing labor movement; the other, a private residence for the Secretary General of the Congo, King Leopold's vast private domain in Africa.

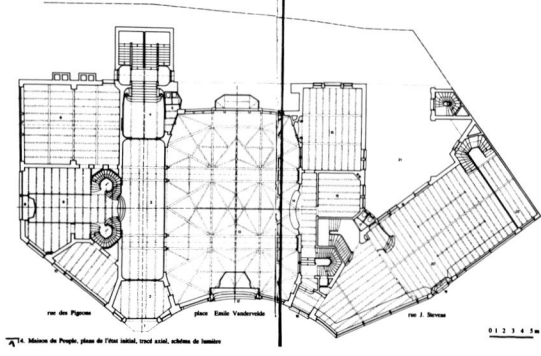

ern architecture as representative of its age.

The Maison du Peuple adhered closely to its lot lines on three sides, but in back it was haphazard. The materials were Horta's usual choice: a stone base, carved to accept metal and glass façades and narrow brick-and-stone piers. Glass and metal predominated, allowing more light inside and curving readily to fit the oval place. Against the sky, a lively roof balustrade held enamel panels blazoning the names of Socialist and Communist leaders. At street level, ample show windows displayed the wares for sale. A series of framed entrances led to different parts of the structure; near the curved center was the entrance to a big, double-height café. Lobbies and halls led to shops, offices, and meeting rooms. The impression of a bustling, diversified center is conveyed in the surviving photographs. At the very top of the building, with wide views from the roof terrace, was the main auditorium with fifteen hundred seats. A light-filled interior showed inclined metal trusses outlining a graceful shell with sides and top in one continuous sweep, an original and harmonious space. Balconies were extended along two levels, the lower for seats, the upper for heating pipes. The heat-guided flow of air and the in-curving ceiling were calculated to assure good acoustics, and they did. This self-contained, readily demountable masterwork was not preserved when the Workers' Party built a banal high-rise on the site.

Edmond van Eetvelde's House (1895–1898) sat on a steep avenue adorned with a central garden strip and rivulet. Facing this amenity Horta raised a flat façade featuring four vertical steel stanchions rising from a cross-beam above the recessed entrance front. The main door lay to the right of center, without framing or other formality. The ends of the party walls were stone-clad, and these and the steel uprights defined three wide and two narrow bays in alternation. The less prominent horizontals were all straight but for segmental arches over the main-floor windows. The topmost floor was recessed, creating a terrace ornately railed. All ironwork was detailed and painted to assure residential character. Spandrels on the front were faced with gently hued mosaic, each showed a simple field bordered by free-flowing whiplash lines, symmetrically disposed. The glass area was noticeably greater than the wall surface. This house front had no antecedents for its arrangement or its materials and required a certain conviction on the part of the client, not shared by his wife. Today, the façade looks clear and graceful, a key work of modern design.

Inside, the Van Eetvelde House, fully furnished by Horta, was equally refreshing. The street door opened to a small vestibule, glass enclosed, whence one saw a marble-walled lobby richly detailed and angled to the left where stairs began to encircle an octagonal space of extraordinary charm. It was once filled with daylight from a glass dome, now unfortunately obscured. This space formed a small mezzanine enclosed with a dado of onyx. Mosaic floors and stairs were inlaid with curvilinear patterns, and balustrades of metal strapwork defined the steps and the hallway. Between balustrade panels rose slender steel posts carrying the glass dome and its encircling barrel vault. The entire steel-and-glass canopy was delicately designed, and electric lamps formed a subsidiary system of brass, carrying flowerlike glass shades. This contrast of structural and nonstructural metals was perfected here by Horta, but has not survived. Originally, this little octagon was one of the most beautiful architectural achievements of its era.

King Leopold created Van Eetvelde a baron, and in 1898 he and the baroness desired more space. A lot next door, at the lowest corner of the avenue, was bought and thus it became possible to enlarge the reception and office areas of the existing house while providing an independent residence for rent. This different use and the shift of floor levels led to facing the new structure in carved stone, unrelated to the steel and mosaic front.

That same year, Horta began work on a house and adjacent office structure for himself; these now serve as the Horta Museum and some spaces for architectural organizations. Horta's remarks about these buildings in his memoirs are fundamental to understanding his future career. He wrote: "Why did I get the impression while finishing [them] that I had reached the acme of my happiness . . . that a course downhill was beginning for me? Gloomy vision . . . how often I had reason to recall it later . . . strange forebodings that presaged new stages of my life." Horta's meaning may be clearer if all three commissions which engaged him at that time are considered: his own house and studio (1898–1911), a country house for the Frison family (whose town residence he had built right after the Tassel House), and the Aubecq House (1899). They are each different, as was not rare in Horta's work. Yet, they are each somewhat in retreat from his early resolve and from his remarkable accomplishment in the years just past.

Horta's Studio building returns to an emulation of Viollet-le-Duc's urban façades, like the Maison Autrique but more accomplished. The stone front of the residence is strictly flat with almost no carving. In front of this hangs a metal harness attached to a square bay projected over the entrance. The ironwork is ingenious and elaborate,

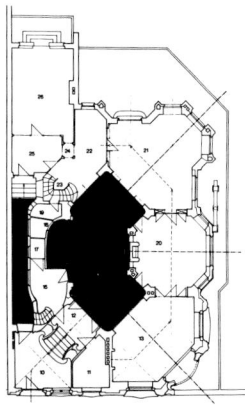

Horta.
Aubecq House (plan of
main floor).
Brussels.
1899

but its main statement seems to be that of strengthening various parts of the bay which ends in a glazed canopy over the door. The stone and metal are skillfully joined, yet each acts separately, unlike Horta's earlier detailing. On the interior, there are striking dissonances, perhaps in part the result of the architect's remodeling in 1911. Altogether, the home and studio are exceptionally restless.

Maurice Frison's chalet shows a side of Horta's work not yet mentioned. His country houses tend to be complex masses angularly shaped in dark brick with plain stone trim, related to the rear façades in town. Roofs are emphasized. In this group the Frison House is notably cottagelike. The house for O. Aubecq was just the opposite. Built on a corner site on the Avenue Louise in Brussels, it displayed a continuous front along two sides, rhythmically accented by projecting bays, but in all only two stories high with a quiet mansard. The stonework was unusually elaborate, and ornamental ironwork was confined to some balconies. The exterior had a distinctly chateau air. On the main floor, the house was planned as a close-packed series of hexagons and octagons yet all partitions were eliminated leaving only piers and making furniture arrangement difficult. No flow of space united the reception area; each part seemed isolated. Was this eccentricity introduced by Horta or by Aubecq? There is no way to guess.

As the century drew to a close Horta evidently was less sure of himself than before for reasons buried in his personality and not scrutable to those who have studied his work. Some have found that Horta's design became weak after 1906, and coldly academic after World War I. Horta's own words and the testimony of his buildings have led scholars to present the years 1898–1900 as the epoch of change. From then on, Horta no longer thought that it was his fate to develop an individual style representative of his times; half his Paris dream had evaporated. But he was still confident in his ability to fulfill the highest needs of the state and of society. He had many years left in which to test that belief.

Horta's exuberant Art Nouveau design flared up one last time in 1901 when he designed the first of several rather varied retail stores in Belgium (and one in Germany). This new field of endeavor was to occupy him for five years. The more elegant shops allowed him to build distinguished stone façades, but the first department store, l'Innovation of 1901 on the rue Neuve in Brussels, was exceptional; it was constructed on a metal skeleton and showed an all-glass front, metal-framed, with fantastic curling ornament. The high central bay was the widest, indicating a main space within; to

either side were narrower three-story bays disposed as balconies. The activity in the shop could be seen from outside, undoubtedly an attraction as was the ingenuity of placing glass at either side to the front while recessing the big central surface. This layering was accented by exterior hanging lamps. The party walls lay behind narrow stone facing which arched across the curved top, an encircling ribbon. Horta's Innovation front was one of several in Europe and the United States which featured a maximum expanse of glass show windows, and it was the most eloquent of all; only Louis H. Sullivan's Chicago store could challenge it. Horta's structure was based on the Bon Marché in Paris; its open front and the pendant lamps recalled the lower floors of Otto Wagner's Neumann Store in Vienna (1895). But the Innovation was a new entity, a fascinating one; in 1967, it was burned down in protest against American merchandise featured within.

Horta's other stores were mediocre by comparison, and his residences became less interesting and less numerous in this period; from 1890 to 1903 he had undertaken twenty-four, but from 1903 to 1915, only six. His efforts were directed elsewhere.

In 1903, Horta was commissioned to build a small museum in Tournai to house a collection of fine arts, a private legacy to the public. Progress was slow, Horta was searching for the right use of fireproof reinforced concrete which he had previously abjured; now he turned to small stone pavilions of the eighteenth century, and it was in this manner that design continued until the outbreak of war. More interesting and demanding was the commission for an extensive medical complex on the outskirts of Brussels, the Brugmann Hospital, first discussed in 1906. The hospital was to replace old city institutions with a thoroughly up-to-date facility; several of Horta's friends and clients, active in politics, were among those concerned. Much time was spent discussing what was required, how to organize it and how to equip it, what it would cost, and how to plan for future needs. Naturally, hospital administrators and medical chiefs were involved. By 1910, a definitive program had been accepted, but nothing had been built when the German army invaded neutral Belgium.

In 1910, Horta was charged with the largest and most complicated assignment of his career. It was focused on a grand, central station for Brussels in which several railways would terminate. The railroad companies had formed a consortium called the Jonction, powerful enough to secure an important site in the heart of the city, below the Royal Palace and major cultural institutions, and crowded with ancient buildings, some of artistic and historic interest. After Horta had exerted himself against this plan to no avail, he accepted the task of determining what the best solution might be. Meanwhile, Horta's obligations at the Free University had grown considerably over twenty years, he was teaching architecture, industrial architecture, the history of architecture, and studio design courses. In 1912 a program was launched to reorganize aspects of the curriculum. Horta was passed over in favor of another professor to lead this work; he resigned, accepting the title of professor emeritus. That same year he became professor at the Academy of Fine Arts in Brussels, and the year following he was named Correspondent for Fine Arts to the Royal Academy of Belgium.

In 1913 basic planning for the Central Station was begun. The site was sloping, and because strict limitations were placed on height to avoid infringing the amenities of the Royal Palace and the museum complex, it became clear that excavation was required. What was feasible and what was affordable were major considerations. How to give some dignity and order to the streets that would be formed, how to create a logical disposition of the interior for rail passengers, freight requirements, and postal traffic, all this had to be discussed with the many involved authorities. Horta also knew that a new arts center for exhibitions, concerts, and lectures probably would be proposed adjacent to the station. His role was to bring order out of this chaos while working within the strict given limitations. In August 1914, war erased these preoccupations.

In 1915, Horta visited London, to work with planners preparing for the problems of rebuilding Belgium after the war. Joined by his wife, Horta then went to the United States, charged with fomenting sympathy and support for their countrymen. Three years in America were hard on them both. Horta found little resonance to his work and little to stir him in the local practice. He tried to lecture on architecture; in 1916, he addressed the students at Cornell University. He was told that more responsive audiences, and ones more helpful to Belgium would be attracted by lectures on Flemish art of the fifteenth and sixteenth centuries. He found himself not only in an alien world, but engaged in an unfamiliar task, tangential to his work and to the real needs of his homeland. At last, in 1919, the Hortas could return to their country house near Brussels; the devastation which they knew by report became shockingly real.

Horta and his colleagues began to re-examine the plans for the Central Station and he started a new chapter of his teaching career as professor at the Advanced Institute of Fine Arts in Antwerp. He was also appointed member for the Fine Arts in the Royal Academy of Belgium. The next year, work was resumed on the art museum at Tournai, and at last the project for the Brussels Arts Center was given formal approval. In 1921, Horta was appointed to the Commission on Monuments and Sites, concerned with extensive plans for war memorials. In the next year, he became president of the faculty at the Antwerp Institute, a post he held for ten years. In 1923, he was planning the program for a school of arts and crafts at Brussels which after more than a decade of consideration was dropped.

Horta.
Central Railway Station.
Brussels.
1911–1937 (completed after
1945)

By 1925, Belgium could see some degree of improvement, and more activity could be felt in many endeavors. Horta was made president of the Fine Arts sector of the Royal Academy of Belgium, and he was elected to lead an independent, international jury that would screen entries in a global competition to design the Geneva headquarters of the newly founded League of Nations. This was to be the symbol of a better world, the architect-jurors representing the highest standards of their respective nations. Some were progressive; others, more conservative; Horta's experience as an organizer was being put to the test of worldwide attention.

The extensive new Brugmann Hospital opened in 1926, creating a maximum of controversy. Many decisions quite outside the architect's purview were attributed to Horta, whether for praise or blame, and he loyally defended the decisions that had been agreed upon. Clearly the Brugmann did not represent the advanced thinking of hospital planners in postwar Europe any more than it represented the rising fashion of building design. Nor was it simply an exercise in antiquated Beaux-Arts architecture. Horta stood alone; he had designed a stiff formation of low, detached structures in particolored brick. He had varied the patterns of the brickwork to emphasize the different uses of each pavilion, yet all shared the same two colors, red and buff. It was not one of Horta's successes.

The League of Nations Headquarters competition occupied much of the jury's time; many entries were examined in numerous sessions. Pressures mounted, not only between the conservative majority of the jurors and the progressives, but also from the outside where national prestige was at stake. Horta, as president of the jury, understood that no one, least of all the League of Nations, stood to gain by confrontation, and turned to two practical devices as the final decision approached, early in 1927. First, the jury could distribute the prize moneys as it saw fit; there was no unalterable first, second, or third prize. Second, the jury distributed the prizes in recognition of merit; the choice of an architect (or several) to build the Headquarters was to be made by a separate League of Nations commission. The jury eventually made nine equal first awards, and a number of second and third awards, for equal amounts each. The top nine ranged from extreme modernism to indurated academism, and four nations were represented: Switzerland, Italy, France, and Germany (newly accepted in the League). The most discussed entry came from two Swiss architects working in Paris, LE CORBUSIER and his cousin PIERRE JEANNERET. Architectural partisans of modernism used to claim that Le Corbusier's entry had been disqualified and that Horta held the balancing vote that was responsible; this is contrary to the record and to Le Corbusier's own attitude. When architects to build the headquarters were chosen from the premiated entrants, politicking made certain that the most conservative talents won the day. In this process, Horta played no role, but he had made it possible for the most progressive entries to receive worldwide attention, even though he admired Le Corbusier's spirit more than his designs, and for German talent to be recognized, recent history notwithstanding.

Later in 1927, Horta was made president of the Academy of Fine Arts in Brussels. In 1928 the little museum in Tournai was formally opened, and so was the Brussels Arts Center (Palais des Beaux-Arts). The former proved to be a rather fussy but well-planned little showpiece of historical allusions. The Arts Center was big, sober, and deeply disappointing as an artistic statement. On the exterior, it was necessary to accommodate retail stores at street level, not only to bring income but to assure continuing life to the streets during the day; the difficulties of the site have been mentioned. Horta chose a reinforced concrete structure, as had been decided for the Central Station. He surely knew the work of AUGUSTE PERRET and his brothers in this material; they were no more concerned than himself with avant-garde architecture and had demonstrated that elegance could be achieved in concrete, even in extensive, repetitious façades. Horta, going his own way, could not equal their successes. The stone facings of his concrete buildings survived in poor condition even though for the Brussels buildings he developed cubical, classicizing details intended to cope with weathering. The neobaroque of Tournai fared worse. The interiors of the Palais des Beaux-Arts were so badly worked that Horta had to forget his plan to display the raw concrete; the walls and ceilings are stuccoed. There is no life in this architecture. Horta must have seen (and heard) that the key examples of his second career as a top-level official architect fell flat. His work of the 1930s and 1940s was remote from the drawing board; he subsided into an eminent and experienced committee man. His bitterness, expressed in the memoirs, is understandable.

In 1929, Horta began a long, fruitless effort to reorganize the art museums of Belgium, and in the next years he resigned from both the Academy of Fine Arts in Brussels and the Advanced Institute in Antwerp; his years of teaching were over. Early in 1932 Horta was created baron by King Albert I, an honor due a faithful servant of Belgium throughout a long career. Plans to reorganize the nation's library system were assigned to him in 1934, without determinable effect. In 1937, at last, work was begun on the Central Station. Horta remained involved but there was only a marginal opportunity for architectural effect, and where there are signs of Horta's refinements they are swamped in the size and heaviness of the whole.

World War II put a stop to all building activity. When at last peace was declared Horta no longer had the energy or the will to continue; he asked that his duties be assigned to one of his former students, Maxim Brunfaut. A bronze plaque was set in the Station as part of an opening ceremony; the architect named was Brunfaut. Before Horta's death, the error was corrected on another plaque. In this atmosphere, when Horta moved his residence in 1945, he sold all his papers for scrap. Two years later, he died.

Horta suffered many adversities, not all of his own making. He was an unusually sensitive designer at his best, a master of effective nuances. The same sensitivity marked his relationships with people, as his memoirs make clear. What was a virtue in his work became a weakness in his professional career.

Horta more than most has been misjudged in order to substantiate a preconceived scenario of architectural history. Modern architecture, as it was canonized, required an ancestry before being accepted into the historical sequence. Architects themselves were ready to deny the Art Nouveau and all its works, but historians were relieved by an insurgent group, the Surrealists. Salvador Dalí especially was enthusiastic about HECTOR GUIMARD and the Paris Métro entrances, which reminded him of the work of his fellow Catalan, ANTONÍO GAUDÍ Y CORNET. From that to a re-evaluation of Horta was a short step. The architecture of Victor Horta in due course was acknowledged as the first flowering of Art Nouveau. Horta was one of the precursors of the Modern movement, and his work was judged in that sense only. Whatever was novel, inventive, and ingenious in it was highlighted, and the relationships to tradition were slurred over. Inevitably, this falsified the work and aims of Horta himself. If he did not, after World War I, design in the latest manner, it was because he had no inclination to become a rebel. He wanted to be a renovator, reviving the spirit of Western architecture after its unhappy rejection of the industrialized world. Continuity, not revolt, was his leading motif. If Horta's works after 1900 became dessicated and empty of the lyricism with which he began, that had little to do with the architecture that swept over Europe and the Americas in the second third of the twentieth century. Horta's faults and virtues were keyed differently, and they will someday contribute to a more equitable view of Western architecture after 1890.

EDGAR KAUFMANN, JR.

WORKS

1889–1905, Lambeaux Sculpture Pavilion; 1890, Mattyn House; 1892–1893, Tassel House; 1893, Autrique House; 1894, Frison Town House; 1894, Monument to Labor (project with Constantin Meunier); 1894–1903, Winssinger House; 1894–1900, Solvay House; 1895–1898, Van Eetvelde Houses; *1895–1899, Maison du Peuple; 1898–1911, Horta House and Studio; 1899, Aubecq House; *1901, L'Innovation Department Store, rue Neuve; 1903, Hallet House; 1903, Wauquez Store; 1903–1928, Tournai Museum; 1906–1930, Wolfers Store; 1906–1926, Brugmann Hospital; 1911–1937, Central Railway Station (completed after 1945 by Maxim Brunfaut); 1920–1928, Palais des Beaux-Arts; Brussels.

BIBLIOGRAPHY

BORSI, FRANCO, and PORTOGHESI, PAOLO 1969 *Victor Horta*. Rome: Edizione del Tritone. Includes hundreds of illustrations and some useful facts, poorly arranged.

DELEVOY, ROBERT L. (1958)1964 *Monographies de l'art belge*. 2d ed. Brussels: Meddens.

HOPPENBROUWERS, A.; VANDENBREDEN, J.; and BRUGGEMANS, J. 1975 *Victor Horta architectonographie*. Brussels: Confédération Nationale de la Construction. The most complete and reliable study of Horta, with good illustrations and a bibliography.

HOSTE, HUIB

Huibrecht Hoste (1881–1957), born in Bruges, Belgium, studied at the University of Ghent and worked for the Belgian architects Charles De Wulf and LOUIS CLOQUET. He traveled in the Netherlands in 1910, 1911, and 1912, finally settling there in 1914 for the duration of World War I. His exposure to recent Dutch brick architecture, notably that of H. P. BERLAGE, favored the overcoming of his earlier historicizing tendencies in design. Having made contact with the major Dutch artists and architects of the early 1900s, Hoste returned to Belgium and became active there in postwar reconstruction efforts. During the 1920s, Hoste was one of the leading Flemish proponents of garden-city planning. On several projects he collaborated with the Belgian urbanist LOUIS VAN DER SWAELMEN. His architecture of this period had a pronounced Dutch character. A stylistic and ideological shift in Hoste's architecture occurred around 1927, the year in which he became a founding member of the Congrès Internationaux d'Architecture Moderne (CIAM). During the 1930s and 1940s, his designs were mostly in the International style.

His own buildings tended to be modest in scale, and his primary importance for the development of European modernism was as a theoretician and propagandist rather than as a builder.

ALFRED WILLIS

WORKS

1910-1920, Saint Joseph Clinic, Bruges, Belgium. 1917, Belgian War Memorial, Amersfoort, Netherlands. 1921-1923, Klein Rusland Garden City (with Louis Van der Swaelmen), Zelzate, Belgium. 1922-1926, Kapelleveld Housing Estate (with Van der Swaelmen and others), Woluwe-Saint-Lambert, Brussels. 1931, House, Stationstraat, Zele, Belgium. 1933, Gombert House, Brussels. *1943, Villa, Haacht, Belgium.

BIBLIOGRAPHY

BONTRIDDER, ALBERT 1963 *L'architecture contemporaine en Belgique.* Antwerp, Belgium: Helios.
CULOT, MAURICE, and TERLINDEN, FRANÇOIS 1969 *Antoine Pompe et l'effort moderne en Belgique.* Ixelles, Belgium: Musée d'Ixelles.
DEVLEIGHER, LUV 1975 *Les maisons à Bruges: Inventaire descriptif.* Tielt, Belgium: Lannoo.
PUTTEMANS, PIERRE 1976 *Modern Architecture in Belgium.* Brussels: Vokaer.
SMETS, MARCEL 1972 *Huib Hoste: Propagateur d'une architecture renouvelée.* Brussels: Confédération Nationale de la Construction.
SMETS, MARCEL 1977 *L'avènement de la Cité jardin en Belgique.* Brussels: Mardaga.
STYNEN, HERMAN 1979 *Urbanisme et société: Louis Van der Swaelmen (1883-1929) animateur du mouvement moderne en Belgique.* Brussels: Mardaga.

HOWARD, EBENEZER

Ebenezer Howard (1850-1928) was the originator of the garden city movement, and his efforts enabled the first garden cities to be built. Born in London, he had a private education, and at the age of fifteen became a clerk in the City. In 1872, for health reasons, he set out with friends for the United States, where he briefly worked on a farm in Nebraska before moving to a stenographers' office in Chicago. He returned to England in 1877. He seems, while in America, to have been impressed by the spiritual values of Walt Whitman and Ralph Waldo Emerson. He also showed an aptitude for mechanics, seeking improvements to the typewriter. In England, Howard continued to be inspired by American thought. In 1881, he read Henry George's *Progress and Poverty* (1879) and was converted to the ideals of land reform. In 1888, a friend in Chicago sent him a copy of Edward Bellamy's *Looking Backward 2000-1887.* This book, with its promise of an imminent change in industrial society, possible through co-operation, spurred Howard into action. Initially accepting that the great changes envisaged by Bellamy could be rapidly realized, he came to see the need for testing the processes of change on a more moderate scale. Hence the garden city, which appeared fully formed in Howard's book *To-morrow: A Peaceful Path to Real Reform* (1898). In his garden city, Howard sought to remedy the evils of urban overcrowding and rural depopulation by bringing both areas into a mutually beneficial proximity. The size of the cities would be limited, and growth would be directed into distinct satellites. Howard's persuasiveness and enthusiasm enabled him to rally support for a Garden City Association—founded in 1899—which by 1903 was able to form a company to develop Letchworth, Hertfordshire, thirty miles from London, as a garden city. In 1919, a second town near London, Welwyn, Hertfordshire, was similarly developed. In both these developments Howard's diagrammatic plans were adapted to the needs of the site. Howard's ideas continued to influence town planning internationally, in Britain finding their fullest expression in the New Towns policy after World War II, when he was knighted.

BRIAN HANSON

BIBLIOGRAPHY

BELLAMY, EDWARD (1888)1967 *Looking Backward 2000-1887.* Edited by John L. Thomas. Reprinted from the corrected manuscript. Cambridge, Mass.: Harvard University Press.
FISHMAN, ROBERT 1977 *Urban Utopias in the Twentieth Century: Ebenezer Howard, Frank Lloyd Wright, and Le Corbusier.* New York: Basic Books.
GEORGE, HENRY (1879)1976 *Progress and Poverty.* London: Dent.
HOWARD, EBENEZER (1898)1965 *Garden Cities of To-morrow.* Edited by F. J. Osborne. With an introductory essay by Lewis Mumford. Reprint of 1946 edition. London: Faber. Originally published with the title *To-morrow: A Peaceful Path to Real Reform.*
MACFADYEN, DUGALD (1933)1970 *Sir Ebenezer Howard and the Town Planning Movement.* Cambridge, Mass.: M.I.T. Press.
PURDOM, C. B. 1963 *The Letchworth Achievement.* London: Dent.

HOWARD, HENRY

Born in Cork, Ireland, Henry Howard (1818-1884) went to New York in 1836 and to New Orleans, Louisiana, in 1837. He worked as a carpenter, studied in 1845 with JAMES DAKIN and Henry Molhausen, and started Madewood Plantation in 1846.

His long, large architectural practice, which

included no contracting, produced Greek Revival, Italianate, and Modern French buildings boldly scaled, handsomely detailed, and occasionally asymmetrically planned and massed.

HENRY W. KROTZER, JR.

WORKS

*1846, Ascension Parish Courthouse, Donaldsonville, La. 1846, Madewood Plantation; *1846, Woodlawn Plantation; Assumption Parish, La. 1849, Pontalba Buildings (exteriors and finishing details); 1850, Robert A. Grinnan Residence; 1851, W. P. Converse Residence; *1851, Crescent Mutual Insurance Building; *1852, Thomas Hale Row; 1852, Thomas Hale Stores; 1852, Thomas Hale Warehouse; *1853, Evan Jones McCall Residence; *1853, Saint Mary's Orphan Boys Asylum; 1854, Jefferson Parish Courthouse; *1854, Saint Elizabeth's Asylum; *1855, First Presbyterian Church; *1855, First District, Public School; New Orleans, La. *1856, Belle Grove Plantation, Iberville Parish, La. 1856, Bonnabel Stores, New Orleans, La. 1856, R. C. Camp Country Residence, Carville, La. *1857, Charity Hospital (syphilitic wards and dissecting rooms; with Albert Diettel), New Orleans, La. 1857, Nottoway Plantation (with Diettel), Iberville Parish, La. *1858, Harrell Foundry (with Diettel); *1858, Second District, Public School (with Diettel); *1858, Third Presbyterian Church (with Diettel); 1859, Cyprien Dufour Residence (with Diettel); New Orleans, La. 1859, Edgewood (with Diettel), Natchez, Miss. 1859, Robert Henry Short Residence (with Diettel); 1860, Louis Mayer double dwelling, 2331-2333 Magazine Street (with Henry Thiberge); 1860, Philip T. Philips Grocery Store, 2139 Saint Charles Avenue (with Thiberge); 1860, Saint Peter's Catholic Church; c.1866, Peter Conery double dwelling; 1867, Importers Bonded Warehouse; 1867, John T. Moore Residence; 1867, Antonio Palacios Residence; *1869, Jewish Widows and Orphans Home (additions and repairs); New Orleans, La. 1870, State Insane Asylum (new wing), Jackson, La. *1871, Louisiana Fair Grounds Buildings; *1872, New Orleans Mutual Insurance Association Building; 1874, George O. Sweet Residence; 1875, Crescent City Billiard Hall (Pickwick Club); 1880, Henry Gardes Building (with Thiberge); New Orleans, La.

BIBLIOGRAPHY

CHRISTOVICH, MARY LOUISE ET AL. 1972 *The American Sector.* Volume 2 in *New Orleans Architecture.* Gretna, La.: Pelican.

CHRISTOVICH, MARY LOUISE; EVANS, SALLY KITTREDGE; and TOLEDANO, ROULHAC 1977 *The Esplanade Ridge.* Volume 5 in *New Orleans Architecture.* Gretna, La.: Pelican.

DUFOUR, CHARLES L. 1952 "Henry Howard: Forgotten Architect." *Journal of the Society of Architectural Historians* 11, no. 4:21-24.

SCULLY, ARTHUR, JR. 1973 *James Dakin, Architect: His Career in New York and the South.* Baton Rouge: Louisiana State University Press.

TOLEDANO, ROULHAC; EVANS, SALLY KITTREDGE; and CHRISTOVICH, MARY LOUISE 1974 *The Creole Faubourgs.* Volume 4 in *New Orleans Architecture.* Gretna, La.: Pelican.

TOLEDANO, ROULHAC, and CHRISTOVICH, MARY LOUISE 1980 *Faubourg Tremé and the Bayou Road.* Volume 6 in *New Orleans Architecture.* Gretna, La.: Pelican.

WILSON, SAMUEL, JR. (editor) 1952 *Henry Howard, Architect: An Exhibition of Photographs of His Work by Clarence John Laughlin.* New Orleans: Louisiana Landmarks Society and Newcomb Art School.

WILSON, SAMUEL, JR., and LEMANN, BERNARD 1971 *The Lower Garden District.* Volume 1 in *New Orleans Architecture.* Gretna, La.: Pelican.

HOWARD, JOHN GALEN

John Galen Howard (1864-1931) was a leader in the American Renaissance movement. He was educated at the Massachusetts Institute of Technology (1882-1885) and the Ecole des Beaux-Arts (1891-1893) and apprenticed with H. H. RICHARDSON (1885-1886) and with McKIM, MEAD, AND WHITE (1889-1891). After practicing in New York, Howard moved to California in 1901 to execute the Hearst Plan for the University of California, Berkeley, and to establish the School of Architecture there. While teaching and designing the university's new buildings, he maintained a sizable practice in San Francisco. Some of Howard's houses were designed in the casual Bay Area tradition, but his commercial and public buildings consistently exhibited his desire to create a progressive classical tradition appropriate for America.

JOAN E. DRAPER

WORKS

1901, Electric Tower, Pan-American Exposition, Buffalo, N.Y. 1901-1907, Hearst Mining Building, University of California; 1902-1903, Greek Theater, University of California; 1903, Berkeley Public Library; 1903-1905, California Hall, University of California; 1903-1907, Gregory House; 1906-1912, Architecture Building, University of California; *1907-1908, Berkeley National Bank; 1907-1917, Doe Library, University of California; Berkeley. 1908-1910, Adam Grant Building, San Francisco. 1908-1910, Sather Gate, University of California; 1908-1911, Boalt Hall, University of California; 1909-1910, McDuffie House; 1911-1914, Sather Tower, University of California; 1912, Howard House; 1916-1917, Hilgard Hall, University of California; 1921-1923, Stephens Hall, University of California; 1923, Women's Faculty Club, University of California; Berkeley.

BIBLIOGRAPHY

CROLY, HERBERT 1908 "The New University of California." *Architectural Record* 23:269-293.

DRAPER, JOAN E. 1972 "John Galen Howard and the Beaux-Arts Movement in the United States." Masters thesis, University of California, Berkeley.

DRAPER, JOAN E. 1976 "The San Francisco Civic Center." *Journal of the Society of Architectural Historians* 35:289–292.

DRAPER, JOAN E. 1979 "The San Francisco Civic Center: Architecture, Planning, and Politics." Ph.D. dissertation, University of California, Berkeley.

HAYS, WILLIAM CHARLES 1915 "Some Architectural Works of John Galen Howard." *Architect and Engineer of California* 40:47–82.

HOWARD, JOHN GALEN 1912 "The Future of Architecture on the Pacific Coast." *Western Architect* 18, Nov.:113–123.

HOWARD, JOHN GALEN 1913 "Outlook and Inlook Architectural." *Architectural Record* 34:531–543.

HOWARD, JOHN GALEN 1898a "The Paris Training." *Architectural Review* (Boston) 5:4–7.

HOWARD, JOHN GALEN 1898b "The Spirit of Design at the Ecole des Beaux-Arts." *Architectural Review* (Boston) 5:25–27.

KELHAM, GEORGE 1917 "The University of California." *The Architect* (San Francisco) 14, Aug.: entire issue.

KOSTOF, SPIRO (editor) 1976 *The Architect: Chapters in the History of the Profession.* New York: Oxford University Press.

PARTRIDGE, LOREN W. 1978 *John Galen Howard and the Berkeley Campus: Beaux-Arts Architecture in the "Athens of the West."* Berkeley: Architectural Heritage Association.

HOWE, GEORGE

After a cosmopolitan upbringing in France, Switzerland, and America, George Howe (1886–1955) attended Harvard College and the Ecole des Beaux-Arts in Paris (1908–1913). Returning to America, he built a remarkable house for himself, *High Hollow* (1914–1916) in Philadelphia, which effectively synthesized the lessons of his French training, his travels in Italy, and the vernacular building techniques of the Philadelphia region. Soon after, Howe joined the already established partnership of Mellor and Meigs, known for its eclectic houses, and developed a fashionable practice (1916–1928), designing houses in a picturesque style influenced by the English Arts and Crafts movement and based in particular on the early houses of EDWIN LUTYENS. In 1928, after an agonizing personal and professional reappraisal, Howe abandoned the historicizing forms of his previous work in favor of those of the International style, just then coming to maturity in Europe. Breaking with his partners, Howe was able to retain as a client the Philadelphia Saving Fund Society (PSFS). His work for the society in 1926–1929, especially the early studies for its new office building, reveal his struggle to balance his traditional architecture with the new forms and compositional techniques. In 1929, Howe entered into partnership with the Swiss modernist WILLIAM LESCAZE. They designed the remarkable PSFS Office Building (1931), now regarded as the canonical International style skyscraper of the period, as well as the Oak Lane School in Philadelphia (1929) and projects for the Museum of Modern Art in New York City (1930–1931). The visible achievement of the PSFS's articulation of its complex program, as well as Howe's impeccable professional and social credentials, proved to be a prestigious advertisement for the fledgling International style in America.

Howe continued to promote the modernist cause with his sponsorship in the 1930s of *T-Square* and later *Shelter* magazines. Contributors included such pioneers as RICHARD NEUTRA, PHILIP JOHNSON, LE CORBUSIER, RUDOLPH M. SCHINDLER, NORMAN BEL GEDDES, and R. BUCKMINSTER FULLER. *T-Square* was the forum for Howe's debate with FRANK LLOYD WRIGHT on the legitimacy of an International style.

Howe and Lescaze dissolved their partnership in 1935 after a period of bitter personal conflict, and Howe returned to domestic architecture. In Whitemarsh, Pennsylvania, Square Shadows (1932–1934), built largely to Howe's designs, meshes a traditional plan with an elementarist massing and an expressive use of reinforced concrete, brick, and local stone. Similarly, Fortune Rock on Mount Desert Island (1937–1939), responds to its seashore site in Maine with an abstract clarity of essentially vernacular forms, a sensitive use of natural and regional materials, and a logical expression of wood construction.

Howe entered into partnership with LOUIS I. KAHN in 1940, designing prototypical housing developments at Pine Ford Acres, Middletown, Pennsylvania, and later, with Kahn and OSCAR STONOROV, Carver Court in Coatesville, Pennsylvania. These efforts were compromised, however, by stringent economics and community opposition to the Modernist aesthetic.

In 1942, Howe was appointed supervising architect to the Public Buildings Administration, the highest governmental post in architecture. Although the war effort precluded any significant construction, Howe's public service marks a break with the previous "official" style of stripped classicism and lent him public prominence as the profession's most eminent spokesman.

Howe became chairman of the department of architecture at Yale University in 1950. His installation, along with that of Joseph L. Albers in the department of art, signaled Yale's re-ascendancy in the visual arts. Howe's preferred teaching method was the formal lecture in which he spoke of the importance of human scale and of faith in the perceptual abilities of architects and laymen alike. His regime was marked by the founding of *Perspecta* magazine and the shift of Yale's building program away from historical revivalism. Kahn's design for the Art Gallery and Design Center was the first tangible result of this shift in policy.

Howe died suddenly in 1955. His work falls into the historical context of the "Philadelphia school," a legacy of influence that includes FRANK FURNESS, WILSON EYRE, PAUL P. CRET, Kahn and ROBERT VENTURI. For Howe, the advent of the International style did not require the abandonment of cultural and traditional values; it was the synthesis of these two attitudes toward building that constitutes Howe's achievement and ensures the continuing vitality of his example.

ROBERT A. M. STERN

WORKS

1914–1916, High Hollow, *1929, Oak Lane Country Day School (with William Lescaze); 1931, Philadelphia Saving Fund Society Building (with Lescaze); Philadelphia. 1932–1934, Square Shadows, Whitemarsh, Pa. 1937–1939, Fortune Rock, Mount Desert Island, Me. 1954–1955, Evening and Sunday Bulletin Building (with Robert Montgomery Brown), Philadelphia.

BIBLIOGRAPHY

HITCHCOCK, H. R. (1932)1970 "Howe and Lescaze." Pages 144–145, 148, 153 in Alfred Barr et al., *Modern Architecture: International Exhibition*. Reprint. New York: Arno.
JORDY, WILLIAM H. 1962 "PSFS: Its Development and Its Significance in Modern Architecture." *Journal of the Society of Architectural Historians* 21, May:47–83.
STERN, ROBERT A. M. 1962 "PSFS: Beaux-Arts Theory and Rational Expressionism." *Journal of the Society of Architectural Historians* 21, May:84–102.
STERN, ROBERT A. M. 1975 *George Howe: Toward a Modern American Architecture*. New Haven: Yale University Press.

HOWELLS, JOHN MEAD

Son of editor and novelist William Dean Howells, John Mead Howells (1868–1959) was born in Cambridge, Massachusetts. After graduating from Harvard University (1891) and from the Ecole des Beaux-Arts, Paris (1897), he practiced architecture in New York with I. N. PHELPS STOKES. Later with RAYMOND M. HOOD, he won the prize for the design of the Chicago Tribune Tower in 1922. He oversaw the rebuilding of the University of Brussels under the Hoover Commission.

An authority on early American architecture, he wrote many articles and also contributed to *Harper's, The Century,* and architectural periodicals.

JANE G. FEAVER

WORKS

1904–1907, Saint Paul's Chapel (with I. N. Phelps Stokes), Columbia University, New York. 1913, Paint Hall (Music Building), Harvard University, Cambridge, Mass. 1923–1925, Chicago Tribune Tower (with Raymond M. Hood). 1928, Beekman Tower (originally Panhellenic Hotel); 1929–1931, Daily News Building (with Hood); 1930, Title Guarantee and Trust Co.; New York.

BIBLIOGRAPHY

BUNTING, BAINBRIDGE, and NYLANDER, ROBERT H. 1973 *Survey of Architectural History in Cambridge, Report Four: Old Cambridge*. Mass.: Cambridge Historical Commission.
GOLDSTONE, HARMON H., and DALRYMPLE, MARTHA 1974 *History Preserved: A Guide to New York City Landmarks and Historic Districts*. New York: Simon & Schuster.
"Howells, John Mead." 1963 Volume 3 in *Who Was Who in America*. Chicago: Marquis.
WEISMAN, WINSTON R. 1970 "A New View of Skyscraper History." Pages 115–160 in Edgar Kaufmann (editor), *The Rise of an American Architecture*. New York: Praeger.
WHITE, NORVAL, and WILLENSKY, ELLIOT 1978 *A. I. A. Guide to New York City*. New York: Macmillan.

HRYNIEWIECKI, JERZY

Jerzy Hryniewiecki (1908–) studied architecture at the Technical University of Warsaw and graduated in 1936. He has been a professor of the history of ancient and modern architecture and design at the Technical University since 1945. He has also lectured at universities in China, the United States, Great Britain, and Iraq. His professional work encompasses graphics, exhibition design, sports buildings, industrial architecture, and town planning. A brilliant design consultant, he is known for his innovative attitude to any design problem. Throughout the many years of his active career as an educator, he greatly influenced the development of architectural thought in Poland.

LECH KŁOSIEWICZ

WORKS

*1937, Polish Pavilion, Exhibition of Decorative Arts, Paris. *1939, Polish Pavilion, World Exhibition, New York. *1948, Western Polish Territories Exhibition, Wrocław, Poland. 1955, Tenth Anniversary Stadium (with M. Leykam and Cz. Rajewski), Warsaw.

BIBLIOGRAPHY

WISŁOCKA, IZABELLA 1968 *Awangardowa Architektura Polska: 1918–1939.* Warsaw: Arkady.

HUBACHER, CARL

The civil engineer and architect Carl Hubacher (1897–) was born and educated in Zurich. He pursued engineering work in Italy between 1924 and 1927. From 1929 to 1936, he was a partner with RUDOLF STEIGER in the architecture-engineering firm of Hubacher and Steiger, Zurich. The firm participated in the Werkbund-Siedlung Neubühl (1930–1932) with PAUL ARTARIA and HANS SCHMIDT, MAX HAEFELI, and WERNER MOSER and ALFRED ROTH. An important example of the work of the Swiss Modern movement, the project displays a humane attitude in the carefully scaled, stepped elevations, the sensitive landscaping, and the wide variety of dwelling types. Since 1936, Hubacher has worked in Thailand, India, Sri Lanka, Greece, Syria, Italy, and Turkey in engineering, planning, and construction management, including power stations, dams, and earthquake structures. Between 1964 and 1968, he was associated with Alfred Roth; since 1975, he has worked with the Bausektor der Schweiz.

SHELLEY SMITH KELLAM

WORKS

1930, Zetthaus; 1930–1932, Werkbund-Siedlung Neubühl (with others), Wollishofen; Zurich. 1931, Weekend House and Boat House (with Rudolf Steiger), Herrliberg, Switzerland. 1933, Haus V. (with Steiger); 1934, Tea House, Mühlehalde (with Steiger); Witikon, Zurich. 1936, General Motors Swiss S.A. (with Steiger), Biel, Switzerland.

BIBLIOGRAPHY

BILL, MAX 1949 *Modern Swiss Architecture: 1925–1945.* Basel: Werner.
KUNSTGEWERBEMUSEUM 1977 *Um 1930 in Zürich: Neues Denken, neues Wohnen, neues Bauen.* Zurich: Schöb.
"Teehaus Mühlehalde bei Witikon-Zürich, Hans V. in Witikon-Zürich und Wochenend- und Bootshaus in Herrliberg: Architekten Hubacher und Steiger BSA, Zürich." 1938 *Das Werk* 25:152–155.
"'Z-Haus' Zürich, Architekten BSA Carl Hubacher und Rudolf Steiger, Zürich." 1934 *Das Werk* 21, Jan.:1–11.

HUBBARD, ELBERT

Elbert Hubbard (1856–1915), author, publisher, and entrepreneur, was a principal proponent of the Arts and Crafts movement in the United States. A businessman until the age of thirty-six, he met WILLIAM MORRIS while traveling and, inspired by him, founded the Roycroft Press in East Aurora, New York, in 1895, and its successor, Roycroft Industries, four years later. Hubbard, a charismatic figure, influenced many, including FRANK LLOYD WRIGHT. He did not design himself but managed and promoted the sizable and widely known Roycroft community. Its products were handmade, typically of oak, beaten copper, or tooled leather, with simple forms incorporating Art Nouveau motifs; they varied in quality, the best of them designed by Dard Hunter. Hubbard died on the *Lusitania* in 1915.

MICHAEL HOLLANDER

BIBLIOGRAPHY

BALCH, DAVID ARNOLD 1940 *Elbert Hubbard: Genius of Roycroft.* New York: Stokes.
CHAMPNEY, FREEMAN 1968 *Art and Glory: The Story of Elbert Hubbard.* New York: Crown.
HUBBARD, ELBERT 1908 *The Roycroft Shop: A History.* East Aurora, N.Y.: Roycroft Shop.
KOCH, ROBERT 1967 "Elbert Hubbard's Roycrofters as Artist-Craftsmen." *Winterthur Portfolio* 3:67–82.
SHAY, FELIX 1926 *Elbert Hubbard of East Aurora.* New York: Wise.

HUBERT, AUGUSTE

Auguste Hubert (1755–1798), or de Saint-Hubert as he was also known, studied both painting and architecture, the latter under LOUIS FRANÇOIS PETIT-RADEL and A. F. Peyre the Younger (see PEYRE FAMILY), before winning the Prix de Rome in 1784. On his return to Paris, he created festive decorations during the Revolutionary period with his future brother-in-law, Jacques Louis David, through whom he became architect of the City of Paris, inspector of the Louvre, and Inspecteur des Bâtiments Nationaux.

DAMIE STILLMAN

WORK

*1793–1795, Festive Decorations, Paris.

BIBLIOGRAPHY

AULANIER, CHRISTIANE 1948,1954 *Histoire du Palais et du Musée du Louvre.* Paris: Editions des Musées nationaux.
HAUTECOEUR, LOUIS 1953 *Révolution et empire: 1792–1815.* Volume 5 in *Histoire de l'architecture classique en France.* Paris: Picard.
J.J.G. 1876 "Auguste Cheval dit Hubert, architecte de la ville de Paris pendant le Révolution (1755–1798)." *Nouvelles Archives de l'Art Français* 4:409–413.
MONTAIGLON, A. DE, and GIUFFREY, J. (editors)

1887–1912 Volume 13, pages 389–390 in *Correspondance des Directeurs de l'Académie de France à Rome avec les Surintendants des Bâtiments*. Paris.

HÜBSCH, HEINRICH

Heinrich Hübsch (1795–1863) can be considered one of the leading representatives of the German *Rundbogenstil,* which he decisively helped to spread and to which he provided a theoretical foundation in his famous treatise, *In welchem Stil sollen wir bauen?* (1828). In this treatise, Hübsch turned against the hegemony of the dogmatic, Doric-oriented classicism which, in the beginning of the nineteenth century, was represented by Alois Hirt and the Prussian-Berlin school. Influenced by French models such as JEAN NICOLAS LOUIS DURAND, Hübsch demanded a historical analysis of the question of style, based on appropriateness of construction and economic rationality. His plea for the *Rundbogenstil* of the Byzantine and Romanesque periods was thus founded not on the authority of the historic model but on its hypothetical relation to modern technical capabilities (vault, brick as building material, etcetera). Among the numerous public buildings which Hübsch, succeeding FRIEDRICH WEINBRENNER, executed as *Baurat* (building adviser) in Karlsruhe, the principles of the *Rundbogenstil* are realized most consistently in the *Trinkhalle* (pump room) in Baden-Baden.

EBERHARD DRÜEKE
Translated from German by
Beverley R. Placzek

BIBLIOGRAPHY

DÖHMER, KLAUS 1976 *In welchem Style sollen wir bauen?* Munich: Prestel.
VALDENAIRE, ARTHUR 1926 *Heinrich Hübsch.* Karlsruhe, Germany: Braun.

HUDNUT, JOSEPH FAIRMAN

The son of a Michigan bank president, Joseph Fairman Hudnut (1884–1968) followed studies at Harvard University with two years as a draftsman in Chicago and by study of architecture at the University of Michigan. In 1912, Hudnut was appointed professor of architecture at Alabama Polytechnic Institute. He spent the next four years as a teacher and practitioner, building houses, a high school, and churches. He earned an M.A. from Columbia in 1916 and served in the army from 1917 to 1919. Thereafter, Hudnut worked in a New York office of a traditional line.

Hudnut became director of the McIntire School of Fine Arts at the University of Virginia in 1923, teaching architecture and painting. He was appointed professor in the School of Architecture at Columbia University in 1926 and became dean in 1933. In 1935, he became dean of the Graduate School of Design at Harvard University.

Though an expert in Georgian Colonial architecture, he was a champion for the new architecture in trying to bridge the gap between the old and the new. Hudnut gained wide recognition and exerted a profound influence on architecture and architectural education by bringing WALTER GROPIUS to Harvard in 1937. Retiring in 1953, he continued his perceptive writing and lecturing.

REGINALD R. ISAACS

BIBLIOGRAPHY

HUDNUT, JOSEPH 1929 *Modern Sculpture.* New York: Norton.
HUDNUT, JOSEPH 1934 "The Gothick University." *Columbia University Quarterly* 26, Mar.:1–10.
HUDNUT, JOSEPH 1937 Preface in Walter Gropius, *The New Architecture and the Bauhaus.* New York: Museum of Modern Art.
HUDNUT, JOSEPH 1941 "The Last of the Romans: Comment on the Building of the National Gallery of Art." *Magazine of Art* 34, no. 4:169–173.
HUDNUT, JOSEPH 1942 "Education and Architecture." *Architectural Record* 92, Oct.:36–38, 90.
HUDNUT, JOSEPH 1946 "The Political Art of Architecture." *Journal of the Royal Architectural Institute of Canada* 23, no. 3:53–54.
HUDNUT, JOSEPH 1949 *Architecture and the Spirit of Man.* Cambridge, Mass.: Harvard University Press.
HUDNUT, JOSEPH (1952)1972 "The Post-modern House." Pages 306–315 in Lewis Mumford (editor), *Roots of Contemporary American Culture.* Reprint. New York: Dover.

HÜLTZ, JOHANNES

Johannes Hültz (?–1449) of Cologne, Germany, took over as architect of the north tower of Strasbourg Cathedral at the death of ULRICH VON ENSINGEN in 1419. With the tower already brought to its octagonal stage, Hültz completed it with a fantastic spire in the form of a transparent pyramid of step towers crowned with a Madonna statue. The tower was consecrated on June 24, 1439.

ALISON LUCHS

WORKS

1419–1439, Strasbourg Cathedral (spire on the north tower; Madonna statue removed in 1488), Germany.

BIBLIOGRAPHY

BIALOSTOCKI, JAN 1972 *Spätmittelalter und beginnende*

Neuzeit. Berlin: Propyläen.

HILGER, HANS PETER 1972 "Eine Statue der Muttergottes aus den Prager Parler-Kreis im Dom zu Köln." *Pantheon* 30:111.

PUCHTA, H. 1975 "Zufallsfunde mitgeteilt von H. Puchta." *Ars Bavarica* 3:115–116.

RECHT, ROLAND 1969 "Dessins d'architecture pour la cathédrale de Strasbourg." *Oeil* 174–175:26–33.

HUNT, RICHARD MORRIS

Richard Morris Hunt (1827–1895) was the most important figure in the development of architectural professionalism in the United States during the nineteenth century. The first American trained at the Ecole des Beaux-Arts, a founder and president of the American Institute of Architects, a respected spokesman for high professional standards, a tireless worker for public recognition of architects as professionals, a designer of many significant buildings, Hunt became known as "the dean of American architecture." At his death he was widely considered the most eminent architect in the United States.

Born on October 31, 1827, in Brattleboro, Vermont, Hunt spent his early years in New England and Washington, where his father, Jonathan Hunt, a wealthy lawyer, banker, and landowner, was a congressman. His family had been prominent in New England for several generations, and Hunt always took pride in his American roots. His oldest brother William Morris Hunt was a noted painter.

After his father's death in 1832, Jane Maria Leavitt Hunt, his mother, settled with her five children in New Haven and later in Boston, so that William might prepare for Harvard College. In 1843, however, seeking to restore William's health, Mrs. Hunt took the entire family to Europe. After a visit to Paris they spent the winter in Italy. When William chose a career in art, the entire Hunt family decided to remain in Europe. While attending school in Geneva Richard Hunt took lessons in architectural drawing from Samuel Darier and began collecting architectural books. He was seriously considering a military career but by mid-1845 he had decided to study architecture.

Settling in Paris, Hunt was soon accepted into the atelier of HECTOR MARTIN LEFUEL. In 1845 he took the entrance examinations for the Ecole des Beaux-Arts but was unsuccessful; however, the following year he gained admission. In 1851 Hunt was advanced from the second to the first class of the Ecole, where he studied intermittently until 1854. He also traveled widely through western Europe and the British Isles, and in 1852–1853 made a lengthy tour through Egypt and the Middle East.

In 1854, when Lefuel was placed in charge of renewed construction on the Louvre Palace, he invited Hunt to join the project as an inspector of works. In this capacity the young American assisted Lefuel in designing the Pavillon de la Bibliothèque. In September 1855, however, Hunt returned to the United States and established himself in New York City, where, he believed, the greatest opportunities for an American architect lay. With his years of study and work at the Ecole and the Lefuel atelier, his extensive travels, and his public works experience, he was undoubtedly one of the best-trained young American architects of the time.

Hunt's first commission was for a New York City townhouse (1855–1857) with studio space for Thomas P. Rossiter, a long-time painter friend. The structure echoed on a small scale and in a simplified way some of the decorative elements of the Louvre pavilion, but Hunt was careless in various construction details. When Dr. Eleazer Parmly, who commissioned the house, refused to pay Hunt's fee, Hunt sued him. The verdict helped affirm a customary fee schedule for architectural work, differentiating trained architects from carpenter–craftsmen, and gave Hunt a reputation in New York for striving to protect professional rights. In 1856, Hunt briefly worked for THOMAS U. WALTER in Washington, on the Capitol extensions, gaining public works experience in this country.

Hunt's most significant early project was the Studio Building (1857–1858), in New York City, the first American building constructed specifically for artists. Upon completion, the Studio Building quickly became the center of the city's artistic life, and the architect himself occupied quarters there, bringing his large library of architectural books. Here, for a few years, he carried on architectural instruction in an atelier modeled after those in Paris. Charles D. Gambrill, GEORGE B. POST, Henry Van Brunt, William P. Ware (see WARE AND VAN BRUNT), and FRANK FURNESS, among others, studied with Hunt. Hunt thus had a formative influence on the development of American architectural education.

More important in the growth of architectural professionalism was the founding of the American Institute of Architects in 1857. The call to establish a professional society was initiated by RICHARD UPJOHN, its first president. Hunt played a prominent role as a founding member, the first secretary, and a frequent spokesman. Although the A.I.A. lapsed for a time during the Civil War, it was reinstituted in 1864 and reorganized in 1867 from a local group to a national society. For several years, Hunt was head of the New York City chapter and also served as vice president of the national organization.

Hunt's marriage in 1861 to Catharine Clinton Howland joined him to a large and wealthy New York shipping and merchant family, several of whose members subsequently commissioned his professional services. Almost immediately after the outbreak of the Civil War, Hunt and his bride sailed for Europe, where they spent more than a year and where their first child, Richard Howland Hunt, was born. Hunt traveled extensively on this visit, viewing architectural sites and doing considerable sketching and painting.

On returning to New York, Hunt designed gateways for the southern entrances to Central Park. The French-inspired designs, however, were rather graceless and most critics considered them grandiose and inappropriate for the new park. Although never built, they added to his reputation for promoting the arts. In 1867, Hunt was named an American judge and fine arts commissioner for the Paris International Exposition. Upon his return, the range of his commissions was exceptionally broad.

The Presbyterian Hospital (1868–1872) and the Lenox Library (1870–1877) in New York City were commissioned by James Lenox, a wealthy merchant, bibliophile, and art collector. For the hospital, Hunt incorporated the latest health planning ideas of detached pavilions, with large windows providing good light and ventilation. The exterior red-brick and white-limestone design of the substantial north pavilion and the administration building, joined by covered corridors, however, struck some contemporary observers as agitated and confused, although the picturesque rooflines adumbrated a feature that Hunt often stressed in his later work. The Lenox Library, by contrast, was dignified and monumental in conception, with the fenestration providing the principal decorative element and with considerable *néo-grec* ornamentation. The large reading rooms of the library were among the grandest interior spaces in the city. The Lenox collection of books and paintings was later consolidated into the New York Public Library, and in 1912 the building was razed and the site given over to the residence and gallery of Henry Clay Frick.

At the Yale Divinity School in New Haven, East Divinity Hall (1869–1870) was arranged with classrooms and a library on the ground floor and students' accommodations above. Characterized as French neo-Gothic in design, the asymmetrical building was dominated on the exterior by a cluttered, splayed corner pavilion, and had a restless

quality to it. Adjoining East Divinity Hall was the small Marquand Chapel (1870–1871), harmonizing with its neighbor but possessing an unpretentious elegance lacking in the larger building. Both structures were razed in 1931 to make way for Calhoun College at Yale. Nearby, for a Yale student secret society, Hunt designed the Scroll and Key Society Clubhouse (1867–1869), Moorish in inspiration, with dark striped masonry, banded columns, a richly decorated impost band, and deep-set stilted arches.

In contrast, Hunt's first Academic Hall (1869–1870) for the newly founded Hampton Normal and Agricultural Institute in Virginia, was little more than a serviceable shell. After this classroom building was destroyed by fire in 1879, Hunt provided plans for a slightly smaller but fireproof replacement building (1880–1881). Virginia Hall (1872–1874), also at the Hampton Institute, was much larger and embodied both Second Empire and Victorian Gothic elements.

A smaller but more striking and original building was the Howland Circulating Library in Matteawan (later Beacon), New York (1871–1872),

Hunt.
Lenox Library.
New York.
1870–1877

Hunt.
Howland Circulating
Library.
Beacon, N.Y.
1871–1872

devised in a "Norwegian style." The multigabled roof surmounts textured polychrome walls of patterned slate and brick set upon a roughly dressed stone base. The interior reading room provides an elaborate interplay of columns, braces, hammerbeams, and arches.

In his commercial commissions, Hunt was able to adapt his ideas to a variety of client needs, while utilizing various new technological advances. Outstanding among these buildings was the first American apartment house, the Stuyvesant Apartments (1869–1870) on East Eighteenth Street in New York City. Before this building was erected, multifamily dwellings had only been used in America for housing the poor, but the elegant and comfortable Stuyvesant Apartments, modeled on an urban French mode, helped make such residences respectable and was an important prototype for a whole new class of structures in American cities. As in the Studio Building, Hunt provided quarters here for artists, with commodious, well-

lighted studios at the attic level. Much larger was Stevens Apartment House (1870–1872) in New York City, later converted into the Victoria Hotel. With its streetlevel shops and three-story mansard, the multiuse building had a decided Parisian look to it.

Two stores by Hunt in New York City embodied the new midcentury cast-iron technology. The façade of the Van Rensselaer Building (1871–1872) was an iron front in Moorish design, colorfully painted and styled to advertise the dry goods and notions firm housed in the building. Directly adjacent was Hunt's Roosevelt Building (1873–1874), with a bolder and more powerful front, though less colorful, embodying *néo-grec* piers, colossal pilasters and columns, delicate colonnettes, and a boldly bracketed cornice.

Also in New York, the Delaware and Hudson Canal Company Building (1873–1876)—a large stone and brick office building, where for a time Hunt maintained his offices—had a solid and dignified appearance, though somewhat sober. The façade of the Guernsey Office Building (1881–1882), in New York, with again sharp color contrasts of brick and stone, had like some other Hunt structures a rather agitated appearance.

The most notable of Hunt's commercial structures was the Tribune Building (1873–1876), facing City Hall Park, for a time the architect's best-known creation. Rising eight main stories above a basement and subcellar and topped by a two-story attic and a tower, at 260 feet it was for some years the tallest edifice in the city, except for the spire of Trinity Church. Although the tower accentuated the building's height, the grouping of the ten stories into five units deemphasized the vertical thrust. In 1881–1883, a narrow wing was added to the north side, and in 1905, in a remarkable engineering endeavor, nine stories were added to the main section. The Tribune Building was razed in 1966.

Domestic commissions also engrossed Hunt's creative energies during these years. In Boston, the Brimmer Houses (1869–1870), built for Hunt's close friend the philanthropist Martin L. Brimmer, prefigured in various decorative details Hunt's later use of French Renaissance elements. In Chicago, the Marshall Field House (1871–1873) soon became one of the showplaces of the city. Dominated by a tall, shingled, third-story mansard, the Second-Empire formality of the street front contrasted markedly with the greater informality of the garden side.

More important were Hunt's early designs in Newport, Rhode Island. The J. N. A. Griswold House (1861–1863), a picturesque, seemingly sprawling structure, initiated Hunt's vernacular, stick-style mode of expression. The George War-

Hunt.
Tribune Building.
New York.
1873–1876

ing House (1870–1871), known as "The Hypothenuse," included a rustic, alpine gable containing a bargeboard arch of perforated wood, a feature used in several of his Newport houses. Among Hunt's other picturesque houses in Newport were those for the famous actress Charlotte Cushman (1870), for Thomas G. Appleton (1870–1871), and for Henry G. Marquand (1872–1873), all of which have been destroyed. The Marquand House, known as Linden Gate, sensitively incorporated a variety of building materials and provided a skillful massing of the primary and secondary forms; it was transitional to Hunt's later Newport palaces. The picturesque mode was also evident in the Travers Block (1870–1871), with small streetfront shops and apartments above. Hunt also remodeled Chateau-sur-Mer, the George Wetmore Mansion (1869–1879), considerably enlarging what was then Newport's largest house.

Hunt's tremendous output of the early 1870s took its toll. To recuperate from a severe illness, he and his family went to Europe in 1874, and for more than a year he was almost completely removed from the demands of a busy office. Following his return, Hunt served as a juror for the architectural exhibits of the Philadelphia Centennial Exhibition of 1876.

For the Princeton Theological Seminary, James Lenox commissioned Hunt to design a new library and two houses for professors. The Lenox Library (1876–1879) had two lower stories as a lean-to against a high and spacious core, lighted from above by twenty large windows ranged as a clerestory. At Princeton College, Hunt built the large Marquand Chapel (1880–1882). A rugged structure of roughly dressed stone, the chapel front was ornamented by an elegant, well-proportioned campanile. Also at Princeton College, Hunt's Chemical Laboratory (1885–1891), a plain, serviceable, classroom–laboratory building, stood in mediocre contrast to the now destroyed Marquand Chapel and Lenox Library.

Hunt's long association with the Vanderbilt family began in the late 1870s. A Queen Anne style country house (1878–1880) at Oakdale, Long Island, for William K. Vanderbilt, and Saint Mark's Chapel and Rectory (1879–1880) at Islip, New York, fashioned in a Scandinavian timberwork style, were early commissions. And the very large New York townhouse (1878–1882) for William K. Vanderbilt became one of Hunt's most admired compositions.

Styled after late-Gothic–early Renaissance French châteaux, the W. K. Vanderbilt Mansion marked the beginning of both Hunt's use of this style and his most characteristic building type— the very large, costly, and ornately decorated pri-

vate dwelling. Finely proportioned, artfully massed, lavishly decorated without and within, the Vanderbilt Mansion, perhaps more than any other dwelling of the Gilded Age, set a mark for Americans of wealth and fashion to emulate. In New York and elsewhere, rich Americans soon vied with one another in creating sumptuous residences, many of them in the château style. The Vanderbilt Mansion was razed in the 1920s when the value of the land made it a prime commercial site.

Other Vanderbilt family commissions soon followed. At the Moravian Cemetery at New Dorp, Staten Island, Hunt's Vanderbilt family mausoleum (1884–1889), a collaborative project with FREDERICK LAW OLMSTED, was a huge tomb, partly underground, the façade of which was styled after that of the Church of Saint Gilles, near Arles, France. For George W. Vanderbilt, one of Hunt's

Hunt.
Griswold House.
Newport, Rhode Island.
1861–1863

Hunt.
William K. Vanderbilt Mansion.
New York.
1878–1882

most important later clients, the architect did alterations on the Vanderbilt homestead on Staten Island as well as created the Jackson Square branch of the New York Free Circulating Library (1887–1888), with a delicately conceived Flemish-style façade.

In sharp contrast to the sumptuous dwelling for W. K. Vanderbilt was the Association Residence for Respectable Aged Indigent Females (1881–1883) in New York, blending both French Second Empire and Gothic Revival elements. Hunt also designed several multifamily tenement houses in New York.

Widely recognized by the 1880s as a leading American architect, Hunt was increasingly called upon to design public monuments and memorials of national significance. Most of Hunt's major monuments were in collaboration with the sculptor John Quincy Adams Ward. Hunt customarily prepared the general ideas, furnished the inscriptions, and planned the pedestals, while Ward created the sculptured figures. The Hunt–Ward projects included the Matthew C. Perry Statue (1868) in Newport, Rhode Island; the Yorktown Monument (1880–1884), with Henry Van Brunt, in Virginia; the Lafayette Statue (1882–1883) in Burlington, Vermont; the Seventh Regiment Monument (1867–1873), the Washington Statue (1883), the Pilgrim Statue (1884–1885), and the Horace Greeley Statue (1881–1890) in New York; the Henry Ward Beecher Statue (1888–1891) in Brooklyn, New York; and the James Garfield Monument (1884–1887) in Washington. More widely viewed than any of these, however, was Hunt's work with Auguste Bartholdi on the Statue of Liberty, the most significant monumental sculpture in the United States and a national symbol. After the Liberty figure had been conceived by Bartholdi and was already largely executed, Hunt was invited to serve as architect in chief for the project, in charge of designing the statue pedestal (1881–1886). Hunt had to provide a base that harmonized with the statue, though not so ornate or massive as to call attention to itself. In the scale of the forms he used, in the subordination of decorative detail, and in the emphasis on massive solidity and vertical thrust, the Liberty pedestal was highly successful.

Hunt's professional importance was recognized by his election as the third president of the A. I. of A. He assumed office in 1888, when the question of amalgamation with the recently established, yet larger, Western Association of Architects, was a central issue. Hunt worked to consolidate the two organizations and was unanimously elected president of the reorganized institute, serving through 1891. As a spokesman for the profession, he devoted himself to the cause of improving the quality of buildings erected by the federal government.

Of the many building types that Hunt employed, he seemed to find the designing of very large private houses his most congenial work. With the extensive resources of wealthy patrons, he was often in the fortunate situation of being able to carry out with no restraints the ideas that seemed most suitable to him and to the life-styles of his clients.

Among his large dwellings, Hunt's residence for Henry G. Marquand, on Madison Avenue in New York City, aroused considerable contemporary interest because of its exterior design, its period rooms, and the valuable art collection they contained. In the Marquand House (1881–1884) and two conjoined houses built as a single unit, Hunt again turned to the sixtenth-century French Renaissance for inspiration. The highly animated façades were harmoniously composed with a myriad of decorative details. Close by on Fifth Avenue, Hunt chose a Venetian Gothic style for the Ogden Mills Mansion (1885–1887). Following up on the ideas he used for the W. K. Vanderbilt Mansion, Hunt provided a smaller and less ornate version in Chicago for William Borden. The Borden Mansion (1884–1889) gave an impression of great strength and dignity; the outstanding decorative feature was a corbelled *tourelle,* placed at the salient angle of the two principal fronts.

Hunt's other mansions helped establish a tone of decorative elegance for New York's upper Fifth Avenue. The William V. Lawrence Mansion (1890–1891), long and very narrow, was dominated by a large conical-roofed tower, a feature characteristic of several of Hunt's houses. The Elbridge T. Gerry Mansion (1891–1894) provided a richness of architectural motifs and details masterfully integrated into an impressive composition. Inspired by French architectural work of the late fifteenth century, the Gerry Mansion also featured a corner tower, toward which the masses on either side were piled. This interesting house was torn down to make way for the Hotel Pierre. Even larger was the double residence for Mrs. William Astor and her son (1891–1895), again looking back for inspiration to the French Renaissance, though later to the mid-sixteenth century. More formal and regular than the Gerry Mansion, with crisply articulated lines, the Astor Mansion included large rooms for public entertaining and was probably the most sumptuous private residence in the city. In the late 1920s the structure was demolished to make way for Temple Emanu-El.

Hunt's domestic commissions of the late 1880s and early 1890s included several country houses. For his close friend Levi P. Morton, vice president

Hunt.
William K. and Alva
*   Vanderbilt Mansion*
*   (Marble House).*
Newport, Rhode Island.
1888–1892

of the United States under Benjamin Harrison, Hunt designed a large house at Rhinecliff-on-Hudson, New York. The Morton Mansion (1886–1887), known as Ellerslie, was characterized by Tudor half-timber work and had a vaguely Elizabethan look. Grey Towers (1884–1886), the Milford, Pennsylvania, summer residence of James W. Pinchot, was created as a highly romantic, rustic looking structure in a late French medieval style, dominated by three squat, conical-roofed towers. The Archibald Rogers Mansion (1886–1889), Crumwold Hall, at Hyde Park, New York, featured similar towers, built up of roughly dressed stone. The architect's interest in wall-surface textures was even more emphasized in the Joseph R. Busk Mansion (1889–1891), rising from a rocky coastal perch in Newport. Here the rugged stone walls seemed to grow right out of the site.

In Newport, Hunt's four great "cottages" set the stage for the turn of the century era of palace construction in the country's most fashionable summer resort. Ochre Court (1888–1892), built for Ogden Goelet, developed the early French Renaissance ideas on a grander scale than in any of Hunt's earlier houses. Ochre Court later became an administration building for Salve Regina College.

Marble House (1888–1892), constructed for William K. and Alva Vanderbilt, was modeled in part on the White House in Washington, and on the Petit Trianon at Versailles. The symmetrical exterior of the white marble mansion, decorated by colossal columns and pilasters, was artfully arranged to give a feeling of great dignity and formality. The interiors, which reportedly cost some

nine million dollars, were the most lavish that Hunt ever executed. The great entrance hall was faced with yellow Sienese marble, while the dining room walls were lined by dark pink Numidian marble. The gold ballroom, the most richly ornamented room of the mansion, included many carvings by Hunt's protégé, the sculptor Karl Bitter.

Belcourt Castle (1891–1894), the residence of Oliver H. P. Belmont, was originally a magnificent stable and carriage house with living quarters and rooms for entertaining. Arranged around a central courtyard, the wings of the mansion include a combination of French, Italian, and English elements.

The Breakers (1892–1895), the largest of the Newport houses, was created for Cornelius Vanderbilt II. Designed in a sixteenth-century Genoese manner, the seventy-room mansion, though formally balanced in many ways, was given an open and airy character suitable to summer living,

Hunt.
Cornelius Vanderbilt II
*   Mansion (The Breakers;*
*   dining room).*
Newport, Rhode Island.
1892–1895

by the arrangement of the rooms and loggias, centering about a large, two-story great hall.

Considerably larger is Biltmore House (1888–1895), in Asheville, North Carolina, a two-hundred-and-fifty-five room summer residence commissioned by George W. Vanderbilt. The château, surrounded by lawns and gardens, was set in some 125,000 acres of grounds, planned and arranged by Olmsted. Using French late Gothic and early Renaissance elements, Hunt created a highly romantic structure, dominated on the principal front by a richly detailed entrance pavilion to which the grand staircase was attached. The principal rooms were elaborately decorated and richly furnished. The banquet hall, the largest room with a ceiling rising seventy feet, focuses on a huge triple fireplace surmounted by a large frieze carved by Karl Bitter. The most lavishly decorated room is the library, also featuring Bitter carvings. In the upstairs hall sitting room are full-length portraits of Hunt and Olmsted, painted by John Singer Sargent.

While Hunt's creative energies in the early 1890s, refreshed by further European visits in 1885–1886, 1889, and 1893, were largely devoted to the great houses, he also was involved in various lesser commissions. For Adelbert College, in Cleveland, Ohio, later Case Western Reserve University, Hunt designed Clark Hall (1889–1892). For Harvard University, he built the Fogg Museum (1893–1895), a highly formal, neoclassical classroom and exhibition building, which was poorly received and eventually demolished in 1973. He designed structures for the United States Naval Observatory (1887–1893) in Georgetown Heights, Washington, to house special astronomical instruments. At the United States Military Academy, West Point, Hunt also designed a gymnasium (1889–1893), an Academic Building (1889–1895), and a small guardhouse (1894–1895), all with rough-textured stone walls and traditional military details to fit in with older buildings on the post. For Trinity Church in New York City, Hunt designed three sets of bronze entrance doors (1890–1894). The principal doors were executed by Karl Bitter, who honored the architect with a portrait head on the right-hand portal.

Another major endeavor for Hunt was his work on the World's Columbian Exposition in Chicago in 1893. As chairman of the board of architects, Hunt helped bring about the unified and harmonious conception of the main buildings. Hunt's Administration Building (1891–1893) was a monumental, neoclassical edifice whose gleaming gold and white dome was visible all over the grounds. Serving as a vestibule to the fair, the Administration Building was given an interior finish on its inner shell. The outer dome, rising some two hundred and seventy-five feet, rested upon a low octagonal drum, which in turn was supported by a high Ionic colonnade. The lower part of the building extended into four corner pavilions having large wall areas of glass, thus giving the effect of a great closed loggia base for the huge structure. This temporary building was no doubt Hunt's best-known work during his lifetime.

Hunt.
George W. Vanderbilt
Mansion (Biltmore
House).
Asheville, North Carolina.
1888–1895

The architect's final major commission was the entrance wing for the Metropolitan Museum of Art (1894–1895), in New York. Hunt conceived of the wing as part of the museum's expansion into a palace of art, covering some eighteen and one-half acres of floor space, completely surrounding the first red-brick museum building and its two extensions and hiding them from view. The Hunt wing houses the great hall, the museum vestibule, also used for display of sculpture. Facing Fifth Avenue, the symmetrical, Beaux-Arts front includes a variety of architectural and sculptural elements admirably arranged and harmoniously composed. The wing was completed by Richard Howland Hunt, after his father's death in Newport on July 31, 1895.

By the 1890s, Hunt was the most honored American architect of his time and one of the most internationally honored Americans. He was an honorary and corresponding member of the Académie des Beaux-Arts of the Institut de France (1882); chevalier of the Légion d'Honneur (1884); member of the Societé Centrale des Architectes Français (1886); honorary and corresponding member of the Royal Institute of British Architects (1886); honorary and corresponding member of the Engineers' and Architects' Society of Vienna (1887); president of the American Institute of Architects (1888–1891); academician of the Society of Saint Luke, Rome (1892); honorary doctor of laws, Harvard University (1892); honorary member of the Society of Architects, Amsterdam (1893); Queen's Gold Medal recipient of the Royal Institute of British Architects (1893); and foreign associate member of the Académie des Beaux-Arts of the Institut de France (1893). A civic monument honoring Hunt was erected on Fifth Avenue in New York in 1898.

Hunt's significance in the history of American architecture comes less in his many building designs than in his work as a molder of his profession. More than any other figure of the latter half of the nineteenth century, he worked to promote high professional standards, and to make architecture a respected profession in the United States. His atelier was a foundation for the development of American architectural education, and his work to promote the arts in general extended considerably beyond his architectural endeavors. In his own building designs, Hunt ranged very widely in building types and stylistic elements, and he stood in the forefront in the use of technological innovations. He was, nonetheless, strongly committed to traditions of the European past, finding in the best work of the past stylistic inspiration and standards of quality for work done in the present.

PAUL R. BAKER

WORKS

*1855–1857, Thomas P. Rossiter House; *1857–1858, Studio Building; New York. 1861–1863, J. N. A. Griswold House, Newport, R.I. 1867–1869, Scroll and Key Society Clubhouse, New Haven. 1867–1873, Seventh Regiment Monument Pedestal, New York. 1868, Matthew C. Perry Statue Pedestal, Newport, R.I. *1868–1872, Presbyterian Hospital, New York. *1869–1870, Academic Hall, Hampton Normal and Agricultural Institute, Va. *1869–1870, Martin L. Brimmer Houses, Boston. *1869–1870, East Divinity Hall, Yale Divinity School, New Haven. 1869–1870, Stuyvesant Apartments, New York. 1869–1879, George P. Wetmore Mansion (alterations); *1870, Charlotte Cushman House; *1870–1871, Thomas G. Appleton House; Newport, R.I. *1870–1871, Marquand Chapel, New Haven. 1870–1871, Travers Block; 1870–1871, George Waring House; Newport, R.I. *1870–1872, Stevens Apartment House (Victoria Hotel); *1870–1877, Lenox Library; New York. 1871–1872, Howland Circulating Library, Beacon, N.Y. *1871–1872, Van Rensselaer Building, New York. *1871–1873, Marshall Field House, Chicago. *1872–1873, Henry G. Marquand House, Newport, R.I. 1872–1874, Virginia Hall, Hampton Normal and Agricultural Institute, Va. 1873–1874, Roosevelt Building; *1873–1876, Delaware and Hudson Canal Company Building; *1873–1876, Tribune Building; New York. *1876–1879, Lenox Library, Princeton, N.J. *1878–1880, William K. Vanderbilt Mansion, Oakdale, N.Y. *1878–1882, William K. Vanderbilt Mansion, New York. 1879–1880, Saint Mark's Chapel and Rectory, Islip, N.Y. 1880–1881, Second Academic Hall, Hampton Normal and Agricultural Institute, Va. *1880–1882, Marquand Chapel, Princeton, N.J. 1880–1884, Yorktown Monument (with Henry Van Brunt), Va. *1881–1882, Guernsey Office Building; 1881–1883, Association Residence; *1881–1884, Henry G. Marquand House; 1881–1886, Statue of Liberty Pedestal; 1881–1890, Horace Greeley Statue Pedestal; New York. 1882–1883, Lafayette Statue Pedestal, Burlington, Vt. 1883, Washington Statue Pedestal; 1884–1885, Pilgrim Statue Pedestal; New York. 1884–1886, James W. Pinchot Mansion (Grey Towers), Milford, Pa. 1884–1887, James Garfield Monument Pedestal, Washington. *1884–1889, William Borden Mansion, Chicago. 1884–1889, Vanderbilt Mausoleum (with Frederick Law Olmstead), Moravian Cemetery, Staten Island, N.Y. *1885–1887, Ogden Mills Mansion, New York. 1885–1891, Chemical Laboratory, Princeton, N.J. *1886–1887, Levi P. Morton Mansion (Ellerslie), Rhinecliff-on-Hudson, N.Y. 1886–1889, Archibald Rogers Mansion (Crumwold Hall), Hyde Park, N.Y. 1887–1888, New York Free Circulating Library. 1887–1893, United States Naval Observatory Buildings, Washington. 1888–1891, Henry Ward Beecher Statue Pedestal, Brooklyn, N.Y. 1888–1892, Odgen Goelet Mansion (Ochre Court); 1888–1892, William K. and Alva Vanderbilt Mansion (Marble House); Newport, R.I. 1888–1895, George W. Vanderbilt Mansion (Biltmore House), Asheville, N.C. 1889–1891, Joseph R. Busk Mansion (Indian Spring), Newport, R.I. 1889–1892, Clark Hall, Adelbert College (later Case Western Reserve University), Cleveland, Ohio. *1889–1893, Gymnasium; 1889–1895, Academic Building; United States Military Academy, West Point, N.Y. *1890–1891, William V. Lawrence Mansion; 1890–1894, Trinity Church (doors); New York. *1891–1893, Administration Building, World's Columbian Exposition, Chicago. 1891–1894, Oliver H. P. Belmont Mansion (Belcourt Castle), Newport, R.I. *1891–1894, Elbridge T. Gerry Mansion; *1891–1895, Mrs. William B. Astor and John Jacob Astor IV Mansion; New York. 1892–1895, Cornelius Vanderbilt II Mansion (The Breakers), Newport, R.I. *1893–1895, Fogg Museum (later Hunt Hall), Harvard University, Cambridge, Mass. *1894–1895, Metropolitan Museum of Art Wing "D" (not completed until 1902 by Richard Howland Hunt), New York.

BIBLIOGRAPHY

Baker, Paul R. 1980 *Richard Morris Hunt.* Cambridge, Mass.: M.I.T. Press.

Burnham, Alan 1952 "The New York Architecture of Richard Morris Hunt." *Journal of the Society of Architectural Historians* 11, no. 2:9–14.

Ferree, Barr 1895 "Richard Morris Hunt: His Art and Work." *Architecture and Building* 23, Dec. 7:271–275.

Paris, William Francklyn 1955–1956 "Richard Morris Hunt: First Secretary and Third President of the Institute." *Journal of the American Institute of Architects* 24:243–249; 25:14–19, 74–80.

Schuyler, Montgomery 1895 "The Works of the Late Richard M. Hunt." *Architectural Record* 5, no. 2:97–180.

Van Brunt, Henry 1895 "Richard Morris Hunt: A Memorial Address." *American Architect and Building News* 50, Nov. 2:53–56.

Van Pelt, John Vredenburgh 1925 *A Monograph of the William K. Vanderbilt House: Richard Morris Hunt, Architect.* New York: The author.

Wallis, Frank E. 1917 "Richard M. Hunt, Master Architect and Man." *Architectural Review* 5:239–240.

HUNT, THOMAS FREDERICK

Employed by the Office of Works from 1813, Thomas Frederick Hunt (c.1791–1831) is best known for his special study of the picturesque Tudor style, on which he published several books. He designed at least two buildings in an elegant neoclassical style: the Burns Mausoleum (1815) and an Episcopalian church in Dumfries, Scotland.

Jill Lever

WORKS

1815, Burns Mausoleum, Saint Michael's Churchyard; Opened 1817, Episcopalian Church (now Wesleyan Church); Dumfries, Scotland. *c.1825, Bifrons, Patrixbourne, Kent, England. 1828, Danehurst, near Danehill, Sussex, England. 1828, Redrice, near Andover, Hampshire, England.

HURTADO IZQUIERDO, FRANCISCO

Francisco Hurtado Izquierdo (1669–1725) was a Spanish baroque architect active in the province of Granada. Details of his early life and training are unknown. He is first documented in 1696 at the Church of San Lorenzo in Córdoba in the position of master joiner. He served as chief architect of both the Cathedral of Córdoba (1697) and the Cathedral of Granada (1705). He began work on the sacristy at Córdoba in 1703. In 1707, he executed the retable of Santiago; the marble pulpits at Granada were done in 1713. A major turning point in his career resulted from his appointment as royal tax commissioner for the town of Priego in 1712. Henceforth, he was able to devote himself to works of his own choosing.

Hurtado's two greatest commissions were undertaken for the Carthusian order, in particular the Sacristy for the Cartuja of Granada, designed between 1703 and 1720 and executed posthumously. His last major Carthusian work was the Sacristy of the Cartuja of Nuestra Señora del Paular in Rescafría of around 1719. Hurtado's work is remarkable for its rich polychrome effects of juxtaposed colored marbles. As an architect of the first period of the Spanish baroque, he anticipated later tendencies. He founded a large workshop of decorators and craftsmen in Priego.

Elizabeth A. T. Smith

WORKS

(A)1693, Camarín, Mausoleum of the Counts of Buenavista, Málaga, Spain. 1696, San Lorenzo (retable); 1699, La Fuensanta Antechamber (reconstruction of stairway); *1700, Houses, calle del Baño (now calle de Céspedes); 1701–1703, Hospital of the Destitute; Córdoba, Spain. 1703, El Carpio (vaulting of side aisles), Spain. 1703, Parish Church (first story of the belfry), Belalcazar, Spain. 1703–1720, Cartuja of Granada (sacristy, executed posthumously), Spain. 1703–?, Córdoba Cathedral (sacristy); 1704, Capilla Mayor of Church La Magdalena (divisionary steps); Córdoba, Spain. 1707, Santiago (retable), Spain. 1713, Granada Cathedral (marble pulpits), Spain. c.1719–1725, Cartuja of Nuestra Señora del Paular (sacristy; not completed until c.1770), Rascafría, Spain.

BIBLIOGRAPHY

Gallego Burín, A. 1956 *El barraco granadino.* Spain: University of Granada.

Kubler, George, and Soria, Martin 1959 *Art and Architecture in Spain and Portugal and their American Dominions: 1500–1800.* Baltimore: Penguin.

Schubert, Otto 1924 *Historia del barroco en España.* Translated from German by Manuel Hernández Alcalde. Madrid: Editorial Saturnino Calleja.

Taylor, R. C. 1950 "Francisco Hurtado and His

School." *Art Bulletin* 32:25–61.

TAYLOR, R. C. 1962 "La sacristía de la Cartuja de Granada y sus autores." *Archivo Español de Arte* 35:135–173.

HUSLY, J. OTTEN

Born in Doetinchem, Netherlands, Jacob Otten Husly (1738–1796) left home at an early age for Amsterdam where he studied at the municipal drawing school. In 1765, he was appointed as one of the directors of the school; in 1769, he became a teacher of architecture there. Husly's work, which shows the influence of ANDREA PALLADIO, marks the beginning of a neoclassical trend in Holland, which lasted until the middle of the nineteenth century.

WIM DE WIT

WORKS

1771–1776, Town Hall, Weesp, Netherlands. *1775, Canal House (façade), 382 Herengracht, Amsterdam. 1775, 1793–1810, Town Hall, Groningen, Netherlands. 1780, Teylers Museum (interior decoration), Haarlem, Netherlands. 1781–1788, Felix Meritis Society Building, Amsterdam.

BIBLIOGRAPHY

LUYKX, P. J. E. 1965 "Het voormalig huis Herengracht 382 en zijn bouwmeester Jacob Otten Husly." *Ons Amsterdam* 1:2–9.

ROSENBERG, JAKOB; SLIVE, SEYMOUR; and KUILE, E. H. TER (1966)1972 *Dutch Art and Architecture: 1600 to 1800.* Rev. ed. Harmondworth, England: Penguin.

VRIEND, J. J. (1938)1949 Part 1 in *De bouwkunst van ons land.* 3d rev. ed. Amsterdam: Scheltema.

WEISSMAN, A. W. 1912 *Geschiedenis der Nederlandsche Bouwkunst.* Amsterdam: van Looy.

HUTCHISON, ALEXANDER COWPER

Alexander Cowper Hutchison (1838–1922) epitomized the generation of native-born, self-taught architects who worked in Montreal during the second half of the nineteenth century. He began his career as a stonecutter, but by 1865, he had gained sufficient training to set up an architectural practice with the Englishman O. Steele. The output of the office was stylistically varied, ranging from the inventive classicism of the Redpath Museum (1880) to the rich Romanesque of the Erskine-American Church (1893–1894), both in Montreal. Not surprisingly, all were notable for the fine detailing of their stonework. Hutchison and Steele's expertise in designing the gargantuan ice palaces for the Montreal Winter Carnivals during the 1880s brought them similar commissions from as far away as Minnesota. The firm was continued into the 1930s by Hutchison's son and son-in-law, under the name of Hutchison, Wood, and Miller.

JULIA GERSOVITZ

WORKS

*1865, American Presbyterian Church (with M. T. Morell), Dorchester Street; *1873, Young Men's Christian Association Building, Victoria Square; *1878, Crescent Street Presbyterian Church; 1880, Redpath Museum, McGill University; *1887–1889, Ice Palace, Winter Carnival; *1889–1891, Lord Strathcona Residence and Guest Houses, Dorchester Street; *c.1892, High School of Montreal, de Maisonneuve Street West; *1892, A. R. Reid Residence, Drummond Street; Montreal. *1893, A. W. Ogilvie Summer Residence, Lasalle, Quebec. 1893–1894, Erskine-American Church, Sherbrooke Street West; 1906, McGill Student Union (with Percy E. Nobbs), Montreal. 1907, MacDonald Agricultural College (with Hutchison, Wood and Miller), Sainte Anne de Bellevue, Quebec.

BIBLIOGRAPHY

American Architect and Building News 1889 25, no. 682:35.

ATHERTON, WILLIAM HENRY 1914 Volume 3, page 277 in *Montreal 1535–1914.* Montreal: S. J. Clarke.

Canadian Architect and Builder. 3, Sept.:102.

HUTTON, ADDISON

Born in Sewickley Township, Pennsylvania, Addison Hutton (1834–1916) was the son of a carpenter, to whom he was apprenticed as a youth. At age sixteen, Hutton started work on his own and subsequently was a draftsman (1857–1861), then a partner (1864–1868), with SAMUEL SLOAN in Philadelphia. He maintained his own office there from 1868 to 1907. Most of Hutton's work exhibits a restrained handling of High Victorian modes.

RICHARD W. LONGSTRETH

WORKS

1868, Lockwood House (Glenloch), Glenloch, Pa. 1868, Philadelphia Saving Fund Society Building; 1870–1878, Ridgway Library; Philadelphia. 1878–1885, Taylor Hall, Bryn Mawr College, Pa. 1885, Clothier House (Ballytore), Wynnewood, Pa.

BIBLIOGRAPHY

TATUM, GEORGE B. 1961 *Penn's Great Town.* Philadelphia: University of Pennsylvania Press.

TEITELMAN, EDWARD, and LONGSTRETH, RICHARD W. 1974 *Architecture in Philadelphia: A Guide.* Cambridge, Mass.: M.I.T. Press.

WEBSTER, RICHARD J. 1976 *Philadelphia Preserved.* Philadelphia: Temple University Press.

YARNALL, ELIZABETH BIDDLE 1974 *Addison Hutton, Quaker Architect, 1834–1916.* Philadelphia: Art Alliance Press.

HUVE, JEAN-JACQUES-MARIE

Son of the architect Jean-Jacques Huvé, the grand prize recipient of 1770 who made an honorable career under Louis XVI, Jean-Jacques-Marie Huvé (1742–1808) studied with his father and with Perrier. In 1817, he was appointed architect of the Madeleine in Paris, for which PIERRE ALEXANDRE VIGNON had already submitted new plans. Active under the Restoration, he was architect of the Hospices of Paris and later worked at the Château of Compiegne under Louis XVIII; he finally became architect of the Postal Administration. Huvé was a neoclassical artist of talent, a talent he had too little occasion to affirm in any truly personal works.

DANIEL RABREAU
Translated from French by
Shara Wasserman

WORKS

1827–1831, Market of the Fat Cows; 1827–1831, Ventadour Theater; Paris.

HUYOT, JEAN NICOLAS

Jean Nicolas Huyot (1780–1840) studied with A. F. Peyre (see PEYRE FAMILY) and won the Prix de Rome in 1807. His drawings of the Temple of Fortune at Palestrina were exhibited at the 1815 Salon. In 1819, Huyot was appointed professor at the Ecole des Beaux-Arts. He twice served as architect of the Arc de l'Etoile.

LISA B. REITZES

WORKS

1817, French hospital, Constantinople. 1823–1825, 1828–1831, Arc du Triomphe de l'Etoile (supervision), Paris.

BIBLIOGRAPHY

DREXLER, ARTHUR (editor) 1977 *The Architecture of the Ecole des Beaux-Arts.* New York: Museum of Modern Art.
HAUTECOEUR, LOUIS 1943–1957 *Histoire de l'Architecture classique en France.* 7 vols. Paris: Picard.

I'ANSON, EDWARD JR.

Edward I'Anson (1812–1888) was the son of an architect and surveyor of the same name. He was educated at Merchant Taylors' School, London, and in France, at the Collège Henri Quatre; he was articled to his father. He designed a number of the early office blocks in London and claimed to be the first architect to use white-glazed bricks for internal courtyards. His designs were in a Renaissance or a Ruskinian (see JOHN RUSKIN) Gothic style, both of which showed Italian and French influence.

He was president of the Royal Institute of British Architects from 1886 until his death. His son E. B. I'ANSON was in partnership with him.

ROGER DIXON

WORKS
*1842–1844, Royal Exchange Buildings; 1866, British and Foreign Bible Society Building; 1869–1870, 69 Cornhill Street; 1878–1879, Saint Bartholomew's Hospital (museum and library); 1879, Garden Corner, 13 Chelsea Embankment (alterations by C. F. A. VOYSEY); 1881, Corn Exchange; London.

BIBLIOGRAPHY
"The British and Foreign Bible Society." 1866 *The Builder* 24:445–447.
DIXON, ROGER, and MUTHESIUS, STEFAN 1978 *Victorian Architecture.* London: Thames; New York: Oxford University Press.
"Edward I'Anson, Jr." 1979 In *Concise Dictionary of National Biography.* London: Oxford University Press.
HITCHCOCK, H. R. (1954)1972 *Early Victorian Architecture in Britain.* 2 vols. Reprint. New York: Da Capo.
"The Late Mr. Edward I'Anson." 1888 *Building News* 54:177–178.
"The Late President of the Institute." 1888 *The Builder* 54:77–78.
"London Street Architecture: Premises in Cornhill." 1871 *The Builder* 29:187.
PEVSNER, NIKOLAUS (1952)1969 *London.* 2d ed. Harmondsworth, England: Penguin.
WARE, DORA 1967 *A Short Dictionary of British Architects.* London: Allen.

IKTINOS

The date and specific place of birth of Iktinos (5th century B.C.) are unknown, although Herodianos implies that he came from Attika. Nothing is known about his life or artistic personality.

However, ancient literary sources attest that, along with KALLIKRATES, he was the architect of the Parthenon, that he drew up a project for the

I

Iktinos.
The Akropolis.
Athens.

Telesterion at Eleusis, and that he was the architect of the Temple of Apollo at Bassai.

The Parthenon. According to two references in Strabo, Iktinos built the Parthenon on the Akropolis of Athens in honor of Athena, with Perikles, the leading Athenian statesman of the period, superintending the work. VITRUVIUS remarks that, like other famous architects, Iktinos was interested in theory and, together with Carpion (otherwise unknown; conceivably his illustrator), wrote a lost volume on the Doric temple of Athena on the Akropolis of Athens. Plutarch adds that Kallikrates was his associate, and it was Iktinos's work on the Akropolis that caused him to be included in Varro's list of seven great architects reported by Ausonius. Kallikrates, responsible for the southern Long Wall from Athens to the Piraeus and other activities on the Akropolis, appears to have served as Iktinos's contractor, his technical director of works. Hence, the designing architect of the Parthenon was Iktinos.

Perikles had named the sculptor Pheidias general overseer of the works on the Akropolis. It was his colossal chryselephantine statue of Athena Parthenos that was the cult image of the Parthenon, a term originally restricted to the lesser chamber of the temple and meaning the chamber of the virgin, which, from the fourth century on, was applied to the entire building. Built between 447 and 438 B.C. and dedicated at the Panathenaic festival in the latter year, it dominated the Akropolis, a lofty, rocky platform in the heart of the city. The site, on the southern side of the Akropolis, had been prepared for a previous temple begun before the second Persian War and sacked by the Persians in their destruction of the buildings and monuments of the Akropolis in 480–479 B.C. Like the extant building, the older Parthenon, as it is known, had two chambers. Its platform or foundation had been completed and the lower drums of many of its columns had been set in place before the Persian sack. Hundreds of additional drums lay

in the vicinity. In designing the new temple, Iktinos used as much as possible of the previous building material, a wise economy of time, transport, and material, even retaining both the previous intercolumniations and the size of their lower diameters—a key figure in the proportion of Greek colonnades. Both the old and the new temples were constructed of the Pentelic marble locally quarried in Athens.

To accommodate Pheidias's colossal cult image, the size and proportions of the new building were altered. Octastyle façades replaced the previous hexastyle façades and an additional column was added on the flanks (8 by 17 columns as opposed to the previous 6 by 16); hexastyle porches within the colonnade replaced the earlier tetrastyle porches before the two chambers of the building. The new plan did not fit the previous platform, hence it was extended on the northern flank, and portions of the east and south sections of the previous platform were left unoccupied. The new proportions of 9:4 (length to breadth) in plan and elevation produced façades of exceptional amplitude and harmony. The breadth of the cella involved the narrowing of the ambulatories between the walls and colonnades of the building. On the façades, wide central metopes give way to narrower metopes toward the corners of the building. No triglyph is centered over any column, thus establishing a perspective effect, like other so-called optical refinements of the temple, that adds to it extraordinary life and vitality. Thus, the steps of the building are characterized by horizontal curvature, that is, on the façades, they descend $2\frac{3}{4}$ inches from the center to the corners and on the flanks, $4\frac{5}{16}$ inches, a curvature repeated throughout all the upper courses of the façade to prevent the horizontal courses from appearing to sag at the center. The vertical columns not only were given entasis in order not to appear concave and tilting inward toward the center, but they were also altered in size, the outer columns seen against space being thickened. The walls of the building were characteristically vertical on the interior and oblique on the exterior. These features, precise and subtle, reveal both the care of the architect and the extraordinary skill of the masons.

Now, for the first time, Ionic elements were introduced into a Doric building: the continuous Ionic frieze high up on the exterior of the building's walls (c.524 feet in length), the frieze itself resting not on an Ionic banded architrave but, in unorthodox and bold fashion, on a Doric architrave crowned by the molding normally found beneath a Doric frieze of metopes and triglyphs (taenia, regulae, guttae), and by the use of what seem to have been four Ionic columns in the interior of the lesser chamber which served as a treasury. Both this chamber and the opisthodomos were closed with grilles.

The length of the original archaic poros temple that preceded the later two structures and was known as the Hekatompedon or hundred-foot temple was retained in the main chamber of Iktinos's building, where Pheidias's colossal statue of Athena Parthenon rose to the full height of the cella. Here Iktinos framed the gigantic statue by a horseshoe double-storied Doric colonnade creating what has been termed the first molded interior space in antiquity. The colonnade itself was elevated on a low step which further defined and articulated the space of the interior. The upper story of the Doric frame supported the ceiling. Bronze grilles were attached between the columns of the lower order, making the outer horseshoe of space inaccessible to the worshiper, seemingly yet another barrier before the cult image forced the visitor to view the statue from a precise area in the cella—another instance of the architect's imaginative anticipation of the visual effect that the building and its cult statue would have on the beholder. Light was admitted into the cella only by a lofty door thirty-two feet in height.

The collaboration of architect and sculptor must have been a happy one. The function of the Parthenon was to house the cult image made by Pheidias. Its ninety-two sculptured metopes, the sculptured frieze that enveloped the exterior walls of the building, its sculptured pediments, floral akroteria and antefixes, that is, the unique presence of sculpture on Iktinos's temple indicates that the architecture of the Parthenon was geared to its sculptural program. Even the atypical sculptured moldings over the metopes and triglyphs and the framing of the raking sima crowning the pediments by nonfunctional sculptured lion's heads reflect the influence and adjustment of the architect to the requirements of the sculptor. The final sculptures were completed in 432 B.C., on the eve of the Peloponnesian War.

At the end of the fourth century A.D., the interior Doric colonnade in the cella was destroyed. The damaged columns were removed to the agora to be drawn on for material needed for new building operations in the lower city. Early in the fifth century, the colonnade seems to have been replaced by a later pagan, Herculius, Praetorian Prefect of Illyricum.

Iktinos.
Plan of the Parthenon.
Athens.
447–432 B.C.

Iktinos.
The Parthenon.
Athens.
447–432 B.C.

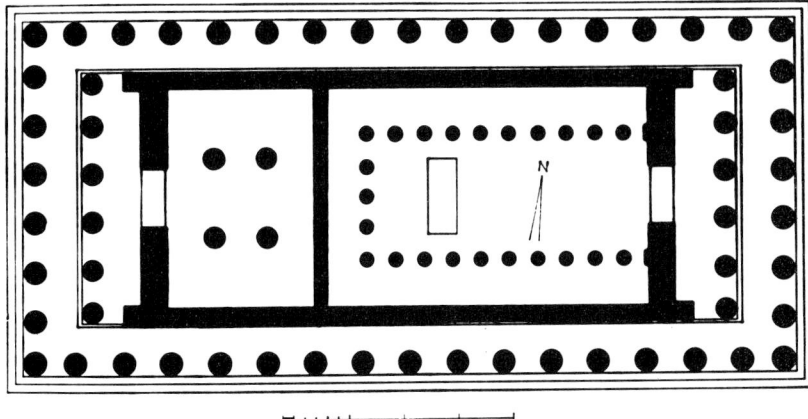

From the end of the sixth century until 1458, the Parthenon was converted to a Christian church dedicated to the Panagia, the Virgin Mary. An apse was added at the east end, displacing the sculptures of the central section of the eastern pediment. After the capture of Athens by the Turks in 1458, the church was converted to a mosque. In 1687, in the course of a conflict between the Venetians and the Turkish garrison on the Akropolis, the Venetians shelled the Parthenon in which the Turks had stored their powder. A great explosion followed in which the interior was destroyed and the columns in the center of the flank colonnades were blown out. Soon afterward, a small mosque was built in the cella, where it stood until 1844. Reconstruction and consolidation of the building began in 1842 and was continued more extensively between 1895 and 1933.

The Telesterion. According to Strabo 9.1.12, "one comes to the city of Eleusis, in which there is a sanctuary of the Eleusinian Demeter and the mystic chapel which was built by Iktinos, a theatre which is large enough to admit a crowd of spectators." Vitruvius 7 *Praef.,* 16, adds: "At Eleusis, Ictinus built the cella of Ceres and Proserpina in the Doric manner and of immense size without exterior columns; it was covered in to afford a convenient space for sacrifice."

Traces of six structures, one overlying the other, are present today at the site of the Telesterion or Hall of Initiation, a famous sanctuary, where individuals were initiated into the mysteries of the Eleusinian Gods. The third Telesterion, built under the Attic statesman Peisistratos in the late sixth century B.C., was a hall some $88\frac{1}{2}$ feet square preceded by a Doric portico. It was entered by three doors. On the remaining three sides, the interior was framed by a flight of seven steps and its roof was supported by twenty-two columns in addition to preserving, in the rear left corner, the location of the previous Anaktoron, a holy of holies entered only by the priest. The Persians set fire to this building as they had to the Parthenon. It was replaced by a building intended to be four times the size of its predecessor and supported by a forest of forty-two columns. Only half of this building was executed, but the project was revived under Perikles, who entrusted the work to Iktinos, seemingly toward 440 B.C. and at the conclusion of his activity on the Akropolis.

Once again, Iktinos had to cope with earlier structures. From cuttings in the rock and the building's rocky steps, the general design of his Telesterion may be deduced, although it, too, was not completed. He doubled the size of the executed portion of the preceding building, thus reverting to the square shape of the late archaic Telesterion. The vast building, c.170 feet square, was to have held some 5,000 worshipers who stood or sat on the eight narrow steps that enclosed all four sides of the building. At and adjacent to the rear wall, they were carved out of the living rock. All four walls were pierced by two doorways, those in the rear wall, embedded in the rocky slope, at a higher level. Iktinos more than halved the previous number of columns, reducing the number to twenty (five in width by four in depth)—a bold scheme that allowed spectators easy vision of the liturgical ceremonies that took place in the center of the building, where the venerable Anaktoron continued to be placed. Above it, he introduced an *opaion* or opening where, at dawn, after the long nocturnal ceremonies, light flooded into the building. Here, as in the Parthenon, the work executed was of the utmost precision and finesse.

This project—in which the demands of the liturgy and the desire for bold spatial effects were so brilliantly solved—proved ill-starred. Whether because of the waning influence of Perikles or the difficulty in coping with its wide spans, Iktinos's Telesterion was abandoned.

In the final building, erected according to Plutarch by three successive architects, Koroibos, Metagenes, and Xenokles, the less venturesome plan of Iktinos's predecessor was again adopted: forty-two columns replaced twenty. Still later, in the late fourth century B.C., PHILON added a portico of Doric columns before the façade. Of gleaming Pentelic marble, they stood on steps of the soft gray stone quarried in Eleusis, that local stone of which the Telesterion itself had been constructed. Somber and austere, it suited the awe-inspiring ceremonies performed within the Hall of the Mysteries.

Under Perikles, an Odeion, a hall for concerts and musical contests, was erected near the Theater of Dionysos in Athens. Indeed, it was the first roofed building for such a purpose in Athens. Although it has never been fully excavated, it is known to have been rectangular and supported on a multitude of columns. Owing to its seeming analogy to the Telesterion, the Odeion has been attributed to Iktinos by some modern writers. This is a purely theoretical attribution inasmuch as no ancient literary source ascribes the building to Iktinos.

The Temple of Apollo at Bassai. Pausanias 8.41.7–9 reports that:

Phigalia is surrounded by mountains, on the left by the mountain called Kotilion . . . the distance from the city to Mount Kotilion is about forty stades. On the mountain is a place called Bassai, and the temple of Apollo Epikourios [the Helper or Ally] which, including the roof, is of stone. Of all the temples in the

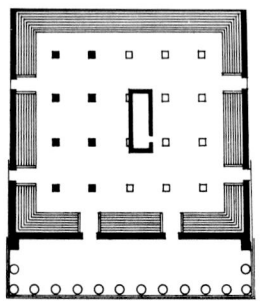

Iktinos.
Plan of project for
the Telersterion.
Eleusis, Greece.
Begun c.440 B.C.

Peloponnesos, this might be placed first after the one at Tegea for the beauty of its stone and its harmony. Apollo received his name from the help he gave in time of plague, just as the Athenians gave him the name of Alexikakos [Averter of Evil] for turning the plague away from them. It was at the time of the war between the Peloponnesians and the Athenians that he also saved the Phigalians, and at no other time; the evidence is that of the two surnames of Apollo, which have practically the same meaning, and also the fact that Iktinos, the architect of the temple at Phigalia, was a contemporary of Perikles, and built for the Athenians what is called the Parthenon.

Encircled by the lofty mountains of southwestern Arcadia, as Pausanias reported, and located on a narrow ridge, the present Temple of Apollo at Bassai is the fourth building on the site. It was preceded by two early archaic forebears lying directly to its south. Oriented north–south and provided with two chambers like the last temple, the first temple was erected c.625 B.C. It was rebuilt some fifty years later and given an opisthodomos. This structure was replaced by a building erected c.500 B.C. and constructed of large, limestone blocks reused for the foundations of the present temple, as has recently been discovered. As in the Parthenon, the building material of the immediate predecessor was not wasted.

Iktinos's temple was set directly on bedrock and was largely built of the hard gray limestone that was locally quarried. His brilliance as an architect reached its zenith at Bassai in his fusion of traditional requirements and bold innovations. Doric on the exterior and provided with two deep porches at each end (pronaos and opisthodomos) each containing two Doric columns in antis, the temple consisted of both the customary cella and a rear chamber or adytum entered by a separate door on the east side of the building. In its atypical north–south orientation, in its old-fashioned retention of the archaic proportion of six by fifteen columns in the Doric colonnade, and even in the retention of archaic features in the design of the columns, it preserved the orientation of its predecessors and features characteristic of archaic architectural practice. The very use of spur walls within the cella had its forebear in the early archaic Temple of Hera at Olympia, the great nearby local sanctuary, as did the use of six sculptured metopes above the porches, which have a prototype in the similar atypical location of the sculptured metopes of the early classical Temple of Zeus in the same sanctuary.

But coupled with the tactful retention of old-fashioned and traditional elements in a provincial area of the Peloponnesos are elements that appear for the first time in the history of Greek architecture. Within the cella, a sculptured marble frieze

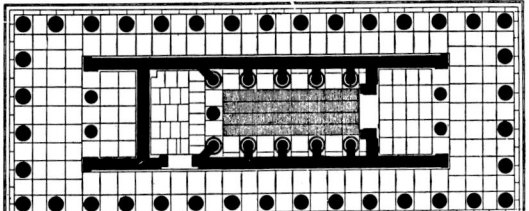

Iktinos.
Plan of the Temple of Apollo Epikourios.
Bassai, Greece.
c.429–427, 414–400 B.C.

Iktinos.
Partial longitudinal section of the Temple of Apollo Epikourios (after Haller von Hallerstein).
Bassai, Greece.
c.429–427, 414–400 B.C.

encloses all four sides of the chamber. Part of a full limestone entablature, it and its backers rested on an Ionic engaged order in which the spur walls of the cella terminated. Like the frieze, the Ionic capitals were of marble and novel in design, lacking the normal abacus and characterized by powerful, swelling outer contours. Flaring, projecting bases exceeded the depth of the half-columns they supported, giving the impression, seen frontally or laterally, of full bases. The spur walls themselves numbered ten: four set at right angles to the wall on each side of the cella and two diagonal spur walls that frame the entrance to the adytum. Most original of all was the free-standing Corinthian column placed between the diagonal spur walls—a wholly new feature destined to have immense influence and popularity in later Greek and Roman architecture. The most luxuriant of the Greek capitals, this first example, now lost and known only from drawings, rose from a leafy base of acanthus leaves whence outer tendrils rose to support the crowning abacus, here painted with a meander pattern; lower, abutting inner tendrils on each face supported a palmette. The base, a modification of the standard Ionic base, projects into the cella less markedly than do those of the engaged Ionic columns.

Echoes of the Parthenon appear at Bassai—the continuous Ionic frieze on the exterior of the walls of the Parthenon can be found at Bassai in the interior of the cella, that is, the introduction of an Ionic element into a Doric building. The framing of the cella by a horseshoe colonnade or pseudo-colonnade were features in both temples. At Bassai, the cult image of Apollo (an akrolith, that is, a wooden statue with marble head, hands, and feet) appears to have stood before the solitary Corinthian column but, in each case, the statue was visi-

ble within a plastic, architectural frame. At Bassai, the niches between the spur walls were used for votive gifts, often suspended from the walls.

Both the main northern door and the lesser door leading into the adytum, whose precise function remains unknown, were closed by grilles. Hence, the visitor might look into the cella when the temple was officially closed.

The coffered ceilings of the building were exceptionally rich and varied in pattern. Five sets of coffers exist, two of limestone—one used in the ambulatories; the other, in the porches—and three of marble placed over the adytum, the niches, and conceivably in the cella. There, the ceiling seems to have been suspended from wooden cross-beams sheathed in marble that spanned its walls. Thus the ceilings of the several sections of the temple were carefully articulated.

Not only were additional sculptured elements of the building, such as the frieze and capitals, of marble (the floral akroteria that, as on the Parthenon, crowned the pediments, and the raking sima that framed them) but also the components of the roof, tiles and antefixes, were of marble, as Pausanias noted—a rare scheme for so sizable a building. Conceivably, this reflects the ingenious tiles which

combine both pan tiles and cover tiles. At Bassai, however, the shallowness of the pediments indicates that there were no pedimental sculptures.

Subtle optical refinements are, again, characteristic of the temple at Bassai—not only the horizontal curvature present on the Parthenon but also the splaying of the ground plan into a trapezoidal shape which countered the old-fashioned length of its archaic plan. Precision of workmanship characterized both the shaping of the blocks and the embellishment of the risers of the steps which are adorned with stippled panels and moldings at the bottom, a scheme that proved popular in subsequent centuries.

As a result of the co-existence in the Temple of Apollo at Bassai of old-fashioned features and brilliant innovations and of the incorrect early twentieth-century re-erection of both the cella walls and the spur walls which contributed to the impression of sloppy execution and modifications to the original plan, many modern scholars have doubted not only Pausanias's date for the temple but the very attribution of the building to Iktinos. Fortunately, the temple has been carefully reinvestigated in recent years. The American archeologist Frederick A. Cooper has re-examined every block at the site and uncovered additional elements of its architecture and sculpture along with further excavation of the site by Nicholas Yalouris of the Greek Archaeological Service. They have established, without any question, that the temple was designed by Iktinos c.429–427 B.C. and that all previous attempts to understand it as the product of successive phases of design carried out over more than half a century are false. The new discovery of the presence of Attic workmen at Bassai judging by inscribed mason's marks on a variety of blocks confirms Pausanias's identification of the architect as Iktinos.

In one respect, however, Pausanias erred—his interpretation of the epithet Epikourios and equation of it with Alexikakos and consequent assumption that the epithets alluded to salvation from the plague which had afflicted the Athenians at the time of the Peloponnesian War. Epikourios not only means helper or ally but, quite specifically, military ally or mercenary. Apollo Bassitas, the original epithet of Apollo at Bassai, was a martial divinity. No objects found at Bassai reflect a cult of healing, but many dedications dating from the seventh century B.C. on consist of miniature bronze weapons—indeed, a foundry was found not far from the temple. The Epikouroi were famous Arcadian mercenary troops employed extensively in the critical years of the Peloponnesian War at the very moment of the plague. Seemingly, late in the fifth century B.C., they adopted as their patron divinity the old war god, Apollo of Bassai. Hence, the new epithet replaced the old. Seemingly, too, they were in a position to commission a splendid new temple by a famous architect. Begun c.429–427, work on the temple was interrupted from 421–414. It was resumed in that year and the building was finally completed c.400 B.C.

The stylistic common denominator of Iktinos's two actually executed buildings and one unexecuted project is their concern for interior space. In the Parthenon, he provided an architectural setting for Pheidias's colossal image; at Bassai, too, the cella was richly articulated by its architectural frame—a new unity was created between the cult image and its architectural setting or environment. In each building, the worshiper was drawn into a precise frame as he faced the cult statue. The wide spaces of the design for the Hall of Initiation at Eleusis, where, via the *opaion*, interior and exterior space were linked, allowed the worshipers sitting or standing at the outer periphery of the building to witness the ceremonies at its center with ease, again drawn toward a precise focal point. Always the visual response of the individual, the spectator, was considered whether in terms of subtle optical refinements or the larger relationship between his

presence and the carefully defined space of the building.

Although no ancient literary source comments on the nature of Iktinos's architectural style, analysis of the three buildings ascribed to him reveals his brilliance as an architect. As an innovator of genius, whether in designing a new form of molding or a new order, his influence on later Greek architecture was profound.

PHYLLIS WILLIAMS LEHMANN

WORKS

447–432 B.C., The Parthenon (partially destroyed and rebuilt), Athens. Begun c.440 B.C., Telesterion, Eleusis, Greece. c.429–427, 414–400 B.C., Temple of Apollo Epikourios, Bassai, Greece.

BIBLIOGRAPHY

English translations of the classical texts can be found in the Loeb Classical Library series published by Harvard University Press, Cambridge, Mass., and Heinemann, London.

AUSONIUS, *Mosella*, lines 305–310.

BECATTI, GIOVANNI 1961 "Iktinos." Volume 4, pages 100–103 in *Enciclopedia dell'arte antica classica e orientale.* Rome: Istututo dell Enciclopedia Italiana.

BERVE, HELMUT, and GRUBEN, GOTTRIED 1963 Pages 351–354, 373–379, 399–404 in *Greek Temples, Theatres and Shrines.* New York: Abrams. Photographs by Max Hirmer.

COOPER, FREDERICK A. 1978 *The Temple of Apollo at Bassai: A Preliminary Study.* New York and London:

DINSMOOR, W. B., SR. 1932–1933 "The Temple of Apollo at Bassae." *Metropolitan Museum Studies* 4:204–227.

DINSMOOR, W. B., SR. (1950)1975 *The Architecture of Ancient Greece: An Account of its Historic Development.* Reprint. London: Batsford. Originally published as a third edition of W. J. Anderson and R. P. Spiers, *The Architecture of Ancient Greece and Rome.* London: Batsford, 1902.

ECKSTEIN, FELIX 1960 "Iktinos, der Baumeister des Apollontempels von Phigalia-Bassai." Pages 55–62 in θεωρια *Festschrift für W.-H. Schuchhardt.* Baden-Baden, Germany: Grimm.

FRANTZ, ALISON 1979 "Did Julian the Apostate Rebuild the Parthenon?" *American Journal of Archaeology* 83:395–401.

HAHLAND, WALTER 1948/1949 "Der Iktinische Entwurf des Apollontempels in Bassae." *Jahrbuch der deutschen archäologischen Instituts* 63/64:14–39.

HERODIANUS, AELIUS 1867 *Herodiani Technici reliquiae.* Edited by Augustus Lentz. 2 vols. Leipzig: Teubner.

HOFKES-BRUKKER, CHARLINE, and MALLWITZ, ALFRED 1975 Pages 7–40 in *Der Bassai-Fries.* Munich: Prestel.

MCCREDIE, JAMES R. 1979 "The Architects of the Parthenon." Pages 69–73 in *Studies in Classical Art and Archaeology.* Locust Valley, N.Y.: Augustin.

MARTIN, ROLAND 1963 "Iktinos." Volume 7, columns 786–788 in *Encyclopedia of World Art.* New York; Toronto; and London: McGraw.

MYLONAS, GEORGE E. 1961 Pages 57, 67–70, 78–90, 111–124, 127–128, 133–135 in *Eleusis and the Eleusinian Mysteries.* N.J.: Princeton University Press.

NOACK, FERDINAND 1927 *Eleusis.* Berlin and Leipzig: Gruyter.

PAUSANIAS *Description of Greece* Book 8, Chapter 41, sections 7–9.

PLUTARCH *Perikles* Book 13, Chapters 4–5

ROBERTSON, D. S. (1929)1964 Pages 169–174 in *A Handbook of Greek and Roman Architecture.* 2d ed, rev. Cambridge University Press.

ROUX, GEORGES 1961 Pages 21–56 in *L'architecture de l'Argolide aux IVᵉ et IIIᵉ siècles avant J.-C.* Paris: E. de Boccard.

ROUX, GEORGES 1976 *Karl Haller von Hallerstein, Le Temple de Bassae.* France: University of Strasbourg Press.

STRABO *Geography* Book 9, Chapter 1, sections 12, 16.

TRAVLOS, JOHN Pages 444–457 in *Pictorial Dictionary of Ancient Athens.* New York: Praeger.

VITRUVIUS *De architectura,* Book 7, Praef. 12, 16.

WINTER, FREDERICK E. 1980 "Tradition and Innovation in Doric Design III: The Work of Iktinos." *American Journal of Archaeology* 84:399–416.

YALOURIS, NICHOLAS 1973 "'Ανασκαφαὶ εἰς τὸν ἐν βάσσαις φιγαλείας ναὸν τοῦ 'Επικουριου 'Απόλλωνος." *Athens Annals of Archaeology* 6:39–55.

ILLESCAS MIROSA, SIXTO

Sixto Illescas Mirosa (1903–) was born in Barcelona, Spain, and graduated from the School of Architecture there in 1928. He began his professional career in a joint office with JOSEP LLUIS SERT and was a cofounder of the Catalan Architectural and Technical Group for the Progress of Contemporary Architecture (GATCPAC) which was the forum for rationalist architecture in Catalonia following WALTER GROPIUS and LE CORBUSIER.

He practiced as an architect only between 1929 and 1935. During the Spanish Civil War, he was a functionary in the Catalan government, and after 1939 he dedicated himself to other industrial activities and to painting and ceramics.

JUAN BASSEGODA NONELL
Translated from Spanish by
Judith E. Meighan

WORKS

1929, Housing, Calle Aribau and Calle Diputación; 1929, Housing, Avenida Meridiana, Calle Pallars; 1929–1931, House, 43 Avenida del Portell; 1934–1935, Housing 96 Calle Padua; Barcelona, Spain.

BIBLIOGRAPHY

BOHIGAS, ORIOL 1970 *Arquitectura española de la Segunda República.* Barcelona, Spain: Tusquets.

HERNÁNDEZ-CROS, J. E. 1978 *Guía de Arquitectura de Barcelona.* Barcelona, Spain: Glegio de Arquitectos.

SOLÀ-MORALES, IGNASI 1980 *Eclecticismo y vanguardia.* Barcelona, Spain: Gili.

IMHOTEP

Historical Background. Until the end of the nineteenth century the credibility of Imhotep (active 2635–2595 B.C.) as a historical personage could be doubted. The posthumous data evoke his personality as a patron of scribes protecting them as a god, a sage, and a leading figure of Egyptian literature, personifying knowledge. The earliest mention of Imhotep occurs in the Papyrus of the Kings, now in the Turin Museum, describing him as son of Ptah and the lady Kherdw'ankh, therefore a demigod. Since the Twenty-Sixth Dynasty, when Imhotep became a god in Memphis, his cult spread throughout Egypt as that of a renowned mediator helping with everyday problems, especially sickness and sterility. His fame rose and his tradition lived on in Hermetic writings. He was known to the Greeks as Imuthes, and later, in Islamic Egypt till contemporary times, he was connected with the so-called Prison of Joseph (Sign Yusef) in Saqqara North.

In 1926, Cecil Firth, during his excavation of the mortuary temple of King Neterikhet (Djeser) from the Third Dynasty at Saqqara, found a base of a royal statue. Though only the two feet of the standing figure remain on the base, with some fragments, this slightly oversized statue (1.80 meters high) was assumed to represent the king standing, wearing a crown, a skirt held by a strap passing over the left shoulder (as that of King Na'rmer's portrait on his palette), a straight beard painted black, an animal's tail reaching to the ground and connected to the two aligned feet. The king held a crook on his left shoulder and two scepters in front of him. He stood barefoot on the nine bows, carved in low relief on the upper face of the base and symbolizing the nine traditional enemies of Egypt; along the front edge of the base there appeared three *rekhit* birds, heraldic symbol for the people of Egypt. The front side of the base, the only one carved, bears in exquisite relief the names and titles of King Neterikhet separated from those of Imhotep to the right of the base by a *djed* pillar, a hieroglyph symbolizing stability. This pillar alternates to the left of the base with the *tit* symbol. In the middle panel is the name of Horus Neterikhet confronted with that of "King of Lower Egypt Senwi," otherwise unknown. The remaining hieroglyphs read "Seal-bearer of the king of Lower Egypt, chamberlain, ruler of the great mansion, hereditary prince, greatest of Seers, Imhotep, carpenter, sculptor . . ." (Gunn, 1926a, pp. 177–196). Only one tip of the sign following shows, the rest having been broken off. Assumed to represent a trowel (Wildung, 1977b, p. 8; Gunn, 1926a, p. 193) and translated "worker with the trowel," it could as well depict a surgical instrument of the type known since the archaic period (Wildung, 1977a), which would then define "surgeon, physician." The latter interpretation would be in line with the other aspect of Imhotep's activity probably understood under the attribute "he causes to live" (Wildung, 1977b, p. 32) together with that of "master builder" in the papyrus of the Kings. This second aspect of Imhotep supersedes his architect's achievements, even to become the only one mentioned in the innumerable invocations by sick and sterile people and in the official inscriptions of temples.

A second monument contemporary with the Third Dynasty is a seal impression on the mortar between the blocks lining chamber B under the Step Pyramid (Lauer, 1936–1939, vol. 1, p. 53). The Horus name Neterikhet repeated thrice alternates with the titles "seal-bearer of the king of Lower Egypt, chamberlain" (twice) and "seal-bearer of the king of Lower Egypt, carpenter of Nekhen" (once). Though Imhotep is not mentioned, he is the only person contemporary with Neterikhet who could have borne these important titles. In the same chamber were found stone vessels inscribed with titles but no name of dedicator. Some inscriptions are identical with those on vessels from the tomb of King Kha'sekhemwy, predecessor of Neterikhet at Abydos. It is surmised that Imhotep could have presented these vessels as gifts to the king (Wildung, 1977b, pp. 9–10). A graffito in black ink on the blocks lining the north side of the enclosure surrounding the unfinished pyramid of King Sekhemkhet, successor of Neterikhet at Saqqara, mentions "seal-bearer of the king of Lower Egypt, Imhotep" (Goneim, 1957, plate 13). The provenance of the title known to be Imhotep's from the statue base and the similarity of the architectural complexes of King Neterikhet and King Sekhemkhet next to it tend to prove that their architect was Imhotep. Were these hypotheses correct, it would follow that Imhotep was responsible for royal projects during a time span of forty years starting with King Kha'sekhemwy (2635 B.C.), then Nebka, Neterikhet, and Sekhemkhet (2600–2595 B.C.). However, none of these projects compares in scope and stylistic influence with the funerary complex Imhotep designed and built for King Neterikhet (2620–2600 B.C.).

Contrasting with the rather meager information about Imhotep as a historical person is the abundant material recording his sweeping rise as demigod since the New Kingdom, and his apotheosis as full deity in the Ptolemaic period. This is not to discredit the importance of Imhotep in the history of Egypt as recorded by the Egyptians themselves, for he is the only nonroyal personage included in the royal lists with the attributes "master-builder, who causes people to live" (Papyrus of the Kings, Ramesside period). Such a unique recognition of Imhotep's wisdom in both architecture and medicine by officialdom is matched or even surpassed by the universal recognition from the scribes or from master builders. The statue of a certain Iahmes (Twenty-Seventh Dynasty; Wildung, 1977b, pp. 33–35) represents him standing, holding a naos containing a figure of the goddess Bastet. The inscription around the naos mentions no less than seven of his priestly titles. An inscription on Iahmes's statue points to the existence of a temple of Imhotep in the Twenty-Sixth Dynasty, and its domain in the district of Memphis, probably at Saqqara North. Its priesthood, which was transmitted from father to son, serviced also other Memphite gods, as well as Kings Neterikhet and Djeser Teti of the Third Dynasty. Also from the Twenty-Seventh Dynasty, a certain Khnumibre' in the year 26 of Darius was priest in Heliopolis and master builder in the whole land. He recorded in the quarries at Wadi Hammamat his genealogy through twenty-two generations of master builders, back to the reign of Ramses II, and still earlier to Rahotep, who derived his glory from Imhotep, the high official of King Djeser

(Sethe, 1902, pp. 106–107). Such an inscription claims historicity through two thousand years and proves the strong link uniting Imhotep and his king, Djeser or Neterikhet.

In the Twenty-Sixth and Twenty-Seventh dynasties, Imhotep is offered a well-organized cult. Another priest, Wahibre', of the same epoch, dedicates a statuette of basalt, the earliest representation of Imhotep, seated, wearing a hair cap, long robe to the calf of his legs, holding with both hands a papyrus roll open on his lap. On the papyrus is an inscription requesting a libation from every scribe. This statue type is characteristic for Imhotep and appears also in his iconography in low relief or drawing and in innumerable bronzes of Greco-Roman time. Imhotep's standard epithet "son of Ptah" appears already in the Ramesside Papyrus of the Kings. Imhotep appears in the company of gods such as Apis in the temple of Ptah, and others (Sokaris, Osiris). A certain Pakaw dedicated a stela, perhaps in the Serapeum at Saqqara (Thirtieth Dynasty), representing him in a hall with palmiform columns offering and praying to the bull-headed god Apis, followed by "Imhotep, son of Ptah, the august god who causes people to live" in front of a statue of "Ptah, beautiful of face" in his shrine. Imhotep had by then reached the status of a full-fledged god having his own myth and a calendar of six festivals: nativity, apotheosis by god Ptah, participation in the war of Sakhmet against the Asiatics, death, embalming, ascent to heaven. A late papyrus of 89 B.C. indicates that a house for embalming was attached to the Asklepion (Imhotep's temple) near Memphis. Under the Ptolemies (third century B.C. to first century A.D.), the cult of Imhotep centered in the district of Memphis where it reached its apex, as proven by the numerous bronze statuettes of Imhotep dedicated by pilgrims in Saqqara. These bronze statuettes, mostly dedicated in Memphis, are all of a remarkable craftsmanship, perhaps indicative of a higher class of devotees. The usual attitude is that of a seated figure unrolling a papyrus with both hands. He is dressed as in his relief portrayals in a long, short, or breast skirt, a mantle, and does not wear a beard. He is "Imhotep the Great, son of Ptah." In contemporary Greek and Latin literature, he is the demigod Imuthes sometimes equated with Asklepios. As a demigod, Imhotep is the hero of several Hellenistic Romans, who related his feats in military expeditions against Mesopotamia in the reign of Djeser. Clemens of Alexandria (second century A.D.) remarked that men of the Egyptians became gods through their earthly reputation, such as Hermes the Theban and Asklepios the Memphite. Hermes was probably AMENHOTEP, son of Hapu, deified in

Thebes as "brother" of Imhotep. The cult of Imhotep lived on after the mid-fourth century A.D., when Ptah and other Egyptian deities had disappeared and superseded that of Sarapis. Arab chronicles of the ninth to the eleventh centuries describe the Prison of Joseph (Sign Yusef) on the hill of Saqqara North, where pilgrims visited in an Egyptian temple (destroyed in the twelfth century) a statue of a sage beautiful of face, holding a book on his lap, in which we recognize the typical Imhotep. Imhotep appears in temples other than Memphite ones, though not as the main figure, in lower Egypt, at Heliopolis, in the Middle Kingdom temple at Medinet Madi in the Fayum, and even in the Hellenistic necropolis of Alexandria and other districts of the Delta (Xois, Mendes). In Upper Egypt, at Hathor's Temple at Dendera, numerous beneficent aspects are ascribed to "Imhotep the Great, son of Ptah" as architect who "renews everything that is destroyed in temples, reckoning everything, knowledgeable as Thot the Great, knowing the course of stars, decreasing famine, versed in the divine words, causing people to live, bringing children to the childless, rejuvenating elders (*ibid.*, 136–140). As healing god he is invoked in inscriptions at Esna (Khnum Temple) and Edfu (Horus Temple). Here, a unique inscription records that Ptolemy IX completed the outer parts of the temple "as specified by the Book of the Order of a Temple, which the chief lector priest Imhotep the Great, son of Ptah, had redacted." This mention of a reference work on temple design comes at the end of a description of various activities carried out by Ptolemy IX in the court, pylon, and enclosure wall of the Horus Temple at Edfu: "the vestibule, its two fronts are carried on lotiform and papyriform columns; it is beautiful as the Great Palace. He erected a forecourt and a pylon with its gate. . . . He protected its entourage with this wall on all four sides." This encyclopedia of temple design, redacted by Imhotep the Great, is recorded in the list of books kept in the library of the temple at Edfu, on whose door embrasure Imhotep is represented before Horus.

Imhotep was known also in marginal sites in the Bahriya oasis and as far off as Ptolemais in Cyrenaica. At Philae Island, on the southern boundary of Egypt, Ptolemy V built a small two-roomed temple entered from the south—the only existing temple dedicated to Imhotep. The façade presents a clear example of harmonic design according to a ratio of 8 (base length) to 5 (height). As other small temples (Khonsu at Karnak), it has a side door opening directly to the sanctuary to allow the priest to have access to pronounce oracles without being seen by the devotees. Only the façade and door frame between the two rooms bear wall scenes—prototypes of those built by the Ptolemies in Nubia (Debod, Kalabsha, Dakka) and the Sudan (Meroë). Inscriptions mention Imhotep's mother Kherdw'ankh and his wife Renpet Nefert. The significance of the temple at Philae is indeed in conjunction with Imhotep's beneficent powers of healing and bringing the yearly flooding, for the sources of the Nile were thought to be in that region. The historical context of the building is, however, evident: Ptolemy V had waited seven long years for a child from his wife Cleopatra I, till the royal couple had their wish fulfilled by Imhotep with the birth of Ptolemy VI in 186 B.C. The Greek dedicatory inscription on the architrave of the entrance doorway is quite unusual and reads: "King Ptolemy and Queen Cleopatra, the Epiphanes gods, and Ptolemy, their son, to Asklepios." Ptolemy must have come south in the same year (186–185 B.C.) to quell a revolt in Thebes. The foundation of Imhotep's temple must be set in conjunction with the dedication of the famine stela at Seheil, relating the beneficent intervention of Khnum, god of the cataract region, who ended a seven-year low Nile period in the reign of Djeser (Neterikhet), after Imhotep had found the causes of this evil in the House of Life at Hermupolis. The stela was probably the work of Ptolemy V and must have echoed a historical event in the reign of Djeser, with Imhotep in the role of bringer of the inundation, as recorded in Greco-Roman temples at Dendera: "I let the Nile come to you at its time," he being "the one who decreases famine"; and in Edfu: "I give thee the Nile in (its) course at the right time." Imhotep's temple at Philae would have been erected in recognition of one aspect of this god as "bringer of child," parallel to another aspect, that of "bringer of the Nile inundation" recorded on the famine stela at Seheil, through the intervention of Imhotep with the god of the cataract, who was also god of creation, modeling the child on his potter's wheel. The historic credibility of the famine stela is thereby enhanced: Imhotep in the reign of Neterikhet had not yet had access to the rank of an independent god and had to refer to Khnum. Another factor adding to the credibility is the exceptional documentation unfolded by Khnum about the rocks (seven types) with which "no one has yet built" and minerals (twenty-two types) "precious stones of which no inlaid eye was made," to be mined and quarried in the cataract region—a documentation which assumes significance in conjunction with the first use of such materials on a large scale by Imhotep.

In Thebes, Imhotep was recognized as a sage since the New Kingdom, a status similar to that of Amenhotep. With the Ptolemies, both personalities became gods, often associated as a pair popular with the middle class of Thebans. Both gods were "brothers" and had the title "the Great," perhaps as assonance after "Imhotep the Great, son of Ptah." Each is represented on either doorjamb flanking the entrance to a shrine, accompanied by a hymn to be recited in his honor (Ptah temple by Tiberius at Karnak) or in the depiction of a naos of Ptah (Amun temple, room XV, Ptolemy IX). In Ptah's temple, there stand on the rear east wall, behind Ptah in his naos, Hathor, Imhotep, and Amenhotep (added)—a whole row of gods lined with gold sheet or enclosed within a wooden shrine abutting against the wall (*ibid.*, pp. 201–206). Imhotep is invited to "thy house, to thy temple in Thebes." The pair appear in a similar row in Tod temple, or alone, with Imhotep confronting Amenhotep (private stela). When set in parallel as on Tiberius's embrasures (Ptah temple), Amenhotep appears on the left (north) and Imhotep on the right (south). There obviously is a parallel, helped by the context of Ptah's temple, between the attribute of an invitation addressed to Imhotep from Memphis to "thy house, thy temple in Thebes," from where he can behold the temple's gods in joy, enjoy the food offering and censing, and Amenhotep "beautiful of face . . . created by Tatenen," engaging in activities similar to those of Imhotep. On the rear east wall of the same temple Imhotep's attribute "wonderful appearance of the gods," used also elsewhere, is balanced by Amenhotep's "beloved servant of Amun." Assimilation is even closer between both deified architects when dealing with their activities in the description of their respective origins, whereby the true sage that was Imhotep looms larger than his "brother" Amenhotep, who rose through his diligent alertness.

Lifework of Imhotep. Although Imhotep has been credited with architectural achievements since the reign of King Nebka or even King Khasekhemwy (*ibid.*, p. 10), the only certainty is that he built the complex of King Neterikhet at Saqqara. The graffito of his name inscribed in cursive signs in black ink on the north side of the enclosure wall of Sekhemkhet's unfinished pyramid (Goneim, 1957, plate 13) could prove, though not definitely, that he was also responsible for this later project, so similar in many respects to that of Neterikhet. The latter is a unique assemblage of several buildings, dominated by the Stepped Pyramid. Against its northern face abuts the funerary temple, where the liturgy of the funeral and the daily ritual for the deceased king were performed. All the other buildings imitated in stone masonry the various structures made of plant stems and mats for the celebration of the jubilee festival of the king, thirty years after his access to the throne. Of the various phases of the festival the most essential ones were the race of the king around two massifs to prove his ability at pursuing his activity, and his appearance on the two thrones of Upper and Lower Egypt, placed on a podium. Neterikhet's complex, with the exception of the royal pavilion and the funerary temple, consists of dummy buildings built of façades enclosing a fill of gravel, sand, and rubble. In two of the façades a doorway opens on to a short bent-up corridor leading to wall niches. It is, therefore, obvious that the purpose of the architecture was to afford a substitute in abiding stone masonry for the original jubilee buildings made of plant stems, intended to be used by Neterikhet in his netherlife. This was the challenge Imhotep faced: to interpret in durable stone masonry the structures of the jubilee festival, called Hebsed in Egyptian, with all their characteristics of design and plant forms, so that they would respond by magic, as did the original ones, to the various episodes of the liturgy. To transfer into stone plant shapes such as posts as tall as 12 meters, topped with drooping leaves or floral capital (papyrus or sedge flower), bundles of stems with ribbed or fluted textures into shafts of columns, rows of tufts crowning the upper edges of partitions into "ornament" friezes (*kheker*), or represent these wattle partitions with their interlace of green glistening stems with green faïence tiles were some of the problems Imhotep had to solve. It asked for more than the ordinary competence of a master builder, for the idea of the project was new, its scope extremely huge, and the tectonic means at hand restricted. It took all the initiative and courage of a genius, though Imhotep did not completely solve them: all the columns are engaged to the façades or at butt ends of transverse walls, built of a masonry of small blocks of fine limestone; all open areas in the original façades of plants are substituted by solid masonry; all elements such as door leaves had to be represented as open; all roofs, whether flat or curved into vaults, had to be transferred with their ribbed underside into stone. To these technological problems aggregated others dealing with forms. Plant elements which had been given stylized shapes before in wood had to be carved in stone, such as column shafts and capitals, friezes of *kheker* ornament. Even animal shapes were stylized such as the standing serpents forming a *uraeus* frieze.

To these problems accrued those of a purely tectonic nature when Imhotep decided to transform the original mastaba (Arabic: built-in bench) superstructure after enlarging it twice, into a pyramid. The purpose of the tomb superstructure was twofold: to allow the deceased to mingle with the circumpolar stars, thus fulfilling his stellar destiny,

and to afford a chapel where the deceased could come out through the false-door and partake of the funerary offering placed on the offering slab in front of it. To achieve the stellar destiny, the spirit would rise in the north passageway issuing at an incline from the sarcophagus chamber toward the circumpolar stars. It was to enhance this ideology of ascent that the pyramid was invented as a substitute for the flat rectangular mastaba superstructure, perhaps with a tinge of the solar cult. Imhotep had to deal with problems unknown before in design, construction, and organization. He succeeded to build a pyramid over the initial mastaba and even to enlarge it northward to a high level of 60 meters. To insure stability and avoid twist he devised a new type of construction using concentric layers of masonry inclined at 74 degrees abutting against a central core and by having the beds of masonry slanting toward the center after a pan-shape fashion. To this pyramid he appended a mastaba superstructure some 200 meters south for the inner organs of the mummy.

This extensive program was achieved during the reign of Neterikhet in twenty years. Much of the complex was destroyed but enough remains to have allowed J.-Ph. Lauer, the French architect, to devote more than fifty years to its study and restoration and present a clear picture. The enclosure wall is in itself a monumental structure measuring 545 x 277.64 x 10.48 meters oriented north–south. Of the earlier royal mastaba tombs of the First Dynasty built of brick at Saqqara it borrowed the ratio 1:2 in the dimensions of the plan and the articulation with recessed paneling consisting of recesses flanked by buttresses, themselves grooved vertically with secondary recesses. Toward the top, small square sunken panels neatly arrayed in superimposed rows give the impression of butt ends of rafters in a timber roof. Fourteen towers project along the periphery of the enclosure. Every tower has a doorway represented, complete with its door leaves and lock, but they are dummies, except for the southernmost one on the east façade. The design using recessed paneling is symbolic for appurtenance to royalty, since it was derived from the elevation of a palace doorway, probably built of timber and mud-brick filling. In the royal tombs of the First Dynasty, the recesses were painted to represent hangings of polychrome mats or rugs stretched between two battens at top and bottom. We do not know if this was the case in the enclosure of Neterikhet. The entrance doorway opens onto a small trapezoid lobby followed by a processional hall. It is in this lobby that a double-leafed doorway is represented ajar: the two leaves askew in plan would have shut in the original structure in such a way as to afford double thickness for extra

protection. On either side of the nave is a row of tall columns with ribbed shaft (4.95 meters) tapering up to an abacus. The shaft stands on a shallow base and its top is smooth to indicate a sheath. The ceiling is ribbed to imitate bundles of reeds set transversely side by side. Upper windows open in the north wall. From the second intercolumniation to the right side starts a corridor running north to give access into the structures of the jubilee festival, at the southeast corner of the jubilee chapels. In the opposite row of engaged columns (tenth intercolumniation) a passage bends up to a statue room where Neterikhet's statue had been (only its base was found).

The location of this statue at the entrance to the complex and its inscriptions recording royal names as well as the name and titles of Imhotep are quite unique and seem to provide enough evidence regarding the authorship of the architectural project. The processional hall widens into a transverse broad hall with two rows of four columns each before opening up on to the great court. This forms the most extensive open area of the complex, oriented north–south in the axis of the final pyramid. Its funerary purpose is determined by its location between the south face of the pyramid and the southern mastaba tomb along its south side and also by its direct connection through a long passageway with the funerary temple. In the court, along the axis of the initial pyramid are an altar and two massifs of masonry on a B-shaped plan, built at a third and two-thirds of the length. These are the two markers forming the boundaries around which Neterikhet had to race during the jubilee. A portrayal of the king racing is preserved on two of the plaques in the underground chambers of both the pyramid and the mastaba. In the southwest corner of the great court, a projecting rectangular structure is entered through a central door opening onto that of the bent-up corridor probably reaching a statue room—an arrangement similar to the one in the funerary temple. Behind stood the superstructure of the mastaba proper (160 x 25 cubits of 0.523 meters) in which an east–west stairway descends axially to the shaft, identical to that under the pyramid, containing at 28 meters' depth a granite burial chamber (1.60 meters square, 1.30 meters high), to which is adja-

Imhotep.
Restored elevations of North
and South Palaces.
Neterikhet's Complex.
Saqqara, Egypt.
2620–2600 B.C.

Imhotep.
Perspective of model of
Neterikhet's Complex.
Saqqara, Egypt.
2620–2600 B.C.

cent an apartment for the *ka* or "vital forces," identical to that of the pyramid. Above the burial chamber is a room for handling and lowering in place its roofing blocks. The *ka* apartment was lined with small green faïence tiles in rows, alternating with white limestone bands carved as rope bindings. Some of these linings are designed around doorways, with carved doorposts and a transom window in the shape of a lunette. With an eye to aesthetics, the open-work elements of the lunette featuring nine *djea* pillars symbolizing stability are shaped so that their top quadruple abacus follows the flat curve of the lunette. In three niches on the west wall were plaques carved in fine relief representing Neterikhet wearing the white crown of Upper Egypt and racing, and twice striding, wearing either the white or the red crown. At the back of the plaques are dummy doors representing those of the palace. The purpose of the south mastaba was to provide a burial apartment for the so-called Canopic jars containing the inner organs of Neterikhet—perhaps a reminiscence of the custom of Archaic kings to be buried at Saqqara and have a cenotaph at Abydos.

Along the west side of the enclosure there stands a massif 25 x 400 meters, similar to the one on the north side. Its roof was in the shape of a flat curve; three underground parallel north–south galleries run below it. The central gallery, 2.8 meters wide, is connected to the two lateral ones, flanked each by a series of contiguous deep narrow rooms, totaling around four hundred. Access to the galleries was through a stairway at the north end, a shaft at either end of the main gallery, and other subsidiary shafts. The enclosure wall proper to the west of the massif consisted of two parallel walls (the east wall being 5 meters thick and the west wall 6 meters) retaining a fill in the intervening space 17.60 meters broad between them.

The walls of the great court are articulated with primary recessed paneling topped with a frieze of *uraei*. At the upper end of each recess is a drum representing a rolled-up mat that closed the doors in the original plant stems structure. The pyramid stands at the focal, not the geometrical, center of the enclosure. In its final stage, its sides measured 121 x 109 meters, and it rose 60 meters in height. Its profile in six steps echoes the construction, each step formed by the upper ends of two accretion layers 2.6 meters thick each. The initial mastaba (63 meters square, 8 meters high) consisted of coarse limestone blocks bedded in thick clay mortar and faced with fine limestone from Tura, built in courses 0.3 meter high and battered 8 degrees to the vertical. This initial superstructure was surrounded by a continuous casing on four sides lengthening it to 71.5 meters. In its third stage, the superstructure was enlarged east to cover eleven shafts leading down 33 meters below ground level to five galleries with burials of royal relatives and six magazines. At that point, marked by Imhotep's initiative, a new type of superstructure was started in the shape of a stepped pyramid covering the third mastaba, then enlarged to the north and west to reach its final dimensions. Whereas the masonry of the mastaba was in horizontal courses, that of the pyramid was in layers at a slant perpendicular to the casing blocks. This system of "accretion layers" insured much stability to the structure designed to rise to a considerable height—a system maintained in all later pyramids, even those with smooth faces, though the latter's layers were single and in horizontal courses. The casing blocks in the two pyramid stages increased to 0.38 meter and 0.50 meter, respectively. The pyramid of massive masonry covers two groups of underground apartments. The one accessible from the north through a trench followed by a tunnel contains a shaft 7 meters square and 28 meters deep, at the bottom of which was the royal burial chamber. This chamber (2.96 x 1.65 meters) was built within five courses of pink granite and was accessible through a north hole in its ceiling, blocked by a huge granite plug weighing 3.5 tons and measuring 1.75 meters in height and 1 meter in diameter. Only fragments of Neterikhet's mummy were found. Above the chamber there must have existed a room whence the mummy could be lowered and the granite plug set in place. At the level of the burial chamber four galleries start at right angles to the sides of the shaft. Three end to a transverse branch out of which open four magazines for the storage of vessels. The fourth gallery leads west to an apartment of four rooms whose walls were lined above a plinth 0.40 meter high with blue–green faïence tiles (5.8 x 3.6 centimeters) imitating wattlework topped with panels containing *djed* pillars or enclosing three niches each containing a limestone relief portraying Neterikhet performing a phase of the jubilee festival. This apartment is identical to that under the south mastaba. The eleven shafts, 33 meters deep, along the east edge of the mastaba descend each to an east–west gallery about 30 meters long. The five northern ones were lined with timber planks as shoring and contained rests of burials such as wooden plaques, alabaster sarcophagi, stone vessels and gold nails. The six other galleries were used for the storage of approximately thirty-six thousand vessels of alabaster, breccia, diorite, dolerite, porphyric rocks, granite, dolomite, shist, aragonite, and quartz inscribed with the names of kings of the First and Second Dynasties. On the inner wall of the vases were inscriptions in ink recording the name of the donor, material contained, and manufacturer. Perhaps these vessels were stored in Neterikhet's monument to salvage them from further depredation.

The funerary temple that abuts against the middle of the north face of the pyramid consists of a duplicated deep court with a pillared portico at the rear and further rooms along the west. The two courts are probably echoing the dual aspect of kingship in the funerary liturgy. Before the southeast corner a statue room contained the limestone statue of Neterikhet seated, facing north. Lauer noted several characteristics common to this temple and the much earlier one of King Qaya at Saqqara: eastern entrance, north ambulatory leading to cult rooms and ending into a butt end, and bent-up approaches. A broad doorway represented ajar opened onto the north ambulatory and originally to a bent-up corridor leading to a south ablution room and farther to a north one, dedicated to the funerary ritual for Upper and Lower Egypt. The two courts connected at their north end each have a southern portico with columns engaged to two intercolumnar walls. They are simple fluted shafts of a type known from models of the First Dynasty. A square room abutting against the side of the pyramid might have contained the main cult statue of Neterikhet (now in the Cairo Museum).

Against the inner face of the north enclosure wall is a square (15 meters) platform 2 meters high, probably an altar where the offerings were exposed before they were stored in the underground magazines west of the area. These magazines stretch as a gallery with branching off side chambers beneath a massif containing contiguous rooms abutting along the north wall of the enclosure. There were stored grain (wheat, barley, lentils), fruit (sycamore figs, grapes), and bread. Perhaps they were stored temporarily in the rooms of the magazines before being transferred into the underground chambers.

The second part of the complex, accessible directly from the entrance, comprises the components for the celebration of the Hebsed jubilee festival. Before these components proper, a small structure, the only one in addition to the funerary temple to have real accessible apartments, was probably a royal pavilion where Neterikhet could rest. It is on a tripartite plan similar to that of a contemporary brick house of smaller size built on the west side of the enclosure (Badawy, 1954, p. 54). The same arrangement in two longitudinal strips—a small side room next to the entrance, a reception room with two engaged columns followed by a cruciform room lit by clearstory windows—precedes the living room, and at the very

rear there is a secluded room. Conspicuous are the torus molding along the edge of the façade and the fluted columns.

The court of the jubilee chapels, a long, narrow north–south area bordered east and west by a row of contiguous independent chapels, is the first component of the jubilee compound. The chapels to the west are more important, with a two-columned façade on a podium roofed with a flat vault. The columns have the typical fluted shaft topped with drooping leaves. The two southernmost façades show a niche accessible from a few steps, containing a seated statue of Neterikhet. Every shrine is preceded by a small court flanked by a dummy stockade carved in bold relief. The eastern shrines have flat horizontal roofs. The two groups might represent the nomes participating in the jubilee festival. At the southwest end of the court, a small platform accessible by two flights of steps rising to its east face carried the two thrones beneath two baldachins, side by side, marking one stage of the jubilee when the king sat in state, wearing the white crown of Upper Egypt or the red crown of Lower Egypt. For some unclear reason the lowest step has a curved front, and all goings are, as elsewhere, slightly slanting up.

To the north of this court is the so-called court of the South Palace, having at its rear a façade 12 meters tall featuring four slender fluted shafts topped with drooping leaves and carrying a flat vault. On either corner a broad-ribbed pilaster gave stability to the original flimsy tentlike structure. The open area above a low partition crowned with a *kheker* frieze is rendered with solid walls. A doorway opens slightly off center to take advantage of the solid abutment of a column, marking again the flimsy prototype. Behind starts a bent-up corridor to a roomlet with three niches for crowns. On the east side of the court a slightly recessed arched façade featured one central column probably topped with a sedge capital, heraldic symbol for Upper Egypt, on the analogy of a similar recess in the next court north featuring three papyriform columns, heraldic symbol for Lower Egypt. The façade of the North Palace is nearly identical to that of the one for Lower Egypt, though lacking the two corner posts semicylindrical in plan, but crowned with a cavetto cornice.

Interpretation. In creating this unique architectural ensemble Imhotep recorded in abiding material and to a natural scale the *style* of plant stems structures. There is no doubt that the flimsy tentlike façades with slender columns as tall as twelve meters carrying flat vaults originally could be built only of timber and bundles of plant stems. The recessed paneling of the enclosure wall denotes a mixed construction of mud brick in a timber frame. In the design of the plan certain norms prevail such as zoning in two separate groups of buildings: funerary to the west, the jubilee to the east. The components conform to north–south axes, balanced on either side east and west of the courts. Such a rich assortment of architectural style needs interpretation. Some of its elements are direct copies from the original plant models (open door leaves, timber fence), others are halfway stylized (cavetto cornice, torus, drooping leaf caps), and still others, nonexistent in the prototypes, are introduced to cope with the nature of stone construction in its initial immature stage (columns engaged, walls filling in open areas).

In the fence represented on the walls of the courts fronting the chapels the vertical posts are tapering down to a pointed bottom allowing them to be driven into the ground—a representation true to nature, though engaged to, and boldly projecting from the wall. The two doorways at both ends of the processional hall—and some two hundred others—copy wooden leaves left ajar, the one to the front entrance east being double so that the two single leaves only 1 meter wide would have overlapped the one behind the other when closed.

The columns certainly qualify as the most representative of stylized elements, though they were all subjected to being engaged in a façade or at the butt ends of a special transverse wall. Both height and type of columns could be determined by Lauer through anastylose. All columns, with the exception of the two floral specimens, papyrus and sedge, have bundle shafts either ribbed (processional hall) or fluted (royal pavilion, north and south Palaces, jubilee chapels, funerary temple). Some of the columns are fluted shafts carrying an abacus (funerary temple). Others are wrapped at the top with a smooth sheath made of hide or wickerwork (processional hall). More sophisticated shafts are capped with two drooping leaves strongly stylized into a bulbous shape, sometimes labeled coniferous (palaces, chapels) and provided with a wooden bracket carrying an emblem. The most original creation is, however, the floral column such as the papyriform one (side façade in North Palace court) whose shaft imitates a stem, triangular in cross-section, and the capital as a strongly stylized open papyrus flower. Proportions and forms of the most refined and successful type of column were thus defined for the first time in stone by Imhotep. He similarly stylized ceilings made of bundles of reeds set side by side, so that they show ribbed articulation (processional hall)—a lasting form that appears much later in the ceiling of Askut's Fortress. Flat vaults to counteract sagging were sometimes edged with a cavetto cornice (North Palace, chapels). Though

following the roof curvature, this type of cavetto cornice shows the same rectilinear flaring-out profile deriving from a theriomorphic shrine hut (Badawy, 1948, pp. 31–35; 1954, p. 80) and appearing here for the first and only time in stone. In the Fourth Dynasty, the cavetto softened into a smooth curve. Another element crowning a wall assumes the shape of a *kheker* frieze stylized from the tips of a vertical stem bundle of bulging profile. On outer faces of walls Imhotep adapted the recessed paneling articulation already perfected since the First Dynasty mud-brick tombs of kings at Saqqara: a series of buttresses and recesses with secondary faceting (enclosure wall) or topped with a frieze of upright foreparts of serpent *uraei,* protectors of kingship (wall around great court). Imhotep wielded the process of stylization as successfully when dealing with animal forms as he did with plant ones. Imhotep's ability at designing sculpture in stone and carving extensive friezes in stylized, even geometrized iteration reminds us of his two titles inscribed on Neterikhet's statue "carpenter, sculptor." The blue-green, slightly convex tiles convey a close impression of the green plump stems stylized into a regular pattern—an impression enhanced by the white double bands carved in the fine limestone to imitate rope bindings. Even rolled-up mats and open-work transverse windows were made in the same faïence.

Focusing our investigation on the tectonics, we are surprised at the able versatility displayed in faïence and wood crafts. There is no doubt that such a huge project as Imhotep's needed a whole set of drawings, surveying, and measuring as preparation before building. Of these, as for later architecture, we are left in the dark, except for a shard inscribed in black ink with the diagram of half a curve (Gunn, 1926b, pp. 197–202). This unique document found on the site proves that the graphical method of representing geometrical curves with abscissae and coordinates has hardly progressed since Imhotep. Jotted down in cursive hieroglyphs along the verticals are their dimensions in cubits and fractions thereof. A cross-section of one of the smaller superstructures compares closely with the old curve. The reason for the inability of Imhotep's masons, already noted when dealing with columns, becomes apparent upon a closer investigation of the masonry. The method of building up a shaft in drums had not yet been invented, and the same type of masonry was used for both wall and projecting shaft. Carved on the outer face with flutes or ribs, the small blocks showed the basic defects of looseness brought by joints, tight on the exterior but opening up within the body of the wall. There were some attempts at insuring stability of the projecting shafts, such as alternating stretchers with deep headers above. Dealing with major problems of stability in the building of a pyramid, Imhotep devised a method of making courses slant down toward the axis of the monument instead of horizontal ones used in the south mastaba. This type of pan-shaped course was followed in later pyramids (Meydum, Dahshur). The design of inner masonry consisting of a series of accretion layers abutting in pairs at 74–75 degrees against the four sides of a core was an essential invention of Imhotep, followed throughout pyramid building during the Old Kingdom and abandoned only in the statics of the Middle Kingdom pyramids based on framework construction. Statics based on massiveness as invented by Imhotep culminated in the Fourth Dynasty pyramids and temples at Giza, perfected with the development of quarrying and erecting huge monoliths of soft or hard rocks alike. Imhotep's sensitive design of wattlework patterns made of faïence had to be matched with the most careful execution. The choice of the material and its molding—faïence enameled blue-green and shaped with convex faces—allowed a close interpretation of the lush aspect of green stems, enhanced by the superb quality of the design. The extraordinary tectonics of assembling the tiny tiles (5.8 x 3.6 centimeters) to form horizontal rows simulating plant stems and securing them within the channels precut in the wall face to receive them without any apparent means of fixation, rose to the level of both design and material. Both edges along the channel were carved as thin straight bands imitating white ropes. The tiles were then inserted, the one next to the other, connected by fibers passing through holes in the boss at the back of every tile, and embedded in mortar so that they looked like a continuous green stem.

Lining walls with timber had been used ever since the prodynastic burials (Me'adi) and in royal cenotaphs at Abydos. Sarcophagi to bury crouching bodies were also made of timber. Imhotep resorted to that ancient technique to achieve a smooth clean wall face shoring. With an eye to economy, planks, assembled to match individual shapes, were secured together by thongs passing in pairs of thin mortises. Planks joined at right angles along the meeting line of ceiling and wall asked for a quite elaborate system.

The incomplete pyramid complex of King Sekhemkhet stands within a rectangular enclosure (545 x 190 meters) as long as, though narrower than that of Neterikhet, oriented $11\frac{1}{2}$ degrees west of north—a unique derogation to the typical north-south orientation. The articulation with buttresses and recesses is identical to Neterikhet's but carried out in courses 0.5–0.52 meter high only

one block thick (0.3–0.5 meters; compare Neterikhet's wall, 2.3–4.7 meters thick, in courses 0.22–0.26 meters high). The masonry of the pyramid was in courses slanting perpendicularly to the face of the accretion layers, as Neterikhet's. The access to the underground apartment through a trench continued by a tunnel descending from the north in the north–south axis of the complex intercepted by a vertical shaft was also similar. From this shaft a subsidiary gallery runs horizontally north to meet a system of U-shaped galleries (150 meters east–west, 100 meters north–south, 2 meters tall) flanked on both sides by a regular series of small rooms, those on one side offset with respect to the ones opposite. The blocked burial chamber, 32.10 meters below the base of the enclosure wall and in the axis of the pyramid, measures 9 x 4.5 meters and contained an alabaster sarcophagus. Though still closed by a unique type of trap door, it was empty. The apartment around the chamber consisted of one long room east and west, a butt-end corridor proceeding south and a small north room connected to the tunnel. The only significant finds, besides a few hundred stone vases at the bottom of the shaft, were gold bracelets, a shell-shaped unguent box, pearls, and an ivory plaque inscribed with a list of clothes and the name of a princess, Nebty Djeseretankh.

Conclusion. It appears that Imhotep achieved a unique feat in architecture. Ever since the First Dynasty there had been isolated attempts at adding elements not essential to the funerary cult north of some royal tombs at Saqqara: a whole group of silos at reduced scale and a boat of mud brick (King Aha), a boat (Queen Merneith), silos (King Adjib), an extensive system of underground magazines (King Wdimw), and even a funerary temple (King Qaya). Imhotep was the first and only architect who integrated into the program of the funerary temple in stone a whole complex of jubilee festival. Later, royal temples represented in low relief phases from the jubilee. Imhotep also invented the pyramid rising higher than a mastaba to fulfill more adequately the stellar destiny of the king. This inventiveness manifested itself therefore in both style and construction. Both required the daring initiative of a genius. Architectural design was adapted to stone in composition and elements, still close to the plant stems prototypes. Tectonic means did not allow more than dummy structures, but they were developed considerably for pyramid construction—a development showing in the final stages with the use of larger blocks in masonry, continued in the pyramid complex of Sekhemkhet: larger blocks and taller courses, matched by a sense for economy in material. The style initiated by Imhotep was developed only partly in the Fourth Dynasty, in contrast with the outstanding growth of tectonic methods that allowed the use of monoliths and the building of huge massive pyramids at Giza. During the Fifth Dynasty, the floral style was resumed and fully perfected, making use of monoliths of granite and an extensive repertoire of wall scenes, carved and painted. This abundance of representational means lacks, however, Imhotep's feeling for texture transferred from plant stems into a unique material, faïence lining, not used after him.

The architectural achievements of Imhotep are only one aspect of his genius, which must have been paralleled by proficiency in medicine, and his rise to the status of a demigod. It is certainly unfortunate that the same inscription on Neterikhet's statue that identifies Imhotep as an architectural genius stops short of other promising titles. There seems to have existed a strong affinity between architecture and medicine, for Amenhotep, who was a career master builder establishing a sense for colossal architecture and statuary, was invoked as a healing god in Thebes soon after his death. Much earlier, the architect Ankhmahor (Sixth Dynasty), who is known to have controlled the program of wall scenes in his funerary chapel at Saqqara, manifested his interest in medicine in having scenes of circumcision (one of the only two known), massaging hands and feet, and fainting mourners represented.

ALEXANDER BADAWY

BIBLIOGRAPHY

BADAWY, ALEXANDER 1948 *Le dessin architectural chez les anciens Egyptiens.* Cairo: Service des Antiquités tiquités de l'Egypte.

BADAWY, ALEXANDER 1954 *From the Earliest Times to the End of the Old Kingdom.* Volume 1 in *A History of Egyptian Architecture.* Cairo: The author.

FIRTH, CECIL 1926 "Preliminary Report on the Excavations at Saqqara (1925–1926)." *Annales du Service des Antiquités de L'Egypte* 26:98–101, plate 1.

FIRTH, CECIL 1927 "Excavations of the Service des Antiquités at Saqqara (November 1926–April 1927)." *Annales du Service des Antiquités de L'Egypte* 27:106–111.

GONEIM, MOHAMMED ZAKARIA 1957 *Horus Sekhemkhet.* Cairo: Institut français d'archeologie orientale.

GUNN, BATTISCOMBE 1926*a* "An inscribed statue of King Zoser." *Annales du Service des Antiquités de L'Egypte* 26:177–196.

GUNN, BATTISCOMBE 1926*b* "An Architect's Diagram of the Third Dynasty." *Annales du Service des Antiquités de L'Egypte* 26:197–202.

HURRY, J. B. (1926)1928 *Imhotep, The Vizier and Physician of King Zoser.* 2d ed., rev. London: Oxford University Press.

LAUER, JEAN PH. 1936–1939 Volumes 1 and 3 in *La Pyramide à Degrés.* Cairo: Institut français d'archéologie orientale.

LAUER, JEAN PH. 1962 Volume 1 in *Histoire Monumentale des Pyramides d'Egypte.* Cairo: Institut français d'archéologie orientale.

LECA, ANGE P. 1971 *La médecine égyptienne au temps des pharaons.* Paris: Dacosta.

SETHE, KURT 1902 *Imhotep, der Asklepios der Ägypter.* Leipzig: Hinrichs.

WILDUNG, DIETRICH 1977*a* "Imhotep." Volume 3, columns 145–148 in Wolfgang Helck and Wolfhart Westerdorf (editors), *Lexikon der Ägyptologie.* Wiesbaden, Germany: Harrossowitz.

WILDUNG, DIETRICH 1977*b* *Imhotep und Amenhotep.* Munich: Deutscher Kunstverlag.

INWOOD, WILLIAM, and INWOOD, HENRY W.

William Inwood (1771?–1843) and his son, Henry William Inwood (1794–1843), excelled in the Greek Revival. They built Saint Pancras New Church, London (1819–1822), incorporating Erechtheum caryatid porticoes; All Saints, Camden Town (1822–1824); and Saint Peter's, Regent Square (1822–1825). William was born in London, served as a surveyor, and published *Tables for the Purchasing of Estates* (1811). Henry, also born in London, was trained by his father, whose other pupils included William Railton and, briefly, WILLIAM BUTTERFIELD. He exhibited at the Royal Academy from 1809, traveled in Italy and Greece (1818–1819), published *The Erechtheion at Athens* (1827), and a short essay on ancient design, *The Resources of Design in the Architecture of Greece, Egypt and Other Countries* (1834). His neo-Gothic buildings, including New Westminster Hospital, London (1832–1834), are meager. Latterly collaborating with his pupil, Edward N. Clifton, Henry drowned on passage to Spain, March 1843; William died in London the same year in poverty.

R. WINDSOR LISCOMBE

WORKS

1812, Radwinter Rectory, Essex, England. 1819–1822, Saint Pancras New Church; 1822–1824, Camden Chapel (All Saints), Camden Town; *1822–1825, Saint Peter's Chapel, Regent Square; *1824, Woburn Lodge, Upper Woburn Place; 1824–1827, Saint Mary's Chapel, Somers Town; *1832–1834, New Westminster Hospital; 1837–1838, Saint James's Church, Holloway; 1837–1839, Saint Stephen's Church, Islington; London.

BIBLIOGRAPHY

BRITTON, JOHN, and PUGIN, AUGUSTUS CHARLES 1825 Volume 1, pages 151–165 in *Illustrations of the Public Buildings of London.* London: J. Taylor.

INWOOD, HENRY 1827 *The Erechtheion at Athens.* London: J. Carpenter.

INWOOD, HENRY 1834 *The Resources of Design in the Architecture of Greece, Egypt and Other Countries.* London.

INWOOD, WILLIAM (1811)1880 *Tables for the Purchasing of Estates.* 21st ed. London.

PATON, JAMES MORTON (editor) 1927 *The Erechtheum.* Cambridge, Mass.: Harvard University Press.

SUMMERSON, JOHN (1962)1979 *Georgian London.* 3d ed. Baltimore: Penguin.

IOFAN, BORIS M.

Born in Odessa, Russia, Boris Mikhailovich Iofan (1891–) graduated from the local art school (1911), worked in St. Petersburg as a construction supervisor (1913–1914), and then studied in Rome at the Regio Instituto Superiore di belle arti (1914–1916) and at the Scuola d'aplicazione per gli ingeneri (1917). Joining the Italian Communist Party (1921) and practicing in Rome since 1917, Iofan designed the Soviet Embassy there (1923), the first Soviet structure abroad. This geometricized classical building surmounted by a large symbolic sculpture was the prototype of Iofan's Soviet pavilions for the Paris (1937) and New York (1939) International Expositions, as well as of his winning project for the Palace of the Soviets (1931–1939, VLADIMIR A. SHCHUKO and V. G. Gelfreikh).

Working in the Soviet Union since 1924, Iofan succumbed to Russian Constructivism during the late 1920s. Subsequently, as a leader of Socialist Realism, he received Stalin's award (1941), became an honorary citizen of New York (1939), headed Mossoviet's Architectural Studio, and authored numerous architectural and planning projects. Iofan practiced long enough to witness the rejection of Socialist Realism (mid-1950s) and the return of Soviet architecture to the modern idiom.

MILKA T. BLIZNAKOV

WORKS

*1923, Soviet Embassy, Rome. 1927–1928, Experimental Station, Karpov Chemistry Institute; 1928–1931, Housing Complex, Serafimovich Street; Moscow. 1929–1933, Sanatorium, Barvikha, near Moscow. *1937, USSR Pavilion (with V. T. Mukhina), International Exposition, Paris. *1939, USSR Pavilion (with D. M. Iofan, K. S. Alabian, and V. A. Andreev), International Exposition, New York. 1939–1944, Subway Station Baumanskaya; 1944–1947, Physics Institute Laboratory (with E. N. Stamo and G. A. Aseev), Academy of Sciences of the Union of Soviet Socialist Republics; Moscow. 1945, Master Plan for the Center of Novorossiisk, Union of Soviet Socialist Republics. 1962, Housing Complex, Shcherbakov Street; 1964–1974, State Central Institute for Physical Culture, Izmailov District; Moscow.

BIBLIOGRAPHY

AFANASIEV, K. N. (editor) 1970 *Iz istorii Sovetskoi arkhitektury.* Moscow: Akademiia Nauk SSSR.

BARKHIN, M. G. (editor) 1975 Volume 2, pages 211–244 in *Mastera sovetskoi arkhitektury ob arkhitekture.* Moscow: Iskusstvo.

DE FEO, VITTORIO 1963 *URSS architettura: 1917–1936.* Rome: Riuniti.

IOFAN, BORIS M. 1933 "Kak ia rabotaiu nad proektom Dvortsa sovetov." *Arkhitektura SSSR* 5:30–31.

IOFAN, BORIS M. 1935 "Ploshchad i prospekt Dvortsa sovetov." *Arkhitektura SSSR* 10–11:25–27

IOFAN, BORIS M. 1971 "Tsentr stolitsy: Kakim emu byt'? Nekotorye itog i konkursa na eskiz-ideiu." *Stroittelstvo i arkhitektura Moskvy* 4:4–11.

Istoriia Russkogo iskusstva, vol. 12 1961.

KOPP, ANATOLE 1978 *L'architecture de la période Stalinienne.* Grenoble, France: Presses Universitaires.

KORNFELD, YA. A. 1953 *Laureaty Stalinskikh premii v arkhitekture: 1941–1950.* Moscow: Izd. lit. po stroitelstvu i arkhitekture.

IONESCU, GRIGORE

Grigore Ionescu (1904–) graduated from the School of Architecture in Bucharest in 1930, after which he attended the Rumanian Academy in Rome to study the history of architecture and monument preservation. On his return to Rumania, he became a professor at the Institute of Architecture in Bucharest where he taught from 1934 to 1973. His architectural works are characterized by the sobriety of the International style idiom.

Ionescu is best known as an architectural historian and as such has written countless articles and participated in many seminars across Europe.

CONSTANTIN MARIN MARINESCU

WORKS

1936, Tuberculosis Sanatorium, Covasna, Rumania. 1937, Sanatorium, Bîrnova-Iaşi, Rumania. 1940, Tramway Yard and Administration Building; 1950, Emilia Irza Institute of Pediatrics; 1960, Engineering Institute of Roads and Bridges; Bucharest.

BIBLIOGRAPHY

IONESCU, GRIGORE 1935 "La Chiesa pugliese a tre cupole." *Ephemeris Dacoromana* 6:50–128.

IONESCU, GRIGORE 1937 *Istoria arhitecturi româneşti din cele mai vechi timpuri până la 1900.* Bucharest: Cartea Românească.

IONESCU, GRIGORE 1934 *Rumänische Bautätigkeit in Siebenbürgen von 1919–1940.* Bucharest: Institut für Romanische Geschichte.

IONESCU, GRIGORE 1957 *Arhitectura populara*

romîneasča. Bucharest: Editura Tehnică.

IONESCU, GRIGORE 1965 Volume 2 in *Istoria Arhitecturii in Romania.* Bucharest: Editura Academiei Republicii Romañe.

IONESCU, GRIGORE 1969 *Arhitectura in Romania: Perioda anilor 1944–1969.* Bucharest: Editura Academiei Republicii Socialiste Romañia.

IONESCU, GRIGORE 1972 "Saptezeci si cinci de ani de la infiintarea invatamintului de arhitectura din Romania." *Arhitectura* 20:35–42.

MAMBRIANI, ALBERTO 1969 *L'Architettura Moderna nei Paesi Balcanici.* Bologna, Italy: Capelli.

PATRULIUS, RADU 1973–1974 "Contributii Romanesti in Arhitectura Anilor Anilor '30." *Arhitectura* 21, no. 6:44–52; 22, no. 1:53–59.

SASARMAN, GHEORGHE 1972 "Inceptile gindirii teoretice in architectura româneasča (1860–1916)." *Arhitectura,* 20, no. 6:44–46.

IORDANOV and OVCHAROV

Iordan Dimitrov Iordanov (1888–1968) and Sava Dimov Ovcharov (1892–1964) were among the most prominent Bulgarian architects of the second quarter of this century. Practicing in partnership between 1920 and 1948, they won numerous design competitions for such important civic buildings as the City Hall in Sliven, Bulgaria (1931), the Bulgarian Bar Association Building (1932–1933), and the Macedonia Cultural Center (1938–1939), all in Sofia, the Hot Springs Spa Resort of 1937–1939 in Bania, Karlovsko, Bulgaria, and many more.

Born in Sliven, Bulgaria, Iordanov graduated in 1911 from the Polytechnic Institute in Munich. Ovcharov was born in Kalofer, Bulgaria, studied architecture (1910–1916) in Vienna, and worked shortly with Kraus before returning to Bulgaria to participate in World War I.

Although in their early buildings Iordanov and Ovcharov often used classical proportions and details, by the mid-1930s they had joined the Modern movement. But with the official rejection of modernism in Bulgaria after World War II, they turned to nineteenth-century Bulgarian folk architecture for inspiration and interpretations. From 1948 on, Iordanov and Ovcharov led architectural teams in state design organizations. Between 1948 and 1950, Iordanov was director of the Urban Design Organization, and between 1950 and 1959, he was department chairman of the Institute of Urban Design and Architecture at the Bulgarian Academy of Science in Sofia. Ovcharov chaired a design studio at the Central Architectural Design Organization, Sofia, from 1948 until his retirement in 1962.

MARIA POPOVA

WORKS

*1920–1921, Office Building, Gurko and Levski Streets, Sofia. 1922–1929, Theater and Library, Iambol, Bulgaria. 1930, Bulgarian Academy of Science (additions and meeting halls), Sofia. 1931, City Hall, Sliven, Bulgaria. 1933–1934, Popular Bank, Stanke Dimitrov, Bulgaria. 1935–1937, Central Post Office, Plovdiv, Bulgaria. 1937–1939, Hot Springs Spa Resort, Bania, Karlovsko, Bulgaria. 1938–1939, Teacher's Mutual Insurance Company, Sofia. 1947, Central Post Office (with A. Stoichkov and M. Milkov), Pleven, Bulgaria.

BIBLIOGRAPHY

"Arkhitekt I. D. Iordanov." 1969 *Arkhitektura* 1:44.

BŬLGARSKA AKADEMIÏA NA NAUKITE 1965 *Kratka Istoriïa na Bŭlgarskata Arkhitektura.* Sofia: The academy.

IORDANOV, IORDAN 1947 "Blagoustroistvo na Seloto." *Arkhitektura* 1947:1–3.

IORDANOV, IORDAN 1953 *Arkitektura i Stroitel'stvo* 1953:1–7.

IORDANOV, IORDAN 1956 *Proektirane na Tipnichni Obshchestveni Sgradi v Bulgaria.* Sofia: Tekhnika.

KUTEVA, SABINA 1965 "Arkhitekt Sava Ovcharov, 1892–1964." *Arkhitektura* 9–10:16–20.

MAMBRIANI, ALBERTO 1969 *L'architettura moderna nei paesi Falcanici.* Bologna, Italy: Cappelli.

NENKOV, BORIS 1952 "Bŭlgarskata Arkhitektura Sled Purvata Svetovna voina." *Arkhitektura i stroitel'stvo* 1952:9–14.

IRWIN, HARRIET MORRISON

In 1869 Harriet Morrison Irwin (1828–1897) became the first American woman to patent an architectural design. It was for an hexagonal house whose principal rooms were also hexagonal. A version of her house design was erected at 912 West Fifth Street in Charlotte, North Carolina, around 1869.

Irwin believed that a hexagonal dwelling could promote physical well-being; she discussed ideas on health, the out-of-doors, and hexagonal architecture in her major literary effort, a novel *The Hermit of Petraea* (1871). Although she publicized her patent design, it did not catch the public fancy as had the earlier (1848) octagonal house design conceived by Orson S. Fowler.

BEVERLY HEISNER

WORK

*c.1869, House, 912 West Fifth Street, Charlotte, N.C.

BIBLIOGRAPHY

COLE, DORIS 1973 *From Tipi to Skyscraper: A History of Women in Architecture.* New York: Braziller.

FOWLER, ORSON S. (1854)1973 *The Octagon House: A Home for All.* Reprint. New York: Dover. Originally published with the title *A Home for All; or: The Gravel Wall and Octagon Mode of Building.*

HEISNER, BEVERLY 1981 "Harriet Morrison Irwin's Hexagonal House: An Invention to Improve Domestic Dwellings." *North Carolina Historical Review* 58, no. 2:105–124.

IRWIN, HARRIET MORRISON 1871 *The Hermit of Petraea.* Charlotte, N.C.: Hill & Irwin.

STERN, MADELEINE BETTINA (1962)1974 *We the Women: Career Firsts of Nineteenth Century America.* New York: Artemis.

TORRE, SUSANNA 1977 *Women in American Architecture.* New York: Whitney Library of Design.

IRWIN, LEIGHTON

Leighton Francis Irwin (1892–1962), born in Mitcham, South Australia, and educated at Haileybury College, Melbourne, was articled to the firm of Klingender and Alsop from 1910 to 1912. Irwin served in Europe in World War I, and remained there to study at the Architectural Association in London. Returning to Australia, he commenced private practice and then formed a partnership with Roy Kenneth Stevenson from 1921 to 1934. This partnership received the R.V.I.A. Street Architecture Award for the Royal Australasian College of Surgeons Building, Melbourne (1937).

Irwin's great contribution to his profession was the development of the Architectural Atelier into the world-renowned school of architecture at the University of Melbourne. He was director of the Atelier for many years. After an overseas study tour on advanced hospital design, Irwin appointed engineers onto his staff and soon established his firm as the leading hospital architects in Victoria.

PETER NAVARETTI

WORKS

1921, Townsville Town Hall, Queensland, Australia. 1924, South African War Memorial; 1929, Public Library Extensions; 1932, National Art Gallery Extensions; 1933, Royal Australasian College of Surgeons; 1935, Prince Henry's Hospital; Melbourne. 1936, Saint George's Hospital (with Louis R. Williams), Kew; 1939, Omeo Hospital; 1940, Heidelberg Repatriation Hospital; Victoria, Australia. 1940, Hobart Public Hospital, Tasmania, Australia. 1947–1958, Box Hill and District Hospital; 1950–1957, Portland and District Hospital; 1957, Southern Memorial Hospital, Caulfield; Victoria, Australia. 1958, Blacktown District Hospital, New South Wales, Australia.

BIBLIOGRAPHY

Additional information on Francis Leighton Irwin is available from Architectural Records, Office of Leighton Irwin & Co. Pty. Ltd., Melbourne, Victoria, Australia.

FREELAND, JOHN MAXWELL 1971 *The Making of a Profession.* Sydney: Angus & Robertson.

NAVARETTI, PETER Y. 1971 "Architects of Melbourne and Their Work." Unpublished B.A. thesis, Leighton Irwin Memorial Library, University of Melbourne.

ISIDOROS

An architect, engineer, geometer, and scholar, Isidoros (first half of the sixth century) was born in the ancient city of Miletus in Asia Minor (Turkey) and was presumably educated in Constantinople (Istanbul). He worked closely with ANTHEMIOS, with whom he created the Hagia Sophia (532–537). Their names are coupled several times in the writings of contemporaries, where there are references to their consulting activities and to widespread practice both in the capital and in the provinces. Only the Hagia Sophia, however, is named there as their creation. A later text, of the tenth century, credits them with the Church of the Holy Apostles, built in Constantinople during the 540s and 550s, also for Justinian; the tomb–church of the Byzantine emperors, it was destroyed by the Turks after the conquest of 1453.

Modern writers have tended to make Isidoros Anthemios's engineer, but, given Anthemios's

Isidoros.
Hagia Sophia (higher dome completed with Isidoros the Younger).
Constantinople (Istanbul), Turkey.
563

expertise in such fields as applied physics and advanced geometry, it seems more likely that both men were architect–engineers, a combination common in antiquity as the writing of VITRUVIUS and the career of APOLLODORUS make clear. The Greek words used in the texts for professional competency in architecture and engineering do not settle the matter because they chiefly derive from the root of the word *mechanikos,* which means inventive, full of resource, and, by extension, connected with machines. However Anthemios seems to have been the senior man— his name is always given first, and Procopius, in his work *On the Buildings* (of Justinian), gives his abilities the greater emphasis. The likely inference is that they were partners and that Anthemios was older than Isidoros; in a description of the rebuilding of the dome of Hagia Sophia after the earthquake of 558, another writer speaks of Anthemios as then being long dead. It is impossible now to tell what each man was responsible for at the Hagia Sophia. The passage in Procopius mentioned above is about all there is to go on: "Anthemios of Tralles, the most learned man in . . . the art of building . . . duly (regulated) the tasks of the various artisans, and (prepared) in advance the designs of the future construction; and associated with him was another master-builder, Isidoros by name, a Milesian . . . intelligent and worthy . . . (1.1.24)."

Isidoros's contemporaries valued his learning as much as his architectural and engineering expertise. He was a diligent student of the work of Archimedes and a respected teacher thereof. He appears as an authority on advanced geometry in one of the supplementary books added to the Euclidian canon, where he is called a "great master." He was also an inventor, for example of compasses for constructing parabolas. His architectural studies were attested to by a commentary he wrote, now lost, on a treatise on vaulting by Heron of Alexandria (probably of the first century), a prolific writer on mechanics, surveying, geometry, metrology, automata, and so on—subjects close to the center of the work of professionals like Anthemios and Isidoros. Not only did such men help keep classical and Hellenistic thought and practice in these areas alive, but they also, in the case of Anthemios and Isidoros, possessed the daring and ability to put their hard-won knowledge to the test in highly original, monumental buildings such as the Hagia Sophia. That building and its many progeny are the most significant tangible descendants of the masterful Greek exploration of mathematics and physics.

Given the meager information we have about Isidoros it is tempting to see him as the designer and constructor of the splendid vaults of the Hagia Sophia and other Justinianic buildings such as Saints Sergius and Bacchus (c.530) in Constantinople. The shallow first dome of the Hagia Sophia was pared down to the limits of the structural possibilities, and behind that ambitious design one may sense Isidoros's and Anthemios's calculations and theoretical knowledge. The Hagia Sophia's huge pendentives—the first monumental examples of that quintessentially Byzantine architectural form—also express the studies and predispositions of the geometer. Many of the major new churches of the period of which we have knowledge— Hagia Sophia, Saints Sergius and Bacchus, the Holy Apostles (judging from existing descriptions), and perhaps Saint Polyeuktos, all in Constantinople, as well as Saint John at Ephesus and some other buildings far away—embody results of practical and theoretical studies of the kind in which Isidoros was immersed.

The daringly designed dome that he and Anthemios provided for the Hagia Sophia collapsed in an earthquake in 558. Anthemios had died some time before, and Isidoros had either ceased to practice or was also deceased, for it was his nephew, Isidoros the Younger (also from Miletus), who was put in charge of rebuilding the dome during Justinian's old age. In a Syrian inscription the younger man is called "most magnificent and illustrious." He made the new dome less flat in section, and surely more stable, by raising it some twenty feet higher than the original one. Agathias, who knew both versions, remarks in his *Histories* that the result was not entirely pleasing: "But despite the fact that it is straighter, despite its balanced curves and regular outline, it has become narrower, its lines have hardened and it has lost something of its old power to inspire awe and wonder in the beholder. It is, however, much more firmly and securely fixed (5.9.5)."

It is substantially this vault that exists today, though there was further serious damage to the superstructure in 989 and again in 1346, necessitating partial reconstruction on both occasions.

WILLIAM L. MACDONALD

WORKS

532–537, Hagia Sophia (with Anthemios); *540s–550s, Church of the Holy Apostles (with Anthemios); 563, Hagia Sophia (higher dome completed with Isidoros the Younger); Constantinople (Istanbul), Turkey.

BIBLIOGRAPHY

AGATHIAS, *The Histories,* Book 5. Quotations in the text are from the translation by J. F. Frendo, published in Berlin and New York by de Gruyter in 1975.

DOWNEY, GLANVILLE 1946–1948 "Byzantine Architects, Their Training and Methods." *Byzantion* 18:99–118.

HUXLEY, G. L. 1959 *Anthemius of Tralles: A Study in Later Greek Geometry.* Cambridge, Mass.: Harvard University Press.

PAUL THE SILENTIARY, *Description of the Hagia Sophia.* Quotations in the text are from the translation on pages 80–91 in Cyril A. Mango, *The Art of the Byzantine Empire, 312–1453.* Englewood Cliffs, N.J.: Prentice-Hall.

PROCOPIUS, *On the Buildings,* Books 1.1 and 2.3. Quotations in the text are from the translation by H. B. Dewing and Glanville Downey, published in 1940 by Harvard University Press and Heinemann as part of the Loeb Classical Library series.

ITALIA, ANGELO

Angelo Italia (1629–1700), born in the Sicilian town of Licata near Agrigento, was a Jesuit who designed both buildings and cities in late seventeenth-century Sicily. His activity during the first forty years of his life remains largely a mystery. On the basis of an eighteenth-century history of the *chiesa madre* of Palmaldi Montechiaro, published by Giosuè Fiorentino, Italia is credited with its design. The graceful twin-towered church façade, begun in the 1660s, may be by Italia. Its design is not antithetical to his style. Yet, inconsistencies in the style of the church as a whole and its protracted construction history make Italia's contribution problematical.

Italia's activity becomes clearer in the 1670s when he joined the Jesuit order. From 1678 through 1681, he worked as an architect while he was attached to the Jesuit College in Palermo. For the next three years, he worked under Giacomo Napoli at Mazara del Vallo, returning to Palermo in the 1680s.

In 1684, Italia designed San Francesco Saverio (1684–1700) in Palermo, a unique church in which a domed, Greek-cross central space is juxtaposed with four chapels, each placed between the arms of the cross. The entablature which bends around the central Greek cross is counterweighted by the entablatures and supporting columns of each of the chapels. The chapels rise above the entablatures and their domes can be seen through relieving arches from the central portion of the church, creating a play between the exterior wall of the whole building and the column screen and arches that separate the central Greek cross from the chapels. Perhaps Italia derived this idea from GUARINO GUARINI whose drawings for the Somaschi Church in Messina he may have known. But the style of the ornament, the composition of the building, and the relative conservatism of its elements suggest that Italia worked it out independently. Italia repeated his scheme for San Francesco Saverio in the more restrained and less effective church of the Jesuit College of Polizzi Generosa in Sicily which he redesigned in 1689.

A work of quite a different sort is the lavishly decorated Cappella del Crocifisso in the Cathedral of Monreale. First planned by Giovanni da Monreale, a Capuchin monk, the chapel was redesigned and built by Italia from 1688 to 1692. The chapel's magnificent polychromy and multiplicity of textures show Italia's close ties to contemporary Spanish design which does not otherwise appear in his work.

Shortly after the destructive earthquake of 1693, Italia was called to Catania to rebuild the Jesuit College there. While in Catania, he accepted the task of selecting a new site for the severely damaged city of Avola. He carefully surveyed the terrain and decided to move the city to a new location. For a city plan, he decided upon a hexagon with an enormous central piazza, perhaps conceived as a refuge in and after earthquakes. The uniqueness of his plan may have sparked the interest of the citizens of nearby Noto. After the earthquake, Italia had suggested a location for Noto's new city but his first conception did not meet with the Spanish government's full approval. After several ad hoc solutions were tried, he was called back to Noto to put the city into a more orderly plan, which he did by coordinating the open spaces and locations of religious institutions.

After this creative and probably difficult period of city planning, Italia returned to Palermo in 1699. In the same year, he journeyed to Alcamo where he designed the Chiesa Madre, the last recorded work before his death in 1700.

STEPHEN TOBRINER

WORKS

1684–1700, San Francesco Saverio (not completed until 1710), Palermo, Italy. 1688–1692, Cappella del Crocifisso, Cathedral of Monreale, Italy. c.1689, Church of the Jesuit College, Polizzi Generosa, Italy. 1693–1700, Avola Town Plan, Italy. 1693–1700, Noto Town Plan, Italy. 1693–1700, Church of San Francesco Borgia and Jesuit College (not completed until 1754), Catania, Italy. 1699, Chiesa Madre, Alcamo, Italy.

BIBLIOGRAPHY

BLUNT, ANTHONY 1968 *Sicilian Baroque.* London: Weidenfeld & Nicolson.

CARONIA ROBERTI, SALVATORE 1935 *Il Barocco in Palermo.* Palermo, Italy: Ciuni.

FIORENTINO, GIOSUÈ 1932 "La Chiesa Madre di Palma di Montechiaro." *Archivio Storico per la Sicilia Orientale* 28:492–498.

MILLUNZI, GAETANO 1907 "La Cappella del Crocifisso nel Duomo di Monreale." *Archivio Storico Siciliano* 32:459–524.

STELLA, MARIA LUIGIA 1968 "L'architetto Angelo Italia." *Palladio* 28, nos. 1–4:155–176.

TOBRINER, STEPHEN 1982 *The Genesis of Noto; An Eighteenth Century Sicilian City.* Berkeley: University of California Press; London: Zwemmer.

ITTAR, STEFANO

Stefano Ittar (?–1790) was an influential architect in late eighteenth-century Catania, Italy. His Tuscan family, called Guidone da Hittar, had moved to Rome, where the young Ittar was brought up. Although Ittar's early training is undocumented, it is clear from his later buildings that he was deeply influenced by the circle of CARLO FONTANA, whose late baroque classical style was so pervasive in early eighteenth-century Rome. On a visit to Catania in 1765, Ittar met Ignazio Paterno, the prince of Biscari, a powerful local aristocrat and noted collector of antiquities. Persuaded by Biscari to remain in Catania, Ittar married the daughter of FRANCESCO BATTAGLIA, one of Catania's most active architects. The son from their union, Sebastiano Ittar, became an illustrator of classical antiquities in the Catania area. Stefano Ittar worked as an architect in Catania until the 1780s, dying in Malta where he was directing the construction of a library for the Knights of Malta in 1790.

Ittar's two noteworthy buildings in Catania are the façade of the Collegiata (1767) and the Church of San Placidio (1769), both of which illustrate his ties with baroque architecture in Rome. The striking combination of the cupola raised over a deep niche in the Collegiata façade is based on a proposed design for the façade of San Giovanni in Laterano in Rome by ANDREA POZZO. Ittar crowned his façade with an interpretation of FRANCESCO BORROMINI's lantern of Sant' Ivo della Sapienza, showing his appreciation of the seventeenth-century master. Otherwise, the organization and ornamentation of the façade with its gentle curves, denatured volutes, and column-pilaster progressions relies on Carlo Fontana's façade for San Marcello al Corso in Rome.

STEPHEN TOBRINER

WORKS

1767, Collegiata (façade); 1768–1783, Benedictine Monastery (work); 1768–1783, San Nicola (dome); 1769, City Gate (Porta ferdinandea); 1769, San Martino ai Bianchi; 1769, San Placidio; 1769, Santissima Trinità (second order of the façade); Catania, Italy. 1784, Knights of St. John of Jerusalem Library, Valetta, Malta, Italy.

BIBLIOGRAPHY

BLUNT, ANTHONY 1968 *Sicilian Baroque.* London: Weidenfeld & Nicolson.

ROSCARINO, SALVATORE 1961 *Studi e rilievi di architettura siciliana.* Messina, Italy: Raphael.

IVORY, THOMAS

Thomas Ivory (c.1732–1786) was probably born in Cork, Ireland, and was apprenticed to a carpenter and a gunsmith. Around 1760, he was appointed master of the Dublin Society's Drawing School. He competed in the Royal Exchange competition of 1769, and won the competition for the King's Hospital School, which he built in 1773. His other works include the Newcomen Bank, Dublin, the bridge at Lismore, and Kilcarty, County Meath.

MAURICE CRAIG

BIBLIOGRAPHY

McPARLAND, EDWARD 1973 *Thomas Ivory: Architect.* County Cork, Ireland: Ballyotton.

IVORY, THOMAS OF NORWICH

The birthplace of Thomas Ivory (1709–1779) is unknown. He purchased the Freedom of Norwich, England, in 1745 and worked there all his life. He was a carpenter at the Great Hospital in 1751 and then became a builder and timber merchant. He designed important civic buildings and put up merchants' houses as a speculation in a good provincial Georgian style. His son William succeeded him in business.

JILL ALLIBONE

WORKS

1751–1753, The Great Hospital, Norwich; *1751–1753, The Methodist Meeting House, Bishopsgate; 1754, The Assembly Rooms, Norwich; 1754–1756, The Octagon Chapel, Colegate, Norwich; *1757, Norwich Theater; 1761–1762, 29–35 Surrey Street, Norwich; Norfolk, England. *1764, Colchester Theater, Suffolk, England. 1767–1779, Blickling Hall; 1770–1773, 25–27 Surrey Street, Norwich; 1771–1772, The Artillery Barracks, Norwich; Norfolk, England.

BIBLIOGRAPHY

WEARING, STANLEY J. 1927 *Georgian Norwich: Its Builders.* Norwich, England: Jarrold.

ʿIWAḌ

ʿImād al-Dawla wa ʾl-Dīn Ḥājjī ʿIwaḍ b. Akhī Bāyazīd, Ottoman Turkish architect, soldier, and bureaucrat, was active in the first decades of the fifteenth century. Born into modest circumstances in the village of Beg Ovasi near Tokat in Anatolia, it is probable that ʿIwaḍ was trained as a young man to become a Muslim theological scholar. In 1421, he was appointed district governor (*subāshī*) of Kazabad (Kazova) in the province of Tokat, and two years later, in 1423, he was made governor of the Ottoman capital, Bursa. Subsequently, the Ottoman ruler Sultan Meḥmed I appointed ʿIwaḍ to the rank of pasha and made him one of his viziers.

As vizier, ʿIwaḍ was in charge of the construction in Bursa of Sultan Meḥmed's imperial mosque (1414–1424), his tomb (1421), and very likely his madrasah (theological college [c.1420]) and ʿimārat (public soup kitchen [c.1420]) as well. ʿIwaḍ's involvement in these projects went beyond mere administrative supervision, for in an inscription on the portal of the mosque, he describes himself as "he who designed it, organized it and fixed its proportions."

Whereas in terms of planning Meḥmed's mosque and tomb conform to well-established Ottoman types—the T-plan mosque and tomb tower—in terms of decoration they break radically with the past. The lavish use of turquoise faïence for surface decoration, as a result of which Meḥmed's foundations are called the Yeşil (Green) Mosque and Tomb, is without precedent in Ottoman architecture, and draws on models then current in Timurid Iran and Central Asia. The Timurid inspiration for the decorative program of Meḥmed's buildings is further emphasized in certain of their inscriptions, in which mention is made of craftsmen of Iranian origin or training, including the decorator ʿAlī b. Ilyās ʿAlī, the woodcarver ʿAlī b. Ḥājjī Aḥmad Tabrīzī, and the anonymous tile workers who signed their work "The Masters of Tabriz."

ʿIwaḍ also built the Mosque of Çelebi Sultan Meḥmed (1421) for the Ottoman ruler at Dimetoka in Thrace. Square in plan, with a porch along its north façade, it is covered with a 13-meter dome carried on four massive piers and attests to the growing Ottoman interest in exploiting the possibilities of ever larger domical vaults.

ʿIwaḍ is also popularly credited with the construction of a bridge at Ulubad near Bursa (c.1420) and the building of a water supply system connecting the Tunca river with the city of Edirne in Thrace (c.1420). In addition, he endowed numerous pious foundations (*wakf*), among them a

ʿIwaḍ.
Tomb of Meḥmed I (Yeşil Turbe).
Bursa, Turkey.
1421

mosque, *madrasa, zāwiya* (dervish convent), and two *khāns* (large commercial buildings) in Tokat, a mosque and *madrasa* in Bey Ovasi, the Imadiye complex (mosque, *madrasa,* primary school, and market), Ivaz Paşa Mosque, Sandıkcılar Hanı, and Geyve Hanı, all in Bursa, and, presumably, the Haci Ivaz Mosque in Ankara. Of these, only the last two are still standing in their fifteenth-century form. Whether ʿIwaḍ was the architect of any or all of them is unknown.

On the death of Sultan Meḥmed in 1421, his successor, Sultan Murād II, retained ʿIwaḍ as one of his viziers, and ʿIwaḍ was one of the commanders of the sultan's army in the battle at Ulubad (1422). Subsequently, however, ʿIwaḍ seems to have lost Murād's favor, was dismissed from office, and was, according to some accounts, blinded. The epitaph on his tombstone in the cemetery of Pinarbaşı, outside Bursa, gives the date of his death as August 20, 1428.

ʿIwaḍ is notable less for his planning concepts, which for the most part reproduce accepted Ottoman models, than for his innovations, in the area of architectural decoration. Indeed, the mosque and tomb of Meḥmed I in Bursa are the first Ottoman buildings in which ceramic faïence was used extensively, and they witness to ʿIwaḍ's importance as introducer of the Timurid-Iranian style of decoration to Ottoman architecture.

HOWARD CRANE

WORKS

1414–1420, Mosque of Meḥmed I (Yeşil Cami); (A)c.1420, Public Soup Kitchen; (A)c.1420, Theological College; Bursa, Turkey. (A)c.1420, Ulubad Bridge, Turkey. 1421, Mosque of Çelebi Sultan Meḥmed,

Dimetoka, Greece. 1421, Tomb of Mehmed I (Yeşil Turbe) and Mosque, Bursa, Turkey.

BIBLIOGRAPHY

AYVERDI, EKREM HAKKI 1972 Pages 46–118, 136–150 in *Osmanlt Miᶜmârîsinin Çelebi ve II. Sultan Murad Devri, 806–855 (1403–1451)*. Istanbul, Turkey: Baha Matbaası.

GABRIEL, ALBERT 1958 Pages 79–104 in *Une Capitale turque: Brousse—Bursa, I.* Paris: E. de Boccard.

TAESCHNER, FRANZ 1932 "Die Ješil Ǧamiᶜ in Brussa, ihre historischen Inschriften und ihre Künrtler." *Der Islam* 20:139–168.

UZUNÇARŞILI, İSMAIL HAKKI 1959 "Haci Ivaz Paşa Dâir." *Tarih Dergisi* 10:25–38.

JACKSON, JOHN

John Jackson (c.1602–1663) was a master mason, active mainly in Oxford. Evidently esteemed and successful, he was employed on some of the outstanding Oxford buildings of the mid-seventeenth century, but his status as a designer is uncertain. Of the works listed below, the chapel at Brasenose College, a fairly sophisticated mixture of Gothic and classical elements, has the best claim to be Jackson's own design; the design of the porch of Saint Mary the Virgin (1637) is usually credited to NICHOLAS STONE.

IAN CHILVERS

WORKS

1634–1636, Canterbury Quadrangle (completion), Saint John's College; 1637, Church of Saint Mary the Virgin (porch); 1656–1666, Chapel and Library, Brasenose College; Oxford.

BIBLIOGRAPHY

ROYAL COMMISSION ON HISTORICAL MONUMENTS, ENGLAND 1939 *An Inventory of the Historical Monuments in the City of Oxford.* London: H.M. Stationery Office.

SHERWOOD, JENNIFER, and PEVSNER, NIKOLAUS 1974 *The Buildings of England: Oxfordshire.* Harmondsworth, England: Penguin.

JACKSON, THOMAS GRAHAM

Thomas Graham Jackson (1835–1924) was born in Hampstead, England, and was educated at Brighton College and Oxford. After spending four years as a pupil of GEORGE GILBERT SCOTT, he set up in practice in 1862. A poor planner but a decorator of exceptional skill, he did many restorations and remodelings. For his nonecclesiastical works he used a style which he called refined English Renaissance.

PETER HOWELL

WORKS

1861–1863, Send Vicarage, Surrey, England. 1863, Ketton Church (restoration of chancel), Rutland, England. 1868, Ellesmere Memorial, Walkden, Lancashire, England. 1872, Annesley Church, Nottinghamshire, England. 1872–1874, Hornblotton Church, Somerset, England. 1875, Patteson Memorial Church, Norfolk Island. 1876–1883, Examination Schools, Oxford. 1877, Lime Tree Walk (Twenty-four Cottages), Sevenoaks, Kent, England. 1879–1881, High School for Boys; 1879–1881, High School for Girls; 1880–1883, Grove Building, Lincoln College; 1883–1887, Trinity College (front quad and president's lodgings); Oxford. 1885–1890, Stratton Church, Hampshire, England. 1886–1889, 1909–1911, Brasenose College (new quadrangle),

Oxford. 1887–1890, Northington Church, Hampshire, England. 1887–1914, Hertford College (new buildings, including the chapel, and the bridge), Oxford. 1889, Blenheim Palace Chapel (alterations and refitting), Oxfordshire, England. 1889–1893, Zadar Cathedral (new campanile), Yugoslavia. 1894–1896, Church of Saint Mary the Virgin (restoration of spire), Oxford. 1897–1901, Giggleswick School Chapel, Settle, Yorkshire, England. 1899, Burlington House (entrance hall remodeled), London. 1899, Sedgwick Museum, Cambridge. 1905–1911, Winchester Cathedral (underpinning), Hampshire, England. 1908–1910, Electrical Laboratory, Oxford. 1914–1918, Holy Trinity Church (restoration), Coventry, England. 1922, Radley College (War Memorial Gateway), Oxfordshire, England.

BIBLIOGRAPHY

JACKSON, BASIL H. (editor) 1950 *Recollections of Thomas Graham Jackson.* London: Oxford University Press.

JACKSON, THOMAS GRAHAM 1873 *Modern Gothic Architecture.* London: King.

JACKSON, THOMAS GRAHAM 1887 *Dalmatia, the Quarnero, and Istria.* 3 vols. Oxford: Clarendon.

JACKSON, THOMAS GRAHAM 1893 *Wadham College.* Oxford: Clarendon.

JACKSON, THOMAS GRAHAM 1897 *The Church of St. Mary the Virgin, Oxford.* Oxford: Clarendon.

JACKSON, THOMAS GRAHAM 1906 *Reason in Architecture.* London: Murray.

JACKSON, THOMAS GRAHAM (1913)1920 *Byzantine and Romanesque Architecture.* 2d ed. Cambridge University Press.

JACKSON, THOMAS GRAHAM 1915 *Gothic Architecture in France, England and Italy.* 2 vols. Cambridge University Press.

JACKSON, THOMAS GRAHAM 1917 *A Holiday in Umbria.* London: Murray.

JACKSON, THOMAS GRAHAM 1921–1923 *Renaissance of Roman Architecture.* 3 vols. Cambridge University Press.

JACKSON, THOMAS GRAHAM 1923 *Memories of Travel.* Cambridge University Press.

JACKSON, THOMAS GRAHAM (1925)1932 *Architecture.* London: Macmillan.

Jacobensen.
Rødovre Town Hall.
Copenhagen.
1955

JACOBSEN, ARNE

Arne Jacobsen (1902–1971) graduated from the Technical School in Copenhagen in 1924. Earlier, in 1919, he had started his education at the Royal Academy, where his teachers were KAY FISKER, Ivar Bentsen, and Kaj Gottlob. Jacobsen was a distinguished designer from the very beginning; he knew how to use watercolor, and he was a born prize winner. He was educated in the spirit of the Klint school (see KAARE KLINT)—to find the simplest and most logical solution with an honest awareness of the nature of materials. Jacobsen combined an individual conception of design with the main features of contemporary thinking and Danish functional tradition, in which style he built his first private houses. His inspiration was a highly admired cottage from 1805 by the Danish sculptor and architect Nicolai Abildgaard, named Spurveskjul, but when in 1928 he built for himself, he had adopted the new white cubic style of the Weissenhofsiedlung in Berlin. The plastered brickwork was to be taken for concrete and the plan was traditional. The International style was met with criticism; to the Danes it was just another style, good for bathrooms and beach areas. The best samples, however, were designed by Jacobsen: the House of the Future (1929) with a circular plan; the Rothenborg House in Copenhagen (1931) which lies like a steamship in the garden; and the housing, restaurant, and theater at Bellevue, Copenhagen (1933–1934), where he also had the opportunity to make the landscaping and interior decoration an integral part of the architecture. In the 1930s, ERIK GUNNAR ASPLUND was most influential; when Jacobsen worked on Aarhus Town Hall he sent the drawings to Asplund for his opinion. The German occupation and the prosecution of the Jews forced Jacobsen to go to Stockholm in 1943 where he was welcomed by his friend ALVAR AALTO. In Sweden, Jacobsen had great success with his textile and wallpaper patterns.

The response to the German occupation was a strengthening of the Danish functional tradition to the disadvantage of the position of modernism, and the shortage of building materials, in particular steel, kept the brick tradition alive. A sensitivity to texture and a wish for human scale and unpretentiousness became the characteristic of Danish design. Jacobsen's buildings at Bellevue, from the theater to the Søholm rowhouses, and the Munkegaard School in Copenhagen (1952–1956) are outstanding examples of that development. The most influential inspirations after the war came from the United States, with modular planning and a higher degree of industrialization.

Rødovre Town Hall (1955) and the SAS Hotel Royal (1958–1960), a tower block of the Lever House type by SKIDMORE, OWINGS, AND MERRILL, introduced the idiom of LUDWIG MIES VAN DER ROHE to Denmark. For the SAS Hotel, Jacobsen carried out the design as well as pieces of furniture, tableware, and light fixtures. His very popular bent-plywood stacking chair, the *Violin*, designed in 1952 for Fritz Hansen, is still being made.

LISBET BALSLEV JØRGENSEN

WORKS

1927, Private House, 5 Krathusvej; 1928, Arne Jacobsen House; 2 Gotfred Rodesvej; 1929, House of the Future (with Flemming Lassen), Exhibition in Forum; 1931, Rothenborg House, 37 Klampenborgvej; 1931–1937, Bellevue Lido and Summer Theater; 1933–1934, Bellavista Housing, Bellevue; Copenhagen. 1937–1942, Town Hall (with Erik Møller), Aarhus, Denmark. 1941–1942, Søllerød Town Hall (with Lassen), Copenhagen. 1943, Smokehouse, Odden, Denmark. 1950–1952, Bellevuekrogen (rowhouses), Søholm; 1952–1956, Munkegaard Primary School, 178 Vangedevej; 1955, Rødovre Town Hall; 1958–1960, SAS Hotel Royal and Air Terminal; 1960–1962, Tom Chocolade Factory, Ballerup; 1961–1978, National Bank of Denmark (with Hans Dissing and Otto Weitling), Copenhagen. 1970, Hamburg Electricity Supply Company Head Office (with Weitling), Germany. 1970–1973, Town Hall (with Weitling), Mainz, Germany. 1973–1976, Central Bank of Kuwait (with Dissing and Weitling).

BIBLIOGRAPHY

"Arne Jacobsen: Projekter." 1964 *Arkitektur* 8:181–206.

"Central Bank of Kuwait." 1980 *Arkitektur* 24, no. 2:62–67.

DYSSEGAARD, SOREN 1971–1972 *Arne Jacobsen: A Danish Architect.* Copenhagen: Ministry of Foreign Affairs. Originally published in Danish.

FABER, TOBIAS 1964 *Arne Jacobsen.* Translated from Danish by E. Rockwell. New York: Praeger.

FABER, TOBIAS 1978 *A History of Danish Architecture.* Copenhagen: Det danske Selskab.

"Foyer i Hannover-Herrenhausen, Landskrona idrætshal, Castrop-Rauxel bycenter, Christianeum, et gymnasium i Hamburg, Østersøbadet Burg på Fehmarn." 1966 *Arkitektur* 10, no. 5:177–199.

KASTHOLM, JØRGEN 1968 *Arne Jacobsen.* Copenhagen: Høst. Originally published in Danish.

"Ved Bellevue Bugt." 1962 *Arkitektur* 6, no. 1:1–9.

"St. Catherine's College, Oxford." 1964 *Architectural Review* 136, no. 9:188–195.

JACOBSEN, HOLGER

Holger Jacobsen (1876–1960) entered the Royal Academy in Copenhagen in 1898 and graduated in 1905. As a pupil of HANS JØRGEN HOLM, he was trained to find his own way among the styles. Influenced by the art historian Vilhelm Wanscher, MICHELANGELO and the Roman Magnificenza became his ideals. To a certain extent, his idiom was that of Art Nouveau, but without its organic nature. After HACK KAMPMANN's death in 1920, Jacobsen finished the Police Headquarters in Copenhagen together with Aage Rafn, and he is certainly responsible for the expressionistic classicism of the details. His most ambitious work is the new building for the Royal Theater in Copenhagen (1919–1931), called Stærekassen (bird house) by the Danes.

LISBET BALSLEV JØRGENSEN

WORKS

1905–1907, Bispebjerg Crematorium; *1914, Circus Building; 1918–1924, Police Headquarters (with Aage Rafn and Christian Kampmann), Hack Kampmann; 1926, Holger Jacobsen House, Rosbæksvej; 1919–1931, Royal Theater (Stærekassen), Tordenskjoldsgade; 1933–1934, Villa, Henningsens allé; Copenhagen.

BIBLIOGRAPHY

JØRGENSEN, A. G. 1949 Volume 2, pages 18–19 in *Weilbachs Kunstnerleksikon.* Copenhagen: Aschehoug Dansk Forlag.

JØRGENSEN, LISBET BALSLEV 1979 Page 131 in *Enfamiliehuset.* Copenhagen: Gyldendal.

MILLECH, KNUD 1960 "Obituary." *Arkitekten* 62, no. 10:179.

JACOBSEN, VIGGO

Viggo Jacobsen (1885–1975) entered the Royal Academy in Copenhagen in 1905 and graduated in 1918. He started his career designing two wooden houses in a neoclassical revival style: Klelund (1920) in Esbjerg was a polychrome building inspired by MICHAEL GOTTLIEB BINDESBØLL's Thorvaldsen Museum project of 1837, and Skramsø (1921) in Randers was gray and white and looked just like a house from 1800. Jacobsen knew how to employ the architectural clichés of the day and was successful with his cinema interiors. From the 1930s on, his buildings were devoid of classical ornamentation, and with the Kirkebjerg School (1943) in Copenhagen, the transition to functionalism was complete.

LISBET BALSLEV JØRGENSEN

WORKS

1920, Klelund (with Albert Oppenheim), Esbjerg, Denmark. 1921, Skramsø (with Oppenheim), Randers, Denmark. *1924, Metropol Cinema (interior); 1936, Bellahøj School; 1943, Kirkebjerg School; Copenhagen.

BIBLIOGRAPHY

R.E.D. 1949 Volume 2, pages 22–23 in *Weilbachs Kunstnerleksikon.* Copenhagen: Aschehoug Dansk Forlag.

JACQMAIN, ANDRE

A student of Henry Lacoste at the Académie des Beaux-Arts of Brussels, André Jacqmain (1921–) retained his master's predilections for extreme refinement and architectural gesture. His earliest works, influenced by FRANK LLOYD WRIGHT as much as by Expressionism, illustrate his desire to create a new, monumental architecture. Considered the leader of the young Belgian architects of the 1960s and 1970s, Jacqmain embodies their propensity for deliberate originality.

MAURICE CULOT
Translated from French by
Shara Wasserman

WORKS

1960, Urvater House and Museum, 59 Avenue Lequine, Rhode-Saint-Genese; 1962–1967, Glaverbel Principal Seat, Hulpe Highway, Boitsfort; Brussels. 1962–1968, University of Liège (restaurant and student housing), Sart-Tilman, Angleur-Tiliff, Belgium. *1967–1970, Belgian Pavilion, Universal Exposition, Osaka, Japan. 1970–1977, Library; 1970–1977, Science Square (remodeling); Louvain-la-Neuve, Ottignies, Belgium. 1976–1981, University of Liège (Department of Law, Economics, and Social Sciences), Sart Tilman, Angleur–Tiliff, Belgium.

JADOT, JEAN NICOLAS

Jean Nicolas Jadot (1710–1761) trained with GERMAIN BOFFRAND. His career was intimately tied to Duke Franz Stephen (later Emperor Franz I of Austria) for whom his first designs were occasioned by the duke's marriage to Maria-Theresa. Following the duke, first to Vienna and then to Tuscany, where he provided needed pomps, and in 1750 again to Vienna, being now named *Hofbauinspector,* he finally gained the opportunity to design public buildings. He spent the last years of his life in less artistic activities as the *contrôleur de change* for the duke's brother in Brussels.

JUANITA M. ELLIAS

WORKS

*1737, Temple to Hymen and Pease, Nancy, France. 1739, Arch of Triumph, near the Porta San Galla, Florence. 1756, Alte Universität (later Akademie der Wissenschaften); 1750s, Michelerplatz (façades); Vienna.

BIBLIOGRAPHY

HAUTECOEUR, LOUIS 1950 *Première moitié du XVIIIᵉ siècle: Le style Louis XV.* Volume 3 in *Histoire de l'architecture classique en France.* Paris: Picard.

JAMES, JOHN

John James (1672?–1746) began his career as a carpenter after training under Matthew Bancks, master carpenter to the Crown. His lengthy career as a clerk of works and surveyor began at Greenwich in 1705 and was followed by appointments at Saint Paul's Cathedral and Westminster Abbey. He also served as a surveyor to the Commissioners for Building 50 New Churches. His considerable private practice shows him to have been an architect of competence, building, despite his admiration for INIGO JONES, in a sober version of the English baroque style learned from CHRISTOPHER WREN. He published English translations of the architectural treatises of ANDREA POZZO (1707) and CLAUDE PERRAULT (1708).

JOHN BOLD

WORKS

*1700–1704, Herriard Park, Hampshire, England. 1701–1713, Appuldurcombe House, Isle of Wight, England. *1710, Orleans House, Twickenham; 1713–1715, Saint Mary's Church, Twickenham; 1714–1716, Saint Lawrence's Church, Whitchurch; Middlesex, England. 1714–1733, Saint George's Church, Tiverton, Devon, England. 1717–1719, Park Hall, Crooms Hill, Greenwich, England. 1720?, Hursley Lodge, Hampshire, England. Saint George's Church, Hanover Square, London. (A)1722–1724, Iver Grove, Buckinghamshire, England. 1724, Warbrook House, Eversley, Hampshire, England. 1725?, Wricklemarsh, Blackheath, Kent, England. 1727–1733, Saint John's Church (with Nicholas Hawksmoor), Horsleydown; 1727–1733, Saint Luke's Church (with Hawksmoor), Old Street; London.

BIBLIOGRAPHY

DOWNES, KERRY 1966 *English Baroque Architecture.* London: Zwemmer.
LEES-MILNE, JAMES 1970 *English Country Houses: Baroque.* Feltham, England: Country Life.
WREN SOCIETY 1924–1943 20 vols.

JANÁK, PAVEL

Pavel Janák (1882–1956), born in Prague, Czechoslovakia, was a representative of Prague avantgarde cubism. He issued from the Wagnerian (see OTTO WAGNER) modern trend; soon, however, he felt the danger of uniformity in the rationalistic style. In 1911, he founded, together with other architects including JOSEF GOČÁR and JOSEF CHOCHOL, painters, and sculptors, a group of artists who prepared and published the Manifestoes of Cubism. Janák was the leading theoretician of this movement; he postulated a spiritual architecture characterized by a three-dimensional shaping of façades. The one-sided concentration of architects on façades resulted after World War I in a national academic style, the so-called rondo-cubism, where angular and pyramidal shapes were replaced by circular elements. Janák applied these principles in the Riunione Adriatica di Sicurta Palace in Prague and in the Pardubice Crematorium (both structures were built in 1921–1923). It was only after this period that Janák, under the strong influence of Dutch brickwork architecture, developed his functionalist style.

In 1936, he succeeded JOSEF PLEČNIK in his position as chief architect of Prague Castle, and the renovaton of historical monuments became another field of interest. Reconstructions of the Černínský Palace, the Theresian Wing of Prague Castle, the Ball Game House, the Riding Hall, and the Belvedere Palace, carried out from the late 1930s until his death, were his greatest achievements in this field of architectural activity.

VLADIMÍR ŠLAPETA

WORKS

1909–1911, Hlávkův Bridge, Prague. 1911–1912, House, Jičín, Czechoslovakia. 1914, Weir, Předměřice, Czechoslovakia. 1921–1923, Crematorium, Pardubice, Czechoslovakia. 1921–1923, Riunione Adriatica di Sicurta Palace; 1925–1926, Škoda Works Administration Building; Prague. 1927–1929, Mariánské Lázně Airport, Czechoslovakia. 1927–1933, Černín Palace (reconstruction and extension); 1927–1933, Juliš Hotel; 1932, Pavel Janák Residence, Baba Estate; 1948–1950, Prague Castle (reconstruction of Riding Hall); 1948–1952, Hvězda Palace (reconstruction); 1950, Prague Castle (reconstruction of Ball Game House); 1952–1955, Belvedere Palace (reconstruction), Hradčany District; 19?–1956, Prague Castle (reconstruction of Theresian Wing).

BIBLIOGRAPHY

BENEŠOVÁ, MARIE 1959 *Pavel Janák*. Prague: Nakladatelství československých výtvarných umělců.
JANÁK, PAVEL 1933 *Sto let obytného nájemného domu v Praze*. Prague: Styl.
KOŽELKA, KAREL 1942 "Pavel Janák a Skola." *Architektura* 4:90–93.
STARÝ, OLDŘICH 1942 "Architekt Prof. Pavel Janák." *Architektura* 4:81–85, 107–114.
STEFAN, OLDŘICH 1942 "Pavel Janák—Theoretik Architektury." *Architektura* 4:86–89, 118.
WAGNER, VÁCLAV 1942 "Pavel Janák a Staré Umění." *Architektura* 4:115–118.

JANSSEN, BERNARD

Bernard Janssen (Johnson) (16th–17th centuries) was a sculptor and surveyor, a son of the Amsterdam sculptor Gerrit Janssen (Gerard Johnson), who had settled in England in about 1567. The younger Janssen's only surviving documented work is an altar–tomb (c.1620) supporting NICHOLAS STONE's effigies of Sir Nicholas and Lady Bacon in Redgrave Church, Suffolk. Stone's greatnephew, Charles Stokes, however, told the celebrated antiquary George Vertue that Janssen was the surveyor of Northumberland House, London; Audley End, Essex; and "many other buildings." In spite of partial demolition, Audley End remains, in John Summerson's words, "the most powerful and impressive of Jacobean houses" (Summerson, 1953).

IAN CHILVERS

WORKS

c.1603–1616, Audley End (partially demolished), Essex, England. *c.1605–1609, Northumberland House, Strand, London.

BIBLIOGRAPHY

CLAPHAM, ALFRED W. and GODFREY, WALTER H. 1913 "Northumberland House, Shand." Pages 179–195 in *Some Famous Buildings and Their Story*. London: Technical Journals Ltd.
DRURY, P. J. 1980 "No Other Palace in the Kingdom Will Compare With It." *Architectural History* 23:1–39.
LONDON CITY COUNCIL 1937 "Northumberland House." Chapter 2 in *The Strand*. Volume 18 in *Survey of London*. London County Council.
SPIERS, WALTER LEWIS 1918–1919 "The Note-Book and Account-Book of Nicholas Stone." *Walpole Society* 7:52.
SUMMERSON, JOHN (1953)1977 *Architecture in Britain: 1530 to 1830*. 6th ed., rev. Harmondsworth, England: Penguin.
VERTUE, GEORGE 1931–1932 "Note-Books" (Volume 2). *Walpole Society* 20:49.
WALTER, R. J. B. ET AL. 1973 *Audley End, Essex*. London: H.M. Stationery Office.

JAPPELLI, GIUSEPPE

Giuseppe Jappelli (1783–1852) was the most eclectic Italian architect of the first half of the nineteenth century. His works borrow motifs from the entire range of historical styles. He is most commonly labeled a Romantic but his more severe works might give one cause to question this appellation. He was quite knowledgeable in the latest architectural works as a result of his frequent trav-

Jappelli.
Caffé Pedrocchi.
Padua, Italy.
1816–1831

els, most often to Belgium, England, France, and Germany, in addition to his native Italy.

Jappelli was born in Venice and received his architectural education at the Accademia Clementina in Bologna. In 1803, when he was twenty, he returned to Venice and entered the studio of GIOVANNI ANTONIO SELVA, who may have inspired Jappelli's eclecticism and encouraged his travels. For several years, Jappelli was involved in hydraulic engineering, and in 1816, he began work on what was to be his best-known and most important work: the Caffé Pedrocchi in Padua (1816–1831). Henry-Russell Hitchcock has called this building "the handsomest nineteenth century cafe in the world and about the finest Romantic Classical edifice in Italy." The Caffé is basically triangular in plan, with Doric porches on each of the corners. The main entrance is a square U-shape, with projections made by two of the porches. The center recessed area is a loggia made up of a giant Corinthian order over a rusticated ground story. This motif is continued with giant order pilasters on the street side and draws from the Palladian (see ANDREA PALLADIO) tradition of the Veneto, which served Jappelli well throughout his career.

The interior of the Caffé Pedrocchi is drawn from many sources. There is an Empire-style ballroom, a Gothic suite, and an Egyptian lodge room. Jappelli continued to be involved with the Caffé throughout his life. In 1837, after traveling to England, he built *Il Pedrocchino*, a wing added to the Caffé on the diagonal side of the triangular plan. This was constructed in an English Gothick style, in the manner of Strawberry Hill or Arbury Hall. He also constructed a Casino for the Caffé in 1842.

One of Jappelli's more extensive commissions was the Villa dei Conti Cittadella Vigodarsene (1817–?) near Saonara where he built the house, the chapel, and the gardens. The chapel betrays

Jappelli's interest in Palladio once again; its Pantheon-like cylinder base, low dome, and temple front recall the chapel at the Villa Barbaro at Maser. But its size has made more than one observer also recall Chiswick House, near London, one of the finest examples of English Palladianism. Whereas the chapel speaks of its architectural precedents, the villa itself is a lecture on spareness. Indeed, it looks almost unfinished in its pure rigorist forms. There are fifteen bays of rectangular fenestration and virtually no ornament of any kind. One might be tempted to see in this villa the logical (or perhaps illogical) simplification of another design by Palladio—the Villa Godi. Jappelli's structure lacks the plasticity and ornament of the Villa Godi but both houses have stark, light-colored walls with rectangular windows. Jappelli rejected two motifs used by Palladio: a recessed center section and arched openings. What makes the whole Saonara complex even more interesting is its setting. The buildings stand in a Romantic park from which Jappelli had cleared away long avenues to place an English meadow with clumps of trees, an artificial lake, and many minor Picturesque structures such as a Gothic cellar, grottoes, and temples, all in the tradition of the English garden architects HUMPHRY REPTON and CAPABILITY BROWN. Jappelli continued to receive many garden commissions throughout his career.

Jappelli's reputation was that of an architectural eclectic but his works also show him to be an architectural scholar. His Padua Meat Market (1821; now an art school) in a Greek Revival style, the neoclassical façade of the Theater at Cittadella (1828), his Moorish Greenhouse at the Villa Torlonia (1840s), and the Empire/rococo remodeling of Padua's Teatro Nuovo (1847), not to mention the Gothick Pedrocchino at the Caffé Pedrocchi, all display a sound knowledge of the styles Jappelli used, a quality absent in many of his contemporaries.

After Jappelli's death in Venice, he was praised by Pietro Estense Selvatico in *Scritti d'arte* for his eclecticism and especially for initiating the study of Lombard architecture and other medieval Italian styles, since the trend of the day was heavily dependent on Cinquecento imitation, something Jappelli seems to have successfully avoided.

JOHN H. WILSON

WORKS

1816–1831, Caffé Pedrocchi, Padua, Italy. 1817–?, Villa dei Conti Cittadella Vigodarsene (chapel and gardens), near Saonara, Italy. 1821, Meat Market, Padua, Italy. 1825, Hotel Reale Orologio (façade), San Lorenzo, Italy. 1827, Villa Gera, Conegliano, Italy. 1828, Theater (façade), Cittadella, Italy. 1829, Restaurant, Acqua Raineriana, Italy. 1837, Caffé Pedrocchi (Il Pedrocchino, wing), Padua, Italy. 1840s, Greenhouse, Villa Torlonia, Italy. 1842, Caffé Pedrocchi Casino; 1847, Teatro Nuovo (remodeling); Padua, Italy. 1848, Museo Atestino (gardens), Este, Italy.

BIBLIOGRAPHY

DAMERINI, GINO 1934 *Un Architetto veneziano dell'ottocento: Giuseppi Jappelli.* Venice.
FIOCCO, GIUSEPPE 1931 *Giuseppe Jappelli: Architetto.* Padua, Italy: Stedir.
LAVAGNINO, EMILIO (1956)1961 *L'arte moderne dai neoclassici ai contemporanei.* Turin, Italy: Unione tipografico-editrice torinese.
MANTIGLIA, ROBERTO C. 1955 "Giuseppe Jappelli architetto." *L'Architettura* 1, Nov.–Dec.:538–552.
MEEKS, CARROLL L. V. 1966 *Italian Architecture: 1750–1914.* New Haven: Yale University Press.
SELVATICO, PIETRO ESTENSE 1859 *Scritti d'arte.* Florence: Bianche.

JARDIN, NICOLAS

Nicolas Henri Jardin (1720–1799) was significant as an early neoclassical architect. Educated in Paris, he won the Prix de Rome in 1741 and lived in Rome from 1744 to 1748. In 1754, on the recommendation of his friend, the sculptor Jacques Saly, he was called to Denmark by Frederick V and appointed first professor at the Art Academy and, a year later, architect of the Frederickskirken. None of his designs for this was executed, but while he was in Denmark he worked on a number of buildings that had great influence on later Danish architecture. On his return to France in 1771, he was appointed professor at the Academy and worked in and around Paris.

DAVID CAST

WORKS

1764, Gule Palae; 1765–1769, Sölvgaden-Kaserne; Copenhagen. 1768, Schloss Marienlyst, Helsingör, Denmark. 1776–1786, Hospital, Lagny, France. 1783, Hôtel de Ville, Cambrai, France.

BIBLIOGRAPHY

HAUTECOEUR, LOUIS 1946 Volume 4 in *Histoire de l'architecture classique en France.* Paris: Picard.
HØLLER, VIGGO STEN 1973 *Amalienborg.* Copenhagen: Rhodas.
REDSLOB, EDWIN (editor) 1922 *Alt-Dänemark.* Munich: Delphin.

JAUSSELY, LEON

Born in Toulouse, France, Léon Jaussely (1876–1933) studied first in his home town with Curvale, then in Paris under Daumet, winning the Premier

Grand Prix de Rome in 1903. Jaussely achieved widespread recognition in the first two decades of the twentieth century for his urban planning designs, including one for Paris that gained him the Premier Prix.

PETER L. DONHAUSER

WORKS

1931, Musée des Colonies (with ALBERT LAPRADE), Vincennes, France. 1933, Post Office, Paris.

BIBLIOGRAPHY

HENRY, FRÉDÉRIC 1933 "Léon Jaussely." *L'Architecture* 46:37–40.
JAUSSELY, LÉON, and BUKIET, J. 1933 "Le Bureau de Poste de Paris." *L'Architecture* 46:41–44.
LAPRADE, ALBERT 1933 "Léon Jaussely (1857–1933)." *Urbanisme* 1933:102–103.

JAY, WILLIAM

William Jay (c.1793–1837), an English-born Regency architect, executed his major commissions in the United States. Jay trained and worked in London until 1817 when he traveled to America, where he designed several distinctive houses, combining late neoclassical clarity of form with Regency elegance. He returned to England in 1824 but departed for Mauritius in 1836 to assume the position of assistant chief architect.

BRIAN LUKACHER

WORKS

1815–1816, Albion Chapel, London. 1818, Richard Richardson House; 1819, William Scarborough House; Savannah, GA.

BIBLIOGRAPHY

GOODFELLOW, G. L. M. "William Jay and the Albion Chapel." *Journal of the Society of Architectural Historians.* 22:225–227.
NICHOLS, FREDERICK DOVETON 1976 *The Architecture of Georgia.* Savannah, Ga.: Beehive Press.

JEAN DE LOUP

See JEAN D'ORBAIS.

JEAN DES CHAMPS

Jean des Champs (13th century) was a French master mason of the Gothic period credited by one or more authors with the design of the cathedrals of Notre-Dame at Clermont (now Clermont-Ferrand), Saint-Etienne at Limoges, Saint-Just at

Narbonne, Notre-Dame at Rodez, and Saint-Etienne at Toulouse, as well as the Church of the Cordeliers at Clermont and the Church of Saint-Nazaire at Carcassonne. EUGÈNE EMMANUEL VIOLLET-LE-DUC first noted the similarities of plan and design of Clermont, Limoges, and Narbonne and attributed all three to Jean des Champs. The other attributions to him have been made by more recent authors, most especially Emile Mâle (1926).

Virtually nothing is known about the life or career of Jean des Champs, and he can be associated by documentation only with Clermont and Narbonne. It is unknown when he was born, or whether he was a native of Auvergne, as has been assumed. In 1287, Jean des Champs served as a witness to the signing of a capitular document at Clermont.

The association of Jean des Champs with Clermont is known only through two late transcriptions of a copy of his tomb inscription. In the seventeenth century, Canon Jean Dufraisse and, in the eighteenth century, Canon Pierre Audigrier each recorded an inscription made about 1400 when Jean des Champs's tomb was destroyed. Both report that Jean des Champs began the cathedral at Clermont in 1248 and that he was buried with his wife and children in front of the Portal of Saint Mary of Grace. However, since neither the original inscription nor the copy made around 1400 survives, the accuracy of the later transcriptions cannot be verified.

If Jean des Champs was master at Clermont as early as 1248 and was still alive in 1287, he was associated with the church for thirty-nine years at least, a tenure comparable to that of Bernard de Soissons who was master at Reims for thirty-five years. Robert Branner (1965) has proposed that although the intention to rebuild at Clermont may have been made as early as 1248 and some planning carried out at that time, actual construction began only in or after 1262 when Louis IX the Saint was at Clermont for the marriage of his son and heir, the future Philippe III le Hardi, to Isabella of Aragon. It is reported that at the time of his visit Louis gave the cathedral chapter funds to undertake construction of its cathedral.

As first master of Clermont, Jean des Champs was responsible for importing into southern France the Court or Rayonnant style from the region of Paris. He combined a number of northern features into his design concept: "cathedral plan" of such buildings as Amiens and Reims (but the nonprojecting transept of Paris), High Gothic three-story elevation, piers from Saint-Denis, gabled triforium openings of Amiens or Saint-Nicaise at Reims, and a clearstory design combining features found at Amiens, Le Mans, and the

Sainte-Chapelle in Paris. Jean des Champs was responsible for the chevet only at Clermont, and construction of that was completed by one Pierre des Champs, possibly a relative (son or nephew?), in the early fourteenth century.

The only building other than Clermont associated by documentation with Jean des Champs is Narbonne. An inventory of cathedral capitular acts made in 1680 records that on the fourth of the kalens of December (28 November), 1286, the chapter agreed to give Jean des Champs, principal master of the works of the church (*magister principalis operis ecclesie*), each day he was present in Narbonne, including feast days, three *solidi* for his gloves, 100 *solidi* for the maintenance of the house where he lived in Narbonne, and ten *livres* annually for his clothes. The text does not mention that the Jean des Champs (Johannes de Campis) in question was associated with or was from Clermont. However, it is clear from the wording of the text that Jean des Champs was not in permanent residence in Narbonne. It seems likely that the text anticipates that Jean des Champs would be "commuting" to Narbonne from somewhere (Narbonne is about 200 miles south of Clermont). In the second half of the thirteenth century, individual master masons did occasionally direct construction at two different sites simultaneously, for example, Godefroi de Varinfroi at the cathedrals of Evreux and Meaux.

The cornerstone at Narbonne was laid on 13 April 1272, but construction above ground came only in the 1280s. Narbonne is similar in plan and in design to Clermont and displays Jean des Champs's special Leitmotiv, an unglazed panel triforium linked with the clearstory, both contained between narrow vertical sections of wall erected beside the main vault responds. This particular design is found in early buildings of the Parisian Court style, for example, at Royaumont. Narbonne proves itself to be more modern than Clermont in the design of its main arcade piers and arches. At Clermont, the main arcade arches spring from capitals atop the main arcade piers. At Narbonne, they emerge directly from the piers themselves, a treatment dating from the 1270s (Saint-Germain at Auxerre, choir, 1277).

It is the similarity of cathedral plans with ambulatory and radiating chapels, three-story elevation of main arcade, triforium, and clearstory, and especially the combination of unglazed triforium linked with clearstory, found at Limoges, Rodez, Toulouse, and elsewhere in these southern French cathedrals and churches, that has led to the attribution of so many of them to Jean des Champs. Yet, it must be stressed that he can be associated only with Clermont and with Narbonne by documentation, and it is not assured beyond all doubt that the Clermont and the Narbonne Jean des Champs are the same individual, although this seems likely. The reference in an early fourteenth-century document at Rodez to a certain *Maestre dels Cams* cannot be taken seriously as specifying Jean des Champs.

Although Jean des Champs cannot be associated specifically with all the buildings traditionally attributed to him, this does not diminish his significance. His design at Clermont had great influence in the south of France. As was written of Narbonne in 1268 by Clement IV, a former archbishop of Narbonne, the building was an attempt "to imitate the noble and magnificently worked churches . . . which are constructed in the Kingdom of France." Jean des Champs's designs were not, as is sometimes said of them, either unimaginative or academically dependent on ideas a generation old. The significance of Jean des Champs has been summarized best by Robert Branner (1965): "Jean des Champs opened up the vast provinces of central and southern France to the Parisian mode [of architecture], and if some of the monuments where he and his immediate successors worked bear a strong resemblance to one another, that is more a proof . . . that personal styles changed slowly in the thirteenth century, than it is evidence of an academic mentality."

CARL F. BARNES, JR.

BIBLIOGRAPHY

BRANNER, ROBERT 1965 Pages 97–101, 141–142 in *St. Louis and the Court Style in Gothic Architecture.* London: Zwemmer. Concerns the redating of Clermont.

DAVIS, MICHAEL T. 1981 "The Choir of the Cathedral of Clermont-Ferrand: The Beginning of Construction and the Work of Jean des Champs." *Journal of the Society of Architectural Historians* 40:181–202. In this article, Davis dates the choir of Clermont-Ferrand to the years 1248–1280 and places Jean des Champs's tenure at the beginning of the work, rejecting the late dating proposed by Branner.

DU RANQUET, HENRI 1912 "Les Architectes de la cathédrale de Clermont." *Bulletin monumental* 76:70–124. Contains the Dufraisse and Audigrier Clermont transcriptions.

MÂLE, EMILE 1926 "L'Architecture gothique du midi de la France." *Revue des deux mondes* Series 7 31:827–857. Includes the maximum number of unsubstantiated attributions to Jean des Champs.

NARBONNE, LOUIS 1901 *La cathédrale de Saint-Just de Narbonne.* Narbonne, France: Caillard.

DU REY, RAYMOND 1954 "La Cathédrale de Narbonne." *Congrès Archéologique de France* 112:446–475. Includes the text by Clement IV.

STEIN, HENRI (1909)1929 Pages 95 and 99 in *Les Architectes des cathédrales gothiques.* Rev. ed. Paris: Laurens. Gives standard misattributions to Jean des Champs.

VIOLLET-LE-DUC, EUGÈNE 1854–1868 Volume 2, page 373 and volume 9, page 298 in *Dictionnaire raisonné de L'Architecture française du XIe au XVIe siècle.* Paris: Bance. Gives the first attribution of Limoges and Narbonne, in addition to Clermont, to Jean des Champs.

JEAN D'ORBAIS

Jean d'Orbais (active c.1210–c.1220), together with Jean (de) Loup, Gaucher de Reims, Bernard de Soissons, Robert de Coucy, and a certain Adam (de Reims) are believed to have been the architects responsible for design and construction of the Cathedral of Notre-Dame at Reims, France, between 1211 and c.1310. However, documentation for this is tenuous and controversial and has been subject to a variety of contradictory interpretations. Of the six, only Bernard de Soissons and Robert de Coucy are more than quasimythological figures whose existence is assured by noncontroversial sources. In no case can the architectural activities of any one of the six be precisely determined.

The names of the first four are known only on the basis of a labyrinth installed in the nave floor at Reims c.1290/1300 which honored them with images and inscriptions. However, this labyrinth was destroyed in 1779 and is known only by secondary accounts and depictions, especially the drawing by Jacques Cellier made between 1583 and 1587 (Paris, Bibliothèque nationale, Ms fr. 9152, fol. 77). The four are shown at the outer corners of the design in this order (clockwise from the upper right corner): Jean d'Orbais, Bernard de Soissons, Gaucher de Reims, and Jean (de) Loup.

Outside these images were inscriptions concerning each which were copied or paraphrased five times between 1645 and 1779 when they were destroyed. These transcriptions do not agree in detail, adding additional confusion to the question of the tenure and activities of each individual. No inscription identified the figure in the center of the labyrinth which has been subject to a considerable variety of interpretations.

In 1884 Louis Demaison first recognized that the architects shown in the labyrinth were those of the cathedral, and he proposed the following sequence and tenures: Jean d'Orbais, 1211–1231; Jean (de) Loup, 1231–1247; Gaucher de Reims, 1247–1255; and Bernard de Soissons, 1255–1290. Only the latter is supported by external documentation, for Bernard appeared in Reims tax rolls in 1282 and 1287. However, since Demaison's article appeared, various scholars have concluded every alternative possibility of sequence with the exception of Bernard de Soissons. For summary, see

Branner (1962) and Salet (1967).

Both Branner and Salet have insisted correctly that the information from the labyrinth alone is inadequate for determining either the sequence of the four or their tenures and activities. Both also claim convincingly that the labyrinth should not be the point of departure for study of Reims.

The history of these four architects is complicated by two other factors. It is possible that the unidentified figure in the center of the labyrinth is either a cleric or an architect. If a cleric, he could be the archbishop under whom the cathedral was begun (Aubri de Humbert) or the Archbishop of Reims when the labyrinth was installed c.1300 (either Pierre Barbette or Robert de Courtenai). If an architect, he could be Robert de Coucy who died in 1311 and to whom most writers attribute installation of the labyrinth. However, in 1642 a tomb was discovered outside the Reims choir with the inscription "HERE LIES MASTER ADAM WHO WAS MASTER OF THE WORK." Several scholars, most notably Emile Mâle, propose that this unidentified figure represents the first architect of the cathedral, possibly this Master Adam.

Making the best of the recorded labyrinth inscriptions and the attributes shown by Cellier, the following may be claimed: Jean d'Orbais, shown laying out a plan (according to Branner 1962) *may* have been the first architect of the cathedral and *may* have designed the choir plan; Jean (de) Loup, shown with a mason's square, was master for sixteen years and worked on portals, possibly those of the north arm of the transept; Gaucher de Reims (unidentifiable attribute), for an indefinite period worked on portals and some vaults; Bernard de Soissons, shown inscribing a large circle, was responsible for five vaults in the nave and the western rose during a long tenure of thirty-five years. Of these four, only the work and approximate dates for Bernard de Soissons are reasonably confirmed.

In sum, Jean d'Orbais, Jean (de) Loup, Gaucher de Reims, and Bernard de Soissons, plus Robert de Coucy and possibly the enigmatic Master Adam, collectively created, over a century, one of the most splendid and uniform of the great High Gothic cathedrals of France. But it is unlikely that the specific contributions of each will ever be determined beyond all doubt.

CARL F. BARNES, JR.

BIBLIOGRAPHY

BRANNER, ROBERT 1961 "Jean d'Orbais and the Cathedral of Reims." *Art Bulletin* 43:131–133.
BRANNER, ROBERT 1962 "The Labyrinth of Reims Cathedral." *Journal of the Society of Architectural Historians* 21:18–25.
DEMAISON, LOUIS 1948 "Les architectes de la cathédrale de Reims." *Bulletin archéologique* 1884:1–40.
MÂLE, EMILE 1921 "La Cathédrale de Reims." *Gazette des Beaux-Arts.* 5th series 3:73–88.
SALET, FRANÇOIS 1967 "Chronologie de la cathédrale [de Reims]." *Bulletin monumental* 125:347–394.
STODDARD, WHITNEY S. 1966 Pages 204–205 in *Monastery and Cathedral in France.* Middletown, Conn.: Wesleyan University Press.

JEANNERET, PIERRE

Arnold André Pierre Jeanneret-Gris (1896–1967) was born in Geneva and grew up there, but during the course of his architectural career spent much of his time away from Switzerland. After attending the Ecole des Beaux-Arts in Geneva, he was in the military and completed architectural training before leaving for Paris to work in the firm of Auguste and Gustave Perret (see AUGUSTE PERRET), an efficacious prelude to his long and fruitful collaboration with his distant relative, LE CORBUSIER, the exact nature, extent, and impact of which remains to be assessed.

During their first period of joint effort (1921–1940), Jeanneret and Le Corbusier produced works of architecture, urbanism, and furniture design, many of which were the classic creations of the Modern movement, such as the Pavillon de L'Esprit Nouveau (1925), their houses for the Weissenhof Siedlung in Stuttgart (1927), their project for the Palace of the Society of Nations in Geneva (1927), the Villa Savoye at Poissy (1928–1931), and the apartment house Clarté in Geneva (1930–1932).

Although the atelier debates of the two men have become legendary, most of the theoretical and polemic writings published at this time were signed by Le Corbusier; many significant texts, however, were signed jointly, such as their succinct formulation of "The Five Points to a New Architecture," the basic statement of their design philosophy. Design work was usually credited to both men, and together they participated in events significant in the ideological development of the period, for example, the founding of the Congrès Internationaux d'Architecture Moderne (CIAM) in 1928 and its subsequent meetings, during which Jeanneret was known to let his voice be heard. Three French patents were held jointly with Le Corbusier: the framework for a horizontal sliding window (1926); a *chaise longue* (1929; with CHARLOTTE PERRIAND); and a sanitary installation (1937; with Charlotte Perriand). Throughout this early period, even Le Corbusier acknowledged that Jeanneret's interests in "Taylorization" and rationalization were even stronger than his own.

World War II led the two architects in separate directions. After a short period in Ozon in the Pyrénées in 1940, Jeanneret went to Grenoble to work with the Bureau Central de Construction founded that autumn by Georges Blanchon. This organization was concerned with the rapid construction of housing and other facilities for firms displaced to the southern free zone of France because of the war. During these war years, Jeanneret's architectural preoccupations were with prefabrication, work in light metals and wood, demountable construction techniques, transportable housing with fold-out elements, and central-drainage mushroom-roof units subject to combination for multipurpose use. When the war ended in France in 1944, Jeanneret set up his own architectural office in Paris; most of the work, however, remained in the project stage. One such project, for a 200-unit apartment house (1946–1947), bore resemblance to Le Corbusier's *unités d'habitation* in that the apartment units ran the full depth of the block; they had the additional refinement, however, of being V-shaped, which would have provided a significant difference in the penetration of the sun in the course of the day. In the late 1940s, at the suggestion of JOSEP LLUIS SERT, Jeanneret was called to New York by the firm of Hans and Florence Knoll to design furniture; he spent almost a year in New York and "chair 92" went into production, joining those of other designers such as Isamu Noguchi and EERO SAARINEN.

Collaboration with Le Corbusier began anew in 1951, when Jeanneret joined the Chandigarh team which also included Maxwell Fry and JANE DREW. After his arrival in India in March 1951, it was not long before his practicality helped him to adapt his work to difficult conditions and construction methods, and his successes gave him renewed confidence in his own accomplishments; he remained after his colleagues left in 1954.

At Chandigarh, he served as the director of the Capital Project Office, and among his many responsibilities was the supervision of the construction of Le Corbusier's buildings. He designed a wide range of building types for the city: hospitals, the Junior Secondary School for Boys in Sector 22, a primary school in Sector 15, shops and offices on V4 (with B. P. Mathur and S. D. Sharma), and the State Library and Town Hall (with M. N. Sharma). His inventiveness was particularly challenged in the designing of many types of dwellings, from Type 14, the most modest, to Type 1, for the Chief Minister; he also did the MLA flats (for members of the legislative assembly), the Deputy Ministers' Houses in Sector 7 (with Mrs. U. E. Chowdury, 1962), the Circuit House, the Governor's Palace, and a private house for Nayantara Sahgal. Jeanneret was appointed chief architect and town planning adviser to the government of Punjab, and was in charge of the design and construction of the University of Punjab at Chandigarh. He also did architectural and urbanistic work in other areas, including Pandoh, Sundernager, Slapper, Ahmedabad and two new townships—the Beas-Sutlej link and Talwara.

While in India, Jeanneret's interests were varied. He designed lightweight furniture made from simple materials, promoted architectural education (especially at the School of Architecture at Chandigarh where he taught on occasion), and significantly influenced the development of modern architecture in remote northern areas. Concerned as he was with designing for the greatest common good, he was constantly searching for new solutions to the problems of low-cost housing and the control of sun, water, wind, and heat with natural rather than mechanical means, through the use of screens, shade-giving elements, wind-catchers, sun-breakers, and other climate control devices. He popularized the inventive use of unstuccoed brick (the least expensive local building material) for grillwork as well as for load-bearing walls. In his work, rough stone walls were often contrasted with surfaces of smooth texture, and reinforced concrete was reserved for special structural features and for buildings of larger size. His love for beautiful forms that were the result of natural structuring processes led him to search for and photograph examples in the Indian landscape on rambles reminiscent of those of the mid 1930s in France in the company of Charlotte Perriand and Fernand Léger.

Outstanding buildings from this period in India include the Bhawan dedicated to the memory of Mahatma Gandhi (c.1960), placed in a reflecting pool where the play of changing light on the water echoes the animated forms of its profile, and the Administration Building of Punjab University (1961). Although the structural forms of the latter are somewhat reminiscent of work from the late 1920s—such as the Villa Baizeau at Carthage, Tunisia (1928)—with its forms set back from the supporting pilots (that is, in both cases, a design solution suitable for buildings in hot climates), in the Indian design, there is an overriding symmetry of the main façade and a boldness in the cantilevered elements.

Jeanneret returned to Europe for eye treatments in 1964, but made another trip to India for work at Talwara. Due to ill health, he left India for good in August 1965.

Even though Jeanneret could claim a very successful independent career in India—achieving more in a short time span than many architects in a lifetime—he never forgot his long years as a master figure in the atelier at 35 rue de Sèvres in Paris. Respected for his civility, his good sense, and his facility with and dedication to technical matters, Jeanneret maintained a modest and flexible attitude toward the often conflicting views of Le Corbusier. In 1965, Jeanneret still felt that no other designer had embraced the spirit and philosophy of Le Corbusier's work as much as he when he declared, "it seems surprising to me that despite the fundamental differences between the two of us (he, order and organization, me, ideas that were always a little anarchical), I am the closest [architect] to him in terms of plan of action." Le Corbusier may have viewed the relationship with a little less tolerance, when he said, "I am the sea, he [P. J.] the mountain, and anyone knows that the two do not meet" (1965, p. 110). But Le Corbusier also wrote: "My architectural work exists only because team-work existed between Pierre Jeanneret and me. . . . Pierre Jeanneret is without doubt the person who has been closest to my work. That is important. What is more important is that he was and still is my friend. Life without friends of that caliber would not be possible" (Petit, 1967, p. 17).

Jeanneret was greatly admired by his Indian collaborators for his significant contribution to contemporary design in India. It is only fitting that his ashes were transported there in 1970 by his niece Jacqueline Vauthier Jeanneret. In the presence of the governor of Punjab, his friends, close associates, and the citizens of the city he helped to create, his remains were scattered in the Lake of Chandigarh.

Mary Patricia May Sekler

WORKS

For works done with Le Corbusier, see entry under Le Corbusier.

1940, Buildings (primarily housing, from light-weight, prefabricated elements; with Charlotte Perriand, Jean Prouvé, Georges Blanchon, and André Masson), Issoire, France. 1941–1944, Housing, offices, meeting halls (prefabricated, primarily in metal frame with wood in-fill, later all wood; with the B.C.C. at Grenoble and Jean Prouvé; for Pechiney- Aluminum Français), Saint-Auban, Gardanne, Salindres, Brignoles, Lunel, Bedarieux, France. 1948–1949, Jean Pluet House (with Georges Blanchon), Île de Bréhat, France. 1949–1950, Technical School (with Dominique Escorsa and the Atelier Jean Prouvé), Béziers, France. 1960, The Gandhi Bhawan (with B. P. Mathur), Chandigarh, India. 1961, The Library, the Administration Building; Punjab University, Chandigarh, India.

BIBLIOGRAPHY

For additional material on Pierre Jeanneret, see the bibliography under Le Corbusier.

Barbey, Gilles 1968 "Pierre Jeanneret." *Werk* 55, no. 6:390–396.

Chowdhury, U. E. 1964 "Pierre Jeanneret of Chandigarh." *Design* 8, no. 9:17–24.

Chowdhury, U. E. 1964 "Recent Work of Pierre Jeanneret." *Progressive Architecture* 45, no. 2:148–153.

"French System of Prefabrication. Architect: P. Jeanneret. Engineer: Jean Prouvé." 1946 *Progressive Architecture* 103:487–491.

"Hommage à Pierre Jeanneret." 1968 *Werk* 55, no. 6:377–389.

Jeanneret, Pierre 1945 "Maison Transportable." *L'Architecture d'aujourd'hui* 16, no. 2:62–63, 74.

Jeanneret, Pierre 1957 "Chandigarh: Symposium, 1." *Mārg* 10, no. 2:48–49.

Jeanneret, Pierre 1961 "Aesthetic: Reflections on Beauty of Line, Shape and Form." *Mārg* 15, no. 1:56–57.

Jeanneret, Pierre and Hervé, Lucien 1956 "La Maison de Pierre Jeanneret à Chandigarh." *Aujourd'hui art et architecture* 2, no. 9:62–67.

Jeanneret, Pierre and Le Corbusier 1927 "Fünf Punkte zu einer neuen Architektur." Pages 5–7 in Alfred Roth, *Zwei Wohnhäuser von Le Corbusier und Pierre Jeanneret*. Stuttgart, Germany: Wedekind.

Jeanneret, Pierre and Le Corbusier 1930 1930 "Le Problème de la 'Maison Minimum'." Pages 5–15 in 3d Series, *Le Corbusier et Pierre Jeanneret*. Paris: Morancé.

Jeanneret, Pierre and Le Corbusier 1932 "Plan d'Aménagement de la Ville d'Alger, 1931–1932." Pages 5–9 in 5th Series, *Le Corbusier et Pierre Jeanneret*. Paris: Morancé.

Jeanneret, Pierre and Le Corbusier 1933 "L'immeuble 'Clarté' à Geneve." *L'Art en Suisse* 4–5:special issue.

Jeanneret, Pierre and Le Corbusier 1938 *L'Ilot Insalubre No. 6*. Paris: Tournon.

Petit, Jean 1967 *Le Corbusier Parle*. Geneva: Forces-Vives.

"Pierre Jeanneret, 1896–1967." 1968 *L'Architecture d'aujourd'hui* 39, no. 136:v–vii, xii.

"Talwara Town, Punjab." 1963 *Design* 7, no. 6:21–24.

JEANNERET-GRIS, CHARLES-EDOUARD

See Le Corbusier.

JEFFERSON, THOMAS

Thomas Jefferson (1743–1826), the third president of the United States, was the greatest native born architect of his time in America. His most distinguished contemporary, Benjamin H. Latrobe, was born and trained in England and did not come to the New World until 1796. Jefferson designed, built, and in some cases supervised the construc-

tion of at least seven houses, at least two documented courthouses, one state capitol, a church, and the greatest complex of buildings for any American university. Then there are the designs which were never executed. These include a domed Governor's House for Virginia, an octagonal church, a prison, and an extension for the College of William and Mary. One of his final designs was for his own tombstone, the original of which is now at the University of Missouri; a copy marks the grave at Monticello.

In order to produce this large body of work, Jefferson made many supportive sketches—both preliminary and development drawings. He retained a copy of each of his 460 architectural drawings, the largest oeuvre by far of any American architect up to that time with the exception of Latrobe. The latter was, of course, primarily an architect and an ingenious engineer, whereas Jefferson's avocation as an architect was incidental to his primary occupations as lawyer, farmer, diplomat, revolutionary statesman, and educator.

Jefferson was a self-taught architect. Having become interested in the field when he was a student at the College of William and Mary, he purchased the first of what was to be a great collection of architectural pattern books, probably GIACOMO LEONI's *Quatri Libri* of ANDREA PALLADIO. There were no architectural schools in the United States at that time and Jefferson had one of the finest architectural libraries in the country, including five editions of Palladio, among them the French portable edition published in 1766. As this was the

small octavo edition, he could carry it in his pocket on inspection trips.

In 1767, Jefferson wrote the word "Hermitage" in his garden book. Then he crossed it out and wrote "Monticello." From that day on, Monticello was indeed his home where all his wishes ended and where he hoped his life would end. He began grading his little mountain top the following year and commenced actual work on the house in 1768. For forty years Monticello was used as Jefferson's building laboratory. As he said, "building up and pulling down are the delights of my life," and there was nothing he enjoyed more. Monticello is the first American house to have complete working drawings in the modern sense.

In 1782, the first house was essentially complete. Jefferson had used porticoes and classical cornices from different Roman buildings in each room. The Marquis de Chastellux remarked that his host was the first American who had used the fine arts to shelter himself. This house as planned was essentially a Palladian layout with washroom, carriage room, stable for horses, tack room, ice house (circular in form like most of the Virginia ice houses), and a kitchen with wine, beer, and rum cellars and a cook's room all in the basement. An underground passage connected these service buildings together in a U-shaped arrangement and was patterned after the service buildings at Palladio's great villas in the Veneto. But as always, Jefferson had one eye on the aesthetic and one eye on the functional; he set the service buildings into the side of the hill so they would not interrupt his

Jefferson.
Monticello.
Near Charlottesville,
Virginia.
1768–1782 (remodeled
1796–1809)

splendid 360-degree view from the top of Monticello mountain. This version of the house was the bachelor's pavilion, having only a parlor, dining room, and bedroom, with a stair from the front hall to the large library and two small bedrooms on the second floor. Jefferson designed for it a pair of two-story porticoes, with a Doric order under the Ionic, patterned after the example by Palladio at the Villa Pisani at Montagnana.

During the construction of Monticello while wartime governor of Virginia, Jefferson also found time to redesign and add to several buildings in Williamsburg. He planned to enlarge the College of William and Mary by completing the courtyard, adding dormitories and tutors' rooms to approximately double the amount of space. Jefferson's own drawing for this addition survives and he got as far as the foundations: some years ago the land was excavated and it was discovered that the foundations had been put down. Apparently, the Revolution interrupted the work, which was then never resumed.

If Jefferson had had his way, the old Palace in Williamsburg would have been a neoclassical templeform building with two porticoes, one at the front and one at the rear. In that case it would have been the first templeform building in Virginia, preceding the State Capitol by Jefferson which was constructed after 1785. Also, at that time, Jefferson planned an octagonal chapel for Williamsburg, which was to have been surrounded by a peristyle of columns with a lectern or pulpit in the center of the room. This very interesting proposal was never realized.

In 1784, Jefferson was to receive one of the most fortunate stimulants to his architectural career in his appointment as the second American Minister to Paris. This was the time when all of Europe was going to Paris to study the arts—the so-called First School of Paris. While Jefferson was busy with his official duties, he also found time to study carefully the work of the avant-garde architects, inviting them to dinner at the Embassy to discuss theories and their latest projects. This training was to complete his architectural education; not only did it broaden Jefferson's vision with the greatness of the French urban building tradition, but it also brought him in touch with the younger thinkers.

Jefferson rented one of the most beautiful houses in Paris for his embassy: the Hôtel de Langeac, located on the Champs Elysées at the Ronde Pointe. Constructed by the famous neoclassical architect JEAN FRANÇOIS CHALGRIN, it was a revelation to Jefferson, containing long French windows, panels of neoclassical sculptural decoration, a balustrade to hide the roof, and an interior rich with the play of cylindrical and oval rooms. In comparison with the casual quality of life in America, where there was little or no privacy, each bedroom in the embassy had its own private stair, dressing room, study, and flush toilet. Nonetheless, as in every other house where he lived, Jefferson redesigned it. The garden stretched along the Rue de Berri and was to have been a miniature *jardin des Anglais* after the latest style with tiny vistas, eye-catching temples and outbuildings, and wandering, irregular paths.

Jefferson persuaded John Adams, then America's first envoy to the court of Saint James, to go on a two-week English garden tour with him in 1786. They took with them Thomas Whateley's book on English gardens, and both wrote in their diaries their comments upon the gardens, generally consisting of ideas as to whether or not Whateley's comments were correct. The informal *jardins des Anglais,* in contrast to the strict formality of those of ANDRÉ LE NOSTRE and the French garden designers, were the rage thoughout Europe, and they were particularly fashionable in France at this time. On this tour, Jefferson and Adams visited Blenheim Palace (before the changes of CAPABILITY BROWN), Stowe, Hagley (over the mantel of which there is still a portrait of Alexander Pope, the literary mentor of the movement whose garden at Twickenham was a small essay in the style), Wotton, Esher, Clermont, Chiswick (LORD BURLINGTON's pavilion and great house), and the Leasowes.

Jefferson used every spare moment to study the new buildings while in Paris. He admired the work of CLAUDE NICOLAS LEDOUX, one of whose barrières was diagonally across the street from the embassy. Jefferson's great friend, the Countess de Tesse, had built Chaville on the outskirts of Paris as designed by ETIENNE LOUIS BOULLÉE; it was here that he first saw the new skylights which were to interest him so much when he returned to America. The lightweight wooden dome of JACQUES MOLINOS and Etienne Le Grand on the Halles au Blé in Paris fascinated him. He also knew the Baron Grimm, the leading art critic of Paris and an architectural commentator.

Jefferson was fortunate as well in arriving in Paris at the time the architect PIERRE ROUSSEAU was beginning work on the beautiful Hôtel de Salm. It was this building that Jefferson described when he remarked about "loving a building so much that he gazed at it long hours like a lover at his mistress." Many of the new ideals were worked out in this building. The main portion of the house was one story, facing the Seine, with its central room capped by a dome, a concept which Jefferson was to use at Monticello. The most fashionable Parisian houses were Roman in concept by virtue of this single main story with mezzanine. The Hôtel de Salm also had the long French windows with circular niches for busts above them. Being a practical American, Jefferson realized the difficulty of using busts in the new American buildings and so achieved a similar effect by substituting circular or octagonal windows above long French windows or in the drum of the dome. Other features Jefferson admired were the entrance courtyard surrounded by a colonnade and, as a final tribute to antique Rome, the gates themselves, which were a Roman triumphal arch.

One of the other houses and gardens which Jefferson particularly admired was Le Désert de Retz. This had been built in the form of a ruined column with trees growing upon the roof. There were three main floors consisting of oval rooms set around a circular staircase. One of the most famous gardens of Paris surrounded the house, containing everything from a grotto to classical temples and even a wooden Chinese temple. Jefferson and Maria Cosway visited it and commented in letters to each other about the beauties of the interior of Le Désert. The oval rooms inscribed within the cylinder of the house were to provide the inspiration of the oval rooms at the Rotunda when Jefferson designed the University of Virginia.

JACQUES-GERMAIN SOUFFLOT's Pantheon in Paris, built in the form of a cross and boasting a graceful dome on a colonnade, was another building which Jefferson admired. He sketched the Pantheon and mentioned in his notes that it might prove the prototype for one of the new public buildings in Washington; however, this did not come to pass.

Jefferson watched with great interest the modernization program of the city. The medieval bridges which had stretched across the Seine were pulled down, filled though they were with houses and shops. It is also characteristic of Jefferson's architectural thinking that the great formal garden at Versailles, which had been designed and developed as a hunting garden, would provide inspiration for the design of the new capital city in the District of Columbia—from it he drew the ovals and diagonal streets.

Upon his return to America, Jefferson brought some two dozen engraved plans of European cities, many of which he had visited. He recommended to two students that, in order to understand a city, a visitor should first climb the highest tower to get a good idea of the general layout, and then proceed from there to visit the various sections of the town. While PIERRE CHARLES L'ENFANT was designing the District of Columbia, Jefferson also made suggestions and even did several drawings.

These included his version of the mall with attendant buildings and one showing Pennsylvania Avenue as a triple roadway with sidewalks and plantings of Lombardy poplar.

While still in Paris, Jefferson was responsible for another important building—the Virginia State Capitol (1785–1799). He had presented a bill to the House of Delegates in 1776 for the design of the new Capitol in Richmond. It was a revolutionary bill which, for the first time, provided separate buildings to house the various branches of the government. In 1780, it was determined that the new public buildings should be erected and Jefferson was appointed head of a committee for this purpose. He displayed his interest in town planning by drawing up plans for enlarging Richmond with some four hundred new lots on a grid plan with four lots to a block. As he said later:

I have supposed it practicable to prevent its generation [the generation of yellow fever] by building our cities on a more open plan. Take, for instance, the chequerboard for a plan. Let the black squares only be building squares, and the white ones be left open, in turf and trees. Every square of houses will be surrounded by four open squares, and every house will front an open square. . . . (Jefferson to C. F. C. Volney, February 8, 1805)

He also made drawings for the Halls of Justice and then began his studies for the Capitol in Richmond. These show a templeform building and, except for the studies for remodeling the Palace in Williamsburg, they indicate that he was the first in the Western world to reintroduce the templeform for public buildings. His design for the Richmond Capitol dates some twenty-two years before the Madeleine was begun in Paris in 1807. Before going to Europe and visiting the Maison Carrée in Nîmes, before projecting templeform buildings, Jefferson explained in his autobiography that he believed he would improve the taste of his countrymen by "introducing into the State an example of architecture in the classic style of antiquity."

Jefferson.
Virginia State Capitol.
Richmond.
1785–1799

When the commissioners finally wrote to him requesting a design for the Capitol, Jefferson engaged JACQUES-LOUIS CLÉRISSEAU, the great French archaeologist–architect, to assist him with the model. The only French touches in the final design were the panels between the windows, enriched with swags.

Another advanced idea in which Jefferson was interested at this time was a new system for rehabilitating criminals. Believing that solitary confinement was the best course to pursue so that older criminals would not corrupt younger ones, Jefferson described in his autobiography what he had in mind:

With respect to the plan of a Prison . . . I have heard of a benevolent society, in England, which had been indulged by the government in an experiment of the effect of labor, in *solitary confinement,* on some of their criminals; which experiment had succeeded beyond expectation. The same idea had been suggested in France, and an Architect of Lyons [P.-G. Bugniet] had proposed a plan of a well-contrived edifice on the principle of solitary confinement. I presented a copy, and as it was too large for our purposes, I drew one on a scale less extensive. . . . Its principle . . . but not its exact form, was adopted by Latrobe in carrying the plan into execution.

When Jefferson returned to America in 1789, he was named secretary of state. In the years that followed, he used every possible opportunity to see that the buildings under construction in the future capital city of Washington were of classical architecture. There is a sketch plan, now in the Library of Congress, which shows his designs for the streets, the Capitol, the President's House, the offices, and public walks. He planned the whole community, and the design of the buildings was to be controlled by regulations and by land acquisition. He indicated the sites of the President's House and the Capitol, and it is of interest that these are now located in roughly the same relationship as that in which he planned them. Lot sizes were to be fifty feet by the diagonal of the square but he did not propose setbacks, believing that a dull monotonous uniformity would be the result. He had many good reasons for uniform building heights, such as that they kept down the price of land, improved the houses, made the streets light and airy, and reduced the difficulty of fighting fires.

Jefferson entered the design competition for the President's House under an assumed name, Abraham Faw. His design was based on the Villa Rotonda, by Palladio, near Vicenza, Italy, which he had earlier suggested for the Governor's House in Richmond. At that time he had added two wings which were inharmonious with the strongly unified original design; the plans for the President's House eliminated this flaw. He had very strong ideas as to the designs of the new buildings in Washington. As he wrote to L'Enfant, he preferred for the Capitol "the adaption of some model of antiquity which had the approbation of thousands of years . . . such are the Galerie du Louvre [CLAUDE PERRAULT's great colonnade], the Gardes meubles, and the two fronts of the Hôtel de Salm."

Jefferson's love of the French architecture being erected during the reign of Louis XVI led him to see his earlier version of Monticello, with its pair of two-story porticoes as very old-fashioned. He determined to make Monticello look like an elegant Parisian pavilion. In 1793, he began plans for the enlargement and alterations. He described the effect after which he was striving:

In Paris particularly all the new and good houses are of a single story. That is of the height of 16 or 18 f. generally, and the whole of it given to rooms of entertainment, but in the parts where there are bedrooms they have two tiers of them of from 8 to 10 f. high each, with a small private staircase. By these means great stairways are avoided, which are expensive and occupy a space which would make a good room in every story. (Jefferson to John Brown of "Liberty Hall," Frankfort, Kentucky, April 5, 1797).

This, then, is his answer to the question often asked as to why he made his stairs small and hidden. He also added skylights and "the alcove bedrooms to which I am much attached." Jefferson was thus the father of the American one-story house.

The new Monticello was to be doubled in width with a transverse hall running down the middle of the new house with four bedrooms on the entrance side. At either end of this hall were to be the small stairs. The portico on the entrance side was moved out to take care of his entrance hall, or his "museum," as he called it. This new plan offered great privacy, as Jefferson was a very private person and had several times been appalled at the customs of the day whereby an inn would provide only part of a bed and the traveler retired with his clothes on, not knowing who might join him during the night!

Jefferson's own suite consisted of his bedroom with a closet above an alcove bed open on both sides for ventilation and a private toilet whose pot could be emptied by means of pulleys though an outside tunnel so that the waste did not have to go through the house, his greenhouse where he raised his beloved plants and seeds, a dressing room, and a study with most of his books.

The cornices for the rooms of Monticello were taken from Jombert's 1766 edition of Errard and de Chambray's *Parallèle de l'architecture antique et moderne.* The plates, in Jefferson's copy marked in his hand, are now with the remainder of his library at the Library of Congress, to which his books were sold in 1815. The dome on the Hôtel de Salm which had so impressed Jefferson found its way onto Monticello, with the room beneath it being referred to as his "sky room." According to family tradition, this was built for a billiard room but was never used as such.

On the front of the house, Jefferson tied his windows together with single frames so as to create an apparent single story—he added a single pivoting sash for the mezzanine bedrooms above the first-floor double-hung window. He also removed the two-story portico—if indeed it had ever been completed—and on the garden front he adapted a garden temple. This temple originally appeared in JAMES GIBBS's *Book of Architecture* (1728), and was adapted in ROBERT MORRIS's book, *Select Architecture* (1757), from which Jefferson drew the design, adapting it in his turn.

Such was Jefferson's fame that many of his friends asked for plans or for assistance in remodeling their existing homes. Although many houses around Charlottesville have been credited to Jefferson, he designed only seven, including Monticello. One of the earliest was Edgemont, completed by 1797, a beautiful one-story wooden house with a typical Jefferson plan—transverse hall, an octagonal drawing room, and four porticoes. For his daughter Martha he began a one-story house at Edgehill before 1798. This was later moved and a two-story house of brick was erected on the site in 1828.

For his friend George Divers, he designed an addition to Farmington (1802–1808), near Charlottesville. An old plantation of the typical townhouse type, with a sidehall and pair of drawing rooms, Farmington had been built in such a way that the owner could add on to it. As Jefferson designed it, there was a two-story octagonal drawing room with a one-story dining room and a small mezzanine bedroom above, very much after Jefferson's typical exteriors. It had a two-story Doric portico, circular stone windows imported from Portland, England, and a Chinese trellised balcony on the roof. Jefferson returned home from a trip and found that the capitals were too small for the columns. He stopped work and the house was not finished until about 1850 when the black marble mantles, the front door, and the connecting wings to the servants' quarters were added.

Bremo (1818–1820), described by TALBOT HAMLIN as "the most Jeffersonian house not by Jefferson," contains the name James Neilson in the cornerstone. Neilson was one of the two expert housewrights whom Jefferson imported from Philadelphia and whom he trained so thoroughly that the houses they built have every appearance of being done by Jefferson's own hand. The exteriors with the four porticoes, the low-pitched roof with wooden balustrade, the use of Jefferson's favorite Tuscan order as well as his preferred siting—with the house on the edge of a hill with a one-story front and a two-story back, all betray the master's guidance. Jefferson had told his friend General John Hartwell Cocke, builder of Bremo, that he could not design it for him because he "did not have [his] books with [him] at the time" when Cocke asked him to draw the plans.

Bremo has a typical Jefferson plan, even including alcove beds in the bedrooms, mezzanine bedrooms on the front of the house, while the two great bedrooms and the drawing room are two-story rooms on the riverfront of the house. The two great bedrooms are cubes approximately 30 by 30 by 30 feet, with a drawing room between them that has a small portico protected by fixed jalousies. In the drawing room are a handsome marble mantle and a marbleized baseboard. One of the most charming things about Bremo is that it has much of its original furniture, including a few fine pieces from Monticello. On the ground floor are the marble-floored dining room, a large pantry, and the library, which has some of its bookshelves covered with tambours.

Bremo boasts a superb collection of outbuildings, among them the only barn in American architecture that is enriched with a portico. Built of stone, the barn contains in the belfry of its cupola a bell that was given to General Cocke by Lafayette on his last tour of America. There was also an experimental house on the grounds that Jefferson and Cocke were both interested in, built of pisé. Made of puddled mud bound with straw, the house survived very well because, according to the old English saying of mud houses, "its head and its feet were protected and kept dry" (that is, it had a good roof with a good overhang). Additionally, there is an outside kitchen and schoolroom, with furnishings largely intact, built by Cocke, for the instruction of his slaves so that when freed, they would be able to function in society. A superb Greek Revival garden gazebo with curving steps opens onto a reflecting pool. At the end of the pool is General Cocke's great cast-iron pitcher which was originally located at the spring near the canal so that travelers could refresh themselves from the cold springwater which gathered in the pitcher. Cocke was also responsible for the design of the Palmyra Courthouse, which sits on its own Acropolis, and for Temperance Hall at the University of Virginia, which was to encourage the students to drink water instead of spirits. Neither the pitcher for springwater nor Temperance Hall had any success whatsoever.

For more than thirty years, whenever he was free of his official duties, Jefferson was constantly preoccupied with the repair and enlargement of his beloved Monticello. By 1792, he was ordering materials, but the work went so slowly that in 1798 he brought a skilled housewright from Philadelphia, James Dinsmore. Another skilled workman, James Oldham, was employed in 1801, and work began to proceed at a faster pace. In 1804, Jefferson brought in James Neilson. All of these men also worked on the houses Jefferson designed or for which he made suggestions, and they were essential in the building of the University of Virginia.

Before Monticello was finished, Jefferson proposed a garden in the landscape style. The top of the mountain was to be laid out with lawns, orchards, and groves of trees arranged to frame the views from the roundabouts or the roads that spiraled down the mountain. There was to be a labyrinth of broom with dells and glens. If he had had the money, he would have built a Gothic garden gazebo, a model of the Pantheon, a Chinese pavilion, a model of the Maison Carrée, and also of the Monument of Lysikrates. Jefferson did build the groves, the orchards, and the roundabouts, and even the most simplified garden reflects his great interest in horticulture and garden design.

Monticello was essentially completed in 1809, although the railings were not finished until much later. As it stands, it is a tribute to Jefferson's design ability and to his love of the French pavilion style. It is, above all, one of the most personal houses in the world; in it, one can read Jefferson's lifestyle, as well as his character and interests.

Before the completion of Monticello, Jefferson began plans for Poplar Forest in Bedford County (1806–1812). He was to spend a month in the fall and in the spring there, usually with one or two grandchildren. The house is an octagon and the terraces reflect the same form; so, too, do most of the rooms, and even the privies are octagonal, carrying out the theme. The plan has a large parlor and two large bedrooms with open alcove beds, like his own at Monticello, all octagonal. There are two little pavilions on each side of the house for stairs, as usual not apparent to the visitor. But the brilliant design of the dining room is the cynosure: it is a square room in the middle of the house lit by one of Jefferson's skylights, with a strong diagonal thrust, focusing on the fireplace. In a completely symmetrical composition, this diagonal is the one relieving element which adds variety to the composition.

The great triumph of Jefferson's architectural career was his design for the University of Virginia (1817–1826). His first scheme consisted of nine pavilions for faculty arranged around an open square filled with grass. Each was to have two rooms for the professor and his schoolroom on the main floor, to be connected with the others by students' rooms, with all three sides to have covered passages for communication. The third side was left open. He sent this sketch to both WILLIAM THORNTON and Latrobe, who made some useful suggestions, but most of the ideas were his. Latrobe suggested a focal building and a rectangular lawn. These ideas were eagerly accepted by Jefferson. Jefferson determined to use the Pantheon, with its proportions reduced to one-half scale, as his focal building. The carefully designed Dome Room, also at one-half scale, was to house the library. The general scheme may have been based on that of Marly-le-Roi, the favorite château of Louis XIV, where the king went to escape the intrigues and crowds at Versailles. Jefferson knew Marly well, as he liked to picnic there.

The cornerstone of the university was laid in 1817, in the presence of three presidents—Jefferson, James Madison, and James Monroe, when Jefferson was seventy-four. Its design admirably reflects Jefferson's curriculum, which—along with the design, the construction, the building funds, the books for the library, and the professors—were all the responsibility of its founder. The university was indeed, as it has been called, the lengthened shadow of one man.

On October 7, 1822, five years after the cornerstone was laid, Jefferson reported that all the buildings were finished with the exception of the Rotunda, which was to be used for religious worship, public examinations, a library, classes in dancing and drawing, and any "of the other polite adornments of civilization." The completed buildings in 1822 included ten houses or pavilions, each of which had its own lecture room (there were ten professors, each of whom taught in a separate school) with four other apartments and accommodations for a professor and his family. Each pavilion also had a garden and necessary outbuildings such as a privy and smokehouse. There were six hotels for feeding the students in which a different language would be spoken at table. Arranged in four rows between the six hotels on the ranges and the ten pavilions on the lawn were 109 student rooms, each accommodating two students. In the case of the range rooms, the covered passages joining them were brick arcades; those on the lawn were brick colonnades, stuccoed. All was completed except for some plastering, the gardens and garden walls, and some columns. The columns were those of the Ionic and Corinthian orders which had not yet come from the quarry at Carrara near Florence. Those of the Doric order could be run in plaster and were within the capacities of the local workmen. Finally in 1823, funds were obtained for the Rotunda, and it was far enough along in 1825 that the university could open and Lafayette could be entertained in it.

Jefferson applied the lessons he had learned from the French visionary architects in the design of the Rotunda. He agreed wholeheartedly with their aims to promote the public welfare with large, splendid building projects; to base designs on geometry because mathematics was a natural science; and to recall the buildings of ancient Rome, which had been admired for some two millennia. The design of the much admired Rotunda was based on the Pantheon in Rome, the interior of the Dome Room is exactly one-half the size of the original. In Jefferson's view, the Rotunda was the capstone of the university because it housed the library.

Another innovative and subtle design detail employed at the university was the use of the old Virginia plantation garden motif of three "falling terraces" to lead the eye to the distant view of the Ragged Mountains. He also emphasized the view by means of gradually enlarging the spaces between the pavilions by adding an additional student room between Pavilions I and III, then two additional rooms between Pavilions III and V, three rooms between V and VII, and four rooms between VII and IX. Thus, the subtle enlargement of the length of the lawn, with the expanding hierarchy of the spacing, represents Jefferson's belief in the limitless freedom of the educated mind. The schoolroom in each of the professor's pavilions represented the close contacts with students and teachers which he expected, but by placing the professors' drawing rooms on the second floor along with terrace passages between houses, they were provided some privacy from the students. The grass represented his concern with the environment (he had bought the Natural Bridge near Lexington, Kentucky, to preserve it). He provided a gymnasium under the Rotunda terraces for the students to exercise in bad weather. He provided large meeting rooms for teaching and religious purposes in the Rotunda, and he wanted the students to be learning even at mealtimes, when they were to speak only the foreign language they were studying at that time. It is the brilliant reflection of one man's strong beliefs and of his love of learning.

The care with which he designed and furnished the university attests to its supreme importance in Jefferson's mind. He adapted the design of Marly-le-Roi to the lawn. Marly had a Rotunda set in a rectangle for the Sun King's own quarters, and a central space closed on two sides with six small pavilions, one for each of the twelve months; on the other side, opposite the retreat of Louix XIV, was a view to the distant hills. The falling terraces and the increase in the spaces between the pavilions were Jefferson's own ideas to enrich the importance of the view.

The ingenious design of the Rotunda is based on the idea of a sphere inscribed in a cylinder. The top of the dome is the top of the sphere and the base of the sphere is the ground floor. With its three great oval rooms on the main floor and its free-form hall, the Rotunda has the finest suite of oval rooms in America. The design of the oval rooms set in a cylinder was probably derived from Le Désert de Retz. The interior of the Rotunda

Jefferson. Rotunda, University of Virginia. Charlottesville. 1817–1826

was restored to its original form in 1972–1976, replacing the interior which STANFORD WHITE introduced during the rebuilding of the Rotunda after the fire of 1895. White had also closed the vista at the south end of the lawn which Jefferson had so carefully designed as an integral part of his complex of buildings. Cabell Hall now seems to be rising out of the ground when viewed from the bottom of the Rotunda steps, and one wonders why Charles F. McKim (see McKIM, MEAD, AND WHITE), the great American classicist, should have permitted his partner to spoil the vista and the interior of one of America's most magnificent buildings.

Each of the pavilions of the university had an order from a different Roman temple, so there would be not only variety but also examples for the architectural lecturer to discuss. Almost every pavilion plan is different, but all had a school room on the main floor, and Jefferson was careful to set all the drawing rooms of the pavilions on the south side of the buildings. It is this variety within a unified scheme that gives the lawn much of its charm.

Sir John Wheeler-Bennett, a distinguished scholar and historian, referring in his autobiography to his first visit to Jefferson's university in 1923, declared that he recognized it immediately for what it was—"namely the most beautiful man-made thing in the United States, an opinion I was later to have authoritatively confirmed by Kenneth Clark." The university has appealed to laymen of all generations for its serene classical beauty, and to students and teachers for its unity as an academic community. Professional architects, interested in its functionalism and aesthetics and in Jefferson's highly personal and sometimes amateurish adaptations, gave it an extraordinary accolade in America's bicentennial year. In a 1976 poll by the American Institute of Architects, a lopsided majority named the university as the greatest architectural creation of the nation's first two hundred years.

Jefferson's architecture is both aesthetic and practical. For example, Monticello is the best-insulated house in America. There is brick nogging between all floors and ceilings; he seems to have been the first to use storm sashes—every bedroom door and the parlor doors were double; he used Rumford fireplaces and Franklin stoves extensively to conserve heat; and his greenhouses had masonry floors to act as passive solar heat retainers. He liked octagons because they provided much light and the sun's rays in winter, but were protected from the summer heat by the porticoes. Jefferson was among the first to use tin roofs, believing they would last one hundred years if properly painted

and maintained. Some of his metal roofs are still on the university and Monticello! He did not wish to weaken his brick columns by using them to support his balconies on the lawn, so he was among the first to use suspension rods for support.

Certainly architecture was one of Jefferson's greatest achievements. But he could also write the Declaration of Independence and fifty thousand letters, many of them among the great letters of his age, assemble three great libraries, render learned professional opinions on points of law, acquire through diplomacy and purchase a vast continental empire for his country without firing a shot, preside over affairs of state, and design an innovative mould board plow. Believing that most of the problems of mankind had been discussed or solved by the Greek and Romans, he read Greek and Latin, loving their literature and believing that the past was one of the best guides to the future. He admired Palladio as the ideal interpreter of the architecture of the ancient world, whose designs were based on mathematics and natural laws. Jefferson himself was such an interpreter. He seems to have found time for everything, even for designing his own tombstone and for planning its inscription:

Here was buried
Thomas Jefferson
Author of the Declaration of Independence
Of the Statute of Virginia for Religious Freedom
And Father of the University of Virginia.
Born April 2, 1743 O.S. Died July 4, 1826.

When some of his friends were concerned that he had left out other achievements: wartime governor of Virginia, secretary of state, vice-president, ambassador to France, and president, Jefferson replied that those were the honors which the people had given him; he wished to be remembered only for those things he had given to the people of his country—the foundations for political, religious and intellectual freedom.

FREDERICK D. NICHOLS

WORKS

1755–1797, Montpelier (remodeled 1797–1812), near Orange, Va. 1768–1782, Monticello (remodeled 1796–1809), near Charlottesville, Va. 1785–1799, Virginia State Capitol, Richmond. 1793, Woodbury Forest; 1795–?, Belle Grove; c.1797, Edgemont House; before 1798, Edgehill House (second house, 1828); 1802–1808, Farmington House (addition); near Charlottesville, Va. 1806–1812, Poplar Forest House, Bedford County, Va. 1809, House, Farmington, Ky. 1817–1822, House, Barboursville, Va. (now W.Va.). 1817–1826, University of Virginia, Charlottesville. *1818, Botetourt County Courthouse, Fincastle Va. 1820, House, Oakhill, Va. (now W.Va). *1821, Buckingham County Courthouse, Buckingham, Va. *1824–1826, Christ Church, Centerville, Va.

BIBLIOGRAPHY

BERKELEY, FRANCIS LEWIS, JR., and THURLOW, CONSTANCE E. (compilers) 1950 *The Jefferson Papers of the University of Virginia.* Charlottesville: University of Virginia Library, with assistance from the Research Council of the Richmond Area University Center.

BOYD, JULIAN P. (editor) 1950– *The Papers of Thomas Jefferson.* 19 vols. N.J.: Princeton University Press.

GIBBS, JAMES (1728)1968 *A Book of Architecture.* Reprint. New York: Blom.

JEFFERSON, THOMAS 1959 *Autobiography.* Introduction by Dumas Malone. New York: Capricorn.

KIMBALL, SIDNEY FISKE (1916)1968 *Thomas Jefferson Architect.* Introduction by Frederick Doveton Nichols. Reprint. New York: Da Capo.

KIMBALL, SIDNEY FISKE (1922)1966 *Domestic Architecture of the American Colonies and of the Early Republic.* Reprint. New York: Dover.

LEHMAN, KARL (1947)1980 *Thomas Jefferson, American Humanist.* Reprint. University of Chicago Press.

MALONE, DUMAS 1948–1974 *Jefferson and His Time.* 5 vols. Boston: Little, Brown.

MAYO, BERNARD (editor) (1942)1970 *Jefferson Himself: The Personal Narrative of a Many-Sided American.* Charlottesville: University Press of Virginia.

MORRIS, ROBERT (1757)1973 *Select Architecture: Being Regular Design, of Plan and Elevation Well Suited to Both Town and Country.* Reprint. New York: Da Capo.

NICHOLS, FREDERICK D. (compiler) (1961)1978 *Thomas Jefferson's Architectural Drawings.* 4th ed., rev. & enl. Boston: Massachusetts Historical Society.

NICHOLAS, FREDERICK D., and BEAR, JAMES A., JR. 1967 *Monticello.* Monticello, Va.: Thomas Jefferson Memorial Foundation.

O'NEAL, WILLIAM BAINTER 1956 *Jefferson's Fine Arts Library for the University of Virginia.* Charlottesville: University Press of Virginia.

O'NEAL, WILLIAM BAINTER 1960 *The Rotunda.* Volume 1 in *Jefferson's Buildings at the University of Virginia.* Charlottesville: University Press of Virginia.

JEKYLL, GERTRUDE

Gertrude Jekyll (1843–1932) was an artist, gardener, and craftswoman. She also had a large literary output from around 1899. In 1861, she went to the South Kensington School of Art, and throughout the 1860s and 1870s painted, traveled, and executed embroidery. In 1883, she developed a garden site at Munstead Wood and began a parallel interest in horticulture and old Surrey crafts. In 1889, she met EDWIN LUTYENS, who designed her house, Munstead Wood, in 1896. From then until around 1930, she designed the planting of many gardens with him and other architects. She was the first horticultural Impressionist, translating gardening into terms of painting.

MARGARET RICHARDSON

WORKS

In this list, the asterisk indicates gardens where the original planting does not survive, but the garden itself does.

*1893, Garden (with Edwin Lutyens), Chinthurst Hill, Wonersh; *1896, Garden, Munstead Wood; *1897, Garden (with Lutyens), Orchards, Godalming; Surrey, England. 1906, Garden (with Lutyens), Hestercombe House, Taunton; 1917, Garden (with Forbes and Tait), Barrington Court, Ilminster; Somerset, England.

BIBLIOGRAPHY

BROWN, JANE 1982 *Gardens of a Golden Afternoon: The Story of a Partnership, Edwin Lutyens and Gertrude Jekyll.* Harmondsworth, England: Penguin.

JEKYLL, FRANCIS 1934 *Gertrude Jekyll: A Memoir.* London: Cape.

JEKYLL, GERTRUDE (1899)1938 *Wood and Garden.* London: Longmans, Green.

JEKYLL, GERTRUDE (1900)1926 *Home and Garden.* London: Longmans, Green.

JEKYLL, GERTRUDE (1901)1903 *Lilies for English Gardens.* 2d ed. London: Country Life.

JEKYLL, GERTRUDE 1904 *Old West Surrey.* London: Longmans, Green.

JEKYLL, GERTRUDE (1908)1934 *Children and Gardens.* New ed. London: Country Life; New York: Scribners.

JEKYLL, GERTRUDE, and HUSSEY, CHRISTOPHER (1918)1927 *Garden Ornament.* 2d ed., rev. London: Country Life.

MASSINGHAM, BETTY 1973 *Miss Jekyll: Portrait of a Great Gardener.* Newton Abbot, England: David & Charles.

JELLICOE, GEOFFREY

Geoffrey Jellicoe (1900–) has practiced architecture, town planning, and landscape architecture, but it is as a landscape architect that he acquired his international reputation and it was for his contribution to that art that he was awarded a knighthood in 1979.

Jellicoe was born in London and has lived there for most of his life. He was educated at Cheltenham College. In later life, he was to return there to design a Sports Centre in a landscape setting. He received his architectural training at the Architectural Association School before the Modern movement in architecture was recognized in Britain, most students' ideas of "modern" being the Swedish Romantic movement as typified by Stockholm Town Hall. Jellicoe subsequently took no part in the formation of MARS, the English branch of the

International Union of Architects, and he has not been consciously influenced by the Modern movement in architecture.

Jellicoe enjoys architecture too much to accept the aesthetic discipline of a movement and is just as happy designing a Palladian (see ANDREA PALLADIO) mansion in coral as a row of flat-roofed workers' cottages in brick and timber. The early years of his practice saw the growth of his reputation as a landscape architect, his best-known work being Ditchley Park (1935), probably the last great classical garden in England. He was a founder member of the Institute of Landscape Architects, became its president in 1939, and kept it alive during the war years. He was later active in the formation of the International Federation of Landscape Architects. After the war, Jellicoe always practiced architecture with partners who were also designers, and it is not possible to attribute their housing schemes, schools, and important buildings like Plymouth Town Hall to any individual. They were not innovators and the practice did not produce any consistent architectural style.

Jellicoe is one of a few well-known architects who are also qualified town planners, and in consequence he became involved in postwar reconstruction. He prepared town plans for Guildford and Wellington, and a comprehensive plan for the central area of Gloucester, but his most important commission was the Master Plan for Hemel Hampstead new town, a design based on the valley form of the topography. Although he did not remain with the Development Corporation, he was commissioned to design the splendid water garden adjacent to the town center—by far the greatest contribution to the character of the town.

Jellicoe has published many books, mostly on the philosophical basis of landscape design and his own experience as a practitioner, but his great work, on which his wife, Susan, collaborated over many years, is undoubtedly *The Landscape of Man* (1975).

FREDERICK GIBBERD

JENNEY, WILLIAM LE BARON

William Le Baron Jenney (1832–1907), a Chicago architect who played a major role in the development of the modern steel-framed skyscraper, was born in Fair Haven, Massachusetts, on September 25, 1832. The family belonged to the local mercantile aristocracy, and its prosperity was based primarily on the ownership of a fleet of whaling vessels. Jenney's interest in the building arts began when he was a student at the Phillips Academy in Andover, Massachusetts. During a Pacific voyage in 1849, he was, according to a later recollection, impressed by the strength and the storm resistance of native houses constructed of light bamboo frames in the Philippine Islands. According to his partner William B. Mundie, this memory contributed to early enthusiasm as a practicing architect for iron-framed rather than traditional bearing-masonry structures. In 1850, he entered the Lawrence Scientific School at Harvard University, where he was dissatisfied with the engineering and scientific program. Jenney took the unprecedented step for an American student of enrolling in the prestigious Ecole Centrale des Arts et Manufactures in Paris in the fall of 1853. He graduated with honors in 1856. The curriculum, which included a number of architectural courses in a predominantly engineering program, left an influence on Jenney that bore remarkable architectural fruit twenty years after his graduation.

The theory of architecture that was taught at the Ecole Centrale was set forth in the lectures of Professor Louis Charles Mary, but it was in fact derived from the doctrines advanced by the influential theorist and designer JEAN-NICOLAS-LOUIS DURAND. Durand had reached a wide audience through his lectures on architecture at the Ecole Polytechnique, which were subsequently published. The essential principle of his teaching, as stated by Mary, was that the structural system embodied in a building and its formal architectural dress are interdependent aspects of the building art, and can be separated only by arbitrary, or even deceptive, means. The process of architectural design, according to Mary, must as a consequence represent a unification of planning and formal expression with structural techniques, which in turn must evolve from the materials of construction and the function for which the building is intended. The evidence is persuasive, therefore, that the empirical and pragmatic spirit that Jenney later brought to architectural practice in Chicago was instilled in him directly and indirectly by French theorists. As a result of this education which was followed by practical experience gained in various ateliers of Paris in 1858–1859, Jenney was receptive to the influences of the warehouse of the St. Ouen Docks in that city (1865–1866). This structure, the first multistory, iron-framed, concrete-floored, curtain-walled, fireproofed building, embodied all the ingredients of the skyscraper.

Jenney's early career lacked any clear direction, although he derived useful experience from his engineering activities. Between his graduation from the Ecole Centrale and his return to Paris, he served as an engineer with the Tehuantepec Railroad Company (1857–1858), then engaged in constructing a rail line across the Isthmus of Tehuantepec in lower Mexico. Shortly after his return to the United States, the Civil War and its aftermath interrupted his professional plans for five years. In 1861 he became a captain in the United States Army, Corps of Engineers; served on the staff of General U. S. Grant during the Mississippi campaign (Cairo, Illinois, to Corinth, Mississippi) and with General William T. Sherman in Tennessee; and was honorably discharged with the rank of major in 1866. He went to Chicago in the following year and opened an independent architectural office in 1868. His activities expanded through a partnership with Mundie in 1891. He added Elmer Jensen as a third partner in 1905 because of poor health as well as the burdens of his office. Jenney served as the landscape engineer for the West Park District of Chicago in 1870–1871, when he played a major role in planning the once distinguished West Park boulevard system. He lectured at the University of Michigan in 1876, but except for these brief hiatuses and the writing of a few articles, he devoted his time entirely to architectural design until his retirement and his subsequent move to Los Angeles in 1905. He died in that city on June 15, 1907. He influenced the architects of Chicago through his buildings and through his training of a number of young architects, among whom the most notable were LOUIS H. SULLIVAN, William HOLABIRD AND Martin ROCHE, DANIEL H. BURNHAM, and Enoch H. Turnock.

Jenney's first work to simultaneously reflect the teachings of the Ecole Central and suggest a new architectural direction was a project executed in 1876 for a narrow four-story commercial building, the façade of which was opened almost entirely to glass, interrupted only by cast-iron columns at the base and extremely attenuated iron mullions above the second floor. It was a prophetic work, and the architect was shortly able to give physical embodiment to his principles in the timber and iron frame and in the cagelike street elevations of the first Leiter Building (1879). Jenney almost achieved complete skeletal construction in this design, but a small portion of the outer floor and roof loads fell on the brick piers disposed along the street walls. This modest work marked a step toward the most famous, the most influential, and the most discussed of Jenney's achievements.

The Home Insurance Building (1884–1885), designed in association with the engineer George B. Whitney, was an early skyscraper, originally nine stories in height but raised to eleven in 1891. The primary structural system was composed of columns of both cast and wrought iron, girders

and floor beams of wrought iron up the sixth floor, and spandrel girders of steel above that level, which marked the first use of the metal in a structure other than a bridge. The columns were founded on spread footings of stone carried by reinforced concrete rafts resting in turn on a shallow layer of hardpan clay. All connections between framing members were bolted. The question, whether the Home Insurance Building was the first work of complete skeleton construction or the first fully iron-framed skyscraper, has been debated at length over the years, and the conclusion reached by all who had investigated the matter, the editors of *Engineering Record* (1896), Woltersdorf (1924), Mujica (1929), Giedion (1941), among others, was that Jenney had created the skeleton frame appropriate to high-building construction for this work. Since a portion of the total load, however, was carried by granite piers and brick party walls, and since no windbracing was incorporated in the frame, the building must be regarded as a protoskyscraper, or as a very long step in the direction of the mature form rather than the ultimate achievement itself. The truth is that there is no such thing as the first skyscraper: a number of architects in Chicago and New York were involved in the evolution of the high skeleton structure from 1882 to 1889, and it is impossible to single out one work that unambiguously takes precedence over all its forerunners. An eastern counterpart to the Home Insurance Building, for example, was the New York Produce Exchange (1882–1884), designed by GEORGE B. POST.

The Home Insurance Building can hardly be regarded as an architectural triumph, but Jenney's formal mastery of the new structural technique came rather suddenly with a galaxy of buildings

Jenney.
Home Insurance Building.
Chicago.
1884–1885

Jenney.
Leiter Building.
Chicago.
1879

designed and erected in Chicago over the two highly productive years from 1889 to 1891. The Manhattan Building (1889–1890), the product of a collaboration between the architect and the engineer Louis E. Ritter, is the first structure to embody full skeleton construction, calculated to support all floor, wall, roof, and wind loads without masonry adjuncts. The framework of cast iron, wrought iron, and steel, all the ferrous metals in structural use around 1890, represented the frontier of building technology at the time, but the overly busy façade of granite, brick, and metal, chiefly marked by heavily delineated oriel bays of two different shapes, indicates a less sure architectural hand. The architectonic possibilities of the steel and iron frame are best expressed in the huge Sears, Roebuck and Company Store, erected in 1890–1891, but in the stage of advanced planning as early as 1889. The strongly articulated street elevations, clothed in an envelope of granite, clearly reflect the underlying geometry of the metal skeleton. The variations in the width of the piers, the four-part horizontal composition, the massive parapet, and other formal elements are well subordinated to the ruling pattern and add the visual interest of changing rhythms to what might otherwise have been a monotonous blocklong wall. For elegance and purity of over-all form combined with great delicacy of ornamental detail, all conceived within the limits of the empirical approach that Jenney favored, the architect's prize design is the Ludington Building, also completed in 1891. Indeed, it represents the artistic high point of Jenney's career.

The Fair Store (1891–1892), although revealing an obvious attempt to exploit the formal possibilities of steel framing, was disfigured by heavy-handed ornament and irrational horizontal divisions of the street elevations. Later works are distinctly anticlimactic compared to the Luding-

ton; only the Morton Building (1896) and the Chicago Garment Center (1904–1905), the last work to be completed before Jenney's retirement, suggest something of the creative powers and the innovative spirit that distinguished the buildings of the 1891 group.

CARL W. CONDIT

WORKS

*1872, Portland Building; *1879, Leiter Building; 1884–1885, Home Insurance Building; 1889–1890, Manhattan Building; 1889–1891, Sears, Roebuck and Company Store; 1891, Central Young Men's Christian Association; 1891, Ludington Building; 1891–1892, Montgomery Ward and Company (Fair) Store; *1893, Horticultural Building, World's Columbian Exposition; 1896, Morton Building; 1904–1905, Chicago Garment Center; Chicago.

BIBLIOGRAPHY

CONDIT, CARL W. 1964 *The Chicago School of Architecture: A History of Commercial and Public Building in the Chicago Area, 1875–1925.* University of Chicago Press.

JENNEY, WILLIAM LE BARON 1885 "Construction of a Heavy Fireproof Building on Compressible Soil." *Engineering Record, Building Record and Sanitary Engineer* 13:32–33.

JENNEY, WILLIAM LE BARON 1891 "The Chicago Construction, or Tall Buildings on a Compressible Soil." *Inland Architect and News Record* 18:41.

"Jenney, William Le Baron." 1943 Volume 10, page 55 in *Dictionary of American Biography.* New York: Scribner.

MUJICA, FRANCISCO 1929 *History of the Skyscraper.* Paris: Archaeology and Architecture Press.

RANDALL, FRANK A. 1949 *History of the Development of Building Construction in Chicago.* Urbana: University of Illinois Press.

TURAK, THEODORE 1970 "Ecole Centrale and Modern Architecture: The Education of William Le Baron Jenney." *Journal of the Society of Architectural Historians* 29:40–47.

WEBSTER, J. CARSON 1959 "The Skyscraper: Logical and Historical Considerations." *Journal of the Society of Architectural Historians* 18:126–139.

WOLTERSDORF, ARTHUR 1924 "The Father of the Skeleton Frame Building." *Western Architect* 33: 21–23.

Jenney.
Ludington Building.
Chicago.
1891

JENSEN, ALBERT

Albert Jensen (1847–1913), a Danish architect, belonged to a circle of rather academic architects with an international outlook. He designed a number of splendid buildings in the Danish capital, most of them in collaboration with another leading figure of the group, FERDINAND MELDAHL, such as the Marble Church (1874–1894), the exhibition building at Charlottenborg and the department store Magasin du Nord, Kongens Nytorv.

VILLADS VILLADSEN

JENSEN-KLINT, PEDER VILHELM

Peder-Vilhelm Jensen-Klint (1853–1930) graduated from the Technical University of Denmark in 1877 as a building engineer. He entered the Royal Academy in Copenhagen in 1878 to become a painter, but after several years he chose architecture as his artistic medium. His ideas had deep roots in N. F. S. Grundtvig's philosophy and the Grundtvigian Folk High School. From JOHAN DANIEL HERHOLDT, who was a teacher in building construction at the University of Denmark, he learned the sculptural context of volumes, the honest expression of the nature of materials, and the importance of continuity of craftsmanship. The vernacular should not vanish, being a fruit of long and hard-won knowledge. Jensen-Klint had seen the influence of the craftsman decline in favor of the academic architect, whose knowledge came from photographs and prints. He wanted to "give architecture back to the people" and to create a "real architecture" comparable to that of the Middle Ages. He proclaimed most emphatically the importance of continuity. Architecture and craftsmanship must be one and the same thing. The architect creates the tradition to be, while the craftsman maintains and improves upon it. The architectural student should be trained to build rather than to design. He should study the landscape of dolmens, churches, manors, and farms, and when all these architectural manifestations of his ancestors have become part of him, he can give them back reborn, without copying, because then he gives himself. Jensen-Klint detested the abstractions of academic neoclassicism and its outward applications of paint and plaster. His first house, Villa Holm, is a manifesto of his expressionistic mysticism: a man's production should be an organic whole, growing according to the laws of nature. The limestone lintels are recreated by the sculptor's chisel into the shape of shells, thus symbolizing his aim of creating timeless architectural forms. He called himself a master mason (*bygmester*) and he preferred to call architecture "building culture." His most important work is the Grundtvig's Church, a magnified expressionistic paraphrase of the typical Danish country church, surrounded by dwellings in human scale, all in brick and tile. Jensen-Klint was most influential; a flock of devotees spread his message which became the Danish Functional Tradition and the Klint school.

LISBET BALSLEV JØRGENSEN

WORKS

1896, Holm Villa, 27 Sofievej; 1897–1898, Rasmussen Gymnastic Institute, 49 Vodrofsvej; 1905–1906, Villa Rødsten, 12 Onsgårdsvej; Copenhagen. 1907, Aagaard House, Ryslinge, Denmark. 1913–1930, Grundtvig Church and surrounding housing (not completed until 1940 by KAARE KLINT), Copenhagen.

BIBLIOGRAPHY

FISKER, KAY 1963 "Den Klintske skole." *Arkitektur* 7:entire issue.
JENSEN-KLINT, PEDER VILHELM 1911 *Bygmesterskolen.* Copenhagen: Gyldendal.
JØRGENSEN, LISBET BALSLEV 1979 *Enfamiliehuset.* Copenhagen: Gyldendal.
MILLECH, KUND 1947 "Jensen-Klint, Peder Vilhelm." Volume 2, pages 57–60 in *Weilbachs Kunstnerleksikon.* Copenhagen.
MILLECH, KNUD 1951 *Danske arkitekturstrømninger: 1850–1950.* Copenhagen: Østifternes kreditforening.
RASMUSSEN, STEEN EILER 1931 "Om P. V. Jensen-Klints Arkitektur." *Tilskueren* 48:2.

JERMAN, EDWARD

Born into a family of London carpenters, Edward Jerman (?–1668) was master of the Carpenters' Company from 1653 to 1657. Working essentially within the City of London itself, he was surveyor to the Fishmongers from 1654 to 1668. After the Great Fire of London in 1666, he was appointed surveyor along with ROBERT HOOKE and PETER MILLS to control the reconstruction of devastated areas, working with CHRISTOPHER WREN, HUGH MAY, and ROGER PRATT.

Jerman designed several Companies' Halls in the City artisans' manner, featuring the finest carpentry and joinery of the period. The Royal Exchange (1667–1671) was his most important work; it was inspired by the Charles I style rather than reflecting new tendencies by Pratt, Hooke, and Wren.

MARC DILET

WORKS

1667–1669, Weavers' Hall, Basinghall Street; 1667–1771, Barber–Surgeons' Hall, Monkwell Street; 1667–1771, Royal Exchange; 1667–1672, Fishmongers' Hall, London Bridge; 1667–1772, Goldsmiths' Hall, Foster Lane; 1668–1670, Wax Candlers' Hall, Maiden Lane; 1668–1671, Drapers' Hall, Throgmorton Street; 1668–1672, Mercers' Hall and Chapel, Cheapside; London.

JEWELL, RICHARD ROACH

Richard Roach Jewell (1810–1896) was born in Barnstaple, England. His education is obscure. He migrated to the colony of Western Australia in 1852 and was appointed first foreman of public works and then supervisor (1853). He retired in 1884. Jewell is credited with the design of many public buildings in Perth.

JOHN WHITE

WORKS

1854, Courthouse and Jail; 1863, Pensioner's Barracks; 1864, Trinity Congregational Church; 1867, Town Hall; 1874, Public Offices; 1877, Perth Girls' School; Perth, Western Australia.

BIBLIOGRAPHY

OLDHAM, RAY, and OLDHAM, JOHN (1961)1978 *Western Heritage.* Reprint. Perth: University of Western Australia Press.

PITT MORISON, M., and WHITE, JOHN (editors) 1979 *Western Towns and Buildings.* Perth: University of Western Australia Press.

JOHANSEN, JOHN M.

John Maclane Johansen (1916–) is an American architect who developed an innovative and highly forceful style during the 1960s after persistent experiment with various vocabularies. Johansen was born in New York and graduated with an architectural degree from Harvard University in 1942. He worked for MARCEL BREUER, and for SKIDMORE, OWINGS, AND MERRILL in New York before opening his own practice in New Canaan, Connecticut, in 1948. For many years, his work was eclectic: the United States Embassy in Dublin (1963) incorporates twisting precast concrete frames; Clowes Hall, a severely formal theater in Indianapolis, Indiana (1964), consists of staggered shafts of limestone and glass; while the Taylor House in Westport, Connecticut (1966), em-

bodies interlocking, cavelike spaces.

His mature work is exemplified by the Mummer's Theater in Oklahoma City, Oklahoma (1970), a cluster of axially splayed volumes systematically differentiated according to their enclosed functions and connected by long-spanning tubular passageways and mechanical service enclosures. Its unique industrial-looking composition reflects the informality of early British Archigram projects and the Brutalist character of much contemporaneous building.

Johansen moved his office to New York in 1968 and, two years after, formed a partnership with Ashok M. Bhavnani, Johansen and Bhavnani. His commissions at this time broadened to include multistory housing and academic complexes; in the late 1970s he designed several private residences.

MICHAEL HOLLANDER

WORKS

1957, Warner House, New Canaan, Conn. 1963, United States Embassy, Dublin. 1964, Clowes Hall (with Evans Woollen), Indianapolis, Ind. 1966, Taylor House, Westport, Conn. 1967, Morris Mechanic Theater, Baltimore. 1968, Goddard Library, Clark University, Worcester, Mass. 1970, L. Francis Smith School, Columbus, Ind. 1970, Mummer's Theater (now the Oklahoma Theater Center), Oklahoma City. 1974, Johansen House II, Stanfordville, N.Y. 1975–1976, Roosevelt Island Neighborhood (with Ashok Bhavnani), New York.

BIBLIOGRAPHY

BLAKE, PETER 1971 "The Mummer's Theater." *Architectural Forum* 134, no. 2:30–37.

HEYER, PAUL 1966 *Architects on Architecture: New Directions in America.* New York: Walker.

JOHANSEN, JOHN 1961 "Act and Behavior in Architecture." *Perspecta* 7:43–50.

JOHANSEN, JOHN 1966 "An Architecture for the Electronic Age." *American Scholar* 35.

JOHNSON, JOHN

Born in Leicester, in the English Midlands, John Johnson (1732–1814) spent most of his career in London and, from 1782 to 1812, as surveyor for the county of Essex. In the latter capacity, he designed the Shire Hall at Chelmsford (1789–1791) along with other public buildings, including bridges. He was also responsible for a substantial number of country houses as well as London townhouses, various buildings in his native Leicester, and public buildings elsewhere, most of them in a refined neo-classical manner.

DAMIE STILLMAN

Johansen.
United States Embassy.
Dublin.
1963

WORKS

1771–1772, The New Rooms (since refronted), Newmarket, Suffolk, England. c.1772–1778, Terling Place, Essex, England. 1773–1775, Sadborow House, Dorset, England. 1774–1775, Kingsthorpe Hall, Northamptonshire, England. *c.1775, Clasmont, Glamorganshire, Wales. c.1775, Pitsford Hall (since altered), Northamptonshire, England. *1775–1776, 19 Charles Street, Saint James's Square, London. c.1775–1778, Holcombe House, Mill Hill, Middlesex, England. 1776, Woolverstone Hall, Suffolk, England. 1776–1777, 61 and 63 New Cavendish Street, London. *c.1776–1778, Gnoll Castle, Glamorganshire, Wales. *1777–1781, Carlton Hall, Northamptonshire, England. *1778–1779, Killerton Park, Devon, England. *c.1779, Palliser House, Pall Mall; *Before 1780, 63 and 68 Harley Street; London. 1781–1786, Bradwell Lodge; *1782, Langford Grove; Essex, England. *c.1785, Benhall Lodge, Suffolk. England. *c.1787, Dedham Bridge; 1787, Moulsham Bridge, Chelmsford; Essex, England. *1787–1788, Wimbledon Church, Surrey, England. 1789–1791, Shire Hall, Chelmsford; *1791–1792, House of Correction, Barking; Essex, England. *1792–1793, Consanguinitarium; *1792–1793, Gaol; Leicester, England. 1792–1794, Hatfield Place, Essex, England. *1792–1800, County Rooms; *1800, Theatre; Leicester, England. *c.1801, Saint Leonard's Lodge, Sussex, England. 1801–1803, Saint Mary's Church (alterations to nave; now a cathedral), Chelmsford; *1802–1807, House of Correction, Chelmsford; *c.1805, Forest Hall; c.1808, Broomfield Lodge; Essex, England. 1808–1812, County Hall, Lewes, Sussex, England.

BIBLIOGRAPHY

NICHOLS, JOHN 1795–1815 *The History and Antiquities of the County of Leicester.* 4 vols. London: Nichols.

SIMMONDS, JACK 1949 "Notes on a Leicester Architect: John Johnson, (1732–1813)." *Transactions of the Leicestershire Archaeological and Historical Society* 25:144–159.

JOHNSON, PHILIP

A notable critic and historian both before and during his long, active career as architect, Philip Johnson (1906–) was born in Cleveland, Ohio. He graduated from Harvard University (1927) with a degree in the classics. His interests in the new European architecture were stimulated during travels immediately following graduation. At an early date he became a devotee of three remarkable architects: the romantic classic KARL FRIEDRICH SCHINKEL, the nineteenth-century American H. H. RICHARDSON, and the contemporary pioneer LUDWIG MIES VAN DER ROHE. These selective enthusiasms have persisted, shaping and coloring his keen taste and effervescent wit.

Associated with the Museum of Modern Art

Johnson.
Philip Johnson Glass House.
New Canaan, Connecticut.
1949

from an early date, Johnson was in charge of its unique, innovative department of architecture from 1932 to 1934 and resumed this position briefly after World War II. An adventurous collector of contemporary art, he has been an important donor to the museum's collection of painting and sculpture and has long served as a trustee. He was the architect of the museum's distinctive sculpture garden (1953) as well as of two additions (1950, 1964) to its original structure (the first of these additions being demolished in 1979 to make way for expansion). It was at MOMA in 1932 that Johnson, in collaboration with the pioneer historian, H. R. Hitchcock, and with the encouragement of the director, Alfred H. Barr, Jr., organized the epochal exhibition, "Modern Architecture." Simultaneously he coauthored the influential book, *The International Style* ([1932]1966), which singled out one particular strain of radical, vanguard architecture of the 1920s associated with the names of WALTER GROPIUS, LE CORBUSIER, and Mies.

Returning to Harvard at the end of the decade, he completed a professional degree in architecture in 1943. While a student, he built a small brick and glass house for himself in Cambridge (1942), a design derived from the 1930s "court house" projects of Mies. In the later 1940s, while again a director at MOMA, he worked successively upon a critical monograph of Mies, published in 1947, and, for a space of three years, on a series of designs for what ultimately proved to be his Glass House, New Canaan, Connecticut (1949), a building which, in Johnson's distinctive fashion, served both as a creative act, a critical commentary, and a historical exegesis. It was based upon several Mies projects for a completely transparent building, including the Farnsworth House project, but ironically was actually built before its source of inspiration was completed. Widely commented upon, alternately admired and ridiculed, Johnson's Glass House remains a key landmark in postwar architecture. It signaled the entry of modern architecture into a self-conscious, reflective period, one in

Johnson.
New York State Theater.
1964

which architects were no longer fearful of admitting to specific historical sources. The door to subsequent twentieth-century revival and eclectic styles was opened here, even though the Glass House looked every inch an unflinchingly modern, contemporary structure.

Johnson.
A.T.&T. Headquarters Model (with Burgee).
New York.
1980–

During the early 1950s Johnson continued to employ a variety of Miesian paradigms, leading finally to his association with the master in the construction of the Seagram Building in New York (1956). However, by the end of the decade, the latent neoclassic formulae underlying his early houses and other projects became more conspicuous. The characteristically simple, light volumes of familiar modernism were banished in favor of weightier elements. The Kline Science Tower of Yale University, New Haven (1965), and the New York State Theater at Lincoln Center (1964), represent in their diverse ways a new monumentality which Johnson as well as his critics termed eclectic. The formalist style of this middle period was diverse, manifesting original, idiosyncratic shapes that often differed from scheme to scheme. His attitude at this juncture was typical of the stylistic *wanderlust* manifested by many of his important contemporaries. The 1960s were a period of creative uncertainty, following in the wake of an abrupt disenchantment with ideals and values of modernism, especially as they had been narrowly defined by the International style and Johnson's own early work. This monumental phase reached its apogee in the new wing of the Boston Public Library (1973), a forceful contemporary design which manages to pay homage to the robust style of Richardson with its broad round arches and simultaneously to the delicate detailing of Charles McKim's (see McKim, Mead, and White) academic classicism in its sharp contours and precise proportioning.

To a degree, the later 1970s mark yet another distinctive period in Johnson's *oeuvre*. Reflective glass skins, seen in several skyscrapers or in a large church, are once again commonplace, but now in distinctive, prism-shaped forms frequently evoking the Expressionist architecture of the earlier twentieth century. Once again, Johnson's resourcefulness, his susceptibility to change and ability to stay in the vanguard of stylistic evolution is an index of his restless nature. His descip[l]ined inventions, whatever the period, are more than mere responses to fashion. Rather, they indicate an ever enlarging understanding of the diverse strands of the historical period of which he is both master and chronicler. Thus, it should come as no surprise (and yet it did) that at the very end of the 1970s he would respond to the most recent prevailing current, that of post-modernism, with the design of the American Telephone and Telegraph skyscraper in New York (1980). It is a building that once more dispenses with the glass envelope, whether that of the 1950s or the 1970s, in favor of a masonry clad, vertical mullioned, pedimented tower that evokes both the radical skyscraper style of LOUIS H. SULLIVAN and the academic counterpart of McKim of nearly a century before. A.T.&T. represents but one more turn in Johnson's embracing of history, and another perplexing, unforeseen twist in the career of this paradoxical designer who has so effectively surprised and irritated and instructed his contemporaries. In recognition of his unique contribution, he was awarded the Gold Medal of the American Institute of Architects in 1978.

JOHN JACOBUS

WORKS

1942, Philip Johnson House, Cambridge, Mass. 1949, Philip Johnson Glass House, New Canaan, Conn. 1950, John de Menil House, Houston, Tex. 1950, Mrs. John D. Rockefeller 3rd Guest House, New York. 1951, Richard Hodgson House (with LANDIES GORES), New Canaan, Conn. 1951, George C. Oneto House (with Gores), Irvington, N.Y. 1952, Richard C. Davis House, Wayzata, Minn. 1953, The Abby Aldrich Rockefeller Sculpture Garden, The Museum of Modern Art, New York. 1953, Robert C. Wiley House; 1956, Eric Boissonnas House; New Canaan, Conn. 1956, Kneses Tifereth Israel Synagogue, Port Chester, N.Y. 1956, Robert C. Leonhardt House, Lloyd's Neck, N.Y. 1956, Seagram Building (with Ludwig Mies van der Rohe), New York. 1957, University of St. Thomas (auditorium and classroom buildings), Houston, Tex. 1959, Asia House; 1959, Four Seasons Restaurant; New York. 1960, Museum, Munson-Williams-Proctor Institute, Utica, N.Y. 1960, Nuclear Reactor, Rehovot, Israel. 1960, Roofless Church, New Harmony, Ind. 1961, Amon Carter Museum of Western Art, Fort Worth, Tex. 1962, Philip Johnson Pavilion, New Canaan, Conn. 1963, Museum for Pre-Columbian Art, Dunbarton Oaks, Washington. 1963, Sheldon Memorial Art Gallery, University of Nebraska, Lincoln. 1964, Eric Boissonnas House, Cap Bénat, France. 1964, Kline Geology Laboratory (with Richard Foster), Yale University, New Haven. 1964, The Museum of Modern Art (East wing, Garden wing, remodeled Sculpture Garden, and Upper Terrace), New York. 1964, New York State Pavilion (with Foster), Flushing, New York. 1964, New York State Theater, New York. 1965, Epidemiology and Public Health Building, Yale University, New Haven. 1965, Philip Johnson Painting Gallery, New Canaan, Conn. 1965, Kline Science Center, Yale University, New Haven. 1965, Henry L. Moses Institute, Montefiore Hospital, Bronx, New York. 1966, John F. Kennedy Memorial, Dallas, Tex. 1968, Bielefeld Art Gallery, Germany. 1970, Philip Johnson Sculpture Gallery, New Canaan, Conn. 1971, Albert and Vera List Art Building, Brown University, Providence, R.I. 1972, Art Museum of South Texas (with John Burgee), Corpus Christi. 1972, Burden Hall (with Burgee), Harvard University, Cambridge, Mass. 1972, André and Bella Meyer Hall of Physics (with Foster), New York University. 1972, Neuberger Museum, State University of New York, Purchase. 1972, Tisch Hall (with Foster), New York University. 1973, Boston Public Library (addition; with Burgee). 1973, I.D.S. Center (with Bur-

gee), Minneapolis, Minn. 1974, Niagara Falls Convention Center (with Burgee), New York. 1975, Fort Worth Water Garden (with Burgee), Tex. 1975, Morningside House (with Burgee), Bronx, N.Y. 1976, Avery Fisher Hall (interior; with Burgee), New York. 1976, Pennzoil Place (with Burgee); 1976–1978, Post Oak Central I & II (with Burgee), Houston, Tex. 1977, Century Center (with Burgee), South Bend, Ind. 1977, Fine Arts Center (with Burgee), Muhlenberg College, Allentown, Penn. 1977, General American Life Insurance Company Building (with Burgee), St. Louis, Mo. 1977, Thanksgiving Square (with Burgee), Dallas, Tex. 1978, 80 Field Point Road (with Burgee), Greenwich, Conn. 1978, 1001 Fifth Avenue (façade; with Burgee), New York. 1978, Studio Theatre (with Burgee), Kennedy Center, Washington. 1980 (under construction), A.T.&T. Headquarters (with Burgee), New York. 1980 (under construction), Civic Center (with Burgee), National Center for the Performing Arts, Bombay. 1980 (under construction), Civic Center (with Burgee), National Center for the Performing Arts, Peoria, Ill. 1980, Crystal Cathedral (with Burgee), Garden Grove Community Church, Calif.

BIBLIOGRAPHY

HITCHCOCK, H. R. 1966 *Philip Johnson, Architecture, 1949–1965.* New York: Holt.

HITCHCOCK, H. R., and JOHNSON, PHILIP (1932)1966 *The International Style: Architecture Since 1922.* New York: Norton.

JACOBUS, JOHN 1962 *Philip Johnson.* New York: Braziller.

JOHNSON, PHILIP 1979a *Johnson/Burgee: Architecture.* Text by Nory Miller and photographs by Richard Payne. New York: Random House.

JOHNSON, PHILIP 1979b *Writings.* New York: Oxford University Press. Includes a forward by Vincent Scully, an introduction by Peter Eisenmann, and a commentary by Robert A. M. Stern.

JOHNSON, RICHARD NORMAN

Richard Norman Johnson (1923–), an Australian architect, attended the University of Sydney (1946–1950). He became a partner in the firm of McConnel Smith and, in 1971, a director. A winner of numerous awards, Johnson considers his buildings a product of group effort, not a monument to one architect.

Johnson stands apart from his professional peer group as an architect with a humanistic bent, his aim being to satisfy not only his client but also those who may pass through the building for whatever reason. Not concerned with style for style's sake, Johnson exhibits a sense of logic and intelligence in his structures. An example is the Federal-State Law Courts Building in Sydney (1977) where an investigative approach led to the creation of the hexagonal-shaped courtroom, a more intimate and direct design than the traditional and formal rectangle. Johnson is also noted for his clever solutions to energy conservation problems and for his respect for the environment, evident in his Benjamin Government Building (1979) in Belconnen, Canberra, a building advantageously positioned with regard to the intense sunlight and the surrounding scenery.

LYNDA GREENBERG

WORKS

1965, Sydney Water Board Building; 1977, Federal-State Law Courts Building; Sydney. 1979, Benjamin Government Offices, Belconnen, Canberra.

BIBLIOGRAPHY

"Architect's Own House—Chatswood, Australia." 1963 *Architecture in Australia* 52, no. 4:80–83.
"Commonwealth State Law Courts Building." 1978 *Architecture Australia* 66, no. 6:56–57.
"Commonwealth State Law Courts, Sydney." 1978 *Architecture Australia* 67, no. 2:46–51.
SNOWDEN, HARVEY (editor) 1968 *Towards an Australian Architecture.* Sydney.
"World: Sydney Domestic." 1964 *Architectural Review* 135, no. 804:83.

JOHNSTON, FRANCIS

Francis Johnston (1760–1829) was trained by THOMAS COOLEY whom he succeeded in the patronage of Richard Robinson, archbishop of Armagh. Though a competent neoclassicist, he never traveled on the mainland of Europe. He was influenced by JAMES WYATT, and also by JAMES GANDON whom he replaced—jointly with Richard Morrison—at the head of the architectural profession in Ireland after Gandon's retirement around 1808.

Johnston was eclectic and stylistically versatile. His classical work ranges from the Gibbsian (see JAMES GIBBS) Church of Saint George's, Dublin (1802–1817) to the refined neoclassical severity of Townley Hall (begun 1794), a severity which shades into the bleakness of his institutional work such as the Richmond Penitentiary (1812–1816). He toyed with Greek and primitivist orders, but held back from exploiting their expressive potential to the full. His Gothic work includes the Chapel of Dublin Castle (1807–1814) in the manner of Strawberry Hill, and a number of castles which, like Charleville Forest (1801–1812) pioneer, albeit tentatively, the architecture of the picturesque in Ireland.

In 1805, he was appointed architect of the Board of Works and Civil Buildings and in 1823

he was a founder member of the Royal Hibernian Academy of which he was president (1824–1829), and whose premises in Dublin he designed and built at his own expense.

EDWARD MCPARLAND

WORKS

Begun 1794, Townley Hall; 1796–1806, Cornmarket, Drogheda; County Louth, Ireland. 1800–1807, Saint Andrew's Church (completion), Dublin. 1801–1812, Charleville Forest, County Offaly, Ireland. Begun 1802, Killeen Castle, County Meath, Ireland. 1802–c.1817, Saint George's Church; 1804–1808, Bank of Ireland (conversion from Parliament House); 1807–1814, Chapel, Dublin Castle; Dublin. Begun 1809, Courthouse, Armagh, Ireland. 1812–1816, Richmond Penitentiary; 1815–1818, General Post Office; 1824–1826, Royal Hibernian Academy; Dublin.

BIBLIOGRAPHY

"A Letter from Francis Johnston." 1963 *Quarterly Bulletin of the Irish Georgian Society* 6, no. 1:1–5.
MCPARLAND, EDWARD 1969 "Francis Johnston, Architect, 1760–1829." *Quarterly Bulletin of the Irish Georgian Society* 12, nos. 3–4:61–139.

JOHNSTON, WILLIAM L.

William Johnston (1811–1849) is remembered principally, but perhaps erroneously, for his part in the design of the Jayne Building (1848–1850), which stood on Philadelphia's lower Chestnut Street until 1957, when it was demolished as being out of keeping with its better-known colonial neighbors. Although its eight stories made Dr. Jayne's Granite Building one of the tallest structures of its day, historians have been most interested in the form of its façade. By emphasizing the piers and suppressing the lintels, the designer gave vertical expression to a tall building in a way that presaged the solution for which LOUIS H. SULLIVAN was hailed nearly half a century later.

Like many another in an era that put a premium on picturesque effects, Johnston approached the architectural profession through his skill as a draftsman, but the little that has come to light concerning his career is compromised by differences in the spelling of his name. After the Carpenters' Company of the City and County of Philadelphia reorganized its short-lived architectural school in 1835, one of the instructors subsequently hired was a William Johnston, and as late as 1839 the Philadelphia *Directory* lists a "Carver, John E. & Johnston, drawing school" in Carpenters' Court. Presumably in both cases this is the same William Johnston who in 1840 and again in 1842 entered watercolors of architectural subjects in the exhibition sponsored by the Artists' Fund Society of Philadelphia. Probably to avoid confusion with others, about 1839 Johnston began to insert the "t" in his name and to use the middle initial "L." Evidence for this is found in the Philadelphia directories for the years 1837 through 1849. There, as early as 1841, a William L. Johnston appears as "architect" and " William Johnson, house-carpenter" is no longer listed as living at the same address.

When Johnston succumbed to tuberculosis in his thirty-eighth year, Dr. Jayne found another Philadelphia architect in the person of THOMAS U. WALTER, for whom his biographers would claim a larger role in the final form of the Jayne Building than has been generally assumed. Certainly, the Venetian elements of the façade have no parallels in other Philadelphia structures with which Johnston's name has been associated. The Ionic order of the First Methodist Chapel (1840–1841) may have been derived from Greek sources, but the Mercantile Library (1844) made free use of the Roman forms of the Renaissance Revival then coming into vogue, and much the same might be said of both the Odd Fellows' Hall (1845–1846) on Sixth Street, and the original portion of the handsome Commissioners' Hall (1848) in the district of Spring Garden.

In view of the comparatively early date, it is not surprising that the wholesale druggist George W. Carpenter credited Johnston only with drafting the details—and not with serving as architect, as is sometimes claimed—for Phil-Ellena (1841–1844), the former's grandiose neoclassical residence in Germantown. But in the course of his brief career Johnston must have designed a number of Philadelphia residences that still await identification. Possibly, he was himself responsible for the row of "elegant dwellings" on Logan Square that he drew about 1847 for P. S. Duval's lithograph; at least by that time he was sufficiently well-established as a domestic architect to justify his selection as the designer of the Gothic house at the Louisiana plantation of Thomas Asheton Morgan, a client with close Philadelphia ties through his wife and merchant father.

Morgan's Orange Grove (1847–1849) is today a ruin, and except for the Central Presbyterian Church of Philadelphia (c. 1845), a small Italianate structure on Lombard Street, the only work by Johnston known to survive intact is the entrance to Hood Cemetery (1849) in Germantown. With its Moorish arch in an otherwise neobaroque setting, it provides an intriguing glimpse of the artistic imagination of its young designer who died so prematurely and about whom so little is known.

GEORGE B. TATUM

Johnston.
Dr. Jayne's Granite
  Building (with others).
Philadelphia.
1848–1850

WORKS

*1840–1841, First Methodist Protestant Chapel; *1844, Mercantile Library; c.1845, Lombard Street Central Presbyterian Church (now the Pentecostal Bridegroom Church); *1845–1846, Odd Fellows' Hall; Philadelphia. *1847–1849, Orange Grove, Braithwaite, La. *1848, Commissioners' Hall (with others), Spring Garden; *1848–1850, Dr. Jayne's Granite Building (with others); 1849, Hood Cemetery (entrance), Germantown; Philadelphia.

BIBLIOGRAPHY

CULLISON, WILLIAM R. III 1969 "Orange Grove: The Design and Construction of an Ante-Bellum neo-Gothic Plantation House on the Mississippi River." Unpublished M.A. thesis, Tulane University, New Orleans, La.

IWANICKI, EDWIN 1966 "Phil-Ellena: The Country-seat of George W. Carpenter." *Germantown Crier* 18:73ff.

MASSEY, JAMES C. 1955 "Carpenters' School, 1833–42." *Journal of the Society of Architectural Historians* 14, no. 2:29–30.

PETERSON, CHARLES E. 1950 "Ante-Bellum Skyscraper." *Journal of the Society of Architectural Historians* 9, no. 4:27–28.

RUTLEDGE, ANNA WELLS (editor) 1955 *Cumulative Record of Exhibition Catalogues: The Pennsylvania Academy of the Fine Arts, 1807–1870; The Society of Artists, 1800–1814; The Artists' Fund Society, 1835–1845.* Philadelphia: The American Philosophical Society.

SMITH, ROBERT C. 1951 "The Jayne Building Again." *Journal of the Society of Architectural Historians* 10, no. 1:25.

WAINWRIGHT, NICHOLAS B. 1958 *Philadelphia in the Romantic Age of Lithography.* Philadelphia: The Historical Society of Pennsylvania.

WEBSTER, RICHARD J. 1976 *Philadelphia Preserved: Catalog of the Historic American Buildings Survey.* Philadelphia: Temple University Press.

WEISMAN, WINSTON 1961 "Philadelphia Functionalism and Sullivan." *Journal of the Society of Architectural Historians* 20, no. 1:3–19.

JONES, A. QUINCY

A. Quincy Jones (1913–1979) was born in Kansas City, Missouri. His early reputation in small house design led to tract planning (Mutual Housing, a cooperative, Los Angeles [1948–1950] with Whitney R. Smith and Edgardo Contini, and several thousand houses for Eichler Homes, throughout California, with Frederick E. Emmons, in the 1950s). Beside housing, education was a major concern, and much late work was in planning new campuses (State University, Dominguez Hills, Carson, California [1965]) and university buildings (Annenberg School of Communications [1971–1976], University of Southern California, where he served as dean of the school of architecture and fine arts).

ESTHER McCOY

JONES, HUGH

Hugh Griffith Jones (1872–1947) was born in Randolph, Wisconsin, and studied at the University of Minnesota and with George E. Bertrand, Minneapolis. He practiced in Chicago and New York as a designer and renderer in the American Beaux-Arts tradition. He went to Montreal in 1908 and became assistant chief architect for the Canadian Pacific Railway. His principal works are the Union Station, Toronto, with JOHN M. LYLE (1912); Canadian Pacific Railway Station, Moose Jaw (1922); Montreal Terminal Development (1923); Dominion Douglas Church, Montreal (1926); and Pavilion Tower Jacques Cartier Bridge, Montreal (1928). Griffith was an accomplished water colorist and pictorial photographer. In collaboration with Edmund Dyonnet he prepared an unpublished history of the Royal Canadian Academy.

JOHN BLAND

JONES, INIGO

The early life of Inigo Jones (1573–1652) is shrouded in mystery. There are many legends, but his baptism on July 19, 1573, in Saint Bartholomew's the Less, Smithfield, London, is a fact. He may have been one of eight children, and his father was a clothworker. The family could not have been much more than humble. Nearly everything else that is known about Jones's family is enigmatic. Jones never married. When he died on June 21, 1652, at Somerset House, he was buried at Saint Benet's. In his will he left £2000 to a kinswoman Anne, the wife of JOHN WEBB, Jones's principal and personal assistant. In the sense of mystery about lost years and upbringing there is a definite parallel to Shakespeare, whom Jones would certainly have known during the years up to about 1610, and like Shakespeare, Jones was a genius. Indeed, the quality of genius must feature strongly in any assessment of Jones, for he was undoubtedly a man unique in his time, of an intellect rare even in Europe.

In 1603, Jones was referred to as a "picture-maker," a term which then described a portrait painter, and the most likely explanation is that he had been apprenticed to a late Elizabethan painter such as Marcus Gheeraerts around 1590. The death of his father in 1597 meant perhaps a little money, but more likely it provided the incentive to break loose from family ties. It is probable that in 1598 he was attracted to the service of Francis Manners, Lord Roos, brother of Roger, fifth earl of Rutland, and the future sixth earl. When in 1605 Jones was described as a "great traveller," this must refer to his years in Europe between 1598 and 1603 studying painting and to a lesser extent architecture. He probably bought his copy of ANDREA PALLADIO's *Quattro Libri dell' Architettura* (1570) in Venice in 1601, where he probably met Henry Wotton, and the earl of Essex. Jones may well have been able to spend these five years in Italy studying the "arts of design" by virtue of his friendship with what could be described as dandified Elizabethans, although it would be unwise to say that Jones was a homosexual in the modern sense of that word. He may well have been patronized solely on the grounds of his obvious genius. How this was expressed is not clear, for nothing survives of his work before 1605. He must have begun, however, to study the Bolognese masters such as Parmigianino whom he "so loved."

Queen Elizabeth died in 1603, and this event brought courtiers scurrying home to England. James I was now king, and in this year Jones was paid as "picture-maker" for his "paynes" accompanying the fifth earl of Rutland's train to Denmark to present the Order of the Garter to Christian IV, whose sister was James's Queen. Jones is recorded at a banquet in Copenhagen, and it is likely that he was there, not as a portrait painter, but as a deviser of masques. The next recorded event in Jones's life occurred in October 1604 when he was busy on the settings and costumes for *The Masque of Blackness*, performed for Queen Anne in January 1605. Seven more entertainments or masques took place before the end of 1607, and for most of these productions Jones devised a stage that was quite new to England, employing complex machinery and illusionistic settings and lighting, with a knowledge of perspective that was unrivaled. It was at this time that Jones formed a partnership with Ben Jonson, who provided the allegorical and political content and meaning, embodying Renaissance beliefs in the character of kingship and royalty.

Perhaps the most magical survival from these early years is the monument to Lady Cotton at Norton-in-Hales, Shropshire, the first real structure by Jones. Were it not for a surviving design, association with Jones might never have been guessed. Just as the drawing is like a masque design, so is the monument like a setting upon the stage. To enter this lonely rural church and find the earliest surviving work by Jones is a moving experience.

In 1608, Robert Cecil, first earl of Salisbury, acquired land on the Strand, London, to build an Exchange in response to the recently completed Amsterdam Exchange. In July of this same year, Cecil was on the Commission to survey the old Cathedral of Saint Paul and have a new spire built. Jones provided designs for both projects, and the most flattering thing that can be said about them is that Jones had not yet fully developed his genius. They are composed of bookish elements derived from SEBASTIANO SERLIO as well as engraved sources such as Giuliano da Sangallo's (see SANGALLO FAMILY) for St. Peter's in Rome. The Exchange as built was by Simon Basil, then surveyor of the works, but the chasteness of the lower parts of the elevation is in stark contrast to the rather old-fashioned style of Basil's known works and may well have been influenced by Jones. He may well have been acting the role of *éminence grise*, one that he was to play so often in his life.

In the summer of 1609, Jones visited France carrying "letters for his Majesty's service," and this visit sparked off an infusion of new ideas derived from French mannerist architecture as exemplified by PHILIBERT DELORME. He may even have visited Delorme Chateau d'Anet. Certainly by April 1610, the old-fashioned design by Robert Liming for the south front of Cecil's Hatfield House had been revised by another, certainly Jones's, with the insertion of classical windows derived from Delorme. By the fall of 1610, Jones was at work on the settings for the masque *Oberon, the Fairy Prince* performed in January 1611 for Henry, Prince of Wales. The scenery in this masque is strongly

Jones.
Design for Lady Cotton
*   Monument.*
Norton-in-Hales,
*   Shropshire, England.*
c.1608

marked by French influences. In 1611, Jones became surveyor to Prince Henry, but as the prince died in 1612, little was effected except for some work at Saint James's Palace. It seems that the prince was more attracted to Costantini de Servi, a Medicean architect from Florence, and to Salomon de Caus, a French garden designer and hydraulics expert. It may well be that Jones was more favored by Prince Charles, but this is unclear. What is certain is that a solid friendship had been forged between Jones and Thomas Howard, second earl of Arundel, one of Prince Henry's supporters and a friend, too, of Prince Charles. This friendship was the augury of great events.

The first of these events was to follow the wedding of Princess Elizabeth and the Elector Palatine in February 1613. In one of the masques, *The Memorable Masque* by George Chapman, Jones is referred to as "our kingdom's most artfull and ingenious architect," quite a hyperbole considering that nothing substantial by him existed at this time. On April 27, 1613, Jones was granted the reversion of the office of surveyor of the king's works. Soon after this, he and Arundel set off with Princess Elizabeth and her Prince Palatine for Heidelberg, and this was the start of Jones's second Italian journey.

Jones was one of the first Englishmen to travel in an intellectual manner, probably carrying a library with him, and all the time consciously guiding Arundel in his quest for connoisseurship, for Arundel was one of the very first to collect in the Renaissance manner, creating cabinets out of paintings, drawings, antique sculpture, coins, and

Jones.
Edward Cecil's House
(design for entrance).
The Strand, London.
c.1618

bronzes. Jones must have been a great encourager for Arundel to mass his collection of drawings by Parmigianino. Mariette has observed that Jones himself collected the work of Schiavone. In Venice, they made their greatest coup when they met the aged and infirm VICENZO SCAMOZZI, from whom they probably bought most of the designs for private and public buildings by Palladio and the designs by Scamozzi which were contained in two chests in Arundel's collection in the 1650's but were subsequently lost or destroyed. Also on this tour, Lafreri's great *Speculum Romanae* was acquired by Arundel, and this must have been of crucial interest to Jones, representing as it did in engravings the twin polarities of ancient and modern Rome. After criss-crossing Italy, they returned to London in January 1615.

On Basil's death in 1615, Jones became surveyor of the works and began his twenty-five years of activity for the Crown. In all this time, he did not delegate a single design. Jones dealt with every job personally in that all the designs were made by Jones and were not allowed to be altered in execution by any subordinate. But then no subordinate understood Jones or the basis or canon of his style. This is borne out by an examination of those subordinates, the principals in Jones's royal office. His second in command, the comptroller, was Thomas Baldwin, whose Jesus Hospital, Bray, Berkshire, is Jacobean in style, yet it was built in 1623, the year of Jones's royal chapel at Saint James's Palace. His master mason was William Cure, a dyed-in-the-wool Elizabethan, incapable of executing the stonework of the Whitehall Banqueting House in 1619, so that NICHOLAS STONE had to intervene; but even Stone, master mason from 1632, built in a decidedly Northern mannerist style more familiar to Antwerp than to Vicenza. With a few exceptions, Arundel being one, Jones's contemporaries could not tell the difference between a work of Jones's maturity and one in a subordinate or artisan style by the likes of Stone. When the exalted marquis of Buckingham needed an official lodging in Whitehall, Jones as surveyor was responsible for designing it, and if we are to judge by its dining room ceiling design, it was fully in Jones's manner, being based upon the Temple of Venus and Rome via Palladio's Fourth Book. But when the duke (as he had become) wanted a grand addition to his house off the Strand, BALTHASAR GERBIER built it in 1624–1625 in an artisan-mannerist style. This was true of nearly all buildings carried out for courtiers as private commissions by Jones's subordinates.

Paradoxically, however, Jones contributed to this subordinate or artisan style, for after 1615 there were two or three years in which his work

was of a transitional nature, as if he was testing his abilities. Sir Fulke Greville's House in Holborn was built before 1619 and reminds us of similar façades in Augsburg with an attic divided from the lower elevation by an emphatic cornice and capped by a shaped gable topped with a pediment. Greville's house also had a window with an iron-work balcony, called by Jones a "Pergular." There was one on Colonel Cecil's House in the Strand for which Jones designed it as the balcony above an arched entrance. Much of this early work drew upon Serlio, especially for gateways, but Cecil's was purloined from JACQUES FRANCART's *Livre d'Architecture* of 1616. In these borrowings Jones was not always a copyist; rather, he tended to refine upon the originals. This transitional period seems to be the only one in Jones's life when he was willing to deal with courtiers, but he was, after all, an architect at the beginning of his new career, and he was obviously anxious to please. His two most important works of this period may have concerned a theater and a country house. The latter was the house built by Mary, dowager countess of Pembroke, at Houghton Conquest, Bedfordshire. She had begun a traditional Basil-style house in 1615, but before she died in 1621 the house had received two astonishingly classical frontispieces to the north and west fronts, so classical that no one in England bar Jones could have designed them. The theater exists as two designs, a plan and elevation and two sections, that have conclusively been associated with the Phoenix Theatre in Drury Lane, converted from an oval cock-fighting pit in 1617. If these designs were executed, and there is no evidence one way or the other, the Phoenix could be considered as one of the most important small theaters in Europe. Even if the designs are among the most precious of their type in Europe, it would be hazardous to concur in their execution. As designs they only confirm Jones's genius, and it should be said that it would have been natural for the greatest masque designer in England to have been asked to design a theater. They are a trial run for the conversion of the Whitehall cock pit into a small court theater in 1629. Architecturally, this was based on the Teatro Olimpico in Vicenza as designed before 1580 by Palladio and not with the deep perspectives by Scamozzi.

One other project needs discussion in this account of the transitional period, namely, the Star Chamber in Westminster Palace designed in 1617. In Jones's hand only a plan survives, and this accompanies an elevation drawn by John Webb, therefore drawn after about 1627 or 1628 at the earliest. The elevation appears derivative and stilted in composition, as if by Webb himself, and must be dealt with cautiously. It has an academic quality that is suspiciously close to Webb's own work of the late 1640s. He may well have been attempting to reconstruct Jones's elevation upon the original plan of 1617. Also belonging to this period may be a Brew House and a Stable for Newmarket Palace, but it is not certain if the Scamozzian design that has been associated with the Brew House is of this date, for Scamozzi's *L'Idea della architettura universale* appeared only in 1615. The stable design, however, is a most beautiful and limpid drawing, of masquelike character, demonstrating that Jones was the greatest draftsman in England, a reputation that was never questioned or exceeded. The so-called transitional period also encampasses the beginning of the Queen's House at Greenwich in 1616, a major work for Queen Anne of Denmark, for whom Jones had built gateways at her palace of Oatlands in Surrey and for whom he may have added a two-story classical portico to her palace at Byfleet in the same county, both probably in 1617. The Queen's House has gone down in legend as one of Jones's earliest works, and therefore its classical style as evident today has been seen as bursting upon an old-fashioned court; but this is not so, for the Queen's House as begun in 1616 was probably a very different building from that completed in 1636 for Queen Henrietta Maria. Queen Anne tragically died in 1619, and work upon the Queen's House stopped at the level of the top of the ground floor. It remained in this incompleted state until 1630. One factor is clear: Jones took the decision to set the new building across the public road that divided palace precincts from the hunting park. He may have toyed with other solutions, such as a Scamozzian rotunda-type villa or an oblong plan inspired by the Villa Aldobrandini or a compact villa of a type common to the early eighteenth century. This last type is represented by one of Jones's most important drawings. The villa design proposed was found by LORD BURLINGTON among Jones's Palladio designs and was thought to be by that master. It was copied for Burlington and has remarkable affinities with the pioneering neo-

Palladian villa of Marble Hill, Middlesex. Jones, in placing his palace across the road, thought of it as a bridge, but in shape it was decidedly of palace proportions, not a villa. Much searching has taken place to find the source of the resultant H-shaped building, but in fact, it is no more than a rearrangement of the rooms in Scamozzi's Villa Molini, where Lord Arundel and Jones stayed in 1614. There is no evidence that the plan of the Queen's House today is that laid down in 1616. Evidence from paintings suggests a ground story elevation on the park side as having a tall arched central doorway flanked on each side by four small arched windows set rather high up in the wall. From a surviving design, one can infer that Jones was also thinking of a different type of elevation, one with porticoes reminiscent of the Villa Molini. The answer must be that in 1630 Jones was reluctant to build or finish a palace begun so many years before in the same early and transitional style.

The question also deserves to be put as to what the Queen's House looked like when it was finished. A precious elevation of the north front survives as a photographic copy of a stolen original; it demonstrates that Jones's façade was far more eclectic in character than the present neoclassical one. The outer pairs of second floor windows were clasped by iron balconies; there were balconies, too, to the windows on the ground floor on each side of the entrance; there was a pediment behind the balustrade over the middle three bays, and the roof was dominated by two large octagonal copulas, almost like tempiettos, that must have been set above the staircases, one over the circular stair, the other over the square back stairs behind the Queen's bedroom. The most fascinating aspect of the lost drawing is the existence of a program of mural painting in the manner of Italian mannerist palaces. This may, of course, only have been an intention, for the drawing could have been especially commissioned for the purpose of some fete or entertainment in the palace precincts. When John Webb or another filled in the spaces of the H-shaped plan in 1661–1662, he continued the

Jones.
Design for a villa façade
*   (perhaps for the Queen's*
*   House).*
c.1616

Jones.
Greenwich Palace (Queen's
*   House).*
Kent, England.
1616–1635

balconied theme to his windows above the bridges on the east and west fronts. The south portico also needs consideration. No designs by Jones before 1630 indicate such a portico, and this too must be seen as a revision of this period. The idea of a portico in antis or loggia fits in with similar porticoes presumed to have been executed at Bagshot 1631 and Hyde Park Lodges in 1634.

This early period, one of assimilation, came to an end with two of the most important commissions in Jones's career: the new Banqueting House in Whitehall, succeeding an earlier one that burned down, and the Prince's Lodging at Newmarket: both were begun within a few weeks of each other in 1619, and both are inextricably linked in the solutions to their façades. There is slight evidence that Jones may have been involved with the previous Banqueting House finished in 1609, for its interior at least was classical, derivative of a Vitruvian (see VITRUVIUS) basilica, and this was unusual for England in 1609. The plan reveals, however, an elevation that must have been Jacobean in style, and therefore not too much importance should be placed upon this episode. The new Banqueting House was completed in 1622 and in its classical purity astounded London, rising as it did from the muddle of medieval and Tudor Whitehall Palace. At first, Jones conceived the exterior as a Palladian townhouse of a Vicentine type, but in two designs the pedimented centerpiece is eliminated in favor of a more equably balanced façade. This elimination of the central emphasis has been related to the banqueting room behind, a single space surrounded by a cantilevered gallery. The true reason is perhaps more interesting, for Jones may well have thought, in the middle of his design processes, that his Banqueting House might one day serve as a unit of a newly rebuilt palace of Whitehall, in which case a townhouse façade with pediment would be much more difficult to integrate than his horizontally disposed elevation. It is also significant that when Rubens was corresponding about the commission to paint the ceiling compartments, he referred to the "new palace," not to a banqueting house. The fact that from as early as 1620 Rubens had been considered for the ceiling is proof indeed that the room was never intended as a place to hold masques, for the smoke from candles would have quickly ruined the paintings. Indeed, immediately after the paintings were set up, a new masquing room had to be built nearby in 1637. What Jones conceived was a *sala grande* in some as yet unbuilt palace of the future. It is perhaps worthwhile at this point to say that none of the surviving schemes for a Whitehall Palace are in Jones's hand. They are mostly by John Webb, and even the "P" scheme generally accepted as reflecting Jones's designs seems to me to be of that bookish academic character more peculiar to Webb. This is not to deny Jones any role in the Whitehall Palace story, but not one single physical document survives in his hand to support his intervention in the Whitehall Palace commissions. Many of the Webb schemes were made in the 1640s and at least one after 1660. The influence of the Banqueting House was profound, not on Jones's contemporaries but on the neo-Palladians and as published in pattern books from 1715 onward.

The Prince's Lodging at Newmarket was built for the races. It possessed, therefore, a street elevation and a side elevation, the latter possibly of a secondary character and known to us only from a detail by Webb of a large architrave-cornice broken by a small segment-headed window. The street façade is another matter, for two designs survive, one of a Palladian townhouse composed with reference to Scamozzi and Serlio, the other far more idiosyncratic, doing away with the orders and creating an astylar façade that adumbrates a type of country house that became common after the 1670s. With Newmarket, Jones rose to a mastership of classical disciplines that on the plane of creation owes little to immediately obvious precedents. This is pure invention of the sort not even achieved by Palladio himself. Unfortunately, no plan of Newmarket survives, but behind the front there may have been an apartment twenty by forty feet, in other words a double cube of the Banqueting House sort. (The Queen's House possessed a galleried entrance hall of forty foot cube, a plan element that exercised a fascination for the neo-Palladians, such as COLEN CAMPBELL at Houghton Hall, Norfolk, 1722.)

There is a stylistic connection between the façade of Newmarket and the west front of the Queen's Chapel at Saint James's Palace, begun in 1623 in anticipation of the Spanish Infanta's visit, but not completed until May 1625 when Charles married Henrietta Maria instead. The Queen's Chapel picks up the proportions of the centerpiece of the Newmarket astylar design, and behind it is also a double-cube hall, covered by a coffered ceiling. It is lit at the east end by a Venetian or Palladian window, possibly the first use of this window in England, although Jones had intended such a window in one of his early studies for the Queen's House. The Chapel is, in effect, a single-space room, galleried at one end, and is thus the prototype for innumerable Georgian box churches, each with their east Palladian window and their west gallery. The Chapel equally influenced CHRISTOPHER WREN in some of his solutions for rebuilding the City churches. In many ways, the Queen's Chapel was a trial for Jones's other important chapel at Somerset House in 1630, although it may have been thought out in tandem with his remodeling of the old Elizabethan chapel in Greenwich Palace, also in 1623. As with the marquess of Buckingham's dining room ceiling of 1619, the coffers of the Queen's Chapel are derived from the Temple of Venus. In 1623 also, the new House of Lords was begun, over which space Jones erected a covering in the form of a plaster barrel vault painted in *trompe l'oeil* with coffers based, not upon a woodcut in Palladio, but on one in Serlio copied from an antique ceiling. In the House of Lords, as well as in the royal closet above the gallery in the Queen's Chapel, there were chimneypieces of a type that Jones popularized: a pedimented overmantel above a chimney surround. The chimneypiece was essentially a northern invention, and the French provided the most admired models. Few patterns could be found in Italian treatises, with Scamozzi providing two of the very few. His "Nappa" was used by Jones for the surround of the Queen's Chapel, but for the overmantel both here and in the House of Lords, Jones appears to have refined upon Jacobean models, in one proposing waisted pilasters. He later turned to the engravings of French designers such as Jean Barbet whose *Livre* appeared in 1633, but his relationship to certain French designers must be examined in the light of Queen Henrietta Maria's patronage of her own nationals. There are numerous instances when Jones was obliged to redraw chimneypiece designs supplied by an anonymous Frenchman. This is the case for the Cabinet Room in the Queen's House in 1637 and for one at Somerset House in 1636. The same unknown hand drew a chimneypiece inscribed "from ye French ambasator" by Jones and dated January 1636—as if the ambassador was the channel for designs from France. This French influence reaches a peak in the 1630s. It can be detected in the handling of the Somerset House Chapel where the screen seems to echo scenes from *Oberon, the Fairy Queen* but is also archaeologizing in the neoclassical sense by incorporating scrolls substituted for triglyphs into its entablature taken from an antique marble then in Lord Arundel's collection at Arundel House. Despite its survival into the 1770s, only the chapel ceiling, its altarpiece, and its screen were measured or engraved. The character of the suites of state apartments can be reconstructed only from the Declared Accounts. Richness was certainly the key. All that can be gained today of such apartments is a canopied painted ceiling of the Queen's Bedchamber in the Queen's House (c.1635), attributed to Matthew Gooderick or John de Critz I, either of whom may also have

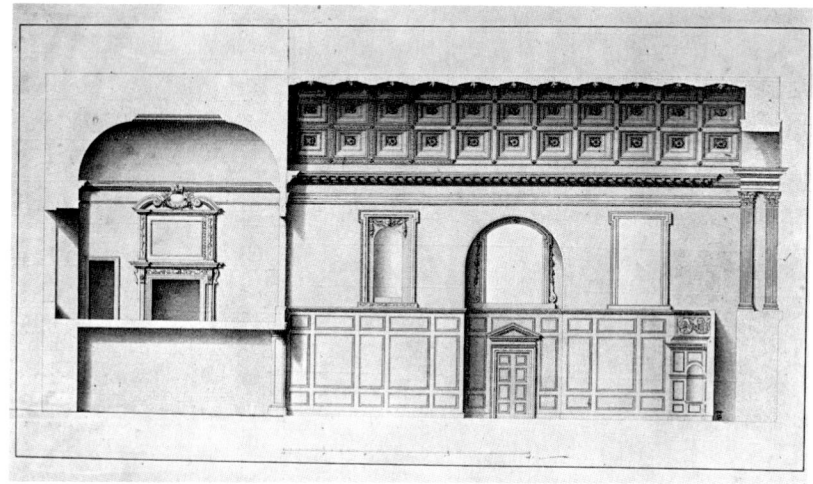

Jones.
Saint James's Palace
 (Queen's Chapel design).
Westminster, London.
1623–1625

painted the ceiling of the Single Cube Room at Wilton House, Wiltshire, for the fourth earl of Pembroke after 1648 and before 1652. Both these ceilings are in a grotesque and arabesque style. The Wilton rooms are, of course, by John Webb, not by Jones. They express perfectly, however, the style of a court interior, and the chimneypieces are as close as anything to the type that Jones designed in the 1630s.

With Somerset House, Jones's work for the Crown began to decrease, although as late as 1640 he was making considerable alterations to Wimbledon House, Surrey, for Queen Henrietta Maria. The two signal works that are unrepresented by

Jones.
Study for a chimneypiece in
 the Queen's House.
c.1635

Jones.
Engraving of screen in
 Somerset House Chapel.

surviving designs are Lodges for hunting: Bagshot Lodge, Surrey, in 1631 and Hyde Park Lodge, London, 1634. Both appear from accounts to have been of the villa type, that is, of five bays divided one-five-one, and both had porticoes in antis. Webb again may come to the rescue with his designs for a lodge in Hale Park, Hampshire, made for John Penruddock in 1638, for they may reflect the style of Jones's lodges.

Parallel with all this activity for the Crown, Jones was equally busy with the court masques. From 1615, he prepared settings and made costume designs for at least thirty-one masques, his last being the *Queen of Aragon* (1640). This was an astonishing achievement, for as with his architecture it was all conceived single-handedly.

It is often forgotten that Webb was not an officer of the royal works and probably represented the executive side of the building process. He was certainly in charge of the renovations and restoration of Saint Paul's Cathedral from 1633 to 1642, which followed stylistically and in time the laying out of Covent Garden and Piazza and Saint Paul's Church there from 1631.

Covent Garden can be seen as a response to the Commission for Building of 1625 that sought to restrict building to brick and stone on old foundations so as to achieve "Uniformitie and Decency." It was as much a precaution against fire and plague as for architectural display. Jones was one of the commissioners, and it was doubtless due to his influence that the fourth earl of Bedford obtained a license in 1631 to build Covent Garden. The idea of a square with an integrated church was derived from the church and piazza at Leghorn that Jones would have seen on his first Italian visit; but there were also the precedents of the Place des Vosges in Paris and, in antiquity, that of San Sebastiano, available to Jones through Palladio. Jones was certainly the designer of Covent Garden, but the actual builder seems to have been ISAAC DE CAUS, the earl's personal architect, and his French presence in this French-looking piazza deserves some consideration. However, as Sir John Summerson has demonstrated, a disciplined Tuscan theme ties together both church and façades, and this must surely be Jones's inspiration. He was required to design a new Protestant church and there was no precedent for this in England. An anecdote by HORACE WALPOLE encapsulates his principles: Lord Bedford, on commissioning Jones, stated that he did not want to go to great expense, so wanted something "not much better than a barn." "Well! then," said Jones, "You shall have the handsomest barn in England." A barn is, of course, a primitive building, and the Tuscan order is the most primitive of the orders. Jones turned, not to the standard exposition of the Tuscan order, but to its most powerful primitive type as published by Daniele Barbaro in his edition of Vitruvius, where the order supports unmolded beams with cantilevers. This appealed to Jones on other grounds, for the plates in the Vitruvius were drawn by Palladio. With his church, Jones created a monument unique in Europe. The Tuscan themes moved around the square: first in the gateways that flanked the church—from the Roman Theater at Verona; then on the fronts of the two ranges, north and west, with a form of pilaster strip terminating in a primitive Tuscan bracketed eaves cornice. Covent Garden was not a complete square, for its southern side was the garden wall of Lord Bedford's house, and behind this was a formal garden with a tempietto that must have been designed by Isaac de Caus. De Caus's role in the actual building of Covent Garden is still not clear. He may have designed the small hipped-roof houses that once stood adjacent to the church gateways. It is worth remarking that soon after Covent Garden was completed, in the middle 1630s, Jones made a design for Lord Maltravers, Lord Arundel's son, for an office and manufactory for minting royal farthing tokens. It is not known if this was built, but in effect it would have been an astylar version of the Covent Garden façades wth fenestration on the ground floor and two entrances. In this prophetic design, Jones was moving close to the idea of the typical astylar terrace house that became the standard London treatment of several dwellings, as pioneered by Colen Campbell on Lord Burlington's estate in the 1720s.

The archaeologizing processes were continued not so far away at another Saint Paul's, this time old Saint Paul's Cathedral. Ever since Jones made his immature design for the spire in 1608, attempts had been made to initiate a restoration program. There was a commission in 1620, but nothing came of it until William Laud became bishop in 1628. By 1631, sufficient funds had been raised to create a new commission, with Jones as architect and Webb as his deputy. By 1642, when work stopped, Jones had recased most of the cathedral except for the central tower and the fourteenth-century Gothic choir. In effect, Jones encased the cathedral in Portland stone, setting at the west front a portico that had few rivals in Europe, one that for Jones had royal connotations because Charles I agreed to pay for it in 1634. Jones took as his model the portico from Palladio's reconstruction of the temple of Venus and Rome, but using the richly decorated order from the temple of Antoninus and Faustina. Its 56-foot height made it one of the marvels of the European world; nothing could match it north of the Alps and little south.

The Corinthian order was appropriate for what was the royal entrance, but as Jones moved around the cathedral in his progressive restoration he attempted to evoke stylistic moods, each representative of an order. Hence, the body of the church was fully rusticated with primitive details that picked up motifs from de Cock's reconstruction of the Baths of Diocletian. Secondary doorways were Doric and greater doorways were Ionic. It was a most subtle and cerebral composition. Again, one has to confess that nothing like it existed anywhere else. It was a mark of Jones's genius, and a lonely genius at that. With the portico complete, Jones saw the approach road, Fleet Street, as a triumphal way. In 1638, the City of London asked him to build a Temple Bar where the City met the boundaries of Westminster, and here Jones would have placed a great triumphal arch of Roman scale, roughly 60 by 60 feet, and based upon the antique Roman arches of Septimius Severus and Constantine. Nothing survives to provide us with a feeling for Jones's handling of the monumental. However, in 1638 Jones designed the choir screen in Winchester Cathedral, like the Saint Paul's portico an act of royal charity. It was demolished in the nineteenth century, but the central bay survives in the Museum of Archaeology in Cambridge, England, as a rare reminder of Jones's monumental handling of the orders.

A myth has grown up about Jones as a country house architect. This was first started by Colen Campbell in his trilogy of *Vitruvius Britannicus* (1715, 1717, 1725), for whom any building of apparently advanced classical style was by Jones. Webb was forgotten and architectural connoisseurship as we know it today was quite unknown. Campbell therefore ascribed to Jones such houses by Webb as Gunnersbury and Amesbury, both built after Jones's death. Before his appointment as surveyor-general of the works, Jones had time to attend to courtiers, but they were nearly all close friends. Typical of this small coterie was Lionel Cranfield, later earl of Middlesex, for whom Jones did minor work at Pishiobury, Hertfordshire, in 1615, and later designed the gateway to Beaufort House, Chelsea, London, in 1621. This is the gateway now re-erected at Chiswick House, Middlesex. Jones was often willing to design gateways, probably finding pleasure in this exercise on a small scale. For the duke of Buckingham, he designed a gateway at New Hall, Essex, in 1623. About the same time, he proposed for the duke of Lennox majestic Vignolesque (see GIACOMO BAROZZI DA VIGNOLA) gateways for Hatton House, Holborn, London, perhaps never actually built. Jones was clearly fascinated by the variety of architectural display possible in these gateways.

It is certainly odd that he never appears to have designed and built a country house in his maturity, but he was essentially an urban man, a man of the court, reluctant to embark upon the bothersome administration of private commissions. Only two houses pass tests of stylistic criteria, and even these are dubiously authenticated. The most famous is, of course, Wilton House, Wiltshire, where the south front was rebuilt for the fourth earl of Pembroke from 1636. It was, however, clearly built by Isaac de Caus, although John Aubrey later claimed that Jones gave his "advice and approbation." A series of ceiling designs by Jones survive in the collection of Worcester College, Oxford, but these are not necessarily for the 1636 house, and I believe them to have been made for the third earl for the interior decoration of the old house. This earl was Jones's true friend, not the fourth nor the fifth, for whom the reconstruction of Wilton was finished after the fire around 1647. Nevertheless, even if Wilton has passed into the mythology of Jones, as

a country house it exercised a profound influence upon the neo-Palladian country houses by the likes of Colen Campbell, Lord Burlington, and WILLIAM KENT. The Palladian tower house became a model as popular as the villa.

The other house that comes close to the Jonesian canon is Stoke Park, Stoke Bruerne, Northamptonshire, begun for Sir Francis Crane around 1630. It appears that only the pavilions and quadrant colonnades were completed in Jones's lifetime. Bridges, in his *History of Northamptonshire* compiled before 1724, writes that Crane "brought the design from Italy, and in the execution of it received the assistance of Inigo Jones." This may well be true, for the pavilions are of advanced classical form, but not in Jones's style. Jones would never have incorporated such literal borrowings as the porches in antis from the Capitoline in Rome. They are too obvious.

This is not to say that Jones never made a design for a country house, but nothing ever got further than the drawing board. There is, however, one house that is composed of parts so close to Jones's own designs as to be virtually by him, although the execution and building were carried out by the owner, Sir Roger Townsend, and his builder, William Edge. This is Raynham Hall, Norfolk, begun about 1622 but built very slowly and perhaps not finished until the 1630s. Its south front is a wonderful synopsis of designs by Jones for Newmarket and for Fulke Greville's house in Holborn, with fenestration based upon Serlian sources as worked out on a sheet of designs by Jones dated April 1619. There is structural as well as documentary evidence that the intervening bays between the gabled wings and the centerpiece were originally one story lower. In other words the center rose out of the body of the house as a true temple, and the relationship to Palladio's Villa Maser is at once obvious. Raynham, however, lacks cohesion, due no doubt to the amateur way in which it was assembled.

To Jones have been attributed several gardens. Again, there is not a scrap of evidence that Jones ever designed a garden. Wilton was definitely the work of Isaac de Caus, and it has been identified with Sir John Danvers's garden at Chelsea as among the most Italianate in England. It may not be a coincidence that in the very year Danvers was laying out his garden, Jones was building the gateway literally next door for Lionel Cranfield. However, Jones as a garden designer is pure speculation, and most of the gardens laid out for the courtiers of the first Stuart Court were either in de Caus's style or had buildings in the style of the artisan or subordinate architects, such as Nicholas Stone.

Just as Jones's early years are shrouded in mystery, so in his last years he fades from the public stage. When civil war broke out in 1642, Jones was already nearly seventy, a considerable age for the seventeenth century. In July 1642, he lent Charles I £500, and three years later was taken prisoner at the sack of Basing House, Hampshire, when "the King's Surveyor, and Contriver of Scenes for the Queen's Dancing Barne" was ignominiously stripped by the soldiery and carried away in a blanket. Although his estate was sequestered, it was restored in 1646 on a total payment of £1045. He died in Somerset House on June 21, 1651, leaving £100 for his monument in Saint Benet's church. This was a sarcophagus tomb with Jones's bust flanked by obelisks and, at each end of the tomb, bas-reliefs, one representing the portico of Saint Paul's Cathedral, the other the Banqueting House. The tomb was demolished after the Great Fire of London in 1666, when Edward Marshall the sculptor "tooke away the bust." It is just possible that Michael Rysbrack's bust (Chatsworth, Derbyshire) is after this lost tomb bust. There are at least three portraits of Jones: the engraved portrait by Francesco Villamena, Rome (c.1614), Anthony Van Dyck's engraved portrait (c.1640), and William Dobson's sad portrait of the disillusioned Jones (c.1644).

John Webb inherited many of Jones's effects, his collection of drawings, and his library. He used them well, but he never rose higher than a competent master in an academic idiom. He was always a witness of his master's genius, the British Vitruvius, who restated the principles of antiquity and the Renaissance theorists in such a way that his buildings were, in his own words, "Solid, proportionable according to the rules, masculine and unaffected."

JOHN HARRIS

WORKS

c.1608, Lady Cotton Monument, Norton-in-Hales, Shropshire, England. (A)1609, Hatfield House (modifications of south front), Hertfordshire, England. (A)c.1615, Houghton House (frontispieces), Bedfordshire, England. 1615–1617, Newmarket Palace (brewhouse, stables, ridinghouse, doghouse), Suffolk, England. 1616–1635, Greenwich Palace (Queen's House; completed by others), Kent, England. (A)c.1617, Byfleet House (remodeling); 1617–1618, Oatlands Palace (great park gate, silkworm house, vineyard gate); Surrey, England. 1617–1618, Saint James's Palace (Prince's Buttery), Westminster; 1617–1618, Somerset House (hall lantern), The Strand; 1618, Arundel House (gateway and probably the Sculpture Gallery), The Strand; c.1618, Edward Cecil's House (entrance), The Strand; 1619?, Fulke Grenville's House, The Strand; 1619–1620, Whitehall Palace (Marquess of Buckingham's lodgings); London. 1619–1621, Newmarket Palace (Prince's lodging and clerk of work's house), Surrey, England. 1619–1622, Whitehall Palace (Banqueting House); 1620–1621, Whitehall Palace (Countess of Buckingham's lodgings); 1621, Beaufort House (gateway), Chelsea; London. 1623, Thoebalds Palace (stable), Hertfordshire, England. 1623, Westminster Palace (House of Lords), London. 1623–1624, Greenwich Palace (remodeling of chapel and great park gate), Kent, England. *1623–1625, Saint James's Palace (Queen's Chapel), Westminster; 1624, Whitehall Palace (park stairs); London. 1625, Thoebalds Palace (Banqueting House), Hertfordshire, England. 1626, Somerset House (Queen's Cabinet Room), The Strand; Saint James's Palace (Sculpture Gallery and perugula to Queen's Withdrawal Chamber), Westminster; 1629, Whitehall Palace (Cockpit Theatre), London. 1630s?, Ascott House (wing and apartment), Buckinghamshire, England. 1630–1635, Somerset House (Queen's Chapel), The Strand; London. 1631, Bagshot Park (lodge); 1631, Oatlands Palace (garden arbor); Surrey, England. 1631, Saint James's Palace (park gate), Westminster; (A)1631–1632, Hale Church, Hampshire, England. 1631–1637, *Saint Paul's Church (burned 1795, rebuilt 1795–1798 by Thomas Hardwick), Covent Garden; *1633–1642, Saint Paul's Cathedral (restoration); 1634–1635, Hyde Park Lodge; London. 1635, Oatlands Palace (balcony to Queen's lodging), Surrey, England. 1635, Somerset House (Cross Gallery), The Strand; 1636–1637, Barber Surgeon's Hall Anatomy Theatre; 1637, Somerset House (new Cabinet Room), The Strand; 1637, Whitehall Palace (new Masqueing Room); London. 1637–1638, *Winchester Cathedral (choir screen; remnant in Museum of Archaeology, Cambridge), England. 1640–1641, Wimbledon House (additions), Surrey, England.

BIBLIOGRAPHY

GOTCH, JOHN 1928 *Inigo Jones*. London: Methuen.

GOTCH, JOHN 1938 "Inigo Jones's Principal Visit to Italy in 1614: The Itinerary of His Journeys." *Journal of the Royal Institute of British Architects* Series 3 46:85–86.

HARRIS, JOHN 1961 "Inigo Jones and His French Sources." *Metropolitan Museum Bulletin* 19:253–264.

HARRIS, JOHN 1967 "A Prospect of Whitehall by Inigo Jones." *Burlington Magazine* 109:89–90.

HARRIS, JOHN 1973a "Inigo Jones and the Courtier Style." *Architectural Review* 154:17–24.

HARRIS, JOHN 1973b "The Link Between a Roman Second-century Sculptor, Van Dyck, Inigo Jones, and Queen Henrietta Maria." *Burlington Magazine* 115:526–530.

HARRIS, JOHN; ORGEL, STEPHEN; and STRONG, ROY 1973 *The King's Arcadia: Inigo Jones and the Stuart Court*. London: Arts Council of Great Britain.

HARRIS, JOHN, and TAIT, A. A. 1979 *Catalog of the Drawings by Inigo Jones, John Webb, and Isaac De Caius at Worcester College, Oxford*. London: Oxford University Press.

KEITH, WILLIAM GRANT 1913 "Some Hitherto Unknown Drawings by Inigo Jones." *Burlington Magazine* 22:218–226.

KEITH, WILLIAM GRANT 1917 "A Theater Project by Inigo Jones." *Burlington Magazine* 31:61–62, 105–111.

KEITH, WILLIAM GRANT 1925–1926 "Inigo Jones as a Collector." *Journal of the Royal Institute of British Architects* Series 3 33:94–108.

LEES-MILNE, J. 1953 *The Age of Inigo Jones*. London: Batsford.

ORGEL, STEPHEN, and STRONG, ROY 1973 *Inigo Jones: The Theatre of the Stuart Court*. 2 vols. London: Sotheby Parke Bernet; Berkeley: University of California Press.

ROWE, C. 1947 "The Theatrical Drawings of Inigo Jones: Their Sources and Scope." Unpublished Ph.D. dissertation, University of London.

SMITH, JOAN SUMNER 1952 "The Italian Sources of Inigo Jones's Style." *Burlington Magazine* 94:200–206.

STONE, LAWRENCE 1957 "Inigo Jones and the New Exchange." *Archaeological Journal* 114:106–121.

STRONG, ROY 1967 *Festival Designs by Inigo Jones*. London: International Exhibitions Foundation.

SUMMERSON, JOHN (1953)1977 *Architecture in Britain: 1530–1830*. 6th ed., rev. Harmondsworth, England: Penguin.

SUMMERSON, JOHN 1964 "Inigo Jones." *Proceedings of the British Academy* 50:169–192.

SUMMERSON, JOHN 1966 *Inigo Jones*. Harmondsworth, England: Penguin.

TAIT, A. A. 1970 "Inigo Jones—Architectural Historian." *Burlington Magazine* 112:235.

WHINNEY, MARGARET 1942–1943 "John Webb's Drawings for Whitehall Palace." *Walpole Society* 33:45–107.

WHINNEY, MARGARET 1952 "Inigo Jones: A Revaluation." *Journal of the Royal Institute of British Architects* Series 3 59:286–289.

WHINNEY, MARGARET 1970 "An Unknown Design for a Villa by Inigo Jones." In Howard Colvin and John Harris (editors). *The Country Seat*. London: Allen Lane.

WICKHAM, GLYNNE 1967 "The Cockpit Reconstructed." *New Theatre Magazine* 7:2ff.

WITTKOWER, RUDOLF 1948 "Inigo Jones: Puritanissimo Fiero." *Burlington Magazine* 90:50–51.

WITTKOWER, RUDOLF 1953 "Inigo Jones: Architect and Man of Letters." *Journal of the Royal Institute of British Architects* Series 3 60:83–90.

JONES, OWEN

Owen Jones (1807–1874), a formidably bearded Victorian, had an intimidatingly clear idea of what architecture should be, but produced little that survives today, working chiefly in commercial architecture and in decorative art. The elevation of art in the broadest sense, nevertheless, was his particular concern.

Jones was born in London, the son of a Welsh

furrier and antiquary. He was educated privately and at Charterhouse (1818–1819), then in 1825 was apprenticed to the architect LEWIS VULLAMY. In 1830, he took a short trip to Paris, Milan, Venice, and Rome, and commenced studies at the Royal Academy. In 1830–1834, he traveled more extensively around the Mediterranean, meeting the young French architect Jules Goury in Athens, where he had arrived as the traveling companion of GOTTFRIED SEMPER, and proceeding on with the latter to Egypt, Istanbul, and finally to the Alhambra in Spain. This was an unexpected itinerary at the end of the neoclassical age, and was consciously Romantic. They saw the Alhambra as the "Palais que les génies ont doré comme un rêve et rempli d'harmonies" (palace gilded by the geniis and filled with the music of the spheres)—a line from Victor Hugo's *Les Orientales* cited by Jones—and they studied it as closely as one might a Greek temple, executing measured drawings, studying the geometric system of its ornament and—most important—reconstructing a brilliant hypothetical color scheme in red, blue, and gold. The study of the polychromatic decoration of the ancient Greek temples begun by Semper and Goury sought to define a higher, quasi-musical chromatic system in pre-Roman building, and at the Alhambra Goury and Jones believed that they had found that system's principal surviving monument.

Goury died of cholera in Spain in 1834, but Jones carried on their work in London, publishing the vast *Plans, Elevations, Sections and Details of the Alhambra* (1836–1845) under joint authorship. It was an early monument of chromolithography printed on a press installed in Jones's house and paid for by the disposal of his patrimony.

During the 1830s and 1840s, as a result of this publication, Jones was sought out as an authority on Oriental design, erecting two Alhambresque villas in Kensington Palace Gardens (1845–1847) for the speculator John Mariott Blashfield, designing a number of Orientalizing interiors, executing tile patterns for Blashfield, and designing books. He gathered about him a circle of friends interested in exotic places and styles of art: JOSEPH BONOMI, Frederick Catherwood, JACOB W. MOULD and JAMES W. WILD (marrying the latter's sister Isabelle in 1842).

Jones's interest in the Alhambra, however, was the precise opposite of escapist. Beginning in the mid-1830s, he was lecturing on the necessity of creating a new, scientific, and industrial style of architecture using iron and decorated according to the universal laws of form and color he had discovered at the Alhambra. The opportunity to demonstrate what he had in mind came in 1850 when he was appointed Superintendent of the Works for the Great Exhibition of the Industry of All Nations to decorate somehow JOSEPH PAXTON's huge iron and glass Crystal Palace. Overcoming considerable resistance, he merely painted the structure's members in narrow stripes of red, blue, and yellow which he intended to blend in the long interior vistas by parallax so as to articulate its size and make it seem as big as it actually was. In the end his decoration was a great success and it led to important opportunities. From 1852, he was employed as an expert and lecturer in HENRY COLE's Department of Science and Art, a government bureau growing out of the Great Exhibition in charge of what came to be the Kensington science and art museums and the schools connected with them. It was for this that Jones compiled his celebrated *Grammar of Ornament* (1856) illustrating all historical styles of ornament and laying down thirty-seven axioms or laws of design that they supposedly documented.

Jones also was invited to project other iron and glass exhibitions, one in 1856 for the Manchester Exhibition of Art Treasures of the United Kingdom, another in 1858–1860 for the "Palace of the People" on Muswell Hill north of London, and a third for Paris about 1862. In 1852–1854, Jones together with Paxton supervised the removal and re-erection of the Crystal Palace at Sydenham. Inside it, Jones, Semper, and MATTHEW DIGBY WYATT erected a series of courts in the various historical styles as part of a permanent industrial exhibition (it burned in a spectacular fire in 1939).

Jones also received a number of private commercial commissions which were actually erected, although all are gone today. First came Saint James' Hall, Piccadilly, in 1855–1858, an orchestra hall with a broad iron barrel vault covered with abstract floral ornament extending down the walls, painted red, blue, and gold, and illuminated by star-shaped gas jets hung below it. Then, in 1858, came the Crystal Palace Bazaar, an iron and glass roofed gallery off Oxford Circus with red, blue, and yellow stained glass illuminated at night from behind. Finally in 1859–1862, came Osler's Glass Shop with mirror-covered walls and another stained glass vault. Jones also designed several shop fronts and country houses, most particularly Eynsham Hall, Oxford, of 1872.

All the while in the 1850s and 1860s, Jones's work as a book designer, interior decorator, and tile and silk designer did not slacken. But he never received a commission for a great public monument. In 1865 he did submit a project in the limited competition for the design of the Saint Pancras Station Hotel (won by GEORGE GILBERT SCOTT) and again in 1866 he submitted a project in the limited competition to rebuild the National Gallery.

DAVID T. VAN ZANTEN

WORKS

*1845–1847, 3 Kensington Palace Gardens; 8 Kensington Gardens (now 24); *1850–1851, Crystal Palace (interior decoration): London. *1852–1854, Re-erected Crystal Palace (redecoration with Joseph Paxton; Greek and Moorish Courts), Sydenham, England. 1855–1858, Saint James' Hall; 1858, Crystal Palace Bazaar; 1859–1862, Osler's Glass Shop (interior); London. 1872, Eynsham Hall, Oxford, England.

BIBLIOGRAPHY

DARBY, MICHAEL 1974 *Owen Jones and the Oriental Influence in Nineteenth Century Design.* Unpublished Ph.D. dissertation, Reading University, England.
DARBY, MICHAEL, and PHYSICK, JOHN 1973 *'Marble Halls': Drawings and Models for Victorian Secular Buildings.* London: H.M. Stationary Office.
DARBY, MICHAEL, and VAN ZANTEN, DAVID 1974 "Owen Jones's Iron Buildings of the 1850's." *Architectura* 1974:53–75.
JONES, OWEN 1854 *An Apology for the Colouring of the Greek Court at the Crystal Palace.* London: Crystal Palace Library and Bradbury & Evans.
JONES, OWEN (1856)1972 *Grammar of Ornament.* Reprint. New York: Van Nostrand.
JONES, OWEN 1863 *Lectures on Architecture and the Decorative Arts.* London: Privately printed.
JONES, OWEN, and GOURY, JULES 1836–1845 *Plans, Elevations, Sections and Details of the Alhambra.* 2 vols. London: Jones.
"The Late Mr. Owen Jones." 1974 *The Builder* 23:383–385.
"Owen Jones." 1974 *Architect* 11:235–236.

JØRGENSEN, EMIL

Emil Jørgensen (1858–1942), a Danish architect, belonged to a group of National Romantic architects. For many years, he worked with more influential personalities such as HANS JØRGEN HOLM and MARTIN NYROP, assisting Nyrop with the building of the Town Hall in Copenhagen. Later, he ran his own office; among his most notable commissions was the county hospital in Gentofte near Copenhagen (1921–1927).

VILLADS VILLADSEN

JØRGENSEN, THORVALD

Thorvald Jørgensen (1867–1946), a Danish architect, started his career strongly influenced by the romantic national tradition, as seen in the Esajas Church in Copenhagen (1903). He soon turned to

a more conventional academic architecture as he was commissioned with the huge and difficult re-erection of Christiansborg Slot (1908), which includes the Parliament, high courts, and royal representative apartments, the whole formed as a baroque pastiche.

VILLADS VILLADSEN

JOSIC, ALEXIS

See CANDILIS JOSIC WOODS.

JOURDAIN, FRANTZ

Frantz Jourdain (1847–1935) was both a writer and an architect most often remembered for the Paris department store La Samaritaine. Jourdain's polemics against official architectural orthodoxy were indispensable in the development of French modernism before World War I. He championed the reintegration and legitimation of the arts and crafts, and he quested for new architectural forms appropriate to the unprecedented realities of modern urban existence. Jourdain's buildings united nineteenth-century bourgeois technology with the decorative legacy of eighteenth-century aristocratic organicism.

Born in Antwerp, Jourdain graduated from the prestigious Lycée Henri IV. Between 1862 and 1867, Jourdain studied with Jules Vallès, a social revolutionary from whom he derived his virulent anti-authoritarian and combative critical style. In

Jourdain. La Samaritaine. Paris. 1907

1867, Jourdain was admitted to the Ecole des Beaux-Arts, where he remained until enlisting as a volunteer in the Franco-Prussian War in 1870.

Despite his identification with the plight of artistic *isolés,* Jourdain held a prominent place in the cultural establishment, and after 1890 became an accepted and celebrated spokesman for artistic reform within official institutions. In his polemical articles, Jourdain criticized the oppressive and dogmatic rule of Greece and Rome within the Ecole des Beaux-Arts, as well as the shackling of the designers' imaginations to the servitude of ancient classicism. He argued that the imitation of past styles denied the imperative that artistic forms adapt to the particular needs of each era.

The cure for *maladie du passé* was not the negation of tradition, but the revitalization of distinctively French aesthetic endowments. Jourdain called for a modernism based on the renewal of the traditions of elegance, charm, and taste, which mark the spirit of the French race, and posited the style nouveau as the modern analogue to decorative rococo elegance. Although in the 1880s he had envisioned a modern architecture as the bold exposure of structural parts, raising the new materials of iron and glass to the surface of light and air, by the 1890s Jourdain called the Eiffel Tower a "metallic carcass," and identified the major goal of the modern style to be the "gracious adornment of the brutalities of modern existence."

In his architectural practice, Jourdain adapted national traditions of gracious adornment to the French modern style. Besides the extended construction of the Samaritaine, Jourdain's work included château restorations and two major commissions. The most important was the design of the top floor (the Grenier) of the house of the brothers de Goncourt in Auteuil, Paris (1886), from which an extensive late nineteenth-century rococo revival originated. In designing the Grenier, Jourdain eliminated the dividing wall, while retaining an awning in the middle section to distinguish the space for social gatherings from the inner sanctum reserved for art objects.

The multiple design and construction of the Samaritaine summarized Jourdain's attempts to articulate a particularly French version of modernism. A lifelong commission for Jourdain, the first project (1891–1907) for the conversion of twenty-three old houses into a single unit for a commercial emporium was followed by additions in 1908, 1909, 1912, and 1914. Each repeated the spatial organization of the original project, which consisted of seven-story structures with vertical iron beams and stanchions, punctuated by large windows. Framing the glass and breaking the iron verticality were a series of polychromatic horizontal panels of encrusted mosaic and ceramic tiling, which alternated between designs of floral garlands and graphic signs advertising the variety of commodities for sale inside. The union of modern architect and decorator in the construction process was particularly appropriate to the melding of tradition and modernity encompassed by the department store. Dependent on intensified production for its merchandise, the Samaritaine represented the peculiarly French capacity to adapt traditional economic practices to the new conditions of a modern commercial capital.

Jourdain's definition of French modernism as the adaptation of the traditions of elegant embellishment to new technical necessities culminated in an architecture befitting a consumer capital which continued to be the citadel of taste and luxury rather than become a crucible of technology and industry.

DEBORA SILVERMAN

WORKS

1886, De Goncourt House (top floor), Auteuil; 1887, Outbuildings, Avenue du Bois de Boulogne; Paris. 1887, Villa, Chelles, France. *1889, Perfumery and Woven Fabrics Section, Exposition Universelle; 1891–1907, La Samaritaine; 1893, Monument to La Fontaine, Square Ranelagh; Paris. 1893, Château de Verteuil (restoration), France. 1897, Chapel for the Ursuline Sisters, Chelles, France. *1900, Moët and Chandon Pavilion and Perfumery, Exposition Universelle; Paris. 1900, Villa, Bouffemont, France. 1902, Tomb of Zola, Montparnasse Cemetery; 1914, La Samaritaine Head Office; 1926–1928, La Samaritaine (new buildings); Paris. n.d., Château de la Roche-Guyen (restoration), Seine-et-Oise, France. n.d., Théâtre des Nouveautés; n.d., Théâtre de Cluny; n.d., Théâtre Sarah-Bernhardt; Paris.

BIBLIOGRAPHY

BOILEAU, L. C. 1900 "Causerie." *L'Architecture* 8:249–255.

BORSI, FRANCO, and GODOLI, EZIO (1976)1978 *Paris 1900.* Translated by J. C. Palmes. New York: Rizzoli.

JOURDAIN, FRANTZ 1893 *L'Atelier Chantorel.* Paris: Charpentier & Fasquelle.

JOURDAIN, FRANTZ 1895 *Les Décorés, ceux qui ne le sont pas.* Paris: Empis.

JOURDAIN, FRANTZ 1896 "Les industries d'art." Pages 72–76 in *Tendances nouvelles, Enquête sur L'évolution des Industries d'Art.* Paris: Floury.

JOURDAIN, FRANTZ 1902 *De Choses et d'autres.* Paris: Empis.

JOURDAIN, FRANTZ 1914 *Propos d'un Isolé en Faveur de son Temps.* Paris: Figuière.

MARX, ROGER 1901 *La Décoration et les Industries d'art à L'Exposition Universelle de 1900.* Paris: Delagrave.

REY, ROBERT 1923 *Frantz Jourdain.* Paris: La Connaissance.

UHRY, EDMOND 1907 "Agrandissements des Magasins de La Samaritaine." *L'Architecte* 2, Feb.:13–14.

JUJOL I GIBERT, JOSEP MARIA

Josep Maria Jujol i Gibert (1879–1949) was a Catalan architect of what has been called the "second modernist generation." Born in Tarragona, Spain, and formed in a period of maturity of *Modernisme,* he inherited from this movement the schism with the eclectic historicists. This rupture permitted the development of subjectivism characteristic of the new architecture of this period, among which Jujol's work stands out clearly as that with the most intense formal imagination.

From 1906, Jujol collaborated with his teacher at the Architectural School in Barcelona, ANTONIO GAUDÍ Y CORNET. His youthful spontaneity—Jujol was thirty years younger than his teacher—his facility, and his great capacity for invention—free from the formal control of the historical architectural movements on the first architects in their search for the "new national style"—would represent a revitalizing element of the first order in the Gaudian work. The primary manifestations of Jujol's talents would develop in the resolution of detail and decoration until achieving an absolutely personal vocabulary. He was a notable sculptor, painter, and draftsman who possessed a profound knowledge of the expressive possibilities of the materials put within his reach by the great development in the applied arts. His work, always under the direction and with the absolute confidence of Gaudí, includes the applied ceramic façade of the Casa Batlló (1906), the polychrome ceramic decorations of Parque Güell (1900–1914), and, in particular, the revetment of the famous undulating benches, realized with a "collage" technique of colored glass fragments arranged according to an abstract expressionist modeling.

That expressive appreciation for texture as well as the appreciation for the absurd in his use of objects out of context—"found objects," as they were named in later years by Dadaists—can be seen in the encrusted soffits in the ceiling of the hypostyle hall of Parque Güell (with elements such as bottles, crystal cups, dolls) or in the balustrade of Casa Negre (1914–1930) incorporating the most common iron farm tools. From this, one can evaluate Jujolian modeling as a significant anticipation of informalism and a premonition of the dream world of surrealism. This quality would go beyond the characteristic essence of his architecture thanks to his spontaneous and intuitive procedure which was little disposed to respect the dictates of any methodological control.

Among his own works, perhaps the Casa de la Creu (1913–1916)—popularly called *Casa dels Ous* (House of Eggs)—shows most clearly how Jujol, at the height of his maturity, could realize a total design from his art of modeling. In contradiction to the rigid interior distribution of the twin houses, the basic concept of the plan developed from the intersection of five circles. In a free interpretation of a Gaudian theme, the transformation of the original plan begins with the first floor. The series of asymmetrical volumes articulated with characteristic logic make difficult the reading of the vertebrate spatial structure around the central openings of the two stairs. Such ambiguities are reinforced in the independent treatment of the roof which is of great plastic interest and spatial complexity similar to the Gaudian solution for the roof of Casa Milá. The concern for the resolution of the roof was to be a constant theme from the Gaudian inheritance. The maximum expression of this theme was achieved in the roof walkway of the Chapel of Vistabella (1918–1923), and, principally, in the extraordinary rationality and expressive capacity of the roof of the Mañach Factory (1916–1922).

Even though Jujol survived all the architects of his generation, he continued always faithful, even in his last works, to the spirit of his own style, expressing his own conceptions at the margin of architectural polemics. In this way, he would construct from baroque inspiration the Fountain of the Plaza de España in Barcelona for the Exposition of 1929. However, the free interpretation of many of the details permits us to discern once again the creative presence of his strong personality. The same happens with the pulpits and the chapel in the Church of Sant Joan Despí (1943) and with the new altar of the Vendrell (1939–1949). The exaggerated survival of faith in the principal students of *Modernisme* indicates to what degree this movement took root in Catalonia, providing impetus for fecund polemics and personal attitudes as subtle and provocative as that of Josep Maria Jujol.

ADOLF MARTÍNEZ I MATAMALA
*Translated from Spanish by
Judith E. Meighan*

WORKS

1900–1914, Parque Güell (garden; with Antonio Gaudí); 1906, Casa Batlló (ceramic façade; with Gaudí); 1909–1910, Casa San Salvador, 89 Calle Nuestra Señora del Coll; *1911, Tienda Mañach, 57 Calle Fernando; 1913–1916, Casa de la Creu (Casa dels Ous), 12 Calle Canalías, Sant Joan Despí; Barcelona, Spain. 1914, Casa Ximenis, 17 Paseo Saavedra, Tarragona, Spain. 1914–1930, Casa Negre (exteriors and alterations), 37 Torrent del Negre, Barcelona, Spain. 1914–1931, Casa Bofarull, Els Pallaresos, Tarragona, Spain. 1916–1922, Talleres Mañach, 39–41 Riera Sant Miquel; 1917, Casa

Queralt, 1 Calle de la Pineda; Barcelona, Spain. 1918-1923, Chapel of the la Vistabella; 1920, Ayuntamiento, Els Pallaresos; 1920, Escuelas, Els Pallarasos; 1920-1927, Casa Fortuny (Ca l'Andreu), Plaza de la Iglesia, Els Pallarasos; Tarragona, Spain. 1923-1924, Casa Planells, 332 Avenida Diagonal, Barcelona, Spain. 1926-1929, Santuario de Montserrat, Montferri, Tarragona, Spain. 1927, Casa Serra-Xaus, 25 Calle Jacint Verdaguer, Sant Joan Despí; 1928-1929, Fuente, Plaza de España; 1932, Casa Propia, 27 Calle Jacint Verdaguer, Sant Joan Despí; Barcelona, Spain. 1939-1949, El Vendrell (altar), Tarragona, Spain. 1941, Monumento a los Caidos, Plaza de Calvo Sotelo, Sant Joan Despí; 1943, Church of Sant Joan Despí; Barcelona, Spain.

BIBLIOGRAPHY

BOHIGAS, ORIOL 1973 *Reseña y Catálogo de la Arquitectura Modernista.* Barcelona, Spain: Lumen.
BOHIGAS, ORIOL 1976a "Josep Maria Jujol (1879-1949)." *Arquitecturas-bis* 12:2-18.
BOHIGAS, ORIOL 1976b "Josep Maria Jujol." Pages 105-127 in *Once Arquitectos.* Barcelona, Spain: La Gaya Ciencia.
FLORES, CARLOS 1972 "Algunas precisiones en torno a la obra de J. M. Jujol." *Hogar y Arquitectura* July-Aug.
JUJOL, JOSÉ MARIA 1969 "Guia de la arquitectura de Jujol." *Hogar y Arquitectura* 84:9-38.
RÁFOLS, J. F. 1950 "Jujol." *Cuadernos de Arquitectura* 13:1-22.
RÁFOLS, J. F.; FLORES, CARLOS; JUJOL, JOSÉ MARIA and TARRAGÓ, S. 1974 *La arquitectura de J. M. Jujol.* Barcelona, Spain: La Gaya Ciencia.

JURKOVIČ, DUŠAN

Dušan Jurkovič (1868-1947), who was born in Turá Lúka, Czechoslovakia, was the founder of modern Slovak architecture. Inspired by folk architecture, he transformed these elements and synthesized them with those of Art Nouveau. His wooden structures of resort and sports constructions are aesthetically pleasing. Of special interest are his projects for World War I cemeteries in Poland. His work of greatest significance and artistic value is the Monument of General Štefánik on the Bradlo (1927-1928).

In addition to architectural, ethnographical, documentary and collector's activities he was active also in literature and theory.

ŠTEFAN ŠLACHTA

WORKS

1897-1899, Hermitage on Radhošť, Beskid Mountains, Czechoslovakia. 1901, Jan House, Luhačovice, Czechoslovakia. 1904, Municipal House, Skalica, Czechoslovakia. 1927-1928, General Štefánik Monument, Hill Bradlo, near Myjaval, Czechoslovakia.

BIBLIOGRAPHY

ŽÁKAVEC, FRANTIŠEK 1929 *Dílo Dušana Jurkoviče Kus dějin československé architektury.* Prague: Vesmir.

JUSSOW, HEINRICH CHRISTOPH

The son of an architect, Heinrich Christoph Jussow (1754-1825) began his architectural training at Kassel in 1778. Initially self-taught, he worked for five years under SIMON LOUIS DU RY, whose English Palladian (see ANDREA PALLADIO) style is mixed with a tendency for purer geometrical composition in Jussow's first independent design, an unexecuted synagogue based on the Pantheon (1781). This more abstract approach to design was strengthened under CHARLES DE WAILLY in Paris in 1784 and by travel to Italy and Sicily. He also visited England in 1786. Jussow's mature career was devoted largely to completing the central wing of Schloss Wilhelmshöhe (1791-1798) and transforming its vast mountainside park into an elaborate picturesque garden. In addition to waterworks and classical temples, he built Schloss Löwenburg (1793-1798). A pioneering monument of the German Gothic Revival—inspired in part by Walpolian (see HORACE WALPOLE) Gothick and castles Jussow visited in England—it was eye-catcher, residence, museum, and Wilhelm's mausoleum. Among his many pupils at the Academy in Kassel, where he taught from 1799, was his nephew G. L. F. LAVES.

BARRY BERGDOLL

WORKS

1785-1791, Lake; 1788-1792, Aqueduct; 1791-1792, Cascade; 1791-1798, Schloss Wilhelmshöhe (central wing and interior of chapel); *1792-1793, Teufelsbrücke (probably with Steinhöfer), Park Wilhelmshöhe; Kassel, Germany. 1793, Hessen Memorial, Frankfurt-am-Main, Germany. 1793-1798, Schloss Löwenburg; 1794, Retraite, Park Wilhelmshöhe; Kassel, Germany. *1798, Hermitage, Park at Riede, Germany. *1802-1808, Church, Unterneustadt; 1803, Wilhelmshöher Tor; *1809, Messhaus, Königstrasse; *c.1810, House, 1 Königstrasse; *1815-1821, Chattenburg; 1817-1818, Jussow-Tempel am Fontänenteich, Park Wilhelmshöhe; 1820, Mausoleum of Kurfürstin Wilhelmine Karoline von Hessen, Luther Cemetery; 1823, Schloss Schönfeld (rebuilding); Kassel, Germany.

BIBLIOGRAPHY

BANGERT, ALBRECHT 1969 "Architektur von Heinrich Christoph Jussow in Kassel um 1800." Unpublished Ph.D. dissertation, Ludwigs-Maximilians-Universität, Munich.
HEIDELBACH, PAUL 1909 *Die Geschichte der Wilhelm-*

shöhe. Leipzig: Klinkhardt & Biermann.

HOLTMEYER, ALOIS 1923 *Kreis Cassel-Stadt.* 2 vols. Volume 6 in *Die Bau- und Kunstdenkmäler im Regierungsbezirk Cassel.* Marburg, Germany: Elwertsche.

KLEIN, JÜRGEN 1975 "Heinrich Christoph Jussow, Erbauer der 'Löwenburg' zu Kassel und die englische Neogotik." *Architectura* 5:138–169.

PAETOW, KARL 1929 *Klassizismus und Romantik auf Wilhelmshöhe.* Kassel, Germany: Bärenreiter-Verlag.

VOGEL, HANS 1958 *Heinrich Christoph Jussow, 1754–1825, Baumeister in Kassel und Wilhelmshöhe.* Kassel, Germany: Hessisches Landesmuseum. Catalogue of an exhibition.

JUVARRA, FILIPPO

Filippo Juvarra (1678–1736), the most accomplished architect of his generation in Europe, was born in Messina, Sicily, and died in Madrid while at work on the designs for the new Royal Palace there.

Juvarra's great achievement lies, first, in continuing a late baroque classical tradition that had been defined for the previous century by GIOVANNI LORENZO BERNINI (and sustained by CARLO FONTANA, Juvarra's teacher). Juvarra also drew upon the criticism of that tradition by MICHELANGELO and FRANCESCO BORROMINI for revitalization and as a source for the rococo.

Throughout his career, Juvarra's work showed an extraordinary simplicity, directness, clarity, and luminosity as well as a steadily increasing concern for attenuated structure, aggregated spaces, and flowing linear shapes and forms. Juvarra also established in his work a new elegant and graceful decorative vocabulary of great strength, freedom, and originality that was to nourish both classical and rococo Piedmontese architects for generations.

With few exceptions, Juvarra's activity in Piedmont took place in the twenty-year period (1714–1734) when he was first architect to Vittorio Amedeo II of Savoy, the new king of Sicily and Piedmont. Before this appointment at age thirty-five, Juvarra seems to have been an able architect and designer in search of a task equal to his talents. He received, however, few commissions resulting in buildings. His attempts to be appointed by Frederick IV of Denmark, Louis XIV of France, Charles XII of Sweden, and Joseph I of Austria came to naught.

In 1714, Juvarra finally secured the position he desired from Vittorio Amedeo II of Savoy who needed an architect of singular ability to realize his ambition to transform Turin from a ducal to a royal capital. In twenty years, Juvarra built or remodeled eight churches, sixteen palaces, and over two dozen altars and prepared designs for many more unrealized projects. His pupil GIOVANNI BATTISTA SACCHETTI compiled a list of Juvarra's commissions from 1714 to 1735, which was published by Adamo Rossi in 1874, together with an Anonymous Life (perhaps by Francesco Juvarra, Filippo's elder brother). Juvarra was a rapid and gifted draftsman who, with seeming facility, designed objects, furniture, interiors, altars, theater scenery, ideal fantastic architectural views, architecture, and urban complexes. Virtually all his designs demonstrate a concern for incident light and luminosity that may have been stimulated by his friendship with painters.

Juvarra preserved many of his drawings, gathered them in related groups, and had some bound in his lifetime following, possibly, the practice of his master, Carlo Fontana. Other groups were bound later. Five albums with over one thousand drawings, including several hundred scene designs, survive from his first ten years in Rome alone. His drawings are held in many public and private collections.

Juvarra, his father, and all four of his brothers who reached adulthood were silversmiths in Messina. Works by the Juvarra family from this period (1693–1701) survive and some have been attributed to Filippo. However, according to the Anonymous Life, Filippo was at this time studying for the priesthood to which he was ordained in 1703. A volume with eight crude engravings depicting monuments erected to commemorate the coronation of Philip V of Bourbon as king of Spain and the Two Silicilies, which appeared in 1701 drawn and engraved (but not designed) by Filippo, confirms his activity as an engraver at this period. According to the Anonymous Life, it was in this period that Juvarra studied architectural treatises and drew from them, which led to his being commissioned to execute some work at the Church of San Gregorio in Messina. According to the Anonymous Life, he embellished the windows, and on the evidence of extant drawings he also designed and perhaps constructed an elevated choir above the main entrance. Shortly thereafter, probably early in 1704, he left for Rome with a letter of recommendation from one of the sisters of the Convent of San Gregorio to her brother, Monsignor Ruffo, the Maestro di Camera of Pope Clement XI.

Ruffo in turn recommended Juvarra to Carlo Fontana, the principal professor of architecture at the Accademia di San Luca, who, astonished at Juvarra's draftsmanship, set him to draw from the works in Rome by Michelangelo, Bernini, Borromini, and other masters.

Early in 1705, already promoted to the final year of study, Juvarra prepared an entry and won first prize in the Concorso Clementino, which that year was a design for a single villa for three individuals of equal rank. Two years later, Juvarra fulfilled a requirement for membership in the Accademia di San Luca by presenting a design for a central-plan church with a pair of campanili. He taught at the Accademia from 1706 to 1708 and again in 1711–1712. But Juvarra had not otherwise been idle. His drawings show that in 1706 alone he made preparatory drawings for the Concorso Clementino of that year; prepared several alternatives for church façades, altars, and scene designs in Naples (on a trip back from Messina); made a trip to Lucca to prepare designs for the completion of the Palazzo Comunale; executed a group of scene designs for Giorgio Törnquist, architect to the king of Sweden, began work on a volume (first published in 1711) of papal and other arms on buildings in Rome; and provided many illustrations for works published by the printers Antonio de Rossi and Giovanni Maria Salvioni.

The Antamoro Chapel (1708–1710) in San Girolamo della Carità in Rome underscored Juvarra's unusual talents. Juvarra sheathed the walls and floor of the small rectangular space (5.1 x 3.2 m) in brown, green, and dark yellow marbles of related tonal value with a dark marble entablature above. The corners were rounded to hold rich, reddish marble Composite columns with bases angled toward the center. Centrality was emphasized by a concave altar with oval steps and, above, a cloister vault with a lantern. The vault, defined by wide ribs with gilded coffers, had white stucco reliefs in the lateral panels. The putti around the oculus, and above and below the white marble altar sculpture of San Filippo Neri by Pierre Legros, and the white marble capitals and bases of the columns and pilasters, were contrasted to the dark tonality of the marble and gilded surfaces of the coffers and garlanded ribs. Behind the figure of San Filippo Neri, a large oval stained-glass window, graded from yellow to orange, cast a glow of glory around the sculpture, seeming to be the moment at which the Holy Spirit appeared to San Filippo Neri as a globe of fire. With this work Juvarra demonstrated a familiarity with chapel design in Rome and with the recent altars of AN-DREA POZZO for the Gesù and Sant' Ignazio in Rome. This chapel led toward a new coloristic conception of the altar and altarpiece that influenced several generations.

Juvarra's interest in antiquity and his archeological knowledge are revealed in a group of extant drawings for a large presentation piece (now lost) of the Campidoglio in antiquity prepared for the projected Roman visit of Frederick IV of Denmark in 1709. Fear of the plague kept Frederick from Rome, and the drawing was sent, through the director of the French Academy, to the duke D'Antin, prime minister of Louis XIV, who thought it quite beautiful but did not recommend the appointment of Juvarra.

The drawings reveal that Juvarra studied ancient coins, medals, literary descriptions, previous reconstructions, and archeological evidence. His reconstructions brought to the Campidoglio an imaginative grandeur, uniformity, scale, and symmetry that it had never had but that an ancient Mediterranean capital of an empire might well be conceived to have had.

In the period 1708–1714, Juvarra was at work on a series of theatrical projects: theater and scene designs for Cardinal Ottoboni; scenes for Queen Maria Casimira of Poland's theater in the Palazzo Zuccaro (1709–1713); designs for the Teatro Capranica (1712–1713); and a project for a new theater near Piazza Sant' Agostino in Genoa (1712–1713). These designs established Juvarra as one of the principal scene designers in Italy, and in 1711 he was asked by Emperor Joseph I of Austria to prepare designs for the opera *Junius Brutus*.

During the later years of his Roman period, Juvarra taught architecture at the Accademia di San Luca. As his fame began to grow, he was asked to prepare designs for the sanctuary of the Virgin of Caravaggio (unexecuted) and for a number of villas and fountains for individuals in Lucca. The range of his mind and his abilities were sufficient to have Domenico d'Aguirre (counselor to Vittorio Amedeo II, new king of Sicily as the result of the Peace of Westphalia), propose Juvarra as royal architect. The king, on an official visit to Sicily, called Juvarra to Messina and requested designs for the completion of the sixteenth-century royal palace in Messina designed by ANDREA CALAMECH.

Juvarra certainly knew Messina well, and as his Concorso Clementino entry and the unrealized palace with eight courtyards (prepared perhaps in 1707 for the prince of Hesse in Kassel) attest, he was adept at composing large palaces. These experiences enabled him to prepare drawings that respected the initial plan form but transformed it to conform to the needs of the eighteenth-century palace through the addition of a columnar atrium, a large axial main salone, grand symmetrically placed pairs of stairs, a large circular-plan chapel, vestibules much larger than any of the principal rooms of the earlier palace, and an extensive, axially oriented garden with parterres, fountains, and periodic lateral axes.

The transformation of the palace preserved the earlier structure yet achieved a sufficient balance between its severity and the necessary contemporary regal grandeur. It secured Juvarra's appointment as royal architect. Vittorio Amedeo had shrewdly gauged Juvarra's talent, and Juvarra would realize both their ambitions. Turin was to become a world capital.

Juvarra sailed from Sicily on September 1, 1714, landed at Savona, and went overland to Turin. On December 12, his appointment was upgraded to first architect, and the royal commissions began. Within two years, he was asked to design the main altar of the Santissima Sindone, the grand gallery of the Venaria Reale, the church and monastery atop Monte Superga, the Church of San Filippo Neri (which had been begun earlier), the church to be added to the Venaria Reale, the façade of Santa Cristina in Piazza San Carlo and, for private patrons, the Palazzo Borgaro and the Palazzo Martini di Cigala.

Juvarra had been in Turin only a few months when Cardinal Albani arranged his return to Rome to complete the drawings and model for his entry in the St. Peter's sacristy competition of 1714 (under Pope Clement XI). Although Juvarra's model was thought to be the best, the sacristy remained unbuilt. Eighteen years later, in 1732, Juvarra was again asked by Cardinal Albani, this time under Pope Clement XII, to work on the sacristy design. The Florentine pope and the *congregazioni* of St. Peter's, however, favored his compatriots and, ignoring Juvarra's earlier designs for both the façade of San Giovanni in Laterano and the Sacristy, enlisted him only as a juror for the Lateran competition (won by the Florentine ALESSANDRO GALILEI) and asked for his opinion of Galilei's proposal for the design of the sacristy. Juvarra's list of the damage that would be done to St. Peter's by the Galilei design may have prevented its construction, but Juvarra did not receive the commission. (The sacristy was eventually built under Pius VI by CARLO MARCHIONNI.)

Juvarra prepared at least five separate alternatives for the sacristy before the model design. In contrast to the earlier alternatives which located the sacristy to the southeast of the transept, Juvarra's model of 1715 aligned the new structure with the axis of the south transept. Two linking passageways from the angled walls to the east and west of the transept led radially to a large concave, colonnaded portico which formed a fan-shaped courtyard between the basilica and the sacristy. The portico led on axis to the main sacristy space, an oval room vaulted at the full height of the building with sixteen large windows at the upper level and free-standing columns at the lower level. The interior decoration, completely executed in the model, displayed Juvarra's mastery of the vocabularly of Roman palace design. The remaining portions of the sacristy complex were arranged behind and to the north and south of the main space as a rectangular palace with two courtyards. To match the angled pavilions that made the juncture of passageway to colonnade, the two outer corner pavilions were turned at a similar angle. The two stories of the pavilions and palace were raised upon a base and articulated by an order of giant pilasters and columns reminiscent of Bernini's Palazzo Chigi-Odescalchi and his designs for the Louvre.

In 1732, Juvarra may have prepared additional designs and a model for the sacristy. The model (now lost) attributed to him (Rovere, Viale, and Brinckmann, 1737, p. 129) shows a much reduced scheme with a two-story circular vaulted structure rising above a lower story of no great extension. In contrast to the model of 1715 with its lush interior, the attributed model of 1732 is a sober, more classical proposal with a central space that includes continuous horizontals at both the lower and upper level, covered by a ribbed dome with gores. Relief sculptural decoration is confined to the gores, to the lunettes below the gores, and to the faces of the ribs and pilasters of the second level. The sculptural decoration on the exterior is more personal, more broadly conceived, and more authoritative than on the earlier model.

An additional attribution, by J. Gaus (1967, p. 77), to Juvarra of a third model, known only from photographs, has been denied by H. Hager (1970, p. 44).

Before leaving for Rome, Juvarra had made a drawing in October 1714 for the main altar of the Sindone Chapel located above and behind the choir of the cathedral, and he may have begun to work on other commissions. He returned to Turin in July 1715 and probably began preparing drawings for the central-plan church and monastery at Superga, the rebuilding of San Filippo Neri, and the façade of Santa Cristina.

In January 1716, the king decided to place a votive church at the top of the Supergan hill, perhaps at Juvarra's suggestion, and requested the city to relinquish its ownership of a church on the site. Vittorio Amedeo II's original intention, perhaps from 1713 or earlier, to build a small church, lower on the hill, was transformed by Juvarra's vision into one of the primary identifying marks of Vittorio Amedeo's reign, a monument to the Savoy family and a pious crown for eighteenth-century Turin (as Monte Cappuccino had been for the seventeenth-century city). A model, still extant, was built in 1716 by C. M. Ugliengo, while demolition, leveling of the mountain top, and construction of a replacement for the former parish church at a new location lower on the slope proceeded.

Juvarra.
Church and Monastery of
Superga.
Near Turin, Italy.
1716–1731

In July 1717, the cornerstone of Superga was laid. The cupola was complete in 1726, the twin campanili were completed in 1727, and the church was sufficiently finished for services to be held in 1731, though it was not consecrated until 12 October 1749. The design as known from the model and associated drawings was altered probably between 1719 and 1721 while construction was underway. The alterations (an extended portico, the monastery lengthened in the opposite direction, and greater relief in its parts, that is, paired columns versus pilasters on the drum) resulted in the lengthier, harmoniously balanced massing of portico, drum and dome, campanili, and monastic building that is compositionally valid both from Turin and from the terrace atop the mountain. As completed, the tall, domed, central-plan church with tetrastyle temple portico was partially embedded in a wider and lower two-story rectangular monastic block that incorporated a pair of flanking campanili.

Juvarra's presentation piece for the Accademia di San Luca of 1707 had also been a central-plan church (an octagon) flanked by campanili placed on the lateral axis. By shifting the towers to the rear, attaching them to the monastic building, extending the portico, and placing the altar against the rear wall of the apse (instead of under a dome in the choir) in the revised design for Superga, Juvarra increased emphasis on the longitudinal direction while maintaining a decisive verticality. In the final design, the vertical dimension of the interior, underlined by salient columns with ressants in the drum, was emphasized beyond the solution chosen for the Accademia di San Luca design by increasing the size of the bays on the main and lateral axes and decreasing those on the diagonals. The wider and higher arches were further extended

by stilting the arches that sprang from the stringcourse, marking an attic above the minor order. Unlike another attic level above the main order to receive the arches (as in the San Luca design), the main order and entablature at Superga rose above the heightened arches on both the interior and the exterior. The additional height on the exterior, coupled with the elimination of the horizontal attic band, enabled Juvarra to realize two full stories within a giant pilaster order in the attached monastic building. The partial disengagement of the body of the church from the monastic block facilitated tracing verticals from the paired pilasters of the lower order of the church through the balustrade, the paired columns of the drum, and the paired ribs of the dome to the lantern.

In the Church of Superga, Juvarra apparently attempted to summarize and boldly restate the design issues of Western church tradition from the Renaissance. The temple portico, with its large vaulted columnless space, seems to emulate, criticize, and improve on the portico of the Pantheon. We are made aware of the encumbrance of the four columns within the portico of the Pantheon. In emphasizing the portico and in recalling the Pantheon, the portico at Superga digests the achievements of Bernini at Ariccia and of Bernini and Carlo Rainaldi in the Piazza del Popolo, and proposes a bolder alternative.

The dome, modeled on St. Peters, is pulled forward, free of the attached complex, visible in its relation to the lower story as St. Peter's was not. Juvarra apparently thought the flanking campanili at Sant' Agnese in Piazza Navona, Rome, merely framed and announced the dome rather than supported and reinforced the reading of the dome as a whole from ground to lantern. The campanili at Superga underline, interlock with, and provide a transition to the retrostanding monastic block. With this building, Juvarra took a place among those defining the mainstream of eighteenth-century Italian architecture.

Juvarra rebuilt the Church of San Filippo Neri in Turin after its dome collapsed in October 1714 before it had been completed. As Sacchetti states and drawings confirm, Juvarra made three designs in 1715 (probably 1715–1717) that at first accepted the original plan (longitudinal with a central dome) but rejected it in the third design (for which a model was built) in favor of a Latin-cross plan with apse, shallow choir, and three-bay nave, but with a wider central bay. Funds were short and work proceeded slowly, so much so that a rough provisional church was built. It walled in the area of the future apse and crossing and added a short narrow nave within the area where the nave foundations were perhaps then under construction. It is uncertain how much of the model design was built, but when work began again in earnest in 1730–1732, an entirely new plan was adopted. In the final design, the sanctuary of the original building was retained, the dome and transepts of the model design were eliminated, the length of the nave was increased and given three bays of equal size, and the nave width was increased by twenty percent. At either end, curved piers narrowed the nave to meet the choir and the entrance wall, and a temple front portico was added. Work was interrupted again in 1738. The last bay of the nave which joined the choir, the sacristy, and the portico up to the level of the vault of the nave, were completed only in the first half of the nineteenth century by GIUSEPPE TALUCCHI, who adhered to Juvarra's design.

The final dimensions of the nave suggest that Juvarra was in this instance revising, updating, and commenting on the Albertian (see LEON BATTISTA ALBERTI) model. The paired pilasters on pedestals, with arches that lead to chapels rising to the full height of the entablature, evoke the memory Sant' Andrea, in Mantua. So do the openings in the piers between the pilasters at the upper and lower levels. However, Juvarra transformed the earlier model from a closed, planar wall architecture of discrete spatial units into an open, skeletal pier construction with spatial continuity. At Sant' Andrea, the height of the vault above the entablature is about half the height below (.48:1). The total height at San Filippo is nearly the same as Sant' Andrea, but the height of the vault (including the attic) above the entablature is almost equal to the height of the main order below (.88:1). Increased emphasis on the vault area was reinforced by the piers which are narrower and salient with ressants above leading to paired arches in the vault. In addition, the piers were pierced by openings at three levels which underlined their skeletal quality. To stress further the skeletal reading, linear columns replaced the wall segments of Sant' Andrea at the entrance to the chapels.

In the vault, there are large penetrations in the area above the chapels filled with sizable, nearly circular openings that, with the banding of arches and moldings of the central panels, differentiate between structure and infill (in contrast to the vault at Sant' Andrea), suggesting lightness and openness in opposition to the massive, closed vault at Mantua.

Spatial unity and continuity of the single, great space is achieved through the piercing of the piers, through the apses of the chapels which return space to the nave, through the chapel vaults with their semidomes high above the arches of the nave (suggesting continuation into the area of the windows of the vault), and through the curved returning of the nave at either end with the consequent closing down of the vault. At Sant' Andrea, the nave transitions at either end are achieved through modest salient piers, pilasters, and arches. At San

Juvarra.
San Filippo Neri.
Turin, Italy.
1717, 1730–1736 (not
* completed until later by*
* others)*

Juvarra.
Santa Cristina (façade).
Turin, Italy.
1715

Filippo, the result is the centralizing of a longitudinal plan.

The appearance of the portico in Juvarra's final scheme may also be a comment on the portico of Sant' Andrea. In both buildings (as Pommer, 1967, has noted) the portico temple front stands lower and forward of the nave, allowing a large opening above in the nave wall at the entrance. Even though Juvarra most likely appreciated Alberti's approximation of the inner order/pier/bay size for the portico of Sant' Andrea, he apparently felt it to be applied rather than integrated. At San Filippo, where the inner and outer orders were also the same height, the slightly salient tetrastyle portico with pediment is held in antis between two supplemental end bays (pierced by arches from the porch and by windows on the façade) which signal the full width of the church.

As in the designs for Superga, Juvarra seems to have restated in San Filippo Neri one of the principal themes of longitudinal churches that derived from Sant' Andrea, merging it, however, with the values of centralized space through the incorporation and reworking of earlier versions of the double-ended oratory or church from Borromini through GUARINO GUARINI.

While preparing the design and models for Superga and San Filippo Neri, Juvarra designed and had a model built for the façade of Santa Cristina in time to begin construction on September 6, 1715. The church, one of two flanking the central street at the south end of Piazza San Carlo, had been built seventy-five years earlier by CARLO CASTELLAMONTE at the request of the Duchess Cristina, but the façade was left unfinished. Its twin, also lacking a façade, had been built somewhat earlier. The queen mother commissioned Juvarra to design façades for both churches. His final design for both churches appears in a view of the piazza dated 1721 engraved by Juvarra's acquaintance in Rome, FILIPPO VASCONI.

Only one façade, that to the east, was executed by Juvarra. The design went through several stages, including a planar, tetrastyle temple front with pairs of free-standing or partially engaged columns (which recall the churches of the Piazza del Popolo in Rome) flanking an entrance portal (below an oval window) which was alternatively either the full width of the church or, with Palladian (see ANDREA PALLADIO) echoes, a temple front confined to the width of the nave, exposing the lower chapels on the flanks. The final, two-tiered, concave-curved façade was initially more broadly conceived, with a single column on the upper level; as constructed, however, a pair of columns flank the oval window. The column set inside at the upper level corresponds to that of the

more salient portico below; the column set outside corresponds to the one displaced laterally below. The columns advance the façade into the piazza, extend its influence laterally, and, with the pilasters behind, suggest extension in depth into the church and down the street alongside.

Juvarra knew well the concave façade of San Marcello al Corso in Rome executed by Carlo Fontana in the last decades of the seventeenth century and learned much from it. At Santa Cristina, the ratio of heights of lower to upper story follows that of San Marcello, but in eschewing pedestals at the lower level (while retaining them on the second level), the columns of the lower level acquired increased verticality, and the accessibility of the church was augmented as appropriate for a sizable public square.

By limiting the salient portico to two columns and by recessing the entablature of the pediment on the second level, Juvarra suggested a greater penetration in depth than had Fontana. Combined with the lateral extension of the lower level, the turning of the pilaster bunches at the edges, and the placement of the sculpted figures and candelabra above in recession to either side, this penetration implied a novel fluidity of mass and spatial extension.

The Castello at Venaria Reale, built in the 1670s on designs by AMEDEO DI CASTELLAMONTE for Carlo Emanuele II, was much damaged in the wars of the late seventeenth century. Vittorio Amedeo II began its reconstruction with designs by MICHELANGELO GAROVE for a grand gallery as a new south wing. Garove died in 1714. In 1715 or 1716, Juvarra was asked to take over. The gallery was redesigned with larger windows in the vault; new stucco decoration of the vault, walls, and piers and splendid entrance portals were added in each apsidal end. In his redesign, Juvarra also relocated the chapel to a piazza planned by Garove and begun in 1716 but never completed. He also added the stables and citroneria from 1720 to 1729.

For the king and his household, the chapel had a royal upper level that encircled a central space. In plan, the Greek cross with four satellite chapels was extended longitudinally by an entrance vestibule, an apse with a semicircular columnar screen, and an annular-vaulted space behind with an oval window on axis. The central piers were pierced at the gallery level and open to the upper level of the satellite chapels. The chapels extended up through both levels to lanterns above. Oval windows in the dome, tall windows in the lower section of the vault over the arms and in the lunettes above the entrance and the altars in the arms, together with light from the domes of the satellite chapels that filtered through piers, richly illuminated an interior that was white and gilded, with contrasting embellished altars and altarpieces.

Juvarra also received commissions for palaces from the nobility (Palazzo Birago di Borgaro and Palazzo Martini di Cigala, both 1716; Palazzo Ghilini (project), 1720; Palazzo Guarene, 1730). The façades of the best of these sober, rectilinear schemes, the Birago di Borgaro and the Guarene, have ground floors with modified rustication and two upper levels united by a giant pilaster order, ultimately derived from the façade of the Palazzo Chigi-Odescalchi by Bernini. At the Birago di Borgaro Palace, a dramatic visual sequence begins with an exterior Doric portico through which one enters a Doric atrium crowned by an elegant oval ribbed vault. The atrium leads through a triple-arched opening to a courtyard shaped by low curved walls which, on axis, separate to reveal, further back against a high wall, a portal of complex form sheltering the standing figure of a female floral deity.

Before Superga, San Filippo, Santa Cristina, and Venaria Reale were much more than begun, Juvarra was asked to prepare plans to complete the Castello at Rivoli (also left unfinished by Garove), design a new façade and wings for the Palazzo Madama to form the east side of a new Piazza Castello, prepare plans for a church dedicated to the archangel Raphael for the queen mother, and begin the church of Santa Croce on Piazza Carlina.

Although Sacchetti omits mention of the designs for San Raffaele (not executed), the drawings are assigned to the period 1718 to 1720 because they are related to the designs for Santa Croce, dated by Sacchetti to 1718. Both churches had central plans. San Raffaele, insistently vertical with the drum and dome more than one and three-quarter times the height of the lower level, was circular with three entrances, two levels of paired columns on the diagonals, attic with oval windows, and ribbed dome with large windows. Santa Croce began with an upper level related to the Antamoro Chapel in Rome but rectangular in plan, including a ribbed dome springing directly from the entablature of the lower order and with axial and lateral arches extending into the area of the dome. As constructed, Santa Croce became a longitudinal oval with a single entrance from the piazza and with chapels on the lateral axis. Pairs of free-standing Composite columns with ressants continue through salient pilasters at the level of the drum/attic to ribs in the coffered dome. On axis leading to the main altar, an arch rises into the second level revealing behind the crowning element of the altar screen, a thermal window giving on the retrochoir. The columns flanking the entrance to the sanctuary are subtly given a one-quarter turn from a ra-

dial alignment to reinforce the direction of the altar. The four piers contain niches at the lower level and oval windows in the drum/attic which alternate with arched rectangular windows on the axes. The altars were not designed until 1730 as the church neared completion.

The drawings for San Raffaele and the early version of Santa Croce were structurally bolder than in execution, as was an early version of the chapel at Venaria Reale. Only after ten to fifteen years of practice did Juvarra achieve some of his more daring and original conceptions in his designs for Sant' Andrea in Chieri (1728), the new cathedral of Turin (1729), Stupinigi (1730), and the Church of the Carmine (1732).

The medieval Castello di Rivoli had been modernized by Carlo Emanuele I, burned by the French in the 1690s and begun again early in the eighteenth century by Vittorio Amedeo II, first using ANTONIO BERTOLA and then Garove as architects. Juvarra's first task was to complete the Garove design. Later, around 1718, Juvarra greatly aggrandized the project and a new model was built (Museo Civico, Turin). Although the Castello was not completed, it was captured in four exterior views painted from drawings supplied by Juvarra, two by G. Pannini (east and south), and two by A. Lucatelli (north and west). Two interiors, one of the salone by M. Ricci and one of the grand atrium and stairs by M. Michele, complete the set. (The paintings, which were originally hung in the Castello, are now in the Museo Civico in Turin and in the Castello Reale at Racconigi.)

The salone alone, oriented north–south and entered from a vestibule at the top of the symmetrical stairs, with its double level of openings, atlantes and caryatids at the upper level, ribbed and frescoed vault (recalling the main hall of the sacristy model for St. Peter's), and paintings and stucco, would have been stunning. Yet, Juvarra's principal achievement at Rivoli, which would

Juvarra.
Painting of the Castello
Reale by Pannini.
Rivoli, Italy.
1718

have provided additional testimony to Vittorio Amedeo's new regal status, was the masterful relationship between the terraces, ramps, and stairs on the hilly slope to the south so splendidly rendered by Pannini and visible in the model as well as in the painting. In the sequence of three levels and diagonal ramps, something of Juvarra's study and reconstruction of the Capitoline Hill in antiquity were brought to fruition.

In February 1718, excavations began for the embellishment and remodeling of the Palazzo

Madama for Maria Giovaanna Battista, window of Carlo Emanuele II and mother of Vittorio Amedeo II. Sited on Piazza Castello at the head of the two main avenues leading east (via Po) and west (via Dora Grossa) and perpendicular to the principal façade of the Royal Palace, the site was a dynastic focal point of the city. Juvarra transformed the Castello, which was itself an enlarged and partially converted towered gateway remaining from the ancient Roman town, into the most regal façade in Turin. His plans included the portion realized—a nine-bay façade and star hall on axis with the avenue to the west (seven bays of which were occupied by the immense vaulted stair hall one bay deep containing the entrance, symmetrical stairs to either side and a landing at the second level); a portion partially achieved—the redesign of the salone and rooms of the piano nobile; and unrealized extensions to the north and south—flanking wings of six bays set back from the stair hall, each terminated by salient three-story pavilions. The wing to the north was to have joined a wing of the Royal Palace. A print, based on a drawing by Juvarra and engraved by Vasconi, shows the entire complex from the west. To judge from the print, Juvarra intended the central trabeated section and the three main arches to either side at the upper level to be unglazed (or to be read as unglazed)—describing a deeply shadowed open entrance portico of royal dimension.

The aggressively regal nature of the building is partly a product of its size and apparent simplicity, partly due to the commanding compositional resolution of the three triple bays each with an added emphasis on its central bay, partly to the association of a rusticated lower floor and giant order, including a second and third level, with royal and princely palaces, and partly to its axial location on the royal square in the center of the city.

The first flight of the stair to the left or right, against the inside wall, leads to an intermediate landing aligned with the central bay of the flanking triads (the bays at either end contain rooms entered from the palace). From there the second flight, now against the façade wall, rises to a central landing at the piano nobile. At this island landing, a bridge crosses the open space between the second flight of stairs and the entrance to the main salone. Overhead, the coffered, ribbed, and stuccoed vault, twice as high as the ascent to the central landing, extends uninterrupted along the entire seven bays of the stair hall enclosing one of the grandest spaces in Europe, articulated and modulated by Juvarra's bold and inventive cream-colored stuccoes, sculpted detail, moldings, and architectural members disposed on a pale green, light-enhancing field.

In these early buildings, Juvarra developed a personal decorative vocabulary that extended his Roman experience of Michelangelo, Borromini, and Bernini. To complete and embellish these buildings, Juvarra secured commissions for altarpieces and other decorations for his acquaintances in Rome. In addition, during these years, he trained a corps of craftsmen in Piedmont to his new manner, men who were to work for him for the remainder of his life and who would continue the Juvarresque decorative tradition for generations.

Late in 1718, Juvarra began a series of voyages that lasted for almost two and a half years. He first went to Paris for unknown reasons and he remained there for about ten months. Shortly after returning to Turin, he left, in November 1719, for Portugal where he was called by King John V. In the year he spent at the court, he is reported to have designed a lighthouse for the port of Lisbon and, near Lisbon at Mafra, a royal palace with adjacent patriarchal palace and church. The vast design is known only through four sketches. In November 1720, Juvarra sailed from Lisbon to England.

He stayed in London with the Portuguese ambassador for about a month before going again to Paris late in 1720 or early in 1721. From Paris he may have gone directly to Rome where in March 1721 he was reported as soon to return to Turin. Aside from the designs for Mafra we know little of his activities during these two and a half years, but he apparently continued to prepare specifications and detail drawings for Superga while on his travels. A number of documents signed by Juvarra, some including drawings by his hand, are dated December 1719 and the spring of 1720 while he was in Lisbon. In fact, work was begun on the new Palazzo del Senato, the Scala delle Forbici in the Palazzo Reale, and the campanile of the cathedral, all following drawings, specifications, or both in Juvarra's hand from the period he was reported to be in Lisbon.

Construction of the Palazzo del Senato was interrupted in 1721 and not taken up again until 1727 following a different design, and this too was abandoned. Work began again in 1741, perhaps following Juvarra's second design, under BENEDETTO ALFIERI. The campanile of the Cathedral was completed through the attic before it, too, was abandoned unfinished.

Of the three works begun in Juvarra's absence, only the Scala delle Forbici, begun in 1720, was completed. Built in three sections, with single, double, and single flights, the stair was placed in a rectangular room adjacent to the Salone degli Svizzeri, the largest reception hall in the palace. It replaced a wooden stair that joined the piano nobile and the second floor of the royal palace. Juvarra transformed what could have been merely another stair into one of the most important stairs of the early eighteenth century, a triumph of spatial manipulation and decorative invention. In Juvarra's first all-white interior, the fluid rise of the stair is contrasted with the massive enclosing walls which are pierced by windows only on one side. The spring lines for the half-arches that form the flights and for the arches that support the landing are deftly concealed behind decorative cartouches, shell motifs, volutes, and wreaths that blur the junctions of planar systems emphasizing continuity of space and surface. The moldings that define the lower edge of the stringer of the third flight break in a three-dimensional curve on either side in mid-flight, to reach the underside of the supporting half-arch where they frame a central medallion. At junctures of flights with landings, moldings, also curved in three dimensions, fuse the two. Curves and countercurves in both the vertical and horizontal planes, proximate and distant, contribute to a consummate sense of controlled manipulation of mass, space, and light. Juvarra used bolder relief on the stringers, soffits, and landings with side lighting while at the upper level, the stucco reliefs were shallow where the openings were doubled and the walls of the stair hall were illuminated directly by the windows opposite. The decorative restraint of the enclosing walls was used as a foil to the exuberance, strength, and lyrical vigor of the stair.

In the early 1720s, Juvarra also designed a pair of altars for Santissima Trinità in Turin and extensively remodeled the Royal Theater in the Palazzo Reale (for which he made many series of scene designs) and the interior of the Oratorio of San Filippo Neri in Turin. He traveled to Lucca in the fall of 1723 and again in February 1724 to present revised plans for the completion of the Palazzo Pubblico, first designed eighteen years earlier, in 1706. While in Lucca, Juvarra prepared designs for an altar in the cathedral, for temporary decorations for a ball in the theater, and for the gardens of the Villa Mansi at Segromigno. In 1725, while in Rome for the Jubilee, Juvarra was asked by Cardinal Albani to design a permanent palace for papal conclaves. The three designs he prepared are preserved, and although the pope is reported to have been pleased enough to appoint Juvarra architect of St. Peter's, none of the designs was executed.

A few years later, perhaps in 1728, Juvarra began work on Sant' Andrea in Chieri. In contrast to his selection of a more conservative solution at both Sant' Uberto and Santa Croce, he realized a bold and revolutionary conception. At Sant' Andrea, Juvarra achieved a greater vertical continu-

Juvarra.
Scala delle Forbici, Palazzo Reale.
Turin, Italy.
1720

ity—through linear structural emphasis in the piers at two levels and in the ribbed dome—than he had in the designs for San Raffaele. His designs for the Duomo Nuovo, Stupinigi, and the Carmine were developments of ideas realized in Chieri.

Instead of a circular plan with emphasis on the diagonals as at San Raffaele, Sant' Andrea was circular with arms that expanded the plan into a Greek cross, isolating the piers on the diagonals. At the sanctuary, the fourth arm was replaced by a large rectangular bay with a dome. As constructed, Sant' Andrea had about the same ratio of width of central space to height (c.1:2.15) as in the design for San Raffaele, but the lateral chapels, entrance arms, and sanctuary were extended upward through the main entablature to the height of the arches at the second level, expanding the space of the church upward and outward.

The audacious windows in the dome and attic level of the design for San Raffaele coalesced at Sant' Andrea into a larger tripartite window that broke downward through the entablature of the second level (linked by a cartouche to the main arches) and expanded laterally to fill the space between the coffered ribs. The ribs, perhaps to avoid a horizontal, sprang directly from the top of the entablature. For further emphasis on openness and lightness at the upper level, Juvarra replaced the paired pilasters of the lower level with paired, salient, three-quarter columns at the second level, thereby de-emphasizing the mass of the pier, and used only a single salient rib in the dome. Although only half the size of Superga, Sant' Andrea was a more coherent, original, and accomplished design, with greater influence. It was destroyed early in the nineteenth century.

In 1728, Vittorio Amedeo II took steps to enlarge the royal chapel that lay between the Palazzo Reale and the Cathedral of Turin. Because enlargement meant destruction of the existing cathedral, Juvarra was asked to prepare several schemes for a new one. Four different designs were developed and sent by the king to the city council, for them to select the most adventuresome. For additional opinions, a report was requested from a knowledgeable noble in Turin, and in Rome from Cardinal Alessandro Albani and a "professor of architecture." All the designs and responses survive. The third of the four designs, a Latin cross with apsidal sanctuary, transepts, and entrance bay, and with single side aisles and chapels (which reminded several of the critics of St. Peter's in Rome), was preferred over two central plans and another longitudinal plan with pairs of side aisles. The new, much larger cathedral was to have been oriented to the south with its façade placed on a new piazza located on the site of the old cathedral. When Vittorio Amedeo abdicated in 1730, the project was dropped.

Nonetheless, as Pommer (1967) has shown, in one of the central-plan projects, Juvarra fused the interest in penetrations, perforations, and modulated sequential spaces of the Venaria Reale with the coherent vertical structure and spatial unity of Sant' Andrea in Chieri. This fusion, although not constructed, was to reappear two years later in the Church of the Carmine.

In the design of the hunting lodge known as the Palazzina di Stupinigi, about 11 kilometers from the center of Turin, there were no pre-existing structures to consider and Juvarra was able to prepare complete plans for the palazzina, its outbuildings, approaches, garden, and avenues lead-

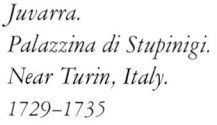

Juvarra.
Palazzina di Stupinigi.
Near Turin, Italy.
1729–1735

ing to the forests. In his design, the oval nucleus and four radiating wings generated the shape of the stairs, terraces, octagonal forecourt, other outbuildings, and garden. From a modest beginning, the palazzina grew under Juvarra and succeeding architects to become one of the most extensive and splendid hunting lodges in Europe.

The palazzina was sited on wooded land belonging to the aristocratic Order of Saint Maurizio and was constructed by the order. The king, as master of the order, instructed the members in April 1729 to build the palazzina according to plans prepared by Juvarra. The next day, documents record, the order returned the drawings to Juvarra for additions and changes that were ordered by the king. Once these were completed, work proceeded rapidly. Early in 1731, the Venetian painters Giuseppe and Domenico Valeriani were engaged to paint the main oval salone following Juvarra's instructions. In November 1731, even though the Valeriani had not completed the vault, the celebration of the feast of Sant' Uberto took place in the salone. Work followed on the outbuildings with further decoration of the main pavilion by more able painters including Carlo Van Loo, Giovanni Battista Crosato, Michele Antonio Milocco, Girolamo Mengozzi-Colonna, and Pietro Antonio Pozzo. The portions Juvarra designed and decorated, including additions made by Carlo Emanuele III in 1733, were completed by 1735 when Juvarra left for Madrid. Further enlargements and extensions continued under the direction of Benedetto Alfieri.

More than a dozen drawings by Juvarra for Stupinigi survive and chronicle the evolution of the design. The palazzina began as a one-story oval pavilion (with mezzanine) somewhat higher than the four one-story radiating wings (also with mezzanines) that were themselves higher than the open arched loggia which linked the main pavilion to the outbuildings of the octagonal forecourt (containing stables and tackle or harness rooms). Four major changes in the design can be observed (all most likely made before construction began) in the following sequence: the first, change probably the result of studies of the interior of the salone (for which a number of drawings are extant), resulted in heightening the mezzanine of the salone to a full story, greatly enlarging the upper windows and providing a balcony on the interior at the upper level; second, the span of the vault was decreased through the insertion of four piers within the oval which resulted in larger and more complex spaces at the upper level; third, an attic level was added to the radiating wings of the central pavilion (confirmed by a pair of drawings in the Promis collection in the Biblioteca Reale in

Turin); and fourth, a level equal in height to the newly added attic of the radiating wings was also inserted in the oval pavilion between the main openings of the lower and upper level, raising once again the height of the central oval above the radiating wings. Coincident with this last heightening, Juvarra added a balustrade capped with urns to the central oval. Through this device, he may have intended to contrast the formal quality of the salone with the residential and utilitarian remainder of the complex.

The transformation of the oval salone by the placement of four piers, combined with the heightening of the salone and penetrations in the peripheral vaults for the enlarged windows of the upper level, resulted in conoid and ovoid vaults on the axes and, at the upper level, in flat triangular soffits between the pier and the outer wall. Were the vaulting and ceilings of the salone not made of wood and plaster, Juvarra would have been forced to seek another solution.

Juvarra.
Palazzina di Stupinigi
   (*salone*).
Near Turin, Italy.
1729–1735

As completed, the salone with its painted fluting, volutes, trophies, moldings, coffering, windows, niches, statues, and other detail and with its hung vaulting, was emphemeral architecture made permanent if not substantial, a stunning stage (even with its raucous painting by the Valerianis) for the king to act or live the hunter/ruler with his audience/court. Juvarra's mastery was apparent both in the approach, hemicycle, and forecourt, which gathered space for the main pavilion, and in the stairs, terraces, and garden which extended it to the woods beyond. The complex is centripetal on approach and, through the salone, centrifugal toward the garden and park. In spite of the sham grandeur of the salone and perhaps because of its theatrical bravura, it is suprisingly convincing. At a level of significance to Europe as a whole, Juvarra realized some of the potential in his earlier unexecuted or abandoned designs for Lucca, Venaria Reale, Rivoli, and Mafra. In Madrid, there would be one further opportunity to work on a grand scale.

The main entries to Turin from the west (Porta Susina) and north (via Milano-Piazza Vittoria) and the enlargement of via Milano between the entrance to the city at Piazza Vittoria to the Palazzo di Città and Torre Civica reveal something of Juvarra's notions of urban design. For the Quartieri Militari, begun at the Susa gate in 1716 and probably initially following a scheme prepared by Garove, Juvarra designed a pair of buildings that formed an arcaded rectangular, U-shaped small entry piazza from which a street ran to the Palazzo di Città between the two structures. An arcaded ground level, which already existed on Piazza Castello, Piazza San Carlo, and along via Po was also endorsed at the Quartieri Militari where Ju-

Juvarra.
Quartieri Militari.
Turin, Italy.
1716

varra suggested it be continued along the façades next to the walls of the city as well as along the thoroughfare leading to the center of Turin. Juvarra used a grand pilaster order on pedestals to unify the open lower arcade and the enclosed upper level, which most strongly recalls Palladio's Loggia del Capitaniato in Vicenza (where, however, half-columns form the giant order). Juvarra made a distinction between the moment of entry (once through the gate) in the piazzetta, articulated by single pilasters, and the continuation of the arcade along via del Carmine, where with the quickened rhythm of passage, the pilasters were doubled.

The larger, more important entry at Piazza Vittoria and via Milano was begun in 1729, probably as part of Vittorio Amedeo's plan to renovate the area to the west of the Palazzo Reale in conjunction with designs for the Duomo Nuovo. From early in the seventeenth century, the main gate from the north led up via Milano to the Palazzo di Città. It seems likely that in 1729 Vittorio Amedeo wished to aggrandize and regalize this entry as he had done earlier at the Porta Susa.

Juvarra fashioned another U-shaped piazza on a larger scale, using a rusticated arcade (with shops and mezzanine behind) and a giant pilaster order above, uniting two main levels with a third tucked into the height of the entablature. The arcaded piazza led into a widened and straightened via Milano. At the cross street site of the Basilica Mauriziana, via Milano opened (to conform to the direction of the façade which followed the pre-existing street direction) into a lozenge-shaped unarcaded piazza with three similar façades to serve as foils to the basilica, the Church of the Order of San Maurizio.

The reshaping of via Milano and the shaping of entries at Piazza Vittoria (where a drawing indicates that Juvarra may have intended a triumphal arch across via Milano) and Porta Susina provided Turin with four regal entrances to the capital as part of Vittorio Amedeo's plan to transform the city.

The Church of the Carmine, built in 1732–1736 along via del Carmine in the enlargement of Turin laid out in the early eighteenth century, two blocks from the Quartieri Militari (and an equal distance from the house Juvarra built for himself in 1723/1724), is perhaps Juvarra's most original and influential design. After a series of drawings that recapitulated some of the ideas studied for San Filippo Neri, Juvarra settled on a simple, double-ended longitudinal nave of five bays with a narrower elongated apsidal sanctuary. Shallower and narrower bays at either end of the nave recall the final solution at San Filippo, also from these years.

If the plan is conventional, the elevation/section is revolutionary. Juvarra's treatment of the shallow chapels in the three bays of the nave surpasses the innovative suggestions partially explored in his studies for Sant' Andrea, Venaria, the Duomo Nuovo, and Stupinigi in his search for vertical spatial and structural continuity, de-emphasis of mass, and vertical lighting to suggest the ethereal.

Juvarra stilted the simple, ribbed barrel vault on a high attic; arches above the chapels reach up into the vault. The rise of the vault and attic is about 80 percent of the height of the main order, slightly less than at San Filippo. But the space of the chapels was extended vertically (through the entablature of the main order which wrapped around the pier and returned to the outer wall) well into the area of the vault.

The arches leading to the chapels remained in the plane of the nave piers independent of the entablature. Behind these arches, pendentives formed an oval cornice ring open to the upper level of the chapel. At the upper level a clearstory window admits light to the nave and chapel below. Behind the arches cut into the main vault, above the chapel, a ribbed oval dome springs from the level of the attic rising to a lantern hidden behind the nave vault. Light from the lantern illuminates the upper level and, through the open oval cornice ring, the chapel altar below. Space and light increase with height.

Although the paired pilasters, barrel vault, and chapels of the Alberti solution at Mantua are retained as they were at San Filippo, the wall of the nave has been further stripped away, leaving linear skeletal piers that are all but free-standing. The vault, while retaining coffers between the paired ribs, has also been reduced by penetrations, and support and infill have been differentiated. The integration of openness and vertical continuity of light and space with vertical structural continuity was one of Juvarra's greatest achievements at the Carmine. Whereas Superga and the Palazzo Madama reaffirmed the achievements of Italian architecture of the sixteenth and seventeenth centuries, Sant' Andrea in Chieri, Stupinigi, and the Carmine altered the direction of its development.

In January 1735, Philip V of Spain asked his former brother-in-law, Carlo Emanuele III, to grant Juvarra leave to come to Madrid to design a royal palace to replace one that burned in September 1734. Permission was granted for a three-year stay, and Juvarra arrived in Madrid in April.

He was immediately asked to embellish a façade of the palace at Aranjuez and, as drawings and documents show, to design the garden façade of the La Granja Palace at San Ildefonso, which was built, however, after his death. Juvarra also set

Juvarra.
Church of the Carmine.
Turin, Italy.
1732–1736

to work on the royal palace in Madrid which was to be sited on steeply sloping ground. Five-hundred-sixty-five meters on a side, it would have made Versailles appear to be a summer retreat. The main palace, to one side of an immense court, 245 x 140 meters, with multiple large courtyards, many smaller light wells, pavilions, and wings, was balanced on the other by the palatine chapel complex. The whole was conceived with Bernini's third design for the Louvre, Juvarra's Rivoli, and his Palazzo Madama in mind, using a giant order enclosing two stories placed on a rusticated base. A large model was built. In January 1736, after impatiently walking to his unheated rooms because the court carriage had not arrived, Juvarra caught a chill and died. He was buried in the Church of Santo Martino in Madrid.

Giovanni Battista Sacchetti, Juvarra's assistant in Turin, was called to Madrid. He built the façade of La Granja following Juvarra's designs but reduced the royal palace by two-thirds at the request of the king's councillors so that it would cover no more than the area of the original palace. Sacchetti added a number of stories to arrive at the areas necessary (two stories on the high side of the rusticated lower level, four stories where the ground dropped off, three within the giant order, another in the attic level, and a top story, with dormers, in the roof). Sacchetti retained, nevertheless, the compositional principle established by Juvarra. Philip V acquired an international palace, a close relative of the palace by Bernini that his grandfather, Louis XIV, chose not to build in Paris.

Juvarra's influence continued in Piedmont and elsewhere for another fifty years. His elaboration and development of the mainstream of the Bernini/Fontana school insured that he would be studied by sober, traditional architects. His achievements were provocative stimuli to innovative architects in Italy, France, and central Europe.

HENRY A. MILLON

WORKS

1708–1710, Antamoro Chapel, San Girolamo della Carità, Rome. 1715, Santa Cristina (façade), Turin, Italy. 1715–1716, Venaria Reale Gallery, Italy. 1715–1717, 1730–1736, San Filippo Neri (not completed until later by others), 1716, Palazzo Birago di Borgaro, Turin, Italy. 1716, Palazzo Martini di Cigala; 1716, Quartieri Militari; Turin, Italy. 1716, Venaria Reale Chapel (not completed), Italy. 1716–1731, Church and Monastery, Superga, near Turin, Italy. 1718, Santa Croce; 1718, Palazzo Madama (stair); Turin, Italy. 1718, Castello Reale (not completed), Rivoli, Italy. 1718–1721, Palazzo Madama (remodeling); 1720, Campanile, Cathedral of Turin; 1720, Scala delle Forbici, Palazzo Reale; Turin, Italy. 1720–1729, Venaria Reale Stables and Citroneria, Italy. *1728?, Sant' Andrea, Chieri, Italy. 1729, Piazza Vittoria, Turin, Italy. 1729–1735, Palazzina di Stupinigi, near Turin, Italy. 1720s, Royal Palace (remodeling of theater); 1730, Palazzo Guarene (façade); 1732–1736, Church of the Carmine; Turin, Italy. 1735, Royal Palace (executed in a reduced form), Madrid. 1736, La Granja Palace (garden façade; not executed until later by others), Sant' Ildefonso, Spain.

BIBLIOGRAPHY

ACCASCINA, MARIA 1956–1957 "La Formazione artistica di Filippo Juvarra." *Bolletino d'Arte* 41:38–52; 42:50–60, 150–162.

BARONI DI TAVIGLIANO, G. 1758 *Modello della Chiesa di S. Filippo per li PP. dell'Oratorio di Torino, inventato e disegnato dall'abate e cav. Don Filippo Juvarra, primo architetto di S.M.* Turin: Stamperia Reale.

BATTISTA, EUGENIO 1958 "Juvarra a San Ildefonso." *Commentari* 9, no. 4:273–297.

BELLA BARSALI, ISA 1964 "Le ville di Lucca dal XV al XIX secolo." *Bollettino del centro di studi per la storia dell'architettura* 20–21.

BENEDETTI, SANDRO 1973 "Una quasi sconosciuta opera Juvarriana: La costruzione settecentesca del palazzo pubblico di Lucca." *Palladio* 23:145–183.

BERNARDI, MARZIANO 1958 *La palazzina di caccia di Stupinigi.* Turin, Italy: Bancario San Paolo di Torino.

BOSCARINO, SALVATORE 1973 *Juvarra architetto.* Rome: Officina Edizioni.

BRINCKMANN, ALBERT E. 1931 *Theatrum Novum Pedemontii, ideen, Entwürfe und Bauten von Guarini, Juvarra, Vittone.* Dusseldorf, Germany: Schwann.

CARBONERI, NINO 1963 "Architettura." Volume 1, pages 44–53 in Vittorio Viale (editor), *Mostra del Barocco Piemontese.* Turin, Italy: Museo Avico.

CARBONERI, NINO 1979 *La Reale Chiesa di Superga di Filippo Juvarra.* Turin, Italy: Ages Arti Grafiche.

CAVALLARI MURAT, AUGUSTO ET AL. 1968 *Forma urbana ed architettura nella Torino Barocca.* 2 vols. in 3. Turin, Italy: UTET.

CHEVALLEY, GIOVANNI 1942 "Vicende costruttive della chiesa di San Filippo Neri in Torino." *Bolletino Storico-Bibliografico Subalpino* 44:63–99.

CHEVALLEY, GIOVANNI 1947 "La formazione della personalità artistica di Filippo Juvarra." *Bolletino della Società Piemontese di Archeologia e Bella Arte* 1:72–82.

FICHERA, FRANCESCO 1935 "Juvarra tra Bernini e Borromini." *Quadrivio* 49.

GRISERI, ANDREINA 1967 *Le metamorphosi del barocco.* Turin, Italy: Einaudi.

GRISERI, ANDREINA 1972 "Il Classicismo Juvarriano." Volume 1, pages 153–172 in *Bernardo Vittone e la disputà fra classicismo e barocco nel settecento.* Turin, Italy: Accademia delle Scienze.

HAGER, HELLMUT 1970 *Filippo Juvarra e il concurso di modelli del 1715 bandito da Clemente XI per la nuova sacrestia di S. Pietro.* Rome: De Luca.

MALLÉ, LUIGI (1962)1973 *Le arti figurative in Piemonte.* Turin, Italy: Casanova.

MALLÉ, LUIGI 1970 *Palazzo Madama in Torino.* Turin, Italy: Tipografia Torinese.

MALLÉ, LUIGI 1972 *Stupinigi un capolavoro del settecento europeo tra barocchetto e classicismo: Architettura, Pittura, Scultura, Arredamento.* Turin, Italy: Tipografia Torinese.

MARCONI, PAOLO; CIPRINANI, ANGELA; and VALERIANI, ENRICO 1974 *I disegni di architettura dell'archivio storico dell'Accademia di San Luca.* 2 vols. Rome: De Luca.

MASINI, LEONARDA 1920 "La vita e l'arte di Filippo Juvarra." *Atti della Società Piemontese di Archeologia e Belle Arte* 9–197ff.

MILLON, HENRY A. 1978 "Vasi, Piranesi, Juvarra." Pages 345–363 in *Piranèse et les Français.* Rome: Académie de France.

MILLON, HENRY A. 1980 "The Antamoro Chapel in S. Girolamo della Carità in Rome: Drawings by Juvarra and an Unknown Draftsman." Pages 261–288 in Henry A. Millon (editor), *Studies in Italian Art and Architecture, 15th through 18th Centuries.* Cambridge, Mass.: M.I.T. Press.

MISCHIATE, OSCAR, and VIALE FERRERO, MERCEDES 1976 "Disegni e incisione di Filippo Juvarra per edizioni romane del primo settecento." *Atti Accademia delle Scienze di Torino* 110:211–274.

MYERS, MARY L. 1975 *Architectural and Ornament Drawings: Juvarra, Vanvitelli, the Bibiena Family and other Italian Draughtsmen.* New York: Metropolitan Museum of Art.

OECHSLIN, WERNER 1972 "Bildungsgut und Antikenrezeption des Frühen Settecento in Rom." In *Studien zum Römischen aufenthalt Bernardo Antonio Vittones.* Zurich and Freiburg im Breisgau: Atlantis.

PASSANTI, MARIO 1945 *Architettura in Piemonte da Emanuele Filiberto al unità d'Italia (1563-1670).* Turin, Italy: Giorgio.

PASSANTI, MARIO 1966 *Lo sviluppo urbanistico di Torino dalla fondazione all' unità d'Italia.* Turin, Italy: Istituto universitario di architettura.

PINTO, JOHN 1980 "Filippo Juvarra's Drawings Depicting the Capitoline Hill." *Art Bulletin* 62:598–616.

PLAZA SANTIAGO, FRANCISCO DE LA 1978 *El Palacio Real Nuevo de Madrid.* Spain: Art History Department, University of Valladolid.

POMMER, RICHARD 1967 *Eighteenth-Century Architecture in Piedmont: The Open Structures of Juvarra, Alfieri, and Vittone.* New York and London: New York University Press.

ROBOTTI, C. 1976 "Rivoli—il Castello." *Restauro* 23:17–24.

ROVERE, LORENZO; VIALE, VITTORIO; and BRINCKMANN, ALBERT E. 1973 *Filippo Juvarra.* Turin, Italy: Crudo.

TAVASSI LA GRECA, BIANCA 1981 "Il decennio romano di Filippo Juvarra." *Storia dell'arte* 41:21–30.

TELLUCCINI, AUGUSTO 1926 *L'Arte dell'architetto Filippo Juvarra in Piemonte.* Turin, Italy: Crudo.

VIALE FERRERO, MERCEDES 1970 *Filippo Juvarra scenografo e architetto teatrale.* Turin, Italy: Pozzo.

VIALE, VITTORIO (editor) 1966 *Catalogo della Mostra di Filippo Juvarra, architetto e scenografo.* Italy: University of Messina.

WITTKOWER, RUDOLF 1949 "Un libro di schizzi di Filippo Juvarra a S. Pietro a Roma." *Bolletino della Società Piemontese di Archeologia e Belle Arte* 3:158–161.

WITTKOWER, RUDOLF (1958)1972 *Art and Architecture in Italy: 1600–1750.* 3d ed. Harmondsworth, England: Penguin.

KAHN, ALBERT

At its peak in the late 1930s, the office of Albert Kahn (1869–1942) employed a staff of over 600, producing 19 percent of all architect-designed industrial building in the United States.

Kahn was born in Rhaunen, Germany, but spent his childhood in the Luxembourg countryside near Echternach. His formal education was terminated when the family emigrated to Detroit, Michigan, in 1880. After joining the Shingle style firm of Mason and Rice (see GEORGE DEWITT MASON) in 1884, Kahn served as the firm's principal residential architect and eventually became chief designer. A $500 scholarship took Kahn to Europe in 1891.

The partnership of Kahn, Nettleton, and Trowbridge, formed in 1896, was dissolved several years later when George W. Nettleton died and Alexander B. Trowbridge accepted a position as dean at Cornell University. In 1902, Kahn formed his own firm, later joined by brothers Julius and Moritz.

The firm's earliest industrial works are relatively conventional. The Packard Motor Car Company Plant (1903–1910) used the standard multistory factory arrangement of its day; the building was distinguished, however, by the straightforward expression of its reinforced concrete structure, developed by Julius Kahn. The George N. Pierce Plant in Buffalo, New York (1906), presaged a significant innovation in factory planning with the use of a single-story structure lighted from above and based on a modular system of potentially limitless extension. Although perfectly suited to the assembly line, the design predates its implementation by Henry Ford and was apparently developed for reasons of lighting and flexibility without regard to the production process. It became the principal prototype for American factory design.

Ford first introduced the powered moving assembly line at his Highland Park Plant (1909–1918), Michigan. This factory, the first of many designed by Kahn for Ford, retained the inefficient multistoried configuration. The Ford River Rouge Plant (1917–1939) in Dearborn, Michigan, was therefore the first to combine innovations in production techniques with the one-story structure best suited for assembly line work. The buildings of the River Rouge complex collectively display the principal features that characterize Kahn's factory design: exposed steel structure, linear disposition of the plan, sawtoothed roof profile, clearstory lighting combined with large window walls, standardized elements, and rapid low-cost construction.

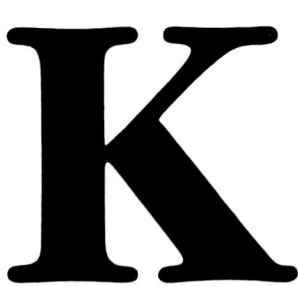

Albert Kahn.
Chrysler Corporation Half-
Ton Truck Plant and
Export Building
(Dodge Division).
Warren, Michigan.
1938

Kahn's straightforward industrial design was ideally suited to the automobile industry, and he quickly became the factory architect for all the major manufacturers. Unlike his contemporaries abroad (PETER BEHRENS, ANTONIO SANT'ELIA, and others) who celebrated the poetic potential of the machine and its architecture, Kahn ignored the symbolic and formal implications of his own work and remained dedicated to the purely pragmatic solution. His factories, provocative images of the nation's industrial capabilities, are more feats of engineering than of architecture.

Although not convinced of its romantic qualities, Kahn nevertheless believed the factory to be a legitimate area of architectural concern. His continued refinement of factory design culminated in the design for the Chrysler Half-Ton Truck Plant (1938) in Warren, Michigan, Kahn's best known work. When the exigencies of war demanded rapid construction of weapon factories, Kahn was able to meet the need immediately through standardization, turning out completed designs in as little as two weeks. The firm's war work was honored in a special certificate of commendation issued by the navy in 1943, after Kahn's death.

Kahn's industrial achievements overshadow his nonindustrial work. Yet, the architect was proudest of his early neoclassical Clements Library (1922) on the campus of the University of Michigan at Ann Arbor. A lifelong association with the university produced such campus landmarks as the Sullivanesque (see LOUIS H. SULLIVAN) Hill Auditorium (1913) and the solid but stylistically conservative Engineering Building (1903), Natural Science Building (1917), and Angell Hall (1922). Kahn's domestic work, exemplified by the Italianate Watson M. Freer House (1895) in Detroit, Michigan, and the Tudor Edsel B. Ford House (1926) in Grosse Pointe, Michigan, are stylistically derivative, following the fashions of the time. His commercial and institutional commissions in the city of Detroit ranged from the Detroit Athletic

Club (1915) designed in the manner of McKIM, MEAD, AND WHITE to the Detroit Free Press (1913), General Motors (1922), and Fisher (1927) Buildings, skyscrapers styled eclectically from Chicago and New York models.

The firm's work in Russia is a unique footnote in the history of international relations. Invited in 1930 to build a tractor plant in Stalingrad, the team of architects and engineers supervised by Moritz Kahn eventually built over 500 factories and in the process trained over 1,000 Soviets in American industrial architecture.

Thus, it is Kahn's industrial work that has had the greatest impact both in the United States and abroad. The stylistic schizophrenia that separates Kahn's industrial from his nonindustrial work can be explained in part by the architect's definition of the appropriate. Yet, it must also be attributed to that peculiarly American contradiction that separates industrial ingenuity from domestic and social conservativism. Kahn was in many ways the prototypical American entrepreneur, the self-made man.

DARALICE DONKERVOET BOLES

WORKS

1895, Watson M. Freer House; *1898, Scripps Library and Art Gallery; 1903, Conservatory, Belle Isle Park; 1903, Temple Beth El; Detroit, Mich. 1903, Engineering Building, University of Michigan, Ann Arbor. 1903–1910, Packard Motor Car Company Plant, Detroit, Mich. 1905, E. Chandler Walker House, Windsor, Ontario. 1905, Country Club of Detroit, Mich. 1906, George N. Pierce Plant, Buffalo, N.Y. 1907, George G. Booth House (now Cranbrook House), Bloomfield Hills, Mich. 1908, Casino, Belle Isle Park, Detroit, Mich. 1908, Henry B. Joy House, Grosse Pointe Farms, Mich. 1909–1918, Ford Motor Company, Highland Park Plant, Mich. 1910, Horace E. Dodge House, Grosse Pointe, Mich. 1910, Dodge Brothers Corporation, Detroit, Mich. 1910, National Theater, Detroit, Mich. 1913, Detroit Free Press Building (now Transportation Building), Mich. 1913, Hill Auditorium, University of Michigan, Ann Arbor. 1915, Detroit Athletic Club, Mich. 1915, Detroit News Building, Mich. 1917, Natural Science Building, University of Michigan, Ann Arbor. 1917, U.S. Aviation School, Laboratory and Hangar, Langley Field, Va. 1917–1939, Ford Motor Company, River Rouge Plant, Dearborn, Mich. 1919, General Library, University of Michigan; 1920, University Hospital; Ann Arbor, Mich. 1921, Fisher Body Company, Cleveland, Ohio. 1922, Angell Hall; 1922, Clements Library; University of Michigan, Ann Arbor. 1922, General Motors Building, Detroit, Mich. 1926, Edsel B. Ford House, Grosse Pointe Shores, Mich. 1927, Fisher Building; 1927, Maccabees Buildings; 1928, Chrysler Corporation Plymouth Plant; Detroit, Mich. 1930, Tractor Plant, Stalingrad, Russia. 1937, Glenn L. Martin Company, Baltimore. 1937, Chrysler Corporation Press Shop De Soto Division, Detroit, Mich. 1938, Chrysler Corporation Half-Ton Truck

Plant and Export Building (Dodge Division), Warren, Mich. *1939, Ford Exposition Building, World's Fair, New York. 1941, Chrysler Corporation Tank Arsenal, Warren, Mich. 1942, Willow Run Bomber Plant, Ford Motor Company (not built until 1943), Ypsilanti, Mich.

BIBLIOGRAPHY

"Albert Kahn, Architect, 1869–1942." 1943 *Architectural Record* 93, no. 1:14–16.

ALBERT KAHN ASSOCIATED ARCHITECTS AND ENGINEERS, INCORPORATED 1948 *Architecture*. New York: Architectural Catalogue.

"Albert Kahn, Inc. Receives Special Award." 1943 *Architectural Record* May:102.

"Albert Kahn, 73, Noted Factory Designer, Dies." 1943 *New York Herald Tribune,* Dec. 9.

DETROIT INSTITUTE OF ARTS 1970 *The Legacy of Albert Kahn.* With an Essay by W. Hawkins Ferry. Detroit, Mich.: The institute.

HILDEBRAND, GRANT 1974 *Designing for Industry: The Architecture of Albert Kahn.* Cambridge, Mass.: M.I.T. Press.

ROTH, LELAND M. 1979 *A Concise History of American Architecture.* New York: Harper.

KAHN, ELY JACQUES

Born in New York City, Ely Jacques Kahn (1884–1972) enjoyed a prolific fifty-year career as one of that city's leading architects. His best-known buildings are the dozens of Art Deco skyscrapers he designed in the 1920s and 1930s when American critics described him as a "militant modernist."

Kahn's architectural education was academic and conservative; after receiving his B.A. from Columbia University in 1903 and a B.Arch. in 1907, he continued his studies in Paris at the Ecole des Beaux-Arts. In 1911 he was the first American to win the *Prix Labarre* and was awarded his *diplôme*. Back in New York, he spent several years as a draftsman and taught at Cornell University for one year (1915). In 1917, he joined Buchman and Fox, an established firm whose principals were anticipating retirement; soon after becoming a partner in 1919, he assumed effective control of the office. In 1929, the firm Buchman and Kahn became Ely Jacques Kahn, Architects; from 1940–1966 he formed a partnership with Robert Jacobs.

The office, considered a model of efficiency, was organized to expedite the design and construction of commercial structures, particularly office buildings and lofts. Although the forms of these buildings were usually predetermined by the economics of rents and the restrictions of the zoning laws, the inventiveness of Kahn's colorful, modernistic ornament and the opulence of his lobbies often transformed them into deco masterpieces. His work assimilated many influences, including the contemporary design he saw at the 1925 *Exposition des Arts Décoratifs* in Paris, the interiors of the Vienna Secession, and his passion for Persian and oriental art and archeology.

A special interest in interior and industrial design led Kahn to organize numerous exhibitions which introduced new ideas in these areas to the American public. Among these were three for the Metropolitan Museum (1929, 1934, and 1940) and the industrial arts section of the Chicago Fair of 1933. Long active in architectural education, he directed the architecture department of the Beaux-Arts Institute of Design and his 1934 international study of schools of art and architecture was published as *Design in Art and Industry* (1935). His work during and after the war included large housing and institutional projects and in general conformed to the aesthetics of International style modernism.

CAROL WILLIS

WORKS

1924–1927, 2 Park Avenue; 1926–1927, Insurance Center Building; 1927, Bergdorf Goodman Store Building; 1929, Film Center Building; 1929, Squibb Building; 1930–1931, 1400 and 1410 Broadway; New York. *1939, Maritime Transportation Building, World's Fair, Flushing, N.Y. 1944, Fort Greene Houses, Section 2, Brooklyn, N.Y. 1969, 1 Astor Plaza, New York.

BIBLIOGRAPHY

Ely Jacques Kahn. 1931 New York: McGraw; London: Whittlesey House.

KAHN, ELY JACQUES 1935 *Design in Art and Industry.* New York: Scribner.

KAHN, ELY JACQUES 1969 *A Building Goes Up.* New York: Simon & Schuster.

KAHN, ELY JACQUES n.d. "Autobiography." Unpublished manuscript, Avery Architectural Library, Columbia University, New York.

SAYLOR, HENRY H. 1931 "Ely Jacques Kahn." *Architecture* 64:65–70.

KAHN, LOUIS I.

Louis Kahn (1901–1974), through a great love of architecture, a lifelong effort, and a few years of intense activity at the end of his life, reintroduced inspirational and spiritual values to an art which had become stereotyped into anonymity and abstractions. His buildings are a luminous testimonial of his beliefs, and, like all great buildings, they challenge time as works of extraordinary beauty.

An immigrant to Philadelphia in 1905 from the small Russian island of Saarama in the Baltic Sea, he was at the same time an immigrant to a new age which slowly had come to recognize the frightening limits of industrialization and technology. A courageous immigrant, he lived his new world intensely, gaining strength from an isolation that made him free from contaminations. He avoided groups and denied himself the hectic consolation of being part of a movement. He was an individual doing his work, and, like all people whose work is outstanding, he was single-minded and quite separate. This separation had one exception, however; he reached for inspiration both in the reality of building and in contacts with the young, saying frequently "the University is my chapel . . ; the profession is in the marketplace." No master has been more of a teacher; no one has been more available to his students.

In physical appearance, Kahn was a singular person: small, with his face badly scarred from an accident during early childhood. He possessed a temperament full of passion, of enthusiasm for his work, and of devotion to a personal discipline focused upon the search for truth. In this search he was uncompromising, which made him a very religious man. He was superbly Jewish in his fundamentalism, in his concept of order, and in his questioning mind. He was always simply but smartly dressed in a bow tie and blazer that he never took off even on the hottest days or in the most tumultuous meeting. His speech was fast, sprinkled with dry humor, his relatively high-pitched voice surprisingly clear when speaking to large groups. He spoke intensely and expressively, communicating by means of parallels and metaphors which could go on at great length, but he was never verbose.

After the period of 1948 until 1957, in which he served as chief critic in architectural design and professor of architecture at Yale University, Kahn divided his time between his office on Walnut Street in Philadelphia and the school of architecture at the University of Pennsylvania, except for the traveling that became extensive in his later years. His real friends were his students, the only ones really capable of questioning him, of arousing his interest. He was always ready to defend their work in review sessions, to see their potential, and to reveal hidden talent. Friends among his colleagues were few, even though he greatly enjoyed camaraderie and good parties, where he relished being at the center of attention. In every sense, Louis Kahn loved life. After school, on weekdays, a small group of teachers frequently met at an apartment near the school of architecture belonging to ROBERT LE RICOLAIS, himself an exceptionally inspiring teacher and an "inventor" of structures, whose thought fascinated Kahn. In those gatherings, as in his reviews of students' work, Kahn sat in long reflective periods of silence, which he punctuated with remarks that gradually mounted to a passionate level.

In practice, Louis Kahn was interested in any architectural challenge and he was prone to accept almost any commission. But he was very conscious of avoiding commercialism and speculative efforts. Of great significance for his thoughts was his contact with India; he maintained a serious admiration for the people he met there. On the other hand, one of his most disappointing experiences was his work from 1962 to 1974 with the Pakistani authorities for the National Assembly of Bangladesh in Dacca. At the dinner given in his honor by the Pakistani ambassador at the United Nations, Kahn did not hesitate in his formal speech to indicate his great distress at the callousness and unresponsiveness of the Pakistani authorities, who were slow in providing payment and who turned to another architect from Japan for a new building in the complex. Such unresponsiveness was one of the causes of the financial indebtedness of his office, a debt which, after his death, could only be resolved with the purchase of his sketches and drawings by the State of Pennsylvania.

In work Kahn saw the sublimation of human values, and in architecture, an uncompromising reflection of them. By his own account, he began making drawings by the age of three, and continued to be recognized and appreciated for that ability among his young friends throughout his youth. From 1912 through 1920, he was educated at the Central High School and Public Industrial Art School in Philadelphia, winning numerous prizes for his drawings, and he graduated in architecture from the University of Pennsylvania in 1924. During that same year, while working in the office of John Molitor, the city architect, he was appointed chief of design for the Sesquicentennial Exhibition of 1926. After traveling in Europe for the first time in 1928, he worked for a brief period in the office of PAUL CRET. In 1935, he went into private practice in Philadelphia, and in 1941 he entered into association with GEORGE HOWE and shortly afterward with OSCAR STONOROV for work on several projects. Both men had an influence on the formation of Kahn's convictions. George Howe in particular introduced Kahn to a refined and elegant version of the Modern movement. With Stonorov, he became involved in the social aspects of architecture, becoming a consultant to the Philadelphia Housing Authority and working on several housing projects with him. During the Depression, Kahn had established friendships with planners such as CLARENCE S. STEIN and HENRY WRIGHT, and he also became acquainted with the philosophy of the "greenbelt towns." His involvement in social projects culminated in the Mill

Creek Redevelopment project in Philadelphia of 1946–1954, developed with Kenneth Day. In total, nearly thirty years were spent by Kahn in what might be called "silent" work.

In the 1950s, Louis Kahn began to emerge as an architect of national prominence. Beginning with an imperfect philosophy, elaborated through experience and expressed aphoristically, he began to develop a coherent theory of architecture which excluded the intransigencies and the abstractions of the International style, but in many ways remained deeply rooted in the tenets of the Modern movement, in fact producing a profound evolution within it. Kahn's memorable statement about the distinction between "servant and served space" in architecture can be seen as a form of sublimation of the postulates expressed by the theorists of the Modern movement with regard to function.

As Kahn's theories unfolded, even more basic principles were exhibited as being embodied in his architecture. Space acquired an essential architectural role, no longer as a mere result of the assembly of functional elements, but as an entity in itself, actually a tangible element capable of giving order to the architectural complex in a hierarchic system. For Kahn, the two concepts of space and place were inseparable, space always possessing the humane connotation of place. As a consequence, the abstractions of modern architecture became translated into an ideology expressed in a fundamental proposition between the environment and a program for life.

"Order" was often appealed to by Louis Kahn as something that manifests itself through art, for man is endowed with a sense of prevalence of order, a common bond among all beings. "Form" was referred to as the potential for making spaces, while "design" is the singular, individual interpretation of the form through shapes and configurations. With such premises, Kahn brought the contemporary discourse about art into focus in architecture, freeing the latter from the limited perceptions of function and technology. In so doing, he reassessed the language of defined and self-suffi-

cient spaces, of solid volumes, and of enclosure versus open spaces in architecture.

The three most important formal contributions to architectural language made by Louis Kahn are centered upon the volumetric aspect of a building and the configuration of its plan. The first consists in the duplication of the peripheral enclosure of a building. His interest in the potentialities of this enclosure for the expression of external sun-control elements appeared as early as his design for the Psychiatric Hospital in Philadelphia of 1944–1946, where deep horizontal slabs with terra-cotta tubes produce a pattern of shading on the slate-clad surfaces of the building elevations. Later, in the project for the U.S. Consular Office in Luanda, Angola (1959–1961), screen walls perforated by arched openings support a roof trellis which extends beyond the glass enclosure of the building. It is in the project for the residences at the Salk Institute at La Jolla, California, of 1959–1965 that circular walls wrap around square rooms, developing a dialectic between the geometry of the openings and that of the volumes. In the National Assembly Building for Bangladesh, this method assumes emphatic proportions, giving an exceptionally monumental configuration to the building. In fact, this method allows retention of sim-

Louis I. Kahn.
Model of Salk Institute
   Laboratory Buildings.
La Jolla, California.
1959–1967

Louis I. Kahn.
National Assembly of
   Bangladesh.
Dacca.
1962–1974

Louis I. Kahn.
Mikveh Israel Synagogue
   Project.
Philadelphia.
1961–1970

ple, synthetic forms for the external volumes, while the inner rooms may assume varied configurations with multiple exposures to daylight. This relationship with daylight was the determining element behind this solution, rather than the formal desire to "create ruins," as some critics have suggested. In the Mikveh Israel Synagogue in Philadelphia, a project of 1961–1970, circular light chambers produce spatial implications of almost baroque nature. In its layers, this building goes beyond the protective and textural devices of a screen: by means of large, deeply shadowed openings, it succeeds in extending the complexities of a building into the environment in what becomes a mutual exchange. In the project for the Hurva Synagogue in Jerusalem (1968–1974), the peripheral elements—the outer layers of the central space—become elements of the city fabric itself.

His second contribution has to do with the release of the corner of a building from being an intrinsic structural component. Emphasis on the corner's strength is inherent in the masonry technology of the past. With the employment of reinforced concrete and steel, the structural importance of the corner is greatly reduced. Kahn sometimes perceived a building as enclosed by "plate-walls," and to give emphasis to this structural form, he interrupted the plates at the corner, leaving a gap between them. The Library at Phillips Exeter Academy in Exeter, New Hampshire (1967–1972), is a classic example of such an attitude. This concept is also embodied in such projects as the design for the Altgar Enterprises office

building in Kansas City, Kansas (1966–1973), and in the residential complex at the Salk Institute. Once again, Kahn appears to intend to place an emphasis on the major elements constituting volume, while at the same time revealing the ambiguity of the structural system with respect to that volume.

A third formal contribution represents a decisive step in the conception of a building plan. This concept is developed in the plan for the Goldenberg House in Rydal, Pennsylvania, of 1959, and especially in a series of sketches for the house in which Kahn identifies "served" and "servant" areas. The sequence of perimetric rooms is interrupted by the formation in plan of a deep opening leading directly to the core of the house. This decision produces an immediate "reading," a comprehensive awareness of all parts of the architectural organism. The same concept is evident in his plans for larger groups of spaces such as the Erdman Hall Dormitories at Bryn Mawr College, Bryn Mawr, Pennsylvania (1960–1965), the Unitarian Church in Rochester, New York (1959–1967), and in the buildings for the National Assembly of Bangladesh. This gesture is in radical apposition to the notion of a contained, discreet volume that characterized the architecture of previous periods. Kahn, however, through the fragmentation and reassembly of the parts, made possible an immediate, existential unfolding of the building's organization to the visitor. A new vitality was thus projected in the architectural composition, a vitality whose potential as a compositional principle became a source of

Louis I. Kahn.
Library, Phillips Exeter
Academy (southwest
façade).
New Hampshire.
1967–1972

inspiration for the following generation of architects.

No great work of art is possible without the assertion of some original concept, and meaningful forms are the inevitable consequence of clear concepts, rather than of aesthetic reactions. These forms are made through the joy of discovery rather than in the rhetoric of citations; an architect cannot demonstrate coherence in his work by repeating formal motives. Of far greater importance is the appearance of certain constants in an architect's work, which, by representing the concept of an idea, are confirmed and clarified in every new design. Two factors generate these constants: a sense of reality of the particular times in which an architect works and a knowledge of the past. We may perceive five constants in the work of Louis Kahn: (1) the sense of composition and integrity of the buildings; (2) the attempt to reveal the character of the building material; (3) the sense of the "room" as the essence of architecture; (4) daylight carefully employed as the "maker" of architecture; and (5) an architecture of connections.

With respect to the first constant, the sense of composition and integrity of the building, Kahn's Bath House in Trenton is especially important. Part of the Master Plan for the Jewish Community Center in Trenton, New Jersey (1954–1959), the Bath House (1955–1956) was the only construction completed from that plan. It is one of the smallest structures that Kahn ever built, yet it is one of the most significant. It is made of four elements, square in plan, and shaded by pitched roofs. The support of the roof is made by articulating the piers, thus forming small rooms which serve both as entrances and services. With a simple statement, the counterpoint of served and servant spaces is announced, a simplicity, however, that relies on the perfect calibration of the single compositional elements. Palladian (see ANDREA PALLADIO) classicity comes to mind, but also LUDWIG MIES VAN DER ROHE's concern for the exact definition of roles for building elements. In this small structure, Kahn makes no concession to descriptive phrases: it directly realizes an architectural composition which demonstrates the aesthetic potentials of his design philosophy.

As illustrated by his designs for the Unitarian Church and the Institute of Management at Ahmedabad, India (1962–1974), Kahn's composite methodology is evident whether embodied in the most simple arrangement of rooms or the most complex system of buildings. It is not a methodology based on axis, spatial sequences, and perspective views according to the recipes of the Beaux-Arts school. Rather than relying on preconceived positions, his methodology involves experience

Louis I. Kahn.
Bath House.
Trenton, New Jersey.
1955–1956

Louis I. Kahn.
Site Model for the Institute
of Management.
Ahmedabad, India.
1962–1974

and the reality of building: his plans invite reflection on both natural and human forces shaping a place.

The second constant in Kahn's work, as noted above, is his search to reveal the character of the building material. His respect for the material is different from the exalting of such material characteristics as color and texture in other periods. Rather, it belongs to the appreciation which the pioneers of the Modern movement had for such characteristics, which together with the celebration of function was the main vehicle of their reaction to the ornamentalism and deceptions of the Beaux-Arts period. In Kahn's work, the attitude toward the characteristics of the material is one of aesthetic refinement, yet it is primarily conditioned by the contribution of these materials to the development of architectural space. Concrete surfaces are generally treated smoothly to exalt the precision of formwork, and wood is often juxtaposed to the finished concrete, developing a continuous, rigid surface. It is as if values of texture and contrast are purposely played down so as not to interfere with the volume of the space.

Two buildings which Kahn designed for Yale University face each other across a street in New Haven. They were built nearly twenty-five years apart, and are instructive about Kahn's use of materials. The Yale Art Gallery, completed in 1953, gave Kahn a sudden renown. The floor structure, made of reinforced concrete tetrahedrons, contains the air distribution system. The northern wall facing the garden is a carefully proportioned mullioned glass wall. The south wall facing the street

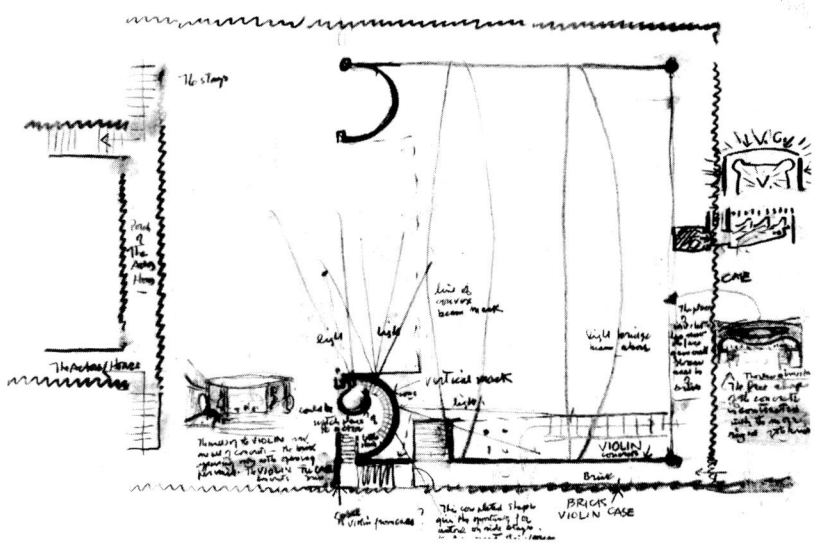

Louis I. Kahn.
Sketches of the Fine Arts
  Center.
Fort Wayne, Indiana.
1965–1974

Louis I. Kahn.
Plan of Erdman Hall
  Dormitories, Bryn Mawr
  College.
Pennsylvania.
1960–1965

and the noise generated by it is of continuous masonry. The Center for British Art and Studies (1969–1974) was constructed with a frame structure of reinforced concrete enclosed by sandblasted stainless steel panels on the exterior and by interior wood panels. In both buildings, the materials used perform an explanatory role: a strength and precise clarity in relation to structural function, orientation, light, and atmosphere. In each case, these materials assume the unique role of transforming spaces from being abstract to being human.

The third constant, space, remains the most important in Kahn's work. In seeing the "beginning" of space in the concept of a room, Kahn revealed the special sense in which he learned from the past saying frequently to his students, "The room is the place of the mind. In a small room one does not say what one would in a large room." Space changes as the perception of the nature of a place changes throughout history, and it is not to be dominated by the tyrannical individuality of the architect. For Kahn, the structure of the space was always more important than the existence of the building; we must remember his phrase, "the Plan—a society of rooms in a place good to live, work, learn." (Giurgola & Mehta, 1975, p. 186)

The Erdman Hall Dormitories at Bryn Mawr College are just such a society of rooms, one which grows from the single residential room into the collective space of the Halls, gradually making that transition through a series of rooms for group activities. As is often the case in Kahn's major spaces, light penetrates at the edges of the rooms via monitors, so that the peripheral walls become strongly illuminated. This tends to enlarge the space while the structure of the ceiling remains in darkness, appearing heavier. It is a singular approach repeated in the Unitarian Church in Rochester, the National Assembly Building of Bangladesh, the Hurva Synagogue of Jerusalem, the Exeter Library, and in the project for the Theological Library for the University of California at Berkeley (1973–1974), among others. It produces a different feeling from that conveyed by a Renaissance dome with its opening at the center. Light for Kahn is more physical than luminescent or all-pervasive.

One beautiful exception exists in his linear vaults at the Kimbell Museum, where light penetrates from the top of the vault, and is distributed along its internal surfaces. But in the Mikveh Israel Synagogue, planned for a Philadelphia congrega-

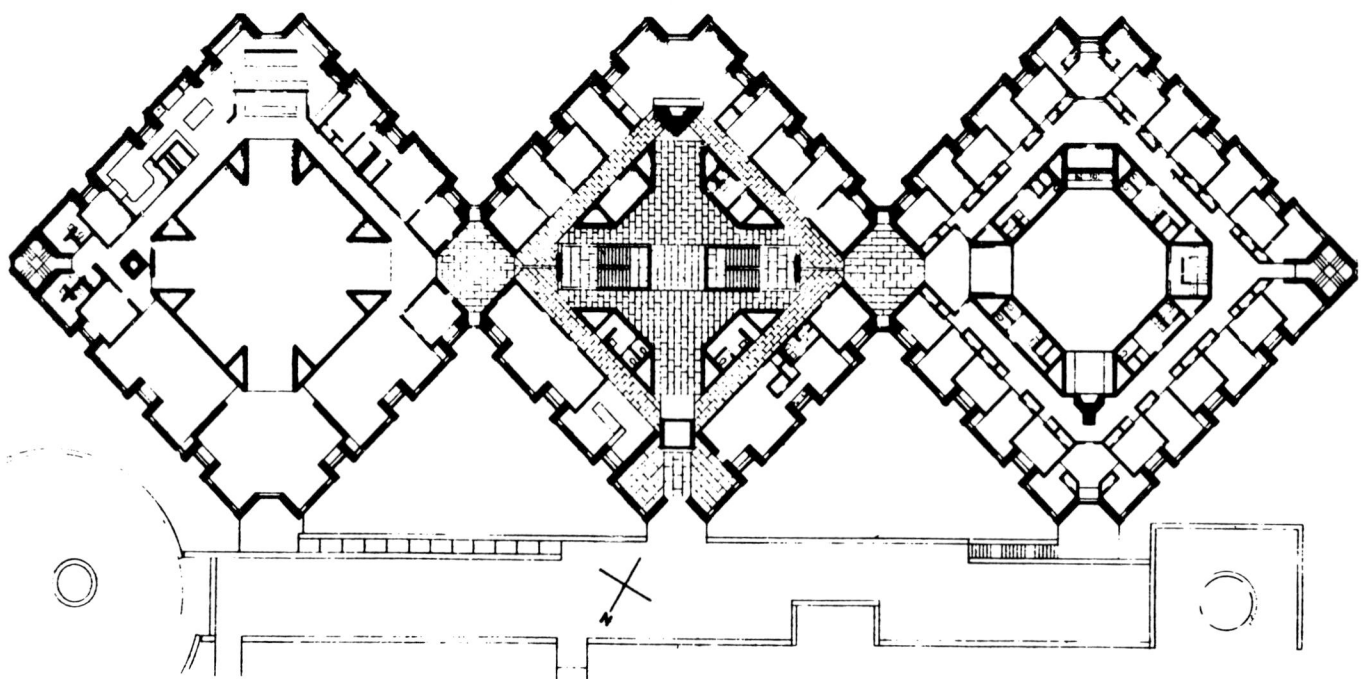

tion (1961–1970), it is the peripheral distribution of light through light chambers that defines the central space. Similar concerns are evident in external spaces carefully built with surfaces facing each other, as in the external "room" of the Roosevelt Memorial project for Roosevelt Island in New York (1973–1974), or the project for the Jewish Martyrs' Memorial in Battery Park, New York (1964–1972), where its space is formed by a symbolic arrangement of glass cubes. It is again in the Institute of Management at Ahmedabad that the external volumes subtly link the entire complex, alternating with the internal voids in a masterful sequence creating a real "treasury of spaces," as Kahn called them.

The fourth constant, the particular and intentional use of daylight with respect to architecture, has already been mentioned frequently in describing the other constants. Like space, it is one of the primary components in the architecture of Louis Kahn. One may define architecture throughout history simply by the degree of subtlety with which daylight defines, reinforces, molds, articulates, and fuses its elements. For example, it is the subtle perception of light that makes the row of columns for a Greek temple become a rhythmically shaded surface that changes color and texture throughout the course of the day; it is the light filtered through the small windows of an early Christian basilica that gives value to the extended wall surfaces transforming the nave into a looming light chamber; and it is the light in a Gothic church that suffuses the atmosphere with an unforgettable glow. It is also the precise juxtaposition of the sources of light that gives the spaces of the

Renaissance their classic sense of the infinite. However, the Beaux-Arts preoccupation with composition and ornament caused those uses of light almost to vanish from the vocabulary of architecture. By contrast, light had a profound structural significance for Kahn, besides being the source of poetic inspiration toward form.

Perhaps more than any of his other buildings, the Kimbell Art Museum (1966–1972) at Fort Worth, a building that has been called a contemporary classic, reveals this concern for the use of daylight in a variety of forms. In Texas, the source of light always appears to be vertical, as if the sun were always at its zenith. In response, the Museum building is linear in form, a parallel system of cycloidal vaults supported by columns spaced at intervals of about one hundred feet. There are two major sources of light: the long fenestration facing the park, which allows a reverberation of "green light" reflected off the park's plantings into the interior, and a slit placed at the center of the vault, which releases "silver light" to the interior. Together they achieve a unique, highly refined human environment in counterpoint to the simplicity of the structure. Buildings of great simplicity have been made before in contemporary architecture, but here there is something decisively new. Here are combined not only the stringent conceptual attitudes of Mies van der Rohe and the poetical imagination of ALVAR AALTO, but also the subtle integration of architectural elements together with a clear process of explanation. Thus, a classical strength is produced, isolating this building as a true masterpiece. The Kimbell Art Museum comes as close as some of the great architec-

Louis I. Kahn.
Kimbell Art Museum.
Fort Worth, Texas.
1966–1972

ture in history to make an ambitious gesture compatible with great economy of means.

The fifth constant, an architecture of connections, is an extension of the first, the sense of composition. Connections in architecture become important when the concept of a complexity is substituted for a single object or building. Buildings today are bound to the demands of a complex society, which requires that they perform and provide a variety of functions. Modern architecture developed a rather simplistic vocabulary of connections made of corridors, bridges, ramps, and so on. Louis Kahn was aware that a serious compositional problem lay in connections. He approached it by assigning himself the task of producing connections related to structure. In the centrifugal arrangement of the Richards Laboratories, connections depend on the location of the columns, while in the Bryn Mawr College dormitory, the connection is made at the corner of the square element in such a way as to maintain the unity of the entire complex. A true case of connection is the project for the Dominican Sisters Convent in Media, Pennsylvania (1965–1968), where single buildings perform this function, as at Hadrian's Villa at Tivoli. Even in three-dimensional terms, the connection reveals the nature of the structure, as in Kahn's project with Anne Tyng for the City Tower Municipal Building in Philadelphia (1952–1957). In this tower of reinforced concrete, the triangulated strut frame is crowned at the intersections by capitals containing mechanical services, which were called the "knuckles" of the structure. Remembering once more the connective columns, vaults, and beams in the Kimbell Museum, each of which is a perfectly calibrated element in its role, one comes to realize how much importance Kahn gave to such transitions in architecture.

Any assessment of Louis Kahn's work, however brief, must include his ideas on the city, a place of "assembled institutions." For him, the solution to the complexities of a modern city was to recapture the directness of thought exhibited by the city's founders, who made the original gesture by giving a place to man's institutions: a place for a church, a town hall, a school, and so on. All of Kahn's mature plans for cities are based on this principle, from the Master Plan for the Gandhinagar Capital in Gujarat, India (1963–1964), to the proposal for the Abbasabad Development in Tehran (1974). Many of his early plans for Philadelphia, as in the Midtown-Penn Center project (1952–1953), reflect the attempt to resolve in an image the crucial problem of separating the car and the realm of the pedestrian. Because the street was for Kahn the essence of urban life, he approached several projects by means of this theme. The street was a "meeting place" in the project for the Independence Mall Area Development in Philadelphia (1972–1974), as well as in the design for the 1976 Bicentennial Exposition in Philadelphia (1971–1974). But all of the images that Kahn made for cities evolve around the city as a building, as a continuum of structures and places of well-being.

These constants, after appearing in Kahn's first works, seem to be confirmed and clarified with each of his subsequent designs, as they represent the concepts of ideas. In Kahn's designs, concepts are never deformed by the existence of nonessential elements; rather, they evolve and become more precise while remaining at the foundation of his work. As already noted, two factors generated those constants: the reality of Kahn's time, and his profound knowledge of the past. As a consequence, his work seems to possess two distinguishable characteristics: a sense of permanency and an unmistakable style. To revisit his buildings after a few years is an experience not dissimilar from the one sensed while visiting the ancient structures of history. In both cases, those buildings seem always to have existed, and yet a unique newness transpires within them.

On March 17, 1974, Louis Kahn died of a heart attack in Pennsylvania Railway Station in New York. Much has happened in architecture since Kahn's death, but his work continues to succeed in a time of incredibly fleeting values because he gave us forms with a sense of permanency, forms which consciously reflect those fundamental values for which mankind is forever searching in different ways, generation after generation. His concern was to anchor architectural concepts to human values, and this most effectively produced the sense both of permanency and of newness in his buildings. We have already noted how the spaces of his buildings unfold with great simplicity and clarity, being almost a process of explanation of their "reason-to-be." Yet, those spaces retain the enigma without which a work of art is impossible. No explanation for those spaces is possible, nor is one required. In fact, we cannot "read" the architecture of Louis Kahn with our intelligence alone; it would not significantly add to our understanding of his buildings. At best, we would know about servant and served spaces, possibly about derivative traits, and, for some critics, about Beaux-Arts connections. But all that would be insignificant, for the reading of Kahn's buildings must be done with something of ourselves, with our "thinking body."

Louis Kahn's architecture is the manifestation of knowledge achieved only through much difficulty and effort. It is the same love of knowledge that is behind Heraclitus's utterances, which respond to his painful sense of his very lack of knowledge. In analogy to Heraclitus, those enigmas produced by contrasting architectural forms find an answer in the unity of Kahn's buildings. Permanency, so improbable today, so vigorously condemned by modernists, and made so ironic by postmodernists with their indulgence in memories, is what distinguishes the architecture of Louis Kahn from that of his contemporaries. It is also what caused his buildings to be linked from the beginning with historicism.

Not unlike great architects before him, Kahn found great inspiration in the forms of Roman structures in their state of ruin. Roman architecture, viewed in such conditions, is significantly different from the original and from the fanciful Beaux-Arts interpretation of it. Indeed, the glory of Roman architecture is in its ruins, in its sense of place, in its spatial dimension. It appeared in this way to Kahn, free from nonessential elements, its conceptual strength undeformed by ephemeral comments. From this particular attitude to the past, a singular stylistic expression emerges, a style bent to clarify a concept in truly classic terms. As in a Greek temple, where the form of a capital belongs to a sequence of explanatory steps which unfold the nature of the building and the beauty of the whole, in Louis Kahn's work a detail is the conclusion of a process of explanations. Details assume a specific role in the formulation of a stylistic language; thus, his style is unambiguous. To each material is assigned a role, often in contrast; and to each space, an evocative strength. It is a style that evolved from the tenets of the Modern movement and enhanced by the eternal experience of the past; a style that gave to modern architecture a sense of maturity and a new-found richness. For such a style no education nor exclusive initiation is necessary, because it basically relies upon the validity of the space: space either accepts or rejects. An education to space is superfluous, just as education to a language that speaks to people about their most vital interests is unnecessary.

It is with such a perception of style that it is possible to understand the fundamental humanism of Kahn's architecture. It is not founded on a view of the universe centered on the valor and dignity of man, for Kahn was an idealist without illusions. Rather, it is based on the value of man's primordial act of realization: in Kahn's words, "I love beginnings; . . . two posts and a lintel, there is the beginning of architecture." For Louis Kahn, those were the signs of human institutions. His contribution to architecture was to rekindle the generating forces of this art in a time in which much of the ideology of modern architecture appears to have failed. He did so by searching in the present as well as in the past. His architecture does not need justifying arguments; it is, as he said, an "offering," beyond events and time.

ROMALDO GIURGOLA
with PAMILLE I. BERG

WORKS

*1924-1926, Buildings for the Sesquicentennial Exposition, Philadelphia. 1944-1946, Psychiatric Hospital, Philadelphia (with Oscar Stonorov). 1946-1954, Mill Creek Redevelopment, Philadelphia (with Kenneth Day). 1948-1949, Morton Weiss House, Norristown, Pa. 1951-1953, Yale Art Gallery, New Haven. 1952-1962, Mill Creek Public Housing, Philadelphia (with others). *1954-1956, Medical Service Building, AFL-CIO, Philadelphia. 1954-1959, Bath House and Master Plan, Jewish Community Center, Trenton, N.J. 1957-1964, Richards Medical Research Building, University of Pennsylvania, Philadelphia. 1958-1961, *Tribune Review* Building, Greensburg, Pa. 1959-1961, Esherick House, Chestnut Hill, Pa. 1959-1965, Salk Institute Laboratory Buildings, La Jolla, Calif. 1959-1967, Unitarian Church, Rochester, N.Y. 1960-1965, Erdman Hall Dormitories, Bryn Mawr College, Pa. 1962-1974, Sher-E-Banglanagar, New Capital of Bangladesh, Dacca. 1962-1974, Institute of Management, Ahmedabad, India. 1965-1974, Theatre of the Performing Arts, Fine Arts Center, Fort Wayne, Ind. 1966-1970, Olivetti-Underwood Factory, Harrisburg, Pa. 1966-1972, Kimbell Art Museum, Fort Worth, Tex. 1967-1972, Library and Dining Hall, Phillips Exeter Academy, N.H. 1969-1974, Center for British Art and Studies, Yale University, New Haven.

BIBLIOGRAPHY

BLAKE, PETER (editor) 1972 "The Mind of Louis Kahn." *Architectural Forum* 137:42-89.

BLAKE, PETER (editor) 1973 "Louis I. Kahn." *Architecture & Urbanism* special issue: 13-17.

GIURGOLA, ROMALDO, and MEHTA, JAIMINI 1975 *Louis I. Kahn.* Boulder, Colo.: Westview.

KAHN, LOUIS I. 1953 "Toward a Plan for Midtown Philadelphia." *Perspecta* 2:10-27.

KAHN, LOUIS I. 1955 "Order and Form." *Perspecta* 3:47-63.

KAHN, LOUIS I. (1962)1973 *The Notebooks and Drawings of Louis I. Kahn.* Edited by Eugene Feldman and Richard Wurman. 2d ed. Cambridge, Mass.: M.I.T. Press.

KAHN, LOUIS I. 1965 "Remarks." *Perspecta* 9-10:303-335.

KAHN, LOUIS I. 1969 *Louis I. Kahn: Talks with Students.* Houston, Tex.: Rice University.

KAHN, LOUIS I. 1970 "Architecture: Silence and Light." In Arnold Toynbee (editor), *On the Future of Art.* New York: Viking.

KAHN, LOUIS I. 1975 *Light is the Theme: Louis I. Kahn and the Kimbell Art Museum.* Edited by Nell Johnson.

Fort Worth, Tex.: Kimbell Art Foundation.

Lepère, Yves 1969 "Louis I. Kahn." *L'Architecture d'aujourd'hui* 142:1–100.

Ronner, Heinz; Jhaveri, Sharad; and Vasella, Alejandro 1977 *Louis I. Kahn: The Complete Works, 1935–1974.* Boulder, Colo.: Westview.

Rowan, Jan 1961 "Wanting to Be: The Philadelphia School." *Progressive Architecture* Apr.:131–163.

Scully, Vincent, Jr. 1962a *Louis I. Kahn.* New York: Braziller.

Scully, Vincent, Jr. 1962b "Wright, International Style, and Kahn." *Arts Magazine* 36, no. 6:67–71.

Scully, Vincent, Jr. 1977 "Yale Center for British Art." *Architectural Record* June:95–104.

Tafuri, Manfredo (1968)1980 *Theories and History of Architecture.* Translated from Italian by Giorgio Verrechio. New York: Harper.

KALLIKRATES

Kallikrates worked mainly in Athens in the third quarter of the fifth century B.C., during the great building program inspired by Perikles. He was probably himself an Athenian, but nothing is known of his life outside his architectural work. Plutarch, a historian of the second century A.D., names Kallikrates (with Iktinos) as architect of the Athenian Parthenon (447–438 B.C.), and says that he also undertook construction of the Middle Long Wall (c.445–443 B.C.), which provided Athens with a fortified corridor to its port of Piraeus. One inscription (c.450 B.C.) calls for Kallikrates to provide designs for a gate and temple for the sanctuary of Athena Nike (Victory) at Athens, while another inscription (c.447/446 B.C.) requires him to improve security on the Akropolis during construction work there.

The second and fourth of these projects are not of great architectural importance, but they have led to suggestions that Kallikrates was the official city architect of Athens, and that he was more concerned with the technical and managerial aspects of architecture than with formal design. Thus he would have assisted Iktinos with the construction of the Parthenon, and with the supervision of building work, but would not have been responsible for aesthetic features. However, there is nothing to suggest that this post, attested in the fourth century, already existed in the fifth, and there is no real evidence that Kallikrates's contribution to the Parthenon was technical.

Rhys Carpenter (1970) has suggested that rather than cooperating with Iktinos, Kallikrates was responsible for an earlier version of the temple with only six columns on the fronts, begun under the patronage of Kimon in c.470–465 B.C.; Iktinos would then have dismantled the unfinished temple in the 440s, reusing much of its material. J. A. Bundgaard (1976) suggests a similar sequence, with stages approximately ten and five years later. Certainly the present Parthenon stands on a platform intended for an earlier temple (probably c.490–480 B.C.), but there is no adequate evidence for an intervening, Kallikratean, Parthenon.

Kallikrates's connection with the temple of Athena Nike provides another line of approach to his work, but here too there are difficulties. The existing temple of Athena Nike was built c.425 B.C., and its style is not that of the 440s. The inscription mentioned above must therefore refer either to an earlier unexecuted project or to the tiny shrine below the existing temple and destroyed by it (Bundgaard, 1976). The new design may also have been by Kallikrates, but there is no positive evidence. Many scholars do make the connection, however, and attribute a number of other buildings to Kallikrates on the basis of style (most notably Shear, 1963).

The sanctuary of Athena Nike occupied a lofty bastion at the west end of the Akropolis. This bastion was enlarged following the building of the Propylaia to the Akropolis (437–432 B.C.); the new temple may have been built to celebrate Athenian defeat of Spartan forces on Sphakteria in 425 B.C. It was dismantled to make a rampart by Turkish defenders on the eve of the Venetian siege (1687), but rebuilt in 1835 and again in 1939. Two notable features of the temple are its plan and its use of the Ionic order. The site is too small for a temple with full surrounding colonnade, and although entrance is from the east, the most important façade was probably the west one which towers above visitors approaching the Akropolis. Thus the temple was given an unusual plan with four columns set prostyle at each end, and its cella is separated from the front portico not by a wall with a solid door, but by two slender piers with grilles between. The Ionic order corresponds closely to the influential version developed in Attica during the later fifth century B.C., with a base profile of convex, concave, and convex members, well-proportioned capitals, a three-fascia architrave, a continuous carved frieze, and no dentil course. The spectacular site and the contrast of orders allow the tiny temple to compete with the more massive Propylaia. Extraordinarily close in design to the Nike temple is a slightly larger one, also in the Ionic order, built near the river Ilissos, just outside of ancient Athens. It was destroyed in 1778 by the Turkish authorities to provide material for a new city wall. The Ilissos temple, like the Nike temple, had porches of four prostyle columns at each end (there was a separate pronaos in front of the cella), and the treatment of the Ionic order is closely similar in both form and proportion. In view of this, many scholars suppose that the Ilissos temple used the designs originally worked out by Kallikrates for the temple of Athena Nike soon after 450 B.C. But the bastion of Athena Nike would not then have had room for the Ilissos temple with an altar, and recent studies of its sculptured frieze suggest a date in the 420s (e.g., Picon, 1978).

Rather less closely related, but again perhaps works of the same architect are: a temple of Apollo on the island of Delos (the "Athenian Temple"), and the Erechtheion in Athens. It is harder to compare the Doric Athenian Temple (c.425–417 B.C.) with the Nike and Ilissos temples, but it too has prostyle porches at each end, allowing the six-columned fronts expected of a major temple to be combined with a cella broad enough for the seven bronze cult statues—in spite of the constricted site. The pronaos is taken over from the Ilissos temple, while the use of rectangular pillars follows the Nike temple. Notable too are the antae articulating the wall of the rear porch, the earliest instance of this device.

The Erechtheion, built to house the age-old statue of Athena, is usually taken to be slightly later. Construction may have begun during the temporary peace between Athens and Sparta from 421, but fragmentary financial accounts exist of its completion in 409–405 B.C. under annually changing architects. After conversion first to a church, then to a harem, it was partly reconstructed between 1902 and 1918. Its design was even more strongly affected by its site, perhaps the holiest one in Athens, with relics like the sacred olive tree of Athena and the tomb of the legendary king Kekrops. Thus although ground level to the west and north was about three meters lower than to the south and east, it was not possible to adopt the usual Greek expedient in such cases and build an artificial terrace on which the temple could stand as on a level site. The result is a unique building with porches, all different, on all four sides, and with the junctions between some elements not wholly satisfactory. A number of scholars have felt that such an irregular building could never have been intended by the architect, but must result from changes forced on him by religious conservatism. On the other hand it is difficult to imagine any fifth-century architect intending to slight such holy places, and without doing so a regular plan could not be achieved within the established conventions of Greek temple design. In fact the Erechtheion as it stands is far from being an aesthetic failure. It stands up to its neighbor the Parthenon remarkably well, chiefly by not competing directly. It sets Ionic against Doric, obvious complexity against apparent simplicity, and elabora-

Kallikrates.
Temple of Athena Nike.
Athens.
c.425–423 B.C.

tion against monumentality. The famous caryatid porch facing the Parthenon is the one most obviously different from it, with its graceful maidens carrying libation dishes; and although the capitals and bases of the other porches are basically related to those of the Nike and Ilissos temples, they are more richly decorated, and there is more extensive use of elegantly carved moldings.

Carpenter (1970) connects Kallikrates with a group of Doric temples in Athens and Attika which have already been attributed to a single architect (the "Theseum Architect") by W. B. Dinsmoor, Sr.: the Hephaisteion above the Athenian agora (c.450–444 B.C.), the temple of Poseidon at Sounion (c.444–440 B.C.), the temple of Ares (c.440–436 B.C., perhaps at Acharnai near Athens, rebuilt in Athens c.5 B.C., then destroyed in the Herulian invasion of A.D. 267), and the unfinished temple of Nemesis at Rhamnous (c.436–432 B.C.). Dinsmoor's attribution has not gone unchallenged, but all four temples share several features, most noticeably the way in which the architrave and frieze of the pronaos continue across to the outer colonnades on the temple sides, so that the area in front of the pronaos is a separately defined space, not just a part of a continuous corridor around the cella building.

Carpenter's identification of the "Theseum Architect" with Kallikrates is based on features which the Hephaisteion shares with the Athenian Temple on Delos or with the supposed Kallikratean Parthenon. Apart from the hypothetical nature of the Kallikratean Parthenon, however, the similarities are not those which unite Dinsmoor's "Theseum" group, and could be ideas current among architects of the same generation in the same city. Indeed since at least four architects are known to have been active in Attica in the third quarter of the fifth century, it would be surprising if almost all the temples not specifically attributed in the written sources were actually the work of only one of those four. Even without the "Theseum" group, we can give Kallikrates a busy career, given the responsibility of classical architects for detailed supervision of construction work. To add four temples and extend his activity back twenty years gives him an improbably long and full life.

Obviously any assessment of Kallikrates's importance as an architect depends on how many of the attributions are correct. If we accept only the firmly attested projects, we can simply say that Kallikrates must have been a competent designer and supervisor of buildings, but had no major buildings to his credit and made no identifiable contribution to the general history of architecture. However, if we suppose that Kallikrates designed the existing Nike temple as well as the earlier project (which is reasonable but unproven), then he becomes a more interesting figure, for we can confidently accept the Ilissos temple as his too, and probably the Athenian Temple on Delos and the Erechtheion as well. All of these involve variations on an unusual temple plan, and all (except perhaps the Ilissos temple) are skillfully adapted to the requirements of awkward sites. In adopting Ionic for three of these four temples, Kallikrates would have been responsible for the gradual acceptance for major temples in Athens of an order previously known there only in secondary roles. Two other features of this group of temples have had a fruitful later history. The antae which articulate the rear wall of the Athenian Temple on Delos lead directly to the pilasters so much loved by Roman and Renaissance architects; and it was in the three Ionic temples that the Attic base profile, even if it originated in the Propylaia, was developed into the satisfyingly yielding form which slowly replaced the earlier Ephesian base, to become almost universal from the second century B.C. onward. For these two contributions alone the Ilissos architect, whether Kallikrates or not, deserves a lasting place in the history of architecture.

J. J. COULTON

WORKS

(A)c.465–460 B.C., South Akropolis Wall; *(A)c.465–449 B.C., Parthenon ("Kimonian phase"); *c.450–447 B.C., Temple of Athena Nike (first project); (A)c.448–442 B.C., Temple of Hephaistos; 447–438 B.C., Parthenon; *c.447/446 B.C., Akropolis (enclosure works); *c.445–443 B.C., Middle Long Wall; Athens. (A)c.442–438 B.C., Temple of Poseidon, Sounion, Greece. *(A)c.438–434 B.C., Temple of Ares, Athens.

*(A)c.434–432 B.C., Temple of Nemesis, Rhamnous, Greece. *(A)c.430 B.C., Temple by the Ilissos; (A)c.425–423 B.C., Temple of Athena Nike; Athens. *(A)c.425–417 B.C., Athenian Temple of Apollo, Delos, Greece. (A)c.421–405 B.C., Erechtheion, Athens.

BIBLIOGRAPHY

BOERSMA, J. S. 1970 *Athenian Building Policy from 561/0 to 405/4 B.C.* Groningen, Netherlands: Wolters-Noordhoff.

BUNDGAARD, J. A. 1976 *The Parthenon and the Mycenaean City on the Heights.* Copenhagen: National Museum of Denmark.

CARPENTER, RHYS 1970 *The Architects of the Parthenon.* Harmondsworth, England: Penguin.

DINSMOOR, W. B., Sr. (1950)1975 *The Architecture of Ancient Greece: An Account of its Historic Development.* Reprint. London: Batsford. Originally published as a third edition of W. J. Anderson and R. P. Spiers, *The Architecture of Ancient Greece and Rome.* London: Batsford, 1902.

MARTIN, ROLAND 1976 "L'âtelier Ictinos-Callicrates au temple du Bassae." *Bulletin de Correspondence Hellénique* 100:427–442.

PICÓN, CARLOS ARTURO 1978 "The Ilissos Temple Reconsidered." *American Journal of Archaeology* 82:47–81.

SHEAR, IONE MYLONAS 1963 "Kallikrates." *Hesperia* 32:375–424.

KALLIMACHOS

As a pupil of the great Pheidias, Kallimachos (?–405 B.C.) was both architect and sculptor. According to an anecdote recounted by VITRUVIUS, he was the inventor of the Corinthian capital, although the tale of the invention itself is clearly fanciful. Kallimachos's name has been attached to the Temple of Apollo at Bassae (c.425 B.C.), where the earliest known examples of the Corinthian capital appeared; and also to the Erechtheion on the Athenian Acropolis (c.421–405 B.C.), for whose interior he designed a golden lamp. The works associated specifically with Kallimachos are now all lost.

B. M. BOYLE

WORKS

c.425 B.C., Temple of Apollo (with IKTINOS), Bassae, Greece. c.421–405 B.C., Erechtheion (with MNESICLES), Athens.

BIBLIOGRAPHY

English translations of the ancient texts can be found in the volumes of the Loeb Classical Library series, published by Harvard University Press and Heinemann.

DINSMOOR, WILLIAM B. (1902)1975 *The Architecture of Ancient Greece.* Reprint of 1950 ed. New York: Norton. Originally published with the title *The Architecture of Ancient Greece and Rome.*

LAWRENCE, ARNOLD W. (1957)1975 *Greek Architecture*. Harmondsworth, England: Penguin.

PAUSANIAS, *Graeciae descriptio*, Book 1.26.

PLINY, *Historia naturalis*, Book 34.92.

VITRUVIUS, *De architectura*, Book 4.1.6–12.

KALLMANN and MCKINNELL

Gerhard Michael Kallmann (1915–) and Noel Michael McKinnell (1935–) together with Edward Frank Knowles won a national competition for the new Boston City Hall in 1962. Kallmann, born in Berlin and living in England from 1936 to 1949, had come to teach at Columbia University, where McKinnell, born in England, came to study in 1959. The aggressive Brutalist aesthetic heralded by Kallmann is developed in the City Hall to dramatize a central permeable public zone, an extension of the surrounding plaza, with business offices buried below and governmental functions lifted above. A rigorous geometry controls the location of "served" and "serving" spaces and of all structural and mechanical components.

Following completion of Boston City Hall (1968), Kallmann and McKinnell established a permanent Boston office with Henry Wood. Both Kallmann and McKinnell have been influential teachers at the Harvard Graduate School of Design. Paths of movement, tied to time and weather conditions by light wells and skylights, more and more have served as "generators of built form" in their buildings. These themes and the monumental expression of structure are evident in the Athletic Facilities, Exeter, New Hampshire (1967–1969). More traditional architectural images are reflected in the American Academy, Cambridge, Massachusetts (1979–1981), where layered spaces surround a pivotal central hall.

THOMAS G. BEDDALL

WORKS

1964–1968, City Hall, Boston. 1967–1969, Phillips Exeter Academy Athletic Facilities, Exeter, N.H. 1967–1970, Government Center Garage; 1967–1974, City Hall Plaza; 1969–1972, Boston Five Cent Savings Bank, School Street; Boston. 1971–1978, Woodhull Medical and Mental Health Center, Brooklyn, N.Y. 1972–1975, Roosevelt Island Motorgate Garage, New York. 1975–1976, Dudley Street Library, Boston. 1979–1981, American Academy of Arts and Sciences, Cambridge, Mass.

BIBLIOGRAPHY

FITCH, JAMES MARSTON 1970 "City Hall, Boston." *Architectural Review* 147, no. 880:398–411.

KALLMANN, G. M. 1959 "The Action Architecture of a New Generation." *Architectural Forum* 111, no. 4:132–137.

KALLMANN, G. M. 1963 Contributions to *Four Great Makers of Modern Architecture: Gropius, Le Corbusier, Mies van der Rohe, Wright.* New York: Columbia University School of Architecture.

KALLMANN, G. M., and McKINNELL, N. M. 1975 "Movement Systems as Generators of Built Form." *Architectural Record* 158, no. 7:105–116.

MORTON, DAVID A. 1972 "Towards the Minimal Shell." *Progressive Architecture* 53, no. 7:54–63.

SCHMERTZ, MILDRED F. 1969 "The New Boston City Hall." *Architectural Record* 145, no. 2:133–144.

SCHMERTZ, MILDRED F. 1971 " A Prep School Athletics Building." *Architectural Record* 149, no. 6:97–106.

SCHMERTZ, MILDRED F. 1981 "A New 'House' for the American Academy of Arts and Sciences." *Architectural Record* 169, no. 15:79–87.

SILVER, ROBERT 1981 "American Academy of Arts and Sciences." *Architectural Review* 170, no. 1016:215–221.

KALŪK IBN ᶜABD ᶜALLĀH

Kalūk ibn ᶜabd ᶜAllāh (13th century) worked under the patronage of the Seljuks of Rum, a Turkish dynasty whose capital was the Anatolian city of Konya. There is no biographical information on him whatsoever; his existence is documented solely by two inscriptions on doorways of important Konya buildings of the mid-thirteenth century. The available evidence of his training and the development of his style stems from the stylistic and technical features of these two buildings, and this evidence, together with the peculiar nature of his name itself, remains a subject of controversy among historians of architecture.

The complex cultural and ethnic mixture of Anatolia under the Seljuks has given considerable difficulty to those who would define that culture in conventional terms bequeathed us by the development of national ideologies of the nineteenth century. In the case of Kalūk and his work, it is the backward projection of current political differences which complicates our attempts to assess his work. Both Armenian and Turkish etymologies have been proposed for the name itself, leading some scholars to use a bare transliteration of the Konya inscriptions (K.LWK) in order to avoid the appearance of taking sides. It seems quite probable that Kalūk may have been a convert to Islam, the conventional rubric "son of the slave of God" (ibn ᶜabd ᶜAllāh) being frequently used in the case of such converts. As the tremendous originality and creative power of Seljuk art in Anatolia is without any doubt the result of cultural synchretism and as its considerable artistic accomplishments are the direct result of the fertile admixture

Kalūk.
Complex of Fakhreddin
*   Sahib Ata.*
Konya, Turkey.
1258

Kalūk.
Madrasah (Ince Minareli).
Konya, Turkey.
n.d.

of many cultural strains under enlightened Turkish patronage, the arguments about Kalūk's racial origins are, from the art historian's point of view, essentially meaningless.

The complex nature of the "Kalūk problem" becomes more evident when we turn to the buildings bearing his name. One of these is the charitable complex built for Fakhreddin Sahib Ata in 1258, consisting of a mosque, tomb, and *hanikah* or gathering-place of dervishes, which bears Kalūk's name on the portal of the mosque. The other is the portal of the undated Ince Minareli or "Slender Minaret" madrasah in Konya. The profound stylistic differences between these two portal structures make it very difficult to define a style particular to Kalūk without assuming that the two buildings are separated by an amount of time sufficient to allow this style to change dramatically. The lack of a readily identifiable style has led to extensive speculation about Kalūk's oeuvre and to the identification of Kalūk with another problemmatical architect of the time, the elusive KALŪYĀN.

The importance of Kalūk's work is beyond question. Sahib Ata was the major architectural patron of his time, founding major endowed architectural complexes in Konya and Sivas and other buildings in other locations between 1249 and 1271. The appearance of Kalūk's name on two of the most important buildings of the Seljuk capital is further testimony to his status and importance, especially as both buildings are original in their layout and decoration. The link with Sahib Ata has prompted Barbara Brend (1975) to attribute other architectural works built under Sahib Ata's patronage to Kalūk, although the arguments used are not completely convincing. If we fall back on the two Konya buildings as the "core" of Kalūk's work, we have two elaborate carved portals of radically

different layout, different material (soft brown stone for the Ince Minareli and white marble for the Sahib Ata portal), and different details of execution. The Sahib Ata portal partakes of the general style of thirteenth-century Seljuk portals in Anatolia, the doorway surmounted by a *muqarnas* niche under a pointed arch and flanked in its deep recess by *mihrab*-like niches on either side. Aside from the intended two minarets, which would have been an innovation for Konya in 1258, and the creative asymmetry in the minaret supports, the Sahib Ata portal cannot be termed a radical work of art. By contrast, the doorway of the Ince Minareli madrasah is in many of its details without precedent in Anatolian architecture, and the overall framing of the portal, the unusual heading of the framing bands, and the shallow niche without *muqarnas* are innovations which call to mind the terms baroque and eccentric.

Given this situation, we might seek the style of Kalūk in other aspects of the two buildings. Certainly, there are considerable similarities in the interior decoration (brickwork enhanced with mosaic tile) and in the plans of the buildings. Both Konya buildings involve an outer decorated façade confronting the urban environment, of which the elaborate portals constitute the most important part, together with an inner core of architectural spaces under roofs, vaults, and domes; the two entities are connected in both buildings by a series of adaptive or adapter spaces in the form of extensions or passageways. It is no coincidence that neither of the Konya buildings bearing Kalūk's name uses the conventional open courtyard with symmetrically placed *eyvans;* Kalūk's architecture involved closed spaces with direct axial links to doorways, and it would appear to be from these characteristics, if anywhere, that the conceptualization of his style must arise.

Of Kalūk's artistic legacy, there are again varying assessments. Rogers sees the gigantic Çifte Minareli madrasah of 1271 in Sivas as the work of Kalūk's atelier, in contradiction to those who would identify Kalūk with Kalūyān, the signature on the exactly contemporary Gök madrasah in Sivas, itself a foundation of Sahib Ata. Until the emergence of a consensus on Kalūk, we are forced into the unusual position of stating that of his importance there can be no doubt, but that the exact nature of his contribution to the development of style in Anatolian architecture of the thirteenth century remains unclear.

WALTER B. DENNY

WORKS

1258, Charitable Complex of Fakhreddin Sahib Ata; n.d., Ince, Minareli; Konya, Turkey.

BIBLIOGRAPHY

BREND, BARBARA 1975 "The Patronage of Fahr addīn ᶜAlī ibn al-Husain and the Work of Kalūk ibn ᶜabd ᶜAllāh in the Development of the Decoration of Portals in Thirteenth Century Anatolia." *Kunst des Orients* 10:160–186.
KURAN, APTULLAH 1969 Volume 1 in *Anadolu Medreseleri.* Ankara: Middle East Technical University, Faculty of Architecture.
ROGERS, J. M. 1974 "Seljuk Architectural Decoration at Sivas." Pages 13–27 in William Watson (editor), *The Art of Iran and Anatolia from the 11th to the 13th Century, A.D.: Colloquies on Art & Architecture in Asia.* University of London, Percival David Foundation of Chinese Art, School of Oriental Studies.
ROGERS, J. M. 1976 "Waqf and Patronage in Seljuk Anatolia: The Epigraphic Evidence." *Anatolian Studies* 26:69–103.

KALŪYĀN

The signature Kalūyān ibn al-Qunawi (literally "good John, son of the Konyaite"), an apparently Greek name in an Islamic form, appears on the portal of the Gök Madrasah in the Anatolian city of Sivas. The building is established by inscription as a foundation of the Seljuk Vizier or minister Fahreddin Ali, called Sahip Ata, one of the foremost architectural patrons of his time, and is dated to 1271. That same year saw the completion of two other madrasahs or theological colleges in Sivas: the gigantic Çifte Minare, financed by Shams al-Din Muhammad Juwayni, and the Bürüciye, the patron of which was Muzaffar ibn Hibatullah of Barujird. Since the Çifte Minare was the work of an Il-Khanid Mongol governor and the Gök Madrasah was supported by a Turkish minister, the political as well as artistic importance of the competition these buildings represent is of considerable interest.

If we accept the premise of J. M. Rogers (1965) that the "signature" of Kalūyān on the Sivas building relates only to the marble portal in which the name is carved and not to the plan, structure, or interior ceramic decoration, then Kalūyān is still an important artist indeed. The façade of the Gök Madrasah, with the extraordinary quality of its carving, the interplay between its two-dimensional pattern and three-dimensional projection, and the elegance of its proportions, is an artistic achievement unequaled in the second half of the thirteenth century in Anatolia, despite Roger's assessment that the building had few artistic heirs.

Of the elusive Kalūyān himself, we can say little more. Some scholars once suspected that he might be identical with the equally enigmatic KALŪK IBN ᶜABD ᶜALLĀH, but on stylistic grounds that seems unlikely. The line of inquiry most likely to deepen our knowledge of the artist involves comparative analysis of the style of the Gök Madrasah portal and other Anatolian portals. Of these, the portal of the Çifte Minare Madrasah of Erzurum resembles it most closely; according to unpublished work by the Turkish scholar A. Özdural, the dimensions of the two portals match exactly. There is no question that the overall similarity between the two suggests a single creator. The differences of stylistic detail between the two, which in the Anatolian decorative spectrum do not loom particularly large, may be explained if

Kalūyān. Gök Madrasah. Sivas, Turkey. n.d.

we accept Rogers's logical dating of the Erzurum building to before 1265.

Kalūyān is clearly an artist working in the tradition of the Seljuk Turkish imperium, and his Sivas portal may indeed be viewed as the summit and the end of a long line of sculpted portals in that tradition. There are two ways in which Kalūyān may acquire a more defined artistic personality. The first, as mentioned, is through comparative analysis such as that of Rogers and Özdural. The second is through the restoration of the Sivas portal, many fragments of which are presently found in the interior of the building. Beyond this stylistic evidence, however, Kalūyān will probably remain, like his near-contemporary Kalūk, a shadowy and uncertain figure.

WALTER B. DENNY

BIBLIOGRAPHY

ROGERS, J. M. 1965 "The Çifte Minare Medrese at Erzurum and the Gök Medrese at Sivas." *Anatolian Studies* 15:63–85.

KAMPMANN, HACK

Hack Kampmann (1856–1920), a Danish architect, assumed an important position among the younger generation of the National Romantic architects. He was commissioned with a number of significant buildings, mostly in Jutland, Denmark, such as the regional archives at Viborg, the custom house in Århus, Århus Theater, and the State Library in Århus. In his later years, he strongly advocated the classicistic trend in which style he designed the Police Yard in Copenhagen, considered the most important building of that period.

VILLADS VILLADSEN

KANTARDZHIEV, PETUR

Born in Sofia, Bulgaria, Petur Stoikov Kantardzhiev (1893–1980) studied philosophy and music in Munich in 1910–1911, participated in World War I, and obtained an architecture degree in Karlsruhe, Germany, in 1920, having studied under HERMAN BILLING.

During his private practice (1923–1944), Kantardzhiev built mostly residences and high-rise apartment buildings, while during the second period of his professional career (1945–1980) he devoted more attention to large-scale civic buildings and urban design. As chief architect of Sofia (1945–1948), he designed its master plan, and he supervised the development of the capital for over thirty years, until his death in Sofia in 1980.

Kantardzhiev was a juror for many architectural competitions, an appreciated and respected administrator, and an organizer of the architectural profession.

MARIA POPOVA

WORKS

1923–1924, Hotel Edelweiss; 1933–1934, Housing Cooperative; 1945–1948, City Hall (with others); 1945–1948, Sports Center (with others), Lozenets; 1946–1950, Lagera Residential Complex (with others); Sofia. 1948–1961, Master Plan (with others), Bansko, Bulgaria. 1950–1951, High Mountain Ski Resort Hotel (with G. Trendafilov and I. Zidarov); 1961–1962, Ski Hotel (with Trendafilov); Pamporovo, Bulgaria.

BIBLIOGRAPHY

ANGELOV, D. 1963 "Arkhitekt Petard Kantardzhiev." *Arkhitektura* 6:24–29.
"Arkhitekt P. S. Kantardzhiev." 1958 *Arkhitektura* 5:34.
BŬLGARSKA AKADEMIIA NA NAUKITE 1965 *Kratka Istoriia na Bŭlgarskata Arkhitektura.* Sofia: The academy.
KANTARDZHIEV, PETUR 1952 *Gradoustroisvoto v Minaloto i pri Sotsializma.* Sofia: Nauka i Izkustvo.
KANTARDZHIEV, PETUR 1960 "Postroiavaneto na Tsentralniia Arkhitekturen Ansambul na Stolitsata." *Arkhitektura* 8–9:6.
KANTARDZHIEV, PETUR 1963 "Diletantstvoto v Arkhitekturata i Negovite Porazheniia u Nas." *Arkhitektura* 7:31.
KANTARDZHIEV, PETUR 1975 "Zarazhdane i Razvitie na Obshchestveno-Tvorcheskite Formi na Organizatsiia na Bulgarskite Arkhitekti." *Arkhitektura* 7:5.

KARFÍK, VLADIMÍR

Vladimír Karfík (1901–) studied at the Technical University in Prague, Czechoslovakia, and worked with LE CORBUSIER and FRANK LLOYD WRIGHT. Among his major works are a hotel (1932) and the seventeen-story office building for Baťa Enterprises in Zlín, Baťa Department Stores in Brno (1930), Bratislava (1931), Liberec (1931), and Amsterdam (1937), and housing developments for Baťa workers in East Tilbury, England and Belcamp, Maryland. In 1945, he became professor of architecture at The Slovak Technical University in Bratislava. His most significant postwar projects include residential areas in Gottwaldov-Zlín and in Bratislava and the first prefabricated residential buildings in Bratislava. Characteristic of his works is their advanced functional, contructional, and artistic conception.

ŠTEFAN ŠLACHTA

WORKS

1931, Baťa Department Store, Bratislava, Czechoslovakia. 1930, Baťa Department Store, Brno, Czechoslovakia. 1931, Baťa Department Store, Liberec, Czechoslovakia. 1932, Baťa Enterprise Offices; 1932, Hotel; Zlin, Czechoslovakia. 1937, Baťa Department Store, Amsterdam. n.d., Housing Development (for Baťa factory workers), Belcamp, Md. n.d., Housing Development (for Baťa factory workers), East Tilbury, Thurrock, England.

BIBLIOGRAPHY

KARFÍK, VLADIMÍR 1975 *Administratívne budovy.* Bratislava, Czechoslovakia: Alfa.
KARFÍK, VLADIMÍR; KARFÍKOVÁ, SVĚTLA; and MARCINKA, MARIÁN 1963 *Nové smery vo výstavbe škôl.* Bratislava, Czechoslovakia: Vydavateľstvo Slovenského fondu výtvarných umení.
ŠLACHTA, ŠTEFAN 1976 "Prof. Ing. arch. Vladimír Karfík 75—rocny." *Projekt* yearbook 18, 202, no. 10:56–58.
ŠLACHTA, ŠTEFAN 1980 "Zlín architecture." *Architese* 6:41–43.

KARPIŃSKI, ZBIGNIEW

Zbigniew Karpiński (1906–) studied architecture at the Technical University in Warsaw and graduated in 1937. He won first prize in the competition for the Warsaw City Center Redevelopment Plan, East Side, and consequently became its chief designer (1958–1968). The project was based on the idea of a pedestrian precinct parallel to the main city street, surrounded by commercial and highrise residential buildings. Many of the individual buildings were designed by other architects, including A. Kaliszewski, J. Kowarski, A. Sierakowski, and Z. Wacławek. The complex as a whole presents a skillful attempt to integrate the remains of the pre-World War II city center fabric with a modest late modern architecture.

Karpiński has taught architecture at the Technical University of Warsaw since 1955.

LECH KŁOSIEWICZ

WORKS

1956–1958, Polish Embassy (with J. Kowarski), Peking. 1958–1968, Warsaw City Center Redevelopment Plan, East Side.

BIBLIOGRAPHY

Warszanska Szkoła Architektury: 1915–1965. 1967 Warsaw: P.W.N.

KATAYAMA, TŌKUMA

Born in Hagi, Yamaguchi Prefecture, Japan, Tōkuma Katayama (1853–1917) achieved his success as a court architect to Emperor Meiji. Educated at the Imperial College of Engineering, he was one of the first graduates from the department of architecture in 1879. Soon thereafter, he started working for the Department of the Imperial Household, and most of his works were buildings for the imperial family and the nobility. He liked the architecture of the classical period and was particularly interested in the baroque style. Katayama's best and largest work is the Akasaka Palace in a neobaroque style (1908) in Tokyo.

TAKASHI HASEGAWA

WORKS

1894, Nara Imperial Museum, Japan. 1895, Kyoto Imperial Museum. 1908, Akasaka Palace (now the National Reception Hall); 1909, Hyōkeikan; Tokyo.

BIBLIOGRAPHY

FUJIMORI, TERUNOBU (editor) 1979 *Nihon-no Kenchiku: Meiji, Taishō, Shōwa.* Tokyo.

KAUFFMANN, RICHARD YITZCHAK

The physical structure of the kibbutzim, the communal agricultural settlements in Israel, was the work of Richard Yitzchak Kauffmann (1887–1958). He was born in Frankfurt and after studies in Darmstadt and Munich (with THEODORE FISCHER) he worked in regional planning in Germany and Norway. An important factor in shaping his thinking was the housing he planned for workers at Krupp Industries in Essen, Germany. In 1920, he went to Palestine. Until the establishment of the State of Israel in 1948, he served as an architect and regional planner for the Jewish Agency, the organization responsible for settling Jews in Palestine. Kauffmann sought to harmonize the Zionist movement's concepts of agricultural settlement with European ideas about garden-cities.

His most impressive work is Nahalal. This cooperative agricultural settlement (*moshav*) is based on a circular design. All the service buildings are concentrated in the center while the dwellings and fields are located around the circumference. Another important project was the planning of Afula as a large urban center designed to serve the local agricultural settlements and to act as a midway point on the railway running between the port of Haifa and Damascus in the East. He also designed suburbs for Jerusalem.

His work is characterized by functional, clear structures, occasionally inclining toward the monumental. It includes small individual dwellings, worker and agricultural settlements, as well as towns and regions. Although Kauffmann laid the ground rules for almost all urban, agricultural, and regional planning in Israel, his name is barely known today.

EDINA MEYER

WORKS

1921, Kibbutz Ein Charod, Israel. 1921, Moshav Nahalal, Israel. 1924, 1925, Moshava Herzliya, Israel. 1925, Talpioth, Beit Hakerem, Jerusalem.

BIE, OSKAR 1928 *Der Architekt Oskar Kaufmann.* Berlin: Pollak.

OSBORN, MAX 1928 *Neue Werkkunst: Oskar Kaufmann.* Berlin: Hübsch.

POSENER, JULIUS 1977 "Oskar Kaufmann." Volume 11, pages 351–352 in *Neue Deutsche Biographie.* Berlin: Duncker & Humblot.

ZUCKER, PAUL 1926 *Theater und Lichtspielhäuser.* Berlin: Wasmuth.

KAUFMANN, OSKAR

Oskar Kaufmann (1873–1956) was one of the leading theater designers of the early twentieth century. Born in Hungary, Kaufmann first studied music at Budapest and then moved on to Karlsruhe in Germany to study architecture. Setting up a private practice in Berlin in 1900, Kaufmann immediately began to specialize in theater design by entering and winning a series of competitions. His first executed design was the Hebbel Theater in Berlin (1907), but the most famous work of his early career was the Freie Volksbühne (Berlin, 1913–1914). These two monumental buildings employed heavy and simplified masonry forms for the exterior, while on the interior they were richly but eccentrically decorated. Kaufmann did not modify the traditional arrangements of his theater interiors, but achieved innovative effects with new surfacing materials and by linking the viewer to the stage through decoration. Kaufmann's work showed some parallels to that of MARTIN DÜLFER and PAUL BONATZ, and some relationship to the German Expressionist movement.

In 1933, Kaufmann fled from Germany to Tel Aviv, where he remained throughout World War II. In 1945, he returned to his native Budapest, and spent his last years helping to rebuild theaters in war-torn Hungary.

BARBARA MILLER LANE

WORKS

1907, Hebbel Theater, Berlin. 1909, Municipal Theater and Museum, Bremerhaven, Germany. 1912, Cinema, Nollendorfplatz, Berlin. 1913, Neue Wiener Stadttheater, Vienna. 1913–1914, Freie Volksbühne (destroyed 1945 and restored in simplified form); 1920s, Office Buildings; 1920s, Houses, Charlottenberg; 1922–1933, Kroll Opera House (reconstruction); 1923, Kurfürstendamm Theater; 1924, Die Komödie; 1926, Renaissance Theater; Berlin. 1927, Neue Schauspielhaus, Königsberg, Germany. 1937, Habimah Theater, Tel Aviv. 1954–?, Madách Theater (with P. Mináry and O. Fábry), Budapest.

BIBLIOGRAPHY

BAB, JULIUS (editor) 1919 *Wesen und Weg der Berliner Volksbühnenbewegung.* Berlin: Wasmuth.

KAZAKOV, MATVEI F.

Matvei Fiodorovitch Kazakov (1738–1812) was born and lived in Russia. He studied architecture under D. V. Ukhtomski, one of the masters of Russian classicism. Kazakov is one of the rare Russian architects of the nineteenth century not to have studied abroad or under foreign masters. His style is stricter and more severe than that of his contemporaries, most of whom worked in St. Petersburg, the capital, a more cosmopolitan town than Moscow where Kazakov established his practice. He designed palaces, hospitals, official buildings, and churches in what is today considered the pure Russian classical style. His palace of the Moscow Senate (c.1780), inside the Kremlin walls, is typical of his manner and also of the disregard which professional architects had for the vernacular Russian architecture as embodied by the Kremlin churches, a stone's throw from Kazakov's palace.

ANATOLE KOPP

WORKS

1777–1788, Church of the Metropolitan Philip; c.1780, Assembly Building of the Nobility; 1796–1812, Golitzki Hospital (not completed until 1881); Moscow.

BIBLIOGRAPHY

Vseobchtchaia istoria arkhitektury. 1963 Moscow.

KECK and KECK

The architecture of the Keck brothers combines a pragmatic approach characteristic of Chicago architecture with a theoretical base derived from European design. Their buildings blend design aspects that are socially conscious, aesthetically progressive, and technologically and environmentally advanced.

Both brothers were born and raised in Watertown, Wisconsin. George Fred Keck (1895–) studied engineering and architecture, respectively, at the Universities of Wisconsin and Illinois. After graduation, he worked for short periods for D. H.

Burnham and Company (see DANIEL H. BURN-HAM) and for Schmidt, Garden, and Erickson (see SCHMIDT, GARDEN, AND MARTIN), and taught at the University of Illinois during 1923–1924. He began an independent practice in 1926.

William Keck (1908–) also studied at Illinois. Graduating in 1931, he joined his brother's practice, becoming a partner in 1946. Other architects who received training under the elder Keck were Leland Atwood, Robert B. Tague, Buford Pickens, RALPH RAPSON, BERTRAND GOLDBERG, and STANLEY TIGERMAN. George Fred Keck further contributed to the training of architects when in 1938, with LÁSZLÓ MOHOLY-NAGY and Gyorgy Kepes, he founded the School of Design in Chicago, where he taught architecture until 1944.

Because of his training in architectural engineering, George Keck readily accepted European modernist design philosophy. He was influenced in his formative years by LE CORBUSIER, FRANK LLOYD WRIGHT, LOUIS H. SULLIVAN, EUGÈNE EMMANUEL VIOLLET-LE-DUC, and R. BUCKMINSTER FULLER. His architecture reveals many of these influences: The Miralago Ballroom (1929) in Wilmette, Illinois, was the first example of the International style in the Chicago area, and its interior was a sophisticated Art Deco design; the House of Tomorrow (1933), done for the Century of Progress International Exposition in Chicago, shows the influence of Fuller's Dymaxion House in its use of advanced technological devices and materials, and in its mode of assembly; his Crystal House (1934), done for the same exposition, was entirely supported by an exterior truss of steel, recalling PETER BEHRENS's Austrian pavilion greenhouse of 1925; his house for Herbert Bruning (1935–1936), with its free-standing helicoidal staircase silhouetted within a semicircular wall of glass brick, brings to mind the glass-enclosed stairways of the Werkbund Model Factory of 1914 by WALTER GROPIUS and HANNES MEYER; his prefabricated Ready-built houses (1942–1946) show the modernists' interest in flexible interior spaces achieved by ceiling-hung, folding walls, recalling the 1927 Weissenhofsiedlung prefabricated houses such as the one by Adolf Rading; and finally, the Chicago Child Care Society Building (1959) uses such classic Corbusian elements as *pilotis*, ramps, and pierced concrete *brise-soleil*.

Though partly inspired by European modernists, the architecture of Keck and Keck was also responsive to American social and technological conditions. Through the 1930s, George Keck was concerned with the social need for housing and concentrated on single and multiple dwellings designed in the spirit of the Machine Age. In 1938, he called for the total mechanization of the house; he willingly worked with developers and he promoted the use of such advanced materials and devices as thermopane glass, radiant heating, central air conditioning, tubular steel furniture, and electric-eye doors.

A common-sense, functionalist approach to housing still characterizes the work of Keck and Keck. The brothers continue today to specialize in thermally efficient and technologically up to date housing design.

FOLKE T. KIHLSTEDT

WORKS

*1929, Miralgo Ballroom and Shops, Wilmette, Ill. 1933, House of Tomorrow; *1934, Crystal House; Century of Progress International Exposition, Chicago. 1935–1936, Herbert Bruning House, Wilmette, Ill. 1937, B. J. Cahn House, Lake Forest, Ill. 1937, Kech–Gottschalk Apartments, Chicago. 1940, Howard M. Sloan House, Glenview, Ill. 1949–1950, Pioneer Cooperative Apartments, Chicago. 1959, Chicago Child Care Society Building. 1961–1962, Normal Weinrib House, Highland Park, Ill.

BIBLIOGRAPHY

COHEN, STUART E. (editor) 1939 *Chicago Architect.* Chicago: Swallow.
"Flats—George Fred Keck." 1940 *Architectural Review* 88:175–178.
"George Fred Keck, William Keck, Architects." 1965 *Inland Architect* 8, July:9–24.
KECK, GEORGE F. 1933 *House of Tomorrow: America's First Glass House.* Chicago: Graham.
KECK, GEORGE F. 1938 "Mayhem in Housing." *Shelter* 3:75, 83.
KECK, GEORGE F., and SCHWEIKER, ROBERT PAUL 1933 "A Chicago Housing Project." *Architectural Record* 73:159–163.
MENOCAL, NARCISO G. 1980 *Keck and Keck—Architects.* Madison, Wisc.: Elvehjem Museum of Art.
MILLER, NORY 1976 "Fred Keck at 81: 'Hit of the Show' After 56 Years." *Inland Architect* 20, May:5–11.
"Miralago Ballroom and Shops." 1930 *Architectural Record* 67:105–109.
"A Portfolio of Modern Houses: George Fred Keck, Architect." 1942 *Architectural Forum* 77:67–82.
SLADE, THOMAS M. 1970 "'The Crystal House' of 1934." *Journal of the Society of Architectural Historians* 29:350–353.
TAGUE, ROBERT B. 1947 *Keck on Architecture.* Colorado Springs Fine Arts Center.

KEELING, E. BASSETT

Enoch Bassett Keeling (1837–1886) was born in Sunderland, Durham, England. A High Victorian architect, he built many brick polychrome churches in London and the southeast of England in the 1860s. An example is the Church of Saint Mark, Notting Hill, London (1862–1864), with its asymmetrical plan, exposed polychrome structural brick, iron piers, and restless timber roof members.

RODERICK O'DONNELL

WORKS

1862–1864, Church of Saint Mark, Notting Hill; *1864, Strand Music Hall; 1864–1865, Church of Saint George; Kensington; 1864–1866, Church of Saint Andrew, Peckham; London. 1864–1866, Church of Saint Paul, Upper Penge, Kent, England.

BIBLIOGRAPHY

CURL, JAMES S., and SAMBROOK, JOHN 1973 "E. Bassett Keeling, Architect." *Architectural History* 16:60–69.
DIXON, ROGER, and MUTHESIUS, STEFAN 1978 *Victorian Architecture.* London: Oxford University Press.

KEELY, PATRICK CHARLES

Patrick Charles Keely (1816–1896) was the patriarch of United States Roman Catholic Church architecture. Keely was born in Kilkenny, Ireland, where his father was a builder. Keely learned the trade from him, and was also influenced by A. W. N. PUGIN, the noted English Gothic ecclesiastical designer.

Keely left Ireland for the United States in 1842, since discrimination against Roman Catholics in Ireland limited his economic growth. He settled in the Brooklyn (N.Y.) Navy Yard district, where a colony of immigrant Irish had already taken root.

In 1847, the Reverend Sylvester Malone, pastor of Saints Peter and Paul's Church in Williamsburgh, Kings County, New York, engaged Keely to submit plans for a new parish church. After difficulties with New York's Bishop John Hughes—who felt the church plan looked too expensive—were overcome, Keely proceeded with the project (1847–1848), which won him a degree of local fame.

Keely's "Annus Mirabilis" followed as his reputation spread among Catholic priests in the northeast. For the next forty-three years, Keely dominated the field of Roman Catholic Church architecture in North America. Although credited with the design of between 600 and 700 buildings, explicit documentation has been found for approximately 150. Keely's churches dot the eastern half of North America from Canada to the Gulf of Mexico and from the Atlantic Coast to Wisconsin.

As his work developed, Keely designed in several styles. At first his parish churches were mostly English Gothic, but after the Civil War, he also designed Romanesque and Second Empire buildings with a few attempts in the Classical Revival mode. He regularly read European publications, including the *London Art Journal,* but did not travel to Europe or take any professional schooling. His Gothic period produced several noteworthy designs including Saint Mary's Church in Newport (1848–1884). Among his finest Gothic parish churches are Saint Anthony's in Brooklyn (1873–1874) and Saint Peter's in Dorchester, Massachusetts (1873–1891). His best completed project was Saint Joseph's Cathedral in Hartford (1875–1892), which was destroyed by fire in 1956.

The Cathedral of the Immaculate Conception (1868) in Brooklyn would have earned Keely a wider degree of architectural immortality, but it was never completed. Based on the Cathedral of Notre Dame in Rouen, Keely's cathedral would have been larger than Saint Patrick's Cathedral in New York. Bishop John Loughlin of Brooklyn, citing other pressing diocesan financial needs, left the cathedral unfinished until its demolition in 1931.

Keely's deeply religious character and conservative, family-oriented personality, coupled with his attention to detail and reputation for uncompromising honesty in business dealings made him a sought after church designer. But Keely sometimes found his clerical clients an albatross: he was often hampered by lack of funds, and frequently his clients were inexperienced in construction. However, when Keely was left to his own element, he was capable of skill and refinement in design.

Keely came under heavy criticism in the last decade of the nineteenth century. Essentially, his time had come and gone, and such critics as RALPH ADAMS CRAM and CHARLES D. MAGINNIS wrote articles taking a dim view of his work. Cram called Keely's Boston cathedral a grouping of "gas pipe columns," and Maginnis, in 1924, called Keely "a man of lesser gifts."

Keely became incapacitated following a stroke in 1890, brought on by the death of his son Charles, whom he hoped would follow him in the family firm. For his labors on behalf of the United States Roman Catholic Church, Keely was awarded the Laetare Medal by the University of Notre Dame in 1884.

ROBERT T. MURPHY

WORKS

*1847–1848, Saints Peter and Paul's Church, Brooklyn, N.Y. 1848–1852, Cathedral of the Immaculate Conception, Albany. 1848–1884, Saint Mary's Church, Newport, R.I. 1851–1852, Saint Joseph's Cathedral, Buffalo, N.Y. 1855, Saint Mary, Star of the Sea, Brooklyn, N.Y.

1866–1875, Cathedral of the Holy Cross, Boston. *1868, Cathedral of the Immaculate Conception (unfinished), Brooklyn, N.Y. 1869–1892, Saint Joseph's Church, New Orleans, La. *1872, Sacred Heart–Saint Stephen's Church; 1873–1874, Saint Anthony's Church; Brooklyn, N.Y. 1873–1891, Saint Peter's Church, Dorchester, Mass. 1874–1875, Holy Name Cathedral (later renovated), Chicago. 1875, Saint Peter's Cathedral, Erie, Pa. *1875–1892, Saint Joseph's Cathedral, Hartford, Conn. 1878–1882, Saint Francis Xavier Church, New York. 1890–1894, Church of Saint John the Baptist, Brooklyn, N.Y.

BIBLIOGRAPHY

Cram, Ralph Adams 1894 "On the Contemporary Architecture of the Catholic Church." *Catholic World* 58:644–654.
Daley, Walter A. 1934 "Patrick Charles Keely: Architect and Church Builder." Unpublished M.A. thesis, Catholic University of America, Washington.
Kervick, Francis W. 1953 *Patrick Charles Keely, Architect: A Record of His Life and Work.* South Bend, Ind.: Privately printed.
Maginnis, Charles D. 1924 "The Work of John T. Comes." *Architectural Review* 55:93–101.
Purcell, Richard J. 1943 "P. C. Keely: Builder of Churches in the U.S." *Records of the American Catholic Historical Society.* 54:208–227.
Wilson, Hult L. 1952 "The Cathedrals of Patrick Charles Keely." Unpublished M.A. thesis, Catholic University of America, Washington.

KEENE, HENRY

Surveyor at Westminster Abbey from 1746, Henry Keene (1726–1776) attracted the patronage of Sir Roger Newdigate, the Gothic Revival enthusiast, who employed him at Arbury Hall (c.1750–1776), Warwickshire, and introduced him to commissions in Oxford. Keene also designed the Gothic Hartwell Church (1753–1755), Buckinghamshire, for Sir William Lee and remodeled Hartlebury Castle Chapel (c.1750) for Bishop Maddox. His classical works include the Guildhall High Wycombe (1757), Buckinghamshire, and, to designs by Theodore Jacobsen, the west front of Trinity College (c.1760), Dublin, Ireland.

MICHAEL MCCARTHY

WORKS

c.1750, Hartlebury Castle Chapel, Worcestershire, England. c.1750–1776, Arbury Hall, Warwickshire, England. 1753–1755, Hartwell Church; 1757, Guildhall, High Wycombe; Buckinghamshire, England. c.1760, Trinity College, Dublin. 1766, Anatomy School, Christ Church; 1766, The Hall, University College; 1773–1776, Provost's Lodgings, Worcester College; Oxford. 1774, Vandelain Tower, Uppark, Sussex, England.

BIBLIOGRAPHY

McCarthy, Michael 1973 "Sir Roger Newdigate: Drawings for Copt Hall, Essex, and Arbury Hall, Warwickshire." *Architectural History* 16:26–36.
Smith, H. Clifford 1945 "Henry Keene: A Georgian Architect." *Country Life* 97:556–557.

KELDERMANS FAMILY

The Keldermans family, also known as the Mansdale family, of architects and sculptors, originally from Mechelin, Belgium, were active in the Netherlands from around 1430 to 1531. Notable are Jan II (1375?–1445), town architect of Mechelin and Louvain, Belgium; Andries (?–c.1480), town architect of Mechelin; Anthonis I (1450–1512), who designed the town hall in Middelburg, Holland; Mathieu I (1425/1450–c.1503), who worked on Antwerp Cathedral from 1487–1498; Mathieu II (?–1526), town architect of Louvain; and Rombout II (c.1460–1531), in 1515 named architect of the Emperor Charles V and town architect of Mechelin, also active in Antwerp, Brussels, and Ghent in collaboration with Domien de Waghemakere (see WAGHEMAKERE FAMILY).

ELIZABETH SCHWARTZBAUM

WORKS

JAN KELDERMANS II

1424–1445, Saint Gommarius, Lier, Belgium. 1439–1442, Town Hall (completed the eastern wing designed by Sulpice von Vorst in 1438), Louvain, Belgium.

ANDRIES KELDERMANS

1475–c.1480, Saint Gommarius, Lier, Belgium.

ANTHONIS KELDERMANS I

c.1480–1512, Saint Rombout (tower), Mechelen, Belgium. 1489, Markiezenhof, Bergen-op-Zoom, Netherlands. 1497–1512, Saint Lawrence (choir), Alkmaar, Netherlands. 1507–1512, Town Hall, Middelburg, Netherlands.

MATHIEU KELDERMANS I

1487–1498, Cathedral of Our Lady (north transept; with Herman de Waghemakere), Antwerp, Belgium.

ROMBOUT KELDERMANS II

1514–1523, Maison du Roy (with Domien de Waghemakere; remodeled in the seventeenth century and rebuilt in 1873–1895), Brussels. 1515–c.1530, Palace of Margaret of Austria, Mechlin, Belgium. 1517–1533, Town Hall (unfinished; with Domien de Waghemakere), Ghent, Belgium. 1521, The Steen (with Domien de Waghemakere); 1531, New Stock Exchange (with Domien de Waghemakere); Antwerp, Belgium.

KELLUM, JOHN

John Kellum (1809–1871) was born in Hempstead, Long Island. In 1842 he moved to Brooklyn and worked in the office of Gamaliel King, who took him into partnership in 1846. In 1859, Kellum and his son joined to create many well-known structures in New York, Kellum is known for his work in iron, which includes the unique cast-iron ferry houses for both Fulton Ferry and South Ferry (1864), and the A. T. Stewart Store (1859–1862), the world's largest iron front building. It had four sides of iron and a metal frame of cast-iron columns and wrought-iron "Cooper" beams. He also planned Stewart's model town for working people, the present Garden City, which was under construction at the time of his death.

MARGOT GAYLE

WORKS

1856, Cary Building (store and offices), 105 Chambers Street; 1858, Friends Meeting House, 18 Gramercy Park; 1859–1860, Ball, Black & Company (stores and offices), 565 Broadway; *1859–1862, A. T. Stewart Department Store (later enlarged), Broadway and 10th Street; 1860, 502 Broadway (store and warehouse); 1861, Condict Saddlers (store and factory), 55 White Street; 1861–1872, New York County Courthouse (completed by Leopold Eidlitz); *1864, Union Ferry Iron Ferry Houses; *1864–1869, A. T. Stewart Residence (Fifth Avenue and 34th Street); *1865, Old Stock Exchange, Broad Street near Wall Street; *1865–1866, Herald Building (editorial offices and printing rooms), Broadway and Ann Street; 1867, 597 Broadway (store and lofts); 1868, McCreery's Silk Store, 801 Broadway; *1869–1870, H. B. Claffin Store, Broadway; *1869–1870, Mutual Life Insurance Building, 140 Broadway; *1869–1870, Tiffany's Jewelry Store, Union Square West; *1869–1877, Working Women's Hotel (later Park Avenue Hotel); New York.

BIBLIOGRAPHY

BURNHAM, ALAN 1956 "Last Look at a Structural Landmark." *Architectural Record* 120, no. 3:273–279.

CANTOR, JAY E. 1975 "A Monument of Trade, A. T. Stewart and the Rise of the Millionaire's Mansion in New York." Pages 167–197 in *Winterthur Portfolio 10.* Charlottesville: University of Virginia Press.

FRANCIS, DENNIS STEADMAN 1980 *Architects in Practice, New York City, 1840–1900.* New York: Committee for the Preservation of Architectural Records.

GAYLE, MARGOT, and GILLON, EDMUND V. 1974 *Cast Iron Architecture in New York; a Photographic Survey.* New York: Dover.

Illustrations of Iron Architecture, made by the Architectural Iron Works of the City of New York. 1865 New York: Baker & Goodwin.

KELLUM, JOHN 1887 Volume 3, page 507 in *Appleton's Cyclopedia of American Biography.* Edited by J. G. Wilson and J. Fiske. New York: Appleton.

New York City Landmarks Preservation Commission 1973 *SOHO Cast Iron Historic District: Designation Report.* New York: The commission.

PIERREPONT, HENRY E. 1879 *Historical Sketch of the Fulton Ferry.* New York: Union Ferry Company.

KEMALETTIN

Kemalettin (1870–1927) was a European-trained Ottoman Turkish architect imbued with nationalism who became the leader of the classical Ottoman Revival. He was a capable engineer who studied at Charlottenburg, Germany, and taught in Istanbul at the engineering school and the Academy of Fine Arts. He was one of a group of architects who replaced the foreign and minority architects who dominated during the nineteenth century. His buildings demonstrate an awareness and acceptance of Western building techniques, together with the legacy of forms from the classical Ottoman tradition.

BEATRICE ST. LAURENT

WORKS

1914, Vakif Han, near Eminönü, Istanbul. n.d., Evkaf Apartment Block, Ankara. n.d., Mosque, Bebek, Turkey. n.d., Mosque, Bostanci, Turkey. n.d., Mosque, Bakirköy, Turkey. n.d., Türbe of Mahmut Sevket Pasa, Sisli, Turkey. n.d., Türbe of Sultan Mehmet V Resat, Eyüp, Turkey.

BIBLIOGRAPHY

CETINTAS, SEDAT 1940 "Mimar Kemalettin Mesleği ve Ülküsü." *Güzel Sanatlar Mecmuası* 5:160–173.

GOODWIN, GODFREY 1971 *A History of Ottoman Architecture.* Baltimore: Johns Hopkins Press.

ÜNSAL, BEHÇET (1970)1973 *Turkish Islamic Architecture.* New York: St. Martin's.

Kellum.
A. T. Stewart Department Store.
New York.
1859–1862

KEMP, GEORGE

George Meikle Kemp (1795–1844), a shepherd's son, trained as a millwright working in Scotland, England, and France. A self-taught Gothic expert, he returned to Edinburgh in 1826 to work for WILLIAM BURN. In 1838, he won the second competition for the Scott Monument in Edinburgh. He accidentally drowned, terminating a promising career.

BRUCE WALKER

WORKS

1836–1840, Maybole West Church, Ayrshire, Scotland. 1840–1846, Scott Monument, Princes Street, Edinburgh.

BIBLIOGRAPHY

D. W. Kemp's research papers on George Meikle Kemp are in the Scottish Record Office (GD1/621).

BONNAR, THOMAS 1892 *Biographical Sketch of George Meikle Kemp: Architect of the Scott Monument, Edinburgh.* Edinburgh and London: Blackwood.

COLSTON, JAMES 1881 *History of the Scott Monument, Edinburgh.* Edinburgh Magistrates and Town Council.

"George Kemp and His Monument." 1929 *Quarterly Illustrated of the Royal Incorporation of Architects in Scotland.* 29, Spring: 2–6.

WRINCH, ANN MARTHA 1971 "George Kemp and the Scott Monument." *Country Life* 150:322–323.

KENT, WILLIAM

Probably born in Bridlington, Yorkshire, and reputed to have been apprenticed to a coach painter, William Kent (1685–1748) attracted the patronage of several noblemen who arranged for him to study in Italy. He left England in 1709 in the company of JOHN TALMAN, whose reputation even then as a connoisseur and collector of drawings was considerable. In return for his patronage, Kent was supposed to buy paintings and objects of *virtu,* but this activity was secondary to his study of painting under Benedetto Luti. His portrait by Luti (1718) is at Chatsworth, a softly feminine face. It is said that he met Thomas Coke, the future builder of Holkham, in Luti's studio, and with Coke toured northern Italy in 1714. His painting on the ceiling of San Giuliano dei Fiamminghi in Rome was executed in 1717 and shows just how mistaken the English were to think him the "English Raphael." In 1715, Kent had met the Earl of BURLINGTON, but the depth of their friendship at this time is uncertain. In 1719, however, it had blossomed to the extent that Burlington brought Kent back to London, installed him for life in Burlington House and Chiswick, and in death shared his vault. It is dangerous to concede a homosexual relationship, for homosexuality as we know it today was not always the same as the deep platonic love that existed between men in Kent's age.

Up to 1719, there is no evidence for Kent's interests in the arts other than painting as a profession. Through Burlington's patronage, Kent was even able to usurp JAMES THORNHILL from the post of Sergeant Painter, and it was Kent, not Thornhill, who painted the staircase and other rooms at Kensington Palace. Compared to Thornhill, Kent was, in truth, mediocre, but he had an easy facility for producing decorative wall and ceiling pictures, more classicizing than Thornhill's baroque style. To eyes used to modern connoisseurship, the ludicrous contrast between Kent's painting and, say, Marco Ricci's in Burlington House, is at once obvious, but it was probably not so to Lord Burlington and his fellow art lovers. At Kensington Palace, there is a "Herculaneum" ceiling, based on antique Roman ceilings of the grotesque sort. Kent is very early in the revival of this neoclassic style which may well owe something to Talman's antiquarian interests in Rome. In many accounts of Kent, he has been judged as a lightweight compared to Lord Burlington, but this is grossly unfair. Evidence is accumulating that Kent was a deeply read man, omnivorous of antiquarian information. He may, for example, have been one of the first English painters to paint historical subjects drawn from the Middle Ages, as witness his Battle of Crecy of 1729 in the Royal Collections.

Kent's years between 1719 and 1724 are inadequately documented, and it is still not known when he designed internal alterations to Burlington House, or whether work there attributed to COLEN CAMPBELL is really by Kent. By 1724, he was certainly designing in a fully Kentian style, as witness his dining room, probably in London, for the second duke of Grafton, dated that year. The style is derivative of the drawings of INIGO JONES and JOHN WEBB acquired by Burlington in 1721 and given to Kent to edit for the *Designs of Inigo Jones, with some Additional Designs* (by Burlington and Kent) published in 1727. The Grafton drawing is also one of the earliest in Kent's idiosyncratic drafting style, using a sepia or bister wash, always freehand (he never used a ruler), and with the sheet ornamented by little whimsical sketches. This is not Kent's style of his Italian years, and he seems to have adopted it quite suddenly without obvious precedent. The only tentative suggestion is that Kent saw the drawings for Claude's *Liber Veritatis* then in the duke of Devonshire's collection just down the road from Burlington House in Piccadilly.

Kent's career developed from painter to inte-

rior decorator, and central to this second phase are the decorations of Chiswick House, Middlesex, and Houghton Hall, Norfolk, both proceeding through the later years of the 1720s. In each case, work began in 1726, although the Chiswick interiors were not finished until the middle 1730s. At Chiswick, Burlington and Kent worked in tandem, but no designs for the decorations there have survived, except for a few architectural details by Burlington. The Corinthian quality of the interiors and the reliance upon ANTOINE DESGODETZ's *Edifices Antiques de Rome* may be attributed to Burlington, and to Kent may be due the more witty character of the decoration, such as the frames with baskets of acanthus, a paraphrase of the Vitruvian (see VITRUVIUS) legend, or the fishtail overdoors. The Blue Velvet Room with the ceiling whose cove is supported by huge double consoles, taken from drawings and engravings by Charles Berard in Burlington's collection may also be by Kent. In effect, and in contrast to Campbell's neo-Palladian interiors, Kent deliberately set out to create an architectonic interior made up of an astonishing variety of sources, many to this day unrecognized. Sometimes, it is as if Kent had a *horror vacui* of bare wall, as in the decoration of the staircase at Houghton. One existing and one lost work of interiors deserve mention, the latter Queen Caroline's Library in Saint James's Palace (1736) for which many ingenious designs survive,

the former, Lady Isabella Finch's 44 Berkeley Square (1742) with its theatrical staircase, a spatial display that has no precedent in England and can stand comparison with the best of its type in Europe.

Kent was also adept at decoration in rococo Gothick, which is always associational, that is, in an earlier, usually Tudor or Elizabethan building. The earliest recorded example is Henry Pelham's Esher Place, Surrey, from about 1732, built around a tower of Cardinal Wolsey's Tudor palace. Surviving fragments of the interior suggest that Esher was a most remarkable Gothick decorative scheme incorporating such Kentian whims as huge plaster scallop shells. Later Gothick interiors occur at Rousham House, Oxon (1738), but the best known Gothick work is the Gothic Gateway in Clock Court, Hampton Court Palace (1732), coeval with Esher, although here interior decoration was minimal. A typical ecclesiastical commission was the Gothic choir screen in Gloucester Cathedral (1741). The influence of Kent's Gothick has been underestimated. Although CHRISTOPHER WREN (at Christ Church, Oxford) and NICHOLAS HAWKSMOOR (the Knights of the Garter stalls in Westminster Abbey) both designed in associational Gothic, Kent's work was widely disseminated by JOHN VARDY in *Some Designs of Mr. Inigo Jones and Mr. William Kent* (1744), as well as through the engravings of Esher Place. Indeed,

Esher Place became the model par excellence of the rococo Gothick country house, directly influencing such large Gothick houses as Milton Abbey, Dorset, and Tong Castle, Shropshire.

Kent emerged as architect and landscape gardener in about 1730. His first country house was Kew House, Surrey, for Frederick, Prince of Wales (1731). The elevation of this betrays a knowledge of the split pediments on the Roman Baths as published by Lord Burlington in his *Fabbriche Antiche* of 1730, and the use of similar sources at Stanwick Park, Yorkshire (c.1730), suggests that this noble house was also by Kent. Its dining room was modeled upon the Blue Velvet Room at Chiswick with the consoled ceiling. The extent to which Kent was responsible for Holkham Hall, Norfolk (1734), for Thomas Coke, later earl of Leicester, is uncertain, for the initial designs were drawn up by Burlington and Kent with the assistance of Coke himself. Most of the staterooms in the main block, although Kentian in their trim, are weak expositions by the inferior MATTHEW BRETTINGHAM I, who was a big-headed clerk of works anxious to demote both Burlington and Kent's involvement. It is certain, however, that Burlington and Kent drew up the general lines and plan of the house, and Kent decorated the family wing. The Hall is certainly Kent's, although it owes much of its inspiration and details from Kent's experiences of Burlington's Assembly Rooms at York and his reading of Roman antiquity. The manner in which the wings are joined to the main block of Holkham creates an elevational composition of advancing and recessing planes, a staccato effect known as concatenation. As a master of the concatenated style, Kent may well have been its initiator.

Surprisingly, Kent was never given the opportunity to design a large country house unaided, unless Stanwick is by him, and his style can now be best judged from two public buildings: the Treasury Buildings, Whitehall (1733), where only the center portion was built, and the Horse Guards, designed by Kent shortly before his death and built by Vardy from 1750. The Treasury is Jonesian, of the Whitehall designs, and the Horse Guards are Holkham brought to town.

Kent is indivisible as architect and landscape gardener, for architecture was a powerful persuasion in his landscapes. His genius as a landscape gardener is unquestioned. He was one of the first to create the archetypal arcadian garden in which the temple is one of the most important elements. He learnt much from JOHN VANBRUGH, who was the first to use the temple and garden building as punctuations in a spatial plan. Kent was at Stowe from 1731 or 1732, for his Temple of Venus appears in ISAAC WARE's *Designs of Inigo Jones and*

Kent.
Holkham Hall.
Norfolk, England.
1734

Others advertised in February 1732, and the creation of the Elysium Fields there (1733) is by Kent. In the Fields, there are characteristic buildings such as the Grotto and the concatenated Temple of British Worthies. His whimsicality was given free reign in garden buildings, such as Congreve's monument at Stowe, or the Shepherd's Cove, or the Hermitage. Kent's most important classical garden buildings all derive from the Rotunda in Carlton Gardens built for Frederick, Prince of Wales, from 1733, and include Worcester Lodge, Badminton, Gloucestershire (c.1740), and the Banqueting House, Euton Hall, Suffolk, 1746.

It should also not be forgotten that Kent designed more than half a dozen important monuments, mostly carved by Michael Rysbrack, including that of the first duke of Marlborough in Blenheim Palace Chapel (1730).

JOHN HARRIS

WORKS

Before 1727, Burlington House (decoration), Piccadilly, London. 1725–1738, Chiswick House (decoration and garden works), Middlesex, England. 1726, Houghton Hall (decorations), Norfolk, England. 1728, Sherbourne House (decoration and furniture), Gloucestershire, England. c.1730, Pope's Villa, Twickenham, England. 1730, Richmond Gardens (garden works), Surrey, England. (A)c.1730, Stanwick Park, Yorkshire, England. 1730–1740, Stowe House (garden buildings and decoration), Buckinghamshire, England. 1731, Kew House (including garden works and State Barge), Surrey, England. 1731, Raynham Hall (decoration), Norfolk, England. 1731, Royal Mews, London. 1731, York Minster (pavement), York, England. 1732, Esher Place (decorations), Surrey, England. 1732, Hampton

Court Palace, Middlesex, England. 1733, Treasury Buildings, Whitehall; 1734, Devonshire House; London. 1734, Holkham Hall, Norfolk, England. Before 1735, Claremont (garden works), Surrey, England. Before 1735, Shotover Park (garden works), Oxfordshire, England. 1735, Aske Hall (Gothic Temple), Yorkshire, England. 1735, Easton Neston (decoration), Northamptonshire, England. *1736, Saint James's Palace (Queen's Library), London. 1738, Rousham House, Oxfordshire, England. 1739, Westminster Hall (Gothic screen), London. c.1740, Worcester Lodge, Badmington, Gloucestershire, England. 1741, 22 Arlington Street, London. 1741, Gloucester Cathedral (choir screen), England. 1741, York Minster (Gothic pulpit and furniture), York, England. c.1742, 16 Saint James's Place; 1742-1744, 44 Berkeley Place; London. 1744, Euton Hall (The Temple); 1746, Banqueting House, Euton Hall, Suffolk, England. c.1748, Wakefield Lodge, Northamptonshire, England. 1749, The Horse Guards, Whitehall, London. n.d., Oatlands House (garden buildings), Surrey, England.

BIBLIOGRAPHY

WITTKOWER, RUDOLF 1945 "Lord Burlington and William Kent." *Archaeological Journal* 102.

KEOUGH, PATRICK

Born in Wexford, Ireland, Patrick Keough (1786-1863) was the first of Newfoundland's contractor-architects. Keough arrived in St. John's as a carpenter and surveyor in 1803 and by 1821 had attained sufficient standing to receive government contracts. In 1830 he built the Harbour Grace Court House—a simple, dignified masonry structure of essentially Regency character. His own St. John's house is a quite straightforward two-and-a-half-story gabled structure of stone. Combining politics and business he supported the mercantile party in Newfoundland's first House of Assembly and, later, in the Legislative Council.

SHANE O'DEA

WORKS

1830-1831, Court House and Jail, Harbour Grace, Newfoundland. 1834, Keough House, St. John's, Newfoundland.

KERR, ROBERT

Born in Aberdeen, Scotland, and articled to John Smith, Robert Kerr (1824-1904) exerted considerable influence upon the British architectural profession, mainly through his writings. After attempting to practice in New York (1843-1844), he became president of the Architectural Associa-

tion, London (1847-1848), where he later lectured (1892-1896), professor in arts of construction at King's College, London (1861-1900), and district surveyor of Saint James's, Westminster (1860-1902). After publication of his satirical *Newleafe Discourses* (1846), he wrote on practical issues especially concerned with domestic design, which relate to his country house architecture. He favored stylistic eclecticism, as propounded in his 1891 edition of JAMES FERGUSSON's *History of the Modern Styles,* notable for its praise of recent American architecture.

R. WINDSOR LISCOMBE

WORKS

1858, Dunsdale, Kent, England. 1860, Great Blake Hall, Essex, England. *1863, National Provident Institution, Gracechurch Street, London. 1865-1874, Bear Wood, Berkshire, England. 1868, Ascot Heath House; 1868, Ford Manor; Surrey, England.

BIBLIOGRAPHY

GIROUARD, MARK (1971)1979 Pages 263-272, 440 in *The Victorian Country House.* Rev. ed. New Haven: Yale University Press.

KERR, ROBERT 1846 *The Newleafe Discourses on the Fine Art Architecture.* London: Weale.

KERR, ROBERT 1864 *The Gentleman's House; or, How to Plan English Residences, from the Parsonage to the Palace.* London: John Murray.

KERR, ROBERT 1866 "On the Problems of Providing Dwellings for the Poor in Towns." *Transactions of the Royal Institute of British Architects* 18:37-80.

KERR, ROBERT 1873 *A Small Country House.* London: John Murray.

KERR, ROBERT 1883 "English Architecture Thirty Years Hence." *Transactions of the Royal Institute of British Architects* 34:218-233.

KERR, ROBERT 1886 *The Consulting Architect: Practical Notes on Administrative Difficulties.* London: John Murray.

KERR, ROBERT 1887 "Observations on the Architect's Function in Relation to Building Contracts." *Transactions of the Royal Institute of British Architects* 37:128-140.

KERR, ROBERT (editor) 1891 *History of the Modern Styles of Architecture* by James Ferguson. Volumes 4 and 5 in *A History of Architecture in All Countries, from the Earliest Times to the Present Day.* 3d ed. London: John Murray.

KERR, ROBERT 1893 "The Problem of National American Architecture." *Architectural Record* 3:121-132.

KERR, ROBERT 1899 Four chapters on "Plan" in F. W. Andrewes, *The Principles and Practice of Modern House Construction.* Edited by George L. Sutcliffe. London: Blackie.

KOUWENHOVEN, JOHN 1953 Page 203 in *Columbia Historical Portrait of New York.* Garden City, N.J.: Doubleday.

LANDY, JACOB 1969 "The Washington Monument

Project in New York." *Journal of the Society of Architectural Historians* 28:292–293.

PEVSNER, NIKOLAUS 1972 Pages 217–221, 224–226, 233–236, 291–314 in *Some Architectural Writers of the Nineteenth Century.* Oxford University Press.

SUMMERSON, JOHN 1947 Page 4 in *The Architectural Association: 1847–1947.* London: Pleiades Press.

SUMMERSON, JOHN 1970 Page 7 in *Victorian Architecture.* New York: Columbia University Press.

KIESLER, FREDERICK

Frederick Kiesler (1890–1965) had a visionary plan: the "Endless," be it house, theater, or museum, whether in the shape of an egg, a shell, a cave, or a whale. Architect, theater designer, and sculptor, Kiesler, who was born in Vienna, dedicated himself to the ideal of enhancing the interaction of man and environment through an architecture based on organic principles.

During the 1920s in Vienna, he worked with ADOLF LOOS, joined the Dutch *De Stijl* group, and experimented with innovative theater productions. He also developed plans for his "Endless": a double-curved shell form molded from reinforced concrete which could enclose any irregularly shaped area within its surface. Designed to escape the limitations of a circular, square, or rectangular plan when applied to house design, the continuous curved surfaces of the "Endless" denied the traditional divisions of floor, wall, and ceiling. Instead, they defined an unrestricted interior which the dweller was free to enclose, open, or alter, as the needs of his life might dictate.

As applied to theater, the "Endless" became a double-spiral stage connected to tracks and continuous runways that were interwoven with rings of spectator seats at various levels. Convinced that isolation threatened the survival of theater, Kiesler wanted to create an environment that encouraged interaction between performers and their audience.

After emigrating to the United States in 1926, Kiesler became associated with the Surrealists, designing installations for their 1947 exhibition in Paris as well as architecture, furniture, and exhibition techniques for Peggy Guggenheim's Art of this Century Gallery in New York. He also completed the World House Gallery in New York (1957) and the Shrine of the Book in Jerusalem (1959). However, the many designs for the Endless House, with its countless modifications and amplifications, never were realized beyond the scope of a full-scale model. For this reason, Kiesler has been described as "the greatest non-building architect of our time" (Huxtable, 1960).

JANET KAPLAN

WORKS

*1925, Austrian Pavilion (City in Space), Exposition International des Arts Décoratifs et Industriels Modernes, Grand Palais, Paris. 1929, Eighth Street Playhouse; 1930, Film Guild Cinema; New York. 1933, Universal Theater, Woodstock, N.Y. 1942, Art of this Century Gallery; 1957, World House Gallery; New York. 1958, Venetian Theater (Caramoor), Katonah, N.Y. 1959, Hospital Section, Albert Einstein Medical Center, New York. 1959, Shrine of the Book, Hebrew University, Jerusalem.

BIBLIOGRAPHY

CONRADS, ULRICH, and SPERLICH, HANS G. 1962 *The Architecture of Fantasy: Utopian Building and Planning in Modern Times.* Translated, edited, and expanded by Christiane C. Collins and George R. Collins. New York: Praeger.

GOODMAN, CYNTHIA 1979 "The Current of Contemporary History: Frederick Kiesler's Endless Search." *Arts* Sept.:118–123.

HUXTABLE, ADA LOUISE 1960 "Architecture on TV: Greatest Non-Building Architect of Our Time Expounds His Ideas." *New York Times* Mar. 27, sec. 2, p. 13.

KIESLER, FREDERICK 1926 "Debacle of the Modern Theater." *International Theatre Exposition* Feb. 27–Mar. 15:14–24.

KIESLER, FREDERICK 1939 "On Correalism and Biotechnique: A Definition and Test of a New Approach to Building Design." *Architectural Record* 86, Sept.:60–75.

KIESLER, FREDERICK 1943 "Design Correlation as an Approach to Architectural Planning." *VVV* Mar.:76–79.

KIESLER, FREDERICK 1950 "Frederick Kiesler's Endless House and Its Psychological Lighting." *Interiors* 110, Nov:123–129.

KIESLER, FREDERICK 1965 "Kiesler by Kiesler." *Architectural Forum* 123, no. 2:64–72.

KIESLER, FREDERICK 1966a "The Grotto for Meditation." *Craft Horizons* 26, no. 4:22–27.

KIESLER, FREDERICK 1966b *Inside the Endless House: Art, People, and Architecture: A Journal.* New York: Simon & Schuster.

"New Display Techniques for 'Art of this Century,' Designed by Frederick J. Kiesler." 1943 *Architectural Forum* 78, no. 2:49–53.

NEW YORK, SOLOMON R. GUGGENHEIM MUSEUM 1964 *Frederick Kiesler: Environmental Sculpture.* New York: The museum.

KIKUTAKE, KIYONORI

The commitment to growth and change that characterizes the design philosophy of Kiyonori Kikutake (1928–) was first indicated in Sky House (1958), Tokyo, Japan, and was developed further in subsequent architectural projects and in his visionary and utopian cities. Rather traditional in its formal vocabulary, Sky House, essentially a single space raised on wall pillars with provisions for suspending additional rooms below the floor slab, was intended to correspond to transformations in the social structure and in modes of living. Kikutake's interest in change derives in part from traditional Japanese philosophy, which does not include the concepts of eternity and perfection. He maintains that the relation between man and architecture is spiritual as well as physical and serves to clarify man's relation to his world generally. Therefore, architecture must contribute to the creation of a new social order based on universal human values. Kikutake defines the task of modern architecture as the discovery and representation of essential principles underlying form. Although he is profoundly interested in the architecture of the past (for example, the Katsura Villa and the Izumo Shrine), Kikutake emphatically denies the use of architectural history as a formal or polemical device.

After receiving a degree in architecture from Waseda University in 1948, Kikutake matriculated in the physical engineering department, graduating in 1950. During his first term, he was awarded third place in a competition for the Hiroshima Peace Memorial Catholic Cathedral, and in 1950 he won the graduate prize in design. After working in various architectural offices, Kikutake established the Kikutake Architecture Laboratory in 1953.

Participation in the International Design Festival in Tokyo in 1960 and the formation of Group Metabolism with Noboru Kawazoe, Mashito Oe, FUMIKO MAKI, and Noriaki Kurokawa led to the publication of *Metabolism/1960: The Proposals for New Urbanism*. The manifesto outlined Metabolism's conception of the organic and cyclical character of cities and included the original schemes for Kikutake's Tower-Shaped Community, comprised of a central service trunk and clip-on cylindrical living units, and for Marine City, the first of a number of plans to extend the living area of Tokyo into the sea.

The Metabolist plans for cities are not extensions of conventional cities. Although the situation in Tokyo served as a point of departure, the cities were conceived as physical representations of a new social order in which the ancient relations between the individual and his world have been modified. Kikutake has continued to develop the idea of floating cities, and the Aquapolis, a pavilion for the International Ocean Exposition in Okinawa of 1975, represents a partial realization.

Kikutake's concern with spatial and formal hierarchies in architecture is best exemplified in his competition entry for the International Conference Palace in Kyoto (unfortunately never executed), in which various functions are integrated within a unified whole rather than allowing specific functions to determine the formal configuration. Kikutake received the Japan Institute of Architects award for the Izumo Shrine Administration Building, which is an outstanding example of his sensitivity to the nature of materials and of his concern for integrating the architecture of the past and the present on a spiritual rather than on a literal or a formal level.

SUSAN STRAUSS

WORKS

1958, Sky (Kikutake) House, Tokyo. 1963, City Hall, Tatebayashi, Japan. 1963, Izumo Shrine Administration Building, Japan. 1964, Asokawa Apartment House, Japan. 1964, Tokoen Hotel, Yonago, Japan. 1966, Pacific Hotel, Chigasaki, Japan. 1968, Iwate Prefectural Library, Morioka, Japan. 1968, Shimane Prefectural Library, Matsue, Japan. 1969, Civic Center, Kurume, Japan. 1970, Tower for Expo '70, Osaka, Japan. 1972, Gymnasium, City University, Shimonoseki, Japan. 1972, Tokoen Hotel (extension), Yonago, Japan. 1974, City Hall, Hagi, Japan. 1975, Aquapolis, International Ocean Exposition, Okinawa, Japan. 1975, City Center (redevelopment), Yamaga, Japan. 1976, Biwako Shopping Center, Otsu, Japan.

BIBLIOGRAPHY

"Architecture of Japan." 1967 *Canadian Architect* 12, Jan.:21–32.
"The Architects." 1962 *Architectural Review* 132:221–230.
BOYD, ROBIN 1968 *New Directions in Japanese Architecture*. New York: Braziller.
KIKUTAKE, KIYONORI 1964 "New Form and Old Tradition." *Arts and Architecture* 81, Dec.: 14–17, 34.
KIKUTAKE, KIYONORI 1973 *Works and Methods: 1956–1970*. Tokyo: Bijutus.
KIKUTAKE, KIYONORI 1975 "The Significance of 'Experience' in Architecture." *Approach* Spring:2–3.
KIKUTAKE, KIYONORI 1978 "Cautious Hopes, and Prophecies." *Japan Architect* 53, Jan.:4–5.
"Kiyonori Kikutake." 1967 *Bauen und Wohnen* 21:256–282.
"Kiyonori Kikutake." 1964 *Japan Architect* 39, Apr.:10–11.
"Kiyonori Kikutake Receives the Auguste Perret Award." 1978 *Japan Architect* 53, Aug.:7.
"Kurume Civic Center." 1969 *Japan Architect* 44, Oct.:21–38.
MURAMATSU, TEIJIRO 1975 "Dialogue Series on Humanity and Architecture." *Japan Architect* 50, Mar.:79–86.
"1963 Pan Pacific Citation Awarded to Japan's Kikutake." 1964 *Architectural Record* 135, Mar.:14–15.
NITSCHKE, GÜNTER 1964 "The Approach of Kiyonori Kikutake." *Architectural Design* 34:507–515.
"Ocean City." 1965 *World Architecture* 2:26–27.

"Office Building for the Izumo Shrine." 1963 *Japan Architect* 38, Nov.:13–26.

ONOBAYASHI, HIROKI 1967 "A Profile of Kiyonori Kikutake." *Japan Architect* 42, Mar.:41–44.

SCHMERTZ, MILDRED F. 1970 "New Developments in Japanese Architecture." *Architectural Record* 148, no. 3:109–128.

"The Shimane Prefectural Library." 1969 *Japan Architect* 44, Oct.:47–54.

"Sky House." 1963 *Kenehiku Bunka* 18, June:63–65.

"The Tanabe Art Museum." 1980 *Japan Architect* 55, Oct.:7–14.

ZEVI, BRUNO 1972 "Megastrutture residenziali come alberi." *L'Architettura Cronache et Storia* 18, no. 8:492–493.

KILEY, DANIEL URBAN

Daniel Urban Kiley (1912–) was born in Boston and attended the Graduate School of Design, Harvard University (1936–1938). He was a draftsman with Warren H. Manning in Cambridge, Massachusetts (1932–1938), and associate town planning architect for the United States Housing Authority, Washington (1939–1940). He has had offices in Washington, Middleburg, Virginia, and Franconia, New Hampshire (1940–1951), and since 1951, with partners, in Charlotte, Vermont. With EERO SAARINEN, he won First Prize in the Jefferson Memorial National Competition, St. Louis (1948).

In Kiley's most typical landscape projects, the buildings surround the gardens rather than vice versa.

MARY D. EDWARDS

WORKS

1951, Federal Reserve Bank (landscaping), Detroit, Mich. 1951, Mill Creek Housing (landscaping), Philadelphia. 1955, Concordia Junior College (landscaping), Fort Wayne, Ind. 1956, International Business Machines Building (landscaping), Rochester, Minn. 1956, Union Carbide Company (landscaping), Eastview, N.Y. 1956, United States Air Force Academy (landscaping), Colorado Springs. 1958, Dulles International Airport (landscaping), Chantilly, Va. 1958, Law Library (landscaping), University of Chicago. 1960, North Court, Lincoln Center (landscaping), New York. 1962, Oakland Museum (landscaping), Calif. 1962, Pennsylvania Avenue (landscaping), Washington. 1963, Stiles and Morse Colleges (landscaping), Yale University, New Haven. 1965, Fredonia College (landscaping), New York. 1966, Snowbird Ski Resort (landscaping), Alta, Utah. 1966, Tufts University (landscaping), Medford, Mass. 1966, University of Lagos (landscaping). 1967, Calgary Place (landscaping), Alberta. 1969, Squibb Corporate Headquarters (landscaping) Lawrenceville, N.J. 1970, Mall and Plazas (landscaping), Dalle Centrale, La Defense, Paris. 1970, Rockefeller University (landscaping), New York. 1971, Blackwell Park (landscaping), Roosevelt Island, N.Y. 1971, National Gallery of Art (landscaping), Washington. 1972, Baltimore Inner Harbor (landscaping). 1974, Minnesota State Capitol (landscaping), Saint Paul. 1975, Detroit Art Institute (landscaping), Mich. 1975, Washington Cathedral (landscaping). 1977, Conservatory surround (landscaping), New York Botanical Gardens.

BIBLIOGRAPHY

KILEY, DANIEL U. 1951 "Site Planning: The Modern Way to Expand Your Living." *Better Homes and Gardens.*

KILEY, DANIEL U. 1962–1963 "Nature: The Source of All Design." *Landscape Architecture* 53:127.

KILEY, DANIEL U. ET AL 1939 "Landscape Design: The Urban Environment." *Architectural Record* 85, no. 5:70–77.

STIRES, ARTHUR McK. 1967 "Dan Kiley." *Vermont Life* 21, no.4:46–51.

KIMBALL, FRANCIS H.

Francis Hatch Kimball (1845–1919), born in Kennebunk, Maine, trained in the Boston office of Louis P. Rogers and studied with WILLIAM BURGES in London. Well known as a theater architect, Kimball also designed several notable churches and experimented in the use of terra cotta. The Manhattan Life Insurance Building (1893), the first New York skyscraper fully framed in iron and steel and set on concrete caissons, was the first product of Kimball's partnership with George Kramer Thompson.

MARJORIE PEARSON

WORKS

*1876–1878, Orphan Asylum, Hartford, Conn. *1879, Madison Square Theater (remodeling interiors); *1881–1882, Casino Theater (with Thomas Wisedell); 1885, Catholic Apostolic Church; New York. 1886–1887, Emmanuel Baptist Church; 1889–1891, Montauk Club; Brooklyn, N.Y. *1890, Harrigan's Theater (later the Garrick); *1891–1892, Fifth Avenue Theater, New York. 1891–1893, Reading Station, Philadelphia. *1893, Manhattan Life Insurance Building (with George Kramer Thompson), New York. 1895, Dobson Building (with Thompson), Philadelphia. 1905–1906, Trinity Building; 1905–1906, United States Realty Building; *1906–1908, City Investing Company Building; 1907, Seligman & Co. Building (with Julian Levi); *1914, Adams Express Company Building; New York.

BIBLIOGRAPHY

A History of Real Estate, Building, and Architecture in New York City. (1898)1967 Reprint. New York: Arno. See especially pages 518–528.

"Kimball, Francis H." (1914)1967 Volume 15, pages 79–80 in *National Cyclopaedia of American Biography.*

Reprint. Ann Arbor, Mich.: University Microfilms.

SCHUYLER, MONTGOMERY 1898 "The Works of Francis H. Kimball and Kimball & Thompson." *Architectural Record* 7:479–518.

KIMBALL, THOMAS ROGERS

Thomas R. Kimball (1862–1934) was educated at the Massachusetts Institute of Technology, where he helped found the *Technology Architectural Review*. Practicing alone and in a variety of partnerships in Boston (1889–1893) and Omaha, Nebraska (1894–1934), Kimball designed many public buildings throughout the Midwest.

GWEN W. STEEGE

WORKS

1897, Burlington Railway Station, Omaha, Neb. 1903–1904, Electric Building, Louisiana Purchase Exposition, St. Louis, Mo. 1905–1916, Saint Cecilia's Cathedral, Omaha, Neb.

BIBLIOGRAPHY

"Kimball, Thomas Rogers." 1936 Volume 25, pages 364–365 in *National Cyclopaedia of American Biography*. New York: White.

STEELE, WILLIAM L. 1934 "An Appreciation." *Octagon* 6:3–4.

KINGSTON, GEORGE S.

Born in Bandon, Ireland, George Strickland Kingston (1807–1880) studied civil engineering in Birmingham, England. He was deputy surveyor in South Australia (1836–1838), and his architectural work began there in 1838, with private and (until 1841) government commissions. After 1851, his interest in politics overshadowed his practice. He was knighted in 1870.

DONALD LANGMEAD

WORKS

*1838–1839, Wesleyan Chapel; 1838–1840, Government House (east wing); *1839–1840, Congregational Chapel; *1839–1841, Public Offices; 1840–1842, Adelaide Gaol; *1842–c.1847, Monument to William Light; Adelaide, Australia. *1846–1847, Burra Hotel, Kooringa, Australia. 1855–1880, Ayers House, Adelaide Australia.

KLAUDER, CHARLES Z.

Charles Z. Klauder (1872–1938) studied architecture as a draftsman in several Philadelphia firms, including COPE AND STEWARDSON, becoming a noted architectural renderer. In 1900, he worked for the firm of FRANK MILES DAY, which became Day and Klauder in 1913. After Day's death in 1918, Klauder continued the firm's nationally recognized work in college design, establishing his own style of strong vertical orientation organized by flat pilasters and shallow wall articulation free of historical detail.

PATRICIA HEINTZELMAN KEEBLER

WORKS

1904, Samuel Wetherill House, Philadelphia. 1913–1938, Chemistry and Liberal Arts Buildings, Pennsylvania State College. 1917–1928, Men's Dormitories and Memorial Cloister, Cornell University, Ithaca, N.Y. 1917–1929, Women's Dormitories, University of Delaware, Newark. 1917–1930, University of Colorado Buildings, Boulder. 1921–1931, Greene Administration Building, Wellesley College, Mass. 1923, Concordia Seminary, St Louis, Mo. 1923–1926, Peabody Museum, New Haven. 1928–1934, Cathedral of Learning, Pittsburgh. 1931, Men's Dormitories, Pennsylvania State College, Pa.

BIBLIOGRAPHY

KEEBLER, PATRICIA 1980 "The Life and Work of Frank Miles Day." Unpublished Ph.D. dissertation, University of Delaware, Newark.

KIDNEY, WALTER C. 1974 *The Architecture of Choice: Eclecticism in America 1880–1930*. New York: Braziller.

KLAUDER, CHARLES Z. 1920 "A House for Practical Convenience." *Architectural Forum* 33:183–186.

"Monographs on Architectural Renderers: The Works of Charles Z. Klauder." 1914 *Brickbuilder* 23:220–222.

"Some Architectural Drawings and Office Studies by Charles Z. Klauder." 1917 *Architectural Review* 5:61–64, 173–179.

KLEIN, ALEXANDER

Born in Odessa, Russia, Alexander Klein (1879–1961) went to the Institute of Technology in St. Petersburg (Leningrad) to study architecture. After graduation, he began his independent practice.

He designed large complexes of buildings, which involved him in city planning work. Besides industrial plants, he designed the municipal hospital for two thousand beds in Saint Petersburg (1904). He also headed the architectural department of the Institute of Technology in Saint Petersburg from 1915 to 1917.

Because of political developments in Russia, Klein settled in Berlin in 1920. He became an important exponent of scientific analysis in housing design. Housing developments in Berlin (1928) and Bad Dürrenberg (1928–1929) served to demonstrate his theories. He rigorously observed a systematic orientation toward all climatic influences and thus became one of the first exponents of a humanistic and comprehensive functionalism.

Klein moved, via France, to Israel in 1935. He became a professor at the Technion, Israel's Institute of Technology in Haifa, and later became the head of their Research Institute for Town Planning and Housing. He worked out several town planning schemes and designed the plan for the Technion campus on Mount Carmel. He lectured widely in many parts of the world. The Technical University at Stuttgart awarded him an honorary doctorate in 1956.

H. H. WAECHTER

WORKS

1904, Peter the Great Municipal General Hospital, Saint Petersburg, Russia. 1928, Housing Development, Zehlendorf, Berlin. 1928–1929, Housing Development, Bad Dürrenberg, Germany. 1939, Kiryat Yam; 1939, Tivon (garden suburb); near Haifa, Israel. 1955, Electrical Engineering Building, Israel Institute of Technology (Technion), Haifa, Israel.

BIBLIOGRAPHY

"Alexander Klein." 1959 *Der Aufbau* (Vienna) 12:503–506

"Arbeiten Alexander Kleins." 1962 *Bauwelt* 53:163–166.

KLEIN, ALEXANDER 1934 *Das Einfamilienhaus-Südtyp.* Stuttgart, Germany: J. Hoffmann.

KLEIN, ALEXANDER 1947 "Man and Town." Volume 6, pages 73–90 in *Technion Yearbook.* New York: American Technion Society.

KLEIN, ALEXANDER 1952 "New Planning and Subdivision Methods." *Journal of the American Institute of Planners* 18:158–163.

KLEIN, ALEXANDER 1952–1953 "New Planning and Housing Methods for Israel." Volume 2, pages 102–108 in *Technion Year Book.* New York: American Technion Society.

WAECHTER, HEINRICH H., and WAECHTER, ELISABETH 1951 Pages 98–99 in *Schools for the Very Young.* New York: Dodge. Plan and discussion of town planning scheme for Wadi Faliq.

KLENZE, LEO VON

More than any other architect of the first half of the nineteenth century—with the possible exception of KARL FRIEDRICH SCHINKEL—Leo von Klenze (1784–1864) formed the image of a German town through his buildings and his plans. With some twenty buildings, he set the monumental scale for the development of Munich into a court city of European rank. The architect's creative and thoroughly successful life work would, however, not have been thinkable without the paramount part played by the crown prince—later King Ludwig I—of Bavaria as client and patron. From the time when he was first called to Munich in 1816 until his death, Klenze found himself in a permanent, usually critical discussion with the king's often conflicting ideas about art and architecture. It was the declared goal of the king to make Munich the first art city of Germany and to connect this undertaking with his own name. With Maecenas as the model for his role, Ludwig I took on the artistic activities of the Medici in the Florence of the Quattrocento. Thus, the discussion between the royal client and the architect centered on their conflicting attitudes toward the architectural system of the early Renaissance and the Grecian classicism emerging at the turn of the century.

Klenze was born in Schladen near Braunschweig and received his first decisive architectural impressions during his studies in Berlin (1800–1803) from the circle around FRIEDRICH GILLY. In Paris, he became acquainted with the architectural theory of JEAN NICOLAS LOUIS DURAND, and for a short time he worked in the atelier of CHARLES PERCIER and PIERRE LEONARD FONTAINE. His worldly and diplomatic demeanor brought him, through contacts, to the court of Napoleon's brother, Jerome, in Kassel. There, he was active until the end of the Napoleonic occupation and was given the opportunity to build his first building, a modest court theater. At the end of the Napoleonic era (1814), he stayed in Paris and Vienna, the diplomatic arenas of political events, and there succeeded in attracting the attention of the Bavarian crown prince. Upon being called by the latter to Munich (1816), he settled there permanently and was immediately charged with drawing up the plans for the expansion of the city toward the north and west, as well as with his first monumental architectural projects.

After seven richly productive years of building activity, he went to Italy in 1823 for several months of study. In Sicily and southern Italy, he was occupied primarily with the reconstruction of the Greek temples (Selinus, Agrigentum, Paestum), the results of which he later published. Here, too, he consolidated his Greco-classicistic architectural vision, which later was to put him in opposition to the Romantic currents of medieval revival and finally left him isolated. His dominant role—also, probably, not entirely free of intrigues—in the building activities of the following decade led finally to a conflict with the king, whose favor, under the pressure of Biedermeyer-romantic middleclass artistic predilections, also turned to architects whose orientation was toward the medieval—above all to their main representative, FRIEDRICH VON GÄRTNER. This being the situation, the king sent Klenze on a diplomatic-political mission to Greece in 1834, where a son of Ludwig had recently been made king. In Athens, Klenze took measures to restore and safeguard the buildings of the Acropolis, the existence of which was threatened by plans to turn them into a royal residence and military installations. At that same time, too, he designed projects for reshaping the city that were fundamental for later realizations. As a consequence of his new international prestige, he was commissioned by the Russian Czar to build an art gallery in St. Petersburg. In the course of its completion, Klenze undertook several trips to Russia (1839 and later). After King Max II ascended the Bavarian throne, Klenze found himself in artistic isolation as the new king's architectural interests were opposed to his own. Klenze's last Munich buildings were privately financed projects for the former king, Ludwig, who had abdicated.

At the time of his death in 1864, Klenze was, in spite of numerous attacks and much criticism, an authority—even if outdated—in European architecture and a member of the most important European academies. Besides his buildings, he left publications on architectural theory and a series of engravings of his works.

When Klenze was called to Munich by the Bavarian crown prince in 1816, substantial parts of the city's expansion outside the baroque belt of fortifications were already fixed. The central issue in these plans was the shaping of the area north of the Schwabinger Tor, which was of primary urbanistic importance because of its nearness to the royal residence, because the connecting road to the summer residence, Nymphenburg, in the west ended there, and because it was the starting point of the road leading north (later Ludwigstrasse), which had yet to be built up. Klenze's fundamentally new idea, as against his predecessors', was to regularize the northern road to make it a straight axial line running out of a rectangular plaza in front of the former city gate (Odeonsplatz). In contrast to the open designs already begun in other areas (pavilion systems, for example, the Karolinenplatz), for this plaza and street Klenze envisioned a closed system of buildings that consistently excluded landscape elements. Thus, the Residenzgarten, which lay to the east of the square, was blocked off from it by a line of walls, opened only by portals and by a gallery to the north.

Generously dimensioned palace buildings were envisioned to line the plaza and the new street. The façades of these were to be designed by Klenze and approved by the king. And here the conflict that determined Klenze's entire building career in Munich came to light, namely, to pattern the plans and aesthetic content of the buildings of a modest court town of 40,000 inhabitants at the start of industrialization on the ambitious scale of the patrician palaces of Renaissance Florence and Rome for which it provided no sociological equivalent. Apart from a small number of aristocrats and members of the upper middle class glad to build, it was thus wealthy artisans who settled in this noble neighborhood. In contrast to the ambitious intent of the crown prince to front several of the small building lots of the new street with single showy façades, Klenze tried to adjust to the sociological constellation by using more modest façade types, derived mainly from the Florentine early Renaissance (houses 1–7 on the Ludwigstrasse). For the further development of the street, the building of the Ministry of War established the tendency to satisfy the representational ambition of the monarch with the erection of public buildings financed by the state.

With his very first building on the edge of the northern expansion of the city, the palace for the duke of Leuchtenberg, Eugène de Beauharnais, a step-son of Napoleon (1816), Klenze created his prototype of a town palace and simultaneously established his own new orientation in opposition to the Palladian (see ANDREA PALLADIO) taste of his Munich contemporaries. The subsequent use of motifs from the palazzi of the Italian Renaissance, which Klenze was the first to implement, was, however, not achieved by imitating any specific model or precisely defined developmental phase. Rather, the motifs appear as abstract patterns of an idealized style set into the plastered wall whose surfaces are emphasized by a frame of rusticated bands at the base and corners and by a slightly protruding cornice. The motifs themselves are a row of eleven aedicula-framed windows over each of three stories, the middle ones being distinguished by triangular gables contrasting with the architraves of the two others. The portico of the portal, carried by double columns—obviously taken from the Farnese Palace in Rome—appears in contrast like a high-relief accent applied to the plane of the wall with its precisely organized ornamentation. The town palaces on the neighboring Wittelsbach Platz (Arco-Palais, 1824, and Alfons-Palais, 1826) are also façade compositions made up of prototypical Renaissance elements, filtered so to speak, through the teachings of Durand.

In the roughly contemporaneous Ministry of War (1826–1830), Klenze achieved a synthesis of balanced planar composition and three-dimensional modeling of the body of the building. In spite of the obvious influence of the Palazzo Pitti in Florence, Klenze managed here to dramatize the architectural theme in ways of his own. The richly instrumented rustication of the three-part building group eloquently suggests the iconology of its purpose. The contrast between the rusticated ground floor with its open pier arcades running the width of the central block and the plastered wall of the upper stories with its round-arched windows framed by rustication—as opposed to the smooth ashlar framing of the ground-floor windows—results in a free play of architectural effects.

In addition to the private commission for the Leuchtenberg Palace at the beginning of Klenze's Munich career, he received an assignment from the crown prince to build a museum of ancient sculpture, the Glyptothek (1816). Klenze's realization of this, a favorite project of the crown prince, came only after a competition in which the designs of Haller von Hallerstein and KARL VON FISCHER stand out; these designs were available to Klenze for his own work. The basic idea of the king was a broadly based complex modeled after the Propylaea of the Acropolis. As the gateway to the treasures of Greek sculpture, it was to be oriented toward the (later) Königsplatz. Klenze's design introduced three variants of stylistic epochs: façades in the Greek, Roman, and Italian Renaissance styles were intended as references to the main holdings of the collection. The version that Klenze built represents a synthesis of these styles. The main side of the roughly square four-wing complex, facing the plaza, is dominated by an eight-column pedimented portico flanked by windowless side wings enriched by aedicula-framed niches. Thus, on the exterior an Ionic temple frontispiece and a Renaissance palazzo (Palazzo del Te) are unified. The spaces in the interior, consisting of vaulted halls and groups of halls, contain mural decorations in the style of RAPHAEL's *grotteschi,* providing an iconographic accompaniment to the program of the collection. The architecture of the museum was thus not only a protective frame for

Klenze.
Ministry of War.
Munich.
1826–1830

the art objects it sheltered but also an important and active element of the total didactic and artistic program.

The painting gallery (Pinakothek, begun 1826) of a decade later shows a comparable tendency toward a *Gesamtkunstwerk.* It, however, was not conceived after the typological scheme of a *Kunsttempel* (temple of art) but rather as a freestanding gallery, built in the tradition of the baroque palace. The body of the building is 127 meters long, with protruding east and west corner pavilions. Two different wall systems, again taken from the Italian Renaissance palazzo, govern the two stories. Above the somewhat soclelike ground floor with its even rhythm of round-arched windows framed by rectangular aediculae, the upper story of the southern, main façade and the outer sides of the corner wings open to fully fenestrated intervals between the half-column protrusions of the classical Roman tabularium. Here, too, the adaptation of various window motifs—using the aedicula frames of the Palazzo della Cancelleria in Rome for the lower story and the tabularium motif in the tradition of DONATO BRAMANTE's Belvedere Court in the Vatican for the main story as Klenze liked to do—leads to a new architectural unity. Unity is further achieved by the classicist principle of a symmetrical arrangement, reinforced by the colonnade motif of the southern, entrance side.

Klenze
Pinakothek.
Munich.
1826–1836

In the Pinakothek, too, the use of motifs from the Italian Renaissance on the exterior is given iconographic correspondence in the decorative program of the interior, which is informed by the then current idealization of Raphael; the cornerstone of the Pinakothek was laid on the birthday of the venerated painter.

Simultaneously with the Pinakothek, Klenze began his alterations of the royal residence. His changes dealt with the façades and the suite of rooms on the south (Königsbau, 1826–1835) and, on the north, with the garden front and the royal festival rooms (Festsaalbau, 1832–1842). In the eastern part of the vast residence complex, the result of five centuries of accretions, Klenze erected his only Munich church, the Allerheiligen-Hofkirche (1826–1837), a domed building the form of which is based on San Marco in Venice, but with exterior motifs deriving from the Romanesque. For the *Königsbau,* Klenze—again his motivation was iconological—chose the Palazzo Pitti in Florence as his model. He refined its powerful rusticated walls ornamentally and, by using the pilaster orders of the Palazzo Ruccelai for the two upper stories together with round-arched windows, transposed the whole into a tension-filled plane.

In addition to the formal motivic similarity to the Palazzo Pitti, its function as a determinant of the plaza made it particularly valuable as a model. As in Florence, the aspect of the royal residence facing the town was defined by the façade of the *Königsbau.* The character of the area allotted to it was already set on the east by the National Theater of von Fischer with its dominant motif of an Ionic pedimented portico (rebuilt by Klenze in 1823–1825 in altered forms). With the rebuilding (1836) of the existing Törring Palace after FILIPPO BRUNELLESCHI's Florentine Ospedale degli Innocenti, Klenze had constructed a further monumental plaza in the immediate vicinity of the city center. In contrast to this, to the north, on the garden façade of the palace, taking the wide garden spaces into account, he placed a dominant sculptural accent: over a five-bay pier arcade there rises a freely transposed colonnade with tabularium motif and strongly molded figures decorating the entablature. Thus, even the remodeling of the Residenz shows Klenze's free use of the Italian paradigms. What is essential is not the correctness of the historic quotation but its free interpretation and adaptation in the respective environmental and iconographic context.

A final group of Klenze's buildings can more clearly than the rest be assigned to the central building concern of the century, namely, the national monument. Although borne on the tide of popular political movements, the actual commissions came from the king: the Walhalla as a temple of fame for the most famous men of the nation (1830-1842), the Ruhmeshalle (hall of fame) in Munich for the great men of Bavaria (1843–1854), and the Befreiungshalle (hall of liberation) near Kelheim on the Danube as a memorial to the dead of the Napoleonic war of liberation (an adaptation of designs by Friedrich von Gärtner, 1842–1863). In the designs for the first two, Klenze could follow revered Greek models: the Walhalla as a Doric periptery, the Ruhmeshalle as a Greek columnar hall similar in form to the as yet unknown Pergamon altar. For the Befreiungshalle he adapted the cupola-crowned round form of the Pantheon, which, however, he dramatized on the outside after the fashion of archaic tumulus buildings.

In one of his last Munich buildings, the Propyläen, forming the eastern end of the Königsplatz (1846–1860), Klenze finally had an opportunity to reproduce the revered model of Greek classical architecture according to his own interpretation. It was the king's wish that it should also represent a monument to the Greek war of liberation. In the oeuvre of Klenze and of the architecture of the century it was, so to speak, a memorial to Doric classicism which had long since fallen victim to the pluralism of other styles.

EBERHARD DRÜEKE
Translated from German by
Beverley R. Placzek

WORKS

1816–1821, Leuchtenberg Palace; 1816–1831, Glyptothek (museum of ancient sculpture); 1823–1825, National Theater (rebuilding), Umbau; 1826–1830, Ministry of War; 1826–1835, Residenz, Königsbau; 1826–1836, Pinakothek (painting gallery); 1826–1837, Allerheiligen-Hofkirche; 1830–1842, Walhalla (Temple of Fame); 1832–1842, Residenz, Festsaalbau; 1836, Törring Palace (rebuilding); Munich. 1839–1851, Hermitage (addition), St. Petersburg, Russia. 1842–1863, Befreiungshalle (Hall of Liberation), Kelheim, Bavaria, Germany. 1843–1854, Ruhmeshalle (Hall of Fame); 1846–1860, Propyläen; Munich.

BIBLIOGRAPHY

HEDERER, OSWALD (1964)1981 *Leo von Klenze—Persönlichkeit und Werk.* Munich: Callwey.

KIENER, HANS 1922 *Leo von Klenze.* Unpublished Ph.D. dissertation, University of Munich.

Klassizismus in Bayern, Schwaben und Franken. Architektur-zeichnungen 1775–1825. 1980 Edited by Winifried Nerdinger. Munich: Münchner Stadtmuseum. Exhibition catalogue.

KLENZE, LEO VON (1822)1833 *Anweisung zur Architektur des christlichen Cultus.* Munich.

KLENZE, LEO VON 1830 *Sammlung architektonischer Entwürfe.* Munich: Cotta.

KLENZE, LEO VON 1843 *Die Walhalla in artistischer und technischer Beziehung.* Munich.
LIEB, NORBERT, and HUFNAGEL, F. (editors) (1977)1979 *Leo von Klenze: Gemälde und Zeichnungen.* Expanded ed. Munich: Residenz.

KLERK, MICHEL DE
See DE KLERK, MICHEL.

KLETTING, RICHARD

Richard Karl August Kletting (1858–1943) progressed from stonecutter in Germany, to draftsman in Paris, to architect in Salt Lake City, Utah (c.1885), from where his prolific practice extended throughout the West. He received national recognition for his Utah State Capitol (1912–1915). He was also interested in zoning and civic planning, technical training programs, and conservation.

GWEN W. STEEGE

WORKS

*1893, Saltair Beach Pavilion; c.1905, Deseret News Building; 1912–1915, Utah State Capitol; Salt Lake City, Utah.

BIBLIOGRAPHY

"Kletting, Richard." 1947 Volume 33, pages 330–331 in *National Cyclopaedia of American Biography.* New York: White.
"New State Capitol: Salt Lake City, Utah." 1916 *Architectural Record* 39:172.
WINKLER, FRANZ K. 1907 "Building in Salt Lake City." *Architectural Record* 22:15–37.

KLINT, KAARE

Kaare Klint (1888–1954) never received an academic education but was trained by his father, Peder Vilhelm Jensen-Klint, the great innovator of Danish vernacular brick architecture, and by CARL PETERSEN, the revivalist of neoclassicism in Denmark. Klint's main interest was furniture design. He taught for thirty years with profound influence at the Royal Academy in Copenhagen. From 1918, he worked on standardization systems and functional analyses. His aim was to simplify and improve traditional forms and constructions and make them fit his time and way of life. Jensen-Klint, Kaare Klint, and Ivar Bentsen developed the vital mainstream Danish architecture that is called the Klint school or Danish functional tradition. Klint was greatly influenced by furniture from China, England, and the United States.

LISBET BALSLEV JØRGENSEN

WORKS

1917–1918, Fåborg Museum (furniture; with Carl Petersen), Denmark. *1921–1942, Thorvaldsens Museum (furniture); 1928, C. L. David's Collection (interior), Kronprinsessegade; 1930–1940, Grundtvig's Church (completion); 1935–1937, Bethlehem Church; Copenhagen.

BIBLIOGRAPHY

ANDERSEN, RIGMOR 1979 *Kaare Klint, Møbler.* Copenhagen: Arkitektens Forlag. Includes a bibliography.
FISKER, KAY 1963 "Den Klintske sokole." *Arkitektur* 17, no. 2:37–80.
RASMUSSEN, STEEN EILER 1949 Volume 2, pages 136–137 in *Weilbachs Kunstnerleksikon.* Copenhagen: Aschehoug Danske Forlag.

KLUMB, HENRY

Henry Klumb (1905–) has produced a genuine tropical architecture using the natural cooling aspects of Puerto Rico's island breezes and interior gardens, bringing to life his statement that "a gradual acceptance of nature becomes in the end a need for nature" (McQuade, 1962, p. 88). In 1944, after a five-year apprenticeship with FRANK LLOYD WRIGHT at Taliesin East and surviving the Depression as an architect for the Los Angeles City Planning Commission, the German-born architect moved his family to Puerto Rico. The eight hundred dollar budget of his first commission, a rural island school, forced immediate realization of Puerto Rico's economical and climatic limitations. Klumb has overcome these obstacles by maintaining Wright's sensitivity toward nature and open planning as well as adapting designs to local building techniques and available materials.

Concrete, the island's most practical building material, has been enriched by Klumb's varied use of sun-screened façades and the introduction of precast elements in 1960 for the Parke-Davis Laboratories and for the award-winning Eli Lilly Plant (1965–1968).

A Puerto Rican enthusiast, Klumb established his architectural firm there in 1945 and has never lacked commissions, which have included the two major Commonwealth University campuses in Rio Piedras (1946–1979) and Mayagüez (1948–1971). In 1964, the American Institute of Architects made him a fellow, recognizing his dedication to solving the architectural problems of a developing tropical island.

ELIZABETH D. HARRIS

WORKS

1946–1979, University of Puerto Rico, Rio Piedras.

1948–1971, University of Puerto Rico, Mayagüez. 1957–1959, IBM Office Building, Santurce, Puerto Rico. 1960, Parke-Davis Laboratories, Carolina, Puerto Rico. 1960–1963, Miramar Condominium, Santurce, Puerto Rico. 1965–1968, Eli Lilly Pharmaceutical Plant, Carolina, Puerto Rico. 1973–1974, U.S. Post Office, Vega Baja, Puerto Rico. 1977–1980, Endo Labs Pharmaceutical Plant, Manati, Puerto Rico.

BIBLIOGRAPHY

CRISP-ELLERT, JoANN 1974 "Henry Klumb in Puerto Rico: Architecture at the Service of Society." *Journal of the American Institute of Architects* 62, July:50–53.
FERNANDEZ, JOSÉ ANTONIO 1965 *Architecture in Puerto Rico.* New York: Architectural Book Publishing.
McQUADE, WALTER 1954 "Henry Klumb Finds an Architecture for Puerto Rico." *Architectural Forum* 101, July:122–127.
McQUADE, WALTER 1962 "Klumb of Puerto Rico." *Architectural Forum* 117, July:86–90.

KNIGHT, J. G.

John George Knight (1824–1892), engineer, architect and administrator, came of a London family of dock engineers and contractors, emigrated to Melbourne in 1852, and joined the Public Works Department, but resigned for private practice in 1854. His partner Peter Kerr is generally given more credit for the design of Parliament House, Melbourne, and especially its magnificent Legislative Council Chamber; however, Knight was much involved in technical aspects. Knight was first president of the Victorian Institute of Architects, 1856–1861, was Victorian manager or representative at various international exhibitions, and in 1873 joined the public service at Darwin, Northern Territory, designing the public buildings of the town in addition to his nonarchitectural duties.

MILES LEWIS

WORKS

1854, Caldwell Train and Company Warehouse (with Thomas Kemp), Port Melbourne, Australia. 1855, Custom House (with Kemp and Peter Kerr); 1855–1856, Legislative Council and Assembly Chambers, Parliament House (with Kerr); Melbourne, 1857, Mechanic's Institute, South Melbourne, Australia. 1858, D'Estaville, Kew, Victoria, Australia. 1859, Synagogue; 1860, Kong Meng and Company Warehouse; 1860, Parliament House Library; Melbourne, Australia. 1877, Government Residence (reconstruction); 1879, Police Station; 1882, Fannie Bay Gaol (cell block); (A)1883, Courthouse; 1883, Town Hall; c.1885, Brown's Labour Mart and Mining Exchange; c.1885, Fannie Bay Gaol (infirmary); Darwin, Northern Territory, Australia.

BIBLIOGRAPHY

FREELAND, JOHN MAXWELL 1971 *The Making of a Profession.* Sydney: Angus & Robertson.
LEWIS, MILES 1972 "Tradition and Innovation in Victorian Building: 1801–1865." Unpublished Ph.D. dissertation, University of Melbourne.
LYALL, D. S. 1965 "The Architectural Profession in Melbourne: 1835–1880." Unpublished M.Arch. thesis, University of Melbourne.
MASON, W. V. 1968 "John George Knight, FRIBA." *Architecture in Australia* 3, no. 57:479–486.
O'NEILL, SALLY 1974 "Knight, John George." Volume 5, page 37 in *Australian Dictionary of Biography.* Carlton, Australia: Melbourne University Press.

KNIGHT, R. P.

Richard Payne Knight (1750–1824), English classicist, connoisseur, and speculative aesthetician, is noteworthy architecturally for one country house, Downton Castle, Herefordshire, designed for and by himself in 1772, and for a textbook of late eighteenth-century aesthetics, *An Analytical Inquiry into the Principles of Taste,* in which he discusses, among other things, contemporary architectural ideas, particularly the Picturesque. Knight was twenty-two when he designed Downton, and his house is a typical youthful work in which the author enjoys being *outré.* The house is neomedieval not classical; it is wilfully, though picturesquely, set on a long ridge, and, most revolutionary of all, it is quite asymmetrical in its plan. Knight claimed that the house was built to look like the architecture in Claude's landscape drawings of which he had a large collection. Picturesquely composed it thus lacks any axis in its plan, and is the first new-built irregular building in the history of English modern architecture. As an amateur, Knight was assisted by the local early Gothic Revival architect THOMAS PRITCHARD of Shrewsbury. The influence of his ideas is keenly marked in the work of JOHN NASH who remodeled parts of the house about 1810.

ALISTAIR ROWAN

WORK

1772–1778, Downton Castle, Herefordshire, England.

BIBLIOGRAPHY

HUSSEY, CHRISTOPHER 1956 Pages 148–152 in *English Country Houses, Mid Georgian, 1760–1800.* London: Country Life.
KNIGHT, RICHARD PAYNE 1794 *The Landscape: A Didactic Poem.* London.
KNIGHT, RICHARD PAYNE (1805)1972 *An Analytical Inquiry into the Principles of Taste.* Reprint. Westmead, England: Gregg.
PEVSNER, NIKOLAUS 1949 "Richard Payne Knight."

Art Bulletin 31:293–320.

ROWAN, ALISTAIR 1970 "Downton Castle, Herefordshire." Pages 170–173 in Howard Colvin and John Harris (editors), *The Country Seat: Studies in the History of the British Country House Presented to Sir John Summerson.* London: Allen Lane.

KNOBELSDORFF, GEORG WENCESLAUS VON

Freiherr Georg Wenceslaus von Knobelsdorff (1699–1753) was born on the Kurckädel Estate in the Cossen (Oder) district of Germany. Beginning his military career in 1714, he rose to the position of captain before illness forced him to resign. Subsequently, the musically gifted Knobelsdorff studied painting at the Berlin Academy under his friend Antoine Pesne and then architecture under A. von Wangenheim and Johann Gottfried Kemmeter. In 1732, he traveled to Dresden, the capital of Saxony. Closely befriended with Crown Prince Frederick of Prussia, he accompanied the prince to Neuruppin (Brandenburg) in 1732 and designed there the Temple of Apollo, a Tuscan monopteros in the prince's Amalthea Garden (1735, altered 1794). At Frederick's urging, Knobelsdorff toured Italy in 1736–1737, remaining for some time in Venice, Florence, and Rome. He principally studied ancient art and architecture and remained largely indifferent to modern Italian architecture. After his return from Italy, he took up residence in the crown prince's court at Rheinsberg (Brandenburg) where he took over the remodeling of the Schloss, which Kemmeter had begun in 1735. Knobelsdorff designed the court façade of the *corps de logis* and its counterpart facing the lake, the open Ionic colonnade galleries, as well as the interiors. Together with the crown prince, whose own taste for French art and for Watteau in particular had been formed by association with Pesne and Knobelsdorff, he drew plans for a "Forum Fredericianum" at the beginning of the Linden Allee in Berlin. Around it were to be placed a new palace, an opera house, and an Academy building. After Frederick II's ascension to the throne, Knobelsdorff was appointed *Oberintendant* (director) of Royal Palaces and Gardens in 1740. He served also as director of theater and music until 1742. A brief trip in the fall of 1740 via Dresden to Paris with a return journey through Flanders served as intense preparation for the future major building tasks and had a decisive influence on Knobelsdorff's architecture. Upon his return, he launched into an active building campaign in Berlin with cooperation of the king. With the erection of the Opera House (1741–1743), he began to realize his Forum

Fredericianum, although this was completed later in a different form (Opernplatz). At the same time, he worked on an extension to Schloss Monbijou (1740–1742) for the queen and the new wing of Schloss Charlottenburg (1740–1743) as a country seat for Frederick the Great. When the king transferred his seat to Potsdam, Knobelsdorff remodeled and redecorated the Stadtschloss there (1744–1751).

The Park of Sanssouci, near Potsdam, was also carried out according to his designs. Following precise instructions from the king, the Weinbergschloss at Sanssouci was constructed, but the planning of this palace resulted in differences with the king and led to Knobelsdorff's estrangement from the crown. Although he was not formally dismissed nor did he resign, Knobelsdorff withdrew from the court and from the supervision of its buildings, which were taken over by his subordinate Johann Boumann the Elder. Knobelsdorff then worked for the court of Anhalt in Dessau (renovation of the Schloss, 1747–1751). Only in 1750 did the king and the ailing architect reconcile their differences, after which Knobelsdorff designed extensions and garden structures for the park of Sanssouci. After returning from a curative trip to a spa, he died in Berlin in 1753. The king's "Eloge de Knobelsdorff" read before the Academy of Sciences in 1754 was a worthy memorial to the architect.

The "Frederician rococo" was created through Knobelsdorff's close cooperation with the dilettante architect king. Based on his own style, which was much influenced by the French architects CLAUDE PERRAULT and JULES HARDOUIN MANSART as well as the theories of the French Academy and ANDREA PALLADIO, it was determined in equal measure by the king's retrospective taste for "historical" architecture and Knobelsdorff's aca-

Knobelsdorff.
Schloss Sanssouci (Neues Palais).
Potsdam, Germany.
1745–1747

demic training. Already in Rheinberg they had developed together the typical motifs of this style: courts and garden spaces bordered by colonnades of paired columns; façades likewise adorned with coupled orders; simple, unornamented articulation of the building mass, determined and proportioned by colossal orders on projected wings; and rich, gay, but clearly articulated rocaille decoration in interiors. Knobelsdorff's style was thenceforth characterized by a simplicity, refinement, and elegance that was reposeful in the restrained use of decorative elements and classically graceful proportions. In its original form, the Opera House in Berlin—the first freestanding structure of its type—best embodied this style. It was a rectangular cubic building, seven by nineteen bays wide and one-and-a-half stories in height. Its main street façade featured a gabled portico of six Corinthian columns in the manner of an ancient temple front. This portico, together with the surrounding base and cornice of the building, determined the principal proportions. Otherwise, the building was articulated only by its window bays and a pilaster relief portico, without gable, in the center of each of the long side façades. Contemporaries viewed this early neoclassical building, equally marked by French Academicism and English Palladianism, as "Greek" because of its simplicity, restraint, and elegance as well as for its written dedication to "Apollo and the Muses" in the pediment. In both form and style, the building suitably embodied its functional and cultural intent. Knobelsdorff's palace exteriors are characterized by the same tendency. In accord with the individual commission, he embodied a worthy solemnity, which suited the king's wishes as well as the preconditions of the task, be it an extension or the remodeling of an older complex.

Knobelsdorff's outstanding achievements as an interior designer have recently been investigated and evaluated by Tilo Eggeling (1980). Taking inspiration from the French rococo, Knobelsdorff placed equal value on the variety and richness of individual ornamental forms and on a clear, easily comprehended arrangement of the over-all decorative system. Within the restrained articulation of the organizing framework, single forms correspond to one another by repetition and mirror-image reversals. The dining room and Green Gallery in the new wing of Schloss Charlottenburg through this manner of decoration achieve a heightened festivity and elegance marking them at once as the richest accomplishment of Frederician rococo and one of the masterpieces of rococo decoration anywhere.

Knobelsdorff's churches—the designs for the Roman Catholic Saint Hedwig in Berlin (1746) and for the French Reformed Church in Potsdam (1752)—were conceived as central plans with vaulted rotundas and pedimented columnar porticoes. Modeled on the Roman Pantheon, they are another example of the conscious, enlightened references to ancient architecture.

Knobelsdorff's most important achievement consists of his felicitous formulation of an unmistakably independent style, uniting early neoclassical tendencies of French and English derivation with elements of the rococo. Next to JOHANN BALTHASAR NEUMANN, he was the most prominent architect of his time in Germany. His architecture and decorative style were influential at the Prussian court even thirty years after his death; his influence spread also to other central German courts such as those at Dessau and Kassel.

FRITZ-EUGEN KELLER and
INA MARIA KELLER
Translated from German by
Barry Bergdoll

WORKS

1735, Temple of Apollo (later altered), Amalthea Garden, Neuruppin; 1737–1740, Schloss Rheinsberg (remodeling); Brandenburg, Germany. *1738–1742, Schloss Monbijou (remodeling and extensions), Berlin. 1740 and later, Rheinsberg (reconstruction after fire damage), Brandenburg, Germany. 1740–1743, Schloss Charlottenburg (new wing); 1741–1743, Opera House (later altered, enlarged, and reconstructed), Berlin. 1744–1746, Schloss (new wing), Zerbst, Saxon Anhalt, Germany. *1744–1751, Stadtschloss; 1744–1753, Sanssouci Park; 1745–1747, Schloss Sanssouci; Potsdam, Germany. *1747–1751, Schloss (reconstruction; never completed), Dessau, Germany. 1747–1773, Saint Hedwig's (executed by Johann Boumann the Elder; later reconstructed in altered form), Berlin. 1750, Lehmann House, Old Market; 1751–1752, House of the Equestrian Bodyguard; 1751–1753, Neptune Grotto and Deer Park Colonnade, Sanssouci Park; 1752, French Church (later damaged); Potsdam, Germany.

BIBLIOGRAPHY

EGGELING, TILO 1980 *Studien zum friderizianischen Rokoko: Georg Wenceslaus von Knobelsdorff als Entwerfer von Innendekorationen.* Berlin.

GIERSBERG, HANS JOACHIM 1975 "Studien zur Architektur des 18. Jahrhunderts in Berlin und Potsdam." Unpublished Ph.D. dissertation, Humboldt Universität, Berlin.

HEMPEL, EBERHARD 1965 Pages 265–271 in *Baroque Art and Architecture in Central Europe.* Harmondsworth, England: Penguin.

KNOBELSDORFF, WILHELM VON 1862 *Georg Wenceslaus von Knobelsdorff.* Berlin.

KÜHN, MARGARETE 1953 *Georg Wenceslaus von Knobelsdorff.* Berlin.

KÜHN, MARGARETE 1955 Pages 57–78 in *Schloss Charlottenburg.* Berlin: Dentscher Verein für Kunstwissenschaft.

KURTH, WILLY 1970 *Sanssouci: Ein Beitrag zur Kunst des Deutschen Rokoko.* Berlin: Henschel.

STREICHHAN, ANNALIESE 1932 *Knobelsdorff und das friderizianische Rokoko.* Burg bei Magdeburg, Germany: Hopfer.

KNOBLAUCH, EDUARD

The first of KARL FRIEDRICH SCHINKEL's followers to devote himself to private architectural practice, Carl Heinrich Eduard Knoblauch (1801–1865)—along with FRIEDRICH HITZIG and FRIEDRICH AUGUST STÜLER—defined the characteristic Italianate style of mid-century Berlin domestic architecture. Knoblauch's plans, incorporating carefully studied and generous lighting and circulation, were seen especially as models. He also designed a series of castellated Gothic country houses. The Berlin Synagogue (1859–1866), a synthesis of Moorish and medieval elements following the lead of GOTTFRIED SEMPER and LUDWIG VON FÖRSTER's synagogues, had interiors by Stüler who, with Knoblauch's son Gustav, took over in 1862 when mental illness forced Knoblauch's retirement. Knoblauch's influence was magnified through the *Architekten Verein* (Architects' Association), which he helped found in 1824, and through his long editorship of the *Zeitschrift für Bauwesen*.

BARRY BERGDOLL

WORKS

*1833, Hossauer House, 28 Kronenstrasse; *1835, Double Villa for the Knoblauch and Stüler Families, 105 Potsdamer Strasse; 1837, Ville Caspar, 16 Bellevuestrasse; *1840–1841, Russian Embassy (remodeling of Princess Amalie's Palace), Unter den Linden; *1841, Werdinger Hospital; *1842–1844, Kroll's Winter Garden (after sketches by LUDWIG PERSIUS and King Friedrich Wilhelm IV); Berlin. 1843, School, Posen, Germany (now Poland). *1846–1847, Knoblauch House, Berlin. c.1850, Anhalt-Dessauische Landesbank, Dessau, Germany. c.1856, Marienberg House, near Rosnowo, Germany. *1857–1858, Arnim-Boytzenburg Palace, Pariser Platz; *1856, Synagogue (remodeling); *1858–1860, Jewish Hospital, 14 Augustrasse; 1859–1866, Synagogue (completed by Friedrich August Stüler and Gustav Knoblauch; only ruins survive); Berlin.

BIBLIOGRAPHY

ASSMANN, G. 1865 "Carl Heinrich Eduard Knoblauch." *Zeitschrift für Bauwesen* 15:427–434.

BÖRSCH-SUPAN, EVA 1977 *Berliner Baukunst nach Schinkel: 1840–1870.* Munich: Prestel.

KNOBLAUCH, GUSTAV, and HOLLEN, F. 1878 *Die neue Synagoge in Berlin.* Berlin: Ernst & Korn.

WALLÉ, PETER 1901 "Eduard Knoblauch." *Centralblatt der Bauverwaltung* 21:469–471.

"Zur Erinnerung an Eduard Knoblauch." 1901 *Deutsche Bauzeitung* 35:486–487, 489–492.

KNOTT, RALPH N.

Born in London, Ralph N. Knott (1878–1929) was articled to Wood and Ainslie and subsequently spent eight years in ASTON WEBB's office. He was only twenty-nine when, in 1908, he won the competition for the new London County Council's County Hall. With Arnold Thornely, he worked on the designs for the Northern Ireland Parliament House, Belfast. From 1921, he was in partnership with E. S. Collins.

GODFREY RUBENS

WORKS

1908–1922, London County Hall, Lambeth, London. 1913, Actor's Orphanage, Langley, Buckinghamshire, England. 1913, Henley Factory, Gravesend, Kent, England. 1913, 18 Upper Brook Street; 1913, 1 and 21 Upper Grosvenor Street; London.

BIBLIOGRAPHY

The Builder 1929 136, no. 2:255.
Journal of the Royal Institute of British Architects. 1928–1929 36:296.

KNOWLES, J. T. SR., and KNOWLES, J. T. JR.

James Thomas Knowles, Sr. (1806–1884) was the son of a glazier at Reigate, Surrey, England. He rose from a late Georgian craft apprenticeship in the 1820s to early Victorian success as an architect of large Grecian country houses before moving in 1839 to Clapham in south London, where in 1845 he built himself an Italianate house. His London reputation rose in the mid-1850s with several urban palazzi. His personal style, with his son's assistance, crystallized in designs for the Grosvenor Hotel at Victoria Station (1860–1862) and for a large villa in Portugal (1863–1865). His "Grosvenor style" was a brief blend of Gothic, Moorish, Renaissance–classical, and Ruskinian (see JOHN RUSKIN) elements; it was notable for "eyelids" of window tracery and much carved foliage on wall surfaces. In subsequent, increasingly conservative work the senior Knowles simplified this style.

James Thomas Knowles, Jr. (1831–1908), also born at Reigate, trained in his father's Gray's Inn office from 1846 to 1853 assisting him from 1855 to 1859. His own works from 1860 on included terraces of large houses, rows of small houses, and new churches in South London, a clubhouse and a block of flats in central London, and Aldworth (1868–1869) in Sussex for Alfred Lord Tennyson. For all but the last, he derived inspiration from his father's Grosvenor style; for the last, under the poet's influence, early Gothic ornament was applied to a late Gothic manor house.

With a flair for fashionable thought and with much nonarchitectural ambition, Knowles meanwhile founded the Metaphysical Society for private discussions of philosophical issues by great men. While still practicing architecture on the side (to c.1885), he edited the *Contemporary Review* until, in 1877, he founded his own monthly review, the *Nineteenth Century,* which he edited until his death. Becoming publicly influential (credited, for example, with stopping schemes for a Channel Tunnel), he was knighted in 1903.

The Knowleses' architectural–historical importance lay in their attempt to reconcile opposing trends in the mid-century battle of styles.

PRISCILLA METCALF

WORKS

J. T. KNOWLES, SR.

*1837, Bramley Park, Surrey, England. *c.1839, Dangstein House, Sussex, England. *1839–1845, Silverton Park, Devon, England. *1845, Friday Grove, Clapham Park, Surrey, England. *1852–1854, Cook Warehouse, Saint Paul's Churchyard; 1854, 15 Kensington Palace Gardens; *1854–1855, Hodgson Auction Rooms and Offices, Fleet Street; 1860–1862, Grosvenor Hotel, Victoria Station; *1862–1863, Tarn's Drapery Shop; London. 1863–1865, Villa Monserrate, Sintra, Portugal. 1865, Hedsor House, Buckinghamshire, England.

J. T. KNOWLES, JR.

1860–1871, Cedars Estate, Clapham Common, and Cedars Road (villas demolished); 1862–1874, (Former) Thatched House Club, Saint James's Street; 1867–1868, Albert Mansions (demolished except west end); London. 1868–1869, Aldworth; 1871–1873, West Brighton Estate (sea-front ranges), Hove; Sussex, England. 1874, Leicester Square (fountain and garden layout); *1874–1875, Kensington House; London. 1879–1880, Royal Sea-Bathing Infirmary (west wing, chapel, and gatelodge), Margate, Kent, England.

BIBLIOGRAPHY

METCALF, PRISCILLA 1978 *The Park Town Estate and the Battersea Tangle.* London Topographical Society.
METCALF, PRISCILLA 1980 *James Knowles, Victorian Editor and Architect.* Oxford: Clarendon Press.

KNUTSEN, KNUT

Knut Knutsen (1903–1969), one of Norway's most important modern architects, attended the architectural section of the Statens Handverks- og Kunstindustriskole (1920–1925), where he became an instructor in 1934. Appointed professor at the Polytechnic Institute, Oslo, in 1966, Knutsen was concerned with domestic architecture suitable for twentieth-century needs.

JUDITH S. HULL

WORKS

*1937, Norwegian Pavilion, International Exposition, Paris. 1947, Collective Housing, Tåsen, Norway. 1952, Norwegian Embassy, Stockholm. 1952, Vacation House, Portør, Norway. 1953, Strandgarden Hotel, Gjøvik, Norway. 1953, Viking Hotel, Oslo.

BIBLIOGRAPHY

"Aørne Korsmo—Knut Knutsen. Arkitekturunstilling Henie-Onstad Kunstsenter." 1972 *Byggekunst* 54, no. 6:162–175.

KOCH, GAETANO

Gaetano Koch (1849–1910), the grandson of the German painter Johan Anton Koch, worked mainly in Rome in the Cinquecento style although he was also inspired by Tuscan and Palladian (see ANDREA PALLADIO) models. His designs are marked by their stylistic restraint as opposed to the more extravagant trends prevalent in the work of his contemporaries.

JOHN H. WILSON

WORKS

1880, Palazzi, Piazza dell'Esedra; 1885–1892, Banca d'Italia, Via Nazionale; 1885–1911, Monument to Victor Emanuel II (completion of GIUSEPPE SACCONI's designs; with Manfredo Manfredi and PIO PIACENTINI); 1886–1890, Palazzo Margherita (Palazzo Boncampagni; now the United States Embassy), Via Veneto; 1887, Biblioteca del Senato; after 1902, Museo Barracco; Rome.

BIBLIOGRAPHY

HITCHCOCK, H. R. (1958)1977 *Architecture: Nineteenth and Twentieth Centuries.* 4th ed., rev. Baltimore: Penguin.
MEEKS, CARROLL L. V. 1966 *Italian Architecture: 1750–1914.* New Haven: Yale University Press.
PORTOGHESI, PAOLO 1968 *L'eclettismo a Roma: 1870-1922.* Rome: de Luca.

KOCHER and FREY

Alfred Lawrence Kocher (1885–1969) and Albert Frey (1903–), working together 1930–1936, pioneered functionalist theory and modern design in America. Born in San Jose, California, Kocher studied medieval history and architecture. Frey, born in Zurich, studied engineering, then turned to architecture, inspired mainly by LE CORBUSIER.

After working for Le Corbusier (1929–1930), Frey sought greater technological opportunities in America, where he met Kocher, the managing editor of *Architectural Record* (1928–1938). Kocher's thorough knowledge of materials complemented Frey's commitment to advanced design. Their Aluminaire House (1931), built in ten days for the New York Architectural League Show, and their Weekend House in Northport, New York (1934), were boldly experimental. The former was the most extreme adaptation of Corbusian principles in America.

Although both had notable careers after 1936, their early cooperative ventures—writing and building—gave timely impetus to the developing modern movement in the United States.

FOLKE T. KIHLSTEDT

WORKS

1931, Aluminaire House, Syosset, N.Y. *1934, Weekend House, Northport, N.Y. 1934–1935, Real Estate Office, Palm Springs, Calif.

BIBLIOGRAPHY

FREY, ALBERT 1939 *In Search of a Living Architecture.* New York: Architectural Book Publishing Company.
KOCHER, A. LAWRENCE 1926 "The Country House: Are We Developing an American Style?" *Architectural Record* 60:385–502.
KOCHER, A. LAWRENCE, and DEARSTYNE, HOWARD 1943 "The Architectural Center." *New Pencil Points* July:26–49.
KOCHER, A. LAWRENCE, and DEARSTYNE, HOWARD 1949 *Colonial Williamsburg: Its Buildings and Gardens.* Williamsburg, Va.: Colonial Williamsburg.
KOCHER, A. LAWRENCE, and FREY, ALBERT 1931a "Windows." *Architectural Record* 69:126–137.
KOCHER, A. LAWRENCE, and FREY, ALBERT 1931b "Real Estate Subdivisions for Low-Cost Housing." *Architectural Record* 69:323–327.
KOCHER, A. LAWRENCE, and FREY, ALBERT 1933 "New Materials and Improved Construction Methods." *Architectural Record* 73:281–293.
KOCHER, A. LAWRENCE, and FREY, ALBERT 1934 "Low-Cost Farmhouse." *Architectural Record* 75:30.

KOHTZ, OTTO

The architectural works and writings of Otto Kohtz (1880–?) indicate that he was among those who pursued certain ideals of modernism within a strong framework of traditionalism. His design training began at the Kunstgewerbeschule and the Baugewerbeschule in Berlin and he concluded studies at the Technische Hochschule in Charlottenburg, Germany. Kohtz, with his partner E. Schütze,

was responsible for numerous commercial office buildings in Berlin and for many homes in the Berlin suburbs. Of his independent work, the best known was his Administration Building of the Imperial Farmer's Union (1911–1912), Berlin-Friedenau; the Home for Bachelors in Berlin-Moabit (1913–1914); and the Scherl Publishing House (1925–1928), Berlin.

The unity of Kohtz's designs is the result of a steadfast reliance upon compositional principles of the academic tradition and a preference for historical models and motifs. Simple, pared-down forms most often of brick and stone, repetitive rhythms, and monumentality are the keynotes of his urban style. Aside from his essays which appeared occasionally in various professional journals, Kohtz published three books, *Gedanken über Architektur* (1909), *Das Reichshaus in Berlin* (1920), and *Büroturmhäuser in Berlin* (1921). In the latter two publications, Kohtz commented on aspects of his work, studies for a Reichshaus on Berlin's Königsplatz and his (and E. Schütze's) multistory office buildings.

Kohtz's book, *Gedanken über Architektur,* is a series of fifty-five uncommissioned drawings with a brief introductory essay. The drawings, created between 1904 and 1909, unite fantasy and academicism, many of the schemes relating to those by contemporary architects such as Otto Rieth, BRUNO SCHMITZ, and WILHELM KREIS. Like those of his contemporaries, Kohtz's imaginary designs for monuments and public buildings reflect a sentiment in Wilhelmine Germany that looked to monuments of powerful scale, dramatic massing, commanding spatial effects, and impressive ornament and sculptural detail as an effective way of communicating something of the imperial might and cultural prowess of Germany. Numerous monuments were erected from the 1880s onward and national competitions for their design were a common procedure. In 1911, Kohtz had entered a competition for a monument to Bismarck near Bingen and won fourth prize. In his imaginary schemes, however, Kohtz was not centering on programs of imperial symbolism but drew freely upon the vocabularies of classical, Byzantine, Oriental, and Mayan architecture as a way of exploring the emotional content of various styles. Contained in the drawings are an additive sequential arrangement of units, a hierarchical rigor, and a breadth of scale that also typified Kohtz's built designs.

A group of eight drawings in the *Gedanken* represented an architecture inspired by natural forms. Like many of his contemporaries within the Arts and Crafts movement, Kohtz claimed that the poetic possibilities of architecture could be amplified by incorporating the laws of other arts and the laws of nature into architectural design. Undoubtedly inspired by the early writings of the journalist, poet, and novelist PAUL SCHEERBART, Kohtz foresaw a time when the earth would be worked freely through incredible synaesthetic effects so as to orchestrate emotions. For Kohtz, the result of such creative efforts would be an architecture produced by both fantasy and reason and one yielding a range of architectural expressions comparable in breadth to that which is found in the natural realm. He even speculated that, comparable to different species of animals and plants, architecture might one day be distinguished by "a land-style, an air-style, a water-style, a style of swiftness and idleness and by gradations of these."

There is an apparent gap between Kohtz's *Gedanken* and his actual output. Although his subsequent designs for buildings and monuments contain compositional ideas first presented in the early drawings, his eloquent call for a new poetry of architecture seems rather distant from his built work. Kohtz's career is but one example of the strong role of tradition in modern architecture.

EUGENE A. SANTOMASSO

WORKS

1906–1907, Electrical Plant Southwest, Schöneberg; 1911–1912, Imperial Farmer's Union Administration Building, Friedenau; 1913–1914, Home for Bachelors, Moabit; 1922–1923, Otto Kohtz House, Dahlem; 1925–1928, Scherl Publishing House; Berlin. 1929, Universum-Film Subsidiary Sound Studios, Neubabelsberg, Germany.

BIBLIOGRAPHY

CONRADS, ULRICH, and SPERLICH, HANS G. 1962 *The Architecture of Fantasy: Utopian Building and Planning in Modern Times.* Translated, edited, and expanded by Christiane C. Collins and George R. Collins. New York: Praeger.
KOHTZ, OTTO 1909 *Gedanken über Architektur.* Berlin: Baumgärtel.
KOHTZ, OTTO 1920 *Das Reichshaus in Berlin.* Berlin.
KOHTZ, OTTO 1921 *Büroturmhäuser in Berlin.* Berlin.
KOHTZ, OTTO 1930 *Otto Kohtz.* With an introduction by Werner Hegemann. Berlin: Hübsch.
PONTEN, JOSEF 1925 *Architektur die nicht gebaut wurde.* 2 vols. Stuttgart, Germany: Deutsche Verlags-Anstalt.
WHITTICK, ARNOLD 1950–1953 *European Architecture in the Twentieth Century.* 2 vols. London: Lockwood.

KONSTANTINIDIS, ARIS

Born in Athens, Aris Konstantinidis studied architecture in Munich. He was employed by the Greek state from 1938 until 1967. He taught in Zurich from 1967 to 1970. In the steps of D. A. PIKIONIS, Konstantinidis formulated his theory for a "true architecture," one that seeks to adapt simplicity, tradition, and technology to public demands for housing.

VASSILIA PH. PETSAS

WORKS

1956, Workers' Housing, Aghios Ioannis Rentis, Athens. 1958, Xenia Hotel, Andros, Greece. 1959, National Tourism Organization Pavilion, at the International Trade Fair, Thessaloniki, Greece. 1965, Archeological Museum, Ioannina, Greece. 1967, Archeological Museum, Komotini, Greece.

BIBLIOGRAPHY

KONSTANTINIDIS, ARIS 1962 "Aris Konstantinidis." *Zygos* 82–83, Sept.–Oct.: 27–50.
KONSTANTINIDIS, ARIS 1964 "Architecture." *Architectural Design* 34, no. 5:212–235.
KONSTANTINIDIS, ARIS 1975 *Elements for Self-knowledge.* Translated by Kay Cicellis. Athens.
KONSTANTINIDIS, ARIS 1978 *Synchrone Alethine Architektonike.* Athens.

KÖRNER, EDMUND

Edmund Hermann George Körner (1875–?) was a leading architect in Essen, Düsseldorf, and Darmstadt, Germany, from the first decade of the twentieth century. After studying at the Technische Hochschulen in Dresden and Berlin-Charlottenburg, Körner entered the municipal building administration of Essen, where he built many municipal buildings, office buildings, and factories. Körner taught briefly at the Künstlerkolonie in Darmstadt, from 1911 to around 1914, and maintained close relations with Bernhard Hoetger and other Expressionist architects. He was best known for cemetery design and for his overwhelming and massive Synagogue (Essen, 1913), executed in rough-cut masonry and entirely devoid of historical references.

BARBARA MILLER LANE

WORKS

1913, Synagogue, Essen, Germany. *1914, Buildings, Exhibition of Darmstadt Künstlerkolonie, Germany. 1914?, Building Trades School; 1914?, Waldhausen House; 1925, Bourse; 1925–?, Folkwang Museum Extensions; Essen. n.d., Arenberg A-G Offices, Essen, Germany. n.d., Bank, Düsseldorf, Germany. n.d., Church, Frillendorf, Germany. n.d., Church of Saint Peter, Althenesson, Germany. n.d., Dippelshof Estate (with Bernhard Hoetger), near Darmstadt, Germany. n.d., Factory, Magdeburg, Germany. n.d., Gewerkschaft Helene-Amalie Offices, Essen, Germany. n.d., Girardet

Publishing House, Düsseldorf, Germany. n.d., Housing Development, Althenessen, Germany. n.d., Housing Development, Camillo Sitte-Platz, Essen, Germany. n.d., Housing Development; n.d., Mackensen Offices; Magdeburg, Germany. n.d., Meerenbusch Estate, near Düsseldorf, Germany.

BIBLIOGRAPHY

HOFF, AUGUST 1925 "Die neue Börse in Essen." *Deutsche Bauzeitung* 59:429–434, 437–443.
KLAPHECK, RICHARD 1914 *Die neue Synagoge in Essen.* Berlin: Wasmuth.
Wasmuths Monatshefte für Baukunst und Städtebau 1914–1915 1:92.

KORNHÄUSEL, JOSEF

Josef Kornhäusel (1782–1860) was not only one of Vienna's most important and productive architects but also a well-known figure of the time before the revolution of 1848.

Kornhäusel's father owned a construction company, where he at first was educated and which he later took over. Nothing is known about his academic career, but in 1808 he was a member of Vienna's Academy. His studio was at times a meeting place for Viennese society. At the beginning of his career as an architect, he designed primarily housing projects in Vienna and its surroundings (1802), using a nondecorative neoclassicism. As Joseph Hardtmuth's successor, he directed building activity for Prince Johann of Liechtenstein from 1812 to 1818, designing several projects for the latter's palace in Lednice, Czechoslovakia.

After several other projects in Vienna and its surroundings, he built his major work of architecture, the Palace of Weilburg in Baden near Vienna for Archduke Carl. The cubic monumentality of this building owes much to KARL VON MOREAU. In his late work, Kornhäusel was mainly concerned with several monasteries in Vienna. The clear form of these buildings, well suited to their purpose, greatly influenced Vienna's future style in housing architecture. He also built the main synagogue for the Vienna Jewish community (1825–1826). His last piece of work was the completion of the baroque monastery of Klosterneuburg near Vienna (1834–1842). In 1840, he seems to have stopped working.

Kornhäusel's numerous buildings throughout Vienna and its surroundings, especially the city of Baden, constitute a characteristic feature of early nineteenth-century townscape in this area. The simplicity of decor in his neoclassicistic architecture put its mark on Vienna's architecture in the Biedermeier period.

ECKART VANCSA

WORKS

*1807–1808, Circus Bach, Vienna. 1812, Husarentempel, near Mödling, Austria. 1815, Townhall; *1820–1823, Weilburg; Baden, Austria. 1822, Albertina Palace (decoration of rooms); 1825–1826, Synagogue; 1827–1835, Schottenstift; 1836–1837, Mechitaristenkloster; Vienna. 1834–1842, Monastery (completion), Klosterneuburg, Austria.

BIBLIOGRAPHY

HERZMANSKY, HEDWIG 1964 "Josef Kornhäusel: Eine Künstlermonographie." Unpublished Ph.D. dissertation, University of Vienna.
RIZZI, GEORG W., and SCHACHEL, ROLAND L. 1979 *Die Zinshäuser im Spätwerk Josef Kornhäusels.* Vienna: Verein für Geschichte der Stadt Wien.
WAGNER-RIEGER, RENATE 1970 *Wiens Architektur im 19. Jahrhundert.* Vienna: Österreichicher Bundesverlag.

KOTĚRA, JAN

Jan Kotěra (1871–1923) was born in Brno, Czechoslovakia. The first period of his professional career (1898–1905), in which his work was strongly influenced by the Vienna Secession, Czech folk art, and the English architecture and way of life, started with the Peterka House on Prague's Venceslas Square (1899–1900) and was closed by the National House at Prostějov (1905–1907) which already exhibited certain features of a functionalistic conception of space and material. His visit to the United States in 1903, where he attended the World Exhibition in St. Louis and became acquainted with FRANK LLOYD WRIGHT's early work, and on trips to Holland and England found its reflection in the second and most fruitful period of Kotěra's professional career (1906–1914). During that time, Kotěra introduced in Bohemia the red brick architecture and—particularly in the Hradec Králové Town's Museum (1906–1912)—Wright's dynamic conception of space. Kotěra covered all areas of architecture, from large-scale designs intended for the University of Prague, (1906–1923) and garden cities (Louny, 1909), to public buildings, villas and various residential forms, furniture, industrial devices (trams), and even glass. As teacher, he formed two generations of Czech architects: the cubist (JOSEF GOČÁR, OTAKAR NOVOTNÝ) at the School of Industrial Arts, and, at the Academy of Fine Arts, the functionalist generation (BOHUSLAV FUCHS, JAROMÍR KREJCAR, ADOLF BENŠ). Largely through Kotěra's influence, Czech art lost its provincial character and dependence on Vienna and became an important focus of Europe's avantgarde.

VLADIMÍR ŠLAPETA

WORKS

1899–1900, Peterka House; Venceslas Square; 1901–1902, S. V. U. Mánes Exhibition Pavilion, Auguste Rodin Exhibition; Prague. 1902, Mácha House, Bechyně, Czechoslovakia. 1904, Sucharda House; Prague. 1905–1906, Tonder House, Saint Gilgen, Austria. 1905–1907, National House, Prostějov, Czechoslovakia. 1906–1907, Water Tower, Michle District, Prague. 1906–1912, Town Museum, Hradec Králové, Czechoslovakia. 1907–1908, Chamber of Commerce and Trade Pavilion, Jubilee Exhibition; 1908–1909, Jan Kotěra House, Vinohrady District, Prague. 1908–1909, Kratochvíl House, Černošice, Czechoslovakia, 1908–1909, Laichter House, Vinohrady District, Prague. 1909–1913, Worker's Garden Colony, Louny, Czechoslovakia. 1911, Tomáš Baťa Residence (reconstruction), Gottwaldov-Zlín, Czechoslovakia. 1911–1912, Slávia Bank, Sarajevo, Yugoslavia. 1911–1913, Mandelík Mansion, Radboř, Czechoslovakia. 1911–1913, Mozarteum, Prague. 1913–1914, Lemberger Palace, Vienna. 1921, Štenc Summer Villa, Všenory, Czechoslovakia.

BIBLIOGRAPHY

FUCHS, BOHUSLAV 1972 *In margine uměleckého odkazu Jana Kotěry.* Brno, Czechoslovakia: Dům umění města Brno.

KOTĚRA, JAN 1902 *Meine und meiner Schüler Arbeiten: 1898–1901.* Vienna: Schroll.

MÁDL, KAREL B. 1922 *Jan Kotěra.* Prague: Štenc.

NOVOTNÝ, OTAKAR 1958 *Jan Kotěra a jeho doba.* Prague: Státní nakl adatelstuí krásné literatury, hudby a umění.

ŠLAPETA, VLADIMÍR, and MAREK, PAVEL (1978)1980 *Národní dům v Prostějově.* 2d ed. Czechoslovakia: Prostějov National House.

KOUZMANOFF, ALEXANDER

Alexander Kouzmanoff (1915–) was born in Chicago and received a master's degree in architecture from the University of Illinois (1940). He was a designer with the firm of Shaw, Naess, and Murphy, Chicago (1940–1943); after serving in the U.S. Army, he joined HARRISON AND ABRAMOVITZ, New York (1947–1952).

Kouzmanoff joined the faculty of the Graduate School of Architecture and Planning at Columbia University in 1954. He designed housing prototypes in Iran, El Salvador, and Lebanon and a new town in Iraq for the International Business Economic Group (IBEC) (1952–1957). He published a study on the revitalization of the Hudson River (1964). He was chairman of the division of architecture 1970–1976.

Kouzmanoff's design approach is intuitive; he has been influenced by medieval town form and, like the Dutch architect ALDO VAN EYCK, advocates a poetic realization of a sense of place. At the Old Westbury campus of the State University of New York (master plan in association with Albert Christ-Janer and JOHN M. JOHANSEN, 1965–1967; updated by Kouzmanoff, 1973), the first cluster college is a dense, irregular, academic "medieval town" (completed 1970).

The first phase of Kouzmanoff's central-core building at Old Westbury (1970–1975) is organized along a 265-foot long skylit gallery as a kind of "town center" for the five colleges ultimately contemplated.

In his extension of Avery Hall, the architecture school at Columbia, Kouzmanoff created a skylit central meeting place which flows around the new auditoria (1970–1977).

In addition to his private practice, Kouzmanoff continues to teach architecture at Columbia University.

JAMES RUSSELL

WORKS

1965–1970, First Cluster College (with Albert Christ-Janer and John Johansen); 1970–1975, Central Core Building (phase 1); Old Westbury College, State University of New York. 1970–1977, Avery Hall (extension), Columbia University, New York. 1976–1982, Central Core Building (phase 2), Old Westbury College, State University of New York.

BIBLIOGRAPHY

ABERCROMBIE, STANLEY 1973 "Hill Town on Long Island: A New College Campus in Old Westbury." *Architecture Plus* 1, no. 11:56–67.

BLEEKER, SAMUEL A. 1981 *The Politics of Architecture: A Perspective on Nelson Rockefeller.* New York: Rutledge.

KOUZMANOFF, ALEXANDER 1964 *Break-through to the Hudson: A Plan for Yonkers to Peekskill.* New York: Columbia University School of Architecture.

KOUZMANOFF, ALEXANDER 1970 "A Solution to Garbage Disposal with Park Land as the Bonus." *Architectural Forum* 133, no. 4:60–62.

KOUZMANOFF, ALEXANDER 1978 "Campus Architecture." *Progressive Architecture* 59, no. 3:53–75.

KOZMA, LAJOS

Lajos Kozma (1884–1948), architect, applied artist, graphic artist, designer, writer, and pedagogue, was one of the most original personalities in Hungarian art in the first half of the twentieth century.

After graduating from the József Nádor Technical University, Budapest, in 1906, he became a member of a group of architects known as the "Young People," which applied the motifs of Hungarian folk art to architecture.

Kozma worked in the office of Béla Lajta. In

1913, he opened a new workshop in the capital entitled "Budapest Workshop," serving the branches of applied arts, furnishings, and furniture art, similar to the Wiener Werkstätte.

In his graphic and book art, he excelled in the application of the motifs of Hungarian folk art. The beauty of his typographic art can be compared with the works of WILLIAM MORRIS. At this time, he was engaged mostly in the designing of furniture and interiors in a style showing baroque reminiscences. Indeed, this style became known under the name "Kozma Baroque," especially in Germany where many of his works were published in the journal *Deutsche Kunst und Dekoration*.

In the 1930s, Kozma prepared several designs in constructive architecture conceived in the views of the Bauhaus. In Budapest, several family houses, villas, and also some apartment houses show his constructive design of space and form, supplemented with accessories executed in a carefully accomplished craftsman's technique. The constructive furniture and interiors for these were also designed by Kozma.

In 1946, Kozma became director of the School of Arts and Crafts, Budapest. He did see the construction of his only public building, the Public Elementary School (1946–1947), Budapest.

Kozma published many works in which he expounded the historical, theoretical, and practical aspects of architecture, applied arts, industrial design, graphic art, and typography.

JUDITH KOÓS

WORKS

1913, Béla Lajta House (furnishings); *1913, Rózsavölgyi Book and Music Shop; 1920–1930, Houses and Villas (reconstruction); 1920–1930, House of Patron of Art; Budapest. 1930–1940, Kozma Summer Residence, Lupa Island, Hungary. 1930–1940, Villas (Bimbó Road, Pusztaszeri Road, Berkenye Street); 1936, Atrium House; 1938, Régiposta Street Apartment House; 1946–1947, Public Elementary School (completed posthumously); Budapest.

BIBLIOGRAPHY

KOÓS, JUDITH 1961a *Kozma Lajos: 1884–1948; Könyvmüvészete és alkalmazott grafikái* ("Typographical Art and Applied Illustrations of Lajos Kozma"). Budapest: Hungarian Bibliophile Society.

KOÓS, JUDITH 1961b "Kozma Lajos/Vázlatok egy tanulmányhozn" ("Lajos Kozma/Sketches to a Study") *Kortars* 5:382–391.

KOÓS, JUDITH (1964)1967 "The Influence of the Secession/Art Nouveau, Jugendstil/in Hungary. The Relation between Hungary and the Other European Countries around 1900." Volume 1, pages 265–270 in *Stil und Überlieferung in der Kunst des Abendlandes*. Berlin: Mann.

KOÓS, JUDITH 1965a "Kozma Lajos: Helye és szerepe a XX. századi müvészet történetében" ("Lajos Kozma: His Place and Role in the History of Art of the Twentieth Century"). *Müvészettörténeti Értesitő* 14, no. 4: 274–280.

KOÓS, JUDITH 1965b "Parallelerscheinungen in der Tätigkeit der Wiener Werkstätte und der Budapester Werkstatt." *Iparmüvszéti Muzeum Évkönyvei* 8:59–82.

KOÓS, JUDITH 1969a "Die Auswerkungen des Jugendstils in Ungarn." *Alte und moderne Kunst* 14, no. 102:23–31.

KOÓS, JUDITH 1969b "Motifs in the Iconography of Art Nouveau." Volume 2, pages 313–318, 423–428, in *Evolution générale et développement régionaux en histoire de l'art*. Budapest: Akadémiai Kladó.

KOÓS, JUDITH 1975 *Kozma Lajos munkássága: Grafica, iparmüvészet és épitészet* ("Activity of Lajos Kozma: Graphic Art, Applied Arts and Architecture"). Budapest: Akadémiai Kladó.

KOÓS, JUDITH 1977 "A Comparative Examination of the Characteristics of National and International Elements in Art Nouveau." *Acta Historiae Atrium* 23, no. 1–2:135–157.

KOÓS, JUDITH 1979 *Style 1900: A szcesszió iparmüvészete Magyar-országon* ("Style 1900: Applied Arts of the Art Nouveau in Hungary"). Budapest: Kepzőmüv.

KOZMA, LAJOS 1922 *Randmerkungen eines ungarischen Buchkünstlers*. Gyoma, Hungary.

KOZMA, LAJOS 1926 *Möbel und Raumkunst, mit einer Einleitung von Ernst Kállai*. Leipzig and Vienna: Hübsch.

KRAEMER, FRIEDRICH WILHELM

Friedrich Wilhelm Kraemer (1907–) is a prominent West German architect and educator of the postwar era. As professor in Braunschweig (1947–1974) and working in partnership as Kraemer, Sieverts und Partner (Braunschweig, 1962–1974, and Cologne since 1974), he has attained a reputation for meticulous expression of modern structural technology in designs for corporate headquarters.

RON WIEDENHOEFT

WORKS

1948, NWDR Radio Station, Hannover, Germany. 1957, Landeszentralbank, Düsseldorf, Germany. 1958, BASF Building, Ludwigshafen, Germany. 1960, Centennial Hall, Hoechst Dyeworks, Hoechst, Germany. 1964, British Petroleum Headquarters, Hamburg, Germany. 1966, DKW Insurance Company Headquarters, Cologne, Germany. 1970, Bavarian Insurance Company Headquarters, Munich. 1975, West German Radio Station, Cologne, Germany. 1976, Thyssen Gas Company Building, Duisburg, Germany. 1977, Ministry of Public Works and Housing, Riyadh.

BIBLIOGRAPHY

JOEDICKE, JÜRGEN 1980 "Kraemer, Friedrich Wilhelm." Pages 439–440 in Muriel Emanuel (editor), *Contemporary Architects.* New York: St. Martin's.

KRÁLÍK, EMIL

Emil Králík (1880–1946) is considered the founder of Moravian modern architecture. Born in Prague, Czechoslovakia, he was professor at the State Technical School in Brno from 1906 to 1910. He was also one of the founders of the Architecture School of Brno Technical University where he was professor from 1920 until his death. Králík's works from the period both before and after World War I display a symmetrical design, well-organized space, and noble details made of natural material. The František Kovařík Villa in Prostějov (1910) was one of the very first structures conceived in the so-called *Raumplan,* that is, space diffusion of various dwelling rooms, as postulated by ADOLF LOOS.

VLADIMÍR ŠLAPETA

WORKS

1909, Smetana Spa House, Luhačovice, Czechoslovakia. 1910, F. Kovařík Villa; 1910–1911, J. Kovařík Villa; Prostějov, Czechoslovakia. 1912, Theater, Mladá Boleslav; 1927–1928, State Tobacco Company; 1928, Theater, Exhibition of Modern Culture; 1932, General Pension Office; Brno, Czechoslovakia.

BIBLIOGRAPHY

MARKALOUS, BOHUMIL 1924–1925 "Emil Králík." *Bytová kultura* 1, no. 10:153.

KRAMER, PIETER LODEWIJK

The major works of Pieter Lodewijk Kramer (1881–1961) are bridges which he designed for the Public Works Department of Amsterdam.

In a city like Amsterdam, with all its canals, the bridge is of primary importance, but in addition, Kramer saw each bridge as having "a particular significance. With each bridge I have an intention wholly for myself without the public needing to know something of its needs. All my bridges are attuned to their surroundings and intend to make a contribution in precisely that special area" (*Handelsblad,* June 30, 1951).

Despite his inward-directed method of creating which coincided with his occult religious affinities as a priest for the Sufi, Kramer was very extroverted in his commitments to the communists. Kramer is known to have voiced his sympathies on street corners.

One of the most meaningful relationships Kramer developed was with MICHEL DE KLERK. Their friendship—perhaps because they were contrasting personalities: Kramer outward and vociferous, de Klerk retiring and of few words—began when they were youths attending night classes at the industry school for the working class, which was run by B. W. Wierink who was a designer of toys, among other things. During the day they worked at the office of EDUARD CUYPERS. Around 1912, the two friends were involved in the building of the Scheepvaarthuis, designed by JOHAN MELCHIOR VAN DER MEY. De Klerk and Kramer next collaborated in the communist organization for the housing of workers, *de Dageraad,* an organization for which Kramer probably had a great affinity (it is not known to what extent de Klerk was a leftist sympathizer). Kramer designed proudly monumental housing blocks with dynamic sculptural masses. Placed at a site that was originally designated for a hospital in H. P. BERLAGE's extension plan for Amsterdam, the layout resembles a "Y" with the main masses culminating at two ends where the cup of the "Y" branches off.

SUZANNE FRANK

WORKS

1911, Marine Building, Den Helder, Netherlands. 1913–1914, Shipping House, Amsterdam. 1917–1918, Complex in Bergen Binnen, Netherlands. 1920–1922, De Dageraad, Amsterdam. 1925–1926, De Bijenkorf, The Hague. 1917–1928, Bridges for the Department of Public Works, Amsterdam.

BIBLIOGRAPHY

Nederland bouwt in baksteen: 1800–1940. 1941 Rotterdam: Museum Boymans-van Beuningen.
RETERA, W. K. 1928 *P. Kramer.* Amsterdam: Van Munster.
ROY VAN ZUYDEWIJN, H. J. F. DE 1969 *Amsterdamse Bouwkunst: 1815–1940.* Amsterdam: de Bussy.
VRIEND, J. J. (1938)1949–1950 *De bouwkunst van ons land.* 3 vols. 3d ed., enl. Amsterdam: Scheltema & Holkema.
VRIEND, J. J. 1957 *Nieuwere architectuur.* Bussum, Netherlands: Moussault.
WATTJES, J. G. (1924)1929 *Nieuw-Nederlandsche bouwkunst.* 3d ed. Amsterdam: Kosmos.

KRANZ, JOSEF

Josef Kranz (1901–1968) was a Czech architect working in Brno. His very first work, the ERA Café in Brno, was already excellent. The building exhibits a remarkable lyrical atmosphere in its interior with deep respect and much attention paid to human needs; the front façade displays a smooth nonarticulated surface, whose conception was based on the contradiction between large windows and small-scale ventilation shutters. The façade makes a deep impression by its almost magical two-dimensional graphic solution. From the early 1930s on, Kranz's interest centered on designs of telecommunication and post office buildings.

VLADIMÍR ŠLAPETA

WORKS

1927–1929, ERA Café; 1928–1929, AVIA Cinema; 1930–1931, Slavík Villa; 1933–1935, Kranz House; 1945–1968, Telecommunications Center; Brno, Czechoslovakia.

BIBLIOGRAPHY

ŠLAPETA, VLADIMÍR 1979 *Josef Kranz 1901–1968.* Olomouc, Czechoslovakia: Gallery of Fine Arts. Exhibition catalogue.

KREIS, WILHELM

Unlike most German architects, Wilhelm Kreis (1873–1953) endured three successive political regimes—the Empire, the Weimar Republic, the Third Reich—with relative success. After a brief association with PAUL WALLOT and HUGO LIGHT, Kreis very early won commissions for more than forty national monuments. These massive buildings, constructed in rough-cut masonry, were perhaps initially influenced by Bruno Schmitz, but soon went far beyond Schmitz's work in their simple geometry and abstraction from historical precedent. As a result of their powerful effect and wide appeal, Kreis received many commissions and teaching posts in the years before 1914.

Although Kreis continued to be honored after 1918, receiving the coveted full professorship at the Dresden Technische Hochschule in 1926 and the presidency of the Bund Deutscher Architekten in 1927, his commissions shrank and changed in character. His commercial and exhibition buildings of these years adapted successfully to the austere and antimonumental aesthetic of the fledgling International style, but lacked his earlier innovative originality. Under the Third Reich, Kreis's continuing prestige brought him the presidency of the Reichskammer der bildenden Künste under Goebbels but only a few commissions, which were executed in an unimaginative "stripped classicism." Kreis survived the great disjunctions of modern German history at the expense of his creativity.

BARBARA MILLER LANE

WORKS

1901, Exposition Building, Dresden, Germany. 1901, Monument for German Students' Association (Burschenschafts-Denkmal), Eisenach, Germany. 1904–1908, Friedrich August Bridge; 1906, Sächsisches Haus; Dresden, Germany. 1906, Wollner House, Wachwitz, near Dresden, Germany. 1908–1909, Emscher Genossenschaft Administration Buildings, Essen, Germany. 1909, Bismarck Towers, Lössnitz near Dresden; Zehdenik; Bautzen; Eisenach; Germany. 1909?, Kyffhäuserverband Monument, Rothenberg, Germany. 1910, Family Vault, Witten, Germany. 1911, Town Hall, Herne, Germany. 1911, Villa Oppenheim, Krefeld, Germany. 1911–1916, Provincial Museum of Prehistory, Halle, Germany. 1912, Tietz Department Store, Elberfeld, Germany. 1912–1914, Tietz Department Store, Cologne, Germany. 1913, Knopf Department Store, Karlsruhe, Germany. 1913, Pavilion, Technical Fair, Leipzig. 1913–1915, Bismark Monument, Stettin, Germany. 1913–1915, Schloss Bühlerhohe, Baden, Germany. 1915, Pulp and Paper Factory, Aschaffenberg, Germany. 1917, Rheinmetall Power Station, Düsseldorf, Germany. 1917–1918, War Memorial, Brussels. 1920, Krupp Company Hannibal Mine Coaling Tower, Essen, Germany. 1922–1924, Wilhelm-Marx House, Düsseldorf, Germany. 1923, Bochum Verein Offices, Bochum, Germany. 1926, Gesolei Exposition Buildings, Düsseldorf, Germany. 1930s, Air Force Regional Headquarters, Dresden, Germany.

BIBLIOGRAPHY

ELLENIUS, ALLAN 1971 *Den offentliga konsten och ideologierna.* Stockholm: Almqvist & Wiksell.

KREIS, WILHELM 1927 *Über die Zusammenhänge von Kultur, Zivilisation und Kunst.* Berlin: Hübsch.

LANE, BARBARA MILLER 1968 *Architecture and Politics in Germany, 1918–1945.* Cambridge, Mass.: Harvard University Press.

LANE, BARBARA MILLER 1979 "Changing Attitudes to Monumentality: An Interpretation of European Architecture and Urban Form, 1880–1914." Pages 101–114 in *Growth and Transformation of the Modern City.* University of Stockholm and Swedish Council for Building Research.

MAYER, HANS F., and REHDER, GERHARD 1953 *Wilhelm Kreis; Architekt in dieser Zeit: Leben und Werk.* Essen, Germany: Vulkan.

MEISSNER, CARL 1925 *Wilhelm Kreis.* Essen, Germany: Baedeker.

MITTMAN, T. 1955 *Wilhelm Kreis.* Berlin.

NIPPERDEY, THOMAS 1976 "Nationalidee und Nationaldenkmal in Deutschland im 19. Jahrhundert." Pages 133–173 in *Gesellschaft, Kultur, Theorie: Gesammelte Aufsätze zur neueren Geschichte.* Göttingen, Germany: Vandenhoeck & Ruprecht.

STEPHAN, HANS 1944 *Wilhelm Kreis.* Oldenburg, Germany: Stalling.

KREJCAR, JAROMÍR

Jaromír Krejcar (1895–1949) was an outstanding representative of the Czech avant-garde architecture between the two world wars. Together with the theorist Karel Teige, Krejcar was the main instigator of the Devětsil avant-garde group. He was also editor of *Život II* (1922) where the ideas of purism and Constructivism appeared for the first time in Czechoslovakia. Krejcar was also an active propagandist; his work was based on a clear modular scheme for which he could always find an adequate formal expression corresponding to the given function, with all details well developed. In 1933–1936, Krejcar worked in Moscow where he designed, together with MOISEI YAKOVLEVICH GINSBURG, several spa houses. He later was professor at the Brno Technical University and at the Architectural Association School in London, where he died.

VLADIMÍR ŠLAPETA

WORKS

1923, Olympic Department Store; 1923, Vladislav Vančura Villa, Zbraslav; 1927, Private Clerks Club House, Vinohrady District; 1928, Gibian House, Dejvice District; Prague. 1930–1932, Machnáč Sanatorium, Trenčianske Teplice, Czechoslovakia. 1936–1937, Czechoslovak State Pavilion, Paris.

BIBLIOGRAPHY

FREEMAN, DAVID 1949 "Jaromír Krejcar." *Architectural Association Journal* 65:89–90.
KREJCAR, JAROMÍR (editor) 1928 *L'architecture contemporaine en Tchécoslovaquie.* Prague: Orbis.
KREJCAR, JAROMÍR 1933 "Architektura a společnost." Volume 5, pages 11–21 in *Za socialistickou architekturu: Sborník Svazu socialistických architektů.* Prague: Levá fronta.
PRŮCHOVÁ, ZEDENA 1975 "Krejcar, Jaromír." Pages 241–242 in *Encyklopedie Českého Výtvarného Umění.* Prague: The academy.
TEIGE, KAREL 1933 *Práce Jaromíra Krejcara. Monografie staveb a projektů.* Prague: Vaclav Petr.

KRISTENSEN, SVENN ESKE

Svenn Eske Kristensen (1905–) graduated from the Århus Technical School before he entered the Royal Academy in Copenhagen in 1929, which he attended until 1933. He occasionally worked with KAY FISKER from 1932 to Fisker's death in 1965. In his care for the nature of materials and consistency in design, he is a true pupil of the KLINT school (see KAARE KLINT). His buildings are characterized by simplicity, clear planning, and refined detail work. Although the exteriors are typical for their time, they will never become outdated. Thanks to carefully planned landscaping and a varied façade scheme, Kristensen's blocks of flats and rowhouses, in contrast to the great mass of postwar housing, are never conform or neutral, but friendly, human, and unpretentious in their regional modernism. His extensive production has been rewarded innumerable prizes. A careful planning made Bredalsparken in Copenhagen (1949–1955) with 1595 apartments, shops, and service institutions a great success. Analyses of environmental conditions, light and shadow, and wind and traffic determined the site plan and gave the area a villagelike atmosphere. Almost all his housing is built for nonprofit associations. As most Danish architects of his generation, he builds in a regional or international modern style.

LISBET BALSLEV JØRGENSEN

WORKS

1940–1942, Christiansgården and Dronningegården (with Kay Fisker), Copenhagen. 1944, Skjoldagervej (rowhouses), Gentofte, Denmark. 1949–1955, Bredalsparken; 1952–1953, Store Taffelbay, Strandvejen; 1953–1954, Bellahøj (high-rise housing); 1954–1956, Hvidovrebo VI, Strandmarksvej; Copenhagen. 1956–1957, School, Zanthe, Greece. 1957–1974, Town Hall, Brøndbyerne, Denmark. 1953–1958, Grenhusene (low-density housing), Hvidovrevej, Denmark. 1955–1958, Baltica Assurance Company Building, Bredgade, Denmark. 1962–1963, Rustenborg (housing), Bagsvaerdvej, Denmark. 1962–1967, Central Administration Office Building, Slotsholmsgade, Denmark. 1965–1967, Carlsberg Breweries Silo and Other Buildings; 1967–1969, Carlsberg Breweries Bottling Plant; Copenhagen. 1971, Kastrup and Holmegårds Glass Work, Fensmark, Denmark. 1970–1972, World Health Organisation Regional Office for Europe, Scherfigsvej, Copenhagen.

BIBLIOGRAPHY

HARTMANN, SYS 1980 Pages 180–183 in *Byenshuse Byens plan.* In *Danmarks arkitektur.* Copenhagen: Gyldendal.
KRISTENSEN, SVENN ESKE 1977 *Et liv i byggeriets tjeneste: 1936–1976.* Copenhagen.
LANGKILDE, HANS ERLING 1949 Volume 2, page 175 in *Weilbachs Kunstnerleksikon.* Copenhagen: Aschehoug Dansk Forlag.
LANGKILDE, HANS ERLING 1960 *Arkitekten Kay Fisker.* Copenhagen: Arkitektens Forlag.
SESTOFT, JØRGEN 1979 Pages 157–183 in *Arbejdets bygninger.* In *Danmarks arkitektur.* Copenhagen: Gyldendal.

KROHA, JIŘÍ

Jiří Kroha (1893–1974) was an architect, theorist, scenic designer, and leading representative of the Czech cultural and political avant-garde. His style developed from an initial Cubistic and Expressionistic inspiration to a specific dynamical conception of functionalism which found its manifestation in many architectural works, such as the State Technical School (1922–1926) and the North Bohemia Exhibition Hall (1926) in Mladá Boleslav, and two dwelling houses in Brno: his own residential villa (1930) and the "House under Water Reservoir" (1935). Jiří Kroha's style expressed his social and political program. As a result of a trip to the Soviet Union in 1930, he made an analysis of the dwelling conditions in capitalist society in his theoretical studies "Sociologický fragment bydlení" (Sociological Aspects of Dwelling, 1933) and "Ekonomický fragment bydlení" (Economic Aspects of Dwelling, 1934) which found a great response among the young generation of architects, members of the Left Front. As a result of his procommunist activity, he was dismissed from his position as professor at the Brno Technical University in the mid-1930s and was even sent to jail. In the late 1930s, he attempted to make a synthesis of the dwelling problems in his theoretical study, "Socialist Dwelling," in which he proposed several types of flats and used various technical experiments, such as the audiovisual projection of works of art in living rooms.

After World War II, Jiří Kroha became the founder of socialist realism in Czechoslovakia. In 1948, he was awarded the title of National Artist.

VLADIMÍR ŠLAPETA

WORKS

1922–1926, State Technical School, Mladá Boleslav, Czechoslovakia. 1923–1927, Bridge, Kralupy nad Vltavou, Czechoslovakia. 1926–1927, North Bohemian Exhibition Hall, Mladá Boleslav, Czechoslovakia. 1928, Czechoslovak Werkbund Exhibition (family house); 1929–1930, Kroha House; 1935, House Under Water Reservoir; 1946–1948, Municipal Tenement Houses (with Vilém Kuba and Josef Polášek); Brno, Czechoslovakia. 1948, Exhibition of Slav Agriculture, Prague. 1951, Stalingrad (center), Ostrava, Czechoslovakia. 1952–1956, Palacký University (Medical Faculty Theoretical Institutes), Olomouc, Czechoslovakia.

BIBLIOGRAPHY

CÍSAŘOVSKÝ, JOSEF 1967 *Jiří Kroha a meziválečná avantgarda.* Prague: Nakl. Československých výtvarných umělců.
CÍSAŘOVSKÝ, JOSEF 1964 *Výstava celoživotního díla národního umělce Jiřího Krohy.* Brno, Czechoslovakia: Union of Architects of ČSSR. Exhibition catalog.
KROHA, JIŘÍ 1919–1920 "O prostoru architektonickém a jeho mezích." *Veraikon* 6:33–34.
KROHA, JIŘÍ 1935 *Bytová otázka v SSSR.* Prague: Society for Cultural and Economic Relations with Soviet Union.
KROHA, JIŘÍ 1973 *Sociologický fragment bydlení.* Brno, Czechoslovakia: Institute of the Preservation of Historical Monuments.
KROHA, JIŘÍ, and HRŮZA, JIŘ 1973 *Sovětská avantgarda architektoniká.* Prague: Odeon.
SVRČEK, JAROSLAV B. 1930 *Jiří Kroha.* Geneva: Verlag Meister der Baukunst.
SVRČEK, JAROSLAV V. 1959 *Jiří Kroha.* Prague: Society for Cultural and Economic Relations with Soviet Union.

KROLL, LUCIEN

Born in Brussels, Lucien Kroll (1929–) studied architecture and planning at the Ecole Nationale Supérieure de la Cambre, Brussels, Belgium. Upon completion of his degree, he entered architectural practice with CHARLES VANDENHOVE. During the 1950s he designed a number of private houses in Belgium. In the later 1950s and early 1960s, Kroll became involved with ecclesiastical projects, his first independent commission being the conversion of a cattle barn on the grounds of the Abbey of Maredsous, Belgium, into craft workshops (1957). In this project, Kroll manifested his characteristic interest, destined to deepen over the following decades, in the collective processes by which an architect's concept is given form by human labor and is further transformed as a consequence of the social activities carried on within the finished structure. His preoccupation with this matter has led Kroll to devise methods for intimately involving builders and future occupants of a structure in the processes of its design.

The design of a chapel in suburban Linkebeek, near Brussels (1960–1963), evolved out of a close collaboration between Kroll, diocesan authorities, and, most important, the congregation. The chapel was erected in part by members of the congregation themselves. Its simple but dignified design using ordinary materials is in keeping with its small size and the limited funds allocated for its construction, and contributes to its comfortable integration into a community consisting of houses of conventional appearance.

In 1962, Kroll went to Rwanda to assist in the creation of new buildings for the government of this former Belgian colony. A Presidential Reception Center and Office Building (1962–1970) was executed according to plans developed by Kroll in consultation with President Grégoire Kayibanda. In this and other projects for Rwanda, Kroll achieved a self-consciously noncolonial, cosmopolitan appearance by using local building materials and techniques along with Western techniques of spatial planning and construction where appropriate.

The design of the Family House boarding school (1965–1968) in Braine-L'Alleud, Belgium, for children with learning disabilities was prepared in conjunction with the founder and director of the facility. The problem here was to create an essentially neutral environment in which teachers and children could interact freely in patterns less rigid than those obtaining in an authority-centered institution.

Kroll was selected as architect of the Social Zone of the new campus of the Medical Faculties of the Catholic University of Louvain, Belgium, in 1969 by a student group opposed to the realization of their living environment in the severe and expressionless modern style originally intended by the University's bureaucracy. Conceiving his role as that of consultant more than that of authoritative form giver, Kroll proceeded to organize student committees. Kroll then worked out the technical details necessary for the translation of the students' schematic concept into built reality. The architect also involved construction workers in the determination of many specific details of the partially prefabricated structures proposed for the Social Zone. As "completed," these buildings should retain the possibility of being easily transformed, both in terms of external appearance and of internal organization, according to the changing tastes and proxemic requirements of their future occupants.

ALFRED WILLIS

WORKS

1957, Crafts Workshops (remodeled from barn), Abbey of Maredsous, Belgium. 1960–1963, Chapel, Linkebeek, Belgium. 1961, Chapel, Waharday, Belgium. 1961–1962, Chapel and Ecumenical Center, Chevotogne Monastery, Belgium. 1962–1970, Presidential Reception Center and Office Building, Kigali, Rwanda. 1964, Block of Houses and Offices, Auderghem, Belgium. 1965–1968, Family House School, Braine-L'Alleud, Belgium. 1969, Benedictine Monastery, Ginindamuyada, Rwanda. 1969–?, Social Zone (including housing offices, dining hall, shops, school, and rapid-transit train station), Medical Faculties of the Catholic University of Louvain, Woluwé-Saint Lambert, Belgium. 1969–1972, Church, Biesmerée, Belgium. 1976, Church, Froidmont, Belgium.

BIBLIOGRAPHY

"Atelier Lucien Kroll." 1977 *Architecture Française* 39:4–17.

DEBUYST, FRÉDÉRIC (editor) 1976 "Trois réalisations communautaires de Lucien Kroll." *Art d'Eglise* 174, Jan.–Mar.:entire issue.

DEBUYST, FRÉDÉRIC 1977 L'Eglise Saint-Etienne à Froidment (Brabant)." *Art d'Eglise* 179, Apr.–June:143–148.

FROYEN, HUBERT P. 1976 "Structure and Infills in Practice: Four Recent Projects." *Industrialization Forum* 7:17–26.

GODEBSKI, NICOLAS 1976 "Lucien Kroll: Architecture et Participation." *CREE* 45, Dec.:78–83. English summary of French text.

HUNTZIKER, CHRISTIAN 1976 "Portrait de Lucien Kroll." *Architecture d'Aujourd'hui* 183, Jan.–Feb.:69–80.

JENCKS, CHARLES 1977 *The Language of Post-modern Architecture.* New York: Rizzoli.

JENCKS, CHARLES 1980 *Late-Modern Architecture.* New York: Rizzoli.

KROLL, LUCIEN 1970 "Quelques réalisations religieuses de Lucien Kroll." *Art d'Eglise* 152, July–Sept.:65–81.

KROLL, LUCIEN 1973 "La Nouvelle Eglise de Biesmerée." *Art d'Eglise* 164, July–Sept.:72–79.

KROLL, LUCIEN 1975a "The Soft Zone." *Architectural Association Quarterly* 7, no. 4:48–59.

KROLL, LUCIEN 1975b "Woluwé Saint-Lambert, Bruxelles. Zone sociale, Université Catholique de Louvain." *International Asbestos-Cement Review* 20:54–57.

KROLL, LUCIEN 1980a "Architecture and Bureaucracy." Pages 162–170 in Byron Mikellides (editor), *Architecture for People.* New York: Holt.

KROLL, LUCIEN 1980b "Stadtteilplannung mit den Bewohnern." Pages 160–163 in G. R. Blomeyer and B. Tietze (editors), *In Opposition zur Moderne: Aktuelle Positionen in der Architektur.* Braunschweig and Wiesbaden, Germany: Vieweg.

LEMAITRE, THIERRY ET AL. 1980 *Louvain-en-Woluwé.* n.p.: De Bont et Van de Kerckhove.

MIKELLIDES, BYRON (editor) 1980 *Architecture for People.* New York: Holt.

PUTTEMANS, PIERRE (1974)1976 *Modern Architecture in Belgium.* Translated by Mette Willert. Brussels: Vokaer.

"Quartier des Facultés Médicales à Woluwé St. Lambert—Bruxelles." 1977 *Global Architecture Houses* 3:24–41. English and Japanese texts.

RAGON, MICHEL 1977 *L'architecte, le Prince, et la Démocratie.* Paris: Michel.

STRAUVEN, FRANCIS 1976 "The Anarchitecture of Lucien Kroll." *Architectural Association Quarterly* 9, no. 2:40–44.

TAFURI, MANFREDO, and DAL CO, FRANCESCO (1976)1979 *Modern Architecture.* New York: Abrams.

"Universität Löwen/Belgien." 1977 *Baumeister* 74:49–53.

VOGT, ADOLF MAX ET AL. 1980 *Architektur: 1940–1980.* Berlin: Propyläen Verlag.

KROMHOUT, WILLEM

Soon after he settled in Amsterdam in 1890, Willem Kromhout (1864–1940), born in Rotterdam, Netherlands, started to voice his opposition against the imitation of old styles and instead advocated designs that clearly showed the structure of a building, with limited decoration. Only in this way could the architect be an artist. Kromhout applied these ideas for the first time in his Hotel Americain in Amsterdam (1898–1901) which was built at the same time as H. P. BERLAGE's Exchange (1898–1903) and is the counterpart of its severe rationalism. In his most successful works, Kromhout always combined a clear construction with a visionary design, but because of the visionary features his designs often were not realized. Apart from his architectural practice, Kromhout taught at several schools.

WIM DE WIT

WORKS

1898–1901, Hotel Americain, Leidseplein; 1900, Printing Office De Fakkel, Reguliersbreestraat, Amsterdam. *1908–1910, Dutch Pavilion, World Exhibition, Brussels. 1919, Noordzee Office; 1927–1928, Villa Yperhof; *1930–1932, Heineken Breweries, Office Building, Rotterdam, Netherlands.

BIBLIOGRAPHY

FANELLI, GIOVANNI (1968)1978 *Moderne architectuur in Nederland: 1900–1940.* Translated from Italian by Wim de Wit. The Hague: Staatsuitgeverij.
Nederland bouwt in baksteen: 1800–1940. 1941 Rotterdam, Netherlands: Museum Boymans van Beuningen.
Nederlandse architectuur 1893–1918: Architectura. 1975 Amsterdam: Van Gennep.
RETERA WZN, WILHELMUS 1926 *W. Kromhout Czn.* Amsterdam: Van Munster.
WALENKAMP, H. J. M. 1925 "W. Kromhout Czn." *Maandblad voor Beeldende Kunsten* 2:244–249, 281–287.

KRONFUSS, JUAN

Juan Kronfuss (1872–1944) was a pioneer who tried to create an Argentine national architecture.

Kronfuss was born in Budapest, Hungary. In 1897, he graduated as an engineer and later specialized in architecture at the Königliche Bayerische Technische Hochschule in Munich. Winner of an international design competition for a university building in Argentina, he traveled there in 1910, living first in Buenos Aires and from 1915 in Córdoba. In Córdoba, he developed his most important works, planning both public and private buildings and publishing his writings.

In his publications, he showed a special interest in colonial architecture which he tried to revive through some of his projects (a district of workmen's houses; the house *El cortijo*). He joined other architects and thinkers of the time in a search for old colonial shapes as inspiration for a national architecture in opposition to the eclectic and European architecture developed in Argentina since the second half of the nineteenth century. Nevertheless, Kronfuss could not rid himself of his environ-

ment, and his architectural style, in spite of its qualities, fell into eclecticism.

Kronfuss is to be credited for having documented buildings that were no longer extant and for having initiated the search that occurs periodically for an architecture independent of international movements.

MARINA E. L. TARÁN

WORKS

1905?–1910, Astoria Hotel, St. Petersburg. 1905?–1910, Imperial Hotel, Karlsbad, Germany (now Kar Corey-Vary, Czechoslovakia). 1905?–1910, Tietz Shops; 1905?–1910, Synagogue; Bamberg, Germany. 1911–1921, Hirsch and Zollfre Building; 1911–1921, House Martinez de Hoz (now the Embassy of Turkey); 1911–1921, Wolf and Schorr Building; Buenos Aires. 1916, Emilio Caraffa Provincial Museum of Fine Arts; 1921, Nuestra Señora de la Misericordia Hospital; 1930, El Cortijo House, Jesús María, Córdoba, Argentina.

BIBLIOGRAPHY

KRONFUSS, JUAN (1921) 1980 *Arquitectura colonial en la Argentina.* Córdoba, Argentina: Editorial Raíces Argentinas.
KRONFUSS, JUAN 1922 *Ideas para monumentos funerarios.* Córdoba, Argentina: Talleres Gráficos Biffignandi.
ORTIZ, FEDERICO ED ALTRI 1968 *La arquitectura del Liberalismo en la Argentina.* Buenos Aires: Editorial Sudamericana.
PAULA, ALBERTO DE 1978 "Kronfuss en la Universidad y 'lo nacional' en el diseño arquitectónico." *Documentos para una historia de la arquitectura argentina.* Edited by Marina Waisman and Ramón Gutíerrez. Buenos Aires: Editions Summa.

KROPHOLLER, MARGARET

Margaret Kropholler (20th century) was the first woman architect who "intuitively followed a lyrical and romantic path, fitting in easily with the fantasy element common to designers of the Amsterdam School" (Sharp, 1971).

Several other writers have made observations on her characteristics and abilities. These observations were included in an article on Park Meerwijk in Bergen Binnen (1916–1918) which confirms three designs by her hand (*ibid.*). All seventeen houses were designed in highly individualistic terms and Kropholler's were among the freest with their arcuated thatched roofs and sculptured brick walls.

Most of Kropholler's other designs were highly restrained versions of the Amsterdam school style. Large brick façades were punctuated by small reliefs in the wall and rows of windows that did not follow strict vertical alignments.

An interesting exception in her oeuvre is a store in Amsterdam. A relatively small store front (1931), it nevertheless seems to bespeak the *zakelijkheid* features of *de 8 en Opbouw* with its angularity and large expanse of glass. It was designed in 1931, when the functional style was reaching its ascendancy.

Kropholler added Staal to her name after J. F. STAAL joined forces with her brother. Staal's inspiration was one of the greatest contributions to her design abilities.

SUZANNE FRANK

WORKS

1916–1918, Park Meerwijk, Bergen Binnen, Netherlands. 1922, Apartment, Holendrechtstraat; 1931, Shop, Kalverstraat; n.d., Apartment, Jan van Galenstraat; n.d., Apartment, Orteliusstraat; Amsterdam.

BIBLIOGRAPHY

SHARP, DENNIS 1971 "Park Meerwijk—An Expressionist Experiment in Holland." *Perspecta* 13–14: 176–189.

KRUMBEIN, JUSTUS

Born in Hamburg, Germany, and educated at Hannover Polytechnic School, Justus Krumbein (1847–1907) emigrated to San Francisco in 1869 and moved to Portland, Oregon, in 1871. He had an extensive practice, winning the competition for the State Capitol of Oregon in 1873. His work was in a florid Italianate or Second Empire style; late examples show Richardsonian (see H. H. RICHARDSON) influence.

MARION DEAN ROSS

WORKS

1872, Jacob Kamm House, Portland, Ore. *1873–1876, State Capitol, Salem, Ore. *1884, Kamm Building; *1891–1892, Perkins Hotel; Portland, Ore. *1892–1893, State Capitol (dome), Salem, Ore. 1892–1894, Ancient Order of United Workmen Temple, Portland, Ore.

BIBLIOGRAPHY

BARBER, JOEL CONRAD 1966 "A History of the Old State Capitol Buildings of the State of Oregon." Unpublished M.A. Thesis, University of Oregon, Eugene.
HAWKINS, WILLIAM J., III 1980 "Justus Krumbein, Architect, 1847–1907." *Portland Friends of Cast-Iron Architecture.* Newsletter no. 16. Portland, Ore. Mimeographed publication.
VAUGHAN, THOMAS, and FERRIDAY, VIRGINIA GUEST (editors) 1974 *Space, Style and Structure.* 2 vols. Portland: Oregon Historical Society.

KUEN, JOHANN GEORG

Johann Georg Kuen (1642–1691), who was born and died in Bregenz, Austria, was one of the Vorarlberg masters who adapted Italian baroque architectural ideas to German and Swiss Alpine requirements, especially in designs for Benedictine monasteries. His principal documented activity was at the monastery of Einsiedeln in Switzerland. CASPAR MOOSBRUGGER, the lay brother who later carried on the reconstruction of the whole convent and church, worked as a stonemason under Kuen.

ALISON LUCHS

WORKS

1674–1676, Choir (rebuilt in 1746–1751 by Franz Anton Kraus); 1676–1684, Confessional Church and Sacristy; 1680–1684, Magdalen Chapel; 1684–1686, Liebfrauen-Brunnen (fountain; completely rebuilt in 1893); Einsiedeln Monastery, Switzerland.

BIBLIOGRAPHY

HEMPEL, EBERHARD 1965 *Baroque Art and Architecture in Central Europe.* Baltimore: Penguin. See pages 168–169 for confusion concerning Einsiedeln dates.
LIEB, NORBERT (1960)1976 *Die Vorarlberger Barockbaumeister.* 3d ed. Munich and Zurich: Schnell & Steiner.
OECHSLIN, WERNER (editor) 1973 *Die Vorarlberger Barockbaumeister.* Einsiedeln. Exhibition catalogue.
SANDNER, OSCAR 1962 *Die Kuen: Bregenzer Baumeister des Barock.* With photographs by Peter Hütter. Constance, Germany: Thorbecke.

KUMLIEN, AXEL, and KUMLIEN, HJALMAR

The partnership of Axel Kumlien (1833–1913) and Hjalmar Kumlien (1837–1897) offers a striking example of the late nineteenth-century combination of comprehensive practice and increasing specialization. Educated in Göteborg, Sweden, and in Germany, the Kumlien brothers ran a prosperous and all-round architectural firm in Stockholm from 1872 to 1891, and after 1891 Axel Kumlien—who seems to have been the most important of the two—continued alone until about 1910.

The most striking building of the firm, from an artistic point of view, was the neo-Renaissance building of Jernkontoret (Ironmasters' Association) in Stockholm (1875), whose plastered façades are typical for the 1870s. From 1880 on, red brick façades dominated the production of the firm.

From 1874, Axel Kumlien was the architectural adviser of the National Board of Health and became a specialist in hospital planning, designing some thirty-five hospitals and other social institutions.

ANDERS ÅMAN

WORKS

1870, Täcka Udden House, Djurgården; 1874, Grand Hotel (later remodeled); 1875, Lusthusporten House, Djurgården; 1875, Ironmasters' Association; 1876, Saint Paul's Methodist Church; Stockholm. 1880, 1900, Saint Lars Mental Hospital, Lund, Sweden. 1881, Railway Station (Bergslagsbanan), Göteborg, Sweden. 1882, Court House; 1887, Mariebergs Mental Hospital; Kristinehamn, Sweden. 1889, Sofiahemmet; 1893, Serafimerlasarettet, Stockholm. 1900, Hålahult Tuberculosis Hospital, Sweden.

BIBLIOGRAPHY

ÅMAN, ANDERS 1976 *Om den offentliga vården: Byggnader och verksamheter vid svenska vårdinstitutioner under 1880- och 1900-talen.* Stockholm: Liber Förlag.
KUMLIEN, HJALMAR 1894 *Svenska herrgårdar och villor af svenska arkitekter.* Stockholm: Norstedts.
LUNDBERG, CARINE 1977 "Axel o Hjalmar Kumlien." Volume 21, pages 684–691 in *Svenskt biografiskt lexikon.* Stockholm: Norstedts.

KYSELA, LUDVÍK

Ludvík Kysela (1883–1960) was a Czech architect working mostly at the Prague Municipal Town Planning and Architectural Office. With the department stores of Lindt (1924–1926), Baťa (1928; together with JOSEF GOČÁR and the Baťa Construction Office), and Alfa (1929) on Venceslas Square, the central boulevard of Prague, Kysela created a new, constructivist type of department store intended for big cities, with a passage on the ground floor and glazed corbels projecting from the façades.

VLADIMÍR ŠLAPETA

WORKS

1924–1926, Lindt Department Store; 1928, Baťa House; 1928, Department Store; 1928, Patria Department Store; 1929, Alfa Department Store; Prague.

BIBLIOGRAPHY

KUBIČEK, ALOIS 1960 "Ludvík Kysela zemřel: 24.4.1883–10.2.1960." *Architektura ČSR* 19, no. 6:410–413.
PODESTA, ATTILIO 1937 "Architetture di Ludvík Kysela." *Casabella* 111:18–23.

LABATUT, JEAN

Jean Labatut (1899–) was born in Martres-Tolosane, France. He attended the Ecole des Beaux-Arts, Paris, where he received his *diplôme* in 1924. Labatut was influenced by, among others, VICTOR A. F. LALOUX, of whose atelier he was a member, and the landscape architect and city planner Jean Claude Nicolas Forestier, with whom Labatut practiced.

Labatut's reputation rests largely on his tenure at the Princeton University School of Architecture, where from 1928 to 1967 he was chief design critic and director of graduate studies. Former Labatut students of note include CHARLES MOORE and ROBERT VENTURI.

CHRISTINE YELAVICH

WORKS

Begun 1926, Plaza Park and Monument to Jose Marti, Havana. 1831, Town Church (residence and gardens), Castillega de Guisman, near Seville, Spain. 1939–1940, Fountains and Fountain Spectacles, New York World's Fair. 1964, Stuart County Day School of the Sacred Heart, Princeton, N.J.

BIBLIOGRAPHY

"Adventure in Light-Color-Polychromy, a Church Prototype." 1951 *Liturgical Arts* 20, Nov.:2–8.
LABATUT, JEAN 1944 *The Universities' Position with Regard to the Visual Arts.* N.J.: Princeton University Store.
LABATUT, JEAN 1958 "Environment for Business and Industry." *Journal of the American Institute of Architects* 30, Dec.:15–17.
LAVANOUX, MAURICE 1965 "An Exercise in Architectural Humanism." *Liturgical Arts* 33, Feb.:38–47.
Princeton Beaux-Arts and Its New Academicism, from Labatut to the Program of Geddes, an Exhibition of Original Drawings over 50 Years. 1977 Princeton Junction, N.J.: PDQ Press.
SMITH, C. RAY 1977 *Supermannerism: New Attitudes in Post-modern Architecture.* New York: Dutton.
"Symphonies in Sight & Sound." 1939 *Magazine of Art* 32:290.

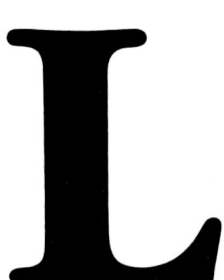

LABISI, PAOLO

Paolo Labisi (1720?–1798?) was educated, worked as an architect, and died in his native city of Noto in southeastern Sicily. Born into an aristocratic family, Labisi was probably the pupil of Francesco Sortino, who taught philosophy, mathematics, and fine arts in Noto. He became active as an architect in the 1740s. In 1750, he designed a major building complex, the church and house of the Crociferi fathers. Problems relating to its construction would occupy him for the rest of his life. He wrote an interesting treatise on architecture in which he dwells on legal problems relating to his profession. As he was a very litigious man himself, the subject matter of this treatise is apt. He served from 1760 to 1787 as royal engineer and architect of the city of Noto.

STEPHEN TOBRINER

WORKS

1748, Oratory of San Filippo Neri (portions); 1750–1790?, Crociferi Fathers House; 1775, Sant'Agata; Noto, Italy.

BIBLIOGRAPHY

LABISI, PAOLO 1773 "La scienza dell'architettura civile." Unpublished manuscript, Biblioteca Comunale di Noto, Italy.

TOBRINER, STEPHEN 1982 *The Genesis of Noto: An Eighteenth Century Sicilian City.* London: Zwemmer; Berkeley: University of California Press.

LABO, MARIO

Mario Labo (1884–1961), who was born in Genoa, Italy, received his degree at the Polytechnic Institute of Turin and apprenticed in the workshop of ANNIBALE RIGOTTI. He was a member, in 1930, of the interregional group of MIAR (Italian Movement for Rational Architecture), and his expressive language evolved along this line. His activity focused on urbanistic themes (from 1945 to 1947, he was a member of the urbanistic committee of the town of Genoa); on the production of industrial art (ceramics, carpets, furniture) with the intention of disseminating modern interior design and furniture; and on the construction of theaters, movie houses, and bathing establishments.

But Labo's role as a man of culture, architectural historian, translator, and scholar is much more important. He wrote for all major periodicals and was the author of numerous entries in the Thieme-Becker *Künstler Lexicon.* In 1954, he translated into Italian *The Culture of the City* by Lewis Mumford and *Space, Time and Architecture* by SIEGFRIED GIEDION. In his monument to Italians who died at Mauthausen, Austria (1963), he was able to fuse his personal suffering (one of his sons was murdered by the Nazis) with the universal suffering of the concentration camp victims.

SILVIA DANESI SQUARZINI
Translated from Italian by
Shara Wasserman

WORKS

1930, Caffè del Parlamento, Rome. 1932, Villa Rosselli, Albisola Capo, Italy. 1935, University Library (remodeling), Genoa, Italy. 1935–1938, Bathing establishments, Pegli; Bagni Mirasole; Stella d'Italia; Italy. 1939, Villa della Ragione, Genoa, Italy. 1963, Monument to the Dead Italians, Mauthausen, Austria.

LABRO, GEORGES

Born in Paris, Georges Labro (1887–?) was a winner of the 1927 design competition for the League of Nations Building in Geneva, although the plan was never realized. His design for Le Bourget Airport near Paris in 1937 has been widely acclaimed for both its planning and its engineering qualities. After World War II, he was responsible for a number of other engineering schemes including an important river dam at Chastang-sur-Dordogne, France.

PETER L. DONHAUSER

WORKS

1933, Centrale Téléphonique Ornano; 1937, Terminal Building, Le Bourget Airport; *1937, Pavilion for Thermal Energy, World's Fair; Paris. 1938, Centrale Téléphonique Daumesnil, Vincennes, France.

BIBLIOGRAPHY

BRAIVE, ANDRÉ 1938 "Le Centrale Téléphonique Daumesnil à Vincennes." *Construction Moderne* 53:461–464.

CLEMENT-GRANDCOUR, CHARLES 1937 "La Nouvelle Aérogare du Bourget." *Construction Moderne* 53:75–84.

CLEMENT-GRANDCOUR, CHARLES 1938 "Le Pavillon des Stations Thermales, Climatiques et Balnéaires à l'Exposition de 1937." *Construction Moderne* 53:213–216.

LABRO, GEORGES 1937 "Terminal Building, Le Bourget Airport." *Architect and Building News* 152:252–255.

LABROUSTE, HENRI

Pierre-François-Henri Labrouste (1801–1875) was born in Paris, the son of François-Marie-Alexandre Labrouste, a legislator in the Revolutionary and Directory governments and, during the Restoration, *premier commis* in the *Ministère des Finances.* Henri had a sister and four brothers, including THEODORE LABROUSTE—two years older, architect, and Grand Prix of 1827—and Alexandre, from 1838 director of the Collège Sainte-Barbe. Henri, like his brothers, attended the Collège Sainte-Barbe. In 1819, he entered the Ecole des Beaux-Arts as a student of A.-L.-T. VAUDOYER and LOUIS HIPPOLYTE LEBAS, competing for the Grand Prix in 1821 (placing second) and winning it in 1824 at the unusually early age of twenty-three.

Labrouste's Grand Prix design for a *Cour de*

Cassation is remarkable for its Doric simplicity and subtlety. Eschewing the expressive projections in plan and silhouette of his older competitors, Labrouste inscribed his plan firmly in a square and linked its elements with the simplest pattern of axes. It could be mistaken for bald or naive, as it would seem to have been by the Académie des Beaux-Arts when they placed the *esquisse* last at the beginning of the competition, but upon closer inspection it proves brilliant in its display of perfectly adjusted relationships unconfused by rhetorical flourishes. Subsequent publications of the Grand Prix projects have started with Labrouste's design and with the more elaborate but equally uncompromising project of 1823 by his friend FELIX DUBAN.

From late 1824 to early 1830, Labrouste studied at the French Academy in Rome. Gathering there were four like-minded architects who became a tight group of friends exploring Romanticism and rationalism together: Duban, Labrouste's predecessor; LOUIS DUC, Grand Prix of 1825; and LEON VAUDOYER, Grand Prix of 1826. They received a sympathetic reception from their immediate predecessors, ABEL BLOUET (1821) and Emile Gilbert (1822), and left behind them a fierce group of younger partisans: Théodore Labrouste (1827), Marie-Antoine Delannoy (1828), Simon-Claude Constant-Dufeux (1829), and Pierre-Joseph Garrez (1830).

This group began to formulate a new, Romantic rationalist architecture in Rome during the late 1820s and to embody their ideas in their *envois* sent back annually to the Académie des Beaux-Arts to demonstrate their progress. Labrouste was seen as the *pensionnaires'* leader and instigator. His penultimate, fourth-year *envoi* was a reconstruction of the three Doric monuments at Paestum, seemingly precise studies of these well-preserved Greek temples but in fact, as EUGÈNE EMMANUEL VIOLLET-LE-DUC was to state, "simply a revolution on several folio sheets of paper" (1877). The Académie criticized the project harshly; young architects cried scandal. The director of the Academy in Rome, Horace Vernet (a painter sympathetic to Romanticism), traveled to Paestum to confirm Labrouste's measurements, then offered his resignation. The stated issue was the accuracy of certain details but this was understood to conceal a point of principle—a point quite variously stated in subsequent histories, but deciphered by Neil Levine (1975) as hinging on the implication in Labrouste's project that the Greek orders at Paestum could be seen to have decomposed under the influence of local cultural and structural forces. The key is the so-called Basilica which Labrouste set at the end of his chronological sequence (instead of at the beginning as had previously been done) and which he restored as an unpedimented meeting hall, not a temple at all.

Labrouste's fifth-year *envoi* of 1829 is disconcertingly reticent, a small bridge at the Franco-Italian border. The Académie des Beaux-Arts intended that the *pensionnaires* in their last projects would demonstrate their skill at large-scale planning (as, for example, VICTOR BALTARD would do in 1839 with his project for a Conservatory of Music). Some of the Romantic *pensionnaires* sent statement of their faith, as Duban had done the year before with his *Temple Protestant* and as Constant-Dufeux would do in 1834 with his Chamber of Deputies. Labrouste, however, hesitated: he sent almost nothing. Léon Vaudoyer would seem to have indicated Labrouste's thoughts when in 1831 he wrote about the fifth-year *envois*: "If it is required that one produce a vast scheme, I declare: I am not an architect; my studies are not completed, and this because art is not taught in France as it should be" (letter to his father of November 17, 1831, private collection, Paris). Labrouste was working to rebuild his understanding of architecture from its foundations. His *envois*, like his Grand Prix design, were as understated as they were resolute. But sketchbooks he kept while in Rome show that privately he was plunging onward formulating two *envois* he had not been ready to submit: a vivid reconstruction of a Greek hill fortress with painted temples and tombs of Gothic bizarreness, and projects for a vaulted church with intricate spaces enfolded in variously shaped shells of masonry.

Soon after his return from Rome in early 1830, the conservative Bourbon regime was overthrown, giving rise to an outburst of Liberal and Romantic euphoria in culture and art. In late spring, a group of the most radical students in A.-L.-T. Vaudoyer's atelier—JEAN LASSUS, Klotz, Gréterin, Dupuis, Carville, Marcel, Penavère, Dumesnil, and Petiau—presented themselves to Labrouste, asking him to open an atelier for them. He accepted hesitantly, and only after Vaudoyer had formally invited him to do so. He made a declaration of his principles:

Let me state my thoughts, my thoughts in their entirety, in a few words. If the elements of architecture cannot remain unchanging because of our new needs and because of the new means put at our disposal by industry to satisfy them, they nonetheless cannot be handled capriciously. These elements—the veritable organs of a being—are modified according to the functions they are made to serve and thus demand the selection of materials most appropriate for enabling them to satisfy these functions. The particular qualities of these materials thus exert the most direct influence on the

Labrouste.
Bibliothèque Sainte-
   Geneviève.
Paris.
1838–1850

Labrouste.
Bibliothèque Sainte-
   Geneviève.
Paris.
1838–1850

form which it is appropriate to give each element so that decoration is intimately tied to construction. The beauty of a monument resides in the expression of a harmony between needs and means used to satisfy them [L. Labrouste, 1902, pp. 214–215].

Labrouste's atelier opened on August 1, 1830, and became the school of a whole generation of Romantic rationalist architects—Eugene Millet, Juste Lisch, Jules Guadet, ANATOLE DE BAUDOT, Emile Boeswillwald, PIERRE BOSSAN, Victor-Francois Hügelin, Louis-Ernest Lheureux, Bouwens van der Boijen. They received few academic honors at the Ecole des Beaux-Arts, however, and when Labrouste closed the atelier a quarter-century later in 1856, not one of his students had even been *en loge* in the Grand Prix competition. He refused to name a successor, suggesting that certain of his students go to Viollet-le-Duc, others (Guadet, for example) to Jules André.

An opportunity to practice architecture came more slowly. Only on November 9, 1838, after eight years as Duban's *inspecteur* for the reconstruction of the buildings of the Ecole des Beaux-Arts, was Labrouste commissioned to design a new structure for the Bibliothèque Sainte-Geneviève, to be erected on the north side of the Place du Panthéon. He submitted a preliminary project on December 19, 1839. It received final approval from the Conseil des Bâtiments Civils on January 15, 1843, was funded by a bill passed on July 19 of that year, and commenced in August. Work was completed on December 15, 1850.

His design is as simple, direct, and effective as his Grand Prix project of fourteen years before. His problem was to house the nationalized monastic library on a small, narrow site, and his solution was to divide the books between those less frequently and those more frequently used, placing the former in a closed stack area occupying the ground floor, and the latter around the walls of a single, tall reading room above. The structure was to be gas-lit, so it could be open in the evening, and thus had to be fireproof, obliging Labrouste either to vault it in stone or to experiment with the new material iron. He boldly chose the latter course, in spite of the hesitations of the Conseil des Bâtiments Civils, and dropped a light metal cage into the building's stone shell, with iron girders supporting the floor of the reading room and iron vaults on a file of slim, exposed iron columns forming its ceiling. Not only was this system of fireproof construction lighter, Labrouste pointed out, but it was also faster to erect, since the ironwork could be fabricated while the masonry shell was being laid up, then swiftly mounted in position. This was the first use of an exposed iron frame in a monumental building.

Labrouste's ornamental articulation of this simple spatial and structural scheme brings out its particular qualities rather than filtering them through the conventional columnar dress of neoclassicism. There are no breaks in the wall plane or pediments or pavilions on the silhouette. There are no pilasters or projecting window surrounds (two columns flanking the main door in the preliminary project disappeared during construction), and the only capitals are collars of Labrouste's invention around the piers of the reading room window arcade. Otherwise, ornament has sunk back into the structural surfaces—for example, the names of great authors articulating the curtain walls of the upper arcade, like the book spines of the shelves behind them, or the flaming lamps flanking the door and commemorating the illumination of the library so that it could be open at night. Instead of the richly varied shadows of a deeply sculpted neoclassical building surface, Labrouste used the flat, even shadows cast by bevels, right-angle projections, and simple cyma rectas to make palpable the solidity of the actual stone surfaces.

Discreet as this ornamentation is on the Bibliothèque Sainte-Geneviève and subordinate as it is to the expression of the spatial and structural facts of the building, it nonetheless remains of great importance in communicating these facts to the beholder. Labrouste and his contemporaries abandoned the conventional vocabulary of ornamental motifs and molding profiles to create a new one of realistic signs and expressive profiles. The cut-stone tomb in their hands became a piece of abstract sculpture in which each surface, silhouette, and molding was modulated and formed to communicate an idea. Labrouste's project for the tomb of Duban might be analyzed as his son, Léon, analyzed Louis Duc's similar, executed design:

In front, where the corpse is laid, a series of horizontal lines constitute a solid base, topped by lines converging in the form of a roof: lines recalling the stillness of death and protecting the sanctified ground where rest the remains of the departed . . . . The vertical marker is completely different in expression. This, rising at the head, communicates to us the will, the intellectual strength of the thinker. This stele, by the graceful and firm curve of its silhouette, thrusts up from the socle, breaking the horizontal lines . . . . In this dominating element these vertical lines express combat, righteousness, correctness, life [L. Labrouste, 1902, p. 226].

The Bibliothèque Sainte-Geneviève placed Labrouste in the front rank of French government architects. As architect of the library, he was in the service of the *Ministère de l'Education Publique et des Cultes,* and a number of further appointments presented themselves. In 1853, he was named architect of the new seminary at Rennes (erected 1857–1875); in 1854, he was named LUDOVICO VISCONTI's replacement as architect of the Bibliothèque Nationale (then Bibliothèque Impériale); and in 1858, he was appointed an *inspecteur général* of the *Edifices Diocésains.* He also, since 1838, had been a member of the Commission des Monuments Historiques and now, off and on, was a *membre temporaire* of the Conseil des Bâtiments Civils as well as a member of the jury of the Exposition des Beaux-Arts (1849–1855; 1867–1874). In 1867, he was at last elected to the Académie des Beaux-Arts replacing JACQUES IGNACE HITTORFF. A number of important private commissions now also came his way: a large house in Paris for the Minister of Finance, Achille Fould (1856–1858); the Hôtels Thouret (1860) and Rouvenat (1861) in Neuilly; administrative offices for the Paris-Lyon-Méditerranée Railroad in Paris (1862); and the Hôtel Vilgruy on the Place

Francois Ier in Paris (1865). In 1856, Labrouste closed his atelier, in part because of the little success his students were having at the Ecole, in part perhaps also because of the press of work. He spent his time henceforth either providing drawings and overseeing work at Rennes and at the Bibliothèque Nationale or writing reports and attending the twice-weekly meetings of the *inspecteurs généraux* of the *Edifces Diocésains* and the Conseil des Bâtiments Civils. He had become an architectural bureaucrat, just as his brother Théodore had working in the *Administration des Hôpitaux et Hospices* or his father had at the *Ministère des Finances* before them. And he was dutiful: the records show that he rarely missed a meeting and accepted unusually heavy assignments of projects to analyze. Many of his contemporaries—Duban in particular—were not so patient. This bureaucratic mechanism, in these early days, however, was a tool for the improvement of the quality of public design, no less significant for the discipline of the profession than the foundation of the Société Centrale des Architectes which Labrouste worked to bring about in 1840 and of which he was vice-president from 1849 to 1873, when he became president just before his death. This rationalization of the management of architecture was as important to him as the rationalization of its engineering and its ornament.

In this context, it is all the more startling and impressive to see what a wonderful fantasy in iron, glass, and glazed tile Labrouste created as the reading room of the Bibliothèque Nationale between 1860 and 1867. The space is surrounded by the masonry shell of the old Palais Nazarin, with the former *cour d'honneur* to the north and a huge book stack to the south—a tightly fitted cage of iron shelves and glass platforms, the first of the now familiar type ever erected. The reading room itself is illuminated by three broad windows in its north wall and by nine round skylights in the centers of domes of brilliantly glazed ceramic tiles supported on a light armature of iron arches and columns. This is all very efficient, but in its form and in the seemingly impossible lightness of its ironwork it is also strangely unreal. The windows at the north are carried down the east and west sides of the room as two rows of lunettes illusionistically painted open to reveal vistas of treetops and blue sky. The space is thus opened on three sides to a great fictive park while the breeze which might be imagined rustling the surrounding sea of leaves also seems to be holding aloft the billowing white, clothlike domes of the room as if they were awnings, tied down by the spindly iron columns rather than held up. Just as Labrouste's imaginative cutting of the stone exterior of the Bibliothèque Sainte-Geneviève makes it seem heavier and more

Labrouste.
Bibliothèque Nationale
(reading room).
Paris.
1854–1875

most spectacular of the Romantic age, but each devolved perfectly from the ideas and facts he was dealing with. Seeking not to astonish or outrage but merely to assert clearly and unequivocally, Labrouste solved the most basic problems of his calling with all the force of a sublime imagination and all the restraint of lucid reason so that his compelling designs are amazing while seeming obvious.

DAVID T. VAN ZANTEN

WORKS

1837, Ridèle and Brunet Tombs, Montparnasse Cemetery; 1838–1850, Bibliothèque Sainte-Geneviève; 1840–1841, Collège Sainte-Barbe (with Théodore Labrouste); *1853, Antoine Albouse Tomb, Montparnasse Cemetery; Paris. 1853–1875, Seminary, Rennes, France. 1854–1875, Bibliothèque Nationale; *1856–1858, Hôtel Fould; Paris. 1856, Clugny Tomb, Fontenay-aux-Roses, France. 1860, Hôtel Thouret; 1861, Hôtel Rouvenat, Neuilly-sur-Seine, France. 1862, Paris-Lyon-Méditerranée Railroad Administrative Offices; 1865, Hôtel Vilgruy; 1865, Zolla Tomb, Montparnasse Cemetery; 1872, Thouret Tomb, Montmartre Cemetery; Paris.

BIBLIOGRAPHY

BAILLY, ANTOINE-NICOLAS 1876 *Notice sur M. Henri Labrouste.* Paris: Firmin-Didot.

DELABORDE, HENRI 1878 *Notice sur la vie et les ouvrages de M. Henri Labrouste.* Paris: Firmin-Didot.

DREXLER, A. ET AL. (editors) 1977 *The Architecture of the Ecole des Beaux-Arts.* Cambridge, Mass.: M.I.T. Press.

LEVINE, NEIL A. 1975 "Architectural Reasoning in the Age of Positivism: The Neo-Grec Idea of Henri Labrouste's Bibliothèque Ste.-Geneviève." Unpublished Ph.D. dissertation, Yale University, New Haven.

LABROUSTE, HENRI 1877 *Les Temples de Paestum.* Volume 3 in *Restaurations des monuments antiques par les architectes . . . de l'Academie de France à Rome.* Paris: Firmin-Didot.

LABROUSTE, LÉON 1885 *La Bibliothèque Nationale: Son début et ses accroissements, ses bâtiments et ses constructions, ses agrandissements, ses travaux.* Paris: Lutier.

LABROUSTE, LÉON 1902 *Esthétique monumentale.* Paris: Schmid.

MILLET, EUGÈNE 1882 *Henri Labrouste, sa vie, ses oeuvres.* Paris: Marpon.

SADDY, PIERRE 1977 *Henri Labrouste, architecte, 1801–1875.* Paris: Caisse nationale des monuments historiques.

Souvenirs d'Henri Labrouste: Notes recueillées et classées par ses enfants. 1928 Fontainebleau, France: Cuënot.

solid, so here his illusionistic elaboration of the iron construction makes the interior seem lighter and opens before the readers' minds quiet, reassuring vistas.

Henri Delaborde remarked that Labrouste's character could be summed up in one word: *Fixité* (*Notice sur la vie et les ouvrages de M. Henri Labrouste,* 1878). What he fixed upon so simply and unrelentingly—from his simple, square Grand Prix design of 1824 to his simple, square Bibliothèque Nationale reading room of 1860–1867—was the perfect balance of functional and imaginative forces so that they would not merely coexist, but that they would echo each other, reinforce each other, and finally become completely merged in each other. In the last design, the structure leads on to the illusion, and the illusion leads back to the structure. He did not use iron as adventurously as possible—for that one must look at the work of his friend HECTOR HOREAU—but he did use it precisely as its characteristics suggested to solve the specific problem he faced. His expressive stonecutting or his iron-and-tile illusionism was not the

LABROUSTE, THEODORE

François-Marie-Théodore Labrouste (1799–1885) was the older brother of HENRI LABROUSTE, of whom he was at first a powerful partisan, but whose brilliance eventually cast him in shadow and led to his retreat to the bureaucracy of the *administration des hôpitaux et hospices*. The two brothers were Parisians, educated at the Collège Sainte Barbe and trained as architects at the Ecole des Beaux-Arts in the atelier of A.-L.-T. VAUDOYER and HIPPOLYTE LEBAS. Théodore was *en loge* in the Grand Prix competition in 1822 and won the prize on a second try in 1827—only after Henri, in 1824, had won on his second attempt. Arriving at the French Academy in Rome late in 1827, Theodore joined Henri and other young radical rationalists in that brilliant circle—FÉLIX G. J. DUBAN, LOUIS JOSEPH DUC, and LÉON VAUDOYER. His *envois* immediately reflected their fresh, realistic vision of ancient architecture, particularly his second-year reconstruction of the Temple of Vesta at Tivoli with internal painted murals in the style of the recently discovered Etruscan tombs and his fourth-year reconstructions of the temples at Cori painted and hung about with awnings and ex-votos like a primitive fetish. He made explicit what his brother Henri had only suggested.

Returning to Paris in 1832, Théodore received several important opportunities. He was appointed *inspecteur* under Charles Rohault de Fleury (see ROHAULT DE FLEURY FAMILY) at the Musée de l'Histoire Naturelle and seems to have altered the design from a conventional classical one to an expressive functional conception. (Simon Girard, 1885, writes that suspicion of Labrouste's actual authorship denied Rohault the *legion d'honneur* for his work.) Théodore also produced unexecuted projects for a fountain on what became the site of Sainte-Clothilde, for lamps on the Pont de la Concorde (1836–1840; with Henri), and for the Bibliothèque de l'Arsenal, of which he was appointed architect in 1841. In 1840–1841, in collaboration with his brother, he designed and erected a new complex of buildings for the Collège Sainte-Barbe behind the Bibliothèque Sainte-Geneviève. All of these early works were in the delicate Quattrocento-Percieresque style characteristic of Labrouste's circle.

In 1844, Théodore Labrouste entered the *Administration des hôpitaux et hospices* as an *architecte divisionnaire,* and in 1853 he was appointed its *architecte en chef.* Here he emerged, somewhat late in his career, as an important hospital architect, designing the new Hospice des Incurables at Ivry (1854–1859) and the Maison Dubois at Saint Denis (c.1856) as well as making additions to other structures, particularly the Hôpital Laennec in Paris. In 1856, he designed and erected the Administration's headquarters, forming one half of the west side of the Place de l'Hôtel de Ville. In 1868, he also finally carried out the enlargement of the Bibliothèque de l'Arsenal.

DAVID T. VAN ZANTEN

WORKS

1840–1841, Collège Sainte-Barbe (with Henri Labrouste), Paris. 1854–1859, Hospice des Incurables, Ivry, France. 1856, Administration des Hôpitaux et Hospices Headquarters, Paris. c.1856, Dubois House, Saint Denis, France. 1868, Bibliothèque de l'Arsenal (enlargement), Paris.

BIBLIOGRAPHY
GIRARD, SIMON 1885 "Théodore Labrouste: Sa vie—ses oeuvres, 1799–1885." *Bulletin de la Société centrale des architectes* 1885.

LACHERT, BOHDAN

Bohdan Lachert (1900–), who was born in Moscow, studied architecture at the Technical University in Warsaw and graduated in 1926. In collaboration with Josef Szanajca, Lachert produced numerous functionalist designs between 1926 and 1939, when Szanajca died. Lachert was a founder member of the Polish avant-garde group "Praesens" in 1926. Between 1949 and 1955, he turned to freely interpreted decorative forms for the façades of some of his buildings. In others, he aimed for a classically inspired axiality.

LECH KŁOSIEWICZ

WORKS

*1929, Centro-Cement Exhibition Pavilion, Poznan, Poland. 1930–1939, Apartment Building (with J. Szanajca), 25 Mickiewicza Street; 1930–1939, Rowhouses (with Szanajca and R. Piotrowski), 25–43 Promyka Street and 12–23 Dziennikarska Street; 1949–1952, Muranow Residential Development; Warsaw.

BIBLIOGRAPHY
The Polish Avant-Garde: 1918–1939. 1981 Paris: Moniteur; Warsaw: Interpress. Exhibition catalogue.
Warszawa Szkoła Architektury: 1915–1965. 1967 Warsaw: P.W.N.
WISŁOCKA, IZABELLA 1968 *Awangardowa Architektura Polska: 1918–1939.* Warsaw: Arkady.

LADOVSKY, NIKOLAI A.

Nikolai Aleksandrovich Ladovsky (1881–1941), a man of foresight and erudition, was the pioneer of contemporary architectural education in Russia, a theoretician of architectural rationalism, and founder of the first avant-garde architectural and urban design associations.

Born in Moscow, Ladovsky evidenced a proclivity for architecture before starting his formal education in 1914 at the Moscow Institute of Painting, Sculpture, and Architecture. While still a student, he joined in 1918 the Architectural Studio of Mossovet headed by IVAN V. ZHOLTOVSKY and ALEKSEI V. SHCHUSEV. As these architects solved tomorrow's problems with yesterday's answers, Ladovsky realized the urgency for a fresh, contemporary approach to design.

An avant-garde architecture, Ladovsky maintained, must originate from the convergence of avant-garde arts and be anchored to sound, scientific principles. Accordingly, he cofounded the Commission for Painting-Sculpture-Architecture Synthesis (*Zhivskulptarkh*) in 1919, coorganized the Institute of Artistic Culture (*Inkkuk*) in 1920, and initiated the Institute's "working group of architects" (1921).

Ladovsky's so-called psychoanalytical method of architectural education was developed in the United Studios (OBMAS), created in 1920 within the innovative Higher State Art and Technical Studios by Ladovsky, Vladimir F. Krinsky, and Nikolai V. Dokuchaev. They aimed at defining the influence of colors, forms, and spaces on the human psyche and, consequently, at economizing man's psychophysical energy in memorizing his environment. Their principles, named "architectural rationalism," were the scholarly foundation for architectural and urban design.

In 1923, Ladovsky organized the Association of New Architects (ASNOVA) for like-minded colleagues, and began the magazine *Izvestiia Asnova* with ELEAZAR LISSITZKY. In 1928, he initiated the Union of Architects-Urbanist to deal with planning and urban design issues.

Ladovsky practiced extensively but completed few designs. Persecuted by the Soviet authorities, he faded into oblivion, yet his numerous students and followers kept his legacy alive.

MILKA T. BLIZNAKOV

WORKS

1927–1929, Industrial Town, Kostino, near Moscow. 1928–1931, Housing Cooperative, Tverskaya Street; 1935, Lermontovskaia Subway Station; 1935–1936, Dzerzhinskaia Subway Station (interior hall now remodeled); Moscow.

BIBLIOGRAPHY

AFANASIEV, K. N. (editor) 1963–1970 *Iz istorii Sovetskoy arkhitektury.* 2 vols. Moscow: Akademiya Nauk SSSR.

Art and Architecture, USSR: 1917–32. 1971 New York: Wittenborn. Exhibition catalogue.

BARKHIN, M. G. (editor) 1975 Volume 1, pages 337–364 in *Mastera sovetskoi arkhitektury ob arkhitekture.* Moscow: Iskusstvo.

BLIZNAKOV, MILKA T. 1971 "The Search for a Style: Modern Architecture in the U.S.S.R., 1917–1932." Unpublished Ph.D. dissertation, Columbia University, New York.

BLIZNAKOV, MILKA T. 1973 "The Rationalist Movement in Soviet Architecture of the 1920s." In Stephen Bann and John Bowlt (editors), *Russian Formalism.* Edinburgh: Scottish Academic Press.

BLIZNAKOV, MILKA T. 1976 "The Constructivist Movement in Architecture." *Soviet Union/Union Sovietique* 3, part 2:210–222.

BLIZNAKOV, MILKA T. 1980 "Nikolaj Ladovskii: The Search for a Rational Science of Architecture." *Soviet Union/Union Sovietique* 7, parts 1–2:170–196.

CHAN-MAGOMEDOV, S. O. 1978 "Nikolai Ladovskij: An Ideology of Rationalism." *Lotus international* 20:104–126.

FRAMPTON, KENNETH 1968 "Notes on Soviet Urbanism: 1917–1932." *Architects' Yearbook* 12:238–252.

KHAN-MAHOMEDOV, S. O. 1970 "N. A. Ladovsky." *Architectural Design* 40, Feb.:86–87.

LADOVSKY, N. A. 1930 "Moskva istoricheskaya i sotsialisticheskaya." *Stroitel'stvo Moskvy* 1:17–20.

LADOVSKY, N. A. 1931 "Planirovka Avtostroiya i Magnitogorska v vuze." *Sovetskaya arkhitektura* 1–2:21–22.

LADOVSKY, N. A. 1934a "Golovnaya ploshchad' dvukh Ordynok." *Arkhitektura SSSR* 2:17.

LADOVSKY, N. A. 1934b "Proekt pasazherskoi ostanovki vodnogo transporta na prichal'noi naberezhnoi." *Arkhitektura SSSR* 4:25.

LADOVSKY, N. A. 1934c "Baza tvorcheskoi raboty." *Arkhitektura SSSR* 9:13–14.

SENKEVITCH, ANATOLE, JR. 1974 "Trends in Soviet Architectural Thought, 1917–1932: The Growth and Decline of the Constructivist and Rationalist Movements." Unpublished Ph.D. dissertation, Cornell University, Ithaca, N.Y.

ZYGAS, KESTUTIS PAUL 1978 "The Sources of Constructivist Architecture: Designs and Images, 1918–1925." Unpublished Ph.D. dissertation, Cornell University, Ithaca, N.Y.

LAFARGE, C. GRANT

See HEINS and LAFARGE.

LAFEVER, MINARD

The significance of Minard Lafever's (1798–1854) contribution to American nineteenth-century architecture was twofold. As one of the pioneer eclectics in New York, his extensive architectural practice included works in the various revival styles, particularly Gothic, which prevailed in the pre-Civil War period. Lafever also played an influential role in spreading Greek Revival motifs nationwide through his extremely popular builders' guides.

Although he was self-taught as an architect, Lafever was a well-trained carpenter and an experienced builder. Of French Huguenot descent, he was born near Morristown, New Jersey, but grew up in the Finger Lakes region of western New York. He was educated in the public schools of Ovid and may also have worked at carpentry. In the years that followed he absorbed the Late Colonial Georgian and Early Republican architectural traditions of that area. In 1820 Lafever married Pamelia Laraway, the first of three wives and with whom he had six children. Four years later he moved his family to Newark, New Jersey, where he worked as a carpenter during the day and spent his evenings drawing plans and details of buildings. About 1827 or 1828 Lafever moved to New York where he participated in the building boom of the late 1820s and the early 1830s as a draftsman supplying architectural drawings for builders.

Lafever's own transition from builder to architect was marked by the publication of his *Young Builder's General Instructor* (1829) and by his unadopted competition design for the Albany City Hall. He was listed in New York City directories as a builder and carpenter until 1831–1832, but thereafter as "architect." Lafever had very brief partnerships with Lewis M. Lindsley (1829), JAMES GALLIER SR. (1832–1834), Charles L. Bell (1835) and, later, with Benjamin F. Smith (1848–1850). Early in his career Lafever was a member of the American Institution of Architects, organized in 1836, which was the precursor of the later American Institute of Architects.

Following current English trends, Lafever's stylistic development began with an early Regency phase which led diretly into the Greek Revival, a transition that can be traced in his first three publications. Lafever's mature and later works were Early Victorian and included several Renaissance Revival examples as well as continuous Gothic Revival structures.

Lafever's fully developed Greek Revival work is best seen in *The Modern Builder's Guide* (1833) and *The Beauties of Modern Architecture* (1835). His designs for temple-type houses and decorative detail, while obviously Greek inspired, were never merely archeological copies. Lafever tried to express the delicacy and restraint of Grecian decorative motifs in his own freely conceived American versions. There is a noteworthy stylistic sequence from his relatively crude adaptations of classical detail to contemporary architectural forms in *The Young Builder's General Instructor,* to his more mature taste revealed in *The Modern Builder's Guide* and, finally, to his sophisticated and sensitive designs in *The Beauties of Modern Architecture.* These were the sources of inspiration for much of the fine wood and plaster detail that characterized houses of the Greek Revival movement.

A basic source for Lafever's knowledge of Greek architecture was the four volume *Antiquities of Athens* (1762–1816) by the English architects–archeologists JAMES STUART and NICHOLAS REVETT. Also helpful were the English builders' guides of PETER NICHOLSON, particularly for technical information, as in Lafever's *Modern Practice of Staircase and Handrail Construction* (1838).

Ironically, Lafever made very limited use of the Greek Revival style in his own architecture. An early major work was the First Reformed Dutch Church (1834–1835) in Brooklyn, with the assistance of his partner Gallier. Here Lafever used a pure Greek temple form with monumental octastyle porticoes at front and rear. A comparable design, attributed to Lafever (Shepherd, 1976), appears in the main building of Sailors' Snug Harbor (1831–1833), a home for retired seamen on the north shore of Staten Island. By the end of the 1830s, Lafever, like RICHARD UPJOHN, gave up the Grecian mode.

Lafever's major contribution to the architecture of New York was a series of churches which, together with the efforts of Upjohn, JAMES RENWICK, and the firm of ITHIEL TOWN and ALEXANDER JACKSON DAVIS, established the popularity of the Gothic Revival style in the 1840s and 1850s. The first of these was the New Dutch South Reformed Church on Washington Square (1839–1840), at University Place and Washington Place, New York. The Perpendicular design of the twin-towered façade was based on that of WILLIAM TITE's National Scotch Church (1824–1827) in London which, in turn, was influenced by the façade of York Cathedral. Lafever's desire for authenticity was a reaction against the eighteenth-century English picturesque "Gothick" mannerisms of BATTY LANGLEY and HORACE WALPOLE. He was not, however, among the many American architects in the 1840s who were adopting the doctrinaire views of ecclesiological correctness in church building put forth by A. W. N. PUGIN and the Cambridge Camden Society in England.

For the First Baptist Church on Broome Street (1841–1842) in New York, and the Pierrepont Street Baptist Church (1843–1844) in Brooklyn, Lafever used a "Collegiate Goth_ " style which may have been directly influenced by the New York University building (1833–1836) by Town and Davis. All were ultimately derived from the façade composition of King's College Chapel in Cambridge which had been recommended as a model for American churches by the Reverend John Henry Hopkins in his influential *Essay on Gothic Architecture* (1836). One of Lafever's major

works, and his most sensitively designed Gothic Revival structure, was the Church of the Saviour (1842–1844) in Brooklyn Heights, now known as the First Unitarian Church. The twin-tower façade was an elaborated version of the King's College Chapel type, while its simulated ribbed vault was typical of the American "Plaster Gothic School."

Lafever's most ambitious Gothic Revival building was the Church of the Holy Trinity (1844–1847) also in Brooklyn Heights. A description and illustrations of the church were included in Lafever's last book, *The Architectural Instructor,* published posthumously in 1856. Its magnificence was due to Edgar John Bartow, who financed the construction and who insisted upon an elaborate and impressive design. Although Perpendicular window tracery was intended originally, Lafever used the Decorated style throughout. The tower and spire (the latter taken down in 1906 after steady deterioration) were not completed until 1867. Much of the opulent quality of the interior was contributed by the elaborately traceried stained glass windows executed by the English designers William Jay Bolton and John Bolton.

In the same years, with his already considerable reputation enhanced by the building of Holy Trinity, Lafever received other commissions for more modest Gothic Revival churches. One of these was for the Second Presbyterian Church (1846–1848)

in Richmond, Virginia, noteworthy for its hammerbeam roof which Lafever was to use again in his last Gothic works. In New York, Lafever designed the Church of the Divine Unity (1844–1845) which fronted on Broadway, and extended through a long passageway to the main church building with another entrance on Crosby Street.

In the 1840s Lafever enriched his eclectic repertoire with Egyptian and Italian Renaissance forms. Characteristically, his emphasis was on invention rather than archeological accuracy. A number of his own works, as well as projects for cottages, villas, and mansions in Italian, Tuscan, Gothic, Grecian, and Roman styles were illustrated in *The Architectural Instructor.* The only executed Egyptian Revival monument was a sepulchral obelisk in brownstone for Ada Augusta Shields (1845) in Greenwood Cemetery, Brooklyn. The same Egyptian obelisk form, more ornate and colossal in scale, was used by Lafever in his accepted but never completed competition design for a monument to George Washington (1847) in New York (Landy, 1969).

A major Egyptian Revival work was the Whalers' (First Presbyterian) Church (1843–1844) in Sag Harbor, Long Island, where Lafever spent some time in 1843 personally supervising its construction. The façade had an Egyptian pylon form with battered walls, but interior details were still Greek Revival, while the steeple (destroyed by a hurricane in 1938) was the English baroque type developed by CHRISTOPHER WREN in his London city churches.

Lafever's use of the Italian style was confined to the more formal types of fifteenth- and sixteenth-century Renaissance architecture. For the Episcopal Church of the Holy Apostles (1846–1848) in New York, the Tuscan Doric manner of the fifteenth century was used for the interior. The exterior, of red brick, was again a simplified version of Wren's city church type, with a prominent single tower and wood spire. Several years later Lafever repeated the design of the Church of the Holy Apostles for two other churches, the Reformed Protestant Dutch Church (1851–1852) in Kingston, New York, and the Pearl Street Congregational Church (1851–1852) in Hartford.

Also Renaissance, in a freely treated Italianate version, was the old Brooklyn Savings Bank (1846–1847) in Brooklyn Heights. While not a pure example of the new Italian Renaissance Revival, it was, with the A. T. Stewart Store, one of the earliest buildings in that style to appear in New York. More specifically Palladian was Lafever's Reformed (Protestant Dutch) Church on the Heights (1850–1851) near Monroe Place, in Brooklyn Heights. The interior was intended to emulate that of the Church of the Madeleine (1808–1843) in Paris. For an approach to the proposed ferry from the foot of Montague Street in Brooklyn Heights to Wall Street in lower Manhattan, Lafever was commissioned by Edgar John Bartow to design a stone archway, bridge, and terrace. Not in any of the current revival styles, Lafever's arched bridge (c.1847–1853) was a severe unadorned structure.

In most of his late works Lafever continued his fundamental adherence to the Gothic Revival style. For the Church of the Neighbor, originally called Church of the Restoration (1848–1850) in Brooklyn Heights, Perpendicular Gothic was combined with some Decorated details. In the same years Lafever designed three churches, a commercial building, and a house in Syracuse, New York. Of these, the First Presbyterian Church (1848–1850) was in the Early English Gothic style, while the First Baptist Church (1848–1850) and the First Dutch Reformed Church (1849–1850) were in the Italian Renaissance mode.

Except for a school building in Elbridge, New York, Lafever's last Gothic Revival works were built in Brooklyn, where he died. He came closest to the spirit of an English parish church of the Decorated period in the Strong Place Baptist Church (1851–1852) just south of Brooklyn Heights. Although Lafever is not known to have had any particular sympathy with the tenets of the Puginians, his design did coincide in time with the ecclesiological parish church revival fostered in the late 1840s by Upjohn, JOHN NOTMAN, and FRANK WILLS. The "open timber roof" motif of the interior was repeated by Lafever in Packer Collegiate Institute (1854) in Brooklyn Heights. This was Lafever's last commission, and one for which he was personally selected by the school's benefactor, Harriet L. Packer. To suggest the educational purpose of the structure, Lafever chose the Tudor Gothic style which he also used for another school building, the Munro Academy (1854) in Elbridge, New York.

Although Lafever was credited with the design of some forty churches and a large number of houses and public buildings, only about half of the churches and very few other buildings have been documented. The amount and quality of the work that is known, however, as well as the importance of his popular builders' guides in the development of the Greek Revival movement, establish Lafever's significance in the history of American architecture during the pre-Civil War period.

JACOB LANDY

WORKS

(A)1831–1833, Sailors' Snug Harbor, Staten Island, N.Y. *1834–1835, First Reformed Dutch Church (with James Gallier, Sr.), Brooklyn, N.Y. *1839–1840, New Dutch South Reformed Church on Washington Square; *1841–1842, First Baptist Church on Broome Street; New York. 1842–1844, Church of the Saviour (now the First Unitarian Church); *1843–1844, Pierrepont Street Baptist Church; Brooklyn, N.Y. 1843–1844, Whalers' (First Presbyterian) Church, Sag Harbor, N.Y. *1844–1845, Church of the Divine Unity, New York. 1844–1847, Church of the Holy Trinity; 1845, Tomb Monument for Ada Augusta Shields; Brooklyn, N.Y. *1846–1847, Brooklyn Savings Bank, N.Y. 1846–1848, Episcopal Church of the Holy Apostles, New York. 1846–1848, Second Presbyterian Church, Richmond, Va. *1847, Monument to George Washington (never completed), New York. *c.1847–1853, Arched Bridge and Terrace; *1848–1850, Church of the Neighbor; Brooklyn, N.Y. *1848–1850, First Baptist Church; *1848–1850, First Presbyterian Church; *1849–1850, First Dutch Reformed Church; Syracuse, N.Y. *1850–1851, Reformed (Protestant Dutch) Church on the Heights, Brooklyn, N.Y. *1851–1852, Pearl Street Congregational Church, Hartford, Conn. 1851–1852, Reformed Protestant Dutch Church, Kingston, N.Y. 1851–1852, Strong Place Baptist Church, Brooklyn, N.Y. *1854, Munro Academy, Elbridge, N.Y. 1854, Packer Collegiate Institute (not completed until 1856), Brooklyn, N.Y.

BIBLIOGRAPHY

BROWN, ROSCOE C. E. 1922 *Church of the Holy Trinity: Brooklyn Heights in the City of New York, 1847–1922; A Historical Sketch Commemorating the Seventy-fifth Anniversary of the Opening of the Church.* New York: Dunlap.
HAMLIN, TALBOT (1944a)1964 *Greek Revival Architecture in America.* Reprint. New York: Dover.
HAMLIN, TALBOT 1944b "Minard Lafever." Volume 21, pages 479–481 in *Dictionary of American Biography.* Supplement One. New York: Scribner.
LAFEVER, MINARD 1829 *The Young Builder's General Instructor.* Newark, N.J.: Tuttle.
LAFEVER, MINARD (1833)1969 *The Modern Builder's Guide.* Reprint. New York: Dover. Introduction to the reprint edition by Jacob Landy.
LAFEVER, MINARD (1835)1968 *The Beauties of Modern Architecture.* Reprint. New York: Da Capo.
LAFEVER, MINARD 1838 *The Modern Practice of Staircase and Handrail Construction, Practically Explained, in a Series of Designs.* New York: Appleton.
LAFEVER, MINARD 1856 *The Architectural Instructor.* New York: Putnam. Published posthumously.
LANDY, JACOB 1969 "The Washington Monument Project in New York." *Journal of the Society of Architectural Historians.* 28:291–297.
LANDY, JACOB 1970 *The Architecture of Minard Lafever.* New York: Columbia University Press.
McKEE, HARLEY J. 1956 "Minard Lafever in the Syracuse Area." *Straight Edge* 9:3–5.
SHEPHERD, BARNETT 1976 "Sailors' Snug Harbor Reattributed to Minard Lafever." *Journal of the Society of Architectural Historians* 35:108–123.

LAFFERTY, JAMES V.

Patenting an elephant building design in 1882, James V. Lafferty (c.1860–?) built hotels with porthole eyes, disposal chute in the trunk, and stairwells in the legs and belly. The first, in Coney Island, New York, was destroyed by fire in 1896. The Elephant Hotel in Margate City, New Jersey, includes a howdah eighty-five feet high which offers a view of the sea.

JANET KAPLAN

WORKS

*1882–1896, Elephantine Colossus, Coney Island, New York. 1883, Elephant Hotel, Margate City, N.J.

BIBLIOGRAPHY

LANCASTER, CLAY 1960 Pages 186–196 in *Architectural Follies in America; or, Hammer, Sawtooth and Nail.* Rutland, Vt.: Tuttle.

LA GUÊPIERE, PIERRE LOUIS PHILIPPE DE

Pierre Louis Philippe de La Guêpière (c.1715–1773) studied architecture with his uncle, the academician Jacques de La Guêpière. Among his associates were JACQUES FRANÇOIS BLONDEL, whose precepts influenced his work, and Leopoldo Retti, who secured his appointment to the court of the margrave of Bade-Durlach (1750) and whom he succeeded as architect to the duke of Wurttemberg (1752–1768). Besides the buildings realized for the duke, de La Guêpière's reputation rests on his fantastic projects of the 1750s published in the *Recueil.* He was a corresponding member of the French Academy and held memberships in the academies of Berlin, Augsburg, and San Luca in Rome.

RICHARD CLEARY

WORKS

1752 Ducal Palace (completion), Stuttgart, Germany. *1752, Margrave's Palace (completion), Karlsruhe, Germany. 1759–1760, Ducal Palace (completion), Ludwigsburg, Germany. 1760–1765, Mon Repos, near Stuttgart, Germany. 1763–1767, La Solitude; *1764–1765, Theater, Ducal Palace; Ludwigsburg, Germany.

BIBLIOGRAPHY

COLOMBIER, PIERRE DU 1956 *L'Architecture française en Allemagne au XVIIIe siècle.* 2 vols. Paris: Presses Universitaires de France.
HAUTECOEUR, LOUIS 1950 *Première moitié du XVIIIe siècle: Le style Louis XV.* Volume 3 in *Histoire de l'architecture classique en France.* Paris: Picard.
HAAS, WALTER 1960 "Die Architekten Retti und La Guêpière am neuen Schloss in Stuttgart." *Deutsche Kunst und Denkmalpflege* no. 1:30–38.
KLAIBER, HANS ANDREAS 1959 *Der württembergische Oberbaudirektor Philippe de La Guêpière: Ein Beitrag zur Kunstgeschichte der Architektur am Ende des Spätbarock.* Stuttgart, Germany: Kohlhammer.
LA GUÊPIÈRE, PHILIPPE DE 1759 *Recueil d'esquisse d'architecture, représentant plusieurs monumens de composition, dont partie sont construits.* Stuttgart, Germany: Cotta.
"Der Wiederaufbau des neuen Schlosses zu Stuttgart." 1966 *Deutsche Kunst und Denkmalpflege* no. 2:117–127.

LAINEE, THOMAS

Thomas Lainée, or Lainé (1686–1739), decorator and architect, trained in Paris, but first worked with ROBERT DE COTTE, JULES HARDOUIN MANSART, and ANGE JACQUES GABRIEL as decorator at Versailles and Fontainebleau. After 1712, when royal commissions ceased, he relocated in southern France, working initially as decorator under the Avignon architect JEAN-BAPTISTE FRANQUE, and then as an independent architect.

JUANITA M. ELLIAS

WORKS

1708, Cathedral of Notre-Dame (choir stalls), Paris. 1708, Chapel (column bases and plaster confessionals), Versailles, France. 1716, Hôtel de Forbin de Sainte-Croix; 1732, Hôtel de Rochegude, 4–6 Rue des Trois-Faucons; 1732, Salle de Comedie, Place de l'Oulle; 1736, Chapel of Pénitents Noirs (façade); Avignon, France.

BIBLIOGRAPHY

HAUTECOEUR, LOUIS 1950 *Première moitié du XVIIIe siècle: Le style Louis XV.* Volume 3 in *Histoire de l'architecture classique en France.* Paris: Picard.
LAINÉE, THOMAS 1740 *Le Livre de divers desseins d'ornements . . . inventé par Mr. Lainé.* With engravings by J. J. Balechou. Aix en Provence, France: Viale.
LAVEDAN, PIERRE 1963 "La Chapelle des Pénitents Noirs à Avignon." *Congrès Archéologique de France* 121:125–131.

LALLERSTEDT, ERIK

Erik Julius Lallerstedt (1864–1955) studied architecture at the Royal Institute of Technology, Stockholm (1882–1886) and in 1889 graduated from the Royal Academy of Art, Stockholm, where he studied under Claes Grundström.

Lallerstedt contributed to modern Swedish design as a leading exponent of Art Nouveau and National Romanticism. However, his career encompasses many styles, including, at the end, functionalism. He was particularly important as a professor at the Kungsholmen Tekniska Högskola between 1907 and 1929, where he was considered I. G. CLASON's successor and where he trained many future architects.

His largest independent work, the Royal Institute of Technology (1911–1922), was also his most outstanding. Formally planned and connected by courtyards, the original complex of buildings was completed in 1922; Lallerstedt continued to add buildings until 1940. The flat surfaces and concrete blocks are modern, but they are offset by traditional elements of Swedish architecture, such as the main tower, the sculptural details, and the steep, pitched roofs. Similar syntheses of old and new occurring in his work before 1930 represent a search for modern architecture expressive of the age, of Swedish heritage and Swedish needs. His writings on architecture appeared frequently in the periodicals *Tekniska Tidskrift* and *Byggmastären Arkitektur*.

Besides his early collaborative efforts with LUDWIG PETERSON, Lallerstedt worked with SIGURD LEWERENTZ and David Helldén on the Malmö City Theater (1935–1940) and during the late 1930s and 1940s with his son Lars Erik Lallerstedt.

JUDITH S. HULL

WORKS

1887–1897, Royal Academy of Art (alterations and extension); 1898–1900, G. E. Broms House (with Ludwig Peterson); 1899, Saint Peter's Church; 1901, Matteus Church; 1902–1909, Bergslagens Railroad Offices; 1906–1909, Tryggs Assurance Limited Building; 1911–1922, 1922–1940, Royal Institute of Technology; 1915, Thule Life Assurance Limited Building; 1918–1926, Humanities and Law Buildings, Stockholm University; Stockholm. 1935–1940, Malmö City Theater (with David Helldén and Sigurd Lewerentz), Sweden.

BIBLIOGRAPHY

AHLBERG, HAKON 1929 "Erik Lallerstedt's undervisning i arkitektur." *Byggmastären Arkitektur* 8:157ff.
BEDOIRE, FREDERIC 1978 "Erik Julius Lallerstedt." Volume 22, pages 190–194 in *Svensk Biografiskt Lexikon.* Edited by Erik Grill. Stockholm: Norstedts Tryckeri.

he became architect of the Cour de Cassation and the Ecole Nationale des Mines. Later, he was Inspecteur Général des Bâtiments Civils et Palais Nationaux. He opened an atelier in 1890, and taught up to the time of his death, a favorite of American students. His first important work was Romanesque, but he was famous rather for his grand and expansive, almost ebullient, classical style.

R. D. MIDDLETON

WORKS

1883–?, Apartment Block, 9 rue Lemoult (rue Saint Christophe); 1885, House, 177 rue Croix-Nivert; Paris. 1887–1924, Basilique Saint Martin, Tours, Indre et Loire, France. c.1890, Apartment Block, rue Bosquet, Paris. 1895–1898, Gare, Place Général Leclerc, Tours; 1896–1904, Hôtel de Ville, Place Jean-Jaurès, Tours, Indre et Loire, France, 1898–1900, Gare du Chemin de Fer d'Orléans and Hôtel Terminus (Gare d'Orsay; completed by Lucien Magne), rue de Bellechasse, Paris. 1905–1911, Hôtel de Ville, Bourse and Chambre de Commerce, Grande Place, Roubaix, Nord, France. 1908–1909, Crédit Lyonnais (glazed dome and gallery with André Felix Narjoux), 18 rue du Quatre Septembre; n.d., Apartment Block, 64 rue des Petits Champs; Paris. n.d., Château of Sancourt (restoration and extension), Nord, France. *n.d., Villa des Bambous, Boulevard de la Croisette, Cannes, Alpes Maritimes, France.

BIBLIOGRAPHY

COX, H. BARTLE 1920 "M. Victor Laloux: The Man and His Work." *Architects' Journal* 51:555–557, 609–611, 639–640, 731–732.
CURINIER, C. E. 1899–1906 Volume 2, pages 36–37 in *Dictionnaire nationale des contemporains.* Paris: Office Générale d'Edition.
"Hommage à Laloux, de ses élèves américains." 1937 *Pencil Points* 18:621–630.
LALOUX, VICTOR A. F. 1888 *L'Architecture Grecque.* Paris: Quantin.
LALOUX, VICTOR A. F., and MONCEAUX, PAUL 1889 *Restauration d'Olympie: L'histoire—les monuments—le culte et les fêtes.* Paris: Quantin.
LEMARESQUIER, CHARLES HENRI CAMILLE 1938 *Institut de France. Académie des Beaux-Arts: Notice sur la vie et les travaux de Victor Laloux.* Paris: Firmin-Didot.

LALOUX, VICTOR ALEXANDRE FREDERIC

Born at Tours, Victor Alexandre Frédéric Laloux (1850–1937) entered the Ecole des Beaux-Arts in 1869. A pupil of Louis Jules André, he won the Grand Prix of Rome in 1878. Returning to Paris,

LAMB, CHARLES ROLLINSON

Born in New York City, Charles Rollinson Lamb (1860–1942) was an energetic and charismatic leader in the city's art and civic organizations from the late 1880s through the 1910s. At sixteen, he left college to work for his father at J. and R. Lamb Studios, the family firm which specialized in interiors for ecclesiastical and memorial architecture, particularly stained glass and mosaics. Later, he managed the company, working with his wife, the painter Ella Condie Lamb, and his younger brother Frederick Stymetz Lamb, the principal designer. Drawing on the art of the past and the aesthetics of the Arts and Crafts movement, their lapidary interiors are characteristic products of the American Renaissance.

Although known as an architect, Lamb built only two structures, both in 1899: his house in Cresskill, New Jersey, and the temporary Admiral Dewey Arch in New York, a collaboration with prominent sculptors which won him national recognition. He also planned the Court of Honor for the Hudson-Fulton Celebration in New York in 1909.

Lamb devoted much time to city planning, both practical and visionary. As a member of the Municipal Art Society, city commissions, and business associations, he promulgated the City Beautiful. His own proposals were generally more inventive and specific than most formal City Beautiful planning; they include pioneering schemes for a setback skyscraper (1898) and pedestrian "streets in the air" connecting tall buildings at upper floors. Though he persistently presented his ideas in journals and newspapers, none were implemented, and he grew increasingly discouraged and silent after 1910. His ideas, however, were not so much impractical as premature, for they reappeared, without credit, in the futuristic renderings of 1920s visionaries such as HUGH FERRISS and HARVEY WILEY CORBETT.

CAROL WILLIS

WORKS

*1899, Admiral Dewey Arch, New York. 1899, Charles R. Lamb House, Cresskill, N.J. 1901, Chapel in the Mission Building, Pan-American Exposition, Buffalo, N.Y. 1904, Flower Memorial (interior), Watertown, N.Y. 1910, Lakewood Memorial Chapel (interior), Minneapolis, Minn. 1910, Sage Memorial Chapel (interior), Cornell University, Ithaca, N.Y.

BIBLIOGRAPHY

COLLINS, GEORGE R. 1979 *Visionary Drawings of Architecture and Planning: 20th Century through the 1960s.* Cambridge, Mass., and London: M.I.T. Press.
LAMB, CHARLES ROLLINSON 1898 "Civic Architecture from Its Constructive Side." *Municipal Affairs* 2:46–72.
LAMB, CHARLES ROLLINSON 1900 "New York—The City Beautiful." *Metropolitan Magazine* 12, no. 5:593–600.
LAMB, CHARLES ROLLINSON 1904 "City Plan." *The Craftsman* 6, no. 1:3–13.
SKY, ALISON, and STONE, MICHELLE 1976 *Unbuilt America.* New York: McGraw-Hill.

LAMB, E. B.

Edward Buckton Lamb (1806–1869) was one of the most perverse and original of mid-Victorian British architects and was characterized as a "Rogue architect" by H. S. GOODHART-RENDEL. His centralized church plans in the tradition of CHRISTOPHER WREN and the eclectic eccentricity of his architectural forms earned Lamb unremitting criticism in *The Ecclesiologist.* Largely unaffected by the stylistic and liturgical orthodoxies established by A. W. N. PUGIN and the Cambridge Camden Society, his attitude to architecture was essentially Picturesque.

The son of an artist, Lamb was articled to L. N. Cottingham and worked as a draftsman for JOHN CLAUDIUS LOUDON. Lamb undertook domestic as well as church work, and he remodeled Hughenden Manor (1863–1866) for Benjamin Disraeli. Having built a large house for himself (1866–1868), Lamb died bankrupt.

GAVIN M. STAMP

WORKS

*1831–1832, Saint Philip's Church, Clerkenwell, London. c.1837–1840, Chequer's Court (lodge and cottage), Buckinghamshire, England. c.1838, King of Würtemberg's House, Stuttgart, Germany. 1839, Ellesborough School, Buckinghamshire, England. 1839–1857, Schloss Hradek, Nechanic, Czechoslovakia. 1840, Saint George's Church, Quarry Hill, Sowerby, Yorkshire, England. 1848–1849, Holy Trinity Church (school and vicarage), Prestwood, Buckinghamshire, England. 1854–1858, Schloss Prugg, Bruck-an-der-Leitha, Austria. 1855, 1863, Royal National Hospital, Bournemouth, England. 1857, Town Hall, Eye, Suffolk, England. 1862, Monument to Isaac d'Israeli, Hughenden; 1863–1866, Hughenden Manor (remodeled and refaced); Buckinghamshire, England. 1866–1868, The Plaisance, Fawkham, Kent, England. 1868, Church of Saint Mary Magdalene, Addiscombe, Surrey, England.

BIBLIOGRAPHY

GIROUARD, MARK (1971)1979 *The Victorian Country House.* Rev. ed. New Haven: Yale University Press.
GOODHARD-RENDEL, H. S. 1949 "Rogue Architects of the Victorian Era." *Journal of the Royal Institute of British Architects* Series 3 66:251–259.
LAMB, E. B. 1830 *Etchings of Gothic Ornament.* London.
LAMB, E. B. 1834–1838 *Architectural Magazine.* Includes many articles by Lamb.
LAMB, E. B. 1843 *A Memoir of J. C. Loudon.* London.
LAMB, E. B. 1846 *Studies of Ancient Domestic Architecture.* London: Weale.
LAMB, E. B. 1860 "Architectural Composition." *Building News* 6:439.
LAMB, E. B. 1861 "Architectural Progression." *Building News* 7:188.
"Obituary." 1869 *The Builder* 27, Sept. 11:720.

SUMMERSON, JOHN   1970   "Two London Churches."
In *Victorian Architecture: Four Studies in Evaluation.*
New York: Columbia University Press.

LAMB, THOMAS W.

Thomas White Lamb (1871–1942) is best known
for his work as a theater designer. Born in Dundee,
Scotland, Lamb came to America as a child and
was educated at Cooper Union in New York. During his career, he designed stage and movie theaters throughout the United States and abroad. In
1932, he won honorable mention in the Palace of
the Soviets competition.

DENNIS MCFADDEN

WORKS

1912, Cort Theater; 1919, Rivoli Theater; 1922, Loew's
State Theater and Offices; 1927, Pythian Temple; New
York.

BIBLIOGRAPHY

Numerous articles on Thomas W. Lamb are in *Mar-
quee: Journal of the Theater Historical Society.*
"Thomas W. Lamb Dies: Designed the Garden and 300
Theaters."   1942   *New York Herald Tribune,* Feb. 27,
p. 16.

LAMB, WILLIAM F.

See SHREVE, LAMB, and HARMON.

LAMB and RICH

The firm of Lamb and Rich was active in New
York City from 1882 to 1899. A partnership between the Scots-born Hugh Lamb (1849–1903)
and Charles Alonzo Rich (1855–1943), a native of
Beverly, Massachusetts, the firm was well known
for its work for educational institutions. Examples
of Lamb and Rich's work in this vein are the Main
Building at Pratt Institute in Brooklyn, New York
(1887), and Millbank, Brinkerhoff, and Fiske Halls
at Barnard College in New York (1890, 1896, and
1897). The firm also designed many residences in
and around New York, including urban rowhouses and such country houses as *Sagamore Hill* in
Oyster Bay, New York, built in 1893 for Theodore
Roosevelt.

DENNIS MCFADDEN

WORKS

1887, Main Building, Pratt Institute, Brooklyn, N.Y.
1890, Millbank Hall, Barnard College, New York. 1893,
Sagamore Hill (Theodore Roosevelt House), Oyster
Bay, N.Y. 1896, Brinkerhoff Hall; 1897, Fiske Hall; Barnard College, New York.

BIBLIOGRAPHY

"Barnard College, New York."   1898   *American Archi-
tect and Building News* 62:82.
"House of Theodore Roosevelt."   1893   *American
Architect and Building News* 39, no. 395:110.
LANDAU, SARAH BRADFORD   1975   "The Row Houses
of New York's West Side." *Journal of the Society of
Architectural Historians* 34:19–36.
"The Pratt Institute."   1887   *American Architect and
Building News* 22:112.

LANE, HENRY BOWYER

Interrupting an obscure career in England to live
briefly (1841–1847) in Canada, Henry B. Lane
(19th century) secured commissions with the aid
of the influential Boulton family to design several
important buildings in Toronto, including the
City Hall and Market (1844–1845), additions and
alterations to Osgoode Hall (1844–1845), and
three churches.

STEPHEN A. OTTO

BIBLIOGRAPHY

*Material on Henry Bowyer Lane is available in the manu-
script Journal of John George Howard, Baldwin Room, Met-
ropolitan Toronto Reference Library, and the Strachan Pa-
pers, Ontario Archives, Toronto. See also the newspapers listed
below on the specific dates noted.*
British Colonist (Toronto) Aug. 20, 1944.
The Church May 17, 1844; Oct. 29, 1845.
The (Toronto) Globe Dec. 2, 1845.
Toronto Herald July 27, 1864; May 18, 1845.
Toronto Patriot July 21, 1843; May 7, 1844.

LANFRANCHI, CARLO EMANUELE

Carlo Emanuele Lanfranchi (1632–1721), son of
FRANCESCO LANFRANCHI, worked primarily for
the ducal court in Piedmont, Italy. The Church of
San Giuseppe (1683–1690) is his best work. The
Basilica of Santi Maurizio and Lazzaro (1679–),
attributed to Lanfranchi, is now known to be by
ANTONIO BETTINO.

HENRY A. MILLON

WORKS

*1683–1690, San Giuseppe; *1684–1690, Palazzo Reale
(east wing and Gallery of Daniel); *1713, Palazzo Reale
(Sala di Caffè); Turin, Italy.

BIBLIOGRAPHY

BRAYDA, CARLO; COLI, LAURA; and SESIA, DARIO

1963   *Ingegneri e architetti del sei e settecento in Piemonte.* Turin, Italy: Società Ingegnerie Architettio.

BERNARDI, MARZIANO   1959   *Il Palazzo Reale di Reale.* Turin, Italy.

ROVERE, C.   1858   *Descrizione del Reale Palazzo di Torino.* Turin, Italy.

TAMBURINI, LUCIANO   1968   *Le Chiese di Torino.* Turin, Italy: Le bouquiniste.

LANFRANCHI, FRANCESCO

Francesco Lanfranchi (c.1600–1669), architectural heir of ASCANIO VITOZZI, was from the Piedmont region in Italy. His adaptation of Vitozzi's design concepts resulted in buildings that are heavier in tone. His emphasis on the central-plan church contrasts with the elongated plans of his contemporary, ANDREA COSTAGUTO. Lanfranchi's major work is the extensive Palazzo di Citta, crucial in Turin's urban development and more distinguished than AMEDEO DI CASTELLAMONTE's Palazzo Reale façade. The projects for the façade prove him a good draftsman despite the provincial mixture of Roman, north Italian, and French elements.

MARTHA POLLAK

WORKS

1657–1660, Church of the Visitation; 1659, City Hall; Turin, Italy. 1663–1664, Church of Eremo, Lanzo, Italy. 1668, San Croce, Caramagna, Italy.

Langhans. Brandenburg Gate. Berlin. 1789

BIBLIOGRAPHY

CARBONERI, NINO   1963   "Architettura." *Mostra del barocco piemontese* 1:27–28.

TAMBURINI, L.   1968   *Le chiese di Torino.* Ruin, Italy.

WITTKOWER, RUDOLF   1965   *Art and Architecture in Italy: 1600 to 1750.* 2d ed., rev. Baltimore: Penguin.

LANFRANCO

An early twelfth-century text and an inscription on the apse of Modena Cathedral, Italy, attest to the fact that Lanfranco (11th–12th centuries.), *mirabilis aedificator,* designed that building in 1099. Lanfranco seems to have come from Lombardy; his cultural framework embraced Burgundian architecture and the late classical remains of northern Italy.

CHRISTINE SMITH

WORK

(A)1099, Cathedral of Modena, Italy.

BIBLIOGRAPHY

QUINTAVALLE, ARTURO CARLO   1964–1965   *La Cattedrale di Modena: Problemi di Romanico Emiliano.* Modena, Italy: Bassi and Nipoti.

LANGHANS, CARL GOTTHARD

A native of Silesia, Carl Gotthard Langhans (1733–1808) studied law before beginning his architectural career at Breslau. Numerous country houses and the public buildings he designed as *Oberbaurat* in Silesia are in a neo-Palladian mode (see ANDREA PALLADIO) inspired by FRIEDRICH WILHELM ERDMANNSDORFF's Schloss Wörlitz. A specialist in theater design, his interest in acoustics and sight lines is reflected in a series of galleried, oval-plan Protestant churches.

In 1788, he was named director of the Royal Office of Buildings, in Berlin and, at King Friedrich Wilhelm III's suggestion, turned to Greek propylaea as a prototype for the Brandenburg Gate (1789). Seen by many contemporaries as a statement of pure Grecian classicism, the Doric gate's svelte proportions and solecisms in type have made it emblematic of the transition from the late baroque of the francophile court to Prussian neoclassicism. Langhans's last major work, the National Theater in Berlin (1800–1802)—rebuilt by KARL FRIEDRICH SCHINKEL after it burned in 1817—was the starting point for his son KARL FERDINAND LANGHANS's long career in theater design.

BARRY BERGDOLL

WORKS

*1764–1772, Protestant Church, Gross-Glogau, Silesia, Poland. 1766–1786, Palace of Fürst Hatzfeld; *1771, Sugar Refinery; *1774–1776, Friedrichstor; Breslau, Poland. *1777–1779, Poorhouse, Kreuzberg, Silesia, Poland. *1782, Old Theater, Breslau, Poland. 1785, Protestant Church, Gross Waltenburg, Poland. 1785, Protestant Church, Waldenburg, Silesia, Poland. 1785–1787, Pachaly House, Breslau, Poland. 1787, Marienkirche an Neuen Markt (tower); 1787, Opera House (rebuilding); 1787, Schloss Charlottenburg (Theater); 1788, Belvedere (Tea House), Schloss Charlottenburg Park; Berlin. *1788–1789, Hauptwache, Breslau, Poland. 1789, Brandenburg Gate; 1789, Mohrenstrasse Colonnades; 1789–1790, Veterinary School; Berlin. 1791, Orangery, Marmorpalais, Potsdam, Germany. 1794–1795, Royal Palace (extension), Breslau, Poland. *1800–1802, National Theater (rebuilt by Karl Friedrich Schinkel), Berlin. 1803–1808, Protestant Church, Rawitsch, Posnania, Germany.

BIBLIOGRAPHY

BAUCH, KURT 1966 *Das Brandenburger Tor.* Cologne, Germany: Freunde des Wallraf-Richartz-Museum.

GRUNDMAN, GÜNTHER 1943 "Die Richtungs-änderung in der schlesischen Kunst des achtzehnten Jahrhunderts." In Hans Tintelnot (editor), *Kunstgeschichtliche Studien.* Breslau, Poland: Ganverlag-NS-Schlesien.

HINRICHS, WALTHER 1909 *Carl Gotthard Langhans: Ein schlesischer Baumeister, 1733–1808.* Strasbourg, France: Heitz & Mündel.

WERNER, PETER 1970 Pages 55–59 in *Pompeji und die Wanddekoration der Goethezeit.* Munich: Wilhelm Fink.

LANGHANS, KARL

An exact contemporary of KARL FRIEDRICH SCHINKEL, Karl Ferdinand Langhans (1781–1869) was trained under his father, CARL GOTTHARD LANGHANS, and David Gilly, and entered the Royal Buildings Department in Berlin in 1797. His lifelong concern with theater architecture began in 1800–1802 working on his father's National Theater. After traveling to Italy and Vienna (1807–1808), he established himself in Breslau where he received an official post in 1815. His own villa (1816–1819) and public buildings there reflect the severe neoclassicism of HEINRICH GENTZ, although in two churches he turned to exposed brick and Romanesque forms. In 1810, Langhans published the first of numerous works on theater design in which acoustics were systematically studied as the basis for design. In 1817, he lost to Schinkel in a bid to rebuild the National Theater; but he returned to Berlin after his design for a palace on Unter den Linden (1834–1836) was se-lected. Nonetheless, Langhans remained outside the dominant Schinkel-trained circle. He devoted himself to designing and advising on theaters, remaining attached to more traditional forms, even reviving rococo interior designs.

BARRY BERGDOLL

WORKS

1810, Pachaly Banking House (addition); 1813, House, 16 Albrechtstrasse; 1816–1819, Loge Friedrich zum goldenen Szepter, 10 Antonienstrasse; 1816–1819, Langhans Villa, Sandbrücke; 1818–1827, Blücher Monument (base); 1821–1823, Elftausendjungfrauenkirche; *1822–1824, Old Stock Exchange; Breslau, Poland. 1822–1824, Chapel, Heiligen Berg, Osswitz, Poland. 1827, Dianabad, 80 Klosterstrasse, Breslau, Poland. *1834–1836, Palace of Prince Wilhelm, Unter den Linden, Berlin. 1838–1841, Actor's Guild Theater, Breslau, Poland. 1841–1842, Municipal Theater, Liegnitz, Germany. *1843–1844, Opera House (remodeling), Berlin. 1846–1849, Theater, Stettin, Poland. *1848, Schilling House, Exerzierplatz; *1852, Palace of Graf Schwerin, Unter den Linden; *1854, Victoria Theater (built by E. Titz); Berlin. 1855–1856, Theater, Dessau, Germany. 1864–1868, Theater, Leipzig. *1869, Opera House (addition for Garderobe), Berlin.

BIBLIOGRAPHY

BÖRSCH-SUPAN, EVA 1977 *Berliner Baukunst nach Schinkel, 1840–1870.* Munich: Prestel.

LANGHANS, KARL F. 1810 *Über Theater oder Bemerkungen über Katakustik in Beziehung auf Theater.* Berlin: Hayn.

ROHE, WILHELM 1934 *Karl Ferdinand Langhans, ein Theaterbaumeister des Klassizismus.* Bückenburg, Germany: Prinz.

SCHNEIDER, LOUIS, and LANGHANS, KARL F. 1845 *Die Geschichte der Oper und des königlichen Opernhauses in Berlin, mit architectktonischen Beiträgen.* Berlin: Duncker & Humblot.

LANGLEY, BATTY

Batty Langley (1696–1751) deserves to be forgotten as an architect. Perhaps he realized this at an early stage in his career or perhaps he never intended to be one, for as the son of Daniel Langley, a Twickenham gardener, he was trained in his father's profession, and as late as 1741 his portrait by J. Carwitham shows him holding the plan of a garden in the semiformal style. His earliest recorded work was for Thomas Vernon at Twickenham in 1722, but his fame as a gardener rests entirely upon two books; the *New Principles of Gardening* and *A Sure Method of Improving Estates,* both published in 1728, and probably also on his *Pomona* of 1729. Already in *Practical Geometry* (1726) he had given directions for what he described as "arti-natural" designs, and these "regular irregularies" place his among the earliest exponents of irregular gardening. Much of his writing was dependent upon STEPHEN SWITZER's *Ichnographica Rustica* (1718), and this dependence upon the precepts of others runs through all his published works. He was not an original thinker and was often outrageously plagiarist, but he was very quick to sense the new fashions and to exploit these to the full. In 1726 his wanton arti-natural lines, recommended as "exceedingly beautiful in building, as in ceilings, parquetting, painting, paving, &c" adumbrate Hogarth's "Line of Beauty" and are a decisive step toward the rococo style in England. There is no doubt at all that Langley is Hogarth's equivalent in architecture, and as Eileen Harris writes, "he was a Rococo pioneer, the leading spokesman of the opposition to the Burlington establishment, a champion of English craftsmen; above all an avid freemason, passionately devoted to the education of his brethren."

It is as a freemason that Langley's achievement in the profession of architectural pattern book compiler and pamphleteer must be judged. No study of Langley's books can be made without extensive reference to an astonishing range of books and engravings, and these are listed in his "advertisement" at the end of the last part of *Ancient Masonry* (1736) in which, incidentally, he first advertised his services for building. *Ancient Masonry* was the largest of English architectural books, but nearly all its five hundred or more plates were plundered from the works of others. Freemasonry was formally organized in England in 1717, and Langley dedicated *Practical Geometry* (1726) to Lord Paisley who had been installed as Grand Master in 1725. In his *Builder's Chest-Book* (1727) the "Dialogue" is in an early form of masonic catechism. *Ancient Masonry* was dedicated to Francis, duke of Lorrain, the first royal freemason; *The Builder's Compleat Assistant* (1738) was subscribed to by the Sun Lodge of Saint Paul's Church-Yard; the *Builder's Jewel* (1741) carries a masonic frontispiece; and *Ancient Architecture* (1742) has as dedicatees two eminent freemasons, the dukes of Richmond and Montagu. There can be no doubt as to Langley's devotion to the fraternity, and should any doubt remain, it will be dispelled by the revelation that his four innocent sons were named Euclid, Vitruvius, Archimedes, and Hiram.

For inventing five Gothic orders in *Ancient Architecture*, Langley was ridiculed by his contemporaries. The initiative to do so was again masonic, especially because the Gothic style was so English and therefore nationalistic. The Gothic designs presented by Langley might have been frivolous, but they were immensely influential, and throughout Britain there are doors, windows, and chimney pieces derived from his book. It may not have been a coincidence that two years later, in 1744, JOHN VARDY published his *Some Designs of Mr Inigo Jones and Mr Wm Kent,* the principal source for Kent's Gothick designs.

Langley was far more influential than WILLIAM HALFPENNY as a pattern book producer, for he was more eclectic in his choice of subjects and produced many small books available to carpenters and builders all over the country. We would agree with Langley's pride in the "great advantages" to be accrued to "Builders and Workmen of all kinds" from his vast output of books and that they are proof of "English capacities in the business of building."

JOHN HARRIS

BIBLIOGRAPHY

LANGLEY, BATTY (1720)1729 *Sure Guide to Builders.* London: Wilcox & Heath.

LANGLEY, BATTY 1724 *An Accurate Description of Newgate.* London: T. Warner.

LANGLEY, BATTY 1726 *Practical Geometry.* London: Innys.

LANGLEY, BATTY (1727)1739 *The Builder's Chest-Book.* 2d ed. London: Wilcox & Hodges.

LANGLEY, BATTY (1728a)1971 *New Principles of Gardening.* Reprint. Farnborough, England: Gregg.

LANGLEY, BATTY 1728b *A Sure Method of Improving Estates.* London: Clay & Browne.

LANGLEY, BATTY 1729 *Pomona.* London: Straham.

LANGLEY, BATTY (1730)1734 *Young Builder's Rudiments.* London: Millan.

LANGLEY, BATTY 1736a *Ancient Masonry.* 2 vols. London: The author.

LANGLEY, BATTY 1736b *A Design for the Bridge at New Palaceyard, Westminster.* London: The author.

LANGLEY, BATTY 1737 *A Reply to Mr. John James's Review.* London: The author.

LANGLEY, BATTY (1738)1738 *The Builder's Compleat Assistant.* 2d ed. London: Ware. Originally published with the title *The Builder's Compleat Chest-Book.*

LANGLEY, BATTY (1740)1922 *The City and Country Builder's and Workman's Treasury.* Reprint of 1950 ed. Boston Architectural Club.

LANGLEY, BATTY (1741)1970 *The Builder's Jewel.* Reprint of 1757 ed. New York: Blom.

LANGLEY, BATTY (1742a)1972 *Gothic Architecture.* Reprint of 1747 ed. New York: Blom. Originally published with the title *Ancient Architecture.*

LANGLEY, BATTY 1742b *The Measurer's Jewel.* London: Wilcox.

LANGLEY, BATTY (1747a)1970 *The Builder's Director or Bench-Mate.* Reprint of 1751 ed. New York: Blom. Originally published with the title *The Builder's Bench-Mate.*

LANGLEY, BATTY (1747b)1750 *London Prices of Bricklayers.* 2d ed. London: Adams. Originally published with the title *Exaction Detected.*

LANGLEY, BATTY 1748 *Survey of Westminster Bridge.* London: Cooper.

LANGLEY, BATTY 1749 *Observations on a Pamphlet . . . by Charles Marquand.* London: The author.

LANGLEY, BATTY 1756 *The Workman's Golden Rule.* London: Ware.

LA PADULA, ERNESTO BRUNO

After taking his architecture degree from the University of Rome in 1931, Ernesto Bruno La Padula (1902–1969) became a member of the Roman group of the Italian Movement for Rationalist Architecture. In the decade that followed, he realized his two most significant works: the monumental Palace of Italian Civilization (1938–1939), a collaborative effort later nicknamed "The Square Colosseum" which was to be part of the fascist regime's 1942 Universal Roman Exposition, and the Knights of Columbus Foundation (1934), his finest work and one of the outstanding examples of rationalism in Rome.

La Padula's career in Italy was broken up by a fourteen-year stay at the University of Cordoba, Argentina, where he held the chair of town planning and architectural composition from 1949 to 1963. In both Argentina and Italy, La Padula distinguished himself as an excellent architect, teacher, and urban planner.

ELLEN R. SHAPIRO

WORKS

1931, Casa Balilla (Fascist Party Youth Cadres Center), Cattolica Eraclea, Italy. 1931, Pavilion, Exposition of Mining Products, Rome. 1934, Church of San Rocco, Pisticci, Italy. 1934, Knights of Columbus Foundation; 1938, Mineral Pavilion (with others), Autarchic Exhibition of Italian Minerals; 1938–1939, Palace of Italian Civilization (with others); Rome. 1941, Exhibition of Armed Forces; 1941, Exhibition of Bank of Italy; Naples. 1947, Rimini (master plan for reconstruction), Italy. 1948, Bracciano (master plan), Italy. 1950, Cordoba and province (master plan), Argentina.

BIBLIOGRAPHY

CENNAMO, MICHELE (1973)1976 *Materiali per l'Analisi dell'Architettura Moderna-/Il M.I.A.R.* 2d ed. Naples: Società Editrice Napoletana.

ISTITUTO NAZIONALE DI URBANISTICA (1952)1954 *Urbanisti Italiani.* Rome: Castaldi.

"Mostra delle Forze Armate: Esercito, Marina e Aeronautica Architetto Bruno La Padula." 1941*a* *Architettura* 19, nos. 1–2:20.

"Mostra della Banca d'Italia Arch. B. La Padula." 1941*b* *Architettura* 19, nos. 1–2:75.

PIACENTINI, MARCELLO 1937 "Mario Ridolfi, V. Cafiero, E. La Padula, E. Rossi: Progetto per la Casa Littoria in Roma, segnalato a Titolo di Lode." *Architettura* 16, no. 12:728–732.

LAPIDUS, MORRIS

Morris Lapidus (1902–) graduated from the Columbia University School of Architecture in 1927. In 1930, he joined the firm of Ross Frankel, where he designed stores and offices. Lapidus went into private practice in 1943 and continued to design primarily retail spaces. However, in 1948 he became the interior designer and associate architect for the San Souci Hotel in Florida. This project was followed by many other hotel commissions in Florida and other locations. Lapidus has also designed office buildings, concert halls, and housing complexes. He has written two books: *Architecture: A Profession and a Business* (1967) and *An Architecture of Joy* (1979).

Much of Morris Lapidus Associates' work has been controversial. The firm's objective has been to satisfy and please public sensibilities rather than appeal to architectural criticism. In many projects, the rectangular forms of most conventional, contemporary architecture were abandoned for the sweeping curves of a more dramatic and emotional style.

PATRICIA C. PHILLIPS

WORKS

1952–1954, Fontainebleu Hotel, Miami, Fla. 1961, Summit Hotel, New York. 1964, Variety Children's Hospital, Miami, Fla. 1966, Americana Hotel, New York. 1969, People's Pools-Park, Bedford Stuyvesant, Brooklyn, N.Y. 1972, Gusman Concert Hall, University of Miami, Fla.

BIBLIOGRAPHY

COOK, JOHN W., and KLOTZ, HEINRICH 1973 *Conversations with Architects.* New York: Praeger.

LAPIDUS, MORRIS 1979 *An Architecture of Joy.* Miami, Fla.: Seemann.

SKY, ALISON, and STONE, MICHELLE 1976 *Unbuilt America.* New York: McGraw-Hill.

LAPPO, OSMO

Osmo Lappo (1927–) has been labeled a Finnish Brutalist, mainly because of his projects for the Finnish army, for which he received the Finnish State Prize in Architecture in 1978. A limited budget and the need for resistance to unusually hard wear resulted in a bold, articulate language and the use of concrete, brick, and wood. One can find influences from HEIKKI SIRÉN's use of simple forms and natural materials and from VILJO

REVELL's rationalist approach in Lappo's architecture; he worked for them after his graduation from Helsinki University of Technology in 1953.

PIRKKO-LIISA LOUHENJOKI

WORKS

1957–1959, Non-commissioned Officers' School (annex), Lappeenranta, Finland. 1962–1968, Garrison Center, Kajaani and Säkylä, Finland. 1968–1974, Garrison Center, Vekarajärvi, Valkeala, Finland. 1973, Sylvää School, Vammala, Finland. 1973, Myllyhaka School, Nokia, Finland. 1979, IBM Office Building, Helsinki. 1980, Swimming Stadium, Riihimäki, Finland. 1981, Government Palace (annex), Helsinki.

BIBLIOGRAPHY

Finnish Architecture. 1975 The Hague: Museum of Finnish Architecture and the Netherlands Congress Center. Exhibition catalogue.

LAPRADE, ALBERT

Albert Laprade (1883–1978) was the last grand architect-planner graduate of the Ecole des Beaux-Arts in Paris. He worked in Morocco and Tunisia and designed the Genissiat Dam on the Rhône in France (1939–1940). He designed pavilions for the 1925 Exposition des Arts Décoratifs et Industriels and the Exposition Coloniale of 1931, both in Paris, but his largest creative output was in publications.

ELIZABETH MCLANE

WORKS

*1925, Pavillon des Jardins et des Lacs, Exposition des Arts Décoratifs et Industriels; *1925, Pavillon du Louvre, Exposition des Arts Décoratifs et Industriels; *1931, Musée des Arts Africains (with Janniot), Exposition Coloniale; Paris. 1939–1940, E. D. F. Hydro-electric Dam, Genissiat-sur-le-Rhone, France.

BIBLIOGRAPHY

"Le Barrage de Genissiat." 1949 *L'Architecture Française* 10, nos. 85–86:6–8.
"Genissiat." 1953 *Techniques et Architecture* 12, nos. 5–6:91.
LAPRADE, ALBERT 1939a "L'Architecture dans nos Provinces Françaises: L'Oeuvre de Henri Drobecq dans le nord." *L'Architecture* 52, Feb.
LAPRADE, ALBERT 1939b L'Oeuvre de Jean-Charles Moreux." *L'Architecture* 52, July:239–246.
LAPRADE, ALBERT 1947 "Maisons Ouvrières." *Construction Moderne* 3, May:785–788.
LAPRADE, ALBERT 1952a "The 'Beaux-Arts' Spirit." *Société des Architectes Diplomés par le Gouvernement Bulletin Mensuel* 7, May:7–8.
LAPRADE, ALBERT (1942)1952b *Croquis.* 2 vols. Paris: Fréal.
LAPRADE, ALBERT 1967 *Croquis.* Paris: Fréal.

"Les Salons de 1910." 1910 *Gazette des Beaux-Arts* 4:41.
"Les Salons de 1925." 1925 *Gazette des Beaux-Arts* 12:13.

LASSURANCE, PIERRE

Pierre Cailleteau, known as Lassurance (1660–1724), was the chief assistant of JULES HARDOUIN MANSART at the Palace of Versailles from 1684 to 1700. The duc de Saint-Simon's claim that Lassurance was the *architecte-sous-clef* from whom Mansart derived his architectural ideas was an extreme exaggeration. However, Lassurance contributed many ideas to the French interior, notably the lavish use of mirrors in interiors of the château and its dependencies.

When Lassurance was moved to Paris in 1702 as overseer of construction at the Hôtel des Invalides, he embarked on a career as one of the foremost builders of private residences in the western boundary of the city. In a series of remarkable town houses, he imbued the standard form of the *hôtel particulier* with modern features, thus opening a new phase in domestic architecture. The Hôtel Desmarets (1704) was a logical development of the work of Mansart in its symmetrical arrangement of spaces around a central vestibule and salon and in its sparse elevations concentrating enrichment on the central pavilion. The tall, closely spaced windows and the compact volumes of the main block were motifs much exploited by such contemporaries as GERMAIN BOFFRAND and ROBERT DE COTTE.

ROBERT NEUMAN

WORKS

1700, Hôtel de Rothelein; *1704, Hôtel Desmarets; *1708, Hôtel d'Auvergne; *1708, Hôtel de Béthune-Neufchatel; 1708, Hôtel de Maisons-Soyecourt; 1715, Hôtel de Pussort-Noailles (remodeling); 1719, Hôtel de Montbason; 1722, Hôtel de Roquelaure (Ministry of Public Works); 1722, Hôtel de Lassay (completed by JEAN AUBERT), Paris.

BIBLIOGRAPHY

BLONDEL, JACQUES-FRANÇOIS (1752–1756)1904–1905 *L'architecture française.* 4 vols. Reprint. Paris: Levy.
HAUTECOEUR, LOUIS 1950 *Première moitié du XVIIIe siècle: Le style Louis XV.* Volume 3 in *Histoire de l'architecture classique en France.* Paris: Picard.
KALNEIN, WEND GRAF, and LEVEY, MICHAEL 1972 *Art and Architecture of the Eighteenth Century in France.* Baltimore: Penguin.
KIMBALL, FISKE (1943)1964 *The Creation of the Rococo.* New York: Norton.
RUSSO, KATHLEEN 1976 "Lassurance-the-Younger:

Architect to Madame de Pompadour." Unpublished Ph.D. dissertation, Florida State University, Tallahassee.

LASSUS, JEAN-BAPTISTE-ANTOINE

A pupil of LOUIS HIPPOLYTE LEBAS and HENRI LABROUSTE, from whom he derived his romantic rationalist approach, Jean-Baptiste-Antoine Lassus (1807–1857) turned early to the study of Gothic architecture. Named inspector in 1838, he later became director of the restorations of Saint Germain l'Auxerrois and the Sainte Chapelle in Paris, where his colorful image of medieval interiors was first realized. In 1844, Lassus and EUGÈNE EMMANUEL VIOLLET-LE-DUC began the restoration of Notre Dame Cathedral in Paris, where they trained most of the important French Gothic Revivalists. His church designs—miniature cathedrals—draw especially on Chartres which he restored beginning in 1848, and on his theory of the human scale or module in Gothic. Although he placed third in the 1855 Lille Cathedral competition, his design was selected for execution.

BARRY BERGDOLL

WORKS

1835, Saint Severin (restoration; with A.-G. Grétarin); begun 1838, Sainte-Chapelle (restoration); Paris. 1843–1852, Saint Nicholas (originally designed by L. Piel), Nantes, France. 1844–1857, Notre Dame Cathedral (with Eugène Emmanuel Viollet-le-Duc); 1846–1850, Chapter House, Notre Dame Cathedral; Paris. c.1847, Convent of the Visitation, Montauban, France. c.1847, Petite Seminare, rue Notre Dame des Champs, Paris. 1848, Chapel, Château de Gezaincourt, Somme, France. Begun 1848, Chartres Cathedral (restoration), France. *1848, Hôtel Soltykoff, Avenue Montaigne, Paris. 1849–1881, Sacré-Coeur; Begun 1852, Notre Dame (restoration and construction of the nave [completed by Eugène Millet]); Moulins, France. 1853–1858, Saint Pierre and Sainte Chanial, Dijon, France. 1854–1859, Saint Jean Baptiste de Belleville; c.1855, Apartment House, 41 Rue Taitbaut, Paris. c.1857–1863, Saint Saturnin, Cusset, France. Begun 1856, Notre Dame de Treille (unfinished), Lille, France.

BIBLIOGRAPHY

FOUCART, BRUNO, and NOËL-BOUTON, VÉRONIQUE 1968 "Saint Nicolas de Nantes, Bataille et Triomphe de Néo-Gothique." Congrès Archéologique de France 126:136–181.
GERMANN, GEORG 1972 Gothic Revival in Europe and Britain: Sources, Influences and Ideas. Translated by Gerald Onn. Cambridge, Mass.: M.I.T. Press.
GUILHERMY, FERDINAND 1857 La Sainte-Chapelle de Paris, après les restaurations commencées par M. Duban. Paris: Bance.
GUILHERMY, FERDINAND 186? Monographie de Notre Dame de Paris et de la nouvelle sacristie de MM Lassus et Viollet-le-Duc. Paris: Morel.
LASSUS, JEAN BAPTISTE ANTOINE 1842–1867 Monographie de la Cathedrale de Chartres. Paris: Imprimérie Nationale.
LASSUS, JEAN BAPTISTE ANTOINE 1856 "M. Lassus on Eclecticism in Art." Ecclesiologist 17:284–287.
LASSUS, JEAN BAPTISTE ANTOINE 1858 Album de Villard de Honnecourt. Paris: Imprimérie Nationale.
LENIAUD, J.-M. 1976 "Recherches sur Jean Baptiste Lassus 1807–1857, archéologue et architecte." Thesis, Ecole des Chartres, Paris.
LÉON, PAUL 1951 La Vie des monuments français. Paris: Picard.
MIDDLETON, ROBIN, and WATKIN, DAVID 1980 Neoclassical and Nineteenth-Century Architecture. New York: Abrams.
PHILADELPHIA MUSEUM OF ART 1978 The Second Empire. Philadelphia: The museum. Exhibition catalogue.
TROCHE, N. M. 1857 L'architecte Lassus. Paris: LeClere.
VIOLLET-LE-DUC, EUGÈNE EMMANUEL 1857 "Nécrologie J. B. A. Lassus." Encyclopédie d'Architecture 7:113–116.

LATROBE, BENJAMIN H.

Generally regarded as the founder of the architectural profession and as the father of the Greek Revival in the United States, Benjamin Henry Latrobe (1764–1820) was born near Leeds, England on May 1, 1764. His father, Irish-born Benjamin Latrobe, was one of the leading Moravian clergymen in England, and his mother, Mary Antes, was the daughter of Henry Antes, a prominent Pennsylvania pioneer. Latrobe grew up in a liberal atmosphere and at an early age showed an interest in architecture and an ability at drawing.

In September 1776, Latrobe left England to study at the Moravian Pedagogium at Niesky in German Silesia, and then at the Moravian seminary at Barby in Saxony. An unconfirmed family tradition states that he also spent three years at the University of Leipzig and served briefly in the army of Frederick the Great. His education appears to have been directed toward the ministry, but while still in Germany, Latrobe showed an interest in engineering, observing the levee systems and flood control works along the Elbe and other rivers. Much of his final year abroad was spent traveling in Germany, France, and Italy, a trip that strengthened his idea of becoming an architect and that also influenced his later works. Latrobe returned to England in 1784 an accomplished mathematician, linguist, musician, watercolorist, writer, and advocate of political and social reforms.

After a brief stay as a clerk in the Stamp Office, Latrobe is said to have worked in the office of JOHN SMEATON, and then in the office of the architect SAMUEL PEPYS COCKERELL, designer of the Admiralty Building in Whitehall on which Latrobe worked. During the years of his European education and travel, Latrobe was undoubtedly impressed with the new classicism that was then succeeding the late Renaissance, baroque, and rococo styles in the advanced and imaginative design concepts of architects such as CLAUDE NICOLAS LEDOUX and ETIENNE LOUIS BOULLÉE in France and CARL GOTTFRIED LANGHANS in Silesia. Nothing, however, probably influenced him more than the radical and Francophile style of JOHN SOANE. Simple masses and the geometrical forms of cubes, hemispheres, cylinders, and pyramids, together with striking contrasts of light and shadow, characterized the new architecture of the end of the eighteenth century and were to become the basic elements of Latrobe's own design concepts.

In 1790, Latrobe married Lydia Sellon; they had two children. In 1791, Latrobe opened his own office and began what promised to be a successful career as an architect in England. Besides numerous commissions for alterations to existing buildings, he designed two new houses, still extant. Both Hammerwood Lodge (c.1791) near East Grinstead and Ashdown House (c.1792) in London are characterized by bold, simple masses with restrained classical elements. The former has a large central block of two stories and an attic flanked by lower wings with Doric porticoes, while the latter is an almost square house, also of two stories and an attic, with a one-story semicircular entrance portico consisting of four Ionic columns. Both houses contain many of the elements to be found in Latrobe's later American works and show his imaginative use of geometrical forms and classical details.

In November 1793, tragedy struck with the death of his wife. In addition, building activity was slow because of the French Revolution and there was political unrest in England. In these trying circumstances Latrobe decided to seek a new life and career in the United States, arriving in Norfolk, Virginia, in March 1796.

During his short stay in Norfolk, his charming personality and intelligence won him many friends in the best social circles. He recorded his keen observations of the new American scene in his journals and sketchbooks. A visit to the Dismal Swamp and his professional engineering interest in the projected canal induced him to visit Richmond. On his way he stopped at Williamsburg where he made several sketches that have been of great assistance in the restoration of that colonial capital. He made other trips around Virginia, sketching and recording his impressions in journals, now published by the Maryland Historical Society. Having formed a friendship with Bushrod Washington, the president's nephew, Latrobe visited Washington at Mount Vernon, dining with him and his family and the young Marquis de Lafayette, whom he sketched on the portico of the mansion. Latrobe's sketches of Mount Vernon were the basis for the removal of the Chippendale railing above the portico that had been added in later years.

Latrobe then made Richmond his home for seven years, widening his circle of influential friends. He designed several handsome houses, few of which were ever built. Their plans were all formal, ingenious, and carefully studied with rooms of various shapes cleverly fitted together to create imposing spaces and functional arrangements. Bold, geometric forms, plain surfaces, and decorative elements, usually concentrated in simple classical porticoes, characterized these buildings and continued to be the distinguishing features of his later works.

The largest and most important of Latrobe's Virginia works was his successful competition design for the Richmond Penitentiary (1797), which included some of the most advanced ideas of THOMAS JEFFERSON's concept of humane penology. The entrance was through a massive semicircular archway in a rough stone wall; the cells were arranged around a large semicircular court. A conspicuous Richmond landmark, fragments of the building survived until 1927. This was Latrobe's last Virginia work and the beginning of his professional frustrations in working with public bodies.

Latrobe moved to Philadelphia with his appointment as architect for the new banking house for the Bank of Pennsylvania (1798). In the design of this monumental building, Latrobe established his reputation as the most accomplished architect in the United States. The circular banking room was contained within a central cubical mass, surmounted by a low dome and lighted from above by a handsome cupola or lantern. Six-columned Ionic porticoes extended from the front and rear, setting a precedent for the countless Greek Revival porticoes that followed. The bank also contained the first masonry vaulted monumental interior in the United States.

Latrobe's other major Philadelphia work was as engineer and architect for the Philadelphia Waterworks (1799). He proposed to use steam engines to raise water from the Schuylkill River to a high point in the city, distributing it from a reservoir by pipes. Despite vigorous opposition from proponents of a Delaware and Schuylkill Canal that was also intended to furnish a water supply, Latrobe's proposal was adopted. The waterworks were constructed and successfully operated. Among those who were associated with him on the project were Nicholas Roosevelt, the only major steam engine builder in the country (eventually Latrobe's son in law), and Frederick Graff, who had begun as Latrobe's clerk of the works at the bank and later as chief draftsman on the waterworks.

The pumphouse for Latrobe's waterworks was a handsome and monumental building located in Centre Square, present site of the Philadelphia City Hall. A one-story rectangular base surmounted by a circular domed tower, smoke from the machinery dramatically emerged from the center. The base contained a recessed central porch with two Doric columns and had a single circular head window in a slight recess in the walls flanking the porch. A fountain was spectacularly placed in front of the building as shown in John Lewis Krimmel's noted painting of a Fourth of July celebration in Centre Square. The composition of the building shows many similarities to published designs of John Soane. Both the bank and the waterworks were to be reflected strongly in Latrobe's later works in New Orleans.

In addition to his architectural and engineering activities, Latrobe found Philadelphia a stimulating environment for his intellectual and social interests. The American Philosophical Society published several of his articles and elected him to membership. His Philadelphia friends included the artist Charles Willson Peale, who painted his well-known portrait, and Isaac Hazlehurst, a prominent merchant and friend of Robert Morris.

In 1800, Latrobe married Mary Elizabeth Hazlehurst and brought his two children to the United States. Young Henry Latrobe was to follow in his father's professional footsteps in a promising career cut short by his untimely death in 1817. The eldest son of the second marriage, John Hazlehurst Boneval Latrobe, became a prominent attorney and historian in Baltimore, and the second son, Benjamin Latrobe, Jr. (1806–1878), became a noted engineer for whom the city of Latrobe, Pennsylvania, is named. Shortly after his second marriage Latrobe took up his architectural practice in Philadelphia. During these years, against the opposition of the Carpenters Company of Philadelphia, Latrobe succeeded in establishing architecture as a profession. Of these Philadelphia years he once wrote: "I have changed the taste of a whole city." And elsewhere: "Here I am the only successful architect and engineer. I have had to break the ice for my successors."

Among Latrobe's Philadelphia residential designs was the Edward S. Burd House (1801–1802). A large three-story brick house with one-story

wings, it was a restrained geometrical composition with a minimum of classical detail in the entrance doorway. Although the design of the Burd House must have been unusual to Philadelphians accustomed to the usual Federal or Georgian style, the design of William Crammond's house, Sedgeley (1799), on the banks of the Schuylkill was even more startling. Here Latrobe designed the first Gothic Revival house in America, a rectangular, hipped-roof, two-story structure with one-story square corner pavilions, embellished with pointed windows and other Gothic details. A few years later he designed a building for the Bank of Philadelphia (1808) in a similar, rather superficial Gothic style. Latrobe's attempts in the Gothic idiom, though interesting and imaginative, are among the least successful of his designs.

During his years in Philadelphia Latrobe began to encounter financial difficulties. Because of his innate generosity and friendship and perhaps a lack of financial acumen, he endorsed notes that eventually led to bankruptcy in spite of his professional success.

With his reputation as an architect and engineer firmly established, President Jefferson summoned Latrobe to Washington to design a great covered dry dock for the Navy. Although Congress failed to make the appropriation for its construction, Jefferson was so impressed with Latrobe's design and obvious ability that in March 1803 he appointed Latrobe as surveyor of the public buildings of the United States and charged him with the completion of the Capitol (1803–1817). Latrobe's changes to WILLIAM THORNTON's design led to bitter feelings between the two but resulted in the building upon which is based Latrobe's chief claim to fame as an architect. Work on the Capitol, Latrobe's principal concern for most of the remainder of his life, brought him in close association with Jefferson and later Latrobe offered valuable advice in the design of Jefferson's University of Virginia. He frequently conferred and corresponded with the president on many details regarding the Capitol and is especially noted for the design of the old House of Representatives (now Statuary Hall). In the design of the capitals for the columns of the Senate stair vestibule, Latrobe used the native corn as a motif. In a letter to Jefferson he remarked that "this capital . . . obtained me more applause from the members of Congress than all the works of magnitude. . . . They called it the Corn Cob Capital."

Latrobe continued work on the Capitol under President James Madison, with whom he was on most friendly terms. He also worked on the White House, assisting first lady Dolley Madison with decoration and furnishings. Under Jefferson, La-

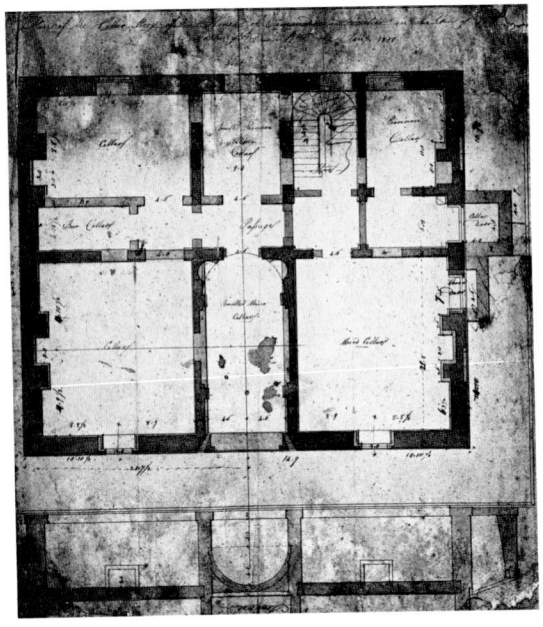

Latrobe.
Plan of United States
Capitol (with others).
Washington.
1803–1817

Latrobe.
Drawing of interior of
United States Capitol
(with others).
Washington.
1803–1817

trobe had designed and laid the foundations for the north and south porticoes of the mansion, but they were not erected until many years later, after the White House and the Capitol had been burned by the British during the War of 1812.

The Capitol project was not without problems, vexations, and even tragedy for Latrobe. On September 21, 1808, his friend and clerk of the works, John Lenthall, was killed when the vault of the Supreme Courtroom in the Capitol collapsed when the centerings were removed. Latrobe also argued with Congress over the cost of the work and successfully sued Thornton for libel. His work on the Capitol ceased on July 1, 1811, when Congress, preoccupied with preparations for the War of 1812, closed down the project.

After the cessation of work on the Capitol, Latrobe took up residence in Pittsburgh, where he built boatways, a forge, and machine shops. He arranged for steam engines for Louisiana sugar planters and for the New Orleans Waterworks, a project he had been engaged on since 1811. He became involved with Robert Fulton and Robert R. Livingston, with whom his son-in-law Nicholas

Roosevelt had been associated in the development of steamboats for the Mississippi rivers. Like most of his financial ventures, Latrobe's Pittsburgh activities were financially disastrous and left him almost penniless and in debilitated health. This, in spite of an active building business that produced both residential and commercial buildings including the Pittsburgh Arsenal (1814), parts of which still stand.

During the years of his working on the Capitol Latrobe designed numerous other buildings in various parts of the country, only a few of which still stand and some so altered as to be scarcely recognizable as Latrobe's design. Some are known only from his extant drawings or old photographs. Among important residences were a house for Senator John Pope (1811) in Lexington, Kentucky; Adena (1805) in Chillicothe, Ohio, for Colonel Thomas Worthington; and Henry Clay's residence, Ashland (1813), in Lexington, Kentucky, still standing but substantially rebuilt in 1857 by T. Lewinski in the Italianate manner.

Latrobe's most important private work during the years before the War of 1812 was the Roman Catholic Cathedral of Baltimore (1804–1818) for which he offered his services without charge. His first design was in the Gothic style, but his second, a domed structure in the Roman style, was chosen by the building committee. The church was not dedicated until after Latrobe's death, but he had lived to see most of the splendid interior completed, its coffered domes and vaults recalling some of his best work at the Capitol in Washington. The towers with their onion-shaped domes were added in 1832, departing somewhat from Latrobe's simpler domical tops. The portico, completed in 1863 under the direction of his son John H. B.

Latrobe.
Adena (now restored).
Chillicothe, Ohio.
1805

Latrobe, follows the original design. The sanctuary was extended in 1890, carefully following the original design. Except for the Capitol, the Baltimore cathedral is undoubtedly Latrobe's most impressive and important extant building.

In 1803, Albert Gallatin, secretary of the treasury, directed Latrobe to design a stone lighthouse for the mouth of the Mississippi river. He sent a young pupil and assistant, Lewis de Mun, a French royalist refugee, to Louisiana to select and survey the site, but no contractor was willing to undertake a stone structure on the unstable soil at the remote river's mouth. The project was abandoned and not again undertaken until 1816 when Latrobe's son Henry, then living in New Orleans, was commissioned to prepare a new design for the lighthouse.

Latrobe's next Louisiana assignment was the design of a customhouse in New Orleans (1807–1809). This small red brick building had a recessed porch with two stone columns, similar to his Centre Square Pumphouse in Philadelphia. The building was raised on an arcaded and vaulted basement. The materials for its construction, including prefabricated items of millwork and stonework, were shipped from Philadelphia. The work was executed by Robert Alexander, a Washington contractor who had worked under Latrobe on the Washington Navy Yard. Due to its inadequate size for the booming business of the port and because of structural difficulties, the building was replaced in 1819. In its design and use of materials, Latrobe's building was something entirely new to New Orleans where almost all buildings were wood or stuccoed on the exterior in the French and Spanish colonial tradition. This was New Orleans's first introduction to the American red brick style which would eventually become common in the city.

Latrobe's major New Orleans project was to provide an adequate water supply to the city, a project urged by Jefferson and the territorial governor, William C. C. Claiborne. His first application for the franchise to the city with water in 1809 was with Alexander. Due to Alexander's lack of knowledge of French when appearing before the predominantly French legislature and city council, the application failed. At Claiborne's request, Latrobe submitted another application but this time sent his son Henry to New Orleans to present it. With his French name and French education by the Sulpicians in Baltimore, his son succeeded admirably.

The New Orleans waterworks project that held such bright prospect of financial success for Latrobe soon brought the same sort of frustrations that had plagued so many of his efforts. First, the

Latrobe.
Roman Catholic Cathedral.
Baltimore.
1804–1818

Latrobe.
Roman Catholic Cathedral.
Baltimore.
1804–1818

site selected for the pumphouse, adjacent to the customhouse, was denied to the city by Congress and a new site at Levee (Decatur) and Ursulines Streets had to be obtained. The pumphouse, erected under Henry Latrobe's direction, was similar to the one in Philadelphia, except that it had a four-column, pedimented portico instead of the recessed porch and an octagonal tower with a pyramid roof instead of the round domed one used in Philadelphia.

Before the steam engines for the system could be completed and shipped to New Orleans, war with England was declared in 1812, preventing the shipment of the machinery from any Atlantic port, imposing a heavy financial loss on Latrobe. Receiving an extension from the city council of two years on his contract, Latrobe and his family moved to

Pittsburgh where he hoped to be able to produce the engines through his association with Robert Fulton and the steamboats. Fulton's death and the War of 1812 prevented that.

The financial losses and the continual frustrations in his Pittsburgh activities were extremely disheartening to Latrobe, the situation being further aggravated by an illness that required a long convalescence. He and his wife wrote to Madison urging that Latrobe be recalled to Washington to rebuild the Capitol, destroyed by the British. These efforts succeeded, and the Latrobes returned to Washington in June 1815.

Although drawings for the rebuilding of the nearly destroyed Capitol occupied most of Latrobe's time, he still found time for other projects. Among these were alterations to Blodgett's Hotel for use as a temporary capitol, the design of Saint John's Church (1816), and the house for Stephen Decatur (1817), the latter two still standing facing Lafayette Square.

Latrobe also designed several other residences in Washington, one for John Peter Van Ness (1816–1817), one of the commissioners of the Capitol before the war. This was Latrobe's largest and perhaps finest residence, the site is now occupied by the Pan American Union Building. He designed Brentwood (1818) for Mayor Robert Brent on Seventh Street Northeast. This house was a square two-story building with a pyramidal roof crowned by a cupola or lantern that lighted an impressive rotunda that extended up through the center of the house. Over the entrance was a handsome Doric portico and at each side one-story wings extended to the rear.

Except for the United States Capitol, Latrobe's largest commission was the design of the Balti-

more Exchange (1816–1818), a commission he received in the summer of 1815 soon after he had returned to Washington from Pittsburgh. In this project he was associated with MAXIMILIAN GODEFROY, a French architect then practicing in Baltimore, a partnership that ended in a bitter misunderstanding. Latrobe also had difficulties with the commissioner of the Capitol and on November 20, 1817, he resigned as architect of the Capitol, to be succeeded by CHARLES BULFINCH of Boston. Latrobe then took up residence in Baltimore to oversee the completion of the Cathedral and the Exchange.

As soon as his projects in Baltimore were sufficiently advanced, Latrobe went to New Orleans in hopes of salvaging some financial security by finishing the waterworks. He sailed from Baltimore in December 1818. Besides erecting a boring mill to produce wooden pipes for the waterworks, Latrobe engaged in other works in New Orleans, designing a house and other works for his friend Vincent Nolte and redesigning the public square (now Jackson Square). The latter project, with monumental entrance gateways, an iron fence, and a center fountain, was only partly carried out and the square was redone in its present form in the 1850s.

Latrobe then purchased a house in New Orleans and briefly returned to Baltimore to complete his work there on the Cathedral and the Exchange and to return with his family overland and by river steamboat to New Orleans, where they arrived on April 4, 1820. The waterworks occupied most of his time, but he also erected a central tower on the old Spanish cathedral and in August 1820 his plans for a new banking house for the Louisiana State Bank were accepted. This proved to be his last design, for he was stricken with yellow fever and died on September 3, 1820.

His plans for the Louisiana State Bank were faithfully carried out, and the building, declared a National Historic Landmark, still stands at the corner of Royal and Conti Streets where it is occupied by an antiques emporium. Curiously, Latrobe's last plan strongly recalls his first major American work, the Bank of Pennsylvania. Each has a domed circular banking room with vaulted office and other spaces front and rear. The simple rectangular form of the New Orleans building with its wrought-iron balconies and semicircular rear center bay and stuccoed walls reflects Latrobe's sensitive appreciation of the design of the earlier buildings of the old French and Spanish city.

Latrobe's influence on the architectural profession in America is incalculable. He set high ethical and design standards which were continued by those who followed, particularly his outstanding

Latrobe.
Stephen Decatur House.
Washington.
1817

students WILLIAM STRICKLAND and ROBERT MILLS. Though many of his works have been destroyed, enough of his major monuments remain to testify to his talents as one of America's leading architects. His significance, however, is not confined solely to his architectural achievements. His sketchbooks and journals, recording in unparalleled detail the early American scene in drawings and vivid writings, are a rare contribution in the recording of the political, social, intellectual, and cultural life of the early years of the American republic. His thousands of letters, meticulously kept in bound volumes from 1803 until 1818, correspondence with the leaders of the nation, artists, artisans, family, and friends, give insight into all phases of life as seen and lived by one of the most observant, sensitive, intelligent, and often controversial men of his day.

SAMUEL WILSON, JR.

WORKS

c.1791, Hammerwood Lodge, East Grinstead, England. c.1792, Ashdown House, London. *1797, Richmond Penitentiary. *1798, Bank of Pennsylvania; *1799, Philadelphia Waterworks; *1799, Sedgeley; *1801–1802, Edward S. Burd House; Philadelphia. 1803, Nassau Hall, Princeton, N.J. 1803, "Old West" Building, Dickinson College, Carlisle, Pa. 1803–1817. United States Capitol (with others), Washington. 1804–1818, Roman Catholic Cathedral, Baltimore. 1805, Adena (now restored), Chillicothe, Ohio. *1805, University of Pennsylvania Medical School, Philadelphia. *1807–1809, United States Customhouse, New Orleans, La. *1808, Bank of Philadelphia. 1808, Christ Church, Washington. *1808–1810, John Markoe House, Philadelphia. 1811, John Pope House, Lexington, Ky. 1811, Long Branch, Clarke County, Va. *1811–1820, New Orleans Waterworks, La. 1813, Henry Clay House (Ashland), Lexington, Ky. 1814, United States Arsenal, Pittsburgh. 1816, Saint John's Church; *1816–1817, John Peter Van Ness House; Washington. *1816–1818, Baltimore Exchange. 1817, Stephen Decatur House; *1818, Brentwood; Washington. 1820, Louisiana State Bank, New Orleans.

BIBLIOGRAPHY

Latrobe's correspondence is in the Maryland Historical Society, Baltimore. Many of his drawings are in the Library of Congress, Washington.

BROWN, GLENN (1903)1970 History of the United States Capitol. Reprint. 2 vols. New York: Da Capo.

CARTER, EDWARD C. II (editor) 1977 The Virginia Journals of Benjamin Henry Latrobe, 1795–1798. 2 vols. New Haven: Yale University Press.

CARTER, EDWARD C. II; VAN HORNE, JOHN C.; and FORMWALT, LEE W. (editors) 1980 Volume 3 in The Journals of Benjamin Henry Latrobe, 1799–1820: From Philadelphia to New Orleans. New Haven: Yale University Press.

CARTER, EDWARD C. II ET AL. 1976 The Papers of Benjamin Henry Latrobe. Microfiche ed. Clifton, N.J.: James T. White.

HAMLIN, TALBOT F. 1955 Benjamin Henry Latrobe. New York: Oxford University Press.

LATROBE, BENJAMIN H. (1905)1971 The Journal of Latrobe; Being the Notes and Sketches of an Architect, Naturalist and Traveler in the United States from 1796 to 1820. Introduction by J. H. B. Latrobe. Reprint. New York: B. Franklin.

NORTON, PAUL F. 1977 Latrobe, Jefferson and the National Capitol. New York and London: Garland.

PADOVER, SAUL K. (editor) 1946 Thomas Jefferson and the National Capital. Preface by Harold L. Ickes. Washington: U.S. Government Printing Office.

STAPLETON, DARWIN H. (editor) 1980 The Engineering Drawings of Benjamin Henry Latrobe. New Haven: Yale University Press.

WILSON, SAMUEL JR. (editor) 1951 Impressions Respecting New Orleans by Benjamin Henry Boneval Latrobe; Diary and Sketches 1818–1820. New York: Columbia University Press.

LAUGIER, MARC-ANTOINE

Marc-Antoine Laugier (1713–1769) was a Provençal born in Manosque, France. At the exceptionally early age of fourteen he entered the Novitiate of the Jesuits in Avignon from where, three years later, he was transferred for further studies to other colleges of the Lyons province, one of which was that of Nîmes. It was here that he intimately came to know the building that in years to come was to give a decisive direction to his ideas on architecture—a small Roman temple, the the so-called Maison Carrée. "Everything here," he wrote later, "accords with the true principles of architecture: a rectangle where thirty columns support an entablature and a roof—closed at both ends by a pediment—that is all; the combination is of a simplicity and nobility which strikes everybody" (1753a, p. 15).

In 1744, he was sent to Paris where he took his final vows and soon made a reputation as a preacher. The wide-ranging humanistic education for which the Jesuits were justly renowned made him susceptible to the intellectual and artistic climate of the metropolis. Over the next few years, his taste and judgment matured, and by 1753 he felt confident enough to publish his views on contemporary art: in that and the following year appeared in quick succession his Essai sur l'architecture (1753a), his most important work; a pamphlet on painting (1753b); and another one on music (1754a). All three anonymously published writings were widely discussed in the circles that mattered, where the author's identity was soon established. Laugier's future as an art critic looked promising, and so did his career as a preacher when, in 1754, he was chosen to preach before the king and his family in the Chapel of Versailles. But this honor proved to be disastrous for him. Acting almost certainly on the orders of his superiors, he referred in his sermon with great vehemence to the political situation of the day. The Society of Jesus, already in a vulnerable and precarious situation, thought it expedient to act as if they disapproved of Laugier's utterances: he was ordered to return to his college in Lyons.

Resentment about the society's failure to stand by him and even more so the banishment from Paris and the literary world which for the last ten years had meant so much to him led Laugier to take the most momentous decision of his life: soon after his arrival in Lyons he tried to obtain, with the help of the liberal-minded Cardinal Passionei, papal permission to leave the society. While waiting for the conclusion of the negotiations in Rome, Laugier replied (1754*b*) to the first critical review of the *Essai* and prepared its second enlarged edition which appeared in 1755 under his name: P. Laugier S. J. In the following year, the release from the Jesuit order and, for form's sake, the transfer to the Benedict order was at last granted. Soon afterward, he was back in Paris.

Lacking now the material support which the society had so far provided, he had to find a post that would give him the financial security needed and yet leave him free for the pursuit of what attracted him most: art criticism and historical research. Sponsored by influential patrons, he soon obtained the post as editor of the official *Gazette de France,* a position he held for several years. During that time he submitted to the *directeur des bâtiments,* the marquis de Marigny, a highly original plan: the publication of a monthly periodical entitled *L'Etat des arts en France,* that would, with him as editor, bring reviews on a wide range of subjects concerning architecture, painting, sculpture, and even the applied arts. But for the opposition of the artists who, believing their privileged position threatened by this emancipation of art criticism, prevented Marigny from giving his approval, the journal as envisaged by Laugier would have been the first of its kind preceding a German art-historical periodical by many years.

His editorial work on the *Gazette* made him known to the various government departments. The most rewarding contact proved to be the one with the ministry of foreign affairs: a recommendation by its minister, the duc de Choiseuil, secured him the profitable post as first secretary to the newly appointed French ambassador at the court of the elector in Bonn. Laugier remained there for over three years, acting at times as chargé d'affaires. His duties left him, however, ample time to attend to his literary work. He had embarked on a most ambitious project: to compose a history of the republic of Venice from the beginning to the present time. The first volume (1759) had already appeared; he now proceeded with the next volumes, though it took almost ten years before the twelfth and last one was published. This work, but above all his fame as author of the *Essai,* earned him the honor of being elected, while still in Bonn, to three Academies, those of Angers, Marseilles, and Lyons. The manuscripts of two discourses to be read at the official reception, one on Renaissance architecture, the other on MICHELANGELO, have survived. When the ambassador was promoted and moved to St. Petersburg, Laugier returned to Paris. With a secure income derived from pensions for the years passed in the diplomatic service and as editor of the *Gazette* he could now afford to move into more fashionable quarters close to the Bibliothèque du Roi and devote his full time to literary work. Soon after his return, he published his second book on architecture, *Observations sur l'architecture* (1765). During the last years of his life, he worked on a number of books of which one, about the peace of Belgrade of 1739, came out a few months before he died, while an art-critical essay on the appreciation of paintings was published posthumously. He died after a short illness on April 15, 1769.

Laugier had been successful as an author. But of all his writings—and they dealt with many different subjects—it was the first, the *Essai,* and of that the preface, the introduction, and the first chapter, that secured him a place in the history of art—sixty-five pages in all, less than a quarter of the whole book. These few pages contain something that had hardly been attempted before: to set out in clear terms and systematic form a precise program of the architecture to come. It was written at a time when, in the philosophical and literary sphere, a longing toward a simpler, more natural form of society made itself felt. Laugier was convinced that this new spirit must pervade architecture, too, if it was to be saved from the impending decadence, and he demanded a return to first principles. In his search for these principles he was led back to "simple nature," to the very beginning when primitive man had built the first shelter out of treetrunks and branches. From this rustic hut, he declared, all the basic elements of architecture evolved: the column, the architrave, and the pediment; they alone form the essential part of a composition to which, out of necessity, must be added the enclosing walls, the doors and windows. In short, he restricted architecture to those formal elements that clearly express function and proscribed those which, because functionally ambivalent, weaken the impact of constructional veracity. The primitive hut had, through VITRUVIUS, found its place in the literature on architectural theory. So far it had been cited either as a curious form of primitive dwelling or as proof for the assumption that Greek stone architecture had derived from wooden structures. For Laugier the hut meant something quite different: he saw the significance of this fictitious dwelling in the influence it could have on present-day architecture by acting as a norm, as a corrective that would eliminate the possibility of deviations, of being led astray from the true path of nature. He had a vision of a new, purified style of architecture, and it was the hut which offered him a seemingly rational justification for the reform he considered necessary. This reform, outlined in the programmatic part of the *Essai,* he then exemplified in one of the following chapters; there he sets out in some detail his conception of an ideal church that would incorporate all the principles which his model, the hut, had revealed to him.

The remaining parts of the book are of less interest. Two chapters deal, in a rather conventional way, with the staple themes of architectural theory—the five orders and the concepts of solidity, convenience, and *bienséance.* Another one on town planning, an unusual subject for an architectural treatise, contains a number of original, though in no way radical observations. In the last chapter, he outlines his views on garden architecture. Although he may have been the first to advocate a synthesis of the formality of the French and the prettiness of the Chinese garden, known to him through the account given by Jesuit missionaries, in this field he evidently lacked the vision that gave so much weight to his architectural doctrine.

The *Essai*—it came out in spring 1753—had a strong impact. It was reviewed in all leading literary journals. A few, mainly older members of the profession, attacked the author for oversimplification, the absurdity of his propositions, and the amateurishness of his church plan. Laugier replied, arguing his case and rebutting with indignation the charge of having done no more than copying what had been stated by another writer, J. L. DE CORDEMOY, in a treatise published more than a generation ago. Since Laugier had frankly acknowledged his indebtedness to this author, the charge of plagiarism was unfounded. No doubt, he had been influenced by Cordemoy's book, but a comparison of the two treatises makes it evident that of the two authors it was only Laugier who, developing his own ideas, was able to visualize the main outlines of the new style soon to come and to reason in a persuasive way about the kind of

*Laugier.
Primitive Hut, Frontispiece
from* Essai sur
l'architecture.
1755

changes called for. In contrast to these critics, Laugier's reasoning found ready response with the younger architects. They were encouraged to hear a writer express in simple, uncompromising terms what they had dimly felt to be their aim, and offer them reasoned justification for discarding the old and sure guidance toward the new. The features prescribed by Laugier—freestanding columns carrying a straight entablature, a barrel vault over a rectangular plan—were soon to appear with ever increasing frequency in French church architecture of the 1760s, mainly the work of architects who were students when the *Essai* appeared. Only in one instance—and it is an important one—can a direct link between book and building be reasonably assumed: the remarkable correspondence between Laugier's description of his church and JACQUES GERMAIN SOUFFLOT's plan for Sainte-Geneviève is unlikely to have been coincidental. Since the *Essai* was published in 1753 while Laugier was still in Paris and Soufflot, summoned from Lyons in 1755, began planning Sainte-Geneviève not before the following year, the conclusion, surprising as it is, can only be that it was the architect who was stimulated by the writer, not the reverse; this, of course, does not mean that Laugier visualized anything like the consummate quality and artistic integration of Soufflot's masterwork. Laugier, no doubt was fully aware of it, and he greatly admired Sainte-Geneviève, convinced that it was going to mark an era in the history of architecture.

The success of the *Essai* soon made the book known abroad. Within two years of its publication, it was translated into English and German. The authors of two major English treatises dealt with Laugier's theory: ISAAC WARE, who accepted it, and WILLIAM CHAMBERS, who rejected it. Fifty years later, England's then leading architect, JOHN SOANE, was greatly influenced in his theoretical outlook by Laugier's writings. In Germany, the *Essai* as well as the *Observations* had been translated and reviewed in all leading journals. That the German public was familiar with Laugier's doctrine is borne out by the curious fact that the young Goethe in his hymn to ERWIN VON STEINBACH, the architect of Strasbourg Cathedral, singled Laugier out when attacking the dogmatism of classical architecture, although ironically, it had been Laugier who had praised this very tower and had demanded the fusion of Gothic gracefulness and classical simplicity. In the *Observations,* on the whole a more conventional book, he also had spoken with admiration of the spatial beauty of Gothic churches due to the uninterrupted vertical lines of their slender pillars. In consequence, he had suggested a design for a modern church in which columns in form of palmtrees, with branches running along the ribs of the vault, replace the classical system of column and entablature. Twenty years later, these palmtree columns appeared in the only building where a particular feature suggested by Laugier was actually carried out: the Nikolaikirche in Leipzig.

The main interest his second book on architecture has for us today rests, apart from numerous judicious remarks about contemporary buildings, on a chapter entitled "On the difficulty to decorate Gothic churches." He could speak here with some authority since, a few years earlier, he had been asked to advise on the redecoration of the choir of Amiens Cathedral, of which he gave a detailed description in his book. Although the plan was not accepted, some of Laugier's suggestions were incorporated in a design submitted by Soufflot and executed in its present form by a local architect.

With the end of neoclassicism, Laugier and the *Essai* were almost forgotten. When at the beginning of the twentieth century the modern movement turned against the decorative excesses of historicism and fought for functional integrity, it is significant that in this situation, akin to the one of 150 years before, the foremost advocate of a reform of architecture, LE CORBUSIER, found the way to Laugier, referred to him frequently, and singled

out, as Laugier had done before him, the hut of primitive man as a guide to a new approach toward architecture.

WOLFGANG HERRMANN

BIBLIOGRAPHY

BRAHAM, ALLAN 1980 *The Architecture of the French Enlightenment.* London: Thames & Hudson.

FICHET, FRANÇOISE (editor) 1979 *La théorie architecturale à l'age classique.* Brussels: Mardaga.

FOUCART-BORVILLE 1974 "Les projets de Charles de Wailly par la Gloire de la cathédrale d'Amiens et de Victor Louis pour le maître-antel de la cathédrale de Noyen." *Bulletin de la Société de l'histoire de l'art français* 1974:131–144.

FRANKL, PAUL 1961 *The Gothic.* N.J.: Princeton University Press.

GERMANN, GEORG 1980 *Einführung in die Geschichte der Architekturtheorie.* Darmstadt, Germany: Wissenshaftliche Buchgesellschaft.

HERMANN, WOLFGANG 1962 *Laugier and Eighteenth Century French Theory.* London: Zwemmer.

LAUGIER, MARC-ANTOINE (1753a)1977 *An Essay on Architecture.* Translated by Wolfgang and Anni Herrmann. Los Angeles: Hennessey.

LAUGIER, MARC-ANTOINE 1753b *Jugement d'un amateur sur l'exposition des tableaux.* Paris: Ouchesne.

LAUGIER, MARC-ANTOINE 1753c "Lettre de l'auteur de l'Essai sur l'Architecture aux auteurs de ces Mémoires." *Journal de Trévoux* Aug.:1864ff.

LAUGIER, MARC-ANTOINE 1754a *Apologie de la musique française contre M. Rousseau.* n.p.

LAUGIER, MARC-ANTOINE 1754b "Réponse du P. Laugier, Jésuite aux remarques de M. Frézier. . . ." *Mercure de France* Oct.:29–51.

LAUGIER, MARC-ANTOINE 1755 "Observations du P. Laugier, Jésuite, sur la nouvelle histoire de la conquête de la Chine." *Mercure de France* Jan.:147ff.

LAUGIER, MARC-ANTOINE 1756 *Oraison funèbre de . . . Louis Auguste de Bourbon . . . le 18 Décembre 1755 par le R. P. Laugier, de la Compagnie de Jésus.* Trevoux, France.

LAUGIER, MARC-ANTOINE 1759–1768 *Histoire de la République de Venise, depuis sa fondation jusqu'à présent.* 12 vols. Paris: Duchesne.

LAUGIER, MARC-ANTOINE 1765 *Observations sur l'Architecture.* The Hague: Desaint.

LAUGIER, MARC-ANTOINE 1768 *Histoire des negociations pour la paix conclue à Belgrade . . . 1739.* Paris: Duchesne.

LAUGIER, MARC-ANTOINE 1771 *Manière de bien juger des ouvrages de peinture par feu M. l'Abbé Laugier. . . .* Edited by Charles Nicolas Cochin. Paris: Joubert.

LE CORBUSIER (1923)1970 *Towards a New Architecture.* Reprint. New York: Praeger.

LE CORBUSIER (1924)1966 *Urbanisme.* Paris: Vincent, Fréal.

LE CORBUSIER 1947 *Oeuvre complète: 1929–1934.* Zürich.

MIDDLETON, R. D., and WATKINS, DAVID 1980 *Neoclassical and 19th Century Architecture.* New York: Abrams.

PETZET, MICHAEL 1961 *Soufflots Sainte-Geneviève und der französische Kirchenbau des 18. Jahrhunderts.* Berlin: de Gruyter.

ROBSON-SCOTT, W. D. 1965 *The Literary Background of the Gothic Revival in Germany.* Oxford: Clarendon.

RYKWERT, JOSEPH 1972 *On Adam's House in Paradise.* New York: Museum of Modern Art.

RYKWERT, JOSEPH 1980 *The First Moderns.* Cambridge, Mass.: M.I.T. Press.

WIEBENSON, DORA 1978 *The Picturesque Garden in France.* N.J.: Princeton University Press.

WILTON-ELY, JOHN 1972 *The Age of Neo-Classicism: Catalogue of the 14th Exhibition of the Council of Europe.* London: Arts Council of Great Britain.

WILTON-ELY, JOHN 1978 *The Mind and Art of Giovanni Battista Piranesi.* London: Thames & Hudson.

ZMIJEWSKA, HELENE 1970 "La Critique des Salons en France avant Diderot." *Gazette des Beaux-Arts* Series 6 76:1–144.

LAURANA, LUCIANO

Luciano Laurana (1420/1425?–1479) occupies a key but sparsely documented role in the shift from the early Renaissance to the high Renaissance architecture of LEONARDO DA VINCI and DONATO BRAMANTE. Modern scholarship has recovered a few facts and produced extensive conjecture.

In his Dalmatian homeland Laurana enjoyed early exposure to Roman buildings. He apparently worked in Venice and Florence, but the first recorded notices are from 1465 when he was working for the Gonzagas in Mantua, where attributions of work at the ducal palace remain open to serious question, and for the Sforzas in Pesaro, where nothing seems to remain of his conjectured work at the ducal palace. In 1465 he supplied a model for the Palazzo Ducale in Urbino where documents place him, although not continuously, from 1466 to 1472, when he left, apparently for good. From 1472 to 1474 he was artillery master at the Castel Nuovo in Naples. Sometime between 1476 and 1479, he worked at the Rocca Costanza in Pesaro, with its clear geometric forms and skillful, harmonious use of brick and stone.

Laurana's fame and importance rest on his activity at the ducal palace in Urbino. He worked under the always close and formative supervision of Federigo da Montefeltro, one of the century's great patrons. Especially important in understanding Laurana's position, perhaps typical during the period, is Federigo's letter patent from 1468 and the claims for Federigo's role found in biographies by Vespasiano da Bisticci and others. Laurana's work must be disinterred from a larger whole. Between 1450 and 1465 a complex incorporating older fabric and including one or more new wings

had taken form under the Florentine Maso di Bartolommeo. Under Laurana after 1465 the palace's definitive character was established: the north wing with its august, vaulted Sala del Trono, the west suite known as the Appartamento del Duca with its complex of small rooms on three floors and its pair of spired towers connected by three superimposed, single-arched loggias overlooking the countryside to the west, and the large courtyard entered from a barrel-vaulted *androne* and next to the grand stairs, the oldest monumental stairs surviving in a Renaissance palace, built between the new north wing and the older work. FRANCESCO DI GIORGIO MARTINI, who had occasionally worked under Laurana at Urbino, took up the project in 1476 after a four-year hiatus, perhaps merely completing Laurana's scheme. He finished the courtyard's upper story, extended a wing to connect or add the so-called *castellare* to the north, and completed the intervening garden; he also began the façade revetment, apparently to his own design, on Laurana's north wing. An additional story containing guest rooms was added in the next century. It effaced Laurana's crenellated silhouette, heightened the two-story courtyard's proportions, and blinded the high south windows in the Sala del Trono.

Laurana's work marks a clear departure from that found in earlier palaces. The palpable formal purity produced by using clear proportional relationships visible in both individual rooms and in the plan's disposition as well as the character of the mouldings and framed openings Salmi (1945) credits to Piero della Francesco's collaboration with Laurana. Others have seen a decisive role for LEON BATTISTA ALBERTI, accessible to Laurana at

Laurana. Palazzo Ducale. Urbino, Italy. 1465–1472

Laurana.
Palazzo Ducale
Urbino, Italy.
1465–1472

an early date through the Gonzagas, Federigo, and Pius II, one of Federigo's ardent sponsors and whom Alberti at least advised in his work at the Vatican and at Pienza. Heydenreich (Heydenreich & Lotz, 1974) was tempted to think that Alberti suggested Pliny's Villa Laurentium as the model for the intimacy, arrangement, and orientation found in the Appartamento del Duca, while Westfall traces the palace's composition back to the Vatican Palace scheme of Nicholas V.

Whatever the sources, the palace, particularly in the courtyard and the larger public rooms, possesses a new gravity (*gravitas*) of structure and richness (*varietà*) of ornamental form unknown in the period's new architecture of Florence, Venice, and northern Italy. Particularly distinctive is the exploitation of a topographically difficult site and the clarity of structure achieved while using the unusually attractive stone and brick available in Urbino and by drawing on ancient Roman structural and ornamental forms. Laurana's work at the palace, by displaying a new potential in using ancient and Renaissance forms and motifs, played an important subsequent role. Perhaps through BACCIO PONTELLI it helped form the style of Roman buildings during the last quarter of the century. It was decisive for the architectural style of Francesco di Giorgio who transmitted the new *romanità* through his buildings and treatises to Leonardo. And it provided Bramante with his first exposure to architecture.

Unresolved is Laurana's connection with the three large tempera panels now in Urbino, Baltimore, and Berlin. Many other artists have also been suggested for their production as have dates extending long after Laurana's death. Undeniable however are the similarities of their architectural forms and spatial composition to similar characteristics first broached in Urbino, for example in paintings by Piero, in intarsia, and in Laurana's sections of the palace. Those similarities, with the enigmatic lack of obvious subject matter other than architectural vistas rendered in perspective, makes them problematic just as was Laurana's role in the palace where he was surrounded by a gang of talented workmen supplying capitals, mouldings, paintings, intarsia, and other ornamental fixtures for a palace in which, as Heydenreich said, "we can recognize the controlling initiative of its patron."

CARROLL WILLIAM WESTFALL

WORK

1465–1472, Palazzo Ducale (major sections), Urbino, Italy.

BIBLIOGRAPHY

HEYDENREICH, LUDWIG, and LOTZ, WOLFGANG 1974 *Architecture in Italy: 1400–1600.* Translated by Mary Hottinger. Harmondsworth, England: Penguin.
ROTONDI, PASQUALE 1950–1951 *Il Palazzo Ducale di Urbino.* 2 vols. Urbino, Italy: Instituto statale d'arte per il libro.
SAALMAN, HOWARD 1971 "The Ducal Palace of Urbino." *Burlington Magazine* 113, no. 814: 46–51.
SALMI, MARIO 1945 *Piero della Francesca e il Palazzo Ducale di Urbino.* Florence: Monnier.
WESTFALL, CARROLL W. 1978 "Chivalric Declaration: The Palazzo Ducale in Urbino as a Political Statement." Pages 20–45 in Henry Millon and Linda Nochlin (editors), *Art and Architecture in the Service of Politics.* Cambridge, Mass: M.I.T. Press.

LAUWERIKS, J. L. M.

J. L. M. Lauweriks (1864–1932) is often mentioned in histories of the Modern movement either for his writing and editorial capabilities in *Der Ring, Architectura,* and *Wendingen* or for his proportional systems which he popularized in writing and lectures, and which he applied in architecture and the applied arts. He is also known for his occult beliefs. Together with K. P. C. DE BAZEL, he left the office of P. J. H. CUYPERS in 1894 and began a lifelong affiliation with theosophy.

Despite Lauweriks's ties to occultism he did not reveal a dependency on it in his writings, which were all more or less clear, although here and there he showed a propensity for the irrational. In a talk given at the Theosophical Association of Haarlem, Lauweriks stressed especially his knowledge of Plato and his geometrical ideas, and he conveyed this "as space symbol of the simplest form; the cube with six equal sides, composed of four side planes of earthly elements, allows itself to be composed for nature." A little later, in 1909, Lauweriks designed an exhibition space with cubes, and that same year, an issue of the magazine *Der Ring* included designs based on the quadrature system.

This issue of *Der Ring* (April 1909) is Lauweriks's single most interesting publication, mainly because of the fascinating intricate nature of the designs. Most of the illustrations are floor plans for a church. They are all rectangular save for one which is square. Almost all resemble DONATO BRAMANTE's plan for that of Saint Peter's in Rome with a centralized dome, but they also resemble later concepts for Saint Peter's with an extended nave. All of the floor plans exhibit a playful experimentation resulting in cosmati decorations.

Lauweriks began teaching architecture when he was sixteen. His attempt to balance individuality of expression with mathematical controlling devices is a notable contribution.

Lauweriks's name comes down to us partly through the reputation accorded him by PETER BEHRENS, K. E. Osthaus, and LE CORBUSIER. Behrens tried to persuade H. P. BERLAGE to come and teach in Düsseldorf, but Berlage did not accept. Lauweriks was asked and did accept, and he apparently became quite close to Behrens. This closeness is evident from the design of a crematorium by Behrens, built in Hagen, Germany, in which the proportional systems of Lauweriks are obvious. Osthaus, an art patron, commissioned Lauweriks to design a series of houses for an art colony in Hagen (1910); the house for Thorn Prikker shows the proportional systems that Le Corbusier mentioned in his *Modular 1*.

SUZANNE FRANK

BIBLIOGRAPHY

"J. L. M. Lauweriks." 1975 Pages 93–111 in *Nederlandse architectuur, 1893–1918: Architectura.* Amsterdam: van Gennep.

TUMMERS, NIC. H. M. 1968 *J. L. Mathieu Lauweriks, zijn werk en zijn invloed op architectuur en vormgeving rond 1910: "De Hagener Impuls."* Hilversum, Netherlands: Uitgeverij F. van Saane.

emigrated to Canada in 1857. With Thomas Stent, he competed successfully for the flanking blocks of Ottawa's Parliament Buildings, and worked in Quebec and Montreal. Laver won one of three first prizes for the New York State Capitol and associated with THOMAS FULLER in its execution (1867–1871). After they were awarded the commission for San Francisco's City Hall (1870–1893), Laver established a prestigious practice there. The earliest western member of the American Institute of Architects, he presided over the Pacific Coast Association of Architects' becoming an A.I.A. chapter.

ANNE BLOOMFIELD

WORKS

1859–1863, Parliament Buildings eastern and western blocks; (with Thomas Stent), Ottawa. *1860, Finlay Asylum (with Stent), Quebec City. 1867–1871, New York State Capitol (foundation and terraces with Thomas Fuller), Albany. *1870–1893, San Francisco City Hall. *c.1876, O'Brian-Montague Building, San Francisco. 1878–1886, Linden Towers (with William Curlett), Atherton, Calif. 1880, James V. Coleman Residence, Menlo Park, Calif. 1886, Ellen Kenna Residence, Oakland, Calif. *1886–1887, Flood Building; 1886–1888, Flood Mansion; 1894, Traynor Flats, 1871–1873, Golden Gate Avenue (with Patrick Mullany); 1897, M. Mullany Residence, 2301 Scott Street (with P. Mullany); San Francisco.

BIBLIOGRAPHY

ARMSTRONG, ALAN H. 1957 "Profile of Parliament Hill." *Journal of the Royal Architectural Institute of Canada* 34, no. 9:327–331.

"Augustus Laver." 1884 *California Architect and Building News* 5, no. 1:9.

HOUGH, FRANKLIN B. 1873 *Gazetteer of the State of New York.* Albany, N.Y.: Boyd.

KIRKER, HAROLD (1960)1973 *California's Architectural Frontier.* Santa Barbara, Calif., and Salt Lake City, Utah: Peregrine Smith.

LANGSAM, WALTER E. 1970 "Thomas Fuller and Augustus Laver: Victorian Neo-Baroque and Second Empire vs. Gothic Revival in North America." *Journal of the Society of Architectural Historians* 29, no. 3:270.

"Obituary." 1898 *California Architect and Building News* 19, no. 3:28.

PHELPS, ALONZO 1881–1882 Volume 2, pages 90–92 in *Contemporary Biography of California's Representative Men.* San Francisco: Bancroft.

LAVER, AUGUSTUS

Augustus Laver (1834–1898) designed monumental High Victorian eclectic buildings. Born in Folkstone, England, he was apprenticed for four years to a London architect and civil engineer. He

LAVES, GEORGES LUDWIG FRIEDRICH

Georges Ludwig Friedrich Laves (1788–1864) was born in Hannover, Germany. He studied in Göttingen and Rome. In Hannover, he designed

the Opera House (1845–1852) and several alterations of the Royal Palace, all in a classicizing style.
Laves also experimented with structural design; in
1850, he submitted a proposal for the Crystal Palace in London.

LISA B. REITZES

WORKS

1817–1830, 1831–1842, Royal Palace (remodeling);
1825–1832, Waterloo Column; Hannover, Germany.
1842–1846, Mausoleum, Herrenhausen, Germany.
1845–1852, Opera House, Hannover, Germany.

BIBLIOGRAPHY
DOLGNER, DIETER 1971 *Die Architektur des Klassizis-
mus in Deutschland.* Dresden, Germany: Verlag der
Kunst.
PEVSNER, NIKOLAUS 1970 "German Crystal Palace."
Architectural Review 148, Oct.:257.

LAVIROTTE, JULES AIME

Jules Aimé Lavirotte (1864–1924) carried the use
of sculpted, glazed bricks further than any of his
contemporaries. Asymmetry and florid sexual motifs characterized both planning and façade designs
of his Art Nouveau Parisian apartment buildings.
In his Paris workers' housing on the other hand,
symmetry and rustic simplicity, derived from neo-
Gothic wood framing, prevailed.

ELIZABETH MCLANE

WORKS

1898, Apartment House, 151 Rue de Grenelle; 1899–
1900, Apartment House, 3 Square Rapp; 1900–1901,
Apartment House, 29 Avenue Rapp; 1903, Apartment
House, 134 Rue de Grenelle; 1906, Low-rent Houses,
Boulevard Lefebvre; 1906, Private House, 23 Avenue de
Messine; c.1907, Apartment House, 6 Rue de Messine;
Paris. c.1910, Etablissement Eaux Thermales du
Châtelet, Evian-les-Bains, France. 1913, Château Saint-
Cyr-Mont-d'Or, near Lyons, France. 1913, Workers'
Housing, Juvisy, France.

BIBLIOGRAPHY
BOILEAU, L. C. 1901 "Causerie." *L'Architecture* 14,
no. 17:141–147.
BORRMANN, RICHARD 1902 *Moderne Keramik
(Monographien des Kunstgewerbes V)*. Leipzig: Seeman.
BORSI, FRANCO, and GODOLI, EZIO 1976 *Paris, 1900.*
Brussels: Vokaer.
"Le Concours de Façades à Paris en 1901—Rapport sur
les Opérations du Jury." 1902 *L'Architecture* 15,
no. 51:453–455.
"Maison Avenue Rapp, à Paris." 1902 *La Construction
Moderne* 17:342–344.
UHRY, EDMOND 1905 "Constructions Récentes de
M. Lavirotte." *L'Art Décoratif* 7:24–32.

LAWRENCE, ELLIS FULLER

Born in Malden, Massachusetts, Ellis Fuller Lawrence (1879–1946) graduated from the Massachusetts Institute of Technology with both bachelor's
and master's degrees in 1902. After work in Maine
and travel in Europe, he headed for California in
1906. He stopped in Portland, Oregon, where he
was persuaded to stay by his friend E. B. Mac-
Naughton. In 1914, he founded the School of Architecture, University of Oregon, Eugene. He remained dean and university architect until his
death.

MARION DEAN ROSS

WORKS

1911–1912, Masonic Temple, Salem, Ore. 1912, Albina
Branch Library; 1912–1914, Westminster Presbyterian
Church; Portland, Ore. 1919–1920, Gerlinger Hall,
University of Oregon, Eugene. 1917–1922, University
of Oregon Medical School, Portland. 1926, Elsinore
Theater, Salem, Ore. 1929–1930, Museum of Art, Uni-
versity of Oregon, Eugene. *1933, Public Market, Port-
land, Ore. 1935–1936, Library, University of Oregon,
Eugene. 1939–1942, State Tuberculosis Hospital, Port-
land, Ore.

BIBLIOGRAPHY
*The Ellis F. Lawrence Papers are in the Special Collections
(592) of the University of Oregon Library, Eugene.*
EMERSON, WILLIAM 1946 "Ellis F. Lawrence,
F.A.I.A., 1879–1946." *Journal of the American Institute
of Architects* 6, no. 1:21–25.
VAUGHAN, THOMAS, and FERRIDAY, VIRGINIA GUEST
(editors) 1974 *Space, Style and Structure.* 2 vols.
Portland: Oregon Historical Society.

LAWSON, R. A.

Robert Arthur Lawson (1833–1902) was born in
Scotland and studied at Perth and Edinburgh. He
went to Melbourne in 1854 and in 1861 won a
design competition for First Church, Dunedin,
New Zealand. He designed many churches and
houses in Gothic Revival style and commercial
buildings such as banks in the classical manner.

JOHN STACPOOLE

WORKS

1868, First Church Manse; 1869, Trinity Methodist
Church; 1870, East Taieri Church; 1871, Larnach's Cas-
tle; 1873, First Church (completion); 1874, ANZ
Bank; 1876, Knox Church; 1877, Seacliff Hospital;
1883, Bank of New South Wales, Oamaru; 1884, Otago
Boys' High School; Dunedin, New Zealand.

BIBLIOGRAPHY
McCOY, E. J., and BLACKMAN, J. G. 1968 *Victorian*

City of New Zealand. Dunedin, New Zealand: John McIndoe.

STACPOOLE, JOHN 1976 *Colonial Architecture in New Zealand.* Wellington: Reed.

LAYBOURNE-SMITH, LOUIS

Louis Laybourne-Smith (1880–1965) was articled in 1899 to the South Australian architect Edward Davies. His major contribution to Australian architecture was the foundation in 1906 of a diploma course in his native Adelaide. Partner in a major practice (1914–1965), he received the Royal Australian Institute of Architects' Gold Medal (1962).

DONALD LANGMEAD

WORKS

1923–1953, Calvary Hospital; 1927, Union Building, University of Adelaide; 1937, Bonython Jubilee Building, School of Mines; Adelaide, Australia.

BIBLIOGRAPHY

WALKLEY, GAVIN 1977 *Louis Laybourne Smith: A Memoir.* South Australian Institute of Technology.

LAZARESCU, CEZAR

Cezar Lazarescu (1923–) graduated from the Institute of Architecture in Bucharest in 1948. He is best known as an urban planner. In 1955, he became the chairman of a group of architects who designed the rehabilitation and development of the Black Sea shore, including all architectural structures for such resorts as Eforie and Mangalia. His work attests to a special concern with contemporary architecture, using advanced building methods and technology. He is the author of many articles and studies.

CONSTANTIN MARIN MARINESCU

WORKS

1950, Urban Development Plan, Navodari, Rumania. 1970, Otopeni International Airport (with others), Bucharest.

BIBLIOGRAPHY

IONESCU, GRIGORE 1965 Volume 2 in *Istoria Arhitecturii in Romania.* Bucharest: Editura Academiei Republicii Romañe.
IONESCU, GRIGORE 1969 *Arhitectura in Romania; Perioda anilor 1944–1969.* Bucharest: Editura Academiei Republicii Socialiste Romañia.
IONESCU, GRIGORE 1972 "Saptezeci si cinci de ani de la infiintarea invatamintului de arhitectura din Ro-

mania." *Arhitectura* 20:35–42.
MAMBRIANI, ALBERTO 1969 *L'Architettura Moderna nei Paesi Balcanici.* Bologna, Italy: Capelli.
PATRULIUS, RADU 1973–1974 "Contributii Romanesti in Arhitectura Anilor '30." *Arhitectura* 21, no. 6:44–52; 22, no. 1:53–59.
SASARMAN, GHEORGHE 1972 "Inceputurile gindirii teoretice in arhitectura româneascâ (1860–1916)." *Arhitectura* 20, no. 6:44–46.

LAZARUS, EDGAR M.

Born in Baltimore, Edgar M. Lazarus (1868–1939) went to Portland, Oregon, around 1892 and had an extensive practice there until after World War I. He was active in the Portland Architectural Club and the American Institute of Architects. His most unusual work, Vista House, Crown Point, on the Columbia River, shows some influence of the *Jugendstil.*

MARION DEAN ROSS

WORKS

1898–1899, Apperson Hall, Oregon State University, Cornvallis. *1904, Ahavai Shalom Synagogue, Portland, Ore. 1904–1907, Clatsop County Courthouse, Astoria, Ore. *1905, Agriculture Building, Lewis and Clark Exposition, Portland, Ore. 1912, Oregon State Hospital, Salem. 1916–1918, Vista House, Crown Point, Ore.

BIBLIOGRAPHY

Further information on Edgar M. Lazarus can be found in the Cachot Therkelson Papers, Special Collections (1029), University of Oregon Library, Eugene.
MARLITT, RICHARD 1978 *Nineteenth Street.* Rev. ed. Portland: Oregon Historical Society.
VAUGHAN, THOMAS, and FERRIDAY, VIRGINIA GUEST (editors) 1974 *Space, Style and Structure.* 2 vols. Portland: Oregon Historical Society.

LEADBETTER, STIFF

Stiff Leadbetter (?–1766) began as a carpenter, builder, and surveyor, and ended up as official surveyor to Saint Paul's Cathedral in 1756. He was a second-generation Palladian whose works lacked flair. Langley Park, Buckinghamshire (1755), Nuneham Park, Oxfordshire (1756), and Newton Park, Somerset (c.1761) are his best houses, and Envills, Surrey (1766) shows he could design charmingly in "Gothick."

JOHN HARRIS

WORKS

1753, Foley House, London. 1755, Langley Park, Buckinghamshire, England. 1756, Nuneham Park, Oxfordshire, England. 1759, Radcliffe Infirmary, Oxford. c.1761, Newton Park, Somerset, England. 1766, Envills, Surrey, England.

LEBAS, LOUIS HIPPOLYTE

Louis Hippolyte Lebas (1782–1867) studied with his uncle, A. Vaudoyer (see VAUDOYER AND VANDOYER), and with Charles Percier (see PERCIER AND FONTAINE). While a professor at the Ecole des Beaux-Arts in Paris (1819–1867), he taught PIERRE FRANÇOIS HENRI LABROUSTE and CHARLES GARNIER. Lebas was also architect of civil works in Paris after 1826; there, he designed the basilican Nôtre-Dame de Lorette (1823–1826) and the prison at the Petite Roquette (1831–1836).

LISA B. REITZES

WORKS

1823–1826, Nôtre-Dame de Lorette; *1827–1830, Statue of Ludwig XVIII (base), Place du Palais Bourbon; 1831–1836, Prison at the Petite Roquette; 1832–1843, Academy of Medicine (remodeling); Paris.

BIBLIOGRAPHY

HAUTECOEUR, LOUIS 1943–1957 *Histoire de l'Architecture classique en France.* 7 vols. Paris: Picard.
SADDY, PIERRE 1977 *Henri Labrouste: Architects, 1801–1875.* Paris: Caisse Nationale des Monuments Historiques et des Sites.

LE BLOND, JEAN

The Parisian architect Jean Baptiste Alexandre Le Blond (1679–1719) was a pupil of both JULES HARDOUIN MANSART and ANDRÉ LE NOSTRE.

Typical of many of the followers of Mansart, Le Blond designed with a simple elegance and intimacy of plan associated with the rococo style. This approach can be seen particularly in the house he designed for Regnault at Chatillon, which highlights an oval salon projecting onto an elaborately terraced garden. This emphasis on the garden was typical of Le Blond, whose abilities as a landscape architect were greatly admired.

Le Blond also did illustrations for a number of books, including J. F. FÉLIBIEN's *Histoire de l'Abbaye Royale de Saint-Denis en France* (1706), Dézallier d'Argenville's *La théorie et la pratique du jardinage* (1709), and CHARLES A. DAVILER's *Cours d'architecture* (1710).

In 1716, he was appointed architect general to Peter the Great of Russia. Accompanied by his family and many assistants, Le Blond took up residence in St. Petersburg in August of 1716. His plans for the city included a network of canals reminiscent of Amsterdam and a summer garden. In addition, he designed the palace and gardens of the summer estate known as Peterhof (1716–1719).

Tragically, Le Blond never lived to see these plans executed. He died of smallpox in 1719 at the age of thirty-nine.

KATHLEEN RUSSO

WORKS

1706, Hôtel de Vendome; *1708–1714, Hôtel de Saissac; Paris. 1716–1719, Peterhof Palace (built posthumously, with later additions by BARTOLOMEO RASTRELLI), St. Petersburg. n.d., Le Cannet Garden, Narbonne, France. n.d., Hoguer House Gardens; n.d., Maison Regnault; Châtillon-sous-Bagneux, France.

BIBLIOGRAPHY

BLONDEL, JACQUES FRANÇOIS 1771–1777 *Cours d'Architecture.* 6 vols. Paris: Desaint.
BRICE, GERMAIN (1752)1971 Volume 4 in *Nouvelle description de la ville de Paris.* Reprint. Geneva: Droz; Paris: Minard.
CONTET, FRÉDÉRIC 1914–1934 Volume 4 in *Les vieux hôtels de Paris.* Paris: Contet.
DAVILER, AUGUSTIN CHARLES (1691)1710 *Cours d'architecture.* Rev. ed. 2 vols. Edited by Jean Baptiste Alexandre Le Blond. Paris: Mariette.
DÉZALLIER D'ARGENVILLE, ANTOINE JOSEPH (1709)1728 *The Theory and Practice of Gardening.* Translated by John James. London: Lintot.
DÉZALLIER D'ARGENVILLE, ANTOINE NICOLAS 1787 *Vies des plus fameux architectes et sculpteurs.* Paris: Debure aîné.
FÉLIBIEN, DOM MICHEL 1706 *Histoire de l'Abbaye Royale de Saint Denis en France.* Paris: Léonard.
GALLET, MICHEL 1972 *Paris Domestic Architecture of the Eighteenth Century.* London: Barrie & Jenkins.
HAUTECOEUR, LOUIS 1950 *Première moitié du XVIIIᵉ siècle: Le style Louis XV.* Volume 3 in *Histoire de l'architecture classique en France.* Paris: Picard.
KIMBALL, FISKE (1943)1980 *The Creation of the Rococo Decorative Style.* Reprint. New York: Dover.
LOSSKY, BORIS 1934 "L'hôtel de Vendome et son architect Alexandre Le Blond." *Gazette des Beaux Arts* Series 6 12:30–41.
LOSSKY, BORIS 1936 "J. B. A. Le Blond, architecte de Pierre le Grand: Son Oeuvre en France." *Bulletin de l'association russe pour les recherches scientifiques à Prague* 3, no. 17:179–216.
MARIETTE, JEAN (1727)1927–1929 Volumes 2–3 in *L'architecture français.* Edited by Louis Hautecoeur. Paris and Brussels: Van Oest.
MARIETTE, PIERRE JEAN 1851–1860 Volume 3 in *Abécédario.* Paris: Dumoulin.
MARSDEN, CHRISTOPHER 1942 *Palmyra of the North: The First Days of St. Petersburg.* London: Faber.
PIGANIOL DE LA FORCE, JEAN AYMAR 1765 Volume 3

in *Description historiques de la ville de Paris et ses environs.* Paris: Les Libraires associés.

WARD, WILLIAM HENRY (1911)1976 Volume 2 in *The Architecture of the Renaissance in France.* 2d ed., rev. New York: Hacker.

LE BRETON, GILLES

A French mason, Gilles Le Breton (1500?–1553) was the eldest son of a Parisian family of master masons. He was trained by his father, with whom he worked on the Château de Chambord and the Gothic chapel of the Château de Vincennes.

His social and professional rise led him to an official appointment as *maître général des oeuvres de maçonnerie* by King François I in 1527. Le Breton's main professional activity throughout his life was his devotion to the Château at Fontainebleau whose construction began in 1528. Working from SEBASTIANO SERLIO's original design, Le Breton extended the Royal Hunting Castle according to the classical ideal of simplicity and clarity in composition of Greek and Roman architecture. The first new buildings were the Entrance Court, the Porte Dorée (1528–1535), the Pavillon for Monsieur les Enfants, and the Chapel. The rebuilding of the main staircase was completed in 1540. The architectonic treatment of windows and pediments and the structural function of columns were original and innovative for the period. His collaboration with PHILIBERT DELORME left hard to define their respective roles in the construction of the Château at Fontainebleau. Le Breton's success brought him many commissions for private hôtels.

Le Breton owned a number of houses in Paris and Fontainebleau, and he also possessed an unusual collection of paintings, sculptures, tapestries, furniture, and books. The source of his funds was unknown, and this led his contemporaries and biographers to questions suggesting foul play. His posthumous inventory did, however, demonstrate his fine taste and interest in expert craftsmanship.

Between 1550 and 1552, Le Breton undertook the rebuilding of the Château at Fleury en Bière; its forecourt wings fully illustrate his mastery as a mason.

MARC DILET

WORKS

1522, Gothic Chapel, Château de Vincennes, France. 1527, Convent of the Trinitaires (remodeling), near Paris. 1528–1552, Château de Fontainebleau (extensions), France. 1547–1550, Hôtel d'Albon; 1547–1550, Hôtel la Guette; 1547–1550, Hôtel Come-Clausse; near Fontainebleau, France. 1550–1552, Château de Fleury-en-Bière (reconstruction), France.

LEBRUN, NAPOLEON

The professional life of Napoleon LeBrun (1821–1901) spanned almost sixty years, first in Philadelphia and then in New York City. Born to French émigré parents in Philadelphia in 1821, he is said to have been apprenticed to THOMAS U. WALTER in 1836. He opened his own office in 1841.

His earliest commissions were for Philadelphia churches, among them the Seventh Presbyterian Church (1842); the German Catholic Church of Saint Peter's (1843–1845), still standing although considerably altered late in the nineteenth century; and major alterations and additions to Saint Augustine's Church (1847). He also considerably enlarged Jefferson Medical College (1845–1846) in Greek Revival style.

LeBrun's ecclesiastical experience as well as the fact that he was a Roman Catholic probably led to his selection, in 1846 or 1847, as the supervising architect for the Roman Catholic Cathedral of Saint Peter and Saint Paul. The cathedral, of enormous size for the time, was not completed until 1864. The archives of the diocese have not been studied to establish definitively the sequence of the building's design. Around 1850, LeBrun was replaced by JOHN NOTMAN, who designed the façade. Subsequently, Notman was dismissed and LeBrun was reinstated. The latter is generally credited with the design of the basilica's Renaissance Revival domed interior.

After his first work on the cathedral, LeBrun designed a courthouse and jail (1850) for Montgomery County in Norristown, Pennsylvania. The courthouse, in somewhat attenuated Classical Revival style, has been much enlarged. The prison, however, with its Gothic Revival quintipartite façade, remains intact. The design, featuring corner turrets and a castellated central pavilion topped with a tower, is obviously derived from Walter's prison for Philadelphia County at Moyamensing.

Prominently sited on Logan Square, the Roman Catholic Cathedral remains one of LeBrun's enduring contributions to the Philadelphia cityscape. His other major surviving landmark building in that city is the Academy of Music (1855–1856), designed in collaboration with Gustave Runge. The commission was awarded after a nationwide competition. With its subdued Italianate exterior and exuberant neobaroque interior, the Academy remains one of the country's foremost concert halls, renowned for its superb acoustics.

LeBrun's Philadelphia practice also encompassed residences and commercial buildings, executed in the fashionable revival styles of the mid-nineteenth century.

In 1864, LeBrun moved to New York, where he lived for the remainder of his life. He established a firm with his sons in the early 1880s, practicing thereafter as N. LeBrun and Sons. During the 1880s, the firm was the official architect of the New York City Fire Department, for which it designed several headquarters buildings and engine houses. These were in a variety of styles, often reflecting the scale and character of the surrounding neighborhood. One of the most notable is a large Châteauesque example for Engine Company 31 (1895).

Late in LeBrun's career, the firm designed two important skyscrapers in New York, the Home Life Insurance Building (1893–1894) and the ten-story Metropolitan Life Insurance Building (1890–1893). The neighboring Metropolitan Life Tower (1909), which still stands, was designed after LeBrun's death in 1901.

CONSTANCE M. GREIFF

WORKS

*1842, Seventh Presbyterian Church; 1843–1845, German Catholic Church of Saint Peter's (later altered); *1845–1846, Jefferson Medical College (alterations and additions); 1846?–1850?, 1854?–1864, Cathedral of Saint Peter and Saint Paul; 1847, Saint Augustine's Church (alterations and additions); Philadelphia. 1850, Montgomery County Courthouse and jail (later enlarged), Norristown, Pa. 1855–1856, Academy of Music (with Gustave Runge), Philadelphia. *1870, Church of the Epiphany; 1884–1896, Fire Department Headquarters; *1890–1893, Metropolitan Life Insurance Building; 1893–1894, Home Life Insurance Building; 1895, Engine Company 31 Building; 1895, Saint Mary the Virgin Church; New York.

BIBLIOGRAPHY

JACKSON, JOSEPH 1923 *Early Philadelphia Architects and Engineers.* Philadelphia: Privately printed.
"The Metropolitan Tower." 1909 *American Architect and Building News* 96:124–129.
SCHUYLER, MONTGOMERY 1910 "The Work of N. LeBrun & Sons." *Architectural Record* 27:365–381.

LE CAMUS DE MEZIERES, NICOLAS

Nicolas Le Camus de Mezières (1721–1789) won the second prize of the French Académie d'Architecture in 1742. Between 1751 and 1792, he was an *architecte expert bourgeois.*

In 1766, he constructed the Varenne House, Rue Mouffetard. He began the Paris Halle au Blé on the site of the old Hôtel de Soissons in 1763, and the building went into use in 1769. Its novel design, free-standing circular form, perfection of elevations, and ingenious vaulting and staircases were praised by contemporaries.

He also built a *hôtel* for the prince of Beauvau in 1769. The Colysée, a famous festival hall on Avenue Matignon near the Rond-point of the Champs-Elysées erected by Louis Denis Le Camus, has been misattributed to Le Camus de Mezières.

He published a *Recueil de différents plans concernant la nouvelle halle aux grains* (1768), *Le génie de l'architecture ou l'analogie des arts avec nos sensations* (1780), a *Guide de ceux qui veulent bâtir* (1781), and the *Traité de la force des bois* (1782).

GÉRARD ROUSSET-CHARNY
*Translated from French by
Richard Cleary*

LE CARPENTIER, ANTOINE MATHIEU

Antoine Mathieu Le Carpentier (1709–1773) became an *architecte du roi* and was appointed to the French Académie d'Architecture in 1756. He worked at the Cour des Comptes under the direction of JACQUES GABRIEL between 1738 and 1740.

Extremely active, he received many commissions from financiers. Around 1755, he built the Pavillon du Roi at Croix-Fontaine (Seine-et-Marne) at the expense of Bouret, an enterprising courtier who reserved this house for the use of Louis XV when the king went hunting in the Sénart forest. He erected the Château de Ballainvilliers for Jacques Samuel Bernard, and then in 1764, the château of the Ferte-Vidame (Eure) for Jean Joseph de Laborde.

He remodeled the *hôtel* of Crozat the Younger on the Rue de Richelieu, which the Duc de Choiseul had received as an inheritance. He designed the Pavillon de La Boissière, Rue de Clichy, completed by Guillaume Couture Le Jeune, an important work marking the transition to neoclassicism.

At Rouen, he designed projects for a new town hall, realized several urban works, and erected the portal of the archbishop's residence. In Paris, he was awarded numerous commissions: the entry to the Palais Bourbon; the church of the Collège de Grandmont, Rue Mignon; the Collège de Navarre, Rue de la Harpe; and the *hôtels* de Boulainvilliers, Rue Bergere, de Lassy or de La Guiche, Rue du Regard, and d'Harcourt-Beuvron.

Between 1754 and 1762, he built the Château of Courteilles (Eure) and the Château of Olweiler in Alsace for Comte Waldner. At Ormesson, he modified the château and built the village church. He also built the buildings of the Abbey of Clairvaux.

GÉRARD ROUSSET-CHARNY
Translated from French by
Richard Cleary

LECHNER, ÖDÖN

Ödön Lechner (1845–1914) was an eminent master of the so-called Hungarian national style, which was closely related to Art Nouveau.

After his studies at the Academy in Pest (1865) and at the Academy in Berlin (1866–1868), he traveled in Italy. Returning home, he initially designed in a strictly historical manner. His new architectural style began with the study and application of the rich tradition of Hungarian popular decorative art. In the ornaments of his buildings Lechner turned more and more toward Hungarian folk art, while relying on Moorish inspiration for the organization of space.

Lechner's main works in the capital and in the country, renovated and restored, show the Hungarian character and originality of his architectural art. His three most famous buildings, the Museum of Applied Arts (1891–1896), the Institute of Geology (1898–1899), and the Postal Savings Bank (1899–1901), all in Budapest, are today historical monuments.

The art of Ödön Lechner started a new period in the history of Hungarian architecture. He had several followers in the young generation of architects. These were the so-called Young People, who carried on Lechner's ideas into the twentieth century.

JUDITH KOÓS

WORKS

1870–1880, Apartment House (since altered), 43 Bajcsy Zsilinszky Road, Budapest. 1882, City Hall, Szeged, Hungary. *1883–1884, Beniczky-Odescalchi Manor House, Zsámbokrèt, Hungary. 1883–1884, Hungarian State Railways Pension Office, Budapest. 1883–1884, Miko House, Szeged, Hungary. 1891–1896, Museum of Applied Arts, Budapest. 1892–1894, City Hall, Kecskemét, Hungary. 1898–1899, Institute of Geology; 1899–1901, Postal Savings Bank; Budapest.

BIBLIOGRAPHY

KISMARTY-LECHNER, JENO 1961 *Lechner Ödön.* Budapest: Képzomüvészeti Alap.
KOÓS, JUDITH 1979 *Style 1900. A szecesszió iparmüvészete Magyarországon* ("Style 1900. Applied Arts of the Art Nouveau in Hungary"). Budapest: Kepzömüv.
LECHNER, ÖDÖN 1906 "Magyar formanyelv nem volt, hanem lesz" ("Hungarian Form of Expression Has Not Been, It Will Be"). *Muveszet* 1906:1–18.
VAGO, JOSEF 1911 "Lechner." *Bildende Kunstler* 12:549–596.
VAMOS, FERENC 1927 *Lechner Ödön, I–II.* Budapest: Amicus Kladas.
VARGA, LASZLO 1964 "Lechner Ödön (1845–1914). Halalanak felevszazados evfordulojan" ("Ödön Lechner, 1845–1914. On the Semi-centennial Anniversary of his Death"). *Magyar Épitomüvészet* 4:52.

LECLERE, ACHILLE

Achille Leclère (1785–1853) won the Prix de Rome in 1808 and was an ardent follower of his teacher, Charles Percier (see PERCIER AND FONTAINE). In 1816, he submitted two grand proposals for the rededicated Madeleine. Leclère also designed residences in a suburb of Paris. His tomb monuments for Luigi Cherubini and Casimir Pierre Périer reflected a taste for archeology.

LISA B. REITZES

WORKS

1819–1820, Residences, Rue Saint Lazare, Paris.

BIBLIOGRAPHY

HAUTECOEUR, LOUIS 1943–1957 *Histoire de l'Architecture classique en France.* 7 vols. Paris: Picard.
SAUNIER, CHARLES 1917 "Deux Projects d'Achille Leclère pour l'achèvement de la Madeleine." *Gazette des Beaux-Arts* 13:349–360.

LECOINTE, J.-F.-J.

An excellent draftsman, J.-F.-J. Lecointe (1783–1858) was JACQUES IGNACE HITTORFF's partner (succeeding FRANÇOIS JOSEPH BÉLANGER) throughout the Restoration in the Menus Plaisirs du Roi administration, designing many festivities and theaters, among them the Salle Favart-Théâtre Italien (1825) and the Ambigù-Comique (1827). He was the partner of E.-J. Gilbert in the design of the July Monarchy's American plan *prison de la nouvelle force* (Mazas) and a noted designer of villas.

DONALD D. SCHNEIDER

BIBLIOGRAPHY

HAUTECOEUR, LOUIS 1955 Volume 6 in *Histoire de l'architecture classique en France.* Paris: Picard.
HITCHCOCK, H. R. (1958)1977 *Architecture: Nineteenth and Twentieth Centuries.* 4th ed., rev. Baltimore: Penguin.
SCHNEIDER, DONALD D. 1977 *The Works and Doctrine of Jacques-Ignace Hittorff (1792–1867).* New York: Garland.

LE CORBUSIER

Le Corbusier (1887–1965) is the architect who next to FRANK LLOYD WRIGHT exerted the single most powerful influence on the architecture of the first three quarters of the twentieth century. He achieved this through a singular combination of talent and indefatigable energy that enabled him to leave behind more than 32,000 architectural and urbanistic drawings and plans (from his own hand as well as those of his associates) dealing with close to 400 projects, some 300 paintings, more than 7,000 drawings, illustrated books, lithographs, engravings, works in enamel, tapestries, and furniture. In addition, he held at least fourteen French patents, dating from 1918 through 1960, which, with few exceptions, testify to a lifelong interest in prefabrication and in the use of standardized modular elements in building. Complementing this activity as a designer was his literary output of innumerable writings in flyer, article, and pamphlet form and the publication of more than forty books; some of these works were translated into as many as eight languages and have affected architectural and urbanistic thinking throughout the world.

Born Charles-Edouard Jeanneret-Gris in La Chaux-de-Fonds in the Canton of Neuchâtel, Switzerland, Le Corbusier was the second son of George-Edouard Jeanneret-Gris and Marie Charlotte Amélie, née Perret. His father, continuing a family tradition of work in the major local industry of horology, was an enameler of watchcases whose avocation was that of a dedicated and accomplished alpinist; his mother was a professor of piano. In 1930, he married Jeanne Victorine Gallis, that same year he became a French citizen.

While as a painter and on some official documents Jeanneret continued to sign with his family name for many years, for other purposes he adopted in 1920 the name of Le Corbusier which, for the sake of simplicity, will be used throughout this article. By the very adoption of this name, Le Corbusier invented a character who invited being addressed in the third person and who, as something of a true alter ego, eventually seems to have taken hold of his inventor's imagination in an uncanny way, greatly helping him in the process of a self-stylization in the service of his ideals.

In looking back on his life, Le Corbusier liked to think that some of his characteristic traits such as perseverance and combativeness were due to his early educational and family background. A member of his family had been involved in the revolutionary uprisings of 1848, and more distant medieval ancestors, according to his belief, were heretic Albigensian Cathars from the south of France.

As far as his education was concerned, it was directed toward the arts from the beginning. Already in 1900, he was taking courses at the local *Ecole d'Art* and by 1902 he was officially enrolled in its program of engraving related particularly to horology. He left this branch in 1905 because of difficulties with his eyesight and had the good fortune to come more fully under the influence of Charles L'Eplattenier who, though relatively new to the community, was already enjoying considerable success as a teacher and an artist. This remarkable man, who had studied in Budapest and in Paris at the Ecole des Beaux-Arts and in the atelier of Luc Olivier Merson and who had seen firsthand the results of the English Arts and Crafts movement which he greatly admired, held deep convictions about the social mission of the artist and about the role of form as a vehicle of symbolic expression. This led him to promote the creation of an art that would express the regional character of the Suisse Romande. At the same time, he gave his students a sound training in the fundamentals of decorative design. With Le Corbusier as one of his pupils, L'Eplattenier in 1905–1906 gave for the first time his *Cours supérieur d'art et de décoration*.

In no small way, Le Corbusier's special contribution to our times stems from the fact that his formative years bridged two centuries, with his youth spent amid artists and artisans whose nineteenth-century heritage made them solid believers in the betterment of society through design and in the ideal of the artist as a bringer of happiness and salvation to mankind, beliefs which made the designer at once servant and master of the society of which he was a part. From an early point in his career, Le Corbusier consciously strove to develop a style of life and action that would fit a self-image modeled on Nietzschean and Ruskinian (see JOHN RUSKIN) conceptions of human grandeur and commitment. Although he grew up in a family where religion played a strong role, he was educated at a time when art and the aesthetic experience were widely taking the place of religion. Certain books read in his youth, such as Henry Provensal's *Art de demain* of 1904 and Edouard Schuré's *Les grands initiés,* first published in 1899, had a profound influence on his life and work. The latter had been the gift of L'Eplattenier.

Le Corbusier's genius lay in his ability to go beyond his teachers and contemporaries in anticipating, reacting to, and influencing the rapidly changing social, economic, and political factors of the twentieth century. He never lost his fundamentally positive attitude toward the designer's role nor his belief in action and in the importance of the dissemination of information through visual and verbal means, all of which had their roots in the activities of his years in La Chaux-de-Fonds.

Le Corbusier experienced international success at an early age when one of his watchcases figured among those winning a Diploma of Honor for the Ecole d'Art at the Milan Exhibition of 1906. But L'Eplattenier lost no time in directing his pupil's interests away from engraving and from a professional preference for painting toward architecture. Already in 1905, Le Corbusier knew the satisfaction of influencing the design of a major new building in La Chaux-de-Fonds, Beau-Site; the suggested changes may represent his first real designs of an architectural nature. L'Eplattenier soon found more positive work for his protégé. By 1906, with help from René Chapallaz, a young architect from Tavannes, Le Corbusier was constructing his first house, the Villa Fallet. This early design bears the strong imprint of L'Eplattenier in its decorative treatment based on rock, plant, and tree motifs from the surrounding Jura, the natural outgrowth of L'Eplattenier's teaching method of the direct observation of natural forms and their structure, the deduction of underlying patterns of growth, the geometrical simplification of the motifs, and the application of the motifs often in repeat patterns based on an underlying grid of varying format. The motifs chosen were not without symbolic content, partly based on the writings of JOHN RUSKIN and OWEN JONES. This infusion of forms with symbolic meaning, though underplayed in certain early phases of Le Corbusier's career when he was rejecting his early training, became, in later phases, the thread which bound his production into one cohesive whole.

Le Corbusier's self-education was as important as any formal training and was given real impetus on early study trips undertaken in emulation of his master with pocket-sized sketchbook in hand. The format of such sketchbooks may have decreased in physical size in later years for the sake of convenience, but their importance never changed, and many survive to bear testimony to his alertness to his environment, his ceaseless questioning, and his extraordinary capacity for seizing relationships amid disparate elements. The most important of these early study trips was an extended tour through northern Italy in the late summer and fall of 1907 in the company of Léon Perrin, a sculptor colleague from the school. Some of Le Corbusier's most handsome watercolors and analytical sketches date from this trip. Objects of sculpture and paintings were recorded as well as works of architecture, with a predilection for pre-Renaissance forms. The Carthusian Monastery of Ema near Florence, visited at this time, with its arrangement of identical dwelling units remained a source of inspiration for Le Corbusier's lifelong concern

with housing modules. The Italian trip, though basically concentrated on works from the past, ended with a visit to the Biennale in Venice and criticism of one's contemporaries.

This contact with the present continued in Vienna during the winter of 1907–1908 where after abortive attempts to enter a recognized school he turned to the design of two new houses for La Chaux-de-Fonds, the Villas Stotzer (1907–1908) and Jaquemet (1907–1908), both again built with the assistance of Chapallaz. Le Corbusier did have brief contact with certain members of the Vienna avant-garde, including JOSEF HOFFMANN and KOLOMON MOSER, but his insufficient familiarity with the German language, his basic lack of understanding of the Viennese movement, and his rejection of form which he perceived to be unrelated to structure led him to turn down a job offer from Hoffmann—whose Wiener Werkstätte was flourishing at the time—in favor of continuing his education in Paris, not Dresden, as L'Eplattenier had suggested. It was not just the need to confer with Chapallaz which led him to stop in Munich and Nuremberg en route, but rather his continuing interest in medieval forms and works in cut stone.

At this period of his life, Le Corbusier was all too well aware of his lack of professional training in architecture, particularly those aspects that concerned structure, construction methods, and calculation. He briefly considered the idea of entering various schools of architecture, including the Eidgenössiche Technische Hochschule (ETH) in Zurich, but eventually he persisted in his autodidactic pursuits. In Paris, along with brief contact with the official schools, these pursuits took the form of copying out Corroyer's *Architecture Romane*, using *Notre-Dame de Paris* as the basis for detailed research, and spending countless hours sketching works in museums. But the highlights of this period were a trip to England with L'Eplattenier in 1908 and, most important of all, part-time employment in the atelier of Gustave and AUGUSTE PERRET. Here, he received firsthand exposure to the most advanced building techniques of the day, particularly in reinforced concrete. Thus, to the ideals of the English Arts and Crafts movement he had shared with L'Eplattenier and to whatever he had absorbed from the Austrian post-Secessionist movement, now was added Auguste Perret's personal blend of French Beaux-Arts composition technique with French rationalist tradition. No wonder one of Le Corbusier's first acquisitions was EUGÈNE EMMANUEL VIOLLET-LE-DUC's *Dictionnaire raisonné de l'architecture française du XIe au XVIe siècle* (1854).

Surviving documents from Le Corbusier's activities at the Perret atelier show that his aptitude as a watercolorist was put to use (as for a rendering of the hunting lodge at Salbris), but also that he drafted plans and elevations for apartment houses, one of these with planted roof terraces, demonstrates in its façade treatment a simplicity and directness usually associated only with works of the 1920s or 1930s. During the period of Le Corbusier's affiliation with the firm, that is, from midsummer 1908 through late 1909, the work of the Perret atelier was characterized by a suppression of classical forms and a tendency toward modular elements almost unknown in later years.

In December 1909, Le Corbusier returned to La Chaux-de-Fonds, but he left again in April 1910, this time for a study and work trip in Germany. One major aspect of this trip was his contact in Munich with the Swiss-born artist and art critic William Ritter, who at the time widened Le Corbusier's awareness of broad currents in the arts and his appreciation for the world of art criticism and who would continue to exert a strong influence over the next few years. Soon after arriving in Munich, Le Corbusier received word that the Commission of the Ecole d'Art had charged him to study the decorative arts in Germany and to prepare a report on professional education; the organization of the art trades; the creation, production, and sale of artistic productions; and art in the city and in architecture. This first critical and analytical publication, the *Etude sur le mouvement d'art décoratif en Allemagne* issued in 1912, was to have little effect locally but was taken up almost immediately in the French and German press and played a significant role in increasing the urgency of the call for a major exhibition of the decorative arts in Paris, a show which, because of the war, would become a reality only in 1925; through the *Etude,* Le Corbusier's name became well-known in the French capital long before he considered going there on a permanent basis.

While in Germany, Le Corbusier was also gathering material for a major study on urban form related to La Chaux-de-Fonds, a study based largely on L'Eplattenier's admiration for the theories of CAMILLO SITTE, with its emphasis on relatively small enclosed public spaces. Le Corbusier's enthusiasm for this project was understandably dampened somewhat by his visit to the 1910 *Städtebau* exhibition in Berlin where his eyes were opened to a still wider framework of inquiry which would be picked up again intensively in 1915 in research at the Bibliothèque Nationale in Paris. Both of these studies gave him good excuse to travel widely and eased introduction to many of the leading figures of the day, such as THEODOR FISCHER, Baron von Pechmann, HERMANN MUTHESIUS, and Karl-Ernst Osthaus. More important, perhaps, they forced him to sharpen his ability to see current happenings both in a wide contemporaneous context and in historical perspective. His sketchbooks from these years are replete with notes on many themes, but particularly cemetery design, concern with landscape, the history of cities, furniture, and recent architecture of note.

The most significant aspect of his stay in Germany as far as architecture was concerned was, of course, his work in the office of PETER BEHRENS from November 1910 through early April 1911 when he could see at first hand what German powers of organization, which he admired so greatly in his *Etude,* were all about. Behrens was, at the time, adviser to the Allgemeine Elektrizitäts-Gesellschaft and had been designing for them everything from lighting fixtures to machine halls. This was not, however, a happy time for Le Corbusier. In spite of his sincere admiration for German accomplishments, particularly in the period since the founding of the Werkbund in 1907, and in spite of the presence in Germany of his brother Albert at the institute of Jacques Dalcroze at Hellerau, Le Corbusier was by temperament a Francophile and was unable to adjust to life in Berlin. He sought new horizons. But the importance of his stay in Germany should not be underestimated; he formed a new knowledge of architectural forms and a heightened awareness of systems of regulating lines and proportion. Above all, he left with a conviction about the importance in the art world of the role of criticism and propaganda which never left him and significantly contributed to the success of his career.

With Auguste Klipstein as travel companion for a large part of the time, Le Corbusier set off in May 1911 for a trip down the Danube that became known as *Le Voyage d'Orient.* En route to Istanbul, major stops were made in Vienna, Budapest, Bucharest, and Adrianopole; the return was through Athos, Athens, Pompeii, Rome, and Florence. This time, he followed partly in Ritter's footsteps rather than L'Eplattenier's. His travel notes (destined for a home-town newspaper but published in totality, in book form, only posthumously) reveal the first powerful unfolding of the poetic aspects of his character which had been largely suppressed during his period of pragmatic searchings in Germany. Tactile and sensual impressions pour forth in a veritable deluge of sensitive descriptive passages. On his trip, as did his contemporaries on similar voyages, Le Corbusier sought design wisdom in vernacular sources and avidly collected what he saw to be the last vestigial remains of handicraft traditions in pottery and in woven and embroidered fabrics. He sketched, analyzed, and admired the myriad forms developed for shelter in the various cultures visited and, especially in the areas leading up to and surrounding the Golden Horn, noted particular design features, including whitewashed walls, cornice treatments, roof terraces, walls adapted to changing levels in terrain, cantilevered building masses, and buildings along the Bosphorus on pilotis; many such elements found echo in his later work. Among the monuments that made the strongest impressions from this trip were the mosque complexes with their dependencies, as well as certain houses and the Forum at Pompeii. He revisited the Carthusian Monastery of Ema and did analytical sketches. But it was the Parthenon and the Acropolis at Athens that held his attention for several weeks as he struggled to render the stark, precise forms in the strong Mediterranean light. Gone was the diffused light of his 1907 Italian watercolors and the soft modeling of forms. The evocation of this experience in essay and image would occupy his attention on numerous occasions and for various reasons during the rest of his life, providing documentation for many a polemic argument. "It made me a revolutionary," he wrote.

Leaving behind this world of new sensory impressions and turning down a chance to return to the Perret atelier, Le Corbusier went home to La Chaux-de-Fonds in November 1911 to become one of several new professors in L'Eplattenier's newly established *Nouvelle Section* of the Ecole d'Art, a teaching program founded in the high aspiration of training professional artists capable of designing everything from a hat pin to an urban plan, with collaborative efforts organized and executed by the Ateliers d'Art Réunis founded already in 1910. Le Corbusier was the official architect of this group and used its offices at 54 Rue Numa Droz as his business address during most of his remaining years in Switzerland. But the revolutionary teaching program of the *Nouvelle Section* proved too advanced, not just for the Ecole d'Art but also for the newly installed Socialist city government, and difficulties ensued. To turn aside accusations of pedagogical incompetence, Le Corbusier, on 6 October 1913, received an official *Brevet de capacité* for the teaching of artistic design in secondary schools. During this period, the Ateliers d'Arts Réunis accomplished such important works as their interiors for the Crematory of La Chaux-de-Fonds and the Observatory at Neuchâtel, and Le Corbusier and L'Eplattenier began to play roles in the arts which extended beyond the local sphere as founding members in 1913 of *L'Oeuvre,* the French Swiss version of the

Werkbund. But inevitably, the *Nouvelle Section* was disbanded. When this occurred in 1914, it was not without reaction. It is typical that Le Corbusier did not accept this defeat in quiet disappointment but accused those responsible for lack of vision. On this occasion, he showed a gift for marshaling forces for a cause that was to prove useful on many later occasions in his life, editing, with others, *Un Mouvement d'Art à La Chaux-de-Fonds* with testimonial letters by Behrens, Osthaus, Fischer, Eugène Grasset, HECTOR GUIMARD, and Rupert Carabin.

During these years in La Chaux-de-Fonds, Le Corbusier took part in architectural competitions, did many interiors, selected and designed furniture for clients (his own somewhat in the style of BRUNO PAUL and carried out in exquisite perfection by the *ébéniste* Jean Egger), took part in a firm for the design and production of lighting equipment, exhibited his watercolors (Neuchâtel, Paris, Zurich), and wrote articles for journals and newspapers. He also acted in many capacities for *L'Oeuvre* as exhibition designer, polemicist, and critic. His official report for this organization on the exhibition of teaching methods shown at the Swiss National Exhibition in Bern in 1914 served later to open the door to the important Parisian artistic circle of the Comité Central Technique des Arts Appliqués et des Comités Régionaux which published sections of it in their bulletin in 1918 and 1919. More and more, Le Corbusier was looked upon in these years as something of an international expert on matters of the applied arts, the organization of ateliers, and teaching methods.

Important architectural works were constructed in the region of La Chaux-de-Fonds during these years: the Villa for his parents (1911–1912) and the Villa Favre-Jacot (1912–1913) (both of which marked a new direction in his work with their extensions into the landscape and their emphasis on greatly simplified form with smooth stuccoed surfaces reminiscent of some of the domestic work of Peter Behrens, Hermann Muthesius, and Josef Hoffmann) and the variety-theater La Scala (1916), a project apparently taken over from Chapallaz and using the same Hetzer prefabricated laminated wooden arches featured at the 1914 Bern Exhibition. But the first building for which he sought international recognition (in *L'Esprit Nouveau* and the *Revue du Beton Armé*) was his famous Villa for Anatole Schwob (1916–1917). The engineers for the structural work of the villa in reinforced concrete and hollow-tile floor slabs were Terner and Chopard of Zurich, the Swiss representatives for the Hetzer system (Le Corbusier would again call upon the expertise of this firm in the late 1920s in conjunction with his project for the Palace of the League of Nations). The villa, with its flat roof terraces with planters dissimulated as heavy cornices, roof drainage to the interior and heated double glazing in the two-story main window, was known in local parlance as the *Villa Turque* (most probably for its use of elements similar to moucharabies known from the Orient trip), and stands as the enigmatic turning point between Le Corbusier as the result of a tradition to Le Corbusier as instigator. Close analysis of the design reveals many elements from past research, particularly its two-level interior parti with spaces extending horizontally and vertically (which he himself related to a small pavilion worked on at the Perret atelier, drawings for which survive), the use of ramps in the garden, and brickwork patterns intended for the panel of the street façade, elements which come from his studies of Marcel Dieulafoy's *L'Art Antique de la Perse,* the same source which provided the model for his later obsession with a square-spiral-shaped museum and reinforced his interest in regulating lines.

Among Le Corbusier's most important architectural works during these years, as would often be the case in his subsequent development, were those not actually constructed. These included the remodeling of Favre-Jacot's Farmhouse, the *Maison du Diable* (1912), a project for a printing establishment (a project for *villes pilotis* [1915]), and his investigations of extendable building units based on multiples and variations of his DOMINO system (1914) which called for a method of construction consisting of horizontal slabs with supports set well back from the exterior skin. Investigations in this method grew from a consideration of reconstruction problems engendered by World War I and went far beyond his earlier large-scale housing scheme for La Chaux-de-Fonds, the Cité Jardin aux Crêtets (1914), which had merely continued the well-established traditional pattern of the English and German garden city. Indeed, such investigations led to the direct consideration of a new building aesthetic derived from new constructional methods and from there to considerations of a new urban aesthetic. During these years Le Corbusier kept in close contact with events elsewhere, attending the *Baufachausstellung* in Leipzig in 1913 and the *Werkbundausstellung* in Cologne Germany, in 1914 just before the outbreak of the war. During the war, in spite of travel restrictions, he managed many trips to Paris for business purposes as well as his research at the Bibliothèque Nationale.

This foment of activity and changing thought processes in the restrictive atmosphere of a small town led to a desire to become involved with work large in scope, importance, and sphere of influence

and formed the natural transition to the new phase of Le Corbusier's career, which began as he gradually shifted his activities to Paris in late 1916. This transition was made possible through his collaboration with Max Dubois of SABA (Société d'application du Béton Armé); he set up a provisional office at 13 Rue de Belzunce, Paris X^e, in early 1917 and moved into 20 Rue Jacob, Paris VIe, which would remain his residence for over a decade. Later that same year, he moved his office to 29 bis rue d'Astorg, Paris VIIIe, the headquarters of SEIE (Société d'entreprises industrielles et d'études) of which he was a directing force. This period saw designs for slaughterhouses, concern for refrigeration techniques, watertowers, powerhouses, continued studies for workers' housing, and an ill-fated attempt to run a brick factory at Alfortville. The end of the war led to many entrepreneurial efforts and dealings in surplus war goods amid the exhilarating if bewildering atmosphere of postwar Paris.

These early Paris years mark a significant change in Le Corbusier's attitudes, accelerated through his contact with the painter AMÉDÉE OZENFANT who, beginning in 1918, exerted a strong influence on his work. Le Corbusier stood somewhat in awe of Ozenfant's worldliness in artistic circles, a worldliness stemming from the days when as editor of *L'Elan* Ozenfant had had contact with the most avant-garde artists of the time, and of his penchant for haute couture and motor cars. Their friendship formed rapidly and led to years of close collaboration on many levels. Ozenfant encouraged him to paint in oil. By December 1918, they held their first joint exhibition and had already published their tract *Après le Cubisme.* This argued against the decorative aspects of cubism and propounded a new art Purisme. In their drawings and paintings, they deliberately took over the standard still-life motifs of bottle, book, glass, carafe, and guitar typical in the works of their contemporaries in order to give them new meaning as the *objets types* of a machine civilization in which immutable laws, as in nature, led to a purification of form. October 1920 saw the publication of the first of twenty-eight issues (1920–1925) of *L'Esprit Nouveau,* "an international review of aesthetics," and in January 1921, the first and only issue of what was to have been a companion publication of the same title devoted to economics was prepared. Much of the content of Le Corbusier's famous early books, with his basic statements of design philosophy, all first appeared in article form in *L'Esprit Nouveau: Vers une Architecture, L'Art décoratif d'aujourd'hui, Urbanisme.*

In spite of problems with his left eye in 1919, Le Corbusier intensified his efforts as a painter. A

Le Corbusier.
Contemporary city for three
   million inhabitants
   (exhibition project).
Paris.
1922

second show of Purist works held with Ozenfant in early 1921 at the Galerie Druet had considerable repercussion in the press and led to a contract with the dealer Léonce Rosenberg. This success in one realm made up for the failure of Le Corbusier's commercial and industrial enterprises, many of which were liquidated in that year. All this activity won many friends as well as enemies. His father recognized this as a natural thing when he wrote in his diary, "but he loves to have adversaries, it's in his temperament." The crystallization of Le Corbusier's thought through intense literary production and the constant refinement of a new formal vocabulary through pictorial investigation provided the framework on which he would begin to hang new architectural and urbanistic searchings.

Suppressing a desire in early 1922 to go to the United States to give lectures on *L'Esprit Nouveau* and to found an American edition, he plunged into a new period of architectural design, his vision enriched from a visit to Vicenza, Italy and to Venice, Italy, where he sketched Palladian (see AN-DREA PALLADIO) churches. That fall at the *Salon d'Automne,* he showed a plaster model of his Maison Citrohan, a variation on pilotis of earlier studies from 1920, and exhibited what would be the basis for continued research in the following decades, his "Contemporary city for 3 million inhabitants," with companion studies of the individual dwelling unit, *la cellule,* and its combination into apartment blocks, *immeubles-villas.* This was the first time that he placed designs before the public which by the boldness and novelty of their approach were bound to create a great deal of interest and controversy. With the *Maison Citrohan*—the name was a deliberate pun on the French car Citröen, implying something about industrial mass production and machinelike efficiency—he had created a basic "type" of housing cell that was to recur in his oeuvre time and again: a box with closed sides, open at the front and rear only and spatially organized in such a way that rooms of regular height on two floors open into a front

room of double height. Another basic "type" created about the same time was the Monol House (1919) with its segmentally vaulted roof. His project for the "Contemporary city for three million inhabitants" combined ideas of A. Perret for tower-houses with those of Hénard, a Parisian traffic expert, and of rectilinear axial planning schemes of the past in a shockingly drastic scheme in the best utopian tradition—except that it was intended realistically.

After the exhibition, the city planning scheme together with supporting material was published in *Urbanisme,* the book which appeared in 1925, two years after *Vers une Architecture.* The latter was written half as a manifesto and half as an interpretation of architectural history. Juxtaposing grain silos, automobiles, steamships, and airplanes with some of the greatest buildings of all times and some of Le Corbusier's own projects, it set out a most convincing argument for his new architecture, little of which had actually been built. With such unforgettable passages as *"L'architecture est le jeu savant, correct et magnifique des volumes assemblés sous la lumière"* and *"Le Parthénon est un produit de sélection appliqué à un standart,"* this book remained a source of inspiration for generations of architects. It also drew the attention of many to its author and his message, among them the industrialist Henry Frugès, who, having in addition seen a Corbusian project for low cost-housing, eventually commissioned him to design workers' housing at Pessac near Bordeaux (1925) with the express intent of achieving an avant-garde solution.

After the impact of *Vers une Architecture* had made itself felt, Le Corbusier began to be known widely as a most aggressive and persuasive advocate of architectural and urbanistic endeavors. The appeal of the cause he championed and the novelty of the forms created began to bring young architects from many parts of the world to his studio, now at 35 Rue de Sèvres where it would remain for the rest of his career. More than 300 designers would pass through this atelier before it was finally closed. But there is general consensus that, in spite of the enthusiasm generated by the constant presence of a young work force and in spite of the expertise of his distant relative PIERRE JEANNERET who had joined him around 1922 and who would supervise the atelier and act as partner through many decades, Le Corbusier remained the undisputed master, coming to the atelier only in the afternoons to review progress and give indications for future work, mornings and all day Sunday being devoted to painting and drawing. The assistance of the others enabled him to increase his output greatly. "Two men who understand one another," he wrote of himself and Pierre Jeanneret, "are stronger than five working independently" (*Oeuvre complète,* vol. 1, p. 12).

At the Paris International Exhibition of Decorative Arts in 1925, which his own *Etude* of 1912 had helped to spawn, Le Corbusier, in protest against the very nature of the exhibition, finally had a chance to construct a demonstration *cellule,* the *Pavillon de L'Esprit Nouveau,* to show the need for rationalized, standardized building methods and types—the very antithesis of the individualized artistic creation. He furnished it with mass-produced items, such as the ubiquitous Thonet chair which he had favored as far back as 1912, and with furniture of his own design along with paintings by Ozenfant and Léger, a Lipchitz relief, and one of his own Purist works. In an annex was the diorama of the *Plan Voisin* of Paris, in which elements were taken from the "Contemporary city for three million inhabitants"; this would have replaced much of the Right Bank beyond the Rue de Rivoli with cruciform skyscrapers and apartment blocks on his *redent* system.

The deliberate "clean sweep" of such gestures must be seen in the context of the postwar period in which the insalubrity of the cities, overcrowded and with outmoded or insufficient sanitary facilities and free space, aggravated by epidemics and high incidence of tuberculosis, took an enormous toll in human life and misery. Le Corbusier was well aware of such social and public health problems from the Lyons habitation congresses of

Le Corbusier.
Villa La Roche (entrance hall).
Paris.
1922–1925

1919, 1920, and 1921, and his contacts with GEORGES BENOIT-LÉVY who published some of his early interiors for workers' housing; however, inspiration for the large-scale nature of his proposals came from his contact with TONY GARNIER. The desire to provide healthy living conditions for large masses of people would remain one of Le Corbusier's prime goals throughout his life, and dwelling types developed early as he worked through various structural systems and constructional methods would show up in his later work.

The very early 1920s were characterized by intensive exploration, formulation of arguments, and establishment of a clearly recognizable avant-garde position, but Le Corbusier built comparatively few actual buildings (Villa at Vaucresson, 1922, Ozenfant Atelier, 1920–1922). The picture changed significantly in the five years between 1923 and 1928. As he became better known through his publications and his participation in exhibitions, his reputation as a designer of modern houses for the cultural elite grew and enabled him to carry through or initiate a number of buildings in which he worked out to his full satisfaction the vocabulary and syntax of a new architecture. Purism visually and reinforced concrete technically were the most important factors in the process; the Villas La Roche-Jeanneret (1922–1925), Cook (1926), Stein–De Monzie (1927), and Savoye (1928–1931) were the outstanding results.

In the Villa La Roche, both a dwelling and a gallery for the owner's collection of contemporary paintings, the triple height of the reception hall and the double height of the gallery with its curving ramp added new refinement and spatial complexity to the artist's architectural language and, for the first time, revealed his concern with the "architectural promenade" inside a building through a carefully ordered sequence of spatial experiences. In the Villa Stein–De Monzie in Garches, France, he succeeded in wedding the spatial liberation that had been the achievement of the Dutch *Stijl* movement with a classical rigor of ordering geometry, while in the Villa Savoye in Poissy, France, he created a stunningly impressive paradigmatic demonstration piece for all his theoretical principles and visual devices, fittingly forming the climactic end-piece for this classic period of "Purist architecture." When the building for which preliminary designs were done in 1928 was finally finished in 1931, Le Corbusier's style had already begun to change.

While he was still approaching the high point of his Purist architecture phase, Le Corbusier in 1926–1927 found himself facing the challenge of a major monumental building: he had decided to participate in the international competition for a palace of the League of Nations, in Geneva. Support from a minority of the jurors (Josef Hoffmann, H. P. BERLAGE, WERNER MOSER, IVAR JUSTUS TENGBOM) was not enough to secure his project the first prize. When it eventually was eliminated, international outrage among progressive architects became one of the contributing factors in the foundation of an organization for the defense and promotion of modern architecture: the Congrès Internationaux d'Architecture Moderne (CIAM) which held its constituting congress at La Sarraz, Switzerland, in June 1928. Le Corbusier became and remained a driving and guiding force in this organization throughout most of its long and stormy life, using it as a testing ground for many of his ideas, especially in the areas of urbanism and housing.

It is indicative of his approach to architectural design and manner of working that he was not satisfied with the creation of successful buildings but in addition felt the need to formulate the principles that informed his work. He defined his vocabulary in "The Five Points to a New Architecture" (1927); he explained syntax in a diagrammatic sketch of four possible types of composition. In a publication that accompanied Le Corbusier's houses at the Weissenhof Siedlung in Stuttgart, the "Five Points" were described as follows: the pilotis for lifting the house off the ground, the roof garden, the free plan, the horizontal strip window and the free façade—made possible by the supporting internal skeleton which freed the outside wall of any carrying function. The four types, as discussed in October 1929 (*Précisions*, p. 135), show the following possible arrangements of a house: one in which the interior "organs" are reflected directly on the exterior, as in the La Roche-Jeanneret houses, and three others in which the exterior conforms to "cubic composition," that is, forms a rectangular geometric solid either with the internal organs forced to conform to the "cube" (Villa Stein–De Monzie), or with organs freely arranged inside the regular geometry

of the openly visible structural skeleton of slabs and pilotis (Villa at Carthage), or with the external purity of the "cube" preserved but with a great freedom of internal arrangement (Villa Savoye). Le Corbusier, in giving such definitions and formulations, clearly felt it was useful to read "in one's own works" since "the consciousness of events is the springboard of progress" (*Précisions*, p. 136). His work in architecture, urbanism, and painting would show more and more of this tendency toward self-critical reflection and the re-examination and re-use in modified form of earlier motifs. One can see this clearly in his paintings where Purist recollections occur time and again later in his career.

Purism had taught Le Corbusier the merits of clarity of outline and geometric order combined with an ambiguity of spatial arrangement, of transparency in the service of dematerialization, and of a restricted palette of broken pastel hues. To one not cowed by the tyranny of historicism in architecture it was perfectly feasible to transfer forms and attitudes toward space from drawing and painting to architecture, without incidentally giving up certain compositional principles acquired while still

Le Corbusier.
Palace of the League of
Nations (competition
project).
Geneva.
1926–1927

Le Corbusier.
Villa Savoye.
Poissy, France.
1928–1931

Le Corbusier.
Villa Savoye.
Poissy, France.
1928–1931

under the sway of classicism. Le Corbusier was very explicit about this point. He wrote: "I have never ceased to draw and paint, searching for the secrets of form where I could find them. One must not search elsewhere for the key to my labours and to my research" (introduction to *Le Corbusier Dessins,* Geneva, Ed. Forces Vives, 1965). He even gave an exact date for the moment at which he succeeded in having complete congruence between all his forms regardless of the medium in which they found expression: "In 1925 the stage [of development] was over. Between the architectural forms . . . and those of his painting, simultaneity is now complete. The spirit of form animates his paintings and his architecture, and even his urbanism" (*Oeuvre complète,* vol. 5, p. 225). If the well-known villas of the late 1920s and the League of Nations project correspond to his Purist paintings in the strict geometry of their composition, avoidance of strong textural effects, layering of parallel slices of space, figure-ground ambiguities, and color schemes, his buildings of the 1930s correspond with equal clarity to the more complex paintings of the post-Purist period, with their organic curves, rich, rough textures and entirely different palette. The outline becomes more changeful, the spatial organization more complex. *Objets à réaction poétique* and, by 1928, human figures make their appearance.

The changes in Le Corbusier's pictorial vocabularly had direct parallels in the treatment of architectural designs. In the project for the Errazuris House (1930), Chile; the De Mandrot House (1930), Le Pradet, France; and the House at Mathes (1935), France; the use of rough, natural materials can be explained by the need to accommodate to the simple building technology in distant rural sites; but no such reason existed at the Swiss Pavilion (1930–1932), Paris. Here, the simple geometry and technological sophistication of the partly glazed steel construction is accompanied

Le Corbusier.
Swiss Pavilion, University
City.
Paris.
1930–1932

in another portion of the building by a curved, textured rubble wall in a crucial position and by sculpturally molded concrete supports instead of the slender pilotis that characterized earlier buildings. The change of architectural intention that becomes apparent here eventually found its culmination in the richly modeled shapes and varied textures of Le Corbusier's architecture after World War II.

In other respects, too, the fundamental themes of Le Corbusier's later architecture as far as basic elements of form and compositional structure are concerned all occur first in his early works, though at times in different contexts. Just as in his paintings, so in his architecture there is a consistency of development that links early and late works, even though superficially they are different in appearance. One of the most telling examples in this context is the transformation of the Monol house type (1919) with its segmentally arched vaults into the later Jaoul houses (1952–1956), Neuilly-sur-Seine, France, and Shodan House (1956); Ahmedabad, India, with the small weekend house at Celle Saint Cloud (1935) and the Rock-et-Rob Project (1949) as intermediary stations. Le Corbusier was well aware that around 1929 a turning point had been reached in his career, and he added a postscript to that extent to his 1930 publication *Précisions: "La révolution architecturale fomentée par les techniques modernes"* was over, the hour of "Grands Travaux" had arrived, and henceforth he would be concerned with the *équipment de la civilisation machiniste."*

By the time the first of what would eventually grow to be eight volumes of his collected works was published in 1930 (German edition, the French to follow in 1937), Le Corbusier was indeed an acknowledged leader among the international avant-garde. A building of major proportions, the Centrosoyous (1928–1934) was rising in Moscow; he was invited as one of twelve architects to a limited competition for the palace of the Soviets, and the Mundaneum (1929), international in function, had been projected for a site near Geneva. The scope of his activities had widened both thematically and geographically. Partly on lecture tours and partly in connection with professional work, he began to travel widely not only throughout Europe, including Russia, but also to South America and North Africa; he finally visited the United States in 1935, a trip he recorded in the book *When the Cathedrals Were White.* In each case, he not only gave demonstrations of how his urbanistic principles might be applied under varying circumstances, but he also observed, noted down, and drew what seemed significant to him, as he had done before during his youthful study tours. In his sketchbooks and in his mind, he thus built up a wealth of images, many of them connected with vernacular architecture from different parts of the world to which he felt especially attracted. In this connection, the CIAM IV Congress, dedicated to the "Functional City," proved a source of additional enrichment since it took place during a Mediterranean cruise and in Athens, with opportunities to visit Greek island architecture. Next to Greece, it was North Africa, linked to France by close political ties, that played a most important role in Le Corbusier's career, both as a source of inspiration—he visited the Algerian Casbah as well as Ghardia and the M'zab in 1931—and as a potential arena of professional activity; over many years, Le Corbusier prepared not only designs for individuals in North Africa (only the villa at Carthage was built) but also, more important, large-scale town planning schemes for the Algiers area.

At the same time that Le Corbusier became increasingly involved with the application of his urbanistic principles to various actual cities, he also began to pursue new directions in building technology. In his early writings, he had often expressed his faith in the positive potential of technology and in a rationalization of the building process through standardization and "Taylorization." It is not surprising, therefore, that in the late 1920s and early 1930s, despite his predilection for and experience with reinforced concrete, he should have turned to an exploration of metal construction. On the one hand, he developed a *maison à sec,* that is, a house type to be built by on-site assembly from prefabricated elements in metal; in the Maison Loucheur project (1929), the elements for the entire building would be trucked from the factory to the site and only the party walls were to be built traditionally in masonry. On the other hand, he used steel skeletons in a number of buildings, as in the dormitory portion of the Swiss Pavilion and most importantly was the Apartment House *Clarté* in Geneva (1930–1932) which was built in direct collaboration with the industrialist-contractor Edmond Wanner. Some of the experience gained here went into the apartment house at 24 rue Nungesser-et-Coli (1933), Paris, which Le Corbusier constructed partly as his own residence.

Metal was also used extensively in three other large-scale projects: the office building of the Centrosoyous in Moscow with its curtain wall; the hostel and multipurpose building for the Salvation Army in Paris (1929–1933), where it was again featured in the glass curtain wall; and the project for the Palace of the Soviets (1930–1931) where it served major carrying functions. In each case, Le Corbusier continued his search for architectural solutions appropriate to the most advanced technology of the time, outdoing the Russian Constructivists at their own game but, in the instance of the Paris building, resorting to a solution that would have demanded a more advanced air conditioning plant than was available and financially feasible. Planned to be hermetically sealed, the building ended up with a drastic remodeling that provided window openings. But with Le Corbusier, one day's failure only led to renewed research, and only a few years later, as architectural adviser to the Brazilian design team, Le Corbusier saw his first *brise-soleil* (sun-breakers) take form in the design of the Ministry of National Education and Public Health Building for Rio de Janeiro (1936–1945).

Le Corbusier's interest in having big industry take over the former functions of the building trades was also reflected in his interest in the potential use of metal in furniture design. Tubular metal was the distinctive feature of the pieces shown at the *Salon d'Automne* of 1929, some of which are still in manufacture, including a variation of the *chaise longue* patented that same year with Pierre Jeanneret and CHARLOTTE PERRIAND. Groupable storage units of standard sizes were also studied in innumerable variations as the necessary elements in the "equipment" of the new technological age.

Much of the technological change in Le Corbusier's work was undoubtedly related to Pierre Jeanneret's adeptness with and love for technical matters. But the general change in the direction of his work had to do with two other important factors. One of these was the state of international political, social, and economic chaos engendered by the crash of 1929. Le Corbusier was much involved with CIAM during this period— many organizational meetings were held in his office—when CIAM was attempting to define dwelling standards on an international basis in order to ameliorate what was perceived to be an international housing crisis. *Le problème de la "Maison minimum"* was read at CIAM II (Frankfurt, October 1929) and at CIAM III (Brussels, November 1930). Le Corbusier lectured on *Le parcellement du sol des villes* (The subdivision of land in cities), circulated a questionnaire, *Air-son-lumière* (Air-sound-light), and exhibited sixteen panels of *La Ville Radieuse* (The Radiant City) which originally were prepared in reply to a questionnaire from the City of Moscow and which a few years later would become the subject of a major polemic work.

Although many of Le Corbusier's proposals were strictly related to basic technological questions, the concerns of CIAM in those years and the content of Le Corbusier's theoretical works, when read in detail, clearly began to go beyond architec-

Le Corbusier.
Unité d'habitation.
Marseilles, France.
1946–1952

ture and urbanism in the traditional sense into the realm of "social engineering." This was the period in which Le Corbusier had great interest in aspects of the radical French labor movement, syndicalism, and participated in two major journals, *Plans* (1931–1932) and *Prélude* (1933–1935), seeking to define a "new order." Le Corbusier's project for agrarian reorganization, *La ferme radieuse* (1934–1938), and his stadium for 100,000 (1936) grew from this context.

Since French parliamentary democracy seemed for a while incapable of dealing with the disastrous financial and social conditions of the early 1930s, it is understandable that Le Corbusier began to scrutinize the alternatives. He was able to gain first-hand experience of Russian communism because of his commission to design the Centrosoyous and because of contacts with architects of the Russian avant-garde, but after the disappointing outcome of the competition for the Soviet Palace it was impossible to have any more illusions about the realities of Stalinistic cultural policies. In a similar manner, despite strong hopes stemming from the brief period when Mussolini supported modern architecture, nothing of consequence came from a visit to Rome in 1934 and contacts with Italian fascism.

The second half of the 1930s, despite a great deal of activity in Le Corbusier's studio, turned out to be a frustrating period since all major projects such as various museums and skyscrapers (perhaps designed as a consequence of impressions from the journey to the United States in 1935) as well as urbanistic propositions remained on paper. The same fate befell several grandly conceived projects in connection with the International Exhibition in Paris in 1937 where all that was built in the end was a small *Pavillon des Temps Nouveaux*. Its significance lay in its tentlike construction which antici-

pated the tension structures of the postwar period, just as another projected pavilion, for exhibitions in San Francisco or Liège, 1939, anticipated postwar developments in its welded steel construction. The plan of the latter was organized around a swastica-arrangement of ramps which introduced a sense of implied rotation or torque, a dynamic motif frequently found in Corbusian compositions and comparable to the spiral arrangements he so often suggested in his plans for "endless" museums.

After the outbreak of the war, Le Corbusier, in contradiction to the request of his books, *Des canons, des munitions? Merci! Des logis . . . S.V.P.,* (1938), was commissioned to do an ammunitions factory, but France was defeated before the project was completed and Le Corbusier left Paris, first to live in a remote village in the Pyrenees and later to go through a brief, unsuccessful interlude as an adviser to the Vichy government. He had hoped to get his urbanistic plans implemented in this fashion, notably his plan for Algiers which was the last in a series of proposals for that city. Nothing came from all of these proposals, but they turned out to be significant as preparation for his postwar work and as inspiration for others.

When the war was over, Le Corbusier, now in his later fifties, was in a uniquely favorable position to accept a major role in the rebuilding that was necessary. Few others could point to such a record of concern with the most urgent problems of postwar France: housing and urbanism. He was commissioned to prepare the urbanistic schemes for Saint Dié (1945) and La Rochelle (1945–1946) and, more important, was charged with the construction of a large housing block in Marseilles (1946–1952). Here, he finally was able to implement the design for what he called an *Unité d'habitation* and what, according to the intentions of its creator, should have been just one in a series of several such large blocks. Lifelong preoccupations, starting with the *immeubles villas* of 1922, came together in the final design: there was the social ideal, Fourierist and Syndicalist in derivation, of combining the places of living and their extensions (shops, laundry, nursery, and so on) in order to create a self-contained social grouping rather than a mere apartment block; there were the freeing of the ground by lifting the building on pilotis and the treatment of the flat roof as a piece of landscape; and finally, there was the provision of ample greenery, true to the ideals of the *Ville Radieuse*.

The architectural language, however, was very different from that of a decade earlier. Where there used to be smooth white surfaces or extended areas of glazing, one now finds very rough concrete and

Le Corbusier.
Chapel Notre-Dame-du-
Haut.
Ronchamp, France.
1951–1955

a strong articulation of surfaces by concrete fins, a variant of the *brise-soleil* as they had been refined already in the skyscraper projects for Algiers. In addition, strong primary colors in lieu of the broken hues so characteristic of prewar schemes enliven the façades and the long corridors inside which the architect envisaged as "internal roads." A consistent system of proportions governs the total design, the result of theoretical considerations that had begun almost at the beginning of Le Corbusier's career and that led to a system of proportionally interlocking dimensions based on the Golden Section and measurements of the human body; it was christened the "Modulor" by its inventor. Modular design, with interrelated standard units, had long been a preoccupation of Le Corbusier; now, through the imposition of the Modulor, it acquired an aesthetic dimension and placed its inventor firmly into a venerable tradition of attempts to express universal harmony through numerical relations.

While the *Unité* was slowly going up, Le Corbusier worked out two other projects which when finished, and together with the *Unité*, had no less revolutionary an effect on contemporary architecture than the buildings of the *Vers une architecture*-period had had in their time: one was a group of two houses for the Jaoul family (1952–1956), in

Neuilly outside Paris; the other, the pilgrimage chapel Notre-Dame-du-Haut at Ronchamp (1951–1955), not far from Belfort. The houses with their rough textures, including brick and wood, strong colors, and strongly modeled vaulted spaces were in such complete contradiction to the image of a "white box on stilts" or a "machine for living" that James Stirling, when reviewing them in 1955, deemed it "disturbing to find little reference to the rational principles which are the basis of the modern movement" (P. Serenyi, 1975, p. 63). To many of Le Corbusier's old friends in CIAM, co-pioneers of a "new architecture," the chapel came as an almost incomprehensible shock. It is only by looking at his previous work as a painter and sculptor (he had his sculptures carved by Joseph Savina, a talented, sympathetic Breton woodworker) that one can begin to understand the derivation of the strongly modeled, complex forms and the intricate colored spaces of Ronchamp. Here, Le Corbusier had achieved symbolic form without overt recourse to historic precedent in a building of dramatic impact, gloriously related to the surrounding landscape and the movement of sunlight and clouds around and above it. With Marseilles, the Jaoul Houses, and Ronchamp, Le Corbusier had opened unsuspected possibilities for modern architecture; in the seventh decade of his life, he showed the capacity for a surprising rejuvenation.

At about the same time that these buildings became known and began to have their effect, the first buildings of the biggest single project in Le Corbusier's whole career—the planning of a whole capital, with detailed architectural projects for many elements, but especially for its government buildings—were going up at Chandigarh in the Punjab (1951–1965). Here finally, Le Corbusier was able to implement the urbanistic precepts he had worked out during a lifetime, though he had to accept the main lines of a preliminary plan established by ALBERT MAYER, a planner from the United States. Le Corbusier organized his plan in roughly rectangular sectors connected by a rectilinear grid of roads with a commercial center in the middle and, at one end of the complex, a monumental government center.

From a sociological point of view, it is easy to fault Le Corbusier's urban schemes, as has been done on several occasions. But to consider Chandigarh from this point of view alone is to overlook the fact that its primary purpose, in the mind of its founders, was that of a symbolic gesture, an assertion of will to progress, of modernity and dignity, and as such it succeeded unequivocally because of the evocative power of Le Corbusier's architecture. The group of capitol buildings, Secretariat, High Court, and Assembly (Parliament) form a magnificent monumental group under the tropical sun although one monument in particular would be needed to help achieve the full effect intended by Le Corbusier: the Open Hand which, in the last years of his life, had become a favorite symbol of his, charged with many meanings and occurring again and again.

As in all his late work, Le Corbusier at Chandigarh strove for that "synthesis of the arts" that had been a subject of discussion at the CIAM VI and VII Congresses of 1947 and 1949. He turned to the design of tapestries, some of vast dimensions, and of colored enamels, and to the creation of bas-reliefs in concrete—the latter produced by attaching wooden cut-outs inside the shuttering before the concrete was poured. The linkage between his work as a painter and as an architect was especially close in those years. Effects of the technique of collage, which he employed widely after the war, are much in evidence in his architecture: the delight with which forms, colors, and rough textures are juxtaposed, as if haphazardly, in many of the late buildings has its direct parallels in his late pictorial work, best summed up in the *Poème de l'angle droit* (1955). This was the title he gave to a sequence of lithographs that combined images and a handwritten text in which he poetically re-evokes all the major concerns and symbols of his life: from the five points of a new architecture and the S-curve of the rising and setting sun to the *Ville radieuse*, the Modulor, and the Open Hand; from the *objets à réaction poétique* to the right angle that reaffirmed his faith in the architect's mission of imposing order.

For the implementation of his intentions at Chandigarh, Le Corbusier could rely on a team of trusted friends, chief among them the partner of his early years, Pierre Jeanneret, and in addition Maxwell Fry and JANE DREW. After Le Corbusier's death, a number of enthusiastic young Indian architects have tried hard to carry on in his spirit. It was during work on site at Chandigarh that, walking around at all hours under the tropical sun, Le Corbusier seriously impaired his health. He had no intention, however, of slowing his pace when he finally found himself an acknowledged leader of world architecture, honored in various ways and the subject of magificent exhibitions in many countries. Commissions now came in increasing numbers and he could afford to turn down those with which he was not in sympathy, as in the case of a luxury hotel for a group of real estate developers or of a church for his native town.

Parallel to the buildings at Chandigarh, Le Corbusier designed another group of buildings in India at Ahmedabad which show his intense interest in responding to the special climatic conditions of a site while at the same time experimenting with free forms set against a geometric framework of strict regularity. The same interest is manifest in his only executed building in the United States, the Carpenter Center for the Visual Arts (1960–1963) at Harvard University, Cambridge, Massachusetts, where, as at the Mill Owners Building in

Le Corbusier.
Palace of the Assembly.
Chandigarh, India.
1953–1963

Ahmedabad (1952–1954), a ramp leads into the core of the building, perhaps as urbanistic metaphor, perhaps just as a recall of an architectural element he had favored ever since he first used it in the 1920s. Construction of the Carpenter Center was supervised by Le Corbusier's former collaborator JOSEP LLUIS SERT. From letters sent to Sert, the meaning Le Corbusier attached to individual architectural elements becomes apparent. He felt that he had worked out a proper language for reinforced concrete construction (smooth columns and floor slabs) as well as for the fenestration of façades, with different elements for different purposes: from the glasspanes to the ventilating louvres (*aerateurs*) and from the modulating, irregularly placed vertical struts (*ondulatoires*) to the sun-breakers (*brise-soleil*). The elements had been invented on different occasions over a considerable period of time but eventually, in Le Corbusier's mind, they became standard elements, to be used as the need arose according to the building type under consideration. The fact that he had such a standardized vocabulary, a system of proportions, a compositional syntax, and a method of composing taken over from painting, enabled Le Corbusier to arrive at design decisions rather quickly and to control a surprising amount of work in his office through personal intervention at crucial moments, though much detail could be left to his small, devoted staff. Like most architects in the later years of their careers, he often took recourse to self-quotations from earlier schemes.

In France, he continued to build *Unités d'habitation* in various locations, while such large schemes as congress buildings for Paris (1961) and Strasbourg, (1962–1964) remained on paper. With a very restricted budget, he managed to construct a large Dominican monastery, La Tourette, at Eveux sur Arbresle (1953–1959) a commission for which he must have had much sympathy since he had expressed admiration for monastic arrangements on various occasions, beginning with his visit to the Carthusian monastery near Florence on his first trip to Italy. La Tourette, like Ronchamp, is a strongly modeled, strongly textured building set on a beautiful site. Reticent on the austere outside, it is full of visual surprises inside and there is the deceptive nonchalance of a collage about the way in which various geometric and free-form elements are put together and sometimes made to jar. As the Ronchamp, the most powerful effects are achieved by the way in which lighting is handled, bringing it into the building dramatically, often through skylights.

The last projects before his death, such as the Boat Club at Chandigarh (1963–1965), the work at Firminy, France, the preliminary designs for a

French Embassy in Brasilia (1964–1965), the Zurich exhibition pavilion (1963–1967), and particularly the great central hospital in Venice (1964–1965), all offer evidence that Le Corbusier still had not reached the end of his stylistic development. At the same time that he was re-introducing a feeling of great geometric rigor and almost classicist severity into his designs, recalling preoccupations of his youth, he was also creating an "open form" capable of extension and change, thus anticipating some of the favorite themes of the later 1960s and the 1970s. Over a creative career of some sixty years, he had kept the capacity to sense vital new directions and to keep himself open to the unexpected dictates of an intuition he had nurtured so carefully in his long sessions with brush and canvas. Even though he always tried to articulate his convictions, to give rational explanations based on analytic thought, and to anchor what he did in a broader social context, he must have been fully aware that, despite his motivation as cultural reformer and his claims as technician, his real strength was in his very personal, intuitive vision. Otherwise, he would not have stipulated in his last will that his studio was to be closed immediately; whatever principles he had conveyed to his followers and whatever methods he had instilled in his collaborators, he knew it would not be enough to carry on after his death. When he died in the Mediterranean off his beloved summer resort at Roquebrune, Cap Martin, he took with him a personal synthesis that was as little transferable as his personal myth.

His buildings and projects in their quality as works of art and his relentless commitment toward

Le Corbusier.
Carpenter Center for the
*   Visual Arts, Harvard*
*   University.*
Cambridge, Massachusetts.
1960–1963

a better, more poetic human environment have remained valid sources of inspiration to later generations and probably will remain so even after his numerous mistakes as a social planner, building technician, or otherwise have been amply demonstrated. His influence was so widespread and so profound that it is probably correct to state that it was he who single-handedly shaped considerable stretches of architectural history in the middle third of the twentieth century. He effected this not only by the example of his work and by his numerous publications and public lectures, but also indirectly through people who worked in his office, became dedicated admirers and disciples, and later assumed important positions themselves in the world of architecture and architectural education. Names such as Alfred Altherr, George Candilis, (see Candilis Josic Woods), BALKRISHNA VITHALDAS DOSHI, Pierre Emery, Guillermo Jullian de la Fuente, Bernard Hoesli, KUNIO MAEKAWA, Oscar Niemeyer, ALFRED ROTH, Otto Senn, Josep Lluis Sert, JUNZŌ SAKAKURA, JERZY SOLTAN, André Wogensky, Shadrach Woods (see WOODS, CANDILIS, AND JOSIC) to cite just a few, indicate to what extent his ideas, methods, and images spread as far as Japan, India, and the United States. Through LÚCIO COSTA, who had been his partner in doing the Ministry Building in Rio de Janeiro, there was a direct connection to South America, and Candilis, Woods, and Soltan provided a direct link to the next generation of avant-garde activists—Team 10—who came from the midst of CIAM and eventually destroyed it.

Many buildings owe more or less large debts to Corbusian models, from being generally inspired to being very direct formal or conceptual copies. The school of architectural thought that went under the label of New Brutalism in the 1960s openly acknowledged its debt to buildings such as the *Unité* in Marseilles with its *béton brut* and the Jaoul houses, just as LOUIS I. KAHN, one of the great figures in the years after Le Corbusier's death, equally did not fail to give credit to Le Corbusier for having opened to him the doors of a new realm. Through teachers in a number of leading schools of architecture, even the generation after Team 10 came in touch with people who formed direct links to the world of Le Corbusier, and it is striking that some of the vigorous proponents of Post-Modernism in architecture took elements from Le Corbusier as their point of departure.

During his lifetime, Le Corbusier received many awards as well as worldwide academic recognition from institutions of higher learning, including honorary degrees from the University and the ETH in Zurich, Cambridge University, the University of Florence, the University of Geneva, and Columbia University. Honorary medals were received from the Royal Institute of British Architects (1953) and the American Institute of Architects (1961). In 1961, he was named *Commandeur de l'ordre du Mérite pour la recherche et l'invention* and in 1963 he became *grand officier* in the French Legion of Honor, having been named *chevalier* as early as 1937. Few architects were awarded so many honors, yet Le Corbusier seemed happiest as "Père Corbu" among his draftsmen and artisans or in his little summer hut, 3.66 m x 3.66 m, close to a few local friends in the nearby bar, overlooking the sea.

It is not easy to characterize the personality of this enigmatic man. He was never an easy person to deal with and, like Frank Lloyd Wright, could be arrogant in his intolerance of mediocrity. He had a harsh side that permitted him on one occasion to dismiss without notice the whole staff of his atelier when he became displeased with the intensity of their work and on another, when asked by assistants for raises, was heard to grumble, "They should have to pay me!" Yet, he had the gift to instill genuine enthusiasm in others and could be a loyal friend. He became suspicious and embittered after the experience of, as he saw it, undeserved failure with the League of Nations project, the Algiers schemes, the project for the United Nations building, and the commission to design the UNESCO building; yet, he remained an optimist to the end.

Generous, selfish, humble, imperious, forthright, devious, courageous, shy, a builder, a destroyer, a visionary, *un fada*—all of these have been applied to Le Corbusier and offer testimony to the complexity of his character. But the early conviction that art was an idealistic struggle and that the artist had to place himself not only in the solitude necessary for artistic creation but also in the embattled solitude of the precursor, enabled him to ignore criticism and remain true to a line of conduct that he perceived to be clearly defined and disinterested, that is, aiming toward his chosen goal regardless of outside pressures and economic recompense. That such thoughts were a gross oversimplification of the actual conditions of his life is immaterial. What is relevant is that he believed in them, just as he remained convinced of the architect's mission to better the human lot. "Architecture, it's a habit of mind, not a profession" (*Oeuvre complète,* vol. 1, p. 5).

There was a continuous tension of unresolved contradictions in his life as in his architecture, yet out of them he was able to achieve harmony because he never lost the gift of faith in man's redemption through poetry; the poetry of form was the quest of his life. But he did not believe that whatever conquests of form he had made could be transmitted to others. What he did transmit was poetically expressed in the *Poème de l'Angle droit* when he wrote *"Pleine main j'ai recu, pleine main je donne."* Since the task of systematically analyzing his life work is only beginning, the fullness of this receiving and the fullness of this giving cannot yet be measured. The process of historical and critical research, based largely on the vast holdings of the Fondation Le Corbusier in Paris, is steadily gaining momentum, producing articles, theses, books, and exhibitions in many parts of the world. Few other architects in history have engendered a similar volume of research and critical debate. As one tries to envisage the results of future research and of the creative exploration of new dimensions with Le Corbusier as their point of departure, it seems likely that despite all future changes in his historical image, the master's stature will remain undiminished. Shortly before his death he philosophized (*Oeuvre complète,* vol. 8, p. 172)," nothing is transmissible except thought."

MARY PATRICIA MAY SEKLER and
EDUARD F. SEKLER

WORKS

1905–1906, Villa Fallet; 1907–1908, Villa Jaquemet; 1907–1908, Villa Stotzer; 1911–1912, Villa Jeanneret; La Chaux-de-Fonds, Switzerland. 1912–1913, Villa Favre-Jacot; Le Locle, Switzerland. 1916, Cinéma La Scala; 1916–1917, Villa Schwob; La Chaux-de-Fonds, Switzerland. 1920–1922, Studio House, Amédée Ozenfant, Paris. 1922, Villa Besnus, Vaucresson, France. 1922–1925, Villas La Roche and Jeanneret, Paris. 1923–1924, ·Villa *Le Lac,* Vevey, Switzerland. 1924, Villa Lipchitz and Villa Miestschaninoff, Boulogne-sur-Seine, France. *1925, Pavillon de L'Esprit Nouveau, Exposition Internationale des Arts décoratifs, Paris. 1925, Housing Development (Cité Frugès), Pessac, France. 1926, Villa Cook, Boulogne-sur-Seine, France. 1926, Maison Guiette, Antwerp, Belgium. 1926, Salvation Army Building, Paris. 1927, Villa Planeix, Paris. 1927, Villa Stein-de Monzie, Garches, France. 1927, Two buildings for the Weissenhof Siedlung Exhibition, Stuttgart, Germany. 1928, Villa Baizeau, Carthage, Tunisia. *1928, Villa Church, Ville d'Avray, France. *1928, Demountable Exhibition Pavilion for Nestlé, Paris. 1928–1931, Villa Savoye, Poissy, France. 1928–1934, Centrosoyous, Moscow, Russia. 1929, Maison de M. X., Brussels. 1929, Work at the Airport of Bourget, Paris. 1929–1933, *Cité de Refuge,* Salvation Army, Paris. 1930, De Beistégui Apartment, Paris. 1930, Villa de Mandrot, Le Pradet, France. 1930–1932, Apartment House Immeuble Clarté, Geneva. 1930–1932, Swiss Pavilion, University City, Paris. *1932–1937, Pavillon des Temps Nouveaux, Exposition Internationale de Paris. 1933, Apartment House (including Le Corbusier's own unit), 24 rue Nungesser-et-Coli, Paris. 1935, Villa on the Atlantic, Les Mathes, France. 1935, Week-end House, La Celle Saint-Cloud, France. 1936–1945, Minis-

try of National Education and Public Health Building (with others), Rio de Janeiro, Brazil. 1946, Factory Claude et Duval, Sainte-Dié, France. 1946–1952, *Unité d'habitation,* Marseilles, France. 1948, Villa Currutchet, La Plata, Argentina. 1951–1955, Chapel Notre-Dame-du-Haut and pilgrims' hostel, Ronchamp, France. 1951–1956, High Court; Chandigarh, India. 1951–1957, Museum, Ahmedabad, India. 1952–1953, *Unité d'habitation,* Rezé-les-Nantes, France. 1952–1954, Mill Owners Association Building; 1952–1955, Villa Sarabhai; Ahmedabad, India. 1952–1956, Maisons Jaoul, Neuilly-sur-Seine, France. 1952–1956, Secretariat, Chandigarh, India. 1953–1959, Convent La Tourette, Eveux-sur Arbresle, France. 1953–1963, Palace of the Assembly, Chandigarh, India. 1956, Villa Shodan, Ahmedabad, India. 1956–1958, *Unité d'habitation,* Berlin-Charlottenburg, Germany. *1956–1958, Philips Pavilion, International Exhibition, Brussels. 1956–1959, Museum of Occidental Art, Tokyo, Japan. 1956–1965, Youth and culture building Maison des Jeunes, Firminy, France. 1957, *Unité d'habitation,* Briey-en-Forêt, Briey, France. 1957–1959 Brazilian Pavilion (with Lúcio Costa), University City, Paris. 1958–1964, Sukna Dam, Chandigarh, India. 1959–1962, Sluice buildings, Kembs-Niffer, France. 1960–1963, Carpenter Center for the Visual Arts, Harvard University, Cambridge, Mass. 1962, Church (unfinished), Firminy, France. 1962–1965, *Unité d'habitation* (not completed until 1968), Firminy, France. 1963–1965, Nautical Club, Chandigarh, India. 1963–1965, Exhibition Pavilion (Maison de l'Homme not completed until 1967), Zurich. 1964–1965, Museum and Art Gallery (not completed until 1968), Chandigarh, India. 1965–1969, Stadium (not completed until 1969), Firminy, France.

BIBLIOGRAPHY

For additional material on Le Corbusier, see the bibliography under Pierre Jeanneret. To understand fully Le Corbusier's own writings, the reader should consult first editions, which often have his own page layout.

ALAZARD, JULES, and HEBERT, JEAN-PIERRE 1961 *De la fenêtre au pan de verre dans l'oeuvre de Le Corbusier.* Paris: Dunod.

L'Architecture d'Aujourd'hui. 1933 Series 3 4:special issue.

L'Architecture d'Aujourd'hui. 1934 Series 4 5:special issue.

L'Architecture d'Aujourd'hui. 1948 Series 18 19:special issue.

Adjourd'hui, art et architecture. 1965 no. 51:memorial issue.

BESSET, MAURICE 1976 *Le Corbusier.* New York: Rizzoli.

BLAKE, PETER 1964 *Le Corbusier: Architecture and Form.* Baltimore: Penguin.

BOESIGER, WILLY (editor) 1972 *Le Corbusier.* New York: Praeger.

BOUDON, PHILIPPE 1972 *Lived-in Architecture: Le Corbusier's Pessac Revisited.* Cambridge, Mass.: M.I.T. Press.

BROOKS, ALLEN (editor) 1982 *Le Corbusier Archive.* 32 vols. New York: Garland.

CHOAY, FRANÇOISE 1960 *Le Corbusier.* New York: Braziller.

DARIA, SOPHIE (editor) 1964 *Le Corbusier: Sociologue de l'urbanisme.* Paris: Seghers.

EARDLEY, ANTHONY, and JULLIAN DE LA FUENTE, GUILLERMO 1975 *Atelier rue de Sèvres 35.* Lexington: University of Kentucky Art Gallery. Exhibition catalogue.

EVENSON, NORMA 1966 *Chandigarh.* Berkeley: University of California Press.

EVENSON, NORMA 1969 *Le Corbusier: The Machine and the Grand Design.* New York: Brazziller.

FISHMAN, ROBERT 1977 *Urban Utopias in the Twentieth Century: Ebenezer Howard, Frank Lloyd Wright, and Le Corbusier.* New York: Basic.

FUSCO, RENATO DE 1976 *Le Corbusier designer: I mobili del 1929.* Milan: Casabella.

GABETTI, ROBERTO, and OLMO, CARLO 1965 *Le Corbusier e "L'Esprit nouveau."* Turin, Italy: Einaudi.

GARDINER, STEPHEN 1974 *Le Corbusier.* New York: Viking.

GAUTHIER, MAXIMILIEN 1944 *Le Corbusier; ou, l'architecture au service de l'homme.* Paris: Denoël.

GEROSA, PIER GIORGIO 1978 *Urbanisme et mobilité.* Basel, and Stuttgart, Germany: Birkhäuser.

GIRSBERGER, HANS 1981 *Im Umgang mit Le Corbusier: Mes contacts avec Le Corbusier.* Zurich: Artemis.

GLAGOLA, JOHN 1976 *Le Corbusier: A Bibliography of Monographs.* Monticello, Ill.: Council of Planning Librarians.

GUITON, JACQUES 1981 *The Ideas of Le Corbusier on Architecture and Urban Planning.* New York: Braziller.

HENZE, ANTON 1956 *Ronchamp: Le Corbusiers erster Kirchenbau.* Recklinghausen, Germany: Paulus.

HENZE, ANTON 1957 *Le Corbusier.* Berlin: Colloquium Verlag.

HENZE, ANTON, and MOOSBRUGGER, BERNHARD 1966 *La Tourette: The Le Corbusier Monastery.* New York: Wittenborn.

HERVÉ, LUCIEN 1970 *Le Corbusier as Artist, as Writer.* Neuchâtel, Switzerland: Griffon.

HILPERT, THILO 1978 *Die funktionelle Stadt: Le Corbusiers Stadtvision.* Braunschweig, Germany: Vieweg.

IZZO, ALBERTO, and GUBITOSI, CAMILLO 1978 *Le Corbusier: Dessins, Drawings, Diesgni.* ROME: OFFICINA EDIZIONI.

JARDOT, MAURICE 1955 *Le Corbusier: Dessins.* Paris: Deux Mondes.

JENCKS, CHARLES 1973 *Le Corbusier and the Tragic View of Architecture.* Cambridge, Mass.: Harvard University Press.

JORDAN, ROBERT FURNEAUX 1972 *Le Corbusier.* London: Dent.

JULLIAN DE LA FUENTE, GUILLERMO 1968 *The Venice Hospital Project of Le Corbusier.* Houston, Tex.: Rice University School of Architecture.

[LE CORBUSIER] JEANNERET, CHARLES-E. (1912)1968 *Étude sur le mouvement d'art décoratif en Allemagne.* Reprint. New York: Da Capo.

LE CORBUSIER (1923)1970 *Towards a New Architecture.* Reprint of the 1927 ed. New York: Praeger. Originally published with the title *Vers une Architecture.*

LE CORBUSIER (1925a)1975 *Almanach d'architecture moderne.* Reprint. Turin, Italy: Bottega d'Erasmo.

LE CORBUSIER (1925b)1978 *L'Art décoratif d'aujourd'hui.* Reprint. Paris: Arthaud.

LE CORBUSIER (1925c)1971 *The City of Tomorrow and Its Planning.* Reprint of the 1929 ed. Cambridge, Mass.: M.I.T. Press. Originally published with the title *Urbanisme.*

LE CORBUSIER (1928)1975 *Une Maison—un palais.* Reprint. Turin, Italy: Bottega d'Erasmo.

LE CORBUSIER (1930)1960 *Précisions sur un état présent de l'architecture et de l'urbanisme.* Reprint. Paris: Vincent, Fréal.

LE CORBUSIER 1930–1970 *Oeuvre complète.* 8 vols. Zurich: Girsberger and Artemis.

Volume 1: *Le Corbusier und Pierre Jeanneret: Ihr gesamtes Werk von 1910–1929.* Edited by O. Stonorov and W. Boesiger. 1930, 10th ed. 1974.

Volume 2: *Le Corbusier et Pierre Jeanneret: Oeuvre complète, 1929–1934.* Edited by W. Boesiger. 1935, 9th ed. 1974.

Volume 3: *Le Corbusier et Pierre Jeanneret: Oeuvre complète, 1934–1938.* Edited by Max Bill. 1939, 9th ed. 1975.

Volume 4: *Le Corbusier, Oeuvre complète, 1938–1946.* Edited by W. Boesiger. 1946, 7th ed. 1977.

Volume 5: *Le Corbusier, Oeuvre complète, 1946–1952.* Edited by W. Boesiger. 1953, 7th ed. 1976.

Volume 6: *Le Corbusier et son atelier, rue de Sèvres 35, Oeuvre complète, 1952–1957.* Edited by W. Boesiger. 1957, 6th ed. 1977.

Volume 7: *Le Corbusier et son atelier, rue de Sèvres 35, Oeuvre complète, 1957–1965.* Edited by W. Boesiger. 1965, 3d ed. 1977.

Volume 8: *Le Corbusier: Les dernières oeuvres; the last works.* Edited by W. Boesiger. 1970, 2d ed. 1973.

LE CORBUSIER 1931 *Requête de MM. Le Corbusier et P. Jeanneret à M. le Président du Conseil de la Société des Nations.* Paris: Imprimerie Union.

LE CORBUSIER (1932a)1937 *Expo. Int. de l'Habitation Paris.* Paris: Imprimerie Union.

LE CORBUSIER 1932b *Salubra Le Corbusier.* Basel: Salubra 323 D.

LE CORBUSIER 1933 *Croisade ou le crépuscule des académies.* Paris: Crès.

LE CORBUSIER 1935a *Aircraft.* London: Studio Publications.

LE CORBUSIER (1935b)1967 *The Radiant City.* New York: Orion. Originally published with the title *La Ville Radieuse.*

LE CORBUSIER (1937)1964 *When the Cathedrals were White.* Reprint. New York: McGraw-Hill. Originally published with the title *Quand les cathédrales étaient blanches.*

LE CORBUSIER 1938 *Des Canons, des Munitions? Merci! Des Logis . . . s.v.p.* Boulogne-sur-Seine, France: Editions de l'Architecture d'Aujourd'hui.

LE CORBUSIER 1939 "Le Lyrisme des Temps Nouveaux et l'urbanisme." *Le Point* 4, Apr. 20:special issue.

LE CORBUSIER 1941a *Destin de Paris.* Paris and Clermont, France: Sorlot.

LE CORBUSIER (1941b)1947 *The Four Routes.* London: Dobson. Originally published with the title *Sur les quatre routes.*

LE CORBUSIER 1942 *Les Constructions "Murondins".* Paris and Clermont-Ferrand, France: Chiron.

LE CORBUSIER (1943a)1973 *The Athens Charter.* New York: Grossman. Originally published with the title *La Charte d'Athènes avec un Discours liminaire de Jean Giraudoux.*

LE CORBUSIER (1943b)1961 *Le Corbusier Talks with Students from the Schools of Architecture.* New York: Orion. Originally published with the title *Entretien avec les étudiants des écoles d'architecture.*

LE CORBUSIER (1946a)1948 *Concerning Town Planning.* New Haven: Yale University Press. Originally published with the title *Propos d'urbanisme.*

LE CORBUSIER (1946b)1971 *Looking at City Planning.* New York: Grossman. Originally published with the title *Manière de penser l'urbanisme.*

LE CORBUSIER 1947 *UN Headquarters.* New York: Reinhold.

LE CORBUSIER 1948 *New World of Space.* New York: Reynal & Hitchcock.

LE CORBUSIER (1950a)1953 *The Marseilles Block.* London: Harvill. Originally appeared as an article in *Le Point* 38, Nov. 7.

LE CORBUSIER (1950b)1968 *The Modulor.* Reprint of the 1954 English ed. Cambridge, Mass.: M.I.T. Press.

LE CORBUSIER 1950c *Poésie sur Alger.* Paris: Falaize.

LE CORBUSIER (1954)1981 *Une Petite Maison.* Zurich and Munich: Artemis.

LE CORBUSIER (1955a)1968 *Modulor 2.* Reprint of the 1958 ed. Cambridge, Mass.: M.I.T. Press.

LE CORBUSIER 1955b *Le Poème de l'angle droit.* Paris: Tériade.

LE CORBUSIER (1955c)1966 *L'Urbanisme est une clef.* Reprint. Paris: Île de France.

LE CORBUSIER 1956 *Les Plans Le Corbusier de Paris: 1956–1922.* Paris: Minuit.

LE CORBUSIER 1957 *The Chapel at Ronchamp.* New York: Praeger.

LE CORBUSIER 1959 *La deuxième collection Salubra par Le Corbusier.* Basel: Salubra.

LE CORBUSIER 1960 *Creation is a Patient Search.* New York: Praeger. Originally published with the title *Le Corbusier: Textes et planches.*

LE CORBUSIER 1965 *Textes et dessins pour Ronchamp.* Paris: Forces Vives.

LE CORBUSIER 1966a *Mise au point.* Paris: Forces Vives.

LE CORBUSIER 1966b *Le Voyage d'Orient.* Paris: Forces Vives.

LE CORBUSIER 1968 *The Nursery Schools.* New York: Orion. Originally published with the title *Les Maternelles vous parlent.*

[LE CORBUSIER] JEANNERET, CHARLES-E.; AUBERT, G.; and PERRIN, L. 1914 *Un Mouvement d'art à La Chaux-de-Fonds à propos de la nouvelle section de l'École d'Art.* La Chaux-de-Fonds, Switzerland: Dubois.

LE CORBUSIER, and PIERREFEU, FRANÇOIS DE

(1942)1948 *The Home of Man.* London: Architectural Press. Originally published with the title *La maison des hommes.*

LE CORBUSIER ET AL. 1938 *Logis et Loisirs.* Boulogne-sur-Seine, France: Éditions de l'Architecture d'Aujourd'hui.

LE CORBUSIER ET AL. 1942 "Il faut reconsidérer l'hexagone français." Pages 5–28 in *Architecture et Urbanisme.* Paris: Publications Techniques.

LE CORBUSIER ET AL. 1943 "Eléments modernes d'une communaté villageoise." Pages 95–108 in *Agriculture et Communauté.* Paris: Librairie de Médicis.

LE CORBUSIER ET AL. 1945 *Les Trois établissements humains.* Paris: Denoël.

Le Corbusier: Images and Symbols: The Late Period, 1947–1965. 1977 Atlanta: Georgia State University. Exhibition catalogue.

"Le Corbusier, 1905–1933." 1979 *Oppositions* nos. 15–16:special issue.

Le Corbusier, 1910–1960. 1960 Edited by W. Boesiger and H. Girsberger. Zurich: Girsberger.

Le Corbusier, 1910–1965. 1967 Edited by W. Boesiger and H. Girsberger. Zurich: Artemis.

"Le Corbusier: 1933–1960." 1980 *Oppositions* nos. 19–20:special issue.

Le Corbusier: Oeuvre Plastique. 1938 Edited by Jean Badovici. Paris: Morancé.

Le Corbusier et Pierre Jeanneret. 1927–1937 Edited by Jean Badovici. 7 series. Paris: Morancé.

Le Corbusier: La ricerca paziente. 1980 Lugano, Switzerland: Città di Lugano e FAS Gruppo Ticino. Exhibition catalogue, Villa Malpensata.

Le Corbusier Sketchbooks. 1981– Edited by the Fondation Le Corbusier and the Architectural History Foundation. 4 vols. Cambridge, Mass.: M.I.T. Press. Volume 1: 1914–1948; Volume 2: 1950–1954; Volume 3: 1954–1957; Volume 4: 1957–1964.

Le Corbusier's Firminy Church. 1981 New York: Rizzoli.

MOOS, STANISLAUS VON 1979 *Le Corbusier: Elements of a Synthesis.* Cambridge, Mass.: M.I.T. Press.

MÜLLER-REPPEN, FRITHJOF (editor) 1958 *Le Corbusier's Wohneinheit "Typ Berlin."* Berlin: Fachliteratur.

L'opera di Le Corbusier. 1963 Florence: Comitato per le manifestazioni invernali a Firenze. Exhibition catalogue, Palazzo Strozzi.

OZENFANT, AMÉDÉE, and [LE CORBUSIER] JEANNERET, CHARLES-E. (1918)1975 *Après le Cubism.* Reprint. Turin, Italy: Bottega d'Erasmo.

OZENFANT, AMÉDÉE, and [LE CORBUSIER] JEANNERET, CHARLES-E. (1925)1927 *La peinture moderne.* Paris: Crès.

PAPADAKI, STAMO (editor) 1948 *Le Corbusier: Architect, Painter, Writer.* New York: Macmillan.

PAULY, DANIÈLE 1980 *Ronchamp lecture d'une architecture.* Paris: Ophrys.

PAWLEY, MARTIN 1970 *Le Corbusier.* With photographs by Yukio Futagawa. New York: Simon & Schuster.

PETIT, JEAN 1955 *Le Corbusier: L'architecte du bonheur.* Paris: Île de France.

PETIT, JEAN (1956)1967 *Ronchamp.* Paris: Piel.

PETIT, JEAN 1957 *Chapelle N.-D. du haut à Ronchamp.* Paris: Forces Vives.

PETIT, JEAN 1958 *Le Poème électronique.* Paris: Minuit.

PETIT, JEAN 1961a *Le Livre de Ronchamp.* Paris: Forces Vives.

PETIT, JEAN 1961b *Un Couvent de Le Corbusier.* Paris: Forces Vives.

PETIT, JEAN 1968 *Le Corbusier, dessins.* Geneva: Forces Vives.

PETIT, JEAN 1970a *Le Corbusier.* Lausanne, Switzerland: Recontre.

PETIT, JEAN 1970b *Le Corbusier lui-même.* Geneva: Rousseau.

"The Philips Pavilion at the 1958 World's Fair in Brussels." 1959 *Philips Technical Review.*

PIERREFEU, FRANÇOIS DE 1932 *Le Corbusier et Pierre Jeanneret.* Paris: Crès.

Projects d'architecture de Le Corbusier. 1977 Paris: Foundation Le Corbusier.

PUOLO, MAURIZIO DI; FAGIOLO, MARCELLO; and MADONNA, MARIA LUISA 1976 *Le Corbusier Charlotte Perriand, Pierre Jeannerett: "La machine à s'asseoir."* Rome: De Luca.

ROTH, ALFRED (1927)1977 *Zwei wohnhäuser von Le Corbusier und Pierre Jeanneret.* Reprint. Stuttgart, Germany: Krämer.

ROWE, COLIN; SLUTZKY, ROBERT; and HOESLI, BERNHARD 1968 *Transparenz.* Basel: Birkhäuser.

SARTORIS, ALBERTO (1935)1936 *Gli elementi dell'architettura funzionale; sintesi panoramica dell'architettura moderna.* With a preface by Le Corbusier. 2d ed. Milan: Hoepli.

SEGAUD, MARION 1969 *Mythe et idéologie de l'espace chez Le Corbusier.* Paris: Centre de Recherche d'Architecture, d'Urbanisme et de Construction.

SEKLER, EDUARD FRANZ, and CURTIS, WILLIAM 1977 *Le Corbusier at Work: The Genesis of the Carpenter Center for the Visual Arts.* Cambridge, Mass.: Harvard University Press.

SEKLER, MARY PATRICIA MAY 1977 *The Early Drawings of Charles-Edouard Jeanneret (Le Corbusier): 1902–1908.* New York: Garland.

SERENYI, PETER 1968 "Le Corbusier's Art and Thought: 1918–1935." Unpublished Ph.D. dissertation, Washington University, St. Louis, Mo.

SERENYI, PETER (editor) 1975 *Le Corbusier in Perspective.* Englewood Cliffs, N.J.: Prentice-Hall.

STEWART, DAVID 1972 "Le Corbusier's Theory of Architecture and L'Esprit Nouveau." Unpublished Ph.D. dissertation, Courtald Institute of Art, London.

TAYLOR, BRIAN BRACE 1972 *Le Corbusier at Pessac: The Search for Systems and Standards in the Design of Low Cost Housing.* Cambridge, Mass.: Carpenter Center for the Visual Arts, Harvard University. Exhibition catalogue.

TAYLOR, BRIAN BRACE 1981 *Le Corbusier: La cité de Refuge, Paris, 1929–1933.* Paris: Équerre.

TURNER, PAUL VENABLE 1977 *The Education of Le Corbusier.* New York: Garland.

WALDEN, RUSSELL (editor) 1977 *The Open Hand: Essays on Le Corbusier.* Cambridge, Mass.: M.I.T. Press.

WEBER, HEIDI (editor) 1968? *Le Corbusier: Oeuvre lithographique.* Zurich: Centre Le Corbusier.

WERNERT, H. K. 1959 *Le Poème Électronique.* Hamburg, Germany: Bluehert.

LEDOUX, CLAUDE NICOLAS

Claude Nicolas Ledoux (1736–1806) constructed more buildings than any other architect of his time, but the vandalism of the nineteenth century destroyed most of them. Toward 1925, the Cubists and Surrealists found in his work affinities with their own. Today, this independent figure is considered one of the great artists of the neoclassical era to which he belongs.

From apprenticeship to mastery. Ledoux was born in Dormans, in the province of Champagne, where his father was a merchant. He completed his general schooling at the age of seventeen and studied architecture in the private school that JACQUES FRANÇOIS BLONDEL had opened in the Latin Quarter of Paris. As a professor, Blondel was passionately attached to certain traditions. The example he held out above all others were the buildings of FRANÇOIS MANSART, in which each story has its own columns and the wings are more modest than the main body. But Blondel kept the atmosphere open to foreign influence. Thanks to Blondel, Hubert Gravelot, and WILLIAM CHAMBERS, some ties were formed with England, so that the students discovered the Palladian (see ANDREA PALLADIO) school across the Channel. In his *L'Architecture française,* a collection of pieces published in 1752–1754, Blondel answered the earlier *Vitruvius Britannicus* of COLEN CAMPBELL. To the superimposed orderings and subtly forced dispositions of a Mansart, Blondel would oppose a colossal order and Palladian taste for open and contrasting volumes. Before submitting himself to the English challenge, Blondel had already crossed the border into Italy, where neoclassical tendencies were on display. He sat by, powerless, as the system that the reign of Louis XIV had brought to perfection came undone.

Ledoux also sought advice from LOUIS FRANÇOIS TROUARD, an older architect pensioned by Louis XV in Rome, who admired Palladio and LUIGI VANVITELLI. We might also hypothesize an internship with PIERRE CONTANT D'IVRY. Whatever the actual case, during a period of several years, Ledoux completed his technical formation and acquired the competence to become an engineer for bridge design.

In 1762, in the Rue Saint-Honoré in Paris, Ledoux decorated the hall of a café reserved for officers from the nobility, which was lodged on the ground floor of a new house. Military trophies and mirrors alternated with bundled pikes fashioned to resemble columns. The journalist Elie Fréron, who had attended Blondel's lectures, recognized a champion of antiquity in Ledoux and lauded his taste.

Two years later, Ledoux married Mademoiselle Bureau, the daughter of an oboe player attached to the company of royal musicians. The happy outcome of this marriage was that a friend of the Bureau family, Masson de Courcelles, obtained for Ledoux the post of architect of waters and forests. In this capacity, Ledoux for some years built village churches, presbyteries, fountains, and bridges in Burgundy and Champagne. This body of work is traditional and respectful of local customs. However, Ledoux decorated the choir of the Gothic cathedral of Saint Germain in Auxerre with brilliance.

Certain authors make him into a misanthropic and solitary figure, but nothing is farther from the truth. Ledoux was a charming man and well-equipped for social relations. While still quite young, he was esteemed by the rich and powerful family of the Farmer-General, Hocquart. For the son of this financier, he built the Château de Montfermeil. For Hocquart's son-in-law, Monsieur de Montesquiou, he restored a property at Maupertuis. It was at Maupertuis that Ledoux took advantage of some unlevel land and rebuilt the château at the summit of the property. He brought up water through an aqueduct and created hydraulic embellishments, an orangery, a pheasantry, and some agricultural appurtenances. At Montfermeil and at Maupertuis, except for the great pilasters of the façades, the architectural conception was still meager in its innovations. However, the Hocquart pavilion at the Chaussée d'Antin (1764) shows that Ledoux opted early for a type of edifice derived from Palladio's Rotunda.

In 1768, a conflict erupted between Blondel and Ledoux that would prove very significant. The young artist had just reconstructed the Parisian residence of the duke of Uzès, in Rue Montmartre. He invited Blondel to visit the construction yard and upset his mentor profoundly with his garrulous, complacent running comments. With some excitement, Blondel criticized the ornate façades for being decorated with "ridiculously colossal" orders, the inconvenience of the interior arrangement, and the great trophies in the drawing room.

At this decisive moment, Ledoux discovered new relationships between volumes, space, and light. He found that in the work of his near contemporary, JACQUES ANGE GABRIEL, the columns were too frail and spaced too far apart, with the result that the ordonnances, as they appeared from a distance, were swallowed up by the light. At the same time as Dumont's book was acquainting his fellow Frenchmen with the temples of Paestum, Ledoux understood the plastic efficacy of those squat supports and straight intercolumniations. At the invitation of Lord Clive of Plassey, he visited England, and there he was to appreciate an architecture with which he was already familiar. By now, the Doric and Palladio's Ionic were his favorite orders.

Toward the time of his trip to England, Ledoux built the Château de Bénouville in Normandy, whose peristyle and staircase retain their charm. With his growing reputation in Parisian circles, he took building commissions from actresses and society ladies. He had moved both his living quarters and his offices over to the Boulevard Saint-Denis, close to the new quarters where the vendors of home furnishings were gainfully plying their trade. The Hôtel Montmorency and the Tabary, Termant de Saint-Germain, and Guimard pavilions belong to this phase of his career, spent among the higher social circles. On an unobstructed site in Louveciennes, between Versailles and Saint-Germain-en-Laye, Ledoux built a Château for Madame Du Barry that remains famous to this day. The decorators he engaged at that time were, among others, Fragonard and the still unknown David. Ledoux was admitted to the Academy of Architecture, and Louis XV made a public show of his esteem for him.

Industrial architecture. For the time of his brief tenure in the waters and forests administra-

Ledoux.
Château for Madame Du Barry (project for extension).
Louveciennes, France.
1771–1773

Ledoux.
Château for Madame Du
Barry (pavilion).
Louveciennes, France.
1771–1773

tion, Ledoux was able to apply his talent to constructions that were useful rather than prestigious. He kept in touch with the administration of bridges and roadways, which controlled public works. In eastern France, some factories that processed mineral salt had to be modernized. Ledoux learned of this and gained the commission for these works. Salt at a time when it alone allowed for the preservation of meat and fish was an important commodity. In the province of Franche-Comté, several towns situated on a salt bank possessed some salt springs and wells. The plants at Salins and Montmorot maintained some caldrons in which the waters yielded their salt after boiling for several hours. The process called for a lot of wood, and the administration hesitated between two courses: either to carry the wood toward the spring, or to guide the salty water toward the forest. When the province wished to build a modern factory, the second solution carried the day. The salt works (1775–1780) were situated between Arc and Senans, at the edge of the Forest of Chaux, where channels fourteen miles long brought the "little waters" there from Salins.

Ledoux gave the salt works a semicircular form. The entrance, some processing buildings, and the two dwellings of the workers closely fit the arching curve. The buildings containing the caldrons stretched along the diameter, framing the director's house, which was placed under the fixed foot of the compass. Such a plan allowed for an easy supervision of the processing.

In order to combat the weakening effects of the light, Ledoux arranged for very narrow spaces between the columns. He adopted the rustic mode, whose effects the Italian Renaissance, and especially BARTOLOMEO AMMANNATI and MICHELE SANMICHELI, had by no means exhausted. In the director's house, alternating cylinders and cubes made up the shaft of the columns, as in the court

of the Pitti Palace. Bossages and projecting keystones produced luminous contrasts. Ledoux wrote that the circular plan imitated the sun in its course, and the salt works were an edifice which the moving play of light transfigured at every moment.

Blondel had taught Ledoux that every ornament should be symbolic. In the salt works, a very simple decoration paid tribute to the mineral kingdom. Under the peristyle of the entrance there was a grotto that seemed carved out of a mountain of salt. In the courtyard, the façades were designed with urns in which the water appears to flow away while crystallizing along the walls. Ledoux professed a philosophy that locates human happiness in the rational exploitation of nature and in the healthy organization of labor.

Theatrical architecture. Until the middle of the eighteenth century, France did not possess any real theaters. In Paris, plays were staged on the enclosed tennis courts of the *Jeux de Paume.* Princes had temporary structures placed in their palaces. In 1755, GERMAIN SOUFFLOT built the theater of Lyons, but in Paris the French players had to wait until 1781 to put on plays in a spacious, well-decorated hall. Ledoux had set up a tiny theater in the apartment of Mademoiselle Guimard, a dancer at the Paris Opera, which was quite elegant and easily disassembled. On the occasion of his trips to Franche-Comté, he was chosen to submit plans for the Theater of Besançon (1771–1773). The prospectus was difficult. He brought into play optics, acoustics, ventilation, heating, police surveillance, and security. Since French society was transforming itself, it was necessary to respect its customs, while at the same time guessing the next step in their evolution. People did not come to spectacles to see but to be seen. The arrangement of the hall had to respect the hierarchy of classes. The nobility remained predominant, but the bourgeoisie demanded some measure of respect, and the common people wished to sit down. Ledoux resolutely accepted this state of things. He dreamed of a society in which spectacles would be a religious act as they had been with the Greeks, in which the theater would be a place of communion and a temple of moral rejuvenation. At Versailles, his ideas were approved by the duke of Duras and the savant Trudaine de Montigny. In Besançon, Ledoux found in La Coré, the intendant of Franche-Comté, a man who was enlightened and prepared to understand him. He wrote the Intendant: "I know what it costs to establish a new religion." This shows that in 1775, his project for social renovation had already taken shape in his mind.

For the hall, Ledoux modeled his design on the inveterate semicircle of the ancients, restored to its place of honor by Palladio. The parterre was adorned with seats reserved for rich theater-goers. The first balcony was designated for officers of the garrison. The nobility occupied the first row of boxes; the middle class, the second. Workers, servants, and ordinary soldiers, who in other times would have remained standing on the parterre, occupied still further seats at the top of the amphitheater. The theater of Besançon, inaugurated in 1784, was extolled in the press. Another project of Ledoux's, for the Theater of Marseille, was not built; but the architect could write in 1794 that he had built some republican theaters under despotism.

Houses.   Like the ones conceived by his contemporaries ETIENNE LOUIS BOULLÉE and FRANÇOIS JOSEPH BÉLANGER, Ledoux's houses illustrated an art of living which was that of French society in the decline of the *ancien regime*. The pavilions at Attilly and d'Espinchal, constructed by Ledoux in 1780, are like noble ancestors of the middle-class villas that appeared like mushrooms in the nineteenth century and the working-class pavilions which in our time lie in a large circle around Paris. Through the spareness and rigor of their forms, Ledoux's pavilions place themselves within that architectural current that leads from the Renaissance Vicenza of Palladio to the Bauhaus of WALTER GROPIUS and LUDWIG MIES VAN DER ROHE. There were individuals, such as the prince of Salm and Beaumarchais, distinguished by the luxury and eccentricity of their dwellings. One such person, Madame Thélusson, the widow of a Swiss banker, was rich enough to permit Ledoux to build a kind of palace for her in the Chaussée d'Antin quarter. The Hôtel Thélusson (1778–1783) gateway, giving on the Rue de Provence, took the form of an arch of triumph with two strongly surbased piles. Here, Ledoux recalled some Roman buildings which the accumulation of earth and ruins had buried to half their height. For his part, Boullée also provided examples of what he would call "a buried architecture." The arcade opened amply upon a garden derived from an English garden and most unlevel. In the background, perched on some sloping rocks, the palace offered in its center a rotunda analogous to that of the later White House in Washington. Behind the palace there extended an inner courtyard reserved for the servants. A rotating movement was prescribed for the arrival and departure of carriages, which left their passengers at the foot of the house. The better part of the principal rooms was illuminated from above. The craftsman Gouthière decorated the chimneys with his bronzes. The painters Callet and Le Barbier decorated walls and cupolas. This home, which resembled none with which

Ledoux.
Hôtel Thélusson, Chaussée d'Antin.
Paris.
1778–1783

they were acquainted, provoked the admiration and astonishment of Ledoux's contemporaries.

After Madame Thélusson, Ledoux found other ostentatious clients in Pradeau de Chemilly and Jean-Baptiste Hosten. The latter was a planter from Santo Domingo. He owned his own residence in Paris and had Ledoux build a collection of individual houses on the same location. The Hosten houses have thus constituted an important landmark in the history of collective residences. Ledoux had gradually broken with the traditional conception of a building ordered around one central, dominant element, an evolution that came to its culmination in the Hosten houses. In these, the architect created the model of an indefinitely extensible ensemble and formed the notion of an architectural series. An English garden passed between stilts beneath one of the houses—another curious anticipation.

Official architecture.   Ledoux was the architect of the Farmers-General, who collected indirect duties for the crown. In Paris, *octroi* rights were imposed on all merchandise entering the city. But the poor organization of the service encouraged smuggling, to the financial disadvantage of the Farmers. Thus, in order to avoid customs inspection, wine was brought into the city by underground channels. In 1785, the Farmers decided to surround Paris with a wall that would be interrupted by some sixty buildings placed at highway crossings. These modest customs offices offered a project that a lot of architects would have treated with disdain. Ledoux turned it into monumental gateways (the Portes de Paris [1784–1789]), which he wished to be worthy of Babylon or Memphis in Egypt. He called them the "Propylaea" of Paris. To overcome the protests of the Parisians, to whom every tax initiative was intolerable, he carried out the operation with unbelievable haste. In three years, fifty gates were completed despite the uneasy atmosphere that presaged the Revolution.

Certain of these gateways were enclosed by two such offices. Others had but a single building. The plans offered numerous variations on some prototypes. The offices of Monceau and Reuilly were rotundas. At la Villette and La Rapée, the rotunda occupied the center of a cross. The office of Picpus was a cube enclosed by four peristyles. The entry to the office of Bonshommes opened up to a sort of vaulted apse of columns: a severe version of the portal to the Guimard Apartments, for Ledoux would constantly take up the same motifs again. The buildings at Gentilly and at Courcelles presented themselves like Greek temples. At Le Trône, Ledoux erected two high columns. The offices of l'Etoile were cubes surrounded by peristyles. The Doric order and the bossages of rustic architecture were ubiquitous. Here and there, the triple Palladian opening (Venetian windows) tempered this robust and grave style. He would sometimes use arcades to enclose a cylindrical building.

These constructions were judged ruinous, and Ledoux was relieved of his duties in 1789.

Utopian work. Energetic and penetrating, as his professional success proves, Ledoux was also a dreamer, sentimental and full of solicitude for women. The reign of Louis XVI was an epoch in which sensibility recovered its rights over the cold reason that had been exercised in the age of the encyclopedists. Ledoux was open to the most irrational currents of thought. All around him, many artists and gentlemen were members of secret societies, and Ledoux doubtless belonged to the Rosicrucians. Before editing his book, *Architecture,* he took comfort in some mysterious ceremonies, like the one about which his friend WILLIAM BECKFORD has left a most curious account.

Ledoux.
Portes de Paris (Propylées;
* Barrière de la Villette).*
Paris.
1784–1789

The French aristocracy at that time was arranging gardens in which art and nature united their seductions in order to touch the already Romantic sensibilities of the readers of Richardson and Rousseau. Ledoux did a study for Monsieur de Chemilly of the gardens of Bourneville. Among his friends were the poets Saint-Lambert and Delille, who celebrated the art of gardens. In the bosom of nature, as these authors understood it, the corrupt soul of the city dweller would experience the benefits of the pastoral life, would rediscover the innocence of earlier ages, and would rise toward the Author of Creation. In composing the designs that would lull the dreamer of such reveries, the architect would return as well to the origins of his art, to those times beyond memory when the hut was the ancestor of the temple and the tree trunk preceded the column.

From 1787 on, a succession of unpleasant events sharpened Ledoux's character and influenced his philosophy. At the moment when he might have hoped to advance to the nobility, the government disavowed the enterprise of the Propylaea. The architect who was bringing ruin upon the national treasury was marked for public reproach. Emigration dispersed his clientele. The large constructions which he had undertaken at Aix-en-Provence were suspended. The Academy of Architecture was dissolved at precisely the moment when he aspired to conduct his first class. In 1792, he lost his wife. The Revolutionary proceeding against Madame Du Barry recalled the favors that the royal court had heaped upon him. As his fortune (five or six pieces of real estate) drew attention, he was incarcerated during the Reign of Terror and believed himself doomed for the guillotine. During his captivity, his favorite daughter died. His other daughter set in motion a legal suit against him that lasted eight years and poisoned his old age. Freed in the Thermidor period (1794), he practically ceased building and prepared for the publication of his literary work.

Beginning in 1773, he used to have his plans engraved, but the evolution of his style obliged him constantly to modify the image of his past productions. Ceaselessly, he would appeal to his engravers to rework their copper plates, and to destroy the prints that he judged out of date. His architecture became more and more colossal, spare, cubic. The mansard roofs were replaced by terraces. The full took precedence over the empty. The walls finally lost their horizontal joints, and the columns their flutings. To take a single example, the elevation of Bénouville was engraved four times.

After 1775, Ledoux had shown Turgot, the controller general of finances, his sketches for the

town of Chaux, a complex of working-class quarters which he offered to build around the Salt Works. The factory would have to be doubled and take the form of an ellipse, around which public edifices and dwellings would have spread, lacing themselves into a net of concentric rays of buildings. The project was amplified and engraved, leaf by leaf, beginning in 1780. Never had so complete an ensemble been composed to assure the subsistence, the education, the leisure time, and the spiritual life of the laboring population.

During his detention under the Revolution, Ledoux wrote the text which would accompany the engravings. The first volume, the only one to appear while its author was alive, presents the theater of Besançon, the Salt Works, and the urban society of Chaux. This volume is entitled *L'Architecture considérée sous le rapport de l'art, des moeurs, et de la législation* (1804). The remaining engravings left by Ledoux constituted a second volume published by Daniel Ramée, who inherited the copper plates, in 1847. In the text of 1804, brilliant formulations alternate with intentionally obscure passages, in which the author seems to be referring to esoteric tradition. He evokes with bitterness and hatred the events that interrupted his activity as a builder, and he develops a social philosophy. The essential conceptions derive from Rousseau. Man is naturally good, susceptible to progress by means of a judicious education, but corrupted by the invincible immorality of great urban gatherings. Restrained and well-incorporated clusters will assure him of the benefits of labor, without which he is not happy. Air, water, space, and light are the gifts of the Supreme Being, and he will be deprived of none of these. Each family will cultivate its garden and will gather its subsistence. As a health measure, hospitals and slaughterhouses will be kept at a distance from inhabited areas. Chaux features an immense market, a hostelry, an establishment of baths, and numerous buildings for education and leisure activities. Disputes are settled by a judge in the "Pacifery." The *Panarethéon* (place of all virtues) is a school in which virtues are taught. The plan of the church takes up Soufflot's project for Sainte Geneviève. The cemetery is a net of catacombs radiating around a spherical void. To all of these edifices, of legendary beauty, Ledoux owes his fame today.

MICHEL GALLET
Translated from French by Richard Koffler

WORKS

1762, Café (interior decoration), rue Saint Honoré, Paris. c.1762–c.1764, Cathedral of Saint Germain (choir), Auxerre, France. c.1762–c.1764, Château de Maupertuis (restoration), France. c.1762–c.1764, Château de Montfermeil, France. 1764, Hôtel d'Uzes (reconstruction), rue Montmartre; 1764, Pavillon Hocquart, Chausée d'Antin; Paris. c.1764–c.1770, Château de Bénouville, Normandy, France. 1770, Hôtel Montmorency; Paris. 1771–1773, Château for Madame Du Barry, Louveciennes, France. 1771–1773, Pavillon Guimard; 1771–1773, Pavillon Tabary; 1771–1773, Pavillon Termant de Saint Germain; 1771–1773, Theater (apartment of Madame Guimard); Paris. 1771–1773, Theater, Besançon, France. 1775–1780, Salt Works, Arc et Senans, France. *1778–1783, Hôtel Thélusson, Chausée d'Antin, Paris. 1780, Pavillon, Attily, France. 1780, Pavillon d'Espinchal, France. 1784–1789, Portes de Paris (Propylées). n.d., Hôtel Pradeau de Chemilly, Paris.

Ledoux.
Ville de Chaux (project).
France.
After 1775

BIBLIOGRAPHY

GALLET, MICHEL 1970 "La jeunesse de Ledoux." *Gazette des Beaux-Arts* 75, no. 2:65–92.
GALLET, MICHEL 1979 *Ledoux et Paris.* Paris.
GALLET, MICHEL 1980 *Ledoux.* Paris: The author.
HERRMANN, WOLFGANG 1960 "The Problem of Chronology in Claude Nicolas Ledoux's Engraved Work." *Art Bulletin* 26, no. 3:191–210.
KAUFMANN, EMIL 1952 *Three Revolutionary Architects: Boulée, Ledoux, and Lequeu.* Philadelphia: American Philosophical Society.
LANGNER, JOHANNES 1960 "Ledoux' Redaktion der eigenen Werke für die Veröffentlichung." *Zeitschrift für Kunstgeschichte* 23, no. 2:136–166.
LANGNER, JOHANNES 1963 "Ledoux und die 'Fabriques': Voraussetzungen der Revolutionsarchitektur im Landschaftsgarten." *Zeitschrift für Kunstgeschichte* 26, no. 1:1–36.
LEVALLET-HAUG, GENEVIÈVE 1934 *Claude Nicolas Ledoux: 1736–1806.* Paris and Strasbourg, France: Librairie Istra.
MOREUX, JEAN-CHARLES, and RAVAL, MARCEL 1945 *Claude-Nicolas Ledoux: Architecte du roi.* Paris: Arts et Metiers Graphiques.

ROSENAU, HELEN (1959)1975 *The Ideal City and its Architectural Evolution.* New York: Harper & Row.

VIDLER, ANTHONY 1976 "The Architecture of the Lodges: Ritual Form and Associational Life in the Late Enlightenment." *Oppositions* 5:75–97.

LEE, FRANCIS D.

Francis D. Lee (1827–1885) studied with, then became a member of Edward C. Jones's firm in Charleston, South Carolina (1849–1857). An eclectic architect with an apparent preference for the Gothic Revival style, Lee pioneered in cast-iron construction. After the Civil War, he established the firm of Lee and Annan in St. Louis, Missouri.

GWEN W. STEEGE

WORKS

1852–1854, Unitarian Church (remodeled); 1853, S. S. Farrar and Brothers Store; 1853–1854, Farmers' and Exchange Bank; 1859, Saint Luke's Church; Charleston, S.C. 1875, Merchants' Exchange; *1880–1881, Gay's Central Building; c.1883, Roe Building; St. Louis, Mo.

BIBLIOGRAPHY

RAVENAL, BEATRICE ST. JULIEN 1945 *Architects of Charleston.* Charleston, S.C.: Carolina Art Association.

LEE, THOMAS

Thomas Lee (1794–1834), the son of an architect who retired from the profession after becoming independently wealthy, was the pupil of JOHN SOANE and David Laing in the 1810s. His career was launched in 1817 with a giant obelisk monument to the Duke of Wellington at Blackdown Hill, Somerset, the most substantial executed (although unfinished) commemoration of the victor at Waterloo. The balance of his commissions was, however, of a lesser order—some country houses and several inexpensive churches in a variety of styles. Lee drowned off the Devonshire coast in 1834.

GERALD L. CARR

WORKS

1817–1818, Wellington Monument, Blackdown Hill, Somerset, England. 1820–1823, Arlington Court; 1822, Eggesford House, Devonshire, England. 1822–1823, Saint Clement's Church, Worcester; c.1825, Priory Hall, Dudley; 1826–1828, Guildhall, Barnstaple; 1827–1830, Netherton Church; Worcestershire, England.

BIBLIOGRAPHY

PAPWORTH, WYATT (editor) 1852–1892 *The Dictionary of Architecture.* 8 vols. London: Architectural Publication Society.

LEEDS, WILLIAM HENRY

The early life of William Henry Leeds (1786–1866) is obscure. Born in Norfolk, England, he exhibited at the Norwich Society of Artists in 1815 and, from 1829 to 1849, at the Royal Academy and Society of British Artists. Apparently never in practice, he became an architectural critic and journalist, writing regular contributions on "public improvements" in the *Companion to the Almanac* (1838–1850).

R. WINDSOR LISCOMBE

BIBLIOGRAPHY

BOLTON, ARTHUR THOMAS 1927 Pages 416–418 in *The Portrait of Sir John Soane.* London: Butler.

BRITTON, JOHN 1827 *Union of Architecture, Sculpture and Painting.* London: The author.

CLARKE, HYDE 1867 "William Henry Leeds: Architectural Critic." *Building News* 14:681–682, 697–698, 717–718.

HITCHCOCK, H. R. (1954)1972 Pages 14, 395, 434 in *Early Victorian Architecture in Britain.* 2 vols. Reprint. New York: Da Capo.

LEEDS, WILLIAM HENRY (editor and translator) 1836 *Moller's Memorials of German Gothic Architecture: With Additional Notes and Illustrations.* London: Weale.

LEEDS, WILLIAM HENRY 1838 Supplement in John Britton and A. C. Pugin, *Illustrations of the Public Buildings of London: With Descriptive Accounts.* London: Weale.

LEEDS, WILLIAM HENRY 1839 *The Travellers' Club House . . . Accompanied by an Essay on the Present State of Architectural Study and the Revival of the Italian Style.* London: Weale.

LEEDS, WILLIAM HENRY (1848)1904 *Rudimentary Architecture: The Orders and their Aesthetic Principles.* 16th ed. London: Crosby.

LEEDS, WILLIAM HENRY (editor) 1862 *A Treatise on the Decorative Part of Civil Architecture by William Chambers.* London: Lockwood.

LEFRANC, PIERRE BERNARD

Pierre Bernard Lefranc (1795–1856) was trained by Charles PERCIER AND Pierre Leonard FONTAINE. In 1837, he became an architect for the court of Louis-Philippe, for whom he restored the Château at Pau and designed the French Renaissance funerary chapel at Dreux (1843). For the centrally planned Chapel of Saint Ferdinand at Neuilly (1843), Lefranc drew from Byzantine sources.

LISA B. REITZES

WORKS

After 1837, Château at Pau (restoration), France. 1843, Royal Chapel, Dreux, France. 1843, Chapel of the Compassion (Saint Ferdinand), Neuilly, France.

BIBLIOGRAPHY

HAUTECOEUR, LOUIS 1943–1957 *Histoire de l'architecture classique en France.* 7 vols. Paris: Picard.

LEFUEL, HECTOR

Remembered for the new Louvre, Hector Martin Lefuel (1810–1880) was a pupil of JEAN NICOLAS HUYOT at the Ecole des Beaux-Arts in Paris, winning the Grand Prix de Rome in 1839. In 1854, Napoleon III named him architect of the Louvre and the Tuileries, in which capacity Lefuel succeeded LUDOVICO VISCONTI. Using Visconti's plan but his own elevations, Lefuel completed Visconti's joining of the two palaces (construction had begun in 1852) and did further work there all his life. With its mansard roofs and richly decorated walls, the new Louvre is the archetype of the Second Empire style.

RICHARD CHAFEE

WORKS

1853, Theater, Château of Fontainebleau, France. 1854–1880, Louvre and Tuileries (enlargement and alterations), Paris. 1869–1876, Castle of Fürst Henckel von Donnersmarck, Neudeck bei Beuthen, Silesia, Germany. *n.d., Hôtel Fould; *n.d., Hôtel de Nieuwerkerke; Paris.

BIBLIOGRAPHY

HAUTECOEUR, LOUIS 1957 *La Fin de l'architecture classique: 1848–1900.* Volume 7 in *Histoire de l'architecture en France.* Paris: Picard.
HITCHCOCK, H. R. (1958)1977 *Architecture: Nineteenth and Twentieth Centuries.* Baltimore: Penguin.
MIDDLETON, R. D., and WATKIN, DAVID 1980 *Neoclassical and 19th Century Architecture.* New York: Abrams.
PASCAL, J.-L. 1881 "H. Lefuel." *Revue générale de l'architecture* 38:259–265.

LEGEAY, JEAN-LAURENT

In the light of recent discoveries—in particular, in the archives kept today in East Germany—Jean-Laurent Legeay (1710–c.1786) appears, at least on the theoretical level, to have been one of the most important European architects of the eighteenth century. A winner of the *Grand Prix de Rome* (1732) and a contemporary of GIOVANNI BATTISTA PIRANESI in the Eternal City (1737–1742), Legeay exerted a profound influence on his pupils ETIENNE LOUIS BOULLÉE, CHARLES DE WAILLY, PIERRE LOUIS MOREAU-DESPROUX, and A. J. Peyre the Younger (see PEYRE FAMILY). A complex, tormented personality, he has rightly been considered one of those who introduced neoclassical taste to France; on the other hand, he formed fierce attachments all of his life to the strangest flights of invention.

GILBERT EROUART

WORKS

1747, Saint Hedwig Catholic Church, Berlin. 1748–1756, Schwerin Castle (garden); c.1750, Ruhn Castle; 1750–1755, Rostock Castle (ballroom); 1753, Kleinow Castle (belvedere); Mecklenburg, Germany. 1763–1764, Sans Souci (marble terrace wall of the Dutch Garden), Potsdam, Germany.

BIBLIOGRAPHY

ERICHSEN, JENS 1975 "Antique und Grec. Studien zur Function der Antike in Architektur und Kunsttheorie des Frühklassizismus." Unpublished Ph.D. dissertation, University of Cologne, Germany.
EROUART, GILBERT 1978 "Jean-Laurent Legeay: Recherches." Pages 199–212 in Georges Brumel (editor), *Piranese et les Français.* Rome: Edizioni dell' Elefante.
EROUART, GILBERT 1982 *Jean-Laurent Legeay: Un architecte français dans l'Europe des Lumières.* Milan and Paris: Electa Edizioni.
HARRIS, JOHN 1967 "Le Geay, Piranesi and International Neo-classicism in Rome (1740–1750)." Pages 189–196 in Douglas Fraser, Howard Hibbard, and Milton J. Lemire (editors), *Essays in the History of Architecture Presented to Rudolf Wittkower.* London: Phaidon.
KAUFMANN, EMIL 1952 "Three Revolutionary Architects: Boullée, Ledoux and Lequeu." *Transactions of the American Philosophical Society* 42, part 3:431–564.
OECHSLIN, WERNER; ARIZZOLI, PIERRE; and EROUART, GILBERT 1976 "Jean-Laurent Legeay." Pages 179–200 in *Piranese et les Français: 1740–1790.* Rome: Edizioni dell' Elefante. Exhibition catalogue.
PÈROUSE DE MONTCLOS, JEAN MARIE 1969 *Etienne-Louis Boullée, 1728–1799, de l'architecture classique à l'architecture révolutionnaire.* Paris: Arts et Métiers Graphiques.

LEGRAND, JACQUES GUILLAUME

Jacques Guillaume Legrand (1753–1809), a student of JEAN RODOLPHE PERRONET and JACQUES FRANÇOIS BLONDEL, became the son-in-law of CHARLES LOUIS CLÉRISSEAU.

He was in charge of the construction of the bridge at Tours around 1775. In 1783, he and JACQUES MOLINOS built the cupola of NICOLAS LE

CAMUS DE MEZIÈRES's Halle au Blé in Paris. He was assigned the remodeling of the Fontaine des Innocents in 1786. With Molinos, he built a house at 6 Rue Saint Florentin in 1789, the same year he was awarded the construction and decoration of the Hôtel Marbeuf in the Faubourg Saint-Honoré. From 1807 to 1809, he worked in Saint-Denis.

He published the *Parallèle de l'architecture ancienne et moderne* (1789), the text for Clérisseau's *Antiquités de la France* (1804), the *Galerie Antique* (1806), an essay on the history of *L'Architecture* (1809–1810), and a *Description de Paris* written in collaboration with C. P. Landon (1818).

GÉRARD ROUSSET-CHARNY
Translated from French by
Richard Cleary

BIBLIOGRAPHY

ADHÉMAR, JEAN 1933 "La Coupole en charpente de la Halle au Blé et l'influence de Philibert Delorme au XVIIIe siècle." *L'Architecture* 46, no. 7:249–252.

LEITH, GORDON

George Esslemont Gordon Leith (1885–1965) was the dominant South African architect of the interwar years, maintaining the classical tradition established by HERBERT BAKER. Leith was born in South Africa. After working as a clerk to the chief architect of the Railway Department, he was sent to the Architectural Association in London, where he studied from 1906 to 1909. He then worked for Baker back in South Africa and became the first winner of the Herbert Baker Scholarship for travel to the British schools in Rome and Athens. Following service during World War I, Leith became an assistant architect for the Imperial War Graves Commission (1918–1920). He returned to South Africa in 1920 and established an office in Johannesburg. His work became increasingly rationalized and classical, analogous to the development of the style of CHARLES HENRY HOLDEN in Britain.

GAVIN STAMP

WORKS

1918–1920, Terlincthun and Calais Southern War Cemeteries, France. 1920–1940, Barclay's Bank, Pretoria. 1920–1940, Chamber of Mines Hospital; 1920–1940, Esslemont House, Houghton; 1920–1940, General Hospital; Johannesburg. 1920–1940, Pretoria Technical College. 1920–1940, Rand Water Board; 1920–1940, Reid Brother's Building; 1920–1940, Reserve Bank; Johannesburg. 1920–1940, Town Hall, Bloemfontein, South Africa. 1920–1940, Union Corporation Building, Johannesburg. 1920–1940, War Memorial, Pretoria. 1928, Central Railway Station (with Gerard Moerdijk), Johannesburg.

BIBLIOGRAPHY

"Dr. G. E. Gordon Leith, M.C., A.R.I.B.A., M.I.A." 1946 *South African Architectural Record* 31:279–286.
"Gordon Leith; Tributes by Two Colleagues." 1965 *South African Architectural Record* 50:12, 47.
STAMP, GAVIN 1977 *Silent Cities*. London: Royal Institute of British Architects.

LE LORRAIN, LOUIS

Louis Le Lorrain (1715–1759) was a painter of historical and architectural scenes, but his most significant contribution lies in his early manifestation of neoclassicism in designs for festival decorations, furniture, and interiors. A pupil of Jacques Dumont, he won the Prize at the Paris Academy in 1739 and was at the French Academy in Rome from 1740 to 1748. While there, he was responsible for designs for the Festival of Chino (1745–1748). On his return to Paris, at the Salon in 1753, 1755, and 1757, he was one of several artists influenced by the antiquarian, the Comte de Caylus, experimenting with encaustic painting. He employed this in 1756 in a room done for the financier La Live de Jully, for whom he also designed early examples of neoclassical furniture. His dining room for Akero, Sweden (1754) is also seen as one of the earliest in that style. In 1758, he was called to St. Petersburg by the Empress Elizabeth and appointed professor at the newly established Academy there, but he died the following year.

DAVID CAST

WORKS

1754, Akero (dining room), Sweden. 1756–1757, Maison La Live de Jully (decorations and furniture), Paris. 1758, Academy of Fine Arts (decorations in the Room of the Busts), St. Petersburg.

BIBLIOGRAPHY

DUSSIEUX, LOUIS E. 1856 *Les artistes français à l'étranger*. Paris: Gide.
ERIKSEN, SVEND 1961 "La Live de Jully's Furniture 'à la grecque'." *Burlington Magazine* 103:340–347.
ERIKSEN, SVEND 1963 "Om salen paa Akero og dens Kunstler Louis-Joseph Le Lorrain." *Konsthistorisk Tidskrift* 32:94–120.
ERIKSEN, SVEND 1974 *Early Neo-classicism in France*. London: Faber.
EROUARD, GILBERT, and OECHSLIN, WERNER 1976 "Louis-Joseph Le Lorrain." Pages 201–215 in *Académie de France à Rome, Piranesi et les Français, 1740–1790*. Rome: Edizioni dell' Elefante.
HARRIS, JOHN 1967 "Le Geay, Piranesi and International Neo-classicism in Rome: 1740–1750." Pages 189–196 in Howard Hibbard, Douglas Fraser, and Milton J. Lewine (editors), *Essays in the History of*

Architecture Presented to Rudolf Wittkower. London: Phaidon.

PEVSNER, NIKOLAUS (1940)1973 *Academies of Art: Past and Present.* Reprint. New York: Da Capo.

LE MASSON, LOUIS

Brother of the sculptor François Le Masson, Louis Le Masson (1743–1829) was the student of CHARLES LOUIS CLÉRISSEAU and became engineer of the Ponts et Chaussées in Paris.

The Abbé de Balivière, *commendataire* of Royaumont, chose Le Masson to rebuild the abbatial palace from 1785 to 1789. In this elegant building, the architect combined the examples of ROBERT ADAM and WILLIAM CHAMBERS with impressions he had collected in Italy. In 1787, he designed projects for the Church of Guitrancourt, and in 1789, he built the church of Courbevoie. He created a panorama of Rome depicted from San Pietro in Montorio engraved on five plates.

GÉRARD ROUSSET-CHARNY
Translated from French by Richard Cleary

BIBLIOGRAPHY

MOREUX, J. CH. 1951 "Emules et disciples de C. N. Ledoux. I. Louis Le Masson 1743–1830: Château de Royaumont et église de Courbevoie." *Revue des Arts* 1951:31–36.

LEMERCIER, JACQUES

Jacques Lemercier (c.1582–1654) was the eldest of the three leading French architects of the mid-seventeenth century; the other two were FRANÇOIS MANSART and LOUIS LE VAU, and though he has justly been called the least talented of the three, he introduced some interesting ideas, of Italian origin, into his work. He was, moreover, extremely fortunate in his principal patron, the great Cardinal de Richelieu.

Lemercier was the son of a master mason from whom he presumably received his first training. Before 1607, however, Jacques was in Rome where he may have worked under Rosato Rosati. By 1615, he was back in Paris and in 1624 he received an important commission from King Louis XIII to continue the rebuilding of the Square Court of the Louvre Palace in Paris, begun by PIERRE LESCOT. He doubled Lescot's wing on the west side of the court, repeating the original design but, for the central feature, dividing the old and new buildings, he erected the imposing Pavillon de l'Horloge. (This, owing to financial difficulties, was not com-

Lemercier. Pavillon de l'Horloge, Louvre. Paris. 1641

pleted until 1641.) As no order of columns or pilasters could correctly have been introduced above those of Lescot's three story façade design (continued in the lower part of the pavilion), the pediment above the pavilion's fourth story is supported by twin caryatids sculpted by Jacques Sarrazin. The pediment itself is of a complicated tripartite design inspired by GIACOMO DELLA PORTA's entrance to the Church of the Gesù in Rome.

From 1624 to 1636, Lemercier was occupied with a very large town house for Cardinal de Richelieu, the Palais Cardinal (later the Palais Royal). Part of this consisted of older buildings and part was designed by Lemercier. This seems to have been a fairly pedestrian work, but it contained five galleries decorated by leading artists. Later much altered and enlarged, the palace was burned down in 1763. The present Palais Royal is a completely new building; only part of an exterior wall by Lemercier survives, decorated with high-relief sculptures of ships' anchors and prows, a reference to Richelieu's command of the navy. At the Palais Cardinal, Lemercier also built for Richelieu the theater (1639) which was the genesis of the Comédie Française of Paris.

Lemercier was concerned with two other important Parisian town houses, the Hôtel de Liancourt (1623), formerly the Hôtel de Bouillon begun by SALOMON DE BROSSE in 1612, and the Hôtel d'Effiat (1636). Both have disappeared, but the Hôtel de Liancourt is known from DANIEL MAROT's engraved plans and elevations.

The Church of the College of the Sorbonne in Paris was built under Richelieu's patronage and begun by Lemercier in 1626. Its plan is based on that of Rosati's church of San Carlo ai Catinari in Rome, an unusual one with a central domed space, equal-length nave and choir, very shallow transepts, and a chapel within each arm of the cross. The whole would have formed an almost unbroken rectangle, with very shallow breaks forward for the altar–apse, transepts, and western entrance. However, this church had to have two important entrances: one for the public at the west end and one, into the north transept, from the college courtyard. Lemercier achieved an imposing entrance and a satisfying culmination to the courtyard by adding an impressive classical portico to the transept. The western façade, based on the Roman church type, is perhaps less successful, but it was widely imitated. (The Roman-type church façade has two stories, the narrower top one pedimented and

Lemercier.
Church of the Sorbonne.
Paris.
Begun 1626

linked to the lower by consoles or other curving elements). These Sorbonne elevations owe much to Lemercier's Italian training and nowhere more so than in the dome. This is also based on San Carlo ai Catinari, but apparently on a drawing by Rosati for the Roman church, whose dome was not begun until five years after Lemercier left Rome. The drums of both the Sorbonne and San Carlo domes have roundheaded windows separated by clustered pilasters—features unknown in any other dome of the period.

Before returning to Lemercier's secular work, we will consider the much later dome of the Val-de-Grâce Church in Paris, which Lemercier developed from this Sorbonne design. Lemercier took over the construction of the Val-de-Grâce from FRANÇOIS MANSART in 1646, and the dome, entirely Lemercier's design, is a most striking and successful composition, full of drama and upward movement. This is achieved by the shape of the dome and lantern, by the number of piers and ribs (double those of the Sorbonne), and by the statues and candelabra that decorate the drum. Here, Lemercier shows a concentrated power and imagination lacking in much of his other work and certainly less evident in his completion of the rest of Mansart's church.

In 1631, Lemercier began to build a château and a small town for the cardinal on the site of Richelieu's childhood home near Chinon in Poitou. The old house was demolished and a château planned on a vast scale replaced it. By 1642, it was nearly completed, but in that year, without ever occupying it, Richelieu died.

The plan was bold, reminiscent of Charleval, the huge, also never completed palace begun for Charles IX in Normandy in 1570. It had an entrance set in a large semicircular wall (this survives), flanked by pavilions and courtyards. Two further central courtyards were flanked by further service courts, and beyond all this lay the main château, built around three sides of an inner courtyard closed by a screen and entrance pavilion. Beyond the semicircular entrance lay the appendage to this domain, the town of Richelieu.

Only one pavilion from one of the service courts survives, but this is enough to prove what is suspected from the engravings—that in detail Lemercier's elevations were not grand or confident enough for the scale of the whole and that their architecture was undistinguished and somewhat old-fashioned as well. The ensemble was constructed by "adding up" parts which bore little convincing relationship to each other or to the whole. An example of the meanness of design in detail at Richelieu is seen in the windows and dormers of the surviving pavilion; totally undistinguished, they seem dwarfed by the building they articulate. After the French Revolution, in 1805, the château was sold to a building contractor. He and his successors demolished it, a process that continued until, in 1877, a Monsieur Heine bought and restored the small remains. Its plans and elevations are known from a large number of engravings by Marot.

The town of Richelieu is still contained within Lemercier's strictly rectangular layout, forming a grid of streets and squares. In one street, the houses are unified by being continuously roofed from end to end, a new departure for the period. The surviving original buildings, of brick and stone, are charming if not particularly distinguished. The church has a façade akin to the west front of the Sorbonne church, but much less grand.

In founding his town, Richelieu ignored geographical and commercial realities. Ill-placed and economically unnecessary, it neither grew nor thrived and remained within its original limits; with many of its original buildings, it has been preserved as a striking example on a small scale of seventeenth-century town planning.

In 1633, Richelieu acquired another, much smaller, château (begun 1606) at Rueil, between Paris and Saint-Germain, much nearer than Richelieu in Poitou to the centers of political and social life. The château at Rueil was enlarged by Lemercier and seems to have been a conventional structure of brick and stone. It was entirely demolished after 1817. The great glory of Rueil, however, was its gardens, terraces, fountains, and cascades, created under Lemercier's supervision and recorded in engravings by Israël Silvestre and others. Richelieu took a passionate interest in the layout and planting of these gardens.

Like many contemporary architects, Lemercier was also an engineer. He supplied designs for bridges at Lyons (1619) and Rouen (1620). He was frequently called in to advise on building works and also on decorative schemes. As an architect, Lemercier never truly succeeded in integrating the Italian motifs in his work—which influenced his successors—with his native French idiom; instead, he grafted them onto a French style which, at any rate in his secular buildings, was somewhat backward-looking.

ROSALYS COOPE

WORKS

*1623, Hôtel de Liancourt (enlargement); begun 1624, Louvre (rebuilding the north wing of the west side of the Square Court); 1624–1636, Palais Cardinal (later the Palais Royal); begun 1626, Church of the Sorbonne; Paris. Begun 1631, Château and Town of Richelieu, France. *Begun 1633, Château (enlargement) and Gardens, Rueil, France. *1636, Hôtel d'Effiat, Paris. 1639, Theater for Palais Cardinal; 1641, Pavillon de l'Horloge (completion), Louvre; 1646, Church of the Val-de-Grâce (supervision of construction of a church designed by François Mansart); Paris.

BIBLIOGRAPHY

BLOMFIELD, REGINALD (1911)1974 *History of French Architecture.* Reprint of 1921 ed. 2 vols. New York: Hacker.

BLUNT, ANTHONY F. (1953)1977 *Art and Architecture in France: 1500–1700.* Harmondsworth, England: Penguin.

BLUNT, ANTHONY F. 1960 "Two Unpublished Drawings by Lemercier for the Pavillon de l'Horloge." *Burlington Magazine* 102:447–448.

CIPRUT, EDOUARD J., and COLLARD, LOUIS 1963 *Nouveaux documents sur le Louvre.* Paris: Picard.

CRAMAIL, ALFRED 1888 *Le château de Ruel et ses jardins sous le cardinal de Richelieu et sous la duchesse d'Aiguillon.* Fontainebleau, France: Bourges.

MAROT, JEAN (c.1655)1969 *Recueil des plans, profils et élévations de plusieurs palais, chasteaux, églises, sépultures, grotes et hostels bâtis dans Paris.* Facsimile ed. Farnborough, England: Gregg.

MAROT, JEAN (1670)1970 *Architecture française.* Reprint. Paris: Laget.

PILLEMENT, GEORGES 1966 *Paris disparu.* Paris: Grasset.

SAUVEL, TONY 1960 "De l'hôtel de Rambouillet au Palais-Cardinal." *Bulletin Monumental* 118:169–190.

SAUVEL, TONY 1962 "Le Palais Royal de la mort de Richelieu à l'incendie en 1763." *Bulletin Monumental* 120:173–190.

LEMOINE, PAUL GUILLAUME

Paul Guillaume Lemoine (18th–19th centuries) won the Grand Prix de Rome in 1775. He was inspector of the Colysée in Paris built by Louis Denis Le Camus between 1771 and 1774 and became *contrôleur* of the Théâtre Français in 1790. In 1806, he became the contractor for the Church of the Madeleine. He designed projects for the Hôtel de Beaumarchais and also for the Porte Saint-Antoine.

GÉRARD ROUSSET-CHARNY
*Translated from French by
Richard Cleary*

BIBLIOGRAPHY

GALLET, MICHEL 1972 *Paris Domestic Architecture of the 18th Century.* Translated by James C. Palmes. London: Barrie & Jenkins.

LE MUET, PIERRE

Pierre Le Muet (1591–1669) was one of the major theoreticians of early French baroque architecture.

His career spanned the political turbulence of the Thirty-Year War and the eventual rise of Louis XIV. Born in Dijon, France, in 1591, he quickly established himself as an architect, receiving important commissions early in his professional life. In 1623, he published his *Manière de bien bastir pour toutes sortes de personnes,* his most famous theoretical treatise.

The prevailing architectural mode at the end of the sixteenth century throughout most of France was a form of classicism, but in Paris, the architects of Henry IV began to produce an essential prototype for the baroque. In domestic architecture, the principles of the new style were developed in two books, the *Architecture française* of Louis Savot (published in 1624) and the *Manière de bien bastir* by Le Muet. In his writing, Le Muet established design theories for all levels of the social strata, some of his plans for houses having a mere twelve feet of street frontage. Le Muet enlarged his treatise in 1647, proposing plans and elevations for elaborate domestic structures in the second edition.

Although Le Muet lived until 1669, his style was shaped in the early 1620s, and during most of his career he retained certain latent mannerist tendencies. One of his most important buildings, the Hôtel Duret de Chevry-Tubeuf (1635–1641), demonstrates the slightly retardataire elements inherent in his designs. The building was designed by Le Muet and probably built by Jean Thiriot. In this mansion (now a part of the Bibliothèque Nationale), the architect did not attempt to repress the mannerist features. The combination of a highly developed type of rustication and the architect's habitual use of quoins is balanced with low reliefs and a particularly complicated symmetricality which is at once seen as a maintenance of the existing mode and as a premonition of the ensuing style. Le Muet began adding more classical elements in the latter half of his career; however, a deliberate sense of personal involvement is continually noted in his handling of surface. In 1645, Anne of Austria founded the Val-de-Grâce monastery, and FRANÇOIS MANSART was commissioned to build the church and a convent. After slightly more than a year of work, he was dismissed and JACQUES LEMERCIER was assigned the task. The dome and upper order were finally completed by Le Muet in 1655 but he basically conserved the original design, thereby accepting the quasi-Palladian (see ANDREA PALLADIO) classicism.

Le Muet's growing reputation was ultimately given official sanction in 1664 when he and François Mansart were awarded governmental commissions with the rank of royal architect, each receiving a salary of 1,000 *livres.* Pierre Le Muet died in Paris, leaving the following generation with a body of theoretical material that united sixteenth-century planning with seventeenth-century elegance.

JEFFREY HUGHES

WORKS

Begun 1629, Notre-Dame-des-Victoires (completed by Gabriel Le Duc in 1663); 1635–1641, Hôtel Duret de Chevry-Tubeuf; Paris. 1643–1649, Tanlay Castle (rebuilt the central wing), France. 1649, Hôtel de L'Aigle; 1649, Hôtel d'Avaux; 1655, Val-de-Grâce; Paris.

BIBLIOGRAPHY

BENEVOLO, LEONARDO 1978 *The Architecture of the Renaissance.* Boulder, Colo.: Westview Press.
BLUNT, ANTHONY (1953)1970 *Art and Architecture in France 1500 to 1700.* 2d ed. Baltimore: Penguin.
NORBERG-SCHULZ, CHRISTIAN 1971 *Baroque Architecture.* New York: Abrams.

L'ENFANT, PIERRE CHARLES

Although Pierre Charles L'Enfant (1754–1825) is known primarily for his 1791 plan for Washington, the fame of the talented French emigré should not rest only on this influential design. Also, his activity in architecture may have had considerable influence on the development of the post-Georgian style in America.

Born in Paris on August 2, 1754, his father, Pierre L'Enfant, "Painter in Ordinary to the King," worked primarily at the Gobelin tapestry factory. During 1758–1766, however, Pierre L'Enfant painted two large battle scenes at Versailles; thus, at an early age his son became exposed to architecture, sculpture, landscape and garden design, town planning, as well as painting.

In 1771 Pierre Charles L'Enfant became a student at the Royal Academy of Painting and Sculpture, taking courses under his father. There is no indication, however, that L'Enfant ever formally studied either architecture or engineering.

The efforts in 1776 by American envoy Silas Deane in Paris to get aid for the struggling colonies appealed to many Frenchmen of adventuresome spirit; L'Enfant volunteered to serve in America. He sailed on Feburary 15, 1777, arriving in Portsmouth, New Hampshire two months later. We soon find him at Valley Forge, Pennsylvania, with the colonial forces, where he drew portraits of numerous officers, including General George Washington.

It has long been thought that L'Enfant was a regular officer in the French army; however, he was simply a volunteer; he was characterized in fact by General Philippe Du Coudray in 1777 as having no special qualifications, though he indeed had "some talent for drawing figures, . . . but nothing for use of an engineer" (Caemmerer, 1950, p. 41).

Fortunately, in January 1778 Baron Friedrich von Steuben arrived and L'Enfant became friendly with the general's French interpreter. Recognizing L'Enfant's artistic abilities and energetic desire to be of service, von Steuben promised him a captaincy, and set him to work. L'Enfant helped both with drilling troops and in Philadelphia that fall in preparing eight drawings for the training manual. In April 1779 L'Enfant was formally given the rank of captain by Congress, in the Corps of Engineers—probably because it was a noncombat division and the only logical place for an artist.

After the manual was completed, L'Enfant journeyed first to Charleston, then to Savannah, arriving in time to take part in the siege of that city. L'Enfant distinguished himself by his bravery and on October 9 even led an unsuccessful sortie to set the British abatis on fire. Wounded in battle and captured by the British, he was exchanged in January 1780 and seems to have gone to New York. A careful topographical view of West Point inscribed by General Henry Knox as having been done by L'Enfant in 1780 is preserved.

L'Enfant was in Philadelphia by February 1782. His first architectural work dates from July: the temporary pavilion designed at the behest of Washington for the celebration of the birth of the Dauphin. According to a contemporary account, the building was "sixty feet in front and forty feet deep, . . . supported by large painted pillars" and open on all sides (*ibid.,* pp. 87–88). The ceiling was decorated with appropriate symbolic motifs.

Whenever anything of an artistic nature was needed L'Enfant seems to have been thought most qualified. In mid-1783 he was called upon to design both the badge for the Order of the Cincinnati, and also the accompanying engraved certificate. Because L'Enfant was planning to visit Paris, he was asked to help set up the organization there and have the medals made. He did this and returned to Philadelphia in April 1784.

By 1786 L'Enfant had settled in New York City and soon began his most active period of architectural design. He was called upon to superintend the erection of the General Richard Montgomery monument at Saint Paul's Chapel in early 1787. L'Enfant also supplied additional embellishments of a symbolic nature—a rising sun with thirteen rays, an American eagle, and so on (*ibid.,* pp. 100–101). These features do not survive.

Unfortunately the rough stone back of the monument was visible through the window over the altar. To hide the monument L'Enfant designed a "glory" of clouds, connected by rays to

tablets above the altar. The device, drawn from eighteenth century French models, was highly praised. During this same period (1786–1787) he also embellished the interior of the church with garlands on the pulpit and clerk's desk.

L'Enfant's next documented work was the huge pavilion for the celebration held on July 23, 1788 in honor of the proposed federal constitution. The original drawing and plan for the pavilion survives, as does a contemporary drawing. Though too small to tell much about the design, at the center was a baldachin to shelter Washington and other dignitaries; symbolic figures and escutcheons were much in evidence, according to contemporary descriptions.

L'Enfant's most important architectural work in New York was remodeling the old City Hall. This venerable building (completed in 1704) was to be modernized and remodeled to become the first Congress Hall of the new nation. Work was begun in October 1788, and was not quite completed when Washington took the oath of office from its portico in April 1789. Although demolished in 1812, accurate contemporary prints of the building survive, two long descriptions of it were published in 1789, and recent research has reconstructed the plan.

The major changes on the outside were the opening up of the ground floor front as a pedestrian passage, and the filling in of the central three bays (between projecting wings) with a pediment above four Tuscan columns. Though the resulting design bears a strong resemblance to JOHN WEBB's Gunnersby of 1657 (shown in *Vitruvius Britannicus* [1715], vol. 1, plate 18), it is unlikely that L'Enfant turned to books for inspiration. The motifs are ones common enough in Parisian architecture of

L'Enfant. Federal Hall. New York. 1788–1789

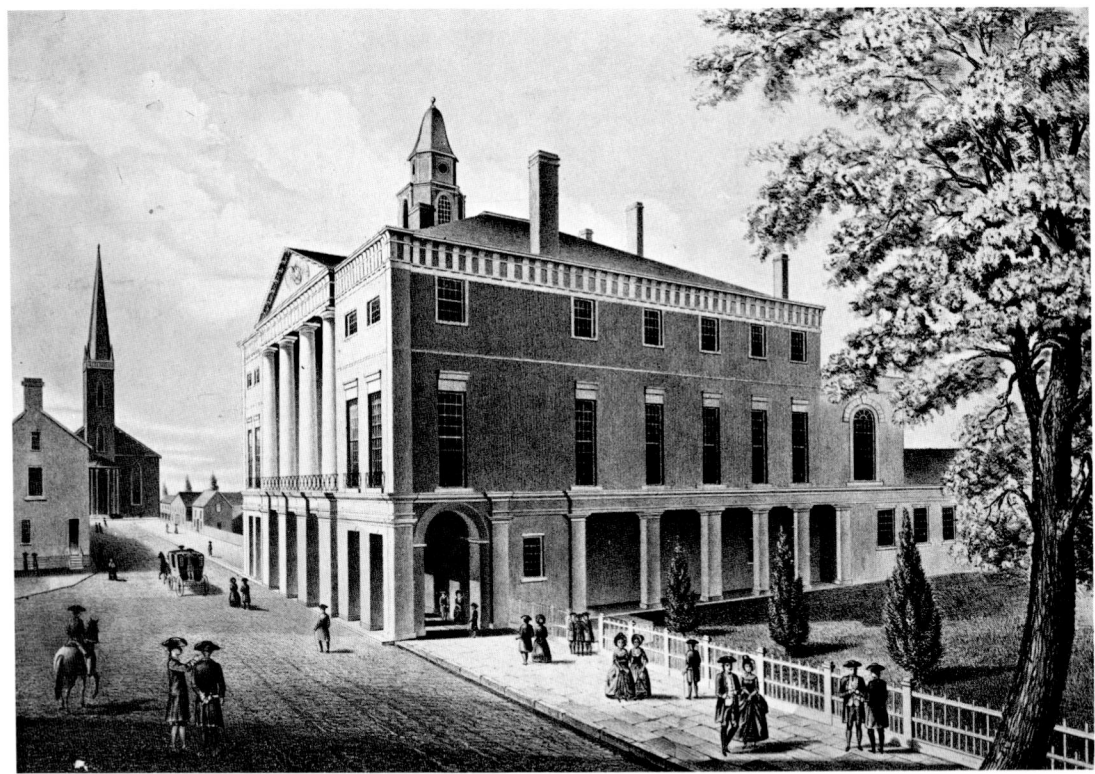

the seventeenth and eighteenth centuries. His pedimented portico, the wide entablature, and the corner piers gave the building a clarity of classical design, and a new over-all unity. His love of symbolic features was most evident in the detailing: stars were placed in the capital necking bands, and also in the thirteen metopes over the porch. Inside this sort of symbolic decoration was carried even further.

After the success of Federal Hall, L'Enfant seems to have been called upon to remodel many older mansions, and even build new ones, during the next several years. Unfortunately, none can be attributed to him with certainty. Although in the 1930s the New York architect William Hindley assigned more than a dozen buildings to L'Enfant on stylistic grounds (*ibid.,* pp. 103–107), Hindley's surviving notes make it clear that his attributions were based mainly on the presence of symbolic details in mantels and other features—the sort of detailing that in fact would have been the domain of the craftsmen—and thus cannot be accepted without further confirmation. Although L'Enfant himself claimed in 1800 that in 1791 he had "proposals already . . . placed under my immediate agency [for] the erecting of Houses to the amount of $1,000,000" (*ibid.,* p. 376) in and around New York, substantiation awaits further research. At present the New York City Landmarks Preservation Commission lists no buildings by or attributed to L'Enfant.

As early as 1789 L'Enfant wrote to George Washington to offer advice on the planning of the new capital. When property on the Potomac had been secured, Washington invited him to examine the site and provide suggestions. L'Enfant arrived on March 9, and submitted his first report three days later.

The planning of Washington, and the possible sources for L'Enfant's design, have been studied by scholars for more than sixty years. Several salient points should be brought out, however, regarding this distinctive and influential plan.

Even in his letter of 1789 L'Enfant emphasized that the plan should be both grand (appropriate to a vigorous new nation), and large in actual size (to accommodate later growth). After inspecting the site he recognized that two prominences, one north of Tiber Creek and the other to the east of it, were the best locations for the major public buildings. On these sites the President's House and the Capitol were later erected. His topographical study (revealed clearly in his "Map of Dotted Lines" of June 1791) showed that his process was to link these prominent spots with sight lines, and also project lines connecting these sites with other prominent features such as the existing main street of adjacent Georgetown, and existing roads leading out of the area. The whole site was given a horizontal and vertical grid which focused on the nodal points where sight lines intersected.

In this way, L'Enfant took full advantage of existing prominences, made his avenues run largely along contour lines, and still provided for the creation of convenient rectangular city blocks. Although he did request THOMAS JEFFERSON to send him a number of maps of European cities, he assured him that he did not plan to imitate them. Indeed, his design was unique, and beautifully adapted to both the site and the needs of the government, though obviously owing much to baroque planning in France, specifically Versailles.

L'Enfant was also to have designed public buildings for the new city. Though nothing came of this, the style might have been quite different from anything seen before in America—more like the monumental classicism of CLAUDE NICOLAS LEDOUX or BENJAMIN H. LATROBE than what was in fact built. A clue to this is provided by L'Enfant's criticism in 1800 of WILLIAM THORNTON's Capitol which instead of being "pretty" he felt should be of a "massy Sullen [and at] the same time grand aspect." He observed further that "the whole composition is of too Slander a Module . . . for having not sufficient masses nor boldness of profile" (*ibid.,* p. 402).

But because of L'Enfant's difficulty in working with the District Commissioners, and many other factors, he was dismissed on February 27, 1792, after which he returned to Philadelphia.

His next project soon followed, however; in July he was called by Alexander Hamilton to assist in the design and establishment of the water system and factories to be built by the Society for Establishing Useful Manufactures in Paterson, New Jersey. L'Enfant met with the directors in August 1792, submitted a plan for the hydraulic system to run the mills, and was appointed Superintendent of the Society August 20. His proposals included a stone aqueduct which turned out to be too costly. Because of many problems, he was dismissed in June; he took with him his plan for the canal system as well as that for the town, both now lost. Thus the present plan of Paterson is probably unrelated to L'Enfant's designs.

The second major documented building by L'Enfant was the mansion for Robert Morris in Philadelphia. Planned in 1793, and begun in 1794, work was halted in 1796 due to Morris's impending bankruptcy. The design was strongly French with a plastic articulation of the exterior wall planes, and a prominent mansard roof. The recessed entrance was apparently to be filled with a portico, probably unpedimented. The lavish use of cut marble, decorative carved panels over the tall French windows, and freestanding classical columns framing façade windows must have astonished local builders still working in the late Georgian vernacular of rectangular brick dwellings. Never lived in by Morris, the house was demolished about 1800.

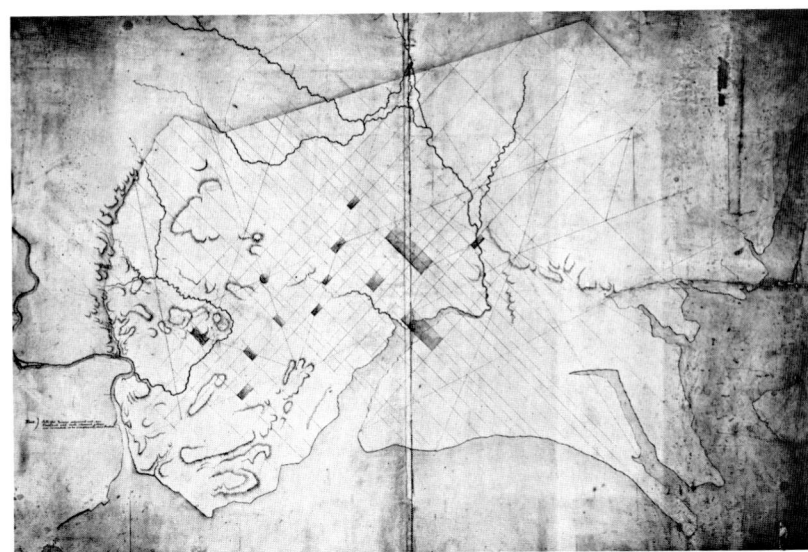

*L'Enfant.
Preparatory study for
Washington (map of
dotted lines).
1791*

L'Enfant was also called upon in 1794 to strengthen Fort Mifflin near Philadelphia, and in 1798 actually supervised some work there; the Commandant's House, a rectangular building of one and a half stories with surrounding pilasters supporting a wide entablature, has been attributed to him.

In 1800 after the death of George Washington, L'Enfant moved to Washington to press claims for proper compensation for his plan of the capital—having declined in 1792 as beneath his notice the offer of $2625 (500 guineas) and "a Lot in a good part of the City." (He had also declined, apparently for similar reasons, payment for the work on Federal Hall, which was to be ten acres at what is now Third Avenue and 68th Street.) For the next decade he lobbied in vain for compensation commensurate with his abilities and achievements.

The last years of his life were spent in reduced circumstances, though he was still highly enough regarded to be offered a professorship at West

*L'Enfant.
Robert Morris House.
Philadelphia.
1794–1796*

Point in 1812, which he declined. In September 1814 he was sent to reconstruct Fort Washington, just south of the city. He supervised work there that fall, and between March and July 1815, but he was then dismissed for not supplying a plan for the work as requested, and subsequent construction was carried on until 1824 by others.

Befriended by the Digges family, he lived with them from 1815 until his death June 14, 1825. Buried first at Green Hill, Maryland, it was only in 1909 that his remains were transferred to Arlington National Cemetery.

Although L'Enfant does not seem to have had a consistent architectural style, from his few documented works it is clear that he favored decorative symbolic and allegorical motifs within a clear classical framework. He also recognized that a building could be conceived as an integrated design with the parts subservient to the over-all form. Introducing European iconography and certain elegant French features undoubtedly provided new ideas for American architecture. Highly regarded by leading men of the day, L'Enfant's designs were undoubtedly studied with care.

Furthermore, in his Washington plan, the importance of an over-all concept for the placing of major buildings, and the integration of the plan to both the site and symbolic needs, raised American city planning to a new level of sophistication.

DANIEL D. REIFF

WORKS

*1782, Dauphin Celebration Pavilion, Philadelphia. 1787, Saint Paul's Chapel (reredos); *1788, Federal Constitution Parade Pavilion; *1788–1789, Federal Hall (remodeling); New York. 1791, Plan for Washington. *1794–1796, Robert Morris House, Philadelphia. (A)1798?, Commandant's House, Fort Mifflin, Pa.

BIBLIOGRAPHY

Many of the unpublished papers, articles, drawings, and sketches of William Hindley are in the collection of the Avery Architectural Library, Columbia University, New York.

CAEMMERER, H. PAUL (1950)1970 *The Life of Pierre Charles L'Enfant, Planner of the City Beautiful, The City of Washington.* Washington: National Republic.

FRIES, RUSSELL I. 1975 "European vs. American Engineering: Pierre Charles L'Enfant and the Water Power System of Paterson, N.J." *Northeast Historical Archaeology* 4:68–96.

KIMBALL, FISKE 1918 "The Origin of the Plan of Washington, D.C." *Architectural Review* New Series 7:41–45.

KITE, ELIZABETH S. (editor) 1929 *L'Enfant and Washington, 1791–1792.* Baltimore: Johns Hopkins University Press.

PADOVER, SAUL K. (editor) 1946 *Thomas Jefferson and the National Capital.* Washington: Government Printing Office.

PARTRIDGE, WILLIAM 1937 "L'Enfant's Vision: A Discussion of Development from a City on Paper to a City in Actuality." *Federal Architect* 7:103–104, 106–107.

PEETS, ELBERT 1927 "The Genealogy of L'Enfant's Washington." *Journal of the American Institute of Architects* 15:115–119, 151–154, 187–191.

PEETS, ELBERT 1932 "L'Enfant's Washington: Notes on a Redrafting of the Autograph Plan." *Architectural Record* 72:158–160.

REIFF, DANIEL D. (1971)1977 *Washington Architecture, 1791–1861: Problems in Development.* 2d ed. Washington. U.S. Commission of Fine Arts.

REPS, JOHN W. 1967 *Monumental Washington: The Planning and Development of the Capital Center.* N.J.: Princeton University Press.

SIMPSON, SARAH H. J. 1925 "The Federal Procession in the City of New York." *New York Historical Society Quarterly* 9:39–57.

SPREIREGEN, PAUL D. (editor) 1968 *On the Art of Designing Cities: Selected Essays of Elbert Peets.* Cambridge, Mass.: M.I.T. Press.

TATUM, GEORGE B. 1961 *Penn's Great Town: 250 Years of Philadelphia Architecture.* Philadelphia: University of Pennsylvania Press.

TORRES, LOUIS 1970 "Federal Hall Revisited." *Journal of the Society of Architectural Historians* 29:327–338.

LENNOX, E. J.

"He did more than any other single individual towards the development of the city," the *Mail*, a Toronto newspaper, said in its obituary of Edward James Lennox (1854–1933). This was no respectful hyperbole: in a prolific career that spanned forty-five years, Lennox had a prominent hand in molding Toronto's essential metropolitan image, which, despite various onslaughts, is clearly evident in the 1980s.

Lennox was not an innovator. He adhered to the fashions of the time—High Victorian, Romanesque Revival, and, later, Beaux-Arts classicism—but it was no slavish adherence. The Lennox hand is always evident—especially in the interplays of gables and arches and in the oppositions of scale and massing. His buildings are also notable for their rich ornament (especially in carved stone) and for their advanced technology (elevators, air conditioning).

Lennox's best work is a blend of English and American influences. His masterpiece, the combined city hall and courthouse (1886–1898), is just this: a marriage of Richardsonian (see H. H. RICHARDSON) Romanesque and the late nineteenth-century English fascination with ornament. The building unashamedly follows Richardson's Allegheny County Courthouse in Pittsburgh (1884–1887) in general plan, but in its polychromatic masonry and rich, free-flowing stone carving it is distinctly English.

DAVID COHEN

WORKS

1878–1879, Bond Street Congregational Church; 1886–1898, Municipal Buildings and Courthouse; 1887–1889, Broadway Tabernacle; 1911–1914, Casa Loma; 1915, Excelsior Life Building; Toronto.

LENOIR LE ROMAIN, SAMSON NICOLAS

Samson Nicolas Lenoir le Romain (1726–1810) studied with JACQUES FRANÇOIS BLONDEL in Paris in 1751 and visited Rome in 1753. Before returning to Paris in 1763 he worked briefly in the provinces. His commercial success in speculative building excluded him from the Academy, but it did not limit his commissions for markets, theaters, exotic pleasure pavilions, and elegant *hôtels* in the neoclassical style.

MYRA DICKMAN ORTH

WORKS

1763, Abbey of Saint Antoine des Champs; *1769, Vauxhall de la Foire Saint Germain; 1773, Hôtel Benoist Sainte Paule; *1773–1775, Halle aux Veaux; Paris. *1774, Vauxhall, Bordeaux, France. *1774–1775, Magasins de la Foire Saint Laurent; 1774, Hôtel de Chestret; *1776, Hôtel Rigoley de Juvigny; 1776, Immeubles Bimont; *1777, Apartment Buildings, rue de Lille; *1780, Apartment Building, rue Montmartre; *1780, Immeuble Choiseul-Gouffier; *1781, Apartments, rue Taitbout; *1781, Magasin des Menus-Plaisirs; *1781, Opéra de la Porte Saint Martin; *1783, Immeuble Giroux de Villette; *1783–1784, Immeuble comte de Tracy; c.1784, Hôtel de la Régie Générale (completed); *1785–1788, Vauxhall de la Rue Saint Thomas du Louvre; *1785, Apartments, rue Bleue; *1787, Bains Chinois; 1787, Eglise de Bagnolet; *1790, Théâtre de la Cité; Paris.

BIBLIOGRAPHY

BRAHAM, ALLAN 1980 *The Architecture of the French Enlightenment.* London: Thames & Hudson.
GALLET, MICHEL 1964 *Les Demeures parisiennes: L'Epoque Louis XVIᵉ.* Paris: Le Temps.
HAUTECOEUR, LOUIS 1952 *Seconde moitié du XVIIIᵉ siècle: Le style Louis XVI.* Volume 4 in *Histoire de l'architecture classique en France.* Paris: Picard.

LENORMAND, LOUIS

Born in Versailles, France, Louis Lenormand (1801–1862) studied under his uncle, JEAN JACQUES MARIE HUVÉ, and under Antoine Fran-

çois Peyre (see PEYRE FAMILY). He was architect of the Cours de Cassation, Paris, from 1838 to 1862; built the church at Le Pollet (1844–1849), near Dieppe; and designed the Pompeian interior of the Hôtel Millaud (1855–1857), Paris. He also restored many Paris *hôtels;* the Church of Saint-Jacques (1842), Dieppe; and the Château de Meillant (1857), Cher.

CHRISTOPHER RIOPELLE

WORKS

1838–1862, Cours de Cassation, Paris. 1842, Church of Saint Jacques (restoration), Dieppe, France. 1844–1849, Church, La Pollet, near Dieppe, France. 1851, Church, La Place, Seine-Inférieure, France. 1855–1857, Hôtel Millaud (interior design), Paris. 1857, Château de Meillant (restoration), Cher, France.

BIBLIOGRAPHY

BAUCHAL, CHARLES 1887 *Nouveau Dictionnaire Biographique et Critique des Architectes Français.* Paris: André, Daly.
DALY, CÉSAR 1861 "Obituary." *Revue Générale de l'Architecture.* 19:242–243.
DAVID DE PENANRUM, LOUIS THÉRÈSE (1895)1907 *Les Architectes Elèves de l'Ecole des Beaux Arts.* Edited by E. Delaire. Paris: Librairie de la Construction Moderne.
HAUTECOEUR, LOUIS 1956–1957 Volumes 6 and 7 in *Histoire de l'Architecture Classique en France.* Paris: Picard.

LE NOSTRE, ANDRE

André Le Nostre or Le Nôtre (1613–1700) was the unequaled master of landscape design in the period of Louis XIV. His grandly formal schemes left an indelible imprint on the face of France and most of seventeenth-century Europe. Le Nostre came easily to his métier as his grandfather, Pierre, was a gardener in the service of Catherine de' Medici. Pierre is mentioned in documents as early as 1572 when he is listed as in charge of six of the garden plots at the Palace of the Tuileries, and by 1583 he is designated *maître jardinier,* living in the Tuileries probably in a house within the actual garden. Jean Le Nostre, André's father, succeeded to Pierre's position at the Tuileries and, at the height of his career, served as *premier jardinier du Roi* under Louis XIII. Thus, the young André was at an early age immersed in garden procedure learned at the knee of his father. He also benefited from the practical wisdom of Claude Mollet, a member of yet another important family of French gardeners, who were working at the Tuileries. From the writings of Olivier de Serres (*Théâtre d'agriculture* [1600]), Le Nostre was able to learn in detail the principles of good agricultural practice, and in the treatise of JACQUES BOYCEAU (*Traité du jardinage selon les raisons de la nature et de l'art* [1638]), he read about the aesthetic principles that should govern the practice of landscape design as they were set forth in print for the first time.

Following Boyceau's counsel that a gardener should know architecture, drawing, painting, and geometry, André Le Nostre set about acquiring the broadest training available to him at the time. In the painting studio of Simon Vouet, he studied draftsmanship and learned the rules of harmonious proportion and color values—aspects of art which he would later apply to his garden practice. It was probably in Vouet's studio that the congenial Le Nostre first came to know as fellow students the painters Charles Lebrun, Eustache Le Sueur, and Pierre Mignard, as well as Adam Pérelle, the engraver. It is a generally acknowledged fact that Le Nostre also studied architecture. His grandiose landscape layouts, so dependent as they were on geometry in bringing architectural harmony to a building site, clearly reflect such training. Although a specific mentor remains unidentified, it seems likely that either JACQUES LEMERCIER, creator of the Château de Richelieu, or FRANÇOIS MANSART, architect of Maison Lafitte, significantly contributed to his education in architecture. André Le Nostre could early have come to Lemercier's attention when his father was working at Richelieu in 1629. That Le Nostre knew Mansart seems equally certain; when Mansart became the architect of Gaston d'Orléans, brother of Louis XIII, Le Nostre is described (by 1635) as *jardinier de M^r frère du roi.*

Le Nostre's broad training was surely supplemented by an intensive study of the treatises on proportions and optics that began to appear in France in the 1630s, especially those of Père Jean-François Niceron (*La perspective curieuse* [1638]) and Girard Desargues (*Manière universelle pour pratiquer la perspective* [1648]). The principles of optical illusion learned from these writings were soon to be applied to the realm of the garden.

Upon his retirement in 1637, Jean Le Nostre was granted permission by Louis XIII to pass along to his son his title of *premier jardinier du Roi au grand jardin des Tuileries*. As a result, Le Nostre found himself working simultaneously for both the king and his brother, Gaston d'Orléans. In 1640, he married Françoise Langlois, daughter of a member of the lesser nobility, and their marriage seems to have been a long and happy one.

By 1643, in his capacity as *dessinateur des plants et parterres de tous les jardins de S. Maj.,* Le Nostre was busy designing new parterre arrangements as well as modifying older ones. For Gaston d'Orléans,

he undoubtedly carried out certain revisions in the parterres designed earlier by Jacques Boyceau in the gardens of the Palace of the Luxembourg. For the duke's daughter, the Grande Mademoiselle, he probably designed the enormous Parterre de Mademoiselle which graced the courtyard of the Palace of the Tuileries. By 1657, Le Nostre's career was further advanced when he assumed the title of *contrôleur général des bâtiments, jardins, tapisseries, et manufactures de France.* His star was clearly on the ascendance when his services were engaged by Nicolas Fouquet, finance minister to the young Louis XIV, to design the gardens of Vaux-le-Vicomte (1656–1661). It is clear that the landscape gardener was not the relative unknown so often described as Fouquet's "discovery." It was, however, at Vaux, most specifically, that Le Nostre was to have the opportunity to create his first acknowledged masterpiece.

The garden and building complex at Vaux provided the young Louis XIV with a format for regal living which he would soon apply to his future pleasure domes. Having finished his work at Vaux, Le Nostre immediately became engaged in redesigning the king's old-fashioned gardens at Fontainebleau (1662–1687); it was while there that his presence in England was requested by Charles II. Although Le Nostre designed at least one garden for the English monarch, namely that at Greenwich (1662), it is doubtful that he ever actually crossed the Channel as he was far too involved on French soil. In 1662, plans were already underway for the modification and expansion of the gardens at Versailles, a project which would occupy the larger part of his long career. The following year saw the initial alterations and additions to the old royal gardens of Saint-Germain-en-Laye and the Tuileries, as well as the commencement of work for the Grand Conde at Chantilly.

The ever increasing demands made upon the landscape gardener necessitated the recruitment of numerous assistants. A workshop system evolved whereby Le Nostre would rapidly commit his initial thoughts to paper and then turn them over to assistants for detailing, clarification, and general refining. Always alert to the possibility of improving a desired visual effect, the gardener constantly made adjustments and readjustments in his own plans and in those of others under his supervision until the last possible moment that a change could be effected. In many cases, he entrusted the actual implementation of his schemes to a clerk of the works drawn from a circle of eager gardeners, the most reliable of whom were certain of his relations. Le Nostre remained, however, the vigilant supervisor of these projects until their completion.

In addition to his title as the king's gardener,

Le Nostre in 1666 was named *conseiller du Roi aux conseils et contrôleur général des bâtiments de Sa Majesté*. This honor brought with it additional duties as it required constant and careful inspection of all newly constructed public buildings. The very fact that Le Nostre was assigned to such a post serves as yet another indication of his firm grasp of architectural matters. On occasion, the gardener may have actually turned architect. He is usually given credit for the designs of the elaborate architectural motifs in the *bosquet* of the Arc de Triomphe at Versailles as well as of the staircases in the Tuileries gardens, and his name is closely associated with the design for a house for M. de Lauzun at Saint-Germain-en-Laye. Listed as a member of the Academy of Architecture as early as 1681, Le Nostre's opinions concerning architecture were constantly sought by the king as well as by practitioners outside the country, including the great Swedish architect Nicodemus Tessin the Younger (see TESSIN FAMILY), his friend and pupil; in 1698 Tessin wrote to the gardener requesting a frank appraisal of his design for the royal palace at Copenhagen.

Ever alert to the importance of introducing new ingredients into his designs, Le Nostre requested and received permission from Louis XIV to visit Italy in 1679. He was charged by Jean-Baptiste Colbert to evaluate the program of the French Academy while in Rome and to relay to the king his judgment of GIOVANNI LORENZO BERNINI's equestrian statue of Louis XIV then in progress. Armed with letters to the duc d'Estrées, the French ambassador, and to Charles Errard, director of the French Academy in Rome, Le Nostre gained easy access to all the villas in and around the city. Because of his discerning eye, he was soon able to write Colbert that he had discovered many novelties which upon his return could be used to advantage in the king's gardens.

The fame of André Le Nostre lies largely in those masterpieces executed for Louis XIV and members of the royal family. In addition to the sites already mentioned, the gardener was actively engaged in the landscaping of Clagny (1674–1676), the Trianons (1670–1687), Maintenon (1675–1678), the Palais Royal (1674), and Saint-Cloud (1665–1678). So desirable was a garden by Le Nostre that every wealthy nobleman and ranking member of the clergy clamored for a plan by his hand. His ongoing commitments and the high costs of realizing his schemes necessarily limited the number of gardens executed by the master. Hence, the myriad gardens ascribed to Le Nostre without positive proof of his actual involvement for the most part turn out to be either products of his workshop or undertakings for which he drew little more than a parterre design.

Even after his official retirement in 1693, Le Nostre continued to advise the king and to draw up plans for eager clients. That very year he was hard at work on the gardens of the Château de Pontchartrain. And as late as 1698, he was found designing a garden for Windsor for the English monarch William III, a work whose execution was entrusted ultimately to Claude Desgots, the gardener's nephew.

Active and alert to the end, André Le Nostre died on September 15, 1700, in his eighty-eighth year. His body was transported with solemn dignity from his house in the Tuileries gardens to Saint-Germain-l'Auxerrois. There he lay in state until the following morning when in the chapel of Saint-André at Saint-Roch, the funeral service and interment took place. The *Mercure de France* noted his passing simply but with considerable feeling: "The King has just lost a man rare and zealous in his service: a man who, very singular in his art, did him great honor" (September 1700, p. 278). Le Nostre enjoyed the love and respect of all who knew him, including the usually vitriolic duc de Saint Simon who wrote at the time of his death that "Le Nostre had an integrity, a correctness, and an uprightness which made him esteemed by all. Never did he overstep his position nor forget himself; he was always completely unselfish . . . he had a charming naiveté and directness" (1885, vol 8, p. 191).

Generous to family and friends, Le Nostre's largess extended to the king himself to whom in 1693 he gave a large portion of his art collection which included sculptures as well as paintings by Nicolas Poussin, Claude Lorrain, Domenico Zampieri (Domenichino), "Velvet" Bruegel, Paul Bril, and others. His collection was so significant and noteworthy that connoisseurs both at home and abroad found their way to his Tuileries residence to view it. The size and quality of the collection attests to both Le Nostre's capacity for sound aesthetic judgment and to his financial success — success which apparently never diluted his pleasant humility.

Le Nostre's directness, vivacity, and generally uninhibited manner appealed to Louis XIV and led to an intimacy between the king and his gardener rare in the monarch's otherwise aloof relationships. Visible signs of royal favor were evidenced in the award to the gardener of the Order of Saint-Lazare in 1679. And later, in 1692, when that Order was rescinded, the king hastened to confer upon Le Nostre the Order of Saint-Michel, an even greater mark of distinction. Assured a generous pension at the time of his retirement, the landscape architect continued to enjoy the king's

Le Nostre.
Château de Vaux-le-
Vicomte (landscaping).
France.
1656–1661

Le Nostre.
Château de Vaux-le-
Vicomte (landscaping).
France.
1656–1661

generosity. Shortly before his death, he could be found riding in a sedan chair alongside his monarch while making a tour of the gardens of Marly. Such was an honor rarely accorded any male member of the court, much less one of Le Nostre's station.

The full scope of André Le Nostre's garden theory and practice was first revealed at Vaux-le-Vicomte. Unencumbered by either existing building or garden complex, Le Nostre and LOUIS LE VAU created an entirely new ensemble. With little consideration for the natural contours of the terrain, the gardener imposed a rigidly formal design upon the site. Borrowing from earlier garden practitioners, he laid out his scheme along a single dominant axis which perfectly bisected the château. From this spine extended transverse and diagonal axes which served to further compartmentalize the landscape. In turn, these larger areas were divided by lesser paths and garden plots. This geometricizing of the terrain thus imposed a sense of strict order on the site.

Le Nostre was ever mindful that the principal function of a garden was to serve as handmaiden to the architecture, setting the building off to best advantage regardless of the direction from which it was viewed. For this reason, he laid bare the château at Vaux-le-Vicomte by placing the trees and shrubs at a distance. He manipulated all the multifarious components of the garden in such a way that they always related to the structure itself, though perhaps not always in the same way. These subtle interrelationships demanded, of course, the most careful collaboration between the architect and the landscape gardener.

The vista from the salon at Vaux or from the terrace immediately before it revealed a vast garden enclosed along its sides by thickly planted trees and shrubs. The principal axis extended outward seemingly to culminate in a gilded statue of Hercules raised upon the top of a distant slope. From this view, the proportions of the garden—the relationship of length to width, for example—and the sizes and slopes of all its components—flower beds, paths, pools, fountains, and sculptures—consorted one with the other to produce a perfectly balanced composition in which there was not a single discordant note. The garden at Vaux thus viewed impressed the rational French mind of the seventeenth century by its very rigid order. It was a landscape controlled by man, a landscape so lacking in ambiguities that the viewer immediately felt in complete intellectual control. Yet, at the same time, the Frenchman of the period, confident in his rationality, enjoyed having his sensibilities quickened, and this Le Nostre was able to accomplish for him in a singularly artful way.

At Vaux-le-Vicomte, endless surprises awaited the visitor to the gardens, surprises which revealed themselves only as the spectator actually walked through the landscape and experienced the space both physically and mentally. The gardens that had appeared relatively flat when viewed from the château, proved, on closer inspection, to be on many levels connected to one another by flights of steps hidden from view of the buildings. These levels concealed walks, flower beds, pools, cascades, sculptures, and other garden embellishments. In addition, the size and shape of pools, beds, and sculptures, when seen from afar, were often found to be very different when viewed closely. These carefully calculated surprises provided great diversity in the midst of apparent congruity and served to draw the visitor to the farthest reaches of the garden, in this case to the figure of Hercules. Only from this vantage point did the raison d'être for Le Nostre's over-all design become apparent. From the Hercules, all the components making up the design came together to provide a perfect frame for the château in the distance.

Along the central axis leading from the statue back toward the building, the garden elements continued to relate purposefully to the body of the château although their relationship to each other changed; a whole series of different visual impressions was thereby provided for the promenader by the skillful designer.

The magnitude and splendor of both the structure and the garden at Vaux-le-Vicomte were soon to be emulated in the great building program at Versailles. For this endeavor, Louis XIV in 1661 enlisted the services once again of Louis Le Vau and André Le Nostre. Initially, the king's aspirations for Versailles were relatively modest, entailing mainly the refurbishing of Louis XIII's old hunting lodge. Le Vau modified the existing building by adding lavish decoration and created new outlying structures along the avenue of approach as well as an orangery, carefully oriented to the south flank of the château. At the same time that these structural revisions were going on, Le Nostre was busy enriching the already existing gardens designed earlier in the century through the collaborative effort of Jacques Boyceau and his nephew, Jacques de Menours. He does not seem to have made any major changes in the essentially axial predisposition of the garden which centered upon the château nor does he appear to have altered the proportions of the existing paths and garden plots, the dimensions of which were calculated to harmonize with the château as built by Louis XIII.

Unlike Vaux-le-Vicomte, which was conceived and executed over a very short period of time, the construction at Versailles extended over more than thirty years, during which time both building and garden were in a constant state of evolution. No sooner was the complex readied in 1664 for the first great fête than the scale of the gardens underwent a significant change which involved the enlargement of the areas along the central axis and those to the north of the château. Such modifications in the grounds immediately surrounding the building not only diminished the subtle balance of proportions that existed between house and garden but also suggested that a château of vastly larger scale was already being contemplated by the architect. In a sense, the grander scale of Le Nostre's design forced the hand of the architect, Le Vau; here it was not a case of the landscape gardener adjusting his proportions to those of a building as at Vaux-le-Vicomte, but rather of the architect being obliged to accommodate his projected architectural additions to the already enlarged scale of the gardens. With the 1665–1670 construction of his famous "envelope" which encased three sides of the Louis XIII structure, Le Vau's design

Le Nostre.
Château de Versailles
(landscaping).
France.
1661–1687

Le Nostre.
Château de Versailles
(Apollo Basin).
France.
1661–1687

partially restored a sense of equilibrium between the château and its surroundings.

The subsequent history of Versailles reflects a continuous interaction between architect and landscape gardener. When the château underwent further enlargements under JULES HARDOUIN MANSART, its proportions continued to be determined in part by the already existing gardens. In like manner, when the scale of Mansart's additions finally exceeded the scale of the gardens, Le Nostre hastened to modify his arrangements so that they harmonized with the new building. Always of paramount importance in the mind of both architect and gardener was the quest for perfect visual bal-

Le Nostre.
Château de Versailles
(landscaping).
France.
1661–1687

Le Nostre.
Château de Versailles
(Grand Canal).
France.
1661–1687

ance and unity between the structure and its vast surroundings.

Except for its sheer magnitude, the mature plan of Versailles differed little from that of Vaux-le-Vicomte; a similar divisioning of the space by transverse and diagonal axes and a strong central axis can be found in the skeletal designs for both gardens. The concept of *forcer la nature* dominated the entire scheme for Versailles. Le Nostre's interest in optical illusion governed the treatment of every axis and was manifest in the invention of myriad surprises which awaited the visitor bold enough to walk the length of his gardens. These illusions were carefully staged so as to produce what seemed to be an endless variety of optical changes depending upon the direction from which a given axis was viewed. The very extent of these broadly proportioned avenues had the power to exhaust the most intrepid walker. To avoid this possibility, Le Nostre provided cloistered retreats carved out of thickly planted squares within the garden. Here were found open air chambers of intimate scale, decorated with an infinite variety of

pools, fountains, sculptures, pavilions, and dense greenery, all calculated to titillate the sensibilities of the beholder.

In the majority of his work, Le Nostre devoted himself to the revamping and enlargement of older garden schemes such as that at Fontainebleau, the hunting lodge-château that had been a favorite retreat of French kings from the time of Francis I. The building and gardens had been enlarged by succeeding monarchs and particularly by Henry IV between 1602–1609 when Jacques Mollet was among those called to work on the garden project. In all the modifications of structure and gardens, little thought seems to have been given to establishing a sense of visual cohesion between the two, due perhaps to the irregularities in the plans for both the architectural complex and the attendant gardens.

Although Le Nostre may be placed at Fontainebleau as early as 1645 when he was at work modifying the Jardin de la Reine, it was not until the fall of 1661 that he seriously addressed the problem of bringing some semblance of unity between the garden and château. This he accomplished in a singularly successful way by creating the Grand Jardin du Roi with its hugely scaled fountain and parterre design. Although the site was fairly irregular in its boundaries, the gardener was able to convey a sense of visual balance by means of subtle optical adjustments. He oriented this garden on two axes, one focusing on one of the principal wings of the château from whose upper windows it would be principally viewed, the other perpendicular to it extending outward to the Grand Canal constructed earlier in the period of Henry IV. The latter axis was reinforced by the creation of the cascades which provided the visual link between the level of the Grand Jardin and that of the canal below. By using a grand scale, Le Nostre eradicated the somewhat finicky character of the earlier arrangements in this part of the gardens. In its sheer size—310 meters by 395 meters—the Grand Jardin du Roi was unique in France at the time. Overwhelmed by the opulence of Vaux-le-Vicomte, Louis XIV was undoubtedly seeking the same kind of majestic grandeur for his gardens at Fontainebleau.

Among the châteaux particularly favored by Louis XIV were those at Saint-Germain-en-Laye. Their landscaping occupied Le Nostre's attention as early as 1663. The Château-Vieux and Château-Neuf were, like Fontainebleau, products of an earlier age. The former dated from the reign of Francis I while the latter was begun around 1556 under Henry II. The Château-Neuf was not completed nor did it receive its terraced gardens extending down to the Seine until the period of

Henry IV. These gardens, constructed between 1597–1605, were the most Italianate in France and reflected the kind of thinking that produced the Villa Lante at Bagnaia and the Villa d'Este at Tivoli. In the layouts of the building complexes at Saint-Germain-en-Laye, there was no thought of over-all unity and hence the later building was conceived as being totally independent of its neighbor.

Le Nostre's first efforts at the site appear to have involved the rebuilding of the earlier terrace gardens several levels of which had collapsed as a result of years of neglect. He simplified the earlier design, thereby lending a new and monumental scale to the garden. As Louis XIV preferred the Château-Vieux which he chose as his actual residence when at Saint-Germain, he charged Le Nostre to redesign the area alongside it. The landscape architect brought focus to bear on the north wing of the building by drawing an axis from its center and extending it outward and into infinity. Along this line, he provided countless enlivening agents in the form of embroidered parterres, pools, and fountains. With judicious planting of trees and shrubs along the axis, Le Nostre was able to conceal the existing irregularities present in the structure and to provide a perfect frame for the building. Again, as at Vaux-le-Vicomte, a number of enticing surprises in the form of concealed levels, unexpected water bodies, etcetera, awaited the visitor, making a tour of this part of the garden an exciting experience.

In 1669, Le Nostre began work on his most imposing undertaking at Saint-Germain-en-Laye, the Grande Terrasse, a vast esplanade 30 meters wide and 2400 meters long which hugged the slope some 62 meters above the Seine. Realizing that an uninterrupted expanse over two kilometers long would discourage any visitor from contemplating a walk down its extent, Le Nostre resorted to optical illusion to conceal its true dimensions. Using a subtle downward slope for the first one-third of the terrace while rendering the last two-thirds absolutely flat, he managed by means of foreshortening to minimize its awesome length. Within the vast limits of this terrace, so many remarkable and diverse visual experiences awaited the visitor that his interest never flagged.

Although Louis XIV never appears to have been particularly fond of Paris, he did undertake to renovate and enlarge the palace and garden of the Tuileries as early as 1664. André Le Nostre, who was brought up in this garden and involved in its maintenance from an early date, must have joined Le Vau in this new venture with special enthusiasm. The palace, the work of PHILIBERT DELORME, was begun by Catherine de' Medici in 1562 but

Le Nostre.
Château de
Fontainebleau
(landscaping).
France.
1662–1687

never finished. The garden was enclosed from the very beginning by a high wall and separated from the palace proper by a busy thoroughfare. Laid out along an axis that bisected the building, the garden was divided into regularized plots which formed a rigid grid. Though these areas were variously decorated, the landscape complex as a whole did not lend itself readily to exciting diversity.

As at Vaux-le-Vicomte, Le Vau and Le Nostre worked in close harmony. The modification of the de L'Orme structure, notably the enlarged scale of the central pavilion with its square dome and the addition of another story to the ranges at its sides, was calculated to increase the scale of the overall design. This new monumentality in the architecture was reinforced by the significant increase in the proportions of the garden by the widening of *allées* and the elimination of small-scale arrangements. With the suppression of the street which had hitherto separated the palace from the garden, Le Nostre was able to erect in front of the building a huge raised terrace planted with elaborate embroidered parterres. From this vantage point as well as from the windows of the palace, the long rectangular garden would have appeared square as a result of optical foreshortening and the pools along the central axis would have seemed to be of identical size and shape, although, in fact, those in the distance were far larger than those closer to the palace. His comprehensive knowledge of optics, therefore, enabled Le Nostre to create a sense of perfect visual equilibrium in this garden, in spite of the considerable disparity existing within the site itself; from the terrace only the garden architect knew that the garden sloped some $1\frac{1}{2}$ meters from north to south. Knowledge of such discrepancies and the ultimate discovery of the real di-

Le Nostre.
Château de Chantilly
*   (landscaping).*
France.
1663–1688

mensions and shapes of the garden's components again required physical participation in the space on the part of the visitor.

Le Nostre's best known modification of the Tuileries garden was the elongation of the central axis. Tearing down the wall that had served as the western terminus to the older garden, he opened up the vista into the distance in an unerringly straight avenue which was to become the Champs-Elysées. Not only was this extended axis designed to harmonize with the established proportions of the Tuileries garden and thus to provide a satisfying visual impression when viewed from the palace, but also, equally important, it was so conceived that it focused perfectly upon the palace when the over-all scheme was seen from afar.

Le Nostre's favorite garden, by his own admission, was that of the Château de Chantilly belonging to the king's cousin, the Grand Condé. Begun in 1663, it demanded the gardener's attention until 1688 or later. With his reliable brother-in-law, Pierre Desgots, in charge of implementing his designs, Le Nostre made many visits to the site refining the optical subtleties which were so integral to his carefully calculated design. The Château de Chantilly had been built between 1528–1534 by Anne de Montmorency, the famous Constable of France. Between 1600–1614, additions were undertaken by his son Henry at which time a large terrace was erected along one side of the architectural complex. In neither period of construction was any serious attempt made to establish visual unity between the château and its surroundings. The resultant arrangement, therefore, was highly irregular, making it impossible for Le Nostre to follow his usual method of orienting his principal axis

upon the central façade of the château. Instead, he elected to focus his avenue of approach on the equestrian figure of the Constable of France placed in the middle of the Grande Terrasse. In his scheme, the statute of Anne de Montmorency was visible from as far as the eye could see when one was approaching the château along the central axis and, once seen, it was never lost from view thanks to a series of optical tricks which the landscape gardener brought into play. Awaiting the visitor along this approach were many garden components which were actually concealed, elements which afforded a succession of unexpected visual impressions and exciting surprises, not the least of which was the presence of a majestic staircase leading down to an immense parterre surrounded by a grandly proportioned body of water; these features came into view only when one reached the level of the Grande Terrasse.

The Grand Canal was perhaps one of the greatest wonders of the garden at Chantilly. The result of rigid channeling of the river La Nonette, the canal was 80 meters wide and extended 1800 meters in a straight line across the landscape. The waterway was preceded by a large circular pool which, because of its emplacement at a higher level, spilled forth its abundant waters into the canal by means of a tiered cascade. Here once again, the element of surprise played a vital role in luring the visitor to this sector of the garden. In the eyes of the beholder, the large pool became a perplexing visual phenomenon; encircling it with a broad path, rows of trees, and thickly planted bushes, Le Nostre cleverly concealed the water source for the pool by using subterranean conduits. The pool appeared to spring up on the landscape as by a miracle.

Unlike Louis XIV, the Grand Condé did not have unlimited funds and hence was compelled to build his garden in stages. Once the principal lines of his scheme were realized, Le Nostre turned to the creation of *bosquets*. Of considerable number and variety, they were notable for the richness of their water effects made possible by the unusual abundance of water on the site.

Le Nostre was also actively engaged in the creation of the gardens of Saint-Cloud (1665–1678). As in a number of his other projects, the gardener initially had to accommodate his design to an already existing structure, parts of which dated back to the late fifteenth and other parts to the early seventeenth centuries. More challenging still was the very nature of the site itself. Markedly uneven, the terrain was cursed with deep, unexpected depressions and steeply sloping hills which rose close to the margins of the Seine. At first, Le Nostre must have been perplexed as to how to go about bringing a sense of order to such a vexatious emplacement. His imaginative solutions to the problem—the result of careful axial planning and often ingenius use of optical illusion—turned the very irregularities of the terrain into assets, and ultimately, Saint-Cloud, in the very diversity of its levels, the beauty of its perspectives, and the fascinating complexities of its harmonies, emerged as one of Le Nostre's most provocative works.

From the early days of his career, the landscape gardener could be found creating small gardens for the townhouses belonging to wealthy Parisians. If the dwelling was built on a regularized plot, such as that belonging to Monsieur de Saint-Poange, a design for the accompanying garden presented little difficulty. Highly formal in nature, the garden would generally be rectangular in shape, laid out on an axis which bisected the dwelling. Usually enclosed by high walls to insure privacy, the wall marking the end of the axis was often screened by thickly planted trees and by elaborate trelliswork forming intricate architectural shapes. The garden itself would be decorated with an elaborate parterre and usually a fountain as well as shrubs planted in earthenware pots or wooden boxes. The over-all impression was one of balance and harmony, evidenced in the scale of the garden and in its components. Some of the larger city residences, such as the Hôtel de Conde (1666), were built on odd-shaped lots, and to these Le Nostre sought to bring a sense of regularity, balance, and over-all order. In the Condé garden, he resorted to the use of elaborate free-standing latticework pavilions which he placed on different levels in such a way as to disguise the actual irregularities existing on the site. In addition, he set up a visual interplay between these pavilions and the intervening spaces separating them from one another. As a result, the visitor was drawn forward into the garden, eager to discover the fascinating surprises which lay ahead.

When in 1670, Jean-Baptiste Colbert, minister of finance to Louis XIV, purchased the barony of Sceaux as a country residence, he retained the old existing château and charged Le Nostre with its landscaping (1673–1677). As was his custom, the gardener was able to orient his avenue of approach on an axis which sliced through the middle of the château to project beyond in a terraced parterre and pool. The avenue of approach was marked by a pronounced slope leading up to a broad, deep area which preceded the building complex. The château, therefore, was completely hidden from view from the bottom of the incline. Only slowly and at distinct stages did it come into view: first, just the chimneys and roofs, then the third story of the central structure, followed in turn by the second story, until finally the whole architectural ensemble was at last revealed. This game of gradually unmasking forms in space is one which Le Nostre played with particular skill in the garden of Sceaux.

Le Nostre's involvement at Sceaux, which began soon after the acquisition of the property by Colbert, continued late into the century when, following the death of the finance minister, the château passed to his son, the Marquis de Seignelay. It was under the aegis of these two owners that Le Nostre created the most remarkable features at Sceaux, the Octagon and the Grand Canal. In both cases, these two large water bodies were born of his desire to gather together the profusion of spring waters which had rendered the site extremely marshy. Both the Octagon and the Grand Canal were located in areas south of the château and because of a pronounced difference in level, they were completely concealed from the building. Le Nostre employed them as terminal motifs for the major cross-axes in the garden. By means of subtle optical adjustments their presence was revealed only by degrees and in diverse ways, assuring the visitor to the garden maximum astonishment and wonder. In the case of the Grand Canal, Le Nostre so designed the paths in front of the garden façade that the visitor was obliged to follow a specific route which led him in a carefully calculated way to a vantage point from which the canal suddenly appeared in all its grandeur. As in so many of the landscape gardener's designs, the major axes revealed new and unexpected visual impressions depending upon the end from which they were viewed.

Between 1679–1680, Le Nostre was actively engaged in modifying and expanding the gardens of the Château de Meudon which belonged to François-Michel Le Tellier, marquis de Louvois. Not far removed from the Château de Saint-Cloud, the site afforded a commanding view of the Seine and the distant spires of Paris. The château, dating from the period of Francis I and even earlier, had been substantially modified over the years. The most significant changes occurred in 1654 when the property was acquired by Abel Servien who held the post of *surintendant des finances* which he shared jointly with Nicolas Fouquet. The Meudon of this period is of special interest, for in addition to Louis Le Vau who was responsible for the revisions in the structure itself, Le Nostre was probably involved in the new landscaping plans. Servien's Meudon then could well have marked the beginning of a collaborative effort between the architect and gardener who were shortly thereafter to pool their talents even more closely at Vaux-le-Vicomte. The creation of the enormous terrace which provided the château with

Le Nostre.
Grand Trianon
    (landscaping).
Versailles, France.
1670–1687

its very straight avenue of approach dates from this period. This axis extended from the garden façade, plunging downward some 58 meters to a valley floor before ascending a high hill opposite to terminate finally in open sky. No sooner had two water basins been executed along this central axis—the future Grand Carré and Hexagone—than work came to a halt as a result of Servien's sudden death in 1659.

Only with the purchase of Meudon by Louvois twenty years later was work on the garden and château resumed. Always taking Le Vau's earlier building modifications into account, Le Nostre laid out the garden along the already projected axis in such a way that there was a constantly changing interplay between the components of the garden and the building. In like manner, he manipulated sizes and shapes of pools and paths as well as varying degrees of slope in order to provide an astonishing variety of optical illusion in the midst of over-all visual harmony.

Unfortunately, the Meudon of Louvois's time no longer survives. The château was torn down in the eighteenth century after another building was erected on an adjoining site. This structure, in turn, was partially destroyed in 1871 and the gardens fell into decay. Today, though the Hexagone still exists, it is surrounded by a high fence. The central axis itself is virtually obliterated by the emplacement of factory buildings and by roads which extend across it. Only from the top of the slope opposite the site of the old château are the grand lines of Le Nostre's scheme still visible.

In 1670, simultaneous with the building by Louis Le Vau of his famous "envelope" for the château at Versailles, there began in the northwest reaches of the park the so-called Trianon de Porcelaine. The new project also coincided with the excavation of the transverse arm of the Grand Canal, whose northern extremity would terminate at Trianon. With the building of this new complex, a pleasant balance was achieved between the Ménagerie at the south end of the transverse arm of the Grand Canal and these new architectural arrangements at the other.

The Trianon de Porcelaine which sprang up virtually overnight, having been begun in the spring and finished in October, was conceived as an intimate retreat where the king and a few favorites might enjoy the intimacy which its smaller scale invited. An exquisite little structure arose on the site, its beauty enhanced by blue glazed faience in the form of vases and architectural decorations.

Although the garden was small in contrast to that of the neighboring château, it was no less formal. Le Nostre employed his usual strict axial orientation, thereby providing an avenue of approach. On the garden side he created his customary embroidered parterre and added an open air orangery. Only beyond these areas did he permit the planting of high trees or shrubs. The axis continued down a relatively narrow path to terminate in a closed perspective very different from the limitless one suggested by the principal axis of the château as prolonged by the Grand Canal. Le Nostre skillfully provided a dual orientation for Trianon—one axis formed by the avenue of approach, the other by the cross arm of the Grand Canal. Although these two axes were not at exact right angles to one another, by means of judicious planting, the gardener obscured this discrepancy, assuring a sense of perfect visual balance and order. The wooded areas to left and right of the central axis were thickly planted with trees and shrubs out of which secluded *bosquets* were carved. At nearly every turn there was a feeling of enclosure designed to reinforce the sense of intimacy and charm which was the essence of this garden.

By 1687, the Trianon de Porcelaine appears to have been outmoded and gave way to the Grand Trianon of Jules Hardouin Mansart. Though the building was new, the garden remained the same in its basic disposition. The most interesting additions lay in the landscaping embellishments for the asymmetrical wing which projected westward before turning north to form the so-called Trianon-sous-bois. For this long single-storied range, Le Nostre conceived a variety of vantage points, orienting every room on some specific feature in the garden always found in a small outdoor chamber. The proportions as well as the shapes of these chambers often echoed the shapes and proportions of the rooms from which they were viewed. Each of these garden features was designed to be seen singly, thereby assuring the highly desirable intimacy of scale which was Le Nostre's particular goal in laying out the Grand Trianon landscape.

The Trianon de Porcelaine and its successor, the Grand Trianon, were renowned for the abundance of flowers whose varieties were chosen not so much for their beauty as for their scent. The assault on the senses of both sight and smell made the garden of the Trianons one of the most popular of the age.

Le Nostre's work at the Château de Pontchartrain which began in 1693 attests to the octogenarian's continuing energy and mental acumen. Here, the diversity of levels and degrees of slope along the central axis which so characteristically bisected the architectural complex of Jules Hardouin Mansart afforded the landscape designer the opportunity to create startling optical effects. As in many of Le Nostre's designs, the true size and shape of the garden could be grasped only by actually walking through the space and experiencing what was happening therein. At Pontchartrain, with the château itself ever the focal point, the interaction and constantly changing relationships between near and far objects in the landscape reached an exciting intricacy. The Pontchartrain complex serves as a fitting climax to the long career of Le Nostre.

There is no question that André Le Nostre's influence was broadly felt. A number of crowned heads and noble families of Europe enjoyed his counsel, and his pupils were soon at work in countries as widespread as Portugal, England, Sweden, Germany, and Russia. Indeed, the face of Europe was for a time transformed by those who hastened to imitate the glories and grandeur of the seventeenth-century French landscape.

F. HAMILTON HAZLEHURST

WORKS

1654?, 1679–1682, Château de Meudon (landscaping; partially destroyed), France. 1656–1661, Château de Vaux-le-Vicomte (landscaping), France. 1661–1687, Château de Versailles (landscaping), France. 1662, Gardens, Greenwich, England. 1662–1687, Château de Fontainebleau (landscaping), France. 1663–1673, Château de Saint-Germain-en-Laye (landscaping), France. 1663–1688, Château de Chantilly (landscaping), France. 1664–1679, Palais de Tuileries (landscaping), Paris. 1665–1678, Saint-Cloud (landscaping), France. 1666, Hôtel de Condé (garden), Paris. 1670–1687, Trianon de Porcelaine and Grand Trianon (landscaping), Versailles, France. 1673, Château de Conflans (landscaping), France. 1673–1677, Château de Sceaux (landscaping), France. 1674, Palais Royal (landscaping), France. 1674–1676, Château de Clagny (landscaping), France. 1675–1678, Château de Maintenon (landscaping), France. *1679–1680, Château de Meudon (landscaping), France. Begun 1685, Convent School (landscaping), Saint-Cyr, France. 1691–1692, Château de Gaillon (landscaping), France. 1693–1698, Château de Pontchartrain (landscaping), France.

BIBLIOGRAPHY

ADAMS, W. H. 1979 *The French Garden, 1500–1800.* New York: Braziller.

BERRALL, JULIA S. 1978 *The Garden: An Illustrated History.* New York: Viking.

BOYCEAU DE LA BARAUDERIE, JACQUES 1638 *Traité du jardinage selon les raisons de la nature et de l'art.* Paris.

CORPECHOT, LUCIEN 1937 *Parcs et jardins de France.* Paris: Librairie Plon.

DESARGUES, GIRARD 1648 *Manière universelle pour pratiquer la perspective.* Paris: Deshaye.

DESMOLETS, PIERRE NICOLAS 1730 Volumes 8 and 10 in *Continuation des mémoires de littérature et d'histoire.* Paris.

FOX, HELEN M. 1962 *André Le Nôtre, Garden Architect to Kings.* New York: Crown.

The French Formal Garden. 1974 Volume 3 in Dumbarton Oaks Colloquium on the History of Landscape Architecture. Edited by E. B. MacDougall and F. H. Hazelhurst. Washington: Dumbarton Oaks.

GANAY, ERNEST DE 1962 *Andre Le Nostre, 1613–1700.* Paris: Vincent, Fréal.

GOTHEIN, MARIE LUISE (1919)1928 *A History of Garden Art.* Rev. ed. Translated by Mrs. Arthur-Hind. London: J. M. Dent. Originally published with the title *Geschichte der Gartenkunst.*

GUIFFREY, JULES 1912 *André Le Nostre.* Paris: Laurens.

HAZLEHURST, F. HAMILTON 1980 *Gardens of Illusion: The Genius of Andre Le Nostre.* Nashville, Tenn.: Vanderbilt University Press.

NICERON, PÈRE JEAN-FRANÇOIS (1638)1663 *La perspective curieuse.* Paris: Du Puis.

"Obituary." 1700 *Mercure de France* September:278–281.

SAINT-SIMON, LOUIS DE ROUVROY 1855 Volume 8, page 191, in *Mémoires de Saint Simon.* Edited by A. de Boislisle. Paris: Hachette.

DE SERRES, OLIVIER (1600)1804–1805 *Théâtre d'agriculture.* New ed. Paris: Madame Huzard.

LEO, LUDWIG

Ludwig Leo (1924–), practicing independently in Berlin after working with Hans and Wassili Luckhardt from 1953 to 1955, has developed formal solutions to particular building tasks through technological rationalization. His poetic rigor has created unique structures imbued with respect for the activities accommodated, especially the Circulation Tank (1969–1972) and the DLRG Boathouse (1969–1972), Berlin.

THOMAS G. BEDDALL

WORKS

1958, Kindergarten, Loschmidstrasse; 1959, Eichkamp Students Residence (with Müller and Heinrichs); 1962–1963, Sports Hall, Charlottenburg; 1968–1970, Märkisches Viertel Development; 1969–1972, Circulation Tank, Institute for Waterways and Shipbuilding, Tiergarten; 1969–1972, Deutsche Lebens Rettungs Gesellschaft Multi-purpose Station, Spandau; Berlin.

BIBLIOGRAPHY

CARLINI, ALESSANDRO 1972 "Progetti di Ludwig Leo a Berlino." *Controspazio* 4, nos. 11–12:4–17.
COOK, PETER 1981 "Ludwig Leo: Berlin Mysteries." *Architectural Review* 169, no. 1012:371–373.
"Leo: Architekturdokumente." 1979 *Kunstwerk* 32, Apr.–June:98–103.
"Serious Sport." 1966 *Architectural Review* 140, no. 833:1–2.

LEONARDO DA VINCI

Leonardo da Vinci (1452–1519) had no formal training as an architect, but his accomplishments both in architectural theory and planning show that he is fully entitled to be considered as an architect, and this precisely in the sense postulated by such Renaissance theorists as LEON BATTISTA ALBERTI and GIORGIO VASARI, for whom all that the architect ought to be concerned with is the "design," while the models and the execution of the actual buildings are merely the work of carvers and masons. And yet the training that Leonardo received as a painter and a sculptor in Verrocchio's studio (c.1469–c.1476) must have taught him the importance of approaching art with a scientific mind. He learned to recognize the need of an extensive and systematic daily practice in acquiring dexterity of hand and built up a visual vocabulary of forms in the full range of their natural varieties. Thus, the artist's ability to reproduce natural forms in conceptual images, both human figures and the architectural setting that human figures require, in a painting as a convincing representation of the figure's habitat or environment and not simply as a decorative stagelike backdrop derives directly from this training. Significantly enough, the tool that Florentine artists of the end of the *quattrocento* looked on as the greatest achievement of the earlier generation—artificial perspective—was the invention of the first Renaissance architect, FILIPPO BRUNELLESCHI, the already legendary figure who was to have so much appeal for the young Leonardo, not only for the classical purity and clarity of his architectural forms, but above all for his daring, ingenious, and astounding technological innovations. It is in fact this particular aspect of Brunelleschi's work that only recently has been shown to have had a strong and everlasting impact on Leonardo's exuberant technical inventiveness.

Leonardo's earliest sheets in the Codex Atlanticus, which can be shown to date from about 1478–1480, record a number of devices and machinery invented by Brunelleschi for the construction of the dome of Florence Cathedral. Next to these drawings are studies of the system of lifting the copper sphere on top of the lantern of the dome, and these refer to a commission that Verrocchio had received in 1469 and that Leonardo himself mentions in a later record, thus suggesting the earliest date of his association with Verrocchio's studio. So intimate was Leonardo's knowledge of Brunelleschi's technology during the first Florentine period of his activity that he was soon to apply that technology to a variety of uses, including ways of exerting great power by means of screw devices that could be employed in lifting and carrying enormous weights, in breaking the iron bars in the windows of a prison, and even in causing the bottom of ships to split open. Around 1480–1485, in fact, Leonardo became concerned with new aspects of naval warfare, engaging divers equipped with a screw device similar to one invented by Brunelleschi. Later, about 1490, he studied a kind of submarine which had nothing to do with what was thought to be a project for attacking the Turkish fleet in 1500, but which was probably the same kind of ship described by CESARE DI LORENZO CESARIANO in his 1521 edition of VITRUVIUS as having been used in the moats of the Sforza Castle at Milan and in the Lake of Como.

Leonardo Da Vinci. Early architectural study. c.1485

In participating with Verrocchio in the completion of Brunelleschi's greatest architectural undertaking, Leonardo must have become aware of the lantern having the characteristics of a self-contained, individual "building" on a centralized plan that could be related to another Brunelleschi building, Santa Maria degli Angioli, which came to be joined to it by a visual axis that integrated the two architectural conceptions in the same urban setting.

Among the earliest records of Leonardo's activity before he moved to Milan in 1482 are the somewhat fanciful accounts of Vasari about the great many ideas and models pertaining to an early project of regulating the course of the Arno River, the excavation of canals, and in general the use of water as motive power in operating a great variety of instruments and machines, with some hint at an aspect of naval architecture that shows an awareness of Brunelleschi's patented device—the famous "Badalone"—the river boat that was to carry the loads of marble from Pisa to Florence upstream on the Arno River. It was apparently during the same early period that Leonardo had proposed the seemingly impossible task of lifting the Baptistery of Florence Cathedral in order to set it on a base with marble steps. Again, the information comes from Vasari as an anecdote, but once it is viewed in a historical, cultural, and technological context which again refers back to Brunelleschi's visionary innovations, it may contain some truth if not feasibility. The only reflection, however, would be in Vincenzo Borghini's later "archeological approach" to the Florentine monument in terms of an antique temple set on a base with marble steps.

Leonardo's first exposure to architectural theory and practice during the time of his training in Florence provided him with the impulse to approach major architectural problems in Lombardy, where he moved about 1482. It was there that he came in contact with a strong and long established Gothic tradition that the local architects—for example, the SOLARI FAMILY—strove to maintain with little concession to Renaissance ideas which by the middle of the fifteenth century had spread to North Italy. It was not until about 1470, however, that those ideas became more pressing with the work of Alberti at Mantua. In 1487, Alberti's assistant LUCA FANCELLI came to be directly involved with the final phase of planning the tiburio (tower over the crossing) of Milan Cathedral. Leonardo's participation in that project is documented, but the complex accounts of the completion and the discussions related to it, which involved local as well as foreign architects, hardly allows for a clear definition of Leonardo's contribution. However, whatever is left in his manu-scripts in the way of preliminary studies which were to lead to the preparation of a wooden model must be considered in relation with the work of DONATO BRAMANTE, GIOVANNI GIACOMO DOLCEBUONO, Pietro da Gorgonzola, and Solari first, and then with the work of FRANCESCO DI GIORGIO MARTINI, with whom Leonardo was to come in close contact in 1490. The contact was in fact so close that the suggestion is put forward that Leonardo allowed his colleague to take over his own model, which, with some modification, was then approved and carried out. In 1490, Leonardo and Francesco di Giorgio were both consulted in Pavia on problems pertaining to the construction of the Cathedral there, which was begun in 1488 based on a project apparently inspired by both Leonardo and Bramante. Much new evidence of Leonardo's involvement in that project has been provided by an extensive investigation of Leonardo's drawings at Windsor Castle, on which a wealth of hitherto unknown details (mostly of architectural studies) have recently been revealed through ultra-violet photography. The result of this investigation has been published as a commentary to the sheet in the Codex Atlanticus on which Leonardo recorded his relation with persons and events in Milan and Pavia in 1489. This document also contains Leonardo's first known mention of Bramante, whose *opinio* on the construction of the tiburio of Milan Cathedral can provide a better explanation of Leonardo's contribution to the project. From then on, that is from 1490 on, Leonardo's activity as an architect in Milan is one of an increasingly closer association with Bramante, an association, in fact, that seemed to have developed into a friendship based on identity of aims and interests, fostered by the enthusiastic and far-reaching views of their mutual patron, Lodovico Sforza.

Under the aegis of Lodovico Sforza, a bold and drastic plan of urban renewal was undertaken in Milan and in other Lombard centers beginning about 1490, when both the Cathedral and the Sforza Castle came to be viewed as focal points in an urban setting that was to organize city life in terms of stimulated industrial and commercial activities, thus complying with a political design that aimed at expanding and strengthening the Milanese dukedom. Leonardo developed the overall plan about 1493 with the idea of enlarging the city with an additional ring much in the way in which it was actually carried out in the sixteenth century. Leonardo's practical proposal was to test the ambitious plan with a "pilot project" involving the periphery between two city gates. With this plan Leonardo developed ideas already presented theoretically in an earlier manuscript (MS. B, c.1487–1490), departing in fact from the

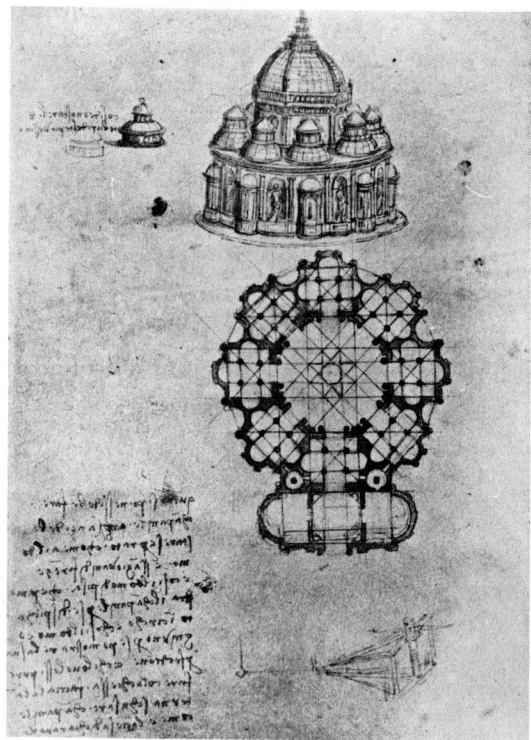

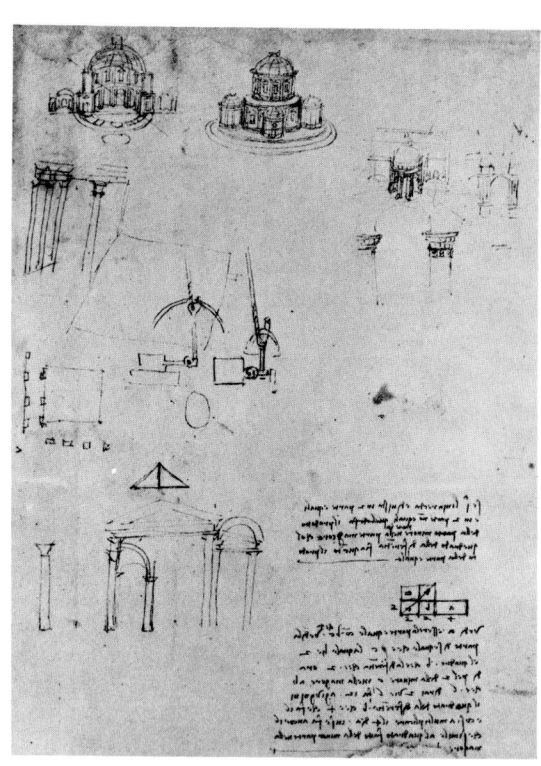

somewhat stereotyped schemes of the "ideal city" as suggested by *quattrocento* theorists such as IL FILARETE and Francesco di Giorgio. Leonardo faced the problem with a keen awareness of its political implications, thus anticipating Machiavelli's shrewdness and broad-mindedness in proposing an organization of city life that went beyond the idealized approach of the humanists (for example, Matteo Palmieri) to pave the way for the concept of the modern state.

It was with this structural approach to urbanism that Leonardo gave free rein to his imagination in visualizing buildings as proportionately related to streets and piazzas and linked to gardens and parks according to principles of axial planning that were to be fully exploited by the architects of the next generation in Italy and France. The buildings thus conceived were given more festive connotations which were in keeping, however, with the classical solemnity of their geometrically reorganized urban setting. Again, it was Bramante, with his stagelike views of about 1495 which are reflected in some of Leonardo's drawings, who interpreted the pervading atmosphere of city renewal at the turn of the century, when he and Leonardo, urged by Lodovico Sforza's political design, were gradually giving shape to architectural ideas long dreamed about in Florence and Urbino, and fostered in Naples and Ferrara.

Centers outside Milan, such as Vigevano and Pavia, could well have provided the necessary testing ground for such ideas, and Leonardo's manuscripts of about 1493–1494 are precious testimony

to the hectic activities in building construction and decoration at that time not only of Leonardo and Bramante but also of a Ferrarese architect, Iacomo Andrea da Ferrara, whose untimely death in 1500 ended abruptly the brilliant career of a devoted student of Vitruvius and—as Pacioli tells us—one of Leonardo's dearest friends, "almost a brother to him."

The program visualized by Lodovico Sforza in consultation with his architects was soon to engage the full cooperation of prominent citizens and members of his court and government. An area of special development was to stretch from the Sforza Castle in the direction of the convent of Santa Maria delle Grazie (soon to be transformed into a Sforza Mausoleum) outside of Porta Vercellina. This was to be turned into a luxurious, residential area, with majestic buildings planned for such prominent citizens as the Atellani, the Sanseverino, and the Guiscardi, while in the neighboring area toward Porta Comasina was built the suburban residence of Lodovico's treasurer Gualtiero Bascapé, a building later expanded into the better known Villa Simonetta. Leonardo seems to have been involved in the design of nearly everyone of these buildings. There is clear evidence of his extensive study of the area from the point of view of land plotting as part of an overall plan; there are also studies of individual buildings and several drawings of architectural details which consistently refer to constructions in the area of Santa Maria delle Grazie and which are full of anticipations of High Renaissance forms.

At times, a project afforded him the opportunity to digress into theoretical considerations, as was the case with the project of a house for Mariolo de' Guiscardi (c.1497), which was also a unique document of the relationship between architect and patron in that it recorded the latter's specifications to the former. The project seemed to anticipate much of Leonardo's attitude if not ideas in later planning, as expressed in projects for the villa of Charles d'Amboise, the French governor of Milan (c.1506–1508), the enlargement of the Villa Melzi at Vaprio (c.1513), a new Medici Palace at Florence (c.1515), and above all the new royal residence at Romorantin in France (c.1517–1519), the latter with notes which would be suitable for a treatise on architecture.

Not much is known of Leonardo's possible involvement with the remodeling of the old Carmagnola palace (the present Broletto) that Lodovico Sforza in 1490 donated to his mistress, Cecilia Gallerani, the highly sophisticated and learned lady whose portrait Leonardo had painted about 1485. Lodovico himself inspected the place in 1491 together with "a few engineers" in order to plan with them its restoration and beautification. Other documents give the names of headmasters involved in the actual work, including a Battista Alberti who was also engaged by Bramante at Santa Maria delle Grazie. It was this Alberti who later recalled having been in relationship with Leonardo and Andrea da Ferrara, and so there is strong circumstantial evidence that Leonardo too was called in to look into the project for Cecilia Gallerani, especially in view of the fact that Cecilia herself, writing to Isabella d'Este in 1498, refers to Leonardo as an artist "who has no equal," while Sabba da Castiglione's account of Leonardo's activity in those years stresses the point that "when Leonardo was supposed to work at painting, in which he would have turned out to be a new Apelles, he devoted himself entirely to geometry, architecture, and anatomy."

In Leonardo's notebooks of about 1495–1497, at the time of his work on the *Last Supper* and therefore before the decoration of the *Sala delle Asse* at the Sforza Castle (1498), there are several studies of knots and vegetable motifs as well as geometrical patterns suitable for ceiling and wall decoration. There is some evidence that motifs of this kind were found in the remodeled house of Cecilia Gallerani, and it may be surmised that this would have been in keeping with her refined taste since the same decorative motifs appear in her dress in Leonardo's portrait. There is also some indication that the garden side of the Carmagnola palace had towers, and it could well be that Leonardo had thought of transforming them into fanciful, pavil-

Leonardo Da Vinci.
Study of a palace.
c.1517

Leonardo Da Vinci.
Study of villa, with details
of wall articulation.
c.1506

ionlike adjuncts with a stress on their decorative function, which seemed to anticipate the French taste manifested in Leonardo's later studies for the Villa Melzi or even GIACOMO BAROZZI DA VIGNOLA's first project for the casino of Villa Giulia. A reflection of such a suggestion is again in the notebooks of 1495–1497 and above all in the famous and splendid study for an apostle of the *Last Supper.* Leonardo's work on the *Last Supper,* between 1495 and 1497, brought him even closer to Bramante, and in fact there is now evidence of his involvement with Bramante's project of rebuilding Santa Maria delle Grazie, so that the suggestion of Leonardo's active participation in that project is not simply based on elements of architectural theory and style. In one of Leonardo's notebooks of 1497 is found, almost concealed by superimposed writing, the ground plan of the new apse

Leonardo Da Vinci.
Villa Melzi (enlargement;
possibly undertaken and
abandoned).
Vaprio, Milan.
c.1513

Leonardo Da Vinci.
Study of Trivulzio
Monument.
c.1508–1510

of Santa Maria delle Grazie with specification of the method that either Leonardo or Bramante (or both) had thought to adopt in linking it to the new nave of the church—a method consisting in narrowing the transitional area so as to convey to the apse the effect and character of a freestanding, centrally planned building, one that would be suitable as a Sforza Mausoleum according to a possible precedent inherent in Alberti's project of transforming the church of San Francesco at Rimini into the Tempio Malatestiano.

The tribune of Santa Maria delle Grazie has no crypt, but there is full documentary evidence that the "Sforza Sepulchre," that is, the tomb for Lodovico Sforza and his wife Beatrice d'Este, was planned to be built at its center, while other members of the family would be placed in other points of the great apse. The tomb was actually built, and the twin sarcophagus was set in place in 1497, at Beatrice's death, when Lodovico urged his sculptors and architects to give top priority to the project. By then Bramante's apse as well as Leonardo's *Last Supper* had just been completed, and the next phase of the architectural project consisted in the reconstruction of the nave and in the design of a new façade. Nothing of all this was accomplished, possibly on account of the political situation, which shortly afterward, in 1499, was to bring about the end of the Sforza dynasty.

All that is left of the intended "focal point" of the rebuilt church of Santa Maria delle Grazie, a focal point which was to be both liturgical and political, is the sarcophagus lid with Cristoforo Solari's effigies of Lodovico and Beatrice, now at Pavia, the only surviving portion of a tomb that was dismantled in 1568 in compliance with the decrees of the Council of Trent. Contemporary mentions of the monument are scanty and vague, and these, taken in conjunction with the few documents pertaining to its construction, seem to suggest that it was not completed. On a sheet of Leonardo's technical studies of 1497 there are sketches

of an architectural structure resembling the canopy of a bed, which is now identified as pertaining to the project of the Sforza Sepulchre. Other hints of the same project may be gleaned in other Leonardo sheets and notebook pages dating from the same time; but above all, a reflection of it can now be recognized in some of Leonardo's later studies for the Trivulzio Monument.

Leonardo's small drawings for the Sforza Sepulchre can be taken as a summation of architectural ideas which he had been testing since the time when he first collected an extensive repertory of models of ecclesiastical buildings, with variations on the theme of the centralized plan which seems to combine the Brunelleschian model of Santa Maria degli Angioli and an earlier Filarete project for a Sforza Mausoleum.

Milanese sculptors and architects in the second half of the fifteenth century were much involved in projects of funerary monuments, and Leonardo must have been well familiar with their work. Even the altarpiece that was to include Leonardo's *Virgin of the Rocks* in the Church of San Francesco Grande at Milan was conceived as an architectural structure reminiscent of a triumphal arch that was to provide the frame for a symbolic sarcophagus; a reflection of this can be seen in Tullio Lombardo's Vendramin Tomb at Venice of 1492–1495. The commission for the altar in San Francesco engaged workers who were also employed by Bramante at San Satiro at the same time that Bramante was working on the fresco decoration of the nearby Panigarola house, which may provide further evidence of his association with Leonardo. This association is now documented by the identification of Bramante as the author of the *Antiquarie prospettiche romane,* a booklet on Roman antiquities published about 1500 and dedicated to Leonardo with an invitation to join the author—the "Milanese prospectivo depintore"—in Rome. This publication, known in a unique copy now in the Casanatense Library in Rome, can be taken to underline the role of Bramante and Leonardo in the study of antiquity at a turning point in the development of Italian art and architecture.

Leonardo returned to Florence after the fall of the Sforza dynasty in the autumn of 1499 by way of a detour that took him and his friends LUCA PACIOLI and Salai to Mantua first and then to Venice for a period of approximately four months. Any newly discovered information pertaining to this brief period of Leonardo's life would add greatly to our knowledge of the development of his art. A gradual change of style is apparent in his drawings, including the technical ones, a change in the direction of a greater emphasis on structure and form so as to represent function more effectively. This undoubtedly had a bearing on Leonardo's architectural conceptions after 1500, as first manifested in the villa project on the cover of the *Codex on the Flight of Birds* of 1506, which can be taken to codify architectural principles of the High Renaissance as introduced in Bramante's and RAPHAEL's later Roman buildings—a volumetric approach to structure and form conceived both in sculptural and coloristic terms. Such devices as the cluster of columns and columns recessed in the thickness of the wall make their "official" appearance only later, with MICHELANGELO at the Laurentian Library. But even before this extraordinary drawing, and in fact soon after Leonardo's visit to Venice where he was consulted as a military architect, there appeared in his architectural sketches revealing hints of forms and details that show the direction that Italian Renaissance architecture was to take with Bramante in Rome and the SANGALLO FAMILY in Tuscany in the first two decades of the sixteenth century. It may be significant that Leonardo's first design after he had returned to Florence—the monumental altar at the entrance of the tribune of the Santa Annunziata, nothing of which is left—was to be carried out by an architect—Baccio d'Agnolo—much responsible for the introduction of the High Renaissance style in architecture in Florence.

Leonardo's architectural work in the Veneto—fortification, river control, naval architecture—led to his activity in the service of Cesare Borgia in Romagna two years later, and then, again as a military architect, in the service of Iacopo IV Appiani at Piombino in 1504. His fortification studies at that point were taking into account the increased power of artillery fire, thus applying amortization and deflecting techniques in the round and squat forms of bastions and curtains. The concept seemed to add a new sense of vitality and dynamics to architectural structures that were conceived in relation to the trajectories of gun fire, and the same sense of energy was soon to be projected onto pala-

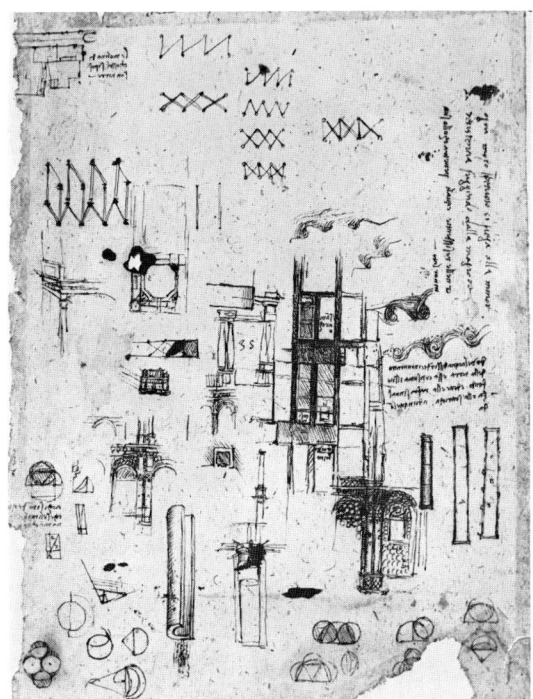

Leonardo Da Vinci. Studies for new Medici Palace in Florence. c.1515

tial architecture, with such ultimate results as shown in the lively articulated, massive forms of the new Medici palace in Florence (c.1515) and in the Romorantin palace in France (c.1517–1519).

The technical drawings, like the architectural ones, also acquired an unprecedented dynamic dimension; suffice it to mention the powerful images of mechanical devices in the recently discovered *Madrid Codices* and the famous drawings of machines for the excavation of canals. The latter are now shown in their originally intended "contextual view," that is, they are joined together to show that the two machines are operating on the same canal, thus stressing the innovation of Leonardo's system (motive power provided by counterweights) as opposed to the traditional system recorded by Vitruvius (motive power provided by a treadmill).

Just before and during Leonardo's work on the *Battle of Anghiari,* a composition which incorporates much of his views on the dynamics of forms in space, he made occasional notations of buildings and architectural details that may be related to specific commissions. This is the case with the drawings on the theme of the rural house, which seem to be linked to a request received in 1501 for a design for Mantua of a replica of the Villa Tovaglia built near Florence by Lorenzo da Monteacuto about 1480. Leonardo was not too keen about divorcing a building of its ambient, and nothing seems to have come of a project which consisted of Leonardo's large-scale plan and elevation drawings, now lost. Likewise, only hints are left of another project involving palatial architec-

Leonardo Da Vinci.
*Studies for enlargement of
Villa Melzi.*
Vaprio, Milan.
c.1513

ture within the fortress of Imola in 1502. Nevertheless, Leonardo's pictorial and architectural visions at that time were increasingly broadened to encompass a wider territorial range of activity, hence the extensive work of land surveying resulting in the magnificent maps of Tuscany and Romagna, and of course of the city of Imola, which can be taken as the first city map known to have been made according to the same scientific method of surveying later described by Raphael in his letter to Leo X on the study of Roman antiquities.

Land surveying was indeed Leonardo's major occupation during the years of his activity as a military architect in the service of Cesare Borgia and of the Florentine Republic, both in connection with military operations and with canalization. As a synthesis of the various aspects of this type of field activity came his involvement with "La Verruca," the fortress at the top of a high hill overlooking Pisa and the Arno valley. The site itself—aside from all problems of military architecture involved—afforded him the opportunity of sharpening his own awareness of the relationship between artificial, that is, man-made, and natural forms. The majestic and terrifying peaks in which the fortress was embedded, juxtaposed as they were with a compelling view of rolling hills and of the winding river, became the symbol of his concept of the workings of nature—a concept which was latent in his mind at the time of his first drawing of the Arno landscape of 1473, and which was given full expression in the later landscapes of the *Mona Lisa* and *Saint Anne,* or in the turbulence of the unbridled forces of nature in his final visions of the *Deluge.*

A manuscript copy of Francesco di Giorgio's treatise on architecture was recorded by Leonardo

himself in a list of books that he owned in 1504. This copy has been identified as the Ashburnham MS. 361 in the Laurentian Library, Florence, which in fact has a number of marginal notes by Leonardo. These can be shown to date from about 1506, the beginning of what one may call the later period of Leonardo's activity, corresponding approximately to the last twenty years of his life. The question now is whether this should be considered a period of decline or one of ultimate accomplishments. This was indeed a period of Leonardo's very intense architectural activity and it has been the subject of much scholarly research in recent years. So much, in fact, is now known of his later architectural projects that they can be better evaluated in a comprehensive survey aiming at placing them in the context of his general development as an artist and at viewing them as a summation of a lifelong dedication to problems of architectural theory and practice. This is also a period which shows how the impact of Leonardo's architectural ideas began to be felt not only in Italy but also in France. His project for the villa of Charles d'Amboise in Milan (c.1506–1508), linked as it was to such *quattrocento* models as Poggioreale in Naples, was nevertheless full of anticipations of High Renaissance ideas which placed a stress on axial planning. This and the project that immediately followed—the enlargement of the Villa Melzi at Vaprio—showed a movement in the direction of BALDASSARE PERUZZI and Raphael in Rome, prefiguring, at the same time, the imaginative inventiveness PHILIBERT DELORME in France. Leonardo himself eventually moved to Rome (1513) and was lodged in the Vatican next door to one of the greatest collections of antiquities—the statue court of the Vatican Belvedere. This was not a dramatic change of scene. Bramante's unfinished Belvedere and other papal palaces, which were conceived in terms of a revival of Roman grandeur, must have been seen by Leonardo as the obvious outcome of the ideas that had been advocated so passionately in Milan some twenty years earlier, the legacy of which, in the works of Bramante's followers in Milan, Bramantino and Cesariano, was gradually sliding into a tame classicism bordering on mannerism. For Leonardo as for Bramante, the study of antiquity was a means of acquiring excellence ("even nobility," according to Cesariano), and not an end in itself. Thus, they were both capable of dominating the classical idiom and to incorporate it into their own vocabulary. In Rome and, during the same period, in Florence, Leonardo's architectural projects stemmed from a lineage that can be traced back to his first conceptions in Milan in the early 1480s, with no drastic change of style except for a greater richness in wall articulation, which deliberately expressed natural forms—rocks and plants—as was the case with the design of the new Medici Palace. Natural forms and their inherent dynamics were incorporated in the architecture of stage sets, as was the case with the mountain that opened in a play staged for Charles d'Amboise.

But finally, just before the French plans for Romorantin, there came Leonardo's approach to classical forms—arches and arenas—in terms of their essential, purely abstract geometrical structures. This particular phase of Leonardo's architectural thought seems to have originated with a meditation on the theme of the temple façade, perhaps in relation to temporary architecture of the kind organized in Florence in 1515 on the occasion of the entry of Leo X, or perhaps in the aftermath of the discussions about the projected façade of San Lorenzo, or more probably as theoretical digressions on the models proposed by Bramante in Lombardy and resumed by Peruzzi at Carpi. As a result of these experiments in manipulating classical forms in terms of their geometrical components, Leonardo did an extraordinary stereometric analysis of Bramante's St. Peter's, shown in an exploded view of its essential elements as if to illustrate the concept of the compenetration of forms generated by the cube—an idea which can rightly be taken to symbolize the architecture of the High Renaissance.

In the last three years of his life, in France, Leonardo was engaged in planning a new royal residence at Romorantin, which involved the systematization of the whole region with a set of canals which ultimately aimed at joining the British Channel to the Mediterranean. According to a recent interpretation, this plan—a modern equivalent would be the Tennessee Valley Authority—was beginning to emerge as Leonardo the engineer allowed himself to be carried away by the immense possibilities of the Romorantin scheme, a scheme that represented the first proposal of multipurpose waterway control which would be realized, in fact, only in the twentieth century.

Leonardo as designer. The modern concept of "designer" could well be applied to Leonardo as an architect whose interests and preoccupations went well beyond the problems of palatial and ecclesiastical architecture and even urban planning. The *architectura ficta,* that is, the architectural backgrounds in his paintings, are a case in point. Leonardo used perspective to suggest depth with a sense of acceleration that enhances the physical and spiritual stature of the foreground figures, as in the *Last Supper.* It could well be that such backgrounds were depicting a flattened relief as in Piero della Francesca's Brera altarpiece, thus prefiguring a visual device that was later to be applied in stage design and ciboria. But even in paintings where the background is not architectural, Leonardo conceived of the human figure—single or in a group—as the center of a surrounding natural setting, which is reminiscent of Bramante's concept of a building centrally planned as the nucleus of an enveloping architectural setting. The perspective of measurable architectural elements in the background of Leonardo's paintings can be taken as a means to reconstruct the represented space in ground plan and elevation as well as in isometric projection.

For related problems in the organization of space according to illusionistic effects, one must also consider Leonardo's involvement with stage architecture, festivals, theatrical representations, and costume design from about 1490 to his last years in France, which expressed many of his views on urban planning and garden design, especially in the later phase of his work in Italy and France, reflecting the contemporary aspiration of recreating the grandeur and scenery of imperial architecture as in Bramante's Vatican Belvedere.

Leonardo's numerous and well-known decorative designs consisting of a geometrical play of interlacing cords or ribbons often interwoven with vegetable elements acquire architectural connotations as soon as they are considered for their intended function of organizing space symbolically, as in the decoration of the walls and ceiling of the *Sala delle Asse* in the Sforza Castle in Milan (c.1498). This can be shown to be directly related to a series of engravings designated as "Academia Leonardi Vinci"—those extraordinary geometrical exercises in abstract design that had been taken in the past as the emblems of a school established by Leonardo in Milan for the study of architecture. The "Leonardo knots" or "Bramante's knots," as Leonardo himself called them, might have been intended for pavement design as well, and there is in fact some evidence of Leonardo's having thought of applying them to the geometrical framework that relates the peripheral elements of a centrally planned building to the star motif in its core. This is reminiscent of Isidor of Seville's cosmological diagram that Michelangelo was to apply to the design of the piazza of the Capitol. And with this comes Leonardo's possible intention of using pictographs as a substitute for epigraphy as it was done by Bramante at the Vatican Belvedere. It is again a playful approach to architectural symbolism by way of ideograms or hieroglyphics, which are the essence of allegory. And so it is perhaps not a coincidence that Leonardo's allegorical drawings should often include architectural elements which reflect contemporary theory and practice. Even a lamp or a portable inkwell as shown in two of Leonardo's emblems may take up architectural connotations suggesting a Bramantesque *tempietto* or the more obvious form of a well.

Leonardo's lifelong involvement with technology can also be related to his architectural activity. The Renaissance term "ingegno" for machine explains etymologically the designation of "engineer" in a classical sense—which is retained somewhat in the English language—of one who is dealing with the technological aspects of architecture in general and of military architecture in particular. The invention of war machines, of devices to lift and transport weights, of mills, fountains and pumps, and even clocks, pertains to the architect in his capacity of engineer, that is, the engine maker.

Fountains are often intended to provide a monumental accent to the focal points in open or enclosed spaces, and Leonardo showed a fascination for the visual and even musical play of water which to him seemed to revive an aspect of technological virtuosities in antiquity as known from Heron's *Spiritali,* and which were a prelude to the festive exuberance and pomp of the Baroque.

The musical components of architecture, aside from the less sensory elements of harmonic proportions, are implied in the mechanisms pertaining to clocks and bells. One of the earliest records of Leonardo's activity refers to the painting of a sun-dial or clock face for the convent of San Donato at Scopeto near Florence (for which Leonardo also was to paint the *Adoration of the Magi*), and it reminds one of Uccello's precedent at Florence Cathedral, just as Leonardo's later studies of clocks remind one of Brunelleschi's involvement with the principles of "multiplication of power" inherent in the wheel mechanisms of clocks. These principles are similarly applied by Leonardo in devising vehicles for lifting and transporting great weights, such as bells, artillery, or columns. And with this Leonardo comes again in contact with a classical tradition of *semoventi* machines, vehicles that move by themselves, that is, by a motive power generated within themselves—a power that can only be provided by a system of descending weights and counterweights or by springs. Hence Leonardo's invention of automata, such as carts for festivals, bell-ringer devices for palaces, and of course the famous mechanical lion for the king of France. There is even some indication that he built a robot, a mechanical man in a suit of armor, with articulated limbs and even with a movable mandibula as if to imply that it was to speak! It appears that Leonardo was wondering whether anything like this was ever built in Rome (as in fact it was). And so it may be that after Brunelleschi's epoch-making achievement with the invention of *perspectiva artificialis,* Leonardo had thought of building a human simulacrum as a demonstration of *anathomia artificialis,* thus surpassing the technological ingenuity of antiquity. This excursus must conclude with a consideration of what may be called Leonardo's "industrial design"—a category which includes a wealth of ideas in the invention of tools and instruments and in the design of fanciful yet functional forms for objects of daily use both in the house and in the trade. And here Leonardo the architect comes to the assistance of Leonardo the painter with projects of screened lamps and even of a studio with movable walls to control the direction of light. This brings the human side of Leonardo's genius into focus.

CARLO PEDRETTI

WORKS

Leonardo's drawings in the Royal Library at Windsor Castle are reproduced by gracious permission of Her Majesty Queen Elizabeth II. Those in the Codex Atlanticus *and in other collections are reproduced by permission of the libraries and institutions in which they are kept. The photographs have been provided by the author.*

*c.1497, Mariolo de' Guiscardi House, Milan, Italy. *1502, Fortification Work (primarily in the Imola Fortress), Romagna, Italy. *1504, Fortification Work, Piombino, Italy. *1504, La Verruca Fortress (restoration), near Pisa, Italy. *c.1506–1508, Charles d'Amboise Villa (possibly undertaken and abandoned); *c.1513, Villa Melzi (enlargement; possibly undertaken and abandoned), Vaprio; Milan. *c.1517–1519, Royal Residence (undertaken and abandoned at Leonardo's death), Romorantin, France.

BIBLIOGRAPHY

ARATA, GIULIO ULISSE 1953 *Leonardo architetto e urbanista.* Milan: Museo Nationale della Scienza e della Tecnica.

BELTRAMI, LUCA 1903 *Leonardo da Vinci negli studi per il tiburio della cattedrale di Milano.* Milan: Tipografia U. Allegretti.

BRIZIO, A. M. (1970)1974 "Bramante e Leonardo alla corta di Lodovico il Moro." Pages 1–26 in *Studi Bramanteschi: Atti del Congresso internazionale.* Rome: De Luca.

CALVI, I. 1943 *L'architettura militare di Leonardo da Vinci.* Milan: Libreria Lombarda.

FERGUSSON, FRANCES D. 1977 "Leonardo da Vinci and the tiburio of the Milan Cathedral." *Architectura* 7:175–192.

FIRPO, L. (editor) 1963 *Leonardo: Architetto e urbanista.* Turin, Italy: Unione Tipografico Editrice Torinese.

HEYDENREICH, LUDWIG-HEINRICH (1929)1971 *Die Sakralbau-Studien Leonardo da Vincis.* Rev. ed. Munich: Fink.

LANG, S. 1968 "Leonardo's Architectural Designs and the Sforza Mausoleum." *Journal of the Warburg and Courtauld Institutes* 31:218–233.

MALTESE, CORRADO 1954 "Il pensiero architettonico e urbanista di Leonardo." Pages 333–358 in *Leonardo Saggi e Ricerche.* Rome: Instituto Poligrafico dello Stato.

MURRAY, PETER 1963 "Leonardo and Bramante: Leonardo's Approach to Anatomy and Architecture and Its Effect on Bramante." *Architectural Review* 134:346–351.

PEDRETTI, CARLO 1962 *A Chronology of Leonardo's Architectural Studies after 1500.* Geneva: Droz.

PEDRETTI, CARLO 1972 *Leonardo da Vinci: The Royal Palace at Romorantin.* Cambridge, Mass.: Harvard University Press.

PEDRETTI, CARLO 1973a "The Original Project for S. Maria delle Grazie." *Journal of the Society of Architectural Historians* 32:30–42.

PEDRETTI, CARLO 1973b "Newly Discovered Evidence of Leonardo's Association with Bramante." *Journal of the Society of Architectural Historians* 32:223–237.

PEDRETTI, CARLO 1977–1978 "The Sforza Sculpture." *Gazette des Beaux Arts* 69:121–131; 70:1–20.

PEDRETTI, CARLO 1978 *Leonardo architetto.* Milan, Electa.

LEONI, GIACOMO

Although he described himself as a Venetian, Giacomo Leoni (1686?–1746) spent most of his working life in England. Before his arrival there, probably around 1713 or 1714, he was in the German Palatinate, where he helped MATTEO ALBERTI in the building of Schloss Bensberg, near Cologne, for the Elector Palatine. Shortly after coming to England, he published (1715–1720) an edition of ANDREA PALLADIO's *Four Books on Architecture,* which was to be very influential in the English Palladian revival, though he never seems to have secured the patronage of that movement's guiding spirit, LORD BURLINGTON. In 1726, he published his three-volume translation of *The Architecture of L. B. Alberti.* As an architect, Leoni was especially concerned with country houses, introducing certain baroque features into his Palladian designs, in contrast to the designs of Burlington's followers.

ANNE RICHES

WORKS

1721–1723, Queensberry House, 7 Burlington Gardens; 1723, Argyll House, Chelsea; London. 1725–1735, Lyme Park (remodeled), Cheshire, England. *1728–1745, Moulsham Hall, Essex, England. 1735–1736, Alkrington Hall; c.1740, Lathom House; Lancashire, England.

BIBLIOGRAPHY

COLLINS, PETER 1960 "New Light on Leoni." *Architectural Review* 127:225–226.

HUDSON, TIMOTHY 1975 "A Venetian Architect in England." *Country Life* 157:830–833.

LEONI, GIACOMO (1716–1720)1742 *The Architecture of A. Palladio, Revis'd, Design'd, and Publish'd by Giacomo Leoni, a Venetian: Architect to His Most Serene Highness, the Elector Palatine.* London: Ward. With notes by Inigo Jones.

LEONI, GIACOMO (editor) (1726)1755 *The Architecture of Leon Battista Alberti.* 3d ed. London: Owen.

WITTKOWER, RUDOLF 1954 "Giacomo Leoni's Edition of Palladio's 'Quattro libri dell'architectura'." *Arte Veneta* 8:310–316.

LEONIDOV, IVAN IVANOVICH

Ivan Ivanovich Leonidov (1902–1959) was born in Vlasikh near Kalinin, Russia. After working as a docker and farmhand, Leonidov was first recognized as having artistic talents by an icon painter in Tver', and it was this recognition that enabled him in 1919 to join the Tver' art school. After developing his skill as a painter, he gained admission in 1921 to the Vkhutemas in Moscow, where he fell under the influence of Aleksandr Vesnin (see VESNIN FAMILY) and transferred from painting to architecture. As a third-year architecture student, he began to enter architectural competitions and won several awards, including a project for an improved peasant cottage (1925), a prototypical workers' club (1926), and a housing complex in Ivanov-Voznesensk (1925).

Leonidov came to prominence with his final-year project for the Lenin Institute which was displayed at the first OSA (Association of Contemporary Architects) exhibition held in Moscow in 1927. He followed this public success with an influential article entitled "Summation and Perspective on Contemporary Architecture," published in the journal *Sovremenia Arkhitektura* (Contemporary Architecture). MOISEI YAKOVLEVICH GINSBURG, the founder of the OSA, saw Leonidov's Lenin Institute as having consequences for the future of urbanism. With its glass-clad suspended structures and elevated monorail, it envisaged a form of continuous open-ended regional development.

In part neo-Platonic, in part a Constructivist celebration of advanced technology, Leonidov's unique vision was strongly influenced by the floating imagery of Suprematism, and it is this no doubt that led him to design a dynamic yet nonrhetorical, curtain-walled architecture. An example is the 1930 Palace of Culture projected for the site of the Simonov monastery in Moscow. In this characteristically simple yet powerful composition, Leonidov combined into one complex a pyramidal sports hall *cum* winter garden; a hemispherical, transformable auditorium; and an orthogonal research building. Above these glistening solids hovered an airship and a light steel lattice mooring mast. In the same year, Leonidov made an unusual proposition for a new type of low-rise communal dwelling in his linear city project for Magnitogorsk. As with other Constructivists, Leonidov's style changed decisively after 1932 when elements drawn from traditional Russian iconography began to influence his later somewhat baroque manner, as in the rather emblematic monumentality of his entry for the 1933 Narkomtiazprom competition. After all this activity, Leonidov was to realize only one notable work, namely, the extensively landscaped amphitheater and ornamental stairway built for Ordjonikidze Sanatorium at Kislovodsk in 1932.

KENNETH FRAMPTON

WORK

1932, Ordjonikidze Sanatorium (amphitheater, landscaping, and stairway) Kislovodsk, Russia.

BIBLIOGRAPHY

HRÜZA, J. 1973 "Ivan Leonidov." *Architektura CSR* 32, no. 5:229–236.
KHAN-MAGOMEDOV, S. O. 1964 "Ivan Leonidov." *Sovetskaya Arkhitektura* no. 16:103–116.
KHAN-MAGOMEDOV, S. O. 1970 "I. I. Leonidov: 1902–1959." In O. A. Shvidovsky (editor), *Building in the USSR: 1917–1932.* London Studio Vista; New York: Praeger.
KOPP, ANATOLE 1970 *Town and Revolution.* New York: Braziller.
QUILICI, VIERI, and SCOLARI, MASSIMO (editors) 1975 *Ivan Leonidov.* Milan: Angeli.

LEOPARDI, ALESSANDRO

Alessandro Leopardi (c.1450–1522/1523) played an important part in the introduction of Renaissance architecture to Venice. First recorded as a goldsmith, he was also Master of the dies at the Mint, medal maker, and friend of humanist scholars.

In 1489 he received one of the most important public commissions of the period, casting the bronze equestrian monument of Bartolommeo Colleoni (1489–1496) left unfinished by Verrocchio, and designing the marble plinth. The monument is remarkable for the quality of its lettering and decoration and put Venice in the forefront of contemporary sculpture.

Leopardi is also responsible for the only other great urban bronze of the era, the three flagstaff bases in the Piazza outside Saint Mark's, Venice (1501?–1505). Each base is divided into zones of fluting, applique decoration, and allegorical friezes. The mermaids, nymphs, and tritons of the friezes are perhaps the first examples of the use of pagan antique imagery to glorify the Venetian state, which became one of the main themes of sixteenth-century art. The bases were also models for the nineteenth-century historic decoration, above all street lamps, as on the Embankment, London, with their rich and fancy elaboration.

In 1503–1505 he began another great marble and bronze work, the funerary chapel of Cardinal Zen in Saint Mark's. It is likely that he is responsible for the overall design and the exterior marble screen. After some years as a military engineer (Padua and Treviso), in 1521 Leopardi became architect of Santa Giustina, an important Benedictine foundation in Padua, but he died before he could complete its rebuilding.

HANS BRILL

LE PAUTRE, ANTOINE

Antoine Le Pautre (1621–1679) was born in Paris into a family of artists, artisans, and masons. The son of a master woodworker, he was trained in engraving by his elder brother Jean and in architecture probably by Etienne Martellange. He was first cited as a "mason and architect" in 1643, and in 1644 he acquired the title "architect of the king's buildings."

Among Le Pautre's earliest patrons were the Jansenists, for whom he built the Chapelle de Port-Royal (1646–1648) in Paris. The Hôtel de Fontenay-Mareuil (1646–1647), also in Paris, was commissioned by a marquis who was related to the Jansenist Arnauld family. The chapel as executed and the hotel displayed an austerity in harmony with Jansenist taste. The chapel was largely based on Martellange's Jesuit Novitiate, Paris (1630–1642), which was esteemed by the classicistic group formed around François Sublet de Noyers, Superintendant of the King's Buildings from 1638 to 1643. Le Pautre's choice of prototype reflected his probable training under Martellange and his initial sympathy for French classicism, which was compatible with ascetic Jansenist sensibility.

At the end of 1652 or in 1653 Le Pautre published a book of prints, the *Desseins de plusieurs palais,* which revealed his new dramatic baroque style. Significantly, the book was dedicated to Jules Cardinal Mazarin, whose enthusiasm for contemporary Italian baroque art was well known. The *Desseins* apparently attracted the attention of one member of the court circle—Catherine Bellier

Beauvais, lady in waiting to Anne of Austria—for whom Le Pautre built the Hôtel de Beauvais in Paris (1654–1660). Le Pautre's baroque style appears in this building, as well as in the choir decoration of Saint-Laurent, Paris (1654–1658) and in the north façade of the church of the Jacobins in Lyons (1657–?). All of these works were constructed or begun during the period of Mazarin, when the Italianate baroque was encouraged in France.

In 1659, Le Pautre was appointed architect to Philippe d'Orléans, the king's brother, an indication of his high standing in the profession. Le Pautre's first work for Philippe, the cascade at Saint-Cloud (early 1660s), continued his baroque vein, but about this time his style shifted again—to a rejection of the baroque in favor of much greater simplicity and restraint. This change may be noted in the Château de Seiglière de Boisfranc, Saint-Ouen (1662–1665), the wings of the Château de Saint-Cloud (c.1655–1677), the Château de Clagny (1674), and the Orangery, Saint-Ouen (1678–1679). This final phase largely emerged during the period of Jean Baptiste Colbert (Superintendant of the King's Buildings from 1664–1683), who directed French architecture away from the baroque. Colbert's aims were furthered by the Royal Academy of Architecture, which Le Pautre joined as a founding member in 1671. Le Pautre's entire stylistic development, therefore, echoes the broader evolution of French architecture during the Louis XIV era.

Aside from the historical interest of his artistic development, some of Le Pautre's works have enduring value as highly imaginative creations. These include an ideal château design (from *Desseins*), the Hôtel de Beauvais, and the cascade at Saint-Cloud.

ROBERT W. BERGER

WORKS

*1646–1647, Hôtel de Fontenay-Mareuil; 1646–1648, Chapelle de Port-Royal; 1654–1658, Saint-Laurent (choir decoration); 1654–1660, Hôtel de Beauvais; Paris. *1657–?, Church of the Jacobins (north façade), Lyons, France. Early 1660s, Cascade, Saint-Cloud, France. *1662–1665, Château de Seiglière de Boisfranc, Saint-Ouen, France. *c.1665–1677, Château de Saint-Cloud (south and north wings), France. *1674, Château de Clagny, France. *1678–1679, Orangery, Saint-Ouen, France.

BIBLIOGRAPHY

BERGER, ROBERT W. 1966 "Antoine Le Pautre and the Motif of the Drum-without-Dome." *Journal of the Society of Architectural Historians* 25, no. 3:165–180.

BERGER, ROBERT W. 1969 *Antoine Le Pautre: A*

Le Pautre.
Ideal château design from
  Desseins de plusieurs
  palais.
1652–1653

French Architect of the Era of Louis XIV. New York University Press.

HAUTECOEUR, LOUIS 1948 *Le règne de Louis XIV.* Volume 2 of *Histoire de l'architecture classique en France.* Paris: Picard.

LE PAUTRE, ANTOINE 1652–1653 *Desseins de plusieurs palais.* Paris: The author.

LE PAUTRE, ANTOINE (1681)1966 *Les oeuvres d'architecture d'Anthoine Le Pautre.* Text by Augustin Charles d'Aviler? Reprint. Westmead, England: Gregg.

THIVEAUD, JEAN MARIE 1970 "Antoine Le Pautre (1621–1679)." *Ecole Nationale des Chartes, Paris: Positions des thèses* 1970: 215–223.

THIVEAUD, JEAN MARIE 1974 "Antoine Le Pautre (1621–1691) (sic), architecte de la chapelle de Port-Royal de Paris." *Chroniques de Port-Royal. Bulletin de la société des amis de Port-Royal* 22–23:45–64.

LEPAUTRE, PIERRE

As was not unusual in a society where strong craftsmen's guilds prevailed, Pierre Lepautre (1659?–1716) was one of a family of artists. He was the son of the engraver Jean Lepautre (1618–1682), the nephew of ANTOINE LE PAUTRE, and the brother of Jacques Lepautre, also an engraver. There is no agreement among biographers concerning Pierre's birth date, the earliest personal document seeming to be his marriage license dated 1678, but Louis Hautecoeur (1948, vol. 2, p. 649) gives the date firmly as 1659.

Lepautre's first appointment to a post of importance as engraver and designer to the king came in 1699 when he entered the service of JULES HARDOUIN MANSART, the king's chief architect. Before this time, Lepautre had engraved illustrations for many publications of works by such architects as ANTOINE DESGODETS and CHARLES PERRAULT. From 1699 on, Lepautre, of course, recorded the work of Mansart as well. It is largely through the engravings of Lepautre's own works—suites of designs for tables, chimneypieces, garden furniture, doors, wall decoration, and particularly the magnificent folio of plans, sections, profiles, and elevations for the chapel at Versailles that the extent and quality of his production is appreciated.

Lepautre introduced a new style of interior decoration that immediately became fashionable. In general, the forms were lighter and more slender than those of his predecessors. The paneling, essential to wall decoration in eighteenth-century French taste, became long and vertical, accented at times only by rosettes in the center, rising from the base of the wall to the cornice. A more obvious development took place in the moldings, which Lepautre transformed from simple frames to arabesques and leafy vines dancing over the surfaces in a combination of geometry and fantasy, integrating with the central ornament.

ELAINE EVANS DEE

WORKS

1699, Château de Marly, France. 1701, Château de Versailles (appartements du roi and cabinet du conseil), France. 1702–1706, Cathedral (choir), Orléans, France. 1702–1706, Trianon; 1708–1710, Chapel; 1711, Salon d'Hercule; Versailles, France. 1711, Notre Dame (choir), Paris. 1712–1715, Château de Bercy, France.

BIBLIOGRAPHY

HAUTECOEUR, LOUIS   1948   Volume 2 in *Histoire de l'architecture classique en France.* Paris: Picard.

KALNEIN, WEND GRAF, and LEVEY, MICHAEL   1972 *Art and Architecture of the Eighteenth Century in France.* Harmondsworth, England: Penguin.

KIMBALL, FISKE   (1943)1980   *The Creation of the Rococo.* Reprint. New York: Dover.

LEPERE, JEAN-BAPTISTE

Jean-Baptiste Lepère (1761–1844) is most noted as an architect under Napoleon in Egypt, the architect of Malmaison (1802–1806), with JACQUES GONDOIN of the colonne de la Grande Armée, Vendôme (1806–1810), and of the first designs of the Church of Saint-Vincent-de-Paul in the style of Saint-Philippe-du-Roule (1824–1831). He was the father-in-law of JACQUES IGNACE HITTORFF, who finished the church.

DONALD D. SCHNEIDER

BIBLIOGRAPHY

HAUTECOEUR, LOUIS   1952–1957   Volumes 5 and 6 in *Histoire de l'architecture classique en France.* Paris: Picard.

HITCHCOCK, H. R.   (1958)1977   *Architecture: Nineteenth and Twentieth Centuries.* 4th ed., rev. Baltimore: Penguin.

SCHNEIDER, DONALD D.   1977   *The Works and Doctrine of Jacques-Ignace Hittorff (1792–1867).* New York: Garland.

LE RICOLAIS, ROBERT

Georges Robert Le Ricolais (1894–1977), who was born at La Roche sur Yon, France, studied and worked in France from 1912 to 1951, and taught at the University of Pennsylvania from 1954 to 1975.

World War I prevented the completion of his university studies in mathematics and physics, and World War II hindered the development of his contracting and consulting practices. From 1918 to 1943, he practiced as a hydraulics engineer, exhibited his constructivist air-brush paintings, published his poetry, and wrote two seminal articles concerned with his life's search for structural configurations of "infinite span and zero weight." The first paper, in 1935, "Les Toles composées et leurs applications aux constructions métalliques légères," introduced the concept of corrugated stressed-skins to the building industry; and in 1940, his "Essai sur des systèmes réticulés à trois dimensions" introduced the concept of space frames to architects. In 1962, André Malraux, the French minister of culture, in awarding Le Ricolais the Grand Prix du Cercle D'Etudes Architecturales, said, "Le Ricolais is the father of space structures and his concepts have influenced the greatest architects."

Le Ricolais's influence in the United States comes not from his almost unknown collaboration on eight built projects from 1947 to 1958 but from his "way of thinking" in his structural research at the University of Pennsylvania. His belief that he had "found no better discipline in this unpredictable problem of form than to observe the prodigies created by nature" led to his studies of soap films and radiolariae. His observation that "it is an enormous reservoir of unexploited forms, mathematics and its symbols," led to his unique use of topology. Being against "people eating symbols all the day" and believing that "the contact with things is full of meaning," he insisted on the building and testing of physical models of all concepts. His use of the paradox as a logical construct meant that in his structures "the order of destruction should follow the order of its construction." and in his studies for the partition of urban space he proposed that "the future objective is not how to structure buildings but how to structure circulations."

PETER MCCLEARY

BIBLIOGRAPHY

LE RICOLAIS, ROBERT   1935   "Les Toles composées et leurs applications aux constructions métalliques légères." *Bulletin de la Société des Ingénieurs Civils de France* May–June.

LE RICOLAIS, ROBERT   1940–1941   "Essai sur des systèmes réticulés à trois dimensions." *Annales des*

Ponts et Chaussées 110:63–70; 111:153–165.
LE RICOLAIS, ROBERT 1973 "Survey of Works: Structural Research 1935–1971." *Zodiac* 22:1–56.
MCCLEARY, PETER 1973 "Some Principles of Structure Exemplified in the Work of R. Le Ricolais." *Zodiac* 22:57–69.
"Things Themselves Are Lying, and So Are Their Images." 1973 *VIA* 2:80–109. Interviews with Robert Le Ricolais.

LEROUX, JEAN BAPTISTE

Jean Baptiste Leroux (c.1677–1746) was a prominent architect and decorator of country houses and Parisian *hôtels*. He received his architectural training from FRANÇOIS D'ORBAY, and his rococo interiors reflect the influence of PIERRE LE PAUTRE and, after 1730, NICOLAS PINEAU.

RICHARD CLEARY

WORKS

1714, Maison Fradet; 1721, Hôtel d'Avaray; 1724–1726, 1733, Hôtel de Roquelaure (completion and remodeling); 1729, Hôtel Bourgeois de Boignes; 1731, Hôtel du Prat; *1732, Hôtel de Villars (gallery); 1735, Hôtel d'Etampes (remodeling); 1746, Hôtel Desmares-Villeroy; Paris.

BIBLIOGRAPHY

GALLET, MICHEL 1972 *Paris Domestic Architecture of the Eighteenth Century.* Translated by James Palmes. London: Barrie & Jenkins.
HAUTECOEUR, LOUIS 1950 *Première moitié du XVIIIe siècle, le style Louis XV.* Volume 3 in *Histoire de l'architecture classique en France.* Paris: Picard.
KIMBALL, FISKE (1943)1980 *The Creation of the Rococo Decorative Style.* Reprint. New York: Dover.
LEROUX, JEAN BAPTISTE n.d. *Divers dessins de cheminées de la composition du Sieur Le Roux, architecte.* Paris: Mariette.
LEROUX, JEAN BAPTISTE n.d. *Nouveaux lambris de galeries, chambres, et cabinets.* Paris: Märiette.

LEROY, JULIEN DAVID

Julien David Leroy (1724–1803) was an architectural historian and scholar. Winner of the Rome Prize in 1750, he studied in Italy and traveled in Greece where he drew and measured ancient monuments. His pioneering publication of these measured drawings played an important role in the neoclassical movement, but Leroy was criticized for inaccuracy by GIOVANNI BATTISTA PIRANESI as well as by JAMES STUART and NICHOLAS REVETT. In 1772, Leroy succeeded JACQUES FRANÇOIS BLONDEL as professor at the Academy. He became a respected teacher and was instrumental in saving the School of Architecture, when the Revolutionaries abolished the royal academies in 1793.

CHARLOTTE LACAZE

BIBLIOGRAPHY

BRAHAM, ALLAN 1980 *The Architecture of the French Enlightenment.* Berkeley and Los Angeles: University of California Press.
DUSSAUD, RÉNÉ 1946 Volume 1 in *La Nouvelle Académie des Inscriptions et Belles Lettres.* Paris: Geuthner.
EGBERT, DONALD DREW 1980 *The Beaux-Arts Tradition in French Architecture.* N.J.: Princeton University Press.
ERIKSEN, SVEND 1974 *Early Neo-Classicism in France.* 4th ed. London: Faber.
GALLET, MICHEL (1964)1972 *Stately Mansions.* New York: Praeger. Originally published in French.
HAUTECOEUR, LOUIS 1952 *Seconde moitié du XVIIIe siècle: Le style Louis XVI.* Volume 4 in *Histoire de l'architecture classique en France.* Paris: Picard.
KAUFMANN, EMIL (1955)1968 *Architecture in the Age of Reason.* Reprint. New York: Dover.
LEROY, JULIEN DAVID 1758 *Les Ruines des plus beaux monuments de la Grèce, ouvrage divisé en deux parties, où l'on considère dans la première, ces monuments du côté de l'histoire et, dans la seconde du côté de l'architecture, par M. LeRoy.* Paris: Guerin & Delatour.
LEROY, JULIEN DAVID 1764 *Histoire de la disposition et des formes différentes que les chrétiens ont données à leurs temples depuis le règne de Constantin le Grand jusqu'à nous, par M. LeRoy.* Paris: Dessaint & Seillant.
LEROY, JULIEN DAVID 1767 *Observations sur les édifices des anciens peuples, précédées de réflexions préliminaires sur la critique des "Ruines de la Grèce" publiée dans un ouvrage anglais intitulé: "Les Antiquités d'Athènes" et suivies de Recherches sur les mesures anciennes, par M. LeRoy.* Paris: Merlin.
PÉROUSE DE MONTCLOS, JEAN MARIE 1969 *Etienne-Louis Boulée.* Paris: Arts et Métiers Graphiques.
RYKWERT, JOSEPH 1980 *The First Moderns: The Architects of the Eighteenth Century.* Cambridge, Mass.: M.I.T. Press.
WIEBENSON, DORA 1969 *Sources of Greek Revival Architecture.* London: Zwemmer.
WIEBENSON, DORA 1978 *The Picturesque Garden in France.* N.J.: Princeton University Press.

LESCAZE, WILLIAM

William Edmond Lescaze (1896–1969) is distinguished for his pioneering role in introducing the European International style to the United States. Considered one of the leading architects in the United States in the 1930s, he made one of the first important statements of the new architecture in this country.

Born in Onez, near Geneva, Lescaze received his Master of Architecture degree in 1919 from the

Eidgenössische Technische Hochschule, Zurich, under the direction of KARL MOSER. After working in Arras and in the atelier of HENRI SAUVAGE in Paris, he moved to Cleveland, Ohio, where he worked in the offices of Hubbell and Benes and Walter R. MacCornack. In 1923, he established his own firm in New York. His early modernist style included all the protomodernisms then current, from neoclassicism through the several sources of Art Deco to the International style in the last year of the decade.

Lescaze practiced in a partnership with GEORGE HOWE that lasted until July 1933. Lescaze continued to work under the corporate name, Howe and Lescaze, until March 1935 when he reestablished his private practice. During that time, he produced some of his most important works, influenced by the principles of Constructivism, De Stijl, and Expressionism.

During World War II, Lescaze experimented with new building materials and prefabrication systems. His postwar work, evolving into Miesian (see LUDWIG MIES VAN DER ROHE) classicizing, skeletal structures, consisted mostly of large public, office, and apartment buildings.

LORRAINE WELLING LANMON

WORKS

*1929, Oak Lane Country Day School, Philadelphia. 1929–1932, Philadelphia Saving Fund Society Bank and Office (with George Howe). 1930–1931, Frederick Vanderbilt Field House (with Howe), New Hartford, Conn. 1930–1932, Headmaster's House (Curry House), Dartington Hall, Totnes, Devon, England. 1931–1932, Hessian Hills School (with Howe), Croton-on-Hudson, N.Y. 1932–1936, Churston Estate Housing Development, Devon, England. 1933–1934, Spreter Studio and Garage, Lower Marion Township, Penn. 1933–1934, William E. Lescaze House and Office, New York. *1934–1936, Unity House, near Bushkill, Pa. 1935–1938, Williamsburg Houses (Ten Eyck Houses; with others), Brooklyn, N.Y. 1935–1937, High School, Ansonia, Conn. 1936–1937, Alfred Loomis House, Tuxedo Park, N.Y. 1936–1938, Columbia Broadcasting System Studios and Offices (with E. T. Heitschmid), Hollywood, Calif. *1937–1939, Aeronautics Pavilion; *1938–1939, Swiss Pavilion; World's Fair, New York. 1939–1941, Longfellow Office Building, Washington. 1940–1941, Edward A. Norman House; 1944, West Harlem Housing; N.Y. 1946–1949, Reliance Homes, Fairfax County, Va., and Roslyn, Pa. 1954–1956, Offices, 711 Third Avenue, N.Y. 1959, Swiss Embassy Chancellery, Washington. 1960, Churchill Apartments, Los Angeles. 1960, Civil and Municipal Courthouse (with Matthew Del Gaudio); 1960, Manhattanville Residences; 1961, "Christian Peace" Building and Chapel, United Nations; 1961, U.S. Plywood Building; New York. 1964, Chatham Center, Pittsburgh. 1969, One New York Plaza.

BIBLIOGRAPHY

BARBEY, GILLES 1971 "William Lescaze (1896–1969): Sa carrière et son oeuvre de 1915 à 1939." *Werk* 58:559–563.

COATES, ROBERT M. 1936 "Profiles—Modern: William Lescaze." *New Yorker* Dec. 12:44–50.

FITCH, JAMES MARSTON 1959 "William Lescaze." *Architecture, Formes et Fonctions* 6:96–103.

GIOLLI, RAFFAELLO 1937 "William Lescaze." *Casabella* 10, Jan.:10–21.

HITCHCOCK, H. R. (1932)1970 "Howe and Lescaze." Pages 144–145, 148, 153 in Alfred Barr et al. *Modern Architecture: International Exhibition*. Reprint. New York: Arno.

JORDY, WILLIAM H. 1962 "PSFS: Its Development and its Significance in Modern Architecture." *Journal of the Society of Architectural Historians* 21, May:47–83.

JORDY, WILLIAM H. 1972 Volume 4, chapter 2 in *American Buildings and Their Architects*. Garden City, N.Y.: Doubleday.

LANMON, LORRAINE WELLING 1979 "The Role of William E. Lescaze in the Introduction of the International Style to the United States." Unpublished Ph.D. dissertation, University of Delaware, Newark.

LESCAZE, WILLIAM EDMOND 1942 *On Being an Architect*. New York: Putnam.

POMMER, RICHARD 1978 "The Architecture of Urban Housing in the United States during the Early 1930s." *Journal of the Society of Architectural Historians* 37:235–264.

STERN, ROBERT A. M. 1962 "PSFS: Beaux-Arts Theory and Rational Expressionism." *Journal of the Society of Architectural Historians* 21, May:84–102.

STERN, ROBERT A. M. 1975 *George Howe: Toward a Modern American Architecture*. New Haven: Yale University Press.

WODEHOUSE, LAWRENCE 1976 "Lescaze and Dartington Hall." *Architectural Association Quarterly* 8:3–4.

LESCOT, PIERRE

Although Pierre Lescot (1510/1515–1578) is heralded as the architect who introduced the language of classical architecture to France, few documents have survived to inform us about his life and career. Probably born in Paris of a noble and rich legal family, he inherited the title of Seigneur de Clagny from his maternal ancestors and later enjoyed a privileged position at court. According to Pierre de Ronsard's poem (1560) in praise of Lescot, from the age of twenty, he studied geometry, mathematics, and architecture. Ronsard also emphasized his quality as a painter as did Jean Bodin, who refers to a painting by Lescot in Fontainebleau in the 1560s. There is no evidence that Lescot visited Italy in his youth, though the possibility exists of a journey on an official mission to Rome in 1556 (Blunt, 1977, pp. 78–79). Usually referred to in documents as the "king's overseer" or "supervisor" and more specifically as "director of the buildings of the Louvre," Lescot was architect to Francis I, Henri II, Francis II, Charles IX, and Henri III, as well as their adviser and court chaplain.

In most of his works Lescot collaborated with the sculptor and architect JEAN GOUJON. They worked together on the altar screen of Saint Germain l'Auxerrois in Paris (1541–1544; destroyed in 1750), his first recognized activity. With Goujon he also erected the Fontaine des Innocents (1547–1549); this monument has since been rebuilt, transformed, and moved several times. From 1545–1550, Lescot may have worked with JEAN BULLANT on the Hôtel de Ligneris, now called the Carnavalet; although considerably altered, it is regarded as the only surviving mid-sixteenth-century townhouse in Paris. A few years later, Lescot may have been engaged on the Château de Vallery, only a fragment of which remains; a contract assigns the building, the décor as well as the plan, to Lescot, and stylistic analogies between the garden pavilions and the Louvre have been cited by J. Androuet Du Cerceau (see DU CERCEAU FAMILY) (Baptst, 1912, p. 199; Planchenault, 1963, pp. 252–253). Lescot's architectural activity seems to be confirmed by the fact that he was consulted on the plans of bridges in Paris, the Petit-Pont in 1551 and the Pont-Neuf in 1578.

On August 2, 1546, Lescot was entrusted by Francis I "to build in our château of the Louvre . . . a great *corps d'hostel* on the site of the present grand ballroom"—that is, on the site of the west wing of the old château (Laborde, 1877–1880, I, pp. 439–440) and it is this work that assures his fame, though only the southwest corner of the square court may be ascribed to him with certainty. Lescot's new plan for the Louvre used the site and extant outer walls of Charles V's medieval castle.

Under Henri II, Lescot's post was confirmed by patent letters of the king dated April 14, 1547 and July 10, 1549. The latter authorized the demolition of certain parts of the Louvre already built, "having found that for greater commodity and ease of the said building, it was necessary to complete it otherwise"; new specifications and a new design were drawn up accordingly (Laborde, 1887–1880, I, pp. 440–441). Under Francis I, Lescot's first project for the west wing comprised a two story *corps-de-logis* with a central staircase. Sometime between 1547 and 1551, however, Lescot transferred the staircase to the north end of the wing, so that the ballroom could occupy the entire ground floor. Projecting pavilions were added at both ends for the sake of symmetry. In 1550, Goujon, "follow-

ing a plaster model previously made for him by Sr. de Clagny" and inspired by his own illustrations for the 1547 Martin edition of VITRUVIUS, began work on the Salle des Caryatids (Du Colombier, 1949, p. 96). At this time, a tribune for musicians was provided on the south side to make the proportions of the ballroom more harmonious. The inscription on the entry indicates that most of the work on the inner façade was completed in 1548 (Gebelin, 1927, p. 131).

Lescot soon raised the façade of the court by adding a third story, probably to conform with the greater height of the Pavillon du Roi facing the Seine. The date 1556 was once inscribed on the pediment and a contract of that date for the ceiling of the king's chamber suggests the time of completion.

Batiffol (1930, pp. 276–303) cited fourteen notarial documents relating to the construction of the Louvre; these unedited documents, eleven dealing with Lescot's work, were published by Aulanier in 1951 (pp. 85–100). There are twenty-eight agreements with Lescot and contractors stipulating work to be done and fees to be paid from December 17, 1546 to February 14, 1558.

Was Lescot the author of the "grand design"—the new plan which would quadruple the square court and tie the Louvre to the Tuileries? This grand design superseded that of Francis I's original plan for the building on one wing. Its

Lescot.
Louvre (elevation: West façade of court). Engraving from Les Plus Excellents Bâtiments de France.
Paris.
Begun 1546

Lescot.
Louvre (ground floor and first story). Engraving from Les Plus Excellents Bâtiments de France.
Paris.
Begun 1546

existence is known through an ordinance of Louis XIII dated January 5, 1624 and a letter of Colbert of 1664 (Hautecoeur, 1927, pp. 199–200). Contemporary statements by a Venetian ambassador (1557) and Du Cerceau (1576) attribute the design to Henri II, and today scholars are inclined to see the scheme executed by Lescot in the last years of Henri II's reign as involving a design to build a court enclosed by blocks twice the length of the executed wing, even though the actual plan was not built until the time of Louis XIII and Louis XIV (Blunt, 1977, pp. 198, 220; Batiffol, 1910, pp. 273–298). Batiffol's attribution is based on the plans in the Collection Destailleur which according to him were the work of Lescot. However, not everyone would identify these documents with the designs planned under Henri II. Some scholars believe that they are related to the decisions of January 9, 1595 and February 19, 1603 to renew works on the Louvre rather than to Lescot's design of 1549 (Hautecoeur, 1927, pp. 206–207, 217); Gebelin, noting that the plans include the outer part of the Tuileries and the lodgings provided in the Grand Gallery, both built at the end of Henri IV's reign, concludes that Lescot's 1549 Louvre was but a small palace (Gebelin, 1927, pp. 133–134). Lowry, observing that one of the Destailleur plans bears similarities to SEBASTIANO SERLIO's plan for a city palace in Book VI of Serlio's treatise (Avery and Munich mss.) and to the findings of Louvre excavations in 1866, suggests that it is a refinement of the plan submitted by Lescot in the original competition (1953, pp. 10–11).

Henri Sauval (1724, ii, 25) gives the earliest informed assessment of Lescot's contribution: "this architect was the first who banished from France Gothic architecture, in order to introduce into the country the beauty and grand manner of building here." Indeed, it is the extraordinary classicism of the Louvre court façade, its correct use of orders, that constitutes the significance of this new palace design. But in comparison with the contemporary Farnese courtyard (1546), Blunt notes its general un-Italian character: "the effect is one of ornamental beauty rather than of monumentality" (1977, p. 80). Differences abound: the vertical emphasis, especially marked in the pavilions (almost vestiges of the medieval turrets), the use of ornamental moldings and pilasters with Corinthian and Composite orders. With its double mullion windows and its ornate triangular and curved pediments, the Louvre façade is far more elaborate and complex in its details, lacking the relative simplicity and clarity of the Farnese court façade [though Gebelin (1927) has noted similarities with the exterior façades].

In all Lescot's work, sculpture is an indispensable component of architecture; in fact, Goujon conceived his sculpture to be a perfect complement to Lescot's essentially decorative architecture. This wedding of architecture and sculpture is also a continuation of the French medieval tradition, and it is only in the seventeenth century that architectonic elements rule over decorative ones. Although some authors (Blomfield, Lowry) may consider Lescot but a talented amateur, it was he who assimilated the classical Italian language to late Gothic French architecture and climaxed the immense building activity of Francis I. By the end of the seventeenth century, both CLAUDE PERRAULT and Brice could point to the superior quality of Lescot's plan for the Louvre—his prudence in retaining the contours of the old fortress of Charles V—just as the architects of the east façade in turn would respect the plans of their predecessors (Chastel, 1967, p. 82). As a canon of Notre Dame, Lescot resided in a house of the cloisters, and upon his death in 1578, he was buried in the great cathedral. Perhaps the highest praise was conferred by Ronsard in his "Discours a Pierre Lescot" (1560):

Toi, Lescot, dont le nom jusques aux astres vole . . .
Le Roy François, des lettres amateur,
De ton divin esprit premier admirateur,
T'aima par dessus tout.

NAOMI MILLER

WORKS

*1541–1544, Saint Germain l'Auxerrois (altar screen; with Jean Goujon); c.1545–1550, Hôtel de Ligneris (now the Hôtel Carnavalet; with Jean Bullant); Begun 1546, Louvre (quadrangle cour carée, west side [with Goujon], *south façade, west façade reconstructed); 1547–1549, Fontaine des Innocents (with Goujon; later reconstructed); Paris. *1556, Château de Vallery, France. 1570, Saint Denis (chapel, tomb of the Valois; in charge after death of Primaticcio), Paris. (A)1570, Château and Church, Fleury-en-Bière, France.

BIBLIOGRAPHY

AULANIER, CHRISTIANE 1951 "Le Palais du Louvre au XVIe siècle: Documents inédits." *Bulletin de la Société de l'Histoire de l'Art Français* 1951:85–100.
BAPST, GERMAIN 1912 "Séance du 17 Janvier." *Bulletin de la Société Nationale des Antiquaires de France* 1912:198–199.
BATIFFOL, LOUIS 1930 "Les premières Constructions de Pierre Lescot au Louvre d'après de nouveaux documents." *Gazette des Beaux-Arts* Series 6, 4:276–303.
BAUCHAL, CHARLES 1887 "Pierre Lescot." Pages 370–373 in *Nouveau dictionnaire des architectes français.* Paris: André, Daly.
BERTY, ADOLPHE 1860 *Les grands Architectes français de la Renaissance.* Paris: Aubry.
BLOMFIELD, REGINALD 1910–1911 "Pierre Lescot and Jean Goujon." *Journal of the Royal Institute of British Architects* 18:109–128.

BLOMFIELD, REGINALD (1911)1974 *History of French Architecture, 1494–1661.* Reprint of 1921 ed. 2 vols. New York: Hacker.

BLUNT, ANTHONY (1953)1977 *Art and Architecture in France, 1500–1700.* Harmondsworth, England: Penguin.

CHASTEL, ANDRÉ 1967 "La Demeure Royale au XVIᵉ siècle et le Nouveau Louvre." Pages 78–82 in *Studies in Renaissance and Baroque Art Presented to Anthony Blunt.* London and New York: Phaidon.

DU CERCEAU, JACQUES ANDROUET (1576–1579)1972 *Les Plus Excellents Bâtiments de France.* Reprint. Farnborough, England: Gregg.

DU COLOMBIER, PIERRE 1934 "Les Jubés des Cordeliers et de Saint-Germain l'Auxerrois." *Gazette des Beaux-Arts* 6:143–147.

DU COLOMBIER, PIERRE 1937 "L'Enigme de Vallery." *Humanisme et Renaissance* 4:7–15.

DU COLOMBIER, PIERRE 1949 *Jean Goujon.* Paris: Albin Michel.

GEBELIN, FRANÇOIS 1927 *Les Châteaux de la Renaissance.* Paris: Les Beaux-Arts.

HAUTECOEUR, LOUIS 1927 "Le Louvre de Pierre Lescot." *Gazette des Beaux-Arts* Series 5, 15:199–218.

HAUTECOEUR, LOUIS (1943)1965 *La Renaissance des humanistes (1535/40 à 1569).* Volume 1, part 2, in *Histoire de l'architecture classique en France.* Rev. ed. Paris: Picard.

HAUTECOEUR, LOUIS n.d. *Histoire du Louvre.* Paris.

LABORDE, LÉON DE 1877–1880 *Les Comptes des bâtiments du roi (1528–1571).* 2 vols. Paris: Baur.

LOWRY, BATES 1953 "Château du Louvre." *Renaissance News* 6:10–11.

LOWRY, BATES 1964 "Pierre Lescot." Volume 9, page 238, in *Encyclopedia of World Art.* New York: McGraw.

MILLER, NAOMI 1968 "The Form and Meaning of the *Fontaine des Innocents.*" *Art Bulletin* 50:270–277.

PATTISON, MRS. MARK 1879 Volume 1 in *The Renaissance of Art in France.* London: Kegan Paul.

PLANAT, PAUL 1903 Volume 1 in *Encyclopédie de l'Architecture et de la Construction.* Paris: Dujardin.

PLANCHENAULT, RENÉ 1963 "Les Châteaux de Vallery." *Bulletin Monumental* 121:237–259.

SAUVAL, HENRI 1724 Volume 2 in *Histoire et recherches des antiquités de la ville de Paris.* Paris: Moette.

SAUVEL, TONY 1966 "La Date et l'auteur du 'Dessein' du Louvre." *Bulletin de la Société Nationale des Antiquaires de France* 1966:139–149.

WARD, WILLIAM H. 1909 *French Châteaux and Gardens in the XVIth Century.* London: Batsford.

LETAROUILLY, PAUL MARIE

Born in Coutances, France, Paul Marie Letarouilly went to Paris in 1814 and studied under Charles Percier (see PERCIER AND FONTAINE) and at the Ecole des Beaux-Arts from 1816. In 1819, he was inspector of works at the Théâtre de l'Odéon, Paris. After an Italian sojourn (1820–1824), he served as inspector of construction at the Ministère des Finances, Paris, and from 1831 to 1842 restored and greatly enlarged the Collège de France which had been built by JEAN FRANÇOIS CHALGRIN between 1780 and 1784.

Letarouilly frequently visited Italy where he researched his greatest work, *Edifices de Rome Moderne,* first published in three volumes between 1840 and 1857. Its 355 plates were widely consulted by architects of the Renaissance Revival in France and abroad. He died in 1855, leaving incomplete *Le Vatican et la Basilique de Saint-Pierre de Rome,* which was prepared for press and published in two volumes by Alphonse Simil in 1882.

CHRISTOPHER RIOPELLE

WORK

1831–1842, Collège de France (restoration and enlargement), Paris.

BIBLIOGRAPHY

BAUCHAL, CHARLES 1887 *Nouveau Dictionnaire Biographique et Critique des Architectes Francais.* Paris: André, Daly.

DAVID DE PENANRUM, LOUIS THÉRÈSE (1895)1907 *Les Architectes Elèves de l'Ecole des Beaux-Arts.* Edited by E. Delaire. 2d. ed. Paris: Librairies de la Construction Moderne.

LETAROUILLY, PAUL MARIE (1840–1857)1944 *Buildings of Modern Rome.* Translated by Arthur Broadbent. 3 vols. London: Tiranti.

LETAROUILLY, PAUL MARIE (1878–1882)1963 *The Vatican and the Basilica of St. Peter in Rome.* 2 vols. London: Tiranti.

LETHABY, W. R.

William Richard Lethaby (1857–1931) was born in Barnstaple, north Devon, the son of a craftsman, and in early life was articled to a local architect. In 1879, he became chief assistant to R. NORMAN SHAW, and his superb and learned decorative designs soon made an important contribution to Shaw's style.

Working independently from 1889, he rejected eclecticism and other aesthetic formulae for what, many years later, was to be called Functionalism. He founded the Modern Architecture Constructive Group, which defined architecture as "a developing structural art satisfying the requirements of the time by experiment." He was one of the creators of English Free architecture: his Brockhampton church (1901–1902) is probably the most original, for its date, in the world.

Appointed art inspector (1894) to the Technical Education Board of the nascent London County Council, he initiated the capital's art and craft education, and soon became principal of the new Central School of Arts and Crafts. This, the first of such institutions to have teaching workshops, had a profound influence in Europe (especially Germany) and the United States. Lethaby was also much engaged in the eventually successful attempts to organize architectural education.

Believing that art was the pervasive expression of common life, he was a leading figure in the Arts and Crafts movement, a founder of the Art-Workers' Guild (1884) and the Arts and Crafts Exhibition Society (1888). Later, he was one of the inspirers and founders of the Design and Industries Association (1915) and a leading member of the Society for the Protection of Ancient Buildings. As Surveyor of Westminster Abbey (1906–1927) he applied the society's principle of preservation and pioneered the cleaning and conservation of the fabric as against its "restoration."

Lethaby's social and aesthetic views were shaped by JOHN RUSKIN and WILLIAM MORRIS; more immediately, he learned from PHILIP S. WEBB and Ernest Gimson. But he was his own man. For all his modesty of demeanor, he was a powerful originator, and his influence on the architectural thinking of his time was greater than that of any other Englishman.

GODFREY RUBENS

WORKS

1891–1892, Avon Tyrell, Christchurch, Hampshire, England. *1893–1894, The Hurst, Hartopp Road, Four Oaks; 1899–1900, Eagle Insurance Buildings, Colmore Row, Birmingham; Warwickshire, England. 1899–1900, Melsetter House; 1900, Gatehouse; 1900, Rysa Lodge; 1900, Saints Colm and Mary Chapel; Hoy, Orkney Islands, Scotland. 1901, High Coxlease House, Lyndhurst, Hampshire, England. 1901–1902, All Saints Church, Brockhampton, Hertfordshire, England.

BIBLIOGRAPHY

BLOMFIELD, REGINALD 1932 "W. R. Lethaby: An Impression and a Tribute." *Journal of the Royal Institute of British Architects* 39:293–313.
BRANDON-JONES, JOHN 1949 "W. R. Lethaby: 1857–1931." *Architectural Association Journal* 64:194–197.
LETHABY, W. R. (1904)1912 *Mediaeval Art.* London: Duckworth.
LETHABY, W. R. (1912)1939 *Architecture.* Rev. reprint. London: Butterworth.
LETHABY, W. R. (1922)1957 *Form in Civilization.* Reprint. Oxford University Press.
LETHABY, W. R. (1935)1980 *Philip Webb and his Work.* Rev. reprint. London: Raven Oak Press.
MUTHESIUS, HERMANN (1904)1979 *The English House.* London: Crosby. Originally published in German.
PEVSNER, NIKOLAUS 1961 "Lethaby's Last." *Architectural Review* 130:354–357.
POSENER, JULIUS (editor) 1964 *Anfänge des Funktionalismus: Von Arts and Crafts zum Deutschen Werkbund.* Frankfurt: Ullstein.
ROBERTS, A. R. N. 1957 "The Life and Work of W. R. Lethaby." *Journal of the Royal Society of Arts* 105:355–371.
ROOKE, NOEL 1932 "The Drawings of W. R. Lethaby." *Journal of the Royal Institute of British Architects* 39:314–317.
RUBENS, GODFREY 1975 "William Lethaby's Buildings." In Alastair Service (editor), *Edwardian Architecture and its Origins.* London: Architectural Press.
RUBENS, GODFREY 1976 "William Lethaby and the Revival of Printing." Pages 219–232 in *Penrose Annual.* London: Northwood.
RUBENS, GODFREY 1982 *William Richard Lethaby and His Work.* London: Architectural Press. Forthcoming publication.

LEUTHNER VON GRUND, ABRAHAM

Abraham Leuthner (or Leitner) von Grund (1639?–1700/1701) was born in Grund, Upper Austria. In 1665, he is recorded as citizen of Prague Neustatt. Active at a time when the predominance of Italian architects in Bohemia was declining, Leuthner was the first independent entrepreneur of some standing. His early activity is not yet fully explored. His known career begins with his involvement in the construction of the palace for Count Humbrecht Czernin in Prague. The design for the palace is Francesco Caratti's but Leuthner, together with J. de Capaoli, was hired to do the actual building. In the contract he is mentioned as *Maurer,* that is, stonemason. Work on the palace occupied Leuthner from 1669 to 1676. The Czernin Palace underwent several changes and restorations in later years, but the original appearance is known from engravings by Leuthner.

Leuthner is recorded as independent architect of the Cistercian Abbey Church in Waldsassen (1682–1701). He prepared plans and a model and was assisted in the execution of the building by his students Georg Dientzenhofer and Christoph Dientzenhofer (see DIENTZENHOFER BROTHERS). The design of the church depends on Carlo Lurago's plans for the Cathedral of Passau and the Jesuit Church in Prague, but it also contains new elements. The nave follows the scheme of the wall-pier type church to which a long and narrow rectangular choir is added. The side chapels and the galleries above them are visually connected by means of oval openings in the chapel vault which makes the ceiling of the gallery appear as the ceiling of the chapel and at the same time provides a source of light for these rooms. The façade of the church was designed by Bernhard Schiesser.

During the 1680s, Leuthner was in charge of the fortifications of Eger and eventually was placed in charge of all fortifications in the kingdom of Bohemia. Whether the churches in Neumarkt (Saint John's) and Trepl (Trinity) are his work or were designed by the Dientzenhofers, is a matter under discussion.

Leuthner's treatise, *Grundlegende Darstellung,* which in addition to the obligatory discussion of architectural orders, also contains portals, fountains, church designs, and so on, was extremely influential not only for the formation of the architecture of the Dientzenhofers but also for JOHANN BERNARD FISCHER VON ERLACH.

EGON VERHEYEN

WORKS

1669–1676, Czernin Palace (with Giovanni de Capaoli), Prague. 1680s, Fortification, Eger, Czechoslovakia. 1682–1701, Cistercian Abbey Church (not completed until 1704), Waldsassen, Czechoslovakia.

BIBLIOGRAPHY

BACHMANN, ERICH 1964 "Architektur." Pages 9–124 in Karl Maria Swoboda (editor), *Barock in Böhmen.* Munich: Prestel.
KNOX, BRYAN 1962 *The Architecture of Prague and Bohemia.* London: Faber.
MORPER, JOHANN JOSEPH 1940 *Das Czernin-Palais in Prag.* Prague: Volk & Reich Verlag.
MORPER, JOHANN JOSEPH 1963 *Die Klosterkirche Waldsassen.* Münster, Germany.
WACKERNAGEL, MARTIN 1915 *Baukunst des 17. und 18. Jahrhunderts in den germanischen Ländern.* Berlin: Akademische Verlagsgesellschaft.

LE VAU, FRANÇOIS

François Le Vau (1613–1676) was the younger brother of LOUIS LE VAU. He was active in the 1650s and 1660s as a designer of châteaux. In 1662, he began service as an engineer in the Bridges and Roads Administration, and in 1671, he was named a founding member of the Royal Academy of Architecture. His most important accomplishment is a design (c.1662) for the east façade of the Louvre, featuring a freestanding colonnade of coupled columns, which was the principal source for the final Louvre colonnade (by Louis Le Vau, Charles Lebrun, and CLAUDE PERRAULT; designed and begun 1667).

ROBERT W. BERGER

WORKS

1652–1657, Château de Saint-Fargeau (remodeling), France. *c.1654–1662, Château de Saint-Sépulchre, France. *1656, Château de Lignières, France. Begun 1658, Château de Seignelay, France. After 1658–c.1668, Château de Bercy, France. 1660, Château de Sucy-en-Brie, France.

BIBLIOGRAPHY

HAUTECOEUR, LOUIS 1948 *Le règne de Louis XIV.* Volume 2 in *Histoire de l'architecture classique en France.* Paris: Picard.
LAPRADE, ALBERT 1960 *François d'Orbay, architecte de Louis XIV.* Paris: Vincent, Fréal.

LE VAU, LOUIS

Louis Le Vau (1612–1670) was born in Paris and probably received his early training from his father, Louis Le Vau, a master mason active in Paris and at the royal Château de Fontainebleau. The younger Le Vau began his career in the 1630s as a designer of modest rowhouses and more imposing *hôtels particuliers,* many of which were located in the Île Saint-Louis in Paris. The elder Le Vau collaborated with his son in some of these enterprises.

In his Parisian hotels, Le Vau revealed a sensitivity to the urban context and an innovative approach to interior planning. His houses on normal city streets were built with their *corps-de-logis* at the rear of the court, following traditional practice. But for his houses on the quiet Île Saint-Louis, Le Vau sought river views by building the *corps-de-logis* as the quai façade, by opening up views of the Seine across open gardens, or by extending the hotel toward the river by means of long galleries. Le Vau's innovations in interior arrangement include the use of double ranges of rooms, octagonal and oval rooms, *salons à l'italienne* (vaulted, two-storied rooms), and complex, monumental stairs. His masterpiece in this genre is the Hôtel Lambert (1640–1644) on the Île Saint-Louis, which, in addition to embodying some of the features just described, brilliantly provided for the storage of horses and carriages and their circulation through the building. By 1660, Le Vau's hotels, along with those of his contemporaries FRANÇOIS MANSART and ANTOINE LE PAUTRE, constituted a corpus of domestic urban architecture unrivaled in Europe for ingenious, flexible planning.

About 1640, Le Vau began his first château, Le Raincy (c.1640–c.1645). The *corps-de-logis* was a traditional cluster of separately roofed pavilions, but the central pavilion was an oval unit, containing a severe columnar vestibule with a two-story, richly decorated *salon à l'italienne* directly above, the two rooms linked by a monumental stair. This innovative, dramatic composition was developed with variations at the later Château de Meudon (remodeled 1654–c.1657) and the Château de Vaux-le-Vicomte (1656–1661). Several features of these châteaux suggest relationships with contemporary Italian baroque architecture: the use of oval plans, curved, movemented façades, the combination of monumental vestibule and stair, and the dramatic contrast between rooms.

Le Vau's hotels of the 1630s and 1640s were commissioned by financiers and members of the *noblesse de la robe,* many of whom were royal officials. It is possible that his father, in royal employ at Fontainebleau, was instrumental in attracting these patrons. Le Raincy, Meudon, and Vaux-le-Vicomte were built for men who administered the finances of France. Le Vau, then, was allied with patrons who were committed to monarchical centralization. This record of patronage surely was a factor in his advancement in 1654 to the post of first architect of the King. In his pattern of patronage, Le Vau stood in contrast to his two major rivals, Mansart and Le Pautre, among whose clients were *frondeurs* and Jansenists, enemies of centralization and religious orthodoxy.

Le Vau's baroque style was further developed in the Collège des Quatre Nations, Paris (1662-1674), which features concave wings and an oval-plan chapel. Beginning around 1659, Le Vau produced a series of projects for the east wing of the Louvre. The final scheme featured an internally domed oval vestibule in the central pavilion, flanked by monumental stairs—an outgrowth of the châteaux designs. Possibly because of its baroque style, Jean-Baptiste Colbert (the new Superintendent of the King's Buildings) halted construction of Le Vau's Louvre project in 1664, thus opening up the completion of the Louvre to French and foreign proposals, including the designs of GIOVANNI LORENZO BERNINI. The final Colonnade (designed and begun in 1667) was produced by a committee which included Le Vau, Charles Lebrun, and CLAUDE PERRAULT. The authorship of the Colonnade has been fiercely contested for three hundred years, and it is still not possible definitively to assess the contribution of Le Vau or the other committee members. If Le Vau did play a preponderant role in its design, it would confirm a major stylistic shift in his royal projects of his last years away from the baroque toward classicism, a style also embodied in the garden façades of the *enveloppe* of Versailles (designed 1667 or 1668, built 1668–1670).

This survey of Le Vau's career reveals him as a major mid-century designer of hôtels and châteaux, an exponent of the baroque trend under Jules Cardinal Mazarin and a formulator of a new royal classicism under Colbert. His importance in the history of French seventeenth-century architecture is great, but his critical reputation has suffered, particularly because of his treatment of the classical orders. In 1787, A. N. Dezallier d'Argenville criticized the mixture of colossal and superposed orders on the façades of Vaux-le-Vicomte as "a lack of unity," and this propensity of Le Vau's to mix the scale of orders has also been cited by modern writers as an artistic shortcoming. This viewpoint—formulated in the age of neoclassicism—ignores the architect's artistic intentions. Le Vau recognized the effectiveness of the colossal order for the distant view, and hence employed it in his châteaux (except Meudon, where the sixteenth-century façades were respected) and in the Louvre projects. When designing urban hotels, Le Vau used the colossal order when it could be seen from some distance, as on garden façades; he never displayed it on narrow city street façades or in courtyards (in the latter he typically used superposed orders). Hence, the different façades of a particular hôtel were often differently articulated in response to spectator viewpoint. Some of his buildings, however, display two orders of different scale on the same façade (Vaux-le-Vicomte, Collège des Quatre Nations), and here we are guided to Le Vau's intentions by a document of 1667/1668, written by his architect brother FRANÇOIS LE VAU which suggests a justification of such mixture of the orders by a musical analogy in which the varied orders are compared to the different voices and parts of musical compositions.

These considerations help to clarify Le Vau's artistic aims, but they also pose a problem with respect to the new garden elevations of Versailles.

Le Vau.
Château de Vaux-le-
Vicomte.
France.
1656–1661

Le Vau's practice would lead one to expect the colossal order, and this was indeed proposed by Le Vau in a preliminary design (Nationalmuseum, Stockholm CC 271). But in the executed work, superposed orders were used for the two upper floors. This is uncharacteristic of Le Vau in château design, as is the original villa-massing of the garden front and the juncture of the corner pilasters. For these reasons, the claim of Laprade (1960) that Le Vau's chief assistant, FRANÇOIS D'ORBAY, was the real designer of the *enveloppe* must remain open to scholarly consideration.

ROBERT W. BERGER

WORKS

*1634–1637, Hôtel de Bautru; 1637–1640. Hôtel de Gillier; *1638–1640, Hôtel de Bretonvilliers (completion); *1639–1642, Hôtel Sainctot; 1640–1642, Hôtel Le Vau; 1640–1644, Hôtel Lambert; *c.1640–c.1644, Hôtel Hesselin; Paris. *c.1640–c.1645, Château du Raincy, France. *1642–1646, Hôtel Tambonneau; 1649–1650, Hôtel d'Aumont (continuation of earlier work); Paris. *1654–c.1657, Château de Meudon (remodeling), France. 1654–1661, Château de Vincennes (King's and Queen's pavilions), France. 1656–1657, Hôtel de Lauzun, Paris. 1656–1661, Château de Vaux-le-Vicomte, France. 1656–?, Hôpital de la Salpêtrière; *1659–after 1666, Tuileries (remodeling); *1660–1663, Louvre (south façade I); 1661–1664, Louvre (Galerie d'Apollon); 1662–1664, Hôtel de Lionne; 1662–1674, Collège des Quatre Nations; Paris. *1662/1663–1670, Ménagerie, Versailles, France. 1664–1726, Saint-Louis-en-l'Île; (A)1667, Louvre (colonnade with others); 1668ff., Louvre (south façade II; with others); Paris. 1668–1670, Château de Versailles (enveloppe; not completed until 1673 or 1674); *1670, Trianon de Porcelaine; Versailles, France.

BIBLIOGRAPHY

BERGER, ROBERT W.   1976   "Louis Le Vau's Château du Raincy." *Architectura* 6, no. 1:36–46.
BLUNT, ANTHONY   (1953)1970   *Art and Architecture in France 1500 to 1700.* 2d ed. Baltimore: Penguin.
BOURDEL, NICOLE   1956   "Nouveaux documents sur Louis Le Vau, premier architecte de Louis XIV (1612–1670)." *Mémoires de la fédération des sociétés historiques et archéologiques de Paris et de l'Île-de-France* 8:213–235.
DUMOLIN, MAURICE   1929–1931   *Etudes de topographie parisienne.* 3 vols. Paris.
DUMOLIN, MAURICE   1930   "Notes sur quelques architectes du XVIIᵉ siècle." *Bulletin de la société de l'histoire de l'art français* 1930:11–22.
HAUTECOEUR, LOUIS   1948   *Le règne de Louis XIV.* 2 vols. Volume 2 of *Histoire de l'architecture classique en France.* Paris: Picard.
LAPRADE, ALBERT   1960   *François d'Orbay, architecte de Louis XIV.* Paris: Vincent, Fréal.
TOOTH, CONSTANCE   1967   "The Early Private Houses of Louis Le Vau." *Burlington Magazine* 109:510–518. With notes by Peter Smith.

LEVERTON, THOMAS

Thomas Leverton (1743–1824), son of an Essex builder, achieved early success as the developer and putative designer of Bedford Square, London. One of his clients there Lord Loughborough, later tried to promote him as a penitentiary architect against such contenders as William Blackburn and THOMAS HARDWICK. Leverton is best remembered, however, for his domestic buildings, which feature bland exteriors markedly in contrast with ingenious domical room shapes. Some scholars attribute these interiors to Leverton's gifted assistant JOSEPH BONOMI who trained under ROBERT ADAM. But Leverton's rooms, unlike Adam's, rarely coalesce into coherent planned sequences, and their ornamentation is so liberally applied as to create a contrived effect.

PIERRE DE LA RUFFINIÈRE DU PREY

WORKS

*1771, Woodford Hall, Essex, England. 1772, 65 Lincoln's Inn Fields; 1775–1781, 1, 6, and 13 Bedford Square (interiors and perhaps exteriors); London. 1776, Boyles Court, Great Warley, England. 1777–1782, Woodhall Park, Hertfordshire, England. 1780, Plaistow Lodge, Bromley, Kent, England. 1783, Arch commemorating the American War of Independence, Parlington House, Yorkshire, England. *1784–1794, Phoenix Fire Insurance Company Office and Fire Engine House; *1798–1809, Grocers' Livery Hall; London. 1803, Scampston Hall, Yorkshire, England. 1803, "Sugar" House, New York. *1806, Hamilton Place, London.

BIBLIOGRAPHY

HUSSEY, CHRISTOPHER   1932   "No. 1 Bedford Square." *Country Life* 71:150–156.
HUSSEY, CHRISTOPHER   (1956)1963   *English Country Houses: Mid-Georgian, 1760–1800.* 2d ed. London: Country Life.
NEWMAN, JOHN   1969   *The Building of England: West Kent and the Weald.* Harmondsworth, England: Penguin.
OLSEN, DONALD J.   1964   *Town Planning in London: The Eighteenth and Nineteenth Centuries.* New Haven and London: Yale University Press.
OSWALD, ARTHUR   1954   "Scampston Hall, Yorkshire." *Country Life* 115:946–949, 1034–1038.
RICHARDSON, GEORGE   1802–1808   *The New Vitruvius Britannicus.* 2 vols. London: The author.
SUMMERSON, JOHN   (1945)1978   *Georgian London.* London: Barrie & Jenkins.

LEVI, RINO

Brazilian architect Rino Levi (1901–1965) transformed living habits in his native São Paulo by designing its first large apartment building predicated on Bauhaus functionalism and urban integration. Of Italian heritage, Levi studied architecture at the University of Rome. In 1925, a year before his return to Brazil, he made his first impact on Brazilian architecture by writing a letter to a São Paulo newspaper expounding on the new movement in European architecture which related architecture to an urban network. Levi continued to view architecture as part of an existing continuum as shown in his first commission, the Columbus Apartment Building (1928) and later when planning the UFA Palacio Cinema (1936) and the Central Cancer Hospital (1948) all in São Paulo. He thoroughly studied all aspects of the surrounding urban structure as well as acoustical technology for the theater and administration for the hospital before elaborating his designs.

Levi was innovative in producing brutalist designs with raw concrete for the Parahyba Dairies (1963–1967) and the Santo André Civic Center (1965). His professional activities included being head of the University of São Paulo's department of architecture and urbanism and director of the Brazilian Association of Architects.

ELIZABETH D. HARRIS

WORKS

1928, Columbus Apartment Building; 1936, UFA Palacio Cinema; 1941, Sedes Sapientiae Institute; 1947–1949, Cultura Artistica Theatre; 1948, Central Cancer Hospital; 1950, Edifício Paulista; São Paulo, Brazil. 1936–1967, Parahyba Dairy Plant and Airplane Hanger, São João dos Campos, Brazil. 1965, Santo André Civic Center, São Paulo, Brazil.

BIBLIOGRAPHY

LEVI, RINO 1940 *Rino Levi: Arquitéto Obras 1928–1940.* São Paulo, Brazil: Serviço dos Paises.
LEVI, RINO 1974 *Rino Levi.* Introduction by Roberto Burle-Marx and Nestor Goulart Reis Filho. Milan: Edizioni di Conumità.

LEVI-MONTALCINI, GINO

Gino Levi-Montalcini (1902–1974) was born in Milan. He graduated from the Politecnico in Turin in 1925. A member of the Rationalist movement in architecture during the 1920s and 1930s, he designed buildings in and around Turin. After World War II, he taught in Palermo, Padua, and Turin, where he died.

DENNIS DOORDAN

WORKS

1930, Gualino Office Building (with GIUSEPPE PAGANO), Turin, Italy. 1936–1938, IX Maggio Resort, Bardonecchia, Italy. 1958–1960, Palazzo delle Facolta Umanistiche, Turin, Italy.

BIBLIOGRAPHY

POZZETTO, MARCO 1975 "Gino Levi-Montalcini." *Studi Piemontesi* 4:133–141.

LEWERENTZ, SIGURD

Sigurd Lewerentz (1885–1975), born at Sando, Vasternorrlands, Sweden, graduated from the Chalmers Technical Institute in Göteborg in 1908 and spent two years studying in Germany. He began study at the Royal Academy of Arts, Stockholm, in 1910, but quickly broke away to found an independent architectural school, the Klara School, with several other students. Here RAGNAR ÖSTBERG, CARL BERGSTEN, and IVAR J. TENGBOM taught and offered an alternative to the dessicated classicism of the Academy. They were proponents of National Romanticism and so endorsed the use of indigenous materials and forms; in their concern for authenticity of expression, they opened the door to modern architecture. Their radical students, including OSVALD ALMQVIST and ERIK GUNNAR ASPLUND, collaborated throughout their lives and determined modern Swedish architecture.

From the first, the most influential works by Lewerentz, who had opened an office in 1911, were projects, visible to other architects. The young Danish architect KAY FISKER, at the beginning of a career marked by devotion to modernized traditional architecture, saw Lewerentz's neoclassical project for the Hälsingborg Crematorium exhibited at the Baltic Exhibition in 1914; Fisker subsequently worked for Lewerentz. Lewerentz's prestige abroad is reflected not only in his friendship with LE CORBUSIER and PETER CELSING, but also in his election to the Academy in Copenhagen in 1939, and the Bayerische Akademie in Munich in 1960. At home he received the prestigious Tessin medal in 1962.

Although Lewerentz's famous projects for the Hälsingborg Crematorium and the Woodland Cemetery were neoclassical, he had turned completely to functionalism by the end of the 1920s to achieve his distinctive contribution to the modern. Besides an outstanding villa for the Stockholm Exhibition of 1930, Lewerentz developed the sans-serif graphic style for the banners, program covers, and signs, as well as numerous pavilions, motor vehicles, and the touring boats for visitors to the Exhibition. In the mid-1930s, Lewerentz along with other Swedish architects modified the austerity of the modern and returned to a use of warm materials and picturesque plans. Lewerentz achieved great success in landscaping the Woodland Crematorium, Stockholm, 1914, and the grounds surrounding Eastern Cemetery, Malmö, a work begun in 1916 and accomplished in stages over the next decades.

Lewerentz's contribution to the modern also included industrial design. With Torsten Stubelius, he formed a partnership that specialized in lighting fixtures and other glass products. In the 1920s, he worked with the civil engineer Cläes Kreuger to develop the Ideasta metal window system, and during the 1930s and 1940s, he directed its manufacture at his own factory.

JUDITH S. HULL

WORKS

1913–1914, Färe Glassworks Assembly Rooms (with Torsten Stubelius) Sibbhult, Sweden. 1914, Crematorium, (with Stubelius); Hälsingborg, Sweden. 1914–1915, Worker's Housing, Forsbacka, Sweden. 1916–1958, Eastern Cemetery, Malmö, Sweden. 1920–1925, Burial Chapel, Valdemarsvik, Sweden. 1926, Chapel of the Resurrection (Uppstandelsekapellet), Woodland Cemetery; 1930, Stockholm Exhibition (buildings, motor vehicles, graphic designs); Stockholm. 1932–1944, Theater (with D. Helldén and Erik Lallerstedt), Malmö, Sweden. 1936, Villa Edstrand, Falsterbo, Sweden. 1938–1945, Chapel, Eastern Cemetery, Malmö, Sweden. 1956–1960, Saint Marks Skarpnäck, Stockholm.

BIBLIOGRAPHY

AHLBERG, HAKON 1945 "Sigurd Lewerentz." *Byggmästaren* 19:359–360.
AHLBERG, HAKON 1963 "Sigurd Lewerentz." *Arkitektur* 9:entire issue.
CODRINGTON, JAMES 1976 "Sigurd Lewerentz, 1885–1975." *Architectural Review* 159, no. 950:223.
FISKER, KAY 1963 "Markuskirken i Björkhagen." *Arkitektur* 7:1–17.
JACOBSEN, ARNE 1945 "Kapel og Krematorium i Malmö." *Byggmästaren* 19:360–380.
LINN, BJORN 1979 "Sigurd Lewerentz." Volume 22, pages 640–643 in *Svenskt Biografiskt Lexikon*. Edited by Birgitta Lager-Kromnow. Stockholm: Norstedts Tryckern.

LEWIS, DAVID C.

David Chambers Lewis (1867–1918), born in Portland, Oregon, centered his practice in his native city. He was graduated from Princeton in 1890, did postgraduate work at Columbia University, and studied in Paris for a year before returning to Oregon. His work included noteworthy exposition buildings, fashionable residences, and office buildings. His Railway Exchange Building in Portland, erected in 1910, was the first major office building of reinforced concrete in the city.

ELISABETH WALTON POTTER

WORKS

1900, L. Allen Lewis House; 1904–1906, Trinity Episcopal Church; *1905, Foreign Exhibits Building, Lewis and Clark Centennial Exposition; *1905, Stewart B. Linthicum House; 1906, Couch Building; 1908, Board of Trade Building; 1909, Lewis Building; 1909, Lumbermen's Building; Portland, Ore. *1909, Oregon State Building, Alaska-Yukon-Pacific Exposition, Seattle, Wash. 1910, Railway Exchange Building (with H.G. Beckwith), Portland, Ore. 1915–1916, Thomas McCann House, Bend, Ore.

BIBLIOGRAPHY

MARLITT, RICHARD (1968)1978 *Nineteenth Street.* Rev. ed. Portland: Oregon Historical Society.
PORTLAND, OREGON, CHAMBER OF COMMERCE 1911 *Men of Oregon.* Portland: Chamber of Commerce Bulletin.
VAUGHAN, THOMAS, and FERRIDAY, VIRGINIA GUEST (editors) 1974 *Space, Style and Structure.* 2 vols. Portland: Oregon Historical Society.

LEWIS, JAMES

James Lewis (c.1751–1820) was a representative late eighteenth-century British architect. Little is known about his early training, but in 1770–1772 he traveled to Italy where he met GIOVANNI BATTISTA PIRANESI and formed lifelong continental connections. Although he was surveyor to two major London hospitals (and the architect of one, the sprawling Bethlehem Hospital [1812–1815] and the designer of several distinctive Palladian (see ANDREA PALLADIO) and neoclassical country houses, Lewis is today best known for two volumes—one published in 1779–1780, the other in 1797—of *Original Designs in Architecture*. The texts of these books are related to works by WILLIAM CHAMBERS and ROBERT ADAM, among others, and the high-quality illustrations continue the tradition of COLEN CAMPBELL's *Vitruvius Britannicus* (1715–1725) and JAMES GIBBS's *Book of Architecture* (1728). The subscription list of 1797, including as it does major British and foreign architects and connoisseurs, indicates the breadth of Lewis's audience. He died in London.

GERALD L. CARR

WORKS

1780, Bletchingdon House, Oxfordshire, England.

c.1786, Sutton Park (alterations), Bedfordshire, England. 1790–1794, Lavington House, Sussex, England. c.1797, Nazeing Park (alterations), Essex, England. 1806–1813, Royal College of Surgeons (with George Dance the Younger); 1812–1815, Bethlehem Hospital (now the Imperial War Museum); London.

BIBLIOGRAPHY

CAMPBELL, COLEN (1715–1725)1967 *Vitruvius Britannicus.* 4 vols. Reprint. New York: Blom.

GIBBS, JAMES (1728)1968 *A Book of Architecture.* Reprint. New York: Blom.

LEWIS, JAMES (1779–1797)1967 *Original Designs in Architecture.* 2 vols. in 1. Reprint. Farnborough, England: Gregg.

PAPWORTH, WYATT (editor) 1852–1892 *The Dictionary of Architecture.* London: Architectural Publication Society.

LEWIS, MORTIMER

Mortimer William Lewis (1796–1879) was a London military surveyor who emigrated to Sydney in 1829 and was appointed assistant surveyor. In 1835 he became colonial architect, and in this capacity became Australia's leading exponent of the Greek Revival, the best example being his Darlinghurst Courthouse (1837), Sydney. His duties included the supervision of EDWARD BLORE's castellated Government House, Sydney, and he designed his own Richmond Villa (1850) in a picturesque Gothic, as well as some Gothic churches.

MILES LEWIS

WORKS

1835–1837, Lunatic Asylum, Gladesville, near Sydney. 1837, Darlinghurst Courthouse; 1837, Police Office; Sydney. 1838–1841, Custom House; 1838–1843, Courthouse, Melbourne. 1849, Maitland Gaol, New South Wales, Australia. c.1847–1850, Sydney Museum; 1850, Richmond Villa; Sydney.

BIBLIOGRAPHY

COX, PHILIP, and LUCAS, CLIVE 1978 *Australian Colonial Architecture.* Melbourne: Landsdowne.

HERMAN, MORTON (1954)1970 *The Early Australian Architects and Their Work.* Rev. ed. Sydney: Angus & Robertson.

LEWIS, SCHELL

Schell Lewis (?–1975) was born in Des Moines, Iowa, and educated in St. Louis, Missouri. He came to New York in his teens and entered the office of CHARLES ADAMS PLATT as an office boy. Platt taught him to draw, and Lewis became a great architectural delineator. Lewis worked in Platt's office for seventeen years before opening his own business. In 1931 Lewis won the Birch Burdette Long prize for excellence in delineation.

STEVEN MCLEOD BEDFORD

BIBLIOGRAPHY

"Special Plate Section: A Cross-section of the Present State of the Art of Delineation in America." 1940 *Pencil Points* 21:401–430, 442–446.

LEWIS, WHITFIELD

Born and educated in Wales, Herbert John Whitfield Lewis (1911–) was assistant to ERIC MENDELSOHN and SERGE CHERMAYEFF. He is best known for his work as principal housing architect at the London County Council where he extended the practice of mixing high- and low-rise dwellings in public housing projects.

ELLEN LEOPOLD

WORKS

1945–1947, Saint Pancras Way Housing Scheme; 1950–1959, Seventeen thousand houses (including Ackroyden Estate, Alton Estate, Roehampton Lane Estate, Bentham Road Estate, and Warwick Crescent); London.

BIBLIOGRAPHY

BOR, WALTER 1980 "High Rise Celebrates 25 Golden Years." *Building Design* 500:11.